The Financial Derivatives Reader

The Financial Derivatives
Reader

Edited by

Robert W. Kolb
School of Business Administration
University of Miami

KOLB

Kolb Publishing Company   *Miami, Florida*

The cover photograph appears courtesy of the Chicago Mercantile Exchange and features the S&P 500 futures pit.

A list of sources appears on pages 659–662 at the end of this text.

Printed in the United States of America.

Library of Congress Catalog Card Number   92-90037

ISBN: 1-878975-11-0

XK
KOLB *Kolb Publishing Company*
7175 S.W. 47th Street, Suite 210   Miami, Florida 33155
(305) 663-0550   FAX (305) 663-6579

Preface

The Financial Derivatives Reader presents the most enduring and pivotal articles in the development of our knowledge of financial derivatives. In addition, the *Reader* includes a blend of articles that are accessible to undergraduate students of financial derivatives. In total, the 44 articles in this reader cover the broad waterfront of theory and practical applications of financial derivatives. As such, *The Financial Derivatives Reader* should be of interest to all students of finance, as well as finance professors and finance professionals. By presenting a thorough selection of classic articles, along with many articles focusing on applications, *The Financial Derivatives Reader* is a useful supplement for any course on futures, options, swaps, or financial engineering.

In this text, we interpret financial derivatives to refer to futures, options, options on futures, and swaps that take a financial instrument as the underlying good. This definition includes futures on interest rate instruments and futures on financial indexes, such as the S&P 500 futures contract.

Twenty years ago, there were essentially no financial derivatives—at least not in comparison to the present. In the last two decades, markets for financial derivatives have been founded, and they have flourished. The success of these markets has been so great that we now hear cries that the markets for underlying instruments must be protected from competition with the derivatives that have grown up beside them. For example, the trading of stock index futures and options has been blamed for the Crash of 1987, and critics of financial derivatives claim that the tail (financial derivatives) now wags the dog (the market for underlying financial instruments).

In a limited sense, these critics of financial derivatives are correct, for financial derivatives have become just as important as the markets for the underlying instruments. Further, by many measures, the markets for derivatives are far larger than the markets for the underlying instruments. The greater liquidity and lower transaction costs offered by markets for financial derivatives attract greater trading interest than the markets for the underlying securities, and they promise to grow more rapidly than the markets for underlying instruments. Consistent with the prominent role now captured by derivative markets, many academics and market professionals look first to activity in financial derivatives markets to anticipate the short-term direction of prices on underlying instruments.

Twenty years ago, there were virtually no university courses focusing on financial derivatives. Since that time, spectacular advances in understanding the pricing and uses of financial derivatives has led to a central role for the study of financial derivatives in the finance curriculum.

The 44 readings in this book are organized into six sections, as shown on the next page. Section I sets the stage with broad articles covering the sweep of financial derivative markets and applications. Section II, which is divided into four sub-sections, details pricing principles for each of the different types of derivatives. Sections III and IV focus on equity derivatives, with section III covering the uses of equity derivatives. Section IV considers the role of equity derivatives in the Crash of 1987. Debt market applications are analyzied in Section V, while Section VI focuses on foreign exchange applications.

   I. **Introduction: Financial Derivatives and Financial Engineering**
  II. **Derivative Instruments: Theory and Pricing**
     A. **Forwards and Futures**
     B. **Options**
     C. **Options on Futures**
     D. **Swaps**
 III. **Equity Market Applications**
 IV. **Equity Derivatives and the Crash**
  V. **Debt Market Applications**
 VI. **Foreign Exchange Applications**

I wish to thank the individuals who helped bring this book to life. Joe Rodriguez designed the cover, and the Chicago Mercantile Exchange, through the good offices of Monica Butler and Gail Osten, graciously provided the cover photograph. Kateri Davis managed the entire pre-press effort for the book. The greatest thanks goes to the authors represented here and to the publications where these articles originally appeared. The *Sources* section at the end of this text shows the original place and date of publication for each article. It is customary to praise others for making a book possible. For this book, such praise has special meaning. The creativity of the authors represented in this text really did make this book possible.

Robert W. Kolb
University of Miami

Contents

Section I

Introduction: Financial Derivatives and Financial Engineering

The four articles in this first section of *The Financial Derivatives Reader* provide a broad overview of the range and scope of financial derivatives and their applications. While many traders are attracted to financial derivatives as a vehicle for speculation, the articles in this section emphasize the use of financial derivatives for managing risk. Recent advances in understanding financial derivatives have generated a large leap in applications and have opened up an exciting new field of specialization in finance: financial engineering. These strides have taken place against a background of increasing globalization of financial markets.

In their article, "Managing Financial Risk," Clifford W. Smith, Jr., Charles W. Smithson, and D. Sykes Wilford, address three related issues: measuring the risk of a firm to exchange rates, interest rates, and inflation, determining what financial tools are available for managing risk, and using the financial tools to manage the risk. In the process of exploring these issues, Smith, Smithson, and Wilford show that the process can be simplified considerably by viewing particular financial derivatives as building blocks, each with a particular payoff signature. By combining these simple building blocks, the risk manager can devise a strategy for managing a complex risk that may be quite specific to the firm.

In "Financial Engineering in Corporate Finance: An Overview," John D. Finnerty provides an excellent introduction to this emerging specialization in finance. Financial engineering, as Finnerty explains, is the design, development, and implementation of innovative financial solutions to problems in finance. In most cases, financial engineering involves using financial derivatives to engineer a new financial product with properties designed to control a particular risk. The metaphors of building and engineering are particularly apt, because much of contemporary financial risk management involves the combination of financial derivatives to achieve particular risk management aims.

In "Derivative Assets Analysis," Mark Rubinstein provides a broad overview of the different ways in which finance professionals can understand financial derivatives and employ them to manage risk. Rubinstein emphasizes the way in which one derivative can be used to replicate another. Understanding these replication strategies leads to a deeper understanding of the relationship among different derivatives and their uses in risk management. Rubinstein also includes a useful bibliography showing the range of applications for financial derivatives.

As Peter A. Abken emphasizes by the title of his article, "Globalization of Stock, Futures, and Options Markets," there is a wave of internationalization that is sweeping finance and that promises to be the dominant theme of financial markets in the 1990s. While the United States has been a world leader in the explosion of financial derivatives that began in the early 1970s, other countries are quickly catching up. At present, a major wave of new markets is sweeping Europe and the Orient, with even Russia establishing a futures exchange. Many of the new exchanges throughout the world already lead the United States in the application of electronic trading systems. Abken argues that physical marketplaces are becoming obsolete, and Abken explores the issue of whether electronic trading systems are likely to contribute to unwanted volatility in market prices.

Article 1

MANAGING FINANCIAL RISK

*by Clifford W. Smith, Jr.,
University of Rochester,
Charles W. Smithson, Continental Bank,
and D. Sykes Wilford,
Chase Manhattan Bank**

There is no doubt that the financial environment is a lot more risky today than it was in the 1950s and 1960s. With changes in some macroeconomic institutional structures—notably, the breakdown of the Bretton Woods agreement in 1972—have come dramatic increases in the volatility of interest rates, foreign exchange rates, and commodity prices.

Such increased volatility will not come as "news" to most corporate executives. Since the 1970s, many CEOs and CFOs have watched the profitability of their firms swing widely in response to large movements in exchange rates, interest rates, and commodity prices. What may be news, however, are the techniques and tools now available for measuring and managing such financial risks.

Recognition of the increased volatility of exchange rates, interest rates, and commodity prices should lead managers of the firm to ask three questions:

1. To what extent is my firm exposed to interest rates, foreign exchange rates, or commodity prices?
2. What financial tools are available for managing these exposures?
3. If my firm is significantly exposed, how do I use the financial tools to manage the exposure?

It is with these three questions that the following discussion deals.

*This article is an abbreviated version of Chapters 2, 3, and 19 of *Managing Financial Risk*, forthcoming Ballinger/*Institutional Investor Series*. This material is used with the permission of the publisher.

IDENTIFYING AND MEASURING FINANCIAL RISK

The Risk Profile

U.S. savings and loans (S&Ls) are a widely cited example of firms subject to interest rate risk. Because S&Ls typically fund long-lived assets (e.g., 30-year fixed-rate mortgages) with liabilities that reprice frequently (passbook deposits), their value is negatively related to interest rates. When interest rates rise, the value of S&Ls' assets declines significantly, but the value of their liabilities changes little. So, the value of shareholders' equity falls.

The resulting relation between interest rates and the value of S&Ls is portrayed graphically in a *risk profile* in Figure 1.

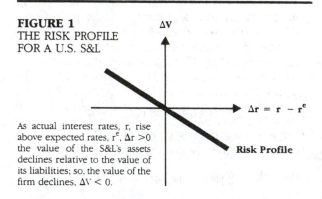

FIGURE 1
THE RISK PROFILE
FOR A U.S. S&L

As actual interest rates, r, rise above expected rates, r^e, $\Delta r > 0$ the value of the S&L's assets declines relative to the value of its liabilities; so, the value of the firm declines, $\Delta V < 0$.

The negative slope reflects the inverse relation between the financial price—i.e., interest rates—and the value of the S&L. The precise measure of the exposure is reflected by the slope of the line; and it is a measure of the slope that the techniques described below will provide.

But before considering the size of the exposure, the first question is: How do we go about identifying such exposures? In the case of S&Ls, the exposure to interest rates is apparent from the firm's balance sheet; the mismatch of maturities between assets and liabilities is obvious. Many companies, however, have economic or "operating" exposures that are not reflected on their balance sheets. Take, for example,

the vulnerability of building products firms to increases in interest rates. Increases in interest rates decrease the demand for building products. As sales and thus cash inflows decline—and to the extent that its costs and liabilities are fixed—the value of a building products firm declines.

We can make a similar observation about foreign exchange risk. In some instances, exposures are apparent. For example, a U.S. importer orders product from Germany and is expected to pay in Deutsche Marks (DM) for the products when they are delivered in 90 days. If, during those 90 days, the price of a DM rises—that is, the value of the dollar declines—the U.S. importer will have to pay more for the product. In this case, an increase in the price of the foreign currency leads to a decrease in the value of the importer.

Since 1972, firms have become adept at dealing with such transaction exposures.[1] However, a firm's exposure to foreign exchange rate risk can be more subtle; even firms that have no foreign receipts or payments may still be exposed to foreign exchange risk. If the dollar is strong, the dollar price of foreign products to U.S. consumers becomes cheaper and foreign firms make inroads into the U.S. market, thereby decreasing net cash flows to the U.S. producers and thus reducing their value. The reverse is true when the value of the dollar falls. Obvious for firms like automakers, this economic or competitive (or "strategic") risk is receiving more attention by the managers of other U.S. firms as well.[2]

Not surprisingly, the same relations appear with respect to commodity price risk. The exposures can be apparent: For example, as the price of oil rises, the costs for an airline rise; so rising oil prices are linked to falling firm values. Or, the exposures can be subtle. For example, a primary input in aluminum production is electric energy. Aluminum manufacturers in Iceland use electricity generated by that country's abundant geothermal energy. As the price of oil rises, the costs of competitors rise while the costs of Icelandic producers remain unchanged, thus improving the competitive position and increasing the value of Icelandic firms. It is when oil prices fall and competitors' costs decline that Icelandic producers worry.[3]

Financial price risk, then—whether caused by changes in interest rates, foreign exchange, or com-

1. A transaction exposure occurs when the firm has a payment or receipt in a currency other than its home currency. A translation exposure results when the value of foreign assets and liabilities must be converted into home currency values.

2. A case in point is Kodak, which has begun to manage "overall corporate performance in the long run." See Paul Dickens, "Daring to Hedge the Unhedgeable," *Euromoney Corporate Finance*, August 1988.

3. For this useful story about Icelandic aluminum producers, we are indebted to J. Nicholas Robinson of Chase Manhattan Bank.

TABLE 1
CALCULATION OF THE
VALUE & DURATION OF
THE BUSINESS LOAN

	(1) Time to Receipt (Years)	(2) Cash Flow	(3) Discount Rate	(4) PV	(5) Weight	(6) Weight × Time
	0.5	90	7.75%	86.70	0.22	0.11
	1.0	90	8.00%	83.33	0.21	0.21
	1.5	90	8.25%	79.91	0.20	0.31
	2.0	90	8.35%	76.66	0.19	0.38
	2.5	90	8.50%	73.40	0.18	0.45
				400.00 Present Value		1.45 Duration

modity prices—consists of more subtle economic exposures as well as the obvious balance sheet mismatches and transactional exposures. And the *risk profile* mentioned earlier, in order to provide a useful measure of a firm's overall economic exposure, must reflect the total effect of both kinds of price risk.

The question that naturally arises, then, is: How do you determine the slope of the risk profile? That is, how do you estimate the change in firm value expected to accompany a given change in a financial price ($\Delta V/\Delta P$)?

Quantifying Financial Risk: A Special Case

Financial institutions, particularly banks, were the first to devote significant attention to quantifying financial exposures. Our S&L example is admittedly an extreme case of interest rate exposure, even for a financial institution. Nevertheless, because some mismatch between the maturities of assets and liabilities almost inevitably occurs in the normal course of their business, all financial institutions generally face some degree of interest rate risk. To measure this exposure to interest rates, financial institutions rely on two techniques: gap and duration.

GAP: The method most financial corporations use to measure their exposure to interest rate changes is called the "maturity gap" approach.[4] The approach gets its name from a procedure designed to quantify the "gap" between the market values of rate-sensitive assets (RSA) and rate-sensitive liabilities (RSL)—that is, GAP = RSA − RSL.[5] The financial institution determines the "gapping period"—the period over which it wants to measure its interest rate sensitivity—say, 6 months, one year, five years, and so forth. Then, for each of these periods, it measures its gap as defined above. In the context of a gap model, changes in interest rates affect a financial institution's market value by changing the institution's Net Interest Income (NII). Hence, once the GAP is known, the impact on the firm of changes in the interest rate can be calculated as follows:

$$\Delta NII = (GAP) \times (\Delta r)$$

Duration: Some financial institutions use an alternative to the GAP approach called "duration analysis" to measure their interest rate exposure.[6] In essence, the duration of a financial instrument provides a measure of when on average the present value of the instrument is received.

For example, let's look at the duration of a business loan with a maturity of 2.5 years and a sinking fund. Because part of the value is received prior to maturity, the duration of the instrument is clearly less than 2.5 years. To find out how much less, we need to ask the question "When on average is the present value received?"

---

4. For a discussion of the maturity gap model, see Alden L. Toevs, "Measuring and Managing Interest Rate Risk: A Guide to Asset/Liability Models Used in Banks and Thrifts," Morgan Stanley Fixed Income Analytical Research Paper, October 1984. (An earlier version of this paper appeared in *Economic Review*, The Federal Reserve Bank of San Francisco, Spring, 1983.)

5. The assets and liabilities that are "rate sensitive" are those that will reprice during the gapping period.

6. For a discussion of duration, see George G. Kaufman, "Measuring and Managing Interest Rate Risk: A Primer," *Economic Perspectives*, Federal Reserve Bank of Chicago. See also Stephen Schaefer, "Immunisation and Duration: A Review of the Theory, Performance, and Applications," *Midland Corporate Finance Journal*, Vol. 2 No. 3, Fall 1984.

Table 1 provides an illustration. Columns 1-4 provide the present value of the bond. To determine *when* the present value will be received, on average, we need to calculate the weighted average time of receipt. Column 5 provides the weights. Multiplying these weights (column 5) by the times the cash flows are received (column 1) and summing gives the duration of this business loan—1.45 years.

The use of duration effectively converts a security into its zero-coupon equivalent. In addition, duration relates changes in interest rates to changes in the value of the security.[7] Specifically, duration permits us to express the percentage change in the value of the security in terms of the percentage change in the discount rate (1 + r) and the duration of the security, as follows:[8]

$$\frac{\Delta V}{V} = \frac{\Delta (1 + r)}{(1 + r)} \times D$$

For example, if the duration of a security is 1.45 years, and the discount rate increases by 1 percent (that is, if $\Delta (1 + r)/(1 + r) = 0.01$), the market value of the 2.5 year business loan will decrease by 1.45 percent. The concept of duration, moreover, can be extended to provide a measure of the interest rate exposure of an entire bank or S&L.

Quantifying Financial Price Risk: The General Case

While gap and duration work well for financial institutions, these techniques offer little guidance in evaluating the interest rate sensitivity of a nonfinancial institution; and, neither gap nor duration is useful in examining a firm's sensitivity to movements in foreign exchange rates or commodity prices. What is needed is a more general method for quantifying financial price risk—a method that can handle firms other than financial institutions and financial exposures other than interest rates.

To get a measure of the responsiveness of the value of the firm to changes in the financial prices, we must first define a measure of the value of the firm. As with interest rate risk for financial institutions, this value measure could be a "flow" measure (gap analysis uses net interest income) or a "stock" measure (duration uses the market value of the portfolio).

Flow Measures. Within a specific firm, estimation of the sensitivity of income flows is an analysis that can be performed as part of the planning and budgeting process. The trade press suggests that some firms have begun using simulation models to examine the responsiveness of their pre-tax income to changes in interest rates, exchange rates, and commodity prices.[9] Beginning with base case assumptions about the financial prices, the firm obtains a forecast for revenues, costs, and the resulting pre-tax income. Then, it considers alternative values for an interest rate or an exchange rate or a commodity price and obtains a new forecast for revenues, costs, and pre-tax income. By observing how the firm's projected sales, costs and income move in response to changes in these financial prices, management is able to trace out a risk profile similar to that in Figure 1.

In making such an estimation, two inherent problems confront the analyst: (1) this approach requires substantial data and (2) it relies on the ability of the researcher to make explicit, accurate forecasts of sales and costs under alternative scenarios for the financial prices. For both these reasons, such an approach is generally feasible only for analysts within a specific firm.

Stock Measures. Given the data requirements noted above, analysts outside the firm generally rely on market valuations, the most widely used of which is the current market value of the equity. Using a technique much like the one used to estimate a firm's "beta," an outside observer could measure the historical sensitivity of the company's equity value to changes in interest rates, foreign exchange rates, and commodity prices.

For example, suppose we wished to determine the sensitivity of a company's value to the following financial prices:
● the one-year T-bill interest rate;
● the Deutsche Mark / Dollar exchange rate;
● the Pound Sterling / Dollar exchange rate;
● the Yen / Dollar exchange rate; and
● the price of oil.

---

7. Note the contrast with the gap approach, which relates changes in the interest rate to changes in net interest income.

8. The calculations in Table 1 are based on the use of MacCauley's duration. If we continue to apply MacCauley's duration (D), this equation is only an approximation. To be exact, modified duration should be used. For a development of this relation, see George G. Kaufman, G.O. Bierwag, and Alden Toevs, eds. *Innovations in Bond Portfolio Management: Duration Analysis and Immunization* (Greenwich, Conn.: JAI Press, 1983).

9. See for instance, Paul Dickens, cited in note 2.

TABLE 2
MEASUREMENTS OF
EXPOSURES TO
INTEREST RATE,
FOREIGN EXCHANGE
RATES, AND OIL PRICES

Percentage Change In	Chase Manhattan		Caterpillar		Exxon	
	Parameter Estimate	T Value	Parameter Estimate	T Value	Parameter Estimate	T Value
Price of 1-Year T-Bill	2.598*	1.56	− 3.221**	1.76	1.354	1.24
Price of DM	− 0.276	0.95	0.344	1.07	− 0.066	0.35
Price of Sterling	0.281	1.16	− 0.010	0.38	0.237*	1.50
Price of Yen	− 0.241	0.96	0.045	0.16	− 0.278**	1.69
Price of WTI Crude	0.065	1.21	− 0.045	0.77	0.082***	2.33

* Significant at 90% single tailed
** Significant at 90%
*** Significant at 95%

We could estimate this relation by performing a simple linear regression as follows:[10]

$$R_t = a + b_1 \left(\frac{\Delta P_{TB}}{P_{TB}}\right)_t + b_2 \left(\frac{\Delta P_{DM}}{P_{DM}}\right)_t + b_3 \left(\frac{\Delta P_{\pounds}}{P_{\pounds}}\right)_t + b_4 \left(\frac{\Delta P_y}{P_y}\right)_t + b_5 \left(\frac{\Delta P_{OIL}}{P_{OIL}}\right)_t$$

where R is the rate of return on the firm's equity; $\Delta P_{TB} / P_{TB}$ is the percentage change in the price of a one-year T-bill; $\Delta P_{DM}/P_{DM}, \Delta P_{\pounds}/P_{\pounds}$, and $\Delta P_y/P_y$ are the percentage changes in the dollar prices of the three foreign currencies; and $\Delta P_{OIL} / P_{OIL}$ is the percentage change in the price of crude oil. The estimate of b_1 provides a measure of the sensitivity of the value of the firm to changes in the one-year T-bill rate; b_2, b_3, and b_4 estimate its sensitivity to the exchange rates; and b_5 estimates its sensitivity to the oil price.[11]

To illustrate the kind of results this technique would yield, we present three examples: a bank, Chase Manhattan, an industrial, Caterpillar, and an oil company, Exxon. For the period January 6, 1984 to December 2, 1988 we calculated weekly (Friday close to Friday close) share returns and the corresponding weekly percentage changes in the price of a one-year

T-bill rate, the dollar prices of a Deutsche Mark, a Pound Sterling, and a Yen, and the price of West Texas Intermediate crude. Using these data, we estimated our regression equation. The results of these estimations are displayed in Table 2.

Given the tendency of banks to accept short-dated deposits to fund longer-dated assets (loans), it is not surprising that our estimates for Chase Manhattan indicate an inverse exposure to interest rates. Although only marginally significant, the positive coefficient indicates that an increase in the one-year T-bill

TABLE 2.A

Bank	Estimated Sensitivity	T-Value
Bank of America	3.2	1.5
Bankers Trust	2.2	1.4
Chase	2.6	1.6
First Chicago	3.0	1.6
Manufacturers Hanover	3.2	1.9

10. In effect, this equation represents a variance decomposition. While it is a multifactor model, it is not related in any important way to the APT approach suggested by Ross and Roll. Instead, it is probably more accurate to view the approach we suggest as an extension of the market model. In its more complete form, as described in Chapter 2 of our book *Managing Financial Risk*, the regression equation would include the rate of return to the market ("beta") as well as the percentage changes in the financial prices, and would thus look as follows:

$$R_t = a + \beta R_{m,t} + b_1 PC(P_{TB}) + b_2 PC(P_{DM}) + b_3 PC(P_{\pounds}) + b_4 PC(P_y) + b_5 PC(P_{OIL})$$

This more complete model is based on a number of earlier studies: French/Ruback/Schwert (1983) ("Effects of Nominal Contracting on Stock Returns," *Journal of Political Economy*, Vol. 91 No. 1) on the impact of unexpected inflation on share returns, Flannery/James (1984) ("The Effect of Interest Rate Changes on Common Stock Returns of Financial Institutions," *Journal of Finance* Vol. 39 No. 4) and Scott/Peterson (1986) ("Interest Rate Risk and Equity Values of Hedged and Unhedged Financial Intermediaries," *Journal of Financing Research* Vol. 9 No. 6)

on the impact of interest rate changes on share prices for financial firms, and Sweeney/Warga (1986) ("The Pricing of Interest Rate Risk: Evidence from the Stock Market," *Journal of Finance* Vol. 41 No. 2) on the impact of interest rate risk on share prices for nonfinancial firms. This model does exhibit the problems of measuring the reaction of firm value to changes in exchange rates, which are described by Donald Lessard in "Finance and Global Competition: Exploiting Financial Scope and Coping with Volatile Exchange Rates," *Midland Corporate Finance Journal* (Fall 1986).

For expositional purposes, we use in this paper the shorter form of the equation. This abbreviated model is acceptable empirically given the small correlations which exist between the percentage changes in the financial prices and the market return.

11. These coefficients actually measure elasticities. Further, had we used the percentage change in the quantity, (1 + one-year T-bill rate), instead of the percentage change in the price of the one-year T-bill, the coefficient b_1 could be interpreted as a "duration" measure.

THE DATA REFLECT THE FACT THAT, AS CATERPILLAR HAS MOVED ITS
PRODUCTION FACILITIES, THE FIRM HAS CHANGED FROM BEING
POSITIVELY EXPOSED TO THE YEN TO BEING NEGATIVELY EXPOSED TO
THE YEN.

TABLE 2.B

	1984	1985	1986	1987	1988
Parameter Estimate for Percentage Change in Price of Yen	1.72	0.15	0.33	-1.08	-0.85
T-Value	1.59	0.31	0.65	1.08	1.53

TABLE 2.C

	1984	1985	1986	1987	1988
Parameter Estimate for Percentage Change in Price of Oil	0.80	0.15	0.09	0.05	-0.01
T-Value	3.94	0.85	2.79	0.37	0.17

rate (or a decrease in the price of the T-bill) is expected to lead to a decrease in the bank's value.

Additional information can be obtained by comparing the coefficient estimates among firms in the same industry. For example, we can compare the estimated sensitivity of Chase's value to the one-year T-bill rate to the sensitivities of other banks as shown in Table 2.A.

In contrast to the bank's inverse exposure, Caterpillar appears to have a positive exposure to the one-year T-bill rate. That is, the negative regression coefficient indicates that increases in the one-year T-bill rate (or decreases in the price of the T-bill) lead to increases in the value of the firm.

Even more surprising, though, given much that has been written about Caterpillar's exposure to foreign currency changes, is the lack of any significant exposure to the yen. This result is more understandable if we break up this 5-year span into shorter intervals and look at Caterpillar's sensitivity to the price of the yen on a year-by-year basis. (See Table 2.B.) The data reflect the fact that, as Caterpillar has moved its production facilities, the firm has changed from being positively exposed to the yen (such that an increase in the value of the dollar would harm Caterpillar) to being negatively exposed to the yen (an increase in the value of the dollar now helps Caterpillar).

Unlike the other two firms, the estimate for Exxon's exposure to interest rates is not statistically significant (not, at least, to the one-year T-bill rate). Exxon does exhibit the expected positive exposure to the price of oil. But our estimates also reflect the now common view, reported in the financial press and elsewhere, that Exxon's exposure to the price of oil has been declining over time—both in size and consistency (as measured by statistical significance). (See Table 2.C.) Given its international production and distribution, as well as its international portfolio of assets, Exxon also exhibits marginally significant exposures to foreign exchange rates. Our estimates suggest Exxon benefits from an increase in the value of the pound but is harmed by an increase in the value of the yen.

Measuring Corporate Exposure: Summing Up

The purpose of this first section, then, has been to outline a statistical technique (similar to that used to calculate a firm's "beta") that can be used to provide management with an estimate of the sensitivity of firm value to changes in a variety of financial variables. Such measures can be further refined by using information from other sources. For example, the same regression technique can be used, only substituting changes in the firm's periodic earnings and cash flows for the changes in stock prices in our model. There are, however, two principal advantages of our procedure over the use of such accounting numbers: (1) market reactions are likely to capture the entire capitalized value of changes in firm value in response to financial price changes; and (2) regression analysis using stock prices, besides being much faster and cheaper, can be done using publicly available information.

THE TOOLS FOR MANAGING FINANCIAL RISK: A BUILDING BLOCK APPROACH[12]

If it turns out that a firm is subject to significant financial price risk, management may choose to hedge that risk.[13] One way of doing so is by using an "on-balance-sheet" transaction. For example, a company could manage a foreign exchange exposure resulting from overseas competition by borrowing in the competitor's currency or by moving production abroad. But such on-balance sheet methods can be costly and, as firms like Caterpillar have discovered, inflexible.[14]

Alternatively, financial risks can be managed with the use of off-balance-sheet instruments. The four fundamental off-balance-sheet instruments are forwards, futures, swaps, and options.

When we first began to attempt to understand these financial instruments, we were confronted by what seemed an insurmountable barrier to entry. The participants in the various markets all seemed to possess a highly specialized expertise that was applicable in only one market to the exclusion of all others (and the associated trade publications served only to tighten the veil of mystery that "experts" have always used to deny entry to novices). Options were discussed as if they were completely unrelated to forwards or futures, which in turn seemed to have nothing to do with the latest innovation, swaps. Adding to the complexities of the individual markets was the welter of jargon that seems to have grown up around each, thus further obscuring any common ground that might exist. (Words such as "ticks," "collars," "strike prices," and "straddles" suddenly had acquired a remarkable currency.) In short, we seemed to find ourselves looking up into a Wall Street Tower of Babel, with each group of market specialists speaking in different languages.

But, after now having observed these instruments over the past several years, we have been struck by how little one has to dig before superficial differences give way to fundamental unity. And, in marked contrast to the specialized view of most Wall Street practitioners, we take a more "generalist" approach—one that treats forwards, futures, swaps, and options not as four unique instruments and markets, but rather as four interrelated instruments for dealing with a single problem: managing financial risk. In fact, we have come up with a little analogy that captures the spirit of our conclusion, one which goes as follows: The four basic off-balance-sheet instruments—forwards, futures, swaps, and options—are much like those plastic building blocks children snap together. You can either build the instruments from one another, or you can combine the instruments into larger creations that appear (but appearances deceive) altogether "new."

Forward Contracts

Of the four instruments, the forward contract is the oldest and, perhaps for this reason, the most straightforward. A forward contract obligates its owner to buy a specified asset on a specified date at a price (known as the "exercise price") specified at the origination of the contract. If, at maturity, the actual price is higher than the exercise price, the contract owner makes a profit equal to the difference; if the price is lower, he suffers a loss.

In Figure 2, the payoff from buying a forward contract is illustrated with a hypothetical risk profile. If the actual price at contract maturity is higher than the expected price, the inherent risk results in a decline in the value of the firm; but this decline is offset by the profit on the forward contract. Hence, for the risk profile illustrated, the forward contract provides an effective hedge. (If the risk profile were positively instead of negatively sloped, the risk would be managed by selling instead of buying a forward contract.)

Besides its payoff profile, a forward contract has two other features that should be noted. First, the default (or credit) risk of the contract is two-sided. The contract owner either receives or makes a payment, depending on the price movement of the underlying

12. This section of the article is adapted from Charles W. Smithson, "A LEGO Approach to Financial Engineering: An Introduction to Forwards, Futures, Swaps, and Options," *Midland Corporate Finance Journal* 4 (Winter 1987).

13. In this paper we do not address the question of why public corporations hedge. For a discussion of the corporate decision whether or not to hedge financial price exposures, see Alan Shapiro and Sheridan Titman, "An Integrated Approach to Corporate Risk Management," *Midland Corporate Finance Journal* 3 (Summer 1985). For other useful theoretical discussions of the corporate hedging decision, see David Mayers and Clifford Smith, "On the Corporate Demand for Insurance," *Journal of Business* 55 (April 1982) (a less technical version of which was published as "The Corporate Insurance Decision," *Chase Financial Quarterly* (Vol.

1 No. 3) Spring 1982); Rene Stulz, "Optimal Hedging Policies," *Journal of Financial and Quantitative Analysis* 19 (June 1984); Clifford Smith and Rene Stulz, "The Determinants of Firms' Hedging Policies," *Journal of Financial* and *Quantitative Analysis* 20 (December 1985).

For some empirical tests of the above theoretical work, see David Mayers and Clifford Smith, "On the Corporate Demand for Insurance: Some Empirical Evidence," working paper, 1988; and Deana Nance, Clifford Smith and Charles Smithson, "The Determinants of Off-Balance-Sheet Hedging: An Empirical Analysis," working paper 1988.

14. See "Caterpillar's Triple Whammy," *Fortune*, October 27, 1986.

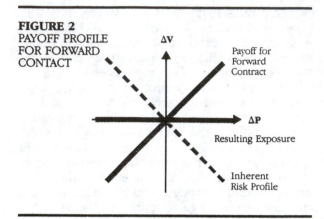

FIGURE 2
PAYOFF PROFILE
FOR FORWARD
CONTACT

asset. Second, the value of the forward contract is conveyed only at the contract's maturity; no payment is made either at origination or during the term of the contract.

Futures Contracts

The basic form of the futures contract is identical to that of the forward contract; a futures contract also obligates its owner to purchase a specified asset at a specified exercise price on the contract maturity date. Thus, the payoff profile for the purchaser of a forward contract as presented in Figure 2 could also serve to illustrate the payoff to the holder of a futures contract.

But, unlike the case of forwards, credit or default risk can be virtually eliminated in a futures market. Futures markets use two devices to manage default risk. First, instead of conveying the value of a contract through a single payment at maturity, any change in the value of a futures contract is conveyed at the end of the day in which it is realized. Look again at Figure 2. Suppose that, on the day after origination, the financial price rises and, consequently, the financial instrument has a positive value. In the case of a forward contract, this value change would not be received until contract maturity. With a futures contract, this change in value is received at the end of the day. In the language of the futures markets, the futures contract is "marked-to-market" and "cash settled" daily.

Because the performance period of a futures contract is reduced by marking to market, the risk of default declines accordingly. Indeed, because the value of the futures contract is paid or received at the end of each day, Fischer Black likened a futures contract to "a series of forward contracts [in which] each day, yesterday's contract is settled and today's contract is written."[15] That is, a futures contract is like a sequence of forwards in which the "forward" contract written on day 0 is settled on day 1 and is replaced, in effect, with a new "forward" contract reflecting the new day 1 expectations. This new contract is then itself settled on day 2 and replaced, and so on until the day the contract ends.

The second feature of futures contracts which reduces default risk is the requirement that all market participants—sellers and buyers alike—post a performance bond called the "margin."[16] If my futures contract increases in value during the trading day, this gain is added to my margin account at the day's end. Conversely, if my contract has lost value, this loss is deducted from my margin account. And, if my margin account balance falls below some agreed-upon minimum, I am required to post additional bond; that is, my margin account must be replenished or my position will be closed out.[17] Because the position will be closed before the margin account is depleted, performance risk is eliminated.[18]

Note that the exchange itself has not been proposed as a device to reduce default risk. Daily settlement and the requirement of a bond reduce default risk, but the existence of an exchange (or clearinghouse) merely serves to transform risk. More specifically, the exchange deals with the two-sided risk inherent in forwards and futures by serving as the counterparty to all transactions. If I wish to buy or sell a futures contract, I buy from or sell to the exchange. Hence, I need only evaluate the credit risk of the exchange, not of some specific counterparty.

The primary economic function of the exchange is to reduce the costs of transacting in futures

15. See Fischer Black "The Pricing to Commodity Contracts," *Journal of Financial Economics* 3 (1976), 167-179.

16. Keep in mind that if you buy a futures contract, you are taking a long position in the underlying asset. Conversely, selling a futures contract is equivalent to taking a short position.

17. When the contract is originated on the U.S. exchanges, an "initial margin" is required. Subsequently, the margin account balance must remain above the "maintenance margin." If the margin account balance falls below the maintenance level, the balance must be restored to the initial level.

18. Note that this discussion has ignored daily limits. If there are daily limits on the movement of futures prices, large changes in expectations about the underlying asset can effectively close the market. (The market opens, immediately moves the limit, and then is effectively closed until the next day.) Hence, there could exist an instance in which the broker desires to close out a customer's position but is not able to immediately because the market is experiencing limit moves. In such a case, the statement that performance risk is "eliminated" is too strong.

FIGURE 3

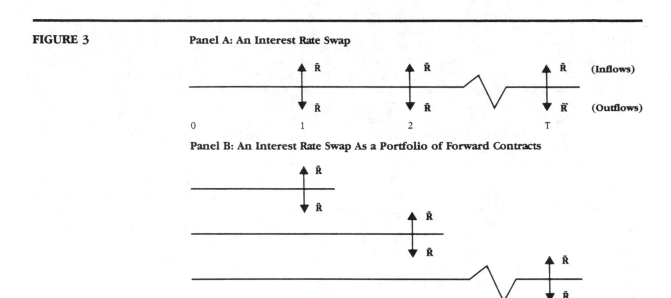

Panel A: An Interest Rate Swap

Panel B: An Interest Rate Swap As a Portfolio of Forward Contracts

contracts. The anonymous trades made possible by the exchange, together with the homogeneous nature of the futures contracts—standardized assets, exercise dates (four per year), and contract sizes—enables the futures markets to become relatively liquid. However, as was made clear by recent experience of the London Metal Exchange, the existence of the exchange does not in and of itself eliminate the possibility of default.[19]

In sum, a futures contract is much like a portfolio of forward contracts. At the close of business of each day, in effect, the existing forward-like contract is settled and a new one is written.[20] This daily settlement feature combined with the margin requirement allows futures contracts to eliminate the credit risk inherent in forwards.

Swap Contracts[21]

A swap contract is in essence nothing more complicated than a series of forward contracts strung together. As implied by its name, a swap contract obligates two parties to exchange, or "swap," some specified cash flows at specified intervals. The most common form is the interest rate swap, in which the cash flows are determined by two different interest rates.

Panel A of Figure 3 illustrates an interest rate swap from the perspective of a party who is paying out a series of cash flows determined by a fixed interest rate ($\tilde{R}$) in return for a series of cash flows determined by a floating interest rate ($\tilde{R}$).[22]

Panel B of Figure 3 serves to illustrate that this swap contract can be decomposed into a portfolio of

---

19. In November of 1985, the "tin cartel" defaulted on contracts for tin delivery on the London Metal Exchange, thereby making the exchange liable for the loss. A description of this situation is contained in "Tin Crisis in London Roils Metal Exchange," *The Wall Street Journal*, November 13, 1985.

From the point of view of the market, the exchange does not reduce default risk. The expected default rate is not affected by the existence of the exchange. However, the existence of the exchange can alter the default risk faced by an individual market participant. If I buy a futures contract for a specific individual, the default risk I face is determined by the default rate of that specific counterparty. If I instead buy the same futures contract through an exchange, my default risk depends on the default rate of not just my counterparty, but on the default rate of he entire market. Moreover, to the extent that the exchange is capitalized by equity from its members, the default risk I perceive is further reduced because I have a claim not against some specific counterparty, but rather against the exchange. Therefore, when I trade through the exchange, I am in a sense purchasing an insurance policy from the exchange.

20. A futures contract is like a portfolio of forward contracts; however, a futures contract and a portfolio of forward contracts become identical only if interest rates are "deterministic"—that is, known with certainty in advance. See Robert A. Jarrow and George S. Oldfield, "Forward Contracts and Futures Contracts," *Journal of Financial Economics* 9 (1981), 373-382; and John A. Cox, Jonathan E. Ingersoll, and Stephen A. Ross, "The Relation between Forward Prices and Futures Prices," *Journal of Financial Economics* 9 (1981), 321-346.

21. This section is based on Clifford W. Smith, Charles W. Smithson, and Lee M. Wakeman, "The Evolving Market for Swaps," *Midland Corporate Finance Journal* Winter (1986), 20-32.

22. Specifically, the interest rate swap cash flows are determined as follows: The two parties agree to some notional principal, P. (The principal is notional in the sense that it is only used to determine the magnitude of cash flows; is is not paid or received by either party.) At each settlement date, 1, 2,..., T the party illustrated makes a payment $\tilde{R} = \tilde{r}P$, where $\tilde{r}$ is the T-period fixed rate which existed at origination. At each settlement, the party illustrated receives $\tilde{R} = \tilde{r}P$, where $\tilde{r}$ is the floating rate for that period (e.g., at settlement date 2. the interest rate used is the one-period rate in effect at period 1).

forward contracts. At each settlement date, the party to this swap contract has an implicit forward contract on interest rates: the party illustrated is obligated to sell a fixed-rate cash flow for an amount specified at the origination of the contract. In this sense, a swap contract is also like a portfolio of forward contracts.

In terms of our earlier discussion, this means that the solid line in Figure 2 could also represent the payoff from a swap contract. Specifically, the solid line in Figure 3 would be consistent with a swap contract in which the party illustrated receives cash flows determined by one price (say, the U.S. Treasury bond rate) and makes payments determined by another price (say, LIBOR). Thus, in terms of their ability to manage risk, forwards, futures, and swaps all function in the same way.

But identical payoff *patterns* notwithstanding, the instruments all differ with respect to default risk. As we saw, the performance period of a forward is equal to its maturity; and because no performance bond is required, a forward contract is a pure credit instrument. Futures both reduce the performance period (to one day) and require a bond, thereby eliminating credit risk. Swap contracts use only one of these mechanisms to reduce credit risk; they reduce the performance period.[23] This point becomes evident in Figure 3. Although the maturity of the contract is T periods, the performance period is generally not T periods long but is instead a single period. Thus, given a swap and a forward contract of roughly the same maturity, the swap is likely to impose far less credit risk on the counterparties to the contract than the forward.

At each settlement date throughout a swap contract, the changes in value are transferred between the counterparties. To illustrate this in terms of Figure 3, suppose that interest rates rise on the day after origination. The value of the swap contract illustrated has risen. This value change will be conveyed to the contract owner not at maturity (as would be the case with a forward contract) nor at the end of that day (as would be the case with a futures contract). Instead, at the first settlement date, part of the value change is conveyed in the form of the "difference check" paid by one party to the other. To repeat,

then, the performance period is less than that of a forward, but not as short as that of a futures contract.[24] (Keep in mind that we are comparing instruments with the same maturities.)

Let us reinforce the two major points made thus far. First, a swap contract, like a futures contract, is like a portfolio of forward contracts. Therefore, the payoff profiles for each of these three instruments are identical. Second, the primary difference among forwards, futures, and swaps is the amount of default risk they impose on counterparties to the contract. Forwards and futures represent the extremes, and swaps are the intermediate case.

Option Contracts

As we have seen, the owner of a forward, futures, or swap contract has an *obligation* to perform. In contrast, an option gives its owner a *right*, not an obligation. An option giving its owner the right to buy an asset at a pre-determined price—a call option—is provided in Panel A of Figure 4. The owner of the contract has the right to purchase the asset at a specified future date at a price agreed-upon today. Thus, if the price rises, the value of the option also goes up. But because the option contract owner is not obligated to purchase the asset if the price moves against him, the value of the option remains unchanged (at zero) if the price declines.[25]

The payoff profile for the party who sold the call option (also known as the call "writer") is shown in Panel B. In contrast to the buyer of the option, the seller of the call option has the *obligation* to perform. For example, if the owner of the option elects to exercise his option to buy the asset, the seller of the option is obligated to sell the asset.

Besides the option to buy an asset, there is also the option to sell an asset at a specified price, known as a "put" option. The payoff to the buyer of a put is illustrated in Panel C of Figure 4, and the payoff to the seller of the put is shown in Panel D.

Pricing Options: Up to this point, we have considered only the payoffs to the option contracts. We have side-stepped the thorniest issue—the valuation of option contracts.

---

23. There are instances in a which bond has been posted in the form of collateral. As should be evident, in this case the swap becomes very like a futures contract.

24. Unlike futures, for which all of any change in contract value is paid/received at the daily settlements, swap contracts convey only part of the total value change at the periodic settlements.

25. For continuity, we continue to use the $\Delta V, \Delta P$ convention in figures. To compare these figures with those found in most texts, treat ΔV as deviations from zero ($\Delta V = V - 0$) and remember that P measures deviations from expected price ($\Delta P = P - P_e$).

BLACK AND SCHOLES TOOK WHAT MIGHT BE DESCRIBED AS A
"BUILDING BLOCK" APPROACH TO THE VALUATION OF OPTIONS...THEY
DEMONSTRATED THAT A CALL OPTION COULD BE REPLICATED BY A
CONTINUOUSLY ADJUSTING PORTFOLIO OF TWO SECURITIES: FORWARD
CONTRACTS AND RISKLESS SECURITIES.

FIGURE 4
PAYOFF PROFILES OF
PUTS AND CALLS

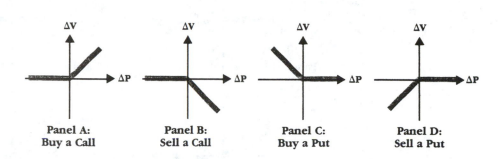

The breakthrough in option pricing theory came with the work of Fischer Black and Myron Scholes in 1973.[26] Conveniently for our purposes, Black and Scholes took what might be described as a "building block" approach to the valuation of options. Look again at the call option illustrated in Figure 4. For increases in the financial price, the payoff profile for the option is that of a forward contract. For decreases in the price, the value of the option is constant—like that of a "riskless" security such as a Treasury bill.

The work of Black and Scholes demonstrated that a call option could be replicated by a continuously adjusting ("dynamic") portfolio of two securities: (1) forward contracts on the underlying asset and (2) riskless securities. As the financial price rises, the "call option equivalent" portfolio contains an increasing proportion of forward contracts on the asset. Conversely, the replicating portfolio contains a decreasing proportion of forwards as the price of the asset falls.

Because this replicating portfolio is effectively a synthetic call option, arbitrage activity should ensure that its value closely approximates the market price of exchange-traded call options. In this sense, the value of a call option, and thus the premium that would be charged its buyer, is determined by the value of its option equivalent portfolio.

Panel A of Figures 5 illustrates the payoff profile for a call option which includes the premium. This figure (and all of the option figures thus far) illustrates an "at-the-money" option—that is, an option for which the exercise price is the prevailing expected price. As Panels A and B of Figure 5 illustrate, an at-the-money option is paid for by sacrificing a significant amount of the firm's potential gains. However, the price of a call option falls as the exercise price increases relative to the prevailing price of the asset. This means that if an option buyer is willing to accept larger potential losses in return for paying a lower option premium, he would then consider using an "out-of-the-money" option.

An out-of-the-money call option is illustrated in Panel C of Figure 5. As shown in Panel D, the out-of-the-money option provides less downside protection, but the option premium is significantly less. The lesson to be learned here is that the option buyer can alter his payoff profile simply by changing the exercise price.

For our purposes, however, the most important feature of options is that they are not as different from other financial instruments as they might first seem. Options do have a payoff profile that differs significantly from that of forward contracts (or futures or swaps). But, option payoff profiles can be duplicated by a combination of forwards and risk-free securities. Thus, we find that options have more in common with the other instruments than was first apparent. Futures and swaps, as we saw earlier, are in essence nothing more than portfolios of forward contracts; and options, as we have just seen, are very much akin to portfolios of forward contracts and risk-free securities.

This point is reinforced if we consider ways that options can be combined. Consider a portfolio constructed by buying a call and selling a put with the

26. See Fischer Black and Myron Scholes, "The Pricing of Options and Corporate Liabilities," *Journal of Political Economy* 1973. For a less technical discussion of the model, see "The Black-Scholes Option Pricing Model for Alterna-tive Underlying Instruments," *Financial Analysts Journal*, November-December, 1984, 23-30.

FIGURE 5

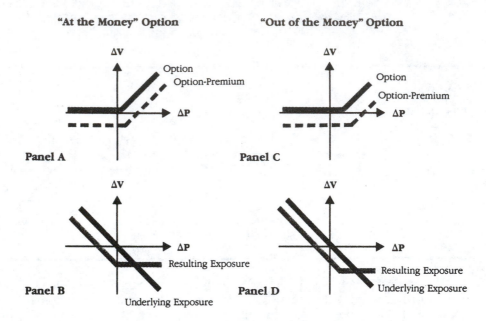

same exercise price. As the left side of Figure 6 illustrates, the resulting portfolio (long a call, short a put) has a payoff profile equivalent to that of buying a forward contract on the asset. Similarly, the right side of Figure 6 illustrates that a portfolio made up of selling a call and buying a put (short a call, long a put) is equivalent to selling a forward contract.

The relationship illustrated in Figure 6 is known more formally as "put-call parity." The special import of this relationship, at least in this context, is the "building block construction" it makes possible: two options can be "snapped together" to yield the payoff profile for a forward contract, which is identical to the payoff profile for futures and swaps.

At the beginning of this section, then, it seemed that options would be very different from forwards, futures, and swaps—and in some ways they are. But we discovered two building block relations between options and the other three instruments: (1) options can be replicated by "snapping together" a forward, futures, or swap contract together with a position in risk-free securities; and (2) calls and puts can be combined to become forwards.

The Financial Building Blocks

Forwards, futures, swaps, and options—they all look so different from one another. And if you read the trade publications or talk to the specialists that transact in the four markets, the apparent differences among the instruments are likely to seem even more pronounced.

But it turns out that forwards, futures, swaps, and options are not each unique constructions, but rather more like those plastic building blocks that children combine to make complex structures. To understand the off-balance-sheet instruments, you don't need a lot of market-specific knowledge. All you need to know is how the instruments can be linked to one another. As we have seen, (1) futures can be built by "snapping together" a package of forwards; (2) swaps can also be built by putting together a package of forwards; (3) synthetic options can be constructed by combining a forward with a riskless security; and (4) options can be combined to produce forward contracts—or, conversely, forwards can be pulled apart to replicate a package of options.

FIGURE 6

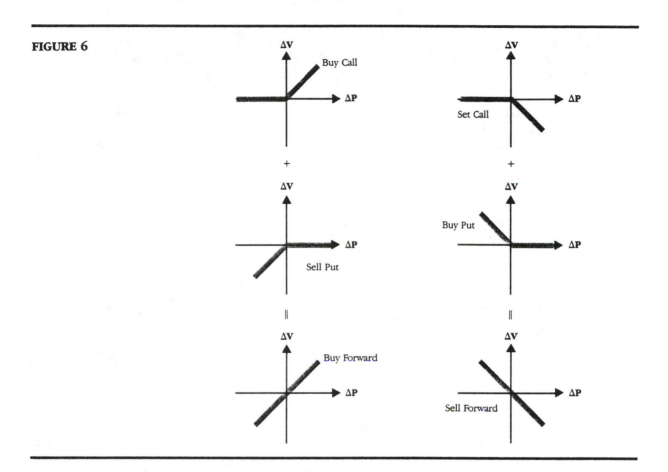

Having shown you all the building blocks and how they fit together in simple constructions, we now want to demonstrate how they can be used to create more complicated, customized financial instruments that in turn can be used to manage financial risks.

ASSEMBLING THE BUILDING BLOCKS

Using The Building Blocks to Manage an Exposure

Consider a company whose market value is directly related to unexpected changes in some financial price, P. The risk profile of this company is illustrated in Figure 7. How could we use the financial building blocks to modify this inherent exposure?

The simplest solution is to use a forward, a futures, or a swap to neutralize this exposure. This is shown in Panel A of Figure 8.

But, the use of a forward, a futures, or a swap

FIGURE 7

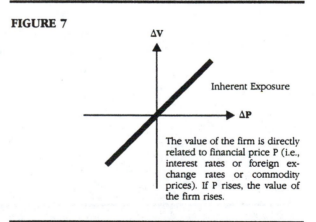

The value of the firm is directly related to financial price P (i.e., interest rates or foreign exchange rates or commodity prices). If P rises, the value of the firm rises.

eliminates possible losses by giving up the possibility of profiting from favorable outcomes. The company might want to minimize the effect of unfavorable outcomes while still allowing the possibility of gaining from favorable ones. This can be accom-

FIGURE 8

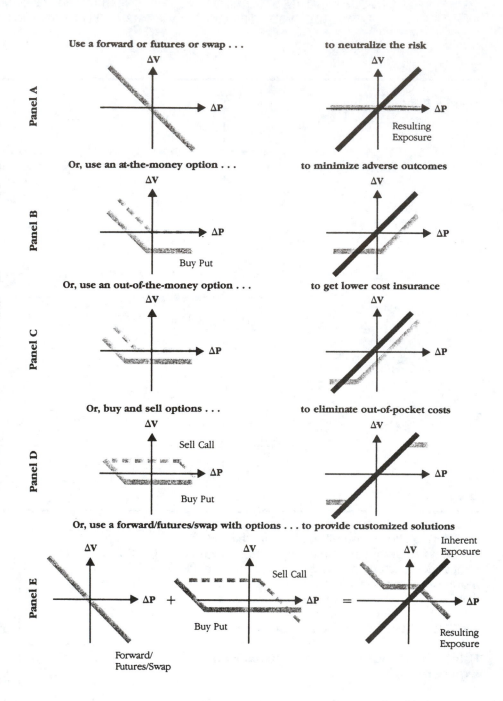

plished using options. The payoff profile of an at-the-money option (including the premium paid to buy the option) is shown on the left side of Panel B. Snapping this building block onto the inherent exposure profile gives the resulting exposure illustrated on the right side of panel B.

A common complaint about options—especially at-the-money options—is that they are "too expensive." To reduce the option premium, you can think about using an out-of-the-money option. As Panel C of Figure 8 illustrates, the firm has thereby given up some protection from adverse outcomes in return for paying a lower premium.

But, with an out-of-the-money option, some premium expense remains. Panel D illustrates how the out-of-pocket expense can be *eliminated*. The firm can sell a call option with an exercise price chosen so as to generate premium income equal to the premium due on the put option it wishes to purchase. In building block parlance, we snap the "buy-a-put" option onto the inherent risk profile to reduce downside outcomes; and we snap on the "sell-a-call" option to fund this insurance by giving up some of the favorable outcomes.

Panel E reminds us that forwards, futures, and swaps can be used in combination with options. Suppose the treasurer of the company we have been considering comes to you with the following request:

I think that this financial price, P, is going to fall dramatically. And, while I know enough about financial markets to know that P could actually rise a little, I am sure it will not rise by much. I want some kind of financial solution that will let me benefit when my predictions come to pass. But I don't want to pay any out-of-pocket premiums. Instead, I want this financial engineering product to pay me a premium.

If you look at the firm's inherent risk profile in Figure 7, this seems like a big request. The firm's inherent position is such that it would lose rather than gain from big decreases in P.

The resulting exposure profile shown on the right side of Panel E is the one the firm wants: it benefits from large decreases in P, is protected against small increases in P (though not against large increases) and receives a premium for the instrument.

How was this new profile achieved? As illustrated on the left side of Panel E, we first snapped a forward/futures/swap position onto the original risk profile to neutralize the firm's inherent exposure. We then sold a call option and bought a put option with exercise prices set such that the income from selling the call exceeded the premium required to buy the put.

No high level math was required. Indeed, we did this bit of financial engineering simply by looking through the box of financial building blocks until we found those that snapped together to give us the profile we wanted.

Using the Building Blocks to Redesign Financial Instruments

Now that you understand how forwards, futures, swaps, and options are all fundamentally related, it is a relatively short step to thinking about how the instruments can be combined with each other to give one financial instrument the characteristics of another. Rather than talk about this in the abstract, let's look at some examples of how this has been done in the marketplace.

Combining Forwards with Swaps: Suppose a firm's value is currently unaffected by interest rate movements. But, at a known date in the future, it expects to become exposed to interest rates: if rates rise, the value of the firm will decrease.[27] To manage this exposure, the firm could use a forward, futures, or swap commencing at that future date. Such a product is known as a *forward* or *delayed start* swap. The payoff from a forward swap is illustrated in Panel C of Figure 9, where the party illustrated pays a fixed rate and receives floating starting in period 5.

Although this instrument is in effect a forward contract on a swap, it also, not surprisingly, can be constructed as a package of swaps. As Figure 9 illustrates, a forward swap is equivalent to a package of two swaps:

Swap 1—From period 1 to period T, the party pays fixed and receives floating.

Swap 2—From period 1 to period 4, the party pays floating and receives fixed.

Forwards with Option-like Characteristics: The addition of option-like characteristics to forward

---

27. For example, the firm may know that, in one year, it will require funds which will be borrowed at a floating rate, thereby giving the firm the inverse exposure to interest rates. Or, the firm may be adding a new product line, the demand for which is extremely sensitive to interest rate movements—as rates rise, the demand for the product decreases and cash flows to the firm decrease.

FIGURE 9

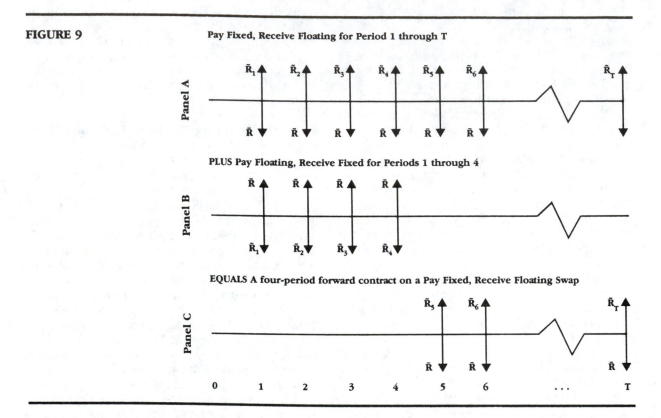

Pay Fixed, Receive Floating for Period 1 through T

PLUS Pay Floating, Receive Fixed for Periods 1 through 4

EQUALS A four-period forward contract on a Pay Fixed, Receive Floating Swap

contracts first appeared in the foreign exchange markets. To see how this was done, let's trace the evolution of these contracts.

Begin with a standard forward contract on foreign exchange. Panel A of Figure 10 illustrates a conventional forward contract on sterling with the forward sterling exchange rate (the "contract rate") set at $1.50 per pound sterling. If, at maturity, the spot price of sterling exceeds $1.50, the owner of this contract makes a profit (equal to the spot rate minus $1.50). Conversely, if at maturity the spot price of sterling is less than $1.50, the owner of this contract suffers a loss. The owner of the forward contract, however, might instead want a contract that allows him to profit if the price of sterling rises, but limits his losses if the price of sterling falls.[28] Such a contract would be a call option on sterling. Illustrated in Panel B of Figure 10 is a call option on sterling with an exercise price of $1.50. In this illustration we have assumed an

option premium of 5 cents (per pound sterling).

The payoff profile illustrated in Panel B of Figure 10 could also be achieved by altering the terms of the standard forward contract as follows:

1. Change the contract price so that the exercise price of the forward contract is no longer $1.50 but is instead $1.55. The owner of the forward contract agrees to purchase sterling at contract maturity at a price of $1.55 per unit; and

2. Permit the owner of the contract to break (i.e. "unwind") the agreement at a sterling price of $1.50.

This altered forward contract is referred to as a *break forward* contract.[29] In this break forward construction, the premium is effectively being paid by the owner of the break forward contract in the form of the above market contract exchange rate.

From our discussion of options, we also know that a call can be paid for with the proceeds from selling a put. The payoff profile for such a situation is

---

28. This discussion is adapted from Warren Edwardes and Edmond Levy, "Break Forwards: A Synthetic Option Hedging Instrument," *Midland Corporate Finance Journal* 5 (Summer 1987) 59-67.

29. According to Sam Srinivasulu in "Second-Generation Forwards: A Comparative Analysis," Business International Money Report, September 21, 1987, break forward is the name given to this construction by Midland Bank. It goes under other names: Boston Option (Bank of Boston), FOX—Forward with Optional Exit (Hambros Bank), and Cancelable Forward (Goldman Sachs)

FIGURE 10

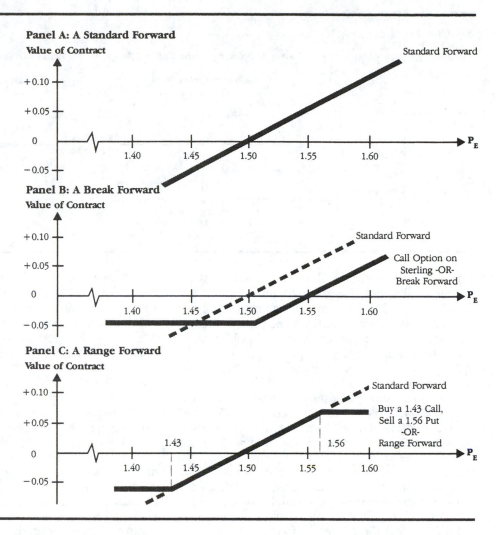

Panel A: A Standard Forward

Panel B: A Break Forward

Panel C: A Range Forward

illustrated in Panel C of Figure 10. In this illustration, we have assumed that the proceeds of a put option on sterling with an exercise price of $1.56 would carry the same premium as a call option on sterling with an exercise price of $1.43.[30]

A payoff profile identical to this option payoff profile could also be generated, however, simply by changing the terms of a standard forward contract to the following:

- at maturity, the buyer of the forward contract agrees to purchase sterling at a price of $1.50 per pound sterling;

- the buyer of the forward contract has the right to break the contract at a price of $1.43 per pound sterling; and

- the seller of the forward contract has the right to break the contract at a price of $1.56 per pound sterling.

Such a forward contract is referred to as a *range forward*.[31]

Swaps with Option-like Characteristics: Given that swaps can be viewed as packages of forward contracts, it should not be surprising that swaps can also be constructed to have option-like

30. These numbers are only for purposes of illustration. To determine the exercise prices at which the values of the puts and calls are equal, one would have to use an option pricing model.

31. As Srinivasulu, cited note 29, pointed out, this construction also appears under a number of names: range forward (Salomon Brothers), collar (Midland Montagu), flexible forward (Manufacturers Hanover), cylinder option (Citicorp), option fence (Bank of America) and mini-max (Goldman Sachs).

FIGURE 11
PAY-OFF PROFILE FOR
FLOOR-CEILING SWAPS

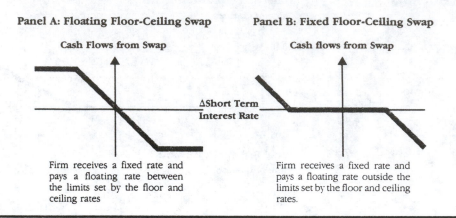

Panel A: Floating Floor-Ceiling Swap

Cash Flows from Swap

ΔShort Term
Interest Rate

Firm receives a fixed rate and
pays a floating rate between
the limits set by the floor and
ceiling rates

Panel B: Fixed Floor-Ceiling Swap

Cash flows from Swap

Firm receives a fixed rate and
pays a floating rate outside the
limits set by the floor and ceiling
rates.

characteristics like those illustrated for forwards. For example, suppose that a firm with a floating-rate liability wanted to limit its outflows should interest rates rise substantially; at the same time, it was willing to give up some potential gains should there instead be a dramatic decline in short-term rates. To achieve this end, the firm could modify the interest rate swap contract as follows:

As long as the interest rate neither rises by more than 200 basis points nor falls more than 100 basis points, the firm pays a floating rate and receives a fixed rate. But, if the interest is more than 200 basis points above or 100 basis points below the current rate, the firm receives and pays a fixed rate.

The resulting payoff profile for this floating floor-ceiling swap is illustrated in Panel A of Figure 11.

Conversely, the interest rate swap contract could have been modified as follows:

As long as the interest rate is within 200 basis points of the current rate, the firm neither makes nor receives a payment; but if the interest rate rises or falls by more than 200 basis points, the firm pays a floating rate and receives a fixed rate.

The payoff profile for the resulting fixed floor-ceiling swap is illustrated in Panel B of Figure 11.

Redesigned Options: To "redesign" an option, what is normally done is to put two or more options together to change the payoff profile. Examples abound in the world of the option trader. Some of the more colorfully-named combinations are *straddles*, *strangles*, and *butterflies*.[32]

To see how and why these kinds of creations evolve, let's look at a hypothetical situation. Suppose a firm was confronted with the inherent exposure illustrated in Panel A of Figure 12. Suppose further that the firm wanted to establish a floor on losses caused by changes in a financial price.

As you already know, this could be done by purchasing an out-of-the-money call option on the financial price. A potential problem with this solution, as we have seen, is the premium the firm has to pay. Is there a way the premium can be eliminated?

We have already seen that buying an out-of-the-money call can be financed by selling an out-of-the-money put. However, suppose that this out-of-the-money call is financed by selling a put with precisely the same exercise price—in which case, the put would be in-the-money. As illustrated in Panel B of Figure 12, the proceeds from selling the in-the-money put would exceed the cost of the out-of-the-money call. Therefore, to finance one out-of-the-money call, one would need sell only a fraction of one in-the-money put.

In Panel B, we have assumed that the put value is twice the call value; so, to finance one call, you need sell only 1/2 put. Panel C simply combines the payoff profiles for selling 1/2 put and buying one call with an exercise price of X. Finally, Panel D of Figure 12 combines the option combination in Panel C with the inherent risk profile in Panel A.

Note what has happened. The firm has obtained the floor it wanted, but there is no up-front premium.

---

32. For a discussion of traditional option strategies like straddles, strangles, and butterflies, see for instance chapter 7 of Richard M. Bookstaber, *Option Pricing and Strategies in Investing* (Addison-Wesley, 1981).

OUR POSITION WITH RESPECT TO "FINANCIAL ENGINEERING" IS THAT
THERE IS LITTLE NEW UNDER THE SUN. THE "NEW" PRODUCTS TYPICALLY
INVOLVE NOTHING MORE THAN PUTTING THE BUILDING BLOCKS
TOGETHER IN A NEW WAY.

FIGURE 12

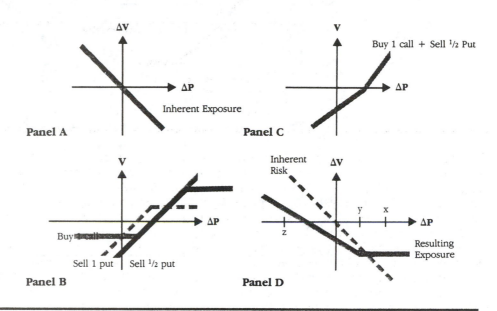

At the price at which the option is exercised, the value of the firm with the floor is the same as it would have been without the floor. The floor is paid for not with a fixed premium, but with a share of the firm's gains above the floor. If the financial price rises by X, the value of the firm falls to the floor and no premium is paid. If, however, the financial price rises by less, say Y, the value of the firm is higher and the firm pays a positive premium for the floor. And, if the financial price falls, say, by Z, the price it pays for the floor rises.

What we have here is a situation where the provider of the floor is paid with a share of potential gains, thereby leading to the name of this option combination—a *participation*. This construction has been most widely used in the foreign exchange market where they are referred to as *participating forwards*.[33]

Options on Other Financial Instruments

Options on futures contracts on bonds have been actively traded on the Chicago Board of Trade since 1982. The valuation of an option on a futures is a relatively straightforward extension of the tradi-

tional option pricing models.[34] Despite the close relation between futures and forwards and futures and swaps, the options on forwards (*options on forward rate agreements*) and options on swaps (*swaptions*) are much more recent.

More complicated analytically is the valuation of an option on an option, also known as a *compound option*.[35] Despite their complexity and resistance to valuation formulae, some options on options have begun to be traded. These include options on foreign exchange options and, most notably, options on interest rate options (caps), referred to in the trade as *captions*.

Using the Building Blocks to Design "New" Products

It's rare that a day goes by in the financial markets without hearing of at least one "new" or "hybrid" product. But, as you should have come to expect from us by now, our position with respect to "financial engineering" is that there is little new under the sun. The "new" products typically involve nothing more than putting the building blocks together in a new way.

33. For more on this construction, see Srinivalsulu cited in note 29 and 31.
34. Options on futures were originally discussed by Fischer Black in "The Pricing of Commodity Options," *Journal of Financial Economics* 3 (January-March 1976). A concise discussion of the modifications required in the Black-Scholes formula is contained in James F. Meisner and John W. Labuszewski,

"Modifying the Black-Scholes Option Pricing Model for Alternative Underlying Instruments," *Financial Analysts Journal* November/December 1984.
35. For a discussion of the problem of valuing compound options, see John C. Cox and Mark Rubinstein, *Options Markets* (Prentice-Hall, 1985) 412-415.

FIGURE 13
USING A SWAP TO
CREATE A REVERSE
FLOATING RATE LOAN

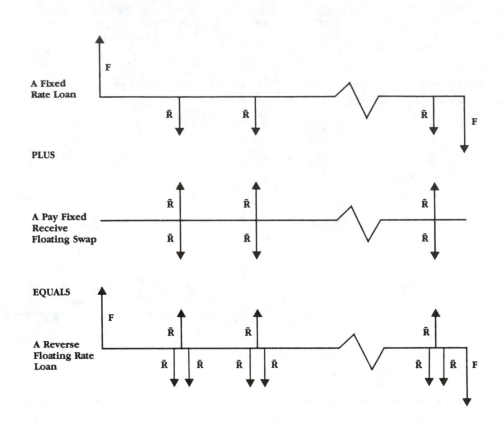

Reverse Floaters: One example of a hybrid security is provided in Figure 13. If we combine the issuance of a conventional fixed rate loan and an interest rate swap where the issuing party pays fixed and receives floating, the result is a reverse floating-rate loan. The net coupon payments on the hybrid loan are equal to twice the fixed rate ($\bar{r}$) minus the floating rate ($\tilde{r}$) times the principal (P), or

$$\text{Net Coupon} = (2\bar{r} - \tilde{r})P = 2\bar{R} - \tilde{R}$$

If the floating rate ($\tilde{r}$) rises, the net coupon payment falls.

Bonds with Embedded Options: Another form of hybrid securities has evolved from bonds with warrants. Bonds with warrants on the issuer's shares have become common. Bond issues have also recently appeared that feature warrants that can be exercised into foreign exchange and gold.

And, in 1986, Standard Oil issued a bond with an oil warrant. These notes stipulated that the principal payment at maturity would be a function of oil prices at maturity. As specified in the Prospectus, the holders of the 1990 notes will receive, in addition to a guaranteed minimum principal amount, "the excess...of the Crude Oil Price...over $25 multiplied by 170 barrels of Light Sweet Crude Oil." What this means is that the note has an embedded four-year option on 170 barrels of crude oil. If, at maturity, the value of Light Sweet Oklahoma Crude Oil exceeds $25, the holder of the note will receive (Oil Price − $25) x 170 plus the guaranteed minimum principal amount. If the value of Light Sweet Oklahoma Crude is less than $25 at maturity, the option expires worthless.[36]

The building block process has also been extended to changes in the timing of the options

---

36. Note that this issue did have a cap on the crude oil price at $40. Hence, the bondholder actually holds two options positions: long a call option at $25 per barrel and short a call option at $40 per barrel.

FIGURE 14   An Off-Market-Rate Bond

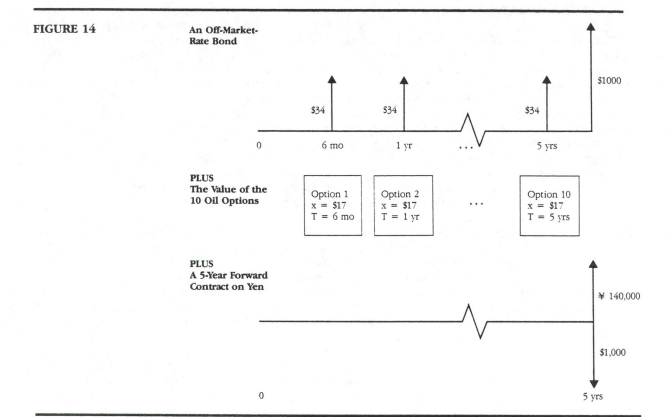

PLUS
The Value of the
10 Oil Options

PLUS
A 5-Year Forward
Contract on Yen

embedded in the bond. For a traditional bond with an attached warrant, there is only one option exerciseable at one point in time. More recent bonds have involved packages of options which can be exercised at different points in time.

The first time we saw this extension was in Forest Oil Corporation's proposed *Natural Gas Interest Indexed Debentures*. As set forth in the issue's red herring prospectus of July 1988, Forest Oil proposed to pay a stipulated base rate plus four basis points for each $0.01 by which the average gas spot price exceeds $1.76 per MMBTU (million British Thermal Units). In effect, then, this proposed 12-year "hybrid" debenture is a package consisting of one standard bond plus 24 options on the price of natural gas with maturities ranging from 6 months to 12 years.[37]

And, if we want to get a little fancier, we can consider the possibility of an *Oil Interest-Indexed, Dual-Currency Bond*.[38] Assume that the maturity of this issue is 5 years, with the semi-annual coupon pay-

ments indexed to the price of crude oil and the final principal repayment indexed to the value of yen. More specifically, assume that, for each $1000 of principal, the bondholder receives the following: (1) the greater of $34 or the value of two barrels of Sweet Light Crude Oil at each coupon date; and (2) 140,000 yen at maturity.

How would we value such a complicated package? The answer, again, is by breaking it down into the building blocks. As shown in Figure 14, this oil-indexed, dual currency bond consists of three basic components: (1) a straight bond paying $34 semi-annually; (2) 10 call options on the price of oil with an exercise price of $17 per barrel ($34/2) maturing sequentially every six months over a five-year period; and (3) a five-year forward contract on yen with an exercise price of 140 yen/dollar. As it turns out, then, this complicated-looking bond is nothing more than a combination of a standard bond, a series of options, and a forward contract.

---

37. As reported in the Wall Street Journal on September 21, 1988, Forest Oil withdrew its Natural Gas Indexed Bond in favor of a straight issue. However, in November of 1988, Magma Copper did issue senior subordinated notes on which the coupon payments were linked to the price of copper in much the same way as Forest's coupons would be linked to the price of natural gas.

38. Unlike the other structures discussed, this one has not yet been issued.

CONCLUDING REMARKS

The world is more volatile today than it was two decades ago. Today's corporate risk manager must deal with the potential impact on the firm of significant month-to-month (and sometimes day-to-day) changes in exchange rates, interest rates, and commodity prices. Volatility alone could put a well-run firm out of business, so financial price risk deserves careful attention. As this summary has demonstrated, there now exist techniques and tools for accomplishing this task.

This article makes three major points:

First, there are simple techniques that allow management (and outsiders as well) to identify and measure a firm's exposures. Besides managing "one-off" exposures (such as interest rate exposures from floating-rate borrowings or foreign exchange transaction and translation exposures), many firms are now recognizing their economic exposures. To measure such economic exposures, we have introduced the concept of the *risk profile*. Using this concept, we have proposed simple methods for quantifying the extent of an individual firm's exposures to interest rates, foreign exchange rates, and commodity prices. In the case of a financial firm's exposure to interest rate risk, the techniques of "gap" and "duration" analysis can be applied directly. For the more general case, we demonstrate how simple regression analysis (the same technique used in calculating a firm's "beta") can be used to measure a variety of exposures.

Second, the tools for managing financial risk are more simple than they appear. These financial instruments can be viewed as building blocks. The basic component is a forward contract. Both futures and swaps are like bundles of forward contracts; forwards, in fact, can be combined to yield futures and swaps. The primary differences between these two instruments are the way they deal with default risk and the degree of customization available.

Even options, moreover, can be related to forward contracts. An option on a given asset can be created by combining a position in a forward contract on the same asset with a riskless security; in short, forwards and T-bills can be combined to produce options.[39] Finally, options can be combined to create forward positions; for example, buying a call and shorting a put produces the same position as buying a forward contract.

Third, once you understand the four basic building blocks, it is a straightforward step to designing a customized strategy for managing your firm's exposure. Once the exposure is identified, it can be managed in a number of ways:
- by using one of the financial instruments—for example, by using an interest rate swap to hedge a building products firm's exposure to rising interest rates;
- by using combinations of the financial instruments—for example, buying a call and selling a put to minimize the out-of-pocket costs of the hedge; or
- by combining financial instruments with a debt instrument to create a hybrid security—for example, issuing an oil-indexed bond to hedge a firm's exposure to oil prices.

Our final point in all of this is very simple. Managing financial price risk with "financial engineering" sounds like something you need a degree from Caltech or M.I.T. to do. Designing effective solutions with the financial building blocks is easy.

---

39. This is most often referred to as a synthetic option or as dynamic option replication.

■ CLIFFORD SMITH

is Professor of Finance at the University of Rochester's Simon School of Business. He is an Editor of the *Journal of Financial Economics*. His research has centered on capital structure (especially on the role of bond covenants), rights offerings as an alternative to underwritings of equity issues, and the options market.

■ D. SYKES WILFORD

is a Vice President with Chase Manhattan Bank in London and deals with risk management products. He is a co-editor (with Bluford Putnam) of the anthology *The Monetary Approach to International Adjustment*.

■ CHARLES SMITHSON

is Vice President of the Risk Management Products division of Continental Bank. His past research, which focused on a wide range of microeconomic issues, has dealt with questions of regulation, production, discrimination in labor markets, natural resources, and issues in the delivery of health care. His current research concerns financial instruments and risk management.

Article 2

Financial Engineering in Corporate Finance: An Overview

John D. Finnerty

John D. Finnerty is Executive Vice President and Chief Financial Officer, College Savings Bank, Princeton, NJ, and is a Professor of Finance, Fordham University, New York, NY.

■ Financial innovation over the past two decades has rapidly brought about revolutionary changes in financial instruments and processes. Almost daily the financial press carries yet another tombstone advertisement featuring a new security. A variety of factors, among the more important of which are increased interest rate volatility and the frequency of tax and regulatory changes, have stimulated the process of financial innovation. The deregulation of the financial services industry and increased competition within investment banking have undoubtedly placed increased emphasis on being able to design new products, develop better processes, and implement more effective solutions to increasing-

The author would like to thank James Ang, Laurence Booth, Marek Borun, Dennis Logue, and the anonymous referees for helpful comments on earlier drafts of the paper. Earlier versions of the paper were presented at Florida State University, the University of Toronto, and the 18th Annual Meeting of the FMA in New Orleans, LA, October 22, 1988.

ly complex financial problems. Financial engineering is the lifeblood of this activity.

Financial engineering involves the design, the development, and the implementation of innovative financial instruments and processes, and the formulation of creative solutions to problems in finance. The term "innovative" is used here to describe a solution that is nontrivial. Innovative financial solutions may involve a new consumer-type financial instrument, such as IRA and Keogh accounts; a new security, such as money market preferred stock; a new process, such as the shelf registration process; or a creative solution to a corporate finance problem, such as the design of customized security arrangements for a project financing or a leveraged buyout.

I. Scope of Financial Engineering

The definition of corporate financial engineering distinguishes three types of activities. The first, securities innovation, involves the development of innovative financial instruments, including those developed primarily for consumer-type applications such as new types of bank accounts, new forms of mutual funds, new types of life insurance products, and new forms of residential mortgages. Innovative financial instruments also include those developed primarily for corporate finance applications such as new debt instruments; options, futures, and other new risk management vehicles; new types of preferred stock; new forms of convertible securities; and new types of common equity instruments.

The second branch of corporate financial engineering involves the development of innovative financial processes. These new processes reduce the cost of effecting financial transactions, and are generally the result of legislative or regulatory changes (for example, the shelf registration process), or of technological developments (electronic security trading).

The third branch involves creative solutions to corporate finance problems. It encompasses innovative cash management strategies, innovative debt management strategies, and customized corporate financing structures such as those involved in various forms of asset-based financing.

II. The Process of Financial Innovation

Miller [38], Silber [46, 47, 48], and Van Horne [53] characterize the process of financial innovation in different terms.1 Miller finds that regulatory and tax factors have provided the major impetus for financial innovation over the past 20 years. He describes financial innovations as "unforecastable improvements" in the array of available financial products and processes that came into being as a result of unexpected tax or regulatory impulses [38, p. 460]. Zero coupon bonds provide a good example of how a tax impulse led to innovation.

Prior to the passage of the Tax Equity and Fiscal Responsibility Act of 1982 (TEFRA), an issuer of zero coupon bonds could have amortized the original issue discount—the difference between the face amount of the bonds and their issue price—on a straight-line basis for tax purposes. Being able to deduct the interest expense faster than the interest implicitly compounded on the bonds produced significant tax benefits, which were greater the higher the bond's offering yield. And,

the higher the bond's offering yield, the deeper the discount. When interest rates rose sharply in 1981 and 1982, there was a flood of zero coupon bond issues to exploit this tax loophole. (See Fisher, Brick, and Ng [24], and Yawitz and Maloney [55].) Zero coupon bonds were not a new financial instrument; it took an external shock (rising interest rates that greatly enhanced the potential tax benefits) to spur their use.

Zero coupon bonds also illustrate the interaction between Kane's regulatory dialectic and financial engineering [31, 32, 33]. Kane defines the regulatory dialectic as a cyclical process in which the opposing forces of regulation and regulatee avoidance adapt continually to one another. Finnerty [19] describes how U.S. corporations responded to TEFRA's closing of the domestic tax loophole by their issuing zero coupon bonds to Japanese investors in order to exploit a Japanese tax loophole. The Japanese regulatory authorities first responded to this activity first by imposing quantitative restrictions on Japanese purchases, and then by threatening to close the tax loophole.

Silber [46, 47, 48] views the process of financial innovation differently from Miller. He characterizes innovative financial instruments and processes as attempts by corporations to lessen the financial constraints they face. In his view, firms maximize utility subject to a number of constraints, some of which are imposed by government regulation, and the balance of which are imposed either by the marketplace or by the firm itself. Innovative activity responds to economic impulses that increase the cost of adhering to a particular constraint. The increased cost stimulates innovative activity to relax the constraint and thereby reduce the cost of adhering to it. For example, banks are capital-constrained. Considerable effort has gone into designing capital notes, which are debt instruments that qualify as "capital" for bank regulatory purposes. Issuing capital notes enables banks to increase the degree of leverage any particular amount of common equity would otherwise support. As a second example, increasingly volatile interest rates raised the cost of adhering to a policy of investing in fixed-dividend-rate preferred stock, which stimulated the innovative activity that led to the development of various forms of adjustable rate preferred stock.

Both Ben-Horim and Silber [5] and Silber [48] report that Silber's constraint-induced model of innovation explains a large percentage of new commercial bank products introduced during the 1952–1982 period. Nevertheless, Silber's model provides only a partial explanation of the process of financial innovation be-

---

1Other noteworthy contributions to the literature on financial innovations have been made by Atchison, DeMong, and Kling [4], Black and Scholes [8], Darrow and Mestres [17], and Friedman [25].

cause it focuses almost exclusively on the securities issuer and leaves investors with an essentially passive role.

Van Horne takes a more critical view of the process of financial innovation than either Miller or Silber. In his 1984 presidential address to the American Finance Association, Van Horne [53] argues that in order for a new financial instrument or process to be truly innovative, it must enable the financial markets to operate more efficiently or make them more complete. If the financial markets were perfect and complete, there would be no opportunities for (nontrivial) financial innovation. Greater efficiency can be achieved by reducing transaction costs, which innovations such as the shelf registration process and electronic funds transfer have accomplished, or by reducing differential taxes and other "deadweight" losses. The financial markets can be made more complete by designing a new security whose contingent after-tax returns cannot be replicated by any combination of existing securities.

Van Horne also notes the excesses that have resulted from the innovative process, citing "innovations" whose only apparent benefit is some sort of desirable accounting treatment (for example, in-substance defeasance) and pointing out the apparently substantial fees that investment bankers and other promoters of financial innovations have reaped.2 How the innovator shares in the rewards to innovation is an interesting empirical question that deserves careful study. In particular, how do the underwriting spreads on innovative securities vary as additional issuers enter the market? How is the net advantage of financial innovation allocated among the various parties to the transaction, and how does this allocation change as the innovative security becomes seasoned and as imitators enter the market? On this last point, Winger et al. [54] found that in the case of adjustable rate preferred stock, later issuers achieved more favorable terms than the initial issuers.

The Miller, Silber, and Van Horne papers suggest that the factors responsible for financial innovation can be classified into 11 categories: *(i)* tax asymmetries that can be exploited to produce tax savings for the is-suer, investors, or both, that are not offset by the added tax liabilities of the other; *(ii)* transaction costs; *(iii)* agency costs; *(iv)* opportunities to reduce some form of risk or to reallocate risk from one market participant to another who is either less risk averse or else willing to bear the risk at a lower cost; *(v)* opportunities to increase an asset's liquidity; *(vi)* regulatory or legislative change; *(vii)* level and volatility of interest rates; *(viii)* level and volatility of prices; *(ix)* academic work that resulted in advances in financial theories or better understanding of the risk-return characteristics of existing classes of securities; *(x)* accounting benefits (which may, and often do, have at best an ephemeral effect on shareholder wealth); and *(xi)* technological advances and other factors. Exhibit 1 lists a broad variety of financial innovations and identifies the factors primarily responsible for each.

III. Consumer-Type Financial Instruments

Exhibit 1 lists 14 innovative consumer-type financial instruments introduced within the past 20 years. Broker cash management accounts, which permit individuals to earn money market rates of interest on funds not currently invested in securities; money market mutual funds and money market accounts offered by banks, which pay current market interest rates on invested cash balances; NOW accounts, which are interest-bearing checking accounts; and debit cards, which enable bank depositors to shift money between accounts or withdraw cash from accounts at remote teller stations; all owe their existence at least partly to rising interest rates, which increased the opportunity cost of maintaining funds in non-interest-bearing checking or passbook accounts. In particular, money market mutual funds circumvented the outmoded Regulation Q interest rate ceilings. Money market accounts and NOW accounts resulted also from relaxed regulatory restrictions on the types of accounts banks could offer.

Municipal bond funds, IRA/Keogh accounts, and all-saver certificates were initiated by legislation. Municipal bond funds enable smaller individual investors to achieve a degree of portfolio diversification more cheaply than they could on their own. IRA/Keogh accounts conveyed special tax advantages to self-directed retirement accounts. All-saver certificates provided a tax incentive to depositing funds in thrifts, which faced funding problems at least partly brought on by high interest rates.

The equity access account was designed to enable individuals to borrow against the equity built up in their

---

2Ricks [43] notes that the SEC is concerned that certain innovative financial products have been misrepresented to investors, for example, the index option has been marketed to retail investors as a conservative hedging product. Ricks raises an interesting issue—whether the evolution of financial instruments has outstripped the ability of brokers to understand what they are selling and of brokerage firms to provide adequate supervision.

Exhibit 1. Factors Primarily Responsible for Financial Innovations

Innovation	Factors Primarily Responsible*	Innovation	Factors Primarily Responsible*
Consumer-Type Financial Instruments			
Broker cash management accounts	7	Money market mutual funds	6,7
Municipal bond funds	2,4,6	Money market accounts	6,7
All-saver certificates	6,7	NOW accounts	6,7
Equity access account	1,6,8	Bull/Bear CDs	2
Debit card	2,7,11	IRA/Keogh accounts	1,6
Tuition futures	4,8	Universal or variable life insurance	1,7,8
Variable or adjustable rate mortgages	7	Convertible mortgages or reduction option loans	2,7
Securities			
Deep discount/zero coupon bonds	1,4,7	Stripped debt securities	1,4,7
Floating rate notes	4,5,7	Floating rate, rating sensitive notes	3,4,5,7
Floating rate tax-exempt notes	4,5,7	Auction rate notes/debentures	2,3,4,7
Real yield securities	2,4,5,8	Dollar BILS	4,7
Puttable-extendible notes	2,3,4	Increasing rate notes	3
Interest rate reset notes	3	Annuity notes	11
Extendible notes	2,4	Variable coupon/rate renewable notes	2,4,6
Puttable/adjustable tender bonds	2,4,7	Variable duration notes	4,7
Euronotes/Euro-commercial paper	2,4	Universal commercial paper	4
Medium term notes	2	Negotiable CDs	2,5
Mortgage-backed bonds	4	Mortgage pass-throughs	2,4,5
Collateralized mortgage obligations	2,4,5	Stripped mortgage-backed securities	4
Receivable-backed securities	4,5	Real estate-backed bonds	4,5
Letter of credit/surety bond credit support	4,11	Yield curve/maximum rate notes	4,6,7
Interest rate swaps	4,6,7	Currency swaps	4,6
Interest rate caps/floors/collars	4,7	Remarketed reset notes	2,3,4
Foreign-currency-denominated bonds	4,7	Eurocurrency bonds	7
Dual currency bonds	4,6	Indexed currency option notes/	
Commodity-linked bonds	4,6,8	Principal exchange rate linked securities	4,6,7
Gold loans	4,8	High-yield (junk) bonds	2,5,7,9
Exchange-traded options	4,9	Foreign currency futures	4,9,11
Interest rate futures	4,7,9	Stock index futures	4,8,9
Options on futures contracts	4,7,9	Forward rate agreements	4,7
Warrants to purchase bonds	4,7	Adjustable rate preferred stock	1,4,5,6,7
Convertible adjustable preferred stock	1,4,5,7	Auction rate preferred stock	1,4,5,7
Remarketed preferred stock	1,4,5,7,11	Indexed floating rate preferred stock	1,4,5,7
Single point adjustable rate stock	1,2,4,5,7	Stated rate auction preferred stock	1,3,4,5,7
Variable cumulative preferred stock	1,2,3,4,5,7	Convertible exchangeable preferred	1,2,10
Adjustable rate convertible debt	1,10	Zero coupon convertible debt	1,11
Puttable convertible bonds	3,4,7	Mandatory convertible/equity contract notes	1,6
Synthetic convertible debt	1,10	Exchangeable auction preferred	1,2,4,5,7
Convertible reset debentures	3	Participating bonds	3,4
Master limited partnership	1	Additional class(es) of common stock	11
Americus trust	4,6	Paired common stock	4
Puttable common stock	3,4,10		
Financial Processes			
Shelf registration	2,6,7	Direct public sale of securities	2,6
Discount brokerage	2,6	Automated teller machines	2,11
Point-of-sale terminals	11	Electronic security trading	2,11
Electronic funds transfer/		CHIPS (same day settlement)	7,11
automated clearing houses	7,11	Cash management/sweep accounts	7,11
Financial Strategies/Solutions			
More efficient bond call strategies	7,9	Debt-for-debt- exchanges	1,7,10
Stock-for-debt swaps	1,7,10	In-substance defeasance	1,7,10
Preferred dividend rolls	1	Hedged dividend capture	1
Leveraged buyout structuring	1,9,11	Corporate restructuring	1,9,11
Project finance/lease/			
asset-based financial structuring	4		

*Notation: 1, tax advantages; 2, reduced transaction costs; 3, reduced agency costs; 4, risk reallocation; 5, increased liquidity; 6, regulatory or legislative factors; 7, level and volatility of interest rates; 8, level and volatility of prices; 9, academic work; 10, accounting benefits; and 11, technological developments and other factors.

own homes. The Tax Reform Act of 1986 limited full interest deductions to mortgage interest, which stimulated the use of this vehicle. Bull and bear CDs pay a variable interest rate that is tied to changes in the Standard & Poor's 500 Index. They give individuals an indirect way of participating in the market for options on the S&P 500 Index. Tuition futures enable families to prepay the future cost of an undergraduate education, which transfers college cost inflation risk to the seller of the tuition futures contract.

The remaining three products are all by-products of the higher level and volatility of interest rates. Universal life insurance and variable life insurance provide a wider choice of investment options than traditional whole life insurance, while retaining the tax deferral of investment earnings that life insurance products provide. Universal life insurance policies build cash value at a stated fixed rate, or according to a stated interest rate formula that the insurance company guarantees. Variable life insurance policies are really families of mutual funds wrapped within a life insurance contract. Current yield and redemption value are tied directly to the particular mutual fund around which the policy is wrapped. Variable rate and adjustable rate mortgages allow the mortgage interest rate to adjust over time, which facilitates thrift asset-liability management in a volatile interest rate environment. Convertible mortgages (also referred to as reduction option loans) give borrowers the option to fix the interest rate on a variable rate or adjustable rate mortgage on one or more specified mortgage rate reset dates, provided the "index" rate has fallen more than two percentage points since the mortgage's issue date. To exercise the option, the borrower pays a fee which is typically smaller than the cost of refunding the original mortgage.

IV. Securities Innovation

There has been a more or less steady flow of security innovations in recent years. The investment banks who develop the new securities herald each new product's introduction along with its advantages, and the financial press dutifully reports them [18, 37]. However, the process is not without its detractors [45, 53].

In addition to the factors discussed in Section II, a change in the industry environment helps account for the revolution in securities innovation. In recent years, the investment banking business has shifted away from what is known as "relationship banking" and become more competitive, and hence, more transactional. Developing an innovative security provides an opportunity for the financial engineer to solicit business from

companies that have traditionally used other investment bankers. A successful innovator is usually awarded a mandate to sell the new security on a negotiated basis, rather than having to bid for securities "off the shelf" as is the case with conventional debt instruments. Investment banks therefore have a strong financial incentive to engineer innovative securities [26, 34].

A new security is truly "innovative" only if it (i) enables an investor to realize a higher after-tax risk-adjusted rate of return without adversely affecting the issuer's after-tax cost of funds, and/or (ii) enables an issuer to realize a lower after-tax cost of funds without adversely affecting investors, than had been possible prior to the introduction of the new security. A new security can accomplish this only if it makes the markets more efficient or more complete. It is not enough for a new security just to be different; there must be some real value added to the issuing company's shareholders.

A. Sources of Value Added

The purpose of securities innovation is to develop positive-net-present-value financing mechanisms [44]. Finnerty [22] develops an analytical framework that indicates three principal sources of value added through securities innovation: features that reallocate or reduce risk and in so doing reduce the required offering yield, characteristics that lead to lower issuance expenses during the period the financial obligation is intended to remain outstanding, and features that create a tax arbitrage for the issuer and investors (at the expense of the Internal Revenue Service). The resulting value added will be allocated among the company's shareholders, the purchasers of the innovative security, and the underwriters through the pricing of the innovative security and the setting of underwriting commissions.

If a company can repackage a security's payment stream so that it either involves less risk or reallocates risk from one class of investors to one that is less risk-sensitive and thus requires a smaller risk premium, and does so in a manner that investors cannot duplicate as cheaply by utilizing existing securities, then shareholder value will be enhanced. Collateralized mortgage obligations (CMOs) and stripped mortgage-backed securities are examples. If a company can issue a security against a diversified portfolio of assets, it can reduce the investor's risk and hence the required yield. If the issuer can accomplish this more cheaply than the investor can by himself, there is opportunity for gain. Some examples are mortgage pass-through securities and

Exhibit 2. Selected Debt Innovations

Security	Distinguishing Characteristics	Risk Reallocation/ Yield Reduction	Enhanced Liquidity	Reduction in Agency Costs	Reduction in Transaction Costs	Tax Arbitrage	Other Benefits
Adjustable Rate Notes and Floating Rate Notes	Coupon rate floats with some index, such as the 91-day Treasury bill rate.	Issuer exposed to floating interest rate risk but initial rate is lower than for fixed-rate issue.	Price remains closer to par than the price of a fixed-rate note of the same maturity.				
Auction Rate Notes and Debentures	Interest rate reset by Dutch auction at the end of each interest period.	Coupon based on length of interest period, not on final maturity.	Designed to trade closer to par value than a floating rate note with a fixed interest rate formula.	Interest rate each period is determined in the marketplace, rather than by the issuer or the issuer's investment banker.	Intended to have lower transaction costs than repeatedly rolling over shorter maturity securities.		
Bonds Linked to Commodity Price or Index	Interest and/or principal linked to a specified commodity price or index.	Issuer assumes commodity price or index risk in return for lower (minimum) coupon. Can serve as a hedge if the issuer produces the particular commodity.					Attractive to investors who would like to speculate in commodity options but cannot, for regulatory or other reasons, purchase commodity options directly.
Collateralized Mortgage Obligations (CMOs) and Real Estate Mortgage Investment Conduits (REMICs)	Mortgage payment stream is divided into several classes which are prioritized in terms of their right to receive principal payments.	Reduction in prepayment risk to classes with prepayment priority. Designed to appeal to different classes of investors; sum of the parts can exceed the whole.	More liquid than individual mortgages.		Most investors could not achieve the same degree of prepayment risk reduction as cheaply on their own.		
Commercial Real Estate-Backed Bonds	Nonrecourse bonds serviced and backed by a specified piece (or portfolio) of real estate.	Reduced yield due to greater liquidity.	More liquid than individual mortgages.				Appeals to investors who like to lend against real estate properties.
Credit-Enhanced Debt Securities	Issuer's obligation to pay is backed by an irrevocable letter of credit or a surety bond.	Stronger credit rating of the letter of credit or surety bond issuer leads to lower yield, which can more than offset letter of credit/ surety bond fees.					Enables a privately held company to borrow publicly while preserving confidentiality of financial information.
Dollar BILS	Floating rate zero coupon note the effective interest rate on which is determined retrospectively based on the change in the value of a specified index that measures the total return on long-term, high-grade corporate bonds.	Issuer assumes reinvestment risk.					Useful for hedging and immunization purposes because Dollar BILS have a zero duration when duration is measured with respect to the specified index.
Dual Currency Bonds	Interest payable in US dollars but principal payable in a currency other than US dollars.	Issuer has foreign currency risk with respect to principal repayment obligation. Currency swap can hedge this risk and lead, in some cases, to yield reduction.					Euroyen-dollar dual currency bonds popular with Japanese investors who are subject to regulatory restrictions and desire income in dollars without principal risk.
Euronotes and Euro-commercial Paper	Euro-commercial paper is similar to US commercial paper.	Elimination of intermediary brings savings that lender and borrower can share.			Corporations invest in each other's paper directly rather than through an intermediary.		
Extendible Notes	Interest rate adjusts every 2-3 years to a new interest rate the issuer establishes, at which time note holder has the option to put the notes back to the issuer if the new rate is unacceptable.	Coupon based on 2-3 year put date, not on final maturity.	Investor has a put option, which provides protection against deterioration in credit quality or below-market coupon rate.		Lower transaction costs than issuing 2 or 3-year notes and rolling them over.		

Security	Distinguishing Characteristics	Risk Reallocation/ Yield Reduction	Enhanced Liquidity	Reduction in Agency Costs	Reduction in Transaction Costs	Tax Arbitrage	Other Benefits
Floating Rate, Rating Sensitive Notes	Coupon rate resets quarterly based on a spread over LIBOR. Spread increases if the issuer's debt rating declines.	Issuer exposed to floating interest rate risk but initial rate is lower than for fixed-rate issue.	Price remains closer to par than the price of a fixed-rate note of the same maturity.	Investor protected against deterioration in the issuer's credit quality because of increase in coupon rate when rating declines.			
Floating Rate Tax-Exempt Revenue Bonds	Coupon rate floats with some index, such as the 60-day high-grade commercial paper rate.	Issuer exposed to floating interest rate risk but initial rate is lower than for fixed-rate issue. Effectively, tax-exempt commercial paper.				Investor does not have to pay income tax on the interest payments but issuer gets to deduct them.	
Increasing Rate Notes	Coupon rate increases by specified amounts at specified intervals.	Defers portion of interest expense to later years, which increases duration.		When such notes are issued in connection with a bridge financing, the step-up in coupon rate compensates investors for the issuer's failure to redeem the notes on schedule.			
Indexed Currency Option Notes/ Principal Exchange Rate Linked Securities	Issuer pays reduced principal at maturity if specified foreign currency appreciates sufficiently relative to the US dollar.	Investor assumes foreign currency risk by effectively selling the issuer a call option denominated in the foreign currency.					Attractive to investors who would like to speculate in foreign currencies but cannot, for regulatory or other reasons, purchase or sell currency options directly.
Interest Rate Caps, Floors, and Collars	Investor who writes an interest rate cap (floor/collar) contract agrees to make payments to the contract purchaser when a specified interest rate exceeds the specified cap (falls below the floor/falls outside the collar range).	Seller assumes the risk that interest rates may rise above the cap (fall below the floor/fall outside the collar range.					
Interest Rate Reset Notes	Interest rate is reset 3 years after issuance to the greater of (i) the initial rate and (ii) a rate sufficient to give the notes a market value equal to 101% of their face amount.	Reduced (initial) yield due to the reduction in agency costs.		Investor is compensated for a deterioration in the issuer's credit standing within 3 years of issuance.			
Interest Rate Swaps	Two entities agree to swap interest rate payment obligations, typically fixed rate for floating rate.	Effective vehicle for transferring interest rate risk from one party to another. Also, parties to a swap can realize a net benefit if they enjoy comparative advantages in different international credit markets.					Interest rate swaps are often designed to take advantage of special opportunities in particular markets outside the issuer's traditional market or to circumvent regulatory restrictions.
Medium-Term Notes	Notes are sold in varying amounts and in varying maturities on an agency basis.	Issuer bears market price risk during the marketing process.			Agents' commissions are lower than underwriting spreads.		
Mortgage Pass-Through Certificates	Investor buys an undivided interest in a pool of mortgages.	Reduced yield due to the benefit to the investor of diversification and greater liquidity.	More liquid than individual mortgages.		Most investors could not achieve the same degree of diversification as cheaply on their own.		
Negotiable Certificates of Deposit	Certificates of deposit are registered and sold to the public on an agency basis.	Issuer bears market price risk during the marketing process.	More liquid than non-negotiable CDs.		Agents' commissions are lower than underwriting spreads.		

Security	Distinguishing Characteristics	Risk Reallocation/ Yield Reduction	Enhanced Liquidity	Reduction in Agency Costs	Reduction in Transaction Costs	Tax Arbitrage	Other Benefits
Puttable Bonds and Adjustable Tender Securities	Issuer can periodically reset the terms, in effect rolling over debt without having to redeem it until the final maturity.	Coupon based on whether fixed or floating rate and on the length of the interest rate period selected, not on final maturity.		Investor has a put option, which provides protection against deterioration in credit quality or below-market coupon rate.	Lower transaction costs than having to perform a series of refundings.		
Puttable-Extendible Notes	At the end of each interest period, the issuer may elect to redeem the notes at par or to extend the maturity on terms the issuer proposes, at which time the note holder can put the notes back to the issuer if the new terms are unacceptable. Investors also have series of put options during initial interest period.	Coupon based on length of interest interval, not on final maturity.		Put options protect against deterioration in issuer's credit standing and also against issuer setting below-market coupon rate or other terms that might work to investor's disadvantage.			
Real Yield Securities	Coupon rate resets quarterly to the greater of (i) change in consumer price index plus the "Real Yield Spread" (3.0% in the first such issue) and (ii) the Real Yield Spread, in each case on a semi-annual-equivalent basis.	Issuer exposed to inflation risk, which may be hedged in the CPI futures market.	Real yield securities could become more liquid than CPI futures, which tend to trade in significant volume only around the monthly CPI announce-ment date.		Investors obtain a long-dated inflation hedging instrument that they could not create as cheaply on their own.		Real yield securities have a longer duration than alternative inflation hedging instruments.
Receivable Pay-Through Securities	Investor buys an undivided interest in a pool of receivables.	Reduced yield due to the benefit to the investor of diversi-fication and greater liquidity. Significantly cheaper for issuer than pledging receivables to a bank.	More liquid than individual receivables.		Security purchasers could not achieve the same degree of diversification as cheaply on their own.		
Remarketed Reset Notes	Interest rate reset at the end of each interest period to a rate the remarketing agent determines will make the notes worth par. If issuer and remarketing agent can not agree on rate, then the coupon rate is determined by formula which dictates a higher rate the lower the issuer's credit standing.	Coupon based on length of interest period, not on final maturity.	Designed to trade closer to par value than a floating-rate note with a fixed interest rate formula.	Investors have a put option, which protects against the issuer and remarketing agent agreeing to set a below-market coupon rate, and the flexible interest rate formula protects investors against deterioration in the issuer's credit standing.	Intended to have lower transaction costs than auction rate notes and debentures, which require periodic Dutch auctions.		
Stripped Mortgage-Backed Securities	Mortgage payment stream subdivided into two classes, (i) one with below-market coupon and the other with above-market coupon or (ii) one receiving interest only and the other receiving principal only from mortgage pools.	Securities have unique option characteristics that make them useful for hedging purposes. Designed to appeal to different classes of investors; sum of the parts can exceed the whole.					
Stripped Treasury or Municipal Securities	Coupons separated from corpus to create a series of zero coupon bonds that can be sold separately.	Yield curve arbitrage; sum of the parts can exceed the whole.					
Variable Coupon Renewable Notes	Coupon rate varies weekly and equals a fixed spread over the 91-day T-bill rate. Each 91 days the maturity extends another 91 days. If put option exercised, spread is reduced.	Coupon based on 1-year termination date, not on final maturity.			Lower transaction costs than issuing 1-year note and rolling it over.		Designed to appeal to money market mutual funds, which face tight investment restrictions, and to discourage put to issuer.

Security	Distinguishing Characteristics	Risk Reallocation/ Yield Reduction	Enhanced Liquidity	Reduction in Agency Costs	Reduction in Transaction Costs	Tax Arbitrage	Other Benefits
Variable Rate Renewable Notes	Coupon rate varies monthly and equals a fixed spread over the 1-month commercial paper rate. Each quarter the maturity automatically extends an additional quarter unless the investor elects to terminate the extension.	Coupon based on 1-year termination date, not on final maturity.			Lower transaction costs than issuing 1-year note and rolling it over.		Designed to appeal to money market mutual funds, which face tight investment restrictions.
Warrants to Purchase Debt Securities	Warrant with 1–5 years to expiration to buy intermediate-term or long-term bonds.	Issuer is effectively selling a covered call option, which can afford investors opportunities not available in the traditional options markets.					
Yield Curve Notes and Maximum Rate Notes	Interest rate equals a specified rate minus LIBOR.	Might reduce yield relative to conventional debt when coupled with an interest rate swap against LIBOR.					Useful for hedging and immunization purposes because of very long duration.
Zero Coupon Bonds (sometimes issued in series)	Non-interest-bearing. Payment in one lump sum at maturity.	Issuer assumes reinvestment risk. Issues sold in Japan carried below-taxable-market yields reflecting their tax advantage over conventional debt issues.				Straight-line amortization of original issue discount pre-TEFRA. Japanese investors realize significant tax savings.	

debt backed by a portfolio of automobile receivables. If a company can securitize a loan so that it becomes publicly tradeable, the lender's liquidity risk is reduced, resulting in a lower required yield. Negotiable certificates of deposit and nonrecourse notes (i.e., mortgages) secured by commercial real estate are examples. Both can be traded in the public securities markets, unlike conventional certificates of deposit and most commercial mortgages. If a company can design a security that reduces the agency costs that would normally arise in connection with a conventional financing, for example costs due to informational asymmetries between the issuer and investors, a lower offering yield can result. Floating rate, rating sensitive notes, whose interest rate increases when the issuer's debt rating decreases, are an example.

Second, if a company can structure a securities issue so that underwriting commissions are reduced, shareholder value will be enhanced. Extendible notes are an example. Their maturity can be extended by mutual agreement between the issuer and investors, effectively rolling over the notes without additional underwriting commissions. Third, if a company can structure a new security so as to reduce investor taxes without increasing corporate income taxes, shareholder value will be enhanced as a result of this tax arbitrage. For example, a company that is not currently a taxpayer can create such an arbitrage by issuing auction rate preferred stock to fully taxable corporate investors in lieu of commercial paper [1, 54]. Fourth, if a company can structure a new security so as to increase the present value tax shields available to the issuer without increasing the investors' tax liabilities, shareholder value can again be enhanced through tax arbitrage. For example, the selling of zero coupon notes to tax-exempt investors before TEFRA resulted in such an arbitrage because the issuer could deduct the original issue discount on a straight-line basis. This tax treatment did not adversely affect tax-exempt investors. The balance of this section describes a number of innovative securities listed in Exhibit 1 in greater detail.

B. Debt Innovations

Most of the financial innovations in recent years have involved debt securities. Some, such as zero coupon bonds, were issued in large volume for a period of time but have become very rare, either because changes in tax law eliminated their advantages or because more recent innovations superseded them. Other debt innovations such as extendible notes, medium-term notes, and collateralized mortgage obligations have had a more lasting impact. Yet others, such as indexed currency option notes, variable duration notes, certain commodity-linked bonds, and annuity notes, have been introduced and disappeared quickly, in some cases after just a single issue. Exhibit 2 lists several of the more significant debt innovations and classifies each innovation's value-enhancing features.

Risk Reallocation/Yield Reduction Most of the debt innovations in Exhibit 2 involve some form of risk reallocation as compared to conventional debt instruments or some other form of yield reduction mechanism. Involving the reapportioning of interest rate risk, credit risk, or some other form of risk, risk reallocation is beneficial when it transfers risk from those who are less willing to bear it to those who are more willing to bear it, in the sense that they require a smaller yield premium to compensate them for bearing the risk. A yield reduction (or equivalently, an increase in the net proceeds that can be realized from the sale of a given debt service stream) results when repackaging a particular debt service stream and selling the component parts yields greater proceeds than selling the original debt service stream intact.

Serial zero coupon bonds, stripped U.S. Treasury securities, and stripped municipal securities illustrate that the sum of the parts can exceed the whole when a particular debt service stream is subdivided and its constituent parts are sold separately. For example, stripping a bearer U.S. Treasury bond creates a serial zero coupon issue. Each zero coupon bond in the series can be sold to the highest bidder. Because the U.S. Treasury did not issue zero coupon bonds, securities firms created them by stripping bearer Treasury securities and earned an arbitrage profit for their effort. As one would expect, the substantial arbitrage profits earned by the securities firms initially involved in stripping were eliminated over time as competitors entered the market.

Mortgage pass-through certificates and receivable-backed securities can be sold in the marketplace at a lower yield than the assets that back them because they provide investors a degree of diversification that many (smaller) investors could not achieve as cheaply on their own. In addition, the issuer often retains a subordinated interest in the collateral pool so that much of the apparent yield reduction results from the investors' senior position with respect to mortgage or receivable pool cash flows. Collateralized mortgage obligations (CMOs) and stripped mortgage-backed securities illustrate the benefits that can result from repackaging mortgage payment streams [50]. Most mortgages are prepayable at par at the option of the mortgagor after some brief period. This creates significant prepayment risk for lenders. CMOs package the mortgage payment stream from a portfolio of mortgages into several series of debt instruments—sometimes more than a dozen—which are prioritized in terms of their right to receive principal payments. In the simplest form of CMO, each series must be repaid in full before any principal payments can be made to the holders of the next series in order to reduce prepayment uncertainty. Thus, CMOs may serve to make the capital market more complete by producing specific payoff streams that were previously unavailable. This occurs especially by achieving a specific allocation of prepayment risk across the different tranches. Stripped mortgage-backed securities divide the mortgage payment stream into two separate streams of claims, in the extreme case, one involving interest payments exclusively and the other involving principal repayments exclusively. The introduction of these securities also enhanced market completeness because of their duration and convexity characteristics. The apparent failure to understand fully the riskiness of these securities led to a substantial and highly publicized financial loss by a major brokerage house [51].

Adjustable rate notes and floating rate notes expose the issuer to floating interest rate risk but reduce the investor's principal risk. This interest rate risk reallocation can be of mutual benefit to issuers whose assets are interest-rate sensitive, such as banks and credit companies, and certain types of investors. Dollar BILS are a special type of floating rate note, one that has zero duration when duration is measured with respect to the specified index to which the floating rate is tied.

A recently introduced mechanism for transferring interest rate risk goes by two different names because it has two different sponsoring securities firms. Yield curve notes and maximum rate notes, collectively "inverse floaters," carry an interest rate that increases (decreases) as interest rates fall (rise) [28, 39, 49]. Typically, the incentive in issuing an inverse floater is to fix the coupon by entering into an interest rate swap agreement. The two transactions together benefit the issuer when they result in a lower cost of funds than a conventional fixed-rate issue. Investors find inverse floaters useful for immunization purposes because of their very long duration, which may exceed the maturity of the security [28, 39, 49].

Three other classes of debt innovations in Exhibit 2 also involve some form of risk reallocation. Credit-enhanced debt securities involve credit risk reallocation through bank letters of credit or insurance company surety bonds. When the letter of credit or surety bond fee is less than the resulting reduction in the yield required to sell the securities, the credit risk reallocation is beneficial to the issuer. Dual currency bonds, indexed currency option notes, and principal exchange rate linked securities illustrate two forms of currency risk reallocation. Bonds that make interest and/or principal payments that are linked to a specified index or commodity, such as the price of oil or the price of silver, are attractive to institutions that are not permitted to invest directly in commodity options and can serve as a hedge for an issuer who is a producer of the commodity.

Reduced Agency Costs Five of the debt innovations in Exhibit 2 are designed at least partly to reduce agency costs. Increasing rate notes, when used in connection with a bridge financing, provide an incentive for the issuer to redeem the notes (out of the proceeds of a permanent financing) on schedule. Interest rate reset notes protect against deterioration in the issuer's credit standing prior to the reset date. Puttable-extendible notes provide a series of put options which protect against deterioration in the issuer's credit standing. The protection that such an option affords investors is not readily available in the options markets because there currently does not exist a well-organized market for long-term corporate bond options. Remarketed reset notes include a put option, which protects against the issuer and remarketing agent conspiring to set a below-market coupon rate, and a flexible interest rate formula (in the event the issuer and the remarketing agent cannot agree on a rate), which provides for a higher interest rate the lower the issuer's credit standing. Similarly, floating rate, rating sensitive notes bear a coupon rate that varies inversely with the issuer's credit standing.

Reduced Issuance Expenses Extendible notes, variable coupon renewable notes, puttable bonds, adjustable tender securities, remarketed reset notes, and euronotes and euro-commercial paper are all designed to reduce issuance expenses and other forms of transaction costs. Extendible notes typically provide for an interest rate adjustment every 2 or 3 years, although other adjustment intervals are possible, and thus represent an alternative to rolling over 2 or 3-year note issues without incurring additional issuance expenses.

Variable coupon renewable notes represent a refinement of the extendible note concept. The maturity of the notes automatically extends 91 days at the end of each quarter—unless the holder elects to terminate the automatic extension, in which case the interest rate spread decreases. A holder wishing to terminate the investment would avoid the reduction in spread by selling the notes in the marketplace. Goodman and Yawitz [28] explain how these features were designed to meet

regulatory investment restrictions that money market mutual funds face.3 In another refinement of the extendible note concept, puttable bonds, adjustable tender securities, and remarketed reset notes give the issuer the flexibility to reset the terms of the security periodically. These securities offer the issuer greater flexibility than extendible notes in the choice of terms on which to extend the maturity of the debt issue.

Euronotes and euro-commercial paper represent the extension of commercial paper to the Euromarket [42]. Transaction cost savings result because corporations invest directly in one another's securities, rather than through banks and other intermediaries, as was the case previously.

Tax Arbitrage Zero coupon bonds, as previously noted, provided a form of tax arbitrage prior to the passage of TEFRA. In addition, the investor bears no reinvestment risk, because interest is compounded over the life of the debt issue at the yield at which the investor purchased the bond.

C. Options, Futures, and Other Interest Rate Risk Management Vehicles

Options, futures, and other interest rate risk management vehicles enable market participants who are averse to certain risks (such as foreign currency risk, interest rate risk, or stock market risk) to transfer that risk to others who are less risk averse, on certain specified terms in exchange for a fee. Miller [38] cites financial futures as the most significant financial innovation of the past 20 years. Block and Gallagher [9] and Booth, Smith, and Stolz [10] catalog the many uses to which interest rate futures may be put for risk management purposes.

Warrants to purchase debt securities, an innovative form of debt option, have been more popular in the Euromarket than in the domestic market. They typically take the form of an option to buy an intermediate-term or long-term bond, and generally have a term of expiration between 1 and 5 years. The warrant issuer is effectively writing a covered call option on the issuer's own debt. Issuing the warrant represents a form of hedging by the debt issuer, and it affords investors

---

3Variable coupon renewable notes have a nominal maturity of one year, which is the maximum maturity permitted money market mutual fund investments. Also, because of the weekly rate reset, variable coupon renewable notes count as 7-day assets in meeting the 120-day upper limit on a money market mutual fund's dollar-weighted average portfolio maturity.

opportunities not available in the traditional options markets.

Interest rate risk management vehicles include interest rate futures, options on interest rate futures, forward rate agreements, interest rate swaps, interest rate caps, interest rate floors, and interest rate collars [3, 6, 13]. The interest rate swap market has exploded within the past five years, and swap activity currently exceeds $400 billion per year. Bicksler and Chen [6] describe the market imperfections that can create comparative advantages among different borrowers in the fixed-rate debt and floating-rate debt markets and across national boundaries, and thereby provide economic incentives to engage in interest rate swaps. Arak et al. [3] provide an alternative rationale for swaps. They state that swaps enable borrowers to fix the risk-free rate so that borrowers who believe their credit standing is about to improve have an incentive to borrow short-term funds and swap into fixed payments. Brown and Smith [13] describe the innovative nature of interest rate caps, floors, and collars, all of which impose limits on an entity's exposure to floating-interest-rate risk.

Miller [38] questions whether diminishing returns to financial innovation have already set in. Much of the innovative activity in recent years has involved the development of new futures products. Reports in the financial press have stated that 80% to 90% of new futures products fail and argued that the financial futures industry has already developed perhaps as much as 90% of the potentially useful futures products [41]. Miller notes that the Chicago Board of Trade and the Chicago Mercantile Exchange spent a combined total of $5 to $6 million developing two distinct futures contracts for over-the-counter stocks, both of which failed in the marketplace. The economics of futures innovation is one area of investigation that might yield at least a partial answer to Miller's question.

D. Preferred Stock Innovations

Preferred stock offers a tax advantage over debt to corporate investors, who are permitted to deduct from their taxable income 70% of the dividends they receive from unaffiliated corporations. Corporate money managers have a tax incentive to purchase preferred stock rather than commercial paper or other short-term debt instruments the interest on which is fully taxable. However, the purchasing of long-term fixed-dividend-rate preferred stock exposes the purchaser to the risk that rising interest rates could lead to a fall in the price of the preferred stock that would more than offset the tax

saving. Exhibit 3 lists a variety of new securities designed to deal with this problem.

Adjustable rate preferred stock was designed to lessen the investor's principal risk by having the dividend rate adjust as interest rates change. The dividend rate adjusts based on a formula. At times the spread investors have required to value the securities at par has differed significantly from the fixed spread specified in the formula, causing the value of the security to deviate significantly from its face amount. Winger et al. [54] document the high volatility of adjustable rate preferred stock holding-period returns relative to those of alternative money-market investments.

Convertible adjustable preferred stock (CAPS) was designed to eliminate this deficiency. CAPS have traded closer to their respective face amounts than adjustable rate preferred stocks. However, there have only been a few CAPS issues, probably because prospective issuers have objected possibly to having to issue common stock or raise a large amount of cash on short notice.

Auction rate preferred stock carried the evolutionary process a step further. The dividend rate is reset by Dutch auction every 49 days, which represents just enough weeks to meet the 46-day holding period required to qualify for the 70% dividends received deduction. (One variation of this security, stated rate auction preferred stock, fixes the dividend rate for several years before the regular Dutch auctions commence.) Alderson, Brown, and Lummer [1] document the tax arbitrage that auction rate preferred stock affords under current tax law. There are various versions of auction rate preferred stock that are sold under different acronyms (MMP, Money Market Preferred; AMPS, Auction Market Preferred Stock; DARTS, Dutch Auction Rate Transferable Securities; STAR, Short-Term Auction Rate; etc.) coined by the different securities firms that offer the product. The names may differ but the securities are the same.

In an effort to refine the adjustable rate preferred stock concept further, there have been at least two attempts to design a superior security, but only one was successful. Single point adjustable rate stock (SPARS) has a dividend rate that adjusts automatically every 49 days to a specified percentage of the 60-day high-grade commercial paper rate. The security is designed so as to afford the same degree of liquidity as auction rate preferred stock, but with lower transaction costs since no auction need be held. However, the fixed dividend rate formula involves a potential agency cost that auction rate preferred stock does not. Investors will suffer

Exhibit 3. Selected Preferred Stock Innovations

Security	Distinguishing Characteristics	Risk Reallocation/ Yield Reduction	Enhanced Liquidity	Reduction in Agency Costs	Reduction in Transaction Costs	Tax Arbitrage	Other Benefits
Adjustable Rate Preferred Stock	Quarterly dividend rate reset each quarter based on maximum of 3-month T-bill, 10-year Treasury, and 20-year Treasury rates plus or minus a specified spread.	Issuer bears more interest rate risk than a fixed-rate preferred would involve. Lower yield than commercial paper.	Security is designed to trade near its par value.			Designed to enable short-term corporate investors to take advantage of 70% dividends received deduction.	
Auction Rate Preferred Stock (MMP/DARTS/ AMPS/STAR)	Dividend rate reset by Dutch auction every 49 days (subject to a maximum rate of 110%, or under certain circumstances 125%, of the 60-day "AA" Composite Commercial Paper Rate). Dividend is paid at the end of each dividend period.	Issuer bears more interest rate risk than a fixed-rate preferred would involve. Lower yield than commercial paper.	Security is designed to provide greater liquidity than convertible adjustable preferred stock.	Dividend rate each period is determined in the marketplace, which provides protection against deterioration in issuer's credit standing (protection is limited by the dividend rate cap).		Designed to enable short-term corporate investors to take advantage of 70% dividends received deduction.	
Convertible Adjustable Preferred Stock	Issue convertible on dividend payment dates into variable number of the issuer's common shares, subject to a cap, equal in market value to the par value of the preferred.	Issuer bears more interest rate risk than a fixed-rate preferred would involve. Lower yield than commercial paper.	Security is designed to provide greater liquidity than adjustable rate preferred stock (due to the conversion feature).			Designed to enable short-term corporate investors to take advantage of 70% dividends received deduction.	
Remarketed Preferred Stock (SABRES)	Perpetual preferred stock with a dividend rate that resets at the end of each dividend period to a rate the remarketing agent determines will make the preferred stock worth par (subject to a maximum rate of 110%, or under certain circumstances 125%, of the 60-day "AA" Composite Commercial Paper Rate). Dividend periods may be of any length, even 1 day. Different shares of a single issue may have different periods and different dividend rates.	Issuer bears more interest rate risk than a fixed-rate preferred would involve. Lower yield than commercial paper.	Security is designed to trade near its par value.			Designed to enable short-term corporate investors to take advantage of 70% dividends received deduction.	Remarketed preferred stock offers greater flexibility in setting the terms of the issue than auction rate preferred stock, which requires a Dutch auction for potentially the entire issue once every 49 days.
Single Point Adjustable Rate Stock	Dividend rate reset every 49 days as a specified percentage of the high-grade commercial paper rate.	Issuer bears more interest rate risk than a fixed-rate preferred would involve. Lower yield than commercial paper.	Security is designed to trade near its par value.		Security is designed to save on recurring transaction costs associated with auction rate preferred stock.	Designed to enable short-term corporate investors to take advantage of 70% dividends received deduction.	
Stated Rate Auction Preferred Stock	Initial dividend period of several years during which the dividend rate is fixed. Thereafter the issuer can elect to have the dividend rate reset every 49 days by Dutch auction.	Issuer bears more interest rate risk than a fixed-rate preferred would involve.	Security is designed to trade near its par value after the initial dividend period has elapsed and the Dutch auctions determine the dividend rate.	The maximum permitted dividend rate, expressed as a percentage of the 60-day "AA" Composite Commercial Paper Rate, increases according to a specified schedule if the preferred stock's credit rating falls.		Designed so as eventually to enable short-term corporate investors to take advantage of 70% dividends received deduction.	
Variable Cumulative Preferred Stock	At the end of any dividend period the issuer can select between the auction method and the remarketing method to have the dividend rate reset.	Issuer bears more interest rate risk than a fixed-rate preferred would involve. Lower yield than commercial paper.	Security is designed to trade near its par value.	The maximum permitted dividend rate, expressed as a percentage of the 60-day "AA" Composite Commercial Paper Rate, increases according to a specified schedule if the preferred stock's credit rating falls.	Security is designed to save on transaction costs the issuer would otherwise incur if it wanted to change from auction reset to remarketing reset or vice versa.	Designed to enable short-term corporate investors to take advantage of 70% dividends received deduction.	Security is designed to enable the issuer to select at the end of each dividend period the method of rate reset it prefers.

a loss if the issuer's managers take actions that cause the issuer's credit standing to deteriorate, because the dividend formula is fixed. Primarily for this reason, there have been at most only a few SPARS issues.

Remarketed preferred stock has a dividend rate that is reset at the end of each dividend period to a dividend rate that a specified remarketing agent determines will make the preferred stock worth par. Such issues permit the issuer considerable flexibility in selecting the length of the dividend period, which may be of any length, even 1 day. Remarketed preferred also offers greater flexibility in selecting the other terms of the issue; in fact, each share of an issue could have different maturity, dividend rate, or other terms, provided the issuer and holders so agree. Remarketed preferred has not proven as popular with issuers as auction rate preferred stock, but that could change due to the greater flexibility remarketed preferred affords.

As a result of the controversy over whether auction rate preferred stock or remarketed preferred stock results in more equitable pricing, variable cumulative preferred stock was invented in order to let the issuer decide at the end of each dividend period which of the two reset methods will determine the dividend rate for the following dividend period.

E. Convertible Debt/Preferred Stock Innovations

Convertible debt innovations share a dominant theme: the creation of additional tax deductions (while preserving the amelioration of moral hazard, which conventional convertible bonds achieve). The creation of additional tax deductions involves a form of tax arbitrage because 80-90% of convertible bond investors are tax-exempt [21]. Exhibit 4 describes seven recent innovations involving convertible securities.

Convertible exchangeable preferred stock consists of convertible perpetual preferred stock that the issuer is permitted to exchange for an issue of convertible subordinated debt, having the same conversion terms and an interest rate that equals the dividend rate on the convertible preferred. The exchange feature enables the issuer to reissue the convertible preferred as convertible debt should it become taxable in the future, but without having to pay additional underwriting commissions. A large volume of such securities have been issued by companies that were not currently taxpayers for federal income tax purposes. Similarly, exchangeable auction preferred stock permits the issuer to exchange auction rate notes for auction rate preferred stock on any dividend payment date.

Adjustable rate convertible debt is a security with a purported tax advantage. The security represented an attempt to package equity as debt. The Internal Revenue Service has ruled that the security is equity for tax purposes, thereby denying the interest deductions and rendering the security unattractive. Zero coupon convertible debt reflects a similar theme [36]. If the issue is converted, both interest and principal are converted to common equity, in which case the issuer will have effectively sold common equity with a tax deductibility feature.

Debt with mandatory common stock purchase contracts represents debt that qualifies as primary capital for bank regulatory purposes because conversion is mandatory. In the meantime, the issuer gets a stream of interest tax deductions that simply selling common stock would not afford. Finnerty [21] and Jones and Mason [30] describe how to package a unit consisting of debt and warrants into synthetic convertible debt, the features of which mirror the features of conventional convertible debt. Synthetic convertible bonds enjoy a tax advantage relative to a comparable convertible debt issue because, in effect, the warrant proceeds are deductible for tax purposes over the life of the debt issue. Lastly, convertible reset debentures protect holders against deterioration in the issuer's financial prospects within two years of issuance through an interest rate reset mechanism.

F. Common Equity Innovations

There are four principal common equity innovations: additional class(es) of common stock whose dividends are tied to the earnings of a specified subsidiary of the issuer, the Americus Trust, the master limited partnership, and puttable common stock. Exhibit 5 indicates the principal benefits resulting from these innovations.

The creation of a new class of common stock that reflects the financial condition and operating performance of a subsidiary is best illustrated by the General Motors Corporation Class E Common Stock. Class E Stock holders are entitled to only one-half a vote per share, and their dividends are dependent on the paid-in surplus attributable to that particular class of stock and to the separate net income of General Motors' Electronic Data Systems Corporation subsidiary. Such a class of stock enables the marketplace to establish a separate market value for the subsidiary while ensuring that the parent company retains 100% voting control and thus the right to consolidate the subsidiary for

Exhibit 4. Selected Convertible Debt/Preferred Stock Innovations

Security	Distinguishing Characteristics	Risk Reallocation/ Yield Reduction	Enhanced Liquidity	Reduction in Agency Costs	Reduction in Transaction Costs	Tax Arbitrage	Other Benefits
Adjustable Rate Convertible Debt	Debt the interest rate on which varies directly with the dividend rate on the underlying common stock. No conversion premium.					Effectively, tax deductible common equity. Security has since been ruled equity by the IRS.	Portion of the issue carried as equity on the issuer's balance sheet.
Convertible Exchangeable Preferred Stock	Convertible preferred stock that is exchangeable, at the issuer's option, for convertible debt with identical rate and identical conversion terms.				No need to reissue convertible security as debt—just exchange it—when the issuer becomes a taxpayer.	Issuer can exchange debt for the preferred when it becomes taxable with interest rate the same as the dividend rate and without any change in conversion features.	Appears as equity on the issuer's balance sheet until it is exchanged for convertible debt.
Convertible Reset Debentures	Convertible bond the interest rate on which must be adjusted upward, if necessary, by an amount sufficient to give the debentures a market value equal to their face amount 2 years after issuance.			Investor is protected against a deterioration in the issuer's financial prospects within 2 years of issuance.			
Debt with Mandatory Common Stock Purchase Contracts	Notes with contracts that obligate note purchasers to buy sufficient common stock from the issuer to retire the issue in full by its scheduled maturity date.					Notes provide a stream of interest tax shields, which (true) equity does not.	Commercial bank holding companies have issued it because it counted as "primary capital" for regulatory purposes.
Exchangeable Auction Preferred Stock	Auction rate preferred stock that is exchangeable on any dividend payment date, at the option of the issuer, for auction rate notes, the interest rate on which is reset by Dutch auction every 35 days.	Issuer bears more interest rate risk than a fixed-rate instrument would involve.	Security is designed to trade near its par value.		Issuance of auction rate notes involves no underwriting commissions.	Issuer can exchange notes for the preferred when it becomes taxable.	Appears as equity on the issuer's balance sheet until it is exchanged for auction rate notes.
Synthetic Convertible Debt	Debt and warrants package structured in such a way as to mirror a traditional convertible debt issue.					In effect, warrant proceeds are tax deductible.	Warrants go on the balance sheet as equity.
Zero Coupon Convertible Debt	Non-interest-bearing convertible debt issue.					If issue converts, the issuer will have sold, in effect, tax deductible equity.	If holders convert, entire debt service stream is converted to common equity.

federal income tax purposes. It can also prove useful for an employee stock option plan or other incentive compensation schemes for employees of the subsidiary.

The first Americus Trust was offered to owners of American Telephone & Telegraph Company common stock on October 25, 1983 [2]. Since then, more than two dozen other Americus Trusts have been formed. An Americus Trust offers the common stockholders of a company the opportunity to strip each of their common shares into a PRIME Component, which carries full dividend and voting rights and limited capital ap-

preciation rights, and a SCORE Component, which carries full capital appreciation rights above a threshold price. PRIMES and SCORES appear to expand the range of securities available for inclusion in investment portfolios.[4]

---

[4]The AT&T Americus Trust was formed prior to the breakup of AT&T. The trust therefore provided an opportunity for investors to acquire units representing shares in pre-reorganization AT&T (i.e., proportionate interests in post-reorganization AT&T and in the seven regional holding companies AT&T spun off) perhaps more cheaply than they could by accumulating the shares of the different entities on their own.

Exhibit 5. Selected Common Equity Innovations

Security	Distinguishing Characteristics	Risk Reallocation/ Yield Reduction	Enhanced Liquidity	Reduction in Agency Costs	Reduction in Transaction Costs	Tax Arbitrage	Other Benefits
Additional Class(es) of Common Stock	A company issues a second class of common stock the dividends on which are tied to the earnings of a specified subsidiary.						Establishes separate market value for the subsidiary while assuring the parent 100% voting control. Useful for employee compensation programs for subsidiary.
Americus Trust	Outstanding shares of a particular company's common stock are contributed to a five-year unit investment trust. Units may be separated into a PRIME component, which embodies full dividend and voting rights in the underlying share and permits limited capital appreciation, and a SCORE component, which provides full capital appreciation above a stated price.	Stream of annual total returns on a share of stock is separated into (i) a dividend stream (with limited capital appreciation potential) and (ii) a (residual) capital appreciation stream.				PRIME component would appeal to corporate investors who can take advantage of the 70% dividends received deduction. SCORE component would appeal to capital-gain-oriented individual investors.	PRIME component resembles participating preferred stock if the issuer's common stock dividend rate is stable. SCORE component is a longer-dated call option than the ones customarily traded in the options market.
Master Limited Partnership	A business is given the legal form of a partnership but is otherwise structured, and is traded publicly, like a corporation.					Eliminates a layer of taxation because partnerships are not taxable entities.	
Puttable Common Stock	Issuer sells a new issue of common stock along with rights to put the stock back to the issuer on a specified date at a specified price.	Issuer sells investors a put option, which investors will exercise if the company's share price decreases.		The put option reduces agency costs associated with a new share issue that are brought on by informational asymmetries.			Equivalent under certain conditions to convertible bonds but can be recorded as equity on the balance sheet so long as the company's payment obligation under the put option can be settled in common stock.

Master limited partnerships are publicly traded limited partnerships that operate much like corporations except for their legal status, and many are listed on the New York Stock Exchange. The partnership structure eliminates a layer of taxation. However, if an entity is profitable and needs to retain the bulk of its earnings, the limited partners will owe tax on their respective pro rata shares of the partnership's income. Collins and Bey [16] show that the master limited partnership structure is best suited for companies with high tax rates and low retention rates, i.e., companies in "mature" industries, but is poorly suited for companies in "growth" industries.

Puttable common stock involves the sale of put options along with a new issue of common stock. The package of securities is comparable to a convertible bond [15]. The put option reduces the agency costs associated with a new share issue and could prove useful in reducing, or perhaps even eliminating, the underpricing of initial public offerings.

V. Innovative Financial Processes

The innovative financial processes listed in Exhibit 1 reflect three basic causal factors: (i) efforts aimed at reducing transaction costs, (ii) steps taken to reduce idle cash balances in response to higher interest rates, and (iii) the availability of relatively inexpensive computer technology to facilitate quicker financial transactions. The shelf registration process, extended to a broad range of corporate issuers by the Securities and Exchange Commission in 1982, has streamlined the process of issuing corporate securities. Kidwell, Marr, and Thompson [34] document the reduction in flotation costs that has resulted from this innovative offering process. Similarly, the direct sale of securities to the public, as evidenced by Green Mountain Power Company's sale of debt securities to its ratepayers beginning in 1970 and Virginia Electric and Power Company's sale of common stock to its ratepayers beginning some ten years later, also reduce transaction costs because the securities are not sold through securities firms. Such offering methods have the potential for reducing a company's cost of capital by appealing to a natural clientele for the company's securities.

Discount brokerage, which resulted from the elimination of fixed commission rates by the Securities and Exchange Commission on May 1, 1975, has substantially reduced brokerage commission charges below the commission rates the "full-service" brokerage houses charge. Essentially, brokerage services have become unbundled. As a result of discount brokerage, individuals can pay separately for transaction execution. Electronic security trading and automated teller machines were also intended to reduce transaction costs.

Electronic security trading, automated teller machines, point-of-sale terminals, electronic funds transfer, CHIPS (Clearinghouse Interbank Payment System), and cash management/sweep accounts have all been made possible by the availability of inexpensive computer technology. The last three were also motivated by a desire to speed cash collection, to speed check processing, and to ensure the investment of excess cash balances, respectively, all in order to reduce idle cash balances, whose opportunity cost increases with rising interest rates. Gentry [27] provides a comprehensive review of recent developments in corporate cash management. It seems likely that further technological advances will lead to more efficient systems for effecting financial transactions and for managing cash balances.

VI. Creative Solutions to Corporate Finance Problems

Although it does not seem reflected in the relatively small number of items listed in that category in Exhibit 1, finding creative solutions to corporate finance problems is an important undertaking. For example, considerable practitioner and academic effort has been expended trying to develop the most efficient strategy for calling high-coupon debt when interest rates decline [11]. Volatile interest rates have also created opportunities for companies to extinguish debt at a discount from its face amount, which produces accounting benefits. Developing techniques for accomplishing this tax-free illustrates the interaction between financial engineering and Kane's regulatory dialectic. The Bankruptcy Tax Act of 1980 eliminated several widely used strategies for obtaining the gain tax-free. Such a gain is the difference between the face amount of the debt and the repurchase price. Investment bankers first developed debt-for-lower-coupon-debt exchanges, and later developed stock-for-debt swaps, in order to achieve tax-free treatment. But the Tax Reform Act of 1984 made the gain realized in such transactions taxable and thereby virtually eliminated all remaining possibilities for refunding discounted debt profitably [20]. Nevertheless, investment bankers came up with in-substance defeasance as a means for extinguishing discounted debt in a tax-free manner. However, Peterson, Peterson, and Ang [40] correctly point out that such transactions are unlikely to enhance shareholder wealth.

Bankers and corporate treasurers have also expended considerable effort to come up with more tax-effective cash management strategies, including preferred dividend rolls (see Joehnk, Bowlin, and Petty [29]) and hedged dividend capture (see Brown and Lummer [12] and Zivney and Alderson [56] and references therein) in addition to the new forms of floating-rate preferred stock discussed earlier.

The third major area of activity encompasses leveraged buyout structuring, corporate restructuring, and project finance/lease/asset-based financial structurings. All involve, among other things, the crafting of contractual and other security arrangements that allocate financial risks and rewards among shareholders and one or more classes of creditors. For example, a leveraged buyout typically involves multiple layers of equity and multiple layers of debt, each with its own particular security arrangements. The capital structure must be engineered to suit the risk-return characteristics of the portfolio of operating assets, to satisfy the risk-return preferences of the various classes of investors, and to minimize potential agency costs.

Recent research has documented the substantial increases in shareholder wealth—on the order of 30%—accompanying the announcements of leveraged buyouts and leveraged recapitalizations [7, 35, 52]. Financial engineering in such cases involves estimating the cash flow stream available to service debt and preferred stock, determining the most appropriate capital structure (including the examining of the advantages of using employee stock ownership plans or other specialized forms of financing to effect the transaction [14]), designing the terms of each issue of securities so as to allocate risks and returns appropriately and minimize potential agency costs, and crafting incentive compensation arrangements for managers to ensure shareholder-wealth-maximizing behavior. Most attention in the financial press has been focused on the restructuring of financially healthy companies, but the same issues arise, and are potentially more challenging, when a troubled company is involved (as for example in the reorganization of First City Bancorporation of Texas into a recapitalized bank holding company and a collecting bank, the latter being given $1.79 billion of nonperforming, past due, and other lesser quality assets that were removed from First City Bancorporation's books [23]).

VII. Conclusion

One of the more important questions raised by Miller is whether the process of financial innovation has reached the point of diminishing returns. If the tax regime remains static, if interest rates stabilize, if the regulatory landscape solidifies, and so on, diminishing returns to financial innovation are bound to set in eventually. But to the extent that financial innovation occurs in response to unexpected economic, tax, and regulatory shocks, such shocks can keep the process of financial innovation going indefinitely without diminishing returns necessarily setting in. Financial innovations symbolize the profit-driven response to the changes in the economic, tax, and regulatory environment. As this environment changes, and as consolidation within the financial services industry intensifies competition, market participants will seek out new ways to conduct financial transactions more efficiently. The rapid pace of financial innovation therefore seems likely to continue.

While much has been written about the process of financial innovation, there has been little empirical analysis of the process. Future research might fruitfully pursue either of two basic lines of inquiry: possible further financial innovations and the economics of financial innovation. With regard to the first line of inquiry, one area that seems particularly fruitful for further investigation is that of mortgage-related securities—specifically, developing the means for further reducing the investor's prepayment risk, and perhaps eventually combining a portfolio of mortgages with options and/or futures and/or interest rate swaps so as to eliminate prepayment risk entirely. Other areas include the

securitization of additional classes of assets and further applications of futures and options to customize securities issues to suit issuer and investor preferences better.

With regard to the economics of financial innovation, the principal issues concern the profitability of securities innovation and how the process of financial innovation operates. In particular, how are the rewards to securities innovation allocated among the financial institution that develops the innovative security, the issuer, and investors? Are the innovator's profits excessive, as Van Horne seems to suggest they might have been in some cases, or are they commensurate with the costs and risks of the process that Miller and others have noted? How are the rewards to the innovator affected as competitors introduce similar products or refinements? Who are the principal innovators: securities firms, banks, securities issuers, the academic community, or others? The answers to these and related questions will promote our understanding of financial engineering, an activity that plays a crucial role in promoting market efficiency.

References

1. M.J. Alderson, K.C. Brown, and S.L. Lummer, "Dutch Auction Rate Preferred Stock," *Financial Management* (Summer 1987), pp. 68–73.
2. Americus Trust for AT&T Common Shares, Series A, Prospectus, October 25, 1983.
3. M. Arak, A. Estrella, L. Goodman, and A. Silver, "Interest Rate Swaps: An Alternative Explanation," *Financial Management* (Summer 1988), pp. 12–18.
4. M.D. Atchison, R.F. DeMong, and J.L. Kling, *New Financial Instruments: A Descriptive Guide,* Charlottesville, VA, Financial Analysts Research Foundation, 1985.
5. M. Ben-Horim and W. Silber, "Financial Innovation: A Linear Programming Approach," *Journal of Banking and Finance* (September 1977), pp. 277–296.
6. J. Bicksler and A.H. Chen, "An Economic Analysis of Interest Rate Swaps," *Journal of Finance* (July 1986), pp. 645–655.
7. B.S. Black and J.A. Grundfest, "Shareholder Gains from Takeovers and Restructurings between 1981 and 1986: $162 Billion is a Lot of Money," *The Continental Bank Journal of Applied Corporate Finance* (Spring 1988), pp. 5–15.
8. F. Black and M. Scholes, "From Theory to a New Financial Product," *Journal of Finance* (May 1974), pp. 399–412.
9. S.B. Block and T.J. Gallagher, "The Use of Interest Rate Futures and Options by Corporate Financial Managers," *Financial Management* (Autumn 1986), pp. 73–78.
10. J.R. Booth, R.L. Smith, and R.W. Stolz, "The Use of Interest Futures by Financial Institutions," *Journal of Bank Research* (Spring 1984), pp. 15–20.

11. W.M. Boyce and A.J. Kalotay, "Optimum Bond Calling and Refunding," *Interfaces* (November 1979), pp. 36–49.
12. K.C. Brown and S.L. Lummer, "A Reexamination of the Covered Call Option Strategy for Corporate Cash Management," *Financial Management* (Summer 1986), pp. 13–17.
13. K.C. Brown and D.J. Smith, "Recent Innovations in Interest Rate Risk Management and the Reintermediation of Commercial Banking," in this issue of *Financial Management*.
14. R.F. Bruner, "Leveraged ESOPs and Corporate Restructuring," *The Continental Bank Journal of Applied Corporate Finance* (Spring 1988), pp. 54–66.
15. A.H. Chen and J.W. Kensinger, "Puttable Stock: A New Innovation in Equity Financing," *Financial Management* (Spring 1988), pp. 27–37.
16. J.M. Collins and R.P. Bey, "The Master Limited Partnership: An Alternative to the Corporation," *Financial Management* (Winter 1986), pp. 5–14.
17. P.H. Darrow and R.A. Mestres, Jr., *Creative Financing in the 1980s*, New York, Practising Law Institute, 1983.
18. J. Dutt, "What's Hot, What's Not," *Investment Dealers' Digest* (March 17, 1986), pp. 20–28.
19. J.D. Finnerty, "Zero Coupon Bond Arbitrage: An Illustration of the Regulatory Dialectic at Work," *Financial Management* (Winter 1985), pp. 13–17.
20. ———, "Refunding Discounted Debt: A Clarifying Analysis," *Journal of Financial and Quantitative Analysis* (March 1986), pp. 95–106.
21. ———, "The Case for Issuing Synthetic Convertible Bonds," *Midland Corporate Finance Journal* (Fall 1986), pp. 73–82.
22. ———, "An Analytical Framework for Evaluating Securities Innovations," *Journal of Corporate Finance* (Winter 1987), pp. 3–18.
23. First City Bancorporation of Texas, Inc., Proxy Statement, January 26, 1988.
24. L. Fisher, I.E. Brick, and F.K.W. Ng, "Tax Incentives and Financial Innovation: The Case of Zero-Coupon and Other Deep-Discount Corporate Bonds," *Financial Review* (November 1983), pp. 292–305.
25. B. Friedman, "Postwar Changes in the American Financial Markets," in M. Feldstein (ed.), *The American Economy in Transition*, Chicago, University of Chicago Press, 1980.
26. W.K.H. Fung and A. Rudd, "Pricing New Corporate Bond Issues: An Analysis of Issue Cost and Seasoning Effects," *Journal of Finance* (July 1986), pp. 633–643.
27. J.A. Gentry, "State of the Art of Short-Run Financial Management," *Financial Management* (Summer 1988), pp. 41–57.
28. L.S. Goodman and J.B. Yawitz, "Innovation in the U. S. Bond Market," *Institutional Investor Money Management Forum* (December 1987), pp. 102–104.
29. M.D. Joehnk, O.D. Bowlin, and J.W. Petty, "Preferred Dividend Rolls: A Viable Strategy for Corporate Money Managers?," *Financial Management* (Summer 1980), pp. 78–87.
30. E.P. Jones and S.P. Mason, "Equity-Linked Debt," *Midland Corporate Finance Journal* (Winter 1986), pp. 47–58.
31. E.J. Kane, "Good Intentions and Unintended Evil: The Case Against Selective Credit Allocation," *Journal of Money, Credit and Banking* (February 1977), pp. 55–69.
32. ———, "Accelerating Inflation, Technological Innovation, and the Decreasing Effectiveness of Banking Regulation," *Journal of Finance* (May 1981), pp. 355–367.
33. ———, "Technological and Regulatory Forces in the Developing Fusion of Financial—Services Competition," *Journal of Finance* (July 1984), pp. 759–772.
34. D.S. Kidwell, M.W. Marr, and G.R. Thompson, "SEC Rule 415: The Ultimate Competitive Bid," *Journal of Financial and Quantitative Analysis* (June 1984), pp. 183–195.
35. R.T. Kleiman, "The Shareholder Gains from Leveraged Cash-Outs: Some Preliminary Evidence," *The Continental Bank Journal of Applied Corporate Finance* (Spring 1988), pp. 46–53.
36. J.J. McConnell and E.S. Schwartz, "LYON Taming," *Journal of Finance* (July 1986), pp. 561–576.
37. G. Miller, "The Knockoff Artists," *Institutional Investor* (May 1986), p. 81ff.
38. M.H. Miller, "Financial Innovation: The Last Twenty Years and the Next," *Journal of Financial and Quantitative Analysis* (December 1986), pp. 459–471.
39. J.P. Ogden, "An Analysis of Yield Curve Notes," *Journal of Finance* (March 1987), pp. 99–110.
40. P. Peterson, D. Peterson, and J. Ang, "The Extinguishment of Debt Through In-Substance Defeasance," *Financial Management* (Spring 1985), pp. 59–67.
41. W. Power, "Many of 1987's New Trading Products Are Failing Despite Spirited Marketing," *Wall Street Journal* (January 4, 1988), p. 26.
42. *Recent Innovations in International Banking*, Bank for International Settlements, April 1986.
43. T.E. Ricks, "SEC Chief Calls Some Financial Products 'Too Dangerous' for Individual Investors," *Wall Street Journal* (January 7, 1988), p. 46.
44. A.C. Shapiro, "Guidelines for Long-Term Corporate Financing Strategy," *Midland Corporate Finance Journal* (Winter 1986), pp. 6–19.
45. D. Shirreff, "Down with Innovation!," *Euromoney* (August 1986), p. 23ff.
46. W.L. Silber (ed.), *Financial Innovation*, Lexington, MA, Lexington Books, 1975.
47. ———, "Innovation, Competition, and New Contract Design in Futures Markets," *Journal of Futures Markets* (No. 2, 1981), pp. 123–156.
48. ———, "The Process of Financial Innovation," *American Economic Review* (May 1983), pp. 89–95.
49. D.J. Smith, "The Pricing of Bull and Bear Floating Rate Notes: An Application of Financial Engineering," in this issue of *Financial Management*.
50. J. Spratlin and P. Vianna, *An Investor's Guide to CMOs*, New York, Salomon Brothers Inc, May 1986.
51. J. Sterngold, "Anatomy of a Staggering Loss," *New York Times* (May 11, 1987), p. D1ff.
52. K. Torabzadeh and W. Bertin, "Leveraged Buyouts and Stockholder Wealth," *Journal of Financial Research* (Winter 1987), pp.

313–321.

53. J.C. Van Horne, "Of Financial Innovations and Excesses," *Journal of Finance* (July 1985), pp. 621–631.

54. B.J. Winger, C.R. Chen, J.D. Martin, J.W. Petty, and S.C. Hayden, "Adjustable Rate Preferred Stock," *Financial Management* (Spring 1986), pp. 48–57.

55. J.B. Yawitz and K.J. Maloney, "Evaluating the Decision to Issue Original Issue Discount Bonds: Term Structure and Tax Effects," *Financial Management* (Winter 1983), pp. 36–46.

56. T.L. Zivney and M.J. Alderson, "Hedged Dividend Capture with Stock Index Options," *Financial Management* (Summer 1986), pp. 5–12.

Article 3

Derivative Assets Analysis

Mark Rubinstein

A *derivative asset* is an asset whose payoffs are completely determined by the prices or payoffs of other underlying assets.[1] While exchange-traded index and interest rate futures and index and equity options are among the most visible examples, many other securities and real assets can also be interpreted as derivative assets (see Appendix).

The increasing importance of derivative assets analysis in modern financial markets is clear. On June 30, 1986, a typical trading day, the total market value of the volume of trading in stocks listed on the New York Stock Exchange was $6.4 billion (160,000,000 shares). Measured in terms of the shares to which an option is a right, the total market value of the volume of trading in exchange-traded equity and index options was $12.9 billion, roughly double the volume of NYSE listed stocks. Measured in terms of the delivery obligation of a futures contract, the total market value of the volume of trading in exchange-traded index futures was $8.1 billion. Comparable figures for Treasury-bond, Treasury-bill and Eurodollar futures were $11.5 billion, $4.2 billion and $22.3 billion, respectively. Outside the United States, Japan's government bond futures market rivals the size of the Eurodollar futures market. Just 14 years ago, these exchange-traded derivative assets did not exist.

[1]This paper uses the term "derivative assets" in place of the common term "contingent claims" used with some variation in meaning in the academic literature. The term "contingent claims" is reserved to mean a class of assets (which includes derivative assets) whose payoffs are completely determined by a predefined set of underlying variables. For example, an inflation future whose payoff depends on realizations of the Consumer Price Index and a Value Line Index future are contingent claims, but they are not derivative assets.

■ *Mark Rubinstein is Professor of Finance, University of California at Berkeley, Berkeley, California.*

Future or forward contract: An arrangement whereby the seller currently agrees to deliver to the buyer a specified underlying asset on a specified future date (delivery date) at a fixed price. In the case of a forward contract, the entire payment occurs on the delivery date; in the case of a futures contract, payment occurs in installments each business day through the delivery date.

European call or put option: A contract giving the buyer the right to buy (in the case of a call) or sell (in the case of a put) a fixed number of units of a specified underlying asset at a fixed price (called the striking price) on a given future date (referred to as the expiration date).

Derivative assets can be used to provide tailor-made patterns of returns stitched from the fabric of their underlying assets to suit the needs of particular investors. For example, suppose an investor would like to buy a particular stock but cannot afford to lose more than 6 percent of the investment should the stock decline. By buying put options on the stock (which may cost 6 percent or less of the stock price), the investor can retain most of the upside potential while at the same time limiting the loss to the cost of the puts. To take another case, suppose an investor knows that some important news is about to be made public (such as the results of a merger negotiation) that would have a significant impact on the market price of a stock. But the investor does not know in advance whether the news will be favorable or unfavorable. Buying a "straddle" (purchasing a call and a put on the underlying stock) might be an appropriate position. This strategy will show a profit whether the stock subsequently moves up or down—as long as it makes a strong move in either direction.

Because of the close relation between the payoffs of a derivative asset and its underlying assets, an investor can often devise a trading strategy using the underlying assets (and possibly a cash or default-free asset) to replicate the payoffs of a desired derivative asset, even if the derivative asset cannot be purchased directly on securities exchanges or in the over-the-counter market. The most important example of "manufactured" derivative assets is portfolio insurance. Just as a life insurance contract must be specifically designed for each individual and is not a standardized traded instrument, insurance against loss on a given investor's portfolio must be tailor-made since no standardized derivative asset is likely to be available with the investor's portfolio as the underlying asset. Even if such an instrument were available, it might not have the desired deductible or maturity. Nonetheless, it is possible to create a type of "insurance" on the investor's underlying portfolio by following a particular trading strategy utilizing only the underlying asset and a cash substitute. Today, it is estimated that at least $50 billion dollars of institutional portfolios are being used to manufacture this type of insurance. As little as five years ago, the term "portfolio insurance" was esoteric academic exotica.

The two key questions surrounding any derivative asset are: how should the derivative asset be valued and how can the payoffs of the derivative be replicated by following a trading strategy using the underlying assets? These questions are closely intertwined. If a trading strategy can be isolated using the underlying assets which provides exactly the same payoffs as the related derivative asset, then, if there are to be no arbitrage opportunities, the current cost of establishing the positions required by the trading strategy must equal the current value of the related derivative asset. This type of insight leads to using underlying assets to manufacture currently non-existent derivative assets by following derived replicating trading strategies.

The existence of replicating arbitrage strategies has permitted techniques for valuing derivative assets to develop independently, for the most part, from the general theory of equilibrium asset pricing. Given the price and probability distribution of an underlying asset, derivative assets analysis may be able to value associated options on that underlying asset. Derivative assets analysis does not provide the equilibrium price of the underlying asset; for that, one needs a general equilibrium model. Moreover, the stochastic process describing how the price of the underlying asset changes over time is usually assumed, rather than derived from more basic hypotheses concerning tastes and technology. Instead, derivative assets analysis shows that in equilibrium there must be certain relationships between the price of the derivative asset and the value of the underlying asset, given that the price of the underlying asset moves according to given rules. Moreover, since many derivative assets can be associated with the same underlying asset (a corporation's stock, bonds, preferred shares, and so on), derivative assets analysis can determine how the values of these securities are related to each other without knowledge of the characteristics of securities issued by other corporations.

Because the task of derivative assets analysis is less ambitious than that of general equilibrium analysis, it is often possible to derive results based on more acceptable assumptions that depend on parameters that are comparatively easy to measure. As long as the assumptions concerning the stochastic processes governing the returns of the underlying asset are consistent with those of general equilibrium analysis, this derivative asset analysis will result in values consistent with those that a full equilibrium model would provide.

Derivative Assets Based on Buy-and-Hold Strategies

The *payoff function* of a derivative asset is a mathematical representation of the relation between the payoffs of the derivative and the prices or payoffs of the underlying assets. One of the simplest and oldest examples is a *forward contract*, an arrangement whereby the seller agrees to deliver to the buyer a specified asset on a specified future date at a fixed price, to be paid on the delivery date. Typically, no money changes hands until the delivery date. For example, the payoff function for a Standard & Poors 500 Index forward contract is

$$C^* = S^* - F$$

where C^* is the value of the forward contract on the delivery date, S^* is the level of the S&P 500 Index at that time, and F is the previously agreed upon forward price. In this case, the seller is obligated to deliver on the future delivery date the cash value on that future date of the S&P 500 Index (S^*), while the buyer is obligated to pay the currently agreed fixed price (F) on the delivery date.

Payoff functions of this type are particularly easy to analyze. The present value of the derivative asset (C) is simply the present value of the future index value, which is defined as $V(S^*)$, minus the present value of paying out the forward price for certain on the delivery date, defined as $V(F)$. Using V, the valuation operator

$$C = V(C^*) = V(S^* - F) = V(S^*) - V(F).$$

The final equality follows from this: if the payoffs from the constituent variables can be purchased and sold separately and no arbitrage opportunities exist, then the present value of the sum of the variables equals the sum of their present values—another version of the whole equaling the sum of its parts and an application of the "value additivity theorem" discussed by Varian in this journal.

The next step is to realize that the present value of the index is its current value (S) minus the amount of money which would need to be set aside currently to pay any dividends (D) through the delivery date. In short, $V(S^*) = S - D$. Moreover, if r is one plus the annualized riskless rate of interest and t is the time to the delivery date, then the present value of paying the forward price for certain on the delivery date is Fr^{-t}. Putting this together

$$V(C^*) = V(S^*) - V(F) = (S - D) - Fr^{-t}.$$

Clearly, the higher F, the amount that must be paid at the termination of the contract, the lower the value (to the buyer) of the contract. In most real-life situations, the forward price F is set so that no money need change hands at the inception of the contract; that is, F is chosen so that the present value of the forward contract is zero. Therefore,

$$V(C^*) = (S - D) - Fr^{-t} = 0 \Rightarrow F = (S - D)r^t$$

and the forward price is determined.

The replicating strategy for the forward contract is clear from the payoff function. The problem is to arrange to receive the index value at the delivery date and simultaneously incur a debt requiring payment of F dollars at that time. To do this an investor could buy the underlying index, sell off rights to any dividends prior to the delivery date, and borrow the present value of the forward price.[2]

More generally, this simple analysis suggests that whenever the payoff function is linear in the prices of the underlying assets, an investor can hope to replicate the derivative asset by a *buy-and-hold* position in the underlying assets, possibly supplemented with riskless borrowing or lending. A proportional payoff function is one in

[2] For this forward contract, or more generally whenever it is possible to store the underlying asset costlessly through the delivery date, the forward price contains no more information about the future price of the underlying asset than is contained in the current price of the underlying asset and the rate of interest. However, if it is either not possible or very costly to store the underlying asset, then the arbitrage argument required for derivative assets analysis breaks down and the forward price may contain information about the future price of the underlying asset that is not available from other sources.

which the payoff is proportional to the price of the underlying asset; a linear payoff function is one in which, in addition, there may be a fixed payoff that does not depend on the price. Thus the payoff to the forward contract is linear, since there is a fixed payment F and the payoff $S^* - F$ increases directly with S^*. Whenever there is a fixed component to the payoff, the valuation result will depend on the rate of interest; that is, the replicating strategy will need a riskless asset to deliver the payoff function. Borrowing will be necessary if there is a fixed payment and lending if there is a fixed receipt.

On the other hand, some derivative assets have a payoff that increases with the price of the underlying asset, but by an amount which is less (or greater) than the increase in the price of the underlying asset. For instance, consider a derivative asset which promises to pay b times the price of the underlying asset. Then the replicating strategy will require purchasing b units of the underlying asset. (If b is negative, the strategy will entail shorting; that is, holding a negative position in the underlying asset.) If the value of a derivative asset with a payoff of S^* is known, the value of a derivative asset paying bS^* will be b times as large. More generally, if the payoff function is of the form

$$C^* = a + b_1 S_1^* + b_2 S_2^*$$

an investor can replicate the derivative asset by risklessly lending ar^{-t} dollars, investing $b_1 S_1$ dollars in the first underlying asset and investing $b_2 S_2$ dollars in the second underlying asset.

Derivative Assets Based on Dynamic Replicating Strategies

Option contracts are a second important type of derivative asset. A *European call option* is a contract giving the buyer the right to buy a fixed number of units of a specified underlying asset at a fixed price at a given future date. The fixed price is colorfully termed the *striking price* and the given future date, the *expiration date*. The act of making the transaction on the expiration date of buying the underlying asset in return for paying the striking price is referred to as *exercising* the call. A purchased forward contract and a European call are thus somewhat similar: both involve exchanging the underlying asset for a specified amount of money on a specified future date. However, there is critical difference. The buyer of the forward contract is committed to make this exchange, while the buyer of the option has the right, but not the obligation, to do so. The buyer of the option contract will presumably only exercise the contract if it pays to do so; that is, if at the expiration date the value of the underlying security S^* exceeds the striking price K. If instead K exceeds S^*, the call will not be exercised, and the return is zero. Thus, the payoff for a European S&P 500 index call option is either 0 or $S^* - K$, whichever is larger. Or more formally

$$C^* = \max[0, S^* - K].$$

That is, the call will pay the difference between the terminal index price and the striking price, or zero, whichever is larger.

The current value of the call (C) is the present discounted value of the payoff $C*$, which as before is written as $V(C*)$

$$C = V(C*) = V\{\max[0, S* - K]\}.$$

Unfortunately, we cannot this time simply use the fact the present value of a sum is the sum of the present values. Instead, the present value of the call will depend on the probability that the future index level will exceed the striking price as well as by how much. While the current index value (S) and the interest rate (r) will provide some information about this value, these numbers cannot capture everything we need to know. In general, finding the present value will require knowing the probability distribution of the rate of return on the index in the area above the striking price, and how the market discounts these uncertain returns. Indeed, since this discount rate will depend on economy-wide attitudes toward risk, it would seem necessary to specify investor preferences for bearing risk. From a theoretical perspective, these requirements would have the unfortunate result of tossing this problem directly into the maelstrom and controversy of general equilibrium asset pricing analysis.

Nonetheless, some tentative conclusions can still be reached about the nature of a replicating strategy (if one exists). First, since an additive negative constant is in the payoff function, we will need to borrow risklessly. Second, since the terminal index value enters positively, we will need to purchase the index. Third, since the call payoff will be relatively insensitive to the index value whenever the index falls below K but relatively sensitive to the index when the index rises above K, we will need to be holding more of the index at high values than at low index values. In contrast to replicating derivative assets with linear payoff functions where only a buy-and-hold position is needed, with a nonlinear payoff function, we will need to follow a *dynamic* strategy. Mere inspection of the payoff function gives clues about the replicating strategy.[3]

Valuing and Replicating Other Derivative Assets

Sometimes we can shortcut the analysis of one derivative asset by showing that it has a payoff function similar to one already analyzed. This procedure will be useful because it can establish relations among the prices of related derivative assets. Establishing such relations is one of the main objectives of derivative assets analysis.

For example, here's how to derive the fundamental relation between a European call and put. A *put* is similar to a call except that it reverses the contracted exchanges: the put buyer has the option of selling a fixed number of units of the underlying asset on the expiration date in return for receiving a fixed price K on the expiration date. Thus, if the price of the underlying asset $S*$ is less than K, the put will be exercised because the put buyer will want to take advantage of the opportunity to sell the

[3]The convexity or concavity of the payoff function also gives us advance notice of the level of portfolio turnover that may be needed to replicate the derivative asset. The faster the payoff function changes in slope as the terminal underlying asset price changes, the more trading will be expected to be required.

underlying asset at a price higher than its market price. The value of the put in that case is just $K - S^*$. On the other hand, if the market price S^* of the underlying asset exceeds K, the put will not be exercised; the right to sell the underlying asset at price K has no value when anyone can sell it at a price of S^* on the market. Thus, the payoff for a European S&P 500 Index put contract is either 0 or $K - S^*$, whichever is larger. That is, the payoff function is

$$\max[0, K - S^*].$$

A little rearrangement shows this payoff is equivalent to

$$\max[0, S^* - K] - S^* + K.$$

To see this, suppose S^* ends up less than K, then the put contract pays off $K - S^*$. The rearranged payoff would then equal $0 - S^* + K$. On the other hand, suppose S^* ends up greater than K, then the put contract will be worth 0 and the rearranged payoff would then equal $S^* - K - S^* + K$, which also nets out to 0. Thus, we are able to rewrite the payoff from a put in terms of the payoff of an otherwise identical call option. Using the valuation operator and the value additivity theorem

$$V\{\max[0, K - S^*]\} = V\{\max[0, S^* - K]\} - V(S^*) + V(K)$$

$$= C - (S - D) + Kr^{-t}.$$

This argument demonstrates that *the present value of a put equals the present value of an otherwise identical call minus the present value of a position in the underlying index, which is not entitled to receive dividends prior to expiration, plus the present value of the striking price.* Academics call this equality the "put-call parity relation" while practitioners call it the "option conversion relationship" since it is used in the market to manufacture puts out of calls.

Consider another derivative asset, known as a "collar", which provides a minimum amount K_1 if the terminal index value is below K_1, the terminal index value itself whenever the index ends up in the middle range between K_1 and K_2, and a maximum amount K_2 if the terminal index value is above K_2. The payoff function for this is

$$\min\{\max[S^*, K_1], K_2\}.$$

A little rearranging shows this can be written as

$$K_1 + \max[0, S^* - K_1] - \max[0, S^* - K_2]$$

which demonstrates that this derivative asset is equivalent to a portfolio consisting of lending $K_1 r^{-t}$, buying an index call with striking price K_1, and selling an index call with striking price K_2.

In each of these cases, the problems of valuing and replicating a particular derivative asset have been converted into the problems of valuing and replicating one or more call options. It remains to find some way of satisfactorily solving our original problem of valuing a single call option.

Black-Scholes Option Pricing Formula

The genesis of the modern approach to the valuation of derivative assets with non-linear payoff functions can be traced to a paper by Kenneth Arrow that was originally presented at a Paris colloquium in 1952, but twelve years passed before the paper was published in English (Arrow, 1964). Among other important results, Arrow developed a theory justifying the general principle that investors may be able to make up for an incomplete set of forward markets if they have enough opportunities to revise their holdings of traded assets prior to a horizon date. This is the essence of the modern Black-Scholes option pricing argument. In Arrow's model, individuals had to be able to predict in advance the prices of the traded assets conditional on "the state of the world." In the Black-Scholes model, investors are assumed to know in advance that the underlying asset price follows a continuous path with a constant variance.

Black and Scholes (1973), probably without realizing the connection to Arrow's work, emphasize a special case of Arrow's model in which only two traded assets (one riskless) are needed to manufacture any derivative asset whose payoff is a deterministic function of the terminal value of the underlying asset price.[4] The previous example of a European index call pointed out that its valuation requires knowing the probability distribution of the rate of return on the index in the area above the striking price. Black and Scholes essentially assumed that the probability distribution of the underlying asset was lognormal, so that it could be completely described by its arithmetic mean and *volatility* (the standard deviation of the natural logarithm of the index price relative). They then derived a self-financing trading strategy using only the underlying index and cash which would exactly replicate the payoffs of the call. Since this argument could all be based on the assumption that no arbitrage possibilities exist, information about investor preferences for bearing risk (data required by a general equilibrium theory of asset prices) was unnecessary. In addition, information about the arithmetic mean return of the index was also not required. Thus, with great ingenuity, Black-Scholes derived a formula for the value of a call depending only on the volatility of the index, as well as the same inputs required for finding the value of a derivative asset with a linear payoff: current price of the index, the striking price, the time to expiration, interest rate, and the pattern of dividends to be paid prior to expiration. .

The Black-Scholes solution to call valuation is the now famous equation (ignoring dividends)

$$C = SN(x) - Kr^{-t}N(x - \sigma\sqrt{t})$$

[4] Robert Merton (1973) extended the Black-Scholes model in many important ways.

where

$$x = \tfrac{1}{2}\sigma\sqrt{t} + \left[\log(S/Kr^{-t})\right]/\sigma\sqrt{t}.$$

Here, σ is the volatility of the index. N is the standard normal distribution function evaluated at x in the first term and at $x - \sigma\sqrt{t}$ in the second term. The N function therefore provides a number between 0 and 1. Recall that the strategy required to replicate the pattern of returns of the option is dynamic; that is, investors will have to change their portfolios at each moment of time. It turns out that the replicating strategy may be read directly from the form of the equation. The number of units of the index in the replicating portfolio is simply the derivative of the current call value (C) with respect to the index level (S). This can be shown to be $N(x)$. Therefore, the first term of the Black-Scholes formula, $SN(x)$, is the currently appropriate dollar amount to invest in the index. Anything left over, $C - SN(x)$, must be invested in cash. So the second term, $-Kr^{-t}N(x - \sigma\sqrt{t})$, is the dollar amount of lending. Observe that the number of units invested in the underlying asset $N(x)$ at each date depends on the time t remaining until expiration. Moreover, unlike the case of linear payoffs, since $N(x)$ also depends on the concurrent underlying asset price S, it will also change stochastically over time.

The mathematical tools employed by Black and Scholes were quite advanced and tended to obscure the underlying economic principles. Fortunately, William Sharpe discovered a way to derive the basic principles of option valuation using only elementary mathematics.[5] He divided the total time prior to expiration of an option into several equally spaced intervals. At the beginning of each interval, an investor managing a replicating portfolio would be allowed to change its proportionate composition between the underlying asset and cash. The investor would not know in advance what the new price of the underlying asset would be at the end of the interval. However (and this was Sharpe's clever idea), Sharpe assumed that over each interval the underlying asset price could only move by a known fixed percentage up or by a known fixed percentage down. With only two possible outcomes over each interval, it is easily shown that any returns an option can have over that interval can be replicated using an appropriate mixture of the index and cash. In turn, this strategy leaves the investor with just the right amount of money to form another mixture of the index and cash to replicate the performance of the option over the next interval. This approach is explained more fully by Varian in this journal.

This technique for valuing derivative assets with nonlinear payoff functions is referred to as the binomial procedure and has become quite popular among traders of exchange-traded options because it provides a natural way to accommodate the effects of potential early exercise. Unlike the European options this paper has considered up to this point, exchange-traded options are "American" in that they can be exercised at any time up to and including the expiration date. Following the binomial procedure, at the beginning of each interval the exercisable value of the option is compared to the

[5]A full treatment of Sharpe's idea appears in Cox, Ross and Rubinstein (1979).

value the option would have if it were held at least one more interval. If the option is more valuable exercised, then the only change in the numerical procedure is to replace the holding value with the exercise value. Of course, this assumes that option buyers will be smart enough to exercise an option when it is in their interest. If anything, investors do not exercise exchange-traded options as soon as they should, so this procedure probably tends to overstate the prices of options.

One other solution procedure has proved very useful for solving problems with European derivative assets (Cox and Ross, 1976). Since neither investor preferences nor expected underlying asset returns enter the replicating strategy developed by Black and Scholes, any convenient assumption about these missing variables is permissible, including the extreme and simplifying assumption of risk-neutrality. In this case, the equilibrium price of any asset equals the sum of its expected payoffs, each discounted at the riskless rate of interest. For the European index call, this assumption implies

$$C = V\{\max[0, S* - K]\} = E\{\max[0, S* - K]\}/r^t.$$

Assuming the probability distribution of $S*$ is lognormal, the expected future value of the call can be found by integration. The result, with some manipulation, yields the Black-Scholes equation for the value of a call. This solution procedure assuming risk neutrality can be used whenever it can be shown from other reasoning that a replicating strategy exists.

Sample Applications

The Appendix lists many applications of derivative assets analysis that have been examined with these techniques. Here, I will take a detailed look at four applications: index futures, equity options, index options, and portfolio insurance.

The omitted applications to corporate securities have recently been surveyed by John Cox and Mark Rubinstein in *Options Markets* (Prentice-Hall, 1985, ch. 7), and the applications to real assets have been surveyed by Scott Mason and Robert Merton in "The Role of Contingent Claims Analysis in Corporate Finance" (*Recent Advances in Corporate Finance*, ed. E. Altman and M. Subrahmanyam, Irwin, 1985).

Index Futures

The valuation and replication of stock index futures would seem to be straightforward. In a futures contract, one party agrees to pay the other the difference between the market price of the underlying asset $S*$ and the futures price F. Thus, futures contracts look very much like the forward contract analyzed in the previous section, but with one important difference. With a forward contract, no money changes hands until the delivery date. Futures, on the other hand, are resettled each day, with the seller (buyer) paying the buyer (seller) any positive (negative) change in the futures price since the close of the previous trading day. Since both the forward and the futures prices must be equal to the price of the underlying asset on the delivery date, if the forward and futures prices also start out equal, the total net payments of the seller to the buyer over the life of the futures contract will equal the amount paid by the seller on the delivery date of the similar forward contract.

Thus, this distinction between forward and futures contracts might at first seem unimportant. However, if the underlying asset rises in price, a buyer will tend to receive a better return from a future than from a forward contract, because although he is paid the same amount, he will receive the money earlier and can reinvest it. For the same reason, the buyer would tend to do better with a forward contract rather than a future when the underlying asset price falls.

From a practical standpoint, how significant is the difference between S&P 500 forward and futures prices likely to be? As an exercise in arbitrage reasoning, it can be shown that if future interest rates are known in advance with certainty, then forward and futures prices must be equal. (For a demonstration, see Cox, Ingersoll and Ross, 1981.) Allowing for realistic uncertain interest rates, the difference between forward and futures prices has been examined both empirically and with Monte Carlo simulation in a number of academic papers and found to be negligible. So fortunately, for the purpose of determining the correct futures price, this paper can ignore the daily resettlement procedure and treat the future as a forward contract.

However, this conclusion does not imply that the difference between forward and futures contracts has no effect on the structure of a replicating strategy.[6] In particular, while the replicating strategy for a forward contract does not require any further trading once the position is initiated, some trading will be needed to replicate a futures contract.

How well does this theory explain actual market prices? While I have not yet seen a study which was careful to correct for all measurement problems, the patterns

---

[6] To see this, let the time to the next resettlement date be h and the time to the delivery date be t. Let the underlying asset and futures prices at the resettlement date be S_1 and F_1, and the current underlying asset and futures prices be S and F. Assume one plus the interest rate is constant and equal to r. In this case of known interest rates, forward and futures prices are equal. Thus, after time h, the cash flow from resettlement (ignoring dividends) will be

$$F_1 - F = S_1 r^{(t-h)} - S r^t.$$

The problem is to find a portfolio of the index and cash which after time t is worth this amount. Consider buying $r^{(t-h)}$ shares of the index and borrowing $S r^{(t-h)}$ dollars. Such a portfolio would be worth $S_1 r^{(t-h)} - S r^{(t-h)} r^h$ after time t, which is exactly the goal. Thus, the replicating portfolio is

$$S r^{(t-h)} \text{ dollars of the index}$$

$$S r^{(t-h)} \text{ dollars of borrowing.}$$

In terms of the futures price, this is F/r^h dollars of the index and F/r^h dollars of borrowing.

Since h is usually one day, for practical purposes, $r^h = 1$. With this approximation, replicating a future requires buying F dollars of the index financed with F dollars of borrowing. Compare this strategy to a forward contract. With no intermediate resettlement, $h = t$, and the strategy is to buy $S \ (= F/r^t)$ dollars of the index financed with S dollars of borrowing. Since F does not equal S, the replicating strategies are not the same.

of deviations of S&P 500 index futures prices from theoretical values are so pronounced that some conclusions are clear. Since S&P 500 index futures were first listed on the Chicago Mercantile Exchange in April 1982, several extended periods have occurred when the futures were consistently trading at levels significantly different than the theory would suggest. In May–June 1982 the futures traded significantly below theoretical value; in September–December 1984 the futures traded above theoretical value; and most recently, prices reverted in September 1986 to below theoretical value (even to the extent of trading below the value of the underlying index itself).

These results are difficult to reconcile with an efficiently functioning securities market. In the early days of the contract, academics were quick to find explanations for the apparent underpricing. First, they pointed out that for arbitragers to correct the mispricing they would need to buy futures and short the underlying index. Shorting the underlying index was difficult and most would short a portfolio of 40 to 50 of the most important stocks in the index. Unfortunately, this partial hedge was fraught with risk since the lack of correlation between the hedge portfolio and the S&P 500 Index could create losses, large in comparison with the predicted profits if the stock portfolio were a perfect hedge. Second, the Tax Recovery Act of 1981 required that unrealized as well as realized gains and losses on futures be taxed at the end of each fiscal year. Thus futures were at a disadvantage relative to holding the underlying stock where an investor could choose to realize losses and postpone taxation of gains. For this reason, it was argued that the futures price should be less than its theoretical value.

Unfortunately, both these arguments are very weak. Investors already holding long positions in stocks, particularly index funds, do not need to short stocks to benefit from futures underpricing. Furthermore, the largest investors are often tax exempt and most traders take only short-term positions. What is worse, these very arguments, if true, would make it even harder to explain how index futures also have periods of significant overpricing. I am forced to the conclusion that even today the growth in index futures trading continues to outstrip the amounts of capital that are available for arbitrage.

Equity Options

More work has been devoted to the problem of valuing equity options than to any other derivative asset. Recall the earlier discussion of options, which explained that valuing an option required an assumption about how the price of the underlying asset changes over time. After the discovery of the Black-Sholes formula, the major thrust of research has been the development of alternative arbitrage-based models with different assumed stochastic processes for the underlying asset. Black and Scholes assumed that the stock price follows a continuous path with a constant volatility. Generalization to a time-dependent but non-stochastic volatility is straightforward. Unfortunately, even with this extension, empirical evidence indicates that although the Black-Scholes formula usually gives values in close agreement with market prices, stock price movements deviate enough from the Black-Scholes assumptions to create significant misvaluation for at least some options.

Stock price behavior may deviate from Black-Scholes assumptions in at least four potentially important ways: (1) the price may occasionally experience large discontinuous jumps to new levels; (2) the volatility over each time interval may depend monotonically on the concurrent level of the evolving stock price; (3) the volatility over each interval may depend on the level of interest rates; and (4) the volatility may itself follow a random process unrelated to stock price or interest rate changes. These types of deviations would show up in prices of call options by causing the market prices of different options on the same underlying stock to appear out-of-line relative to each other. To discuss this phenomenon, a little more terminology is needed. Borrowing from horse racing jargon, a call option is said to be currently "out-of-the-money" if the current stock price is less than the striking price ($S < K$), "at-the-money" if the current stock price equals the striking price ($S = K$), and "in-the-money" if the current stock price is greater than the striking price ($S > K$).

Simulation analysis shows that the first type of deviation would show up in call market prices causing out-of-the-money and in-the-money calls to seem overpriced relative to at-the-money calls, and this overpricing would be relatively greater the nearer an option is to maturity. In contrast, the second type of deviation would show up as a skewing of the call prices around the at-the-money calls, where out-of-the-money calls look either overpriced or underpriced relative to in-the-money calls. The effect of the fourth type of deviation on option prices, which is often empirically difficult to distinguish from the first, depends on how the volatility is assumed to change; for example, changes in the volatility might follow a random walk modified by a tendency to revert some prespecified long-run level.

There are two ways to test for these deviations from Black-Scholes assumptions: examine stock prices directly or perform an indirect test by looking at comparative option market prices. In the latter case, the option market seems fickle, at times pricing options according to one assumption and at times another. However, one deviation from Black-Scholes' predictions tends to be consistent stock for stock and period after period: for out-of-the-money calls, shorter maturity options are overpriced relative to longer maturity options. This relationship probably reflects a jump component to stock price movements that is missing from the Black-Scholes model. The general evidence suggests that a model simultaneously incorporating several of the types of deviations from Black-Scholes assumptions may be necessary to explain the history of option market prices. In addition, because different stocks represent claims on significantly different pools of assets and liabilities, different deviations are more important for some stocks than for others. Unfortunately, it will be hard to keep such an expanded model from becoming a data fitting exercise with little predictive power.

Index Options

Exchange traded index options (first listed in 1983) are similar to their parents, exchange-traded equity options (first listed in 1973). However, many would say that index options are more difficult to value than equity options. An index option is a derivative asset on a portfolio of several underlying assets. If each underlying asset has a lognormal distribution, as Black-Scholes essentially assumes, then a value-weighted index like the S&P 100 will not be lognormal since weighted sums of lognormal random variables are not lognormal. Potentially even worse, as the dollar composition of an index changes, the volatility of an index will be nonstationary in ways that are difficult to predict. For a price-weighted index, like the Dow Jones Industrial Average, this problem could be especially severe.

This position takes as given that lognormality is more reasonable for individual stocks than it is for the market as a whole, which is unlikely to be true. For example, it is an empirical regularity that a large portfolio of stocks experiences less severe price jumps and has greater stability of volatility than the average stock in the portfolio. Ironically, this would seem to make the Black-Scholes model even more appropriate for index options than for individual equity options even though it was clearly equity options that Black and Scholes first had in mind when they developed their formula.

However, certain other technical features of index options complicate the picture. To mention only the most important complications: First, cash dividends for individual stocks are rarely paid more frequently than four times a year, while for an index like the S&P 500, some stock in the index pays dividends about two out of every three trading days. Second, there is a problem of spurious serial correlation of the underlying index which needs to be removed from the estimate of the reported synchronous underlying index value to estimate the value of index options. Third, since the index futures market itself is a natural source of liquidity for trading in the underlying index, option traders usually use index futures rather than a basket of the underlying stocks to hedge their positions in the index options market. This means that index option prices tend to align themselves around the interest rate implied in the index futures price rather than around T-bill or CD rates. Fourth, the decision to exercise an American index option can be delayed until 4:15 p.m. while the exercise is settled based on the 4:00 p.m. price. This gives the option buyer an auxiliary option known as a "wild card."

Readily available empirical evidence on the market pricing of index options is spotty. Sample sizes have been too small both across time and cross-sectionally across the different types of index options. Although transactions and quotation data are available, only closing prices have been examined. None of the studies has dealt properly with the problems created by spurious correlation of the underlying index and the auxiliary wild card option. I regard the current findings as too tentative to justify reporting here. As a result, more work needs to be done before academics will be able to reach definitive conclusions.

Portfolio Insurance

For the student of derivative assets, portfolio insurance and more general dynamic hedging strategies provide an ideal laboratory to refine replication technology. Most commonly, insurers attempt to manufacture a European long-term put option on a stock market index. This places a floor on losses (the difference between the current index level and the striking price of the put) while at the same time retaining most of the profits in a rising market that would have been earned on an investment in the underlying index: hence, the term "portfolio insurance." Ironically, reliance on listed options to create this type of insurance is usually slight since these instruments are typically American, cannot be used to insure the dividend component of stock returns, have very short maturities, may become transactions cost intensive through frequent roll-overs into the next available maturities, and are subject to limits on the size of the position that may be held by a single investor. Instead, insurers manage a position in index futures, buying futures as the market moves up and selling futures as the market moves down. This procedure increases exposure to stock market returns on the upside while at the same time limiting exposure on the downside.

If the Black-Scholes assumptions were met in reality, a precise dynamic replicating strategy for a European long-term put would be easy to construct. However, uncertain interest rates, transactions costs, mispriced futures contracts, potential jumps in market index levels and, most important, uncertain volatility—all assumed away by Black and Scholes—create significant analytical and trade execution problems.

The goals of these new dynamic hedging strategies are predictable upside portfolio returns and control of downside risk. Conditional on the realized return of the underlying portfolio at a given horizon date, one wants to know in advance the payoff function or return of the derivative insured portfolio as precisely as possible. In the standard insurance case, the payoff function is

$$\max[\, aS^*, K\,]$$

where K represents the prespecified desired minimum value of the insured portfolio at the horizon date and a is the proportion of the value of the underlying asset that is captured on the upside consistent with a given initial investment. In terms of call options, this payoff function is equivalent to

$$K + a\max[\,0, S^* - K/a\,].$$

In other words, given a preselected underlying asset with current value S, an insurance period t, and a target minimum value K realized at the end of the period, one determines in advance what will be the *upside capture a*. There is a tradeoff: the greater the value of K, the lower the upside capture. Determining the upside capture for a given value of K is a problem in derivative assets analysis.

Although upside capture depends on the rate of interest, the level of transactions costs, and the extent and direction of futures mispricing, uncertainty about volatility creates the most severe difficulties. So much so that the insurance provides a payoff which explicitly depends on the volatility; for instance, the payoff function is often revised to

$$\max[\, a(\sigma^*)S^*, K\,]$$

where the upside capture a is quoted as a function of the realized market volatility σ^*. Alternative solutions to the problem of uncertain volatility are advocated by different portfolio insurance vendors. Safe to say, these solutions are quite heterogeneous and need further analysis.

Conclusion

Derivative assets analysis enjoys an unusual status; it is a recently developed, relatively complex tool of economic analysis, faithful to the core of economic theory, and widely used to make real-life decisions. For example, most traders on the floors of options exchanges use arbitrage-based option values at least as benchmarks in establishing market prices and in constructing replicating strategies to hedge their option positions.

Despite the excitement on the part of both academics and professional investors engendered by the recent development of derivative assets analysis, one senses that most of the theoretical foundation for derivative assets analysis seems already in place. However, empirical testing of existing models and more sophisticated use of these models by professional investors has a promising future.

Within the scope of applications listed in the Appendix, given their initial promise, the most disappointing have been those involving corporate securities. Despite the level of complexity that can now be handled by derivative assets analysis, the real world of the corporation is significantly more complex. The web of complex capital structures involving many interrelated securities and commitments, the effects of complicated incentive arrangements, the extent of "irrational" (and therefore difficult to predict) behavior on the part of corporate management, and the subtle effects of differential asset composition across firms continues to present one of the most difficult challenges to research in financial economics.[7]

Appendix
Examples of Applications of Derivative Assets Analysis

For each application, one recent publication is cited. In each case, I have tried to cite the most recent acceptable treatment of the related subject. In no sense is this meant to imply that the cited publication is superior to other work not cited.

1. Exchange-traded futures (by type of underlying asset)

A. Treasury bills. Rendleman, R. J. and C. E. Carabini, "The Efficiency of the Treasury Bill Futures Market," *Journal of Finance*, September 1979, *34:4*, 895–914.
B. Treasury bonds
    1. Delivery option. Gay, G. D. and S. Manaster, "The Quality Option Implicit in Futures Contracts," *Journal of Financial Economics*, September 1984, *13:3*, 353–370.

---

[7]Most notorious among these concerns has been the tardiness of corporate management in calling outstanding bonds. For some recent work in this area, see M. Harris and A. Raviv (1985) and Vu (1986).

2. Wild card option. Kane, A. and A. J. Marcus, "Valuation and Optimal Exercise of the Wild Card Option in the Treasury Bond Futures Market," *Journal of Finance*, March 1986, *41:1*, 195–207.

C. Stock market indexes. Figlewski, S., "Hedging Performance and Basis Risk in Stock Index Futures," *Journal of Finance*, July 1984, *39:3*, 657–669.

D. Currencies. Cornell, B. and M. R. Reinganum, "Forward and Futures Prices: Evidence from the Forward Exchange Markets," *Journal of Finance*, December 1981, *36:5*, 1035–1045.

E. Commodities. Brennan, M. J., "The Cost of Convenience and the Pricing of Commodity Contingent Claims," University of British Columbia Working Paper, 1986.

2. Exchange-traded puts and calls (by type of underlying asset)

A. Bonds. Schaefer, S. M. and E. S. Schwartz, "Time-Dependent Variance and the Pricing of Bond Options," University of British Columbia Working Paper, July 1985.

B. Common stocks. Rubinstein, M., "Nonparametric Tests of Alternative Option Pricing Models Using All Reported Trades and Quotes on the 30 Most Active CBOE Option Classes from August 23, 1976 through August 31, 1978," *Journal of Finance*, June 1985, *40:2*, 455–480.

C. Stock Market Indexes. Evnine, J. and A. Rudd, "Index Options: The Early Evidence," *Journal of Finance*, July 1985, *40:3*, 743–756.

D. Currencies. Shastri, K. and K. Tandon, "Valuation of Foreign Currency Options: Some Empirical Tests," *Journal of Financial and Quantitative Analysis*, June 1986, *21:2*, 145–160.

E. Commodities. Hoag, J. W., "The Valuation of Commodity Options," in *Option Pricing*, ed. M. Brenner, D. C. Heath, 1983, pp. 183–221.

F. Stock index futures. Whaley, R. E., "Valuation of American Futures Options: Theory and Empirical Tests," *Journal of Finance*, March 1986, *41:1*, 127–150.

3. Corporate securities

A. Warrants. Emmanuel, D., "Warrant Valuation and Exercise Strategy," *Journal of Financial Economics*, August 1983, *12:2*, 211–236.

B. Callable convertible bonds. Brennan, M. J. and E. S. Schwartz, "Analyzing Convertible Bonds," *Journal of Financial and Quantitative Analysis*, November 1980, *15:4*, 907–929.

C. Bond indenture provisions.

1. Safety covenants. Mason, S. P. and S. Bhattacharaya, "Risky Debt, Jump Processes, and Safety Covenants," *Journal of Financial Economics*, September 1981, *9:3*, 281–307.

2. Priority rules.

    a. Restrictions on financing payouts. Ho, T. and R. F. Singer, "Bond Indenture Provisions and the Risk of Corporate Debt," *Journal of Financial Economics*, December 1982, *10:4*, 375–406.

    b. Sinking funds. Ho, T. and R. F. Singer, "The Value of Corporate Debt with a Sinking Fund Provision," *Journal of Business*, July 1984, *57:3*, 315–336.

D. Secured debt. Stulz, R. M. and H. Johnson, "An Analysis of Secured Debt," *Journal of Financial Economics*, December 1985, *14:4*, 510–521.

E. Preferred stock. Emmanuel, D., "A Theoretical Model for Valuing Preferred Stock," *Journal of Finance*, September 1983, *38:4*, 1133–1155.

F. Leases. McConnell, J. J. and J. S. Schallheim, "Valuation of Asset Leasing Contracts," *Journal of Financial Economics*, August 1983, *12:2*, 237–261.

G. Commodity-linked bonds. Schwartz, E. S., "The Pricing of Commodity-Linked Bonds," *Journal of Finance*, May 1982, *37:2*, 525–539.

H. Executive stock options. Noreen, E. and M. Wolfson, "Equilibrium Warrant Pricing Models and Accounting for Executive Stock Options," *Journal of Accounting Research*, Autumn 1981, *19*, 384–398.

I. Bonds denominated in foreign currencies. Stulz, R. M., "Options on the Minimum or Maximum of Two Risky Assets: Analysis and Applications," *Journal of Financial Economics*, July 1982, *10:2*, 161–185.

J. Option bonds. Stulz, R. M. See previous citation.

K. COLA compensation plans. Stulz, R. M. See previous citation.

L. Stock tender offers. Margrabe, W., "The value of an Option to Exchange One Asset for Another," *Journal of Finance*, March 1978, *33:1*, 177–198.

M. Cash tender offers. Bhagat, S., J. A. Brickley and U. Loewenstein, "The Pricing Effects of Interfirm Cash Tender Offers," University of Utah Working Paper, August 1986.

4. Government securities

A. Treasury bonds. Brennan, M. J. and E. S. Schwartz, "An Equilibrium Model of Bond Pricing and a Test of Market Efficiency," *Journal of Financial and Quantitative Analysis*, September 1982, *41:3*, 301–329.

B. Retractable/extendible bonds. Ananthanarayanan, A. L. and E. S. Schwartz, "Retractable and Extendible Bonds," *Journal of Finance*, March 1980, *35:1*, 31–47.

C. Savings bonds. Brennan, M. J. and E. S. Schwartz, "Savings Bonds, Retractable Bonds and Callable Bonds," *Journal of Financial Economics*, August 1977, *5:1*, 67–88.

D. Inflation-indexed bonds. Fischer, S., "Call Option Pricing when the Exercise Price is Uncertain, and the Valuation of Index Bonds," *Journal of Finance*, March 1978, *33:1*, 169–176.

E. Loan guarantees. Sosin, H. W., "On the Valuation of Federal Loan Guarantees to Corporations," *Journal of Finance*, December 1980, *35:5*, 1209–1221.

F. Farm price supports. Marcus, A. J. and D. M. Modest, "The Valuation of a Random Number of Put Options: An Application to Agricultural Price Supports," *Journal of Financial and Quantitative Analysis*, March 1986, *21:1*, 73–86.

G. Government energy subsidies. Baldwin, C. Y., S. P. Mason and R. S. Ruback, "Evaluation of Government Subsidies to Large Energy Projects: A Contingent Claims Approach," Harvard Business School Working Paper, 1983.

H. Default-free option bonds. Stulz, R. M. "Options on the Minimum or Maximum of Two Risky Assets: Analysis and Applications," *Journal of Financial Economics*, July 1982, *10:2*, 161–185.

I. Defaultible sovereign debt. Gennotte, G. "Sovereign Debt: A Study of Alternative Repayment Schedules," University of California at Berkeley Working Paper, June 1986.

5. Securities issued by financial institutions

A. Fixed-rate bank loan commitments. Bartter, B. J. and R. J. Rendleman, "Fee-Based Pricing of Fixed-Rate Bank Loan Commitments," *Financial Management*, Spring 1979, *8*, 13–20.

B. Equity-linked insurance contracts. Brennan, M. J. and E. S. Schwartz, "The Pricing of Equity-Linked Life Insurance Policies with Asset Value Guarantee," *Journal of Financial Economics*, June 1976, *3:3*, 195–214.

C. Variable-rate loan contracts. Ramaswamy, K. and S. M. Sundaresan, "The Valuation of Floating Rate Instruments: Theory and Evidence," Columbia University Working Paper, May 1985.

D. Fixed-rate mortgages. Kau, J. B., D. C. Keenan, W. J. Muller and J. F. Epperson, "Option Theory and Fixed Rate Mortgages," University of Georgia Working Paper, 1986.

E. GNMA mortgage-backed instruments. Dunn, K. B. and J. J. McConnell, "Valuation of GNMA Mortgage-Backed Securities," *Journal of Finance*, June 1981, *36:3*, 599–616.

F. Revolving credit agreements. Hawkins, G. D., "An Analysis of Revolving Credit Agreements," *Journal of Financial Economics*, March 1982, *10:1*, 59–81.

G. Dual purpose funds. Ingersoll, J. E., "A Theoretical and Empirical Investigation of Dual Purpose Funds: An Application of Contingent Claims Analysis," *Journal of Financial Economics*, January/March 1976, *3:1 / 2*, 83–123.

H. Deposit insurance. Merton, R. C., "An Analytic Derivation of the Cost of Deposit Insurance and Loan Guarantees: An Application of Modern Option Pricing Theory," *Journal of Banking and Finance*, June 1977, *1:1*, 3–12.

I. Rights versus underwriting agreements. Smith, C. W., "Alternative Methods for Raising Capital: Rights Versus Underwritten Offerings," *Journal of Financial Economics*, December 1977, *5:3*, 273–307.

J. Margin deposits. Margrabe, W., "The Value of an Option to Exchange One Asset for Another," Journal of Finance, March 1978, *33:1*, 177–198.

K. Mortgage standby commitments. Margrabe, W. See previous citation.

6. Real assets

A. Natural resources. Brennan, M. J. and E. S. Schwartz, "Evaluating Natural Resource Investments," *Journal of Business*, April 1985, *58:2*, 135–157.

B. Abandonment. Myers, S. C. and S. Majd, "Calculating Abandonment Value Using Option Pricing Theory," M.I.T. Working Paper, 1983.

C. Temporary shut down. McConnell, R. L. and D. R. Siegel, "Investment and the Valuation of Firms When There is an Option to Shut Down," Northwestern University Working Paper, June 1983.

D. Expansion or contraction of size. Mason, S. P. and R. C. Merton, "The Role of Contingent Claims Analysis in Corporate Finance," in *Recent Advances in Corporate Finance* (ed. E. Altman and M. Subrahmanyam), Irwin, 1985, pp. 7–54.

E. Lengthening or shortening of life. Mason, S. P. and R. C. Merton. See previous citation.

F. Sequential or parallel development. Mason, S. P. and R. C. Merton. See previous citation.

G. Time of initiation. Paddock, J. L., D. Siegel and J. L. Smith, "Valuation of Corporate Bids for Hydrocarbon Leases," M.I.T. Working Paper, 1983.

7. Miscellaneous

A. The French prime. Courtadon, G. "A Note on the Premium Market of the Paris Stock Exchange," *Journal of Banking and Finance*, December 1982, *6*, 561–564.

B. Portfolio immunization. Ingersoll, J. E., "Is Immunization Feasible?" in *Innovations in Bond Portfolio Management: Duration Analysis and Immunization*, (edited by G. G. Kaufman, G. O. Bierwag and A. Toevs), JAI Press, 1983.

C. Portfolio insurance. Rubinstein, M. "Alternative Paths to Portfolio Insurance," *Financial Analysts Journal*, July–August 1985, *41:4*, 42–52.

D. Education. Dothan, U. and J. Williams, "Education as an Option," *Journal of Business*, January 1981, *54:1*, 117–139.

E. Capital gains tax recognition. Constantinides, G. M., "Capital Market Equilibrium with Personal Tax," *Econometrica*, *51*, 611–636.

F. Bid-ask spreads. Copeland, T. E. and D. Galai, "Information Effects on the Bid-Ask Spread," *Journal of Finance*, December 1983, *38:5*, 1457–1469.

G. Measurement of market-timing skills. Merton, R. C., "On Market Timing and Investment Performance: An Equilibrium Theory of Value for Market Forecasts," *Journal of Business*, July 1981, *54:3*, 363–406.

H. Investment performance incentive fees. Margrabe, W., "The Value of an Option to Exchange One Asset for Another," *Journal of Finance*, March 1978, *33:1*, 177–198.

I. Generalized linear payoff functions. Ross, S. A. "A Simple Approach to the Valuation of Risky Streams," *Journal of Business*, July 1978, *51:3*, 453–475.

J. Generalized non-linear payoff functions. Cox, J. and M. Rubinstein. *Options Markets*, Prentice-Hall, 1985.

K. Down-and-out options. Cox, J. and M. Rubinstein, See previous citation.

L. Buy-at-the-low, sell-at-the-high. Goldman, M. B., H. B. Sosin and M. A. Gatto, "Path Dependent Options: 'Buy at the Low, Sell at the High'," *Journal of Finance*, December 1979, *34:5*, 1111–1127.

M. Ex-post optimal market-timing. Goldman, M. B., H. B. Sosin and L. A. Shepp, "On Contingent Claims that Insure Ex-post Optimal Stock Market Timing," *Journal of Finance*, May 1979, *34:2*, 401–413.

N. Averaging options. Bergman, Y. Z. "Pricing Path-Dependent Options," University of California at Berkeley Working Paper, 1980.

O. Supershares. Hakansson, N. H., "The Purchasing Power Fund: A New Kind of Financial Intermediary," *Financial Analysts Journal*, November–December 1976, *32*, 49–59.

P. Employment contracts. Abowd, J. M. and S. Manaster, "A General Model of Employment Contracting: An Application of Option Theory," University of Chicago Working Paper, January 1983.

References

Arrow, Kenneth, "The Role of Securities in the Optimal Allocation of Risk Bearing," *Review of Economic Studies*, April 1964, *31:1*, 91–96.

Black, Fischer and Myron Scholes, "The Pricing of Options and Corporate Liabilities," *Journal of Political Economy*, May–June 1973, *81:2*, 637–659.

Cox, John, Jonathan Ingersoll and Stephen Ross, "The Relation Between Forward Prices and Futures Prices," *Journal of Financial Economics*, December 1981, *9:4*, 321–346.

Cox, John and Stephen Ross, "The Valuation of Options for Alternative Stochastic Processes," *Journal of Financial Economics*, January–March 1976, *3:1/2*, 145–166.

Cox, John, Stephen Ross, and Mark Rubinstein, "Option Pricing: A Simplified Approach," *Journal of Financial Economics*, September 1979, *7:3*, 229–263.

Harris, M. and A. Raviv, "A Sequential Signalling Model of Convertible Debt Call Policy," *Journal of Finance*, December 1985, *40:5*, 1263–1281.

Merton, Robert, "Theory of Rational Option Pricing," *Bell Journal of Economics and Management Science*, Spring 1973, *4*, 141–183.

Vu, J. D. "An Empirical Investigation of Calls of Non-Convertible Bonds," *Journal of Financial Economics*, June 1986, *16:2*, 235–265.

Article 4

*G*lobalization of Stock, Futures, and Options Markets

Peter A. Abken

Of the trendy buzzwords to emerge from the 1980s, "globalization" surely ranks high on the list of overused words in the business lexicon, but not without good reason. The word has become associated with financial markets' growing interconnections, facilitated largely by advances in communications and computer technology. Capital moves across national borders primarily as investment flows and secondarily as international trade financing. In dollar terms, global financial transactions today stand at a historically high multiple of world trade volume (John G. Heimann 1989). Record trade imbalances, however, have also contributed to financial interdependence, the most prominent example being the net current account surplus of Japan, leading to large overseas investments of the surplus, and the net deficit of the United States, necessitating borrowing from abroad.

Financial transactions' increasing volume and their decreasing costs have put strong competitive pressures on financial institutions to change the ways in which they intermediate credit and other financial flows. The financial industry has turned to automated securities trading, which is transforming and displacing the face-to-face and mouth-to-telephone methods of making financial transactions and strengthening the globalization or internationalization of securities markets in the process. Automation of trading encompasses a number of innovations that have improved the efficiency of making financial transactions. The technologies range from quotation and communications systems that facilitate traditional trading methods to so-called screen trading systems that supplant them. Their operation can be confined to one organized financial exchange, as the New York Stock Exchange's SuperDot system is, or can link many organized exchanges, as the Chicago Mercantile Exchange's Globex system does. For convenience in this discussion

The author is a senior economist in the financial section of the Atlanta Fed's research department. He would especially like to thank Jim Shapiro of the New York Stock Exchange and Bruce Phelps of the Chicago Board of Trade for helpful comments. However, any errors are the author's responsibility.

of the gradual automation of securities trading, these innovations will be referred to generically as automated trading systems.

This article examines currently running and proposed automated systems for many of the world's principal organized exchanges for common stock, futures, and option contracts. These exchanges are voluntary associations of members who come together to trade securities in auction markets, paying for the right to trade on an exchange—they buy a "seat" on the exchange. They generally trade for their own accounts and for outside customers. In contrast, participants in over-the-counter (OTC) markets, who are geographically dispersed, are brought together by telephone and computer lines. Over-the-counter trades go through dealers, who quote prices to buy and sell. The National Association of Securities Dealers (NASD) is one of several important OTC markets for common stocks in the United States that will be discussed below.

The article concludes with a section on market performance and regulation that takes a broader perspective on globalization. The perceived impact of globalization is closely tied to one's view of market efficiency. Integrating markets through electronic trading may reduce the magnitude of certain kinds of price shocks that propagate across markets because of a lack of information about the sources of such shocks. If markets are efficient, twenty-four-hour trading has the potential to reduce such market volatility. On the other hand, some market observers and participants, believing that markets are inefficient and excessively volatile, have proposed measures to curb speculative activity and the volatility they believe it engenders. The continuing reduction in transactions costs through technological innovation may only exacerbate market volatility. The final section considers this debate.

The Growth of International Securities Trading

Since the 1980s, securities markets of all kinds have been developing rapidly around the world. The volume of equity and bond market transactions has grown steadily, and both American purchases and sales of foreign securities and foreign purchases and sales of U.S. securities have been expanding, as Table 1 shows. A useful indicator of market activity, the growth in transactions volume coincided with in-

creases in volatility of most financial markets, which has been attributed to causes ranging from deregulation of financial markets, fiscal and trade imbalances, and so forth, to out-and-out irrationality and a gambling-casino mentality among traders. Some economists have recommended taxing securities transactions to alleviate the apparently unnecessary volatility.[1] On the other hand, there are substantive reasons for expecting that transactions volume will increase as uncertainty about "fundamentals" rises. For one thing, trading securities is necessary to adjust portfolios optimally in response to changing expected securities' payoffs.[2] In addition, volatility is a prime factor motivating financial risk management, which has spawned a variety of derivative instrument markets. Options and futures markets, for example, deal in contracts that are valued on the basis of stock, bond, and other primary securities prices. A discussion of the growth of primary and derivative securities markets follows.

Equities. Table 1 shows international equity market transactions, comparing activity for selected countries and regions in 1980 with 1990. The sum of purchases and sales, referred to here as transactions volume, measures the total transactions in equity markets by foreigners in U.S. stock markets and by Americans in foreign stock markets.[3] The dollar volume of transactions in 1980 and in 1990 was greater for foreigners transacting in U.S. markets than for Americans dealing in foreign markets. However, the overall margin of foreign volume over domestic volume diminished from 321 percent in 1980 to 43 percent in 1990.[4] The absolute levels of dollar purchases and sales have increased markedly, well in excess of the dollar's inflation rate and twice as fast as the growth of transactions volume on domestic exchanges during this period (Joseph A. Grundfest 1990, 349).

The compound annual growth rate for foreign transactions volume in U.S. securities was 17 percent, while the growth rate for U.S. transactions volume in foreign securities was 30 percent. Japanese transactions in U.S. stock markets grew at a 41 percent compound annual rate, faster than those of all other countries or regions. Japan's percentage share of the international transactions volume has correspondingly risen from 2.5 percent to 16 percent over the decade. The United Kingdom accounts for nearly half the 1990 European volume, up substantially from 1980. Much of its transactions volume probably stems from Middle Eastern and other non-United Kingdom buying and selling of U.S. stocks that occurs through London's markets, which are the preeminent financial

Table 1
Table 1
Transactions Volume in Stocks

	Foreign Transactions in U.S. Securities				U.S. Transactions in Foreign Securities			
	Purchases[a]	Sales[a]	Aggregate Purchases and Sales[a]	Percentage Share of Market	Purchases[a]	Sales[a]	Aggregate Purchases and Sales[a]	Percentage Share of Market
1990								
France	5.82	7.01	12.83	3.55	6.05	5.90	11.95	4.72
Germany	5.90	6.27	12.17	3.37	6.69	7.45	14.14	5.58
United Kingdom	44.94	48.07	93.01	25.74	44.80	45.52	90.32	35.64
Total Europe	84.95	93.53	178.47	49.39	74.53	78.40	152.94	60.36
Japan	27.47	30.38	57.85	16.01	30.89	31.52	62.41	24.63
Canada	19.52	18.63	38.14	10.56	4.78	4.92	9.70	3.83
Total Worldwide	173.04	188.34	361.37	100.00	122.49	130.89	253.38	100.00
1980								
France	2.73	2.24	4.97	6.60	0.47	0.67	1.14	6.36
Germany	2.75	2.56	5.30	7.05	0.24	0.22	0.46	2.57
United Kingdom	7.44	4.94	12.38	16.44	1.38	1.36	2.75	15.38
Total Europe	24.62	21.55	46.16	61.32	3.16	3.62	6.78	37.97
Japan	0.87	1.03	1.90	2.52	0.93	1.77	2.70	15.10
Canada	6.35	5.48	11.83	15.71	3.02	3.66	6.68	37.43
Total Worldwide	40.32	34.96	75.28	100.00	7.89	9.97	17.85	100.00

Compound Annual Growth Rate, 1980-90
(percent)

	Foreign	U.S.
France	9.95	26.53
Germany	8.66	40.88
United Kingdom	22.35	41.81
Total Europe	14.48	36.56
Japan	40.73	36.92
Canada	12.42	3.80
Total Worldwide	16.98	30.38

[a] In billions of U.S. dollars.

Source: Derived by the Federal Reserve Bank of Atlanta from U.S. Department of the Treasury, *U.S. Treasury Bulletin* (Winter 1991), Table CM-V-5; (Winter 1981), Table CM-VI-10.

markets in Europe. From 1980 to 1990, both the United Kingdom and Japan were responsible for net inflows (cumulative excess of purchases over sales) into U.S. equity markets of about 17 billion dollars each.

U.S. transactions volume in foreign equities also grew markedly during the decade, almost twice as fast as foreign volume. This growth rate reflects the low 1980 level of U.S. purchases and sales of foreign stocks relative to foreign participation in U.S. markets. The transactions volume shares in the United Kingdom and Japan realized significant increases from 1980 to 1990, as did the corresponding compound annual growth rates. Though the share of overall volume was still relatively low in 1990, the growth rate for German stock market participation by U.S. investors was about as rapid as the rates for the United Kingdom and Japan.

Chart 1 gives another view of world equity trading, showing the dollar trading volume in major world equity markets. Clearly, the New York and Tokyo markets surpass other world markets. Each of these will be discussed further in connection with automated trading systems.

Bonds. The dollar transactions volume for bonds was approximately ten times as large as that for stocks in 1990; they were roughly comparable a decade earlier. The domestic and foreign bonds included in Table 2 exclude short-term bonds with remaining times to maturity of less than one year. Although there is considerable trading in these short-term securities, much of that trading includes government intervention in foreign exchange markets, leading in turn to sizable purchases and sales of short-term government securities such as U.S. Treasury bills. Long-term securities better gauge the growth in private cross-border capital movements. The securities included in U.S. market transactions are marketable Treasury and federally sponsored agency bonds as well as corporate bonds.

Almost all bonds are traded over-the-counter, though some are traded on organized exchanges. Somewhat less than 10 percent of all U.S. corporate bonds are traded on organized exchanges (Jack Clark Francis 1991, 87). As seen in Table 2, most foreign transactions in U.S. bond markets are in government bonds. Although the bond market is primarily

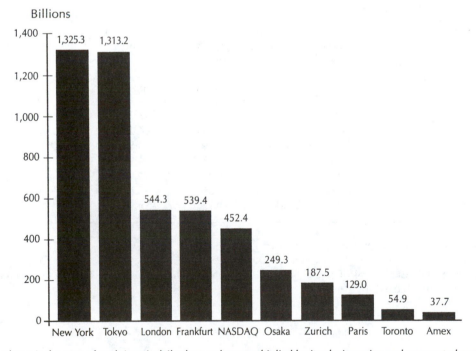

Chart 1
Dollar Trading Volume in Major World Equity Markets in 1990[a]

Billions

Market	Volume
New York	1,325.3
Tokyo	1,313.2
London	544.3
Frankfurt	539.4
NASDAQ	452.4
Osaka	249.3
Zurich	187.5
Paris	129.0
Toronto	54.9
Amex	37.7

[a] Annual trading volume is the sum of each issue's daily share volume multiplied by its closing price and aggregated over all issues and trading days in the year.
Source: NASDAQ (1991).

Table 2
Transactions Volume in Long-Term Bonds[a]

	Foreign Transactions in U.S. Securities				U.S. Transactions in Foreign Securities			
	Purchases[b]	Sales[b]	Aggregate Purchases and Sales[b]	Percentage Share of Market	Purchases[b]	Sales[b]	Aggregate Purchases and Sales[b]	Percentage Share of Market
1990								
France	13.47	12.78	26.24	0.68	14.67	15.50	30.17	4.65
Germany	45.31	39.87	85.18	2.21	15.91	18.23	34.14	5.26
United Kingdom	564.62	555.67	1,120.29	29.08	113.95	114.16	228.10	35.12
Total Europe	804.32	773.85	1,578.17	40.97	185.46	189.78	375.25	57.77
Japan	731.08	744.96	1,476.04	38.32	36.71	43.50	80.21	12.35
Canada	66.81	69.46	136.26	3.54	54.48	56.91	111.39	17.15
Total Worldwide	1,945.19	1,906.80	3,851.99	100.00	313.58	335.93	649.50	100.00
1980								
France	0.71	0.45	1.16	0.94	0.66	0.62	1.28	3.64
Germany	2.54	5.21	7.75	6.31	0.45	0.43	0.88	2.50
United Kingdom	22.36	20.15	42.51	34.60	6.07	6.16	12.23	34.97
Total Europe	30.29	30.37	60.65	49.37	9.09	9.59	18.68	53.39
Japan	2.59	4.21	6.81	5.54	1.35	2.65	4.00	11.44
Canada	0.96	2.39	3.35	2.73	2.20	2.42	4.63	13.22
Total Worldwide	66.61	56.25	122.86	100.00	17.07	17.92	34.98	100.00

Compound Annual Growth Rate, 1980-90
(percent)

	Foreign	U.S.
France	36.66	37.22
Germany	27.09	44.24
United Kingdom	38.70	33.99
Total Europe	38.53	34.99
Japan	71.24	34.96
Canada	44.86	37.46
Total Worldwide	41.13	33.93

[a] *Bonds having maturities of one year or greater.*

[b] *In billions of U.S. dollars.*

Source: Derived by the Federal Reserve Bank of Atlanta from U.S. Department of the Treasury, *U.S. Treasury Bulletin* (Winter 1991), Table CM-V-5; (Winter 1981), Table CM-VI-10.

over-the-counter (and thus not the point of interest in this discussion), the growing number of international transactions in bonds has stimulated derivative securities markets worldwide. Increasingly, derivative securities trade in one country on underlying securities originating in another. Several examples—including the futures contracts on U.S. Treasury bonds that trade on the Tokyo Stock Exchange (TSE) and the German government bond futures that trade at the London International Financial Futures Exchange (LIFFE, pronounced "life")—will be discussed below.

The picture of globalization that emerged from the earlier consideration of equities trading comes into even sharper relief when cross-border bond trading is examined. Aside from the greater magnitude of dollar transactions volume mentioned earlier, the most striking feature is the uniformly high growth rates across countries and regions from 1980 to 1990. Equity market growth rates, particularly for French and German involvement in U.S. markets, do not show this evenness. All but one compound annual growth rate exceeds 30 percent. The transactions volume of Japanese investors in U.S. markets increased 71 percent annually! Similar to the equity data, the Japanese share in transactions volume rose over the decade from 5.5 percent to 38 percent, while the European share declined from 49 percent to 41 percent. U.S. investor participation in foreign bond markets mirrored the increased foreign activity in U.S. markets.

Futures and Options. Exchange-traded futures contracts have a long and—to some—notorious history. Commodity futures originated at the Chicago Board of Trade (CBOT) in the 1860s (see Chicago Board of Trade 1985, 1-4). Not until 1972 were the first financial futures introduced at the Chicago Mercantile Exchange (CME, or the "Merc"). The development of these currency futures reflected the anticipated hedging needs stemming from the decision allowing the dollar and other major currencies to float against one another rather than to be maintained at fixed parities. At the time agricultural contracts accounted for 97 percent of the CME's volume (William J. Brodsky 1990). Many new financial futures and options soon followed. The CBOT established the Chicago Board Options Exchange (CBOE) in 1973 to trade options on listed stocks; they created the Ginnie Mae futures contract in 1975.[5] The CME countered with its Treasury bill futures contract in 1976; the CBOT, with its Treasury bond futures contract in 1977. The latter is the most heavily traded futures contract in the world today.

In the early 1980s, these exchanges developed futures and options contracts on equity indexes, such as the Standard and Poor's (S&P) 500 futures (CME) and S&P 100 options contracts (CBOE). At the time of the market crash of October 1987, the S&P 500 futures achieved a notoriety in the minds of many investors and stock exchange members that lingers to this day. While a number of factors had contributed to the crash, the use of index futures in conjunction with so-called program trading, which uses the automated order-routing system at the New York Stock Exchange, was widely blamed. (This subject will be considered further in a later section.) In any case, many exchanges, including the New York Stock Exchange, greatly expanded capacity through automation to handle future surges in volume.

While volume in other futures contracts has remained generally flat during the 1980s, financial futures volume has grown steadily (see Robert W. Kolb 1991, 23). For example, by 1989 financial futures volume made up 91 percent of the CME's volume, with only the remaining 9 percent accounted for by commodity futures. At all U.S. futures exchanges in 1972, the total annual volume of futures trading measured by the number of contracts traded was 18.3 million. In 1990 this volume had risen to 276.5 million contracts, a compound annual growth rate of 16.3 percent. Though the U.S. exchanges are the world's most established, foreign futures markets are rapidly making inroads in the share of trading volume. For instance, since the opening of the London International Financial Futures Exchange in 1982, thirty options and futures exchanges have opened outside the United States (Brodsky 1991).

The U.S. exchanges are still dominant in the world, but, as Table 3 shows, foreign options and futures markets that emerged in the 1980s are also well represented in the top-twenty ranks. In particular, the Osaka Securities Exchange's Nikkei 225 index futures contract and Tokyo International Financial Futures Exchange's Euroyen contract surged in volume during 1990.

Automation of Equity Markets

Individual stock exchanges everywhere have adopted some degree of automation, reflecting the exigencies of competitive pressures from domestic as well as foreign exchanges. Derivative securities markets have aggressively employed the new technologies to

Table 3
Most Heavily Traded Futures and Options Contracts

Rank 1990	Rank 1989	Contract[a]	Exchanges[b]	Contract Volume 1990	Contract Volume 1989
1	1	T-bond (f)	CBOT	75,499,000	70,303,000
2	2	S&P 100 (o)	CBOE	58,845,000	58,371,000
3	3	Eurodollar (f)	CME	34,694,000	40,818,000
4	4	T-bond (o)	CBOT	27,315,000	20,784,000
5	5	Crude oil (f)	Nymex	23,687,000	20,535,000
6	6	Japanese government bond (f)	TSE	16,307,000	18,942,000
7	7	Notionnel government bond (f)	MATIF	15,996,000	15,005,000
8	30	Euroyen (f)	TIFFE	14,414,000	4,495,000
9	25	Nikkei 225 (f)	Osaka	13,589,000	5,443,000
10	8	S&P 500 (f)	CME	12,139,000	10,560,000
11	18	S&P 500 (o)	CBOE	12,089,000	6,274,000
12	11	Corn (f)	CBOT	11,423,000	9,271,000
13	10	Soybeans (f)	CBOT	10,302,000	9,635,000
14	9	Gold (f)	Comex	9,730,000	9,999,000
15	26	German bond (f)	LIFFE	9,582,000	5,330,000
16	17	Nikkei 225 (o)	Osaka	9,186,000	6,610,000
17	12	Deutsche Mark (f)	CME	9,169,000	8,186,000
18	16	Short Sterling (f)	LIFFE	8,355,000	7,131,000
19	13	Yen (f)	CME	7,437,000	7,824,000
20	15	Notionnel government bond (o)	MATIF	7,410,000	7,177,000

[a] (f) = futures contract; (o) = options contract.
[b] Nymex is the New York Mercantile Exchange; Comex is the Commodities Exchange (New York); other exchanges are described in the text.
Source: *Futures and Options World: 1991 Annual Worldwide Directory and Review* (Surrey, England: Metal Bulletin Journals Ltd., 1991), 9. Data used by permission of the publisher.

link exchanges. The discussion below considers the movement toward automated trading in equity markets and derivative markets.

New York Stock Exchange. U.S. equity markets are the largest and most liquid in the world. The biggest domestic exchange, the New York Stock Exchange (NYSE), is facing mounting competitive pressures from regional domestic exchanges and from foreign stock exchanges. The heart of the New York Stock Exchange is its specialists, charged by the exchange to maintain "fair and orderly" markets in the individual listed stocks assigned to them. The New York Stock Exchange is organized as a continuous two-sided auction market, with the specialist acting as auctioneer for incoming orders to buy or sell a particular stock. The specialist conducts an auction in the sense that he or she continually adjusts a stock's price to balance supply and demand throughout the

trading day. She at times may also need to take the buy or sell side to keep prices from fluctuating too greatly. Overall about 10 percent of share purchases and 10 percent of sales on the NYSE result in specialists' staking their own capital in the trade (New York Stock Exchange 1991a, 17). This role is part of their obligation to the exchange in performing the specialist's function.

Also, the specialist has access to the computerized limit-order book, which displays orders to buy or sell if the market price reaches a specified level. Because of their knowledge, specialists have an informational advantage over traders off the exchange floor.[6] Although they may profit from their inventory position, exchange rules constrain trading for their own accounts. On every trade the specialist also receives the difference between the sale price (the ask) and the purchase price (the bid). Other market participants are willing to incur these costs in order to gain the liquidity specialists provide. However, the specialist's role is being questioned with increasing frequency: How important is it? Is the provision of liquidity worth the price?

Since the rise of institutional trading in the 1960s, the so-called upstairs market has developed, partly insulating the specialists from having to take positions in large blocks of 10,000 or more shares. Such blocks sent directly to the specialists may cause too much price fluctuation and be too risky for them to handle. Instead, block positioners match buyers and sellers and may also take positions in blocks themselves. Blocks are then sent to the specialist post for execution. Because of economies of scale, low commission rates are charged for block transactions. During the latter half of the 1980s, about half the NYSE's volume was accounted for by institutional block trading (NASDAQ 1991, 39). Preferring new, automated mechanisms that are even cheaper, institutional investors are beginning to dispense altogether with using the exchange.

More efficient handling of trading volume led to the development of the NYSE's automated routing system in 1976 called the Super Designated Order Turnaround System (SuperDot). SuperDot routes market orders of less than 2,099 shares to the specialist (or to a floor broker) for rapid execution, usually in less than a minute.[7] The system can also route large orders to the specialist. SuperDot is frequently used by program traders dealing in whole portfolios of stocks; they route lists of stocks through the system to appropriate specialists. The system handles market orders of as many as 30,099 shares and limit orders of as many as 99,999 shares of individual stocks, although the specialists are not obligated to execute these orders as rapidly as the New York Stock Exchange requires for smaller ones. Odd-lot orders of less than 100 shares are executed automatically by SuperDot at the prevailing price quote. About 75 percent of daily NYSE orders are processed through the system (New York Stock Exchange 1991a, 21).

Regionals. Regional exchanges have developed their own versions of automated order-routing and execution systems for small trades. The Midwest Stock Exchange (MSE), Pacific Stock Exchange (PSE), Philadelphia Stock Exchange (PHLX), and Boston Stock Exchange (BSE) use systems named MAX, SCOREX, PACE, and BEACON, respectively.[8] The Cincinnati Stock Exchange (CSE) is in fact an over-the-counter market with competing market makers. All trades on the CSE pass through the National Securities Trading System (NSTS), which is an order-matching system akin to the NASDAQ system to be discussed shortly (U.S. Securities and Exchange Commission 1991, 23-26).

The Securities Act amendments of 1975 mandated the Securities and Exchange Commission (SEC) to establish a national market system with the objectives of increasing competition among market makers at different exchanges and strengthening links among different exchanges (see Francis 1991, 132-33). One major change was that negotiated commissions replaced fixed commissions on securities sales and purchases. Another consequence of the act was the establishment of the "Consolidated Tape," which continuously lists the trades at seven stock exchanges and two over-the-counter markets (NASD and Instinet). Since 1978 the regional exchanges, the American Stock Exchange (Amex), NASD, and NYSE have been linked by the Intermarket Trading System (ITS), which enables a broker or specialist at one exchange to send orders to buy or sell at another exchange showing a better price.

Most of the stocks traded via the ITS communication system are NYSE-listed stocks, and a much smaller number traded are Amex-listed and regionally listed stocks. At the broker's or specialist's discretion, orders are routed to the exchange showing the best bid or offer. Once a small order is received, the BEACON, MAX, and SCOREX systems "expose" it to the specialist for fifteen seconds during which he or she may better the bid or offer price; otherwise, the order is automatically executed at the specialist's quoted bid or offer. (PACE automatically executes all small orders.) The Amex has an order-routing system called Post Execution Reporting (PER) that is very similar to the NYSE's SuperDot. Amex members can send orders for as many as 2,000 shares directly to the specialist using the system and receive an execution report for the trades (U.S. Congress 1990b, 49-50).

The regional exchanges and Amex have only a small slice of the trading-volume pie. Table 4 shows where they stand in relation to the NYSE and NASD, viewed both in terms of share volume and in terms of dollar volumes.

NASDAQ. National Association of Securities Dealers runs a telecommunications network called NASDAQ, for NASD Automated Quotations. In this over-the-counter market NASD dealers compete with one another in making bids and offers on stocks.[9] These OTC securities tend to be smaller capitalization stocks that do not meet exchange listing requirements; only a subset of them are also listed on organized exchanges.[10] To buy or sell a stock, an investor

Table 4
U.S. Equity Markets: 1990 Share and Dollar Volumes

	Share Volume		Dollar Volume	
	Millions	Percent	Millions	Percent
NASDAQ	33,380	39.2	$ 452,430	21.8
NASDAQ/OTC Trading in Listed Securities	2,589	3.0	86,494	4.2
Amex	3,329	3.9	37,715	1.8
Regionals (BSE, CSE, MSE, PSE, and PHLX)	6,208	7.3	178,139	8.5
NYSE	39,665	46.6	1,325,332	63.7
Totals	**85,171**	**100.0**	**$2,080,110**	**100.0**

Source: NASDAQ (1991).

calls a dealer, who checks NASDAQ to find the best quotation from competing dealers in a particular stock at the lowest cost (that is, lowest bid-ask spread and commission). Unlike stock exchange specialists, dealers are not obligated to provide liquidity through their own position-taking. The OTC market instead relies on interdealer competition.

About 13 percent of OTC transactions are handled by NASD's Small Order Execution System (SOES), in operation since 1985. Public buy or sell orders of as many as 1,000 shares go through SOES to the dealer offering the best price quote. However, if there are currently better price quotes on NASDAQ outside SOES, that dealer is required to fill the order at the better price.[11] In 1990 SOES added the capacity to automatically execute matching limit orders entered into the system.

Another NASDAQ system is SelectNet, which allows NASDAQ members to send buy or sell securities orders to other system members' terminals. SelectNet enables market makers to accept and execute orders partially or fully as well as to conduct price and quantity negotiations. System users are therefore not anonymous. NASDAQ securities orders must be for more than 1,000 shares.[12]

NASDAQ leads other domestic exchanges, most notably the New York Stock Exchange, in the indirect trading of foreign equities. This indirect trading is through American Depository Receipts (ADRs). Foreign corporations have American commercial or investment banks buy their equity shares and place them in a trust account, against which ADR certificates are issued. These certificates are negotiable and can be traded on exchanges and through NASDAQ. Investors find ADRs convenient because their purchase and sale and the distribution of dividend payments are entirely in dollars, not foreign currency. Foreign-currency denominated cash dividends are converted into dollars by the trustee, usually a commercial bank, and are passed on to the American Depository Receipts holders. The foreign corporation benefits by not having to comply with the SEC's disclosure requirements and other regulations enforced for domestic corporations (see Francis 1991, 62, 806-7).

In 1990 NASDAQ reached new records in ADR trading with a trading volume of 2.2 billion shares of eighty-seven ADR issues. In comparison, the NYSE had a 1.4 billion share volume for sixty-two ADR issues. NASDAQ dollar volume was 21 billion, while the dollar volume in foreign securities directly listed on NASDAQ was 7 billion.[13] NASDAQ is expanding in 1991 to offer an international quotation network based in the United Kingdom called NASDAQ International.

Instinet. NASDAQ dealers earn their livelihood from the difference in price between what they will pay for stock and their selling price, the bid-ask spread.

That spread has come under pressure to narrow because of an electronic order-execution system called Instinet, owned by Reuters Holdings PLC. Instinet is a screen trading system in that it enables subscribers to trade anonymously. These participants include not only OTC broker-dealers but also institutional investors. For example, NASDAQ dealers can trade with other NASDAQ dealers on Instinet to adjust their inventory of stocks. These trades can be accomplished within the bid-ask spread quoted on NASDAQ so that NASDAQ quotes would be unaffected. Institutional investors have also been trading actively on Instinet at much lower spreads than through NASDAQ dealers or exchange specialists. To stay competitive, dealers have had to cut their spreads.[14]

Most Instinet trades involve OTC and listed U.S. stocks, but an increasing number are in British, French, German, and other European stocks as well. The system, on-line an average of fourteen hours per day, can remain operational almost around-the-clock during periods of heavy trading.[15]

Anonymity is important to traders because a trader's identity can reveal how often and how much he or she is buying or selling, information that could move prices against the trader. For example, traders usually avoid selling large orders at once because doing so may prompt a stock's price to be bid down rapidly in the process of making the trade, on the assumption that some bad news is behind the sale. In that scenario, known as adverse selection risk, large orders will be put on the market in smaller blocks. Instinet allows traders to poll each other almost instantaneously on a prospective trade. They can send anonymous messages over the system to particular traders to negotiate quantity or price. They can see all of the bids and offers on particular stocks at a given time on the Instinet "book."

Madoff Investment Securities. This firm has set itself up in direct competition with NYSE specialists. Madoff makes a market in 350 of the S&P 500 stocks by attracting mainly retail trades from brokers, paying them a penny per share for orders. These orders are executed at prices that match the best quoted on any exchange, as reported through ITS. Madoff operates through the Cincinnati Stock Exchange's National Securities Trading System, which is essentially an over-the-counter market. Because of low overhead costs, his commission costs are much lower than for trades carried out on an exchange floor. According to a recent estimate, this firm alone generates 2 percent of the daily trading volume in NYSE listed stocks (Barbara Howard 1991, 16; William E. Sheeline 1990, 122).

Crossing Networks. To reduce transactions costs, many institutional investors have turned to so-called crossing networks, such as Instinet's The Crossing Network and Posit (Portfolio System for Institutional Trading) of Jefferies & Company, a registered broker-dealer. Many institutional investors deal in indexed equity portfolios—for example, a portfolio mimicking the S&P 500 index. These "passive" portfolio managers are not concerned about the precise timing of trade executions for individual stocks making up an index. For institutional investors seeking to trade in whole portfolios of stocks, crossing networks offer a low-cost alternative to transactions on organized stock exchanges.

The Crossing Network allows whole portfolios of stock to be bought or sold at primary markets' closing prices (for example, NYSE closing prices) and the mean of the bid-ask OTC prices. Because the trades are based on the closing price, and hence passive, there is no "market impact" on the trades themselves—that is, large buy and sell orders are matched or crossed at that price, unaffected by the unfavorable price movement such a trade might ordinarily produce. The price does not adjust to balance supply and demand, so some orders will go unmatched in a single after-hours session.

Posit is a crossing network that operates during trading hours as well as off-hours. Portfolio trades can be executed at the primary markets' opening, at prespecified times of day after the opening, or at closing prices. This system has many options that users can select; their choices affect the cost of their trades. For example, trades not matched through Posit's computer can be canceled, held for matching at a later time, sent to the primary markets for execution, or "price-guaranteed" by Jefferies (that is, Jefferies takes the other side of the trade). These alternatives entail different commission costs. The amount of information about a prospective trade, like the size of the order or identity of the investor, may be revealed or hidden from other system users (U.S. Securities and Exchange Commission 1991, 83-86).

Overseas Trading. The NYSE is also affected by the movement of institutional program trades overseas, particularly to London's over-the-counter market. A common transaction involves a stock-index futures purchase or sale on a U.S. futures exchange with a subsequent exchange-for-physicals (EFP) transaction to unwind the futures position.[16] For example, a portfolio manager who wishes to buy an S&P 500-

indexed portfolio could buy the underlying stocks on the New York Stock Exchange or alternatively buy S&P 500 contracts on the Chicago Mercantile Exchange. In the latter case, the long futures position could then be offset through an EFP over the counter in London by finding a trader (or traders) short the S&P 500 futures who holds the underlying stock portfolio. The cash prices and futures price for the EFP transaction would be determined by negotiation but typically reflect the underlying stocks' closing prices on the New York Stock Exchange, Amex, and OTC markets as well as the futures on the transaction date. The parties have traded stocks outside of the NYSE and have closed out their futures positions off the Chicago Mercantile Exchange exchange floor, saving commissions and market impact costs.[17] Similar over-the-counter program transactions also occur that do not involve index futures.

About 10 to 15 million NYSE shares currently trade after-hours in London every day (Kevin G. Salwen and Craig Torres 1991, C1). This exodus from the exchange floor was spurred in part by a postcrash NYSE rule requiring immediate display of program trades' price and volume.

SPAworks. A new system operated by R. Steven Wunsch takes after-hours trading a step further. He has designed a system, SPAworks, to trade stocks in an after-hours call market, which involves a single-price auction. This institutional arrangement was actually prevalent in the nineteenth century before the advent of continuous auction markets, and many relatively illiquid international exchanges still rely on it (see below). SPAworks has been operational since April 1991.

The system works by allowing buy and sell orders to accumulate after the NYSE closes at 4:00 P.M. (U.S. Securities and Exchange Commission 1991, 73-77; Wunsch 1991). At a predetermined time before the next day's opening, a single computerized auction of each individual stock would be held, whereby trades would be consummated at the price resulting in the largest volume of trade. Participants entering bids above or below the auction price are able to execute their trades at the auction price. Other orders go unmatched. This system saves the cost of paying for the immediate liquidity provided on the exchange floor.

Off-Hours Trading. In response to the inroads these outside trading systems have made, the NYSE announced in May 1991 that it would institute two after-hours sessions. "Crossing Session I" runs from 4:15 until 5:00 P.M. and allows investors to buy and sell at the 4:00 P.M. closing price. Once submitted by NYSE members through SuperDot, single-sided orders are

matched against others based on the times they were submitted. Matched single-sided orders and paired (prearranged) orders are then executed through SuperDot at 5:00 P.M. "Crossing Session II," which operates from 4:00 to 5:15 P.M., specifically accommodates program traders. After the close New York Stock Exchange member firms place paired orders for programs that contain at least fifteen NYSE-listed stocks having a one-million-dollar market value or more. These coupled orders are executed as soon as they are received by the system. To make the new sessions attractive to program traders, the NYSE has granted a

---

Physical marketplaces (the trading floors) are becoming obsolete, while "virtual" marketplaces—networks of computers and computer terminals—are emerging as the "site" for transactions.

---

nine-month exemption from being required to report price and volume information for individual program trades. Only the aggregate volume and dollar value of program trades are disseminated at 5:15 P.M. Single-sided and coupled order volume are each reported separately for Crossing Session I, beginning at 5:00 P.M. (Salwen and Torres 1991, C1; U.S. Securities and Exchange Commission 1991, 36-39; New York Stock Exchange 1991b, 1-5).

Foreign Equity Markets. Many foreign stock markets are considerably less liquid than U.S. stock markets, and their institutional arrangements reflect this fact. The Austrian and Norwegian stock markets simply hold a single daily call auction. Others use a mixed system of call auctions at some times of day and continuous trading at other times. Mixed auctions are prevalent in Belgium, Denmark, France, Italy, Spain, Sweden, and Switzerland.[18] The Australian, British, Canadian, French, and Japanese markets have automated trading systems. Four of the major automated exchanges are relatively well developed.

The Toronto Stock Exchange uses the Computer Assisted Trading System (CATS), which functions as an electronic auction for less actively traded stocks and is being updated to handle more active stocks. Broker-dealers using the system can choose to have their trades executed by either a specialist or computer. CATS currently handles about 75 percent of trades on the exchange, a small volume compared with that of major American exchanges (Hansell 1989, 93; U.S. Congress 1990b, 63; Howard 1991, 15). CATS also displays the best five buy and sell limit orders along with the name of the broker making the order (Hansell 1989, 93; Howard 1991, 15).

The Paris Bourse (stock exchange) relies on a licensed version of CATS, which is also under consideration for use at exchanges in Madrid, Brussels, and Sao Paulo (Hansell 1989, 93, 98; Ian Domowitz 1990, 170). The system used by the French exchange is named CAC, for Cotation Assistée Continu. This exchange, overshadowed by the London market, is much less liquid. In fact, exchange member firms hold a single daily auction in stocks complemented by forward trading in listed stocks using both continuous trading and call auctions in forward contracts (Richard Roll 1988, 29).

The London International Stock Exchange is a dealer market very similar in operation to NASDAQ. The ISE is the most active world market in foreign (non-United Kingdom) stock trading, which makes up slightly more than half of the exchange's volume. The average daily foreign issue volume was 1.3 billion pounds sterling per day in 1990. ISE members have benefited from the migration of some U.S. program trading. The ISE's analog to the NASDAQ quote-display system is the Stock Exchange Automated Quotation System (SEAQ); small orders of fewer than 5,000 shares are automatically executed on the Stock Automated Exchange Facility (SAEF).

The Tokyo Stock Exchange (TSE) has a system similar to Toronto's CATS. Its Computer Assisted Order Routing and Execution System (CORES) now handles all but 150 of the exchange's most actively traded issues; however, the TSE is moving toward a fully automated system. Instead of specialists, the exchange has a group of overseers, called *saitori*, who use computer screens to monitor the trades arranged by the computer and by floor traders and to approve the prices. The saitori can also allow CORES to generate trades automatically within a specified price range. In addition, they act as human circuit breakers on the exchange floor when trading becomes too volatile; they have the authority to suspend trading briefly (Hansell 1989, 97).

Futures and Options Markets

Like prices of exchange-traded stocks, futures prices are established through an auction system, but one with no counterpart to the single individual, the specialist, making a market in a stock. Instead, futures prices are determined by an auction known as the open-outcry system. Exchange members—floor traders—congregate at designated trading pits and shout bids and offers at each other or use hand signals to indicate trading intentions. Exchange officials record the price and amount of each transaction. Effective in providing liquidity, this system is also subject to error and even abuse.[19]

As discussed above, international competition is forcing efficiency-enhancing automation. Many new overseas exchanges are fully or partially automated and trade many of the same contracts as American exchanges, although their volume levels are usually much lower. Systems emerging on futures and options markets harbinger the internationalization soon to come. In particular, the Chicago Mercantile Exchange's Globex (Global Exchange) system is being designed to handle volumes that exceed current open-outcry volume levels at peak trading times.

Globex. Globex, expected to be operable in early 1992, will automate *and link* participating exchanges. To date, the Chicago Board of Trade and Marché à Terme des Instruments Financiers (MATIF), the French financial futures market, are members of Globex. Other exchanges in the Far East are considering joining Globex, including Australia's Sydney Futures Exchange (SFE) and possibly Japan's Osaka Securities Exchange, or OSE (Ginger Szala and Amy Rosenbaum 1990, 44). Globex will operate after-hours, beginning at 6 P.M. Chicago time, when Japanese markets open.

The genesis of Globex lay in efforts to extend the futures trading day. In 1984 the CME established a relationship with the newly founded Singapore International Monetary Exchange (SIMEX), a relationship based mainly on mutual advantages gained from trading compatible Eurodollar and foreign currency futures contracts. The two exchanges set up a mutual offset permitting contracts opened on one exchange to be closed on the other and vice versa. This link effectively lengthened the trading day almost to twenty-four hours, helping the Chicago exchange to secure a foothold in booming East Asian financial markets. SIMEX enjoyed the benefits of the additional liquidity generated by the infusion of Chicago-based trades. Also catering to growing interest from abroad, the Merc's Chicago rival, the Chicago Board of Trade, instituted nighttime trading of its Treasury bond futures contracts in April 1987. However, this insomniac trading, as one observer termed it, and the CME's mutual offset arrangement were regarded as stopgap measures ("Futures Markets" 1988). More efficient and less error-prone electronic trading seems inevitable; the Chicago Board of Trade joined with the Chicago Mercantile Exchange as a Globex partner in 1990. Up to that point the CBOT had been developing its own after-hours system, called Aurora, that would electronically emulate open-outcry trading. (See the discussion below of LIFFE's Automated Pit Trading for a similar system).

The mechanical heart of Globex is a network of computer screens. The system is a joint venture of the "partner exchanges" (CME, CBOT, and MATIF) and Reuters Holdings PLC, which already has a large presence in over-the-counter spot foreign exchange markets. The Reuters network of computer terminals in banks and brokerage firms numbers about 180,000 worldwide. The CME emphasizes that trading via Globex is an alternate method of placing an order on its exchange or on partner exchanges (Brodsky 1990, 621). Because the exchanges do not view Globex as a new kind of futures exchange, they argue that regulatory approval of the system (particularly in Japan) should be straightforward.

Globex automatically matches and executes orders entered into the system. The system first checks the credit standing of the member firm initiating a transaction and then matches orders based on the time an order was submitted and its price. Unlike standard open-outcry trading, Globex does not allow for orders to be executed at the prevailing market price (that is, there can be no market orders); all orders must be good-until-canceled limit orders (the order stays on the book until it is executed or canceled).[20]

Trades are confirmed at participants' screens, prices and quantities are reported through the system, trades are cleared, and buyers' and sellers' accounts are adjusted. Traders on Globex deal anonymously with one another, an important consideration for most participants, as mentioned earlier. However, Globex, like other automated systems, does produce a so-called electronic audit trail, which is regarded as an improvement over the open-outcry system's less accurate recording procedures. Electronic monitoring is expected to give traders more confidence in the trading process and makes the regulator's job easier.

Although trading has not yet begun on Globex, its relative performance compared with the open-outcry auction has been assessed by Domowitz (1991). Using simulated trading experiments, he finds that Globex is the more efficient trading mechanism according to a number of measures. Globex tends to result in lower price volatility and greater market liquidity, and the differences become more pronounced as the size of the market increases.

In contrast, Merton H. Miller (1990) argues that screen trading systems, especially of the order-matching type like Globex, put traders (market makers) at a disadvantage because they cannot observe the order flow on a screen as they can from the trading pit. Traders with more current information can take advantage of previously posted traders' price quotes. For this reason Miller does not believe that electronic systems will ever attract sufficient competing market-maker participation to match the liquidity of the most active trading pits. To date, most screen trading systems have been used at low-volume exchanges or for low-volume contracts. Validation of Miller's or Domowitz's predictions will have to await actual trading through Globex as well as more extensive deployment of other screen trading systems.

Domestic Options Markets. A number of automated trading systems have been introduced to facilitate options trading. The most significant of these is the Chicago Board Options Exchange's Retail Automatic Execution System (RAES), which has been in operation since 1985. The system now handles both index options, including the heavily traded S&P 100 index option, and all CBOE equity options (on individual stocks). About 3.5 percent of contract volume is currently executed through RAES (U.S. Securities and Exchange Commission 1991, 19). The Amex uses a system called AUTO-EX for market and limit orders of as many as twenty equity contracts. The system is designed for use of Amex member firms and exchange specialists. In addition, the Amex has a mutual-offset link with the European Options Exchange in Amsterdam for the stock index options contract on the Amex's Major Market Index, or MMI (U.S. Congress 1990b, 96). The Pacific Stock Exchange has a similar system for equity options called POETS (Pacific Options Exchange Trading System). The Philadelphia Stock Exchange uses AUTOM (Automated Options Market System) for equity options. The NYSE's SuperDot also routes orders for trades on its equity and equity-index options.

Delta Government Securities, a screen-based system for trading options on U.S. Treasury bills, notes, and bonds, is operated jointly by RMJ Securities and RMJ Options, which are a registered clearing agency and registered broker-dealer, respectively. Delta always stands as the intermediary between buyer and seller using the system. It effectively operates like an electronic options exchange, issuing any options traded through the system (U.S. Securities and Exchange Commission 1991, 89).

Foreign Derivatives Markets. There is stiff competition among European futures exchanges. Marché à Terme des Instruments Financiers vies with the London International Financial Futures Exchange primarily over the three-month Euro-deutsche mark futures (a futures on the three-month rate on interbank deutsche mark-denominated deposits). MATIF, Europe's most active futures exchange, joined Globex in November 1989 and plans to list its government bond future (the Notionnel) and its short-term interest-rate future (on PIBOR—Paris Interbank Offered Rate) on the system. Part of the motivation behind MATIF's Globex membership was to boost foreign participation on the exchange and lessen London's advantage of having the offices of almost 600 international banks and brokerage firms (Janet Lewis 1990, 130).

The fact that LIFFE also offers a futures contract on the long-term German government bond, the Bund, in part spurred the creation of the first German futures market, the Deutsche Terminbörse (DTB) in 1990. A consortium of fifty-three institutions, mostly large banks, belong to the DTB. The exchange offers futures contracts to compete with LIFFE's as well as stock options on German firms (Lewis 1990, 130).

The Frankfurt-based exchange is organized as a computer network that matches and processes all trades electronically. The automated trading system employed is based on a similar system used by the Swiss Options and Financial Futures Exchange (SOFFEX), also an entirely automated order-matching system that allows member firms to be market makers, quoting bids and offers. Trades are entered anonymously, so large trades can be anonymously negotiated over the system (Hansell 1989, 93). Five fully automated futures and options exchanges now operate worldwide, as seen in Table 5.

LIFFE has a partially automated system, called Automated Pit Trading (APT), that mimics actual pit-trading (London International Financial Futures Exchange 1991). The after-hours system operates from 4:30 to 6:00 P.M. local time, with access restricted to LIFFE members. APT is not driven by quote-making

dealers but by traders who post bids and offers for specified quantities. By the touch of a computer key, any trader can instantaneously accept bids and offers that appear on the screen. This system is the analog of the open-outcry method, in which bids and offers of floor traders are valid for "as long as the breath is warm." Because the futures exchanges deal in a limited set of futures contracts, liquidity is concentrated and rapid interactions between traders can be emulated on a screen. LIFFE expanded the system in 1990 to include a central limit-order book that enables purchases and sales of futures contracts if the market price reaches the posted limit price.

In Japan financial futures were banned until 1985. Regulators and legislators have gradually been deregulating and expanding their financial and derivative markets, and the Japanese have become very active in developing futures exchanges. Japanese firms are eager to use the new contracts. They may now deal directly in securities on foreign exchanges, and foreign brokerage firms may be members of Japanese futures exchanges (see Szala and Rosenbaum 1990, 42).

The first Japanese contracts were ten- and twenty-year yen bond futures, introduced on the Tokyo Stock Exchange in 1985. As of December 1989 the TSE offered U.S. Treasury bond futures equivalent to those of the CBOT. The Japanese Ministry of Finance, however, requires higher margins to be posted against Tokyo Stock Exchange futures contracts than does the Chicago Board of Trade for comparable positions. The higher margin levels apply even for Japanese firms taking positions in CBOT contracts, so these firms have little incentive to look abroad (Szala and Rosenbaum 1990, 42).

The TSE bond contracts, now the sixth most heavily traded future in the world (see Table 3), can all be traded through CORES. The TSE stock-index future on TOPIX (Tokyo Stock Price Index) is fully automated on CORES. Fully automated trading of a three-month Euroyen contract is conducted on the new Tokyo International Financial Futures Exchange (TIFFE), which competes against SIMEX in Singapore. SIMEX is still dominant in a number of contracts, including yen-U.S. dollar futures and Eurodollar futures, but it lags in Euroyen. Unlike TIFFE, SIMEX is a traditional open-outcry exchange.

The Nikkei 225 futures, the highest-volume Japanese index futures contract, trades at the Osaka Securities Exchange (OSE). The CME has acquired the rights to offer a Nikkei 225 contract on its exchange, though it would prefer to link up with the OSE through Globex (Szala and Rosenbaum 1990,

Table 5
Automated Trading Systems

System Operator	System
Equities	
American Stock Exchange	Post Execution Reporting
Amsterdam Stock Exchange	System based on MSE's MAX
Australian Association of Stock Exchanges	Stock Exchange Automated Trading (SEAT)
Boston Stock Exchange	BSE Automated Communication and Order Routing Network (BEACON)
Cincinnati Stock Exchange	National Securities Trading System (NSTS)
Instinet Corporation	Instinet The Crossing Network
Jefferies & Company, Inc.	Portfolio System for Institutional Trading (Posit)
London International Stock Exchange	Stock Automated Exchange Facility (SAEF)
Midwest Stock Exchange	Midwest Automated Execution (MAX)
National Association of Securities Dealers	Small Order Execution Service (SOES) SelectNet Private Offerings, Resales, and Trading through Automated Linkages (PORTAL)
New York Stock Exchange	Designated Order Turnaround system (SuperDot) Crossing Sessions I and II
Pacific Stock Exchange	Securities Communication Order Routing and Execution System (SCOREX)
Paris Bourse	Cotation Assistée en Continu (CAC)
Philadelphia Stock Exchange	Philadelphia Automated Communication and Execution System (PACE)
Tokyo Stock Exchange	Computer Assisted Order Routing and Execution System (CORES)
Toronto Stock Exchange	Computer Assisted Trading System (CATS)
Wunsch Auction Systems, Inc.	SPAworks
Futures and Options	
American Stock Exchange (equity options)	AUTO-EX
Chicago Board Options Exchange	Retail Automated Exchange System (RAES)
Chicago Board of Trade	Globex
Chicago Mercantile Exchange	Globex
Deutsche Terminbörse	Fully automated, integrated clearing
Irish Futures and Options Exchange	Fully automated, ATS-2
London International Financial Futures Exchange	Automated Pit Trading (APT)

(table continues)

Table 5 (continued)

System Operator	System
Futures and Options	
London Traded Options Market	Associated with LIFFE
Marché à Terme des Instruments Financiers	Globex
New York Stock Exchange	SuperDot
New Zealand Futures and Options Exchange	Fully automated ATS system
Pacific Stock Exchange	Pacific Options Exchange Trading System (POETS)
Philadelphia Stock Exchange	Automated Options Market System (AUTOM)
Stockholm Option Market	Integrated clearing facilities based on electronic trading and telephone brokering
Sydney Futures Exchange	Sydney Computerized Overnight Market (SYCOM)
Swiss Options and Financial Futures Exchange	Fully automated; integrated clearing
Tokyo Stock Exchange	Derivative markets fully automated CORES-F

Sources: U.S. Securities and Exchange Commission (1991); Angrist (1991); U.S. Congress (1990b); Kang and Lawton (1990); Rosenbaum (1990); Hansell (1989).

44). The CME's first overtures to the Ministry of Finance, one of the chief regulators of Japanese exchanges, were made in August 1988 and are still ongoing. The CBOT now lists a Japanese stock-index futures on the TOPIX and several Japanese government bond futures and options.

Market Performance and Regulatory Issues

Regulation of securities markets in the United States is generally intended to ensure that securities trading is conducted openly and based on publicly available information. The Securities Act of 1933 and Securities Exchange Act of 1934 mandated extensive registration and disclosure requirements for firms issuing securities to the public. However, recent policy discussions have shifted regulators' sights to safe-guarding the performance and stability of financial markets.

The Brady Commission's recommendations in the wake of the 1987 crash stand out as the most sweeping proposals for changing the ways financial markets operate and for reorganizing their regulators' responsibilities.[21] To the Brady Commission and to a large number of market observers, the crash was prima facie evidence that private financial markets can fail—spectacularly. Concerns about the flow of information and the ability of participants to act on it superseded traditional questions about fairness and honesty in the marketplace.[22] The crash underscored the potential systemic risk of market failure as trading disruptions spread from one market to another. The problems can engulf the banking system as credit demands mount, for example, because of timing differences between the receipt and disbursement of funds by clearinghouses, straining liquidity and threatening widespread defaults.[23]

An important policy challenge is determining the appropriate mix of government and private-market actions to lessen the risk of securities market failure. It is feared that the electronic globalization of financial exchanges might contribute to systemic risks. The 1987 crash broadened the concerns, touching off a debate about whether a crash in one country's markets can trigger shocks beyond domestic boundaries to other countries' markets. The desirability and feasibility of international regulatory cooperation to contain such potential problems is an open question just beginning to be addressed (see Grundfest 1990; Paul Guy 1990; and U.S. Congress 1990a).

A survey of international regulatory issues is beyond the scope of this article. Rather, the following discussion focuses on the interconnections between markets and proposals to manage the international transmission of volatility. The basic issue to be considered has to do with the source of volatility and arguments for and against counteracting it. Since the stock market crash of October 1987, and even earlier in the decade, regulators and other market observers have become concerned about market volatility and cross-market spillovers.

The increasing prevalence of cross-border trading as well as the opening of new exchanges and deepening of existing ones would seem to imply that world financial markets are becoming unified. However, the evidence of such merging is not clear-cut. In fact, the Brady Commission concluded that through 1987 correlations of price movements from different world markets provide no evidence of closer links: "The correlations between the market in the U.S. and the markets in Germany and Japan appear to form totally random series. . . . [T]here is no evidence to suggest that the association is any closer today than it was a decade ago" (Nicolas F. Brady et al. 1988, II-6). Roll (1988) has observed that the only month in the 1980s in which all major world markets moved together was October 1987.

A number of recent academic papers address the question of world financial market integration. Using a sophisticated model of global equity market equilibrium (an international capital asset pricing model with time-varying moments), Campbell R. Harvey (1991) found evidence of a lack of integration, particularly for Japanese markets with the rest of the world. The basic object of study is the reward-to-risk ratio on equities required by investors. In a world of integrated markets, the reward-to-risk ratio would be the same in every equity market. In fact, this ratio turned out to be twice as large in Japanese markets as in U.S. markets.

In other words, Japanese investors require expected returns on stocks to be double the magnitude expected by U.S. investors. Complete integration across markets would equalize differences in the reward-to-risk ratio across countries because otherwise, for example, U.S. investors would skew their portfolios toward Japanese equities offering better trade-offs between return and risk than domestic equities. Increased U.S. purchases of Japanese stocks would bid up their prices and bid down U.S. stock prices, driving Japanese expected returns down and U.S. expected returns up. There are many subtleties and qualifications in this analysis, but the preponderance of evidence is against the simple hypothesis that world markets have become integrated.

The empirical work of David Neumark, P.A. Tinsley, and Suzanne Tosini reveals that price movements for U.S. stocks listed on New York, Tokyo, and London exchanges are more highly correlated during periods of high volatility than during times of low volatility because "only larger price changes pierce the transaction cost barriers between markets" (1991, 160). These authors noted that ordinarily the stock price volatility for this group of U.S. stocks (which are contained in the Dow Jones Industrial Average) is three times greater during New York trading hours than during London or Tokyo trading hours. In their view, this phenomenon occurs because the largest share of news relevant to the determination of the stock prices is disseminated during New York trading hours. This pattern was disrupted in the aftermath of the October 1987 crash when, in the authors' judgment, news was more globally dispersed and had mostly to do with "the volatile behavior of other investors" (176).

Yasushi Hamao, Ronald W. Masulis, and Victor Ng (1990) conducted another detailed study of intermarket linkages focusing on what they term price "volatility spillovers" among the New York, London, and Tokyo stock markets. For a subperiod that excludes the 1987 crash, they found that, while there was no significant transmission of volatility from Tokyo to either London or New York, the latter two cities' volatility did spill over to trading in Tokyo. When the post-1987 period is included, evidence indicates that all three markets were shocked by "volatility surprises," although Tokyo markets still did not affect New York's.

Mervyn A. King and Sushil Wadhwani (1990) have examined the market events surrounding October 1987 and offer a hypothesis about the worldwide scope of the market crash. To investigate the conundrum of what change in market fundamentals could explain a 23 percent drop in the Dow and similar gigantic declines in other markets around the globe, the authors developed a model in which rational traders in one market have less information about stocks than traders in the home market and must infer information partly from stock price movements abroad. This situation leads to the possibility of price movement "contagion" from one market to another, which will be particularly severe during periods of high market volatility. A sharp decline in a foreign price index is a (noisy) signal of bad news, some of which home market traders may not know from other sources. While the authors' hypothesis does not shed light on the "news" that triggered the October 1987 crash, it does explain why the crash was so uniform around the world despite important differences in markets and economic circumstances.

Gerard Gennotte and Hayne Leland (1990) have also developed a model in which rational traders' lack of information can precipitate a crash. Their concern is with informationless trading associated with hedging strategies like portfolio insurance. Formal portfolio insurance techniques systematically increase exposure to the market as stock prices rise and reduce it as stock prices fall (by shifting a portfolio's mix between index stocks and bonds or by adjusting the size of a short index futures hedge against a stock index portfolio). Although portfolio insurance-related selling is strictly passive, responding to declining stock prices, it could be mistaken for selling based on adverse information, and other traders look to prices and price changes as a way to glean information that they may lack. If nonpassive traders knew that they were taking the buy side of an informationless trade, they would more likely be willing to do so and would thereby supply liquidity to the market.

Gennotte and Leland's model shows how unobserved hedging programs, though only a small proportion of total trading, can destabilize a market. The disturbance may then propagate to other world markets. Their recommendation is that informationless trades should be preannounced and that "[e]lectronic 'open books' should be a seriously considered reform [to show the buy and sell order flow], and other forms of market organization (such as single-price auctions) should be examined" (1990, 1016). Some recent institutional developments are consistent with the authors' recommendations. Toronto's Computer Assisted Trading System displays limit orders to system users, and Wunsch's after-hours single-price auctions help concentrate market liquidity.

The King and Wadhwani and Gennotte and Leland models explain how trading itself can generate intermarket volatility. Joseph E. Stiglitz (1989) and Lawrence H. Summers and Victoria P. Summers (1989), go further by asserting that financial markets are excessively volatile because of irrational traders' speculative activity. Decreasing transactions costs owing to technological innovation and derivative markets promotes this speculation. These authors recommend a transactions tax to "throw sand into the gears" of financial markets (Tobin 1984, cited in Summers and Summers 1989, 263). Each securities purchase or sale would be subject to a "small" tax—for example, 0.5 percent of the stock price. In fact, many governments around the world impose stock transaction taxes, although the trend abroad is toward eliminating such taxes (see Roll 1989, table 4).

The gradual unification of world financial markets and continuing improvement in information flows will probably reduce the information asymmetry that produces contagion effects. However, in the view of those advocating transactions taxes these developments would just exacerbate irrational trading. At the core of their argument is the belief that financial markets are inefficient—that is, asset prices do not reflect "fundamentals." A growing list of so-called market anomalies seems to contradict efficient-markets theory. The apparent excess volatility analyzed by Robert J. Shiller (1989) stands as a challenge to efficient-markets proponents. Nevertheless, the theory is only being challenged, not overturned. Transactions taxes and other remedies for supposed excess trading and excess volatility have been proposed and sometimes implemented with little regard for their efficacy or possible adverse consequences.

Trading halts or circuit breakers, margin requirements, and price limits are also suggested as means of controlling trading. Of all these devices, margin requirements have been the most extensively studied and debated. In essence this work concludes that adjustments to margin requirements have no significant impact on stock market volatility (see David A. Hsieh and Miller 1990). Using data from twenty-three stock markets, Roll (1989) undertook a cross-market study of the effects of transactions taxes, margin requirements, and price limits on market volatility and found that none effectively reduce volatility.

Circuit breakers shut down an entire market temporarily to give participants a "time-out," mainly to avoid a panic selling spree. Both the New York Stock Exchange and Chicago Mercantile Exchange have instituted such circuit breakers (see Franklin R. Edwards 1988, 1989), although evidence is lacking concerning their usefulness. As Gennotte and Leland (1990) point out, the weekend of October 17-18, 1987, was an extended trading halt for the market declines of the previous week, but participants were not inclined to stage a market reversal the following Monday. It is not at all obvious that circuit breakers stabilize prices. To the contrary, they could induce traders to sell earlier and in larger quantities, fearing that a trading-halt price limit will soon be reached. This movement could destabilize prices. Sanford J. Grossman (1990) has argued persuasively that market equilibrium would be restored more quickly without halting trading. Rather than attempting to suppress mispricings, Grossman concludes that the market would be better served by being informed of them, whether they arise from panic or any other source, because better-informed traders would recognize such occurrences as profit opportunities and thus reverse the price movements.

Conclusion

The globalization of financial markets simultaneously fragments traditional financial transactions marketplaces and integrates them via electronic means. Physical marketplaces (the trading floors) are becoming obsolete, while "virtual" marketplaces—networks of computers and computer terminals—are emerging as the "site" for transactions. The new technology is diminishing the role for human participants in the market mechanism. Stock-exchange specialists are being displaced by the new systems, which by and large are designed to handle the demands of institutional investors, who increasingly dominate transactions. Futures and options floor traders also face having their jobs coded into computer algorithms, which automatically match orders and clear trades or emulate open-outcry trading itself.

International capital flows and the trading volume associated with them have been expanding over time. The internationalization of financial markets implies that investment portfolios are becoming more homogenized and creates a demand for worldwide twenty-four-hour trading. Derivative markets also benefit from this trend as multinational corporations need financial services around the clock for hedging and other reasons.

The competitive forces propelling changes in financial markets also compel changes in regulatory oversight of these markets.[24] Technology helps minimize some problems—for example, by making it possible to establish accurate audit trails of trades and thereby discouraging certain kinds of trading abuses—while it creates others, such as business being drawn to markets with the most lenient regulatory standards. Nevertheless, financial marketplaces are perhaps closest to the textbook paradigm of voluntary exchanges for mutual benefit of transacting parties. Competition among the world's financial exchanges as well as among their regulators is likely to be the most efficient way to elicit the best mechanisms for conducting and regulating transactions.

More problematic is the nature of trading and volatility associated with it. Does trading itself generate volatility that interferes with consumption, investment, and other economic decisions, in turn lowering social welfare? This article has given an overview of new automated trading systems and communications networks that are integrating markets. The technology discussed improves market mechanisms and information flows, but it may have the negative side effect of promoting "excess" trading. If markets are efficient, volatility per se is generally regarded as a neutral characteristic of markets. Derivative markets will continue developing to allow any desired degree of hedging against volatility. Only if markets are inefficient can a case can be made for curtailing volatility, but the evidence is ambiguous regarding market inefficiency. Even less clear is the efficacy of measures proposed to safeguard markets against volatility.

1. See Summers and Summers (1989) and the discussion of their proposal below.
2. Frequent trading will be necessary when the number of securities available to "complete markets" is smaller than the number of future "states." See Huang and Litzenberger (1988, chapter 7). This situation will be all the more likely if financial markets are incomplete. However, theory does not give an indication of how much trading is appropriate to allocate wealth over time efficiently.
3. The difference between purchases and sales represents the net capital flow, which is less relevant in considering the growth of securities trading and market liquidity.
4. $321\% = [(75.28/17.85) - 1] * 100$ and $43\% = [(361.37/253.38) - 1] * 100$.
5. See Smith (1991). Ginnie Mae stands for Government National Mortgage Association, a government-chartered agency that makes a secondary market in home mortgages and enhances the liquidity of that market by securitizing individual mortgages into "pass-through" certificates. The futures was on this underlying security.
6. The NYSE is in the process of instituting "A Look at the Book" program that permits public subscribers to the service to view the limit orders for 50 of the 2,370 NYSE-listed stocks. This service will be available through vendors and will show the limit-order book at three fixed times during the trading day. Currently, only the specialists and other NYSE members, such as floor brokers, on the exchange floor have access to the specialists' books.
7. Market orders specify quantity for trade at the current price. Limit orders specify price and quantity.
8. The meanings of the acronyms are given in Table 5.
9. The bid price is the price for which a dealer is willing to buy a stock, and the offer is the price for which he or she is willing to sell the stock.
10. See Bodie, Kane, and Marcus (1989) or Francis (1991) for further institutional details about organized exchanges and OTC markets and such details as listing requirements.
11. This account of SOES is based on Domowitz (1990).
12. See U.S. Securities and Exchange Commission (1991, 69); another NASDAQ system described in this source is PORTAL (Private Offerings, Resales, and Trading through Automated Linkages), which is used in the secondary market for privately placed equity and debt. See note 24 below for further description.
13. See NASDAQ (1991, 14-15). Because of differences in accounting conventions, the NASDAQ figures are inflated compared with the NYSE figures.
14. See Hansell (1989, 102). The amount of institutional participation in NASDAQ stocks as measured by the volume of block trading has been about 43 percent in recent years. See NASDAQ (1991).
15. Instinet-sponsored section in *Institutional Investor* (January 1991).

16. See Kolb (1991, 17-18) for a general discussion of EFP transactions and Miller (1990) for EFPs in connection with the CME's S&P 500 stock-index futures contract.
17. The futures exchange, however, would collect an additional fee for allowing the off-exchange or ex-pit EFP. The Commodity Exchange Act prohibits noncompetitive and prearranged transactions in futures, with the exception of EFPs. See Behof (1990, 2).
18. See Roll (1988, 29). Roll notes that the Spanish market trades groups of stocks continuously for ten minutes at a time. This article contains much interesting information about foreign stock markets.
19. See Kolb (1991, 59-61) for a succinct account of the FBI undercover sting operation at the CME and CBOT, which began in early 1987 and resulted in indictments against forty-seven traders in January 1989.
20. Information on Globex came from 1991 CME promotional literature. Domowitz (1990) provides a detailed description and analysis of the Globex trading algorithm as well as those for two other trading systems.
21. The Brady Commission's basic recommendations were: (1) to have one agency be the overarching regulator of U.S. financial markets; (2) to have a unification of clearing systems of financial exchanges and OTC markets; (3) to have "consistent" margin requirements across different exchanges; (4) to institute coordinated "circuit breakers" across exchanges; and (5) to improve information systems to monitor trading activity in related markets.
22. The Securities and Exchange Act of 1934 authorized the Federal Reserve Board to established initial and maintenance margins to prevent excessive leveraging of securities purchases on securities exchanges. (In practice, the Board has set only minimum initial margin levels.) Part of the rationale for control over margins was to limit massive selling off of leveraged positions during market downturns.
23. See Brady et al. (1988, especially 51-52). Despite the potential dangers, no defaults occurred in the clearinghouse system during October 1987.
24. The SEC's April 1990 approval of Rule 144A is an instance of a change in regulatory standards that reflect changes in the nature of financial transactions. This rule simplifies the SEC's disclosure requirements for private placement issuers (see Chu 1991). Foreign corporations are now able to raise capital in U.S. markets without having to meet the SEC's stringent financial disclosure requirements as long as transactions are limited to large institutional investors. British financial authorities have instituted a similar relaxation of regulations for institutional investors (see Grundfest 1990).

   NASDAQ's new PORTAL system is used for communicating bids and offers on privately placed securities traded under the provisions of Rule 144A.

References

Angrist, Stanley W. "Futures Trade on Screens—Except in U.S." *Wall Street Journal*, May 21, 1991, C1, C14.

Behof, John P. "Globex: A Global Automated Transaction System for Futures and Options." Study by the Federal Reserve Bank of Chicago, June 1990.

Bodie, Zvi, Alex Kane, and Alan J. Marcus. *Investments.* Homewood, Ill.: Irwin, 1989.

Brady, Nicholas F., James C. Cotting, Robert G. Kirby, John R. Opel, and Howard M. Stein. *Report of the Presidential Task Force on Market Mechanisms.* Submitted to the President of the United States, the Secretary of the Treasury, and the Chairman of the Federal Reserve Board, January 1988.

Brodsky, William J. "Futures in the Nineties: Confronting Globalization." In *Proceedings from a Conference on Bank Structure and Competition*, 615-23. Federal Reserve Bank of Chicago, 1990.

_____. "The Future Is Now." *Institutional Investor* 25 (January 1991): 7.

Chicago Board of Trade. *Commodity Trading Manual.* CBOT, 1985.

Chu, Franklin J. "The U.S. Private Market for Foreign Securities." *The Bankers Magazine* 174 (January/February 1991): 55-60.

Domowitz, Ian. "The Mechanics of Automated Trade Execution Systems." *Journal of Financial Intermediation* 1 (1990): 167-94.

_____. "Equally Open and Competitive: Regulatory Approval of Automated Trade Execution in the Futures Markets." Center for the Study of Futures Markets Working Paper #214, forthcoming 1991.

Edwards, Franklin R. "Studies of the 1987 Stock Market Crash: Review and Appraisal." *Journal of Financial Services Research* 1 (1988): 231-51.

_____. "Regulatory Reform of Securities and Futures Markets: Two Years after the Crash." Center for the Study of Futures Markets Working Paper #189, June 1989.

Francis, Jack Clark. *Investments: Analysis and Management.* 5th ed. New York: McGraw-Hill, Inc., 1991.

"Futures Markets Will Let Their Fingers Do the Dealing." *The Economist*, March 19, 1988, 77-78.

Gennotte, Gerard, and Hayne Leland. "Market Liquidity, Hedging, and Crashes." *American Economic Review* 80 (1990): 999-1021.

Grossman, Sanford J. "Institutional Investing and New Trading Technologies." In *Market Volatility and Investor Confidence: Report to the Board of Directors of the New York Stock Exchange, Inc.*, G2-1-17. June 7, 1990.

Grundfest, Joseph A. "Internationalization of the World's Securities Markets: Economic Causes and Regulatory Consequences." *Journal of Financial Services Research* 4 (1990): 349-78.

Guy, Paul. "IOSCO Moves Ahead." *FIA Review* (May/June 1990): 8-10.

Hamao, Yasushi, Ronald W. Masulis, and Victor Ng. "Correlations in Price Changes and Volatility across International Stock Markets." *Review of Financial Studies* 3 (1990): 281-307.

Hansell, Saul. "The Wild, Wired World of Electronic Exchanges." *Institutional Investor* (September 1989): 91ff.

Harvey, Campbell R. "The World Price of Covariance Risk." *Journal of Finance* 46 (1991): 111-57.

Heimann, John G. *Globalization of the Securities Markets.* Statement in hearings before the Senate Subcommittee on Securities of the Committee on Banking, Housing, and Urban Affairs. June 14, 1989, 76.

Howard, Barbara. "The Trade: Technology Aims to Take the Final Step." *Institutional Investor* 25 (January 1991): 15-16.

Hsieh, David A., and Merton H. Miller. "Margin Regulation and Stock Market Volatility." *Journal of Finance* 45 (1990): 3-29.

Huang, Chi-fu, and Robert H. Litzenberger. *Foundations for Financial Economics.* New York: North-Holland, 1988.

Kang, Jane C., and John C. Lawton. "Automated Futures Trading Systems." *FIA Review* (May/June 1990): 6-7.

King, Mervyn A., and Sushil Wadhwani. "Transmission of Volatility between Stock Markets." *Review of Financial Studies* 3 (1990): 5-33.

Kolb, Robert W. *Understanding Futures Markets.* 3d ed. Miami: Kolb Publishing Company, 1991.

Lewis, Janet. "The Euro-Futures War." *Institutional Investor* 24 (March 1990): 129ff.

London International Financial Futures Exchange. *APT Information Package.* 1991.

Miller, Merton H. "International Competitiveness of U.S. Futures Exchanges." *Journal of Financial Services Research* 4 (1990): 387-408.

NASDAQ. *Fact Book 1991.* 1991.

Neumark, David, P.A. Tinsley, and Suzanne Tosini. "After-Hours Stock Prices and Post-Crash Hangovers." *Journal of Finance* 46 (1991): 159-78.

New York Stock Exchange. *Fact Book 1991.* 1991a.

New York Stock Exchange. *Off-Hours Trading.* Brochure. 1991b.

Roll, Richard. "The International Crash of October 1987." *Financial Analysts Journal* 44 (September/October 1988): 19-35.

_____. "Price Volatility, International Market Links, and Their Implications for Regulatory Policies." *Journal of Financial Services Research* 3 (1989): 211-46.

Rosenbaum, Amy. "Scouting Automation: What's the Competition Like?" *Futures* 19 (April 1990): 52-54.

Salwen, Kevin G., and Craig Torres. "Big Board After-Hours Trading May Lead to a Two-Tiered Market." *Wall Street Journal*, June 13, 1991, C1, C17.

Sheeline, William E. "Who Needs the Stock Exchange?" *Fortune*, November 19, 1990, 119ff.

Shiller, Robert J. *Market Volatility*. Cambridge, Mass.: MIT Press, 1989.

Smith, Stephen D. "Analyzing Risk and Return for Mortgage-Backed Securities." Federal Reserve Bank of Atlanta *Economic Review* 76 (January/February 1991): 2-11.

Stiglitz, Joseph E. "Using Tax Policy to Curb Speculative Short-Term Trading." *Journal of Financial Services Research* 3 (1989): 101-15.

Summers, Lawrence H., and Victoria P. Summers. "When Financial Markets Work Too Well: A Cautious Case for a Securities Transactions Tax." *Journal of Financial Services Research* 3 (1989): 261-86.

Szala, Ginger, and Amy Rosenbaum. "Deregulation in Japan May Have Different Meaning." *Futures* 19 (February 1990): 42-44.

Tobin, James. "On the Efficiency of the Financial System." *Lloyds Bank Review*, no. 153 (July 1984): 1-15.

U.S. Congress. Office of Technology Assessment. *Trading Around the Clock: Global Securities Markets and Information Technology—Background Paper*. OTA-BP-CIT-66. Washington, D.C.: U.S. Government Printing Office, July 1990a.

_____. *Electronic Bulls and Bears: U.S. Securities Markets and Information Technology*. OTA-CIT-469. Washington, D.C.: U.S. Government Printing Office, September 1990b.

U.S. Securities and Exchange Commission. *Questionnaire of the Working Party on Regulation of Secondary Markets*. May 29, 1991.

Wunsch, R. Steven. "Single-Price Auctions." *Institutional Investor* 25 (January 1991): 20.

Section II

Derivative Instruments: Theory and Pricing

Section II explores the theory and pricing principles that underlie financial derivatives. Without a thorough understanding of the factors that affect prices of derivatives, it is impossible to use these instruments to manage financial risk. The four major types of financial derivatives are: forwards and futures, options, options on futures, and swaps. The sixteen articles in this section provide a thorough grounding in pricing these instruments. The articles are organized into four subsections, one subsection for each type of derivative.

A. Forwards and Futures

Forwards and futures are closely related instruments, and it is possible to regard futures contracts as a special kind of forward contract. Robert W. Kolb distinguishes these instruments and provides a guide to the pricing principles that govern forwards and futures in his article "An Introduction to Pricing Financial Futures." Kolb begins by showing why futures are a type of forward contract and then explores the no-arbitrage relationships that provide the basic link between prices of goods available for immediate delivery and the price of goods promised for future delivery under futures contracts. In doing so, Kolb briefly explores the pricing of stock index futures and interest rate futures.

Ira Kawaller, Paul Koch, and Tim Koch explore the pricing of the S&P 500 stock index futures contract in detail. Their article, "The Relationship Between the S&P 500 Index and S&P 500 Index Futures Prices," shows that strong economic principles link the spot price and futures price of stock indexes. The authors also explore how deviations from this relationship provide immediate profit opportunities for well positioned traders.

Ira G. Kawaller explores some of the fine points of pricing stock index futures in his article, "Determining the Relevant Fair Value(s) of S&P 500 Futures: A Case Study Approach." The "fair value" of a stock index futures contract is the price that precludes profits from stock index arbitrage. As Kawaller explains, the idea of fair value must be refined to reflect the goals of the user of futures markets. For example, the concept of the fair value must be adjusted depending on whether the goal is to find profitable arbitrage opportunities or to create synthetic money market instruments.

Turning next to interest rate futures, Ira Kawaller and Tim Koch apply the basic no-arbitrage framework of futures pricing to Treasury bills in their paper, "Cash-and-Carry Trading and the Pricing of Treasury Bill Futures." In interest rate futures, no-arbitrage conditions exist that are similar to the idea of a fair value for stock index futures. With Treasury bill futures, the underlying cash market instrument has no cash flows until maturity, thus simplifying the pricing principles. As Kawaller and Koch note, the T-bill futures market exhibits prices that conform well to the no-arbitrage conditions.

B. Options

Option prices depend on the price of the underlying good on which the option is written. This pricing relationship is the key features of options that makes them a financial derivative. By specifying alternative price movement patterns for the underlying stock, financial researchers are able to create different option pricing models. However, if the price movements that are assumed for the underlying good are too complex, it will be impossible to solve the model to determine the option price. Thus, there is a trade-off between mathematical tractability and a sophistication that is adequate to represent the reality of stock price movements. However, even very simple assumptions about stock price movements are sufficient to create very useful models of option prices.

The simplest assumption is that the stock price can rise or fall a given amount in a single period. For example, one might assume that the stock price will rise or fall by 1 percent between the present and one week. Even such simple price movement assumptions are sufficient to create quite useful models. Richard J. Rendleman, Jr., and Brit J. Bartter explore this kind of model in their paper, "Two-State Option Pricing." The two states referred to in the title are the price rise state and the price fall state. This kind of model has received a great deal of attention and has become known as the binomial option pricing model.

In one of the seminal articles of finance, Fischer Black and Myron Scholes develop an exact formula for the pricing of call options. As Black and Scholes show in "The Pricing of Options and Corporate Liabilities," it is possible to compute a theoretical option price by knowing the price of the underlying good, the exercise price of the option, the time until the option expires, the risk-free rate of interest, and the volatility of the underlying good. While the mathematics necessary to derive their model is quite complex, the option pricing model they create is fairly simple to apply. It is not an exaggeration to say that it has revolutionized academic finance and practical finance as well. The Black-Scholes option pricing model is a keystone of modern finance and an integral part of understanding financial derivatives.

In "How We Came Up With the Option Formula," Fischer Black offers his reminiscence of creating the option pricing model. Although their model is now a cornerstone of finance, Black and Scholes had considerable difficulty getting their paper published. Thus, Black both explains the intellectual odyssey that led to the model and provides an interesting tale of the pitfalls that await original work in the game of academic publishing.

Soon after the publication of the Black-Scholes option pricing model, its potential for directing trading strategies became widely apparent. The rush to apply the model to actual markets quickly led to some stumbling blocks, which Fischer Black, details in his article "Fact and Fantasy in the Use of Options." As

Black notes "for every fact about options, there is a fantasy." One of the great fantasies addressed by Black is the widespread belief that covered call writing is almost always a good deal. (A trader writes a covered call by selling a call option on an underlying stock that the trader owns. The goal is to capture the extra income from selling a call, while protecting the position by owning the underlying stock in case the option is exercised against the trader.) This fantasy persists today, almost 20 years after Black's article. As Black is careful to point out, there is no costless strategy for increasing returns, and covered call writing involves sacrifices for the potential increase in income that it offers.

In spite of its widespread acceptance, The Black-Scholes option pricing model does rely on several unrealistic assumptions. In "How to Use the Holes in Black and Scholes," Fischer Black notes that the model "depends on at least 10 unrealistic assumptions." In this article, Black explores the assumptions and the effects that they have on the adequacy of the model. While improving the assumptions may make the model more exact mathematically, Black points out that it does not necessarily make the model more useful in actual markets. Further, Black considers each of the ten assumptions he has identified and suggests how traders can alter their strategies to reflect adjustments to those assumptions.

As we noted above, the Black-Scholes option pricing model shows that the price of a call option depends upon five factors: the price of the underlying good, the exercise price of the option, the risk-free rate of interest, the time until the option expires, and the price volatility of the underlying good. Of these five factors, all are directly observable or easily estimated—except for the volatility. One way to improve estimates of volatility is by using information from option prices themselves to derive a better estimate of volatility. This is exactly the approach that Henry A. Latané and Richard J. Rendleman, Jr., follow in their paper, "Standard Deviations of Stock Price Ratios Implied in Option Prices." Latané and Rendleman view the option price as given, and then use the option pricing model to find a better estimate of volatility. This technique of finding an "implied volatility" has become an important tool in option pricing analysis.

C. Options on Futures

Options on futures take positions in futures contracts as the underlying good. For example, the holder of a long option futures call receives a long position in the underlying futures contract upon exercise. Robust markets for options on futures exist for futures contracts on interest rates, stock indexes, metals, and some agricultural commodities.

Options on futures are also referred to as "commodity options" or "commodity contracts," as in Fischer Black's paper, "The Pricing of Commodity Contracts." In essence, this article applies the techniques of the Black-Scholes option pricing model to determine the value of an option on a futures contract. A slight modification of the original Black-Scholes option pricing model makes the model hold for options on futures, thereby emphasizing the power and generality of the original model.

Robert E. Whaley focuses on S&P 500 futures options in his article, "Valuation of American Futures Options: Theory and Empirical Tests." Whaley first discusses the impact of the early exercise feature of American style futures options, and then compares actually observable market prices with the prices derived from a theoretical model. Whaley finds significant differences between theoretical prices and prices actually observable in the market. However, the price discrepancies are not sufficiently large to cover the transaction costs faced by the typical retail customer.

A key assumption of the Black-Scholes option pricing model and of Black's model for pricing futures options is that the risk-free interest rate is constant over the life of the option. This assumption is unrealistic in any event, but it becomes particularly unrealistic for options on debt securities. Mark Pitts addresses this problem in his paper, "The Pricing of Options on Debt Securities." Pitts considers options on debt instruments themselves and options on interest rate futures contracts. Pitts is able to show how to manage the difficulties that arise in pricing options on debt instruments and options on interest rate futures. In his conclusion, Pitts notes that pricing options on debt instruments faces the familiar tradeoff between making the model more complex by avoiding unrealistic assumptions against making the model too difficult mathematically.

D. Swaps

A swap agreement is a contract in which two parties agree to exchange a series of cash flows over time. As an example, the parties to the contract, called counterparties, may agree for one party to make a series of fixed payments in exchange for a series of payments based on fluctuating interest rates. Generally, the motivation for entering into such an agreement is to reduce an existing risk. For example, one party may be scheduled to receive a series of fixed cash inflows but might prefer that the size of the flows varies with interest rates. The swap just described is the simplest kind of interest rate swap—a "plain vanilla" swap in the jargon of the trade. Other swap agreements include foreign exchange and physical commodities. Starting from a virtually non-existent base a decade ago, the swaps industry has reached enormous proportions. Existing swap agreements cover trillions of dollars of underlying value.

Peter A. Abken provides a survey of the different types of swaps in his article, "Beyond Plain Vanilla: A Taxonomy of Swaps." Starting with a plain vanilla swap, Abken carefully elaborates the various terms of swap agreements that can be altered to allow the swap to deal with more complicated risk exposures. For example, a currency swap normally involves risk dimensions of both interest rates and foreign exchange rates. By systematically explaining the different types of swaps, Abken provides a valuable introduction to the burgeoning world of swap finance.

As noted above, interest rate swap agreements have become very important as a market. The primary purposes of these agreements is to manage interest rate risk. Being newer, however, swaps are probably not understood as well as futures. Larry D. Wall and John J. Pringle, in "Interest Rate Swaps: A Review of the Issues," provide a comprehensive introduction to the nature and function of interest rate swaps, with a particular emphasis on using swaps to manage interest rate risk.

As with all financial derivatives, the price of the instrument depends upon the underlying asset. Kenneth R. Kapner and John F. Marshall tackle the problem of pricing directly in their article, "The Pricing of Swaps." The swaps market has matured rapidly, with swap brokers and swap dealers coming to have increasing importance. A swap broker facilitates swap agreements by finding and matching potential counterparties, but takes no financial position in the swap itself. By contrast, a swap dealer actually acts as a counterparty to a swap agreement to facilitate the transaction. The swap dealer then normally tries to find another counterparty for a new swap agreement in which the dealer can hedge any risk that may have been assumed in the first agreement. Because the swap dealer occupies such a pivotal role in the process of consummating many swaps, an understanding of swap pricing requires an understanding of the dealer function. In this article, Kapner and Marshall provide an integrated discussion of the swap dealer function and the way the dealer sets prices.

Article 5

Pricing Financial Futures: An Introduction

Robert W. Kolb

This article focuses on the Cost-of-Carry Model, which shows that futures prices depend on the cash price of a commodity and the cost of storing the underlying good from the present to the delivery date of the futures contract. The Cost-of-Carry model rests upon the idea of arbitrage, and the model defines the price relationship between the spot price of a good and the futures price that precludes arbitrage. Initially, we assume that futures markets are perfect. In this sanitized framework, we can see more clearly the structure of the pricing relationship defined by the Cost-of-Carry Model. Later we relax the assumption of a perfect market to explore the effect of market imperfections on futures prices.

We focus first on gold as an example of a commodity. While gold is not a financial asset, its simplicity makes it a useful first example. Gold generates no cash flows, yet it behaves in most other respects like the financial assets that underlie financial futures contracts. After initially considering gold, we turn our focus to interest rate futures and stock index futures specifically.

The Cost-of-Carry Model in Perfect Markets

We begin by using the concept of arbitrage to explore the Cost-of-Carry Model or carrying charge theory of futures prices. Carrying charges fall into four basic categories: storage costs, insurance costs, transportation costs, and financing costs. Storage costs include the cost of warehousing the commodity in the appropriate facility. While storage seems to apply most clearly to physical goods such as wheat or lumber, it is also possible to store financial instruments. In many cases, the owner of a financial instrument will leave the instrument in a bank vault. For many goods in storage, insurance is also necessary. For example, stored lumber should be protected against fire, and stored wheat should be insured against water damage.[1]

The carrying charges also include, in some cases, transportation costs. Wheat in a railroad siding in Kansas must be carried to delivery in two senses. First, it must be stored until the appropriate delivery time for a given futures contract, and second, it must also be physically carried to the appropriate place for delivery. For physical goods, transportation costs between different locations determine price differentials between those locations. Without question, transportation charges play different roles for different commodities. Transporting wheat from Kansas to Chicago could be an important expense. By contrast, delivery of Treasury bills against a futures contract is accomplished by a wire transfer costing only a few dollars. In almost all cases, the most significant carrying charge in the futures market is the financing cost. In most situations, financing the good under storage overwhelms the other costs. For financial futures, storage, insurance, and transportation costs are virtually nil, and we ignore them in the remainder of our discussion.

The carrying charges reflect only the charges involved in carrying a commodity from one time or one place to another, and do not include the value of the commodity itself. Thus, if gold costs $400 per ounce and the financing rate is 1 percent per month, the financing charge for carrying the gold forward is $4 per month (1% times $400).

Most participants in the futures markets face a financing charge on a short-term basis that is equal to the repo rate, the interest rate on repurchase agreements. In a repurchase agreement, a person sells securities at one time, with the understanding that they will be repurchased at a certain price at a later time. Most repurchase agreements are for one day only and are known, accordingly, as overnight repos. The repo rate is relatively low, exceeding the rate on Treasury bills by only a small amount.[2] The financing cost for such goods is so low because anyone wishing to finance a commodity may offer the commodity itself as collateral for the loan. Further, most of the participants in the market tend to be financial institutions of one type or another who have low financing costs anyway, at least for very short-term obligations.

Cash and Futures Pricing Relationships

The carrying charges just described are important because they play a crucial role in determining pricing relationships between spot and futures prices as well as the relationships among prices of futures contracts of different maturities. For our purposes, assume that the only carrying charge is the financing cost at an interest rate of 10 percent per year. As an example, consider the prices and the accompanying transactions shown in Table 1.

Table 1
Cash–and–Carry Gold Arbitrage Transactions

Prices for the Analysis:

Spot price of gold	$400
Future price of gold (for delivery in one year)	$450
Interest rate	10%

Transaction	Cash Flow
t=0 Borrow $400 for one year at 10%.	+$400
Buy one ounce of gold in the spot market for $400.	- 400
Sell a futures contract for $450 for delivery of one ounce in one year.	0
Total Cash Flow	$0
t=1 Remove the gold from storage.	$0
Deliver the ounce of gold against the futures contract.	+450
Repay loan, including interest.	-440
Total Cash Flow	+$10

The transactions in Table 1 represent a successful cash-and-carry arbitrage. This is a cash-and-carry arbitrage because the trader buys the cash good and carries it to the expiration of the futures contract. The trader traded at t=0 to guarantee a riskless profit without investment. There was no investment, because there was no cash flow at t=0. The trader merely borrowed funds to purchase the gold and to carry it forward. The profit in these transactions was certain once the trader made the transactions at t=0. As these transactions show, to prevent arbitrage the futures price of the gold should have been $440 or less. With a futures price of $440 for example, the transactions in Table 1 would yield a zero profit. From this example, we can infer the following Cost-of-Carry Rule 1: The futures price must be less than or equal to the spot price of the commodity plus the carrying charges necessary to carry the spot commodity forward to delivery. We can express this rule as follows:

$$F_{0,t} \leq S_0(1 + C)$$ Equation 1

where:

$F_{0,t}$ = the futures price at t=0 for delivery at time=t
S_0 = the spot price at t=0
C = the cost of carry, expressed as a fraction of the spot price, necessary to carry the good forward from the present to the delivery date on the futures

As we have seen, if prices do not conform to Cost-of-Carry Rule 1, a trader can borrow funds, buy the spot commodity with the borrowed funds, sell the futures contract, and carry the commodity forward to deliver against the futures contract. These transactions would generate a certain profit without investment, or an arbitrage profit. The certain profit, would be guaranteed by the sale of the futures contract. Also, there would be no investment, since the funds needed to carry out the strategy were borrowed and the cost of using those funds was included in the calculation of the carrying charge. Such opportunities cannot exist in a rational market. The cash-and-carry arbitrage opportunity arises because the spot price is too low relative to the futures price.

We have seen that an arbitrage opportunity arises if the spot price is too low relative to the futures price. As we now see, the spot price might also be too high relative to the futures price. If the spot price is too high, we have a reverse cash-and-carry arbitrage opportunity. As the name implies, the steps necessary to exploit the arbitrage opportunity are just the opposite of those in the cash-and-carry arbitrage strategy. As an example of the reverse cash-and-carry strategy, consider the prices for gold and the accompanying transactions in Table 2.

In these transactions, the arbitrageur sells the gold short. As in the stock market, a short seller borrows the good from another trader and must later repay it. Once the good is borrowed, the short seller sells it and takes the money from the sale. (The transaction is called short selling because one sells a good that he or she does not actually own.) In this example, the short seller has the use of all of the proceeds from the short sale, which are invested at the interest rate of 10 percent. The trader also buys a futures contract to ensure that he or she can acquire the gold needed to repay the lender at the expiration of the futures in one year. Notice that these transactions guarantee an arbitrage profit. Once the transactions at t=0 are completed, the $12 profit at t=1 year is certain. Also, the trader had no net cash flow at t=0, so the strategy required no investment. To make this arbitrage opportunity impossible, the spot and futures prices must obey Cost-of-Carry

Table 2
Reverse Cash–and–Carry Gold Arbitrage Transactions

Prices for the Analysis:

Spot price of gold	$420
Future price of gold (for delivery in one year)	$450
Interest rate	10%

Transaction	Cash Flow
t=0 Sell one ounce of gold short.	+$420
Lend the $420 for one year at 10%.	- 420
Buy one ounce of gold futures for delivery in one year.	0
Total Cash Flow	$0
t=1 Collect proceeds from the loan ($420 × 1.1).	+$462
Accept delivery on the futures contract.	-450
Use gold from futures delivery to repay short sale.	0
Total Cash Flow	+$12

Rule 2: The futures price must be equal to or greater than the spot price plus the cost of carrying the good to the futures delivery date. We can express this rule mathematically with the notation we introduced earlier:

$$F_{0,t} \geq S_0(1 + C) \qquad \text{Equation 2}$$

If prices do not obey this Cost-of-Carry Rule 2, there will be an arbitrage opportunity. Table 3 summarizes the transactions necessary to conduct the cash-and-carry and the reverse cash-and-carry strategies.

To prevent arbitrage, we have seen that the two following rules must hold:

Rule 1:   To prevent Cash-and-Carry Arbitrage $F_{0,t} \leq S_0(1 + C)$
Rule 2:   To prevent Reverse Cash-and-Carry Arbitrage $F_{0,t} \geq S_0(1 + C)$

Table 3
Transactions for Arbitrage Strategies

Market	Cash–and–Carry	Reverse Cash–and–Carry
Debt	Borrow funds	Lend short sale proceeds
Physical	Buy asset and store; deliver against futures	Sell asset short; secure proceeds from short sale
Futures	Sell futures	Buy futures; accept delivery; return physical asset to honor short sale commitment

Together, Equations 1 and 2 imply Cost–of–Carry Rule 3: The futures price must equal the spot price plus the cost of carrying the spot commodity forward to the delivery date of the futures contract. Expressing Rule 3 mathematically, we have Equation 3:

$$F_{0,t} = S_0(1 + C) \qquad \text{Equation 3}$$

Notice that the relationship of Equation 3 was derived under the following assumptions: Markets are perfect; that is, they have no transaction costs and no restrictions on the use of proceeds from short sales. It must be acknowledged that this argument explicitly excludes transaction costs. Transaction costs exist on both sides of the market, for purchase or sale of the futures. In many markets, however, transaction costs for short selling are considerably more expensive, which limits the applicability of the Reverse Cash–and–Carry strategy.

In a well-functioning market, the implied repo rate must equal the actual repo rate. As we have seen in this section, deviations from this relationship lead to arbitrage opportunities in a perfect market. We now turn to consider the qualifications to the basic conclusion that are required by market imperfections.

The Cost–of–Carry Model in Imperfect Markets

In real markets, the four market imperfections discussed earlier complicate and disturb the relationship of Equation 3. (These imperfections were: transaction costs. restrictions on short-selling, unequal borrowing and lending rates, and lack of storability.) The main effect of these market imperfections is to require adjustments in the identity expressed by Equation 3. Market imperfections do not invalidate the basic framework we have been building. Instead of being able to state an equality as we did in the perfect markets framework leading to Equation 3, we will find that market imperfections introduce a certain indeterminacy to the relationship.

For financial futures, there are few effective restrictions on short selling. In addition, the goods are essentially storable. However, we will see that the coupon payments on bonds and dividend payments on stocks make bonds and stocks somewhat less storable than a commodity like gold. In essence, market imperfections frustrate the Cash-and-Carry and Reverse Cash-and-Carry strategies that we have been considering. We illustrate these effects by considering direct transaction costs.

In actual markets, traders face a variety of direct transaction costs. First, the trader must pay a fee to have an order executed. For a trader off the floor of the exchange, these fees include brokerage commissions and various exchange fees. Even members of the exchange must pay a fee to the exchange for each trade. Second, in every market there is a bid-asked spread. A market maker on the floor of the exchange must try to sell at a higher price (the asked price) than the price at which he or she is willing to buy (the bid price). The difference between the asked price and the bid price is the bid-asked spread. In our discussion, we will assume that these transaction costs are some fixed percentage, T, of the transaction amount. For simplicity, we assume that the transaction costs apply to the spot market but not to the futures market.

To illustrate the impact of transaction costs, we use the same prices with which we began our analysis in perfect markets. Now, however, we consider transaction costs of 3 percent. With transaction costs, our previous arbitrage strategy of buying the good and carrying it to delivery will not work. Table 4 shows the results of this effort. With transaction costs, the attempted arbitrage results in a certain loss, not an arbitrage profit.

Table 4
Attempted Cash–and–Carry Gold Arbitrage Transactions

Prices for the Analysis:

Spot price of gold	$400
Future price of gold (for delivery in one year)	$450
Interest rate	10%
Transaction cost (T)	3%

Transaction		Cash Flow
t=0	Borrow $412 for one year at 10%.	+$412
	Buy one ounce of gold in the spot market for $400 and pay 3% transaction costs, to total $412.	- 412
	Sell a futures contract for $450 for delivery of one ounce in one year.	0
	Total Cash Flow	$0
t=1	Remove the gold from storage.	$0
	Deliver the ounce of gold to close futures contract.	+450.00
	Repay loan, including interest	-453.20
	Total Cash Flow	–$3.20

We would have to pay $400 as before to acquire the good, plus transaction costs of 3 percent for a total outlay of $400(1 + T) = $412. We would then have to finance this total until delivery for a cost of $412(1.1) = $453.20. In return, we would only receive $450 upon the delivery of the futures contract. Given these prices, it clearly does not pay to attempt this "cash-and-carry" arbitrage. As Table 4 shows, these attempted arbitrage transactions generate a certain loss of $3.20. With transaction costs of 3 percent and the same spot price of $400, the futures price would have to exceed $453.20 to make the arbitrage attractive. To see why this is so, consider the cash outflows and inflows. We pay the spot price plus the transaction costs, $S_0(1 + T)$, to acquire the good. Carrying the good to delivery costs $S_0(1 + T)(1 + C)$. These costs include acquiring the good and carrying it to the delivery date of the futures. In our example, the total cost is:

$$S_0(1 + T)(1 + C) = \$400(1.03)(1.1) = \$453.20$$

Thus, to break even, the futures transaction must yield $453.20. We can write this more formally as:

$$F_{0,t} \leq S_0(1 + T)(1 + C) \qquad \text{Equation 4}$$

If prices follow Equation 4, the cash-and-carry arbitrage opportunity will not be available. Notice that Equation 4 has the same form as Equation 1, but Equation 4 includes transaction costs.

In discussing the Cost-of-Carry Model in perfect markets, we saw that futures prices could not be too high relative to spot prices. Otherwise, arbitrage opportunities would be available, as we saw in Table 2. We now explore the transactions as shown in Table 2, except we include the transaction costs of 3 percent. Table 5 shows these transactions.

Table 5
Attempted Reverse Cash–and–Carry Gold Arbitrage

Prices for the Analysis:

Spot price of gold	$420
Future price of gold (for delivery in one year)	$450
Interest rate	10%
Transaction costs (T)	3%

Transaction	Cash Flow
t=0 Sell one ounce of gold short, paying 3% transaction costs.	
Receive $420(.97)= $407.40.	+$407.40
Lend the $407.40 for one year at 10%.	- 407.40
Buy one ounce of gold futures for delivery in one year.	0
Total Cash Flow	**$0**
t=1 Collect loan proceeds ($407.40 × 1.1).	+$448.14
Accept gold delivery on the futures contract.	-450.00
Use gold from futures delivery to repay short sale.	0
Total Cash Flow	**-$1.86**

Including transaction costs in the analysis gives a loss on the same transactions that were profitable with no transaction costs. In the original transactions of Table 2 with the same prices, the profit was $12. For perfect markets, Equation 2 gave the no-arbitrage conditions for the reverse cash-and-carry arbitrage strategy:

$$F_{0,t} \geq S_0(1 + C) \qquad \text{Equation 2}$$

Including transaction costs, we have:

$$F_{0,t} \geq S_0(1 - T)(1 + C) \qquad \text{Equation 5}$$

Combining Equations 4 and 5 gives:

$$S_0(1 - T)(1 + C) \leq F_{0,t} \leq S_0(1 + T)(1 + C) \qquad \text{Equation 6}$$

Equation 6 defines the no-arbitrage bounds—bounds within which the futures price must remain to prevent arbitrage. In general, transaction costs force a loosening of the price relationship in Equation 3. In perfect markets, Equation 3 gave an exact equation for the futures price as a function of the spot price and the cost-of-carry. If the futures price deviated from that no-arbitrage price, traders could transact to reap a riskless profit without investment. For a market with transaction costs, Equation 6 gives bounds for the futures price. If the futures price goes beyond these boundaries, arbitrage is possible. The futures price can wander within the bounds without offering arbitrage opportunities, however. As an example, consider the bounds implied by the transactions in Table 4. With no transaction costs, the futures price must be exactly $440 to exclude arbitrage.

Table 6
Illustration of No–Arbitrage Bounds

Prices for the Analysis:

Spot price of gold	$400
Interest rate	10%
Transaction costs (T)	3%

No–Arbitrage Futures Price in Perfect Markets

$$F_{0,t} = S_0(1 + C) = \$400(1.1) = \$440$$

Upper No–Arbitrage Bound with Transaction Costs

$$F_{0,t} \leq S_0(1 + T)(1 + C) = \$400(1.03)(1.1) = \$453.20$$

Lower No–Arbitrage Bound with Transaction Costs

$$F_{0,t} \geq S_0(1 - T)(1 + C) = \$400(.97)(1.1) = \$426.80$$

Figure 1
No–Arbitrage Bounds

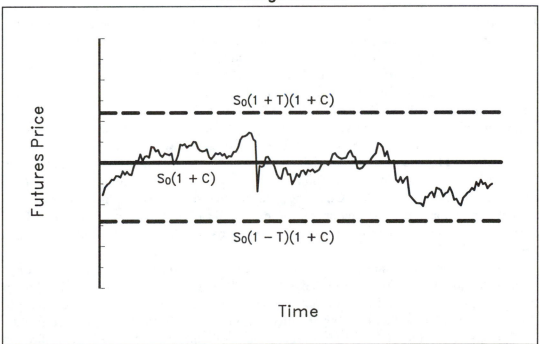

With the 3 percent transaction costs on spot market transactions, the futures price can lie between $426.80 and $453.20 without allowing arbitrage, as Table 6 shows.

Figure 1 illustrates the concept of arbitrage boundaries. The vertical axis graphs futures prices and the horizontal axis shows the time dimension. The solid horizontal line in the graph shows the no–arbitrage condition for a perfect market. In a perfect market, the futures price must exactly equal the spot price times 1 plus the cost of carry, $F_{0,t} =$

$S_0(1 + C)$. With transaction costs, however, we have a lower and an upper bound. If the futures price goes above the upper no-arbitrage bound, there will be a cash-and-carry arbitrage opportunity. This occurs when $F_{0,t} > S_0(1 + T)(1 + C)$. Likewise, if the futures price falls too low, it will be less than the lower no-arbitrage bound. Futures prices that are too low relative to the spot price give rise to a reverse cash-and-carry arbitrage. This opportunity arises when $F_{0,t} < S_0(1 - T)(1 + C)$. Figure 1 shows these no-arbitrage boundaries as dotted lines.

If the futures price stays between the bounds, no arbitrage is possible. If the futures price crosses the boundaries, arbitrageurs will flock to the market to exploit the opportunity. For example, if the futures price is too high, traders will buy the spot commodity and sell the futures. This action will raise the price of the spot good relative to the futures price, thereby driving the futures price back within the no-arbitrage boundaries. If the futures price stays within the boundaries, no arbitrage is possible, and the arbitrageurs will not be able to affect the futures price.

From Figure 1 we can note three important points. First, the greater the transaction costs, T, the farther apart are the bounds. With higher transaction costs, the arbitrage relationships we have been exploring are less binding on possible prices. Second, we have been assuming that all traders in the market face the same percentage transaction costs, T. Clearly, different traders face different transaction costs. For example, a retail trader, who is not an exchange member, can face transaction costs that are much higher than those for a floor trader. It is easily possible for the retail trader to pay as much as 100 times the exchange and brokerage fees paid by a floor trader. Therefore, Figure 1 really pertains to a particular trader, not to every trader in the market. Consider a trader facing higher transaction costs of 2T instead of T. For this trader, the no-arbitrage bounds would be twice as wide as those in Figure 1. Third, we have seen that market forces exist to keep the futures price within the no-arbitrage bounds and that each trader faces his or her own particular bounds, depending on that trader's transaction costs.

Differences in transaction costs give rise to the concept of quasi-arbitrage. Some traders, such as small retail customers, face full transaction costs. Other traders, such as large financial institutions, have much lower transaction costs. For example, exchange members pay much lower transaction costs than do outside traders. Therefore, the quasi-arbitrageur is a potential cash-and-carry or reverse cash-and-carry trader with relatively lower transaction costs. The futures price should stay within the bounds of the lowest transaction cost trader. Once the futures price drifts beyond the bounds of the lowest transaction cost trader, he or she will exploit the arbitrage opportunity. As we have seen, arbitrage activity will drive the futures price back within the no-arbitrage bounds for that trader.

Thus, in the actual market, we expect to see futures prices within the no-arbitrage bounds of the lowest transaction cost trader. This means that traders with higher transaction costs will not be able to exploit any arbitrage opportunities. If prices start to drift away from the perfect markets equality of Equation 3, they will be exploited first by the traders with low transaction costs. This exploitation will take place through quasi-arbitrage, because the low transaction cost trader does not face the full transaction costs of an outside trader. Other market perfections have a similar effect—they widen the no-arbitrage bounds, such as those illustrated in Figure 1.

Pricing Interest Rate Futures Contracts

In this section, we apply the Cost-of-Carry Model to interest rate futures under the initial assumption of perfect markets. In addition, we assume that the only carrying charge is the interest rate to finance the holding of a good, and we assume that we can disregard the special features of a given futures contract. For example, we ignore the options that sellers of futures contracts may hold, such as the option to substitute various grades of the commodity at delivery or the option to choose the exact delivery date within the delivery month, and we ignore the differences between forward and futures prices that may result from the daily resettlement cash flows on the futures contract. Later in this article, we relax some of these assumptions.

Each interest rate futures contract specifies the maturity of the deliverable bond. For example, the T-bill futures contract requires that a deliverable T-bill must have a maturity of 90-92 days. This requirement applies on the delivery date. As we saw earlier, the cash-and-carry strategy involves selling a futures contract, buying the spot commodity, and storing it until the futures delivery date. Then the trader delivers the good against the futures contract. For example, if the futures price of gold is too high relative to the cash market price of gold, a trader could engage in a cash-and-carry arbitrage. Part of this strategy would involve buying gold, storing it until the futures expiration, and delivering the gold against the futures contract.

To apply this strategy in the interest rate futures market, we must be very careful. For example, if a T-bill futures contract expires in 77 days, we cannot buy a 90-day T-bill and store it for future delivery. If we attempt to do so, we will find ourselves with a 13-day T-bill on the delivery date, which will not be deliverable against the futures contract. Therefore, to apply a cash-and-carry strategy, a trader must buy a bond that will still have or come to have the correct properties on the delivery date. For our T-bill cash-and-carry strategy, the trader must secure a 167-day T-bill to carry for 77 days. Then the bill will have the requisite 90 days remaining until expiration on the delivery date.

We illustrate the cash-and-carry strategy with an example. Consider the data in Table 7. The yields used in Table 7 are calculated according to the bond pricing formula. The example assumes perfect markets, including the assumption that one can either borrow or

---

Table 7
Interest Rate Futures and Arbitrage

Today's Date: January 5

Futures	Yield According to the Bond Pricing Formula
MAR Contract (Matures in 77 days on March 22)	12.50%
Cash Bills:	
167-day T-bill (Deliverable on MAR futures)	10.00
77-day T-bill	6.00

---

lend at any of the riskless rates represented by the T-bill yields. These restrictive assumptions will be relaxed momentarily. The data presented in Table 7, and the assumptions just made, mean that an arbitrage opportunity is present. Since the futures contract matures in 77 days, the spot 77-day rate represents the financing cost to acquire the 167-day T-bill, which can be delivered against the MAR futures contract on March 22. This is possible because the T-bill that has 167 days to maturity on January 5 will have exactly 90 days to maturity on March 22.

As the transactions in Table 8 indicate, an arbitrage opportunity exists because the prices and interest rates on the three instruments are mutually inconsistent. To implement a cash-and-carry strategy, a trader can sell the MAR futures and acquire the 167-day T-bill on January 5. The trader then holds the bill for delivery against the futures contract. The trader must finance the holding of the bill during the 77-day interval from January 5 to delivery on March 22. To exploit the rate discrepancy, the trader borrows at the short-term rate of 6 percent and uses the proceeds to acquire the long-term T-bill. At the maturity of the futures, the long-term T-bill has the exactly correct maturity and can be delivered against the futures contract. This strategy generates a profit of $2,235 per contract. Relative to the short-term rate, the futures yield and the long-term T-bill yield were too high. In this example, the trader acquires short-term funds at a low rate (6 percent) and reinvests those funds at a higher rate (10 percent). It may appear that this difference generates the arbitrage profit, but that is not completely accurate, as the next example shows.[3]

Consider the same values as shown in Table 7, but assume that the rate on the 77-day T-bill is 8 percent. Now the short-term rate is too high relative to the long-term rate and the futures yield. To take advantage of this situation, we reverse the cash-and-carry procedure of Table 8, as Table 9 shows. In other words, we now exploit a reverse cash-and-carry strategy. With this new set of rates, the arbitrage is more complicated, since it involves holding the T-bill that is delivered on the futures contract. In this situation, the arbitrageur borrows $955,131 for 167 days at 10 percent and invests these funds at 8 percent for the 77 days until the MAR futures matures. The payoff from the 77 day investment of $955,131 will be $970,894, exactly enough to pay for the delivery of the T-bill on the futures contract. This bill is held for 90 days until June 20 when it matures and pays $1,000,000. On June 20, the arbitrageur's loan on the 167-day T-bill

---

Table 8
Cash–and–Carry Arbitrage Transactions

January 5

Borrow $956,750 for 77 days by issuing a 77-day T-bill at 6%.
Buy 167-day T-bill yielding 10% for $956,750.
Sell MAR T-bill futures contract with a yield of 12.50% for $970.984.

March 22

Deliver the originally purchased T-bill against the MAR futures contract and collect $970,984.
Repay debt on 77-day T-bill that matures today for $968,749.

Profit:

$970,984
− 968,749
$ 2,235

Table 9
Reverse Cash–and–Carry Arbitrage Transactions

January 5

Borrow $955,131 by issuing a 167-day T-bill at 10%.
Buy a 77-day T-bill yielding 8% for $955,131 that will pay $970,984 on March 22.
Buy one MAR futures contract with a yield of 12.50% for $970,984.

March 22

Collect $970,984 from the maturing 77-day T-bill.
Pay $970,984 and take delivery of a 90-day T-bill from the MAR futures contract.

June

Collect $1,000,000 from the maturing 90-day T-bill that was delivered on the futures contract.
Pay $998,308 debt on the maturing 167-day T-bill.

Profit:

$1,000,000
− 998,308
$1,692

---

is also due and equals $998,308. The trader repays this debt from the $1,000,000 received on the maturing bill. The strategy yields a profit of $1,692. Notice in this second example that the trader borrowed at 10 percent and invested the funds at 8 percent temporarily. This shows that it is the entire set of rates that must be consistent and that arbitrage opportunities need not only involve misalignment between two rates.

From our previous analysis, we know that the reverse cash–and–carry strategy involves selling an asset short and investing the proceeds from the short sale. In our example of Table 9, the short sale is the issuance of debt. By issuing debt, the arbitrageur literally sells a bond. A trader can also simulate a short sale by selling from inventory. The same is true for interest rate futures. For example, a bank that holds investments in T–bills can simulate a short sale by selling a T–bill from inventory.

To this point, we have considered a cash–and–carry strategy in Table 8 and a reverse cash–and–carry strategy in Table 9. These two examples show that there must be a very exact relationship among these rates on the different instruments to exclude arbitrage opportunities. If the yield on the MAR futures is 12.50 percent and the 167–day spot yield is 10 percent, there is only one yield for the 77–day T–bill that will not give rise to an arbitrage opportunity, and that rate is 7.15 percent. To see why that is the case, consider two ways of holding a T–bill investment for the full 167–day period of the examples:

1. Hold the 167–day T–bill, or
2. Hold a 77–day T–bill followed by a 90–day T–bill that is delivered on the futures contract.

Since these two ways of holding T–bills cover the same time period and have the same risk level, the two positions must have the same yield to avoid arbitrage. For the examples, the necessary yield on the 77–day T–bill can be found by solving for a forward rate. This Equation expresses the yield on a long-term instrument as being equal to the yield on two short-term positions:

$$(1.10)^{167/360} = (1 + x)^{77/360} (1.1250)^{90/360}$$

This Equation holds only if the rate, x, on the 77-day T-bill equals 7.1482 percent.

We can also express the same idea in terms of the prices of the bills. To illustrate this point, consider the prices of three securities. The first is a 167-day bill that yields 10 percent and pays $1 upon maturity. The second is a T-bill futures with an underlying bill having a $1 face value. With a yield of 12.50 percent, the futures price will be $.970984. Finally, the third instrument matures in 77 days, has a face value of $.970984, and yields 7.1482 percent.

$$P_{167} = \frac{\$1}{(1 + r_{167})^{167/360}} = \frac{\$1}{1.1^{167/360}} = .956750$$

$$P_F = \frac{\$1}{(1 + r_{fut})^{90/360}} = \frac{\$1}{1.1250^{90/360}} = .970984$$

$$P_{77} = \frac{\$.970984}{(1 + r_{77})^{77/360}} = \frac{\$.970984}{1.071482^{77/360}} = .956750$$

The third instrument is peculiar, with its strange face value. However, this is exactly the payoff necessary to pay for delivery on the futures contract in 77 days. Notice also that the 77-day bill and the 167-day bill have the same price. They should, because both prices of $.956750 are the investment now that is necessary to have a $1 payoff in 167 days. The futures yield and the 167-day yield were taken as fixed. The yield on the 77-day bill, 7.1482 percent, is exactly the yield that must prevail if the two strategies are to be equivalent and to prevent arbitrage.

The Financing Cost and the Implied Repo Rate

With these prices, and continuing to assume that the only carrying cost is the financing charge, we can also infer the implied repo rate. We know that the ratio of the futures price divided by the spot price equals 1 plus the implied repo rate. As we have seen, the correct spot instrument for our example is the 167-day bill, because this bill will have the appropriate delivery characteristics when the futures matures. Thus, we have:

$$1 + C = \frac{P_F}{P_{167}} = \frac{.970984}{.956750} = 1.014878$$

Thus the implied repo rate, C, is 1.4878 percent. This covers the cost-of-carry for 77 days from the present to the expiration of the futures. We can annualize this rate as follows:

$$1.014878^{360/77} = 1.071482$$

The annualized repo rate is 7.1482 percent. This exactly matches the interest rate on the 77-day bill that will prevent arbitrage. Therefore, assuming that the interest cost is the only carrying charge, the cost-of-carry equals the implied repo rate. This equivalence between the cost-of-carry and the implied repo rate also leads to two rules for arbitrage.

The Futures Yield and the Forward Rate of Interest

We have seen that the futures price of an interest rate futures contract implies a yield on the instrument that underlies the futures contract. We call this implied yield the futures yield. Now we continue to assume that the financing cost is the only carrying charge, that markets are perfect, that we can ignore the options that the seller of a futures contract may possess, and that the price difference between forward contracts and futures contracts is negligible. Under these conditions, we can show that the futures yield must equal the forward rate of interest.

We continue to use the T-bill futures contract as our example. The T-bill futures, like many other interest rate futures contracts, has an underlying instrument that will be delivered when the contract expires. The SEP 1991 contract calls for the delivery of a 90-day T-bill that will mature in December 1991. The futures yield covers the 90-day span of time from delivery in September to maturity in December 1991. It is possible to compute forward rates from the term structure. Given the necessary set of spot rates, it is possible to compute a forward rate to cover any given period.

To illustrate the equivalence between futures yields and forward rates under our assumptions, we continue to use our example of a T-bill with a 167-day holding period. Let us assume the following spot yields:

For a 167-day bill	10.0000%
For a 77-day bill	7.1482

These two spot rates imply a forward rate to cover the period from day 77 to day 167:

$$(1 + r_{0,167})^{167/360} = (1 + r_{0,77})^{77/360} (1 + r_{77,167})^{90/360}$$

Substituting values for the spot bills and solving for the forward rate, $r_{77,167}$, gives:

$$(1.10)^{167/360} = (1.071482)^{77/360} (1 + r_{77,167})^{90/360}$$

$$(1 + r_{77,167})^{90/360} = \frac{(1.10)^{167/360}}{(1.071482)^{77/360}} = \frac{1.045205}{1.014877} = 1.029884$$

$$1 + r_{77,167} = 1.1250$$

$$r_{77,167} = .1250$$

Therefore, the forward rate, to cover day 77 to day 167, is 12.50 percent. As we saw earlier, the futures yield is also 12.50 percent for the T-bill futures that expires on day 77. Therefore, the futures yield equals the forward rate for the same period. In deriving this result, we must bear our assumptions in mind: markets are perfect, the financing cost is the only carrying charge, and we can ignore the seller's options and the difference between forward and futures prices.

The Cost–of–Carry Model for T–Bond Futures

In this section, we apply the Cost-of-Carry Model to the T-bond futures contract. In essence, the same concepts apply, with one difference. The holder of a T-bond receives cash flows from the bond. This affects the cost-of-carry that the holder of the bond actually incurs. For example, assume that the coupon rate on a $100,000 face value T-bond is 8 percent and the trader finances the bond at 8 percent. In this case, the net carrying charge is zero—the earnings offset the financing cost.

To illustrate this idea, let us assume that, on January 5, a T-bond that is deliverable on a futures contract has an 8 percent coupon and costs 100.00. The trader faces a financing rate of 7.1482 percent for the 77 days until the futures contract is deliverable. Because the T-bond has an 8 percent coupon rate, the conversion factor is 1.0 and plays no role.[4] With an 8 percent coupon, the accrued interest from the date of purchase to the delivery date on the futures is:

$$(77/182)(.04)(100,000) = \$1,692$$

Therefore, the invoice amount will be $101,692. If this is the invoice amount in 77 days, the T-bond must cost the present value of that amount, discounted for 77 days at the 77-day rate of 7.1482 percent. This implies a cost for the T-bond of $100,200. If the price is less than $100,200, a cash-and-carry arbitrage strategy will be available. Under these circumstances the cash-and-carry strategy would have the cash flows shown in Table 10.

The transactions in Table 10 show that the futures price must adjust to reflect the accrual of interest. The bond in Table 10 had no coupon payment during the 77-day interval, but the same adjustment must be made to account for cash throwoffs that the bond holder receives during the holding period.

Interest Rate Futures Pricing: An Example

We conclude our discussion of interest rate futures pricing by applying the Cost-of-Carry Model to actual market data. For this illustration, we consider the difference between the

---

Table 10
Cash–and–Carry Transactions for a T–Bond

January 5
Borrow $100,200 for 77 days at the 77-day rate of 7.1482 percent.
Buy the 8% T-bond for $100,200.
Sell one T-bond futures contract for $101,692.

March 22
Deliver T-bond; receive invoice amount of $101,692.
Repay loan of $101,692.

Profit: 0

SEP and DEC 1989 T-bond futures prices. Under the simplifying assumptions made earlier, we would expect these two prices to be closely related by the financing cost of carrying a bond from September to December 1989. We know that market imperfections, the difference between futures and forward prices, and the seller's options might all disturb this relationship. Nonetheless, we expect the main component of this price difference to be tied to the financing cost from September to December.

To apply this idea to actual data, we use the SEP 1989 T-bill futures contract to provide a proxy for the financing rate to hold a T-bond from September to December 1989. To accept delivery on the SEP 1989 T-bond futures and carry the delivered bond forward to the December delivery involves paying the invoice price to acquire the bond, financing the bond for three months at the SEP 1989 T-bill rate, receiving the accrued interest on the bond, which we estimate as having an 8 percent coupon rate, and selling the DEC 1989 futures. In a perfect market, this strategy should yield a zero profit. In other words, we expect the quantity:

$$F_{0,d} + AI - F_{0,n}(1 + C) = 0 \qquad \text{Equation 7}$$

where:

$F_{0,d}$ = DEC 1989 T-bond futures price
$F_{0,n}$ = SEP 1989 T-bond futures price plus accrued interest due at delivery
C = three month cost-of-carry estimated from SEP 89 T-bill futures
AI = interest accrued from T-bond in December, estimated at $2,000 per contract

Figure 2
Cost–of–Carry Model for SEP and DEC 1989 T–Bonds

Figure 2 graphs the value of Equation 7 for a one contract position. In an absolutely perfect market, we expect the value to be zero. As Figure 2 shows, it is extremely close to zero. The minimum value is –$318, and the maximum value is $105. Thus, the graph of the value of Equation 7 ranges from –3/10 of one percent to +1/10 of one percent. These values are all the closer considering the crude estimate of the accrued interest and the fact that we did not even attempt to find the cheapest-to-deliver bond. Presumably, a more exacting analysis would lead to yet smaller discrepancies.

Stock Index Futures Prices

Like most financial futures, stock index futures essentially trade in a full-carry market. Therefore, the Cost-of-Carry Model provides a virtually complete understanding of stock index futures pricing. When the conditions of the Cost-of-Carry Model are violated, arbitrage opportunities arise. For a cash-and-carry strategy, a trader would buy the stocks that underlie the futures contract and sell the futures. The trader would then carry these stocks until the futures expiration. The cash-and-carry strategy is attractive when stocks are priced too low relative to the futures. In a reverse cash-and-carry strategy, the trader would sell the stocks short and invest the proceeds, in addition to buying the futures. The reverse cash-and-carry strategy is attractive when stocks are priced too high relative to the futures. Thus, any discrepancy between the justified futures and cash market prices would lead to a profit at the expiration of the futures simply by exploiting the appropriate strategy.

The Cost–of–Carry Model for Stock Index Futures

Applying Equation 3 to stock index futures faces one complication—dividends. Holding the stocks gives the owner dividends; however, each of the indexes is simply a price index. The value of the index at any time depends solely on the prices of the stocks, not the dividends that the underlying stocks might pay. Because the futures prices are tied directly to the index values, the futures prices do not include dividends.

To fit stock index futures, Equation 3 must be adjusted to include the dividends that would be received between the present and the expiration of the futures. In essence, the chance to receive dividends lowers the cost of carrying the stocks. Carrying stocks requires that a trader finance the purchase price of the stock from the present until the futures expiration. However, the trader will receive dividends from the stock, which will reduce the value of the stocks. This contrasts directly with the cost-of-carry for holding a commodity like gold. As we have seen, gold generates no cash flows, so the cost-of-carry for gold is essentially the financing cost. For stocks, the cost-of-carry is the financing cost for the stock, less the dividends received while the stock is carried.

As an example, assume the present is time zero and a trader decides to engage in a self-financing cash-and-carry transaction. The trader decides to buy and hold one share of Widget, Inc., currently trading for $100. Therefore, the trader borrows $100 and buys the stock. We assume that the stock will pay a $2 dividend in six months, and the trader will invest the proceeds for the remaining six months at a rate of 10 percent. Table 11 shows the trader's cash flows. In Table 11, a trader borrows funds, buys and holds a stock, receives and invests a dividend, and liquidates the portfolio after one year. At the outset, the stock costs $100, but its value in a year, P_1, is unknown. From Table 11, the trader's cash inflow after one year is the future value of the dividend, $2.10, plus the current value of the stock, P_1, less the repayment of the loan, $110.

Table 11
Cash Flows from Carrying Stock

t=0	
Borrow $100 for one year at 10%.	+ 100
Buy one share of Widget, Inc.	− 100
t=6 months	
Receive dividend of $2.	+$2
Invest $2 for 6 months at 10%.	−$2
t=1 year	
Collect proceeds of $2.10 from dividend investment.	+2.10
Sell Widget, Inc., for P_1.	+ P_1
Repay debt.	− 110.00
Total Profit: P_1 + $2.10 − $110.00	

From this example, we can generalize to understand the total cash inflows from a cash-and-carry strategy. First, the cash-and-carry strategy will return the future value of the stock, P_1, at the horizon of the carrying period. Second, at the end of the carrying period, the cash-and-carry strategy will return the future value of the dividends—the dividend plus interest from the time of receipt to the horizon. Against these inflows, the cash-and-carry trader must pay the financing cost for the stock purchase.

We can now determine the futures price that is consistent with the cash-and-carry strategy. From the arguments advanced earlier, we know that Equation 3 holds as an equality with perfect markets and unrestricted short selling. The cash-and-carry trading opportunity requires that the futures price must be less than or equal to the cash inflows at the futures expiration. Similarly, the reverse cash-and-carry trading opportunity requires that the futures price must equal or exceed the cash inflows at the futures expiration. Therefore, the stock index futures price must equal the cost of the stocks underlying the stock index, plus the cost of carrying those stocks to expiration, $S_0(1 + C)$, minus the future value of all dividends to be received, $D_i(1 + r_i)$. The future value of dividends is measured at the time the futures contract expires. More formally:

$$F_{0,t} = S_0(1 + C) - \sum_{i=1}^{N} D_i (1 + r_i) \qquad \text{Equation 8}$$

where:

$F_{0,t}$ = the stock index futures price at t=0 for a futures contract that expires at time t

S_0 = the value of the stocks underlying the stock index at t=0

C = the percentage cost of carrying the stocks from t=0 to the expiration at time t

D_i = the ith dividend

r_i = the interest earned on carrying the ith dividend from its time of receipt until the futures expiration at time t

Fair Value for Stock Index Futures

A stock index futures price has its fair value when the futures price fits the Cost-of-Carry Model. In this section we consider a simplified example of determining the fair value of a stock index futures contract. We consider a futures contract on an equally weighted index, and for simplicity we assume that there are only two stocks. Table 12 provides the information that we will need.

Based on the data in Table 12, the index value is 110.56, as given by:

$$\frac{P_A + P_B}{\text{Index Divisor}} = \frac{115 + 84}{1.8} = 110.56$$

The cost of buying the stocks underlying the portfolio is simply the sum of the prices of stocks A and B, or $199. For carrying the stocks to expiration, the interest cost will be 10 percent for 76 days or 2.11 percent. Thus, the cost of buying and carrying the stocks to expiration is $199(1.0211) = $203.20. Offsetting this cost will be the dividends received and the interest earned on the dividends. For the stocks, the future value of the dividends at expiration will be:

For Stock A: $1.50(1.0164) = $1.52
For Stock B: $1.00(1.0108) = $1.01

Therefore, the entire cost of buying the stocks and carrying them to expiration is the purchase price of the stocks plus interest, less the future value of the dividends measured at expiration:

Table 12
Information for Computing Fair Value

Today's date:	July 6
Futures expiration:	September 20
Days until expiration:	76
Index:	Equally weighted index of two stocks
Index divisor:	1.80
Interest rates:	All interest rates are 10 percent

Stock A

Today's price	$115
Projected dividends	$1.50 on July 23
Days dividend will be invested	59
r_A	.10(59/360) = .0164

Stock B

Today's price	$84
Projected dividends	$1.00 on August 12
Days dividend will be invested	39
r_B	.10(39/360) = .0108

$$\$203.20 - \$1.52 - \$1.01 = \$200.67$$

In the Cost-of-Carry Model, we know that the futures price must equal this entire cost-of-carry. However, the futures price is expressed in index units, not the dollars of the actual stock prices. To find the fair value for the futures price, this cash value of $200.67 must be converted into index units by dividing by the index divisor, 200.67/1.8 = 111.48. Thus, the fair value for the futures contract is 111.48. Because it conforms to the Cost-of-Carry Model, this fair value for the futures price is the price that precludes arbitrage profits from both the cash-and-carry and reverse cash-and-carry strategies.

Index Arbitrage and Program Trading

In the preceding section we saw how to derive the fair value futures price from the Cost-of-Carry Model. From our earlier discussion, we know that deviations from the theoretical price of the Cost-of-Carry Model give rise to arbitrage opportunities. If the futures price exceeds its fair value, traders will engage in cash-and-carry arbitrage. If the futures price falls below its fair value, traders can exploit the pricing discrepancy through a reverse cash-and-carry trading strategy. These cash-and-carry strategies in stock index futures are called index arbitrage. This section presents an example of index arbitrage using a simplified index with only two stocks. Because index arbitrage can require the trading of many stocks, it is often implemented by using computer programs to automate the trading. Computer directed index arbitrage is called program trading.

Index Arbitrage

Table 12 gave values for stocks A and B, and we saw how to compute the fair value of a stock index futures contract based on an index composed of those two stocks. With the values in Table 12, the cash market index value is 110.56, and the fair value for the futures contract is 111.48, where both values are expressed in index points. If the futures price exceeds the fair value, cash-and-carry index arbitrage is possible. A futures price below its fair value creates an opportunity for reverse cash-and-carry index arbitrage.

To illustrate cash-and-carry index arbitrage, assume that the data of Table 12 hold, but that the futures price is 115.00. Because this price exceeds the fair value, an index arbitrageur would trade as shown in Table 13. At the outset on July 6, the trader borrows the money necessary to purchase the stocks in the index, buys the stocks, and sells the futures. On July 23 and August 12, the trader receives dividends from the two stocks and invests the dividends to the expiration date at 10 percent. Like all stock index futures, our simple example uses cash settlement. Therefore, at expiration on September 20, the final futures settlement price is set equal to the cash market index value. This ensures that the futures and cash prices converge and that the basis goes to zero.[5]

The profits or losses from the transactions in Table 13 do not depend on the prices that prevail at expiration on September 20. Instead, the profits come from a discrepancy between the futures price and its fair value. To illustrate the profits, we assume that the stock prices do not change. Therefore, the cash market index is at 110.56 at expiration. As Table 13 shows, these transactions give a profit of $6.32.

This will be the profit no matter what happens to stock prices between July 6 and September 20. For example, assume the prices of stocks A and B both rose by $5, to $120 and $89, respectively. The cash market cash flows will then come from the sale of

Table 13
Cash–and–Carry Index Arbitrage

Date	Cash Market	Futures Market
July 6	Borrow $199 for 76 days at 10%. Buy stock A and stock B for a total outlay of $199.	Sell one SEP index futures contract for 115.00.
July 23	Receive dividend of $1.50 from stock A and invest for 59 days at 10%.	
August 12	Receive dividend of $1.00 from stock B and invest for 39 days at 10%.	
September 20	**For illustrative purposes, assume any values for stock prices at expiration. We assume that stock prices did not change. Therefore, the index value is still 110.56.**	
	Receive proceeds from invested dividends of $1.52 and $1.01. Sell stock A for $115 and stock B for $84. Total proceeds are $201.53. Repay debt of $203.20.	At expiration, the futures price is set equal to the spot index value of 110.56. This gives a profit of 4.44 index units. In dollar terms, this is 4.44 index units times the index divisor of 1.8.
	Loss: $1.67	Profit: $7.99
	Total Profit: $7.99 – $1.67 = $6.32	

the shares, the future value of the dividends, and the debt repayment:

Sale of stock A	+120.00
Sale of stock B	+89.00
Future value of dividends on stock A	+1.52
Future value of dividends on stock B	+1.01
Debt repayment	-203.20
Futures profit/loss	-2.01

On the futures transaction, the index value at expiration will then equal $116.11 = (120 + 89)/1.8$. This gives a futures loss of 1.11 index points, or $2.01. Taking all of these cash flows together, the profit is still $6.32. The profit will be the same no matter what happens to stock prices.

If the futures price is too low relative to the fair value, arbitrageurs can engage in reverse cash-and-carry transactions. For example, assume that the futures price is 105.00, well below its fair value of 111.48. Now the arbitrageur will trade as shown in Table 14. Essentially, the transactions in Table 14 are just the opposite of those in Table 13. The most important difference is that the trader sells stock short. Having sold the stock short, the trader must pay the dividends on the stocks as they come due.

Table 14
Reverse Cash–and–Carry Index Arbitrage

Date	Cash Market	Futures Market
July 6	Sell stock A and stock B for a total of $199. Lend $199 for 76 days at 10%.	Buy one SEP index futures contract for 105.00.
July 23	Borrow $1.50 for 59 days at 10% and pay dividend of $1.50 on stock A.	
August 12	Borrow $1.00 for 39 days at 10% and pay dividend of $1.00 on stock B.	
September 20	**For illustrative purposes, assume any values for stock prices at expiration. We assume that stock prices did not change. Therefore, the index value is still 110.56.**	
	Receive proceeds from investment of $203.20. Repay $1.52 and $1.01 on money borrowed to pay dividends on stocks A and B. Buy stock A for $115 and stock B for $84. Return stocks to repay short sale.	At expiration, the futures price is set equal to the spot index value of 110.56. This gives a profit of 5.56 index units. In dollar terms, this is 5.56 index units times the index divisor of 1.8.
	Profit: $1.67	Profit: $10.01
	Total Profit: $1.67 + $10.01 = $11.68	

The transactions give the trader a net profit of $11.68. Again, this profit does not depend upon the actual stock prices that prevail at expiration. Instead, the profit comes from the discrepancy between the actual futures price of 105.00 and the fair value of 111.48. Once the trader initiates the transactions in Table 14, the profit will depend only on the discrepancy between the fair value and the prevailing futures price. The profit will equal the error in the futures price times the index divisor: (111.48 - 105.00)1.8 = $11.68.[6]

Program Trading

While we have illustrated the cash-and-carry and reverse cash-and-carry transactions with a hypothetical two stock index futures contract, real stock index futures trading involves many more stocks. The MMI is smallest with 20 stocks, while the S&P 500 contains (of course) 500 stocks, and the NYSE index has about 1,700 underlying stocks. To exploit index arbitrage opportunities with actual stock index futures requires trading the futures and simultaneously buying or selling the entire collection of stocks that underlie the index.

If we focus on the S&P 500 futures contract, we can see that the transactions of Tables 13 and 14 call for the buying or selling of 500 stocks. The success of the arbitrage depends upon identifying the misalignment between the futures price and the fair futures price. However, at a given moment the fair futures price depends upon the current price of 500 different stocks. Identifying an index arbitrage opportunity requires the ability to instantly find pricing discrepancies between the futures price and the fair futures price reflecting 500 different stocks. In addition, exploiting the arbitrage opportunity requires trading 500 stocks at the prices that created the arbitrage opportunity. Enter the computer!

Large financial institutions can communicate orders to trade stock via their computer for very rapid execution. Faced with a cash–and–carry arbitrage opportunity, one of these large traders could execute a computer order to buy each and every stock represented in the S&P 500. Simultaneously, the institution would sell the S&P 500 futures contract. The use of computers to execute large and complicated stock market orders is called program trading. While computers are used for other kinds of stock market transactions, index arbitrage is the main application of program trading. Often "index arbitrage" and "program trading" are used interchangeably. Program trading has been blamed for much of the recent volatility in the stock market, including the crash of October 1987.

Predicting Dividend Payments and Investment Rates

In the example of computing fair value from Table 12, we assumed certainty about the amount, timing, and investment rates for the dividends on stocks A and B. In the actual market, these quantities are highly predictable, but they are not certain. Dividend amounts and payment dates can be predicted based on the past policy of the firm. However, these quantities are far from certain until the dividend announcement date when the firm announces the amount and payment date of the dividend. In practice, there is quite a bit of variability in the payment of dividends depending on the time of year. Further, dividends tend to cluster on certain days in early March, June, September, and December.[7]

In actual practice, traders follow the dividend practices of firms to project the dividends that the stocks underlying an index will pay each day. This problem varies in difficulty from one index to the next. The MMI has only 20 very large firms with relatively stable dividend policies. By contrast, the NYSE index has about 1,700 firms. Many of these firms are small and may have irregular dividend payment patterns. Therefore, it is more difficult to predict the exact dividend stream for the NYSE or the S&P 500 index. While the difficulties in predicting dividends may introduce some uncertainties into the cost–of–carry calculations, projections of dividends prove to be quite accurate in practice.

In our example of computing the fair value of a stock index futures contract and in our arbitrage examples, we also assumed that dividends could be invested at a known rate. In practice, it is difficult to know the exact rate that will be received on invested dividends. While knowing the exact rate to be received on invested dividends is difficult, good predictions are possible. For the most part, the futures expiration date is not very distant, so the current short–term interest rate can provide a good estimate of the investment rate for dividends.

Market Imperfections and Stock Index Futures Prices

Earlier, we saw that four different types of market imperfections could affect the pricing of futures contracts, and we also saw that the effect of these market imperfections is to create a band of no-arbitrage prices within which the futures price must fall. In this section we consider these imperfections briefly in the context of stock index futures.

Direct transaction costs affect stock index futures trading to a considerable extent. Relative to many goods, transaction costs for stocks are low in percentage terms. Nonetheless, stock traders face commissions, exchange fees, and a bid-asked spread. In general, these costs may be about one-half of 1 percent for stock market transactions. Even with such modest transaction costs, we cannot expect the Cost-of-Carry Model to hold as an exact equality. Instead, these transactions costs will lead to a no-arbitrage band of permissible stock index futures prices.

Unequal borrowing and lending costs, margins, and restrictions on short selling all play a role in stock index futures pricing. In the stock market, the restrictions on short selling are quite explicit. The Federal Reserve Board will not allow a trader to use more than 50 percent of the proceeds from a short sale. The short seller's broker may restrict that usage to an even smaller percentage. As we have seen, these factors all force slight discrepancies in the Cost-of-Carry Model. The pricing relationship of Equation 8 holds as an approximation, not with exactitude. Thus, these market imperfections create a no-arbitrage band of permissible futures prices. However, a highly competitive trading environment and low transaction costs keep this no-arbitrage band quite tight around the perfect markets theoretical fair value of Equation 8.

Because the stocks of the MMI, S&P 500, and NYSE indexes are so widely held by financial institutions with low transaction costs, quasi-arbitrage is a dominant feature of stock index futures trading. As an example of the importance of quasi-arbitrage, consider the differential use of short sale proceeds for a retail customer and a pension fund with a large stock portfolio. Assume that the retail customer must sell a stock short through her broker. This customer will be able to use only half of the proceeds of the short sale. By contrast, we will assume that the pension fund already owns the stocks necessary to sell short for the reverse cash-and-carry transaction. In this situation, the pension fund can simulate a short sale by selling a portion of its stock portfolio. Because the pension fund is actually selling stocks, not technically selling short, it receives the full use of its proceeds. However, selling stocks from a portfolio is a perfect substitute for an actual short sale. Thus, the pension fund faces substantially lower transaction costs than the retail customer for engaging in reverse cash-and-carry arbitrage. A similar conclusion emerges from considering program trading. A small retail trader faces enormous transaction costs in attempting to engage in index arbitrage. The quasi-arbitrage opportunities enjoyed by financial institutions ensure that no individual could ever engage in index arbitrage.

Notes

1. In many cases, the owner of these goods will choose to insure these goods for himself or herself. Nonetheless, there is an implicit cost of insurance even when the owner self-insures.

2. For a very informative and readable account of repurchase agreements, see Bowsher, "Repurchase Agreements," *Instruments of the Money Market*, Richmond: Federal Reserve Bank of Richmond, 1981.

3. For studies of this approach to pricing T-Bill futures, see I. Kawaller and T. Koch, "Cash-and-Carry Trading and the Pricing of Treasury Bill Futures," *The Journal of Futures Markets*, 4:2, Fall 1984, pp. 115-123.

4. The T-bond futures contract is quite complex, and our discussion abstracts from many of its features. For a comprehensive discussion of the features of the contract, see Robert W. Kolb, *Understanding Futures Markets, Third Edition*, Miami: Kolb Publishing Company, 1991.

5. Trading for the S&P 500 and the NYSE futures contracts ends on one day, and the final settlement price is set at the next day's opening price.

6. These calculations are sometimes off by a penny or two due to rounding.

7. G. Gastineau and A. Madansky, "S&P 500 Stock Index Futures Evaluation Tables," *Financial Analysts Journal*, 39:6, November–December 1983, pp. 68–76, were among the first to recognize the importance of the daily dividend flows for stock index futures pricing.

Article 6

Ira. G. Kawaller, Paul D. Koch and Timothy W. Koch

The Relationship Between the S&P 500 Index and S&P 500 Index Futures Prices

The Standard and Poor's 500 Index and the related index futures prices are influenced by their own histories, each other's movements, and current market information. This study explores the temporal relationship between these two important market indicators and measures the change in this relationship as futures expiration day approaches.

The advent of markets for stock index futures and options has profoundly changed the nature of trading on stock exchanges. These markets offer investors flexibility in altering the composition of their portfolios and in timing their transactions. Futures and options markets also provide opportunities to hedge the risks involved with holding diversified equity portfolios. As a consequence, significant portions of cash market equity transactions are now tied to futures and options market activity.

The effect of the stock index futures and options markets on traditional stock trading has aroused both the ire of critics and the acclaim of supporters. Critics allege that futures trading unduly influences the underlying equity markets especially on days when futures contracts expire. For example, on various expiration days from 1984 to 1985, the stock markets closed with equity prices either rising or falling dramatically during the final hour of trading.[1] The phenomenon of sharp price swings and the seeming relation to futures market activity has, especially in the wake of the October 19, 1987, stock market crash, prompted various suggestions for modifying the design of the contracts to lessen their impact on the market.[2]

Proponents of futures markets, on the other hand, do not view the final-day price swings as a problem, since the swings are generally temporary and nonsystematic. In fact, proponents argue that such markets provide an important price discovery function and offer an alternative marketplace for adjusting equity exposure. The term *price discovery function* refers to the ability to use a certain market indicator—in this case, stock index futures—to forecast upcoming changes in the prices of securities. For the price discovery function to be most helpful, though, an investor must be able to determine *when* a change in the futures market will be reflected in the underlying market.

This article addresses some basic questions that have a fundamental bearing on the debate between the critics and advocates of futures markets. Do intraday movements in the index futures price provide predictive information about subsequent movements in the index,

or do movements in the index presage futures price changes? Is the price relationship different on expiration days and the days leading up to expiration?

Analysis of the Standard and Poor's (S&P) 500 futures and the S&P 500 index can help answer these questions. This article shows that lags exist not only between movements in the index, but also between the index and subsequent index futures prices, though these lags are not symmetrical. The index lags behind the index futures price by up to 45 minutes, but the index futures price tends to trail the index only briefly. Examination of the lagged relationships on expiration days and the days prior to them indicates that the relationships are remarkably stable, implying that neither expiration day volatility nor the climate preceding these days interferes with the price discovery function that index futures seem to offer.[3]

An Overview of the S&P 500 Index and Index Futures

The S&P 500 stock index represents the market value of all outstanding common shares of 500 firms selected by Standard and Poor's. Prior to April, 1988, this group consisted of 400 industrials, 40 financial institutions, 40 utilities, and 20 transportation firms.[4] Though all of the shares are not traded on the New York Stock Exchange (NYSE), the cumulative market value equals approximately 80 percent of the aggregate value of NYSE-listed stocks. The index changes whenever the price and thus the cumulative market value of any underlying stock changes.

---

[1] The term "triple witching hour" was used to describe this trading period because the Chicago Mercantile Exchange's (CME) S&P 500 futures, the Chicago Board of Trade Options Exchange's (CBOE) S&P 100 options, and contracts on individual stock options all expired on the third Fridays of March, June, September, and December. After March 1987, the final day of trading for S&P 500 futures was moved to the day prior.

[2] The Securities and Exchange Commission, the Government Accounting Office, and the executive branch (the Brady Commission), as well as various exchange and private research groups, are currently studying the relation of price swings to futures market activity.

[3] These results do not explain expiration day swings, nor do they suggest that such swings are desirable.

[4] Standard and Poor's has recently announced that the composition of the S&P 500 will now be flexible.

An S&P 500 futures contract represents the purchase or sale of a hypothetical basket of the 500 stocks underlying the S&P 500 index, set in a proportion consistent with the weights set by the index, with a market value equal to the futures price times a multiplier of 500. The futures price should be tied to the cost of investing in and carrying an S&P 500 look-alike basket of stocks until the expiration of the index futures. The cost of carry incorporates transaction fees, taxes, and the expense of financing the investment, minus the dividends derived from the basket of stocks and any additional reinvestment income.

As a requirement for gaining access to the market, traders must post an initial margin deposit or collateral equal to a fraction of the futures contract market value (price x 500). Futures prices change intermittently throughout each trading day, and at day's end traders must cover any losses when prices move against them. Alternatively, they may withdraw any profit in excess of their initial margin requirement should prices move favorably. During the period from which data for this study were drawn, contracts expired on the third Fridays of March, June, September, and December, with the futures contracts marked to the closing index value at 4:15 p.m., Eastern time.[5]

Basic Functions of Stock Index Futures

Stock index futures typically serve three functions: trading, hedging, and arbitrage. First, traders can take speculative positions in futures to take advantage of anticipated broad market price movements. Second, hedging, which involves the purchase or sale of index futures in anticipation of an intended cash market trade, compensates for adverse price moves in the cash market, and thus reduces aggregate risk. Simple hedges typically involve the purchase (sale) of an asset in the cash market and sale (purchase) of futures contracts on the same asset. As long as the cash-futures spread remains the same and the costs of effecting and financing the transaction are covered, gains (losses) on the cash market purchase are countered by losses (gains) on the futures. The investor thus may mitigate the risk of loss and the possibility of gain on the cash market purchase.

Arbitrage is a third strategy served by stock index futures. It involves the simultaneous purchase and sale of stocks and futures and subsequently enables an investor to capture profits from realignments of relative prices following an apparent inconsistency in the index and the index futures price. When the index futures price moves outside the range determined by the cost of the look-alike basket and the cost-of-carry, arbitrage will tend to drive the futures price and the index toward their cost-of-carry relationship. If the actual futures price is higher than the cost of the look-alike basket and the cost of carry, the futures contract is overvalued, justifying the purchase of the look-alike basket of stocks and the simultaneous sale

of the futures contract. If the futures price falls below the price of the look-alike portfolio plus the cost of carry, the futures contract is undervalued, and the reverse trade would be profitable. In both cases, the arbitrage transactions realign the futures price and the index.

Because physical delivery does not take place, the futures contract is said to be "settled in cash." Cash settlement is an important feature of stock index futures. An arbitrageur who has sold futures and bought the underlying basket of stocks does not deliver the basket of stocks to the investor who bought futures. Instead the arbitrageur must sell the basket of stocks. Any open futures positions are marked to the final settlement index calculation when the futures expire. Once the arbitrageur pays or receives the value of the futures price change from the prior day, the position is closed. A common practice for arbitrageurs, however, is to trade large blocks of stocks or whole portfolios at prices tied to closing prices on the futures expiration days. As a result, these large volumes of orders late in the day have tended, on some occasions, to create at least temporary imbalances in the cash equity markets.

Movements in Futures Prices

Numerous studies have explained the price relationship between stock index futures and the underlying stocks in terms of arbitrage behavior. Futures prices normally vary relative to stock prices within ranges that are not sufficient to trigger arbitrage. In fact, arbitrage opportunities are often not available. A number of scholars have attempted to identify and measure arbitrage trading boundaries.[6] Their results indicate that the futures to cash price differential, referred to as the basis, should fall within boundaries determined by the cost of carry. Because market interest rates have historically exceeded the dividend rate on common stocks, the "fair value" or theoretical stock index futures price normally exceeds the stock index.[7]

---

[5]Since this study, the final settlement procedures for S&P 500 futures have changed. Contracts currently expire one business day prior to the third Friday of the contract month, with the final settlement price based on a special calculation of the Friday opening prices for each of the 500 stocks. Upon expiration, one final cash adjustment is made to reflect the last day's gains or losses.

[6]Cornell and French (1983a,b); Modest and Sundaresan (1983); and Stoll and Whaley (1986).

[7]The theoretical upper and lower bounds are discussed extensively in the literature. For example, see Stoll and Whaley (1986): 8-10, or Kawaller (1987): 447-49.

Conventional wisdom among professional traders dictates that movements in the S&P 500 futures price affect market expectations of subsequent movements in cash prices. The futures price presumably embodies all available information regarding events that will affect cash prices. Purchase or sale of index futures requires one transaction, while purchase or sale of a look-alike portfolio generally involves 200 or more stocks and a minimum $5 million investment. Consequently, the index futures price is likely to respond to new information more quickly than cash market prices in general and, thus, more quickly than the S&P 500 index. This lag of the index behind the futures price results because the underlying stocks must be traded in order for the index to reflect a change in value. Since most index stocks do not trade each minute, the cash market responds to the new information with a lag.[8] S&P 500 index movements may similarly convey information about subsequent price variation in the futures contract; however, the lag of the futures price behind the index is likely to be much shorter than the lag of the index behind the futures price.

If new information on the health of the economy is bullish, a trader has the choice of buying either S&P 500 futures or the underlying stocks. While the futures trade can be effected immediately with little up-front cash, actual stock purchases require a greater initial investment and may take longer to implement since they require a subsequent stock selection. This preference for index futures as a vehicle for speculative transactions explains why changes in futures prices may thus provide an indicator of forthcoming cash prices, which follow when investors who are unwilling or unable to use futures incorporate the same information that led to changes in futures prices into their own cash market transactions.

Changes is the S&P 500 index can also lead changes in the futures price, if the value of the index conveys information that affects futures prices. Futures traders are likely to incorporate recent changes in the index in their pricing decision. For example, if the index declines because investors are selling stocks, for whatever reason, the decline may induce a change in sentiment that is reflected in subsequent futures prices.

Potential lead and lag patterns between index futures and the index are complicated by two more possible relationships: the futures and the index may move together as new information affects both index futures and cash market trades. Each measure may lead the other as market participants find clues about impending values of index futures and broad market movements in previous futures prices and broad cash market movements, respectively. Technical analysts, or chartists, rely heavily on patterns of relationships between past and future values of series such as the S&P 500. A summary of possible relationships between the S&P 500 index and S&P 500 futures prices is shown in Table 1.

Table 1
Possible Effects of Movements in the S&P 500 Index and S&P 500 Index Futures

Movement in the S&P 500 Index	
may be affected by	may affect
• prior index levels	• upcoming index levels
• current futures prices	• upcoming futures prices
• prior futures prices	
• other market information	

Movement in S&P 500 Index Futures Prices	
may be affected by	may affect
• prior futures prices	• upcoming futures prices
• current index levels	• upcoming index levels
• prior index levels	
• other market information	

Tests of the Intraday Relationship Between S&P 500 Futures and the S&P 500 Index

A complex set of potential relationships could exist between S&P 500 futures and the S&P 500 index prices. Movements in each are thought to be influenced by the past and current movements of both as well as by other market information. The study reported on in this article tried to gauge the magnitude and variability of the relationships between the index and the futures by estimating distributed lags between the two prices. Distributed lags employ a method of weighing past data to determine their effects on the data under study.

The pattern of lags between index futures and the index may not be constant over time. While shifting patterns are conceivable throughout the life of the futures contract, the focus of interest on expiration effects begs the question of whether these temporal relationships show any differentiation on those days. On expiration days, the traders' need to close positions may generate market imbalances that could conceivably overwhelm the mechanism by which new information influences index futures and cash market prices. An expiration-day

---

[8]New information could affect a subset of index stocks disproportionately relative to the entire stock market. In such cases, not all index stocks must be traded each minute for the index to adjust completely and quickly to new information.

breakdown in this mechanism would diminish the benefits of the index futures market—at least on expiration day—as a medium for discovery.

The data are minute-by-minute prices of index futures contracts and the S&P 500 index on all trading days in 1984 and 1985. The Chicago Mercantile Exchange provided the data.[9] Pairing the reported index with the last index futures price quoted during the minute that the index appeared yielded 360 pairs of index and futures observations per hour (six-hour trading day X 60 observations per hour). To judge whether the index futures-index relationship changes as the expiration day approaches, lags were estimated for six trading days in each quarter beginning in the second quarter of 1984 and ending with the last quarter of 1985.[10] The days are 88,60,30 and 14 days prior to expiration, and expiration day. These days were chosen to represent the approach of expiration and the effect of this approach on the index futures-index relationship.

The nature and extent of the lead/lag relationships between index futures prices and the index were measured using a number of analyses. First, a time series analysis was performed to study the movements of futures prices relative to prior futures prices. Next, the same method of analysis gauged movement of the S&P 500 index based on past index performance. These time series analyses studied the minute-to-minute changes in both the index and the futures prices. The next step in the analysis was to construct a model to describe the dynamic intraday price relationships between the index and the futures prices. In this model, index movements depend on their own past movements, current and past movements in the futures price, and other relevant market information (see Table 1). Likewise, futures price movements are modeled to depend on their own past movements, current and past movements in the index, and other relevant market information.[11]

Consistent evidence on both the form of the lag relationships and their stability over time emerges from these tests: first, the contemporaneous relationship between futures prices and the index is quite strong—dwarfing the lagged relationships. In fact, the futures and index move almost in lock step. Second, lags between index futures prices and the index are not symmetrical. The index lags behind the index futures price by up to 45 minutes, while the futures price lags behind the index only briefly if at all. This result supports the contention that index futures do, in fact, serve a price discovery function. Third, the lagged relationships do not appreciably change as expiration day approaches or on expiration day itself.

Different patterns of lagged relationships between S&P 500 futures and the S&P 500 index are given in Chart 1. It shows the distributed lag coefficients for two days in the fourth quarter of 1984; results for other days in this contract period, as well as days in other contract periods, are quite similar. Typically, the first coefficient,

which describes the contemporaneous relationship, is the greatest, or one of the greatest, on each day. In the panels showing lags from futures to the index, relatively large and statistically significant coefficients show up with lags as long as 45 minutes. Panels showing lags from the index to futures typically show the one-minute lag as the largest coefficient and the only one that is significant. These results parallel evidence garnered from earlier time-series analyses.[12]

Chart 1 also shows quite similar patterns in the distributed lag coefficients 88 days prior to expiration day. Coefficients showing the lead from futures to the index continue to be mostly positive even on expiration day. They are significant or nearly significant through 20 to 30 minutes on each day, though the lag appears somewhat less on expiration day. Other quarters record quite similar patterns.

Implications

Evidence uncovered in the tests of lagged relationships between S&P 500 index futures prices and the S&P 500 index points to the usefulness of the futures as a predictor of broad equity market movements measured by the index. The S&P 500 futures price and underlying index evidently respond to market information simultaneously, and the index shows lags of up to 45 minutes behind the futures. Importantly, the magnitudes of the contemporaneous effects on different days are consistently much larger than the lagged effects. Thus, though the price discovery function has been demonstrated, the indications of forthcoming cash market changes provided by past futures prices are not sufficient to provide an exploitable trading strategy.

---

[9] At the time of this study, the index was available only each minute. Since then, index quotations have been calculated and disseminated at about 15-second intervals.

[10] Prior to the June 1984 contract, S&P 500 futures expired on Thursdays. This article's sample is restricted to the last three contracts in 1984 and all contracts that expired in 1985. Also note that futures trade for 15 minutes after the stock markets close. Quotes from these 15 minutes are not considered in this analysis. Finally, since September 30, 1985, quotes are available beginning at 8:30 a.m., but the analysis is restricted to the six hours (360 observations) from 9:01 a.m. to 3:00 p.m. so that results can be compared across quarters.

[11] In the context of this model, zero restrictions are tested on the distributed lag coefficients, allowing, alternately, the contemporaneous coefficient and the coefficient at lag one minute to remain unconstrained. See Kawaller, Koch and Koch (1987) for details.

[12] The tests with no restrictions on the contemporaneous and first coefficients also confirm the longer lags from the index to the futures.

Chart 1.
Sample Distributed Lags for the
S&P 500 Index and S&P 500 Index Futures Prices

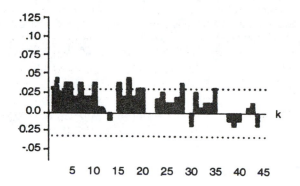

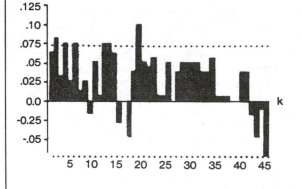

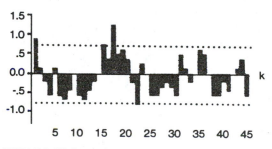

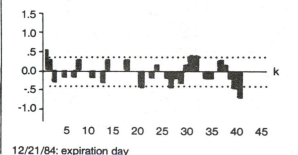

09/24/84: 88 days prior to expiration

12/21/84: expiration day

Chart 1 shows the relationship between minute-to-minute movements in the S&P 500 futures price and the S&P 500 index. The top graph in each set shows how past minute-to-minute movements in the futures price affect current movements in the index, and the bottom figure shows how past movements in the index affect current movements in the futures price.

The vertical axis in each figure represents the magnitude of the minute-to-minute impacts of each value on the other. The horizontal axis charts the number of minute-to-minute lags incorporated into the model. For example, for k=1 minute lag, the value plotted in the top graph shows the impact of the futures price change one minute earlier on the current index value. At the number '20' on the horizontal axis, the effect on the current index value of the futures price 20 minutes earlier is plotted.

When the vertical lines within the graph fall be-tween the two dotted horizontal lines, the magnitude of the distributed lag coefficient is less than twice its standard error, and thus is not statistically significant. When the vertical lines within the graph fall outside the dotted lines, the magnitude of the distributed lag coefficient is more than twice its standard error, and, thus, is statistically significant.

When the vertical lines are concentrated in the positive portion of the figure (above 0.0), most of the lagged impacts of one price on the other are positive; that is, increases in one price are then followed by increases in the other price.

When the vertical lines are concentrated in the negative portion of the figure (below 0.0), most of the lagged impacts of one price on the other are negative; that is, increases in one price are then followed by decreases in the other.

Consistency in the lagged relationships over the days approaching expiration day and on expiration day also indicates that the pattern of lags between futures and the index is not disturbed by the closing out of arbitrage positions. This consistency implies that index futures trading continues to make its contribution to price discovery, even on expiration days that transpired without market activity restrictions.

Bibliography

Cornell, Bradford, and Kenneth French. "The Pricing of Stock Index Futures." *Journal of Futures Markets* 3 (Summer 1983a): 1-14.

_____, and _____. "Taxes and the Pricing of Stock Index Futures." *Journal of Finance* 38 (June 1983b): 675-94.

Elton, Edwin J., Martin J. Gruber, and Joel Rentzler. "Intra-day Tests of the Efficiency of the Treasury Bill Futures Market." *Review of Economics and Statistics* 66 (February 1984): 129-37.

Figlewski, Stephen. "Explaining the Early Discounts on Stock Index Futures: The Case for Disequilibrium." *Financial Analysts Journal* 40 (July-August 1984a): 43-47.

_____. "Hedging Performance and Basis Risk in Stock Index Futures." *Journal of Finance* 39 (July 1984b): 657-69.

_____. Hedging with Stock Index Futures: Theory and Application in a New Market." *Journal of Futures Markets* 5 (Summer 1985): 183-99.

Gastineau, Gary, and Albert Madansky. "S&P 500 Stock Index Futures Evaluation Tables." *Financial Analysts Journal* 39 (November-December 1983): 68-76.

Geweke, John. "Testing the Exogeneity Specification in the Complete Dynamic Simultaneous Equations Model." *Journal of Econometrics* 6 (April 1978): 163-85.

Granger, Clive W. "Investigating Causal Relations by Econometric Models and Cross-Spectral Methods." *Econometrics* 37 (July 1969): 423-38.

Haugh, Larry D. "Checking the Independence of Two Covariance-Stationary Time Series: A Univariate Residual Cross-Correlation Approach." *Journal of the American Statistical Association* 71 (June 1976): 378-85.

Kawaller, Ira G. " A Comment on Figlewski's Hedging with Stock Index Futures: Theory and Application in a New Market." *Journal of Futures Markets* 5 (Fall 1985): 447-49.

_____. "A Note: Debunking the Myth of the Risk-Free Return." *Journal of Futures Markets* 7 (June 1987): 327-31.

_____. Paul D. Koch, and Timothy W. Koch. "The Temporal Price Relationship Between the S&P 500 Futures and the S&P 500 Index." *Journal of Finance* 5 (December 1987): 1309-29.

Koch, Paul D., and James F. Ragan, Jr. "Investigating the Causal Relationship Between Wages and Quits: An Exercise in Comparative Dynamics." *Economic Inquiry* 24 (January 1986): 61-83.

Koch, Paul D., and Shie-Shien Yang. "A Method for Testing the Independence of Two Time Series that Accounts for a Potential Pattern in the Cross-Correlation Function." *Journal of the American Statistical Association* 81 (June 1986): 533-44.

Modest, David, and Mahadeaum Sundaresan. "The Relationship between Spot and Futures Prices in Stock Index Futures Markets: Some Preliminary Evidence." *Journal of Futures Markets* 3 (Summer 1983): 15-41.

Stoll, Hans R, and Robert E. Whaley. "Expiration Day Effects of Index Options and Futures." Vanderbilt University, March 1986.

U.S. Securities and Exchange Commission. Letter to the Honorable John D. Dingell, June 13, 1986a.

_____. Letter to Mr. Kenneth J. Leiber and others, June 13, 1986b.

_____. *Roundtable on Index Arbitrage*, July 9, 1986c.

The authors are Vice President and Director of the New York office of the Chicago Mercantile Exchange; Associate Professor of Finance at the University of Kansas and former visiting scholar at the Federal Reserve Bank of Atlanta; and Chair of Banking at the University of South Carolina, respectively.

The article is printed with permission from the Federal Reserve Bank of Atlanta. It appeared in the Federal Reserve Bank of Atlanta's *Economic Review*, May/June 1988. In turn, the Atlanta Federal Reserve Bank's article was based on research which was originally published in the *Journal of Finance* (Kawaller, Ira G.; Koch, Paul D.; Koch, Timothy W. "The Temporal Price Relationship Between S&P 500 Futures and the S&P 500 Index", *The Journal of Finance*, December 1987).

Article 7

Ira G. Kawaller

Determining the Relevant Fair Value(s) of S&P 500 Futures: A Case Study Approach

A fundamental consideration for potential users of stock index futures is the determination of the futures' break-even price or fair value. Conceptually, being able to sell futures at prices above the break-even or buy futures at prices below the break-even offers opportunity for incremental gain. This article points out an important, though widely unappreciated caveat. That is, no single break-even price is universally appropriate. Put another way, the break-even price for a given institution depends on the motivation of that firm as well as its marginal funding and investing yield alternatives.

In this article five differentiated objectives are identified, and the calculations of the respective break-even futures prices are provided. The various objectives are (a) to generate profits from arbitrage activities, (b) to create synthetic money market instruments, (c) to reduce exposure to equities, (d) to increase equity exposure, and (e) to maintain equity exposure using the most cost effective instrument via stock/futures substitution. All these alternative objectives have the same conceptual starting point, which relates to the fact that a combined long stock/short futures position generates a money market return composed of the dividends on the stock position as well as the basis[1] adjustment of the futures contract. Under the simplified assumptions of zero transactions costs and equal marginal borrowing and lending rates, the underlying spot/futures relationship can be expressed as follows:

$$F = S \left(1 + (i - d) \frac{t}{360} \right) \quad (1)$$

Where
- F = break-even futures price
- S = spot index price
- i = interest rate (expressed as a money market yield)
- d = projected dividend rate (expressed as a money market yield)
- t = number of days from today's spot value date to the value date of the futures contract.

In equilibrium, the actual futures price equals the break-even futures price, and thus the market participant would either have no incentive to undertake the transactions or be indifferent between competing tactics for an equivalent goal.

Moving from the conceptual to the practical simply requires the selection of the appropriate marginal interest rate for the participant in question, as well as precise accounting for transactions costs. This paper demonstrates that these considerations foster differences between the break-even prices among the alternative goals considered. Each goal is explained more fully, and the respective theoretical futures prices are presented.

I. Generating Profits From Arbitrage Activities

Generally, arbitrage is explained as a process whereby one identifies two distinct marketplaces where something is traded and then waits for opportunities to buy in one market at one price and sell in the other market at a higher price. This same process is at work for stock/futures arbitrage, but these market participants tend to view their activities with a slightly different slant. They will enter an arbitrage trade whenever (a) buying stock and selling futures generates a return that exceeds financing costs, or (b) selling stocks and buying futures results in an effective yield (cost of borrowing) that falls below marginal lending rates. Completed arbitrages will require a reversal of the starting positions, and the costs for both buying and selling stocks and futures must be included in the calculations.[2] Thus, the total cost of an arbitrage trade reflects the bid/ask spreads on all of the stocks involved in the arbitrage, the bid/ask spread for all futures positions, and all commission charges on both stocks and futures.[3]

Table 1 (see page 2) calculates these arbitrage costs under three different scenarios. In all cases, the current starting value of the stock portfolio, based on last-sale prices, is $100 million and the S&P 500 index is valued at 335.00. The hedge ratio is calculated in the traditional manner:[4]

The author appreciates helpful comments from Dan Siegel and two anonymous reviewers.

[1] "Basis" in this paper is defined as the futures price minus the spot index value. Elsewhere, the calculation might be made with the two prices reversed.

[2] If any fees or charges apply to the borrowing or lending mechanisms, these, too, would have to be incorporated in the calculations. Put another way, for the calculations that are presented in this article, the marginal borrowing and lending rates are effective rates, inclusive of all such fees.

[3] Brennan & Schwartz note that the cost of closing an arbitrage position may differ if the action is taken at expiration versus prior to expiration. Thus the appropriate arbitrage bound should reflect whether or not the arbitrageur is expecting (or hoping) to exercise his "early close-out option."

[4] See Kawaller (1985) for a discussion of the justification for this hedge ratio.

Table 1: Arbitrage Break-Evens

Arbitrage Costs	A	B	C
Index Value	335.00	335.00	335.00
Size of Portfolio	100,000,000	100,000,000	100,000,000
Average Price Per Share	67	67	67
Number of Shares	1,492,537	1,492,537	1,492,537
Commission Per Share of Stock	0	0.02	0.02
Stock Commissions Per Side	0	29,851	29,851
Stock Commissions (Rnd Trn)	0	59,701	59,701
Bid/Ask Per Unit of Stock	0	0.125	0.5
Bid/Ask Stock	0	186,567	746,269
Contracts	597	597	597
Commissions Per Round Turn	0	12	12
Futures Commissions	0	7,164	7,164
Bid/Ask Per Futures Contract	0.00	0.05	0.50
Bid/Ask Futures	0	14,925	149,250
Dollar Costs	0	268,358	962,384
Index Point Cost	0.00	0.90	3.22
Marginal Borrowing Rate	9.00%	9.00%	9.00%
Marginal Lending Rate	8.00%	8.00%	8.00%
Dividend Rate	3.50%	3.50%	3.50%
Shorter Horizon (Case a):			
Days to Expiration	30	30	30
Upper Bound	336.54	337.43	339.76
Lower Bound	336.26	335.36	333.03
No-Arbitrage Range	0.28	2.08	6.73
Longer Horizon (Case b):			
Days to Expiration	60	60	60
Upper Bound	338.07	338.97	341.29
Lower Bound	337.51	336.61	334.29
No arbitrage range	0.56	2.36	7.01

$$H = \frac{V \times Beta}{S\&P \times 500}$$

Where

H = hedge ratio (number of futures contracts required)

V = value of the portfolio

Beta = portfolio beta

S&P = spot S&P 500 index price.

The average price per share is estimated to be the S&P 500 index divided by five.

In column A, transactions are assumed to be costless, reflected by zero values for bid/ask spreads as well as zero commissions. In column B, more typical conditions are shown. Commissions on stock are assumed to be $.02 per share; bid/ask spreads on stocks are assumed to be 1/8th ($.125 per share); commissions on futures are assumed to be $12 on a round-turn basis (i.e. for both buy and sell transactions); and bid/ask spreads on futures are assumed to be 1 tick or 0.05, worth $25.[5] Column C assumes the same commission structure as that of column B; but bid/ask spreads are somewhat higher, reflecting a decline in liquidity relative to the former case. This scenario might also be viewed as representing the case where impact costs of trying to execute a stock portfolio were expected to move initial

bids or offers for a complete execution. The index point costs in all cases reflects the respective dollar costs on a per contract basis.

The arbitrageur would evaluate two, independent arbitrage bounds: an upper bound and a lower bound. During those times when futures prices exceed the upper arbitrage boundary, profit could be made by financing the purchase of stocks at the marginal borrowing rate and selling futures. When the futures prices are below the lower bound, profits could be made by selling stocks and buying futures, thus creating a synthetic borrowing, and investing at the marginal lending rate. In both cases, the completed arbitrages would require an unwinding of all the original trades.

The upper bound is found by substituting the arbitrage firm's marginal borrowing rate in equation (1) and adding the arbitrage costs (in basis points) to this

---

[5] In practice, it may be appropriate to assume two different cost structures for the upper- and lower-bound break-even calculations, as costs differ depending on whether the trade starts with long stock/short futures or vice versa. The difference arises because initiating the short stock/long futures arbitrage requires the sale of stock on an uptick. The "cost" of this requirement is uncertain because the transactions price is not known at the time the decision is made to enter the arbitrage. No analogous uncertainty exists when initiating the arbitrage in the opposite direction.

calculated value. In the case of the lower arbitrage boundary, the marginal lending rate is used for the variable *i* in equation (1), and the arbitrage costs are subtracted. The calculations in Table 1 assume marginal borrowing and lending rates of 9% and 8%, respectively, and a dividend rate of 3.5%. The upper and lower arbitrage boundaries are given for the three alternative cost structures. For comparative purposes, two sets of arbitrage boundaries are generated for two different terms.

Most obvious is the conclusion that an arbitrageur with a higher (lower) cost structure or a wider (narrower) differential between marginal borrowing and lending costs would face wider (narrower) no-arbitrage boundaries. In addition, Table 1 also demonstrates the time-sensitive nature of the difference between the two bounds, or the no-arbitrage range. As time to expiration expands, this range increases, monotonically, all other considerations held constant.

II. Creating Synthetic Money Market Securities

The case of the firm seeking to construct a synthetic money market income security by buying stocks and selling futures is a slight variant of the arbitrage case described in the prior section.[6] In this situation, too, the firm will seek to realize a rate of return for the combined long stock/short futures positions, but the relevant interest rate that underlies the determination of the break-even futures price is different. While the arbitrageur who buys stock and sells futures will do so whenever the resulting gain betters his marginal borrowing rate, the synthetic fixed-income trader will endeavor to outperform the marginal lending rate. For both, however, the imposition of transaction costs will necessitate the sale of the futures at a higher price than would be dictated by the costless case.

Not surprisingly, the break-even price for this player is directly related to both transaction costs and time to expiration. What may not be quite as readily apparent is the fact that, at least theoretically, situations may arise that provide no motivation for arbitrageurs to be sellers of futures, while at the same time offering a motivation for a potentially much larger audience of money managers to be futures sellers. Put another way, large scale implementation of the synthetic money market strategy by many market investors could certainly enhance these players' returns but also have the more universally beneficial effect of reducing the range of futures price fluctuations that do *not* induce relative-price-based trading strategies.

Yet another seemingly perverse condition that is highlighted by these calculations is that firms that operate less aggressively in the cash market, and thereby tend to have lower marginal lending rates, will likely have a greater incremental benefit from arranging synthetic securities than will firms that seek out higher cash market returns. For example, assume Firm A has access

to Euro Deposit markets while Firm B deals only with lower yielding U.S. domestic banks; and assume further that the difference in marginal lending rates is .25%. Firm B's break-even futures price necessarily falls below that of Firm A. At any point in time, however, the current futures bid is relevant for both firms. Assuming the two firms faced the same transaction cost structures, this futures price would generate the same effective yield for the two firms. Invariably, Firm B will find a greater number of yield enhancement opportunities than will Firm A; and any time both firms are attracted to this strategy simultaneously, B's incremental gain will be greater.

III. Decreasing Equity Exposures

The case of the portfolio manager who owns equities and is looking to eliminate that exposure requires a further determination before the break-even calculation can be made. That is, two different break-evens would result depending on whether the desired reduction in equity exposure were expected to be permanent or temporary.

First, consider the case where the shift out of equities is expected to be permanent. Hedging with futures simply defers the actual stock transaction. At the same time, it introduces futures transactions costs that would otherwise be saved if the immediate sale of stock were chosen. The determination of this break-even, therefore, requires an evaluation of the return that one could realize by liquidating stock today and investing the resulting funds in some money market security maturing at the futures value date, versus the return of hedging the stock portfolio today and subsequently liquidating it on the futures value date.

In calculating the returns from the traditional sell stocks/buy money market securities tactic, one should recognize that the liquidation cost effectively "haircuts" the portfolio. For example, the liquidation of a $100 million portfolio involves an immediate expense such that some amount *less than* the original $100 million becomes available for reinvestment. Thus, the portfolio manager realizes a lower fixed income return than the nominal yield on the proposed money market security. The break-even futures price would be that price which, when including all transactions costs, generates the same realized yield as the net money market return available from the shift into money market instruments.

In Table 2 (see page 4), the haircut is estimated to reflect half of the bid/ask spread as well as the stock commissions. The same commission and bid/ask structure is assumed as that which faces the firms analyzed in the prior section; and, similarly, the same marginal investment rate (8%) is incorporated. Under these conditions, the manager who chooses the liquidation of the stock portfolio and the investment of the proceeds at 8% (rather than hedging) realizes an effective net money market return of 6.51% for 30 days or 7.25% for 60 days. Respective break-even futures prices are 336.33 and 337.58.

---

[6] Section III of this article covers the case where the firm already holds the stock.

Table 2: Reducing Equity Exposures : Permanent Adjustment

Short Hedging Considerations

Index Value	335.00
Size of Portfolio	100,000,000
Portfolio Beta	1.0
Average Price Per Share	67
Number of Shares	1,492,537
Commission Per Share	0.02
Commissions Per Side	29,850.74
Bid/Ask Per Stock	0.125
1/2 Bid/Ask Stock	93,283.56
Total Stock Costs	123,134.30
Investable Funds	99,876,865.70
Money Market Return	8.00%
Hedge Calculations	597.0
Number of Futures Contracts	597
Commissions (Rnd Trn)	12.00
Futures Commissions	7,164.00
Bid/ask Per Contract	0.05
Bid/ask Futures	14,925.00
Total Futures Costs	22,089.00
Total Stock Costs	123,134.30
Dollar Costs/Contract	243.26
Index Point Cost	0.49
Dividend Rate	3.50%

Shorter Horizon (Case a):

Days to End Point	30
Ending Value	100,542,711.47
Net Money Market Return	6.51%
Break-even Futures Price	336.33

Longer Horizon (Case b):

Days to End Point	60
Ending Value	101,208,557.24
Net Money Market Return	7.25%
Break-Even Futures Price	337.58

The case where the decision to reduce exposure is more likely to be temporary involves a minor modification to the above calculations. That is, operating exclusively in the arena of stocks would add the cost of repurchasing a portfolio, thereby lowering the net money market return even further. In contrast, the hedging alternative generates no stock charges. As a consequence, the break-evens in this case are substantially below the break-evens required for the former example.

IV. Increasing Equity Exposure

Perhaps the easiest situation to explain is the choice between buying today at the spot price versus buying in the future at the futures price. This determination simply requires calculating the forward value of the index, which, in turn, reflects the opportunity costs of foregoing interest income of a fixed income investment alternative as well as an adjustment for transactions costs of futures, alone.[7] For the case of the same prototype firm discussed in the earlier sections, and given the same

portfolio, the opportunity cost is generated using the marginal lending rate of 8.0%. Futures costs total $14,925 or slightly more than seven basis points per contract.

Thus, the portfolio manager would be indifferent between buying stocks now and hedging for a future purchase if the futures were cheaper than the price calculated from equation (1), inputting 8.0% for i. In this case, with the spot S&P 500 index at 335.00 and 30 days to the futures value date, the break-even price is 336.18. For a 60-day horizon, the break-even becomes 337.44.

V. Maintaining Equity Exposure in the Most Cost Effective Instrument

Consider the case of the portfolio manager who currently holds equities, with the existing degree of exposure at the desired level. Even this player may find using futures to be attractive if they are sufficiently cheap. At some futures price it becomes attractive to sell the stocks and buy the futures, thereby maintaining the same equity exposure. The break-even price for this trader, then, would be the trigger price. That is, any futures price lower than this break-even would induce the substitution of futures for stocks and generate incremental benefits.

Like the prior case, this strategy rests on the comparison of present versus future values; and again, the firm's marginal lending rate is the appropriate discounting factor. Regarding trading costs, commissions and bid/ask spreads for both stocks and futures must be taken into account, as the move from stocks to futures would be temporary. Thus, the break-even price would be lower than the zero-cost theoretical futures price by the basis point costs of the combined commissions and bid/ask spreads.

For the prototype firm with the marginal lending rate of 8.00%, under the same normal market assumptions used throughout, the break-even price for 30-and 60-day horizons becomes 335.36 and 336.61, respectively.[8]

---

[7] Stock costs would be roughly comparable whether one were to buy now or later, so they do not enter into the calculation. This treatment, admittedly, is not precise. For example, with a significant market move, the number of shares required may vary, as may the average bid-ask spreads; so some differences may arise. Moreover, the statement ignores the fact that although absolute magnitudes may be identical in both the buy-now or buy-later cases, the present values of these charges may differ. This consideration, if taken into account more rigorously, would bias the decision toward a later purchase. For the purposes of this analysis, however, these differences are ignored.

[8] This result happens to be identical to that shown for the lower arbitrage bound of the firm operating with the same cost structure. As explained in footnote 5, however, the arbitrage firm that sells stock short has additional costs that do not apply to the stock/futures substituter. Thus, in practice, the break-even for the substituter is likely to be a higher price than the lower bound for the equivalent firm involved with arbitrage.

Table 3: Alternate Break-even Prices

	Days to Expiration	
	30-Days	60-Days
Lower Arbitrage Boundary*/Futures Substitution Break-even	335.36	336.61
Temporary Equity Adjustment (Short Hedge) Break-even	335.50	336.76
Long Hedge Break-even	336.18	337.44
Permanent Equity Adjustment (Short Hedge) Break-even	336.33	337.58
Synthetic Fixed Income Break-even	337.16	338.41
Upper Arbitrage Boundary	337.43	338.97

*Not reflective of costs associated with the uptick rule.

VI. Consolidation and Summary

The respective break-even prices that are relevant to the various applications discussed in the article are shown in ascending order. All calculations relate to a firm with a marginal borrowing rate of 9.00% and a marginal lending rate of 8.00%. Break-even prices are given for two different time spans for the hedging period: 30-days and 60-days. Further, these calculations reflect the additional assumption of "normal" transactions cost and bid/ask spreads.

The highest price for which it becomes advantageous to take a long futures position is the long hedger's break-even price; and if prices decline sufficiently from this value, such that they fall below the lower arbitrage boundary, additional market participants — namely arbitrageurs — will be induced to buy futures, as well. The lowest price for which it becomes advantageous to sell futures would be the break-even for the temporary short hedger; and, in a similar fashion, if prices rise sufficiently above this level, additional short sellers will be attracted to these markets.

Note that regardless of the time horizon, the lowest price for which buying futures is justified (336.18 or 337.44) is higher than the highest price for which selling futures is justified (335.50 or 336.76). Thus, at every futures price there is at least one market participant who "should" be using this market. Moreover, it is also interesting that if the futures price enables the arbitrageur to operate profitably, at least one other market participant would find the futures to be attractively priced as well. For example, if the futures were below the lower arbitrage bound, aside from the arbitrageur, the long hedger would certainly be predisposed to buying futures rather than buying stocks; and if the futures price were above the upper arbitrage bound, willing sellers would include arbitrageurs, both temporary and permanent short hedgers, and those constructing fixed income securities.

The overall conclusion, then, is that it pays (literally) to evaluate the relevant break-even prices for any firm interested in any of the above strategies — a population that includes all firms that manage money market or equity portfolios. At every point in time, at least one strategy will dictate the use of futures as the preferred transactions vehicle because use of futures in the given situation will add incremental value. Failure to make this evaluation will undoubtedly result in either using futures at inopportune moments or, more likely, failing to use futures when it would be desirable to do so. In either case, neglecting to compare the currently available futures price to the correct break-even price will ultimately result in suboptimal performance.

Bibliography

Brennan, M. and Schwartz E., (1990): "Arbitrage in Stock Index Futures," *Journal of Business* 63:S7-S31.

Cornell, B. and French, K. (1983, Spring): "The Pricing of Stock Index Futures," *The Journal of Futures Markets*, 3:1-14.

Figlewki, S. (1985, Summer): "Hedging with Stock Index Futures: Theory and Application In A New Market," *The Journal of Futures Markets*, 5:183-199.

Hansen, N.H., and Kopprasch, R.W. (1984): "Pricing of Stock Index Futures," Fabozzi, F.J., and Kipnis, G.M. eds., *Stock Index Futures*, Dow Jones-Irwin, 6:65-79.

Kawaller, I. G., (1985, Fall): "A Comment on Figlewski's Hedging with Stock Index Futures: Theory and Application in a New Market," *The Journal of Futures Markets*, 5:447-449.

Kawaller, I.G., (1987, June): "A Note: Debunking the Myth of the Risk-Free Return," *The Journal of Futures Markets*, 7:327-331.

Ira G. Kawaller is Vice President-Director of the Chicago Mercantile Exchange's New York office.

This article originally appeared in the August 1991 issue of *The Journal of Futures Markets*, pp. 453-460.

Article 8

Cash-and-Carry Trading and the Pricing of Treasury Bill Futures

Ira G. Kawaller
Timothy W. Koch

Considerable effort has been devoted to examining whether the Treasury bill futures market is efficient. Most studies have compared futures yields to coincident forward yields implied by the term-structure of spot market bills, and many have found that numerous arbitrage possibilities were available. The existence of statistically significant differences has been attributed to market inefficiency whenever the differences could not be explained, but numerous explanations have been offered.

Early research focused on the impact of differential transactions costs (Poole, 1978; Rendleman & Carrabini, 1979), daily settlement for futures trades (Morgan, 1978), differential tax influences (Arak, 1980), and the cost of guaranteeing performance in futures trades (Kane, 1980). More recently, Chow and Brophy (1982) have argued that futures contracts incorporate a differential "habitat premium" which reflects investors' preferences for the more speculative futures transactions. Regardless of the presumed causal factors incorporated in their analyses, many researchers have concluded that arbitrage opportunities have consistently been available over time.

An entirely different focus on the futures-forward yield relationship was provided by Vignola and Dale (1980). They used Working's theory of storage costs to evaluate the impact of financing costs in establishing equilibrium futures prices under pure arbitrage conditions.[1] Working (1949) originally examined commodity prices and argued that the difference between cash and futures prices could be attributed to carrying charges including transportation, insurance, and warehouse costs as well as interest. Vignola and Dale applied Working's analysis to Treasury bill futures by comparing actual futures prices to equilibrium futures prices con-

---

[1] In pure arbitrage situations a cash position is financed with borrowed funds. This contrasts with quasi-arbitrage transactions which incorporate securities actually owned. Rendleman and Carrabini (1979) and Vignola and Dale (1980) elaborate on this distinction.

Ira G. Kawaller is Director of the New York Office of The Chicago Mercantile Exchange.

Timothy W. Koch is the Continental National Bank Professor of Banking, Texas Tech University.

structed under the assumption that arbitragers borrow the deliverable bills when trading futures. They concluded that carrying costs provide a better explanation of futures prices than unbiased expectations and the term-structure.

This study extends recent research concerning the role of carrying costs and Treasury bill futures. In particular, we examine the pricing of nearby Treasury bill futures with regard to pure arbitrage. Variations in the differential between rates on nearby futures contracts and corresponding forward rates are explained in terms of the spread between rates on term and overnight repurchase agreements. The futures to forward differential, which is typically associated with futures market efficiency, reflects trading strategies employed primarily by U.S. government securities dealers. The arbitrage that drives these rates, the cash-and-carry trade, involves comparing a holding period yield with a financing rate. Traders buy a deliverable Treasury bill and short the corresponding futures contract whenever the yield realized from purchasing the bill, holding it to delivery and ultimately surrendering the bill in fulfillment of the short contract exceeds their financing cost. Conversely, they borrow the deliverable bill via a reverse repurchase agreement, sell it, and go long the futures contract whenever the holding period yield is less than the financing cost.[2]

Although the decision rule appears to be straightforward, a variety of financing alternatives reflecting various repurchase agreements (RPs) leads to different trading decisions. It is the purpose of this article to discuss the different approaches to financing the cash-and-carry trade and to demonstrate that prices on nearby Treasury bill futures are set at the margin via this arbitrage. The analysis helps explain much of the seemingly inefficient behavior in the nearby futures markets described in earlier research.

The remainder of the article is structured as follows. Section I describes the arbitrage in more detail and explains why the futures-forward rate differential varies over time. Section II uses daily data to test whether the differential can be explained in terms of speculative arbitrage, and the final section summarizes the results and compares the conclusions with previous studies.

I. NEARBY FUTURES ARBITRAGE

Market efficiency suggests that traders arbitrage away any differences between the forward rate implied by two spot Treasury bills of different maturities and the futures rate. Inequalities suggest the possibility of arbitrage opportunities. Most studies have thus tested for efficiency by constructing forward rates from yield curve data and comparing these rates with coincident futures rates via mean difference *t*-tests.

While we accept the theoretical soundness of the approach, the arbitrage implied by the futures-forward rate comparison is not the predominant one in the marketplace. The calculation of forward rates focuses on the period beginning with the

---

[2] We focus on nearby futures contracts and the 91 days prior to delivery because deliverable Treasury bills are always available in the arbitrage. This provides traders the option to lock-in a profit whenever they finance to term. Prior to the June 1983 Treasury Bill futures cycle, the arbitrage was not always possible farther from delivery. After June 1983, however, the calendar of delivery dates is adjusted to permit the delivery of previously issued one-year bills with 13 weeks remaining life. Vignola and Dale (1980) examine prices beyond 91 days to delivery and do not address the speculative aspects of this pure arbitrage during the time of their investigation. We do not analyze quasi-arbitrage activities or pricing discrepancies in this study.

futures' delivery date and ending 91 days forward. Instead, professional traders and government securities dealers focus on the period from the present to the delivery date of the nearby futures contract and compare a holding period yield with a financing rate.[3]

Consider the following time chart (Figure 1). The time line identifies the current date ($t = 0$), the delivery date of the Treasury bill futures contract T days from the present and the maturity date of the cash bill that matures 91 days following the delivery date, $T + 91$ days from the present. Let R represent the discount rate per $100 of face value and the notations T and $T91$ refer to the underlying instrument with maturity of T and $T + 91$ days from the present. The forward rate (RFOR) on a 91-day contract to begin T days from the present is calculated from the following equation:[4]

$$[1 - RFOR(91/360)] = [1 - RT91(T + 91)/360]/[1 - RT(T/360)] \tag{1}$$

It is normally argued that if the futures and spot markets are in equilibrium and no inefficiencies exist, the futures rate (RFUT) would equal the forward rate from Eq. (1) after adjusting for transactions costs. This comparison suggests that traders focus on 91-day returns available T days from the present. In fact, the true focus of active bill traders covers the interval from the present until the delivery of the nearby futures contract. For example, a trader can effectively lock-in a return by purchasing a cash bill with $T + 91$ days to maturity and simultaneously shorting the nearby future, thus fixing the selling price of the cash bill T days after purchase. This rate of return (RT*) is commonly referred to as the "implied RP rate" and is calculated on a discount basis from Eq. (2):[5]

$$[1 - RT^*(T/360)] = [1 - RT91(T + 91)/360]/[1 - RFUT(91/360)] \tag{2}$$

Traders compare the implied RP rate with a financing rate that is typically the actual RP rate available when Treasury securities are used as collateral in a repurchase agreement. Whenever the implied RP rate exceeds the actual RP rate, traders buy the deliverable bill and short the future as characterized above. Whenever the

Figure 1

Time Chart

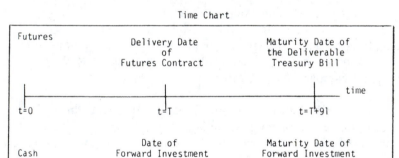

---

[3] Vignola and Dale point out that pure arbitrage is especially applicable to these market participants which, at the time of a 1979 CFTC Survey, held 34% of all outstanding Treasury bill contracts.

[4] For consistency, discount rates are used throughout this article even though some rates are typically quoted on a money market basis. We ignore transactions costs and other influences that may alter effective rates.

[5] Again, in practice, traders tend to calculate this rate on a money market yield basis, but for simplicity, we have chosen to work with a discount rate construction.

actual RP rate exceeds the implied RP rate, traders reverse the transactions by borrowing the deliverable bill via a reverse repurchase agreement, selling it, and going long the nearby futures contract. At delivery, the deliverable Treasury bill is immediately returned to its lender, thereby satisfying the reverse repurchase agreement. In either case any realized difference in the RP rates—implied versus actual—offers a profit opportunity to arbitragers.

With this arbitrage, the futures price is determined at the margin by speculative activity during the three months prior to delivery. Traders buy or sell Treasury bill futures depending on the sign and magnitude of the differential between the implied RP rate and the expected financing rate. Traditional tests of efficiency using forward rates ignore this speculative activity. Instead, it is inferred that futures prices are set relative to 91 day returns available at delivery of the futures contract.

It should be noted, however, that the near-term arbitrage is not entirely risk-free. For example, suppose a trader buys a bill with a six-month remaining life and simultaneously sells a three-month future with a delivery date three-months forward. If interest rates on both the cash and future bill were to fall by 100 basis points, two things would happen: (1) a variation margin payment would be required of $2500 per futures contract and (2) the cash bill would appreciate in value by $5000. The two to one difference reflects a six-month maturity on the cash bill versus a three-month maturity on the future. The added collateral value on the cash instrument, however, might not be realized by the cash-and-carry trader, as the bill has been used in a term RP agreement and it was not in the possession of the trader. The trader must then find additional financing to cover the margin call.

If rates alternatively increased by 100 basis points, the trader would receive $2500 for each futures contract, but *might* be required to add $5000 of collateral to the RP contract. Whether additional financing is required depends upon the margining practice with the RP contract. As these contracts are principal-to-principal agreements, they may be written in a variety of ways. Some allow for marking the collateral to market on a periodic basis as frequently as daily. For others, the terms require only one way margining. When the value of the bills declines, additional collateral is required, but when the bill appreciates, no "excess collateral" is remitted to the "borrower." When financing overnight the asymmetrical valuation effects between the cash bill and the futures can be managed by ratio hedging; that is, by adjusting the ratio of cash bills to futures, the cash-flow asymmetries can be minimized.[6]

An important element of the arbitrage, therefore, is the time for which financing is arranged. If traders finance the transactions to the delivery date using a term RP, they eliminate the risk that borrowing costs might increase over the life of the arbitrage, but they bear the risk of additional costs for financing margin calls. If they finance on a shorter-term basis, they are effectively speculating on future movements in RP rates; however, this strategy may permit better management of cash flow requirements.

When testing for market efficiency, the standard comparison of futures to forward rates is equivalent to a comparison of the implied RP rate with the term RP rate. Our fundamental proposition, however, is that the futures-forward rate dif-

---

[6] For example, taking the six-month cash position against a three-month future, two futures contracts should be used for each million dollars of cash bills. This ratio will decline as the maturity of the cash bill shortens. Thus the cash-and-carry trade becomes an actively managed hedge, where the risks of asymmetrical cash flow considerations can be minimized.

ferential largely reflects traders' practices of financing cash positions on an overnight basis as opposed to any market inefficiencies. In essence, the nearby futures price varies with the overnight RP rate. We hypothesize that whenever the term RP rate is greater (less) than the overnight RP rate (RON), the futures-forward rate differential is positive (negative) with the magnitudes directly related.[7]

In addition, the relationship between the two differentials is likely to be time dependent. The further away is delivery at the initiation of the contracts, the greater is the risk that overnight RP rates will vary prior to delivery—and the wider spread it takes between RP rates to induce traders to speculate.

II. EMPIRICAL EVIDENCE

The empirical analysis consists of an examination of the relationships between actual Treasury bill futures rates and forward rates constructed using different assumed financing rates in the arbitrage. The forward rates reflect either assumed term financing or overnight financing. First, we duplicate previous work by testing for the equality of nearby futures rates and corresponding forward rates from Eq. (1) calculated from the term-structure of Treasury yields. This is equivalent to testing whether term RP finance can explain the difference in futures and forward rates. We then construct adjusted forward rates (RFOR*) by substituting the compounded value of the overnight RP rate (RON*) for RT in Eq. (1) such that

$$[1 - RFOR*(91/360)] = [1 - RT91(T + 91)/360]/(1 - RON*(T/360)) \qquad (3)$$

and we retest for equality between RFUT and RFOR*.[8] RFOR* represents the forward rate that is consistent with overnight financing of securities dealers' arbitrage. A zero difference provides evidence that the futures contract is priced according to the cash and carry arbitrage. In every instance we segment the analysis in terms of the number of days prior to delivery of the nearby futures contract.

The data employed are daily closing quotations for spot and future rates from September 1977 through June 1982. This period covers 18 different cash/futures combinations. Futures rates are based on closing settlement prices from the *Daily Information Bulletin* provided by the International Monetary Market. Rates on outstanding Treasury bills and repurchase agreements are offered rates provided by the Bank of America via Data Resources, Inc. The calculations of RFOR and RFOR* reflect the practice of next day settlement for Treasury bills such that the daily quoted rate actually applies to the following day's transactions.

Table I presents the results of the mean difference *t*-tests. Initially, we analyze the arithmetic differences between futures rates on nearby contracts and the associated forward rates calculated from Eq. (1). Summary statistics are provided in the top part of Table I where the *t*-values reported reflect the hypothesis that the futures rate equals the forward rate. The first column presents the results for the entire sample. The other five columns report similar results for the sample segmented according to the number of days to delivery. Interestingly, the mean difference is zero nearest to delivery, becomes negative after 14 days, and grows increasingly larger

---

[7] Our analysis implicitly assumes that traders expect overnight RP rates to remain constant to term. This treatment is consistent with other studies, such as Hamburger and Platt (1975) which conclude that investors largely act as if they expect future short-term interest rates to equal current short-term rates.

[8] The compounded overnight RP rate (RON*) is calculated as:

$$RON* = (360/T)[1 - (1 - RON/360)^T].$$

Table I
SUMMARY STATISTICS FOR ARITHMETIC DIFFERENCES: FUTURES RATES MINUS FORWARD RATES CALCULATED FROM EQ. (1); DAILY DATA FOR SEPTEMBER 1977 THROUGH JUNE 1982[a]

	Number of Days to Delivery of Futures Contract					
Statistic	Entire Sample	< 15	15-29	30-44	45-59	> 60
Mean	−0.314	−0.006	−0.166	−0.330	−0.434	−0.484
Standard deviation	0.365	0.232	0.288	0.296	0.316	0.387
Number of observations	1126	189	191	194	207	345
t-value	−28.8[b]	−0.3	−8.0[b]	−15.5[b]	−19.8[b]	−23.2[b]

[a] All variables are measured in percentages.
[b] Significantly different from zero at the 1% level.

in absolute terms farther from delivery. The negative means are not surprising given the inverted yield curve that existed over most of the sample period. During that time, overnight RP rates typically exceeded term RP rates so that futures rates were lower than the forward rates inherent in the term-structure. These results would seem to support earlier work that indicated some evidence of market inefficiency.

Similar data are presented in Table II except that the forward rate (RFOR*) used in the comparison is calculated by substituting the compounded overnight RP rate for RT in Eq. (1). In effect we are examining whether the futures rate is determined by RON* as traders generally finance their positions on a continuous overnight basis. If this is the case, the computed differential between RFUT and RFOR*

Table II
SUMMARY STATISTICS FOR ARITHMETIC DIFFERENCES: FUTURES RATES MINUS FORWARD RATES CALCULATED USING THE COMPOUNDED OVERNIGHT RP RATE; DAILY DATA FOR SEPTEMBER 1977 THROUGH JUNE 1982[a]

	Number of Days to Delivery of Futures Contract					
Statistic	Entire Sample	< 15	15-29	30-44	45-59	> 60
Mean	0.030	0.054	0.044	0.013	−0.001	0.037
Standard deviation	0.479	0.212	0.223	0.287	0.309	0.771
Number of observations	1126	189	191	194	207	345
t-value	2.1	3.5[b]	2.7[b]	0.6	−0.1	0.9

[a] All variables are measured in percentages.
[b] Significantly different from zero at the 1% level.

Table III
SUMMARY STATISTICS FOR ARITHMETIC DIFFERENCES: FUTURES RATES MINUS FORWARD RATES CALCULATED USING THE OVERNIGHT RP RATE: DAILY DATA FOR SEPTEMBER 1980 THROUGH JUNE 1982[a]

Statistic	Entire Sample	< 15	15–29	30–44	45–59	> 60
		Number of Days to Delivery of Futures Contract				
Mean	0.041	0.072	0.037	−0.027	0.028	0.072
Standard deviation	0.640	0.288	0.271	0.351	0.379	1.053
Number of observations	588	100	101	100	109	178
t-value	1.6	2.5	1.4	−0.8	0.8	0.9

[a] All variables are measured in percentages.

[b] Significantly different from zero at the 1% level.

should be much smaller than the differential between RFUT and RFOR. In fact, in all cases the mean differences are much smaller using the overnight RP rate than the term RP rate. Moreover the contention of market efficiency generally is supported by the data. The mean rate differential is not significantly different from zero over the entire sample period, but significant differences do appear when data are restricted to less than 30-days prior to the delivery day of the futures contract. These differences may be due to the time difference between the collection of the cash market rate and the future market rate on any given day (roughly 1½ hours). With compounding, such a temporal difference may be more important near the delivery date but less so as the delivery day extends into the future.

Importantly, when the sample was restricted to the period from January 1980 to June 1982, a period when Federal Reserve policy targeted bank reserves and permitted greater interest rate volatility than previously, our results were stronger. As demonstrated in Table III, the mean differences were not significantly different from zero for the entire sample, as well as for each of the time intervals prior to delivery.[9] The results further suggest that one need not appeal to such considerations as transaction costs, variation margin uncertainty, tax treatment, etc. in order to explain futures prices.[10]

The importance of these results is magnified by recent changes in delivery dates for Treasury Bill futures. Except on rare occasions prior to the March 1983 contract, aribitrage opportunities for specific cash/futures combinations were only

[9] The results from September 1977 through December 1979 were comparable to those in Table II.

[10] Using data from 1976 through 1978, Vignola and Dale (1980) demonstrated that mean price differences between futures prices and similarly constructed forward prices cycled around zero. Their study, in contrast, used the federal funds rate as a proxy for overnight carrying costs. We duplicated their tests for the five contracts that overlapped in our sample and obtained comparable results. Comparing price data, actual December 1977 and March 1978 futures prices exceeded projected prices assuming overnight RP financing by an average of $154 and $22, respectively. For the next three contracts, the actual futures prices were $82, $150, and $151 less than the projected prices. These estimates have the same sign as Vignola and Dale's but differ in magnitude. This reflects significant differences in the Federal funds rate and overnight RP rates during each contract period.

available for about 90 days, with a cash market instrument that declined in maturity from, at most, 183 days and the nearby futures contract. Beginning June 1983, the Treasury Bill delivery cycle was altered so that any original one-year bill could satisfy delivery requirements. Thus, the cash-and-carry arbitrage can potentially be extended to nine months. It seems likely that corresponding futures rates on these contracts will come under a greater discipline reflecting this new arbitrage opportunity. Previous studies that have shown significant differences in futures and forward rates on contracts farther from delivery generally have not recognized that the cash and carry trade has not been available.

III. CONCLUSIONS

This study examines the cash-and-carry trade employed by U.S. government securities dealers to explain why futures rates on nearby Treasury bill contracts differ from corresponding forward rates implied by the Treasury yield curve. The nearby contract is the only one for which the actual deliverable bill has been available. Mean difference t-tests are used to demonstrate that futures rates are determined largely by overnight carrying costs. Specifically, futures rates calculated on the basis of compounded overnight RP rates do not differ significantly from observed futures rates on nearby contracts. Thus the nearby futures market is efficient. The availability of deliverable bills on more distant futures contracts suggests that corresponding arbitrage activity will foster greater efficiency in these distant-month contracts than has been found by earlier researchers.

Appreciation is expressed to Robert Klassen for providing computer assistance.

Bibliography

Arak, M. (1980): "Taxes, Treasury Bills, and Treasury Bill Futures," Federal Reserve Bank of New York (March).

Capozza, D., and Cornell, B. (1979): "Treasury Bill Pricing in the Spot and Futures Market," *Review of Economics and Statistics* (November).

Chow, B., and Brophy, D. (1982): "Treasury Bill Futures Market: A Formulation and Interpretation," *The Journal of Futures Markets* (Winter).

Hamburger, M., and Platt, E. (1975): "The Expectations Hypothesis and the Efficiency of the Treasury Bill Market," *The Review of Economics and Statistics* (May).

Kane, E. (1980): "Market-Incompleteness and Divergences Between Forward and Future Interest Rates," *Journal of Finance* (May).

Lang, R., and Rasche, R. (1978): "A Comparison of Yields on Futures Contracts and Implied Forward Rates," *Federal Reserve Bank of St. Louis Review* (December).

Morgan, G. (1978): "Pricing Treasury Bill Futures Contracts," Comptroller of the Currency (June).

Poole, W. (1978): "Using T-Bill Futures to Gauge Interest-Rate Expectations," *Federal Reserve Bank of San Francisco Economic Review* (Spring).

Rendleman, R., and Carrabini, C. (1979): "The Efficiency of the Treasury Bill Futures Market," *Journal of Finance* (September).

Vignola, A., and Dale, C. (1980): "The Efficiency of the Treasury Bill Futures Market: An Analysis of Alternative Specifications," *Journal of Financial Research* (Fall).

Working, H. (1949): "The Theory of Price of Storage," *American Economic Review* (December).

Article 9

Two-State Option Pricing

RICHARD J. RENDLEMAN, JR. and BRIT J. BARTTER[*]

I. Introduction

IN THIS PAPER WE present an elemental two-state option pricing model (TSOPM) which is mathematically simple, yet can be used to solve many complex option pricing problems.[1] In contrast to widely accepted option pricing models which require solutions to stochastic differential equations, our model is derived algebraically. First we present the mathematics of the model and illustrate its application to the simplest type of option pricing problem. Next, we discuss the statistical properties of the model and show how the parameters of the model can be estimated to solve practical option pricing problems. Finally, we apply the model to the pricing of European and American put and call options on both non-dividend and dividend paying stocks. Elsewhere, we have applied the model to the valuation of the debt and equity of a firm with coupon paying debt in its capital structure [9], the valuation of options on debt securities [7], and the pricing of fixed rate bank loan commitments [1, 2]. In the Appendix we derive the Black-Scholes [3] model using the two-state approach.

II. The Two-State Option Pricing Model

Consider a stock whose price can either advance or decline during the next period. Let H_t^+ and H_t^- represent the returns per dollar invested in the stock if the price rises (the + state) or falls (the − state), respectively, from time $t − 1$ to time t, and V_t^+ and V_t^- the corresponding end-of-period values of the option. With the assumption that the prices of the stock and its option follow a two-state process, it is possible to form a riskless portfolio with the two securities. [See Black and Scholes [3] for the continuous time analog of riskless hedging.] Since the end-of-period value of the portfolio is certain, the option should be priced so that the portfolio will yield the riskless interest rate.

The riskless portfolio is formed by investing one dollar in the stock and

---

[*] Both Assistant Professors of Finance, Graduate School of Management, Northwestern University.
[1] Since the original writing of this paper, the authors have learned that a similar procedure has been suggested by Rubinstein [10], Sharpe [11], and Cox, Ross, and Rubinstein [5].

purchasing α units of the option at a price of P_{t-1}. The value of α is chosen so that the portfolio payoffs are the same in both states, or

$$H_t^+ + \alpha V_t^+ = H_t^- + \alpha V_t^-. \tag{1}$$

Solving for α we obtain the number of units of the option to be held in the portfolio per \$1 invested in the stock.

$$\alpha = \frac{H_t^- - H_t^+}{V_t^+ - V_t^-} \tag{2}$$

A negative value of α implies that the option is sold short (written) with the proceeds being used to partially fund the purchase of the stock.

The time $t - 1$ value of portfolio is $1 + \alpha P_{t-1}$. The end-of-period value is given by either side of (1). Discounting the left-hand side by the riskless interest rate, R, and setting the discounted value equal to the present value of the portfolio, a pricing equation for the option is obtained.

$$1 + \alpha P_{t-1} = \frac{H_t^+ + \alpha V_t^+}{1 + R}. \tag{3}$$

Substituting the value of α from (2) into (3), the price of the option can be solved in terms of its end-of-period values.

$$P_{t-1} = \frac{V_t^+(1 + R - H_t^-) + V_t^-(H_t^+ - 1 - R)}{(H_t^+ - H_t^-)(1 + R)} \tag{4}$$

Equation 4 is a recursive relationship that can be applied at any time $t - 1$ to determine the price of the option as a function of its value at time t.

Note that in equation (4) we make a notational distinction between an option's value (V) and its price (P). Assuming that an investor will exercise an option when it is in his best interest to do so,

$$V_t = \text{MAX}[P_t, \text{VEXER}_t], \tag{5}$$

where VEXER_t is the value of exercising the option at time t.

The distinguishing feature among American and European puts and calls is in the definition of their exercisable values. American options can be exercised at any time whereas European options can only be exercised at maturity. Calls are options to buy stock at a set price whereas puts are options to sell. Letting S_t represent the time t price of the stock, X the option's exercise price, and T the maturity date of the option, we obtain

American:

Call $\text{VEXER}_t = S_t - X$ for all t,
Put $\text{VEXER}_t = X - S_t$ for all t,

European:

Call $\text{VEXER}_t = S_t - X$ for $t = T$
  $\text{VEXER}_t = 0$ for $t < T$,
Put $\text{VEXER}_t = X - S_t$ for $t = T$
  $\text{VEXER}_t = 0$ for $t < T$.

Recognizing that for both American and Euopopean puts and calls

$$P_T = 0, \tag{7}$$

since there is no value associated with maintaining an option position beyond maturity, (4–7) represent the formal specification of the two-state model. Through repeated application of (4), subject to (5–7), one can begin at an option's maturity date and recursively solve for its current price.

To illustrate the model, consider a call option on a stock with an exercise price of $100. The current price of the stock is $100 and the possible prices of the stock on the option's maturity date are $110 and $90, implying $H_1^+ = 1.10$ and $H_1^- = .90$. Assuming that the option is exercised if the stock price rises to $110 and is allowed to expire worthless if the stock price falls to $90, the present prices and the end-of-period payoffs of the stock and option can be represented by the following two-branched tree diagram.

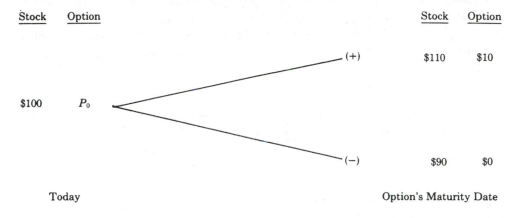

If an investor purchases the stock and writes two call options, the end-of-period portfolio value will be $90 in both states. Equivalently, for every $1 invested in the stock, a riskless hedge requires that $\alpha = (.90 - 1.10)/(10 - 0) = -.02$, or that .02 options are written. Assuming a risk free interest rate of 5%, the present value of the riskless portfolio should be $90/1.05 or $85.71 to ensure no riskless arbitrage opportunities between the stock-option portfolio and a riskless security. Since the riskless portfolio involves a $100 investment in the stock which is partially offset by the two short options, an option price of $7.14 is required to obtain an $85.71 portfolio value. The option price can also be obtained directly from (4):

$$P_0 = \frac{\$10(1 + .05 - .90) + \$0(1.10 - 1.05)}{(1.10 - .90)(1 + .05)}$$

$$= \frac{\$10(.15)}{.2(1.05)} = \$7.14.$$

Although this example is unrealistic, it nevertheless illustrates two of the most important features of the TSOPM. We can observe that the option price does not depend upon the probabilities of the up (+) or down (−) states occurring or the risk preferences of the investor. Two investors who agreed that the stock price is in equilibrium, but had different probability beliefs and preferences, would both view $7.14 as the equilibrium option price. As long as they agreed on the magnitudes of the underlying stock's holding period returns (H^+ and H^-), they would agree on the price of the option.

The example can be extended to a multiperiod framework in which the price of the underlying stock can take on only one of two values at any time t given the price of the stock at $t - 1$. Consider the case in which a non-dividend paying stock's holding period return is 1.175 in all up states and .85 in all down states. Given an initial stock price of $100, these return parameters imply the four-period price pattern shown in Figure 1.

Assume that we wish to value a call option which matures at the end of period 4 and has an exercise price of $100. Given a riskless interest rate of 1.25% per period (5% per year, assuming a one-year maturity), the sequence of option values corresponding to the stock prices in Figure 1 is given in Figure 2.

In Figure 2 the prices $90.61 and $37.89 are the values of the call obtainable by exercising at maturity. For those states at maturity where the price of the stock falls below the exercise price of $100, the option expires worthless. Each of the time 3 option prices is obtained from (4). Similarly, the prices at time 2, 1, and 0 are obtained by recursive application of (4) resulting in a current call option price of $14.41.

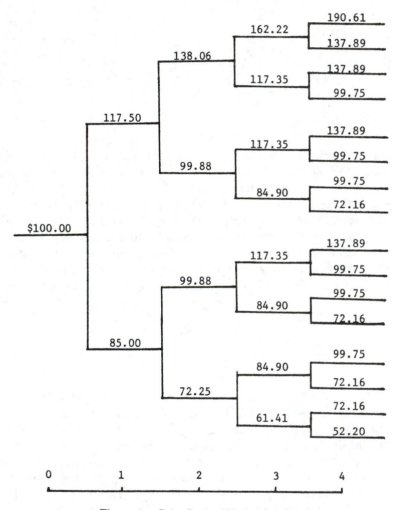

Figure 1.   Price Path of Underlying Stock

Although the above example considers only four periods of time, one can always choose an interval of time to recognize price changes that more realistically captures expected stock price behavior. In Section IV we demonstrate the sensitivity of option prices to the choice of the time differencing interval under the assumption that H^+ and H^- are chosen to hold the mean and variance of the distribution of stock price changes constant over the life of the option. In the Appendix, a generalized formula for the multiperiod case is derived for the situation where R, H^+, and H^- are constant. This formula is extended under the assumption that the two-state process evolves over an infinitesimally small interval of time.

III. Operationalizing the TSOPM

In the TSOPM, the only parameters describing the probability distribution of returns of the underlying stock are the magnitudes of the holding period returns, H^+ and H^-. Although our examples assume that H^+ and H^- remain constant

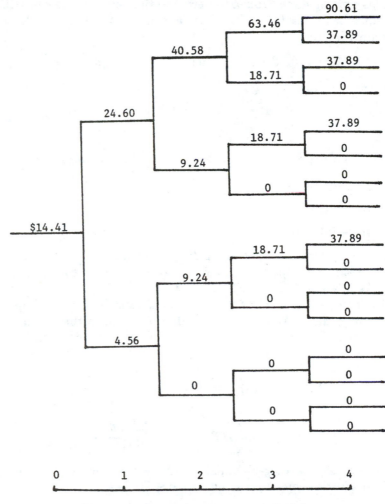

Figure 2. Price Path of European Call Option

through time, this is not a necessary assumption for the implementation of the model. Thus, if one can simply specify the pattern of H^+ and H^- through time, it is possible to value the option.

The TSOPM can be used as a method for obtaining exact values of options when the magnitudes of H^+ and H^- are known in advance. As a practical matter, the values of H^+ and H^- will not be known, but must be estimated. For example, if the probabilities associated with the occurrence of the + and − states remain stable over time along with the magnitudes of H^+ and H^-, then the two-state model implies a binomial distribution for the returns of the stock. It is well known that both the Normal and Poisson distributions can be viewed as limiting cases of the Binomial. Thus, the Binomial distribution can be employed as an approximation procedure for deriving option prices when the actual distribution of returns is assumed to be either Normal or Poisson. We will illustrate how the values of H^+ and H^- can be determined when the binomial distribution is used as an approximation to the lognormal distribution.

If the magnitudes of the relative price changes in our model and their associated probabilities remain stable from one period to the next, then the distribution of returns which is generated after T time periods will follow a log-binomial distribution with a mean

$$\mu = T[h^+ \theta + h^-(1 - \theta)] = T[(h^+ - h^-)\theta + h^-], \tag{8}$$

and variance

$$\sigma^2 = T(h^+ - h^-)^2\theta(1 - \theta), \tag{9}$$

where:

$\theta =$ the probability that the price of the stock will rise

in any period,

$h^+ = \ln(H^+),$

$h^- = \ln(H^-).$

In the last four-period example where $H^+ = 1.175$ and $H^- = .85$, the value of σ and μ for the entire four periods would be .324 and −.003, respectively, if a value of θ equal to .5 is assumed.

It is also possible to determine the values of H^+ and H^- that are implied by the values of μ, σ, θ, and T. By solving (8) and (9) in terms of these parameters and recognizing that $H = \exp(h)$, we obtain the following implied values of H^+ and H^-

$$H^+ = \exp\left(\mu/T + (\sigma/\sqrt{T})\sqrt{\frac{(1 - \theta)}{\theta}}\right) \tag{10}$$

$$H^- = \exp\left(\mu/T - (\sigma/\sqrt{T})\sqrt{\frac{\theta}{(1 - \theta)}}\right) \tag{11}$$

As T becomes large, the log-binomial distribution will approximate a lognormal distribution with the same mean and variance.

IV. Applications of the Model

European Puts and Calls on Non-Dividend Paying Stocks

In this section we price European put and call options on non-dividend paying stocks using the two-state model as an approximation procedure for the case in which stock prices are assumed to follow a lognormal distribution.[2] Given the assumptions of no dividends and lognormal returns, the Black-Scholes [3] model provides the exact values for both types of options, thereby serving as a benchmark to assess the accuracy of the two-state model as a numerical procedure.

In Table 1, we present prices of one-year European put and call options with exercise prices of $75, $100, and $125 assuming a current stock price of $100. The riskless interest rate is assumed to be 5% per year. To conform with the Black-Scholes model, continuous compounding of interest is assumed. Thus, $R = e^{.05/N} - 1$, where N is the number of time intervals per year employed in the analysis. The values of H^+ and H^- are chosen so that the annual standard deviation of the logarithmic return is .324 as in the previous four-period example. The expected value of the logarithmic return is assumed to take on values of .5, .1, 0, −.1 and −.5 per year, and a value of θ equal to .5 is assumed. Finally, option prices are calculated by partitioning the year into 12, 52, and 100 time periods.

Consider the panel of Table 1 in which the stock's growth rate (μ) is assumed to be 0%. When the year is divided into 100 time intervals, the two-state prices of all the put and call options are quite close to their corresponding Black-Scholes prices. With these two parameters ($\mu = 0$, $T = 100$), the greatest absolute percentage difference between the Black-Scholes and two-state prices is .6%. Even if only 12 time differencing intervals are assumed, the two-state and Black-Scholes prices are remarkably close.

For growth rates of 10% and −10%, the two-state prices do not appear to be significantly different from those obtained when a zero growth rate is assumed. Thus, within this range of growth rates, the option price does not appear to be significantly affected by the growth rate.

If extreme growth rates are assumed ($\mu = .5$ and $\mu = −.5$), the two-state model does not appear to provide an accurate approximation to the Black-Scholes price for low T values. However, for 100 time intervals, the two-state and Black-Scholes prices are reasonably close.

The entries in Table 1 reveal that the option price is slightly dependent upon the stock's growth rate. In addition, if θ were varied, we would also discover a slight dependence on investor probability beliefs. These findings seem to contradict the earlier observation that two-state prices are independent of both investor preferences (which would be revealed through μ) and probability beliefs.

This dependence results from the fact that H^+ and H^- are chosen in the two-state model to conform with a given continuous distribution. Since the two-state model is only an approximation, the values of μ and θ implicit in the continuous distribution may be reflected in the two-state solution. In the limit as $T \to \infty$, the two distributions will be identical, and therefore, preferences and probabilities

---

[2] See Brennan and Schwartz [4] and Parkinson [7] for descriptions of alternative numerical procedures for solving option pricing equations.

Table 1

Comparison Between TSOPM and Black-Scholes Option Prices[a]
(European)

μ	X	T	TSOPM Call	TSOPM Put	Black-Scholes Model Call	Black-Scholes Model Put	Percent Difference[b] Call	Percent Difference[b] Put
.5	75	12	29.94	1.28	30.74	2.08	− 2.6	−38.7
		52	30.57	1.91			− .5	− 8.2
		100	30.65	1.99			− .3	− 4.6
	100	12	14.23	9.35	15.14	10.26	− 6.0	− 8.9
		52	14.95	10.07			− 1.3	− 1.9
		100	15.03	10.16			− .7	− 1.1
	125	12	6.05	24.96	6.58	25.48	− 7.9	− 2.1
		52	6.38	25.28			− 3.0	− .8
		100	6.50	25.41			− 1.1	− .3
.1	75	12	30.58	1.93	30.74	2.08	− .5	− 7.6
		52	30.74	2.09			0	0
		100	30.72	2.06			− .1	− 1.1
	100	12	15.37	10.50	15.14	10.26	+ 1.5	+ 2.3
		52	15.12	10.25			− .1	− .2
		100	15.17	10.29			+ .2	+ .3
	125	12	6.78	25.69	6.58	25.48	+ 3.1	+ .8
		52	6.62	25.53			+ .7	+ .2
		100	6.57	25.47			− .1	0
.0	75	12	30.85	2.19	30.74	2.08	− .4	+ 5.2
		52	30.74	2.09			0	0
		100	30.75	2.10			0	+ .6
	100	12	14.88	10.00	15.14	10.26	− 1.7	− 2.5
		52	15.08	10.20			− .4	− .6
		100	15.11	10.23			− .2	− .3
	125	12	6.55	25.46	6.58	25.48	− .3	− .1
		52	6.62	25.52			+ .7	+ .2
		100	6.60	25.50			+ .3	+ .1
−.1	75	12	30.60	1.94	30.74	2.08	− .5	− 7.0
		52	30.73	2.07			− .1	− .8
		100	30.74	2.08			0	− .3
	100	12	15.31	10.43	15.14	10.26	+ 1.1	+ 1.6
		52	15.11	10.23			− .2	− .3
		100	15.16	10.28			+ .1	+ .2
	125	12	6.55	25.43	6.58	25.48	− .8	− .2
		52	6.62	25.48			− .1	0
		100	6.60	25.43			− .8	− .2
−.5	75	12	30.25	1.59	30.74	2.08	− 1.6	−23.6
		52	30.65	2.00			− .3	− 4.2
		100	30.69	2.04			− .2	− 2.4
	100	12	13.85	8.97	15.14	10.26	− 8.6	−12.6
		52	14.87	10.00			− 1.8	− 2.6
		100	14.99	10.12			− 1.0	− 1.5
	125	12	4.65	23.55	6.58	25.48	−29.4	− 7.6
		52	6.12	25.02			− 7.0	− 1.8
		100	6.36	25.27			− 3.4	− .8

[a] $S_0 = 100$, $R = e^{.05/N} - 1$, $\sigma = .324$, $\theta = .5$. In this table, $N = T$ in all cases.

[b] Percent difference between the TSOPM and Black-Scholes (BS) prices is computed according to: (TSOPM-BS)/BS, rounded to the nearest one-tenth of one percent.

should not be reflected in option prices. In the Appendix, we derive the Black-Scholes equation using the two-state model. As expected, neither the growth rate nor probabilities enter the final solution. For practical applications, the two-state model appears to provide an accurate approximation to the Black-Scholes model if 100 or more time differencing intervals are assumed along with any reasonable growth rate. As we show below, however, it is possible to select a growth rate that will closely approximate the value of μ that minimizes the error in the two-state approximation.

Finding the Best Approximation

According to equation (A.11) in the Appendix, the price of a call option in the two-state model can be stated in terms of two binomial pseudo probability distributions. In each distribution, ψ and ϕ are the pseudo probabilities that the price of the underlying stock will rise. These pseudo probabilities are not necessarily equal to the true probability, θ, but nevertheless, the mathematics of probability theory are still applicable.

According to the Laplace-DeMoivre Limit Theorem, it can be shown that the best fit between the binomial and normal distributions occurs when the binomial probability (or pseudo probability in this case) is $\frac{1}{2}$. As a general rule, ψ and ϕ will not be identical. Therefore, it will usually be impossible to simultaneously set both pseudo probabilities to $\frac{1}{2}$. However, since $\psi = \phi(H^+/(1 + R))$, and the term in parenthesis will generally be close to unity, the parameters of the underlying distribution that sets ϕ to $\frac{1}{2}$ will set ψ to approximately $\frac{1}{2}$.

By expanding ϕ in Taylor's series, we find that ϕ is approximately $\frac{1}{2}$ when

$$
\mu = \frac{r - \frac{1}{2}\sigma\sqrt{T}\left[\sqrt{\frac{1-\theta}{\theta}} - \sqrt{\frac{\theta}{1-\theta}}\right] - \frac{1}{4}\sigma^2\left[\frac{1-\theta}{\theta} + \frac{\theta}{1-\theta}\right]}{\left[1 + \left(\sqrt{\frac{1-\theta}{\theta}} - \sqrt{\frac{\theta}{1-\theta}}\right)\Big/\sqrt{T}\right]}. \tag{12}
$$

If the true probability, θ, is $\frac{1}{2}$, this expression simplifies to[3]

$$
\mu = r - \frac{1}{2}\sigma^2. \tag{13}
$$

For the parameters underlying Table 1, we find that (approximately) the best two-state approximation occurs when $\mu = -.002488$. The reasonableness of this result is confirmed by the $\mu = 0$ panel of Table 1.[4]

[3] We wish to acknowledge the referee for suggesting that the best approximation would occur if μ $= r - \frac{1}{2}\sigma^2$.

[4] We repeated the analysis of Table 1 by setting μ to $-.002488$. Although the prices were almost identical to those obtained by setting μ to zero, they were slightly more accurate.

Pricing American Puts and Non-Dividend Paying Stocks

Table 2 shows the prices of American put options along with the value of the premature exercise privilege for the same parameters underlying Table 1, except that only a zero growth rate is assumed. Prices of American call options are not shown since, with no dividends, there will be no added value associated with the ability to exercise the call prior to maturity (see Merton [6]). Prices are shown for put options with exercise prices of 75, 100, and 125 under the assumption that the time differencing interval is 12, 52, 100, and 500 times per year. The differencing interval of 500 times is used as a proxy for the continuous case.

The prices in Table 2 suggest that the two-state model provides a fairly accurate approximation to the value of the premature exercise privilege, even for T values as low as 12. For all practical purposes, 100 time periods appears to provide sufficient accuracy for determining actual American put prices using the two-state model. For the options in Table 2, the prices obtained when $T = 100$ are within $.01 of the $T = 500$ prices.

American and European Puts and Calls on Dividend Paying Stocks

If a stock pays a dividend, it may sometimes pay to prematurely exercise a call option on the stock before the dividend is paid rather than hold the option when the stock is almost certain to decline in value. Thus, one would expect American call options on dividend paying stocks to be worth more than their European counterparts. On the other hand, if a stock is expected to pay a dividend, it is less likely that an American put option will be exercised prematurely since the stock is likely to decrease in value when the dividend is paid due to the ex-dividend effect. The Black-Scholes model has been extended by Merton [6] to price

Table 2

American Put Prices Using the TSOPM[a]

Option Parameters			American Put	Dollar Value of Premature Exercise[b]
μ	X	T		
.0	75	12	2.26	$ .05
		52	2.15	.06
		100	2.16	.06
		500	2.15	.07
	100	12	10.65	.65
		52	10.75	.55
		100	10.77	.54
		500	10.78	.52
	125	12	27.42	1.96
		52	27.40	1.88
		100	27.38	1.88
		500	27.37	1.89

[a] $S_0 = 100$, $R = e^{.05/T} - 1$, $\sigma = .324$, $\theta = .5$.

[b] Dollar value of premature exercise is computed as:

TSOPM [American] Put Price $-$ TSOPM [European] Put Price, assuming $\mu = .0$ in both cases.

European puts and calls when dividends are paid continuously at a constant rate. This model is used in Table 3 as a benchmark for determining the accuracy of the two-state model for pricing European puts and calls.

In Table 3 the prices of European and American puts and calls are shown under the assumption that the underlying stock is expected to pay a quarterly dividend at an annual rate of 4%. The assumptions underlying Tables 1 and 2 are maintained.

The two-state prices of European puts and calls are all within $.03 of the corresponding dividend-adjusted Black-Scholes-Merton prices when the life of the options are partitioned into 100 time intervals. Therefore, with dividends, the two-state model appears to provide an accurate approximation to the lognormal model.

As one would expect, the ability to exercise an American call option on a dividend paying stock prior to maturity can carry a significant premium. For example, for $X = 75$ and $T = 100$, the difference between the prices of American and European calls is $1.03. This premium declines as the option's exercise price increases.

In contrast to the call option, the payment of a 4% dividend significantly lowers the value associated with the ability to exercise the put option prematurely. For example, for $T = 100$ and $X = 100$, the premature exercise premium is $.54 for a non-dividend paying stock but only $.16 if the stock pays a quarterly dividend at an annual rate of 4%.

V. Conclusions

This paper develops a simple two-state option pricing model and demonstrates the application of the model to several complex option pricing problems. Although the mathematics of the model are quite simple, especially when compared to the more conventional continuous time approach, the economics of both approaches to option pricing are essentially the same. Thus, the two-state approach opens the door to the understanding of modern option pricing theory without the added complications associated with the solutions to stochastic differential equations.

In addition to its pedagogic features, the two-state approach can be used as a numerical procedure for solving continuous time option pricing problems for which closed form solutions are unattainable. Moreover, the Black-Scholes equation can be derived from the two-state model as a special case. Admittedly, the mathematics of this derivation are as difficult as stochastic calculus itself, yet one need not carry the two-state model to its continuous limit to derive many interesting insights into both theoretical and practical applications of modern option pricing theory.

Appendix

Derivation of the Continuous Time Version of the TSOPM

In this Appendix we determine the value of a European call option, w_0, using the TSOPM, assuming that the interval of time over which price changes in the underlying stock are recognized is infinitesimally small. This is equivalent to

Table 3

Comparison Between TSOPM and Black-Scholes-Merton Option Prices Including Dividends[a]

	Option Parameters			TSOPM European Prices		TSOPM American Prices		Dollar Value of Premature Exercise[d]		Black-Scholes-Merton Prices[c]	
μ	X	T	INTVL[b]	Call	Put	Call	Put	Call	Put	Call	Put
.0	75	12	3	27.37	2.66	28.15	2.67	$ .78	$ .01	27.30	2.58
		52	13	27.32	2.59	28.29	2.61	.97	.02		
		100	25	27.30	2.59	28.33	2.60	1.03	.01		
	100	12	3	12.85	11.92	13.14	12.10	.29	.18	12.78	11.84
		52	13	12.83	11.89	13.33	12.05	.50	.16		
		100	25	12.80	11.86	13.35	12.02	.55	.16		
	125	12	3	5.40	28.24	5.52	28.93	.12	.69	5.27	28.11
		52	13	5.22	28.07	5.50	28.74	.28	.67		
		100	25	5.24	28.09	5.53	28.75	.29	.66		

[a] $S = 100$, $R = e^{.06/T} - 1$, $\sigma = .324$, $\theta = .5$ and annual dividend yield = .04 for all contracts.

[b] For $T = 12$, a dividend interval (INTVL) of 3 means that a dividend payment is made every 3rd period. If the entire time horizon is one year, then each (T, INTVL) pair implies a typical quarterly dividend payment.

[c] Dividend adjusted Black-Scholes prices are computed by substituting $100 (1 - .04/4)^4$ for the stock price in the Black-Scholes model.

[d] Dollar value of premature exercise is computed as: [TSOPM American price] − [TSOPM European price].

allowing the number of time differencing intervals to become infinite over the fixed life of the option. Before deriving the continuous time version of the model, we will develop a valuation equation for the discrete time case under the assumptions that the distribution of returns of the stock is stationary over time and the stock pays no dividends.

The Discrete Time Model

When the option matures, there will be a one-to-one correspondence between the value of the option and the value of its underlying stock. The value of a call option at maturity, w_T, is $\max(0, S_T - X)$, where S_T is the value of the underlying stock at the maturity date, T, and X is the exercise price of the option. At the period prior to the option's maturity date, the value of the option is given by

$$w_{T-1} = \frac{w_T^+(1 + R - H^-) + w_T^-(H^+ - (1 + R))}{(H^+ - H^-)(1 + R)}. \tag{A.1}$$

Similarly, the value of the option two periods prior to maturity is

$$w_{T-2} = \frac{w_{T-1}^+(1 + R - H^-) + w_{T-1}^-(H^+ - (1 + R))}{(H^+ - H^-)(1 + R)}. \tag{A.2}$$

By substituting equation (A.1) into (A.2) and noting that the term w_t^{+-} is the option value at maturity, given that the price of the underlying stock advances in period $T - 1$ and falls in period T, the value of the option at period $T - 2$ becomes:

$$w_{T-2} = \frac{(w_T^{++}(1 + R - H^-) + w_T^{+-}(H^+ - (1 + R)))(1 + R - H^-)}{(H^+ - H^-)^2(1 + R)^2}$$
$$+ \frac{(w_T^{-+}(1 + R - H^-) + w_T^{--}(H^+ - (1 + R)))(H^+ - (1 + R))}{(H^+ - H^-)^2(1 + R)^2}. \tag{A.3}$$

Equation (A.3) can be simplified by noting that $w_T^{+-} = w_T^{-+}$, since the value of the underlying stock at maturity will be the same whether or not it advances first and then declines, or declines first and then advances. With this substitution, equation (A.3) can be restated as:

w_{T-2}

$$= \frac{w_T^{++}(1 + R - H^-)^2 + 2w_T^{+-}(H^+ - (1 + R))(1 + R - H^-) + w_T^{--}(H^+ - (1 + R))^2}{(H^+ - H^-)^2(1 + R)^2}. \tag{A.4}$$

If this same type of procedure is repeated for a total of T periods, there will always be $T + 1$ terms in the numerator of the option valuation equation. After T periods, there are exactly $\binom{T}{0}$ ways that a sequence of T pluses can occur, there are $\binom{T}{1}$ ways that $T - 1$ pluses can occur along with one minus, there are $\binom{T}{2}$ ways for $T - 2$ pluses and 2 minuses, and so on. In addition, the power to which a term $(H^+ - (1 + R))$ associated with a particular w_T is raised is equal to the number of minus signs associated with the w_T. Therefore, if the valuation procedure is carried back to the present, the value of the option becomes:

$$
w_0 = \left[\binom{T}{0} w_T^{+\cdots+}(1 + R - H^-)^T(H^+ - (1 + R))^0 \right.
$$

$$
+ \binom{T}{1} w_T^{+\cdots+-}(1 + R - H^-)^{T-1}(H^+ - (1 + R))^1 + \cdots
$$

$$
\cdots + \binom{T}{T-1} w_T^{+-\cdots-}(1 + R - H^-)^1(H^+ - (1 + R))^{T-1}
$$

$$
\left. + \binom{T}{T} w_T^{-\cdots-}(1 + R - H^-)^0(H^+ - (1 + R))^T \right] \Big/ [(H^+ - H^-)(1 + R)]^T.
$$

(A.5)

Next, we must determine the value of the option at maturity. If the stock advances i times and declines $(T - i)$ times, the price of the stock will be $S_0 H^{+i} H^{-(T-i)}$ on the expiration date. The option will be exercised if

$$
S_0 H^{+i} H^{-(T-i)} > X, \tag{A.6}
$$

in which case, the maturity value of the option will be

$$
w_T = S_0 H^{+i} H^{-(T-i)} - X.
$$

Otherwise, the option will expire worthless.

Let the symbol a denote the minimum integer value of i in (A.6) for which the inequality is satisfied. This value is given by:

$$
a = 1 + \text{INT} \left[\frac{\ln(X/S_0) - T \cdot \ln(H^-)}{\ln(H^+) - \ln(H^-)} \right], \tag{A.7}
$$

where $\text{INT}[\cdot]$ denotes the integer operator. Thus, the maturity value of the option is given by

$$
w_T = S_0 H^{+i} H^{-(T-i)} - X \quad \text{if} \quad i \geq a
$$

$$
w_T = 0 \qquad\qquad\qquad \text{if} \quad i < a. \tag{A.8}
$$

By substituting (A.8) into (A.5), one obtains a generalized option pricing equation for the discrete time case.

$$
w_0 = \frac{\sum_{i=a}^{T} \binom{T}{i}(S_0 H^{+i} H^{-(T-i)} - X)(1 + R - H^-)^i(H^+ - (1 + R))^{T-i}}{(H^+ - H^-)^T(1 + R)^T}. \tag{A.9}
$$

The Continuous Time Model

In the derivation of the continuous time model, we will determine the option price when $T \to \infty$ assuming that the mean and variance of logarithmic returns of the stock are held constant over the life of the option.

Note that (A.9) can be rewritten as

$$w_0 = S_0 \sum_{i=a}^{T} \binom{T}{i} \left[\frac{(1 + R - H^-)H^+}{(1 + R)(H^+ - H^-)} \right]^i \left[\frac{(H^+ - 1 - R)H^-}{(H^+ - H^-)(1 + R)} \right]^{T-i}$$

$$\frac{-X}{(1 + R)^T} \sum_{i=a}^{T} \binom{T}{i} \left[\frac{1 + R - H^-}{H^+ - H^-} \right]^i \left[\frac{H^+ - 1 - R}{H^+ - H^-} \right]^{T-i}. \quad \text{(A.10)}$$

The two bracketed terms in each term in (A.10) sum to unity and therefore can be interpreted as "pseudo probabilities." Although these pseudo probabilities do not represent the true probabilities that the price of the stock will either advance or decline, we can still apply the mathematics of probability theory to the solution of the problem. Let these pseudo probabilities be represented by

$$\psi = \frac{(1 + R - H^-)H^+}{(1 + R)(H^+ - H^-)}, \quad \text{and}$$

$$\phi = \frac{1 + R - H^-}{H^+ - H^-}.$$

The option price can now be stated as:

$$w_0 = S_0 B(a, T, \psi) - \frac{X}{(1 + R)^T} B(a, T, \phi), \quad \text{(A.11)}$$

where $B(a, T, (\cdot))$ is the cumulative binomial probability that the number of successes will fall between a and T after T trials, where $(\cdot)$ is the probability associated with a success after one trial.

As T becomes large, the cumulative binomial density function can be approximated by the cumulative normal density function. The approximation will be exact in the limit as $T \to \infty$. Therefore,

$$w_0 \sim S_0 N(Z_1, Z_1') - \frac{X}{(1 + R)^T} N(Z_2, Z_2'), \quad \text{(A.12)}$$

where $N(Z, Z')$ is the probability that a normally distributed random variable with zero mean and unit variance will take on values between a lower limit of Z and an upper limit of Z', and

$$Z_1 = \frac{a - T\psi}{\sqrt{T\psi(1 - \psi)}}, \quad Z_1' = \frac{T - T\psi}{\sqrt{T\psi(1 - \psi)}}$$

$$Z_2 = \frac{a - T\phi}{\sqrt{T\phi(1 - \phi)}}, \quad Z_2' = \frac{T - T\phi}{\sqrt{T\phi(1 - \phi)}}.$$

Thus, the price of the option that will obtain when the two-state process evolves continuously is given by:

$$w_0 = S_0(\text{Lim}_{T\to\infty} Z_1, \text{Lim}_{T\to\infty} Z_1') - \frac{X}{\text{Lim}_{T\to\infty} (1 + R)^T} N(\text{Lim}_{T\to\infty} Z_2, \text{Lim}_{T\to\infty} Z_2').$$

$$\text{(A.13)}$$

Let $1 + R = e^{r/T}$ to reflect the continuous compounding of interest. Then,

$$\text{Lim}_{T \to \infty} (1 + R)^T = e^r.$$

We will state without proof that

$$\text{Lim}_{T \to \infty} Z_1' = \text{Lim}_{T \to \infty} Z_2' = \infty.$$

Thus, all that remains in the derivation of the continuous time version of the two-state model is to determine $\text{Lim}_{T \to \infty} Z_1$ and $\text{Lim}_{T \to \infty} Z_2$.

In determining both limits, we will assume that both H^+ and H^- are chosen to hold the logarithmic mean and variance of returns of the stock constant over the option's life. Therefore, we make the following substitutions derived earlier in the text.

$$H^+ = e^{\mu/T + (\sigma/\sqrt{T})\sqrt{(1-\theta)/\theta}}.$$

$$H^- = e^{\mu/T - (\sigma/\sqrt{T})\sqrt{\theta/(1-\theta)}}$$

Substituting H^+ and H^- into a,

$$Z_1 = \frac{1 + \text{INT}\left[\dfrac{\ln(X/S_0) - \mu + \sigma\sqrt{T}\sqrt{\theta/(1-\theta)}}{\sigma/\sqrt{T\theta(1-\theta)}}\right] - T\psi}{\sqrt{T\psi(1-\psi)}}.$$

In the limit, the term $1 + \text{INT}[\cdot]$ will simplify to the term in brackets. To simplify the exposition, we will replace $1 + \text{INT}[\cdot]$ with $[\cdot]$ at this point. With this substitution Z_1 can be restated as

$$Z_1 \sim \frac{\ln(X/S_0) - \mu}{\sigma\sqrt{\dfrac{\psi(1-\psi)}{\theta(1-\theta)}}} + \frac{\sqrt{T}(\theta - \psi)}{\sqrt{\psi(1-\psi)}}. \tag{A.14}$$

Substituting H^+, H^-, and $1 + R = e^{r/T}$ in the expression for ψ and expanding in Taylor's series in T, we obtain

$$\psi \sim \frac{1}{\sqrt{T}} \frac{r - \mu - \frac{1}{2}\sigma^2\left(\dfrac{\theta}{1-\theta}\right) + \sigma^2}{\sigma\left(\sqrt{\dfrac{1-\theta}{\theta}} + \sqrt{\dfrac{\theta}{1-\theta}}\right) + \frac{1}{2}(\sigma^2/\sqrt{T})\left(\dfrac{1-\theta}{\theta} - \dfrac{\theta}{1-\theta}\right) + o\left(\dfrac{1}{T}\right)}$$

$$+ \frac{\sqrt{\dfrac{\theta}{1-\theta}}}{\sqrt{\dfrac{1-\theta}{\theta}} + \sqrt{\dfrac{\theta}{1-\theta}} + \frac{1}{2}\left(\dfrac{\sigma}{\sqrt{T}}\right)\left(\dfrac{1-\theta}{\theta} - \dfrac{\theta}{1-\theta}\right) + o\left(\dfrac{1}{T}\right)} + o\left(\dfrac{1}{T}\right),$$

where $o\left(\dfrac{1}{T}\right)$ denotes a function tending to zero more rapidly than $\dfrac{1}{T}$. [The derivation of the Taylor's series expansions of ψ and ϕ as well as the derivation of the limits below will be made available by the authors upon request.] It can be shown that

$$\mathrm{Lim}_{T\to\infty}\,\psi = \theta \quad \text{and}$$

$$\mathrm{Lim}_{T\to\infty}\,\sqrt{T}\,(\theta - \psi) = -\frac{\sqrt{\theta(1-\theta)}}{\sigma}\left(r - \mu + \frac{1}{2}\sigma^2\right)$$

Substituting $\mathrm{Lim}_{T\to\infty}\,\psi$ for ψ and $\mathrm{Lim}_{T\to\infty}\,\sqrt{T}\,(\theta - \psi)$ for $\sqrt{T}\,(\theta - \psi)$ into (A.14), we obtain:

$$\mathrm{Lim}_{T\to\infty}\,Z_1 = \frac{\ln(X/S_0) - \mu}{\sigma\sqrt{\dfrac{\theta(1-\theta)}{\theta(1-\theta)}}} - \frac{\sqrt{\theta(1-\theta)}\left(r - \mu + \dfrac{1}{2}\sigma^2\right)}{\sigma\sqrt{\theta(1-\theta)}}.$$

$$= \frac{\ln(X/S_0) - r - \dfrac{1}{2}\sigma^2}{\sigma}.$$

The derivation of $\mathrm{Lim}_{T\to\infty}\,Z_2$ closely parallels the corresponding derivation for Z_1. It can be shown that

$$\mathrm{Lim}_{T\to\infty}\,Z_2 = \frac{\ln(X/S_0) - r + \dfrac{1}{2}\sigma^2}{\sigma}.$$

Recognizing that $N(Z, \infty) = N(-\infty, -Z)$, and letting

$$D_1 = -\mathrm{Lim}_{T\to\infty}\,Z_1$$

$$D_2 = -\mathrm{Lim}_{T\to\infty}\,Z_2,$$

the continuous time version of the two-state model is obtained:

$$w_0 = S_0 N(-\infty, D_1) - Xe^{-r}N(-\infty, D_2)$$

$$D_1 = \frac{\ln(S_0/X) + r + \dfrac{1}{2}\sigma^2}{\sigma}$$

$$D_2 = D_1 - \sigma.$$

The above equation is identical to the Black-Scholes model.

REFERENCES

1. Brit J. Bartter and Richard J. Rendleman, Jr.. "Free-Based Pricing of Fixed Rate Bank Loan Commitments." *Financial Management*, forthcoming (Spring, 1979).
2. Brit J. Bartter and Richard J. Rendleman, Jr.. "Pricing Fixed Rate Bank Loan Commitments." (Northwestern University, 1978, unpublished working paper).
3. Fischer Black and Myron Scholes. "The Pricing of Options and Corporate Liabilities." *Journal of Political Economy* (May/June, 1973).

4. Michael Brennan and Eduardo Schwartz. "The Valuation of American Put Options." *Journal of Finance* (May, 1977).

5. John C. Cox, Stephen Ross, and Mark Rubinstein, "Option Pricing: A Simplified Approach." (University of California at Berkeley, September, 1978, Working paper No. 79).

6. Robert C. Merton. "Theory of Rational Option Pricing." *Bell Journal of Economics and Management Science* (Spring 1973).

7. Michael Parkinson. "Option Pricing: The American Put." *Journal of Business* (January, 1977).

8. Richard J. Rendleman, Jr. and Brit J. Bartter. "The Pricing of Options on Debt Securities." *Journal of Financial and Quantitative Analysis*, forthcoming (March, 1980).

9. Richard J. Rendleman, Jr. "Corporate Income Taxes, Valuation, and the Problem of Optimal Capital Structure: A Closer Look." (Northwestern University, 1978, unpublished working paper).

10. Mark Rubinstein. *Option Markets* unpublished book (1977).

11. William F. Sharpe. *Investments* (Englewood Cliffs, New Jersey, Prentice Hall, 1978).

Article 10

The Pricing of Options and Corporate Liabilities

Fischer Black

University of Chicago

Myron Scholes

Massachusetts Institute of Technology

If options are correctly priced in the market, it should not be possible to make sure profits by creating portfolios of long and short positions in options and their underlying stocks. Using this principle, a theoretical valuation formula for options is derived. Since almost all corporate liabilities can be viewed as combinations of options, the formula and the analysis that led to it are also applicable to corporate liabilities such as common stock, corporate bonds, and warrants. In particular, the formula can be used to derive the discount that should be applied to a corporate bond because of the possibility of default.

Introduction

An option is a security giving the right to buy or sell an asset, subject to certain conditions, within a specified period of time. An "American option" is one that can be exercised at any time up to the date the option expires. A "European option" is one that can be exercised only on a specified future date. The price that is paid for the asset when the option is exercised is called the "exercise price" or "striking price." The last day on which the option may be exercised is called the "expiration date" or "maturity date."

The simplest kind of option is one that gives the right to buy a single share of common stock. Throughout most of the paper, we will be discussing this kind of option, which is often referred to as a "call option."

Received for publication November 11, 1970. Final version received May 9, 1972.

The inspiration for this work was provided by Jack L. Treynor (1961a, 1961b). We are grateful for extensive comments on earlier drafts by Eugene F. Fama, Robert C. Merton, and Merton H. Miller. This work was supported in part by the Ford Foundation.

In general, it seems clear that the higher the price of the stock, the greater the value of the option. When the stock price is much greater than the exercise price, the option is almost sure to be exercised. The current value of the option will thus be approximately equal to the price of the stock minus the price of a pure discount bond that matures on the same date as the option, with a face value equal to the striking price of the option.

On the other hand, if the price of the stock is much less than the exercise price, the option is almost sure to expire without being exercised, so its value will be near zero.

If the expiration date of the option is very far in the future, then the price of a bond that pays the exercise price on the maturity date will be very low, and the value of the option will be approximately equal to the price of the stock.

On the other hand, if the expiration date is very near, the value of the option will be approximately equal to the stock price minus the exercise price, or zero, if the stock price is less than the exercise price. Normally, the value of an option declines as its maturity date approaches, if the value of the stock does not change.

These general properties of the relation between the option value and the stock price are often illustrated in a diagram like figure 1. Line A represents the maximum value of the option, since it cannot be worth more than the stock. Line B represents the minimum value of the option, since its value cannot be negative and cannot be less than the stock price minus the exercise price. Lines T_1, T_2, and T_3 represent the value of the option for successively shorter maturities.

Normally, the curve representing the value of an option will be concave upward. Since it also lies below the 45° line, A, we can see that the

FIG. 1.—The relation between option value and stock price

option will be more volatile than the stock. A given percentage change in the stock price, holding maturity constant, will result in a larger percentage change in the option value. The relative volatility of the option is not constant, however. It depends on both the stock price and maturity.

Most of the previous work on the valuation of options has been expressed in terms of warrants. For example, Sprenkle (1961), Ayres (1963), Boness (1964), Samuelson (1965), Baumol, Malkiel, and Quandt (1966), and Chen (1970) all produced valuation formulas of the same general form. Their formulas, however, were not complete, since they all involved one or more arbitrary parameters.

For example, Sprenkle's formula for the value of an option can be written as follows:

$$kxN(b_1) - k^*cN(b_2)$$

$$b_1 = \frac{\ln kx/c + \frac{1}{2} v^2(t^* - t)}{v\sqrt{(t^* - t)}}$$

$$b_2 = \frac{\ln kx/c - \frac{1}{2} v^2(t^* - t)}{v\sqrt{(t^* - t)}}$$

In this expression, x is the stock price, c is the exercise price, t^* is the maturity date, t is the current date, v^2 is the variance rate of the return on the stock,[1] ln is the natural logarithm, and $N(b)$ is the cumulative normal density function. But k and k^* are unknown parameters. Sprenkle (1961) defines k as the ratio of the expected value of the stock price at the time the warrant matures to the current stock price, and k^* as a discount factor that depends on the risk of the stock. He tries to estimate the values of k and k^* empirically, but finds that he is unable to do so.

More typically, Samuelson (1965) has unknown parameters α and β, where α is the rate of expected return on the stock, and β is the rate of expected return on the warrant or the discount rate to be applied to the warrant.[2] He assumes that the distribution of possible values of the stock when the warrant matures is log-normal and takes the expected value of this distribution, cutting it off at the exercise price. He then discounts this expected value to the present at the rate β. Unfortunately, there seems to be no model of the pricing of securities under conditions of capital market

---

[1] The variance rate of the return on a security is the limit, as the size of the interval of measurement goes to zero, of the variance of the return over that interval divided by the length of the interval.

[2] The rate of expected return on a security is the limit, as the size of the interval of measurement goes to zero, of the expected return over that interval divided by the length of the interval.

equilibrium that would make this an appropriate procedure for determining the value of a warrant.

In a subsequent paper, Samuelson and Merton (1969) recognize the fact that discounting the expected value of the distribution of possible values of the warrant when it is exercised is not an appropriate procedure. They advance the theory by treating the option price as a function of the stock price. They also recognize that the discount rates are determined in part by the requirement that investors be willing to hold all of the outstanding amounts of both the stock and the option. But they do not make use of the fact that investors must hold other assets as well, so that the risk of an option or stock that affects its discount rate is only that part of the risk that cannot be diversified away. Their final formula depends on the shape of the utility function that they assume for the typical investor.

One of the concepts that we use in developing our model is expressed by Thorp and Kassouf (1967). They obtain an empirical valuation formula for warrants by fitting a curve to actual warrant prices. Then they use this formula to calculate the ratio of shares of stock to options needed to create a hedged position by going long in one security and short in the other. What they fail to pursue is the fact that in equilibrium, the expected return on such a hedged position must be equal to the return on a riskless asset. What we show below is that this equilibrium condition can be used to derive a theoretical valuation formula.

The Valuation Formula

In deriving our formula for the value of an option in terms of the price of the stock, we will assume "ideal conditions" in the market for the stock and for the option:

a) The short-term interest rate is known and is constant through time.

b) The stock price follows a random walk in continuous time with a variance rate proportional to the square of the stock price. Thus the distribution of possible stock prices at the end of any finite interval is lognormal. The variance rate of the return on the stock is constant.

c) The stock pays no dividends or other distributions.

d) The option is "European," that is, it can only be exercised at maturity.

e) There are no transaction costs in buying or selling the stock or the option.

f) It is possible to borrow any fraction of the price of a security to buy it or to hold it, at the short-term interest rate.

g) There are no penalties to short selling. A seller who does not own a security will simply accept the price of the security from a buyer, and will agree to settle with the buyer on some future date by paying him an amount equal to the price of the security on that date.

Under these assumptions, the value of the option will depend only on the price of the stock and time and on variables that are taken to be known constants. Thus, it is possible to create a hedged position, consisting of a long position in the stock and a short position in the option, whose value will not depend on the price of the stock, but will depend only on time and the values of known constants. Writing $w(x, t)$ for the value of the option as a function of the stock price x and time t, the number of options that must be sold short against one share of stock long is:

$$1/w_1(x,t). \qquad (1)$$

In expression (1), the subscript refers to the partial derivative of $w(x,t)$ with respect to its first argument.

To see that the value of such a hedged position does not depend on the price of the stock, note that the ratio of the change in the option value to the change in the stock price, when the change in the stock price is small, is $w_1(x,t)$. To a first approximation, if the stock price changes by an amount Δx, the option price will change by an amount $w_1(x,t) \, \Delta x$, and the number of options given by expression (1) will change by an amount Δx. Thus, the change in the value of a long position in the stock will be approximately offset by the change in value of a short position in $1/w_1$ options.

As the variables x and t change, the number of options to be sold short to create a hedged position with one share of stock changes. If the hedge is maintained continuously, then the approximations mentioned above become exact, and the return on the hedged position is completely independent of the change in the value of the stock. In fact, the return on the hedged position becomes certain.[3]

To illustrate the formation of the hedged position, let us refer to the solid line (T_2) in figure 1 and assume that the price of the stock starts at $15.00, so that the value of the option starts at $5.00. Assume also that the slope of the line at that point is $1/2$. This means that the hedged position is created by buying one share of stock and selling two options short. One share of stock costs $15.00, and the sale of two options brings in $10.00, so the equity in this position is $5.00.

If the hedged position is not changed as the price of the stock changes, then there is some uncertainty in the value of the equity at the end of a finite interval. Suppose that two options go from $10.00 to $15.75 when the stock goes from $15.00 to $20.00, and that they go from $10.00 to $5.75 when the stock goes from $15.00 to $10.00. Thus, the equity goes from $5.00 to $4.25 when the stock changes by $5.00 in either direction. This is a $.75 decline in the equity for a $5.00 change in the stock in either direction.[4]

[3] This was pointed out to us by Robert Merton.
[4] These figures are purely for illustrative purposes. They correspond roughly to the way figure 1 was drawn, but not to an option on any actual security.

In addition, the curve shifts (say from T_2 to T_3 in fig. 1) as the maturity of the options changes. The resulting decline in value of the options means an increase in the equity in the hedged position and tends to offset the possible losses due to a large change in the stock price.

Note that the decline in the equity value due to a large change in the stock price is small. The ratio of the decline in the equity value to the magnitude of the change in the stock price becomes smaller as the magnitude of the change in the stock price becomes smaller.

Note also that the direction of the change in the equity value is independent of the direction of the change in the stock price. This means that under our assumption that the stock price follows a continuous random walk and that the return has a constant variance rate, the covariance between the return on the equity and the return on the stock will be zero. If the stock price and the value of the "market portfolio" follow a joint continuous random walk with constant covariance rate, it means that the covariance between the return on the equity and the return on the market will be zero.

Thus the risk in the hedged position is zero if the short position in the option is adjusted continuously. If the position is not adjusted continuously, the risk is small, and consists entirely of risk that can be diversified away by forming a portfolio of a large number of such hedged positions.

In general, since the hedged position contains one share of stock long and $1/w_1$ options short, the value of the equity in the position is:

$$x - w/w_1. \tag{2}$$

The change in the value of the equity in a short interval Δt is:

$$\Delta x - \Delta w/w_1. \tag{3}$$

Assuming that the short position is changed continuously, we can use stochastic calculus[5] to expand Δw, which is $w(x + \Delta x, t + \Delta t) - w(x,t)$, as follows:

$$\Delta w = w_1 \Delta x + \frac{1}{2} w_{11} v^2 x^2 \Delta t + w_2 \Delta t. \tag{4}$$

In equation (4), the subscripts on w refer to partial derivatives, and v^2 is the variance rate of the return on the stock.[6] Substituting from equation (4) into expression (3), we find that the change in the value of the equity in the hedged position is:

$$-\left(\frac{1}{2} w_{11} v^2 x^2 + w_2 \right) \Delta t/w_1. \tag{5}$$

Since the return on the equity in the hedged position is certain, the return must be equal to $r\Delta t$. Even if the hedged position is not changed

[5] For an exposition of stochastic calculus, see McKean (1969).
[6] See footnote 1.

continuously, its risk is small and is entirely risk that can be diversified away, so the expected return on the hedged position must be at the short term interest rate.[7] If this were not true, speculators would try to profit by borrowing large amounts of money to create such hedged positions, and would in the process force the returns down to the short term interest rate.

Thus the change in the equity (5) must equal the value of the equity (2) times $r\Delta t$.

$$-\left(\frac{1}{2}w_{11}v^2x^2 + w_2\right)\Delta t/w_1 = (x - w/w_1)r\Delta t. \tag{6}$$

Dropping the Δt from both sides, and rearranging, we have a differential equation for the value of the option.

$$w_2 = rw - rxw_1 - \frac{1}{2}v^2x^2w_{11}. \tag{7}$$

Writing t^* for the maturity date of the option, and c for the exercise price, we know that:

$$\begin{aligned} w(x,t^*) &= x - c, &\quad x \geqslant c \\ &= 0, &\quad x < c. \end{aligned} \tag{8}$$

There is only one formula $w(x,t)$ that satisfies the differential equation (7) subject to the boundary condition (8). This formula must be the option valuation formula.

To solve this differential equation, we make the following substitution:

$$w(x,t) = e^{r(t-t^*)}y\left[(2/v^2)\left(r - \frac{1}{2}v^2\right)\right.$$

$$\left[\ln x/c - \left(r - \frac{1}{2}v^2\right)(t - t^*)\right],$$

$$\left.-(2/v^2)\left(r - \frac{1}{2}v^2\right)^2(t - t^*)\right]. \tag{9}$$

[7] For a thorough discussion of the relation between risk and expected return, see Fama and Miller (1972) or Sharpe (1970). To see that the risk in the hedged position can be diversified away, note that if we don't adjust the hedge continuously, expression (5) becomes:

$$-\left(\frac{1}{2}w_{11}\Delta x^2 + w_2\Delta t\right)\bigg/w_1. \tag{5'}$$

Writing Δm for the change in the value of the market portfolio between t and $t + \Delta t$, the "market risk" in the hedged position is proportional to the covariance between the change in the value of the hedged portfolio, as given by expression (5'), and Δm: $-\frac{1}{2}w_{11}\operatorname{cov}(\Delta x^2, \Delta m)$. But if Δx and Δm follow a joint normal distribution for small intervals Δt, this covariance will be zero. Since there is no market risk in the hedged position, all of the risk due to the fact that the hedge is not continuously adjusted must be risk that can be diversified away.

With this substitution, the differential equation becomes:

$$y_2 = y_{11},\tag{10}$$

and the boundary condition becomes:

$$y(u,0) = 0, \qquad\qquad\qquad u < 0$$

$$= c\left[e^{u\left(\frac{1}{2}v^2\right)/\left(r-\frac{1}{2}v^2\right)} - 1\right], \quad u \geqslant 0.\tag{11}$$

The differential equation (10) is the heat-transfer equation of physics, and its solution is given by Churchill (1963, p. 155). In our notation, the solution is:

$$y(u,s) = 1/\sqrt{2\pi} \int_{-u/\sqrt{2s}}^{\infty}$$

$$c\left[e^{(u+q\sqrt{2s})\left(\frac{1}{2}v^2\right)/\left(r-\frac{1}{2}v^2\right)} - 1\right]e^{-q^2/2}\,dq.$$

$$\tag{12}$$

Substituting from equation (12) into equation (9), and simplifying, we find:

$$w(x,t) = xN(d_1) - ce^{r(t-t^*)}N(d_2)$$

$$d_1 = \frac{\ln x/c + \left(r + \frac{1}{2}v^2\right)(t^* - t)}{v\sqrt{t^* - t}}\tag{13}$$

$$d_2 = \frac{\ln x/c + \left(r - \frac{1}{2}v^2\right)(t^* - t)}{v\sqrt{t^* - t}}$$

In equation (13), $N(d)$ is the cumulative normal density function.

Note that the expected return on the stock does not appear in equation (13). The option value as a function of the stock price is independent of the expected return on the stock. The expected return on the option, however, will depend on the expected return on the stock. The faster the stock price rises, the faster the option price will rise through the functional relationship (13).

Note that the maturity $(t^* - t)$ appears in the formula only multiplied by the interest rate r or the variance rate v^2. Thus, an increase in maturity has the same effect on the value of the option as an equal percentage increase in both r and v^2.

Merton (1973) has shown that the option value as given by equation (13) increases continuously as any one of t^*, r, or v^2 increases. In each case, it approaches a maximum value equal to the stock price.

The partial derivative w_1 of the valuation formula is of interest, because it determines the ratio of shares of stock to options in the hedged position as in expression (1). Taking the partial derivative of equation (13), and simplifying, we find that:

$$w_1(x,t) = N(d_1). \qquad (14)$$

In equation (14), d_1 is as defined in equation (13).

From equations (13) and (14), it is clear that xw_1/w is always greater than one. This shows that the option is always more volatile than the stock.

An Alternative Derivation

It is also possible to derive the differential equation (7) using the "capital asset pricing model." This derivation is given because it gives more understanding of the way in which one can discount the value of an option to the present, using a discount rate that depends on both time and the price of the stock.

The capital asset pricing model describes the relation between risk and expected return for a capital asset under conditions of market equilibrium.[8] The expected return on an asset gives the discount that must be applied to the end-of-period value of the asset to give its present value. Thus, the capital-asset pricing model gives a general method for discounting under uncertainty.

The capital-asset pricing model says that the expected return on an asset is a linear function of its β, which is defined as the covariance of the return on the asset with the return on the market, divided by the variance of the return on the market. From equation (4) we see that the covariance of the return on the option $\Delta w/w$ with the return on the market is equal to xw_1/w times the covariance of the return on the stock $\Delta x/x$ with the return on the market. Thus, we have the following relation between the option's β and the stock's β:

$$\beta_w = (xw_1/w)\beta_x. \qquad (15)$$

The expression xw_1/w may also be interpreted as the "elasticity" of the option price with respect to the stock price. It is the ratio of the percentage change in the option price to the percentage change in the stock price, for small percentage changes, holding maturity constant.

[8] The model was developed by Treynor (1961*b*), Sharpe (1964), Lintner (1965), and Mossin (1966). It is summarized by Sharpe (1970), and Fama and Miller (1972). The model was originally stated as a single-period model. Extending it to a multi-period model is, in general, difficult. Fama (1970), however, has shown that if we make an assumption that implies that the short-term interest rate is constant through time, then the model must apply to each successive period in time. His proof also goes through under somewhat more general assumptions.

To apply the capital-asset pricing model to an option and the underlying stock, let us first define a as the rate of expected return on the market minus the interest rate.[9] Then the expected return on the option and the stock are:

$$E(\Delta x/x) = r\Delta t + a\beta_x\Delta t, \tag{16}$$

$$E(\Delta w/w) = r\Delta t + a\beta_w\Delta t. \tag{17}$$

Multiplying equation (17) by w, and substituting for β_w from equation (15), we find:

$$E(\Delta w) = rw\Delta t + axw_1\beta_x\Delta t. \tag{18}$$

Using stochastic calculus,[10] we can expand Δw, which is $w(x + \Delta x, t + \Delta t) - w(x,t)$, as follows:

$$\Delta w = w_1\Delta x + \frac{1}{2}w_{11}v^2x^2\Delta t + w_2\Delta t. \tag{19}$$

Taking the expected value of equation (19), and substituting for $E(\Delta x)$ from equation (16), we have:

$$E(\Delta w) = rxw_1\Delta t + axw_1\beta_x\Delta t + \frac{1}{2}v^2x^2w_{11}\Delta t + w_2\Delta t. \tag{20}$$

Combining equations (18) and (20), we find that the terms involving a and β_x cancel, giving:

$$w_2 = rw - rxw_1 - \frac{1}{2}v^2x^2w_{11}. \tag{21}$$

Equation (21) is the same as equation (7).

More Complicated Options

The valuation formula (13) was derived under the assumption that the option can only be exercised at time t^*. Merton (1973) has shown, however, that the value of the option is always greater than the value it would have if it were exercised immediately $(x - c)$. Thus, a rational investor will not exercise a call option before maturity, and the value of an American call option is the same as the value of a European call option.

There is a simple modification of the formula that will make it applicable to European put options (options to sell) as well as call options (options to buy). Writing $u(x,t)$ for the value of a put option, we see that the differential equation remains unchanged.

---

[9] See footnote 2.

[10] For an exposition of stochastic calculus, see McKean (1969).

$$u_2 = ru - rxu_1 - \frac{1}{2} v^2 x^2 u_{11}. \tag{22}$$

The boundary condition, however, becomes:

$$
\begin{aligned}
u(x,t^*) &= 0, && x \geqslant c \\
&= c - x, && x < c.
\end{aligned} \tag{23}
$$

To get the solution to this equation with the new boundary condition, we can simply note that the difference between the value of a call and the value of a put on the same stock, if both can be exercised only at maturity, must obey the same differential equation, but with the following boundary condition:

$$w(x,t^*) - u(x,t^*) = x - c. \tag{24}$$

The solution to the differential equation with this boundary condition is:

$$w(x,t) - u(x,t) = x - ce^{r(t-t^*)}. \tag{25}$$

Thus the value of the European put option is:

$$u(x,t) = w(x,t) - x + ce^{r(t-t^*)}. \tag{26}$$

Putting in the value of $w(x,t)$ from (13), and noting that $1 - N(d)$ is equal to $N(-d)$, we have:

$$u(x,t) = -xN(-d_1) + ce^{-rt^*}N(-d_2). \tag{27}$$

In equation (27), d_1 and d_2 are defined as in equation (13).

Equation (25) also gives us a relation between the value of a European call and the value of a European put.[11] We see that if an investor were to buy a call and sell a put, his returns would be exactly the same as if he bought the stock on margin, borrowing $ce^{r(t-t^*)}$ toward the price of the stock.

Merton (1973) has also shown that the value of an American put option will be greater than the value of a European put option. This is true because it is sometimes advantageous to exercise a put option before maturity, if it is possible to do so. For example, suppose the stock price falls almost to zero and that the probability that the price will exceed the exercise price before the option expires is negligible. Then it will pay to exercise the option immediately, so that the exercise price will be received sooner rather than later. The investor thus gains the interest on the exercise price for the period up to the time he would otherwise have exercised it. So far, no one has been able to obtain a formula for the value of an American put option.

---

[11] The relation between the value of a call option and the value of a put option was first noted by Stoll (1969). He does not realize, however, that his analysis applies only to European options.

If we relax the assumption that the stock pays no dividend, we begin to get into some complicated problems. First of all, under certain conditions it will pay to exercise an American call option before maturity. Merton (1973) has shown that this can be true only just before the stock's ex-dividend date. Also, it is not clear what adjustment might be made in the terms of the option to protect the option holder against a loss due to a large dividend on the stock and to ensure that the value of the option will be the same as if the stock paid no dividend. Currently, the exercise price of a call option is generally reduced by the amount of any dividend paid on the stock. We can see that this is not adequate protection by imagining that the stock is that of a holding company and that it pays out all of its assets in the form of a dividend to its shareholders. This will reduce the price of the stock and the value of the option to zero, no matter what adjustment is made in the exercise price of the option. In fact, this example shows that there may not be any adjustment in the terms of the option that will give adequate protection against a large dividend. In this case, the option value is going to be zero after the distribution, no matter what its terms are. Merton (1973) was the first to point out that the current adjustment for dividends is not adequate.

Warrant Valuation

A warrant is an option that is a liability of a corporation. The holder of a warrant has the right to buy the corporation's stock (or other assets) on specified terms. The analysis of warrants is often much more complicated than the analysis of simple options, because:

a) The life of a warrant is typically measured in years, rather than months. Over a period of years, the variance rate of the return on the stock may be expected to change substantially.

b) The exercise price of the warrant is usually not adjusted at all for dividends. The possibility that dividends will be paid requires a modification of the valuation formula.

c) The exercise price of a warrant sometimes changes on specified dates. It may pay to exercise a warrant just before its exercise price changes. This too requires a modification of the valuation formula.

d) If the company is involved in a merger, the adjustment that is made in the terms of the warrant may change its value.

e) Sometimes the exercise price can be paid using bonds of the corporation at face value, even though they may at the time be selling at a discount. This complicates the analysis and means that early exercise may sometimes be desirable.

f) The exercise of a large number of warrants may sometimes result in a significant increase in the number of common shares outstanding.

In some cases, these complications can be treated as insignificant, and equation (13) can be used as an approximation to give an estimate of the warrant value. In other cases, some simple modifications of equation (13) will improve the approximation. Suppose, for example, that there are warrants outstanding, which, if exercised, would double the number of shares of the company's common stock. Let us define the "equity" of the company as the sum of the value of all of its warrants and the value of all of its common stock. If the warrants are exercised at maturity, the equity of the company will increase by the aggregate amount of money paid in by the warrant holders when they exercise. The warrant holders will then own half of the new equity of the company, which is equal to the old equity plus the exercise money.

Thus, at maturity, the warrant holders will either receive nothing, or half of the new equity, minus the exercise money. Thus, they will receive nothing or half of the difference between the old equity and half the exercise money. We can look at the warrants as options to buy shares in the equity rather than shares of common stock, at half the stated exercise price rather than at the full exercise price. The value of a share in the equity is defined as the sum of the value of the warrants and the value of the common stock, divided by twice the number of outstanding shares of common stock. If we take this point of view, then we will take v^2 in equation (13) to be the variance rate of the return on the company's equity, rather than the variance rate of the return on the company's common stock.

A similar modification in the parameters of equation (13) can be made if the number of shares of stock outstanding after exercise of the warrants will be other than twice the number of shares outstanding before exercise of the warrants.

Common Stock and Bond Valuation

It is not generally realized that corporate liabilities other than warrants may be viewed as options. Consider, for example, a company that has common stock and bonds outstanding and whose only asset is shares of common stock of a second company. Suppose that the bonds are "pure discount bonds" with no coupon, giving the holder the right to a fixed sum of money, if the corporation can pay it, with a maturity of 10 years. Suppose that the bonds contain no restrictions on the company except a restriction that the company cannot pay any dividends until after the bonds are paid off. Finally, suppose that the company plans to sell all the stock it holds at the end of 10 years, pay off the bond holders if possible, and pay any remaining money to the stockholders as a liquidating dividend.

Under these conditions, it is clear that the stockholders have the equivalent of an option on their company's assets. In effect, the bond holders own the company's assets, but they have given options to the stockholders to buy the assets back. The value of the common stock at the end of 10 years will be the value of the company's assets minus the face value of the bonds, or zero, whichever is greater.

Thus, the value of the common stock will be $w(x,t)$, as given by equation (13), where we take v^2 to be the variance rate of the return on the shares held by the company, c to be the total face value of the outstanding bonds, and x to be the total value of the shares held by the company. The value of the bonds will simply be $x - w(x,t)$.

By subtracting the value of the bonds given by this formula from the value they would have if there were no default risk, we can figure the discount that should be applied to the bonds due to the existence of default risk.

Suppose, more generally, that the corporation holds business assets rather than financial assets. Suppose that at the end of the 10 year period, it will recapitalize by selling an entirely new class of common stock, using the proceeds to pay off the bond holders, and paying any money that is left to the old stockholders to retire their stock. In the absence of taxes, it is clear that the value of the corporation can be taken to be the sum of the total value of the debt and the total value of the common stock.[12] The amount of debt outstanding will not affect the total value of the corporation, but will affect the division of that value between the bonds and the stock. The formula for $w(x,t)$ will again describe the total value of the common stock, where x is taken to be the sum of the value of the bonds and the value of the stock. The formula for $x - w(x,t)$ will again describe the total value of the bonds. It can be shown that, as the face value c of the bonds increases, the market value $x - w(x,t)$ increases by a smaller percentage. An increase in the corporation's debt, keeping the total value of the corporation constant, will increase the probability of default and will thus reduce the market value of one of the corporation's bonds. If the company changes its capital structure by issuing more bonds and using the proceeds to retire common stock, it will hurt the existing bond holders, and help the existing stockholders. The bond price will fall, and the stock price will rise. In this sense, changes in the capital structure of a firm may affect the price of its common stock.[13] The price changes will occur when the change in the capital structure becomes certain, not when the actual change takes place.

Because of this possibility, the bond indenture may prohibit the sale of additional debt of the same or higher priority in the event that the firm is recapitalized. If the corporation issues new bonds that are subordinated

[12] The fact that the total value of a corporation is not affected by its capital structure, in the absence of taxes and other imperfections, was first shown by Modigliani and Miller (1958).

[13] For a discussion of this point, see Fama and Miller (1972, pp. 151–52).

to the existing bonds and uses the proceeds to retire common stock, the price of the existing bonds and the common stock price will be unaffected. Similarly, if the company issues new common stock and uses the proceeds to retire completely the most junior outstanding issue of bonds, neither the common stock price nor the price of any other issue of bonds will be affected.

The corporation's dividend policy will also affect the division of its total value between the bonds and the stock.[14] To take an extreme example, suppose again that the corporation's only assets are the shares of another company, and suppose that it sells all these shares and uses the proceeds to pay a dividend to its common stockholders. Then the value of the firm will go to zero, and the value of the bonds will go to zero. The common stockholders will have "stolen" the company out from under the bond holders. Even for dividends of modest size, a higher dividend always favors the stockholders at the expense of the bond holders. A liberalization of dividend policy will increase the common stock price and decrease the bond price.[15] Because of this possibility, bond indentures contain restrictions on dividend policy, and the common stockholders have an incentive to pay themselves the largest dividend allowed by the terms of the bond indenture. However, it should be noted that the size of the effect of changing dividend policy will normally be very small.

If the company has coupon bonds rather than pure discount bonds outstanding, then we can view the common stock as a "compound option." The common stock is an option on an option on . . . an option on the firm. After making the last interest payment, the stockholders have an option

[14] Miller and Modigliani (1961) show that the total value of a firm, in the absence of taxes and other imperfections, is not affected by its dividend policy. They also note that the price of the common stock and the value of the bonds will not be affected by a change in dividend policy if the funds for a higher dividend are raised by issuing common stock or if the money released by a lower dividend is used to repurchase common stock.

[15] This is true assuming that the liberalization of dividend policy is not accompanied by a change in the company's current and planned financial structure. Since the issue of common stock or junior debt will hurt the common shareholders (holding dividend policy constant), they will normally try to liberalize dividend policy without issuing new securities. They may be able to do this by selling some of the firm's financial assets, such as ownership claims on other firms. Or they may be able to do it by adding to the company's short-term bank debt, which is normally senior to its long-term debt. Finally, the company may be able to finance a higher dividend by selling off a division. Assuming that it receives a fair price for the division, and that there were no economies of combination, this need not involve any loss to the firm as a whole. If the firm issues new common stock or junior debt in exactly the amounts needed to finance the liberalization of dividend policy, then the common stock and bond prices will not be affected. If the liberalization of dividend policy is associated with a decision to issue more common stock or junior debt than is needed to pay the higher dividends, the common stock price will fall and the bond price will rise. But these actions are unlikely, since they are not in the stockholders' best interests.

to buy the company from the bond holders for the face value of the bonds. Call this "option 1." After making the next-to-the-last interest payment, but before making the last interest payment, the stockholders have an option to buy option 1 by making the last interest payment. Call this "option 2." Before making the next-to-the-last interest payment, the stockholders have an option to buy option 2 by making that interest payment. This is "option 3." The value of the stockholders' claim at any point in time is equal to the value of option $n + 1$, where n is the number of interest payments remaining in the life of the bond.

If payments to a sinking fund are required along with interest payments, then a similar analysis can be made. In this case, there is no "balloon payment" at the end of the life of the bond. The sinking fund will have a final value equal to the face value of the bond. Option 1 gives the stockholders the right to buy the company from the bond holders by making the last sinking fund and interest payment. Option 2 gives the stockholders the right to buy option 1 by making the next-to-the-last sinking fund and interest payment. And the value of the stockholders' claim at any point in time is equal to the value of option n, where n is the number of sinking fund and interest payments remaining in the life of the bond. It is clear that the value of a bond for which sinking fund payments are required is greater than the value of a bond for which they are not required.

If the company has callable bonds, then the stockholders have more than one option. They can buy the next option by making the next interest or sinking fund and interest payment, or they can exercise their option to retire the bonds before maturity at prices specified by the terms of the call feature. Under our assumption of a constant short-term interest rate, the bonds would never sell above face value, and the usual kind of call option would never be exercised. Under more general assumptions, however, the call feature would have value to the stockholders and would have to be taken into account in deciding how the value of the company is divided between the stockholders and the bond holders.

Similarly, if the bonds are convertible, we simply add another option to the package. It is an option that the bond holders have to buy part of the company from the stockholders.

Unfortunately, these more complicated options cannot be handled by using the valuation formula (13). The valuation formula assumes that the variance rate of the return on the optioned asset is constant. But the variance of the return on an option is certainly not constant: it depends on the price of the stock and the maturity of the option. Thus the formula cannot be used, even as an approximation, to give the value of an option on an option. It is possible, however, that an analysis in the same spirit as the one that led to equation (13) would allow at least a numerical solution to the valuation of certain more complicated options.

Empirical Tests

We have done empirical tests of the valuation formula on a large body of call-option data (Black and Scholes 1972). These tests indicate that the actual prices at which options are bought and sold deviate in certain systematic ways from the values predicted by the formula. Option buyers pay prices that are consistently higher than those predicted by the formula. Option writers, however, receive prices that are at about the level predicted by the formula. There are large transaction costs in the option market, all of which are effectively paid by option buyers.

Also, the difference between the price paid by option buyers and the value given by the formula is greater for options on low-risk stocks than for options on high-risk stocks. The market appears to underestimate the effect of differences in variance rate on the value of an option. Given the magnitude of the transaction costs in this market, however, this systematic misestimation of value does not imply profit opportunities for a speculator in the option market.

References

Ayres, Herbert F. "Risk Aversion in the Warrants Market." *Indus. Management Rev.* 4 (Fall 1963): 497–505. Reprinted in Cootner (1967), pp. 497–505.

Baumol, William J.; Malkiel, Burton G.; and Quandt, Richard E. "The Valuation of Convertible Securities." *Q.J.E.* 80 (February 1966): 48–59.

Black, Fischer, and Scholes, Myron. "The Valuation of Option Contracts and a Test of Market Efficiency." *J. Finance* 27 (May 1972): 399–417.

Boness, A. James. "Elements of a Theory of Stock-Option Values." *J.P.E.* 72 (April 1964): 163–75.

Chen, Andrew H. Y. "A Model of Warrant Pricing in a Dynamic Market." *J. Finance* 25 (December 1970): 1041–60.

Churchill, R. V. *Fourier Series and Boundary Value Problems*, 2d ed. New York: McGraw-Hill, 1963.

Cootner, Paul A. *The Random Character of Stock Market Prices*. Cambridge, Mass.: M.I.T. Press, 1967.

Fama, Eugene F. "Multiperiod Consumption-Investment Decisions." *A.E.R.* 60 (March 1970): 163–74.

Fama, Eugene F., and Miller, Merton H. *The Theory of Finance*. New York: Holt, Rinehart & Winston, 1972.

Lintner, John. "The Valuation of Risk Assets and the Selection of Risky Investments in Stock Portfolios and Capital Budgets." *Rev. Econ. and Statis.* 47 (February 1965): 768–83.

McKean, H. P., Jr. *Stochastic Integrals*. New York: Academic Press, 1969.

Merton, Robert C. "Theory of Rational Option Pricing." *Bell J. Econ. and Management Sci.* (1973): in press.

Miller, Merton H., and Modigliani, Franco. "Dividend Policy, Growth, and the Valuation of Shares." *J. Bus.* 34 (October 1961): 411–33.

Modigliani, Franco, and Miller, Merton H. "The Cost of Capital, Corporation Finance, and the Theory of Investment." *A.E.R.* 48 (June 1958): 261–97.

Mossin, Jan. "Equilibrium in a Capital Asset Market." *Econometrica* 34 (October 1966): 768–83.

Samuelson, Paul A. "Rational Theory of Warrant Pricing." *Indus. Management Rev.* 6 (Spring 1965): 13–31. Reprinted in Cootner (1967), pp. 506–32.

Samuelson, Paul A., and Merton, Robert C. "A Complete Model of Warrant Pricing that Maximizes Utility." *Indus. Management Rev.* 10 (Winter 1969): 17–46.

Sharpe, William F. "Capital Asset Prices: A Theory of Market Equilibrium Under Conditions of Risk." *J. Finance* 19 (September 1964): 425–42.

———. *Portfolio Theory and Capital Markets:* New York: McGraw-Hill, 1970.

Sprenkle, Case. "Warrant Prices as Indications of Expectations." *Yale Econ. Essays* 1 (1961): 179–232. Reprinted in Cootner (1967), 412–74.

Stoll, Hans R. "The Relationship Between Put and Call Option Prices." *J. Finance* 24 (December 1969): 802–24.

Thorp, Edward O., and Kassouf, Sheen T. *Beat the Market.* New York: Random House, 1967.

Treynor, Jack L. "Implications for the Theory of Finance." Unpublished memorandum, 1961. (*a*)

———. "Toward a Theory of Market Value of Risky Assets." Unpublished memorandum, 1961. (*b*)

Article 11

How we came up with the option formula

Like many great inventions, it started with tinkering and ended with delayed recognition.

Fischer Black

My paper with Myron Scholes giving the derivation of our option formula appeared in the spring of 1973. We had published a paper on the results of some empirical tests of the formula, however, in the spring of 1972. The work that led to the formula started in the spring of 1969, and the background research started in 1965. Here is the story of how the formula and the papers describing it came to be.

THE SHORT STORY

Before I describe the events surrounding our discovery of the formula, here is the idea behind the formula.

Suppose there is a formula that tells how the value of a call option depends on the price of the underlying stock, the volatility of the stock, the exercise price and maturity of the option, and the interest rate.

Such a formula will tell us, among other things, how much the option value will change when the stock price changes by a small amount within a short time. Suppose that the option goes up about $.50 when the stock goes up $1.00, and down about $.50 when the stock goes down $1.00. Then you can create a hedged position by going short two option contracts and long one round lot of stock.

Such a position will be close to riskless. For small moves in the stock in the short run, your losses on one side will be mostly offset by gains on the other side. If the stock goes up, you will lose on the option but make it up on the stock. If the stock goes down, you will lose on the stock but make it up on the option.

At first, you create a hedged position by going short two options and long one stock. As the stock price changes, and as the option approaches maturity, the ratio of option to stock needed to maintain a close-to-riskless hedge will change. To maintain a neutral hedge, you will have to change your position in the stock, your position in the option, or both.

As the hedged position will be close to riskless, it should return an amount equal to the short-term interest rate on close-to-riskless securities. This one principle gives us the option formula. It turns out that there is only one formula for the value of an option that has the property that the return on a hedged position of option and stock is always equal to the short-term interest rate.

The same argument works for a "reverse hedge," if you assume that you can sell stock short and invest the proceeds of the short sale for your benefit. A short position in the stock combined with a long position in the option (in the right ratio) will be close to riskless. Your equity in that position will be negative, but there is only one formula such that the return on that position is the interest rate — the same formula that we derive from the direct hedging argument.

We can even get the formula by assuming that a neutral spread must earn the interest rate. If you are short one option and long another option on the same stock in the right ratio, you will have a neutral spread. The argument is plausible even for a spread where you take in money, because you are probably in a position to invest the proceeds of a sale of options for your own benefit.

In fact, we can get the formula without assuming any hedging or spreading at all. We just compare a long stock position with a long option position that has the same action as the stock. In our example, the comparable positions would be long one round lot of stock and long two option contracts. These two positions have the same movements for small changes in stock price in the short run, so their returns should differ only by an amount equal to the interest rate times the difference in the total values of the two positions. We can have equilibrium only if investors are indifferent between the two positions. This gives us the same formula as the hedging and spreading arguments.

THE DIFFERENTIAL EQUATION

Jack Treynor was at Arthur D. Little, Inc. when I started work there in 1965. He had developed, starting in 1961, a model for the pricing of securities and other assets that is now called the "capital asset pricing model." William Sharpe, John Lintner, and Jan Mossin developed more or less independent versions of the same model, and their versions began to be published in 1965. Jack's papers were never published, in part because they never quite satisfied the perfectionist in him, and in part (I believe) because he did not have an academic job.

In any case, Jack sparked my interest in finance, and I began to spend more and more time studying the capital asset pricing model and other theories of finance. The notion of equilibrium in the market for risky assets had great beauty for me. It implies that riskier securities must have higher expected returns, or investors will not hold them — except that investors do not count the part of the risk that they can diversify away.

I started trying to apply the capital asset pricing model to assets other than common stock. I looked at bonds, cash flows within a company, and even monetary assets. One of Treynor's papers was on the valuation of cash flows within a company, and he had derived a differential equation to help in figuring this value. His equation had an error because he had omitted some terms involving second derivatives, but we found out how to put in the missing terms and correct the equation.

With this background, I started working on a formula for valuing a warrant. At that time, we thought about warrants more than about options, because the over-the-counter options market was such an imperfect market. I'm not sure when I started work on the warrant problem, but it was probably in 1968 or 1969. I have notes containing the differential equation that are dated June 1969.

Back then, most of the best papers about warrants tried to find the value of a warrant by taking the expected value of the warrant at expiration and discounting it to the present. That method has two problems: you have to know the stock's expected return to find the warrant's expected value at expiration, and you have to choose a discount rate for the warrant. No single discount rate will do, however, because the risk of the warrant depends on the stock price and time. Hence, the discount rate depends on the stock price and time too. None of the papers had dealt with this problem.

One key step in solving the problem is to write the warrant value as a formula that depends on the stock price and other factors. As Treynor had used this approach with his "value equation," I tried it too. And about the same time that I was using this approach, Samuelson and Merton were using it in a paper that appeared in 1969 (although they didn't come up with the same formula).

Another thing that made it possible to solve the problem was to assume away all kinds of complications. I assumed that trading costs are zero, that both borrowing and lending can be done at a single short-term interest rate that is constant over time, and that the volatility of a stock is constant, which means that the future price of the stock follows a lognormal distribution. I made a few other simplifying assumptions, some of which turned out to be unnecessary.

The equation I wrote down said simply that the expected return on a warrant should depend on the risk of the warrant in the same way that a common stock's expected return depends on its risk. I applied the capital asset pricing model to every moment in a warrant's life, for every possible stock price and warrant value. To put it another way, I used the capital asset pricing model to write down how the discount rate for a warrant varies with time and the stock price.

This gave me a differential equation. It was an equation for the warrant formula. It has just one solution, if we use the known value of the warrant at expiration and another condition that I didn't know about at the time.

I spent many, many days trying to find the solution to that equation. I have a Ph.D. in applied mathematics, but had never spent much time on differential equations, so I didn't know the standard methods used to solve problems like that. I have an A.B. in physics, but I didn't recognize the equation as a version of the "heat equation," which has well-known solutions.

I did notice that some of the factors in the original equation were not in the final equation. The warrant value did not seem to depend on how the risk of the stock was divided between risk that could be diversified away and risk that could not be diversified away. It depended only on the total risk of the stock (as measured, for example, by the standard deviation of the return on the stock). The warrant value did not depend on the stock's expected return, or on any other asset's expected return. That fascinated me.

But I was still unable to come up with the formula. So I put the problem aside and worked on other things.

In 1969, Myron Scholes was at MIT, and I had my office near Boston, where I did both research and consulting. Myron invited me to join him in some of the research activities at MIT. We started working together on the option problem, and made rapid progress.

THE FORMULA

First, we concentrated on the fact that the option formula was going to depend on the underlying stock's volatility — not on its expected return. That meant that we could solve the problem using any expected return for the stock.

We decided to try assuming that the stock's expected return was equal to the interest rate. (We were assuming a constant interest rate, so short-term and long-term rates were equal.) In other words, we assumed that the stock's beta was zero; all of its risk could be diversified away.

As we also assumed that the stock's volatility was constant (when expressed in percentage terms) it was easy to figure the likelihood of each possible value of an investment in the stock at the time the option expired. We knew that the stock's terminal value (including reinvested dividends) would have to fit a lognormal distribution.

Other writers on options had made the same sort of assumption about the underlying stock, but they had not assumed an expected return equal to the interest rate. They had, however, assumed a constant expected return, which means a lognormal distribution for the terminal value of a stock that pays no dividends.

If you know the distribution for the stock's terminal value, you can cut it off at the option's exercise price and have the distribution for the option's terminal value. The expected value of that cutoff distribution gives you the expected terminal value of the option.

An article by Case Sprenkle presented a formula for the expected terminal value of an option with these same assumptions, except that Sprenkle allowed the stock to have any constant expected return. By putting the interest rate for the expected stock return into his formula, we got the expected terminal value of the option under our assumptions.

But we didn't want the expected terminal value of the option. We wanted the present value of the option: the value at some time before maturity. So we had to find some way to discount the option's expected terminal value to the present.

Rather suddenly, it came to us. We were looking for a formula relating the option value to the stock price. If the stock had an expected return equal to the interest rate, so would the option. After all, if all the stock's risk could be diversified away, so could all the option's risk. If the beta of the stock were zero, the beta of the option would have to be zero too.

If the option always had an expected return equal to the interest rate, then the discount rate that would take us from the option's expected future value to its present value would always be the interest rate. The discount rate would not depend on time or on the stock price, as it would if the stock had an expected return other than the interest rate.

So we discounted the expected terminal value of the option at the constant interest rate to get the present value of the option. Then we took Sprenkle's formula, put in the interest rate for the expected return on the stock, and put in the interest rate again for the discount rate for the option. We had our option formula.

We checked the formula against the differential equation, and sure enough, it fit. We knew it was right. A few changes, and we had a formula for puts, too.

WORKING TOWARD PUBLICATION

Our first thought was to publish a paper describing the formula. (Later, we thought also about trying to use the formula to make money trading in options and warrants.) As we worked on the paper, we had long discussions with Robert Merton, who was also working on option valuation.

Merton made a number of suggestions that improved our paper. In particular, he pointed out that if you assume continuous trading in the option or the stock, you can maintain a hedged position between them that is literally riskless. In the final version of the paper, we derived the formula that way, because it seemed to be the most general derivation.

Merton started working on a paper on aspects of the option formula. He was able to prove, along with other important points, that if you don't want a constant interest rate in the formula, you should use the interest rate on a discount bond that matures when the option expires.

Scholes and I started thinking about applying

the formula to figuring the values of risky corporate bonds and common stock. Merton began thinking about that too, but neither of us told the other. We were both working on papers about the formula, so there was a mixture of rivalry and cooperation. Scholes and I gave an early version of our paper at a conference on capital market theory sponsored by Wells Fargo Bank in the summer of 1970. We talked then about the application to corporate finance. Merton attended the conference, but he overslept on the morning of our talk, so it was only later that all of us discovered we were working on the corporate finance applications.

The first surviving draft of our paper describing the option formula (dated October 1970) was called "A Theoretical Valuation Formula for Options, Warrants, and Other Securities." I sent it to the *Journal of Political Economy* and promptly got back a rejection letter. They said that it was too specialized for them, and that it would be better in the *Journal of Finance*. I then sent it to *The Review of Economics and Statistics* and promptly got back another rejection letter. They said they could publish only a few of the papers they received. Neither journal had the paper reviewed.

I suspected that one reason these journals didn't take the paper seriously was my non-academic return address. In any case, we rewrote the paper to emphasize the economics behind the formula's derivation. The next draft (dated January 1971) was called "Capital Market Equilibrium and the Pricing of Corporate Liabilities."

Merton Miller and Eugene Fama at the University of Chicago took an interest in the paper. They gave us extensive comments on this draft, and suggested to the *Journal of Political Economy* (which is published there) that perhaps the paper was worth more serious consideration. In August 1971, the *Journal* accepted the paper, conditional on further revisions suggested by the referees.

The final draft of the paper (dated May 1972) was called "The Pricing of Options and Corporate Liabilities." It appeared in the May/June 1973 issue of the *Journal of Political Economy*. Meanwhile, we had written a paper on the results of some empirical tests of the formula, which appeared in the May 1972 *Journal of Finance*.

TESTING THE FORMULA

While we were working on our paper telling about the formula, we began to look for ways to test it on real securities. We started with warrants.

We estimated the volatility of the stock of each of a group of companies with warrants outstanding. We applied the formula in a simple way to these warrants, ignoring some of the ways in which warrants differ from options. We noticed that several warrants looked like very good buys. The best buy of all seemed to be National General new warrants.

Scholes, Merton, and I and others jumped right in and bought a bunch of these warrants. For a while, it looked as if we had done just the right thing. Then a company called American Financial announced a tender offer for National General shares. The original terms of the tender offer had the effect of sharply reducing the value of the warrants.

In other words, the market knew something that our formula didn't know. The market knew that such a tender offer was likely or possible, and that's why the warrants seemed so low in price. Although our trading didn't turn out very well, this event helped validate the formula. The market price was out of line for a very good reason.

It also illustrates a general rule. The formula and the volatility estimates we put into the formula are always based on the information at hand. The market will always have some kinds of information affecting the values of options and warrants that we don't have. Sometimes the values given by the formula will be better than market prices; at other times the market prices will be better than the formula values.

We learned that rule again in our next set of tests. One of Scholes's students managed to get data on the premiums received by a broker's option-writing customers in the over-the-counter options market. The data covered a period of several years.

We used the formula, with some simple volatility estimates, to test trading rules. We wanted to find out how much money we could have made if we had bought the options whose prices seemed lower than our formula's values, and sold the options whose prices seemed higher than our values.

Ignoring transaction costs, our profits seemed to be substantial. As these were over-the-counter options, we assumed the positions were held to maturity. To highlight the profits and losses, we combined each option position with a continuously changing stock position that created a close-to-riskless hedge all the time. The profits were consistent at around fifty cents per day per contract. Nevertheless, transaction costs in the over-the-counter options market could easily wipe out those profits.

We also tried assuming that we bought the underpriced options and sold the overpriced options at the values given by our formula, rather than at the market prices. Then we had losses of around fifty cents per day per contract. In other words, the formula seemed to have some information the market didn't have, but the market had just as much information that the formula didn't have.

Our findings do not mean that you lose if you use the formula for trading. If you trade at market prices, you get the benefit of what the market knows. But it is not a good idea to insist on trading at the values given by the formula. The market may want to trade at prices away from those values for good reasons that the formula cannot consider.

Later, after the CBOE started trading in listed options, Dan Galai wrote a Ph.D. thesis at the University of Chicago in which he tested trading rules based on the formula. Ignoring trading costs, the profits he found in trading listed options were much larger than the profits we found in over-the-counter options, because he assumed that an option position would be changed every time it became underpriced or overpriced.

For example, he tested the profitability of spreads that are kept neutral continuously. A neutral spread is a long position in one option combined with a short position in another option on the same stock. The position is close to riskless. To maintain a neutral spread, you need to change either your long position or your short position (or both) as the stock price and time-to-maturity change.

Galai figures option values using simple volatility estimates, based on past daily data on stock prices. He has only closing prices for the options, but he tries to take out some of their distortions. He assumes that you decide what to do by comparing option values and closing option prices one day, but you execute the trades at closing prices the next day. If closing prices are distorted in the same direction two days in a row, they may still overstate your prices. But if it's possible to trade only at a favorable price, and not at just any next-day's price, then this will understate your profits. This method also ignores profits that market makers can make by opening and closing positions within a single day.

The spreads that Galai looked at involve buying one contract of the underpriced option and selling either more or less than one contract of the overpriced option: whatever is needed to create and maintain a neutral spread. Ignoring transaction costs, the average spread gives a consistent profit of $4.00 or $5.00 per day.

That sounds like a fast way to make money. But it does ignore trading costs, which are especially high for people who have to pay retail commissions. And it does assume trading at the next day's closing prices — a conservative assumption, but one that still may cause profits to be overstated. Finally, the period Galai studied was July 1973 to April 1974. Opportunities like this are harder to come by these days.

One reason for the change is that traders now use the formula and its variants extensively. They use it so much that market prices are usually close to formula values even in situations where there should be a large difference: situations, for example, where a cash takeover is likely to end the life of the option or warrant.

Article 12

by Fischer Black

Fact and Fantasy In the Use of Options

Options trading is where the action is in the securities markets these days.[1] There are some good reasons for the growing popularity of options trading, such as the fact that the brokerage charge for taking a position in options can sometimes be lower than the charge for taking an equivalent position directly in the underlying stock. But for every fact about options, there is a fantasy—a reason given for trading or not trading in options that doesn't make sense when examined carefully. It is sometimes said, for example, that covered option writers almost always gain more than they lose by writing options. This statement focuses on the premium income, and downplays the possible loss of appreciation on the stock if the option is exercised. In fact, careful study shows that an investor who writes call options against his stock will often end up with a worse position than the one he started with.

This article aims at separating fact and fantasy. It will make heavy use of the option formula developed by Black and Scholes, and of the kind of analysis that led to the formula.[2] It will make use of several refinements and extensions of the formula, some of which have been published, and some of which have not yet appeared in final form.[3]

The Option Formula

The option formula (shown in Appendix A) gives the value of a call option for any stock price and time to maturity. The simplest version of the

Fischer Black is Professor of Finance, Graduate School of Business, University of Chicago. He wishes to thank Myron Scholes and Robert Merton for extensive discussions on these issues, and Paul Blair, James Dalton and Joseph Williams for comments on an earlier draft. This work was supported in part by the Center for Research in Security Prices (sponsored by Merrill Lynch, Pierce, Fenner & Smith, Inc.) at the University of Chicago.

formula assumes that the short-term interest rate and the volatility of the stock never change, and that the stock pays no dividends. Thus there are five numbers we need to calculate an option value: (1) the stock price, (2) the time to maturity, (3) the exercise price, (4) the interest rate, and (5) the volatility of the stock.

The tables in Appendix B show the values of an option with a $40 exercise price according to the formula. The option values are arranged in three different ways, so it will be easy to see the effects of changes in any one of the four inputs other than the exercise price. The values for an option with an exercise price other than $40 can be obtained by making proportional changes in the stock price, the exercise price, and the option value.

The big unknown in the option formula is the volatility of the underlying stock. The time to maturity and the exercise price are known. The stock price and the interest rate can be observed. But the volatility of the stock must be estimated. The past volatility of the stock is very helpful in estimating its future volatility, but is not an infallible guide. The volatility of a stock can change over time, and factors other than past volatility can be helpful in predicting it.

Note that the value of an option for a given stock price does not depend on what the stock is expected to do. An option on a stock that is expected to go up has the same value, in terms of the stock, as an option on a stock that is expected to go down. An investor who thinks the stock will go up will think both the stock and the option are underpriced. An investor who thinks the stock will go down won't buy either the stock or the option.

If the price of an option on an exchange is higher than its value, and if the formula is giving the correct value, then an investor who holds the option should sell it, and an investor who doesn't hold the option should write it. If the price of an option on an exchange is lower than its value, and if the formula is giving the correct value, then an investor who doesn't hold the option should buy it, and an investor who has written the option should buy it back.

In other words, the rules for an option buyer are the same as the rules for an option writer. If the option is underpriced, buy it. If the option is overpriced, sell it. An option writer will generally lose if he writes underpriced options, whether he holds the underlying stock or not. His premium income on an underpriced option will be more than offset by his expected losses due to a possible increase in the price of the option over its life.

The writer's gains are the buyer's losses, and the writer's losses are the buyer's gains. If an option is overpriced when it is written, the writer is likely to gain and the buyer is likely to lose. If it is underpriced when it is written, the writer is likely to lose and the buyer is likely to gain. This is true of the writer's options position whether or not he owns the underlying stock.

The hedge ratio is the ratio of the change in the option value to the change in the stock price, for very small changes in the stock price. In Appendix B, the hedge ratios appear in parentheses, under the option values. To see the effects of larger changes in the stock price, we compare two different entries in the same table. We look down a single column at the values of the option for different stock prices.

The hedge ratio tells how to set up a "neutral hedge" between the option and the stock. A neutral hedge is one that is low in risk for small moves in the stock. The hedge ratio is the ratio of stock to option needed for a neutral hedge. For example, suppose the hedge ratio is 0.50. That means that the option value goes up or down about $0.50 when the stock goes up or down $1.00. Then a position that is short two options and long one stock or long two options and short one stock will change in value very little when the stock goes up or down $1.00.[4] The gains or losses on the long position will be offset by losses or gains on the short position. Because large moves in the stock tend to alter the hedge ratio, however, they will bring gains or losses on a fixed hedged position.

In a neutral hedge, the value of the long position need not equal the value of the short position. Suppose, in the above example, that the option price is $5 and the stock price is $40. Then the value of two options is $10, while the value of one stock is $40. The values of the two sides of the position are not even close.

Option versus Stock

The value of an option is closely related to the price of its underlying stock. For small moves in the stock over a short period of time, there is a position in the option that will give almost the same action (in dollars) as a position in the stock. The hedge ratio tells what that position is. If the hedge ratio is 0.33 at a given point in time, then three options will give the same action (in dollars) as one share of stock. This is true for both buyer and seller. Buying three option contracts gives the same action (for small price moves in the short run) as buying one round lot of stock; and selling three option contracts gives the same action as shorting one round lot of stock.

So an investor who wants the action on a stock has two ways of getting it. He can deal directly in the stock, or he can deal in the option. For equivalent dollar action, he usually has to take a larger share position in the option than he would take in the stock.

Changes in the stock price and in time to maturity cause changes in the option position that is equivalent to a stock position. As the stock price goes up, the number of option contracts needed for a position equivalent to one round lot of stock goes down. When the position is way out of the money, it may take ten contracts to give a position equivalent to one round lot. When the option is way in the money, it may take only one contract to give a position equivalent to one round lot.

Sometimes it's better for an investor who wants a position in the stock to take it directly, and sometimes it's better for him to take it via the option. If the option is underpriced—i.e., he can buy it for less than the formula says it's worth—then it may be better to buy the option than to buy the stock. If the commission on an equivalent option position is less than the commission on the stock, it may be better to deal in the option. If the investor wants a short position, it is often better to sell naked calls than to short the stock, because he may get interest on the proceeds of the sale of options. The investor may have to put up less capital to take an equivalent option position, and this can be important if he has limited capital. And finally, there may be tax reasons for dealing in the option instead of the stock.

However, these factors do not always favor options. If it takes ten $100 option contracts to get the equivalent of one round lot of stock, the commission on the ten contracts is $85, under the current commission schedule. But the commission on one round lot of a $40 stock would be about $60. So the fact that multiple option contracts are often needed to get the equivalent of a given stock position can make the option commissions higher than stock commissions.

If options are priced according to the formula, then the "net money" in a stock position is always more than the net money in an equivalent option position.[5] This means that the alternative to a long stock position is a mixture of long option positions and short-term money market instruments. For example, instead of putting up $4,000 for 100 shares of a $40 stock, the investor might pay $1,000 for two option contracts, and put the remaining $3,000 in certificates of deposit.

In the short run, the option position may go up or down just about the same amount as the stock position. In the long run, if the option position is not changed, it will do better than the stock position for large moves in the stock price, and worse than the stock position if the stock price remains about the same. If the stock ends up at the exercise price, the option will expire worthless, and the option position will be down $1,000. But if the stock goes way up, the option position will start moving up twice as fast as the stock position, and will end up with a higher value than the stock position. And if the stock goes way down, the option position will go down a maximum of $1,000, while the stock position can go down any amount up to $4,000.[6]

Thus an appropriate mixture of a long position in options with short-term money market instruments is less speculative from almost any point of view than an investment in the underlying stock. In the short run, the risk in the two positions is the same. And in the long run, the option position comes out ahead for large moves in the stock in either direction. The right mixture of options and CD's has the same expected return as the corresponding stock position, but is surely a more conservative strategy.[7]

Writing Options

Writing naked call options compared with shorting the stock is like buying call options compared with buying the stock.[8] If options are priced according to the formula, and if the hedge ratio is used to set up an equivalent position, then a short position in options will give the same gains or losses in the short run as the equivalent short position in stock. In the long run, the short option position will do better than the short stock position if the stock doesn't move much. But the short option position will do worse than the equivalent short stock position if the stock goes way up or way down and the option position is left unchanged. If buying options is less speculative than buying an equivalent amount of stock, then writing

naked options is more speculative than shorting an equivalent amount of stock.

Writing options against a stock position gives the equivalent of a long position in the stock. An investor who is long 100 shares of stock and short one option contract has a position that will go up in value if the stock goes up, and down in value if the stock goes down. This position can be compared with the two alternatives we have already discussed: a position in the underlying stock without option writing, and a long position in the option.

A position with one round lot of stock long and one option contract short is less risky in the short run than a position with just the one round lot of stock. If a long position in two option contracts is equivalent in the short run to a long position in 100 shares of stock, then a position with 100 shares of stock long and one option contract short will be equivalent to a long position in only 50 shares of stock. Thus the following positions are equivalent in the short run, if the hedge ratio is 0.50: (1) a position that is long 100 shares of stock

Drawing by B. Tobey; © 1958
The New Yorker Magazine, Inc.

"If you want to make a fast buck,
just go in and tell them you want to make a fast buck."

and short one option contract; (2) a position that is long 50 shares of stock; and (3) a position that is long one option contract.

These three positions involve different amounts of net money. Assuming that the stock price is $40 and the option price is $5, the net money involved in each position is: (1) $3,500; (2) $2,000; and (3) $500. To see what happens to the equivalent positions in the long run, we can assume that the investor puts up $3,500, and invests the difference between $3,500 and the net money (if any) in CD's. Thus the investment in CD's in each case is: (1) zero; (2) $1500; and (3) $3000.

The investment in CD's is the limit on the amount the investor can lose. If the stock goes to zero, the investor who buys stock and writes options will lose everything; the investor who buys stock and CD's will end up with $1,500 plus interest; and the investor who buys options and CD's will end up with $3,000 plus interest. Of these three positions, the first is the most speculative (writing covered options) and the last is the least speculative (buying options and CD's).

Writing options against a stock position is speculative because this strategy does worse for large moves in the stock than alternative strategies that have equivalent exposure to the action in the stock for small moves in the stock. If an investor writes options against his stock position and the stock doesn't move, he ends up better off than if he went to an equivalent position by selling some of his stock. But if the stock has a large move, he ends up worse off than if he went to an equivalent position by selling some of his stock.

If the formula gives the correct price for an option, and if an investor writes an option against stock at that price, he is making a fair deal. His possible gains if the stock stays at about the same price are just offset by his possible losses if the stock makes a wide move (relative to selling some of his stock instead). It is not correct to say that an investor can increase his rate of return by writing call options against his stock. In fact, he reduces his "expected return," because he creates a position that is equivalent to selling some of his stock. He creates a position in which he will come out ahead only if the stock doesn't move very much. He will come out behind if the stock moves a lot.

The only way a writer can improve expected return and retain the same exposure to small stock movements is to buy more stock and write overpriced options against his total stock position. The hedge ratio tells how much more stock to buy. If the hedge ratio is 0.50, then writing options against a stock position cuts its exposure in half; so the investor should double his stock position and write overpriced calls on all of it. If the hedge ratio is 0.33, then writing options against a stock position cuts its exposure by a third; so the investor should increase his stock position by 50 per cent, and then write overpriced calls on all of it.

Writing calls makes sense when the calls are overpriced. It does not make sense when the calls are underpriced. The fact that one position is more "speculative" than another is not important in most cases. It becomes important when a large loss has more serious consequences than loss of the money. When a large loss would lead to lawsuits and other complications, it may become important to avoid the more speculative positions. Writing overpriced calls against a stock position makes just as much sense as buying underpriced calls for most investors.

Hedging and Spreading

One way to use options is to hedge options against stock. If the hedge ratio is 0.33, then a neutral hedge will be three option contracts against one round lot of stock. A neutral hedge is achieved by going either long the stock and short the options, or short the stock and long the options. A neutral hedge is neither bullish nor bearish. If the hedge is long stock and short options, it will show gains for small moves in the stock and losses for large moves in the stock in either direction. If the hedge is long options and short stock, it will show losses for small moves in the stock and gains for large moves in the stock in either direction.[9]

When the option is underpriced, then the way to hedge is to go long options and short stock. When the option is overpriced, the way to hedge is to go long stock and short options. The farther out of line the option is, the larger the range of stock prices for which the hedge will end up profitable, and the smaller the range of stock prices for which the hedge will end up unprofitable.

Another way to use options is to spread options against one another. A "money spread" involves buying an option at one striking price and selling an option at another striking price, both on the same stock and with the same maturity. A "time spread" or "calendar spread" involves buying an option at one maturity and selling one at another; both on the same stock with the same striking price. A "butterfly spread" involves buying an option in the middle (in terms of either striking price or time) and selling one on each side, or selling an option in the middle and buying one on each side. More complicated spreads are possible too.

The hedge ratios on two options tell how to create a neutral spread between them. To find the right ratio, just divide the two hedge ratios. For example, if the hedge ratio on an October option is 0.10, and the hedge ratio on the corresponding January option is 0.30, then a neutral hedge would involve three Octobers and one January.

Once the ratio of options in a spread has been figured, the spread can be analyzed more exactly. With a 3:1 spread, we multiply the value of the first option by three, and subtract the result from the value of the second option. This is the value of the spread. Then we multiply the price of the first option by three, and subtract the result from the price of the second option. This is the price of the spread. If the value is greater than the price, it makes sense to sell the first option and buy the second. If the value is less than the price, it makes sense to buy the first option and sell the second.

A spread makes sense, of course, when the long side is underpriced and the short side is overpriced, or when the long side is more underpriced than the short side, or when the long side is less overpriced than the short side. The analysis of a spread is less sensitive to the estimated volatility of the stock than the analysis of a hedge of option against stock; an increase in the volatility estimate will increase the value of all the options on a stock. If an October option seems more overpriced than the corresponding January, and we increase the volatility estimate on the stock so that both now seem underpriced, it is likely that the October will seem less underpriced than the January. The indicated spread will be the same in either case: short the October and long the January in an appropriate ratio.

A spread that is short the near month and long a more distant month is speculative, in the sense that it makes money for small moves in the stock, and loses money for large moves in the stock. Very large moves in the stock can be disastrous if the spread is not changed. This is particularly true when the spread ratio is high. A position with one January long and ten Octobers short has great exposure to potential large losses. Similarly, a spread that is long a more in-the-money option and short a more out-of-the-money option is speculative. A position with one $60 option long and ten $80 options short has great exposure to potential large losses. The greater the difference in the exercise prices, the more speculative it is. It makes sense for an investor who is working with spreads to try to have some that are speculative and some that are conservative. Then if stocks generally move way up or way down, his gains on the conservative spreads will help offset his losses on the speculative spreads; and if stocks generally don't move very much, his gains on the speculative spreads will help offset his losses on the conservative spreads.

Estimating Volatility

The volatility of a stock can be estimated by looking at the size of the typical change in the stock price from day to day. The farther back in time we look, the more data we have to look at. If the volatility of a stock did not change, we would look as far back as possible, and would give as much weight to far distant months as to near months. But the volatility does change, so more weight should be given to recent months, and less weight should be given to distant months.

This means that when a stock seems to have a sharp increase in volatility during a month, our estimate for the future will be higher than it was, but not as high as the apparent volatility in the latest month. Sharp increases and decreases in volatility are often only temporary.

In estimating the volatility of a stock, we can also use information on the price behavior of other stocks. If the latest month shows a sharp increase in volatility for stocks generally, then it makes sense to increase our volatility estimate more for any given stock than we would if it were the only stock showing a sharp increase in volatility. If the latest month shows a sharp increase in the volatility of one of two stocks in the same industry, then the estimated volatility on the other stock should be increased too.

The direction of the price movement in a stock can also be used. A stock that drops sharply in price is likely to show a higher volatility in the future (in percentage terms) than a stock that rises sharply in price.

Sometimes other kinds of information can be useful. If we know that a company with a volatile stock is merging with a large, stable company, we may want to reduce our estimate of the future volatility of its stock. If we know that a company is starting a risky new venture, we may want to increase our estimate of the future volatility of its stock.

An increase in the estimated volatility for a stock will increase the values of all the options on the stock. Thus when the options on a stock seem generally overpriced, it is possible that the "market's estimate" of the volatility of the stock is higher than the estimate used in the formula. When the options on a stock seem generally underpriced, it is possible that the market's estimate of its volatility is lower than the estimate used in the formula. (The other possibility is that the market is simply pricing the options incorrectly.) Since the market may know some things about the future volatility in the stock that we don't know, the volatility estimate implied by the general level of option prices on a stock should be given some weight in estimating the stock's future volatility.

There are times when most traded options seem underpriced, and times when most traded options seem overpriced. Again, there are two kinds of possible explanations for this. It may be that the market is expecting volatilities to be generally lower or generally higher than the estimates used in the formula, or it may be that factors unrelated to option values are affecting the option prices.

Sometimes there should be a different volatility estimate for each option maturity. If the volatility of a stock was unusually high in the latest month, we might project a gradual decline in volatility back to more normal levels. On the other hand, if the volatility of the stock has been increasing in recent months, we might project a continued increase in volatility for a time.

Interest Rates

The interest rate in the option formula is the rate on a very low risk note that matures at the time the option expires. This means that there normally will be a different interest rate for each different option maturity. The rates on CD's and prime commercial paper are given separately for different maturities, so it makes sense to use those rates as inputs to the option formula.

Holding constant all the inputs to the option formula except the interest rate, an increase in the interest rate always increases the value of an option. To get a rough idea of why this is so, note that an increase in the interest rate reduces the present value of the exercise price. Since the exercise price is a potential liability for the holder of an option, this increases the value of the option. A one percentage point change in the interest rate does not generally have much effect on the value of an option. To see the effects of a five percentage point change in the interest rate, see Table 2 in Appendix B.

An increase in the interest rate will have a larger effect on an option with long maturity than on an option with a short maturity. Thus a change in the interest rate will change the relative values of near and far options.

An increase in the interest rate has the same effect as a reduction in the exercise price of an option, when the stock pays no dividends. A one per cent fall in the price of a CD maturing at the same time as the option has the same effect as a one per cent reduction in the exercise price.

In practice, a change in the interest rate will not occur by itself. Over the same period, there may be a change in the stock price and a change in the volatility of the stock. The change in the option price will reflect all of these changes.

Dividends

An option on a stock that pays a dividend is worth less than an option on an identical stock that pays no dividend. The higher the dividend, the less the option is worth. When a stock goes ex-dividend, the stock price usually falls, reducing the likelihood that the stock will be above its exercise price at maturity, hence the value of the option.

If the option will be exercised only at maturity, we can approximate the value of the option on a dividend paying stock by subtracting the present value of the dividends likely to be paid before maturity from the stock price. We use this adjusted stock price instead of the actual stock price in the option formula. We get the present value of the dividends by discounting them at the interest rate we are assuming. For example, if a dividend is due in three months and the interest rate is 12 per cent we discount the dividend by dividing it by about 1.03. (The number will differ slightly from 1.03 because of the effects of compounding.)

Sometimes, however, it pays to exercise an option just before it goes ex-dividend. For all dividends except the last one before the option expires, it can pay only if the annual dividend divided by the exercise price of the option is greater than the interest rate.[10] This condition is rarely satisfied. But it often pays to exercise an in-the-money option just before the last ex-dividend date. The closer the last ex-dividend date is to the expiration date of the option, the more likely it is that exercise just before the ex-dividend date will make sense.

Because there is a possibility that it will pay to exercise the option just before the last ex-dividend date, we can figure an alternative value of the option by assuming that it expires just before the last ex-dividend date. If this gives a higher value of the option than the first calculation, we will use it instead. The fact that we are using a shorter time to maturity tends to reduce the value of the option, but the fact that we are not subtracting the discounted value of the last dividend tends to increase it.

The closer the last ex-dividend date is to the maturity date, the more likely it is that the effect of leaving off the last dividend will dominate the effect of reducing the time to maturity.

Thus to figure the value of an option on a dividend-paying stock, we do two calculations of the value, and use the one that gives the higher value.[11] The first calculation subtracts the present value of all the dividends from the stock price, and uses the actual maturity date for the option. The second calculation subtracts the present value of all dividends but the last, and uses a maturity date just before the last ex-dividend date.

The holder of an option should be careful to decide whether it will pay to hold it beyond the last ex-dividend date. When the stock price is well above the exercise price just before the last ex-dividend date, it will often pay either to exercise or to sell out. This means that the writer should decide whether he wants to close his position by buying in or by having the option exercised against him. If he doesn't buy in before the stock goes ex-dividend, he may find that he has been assigned an exercise notice.

The holder of an option should keep it beyond the last ex-dividend date only if it is worth more "alive" than "dead." The value of the option alive will be its value with the stock price reduced by the dividend, with a time to maturity equal to the time between the last ex-dividend date and the date the option expires. The value of the option dead will be the stock price minus the exercise price.

The writer of an option should decide whether to buy in before the last ex-dividend date on the same basis. If he wants to avoid an exercise notice, and the option will be worth more dead than alive on the ex-dividend date, he should buy in before that date—probably several days before, because the exercise notices will start coming in faster several days before the ex-dividend date.

Transaction Costs

The transaction costs for trading in options will often be lower than the costs of making an equivalent trade in the underlying stocks. For example, assume that a six-month option with a $40 exercise price sells for $5 when the stock price is $40, and has a hedge ratio of 0.60. The round trip public commission for taking a position in the stock is now three per cent or more of the value of the stock. For a round lot of stock, this comes to $120.

To get a position that is equivalent to one round lot of stock in the short run, we need less than two option contracts. (If the hedge ratio were 0.50, we would need exactly two.) The public commission on two option contracts with a premium of $500 for each contract is $37 one way. If the option expires worthless, no further commission will be paid. If it ends up in the money, there will be a commission on the closing transaction. If it is exercised, the commission is based on the exercise price, but is no more than $65.

Taking all these possibilities into account, we get a round trip commission for the option position of around $60, which is about half the commission cost of dealing in the stock directly. This saving, however, applies only to short-term trading. If we try to take the equivalent of a long-term position in the stock by buying or selling options repeatedly, we will end up paying much more in commissions than we would in the stock.

Another element of the transaction cost on either options or stock is the market maker's or specialist's spread: the difference between the highest bid price and the lowest asked price.[12] We should use the hedge ratio to compare spreads on options with spreads on stock, just as we used it to compare commissions. When the hedge ratio is 0.50 on an option, we should compare twice the spread in the option market with the spread on the underlying stock on the stock exchange. Since it takes two option contracts to give the same action as one round lot of stock in the short run, we need to compare the spread for two option contracts with the spread for one round lot of stock.

It would not be surprising to find that the market makers' and specialists' spreads are higher on the options market than the spreads for equivalent positions in the stock market, because "information trading" may tend to shift from the market for a stock to the market for its options.

One reason why a market maker's or specialist's buying price is lower than his selling price is that he doesn't know what information those who trade with him may have. Many of them will have information about the stock that he doesn't have. He does know, however, that those who want to sell to him probably have negative information, and those who want to buy from him probably have positive information. So he protects himself to some extent by quoting a lower price to those who want to sell and a higher price to those who want to buy. He will still lose money trading with those who have important pieces of information, and this will cut into the profits he makes trading with those who do not have valuable pieces of information.

Since an investor can usually get more action for a given investment in options than he can by investing directly in the underlying stock, he may choose to deal in options when he feels he has an especially important piece of information. Also, it is easier to take a short position by writing options than by shorting the underlying stock. So many information traders will go to the options market rather than to the stock market. And many potential information traders will trade on the options market when they wouldn't bother to trade at all if the options market did not exist.

This means that in some cases a market maker or specialist will face a more dangerous trading environment on an options exchange than the specialist on the same stock faces on a stock exchange. A higher proportion of those the market maker trades with will have information that can hurt him. So he may have to set a higher bid-asked spread than the specialist in the stock does (for a corresponding position) just to break even.

The fact that the options market brings out information traders who wouldn't otherwise trade means that the market for the stock will be more efficient than it would be without the options market. Even if a piece of information shows up first on the options market, hedgers will rapidly cause the information to be incorporated in stock prices. Options trading will improve the market in the underlying stock, even if it reduces the volume of trading in the underlying stock. But because hedging brings new trading in the stock, it is unlikely that options trading will reduce the volume of trading in the underlying stock.[13]

Taxes

It appears that gains and losses for an option buyer will be taxed as capital gains and losses, while gains and losses for an option writer who buys his options back will be taxed as ordinary income or loss. A buyer who exercises his option defers realizing a gain or loss, and a writer who has an option exercised against him realizes a capital gain or loss rather than ordinary income or loss.

If everyone were in a 70 per cent tax bracket, then option values would be lower than the values given by the formula. If everyone were in the same tax bracket, then the higher the common tax bracket, the lower the option values would be. The effects of taxes are similar to the effects of dividends on the underlying stock. High taxes reduce option values, and make it profitable sometimes for an option buyer to exercise his option before it expires.

To get a rough idea of the amount by which taxes can affect option values, we can calculate a discount factor as follows. We multiply the interest rate by the common tax bracket. We multiply this by the fraction of a year that remains before the option expires, and add 1.0. We divide the stock price by this discount factor before applying the option formula. Note that the discount factor is applied to the stock price, not to the option value directly.

When the interest rate is 12 per cent, the effect on option values of assuming a common tax bracket of 50 per cent is similar to the effect of assuming that the stock pays a six per cent dividend. The effect is not huge, but it is sometimes significant.

When tax brackets differ, an option will have a different value for an investor in a high tax bracket than for an investor in a low tax bracket. The value will be lower for the investor in a high tax bracket. This means that investors in high tax brackets should more often be writers of options, and investors in low tax brackets should more often be buyers of options. This is true in spite of the fact that investors in high tax brackets who buy options may get the benefit of capital gains taxation of their gains. Investors in low tax brackets also get the benefit of capital gains treatment, and they are taxed at lower rates.

In particular, it means that tax exempt institutions would generally be better off buying options than writing them, so long as they are not overpriced. Hopefully, the push to allow institutions to write options freely will be extended so that they will be allowed to buy options, too. While buying options is often considered imprudent, we have already noted that a mixture of options and CD's is actually less speculative than an equivalent combination of holding stock and writing options.

If the price of an option is $6, it may be worth $7 to a tax-exempt investor, and $5 to a taxable investor. When the taxable investor writes the option at $6, he makes $1. When the tax-exempt investor buys the option at $6, he makes $1. They both gain at the expense of the government.

Taxes affect the hedge ratios, too. An investor in a high tax bracket who wants a neutral hedge that is long stock and short options will have to write more options than an investor in a low tax bracket. Suppose, for example, that the hedge ratio is 0.50. A tax exempt investor would buy one round lot of stock and write two option contracts. But an investor in a 50 per cent tax bracket might write three or four option contracts. If he is going to continue to hold the stock, then he won't realize any gains or losses from the stock. But he will realize his gains or losses from the option. If the option goes up, he will realize an ordinary loss, so the government will pay for half of the loss. If the option goes down, he will realize ordinary income, so the government will take half the gain. In effect, the government is taking half the risk. So he needs to write twice as many options to get the same after-tax risk he would have if he were tax exempt. To get a neutral hedge, he writes four option contracts instead of two against one round lot.

If an investor in a high tax bracket writes in-the-money options, he has an additional possible advantage. If the option goes up, he will have an ordinary loss. If the option expires worthless, he will have ordinary income. But if the option goes down but ends up in the money, he can let the option be exercised against him. He can either deliver the stock he holds or buy new stock in the market, and thus realize a capital gain or loss instead of ordinary income.

To see how options can be used to save taxes, let us consider an extreme example: an option with a zero exercise price. This will allow us to illustrate the principles involved in a relatively simple manner. We will assume a $40 stock, and an option that expires in three months with an exercise price of zero. We will assume that the option can be exercised at any time, so it will have a value equal to the stock price at all times. If the stock goes ex-dividend, the option will be exercised before the ex-dividend day. We will assume no dividends.

Now suppose an investor in a 50 per cent tax bracket owns 100 shares of stock and sells options on 200 shares. He is selling options on more shares than he owns. Suppose further that he plans to keep the stock, but to buy back the options just before they expire. The gains or losses on his stock will remain unrealized, while the gains or losses on the options will become ordinary income or loss. Thus his after-tax gains or losses on the options will be only half of his before-tax gains or losses. Since he has written options on two shares of stock for each share he owns, his position is perfectly hedged. Taking taxes into account, his gains or losses on the options will exactly offset his unrealized gains or losses on the stock.

But the option premiums total $8000, while the investor has only $4000 in the stock. He has $4000 to work with until the options are exercised or until he buys them back. He can invest that $4000. His gain is the interest on $4000 for the life of the option. And he gets that without bearing any risk at all. In effect, he gets an interest-free loan of $4000 for the life of the option. The equity in his hedged position is negative. Of course, he gets this benefit only if he gets interest on the proceeds of the options he wrote naked. If he doesn't get the benefit, his brokerage firm will.

But there is more. The investor doesn't have to buy back all his options at the end. If the price of the stock is lower than it was when the options were sold, he may want to let the options on 100 shares be exercised. This will give him a capital gain or loss, depending on his cost basis for the shares. If it is a capital loss, he is clearly better off letting the options on 100 shares be exercised. If it is a capital gain, he may be better off letting them be exercised, depending on the exact amount of the gain, on whether it is long term or short term, and on how long he is likely to let the gain go unrealized if he buys the options back.

These tax benefits can be shared with the buyer of the options, especially if the buyer is an investor in a low tax bracket. One way to do this is to deal in options that have an exercise price that is not

zero. For example, suppose we have an option on a $40 stock with an exercise price of $10, and suppose that both writer and buyer agree that all transactions in the option will be at the stock price minus the exercise price. A tax-exempt buyer gets the action on a $40 stock for only $30. In effect, he gets a $10 interest-free loan. His gain is the interest on $10 for each share of stock.

Suppose the writer also wants the action on 100 shares. Assuming he will buy back his options at the end, he can accomplish this by buying 200 shares of stock and writing options on 200 shares. Since his gains and losses on the options are taxable at 50 per cent, the options on 200 shares only offset the gains and losses on 100 shares of stock, so he is left with the action on 100 shares. Since the options sell initially for $3000 per 100 shares, he gets $6000 for the options, and pays $8000 for the stock. His net investment is $2000 for the action on $4000 worth of stock. In effect, he is getting a $2000 interest-free loan. His gain is the interest on $2000. Since this interest is taxable, his net gain is the interest on $1000. This is the same as the tax-exempt investor's gain.

Thus both parties to the transaction get an extra three per cent after taxes on their equity, when the interest rate is 12 per cent. They get the return on the stock plus an extra three per cent. And this doesn't count the substantial extra gain that the taxable investor may get by letting his options be exercised if the stock goes down. This should be enough to show, however, that the potential tax advantages from the use of options are truly enormous.

These factors operate on listed options, too. They probably explain why options that are well in-the-money (the stock price is well above the exercise price) often sell at tangible value (stock price minus exercise price). At that price, the option is a clear bargain for a tax-exempt investor. And a taxable investor may be able to make money writing it at the same time.

For an option sold with an exercise price equal to the stock price at the time, the right to let the option be exercised is not worth much to the writer. He will gain if the stock ends up close to the initial price (but above it). If the initial price is $40, and the option sold for $5, and the stock ends up just above $40, then the writer's ordinary income if he buys the option back is just under $5. But if he lets the option be exercised, and if he has held the stock for more than six months, he will have a long-term capital gain of $5. The profit is the same, but it is taxed as long-term capital gains, rather than as ordinary income. But he gets no benefit if the stock ends up above $45 or below

$40. If it's below $40, the option won't be exercised.

But even an option sold with an exercise price equal to the stock price at the time has a tax value to a writer in a high tax bracket. In general, high bracket investors should write options, and low bracket investors should buy them.

Individual listed options may be priced at times so high that even a tax-exempt investor should write them; or so low that even a taxable investor should buy them. The option formula may help in identifying such cases. The ideal strategy might be to use the formula to help taxable investors sell overpriced options and to help tax-exempt investors buy underpriced options.

Margin Requirements

Brokers cannot lend money for the purchase of options. But this is often not a problem, because to get the equivalent of buying a stock on margin, the investor may want to hold a mixture of options and short-term money market instruments. In that case he won't want to borrow to buy options.

The investor who wants the equivalent of a short position in the stock may be much better off writing options than shorting the stock directly. If he can keep both the amount he puts up in margin and the premiums he receives in government securities, then he will be earning interest. Even if he loses interest on one or both of these amounts, they are normally smaller than the amounts he loses interest on if he shorts the stock.

Further, a taxable investor who writes naked options realizes ordinary losses if he is wrong, while an investor who shorts the stock realizes short-term capital losses if he is wrong. Ordinary losses can be used without limit, while capital losses can only be used to offset capital gains plus a small amount of ordinary income. So writing options will be better than shorting stock for both margin reasons and tax reasons.

Actual Prices

The actual prices on listed options tend to differ in certain systematic ways from the values given by the formula. Options that are way out of the money tend to be overpriced, and options that are way into the money tend to be underpriced. Options with less than three months to maturity tend to be overpriced.

Thus the money spreads that make sense usually involve buying an option with a lower exercise price and selling a corresponding option with a higher exercise price. The time spreads that make sense usually involve buying an option with a longer maturity and selling an option with a shorter maturity. The stock option hedges that seem most profitable involve buying the stock and selling out-of-the-money options with only a little time left to go. At least this has been true so far. As time goes on, the pattern may change.

One possible explanation for this pattern is that we have left someting out of the formula. Perhaps if we assumed a more complicated pattern for changes in a stock's volatility, or for changes in interest rates, we would be able to explain the overpricing of out-of-the-money options. But this seems unlikely to give a complete explanation. The underpricing of way in-the-money options is so extreme that they often sell at "parity," where the option price is approximately equal to the stock price minus the exercise price. This means that the market is not giving the remaining time to maturity any value at all. Only tax factors, as discussed above, seem to have any chance of explaining this.

Another possible explanation for the observed pattern is that market makers and other investors have to be induced to take the indicated positions by the promise of substantial profits, because they are so speculative. A market maker who buys one option contract for $1,000 and sells ten contracts at a higher exercise price for $12.50 each is taking a great risk. A sudden large move in the stock price in either direction may give him great losses. If the stock moves down, he can lose all the money he put up. If the stock moves up, he can lose more than all the money he put up.

Those who buy short, out-of-the-money options and mix them with CD's have conservative positions. At most, they can lose all the money they put into the options. Those who write short, out-of-the-money options have speculative positions, even if they hold the underlying stock. They can lose all the money they have invested, and sometimes more. So it may be that those who want conservative positions must pay others to take the speculative positions.

Still another possible explanation is that options give a form of leverage that is otherwise unavailable because of margin restrictions, and that investors bid up their prices because of the leverage they get. This explanation seems very unlikely for two reasons. First, it can't explain why in-the-money options are usually underpriced. They can offer more leverage than the investor can get directly, yet they are underpriced. And second, it can't explain why competition among writers doesn't eliminate the overpricing of out-of-the-money options. There are great numbers of investors who have as much leverage as they want, and would be glad to earn extra money by writing overpriced options if writing options were not so speculative.

At the moment, I think we have to say that we don't know why some kinds of options are consistently overpriced according to the formula and others are consistently underpriced.

Regulation

The SEC seems to be doing a good job in regulating options trading. It has allowed the creation of exchanges that are more advanced in several respects than existing stock exchanges. Clearing facilities are more modern and lower in cost, and short positions are as easy to open as long positions.

However, the Commission has imposed restrictions on the trading of options that are way out of the money. It is hard to see how this can be in the public interest.

Apparently the Commission feels that those who buy way out-of-the-money options are throwing their money away, because there is so little chance that they will be worth anything at maturity. And in fact, the formula suggests that such options are usually overpriced. But we have already noted that careful buyers of such options are actually bearing less risk of catastrophic loss than those who write the options. If the SEC restricts trading, it will hurt those who buy options to reduce their exposure to loss as well as those who buy options to increase their potential gains. Further, no one has to buy these options. Anyone who wants to can write them instead. So this seems like a situation where any possible problems can be adequately solved through additional disclosure. ∎

APPENDIX A. THE FORMULA

The simple option formula is Equation 13 on page 644 of the article by Black and Scholes (1973):

$$w(x, t) = xN(d_1) - ce^{r(t-t^*)}N(d_2)$$

$$d_1 = \frac{ln\frac{x}{c} + (r + \frac{1}{2}v^2)(t^*-t)}{v\sqrt{t^*-t}}$$

$$d_2 = \frac{ln\frac{x}{c} + (r - \frac{1}{2}v^2)(t^*-t)}{v\sqrt{t^*-t}}$$

In this formula, x is the stock price, c is the exercise price, t is the current time, t^* is the time at which the option expires, r is the interest rate, v^2 is the variance rate of the return on the stock (a measure of the stock's volatility), ln is the natural logarithm, N(d) is the cumulative normal density function, and w(x, t) is the value of the option at time t when the stock price is x.

The "hedge ratio" is given by Equation 14 on page 645 of the article by Black and Scholes (1973):

$$w_1(x, t) = N(d_1)$$

In this formula, $w_1(x, t)$ is the derivative of the option formula with respect to the stock price. It is the change in the option value for a small change in the stock price, divided by the change in the stock price. Or it is the number of round lots of stock needed to balance one option·contract to create a hedged position. The other symbols in this formula are defined as they are for the option formula.

APPENDIX B. TABLES OF OPTION VALUES AND HEDGE RATIOS

The tables given below show the values and hedge ratios for an option with an exercise price of $40, for different values of the other inputs to the option formula. There are six different stock prices, three maturities, three interest rates, and nine values of the volatility (annual standard deviation). The hedge ratios are in parentheses.

Table 1 makes it easy to see the influence of stock price and maturity. Reading down, we see how the value of an option changes as the stock price increases. Reading across, we see how the value changes as the maturity increases. An increase in either the stock price or the maturity will always increase the value of the option. Note that while a change of several months in maturity has a substantial effect on the value of an option, a change of a few days or a week usually has only a modest effect on the option value.

Table 2 makes it easy to see the influence of stock price and the interest rate. Reading across, we see how the value changes as the interest rate increases. An increase in the interest rate will always increase the value of the option. Note that even a five percentage point change in the interest rate usually has only a modest effect on the option value. The greatest effect of the interest rate occurs in the longest maturity options.

Table 3 makes it easy to see the influence of stock price and the volatility of the stock. Reading across, we see how the value changes as the volatility increases. An increase in the volatility will always increase the value of the option. Note that when the stock price is well below the exercise price, an increase in the volatility of the stock causes a very large percentage increase in the value of the option.

The figures in Table 2 and 3 are the same as the figures in Table 1. They are just arranged differently.

→

TABLE 1. Option Values and Hedge Ratios for Different Stock Prices and Maturities, by Standard Deviation and Interest Rate.

Annual Std Dev = 0.20   Exercise Price = 40.

Price	Interest Rate = 0.05			Interest Rate = 0.10			Interest Rate = 0.15		
	3 Months	6 Months	9 Months	3 Months	6 Months	9 Months	3 Months	6 Months	9 Months
28.	0.00 (0.00)	0.01 (0.01)	0.07 (0.04)	0.00 (0.00)	0.02 (0.02)	0.12 (0.06)	0.00 (0.00)	0.04 (0.03)	0.20 (0.09)
32.	0.02 (0.02)	0.18 (0.09)	0.44 (0.16)	0.03 (0.03)	0.26 (0.12)	0.65 (0.22)	0.04 (0.04)	0.37 (0.16)	0.93 (0.29)
36.	0.36 (0.19)	0.94 (0.31)	1.50 (0.38)	0.45 (0.23)	1.22 (0.37)	2.01 (0.46)	0.55 (0.26)	1.55 (0.44)	2.61 (0.55)
40.	1.85 (0.57)	2.76 (0.60)	3.51 (0.62)	2.12 (0.62)	3.31 (0.66)	4.35 (0.70)	2.41 (0.66)	3.92 (0.73)	5.27 (0.77)
44.	4.80 (0.87)	5.63 (0.82)	6.38 (0.80)	5.22 (0.89)	6.41 (0.86)	7.49 (0.86)	5.65 (0.92)	7.21 (0.90)	8.64 (0.90)
48.	8.54 (0.98)	9.18 (0.94)	9.83 (0.91)	9.02 (0.98)	10.08 (0.96)	11.11 (0.94)	9.49 (0.99)	10.97 (0.97)	12.39 (0.96)
52.	12.50 (1.00)	13.04 (0.98)	13.60 (0.97)	12.99 (1.00)	13.98 (0.99)	14.96 (0.98)	13.47 (1.00)	14.91 (0.99)	16.30 (0.99)

Annual Std Dev = 0.30   Exercise Price = 40.

Price	Interest Rate = 0.05			Interest Rate = 0.10			Interest Rate = 0.15		
	3 Months	6 Months	9 Months	3 Months	6 Months	9 Months	3 Months	6 Months	9 Months
28.	0.02 (0.01)	0.18 (0.07)	0.45 (0.14)	0.02 (0.02)	0.23 (0.09)	0.59 (0.17)	0.03 (0.02)	0.29 (0.11)	0.76 (0.21)
32.	0.19 (0.09)	0.70 (0.20)	1.27 (0.28)	0.23 (0.11)	0.86 (0.24)	1.58 (0.33)	0.27 (0.12)	1.04 (0.28)	1.94 (0.38)
36.	0.92 (0.29)	1.89 (0.39)	2.72 (0.45)	1.05 (0.32)	2.21 (0.44)	3.25 (0.51)	1.19 (0.35)	2.56 (0.49)	3.84 (0.56)
40.	2.63 (0.56)	3.85 (0.59)	4.84 (0.61)	2.89 (0.60)	4.36 (0.63)	5.59 (0.66)	3.16 (0.63)	4.90 (0.68)	6.40 (0.71)
44.	5.36 (0.79)	6.55 (0.75)	7.54 (0.74)	5.73 (0.81)	7.22 (0.79)	8.50 (0.78)	6.11 (0.83)	7.91 (0.82)	9.49 (0.82)
48.	8.79 (0.92)	9.78 (0.86)	10.70 (0.84)	9.23 (0.93)	10.58 (0.89)	11.82 (0.87)	9.68 (0.94)	11.38 (0.91)	12.94 (0.90)
52.	12.59 (0.97)	13.37 (0.93)	14.18 (0.90)	13.06 (0.98)	14.24 (0.94)	15.41 (0.92)	13.53 (0.98)	15.11 (0.96)	16.63 (0.94)

Annual Std Dev = 0.40   Exercise Price = 40.

Price	Interest Rate = 0.05			Interest Rate = 0.10			Interest Rate = 0.15		
	3 Months	6 Months	9 Months	3 Months	6 Months	9 Months	3 Months	6 Months	9 Months
28.	0.12 (0.05)	0.55 (0.15)	1.09 (0.23)	0.13 (0.06)	0.65 (0.17)	1.30 (0.26)	0.15 (0.07)	0.76 (0.20)	1.54 (0.30)
32.	0.53 (0.17)	1.42 (0.29)	2.26 (0.36)	0.60 (0.19)	1.62 (0.32)	2.62 (0.40)	0.67 (0.20)	1.85 (0.35)	3.02 (0.44)
36.	1.57 (0.36)	2.88 (0.44)	3.96 (0.49)	1.72 (0.38)	3.22 (0.48)	4.49 (0.53)	1.87 (0.41)	3.58 (0.51)	5.06 (0.58)
40.	3.42 (0.56)	4.95 (0.59)	6.17 (0.61)	3.67 (0.59)	5.43 (0.62)	6.87 (0.65)	3.92 (0.61)	5.93 (0.66)	7.60 (0.69)
44.	6.04 (0.74)	7.57 (0.71)	8.82 (0.71)	6.38 (0.76)	8.18 (0.74)	9.67 (0.75)	6.72 (0.78)	8.80 (0.77)	10.56 (0.78)
48.	9.26 (0.86)	10.63 (0.81)	11.83 (0.79)	9.66 (0.87)	11.34 (0.83)	12.82 (0.82)	10.06 (0.88)	12.06 (0.85)	13.82 (0.85)
52.	12.85 (0.93)	14.01 (0.88)	15.11 (0.85)	13.29 (0.94)	14.80 (0.89)	16.21 (0.87)	13.73 (0.95)	15.59 (0.91)	17.31 (0.90)

Annual Std Dev = 0.50   Exercise Price = 40.

Price	Interest Rate = 0.05			Interest Rate = 0.10			Interest Rate = 0.15		
	3 Months	6 Months	9 Months	3 Months	6 Months	9 Months	3 Months	6 Months	9 Months
28.	0.32 (0.11)	1.08 (0.22)	1.88 (0.30)	0.35 (0.11)	1.22 (0.24)	2.14 (0.33)	0.39 (0.12)	1.37 (0.27)	2.42 (0.36)
32.	0.99 (0.24)	2.23 (0.35)	3.32 (0.42)	1.07 (0.25)	2.46 (0.38)	3.71 (0.45)	1.16 (0.27)	2.71 (0.40)	4.12 (0.48)
36.	2.26 (0.40)	3.89 (0.48)	5.20 (0.52)	2.41 (0.42)	4.23 (0.51)	5.73 (0.56)	2.58 (0.44)	4.59 (0.54)	6.28 (0.59)
40.	4.21 (0.57)	6.05 (0.60)	7.49 (0.62)	4.44 (0.59)	6.51 (0.62)	8.15 (0.65)	4.69 (0.61)	6.97 (0.65)	8.83 (0.68)
44.	6.78 (0.71)	8.65 (0.70)	10.13 (0.70)	7.09 (0.73)	9.21 (0.72)	10.92 (0.73)	7.40 (0.74)	9.77 (0.74)	11.72 (0.76)
48.	9.85 (0.82)	11.60 (0.78)	13.07 (0.77)	10.22 (0.83)	12.25 (0.80)	13.96 (0.79)	10.59 (0.84)	12.91 (0.82)	14.87 (0.82)
52.	13.27 (0.89)	14.84 (0.84)	16.24 (0.82)	13.68 (0.90)	15.56 (0.86)	17.23 (0.84)	14.10 (0.91)	16.29 (0.87)	18.22 (0.86)

Annual Std Dev = 0.60   Exercise Price = 40.

Price	Interest Rate = 0.05			Interest Rate = 0.10			Interest Rate = 0.15		
	3 Months	6 Months	9 Months	3 Months	6 Months	9 Months	3 Months	6 Months	9 Months
28.	0.62	1.72	2.76	0.67	1.88	3.05	0.72	2.05	3.35
	(0.16)	(0.28)	(0.36)	(0.17)	(0.30)	(0.39)	(0.18)	(0.33)	(0.42)
32.	1.51	3.09	4.41	1.61	3.33	4.81	1.71	3.59	5.22
	(0.29)	(0.40)	(0.46)	(0.30)	(0.42)	(0.49)	(0.32)	(0.45)	(0.52)
36.	2.96	4.91	6.44	3.12	5.25	6.95	3.29	5.60	7.48
	(0.44)	(0.51)	(0.55)	(0.45)	(0.53)	(0.58)	(0.47)	(0.56)	(0.61)
40.	4.99	7.14	8.81	5.22	7.58	9.43	5.45	8.02	10.07
	(0.58)	(0.61)	(0.63)	(0.59)	(0.63)	(0.66)	(0.61)	(0.65)	(0.68)
44.	7.54	9.74	11.46	7.83	10.26	12.19	8.13	10.79	12.93
	(0.69)	(0.69)	(0.70)	(0.71)	(0.71)	(0.72)	(0.72)	(0.73)	(0.75)
48.	10.52	12.64	14.37	10.86	13.24	15.19	11.20	13.84	16.02
	(0.79)	(0.76)	(0.75)	(0.80)	(0.78)	(0.77)	(0.81)	(0.79)	(0.80)
52.	13.81	15.79	17.47	14.20	16.45	18.38	14.58	17.12	19.28
	(0.86)	(0.81)	(0.80)	(0.87)	(0.83)	(0.82)	(0.87)	(0.84)	(0.84)

Annual Std Dev = 0.70   Exercise Price = 40.

Price	Interest Rate = 0.05			Interest Rate = 0.10			Interest Rate = 0.15		
	3 Months	6 Months	9 Months	3 Months	6 Months	9 Months	3 Months	6 Months	9 Months
28.	0.99	2.42	3.69	1.05	2.60	3.99	1.12	2.78	4.31
	(0.21)	(0.34)	(0.41)	(0.22)	(0.35)	(0.44)	(0.23)	(0.37)	(0.46)
32.	2.08	3.97	5.51	2.19	4.23	5.91	2.30	4.49	6.33
	(0.33)	(0.44)	(0.50)	(0.35)	(0.46)	(0.52)	(0.36)	(0.48)	(0.55)
36.	3.67	5.92	6.67	3.84	6.26	8.16	4.01	6.60	8.67
	(0.46)	(0.53)	(0.58)	(0.48)	(0.55)	(0.60)	(0.49)	(0.57)	(0.62)
40.	5.77	8.23	10.11	6.00	8.64	10.70	6.22	9.07	11.30
	(0.58)	(0.62)	(0.64)	(0.60)	(0.64)	(0.67)	(0.61)	(0.66)	(0.69)
44.	8.32	10.84	12.79	8.59	11.33	13.47	8.87	11.83	14.16
	(0.69)	(0.69)	(0.70)	(0.70)	(0.71)	(0.72)	(0.71)	(0.72)	(0.74)
48.	11.23	13.72	15.69	11.55	14.27	16.45	11.88	14.83	17.21
	(0.77)	(0.75)	(0.75)	(0.78)	(0.76)	(0.77)	(0.79)	(0.78)	(0.79)
52.	14.44	16.81	18.76	14.80	17.42	19.59	15.16	18.04	20.43
	(0.83)	(0.80)	(0.79)	(0.84)	(0.81)	(0.80)	(0.85)	(0.82)	(0.82)

Annual Std Dev = 0.80   Exercise Price = 40.

Price	Interest Rate = 0.05			Interest Rate = 0.10			Interest Rate = 0.15		
	3 Months	6 Months	9 Months	3 Months	6 Months	9 Months	3 Months	6 Months	9 Months
28.	1.42	3.16	4.64	1.49	3.35	4.95	1.57	3.55	5.27
	(0.25)	(0.38)	(0.45)	(0.26)	(0.40)	(0.48)	(0.27)	(0.41)	(0.50)
32.	2.67	4.87	6.62	2.79	5.13	7.01	2.91	5.40	7.42
	(0.37)	(0.47)	(0.53)	(0.38)	(0.49)	(0.55)	(0.40)	(0.51)	(0.57)
36.	4.39	6.93	8.88	4.56	7.26	9.36	4.73	7.60	9.85
	(0.49)	(0.56)	(0.60)	(0.50)	(0.57)	(0.62)	(0.51)	(0.59)	(0.64)
40.	6.55	9.30	11.39	6.77	9.70	11.95	6.99	10.10	12.52
	(0.59)	(0.63)	(0.66)	(0.60)	(0.64)	(0.68)	(0.62)	(0.66)	(0.69)
44.	9.10	11.94	14.11	9.36	12.40	14.75	9.63	12.87	15.39
	(0.68)	(0.69)	(0.70)	(0.69)	(0.71)	(0.72)	(0.70)	(0.72)	(0.74)
48.	11.98	14.81	17.02	12.28	15.33	17.73	12.59	15.85	18.44
	(0.75)	(0.74)	(0.75)	(0.76)	(0.76)	(0.76)	(0.77)	(0.77)	(0.78)
52.	15.11	17.86	20.08	15.45	18.44	20.85	15.80	19.02	21.62
	(0.81)	(0.79)	(0.78)	(0.82)	(0.80)	(0.80)	(0.83)	(0.81)	(0.81)

Annual Std Dev = 0.90   Exercise Price = 40.

Price	Interest Rate = 0.05			Interest Rate = 0.10			Interest Rate = 0.15		
	3 Months	6 Months	9 Months	3 Months	6 Months	9 Months	3 Months	6 Months	9 Months
28.	1.89	3.92	5.61	1.97	4.12	5.92	2.05	4.32	6.24
	(0.29)	(0.42)	(0.49)	(0.30)	(0.43)	(0.51)	(0.31)	(0.45)	(0.53)
32.	3.28	5.77	7.72	3.41	6.03	8.10	3.53	6.30	8.50
	(0.40)	(0.50)	(0.56)	(0.41)	(0.52)	(0.58)	(0.43)	(0.53)	(0.60)
36.	5.11	7.93	10.08	5.27	8.25	10.54	5.44	8.58	11.01
	(0.51)	(0.58)	(0.62)	(0.52)	(0.59)	(0.64)	(0.53)	(0.61)	(0.66)
40.	7.33	10.36	12.66	7.54	10.75	13.19	7.75	11.14	13.73
	(0.60)	(0.64)	(0.67)	(0.61)	(0.65)	(0.69)	(0.62)	(0.67)	(0.70)
44.	9.89	13.03	15.42	10.14	13.47	16.02	10.39	13.92	16.62
	(0.68)	(0.69)	(0.71)	(0.69)	(0.71)	(0.73)	(0.70)	(0.72)	(0.74)
48.	12.74	15.91	18.35	13.03	16.40	19.01	13.32	16.89	19.67
	(0.74)	(0.74)	(0.75)	(0.75)	(0.75)	(0.76)	(0.76)	(0.77)	(0.78)
52.	15.83	18.95	21.41	16.15	19.49	22.13	16.48	20.03	22.85
	(0.80)	(0.78)	(0.78)	(0.81)	(0.79)	(0.79)	(0.81)	(0.80)	(0.81)

TABLE 2. Option Values and Hedge Ratios for Different Stock Prices and Interest Rates, by Standard Deviation and Maturity.

Annual Std Dev = 0.20   Exercise Price = 40.

Price	3 Months			6 Months			9 Months		
	R=0.05	R=0.10	R=0.15	R=0.05	R=0.10	R=0.15	R=0.05	R=0.10	R=0.15
28.	0.00	0.00	0.00	0.01	0.02	0.04	0.07	0.12	0.20
	(0.00)	(0.01)	(0.04)	(0.00)	(0.02)	(0.06)	(0.00)	(0.03)	(0.09)
32.	0.02	0.03	0.04	0.18	0.26	0.37	0.44	0.65	0.93
	(0.02)	(0.09)	(0.16)	(0.03)	(0.12)	(0.22)	(0.04)	(0.16)	(0.29)
36.	0.36	0.45	0.55	0.94	1.22	1.55	1.50	2.01	2.61
	(0.19)	(0.31)	(0.38)	(0.23)	(0.37)	(0.46)	(0.26)	(0.44)	(0.55)
40.	1.85	2.12	2.41	2.76	3.31	3.92	3.51	4.35	5.27
	(0.57)	(0.60)	(0.62)	(0.62)	(0.66)	(0.70)	(0.66)	(0.73)	(0.77)
44.	4.80	5.22	5.65	5.63	6.41	7.21	6.38	7.49	8.64
	(0.87)	(0.82)	(0.80)	(0.89)	(0.86)	(0.86)	(0.92)	(0.90)	(0.90)
48.	8.54	9.02	9.49	9.18	10.08	10.97	9.83	11.11	12.39
	(0.98)	(0.94)	(0.91)	(0.98)	(0.96)	(0.94)	(0.99)	(0.97)	(0.96)
52.	12.50	12.99	13.47	13.04	13.98	14.91	13.60	14.96	16.30
	(1.00)	(0.98)	(0.97)	(1.00)	(0.99)	(0.98)	(1.00)	(0.99)	(0.99)

Annual Std Dev = 0.30   Exercise Price = 40.

Price	3 Months			6 Months			9 Months		
	R=0.05	R=0.10	R=0.15	R=0.05	R=0.10	R=0.15	R=0.05	R=0.10	R=0.15
28.	0.02	0.02	0.03	0.18	0.23	0.29	0.45	0.59	0.76
	(0.01)	(0.07)	(0.14)	(0.02)	(0.09)	(0.17)	(0.02)	(0.11)	(0.21)
32.	0.19	0.23	0.27	0.70	0.86	1.04	1.27	1.58	1.94
	(0.09)	(0.20)	(0.28)	(0.11)	(0.24)	(0.33)	(0.12)	(0.28)	(0.38)
36.	0.92	1.05	1.19	1.89	2.21	2.56	2.72	3.25	3.84
	(0.29)	(0.39)	(0.45)	(0.32)	(0.44)	(0.51)	(0.35)	(0.49)	(0.56)
40.	2.63	2.89	3.16	3.85	4.36	4.90	4.84	5.59	6.40
	(0.56)	(0.59)	(0.61)	(0.60)	(0.63)	(0.66)	(0.63)	(0.68)	(0.71)
44.	5.36	5.73	6.11	6.55	7.22	7.91	7.54	8.50	9.49
	(0.79)	(0.75)	(0.74)	(0.81)	(0.79)	(0.78)	(0.83)	(0.82)	(0.82)
48.	8.79	9.23	9.68	9.78	10.58	11.38	10.70	11.82	12.94
	(0.92)	(0.86)	(0.84)	(0.93)	(0.89)	(0.87)	(0.94)	(0.91)	(0.90)
52.	12.59	13.06	13.53	13.37	14.24	15.11	14.18	15.41	16.63
	(0.97)	(0.93)	(0.90)	(0.98)	(0.94)	(0.92)	(0.98)	(0.96)	(0.94)

Annual Std Dev = 0.40   Exercise Price = 40.

Price	3 Months			6 Months			9 Months		
	R=0.05	R=0.10	R=0.15	R=0.05	R=0.10	R=0.15	R=0.05	R=0.10	R=0.15
28.	0.12	0.13	0.15	0.55	0.65	0.76	1.09	1.30	1.54
	(0.05)	(0.15)	(0.23)	(0.06)	(0.17)	(0.26)	(0.07)	(0.20)	(0.30)
32.	0.53	0.60	0.67	1.42	1.62	1.85	2.26	2.62	3.02
	(0.17)	(0.29)	(0.36)	(0.19)	(0.32)	(0.40)	(0.20)	(0.35)	(0.44)
36.	1.57	1.72	1.87	2.88	3.22	3.58	3.96	4.49	5.06
	(0.36)	(0.44)	(0.49)	(0.38)	(0.48)	(0.53)	(0.41)	(0.51)	(0.58)
40.	3.42	3.67	3.92	4.95	5.43	5.93	6.17	6.87	7.60
	(0.56)	(0.59)	(0.61)	(0.59)	(0.62)	(0.65)	(0.61)	(0.66)	(0.69)
44.	6.04	6.38	6.72	7.57	8.18	8.80	8.82	9.67	10.56
	(0.74)	(0.71)	(0.71)	(0.76)	(0.74)	(0.75)	(0.78)	(0.77)	(0.78)
48.	9.26	9.66	10.06	10.63	11.34	12.06	11.83	12.82	13.82
	(0.86)	(0.81)	(0.79)	(0.87)	(0.83)	(0.82)	(0.88)	(0.85)	(0.85)
52.	12.85	13.29	13.73	14.01	14.80	15.59	15.11	16.21	17.31
	(0.93)	(0.88)	(0.85)	(0.94)	(0.89)	(0.87)	(0.95)	(0.91)	(0.90)

Annual Std Dev = 0.50   Exercise Price = 40.

Price	3 Months			6 Months			9 Months		
	R=0.05	R=0.10	R=0.15	R=0.05	R=0.10	R=0.15	R=0.05	R=0.10	R=0.15
28.	0.32	0.35	0.39	1.08	1.22	1.37	1.88	2.14	2.42
	(0.11)	(0.22)	(0.30)	(0.11)	(0.24)	(0.33)	(0.12)	(0.27)	(0.36)
32.	0.99	1.07	1.16	2.23	2.46	2.71	3.32	3.71	4.12
	(0.24)	(0.35)	(0.42)	(0.25)	(0.38)	(0.45)	(0.27)	(0.40)	(0.48)
36.	2.26	2.41	2.58	3.89	4.23	4.59	5.20	5.73	6.28
	(0.40)	(0.48)	(0.52)	(0.42)	(0.51)	(0.56)	(0.44)	(0.54)	(0.59)
40.	4.21	4.44	4.69	6.05	6.51	6.97	7.49	8.15	8.83
	(0.57)	(0.60)	(0.62)	(0.59)	(0.62)	(0.65)	(0.61)	(0.65)	(0.68)
44.	6.78	7.09	7.40	8.65	9.21	9.77	10.13	10.92	11.72
	(0.71)	(0.70)	(0.70)	(0.73)	(0.72)	(0.73)	(0.74)	(0.74)	(0.76)
48.	9.85	10.22	10.59	11.60	12.25	12.91	13.07	13.96	14.87
	(0.82)	(0.78)	(0.77)	(0.83)	(0.80)	(0.79)	(0.84)	(0.82)	(0.82)
52.	13.27	13.68	14.10	14.84	15.56	16.29	16.24	17.23	18.22
	(0.89)	(0.84)	(0.82)	(0.90)	(0.86)	(0.84)	(0.91)	(0.87)	(0.86)

TABLE 2. Option Values and Hedge Ratios for Different Stock Prices and Interest Rates, by Standard Deviation and Maturity. (Continued)

Annual Std Dev = 0.60   Exercise Price = 40.

Price	3 Months			6 Months			9 Months		
	R=0.05	R=0.10	R=0.15	R=0.05	R=0.10	R=0.15	R=0.05	R=0.10	R=0.15
28.	0.62 (0.16)	0.67 (0.28)	0.72 (0.36)	1.72 (0.17)	1.88 (0.30)	2.05 (0.39)	2.76 (0.18)	3.05 (0.33)	3.35 (0.42)
32.	1.51 (0.29)	1.61 (0.40)	1.71 (0.46)	3.09 (0.30)	3.33 (0.42)	3.59 (0.49)	4.41 (0.32)	4.81 (0.45)	5.22 (0.52)
36.	2.96 (0.44)	3.12 (0.51)	3.29 (0.55)	4.91 (0.45)	5.25 (0.53)	5.60 (0.58)	6.44 (0.47)	6.95 (0.56)	7.48 (0.61)
40.	4.99 (0.58)	5.22 (0.61)	5.45 (0.63)	7.14 (0.59)	7.58 (0.63)	8.02 (0.66)	8.81 (0.61)	9.43 (0.65)	10.07 (0.68)
44.	7.54 (0.69)	7.83 (0.69)	8.13 (0.70)	9.74 (0.71)	10.26 (0.71)	10.79 (0.72)	11.46 (0.72)	12.19 (0.73)	12.93 (0.75)
48.	10.52 (0.79)	10.86 (0.76)	11.20 (0.75)	12.64 (0.80)	13.24 (0.78)	13.84 (0.77)	14.37 (0.81)	15.19 (0.79)	16.02 (0.80)
52.	13.81 (0.86)	14.20 (0.81)	14.58 (0.80)	15.79 (0.87)	16.45 (0.83)	17.12 (0.82)	17.47 (0.87)	18.38 (0.84)	19.28 (0.84)

Annual Std Dev = 0.70   Exercise Price = 40.

Price	3 Months			6 Months			9 Months		
	R=0.05	R=0.10	R=0.15	R=0.05	R=0.10	R=0.15	R=0.05	R=0.10	R=0.15
28.	0.99 (0.21)	1.05 (0.34)	1.12 (0.41)	2.42 (0.22)	2.60 (0.35)	2.78 (0.44)	3.69 (0.23)	3.99 (0.37)	4.31 (0.46)
32.	2.08 (0.33)	2.19 (0.44)	2.30 (0.50)	3.97 (0.35)	4.23 (0.46)	4.49 (0.52)	5.51 (0.36)	5.91 (0.48)	6.33 (0.55)
36.	3.67 (0.46)	3.84 (0.53)	4.01 (0.58)	5.92 (0.48)	6.26 (0.55)	6.60 (0.60)	7.67 (0.49)	8.16 (0.57)	8.67 (0.62)
40.	5.77 (0.58)	6.00 (0.62)	6.22 (0.64)	8.23 (0.60)	8.64 (0.64)	9.07 (0.67)	10.11 (0.61)	10.70 (0.66)	11.30 (0.69)
44.	8.32 (0.69)	8.59 (0.69)	8.87 (0.70)	10.84 (0.70)	11.33 (0.71)	11.83 (0.72)	12.79 (0.71)	13.47 (0.72)	14.16 (0.74)
48.	11.23 (0.77)	11.55 (0.75)	11.88 (0.75)	13.72 (0.78)	14.27 (0.76)	14.83 (0.77)	15.69 (0.79)	16.45 (0.78)	17.21 (0.79)
52.	14.44 (0.83)	14.80 (0.80)	15.16 (0.79)	16.81 (0.84)	17.42 (0.81)	18.04 (0.80)	18.76 (0.85)	19.59 (0.82)	20.43 (0.82)

Annual Std Dev = 0.80   Exercise Price = 40.

Price	3 Months			6 Months			9 Months		
	R=0.05	R=0.10	R=0.15	R=0.05	R=0.10	R=0.15	R=0.05	R=0.10	R=0.15
28.	1.42 (0.25)	1.49 (0.38)	1.57 (0.45)	3.16 (0.26)	3.35 (0.40)	3.55 (0.48)	4.64 (0.27)	4.95 (0.41)	5.27 (0.50)
32.	2.67 (0.37)	2.79 (0.47)	2.91 (0.53)	4.87 (0.38)	5.13 (0.49)	5.40 (0.55)	6.62 (0.40)	7.01 (0.51)	7.42 (0.57)
36.	4.39 (0.49)	4.56 (0.56)	4.73 (0.60)	6.93 (0.50)	7.26 (0.57)	7.60 (0.62)	8.88 (0.51)	9.36 (0.59)	9.85 (0.64)
40.	6.55 (0.59)	6.77 (0.63)	6.99 (0.66)	9.30 (0.60)	9.70 (0.64)	10.10 (0.68)	11.39 (0.62)	11.95 (0.66)	12.52 (0.69)
44.	9.10 (0.68)	9.36 (0.69)	9.63 (0.70)	11.94 (0.69)	12.40 (0.71)	12.87 (0.72)	14.11 (0.70)	14.75 (0.72)	15.39 (0.74)
48.	11.98 (0.75)	12.28 (0.74)	12.59 (0.75)	14.81 (0.76)	15.33 (0.76)	15.85 (0.76)	17.02 (0.77)	17.73 (0.77)	18.44 (0.78)
52.	15.11 (0.81)	15.45 (0.79)	15.80 (0.78)	17.86 (0.82)	18.44 (0.80)	19.02 (0.80)	20.08 (0.83)	20.85 (0.81)	21.62 (0.81)

Annual Std Dev = 0.90   Exercise Price = 40.

Price	3 Months			6 Months			9 Months		
	R=0.05	R=0.10	R=0.15	R=0.05	R=0.10	R=0.15	R=0.05	R=0.10	R=0.15
28.	1.89 (0.29)	1.97 (0.42)	2.05 (0.49)	3.92 (0.30)	4.12 (0.43)	4.32 (0.51)	5.61 (0.31)	5.92 (0.45)	6.24 (0.53)
32.	3.28 (0.40)	3.41 (0.50)	3.53 (0.56)	5.77 (0.41)	6.03 (0.52)	6.30 (0.58)	7.72 (0.43)	8.10 (0.53)	8.50 (0.60)
36.	5.11 (0.51)	5.27 (0.58)	5.44 (0.62)	7.93 (0.52)	8.25 (0.59)	8.58 (0.64)	10.08 (0.53)	10.54 (0.61)	11.01 (0.66)
40.	7.33 (0.60)	7.54 (0.64)	7.75 (0.67)	10.36 (0.61)	10.75 (0.65)	11.14 (0.69)	12.66 (0.62)	13.19 (0.67)	13.73 (0.70)
44.	9.89 (0.68)	10.14 (0.69)	10.39 (0.71)	13.03 (0.69)	13.47 (0.71)	13.92 (0.73)	15.42 (0.70)	16.02 (0.72)	16.62 (0.74)
48.	12.74 (0.74)	13.03 (0.74)	13.32 (0.75)	15.91 (0.75)	16.40 (0.75)	16.89 (0.76)	18.35 (0.76)	19.01 (0.77)	19.67 (0.78)
52.	15.83 (0.80)	16.15 (0.78)	16.48 (0.78)	18.95 (0.81)	19.49 (0.79)	20.03 (0.79)	21.41 (0.81)	22.13 (0.80)	22.85 (0.81)

TABLE 3. Option Values and Hedge Ratios for Different Stock Prices and Standard Deviations, by Maturity and Interest Rate.

3 Months   R = 0.05   Exercise Price = 40.

Price	S.D.=0.20	S.D.=0.30	S.D.=0.40	S.D.=0.50	S.D.=0.60	S.D.=0.70	S.D.=0.80	S.D.=0.90
28.	0.00 (0.00)	0.02 (0.01)	0.12 (0.05)	0.32 (0.11)	0.62 (0.16)	0.99 (0.21)	1.42 (0.25)	1.89 (0.29)
32.	0.02 (0.02)	0.19 (0.09)	0.53 (0.17)	0.99 (0.24)	1.51 (0.29)	2.08 (0.33)	2.67 (0.37)	3.28 (0.40)
36.	0.36 (0.19)	0.92 (0.29)	1.57 (0.36)	2.26 (0.40)	2.96 (0.44)	3.67 (0.46)	4.39 (0.49)	5.11 (0.51)
40.	1.85 (0.57)	2.63 (0.56)	3.42 (0.56)	4.21 (0.57)	4.99 (0.58)	5.77 (0.58)	6.55 (0.59)	7.33 (0.60)
44.	4.80 (0.87)	5.36 (0.79)	6.04 (0.74)	6.78 (0.71)	7.54 (0.69)	8.32 (0.69)	9.10 (0.68)	9.89 (0.68)
48.	8.54 (0.98)	8.79 (0.92)	9.26 (0.86)	9.85 (0.82)	10.52 (0.79)	11.23 (0.77)	11.98 (0.75)	12.74 (0.74)
52.	12.50 (1.00)	12.59 (0.97)	12.85 (0.93)	13.27 (0.89)	13.81 (0.86)	14.44 (0.83)	15.11 (0.81)	15.83 (0.80)

3 Months   R = 0.10   Exercise Price = 40.

Price	S.D.=0.20	S.D.=0.30	S.D.=0.40	S.D.=0.50	S.D.=0.60	S.D.=0.70	S.D.=0.80	S.D.=0.90
28.	0.00 (0.00)	0.02 (0.02)	0.13 (0.06)	0.35 (0.11)	0.67 (0.17)	1.05 (0.22)	1.49 (0.26)	1.97 (0.30)
32.	0.03 (0.03)	0.23 (0.11)	0.60 (0.19)	1.07 (0.25)	1.61 (0.30)	2.19 (0.35)	2.79 (0.38)	3.41 (0.41)
36.	0.45 (0.23)	1.05 (0.32)	1.72 (0.38)	2.41 (0.42)	3.12 (0.45)	3.84 (0.48)	4.56 (0.50)	5.27 (0.52)
40.	2.12 (0.62)	2.89 (0.60)	3.67 (0.59)	4.44 (0.59)	5.22 (0.59)	6.00 (0.60)	6.77 (0.60)	7.54 (0.61)
44.	5.22 (0.89)	5.73 (0.81)	6.38 (0.76)	7.09 (0.73)	7.83 (0.71)	8.59 (0.70)	9.36 (0.69)	10.14 (0.69)
48.	9.02 (0.98)	9.23 (0.93)	9.66 (0.87)	10.22 (0.83)	10.86 (0.80)	11.55 (0.78)	12.28 (0.76)	13.03 (0.75)
52.	12.99 (1.00)	13.06 (0.98)	13.29 (0.94)	13.68 (0.90)	14.20 (0.87)	14.80 (0.84)	15.45 (0.82)	16.15 (0.81)

3 Months   R = 0.15   Exercise Price = 40.

Price	S.D.=0.20	S.D.=0.30	S.D.=0.40	S.D.=0.50	S.D.=0.60	S.D.=0.70	S.D.=0.80	S.D.=0.90
28.	0.00 (0.00)	0.03 (0.02)	0.15 (0.07)	0.39 (0.12)	0.72 (0.18)	1.12 (0.23)	1.57 (0.27)	2.05 (0.31)
32.	0.04 (0.04)	0.27 (0.12)	0.67 (0.20)	1.16 (0.27)	1.71 (0.32)	2.30 (0.36)	2.91 (0.40)	3.53 (0.43)
36.	0.55 (0.26)	1.19 (0.35)	1.87 (0.41)	2.58 (0.44)	3.29 (0.47)	4.01 (0.49)	4.73 (0.51)	5.44 (0.53)
40.	2.41 (0.66)	3.16 (0.63)	3.92 (0.61)	4.69 (0.61)	5.45 (0.61)	6.22 (0.61)	6.99 (0.62)	7.75 (0.62)
44.	5.65 (0.92)	6.11 (0.83)	6.72 (0.78)	7.40 (0.74)	8.13 (0.72)	8.87 (0.71)	9.63 (0.70)	10.39 (0.70)
48.	9.49 (0.99)	9.68 (0.94)	10.06 (0.88)	10.59 (0.84)	11.20 (0.81)	11.88 (0.79)	12.59 (0.77)	13.32 (0.76)
52.	13.47 (1.00)	13.53 (0.98)	13.73 (0.95)	14.10 (0.91)	14.58 (0.87)	15.16 (0.85)	15.80 (0.83)	16.48 (0.81)

6 Months   R = 0.05   Exercise Price = 40.

Price	S.D.=0.20	S.D.=0.30	S.D.=0.40	S.D.=0.50	S.D.=0.60	S.D.=0.70	S.D.=0.80	S.D.=0.90
28.	0.01 (0.01)	0.18 (0.07)	0.55 (0.15)	1.08 (0.22)	1.72 (0.28)	2.42 (0.34)	3.16 (0.38)	3.92 (0.42)
32.	0.18 (0.09)	0.70 (0.20)	1.42 (0.29)	2.23 (0.35)	3.09 (0.40)	3.97 (0.44)	4.87 (0.47)	5.77 (0.50)
36.	0.94 (0.31)	1.89 (0.39)	2.88 (0.44)	3.89 (0.48)	4.91 (0.51)	5.92 (0.53)	6.93 (0.56)	7.93 (0.58)
40.	2.76 (0.60)	3.85 (0.59)	4.95 (0.59)	6.05 (0.60)	7.14 (0.61)	8.23 (0.62)	9.30 (0.63)	10.36 (0.64)
44.	5.63 (0.82)	6.55 (0.75)	7.57 (0.71)	8.65 (0.70)	9.74 (0.69)	10.84 (0.69)	11.94 (0.69)	13.03 (0.69)
48.	9.18 (0.94)	9.78 (0.86)	10.63 (0.81)	11.60 (0.78)	12.64 (0.76)	13.72 (0.75)	14.81 (0.74)	15.91 (0.74)
52.	13.04 (0.98)	13.37 (0.93)	14.01 (0.88)	14.84 (0.84)	15.79 (0.81)	16.81 (0.80)	17.86 (0.79)	18.95 (0.78)

TABLE 3. **Option Values and Hedge Ratios for Different Stock Prices and Standard Deviations, by Maturity and Interest Rate.** (Continued)

6 Months   R = 0.10   Exercise Price = 40.

Price	S.D.=0.20	S.D.=0.30	S.D.=0.40	S.D.=0.50	S.D.=0.60	S.D.=0.70	S.D.=0.80	S.D.=0.90
28.	0.02	0.23	0.65	1.22	1.88	2.60	3.35	4.12
	(0.02)	(0.09)	(0.17)	(0.24)	(0.30)	(0.35)	(0.40)	(0.43)
32.	0.26	0.86	1.62	2.46	3.33	4.23	5.13	6.03
	(0.12)	(0.24)	(0.32)	(0.38)	(0.42)	(0.46)	(0.49)	(0.52)
36.	1.22	2.21	3.22	4.23	5.25	6.26	7.26	8.25
	(0.37)	(0.44)	(0.48)	(0.51)	(0.53)	(0.55)	(0.57)	(0.59)
40.	3.31	4.36	5.43	6.51	7.58	8.64	9.70	10.75
	(0.66)	(0.63)	(0.62)	(0.62)	(0.63)	(0.64)	(0.64)	(0.65)
44.	6.41	7.22	8.18	9.21	10.26	11.33	12.40	13.47
	(0.86)	(0.79)	(0.74)	(0.72)	(0.71)	(0.71)	(0.71)	(0.71)
48.	10.08	10.58	11.34	12.25	13.24	14.27	15.33	16.40
	(0.96)	(0.89)	(0.83)	(0.80)	(0.78)	(0.76)	(0.76)	(0.75)
52.	13.98	14.24	14.80	15.56	16.45	17.42	18.44	19.49
	(0.99)	(0.94)	(0.89)	(0.86)	(0.83)	(0.81)	(0.80)	(0.79)

6 Months   R = 0.15   Exercise Price = 40.

Price	S.D.=0.20	S.D.=0.30	S.D.=0.40	S.D.=0.50	S.D.=0.60	S.D.=0.70	S.D.=0.80	S.D.=0.90
28.	0.04	0.29	0.76	1.37	2.05	2.78	3.55	4.32
	(0.03)	(0.11)	(0.20)	(0.27)	(0.33)	(0.37)	(0.41)	(0.45)
32.	0.37	1.04	1.85	2.71	3.59	4.49	5.40	6.30
	(0.16)	(0.28)	(0.35)	(0.40)	(0.45)	(0.48)	(0.51)	(0.53)
36.	1.55	2.56	3.58	4.59	5.60	6.60	7.60	8.58
	(0.44)	(0.49)	(0.51)	(0.54)	(0.56)	(0.57)	(0.59)	(0.61)
40.	3.92	4.90	5.93	6.97	8.02	9.07	10.10	11.14
	(0.73)	(0.68)	(0.66)	(0.65)	(0.65)	(0.66)	(0.66)	(0.67)
44.	7.21	7.91	8.80	9.77	10.79	11.83	12.87	13.92
	(0.90)	(0.82)	(0.77)	(0.74)	(0.73)	(0.72)	(0.72)	(0.72)
48.	10.97	11.38	12.06	12.91	13.84	14.83	15.85	16.89
	(0.97)	(0.91)	(0.85)	(0.82)	(0.79)	(0.78)	(0.77)	(0.77)
52.	14.91	15.11	15.59	16.29	17.12	18.04	19.02	20.03
	(0.99)	(0.96)	(0.91)	(0.87)	(0.84)	(0.82)	(0.81)	(0.80)

9 Months   R = 0.05   Exercise Price = 40.

Price	S.D.=0.20	S.D.=0.30	S.D.=0.40	S.D.=0.50	S.D.=0.60	S.D.=0.70	S.D.=0.80	S.D.=0.90
28.	0.07	0.45	1.09	1.88	2.76	3.69	4.64	5.61
	(0.04)	(0.14)	(0.23)	(0.30)	(0.36)	(0.41)	(0.45)	(0.49)
32.	0.44	1.27	2.26	3.32	4.41	5.51	6.62	7.72
	(0.16)	(0.28)	(0.36)	(0.42)	(0.46)	(0.50)	(0.53)	(0.56)
36.	1.50	2.72	3.96	5.20	6.44	7.67	8.88	10.08
	(0.38)	(0.45)	(0.49)	(0.52)	(0.55)	(0.58)	(0.60)	(0.62)
40.	3.51	4.84	6.17	7.49	8.81	10.11	11.39	12.66
	(0.62)	(0.61)	(0.61)	(0.62)	(0.63)	(0.64)	(0.66)	(0.67)
44.	6.38	7.54	8.82	10.13	11.46	12.79	14.11	15.42
	(0.80)	(0.74)	(0.71)	(0.70)	(0.70)	(0.70)	(0.70)	(0.71)
48.	9.83	10.70	11.83	13.07	14.37	15.69	17.02	18.35
	(0.91)	(0.84)	(0.79)	(0.77)	(0.75)	(0.75)	(0.75)	(0.75)
52.	13.60	14.18	15.11	16.24	17.47	18.76	20.08	21.41
	(0.97)	(0.90)	(0.85)	(0.82)	(0.80)	(0.79)	(0.78)	(0.78)

9 Months   R = 0.10   Exercise Price = 40.

Price	S.D.=0.20	S.D.=0.30	S.D.=0.40	S.D.=0.50	S.D.=0.60	S.D.=0.70	S.D.=0.80	S.D.=0.90
28.	0.12	0.59	1.30	2.14	3.05	3.99	4.95	5.92
	(0.06)	(0.17)	(0.26)	(0.33)	(0.39)	(0.44)	(0.48)	(0.51)
32.	0.65	1.58	2.62	3.71	4.81	5.91	7.01	8.10
	(0.22)	(0.33)	(0.40)	(0.45)	(0.49)	(0.52)	(0.55)	(0.58)
36.	2.01	3.25	4.49	5.73	6.95	8.16	9.36	10.54
	(0.46)	(0.51)	(0.53)	(0.56)	(0.58)	(0.60)	(0.62)	(0.64)
40.	4.35	5.59	6.87	8.15	9.43	10.70	11.95	13.19
	(0.70)	(0.66)	(0.65)	(0.65)	(0.66)	(0.67)	(0.68)	(0.69)
44.	7.49	8.50	9.67	10.92	12.19	13.47	14.75	16.02
	(0.86)	(0.78)	(0.75)	(0.73)	(0.72)	(0.72)	(0.72)	(0.73)
48.	11.11	11.82	12.82	13.96	15.19	16.45	17.73	19.01
	(0.94)	(0.87)	(0.82)	(0.79)	(0.77)	(0.76)	(0.76)	(0.76)
52.	14.96	15.41	16.21	17.23	18.38	19.59	20.85	22.13
	(0.98)	(0.92)	(0.87)	(0.84)	(0.82)	(0.80)	(0.80)	(0.79)

TABLE 3. Option Values and Hedge Ratios for Different Stock Prices and Standard Deviations, by Maturity and Interest Rate. (Continued)

| Price | 9 Months R = 0.15 Exercise Price = 40. | | | | | | | |
	S.D.=0.20	S.D.=0.30	S.D.=0.40	S.D.=0.50	S.D.=0.60	S.D.=0.70	S.D.=0.80	S.D.=0.90
28.	0.20 (0.09)	0.76 (0.21)	1.54 (0.30)	2.42 (0.36)	3.35 (0.42)	4.31 (0.46)	5.27 (0.50)	6.24 (0.53)
32.	0.93 (0.29)	1.94 (0.38)	3.02 (0.44)	4.12 (0.48)	5.22 (0.52)	6.33 (0.55)	7.42 (0.57)	8.50 (0.60)
36.	2.61 (0.55)	3.84 (0.56)	5.06 (0.58)	6.28 (0.59)	7.48 (0.61)	8.67 (0.62)	9.85 (0.64)	11.01 (0.66)
40.	5.27 (0.77)	6.40 (0.71)	7.60 (0.69)	8.83 (0.68)	10.07 (0.68)	11.30 (0.69)	12.52 (0.69)	13.73 (0.70)
44.	8.64 (0.90)	9.49 (0.82)	10.56 (0.78)	11.72 (0.76)	12.93 (0.75)	14.16 (0.74)	15.39 (0.74)	16.62 (0.74)
48.	12.39 (0.96)	12.94 (0.90)	13.82 (0.85)	14.87 (0.82)	16.02 (0.80)	17.21 (0.79)	18.44 (0.78)	19.67 (0.78)
52.	16.30 (0.99)	16.63 (0.94)	17.31 (0.90)	18.22 (0.86)	19.28 (0.84)	20.43 (0.82)	21.62 (0.81)	22.85 (0.81)

Footnotes

1. For descriptions of options trading, see "New Game in Town" (1974), "Option Plays Are Spreading" (1973), and "The Values in Options" (1973) listed under References, and the current OCC *Prospectus*. Relevant books include Thorp and Kassouf (1967), and Malkiel and Quandt (1969).
2. See Black and Scholes (1972, 1973).
3. For some refinements and extensions, see Merton (1973).
4. More precisely, the position is short two-option contracts and long one round lot of stock, or long two-option contracts and short one round lot of stock.
5. The net money in a position is the value of any stock or options long in the investor's account minus the value of any stock or options that he is short. When he has no short positions, his net money is just the value of the stock or options in his account.
6. In fact, the $3,000 in certificates of deposit will earn interest, so the possible loss in the option position is even less than $1,000.
7. In this paragraph, I am using "speculative" and "conservative" as I take them to be used in ordinary language as related to investments.
8. Writing naked options is writing options without holding the underlying stock.
9. This assumes that the options are priced according to the formula. If they are overpriced, it may be possible to create a hedge that is long stock and short options and that shows losses only for large increases in the stock price.
10. For a proof of this, see Merton (1973, pp. 151-156).
11. This method is only an approximation. It assumes that the dividend is known for sure, and will neither be increased nor decreased. For options that expire in less than a year, this assumption gives a value that is very close to the correct value. When there is a possibility that the option will be exercised before an early ex-dividend date, we do calculations assuming expiration just before every ex-dividend date, and use the one that gives the highest value.
12. For extensive discussions of the role of information trading in determining a market maker's spread, see Bagehot (1971) and Black (1971).
13. For a discussion of the factors affecting the quality of the market for a stock, see Black (1971).

References

Bagehot, Walter. "The Only Game in Town." *Financial Analysts Journal* (March/April 1971), pp. 12-15.

Black, Fischer. "Toward a Fully Automated Exchange." *Financial Analysts Journal,* Parts I and II (July/August and November/December 1971).

Black, Fischer, and Myron Scholes. "The Valuation of Option Contracts and a Test of Market Efficiency." *Journal of Finance* (May 1972), pp. 399-417.

──────. "The Pricing of Options and Corporate Liabilities." *Journal of Political Economy* (May/June 1973), pp. 637-654.

Malkiel, Burton G. and Richard E. Quandt. *Strategies and Rational Decisions in the Securities Options Market.* Cambridge, Massachusetts: MIT Press, 1969.

Merton, Robert G. "Theory of Rational Option Pricing." *Bell Journal of Economics and Management Science* (Spring 1973), pp. 141-183.

"New Game in Town." *Wall Street Journal* (April 22, 1974), p. 1.

"Option Plays Are Spreading." *Business Week* (December 22, 1973), p. 104.

"The Values in Options." *Fortune* (November 1973), p. 89.

Thorp, Edward O. and Sheen T. Kassouf. *Beat the Market.* New York: Random House, 1967.

Article 13

HOW TO USE THE HOLES IN BLACK-SCHOLES

*by Fischer Black, Goldman, Sachs & Co.**

he Black-Scholes formula is still around, even though it depends on at least 10 unrealistic assumptions. Making the assumptions more realistic hasn't produced a formula that works better across a wide range of circumstances.

In special cases, though, we can improve the formula. If you think investors are making an unrealistic assumption like one of those we used in deriving the formula, there is a strategy you may want to follow that focuses on that assumption.

The same unrealistic assumptions that led to the Black-Scholes formula are behind some versions of "portfolio insurance." As people have shifted to more realistic assumptions, they have changed the way they use portfolio insurance. Some people have dropped it entirely, or have switched to the opposite strategy.

People using incorrect assumptions about market conditions may even have caused the rise and sudden fall in stocks during 1987. One theory of the crash relies on incorrect beliefs, held before the crash, about the extent to which investors were using portfolio insurance, and about how changes in stock prices cause changes in expected returns.

THE FORMULA

The Black-Scholes formula looks like this:

$$w(x,t) = xN(d_1) - ce^{-r(t^* - t)}N(d_2)$$

where

$$d_1 = \frac{\ln(x/c) + (r + 1/2v^2)(t^* - t)}{v\sqrt{t^* - t}}$$

and

$$d_2 = \frac{\ln(x/c) + (r - 1/2v^2)(t^* - t)}{v\sqrt{t^* - t}}$$

In this expression, w is the value of a call option or warrant on the stock, t is today's date, x is the stock price, c is the strike price, r is the interest rate, t^* is the maturity date, v is the standard deviation of the stock's return, and N is something called the "cumulative normal density function." (You can approximate N using a simple algebraic expression.)

The value of the option increases with increases in the stock's price, the interest rate, the time remaining until the option expires, and the stock's volatility. Except for volatility, which can be estimated several ways, we can observe all of the factors the Black-Scholes formula requires for valuing options.

Note that the stock's expected return doesn't appear in the formula. If you are bullish on the stock, you may buy shares or call options, but you won't change your estimate of the option's value. A higher expected return on the stock means a higher expected return on the option, but it doesn't affect the option's value for a given stock price.

This feature of the formula is very general. I don't know of any variation of the formula where the stock's expected return affects the option's value for a given stock price.

HOW TO IMPROVE THE ASSUMPTIONS

In our original derivation of the formula, Myron Scholes and I made the following unrealistic assumptions:
- The stock's volatility is known, and doesn't change over the life of the option.
- The stock price changes smoothly: it never jumps up or down a large amount in a short time.
- The short-term interest rate never changes.
- Anyone can borrow or lend as much as he wants at a single rate.
- An investor who sells the stock or the option short will have the use of all the proceeds of the sale and receive any returns from investing these proceeds.

- There are no trading costs for either the stock or the option.
- An investor's trades do not affect the taxes he pays.
- The stock pays no dividends.
- An investor can exercise the option only at expiration.
- There are no takeovers or other events that can end the option's life early.

Since these assumptions are mostly false, we know the formula must be wrong. But we may not be able to find any other formula that gives better results in a wide range of circumstances. Here we look at each of these 10 assumptions and describe how we might change them to improve the formula. We also look at strategies that make sense if investors continue to make unrealistic assumptions.

Volatility Changes

The volatility of a stock is not constant. Changes in the volatility of a stock may have a major impact on the values of certain options, especially far-out-of-the-money options. For example, if we use a volatility estimate of 0.20 for the annual standard deviation of the stock, and if we take the interest rate to be zero, we get a value of $0.00884 for a six-month call option with a $40 strike price written on a $28 stock. Keeping everything else the same, but doubling the volatility to 0.40, we get a value of $0.465.

For this out-of-the-money option, doubling the volatility estimate multiplies the value by a factor of 53.

Since the volatility can change, we should really include the ways it can change in the formula. The option value will depend on the entire future path that we expect the volatility to take, and on the uncertainty about what the volatility will be at each point in the future. One measure of that uncertainty is the "volatility of the volatility."

A formula that takes account of changes in volatility will include both current and expected future levels of volatility. Though the expected return on the stock will not affect option values, expected changes in volatility will affect them. And the volatility of volatility will affect them too.

Another measure of the uncertainty about the future volatility is the relation between the future stock price and its volatility. A decline in the stock price implies a substantial increase in volatility, while an increase in the stock price implies a substantial decrease in volatility. The effect is so strong that it is even possible that a stock with a price of $20 and a typical daily move of $0.50 will start having a typical daily move of only $0.375 if the stock price doubles to $40.

John Cox and Stephen Ross have come up with two formulas that take account of the relation between the future stock price and its volatility.[1] To see the effects of using one of their formulas on the pattern of option values for at-the-money and out-of-the money options, let's look at the values using both Black-Scholes and Cox-Ross formulas for a six-month call option on a $40 stock, taking the interest rate as zero and the volatility as 0.20 per year. For three exercise prices, the value are as follows:

Exercise Price	Black Scholes	Cox-Ross
40.00	2.2600	2.2600
50.00	0.1550	0.0880
57.10	0.0126	0.0020

The Cox-Ross formula implies lower values for out-of-the-money call options than the Black-Scholes formula. But putting in uncertainty about the future volatility will often imply higher values for these same options. We can't tell how the option values will change when we put in both effects.

What should you do if you think a stock's volatility will change in ways that other people do not yet understand? Also suppose that you feel the market values options correctly in all other respects.

You should "buy volatility" if you think volatility will rise, and "sell volatility" if you think it will fall. To buy volatility, buy options; to sell volatility, sell options. Instead of buying stock, you can buy calls or buy stock and sell calls. Or you can take the strongest position on volatility by adding a long or short position in straddles to your existing position. To buy pure volatility, buy both puts and calls in a ratio that gives you no added exposure to the stock; to sell pure volatility, sell both puts and calls in the same ratio.

Jumps

In addition to showing changes in volatility in general and changes in volatility related to changes in stock price, a stock may have jumps. A major news development may cause a sudden large change in the stock price, often accompanied by a temporary suspension of trading in the stock.

When the big news is just as likely to be good as bad, a jump will look a lot like a temporary large increase in volatility. When the big news, if it comes, is sure to be good, or is sure to be bad, the resulting jump is not like a change in volatility. Up jumps and down jumps have different effects on option values than symmetric jumps, where there is an equal chance of an up jump or a down jump.

Robert Merton has a formula that reflects possible symmetric jumps.[2] Compared to the Black-Scholes formula, his formula gives higher values for both in-the-money and out-of-the-money options and lower values for at-the-money options. The differences are especially large for short-term options.

Short-term options also show strikingly different effects for up jumps and down jumps. An increase in the probability of an up jump will cause out-of-the-money calls to go way up in value relative to out-of-the-money puts. An increase in the probability of a down jump will do the reverse. After the crash, people were afraid of another down jump, and out-of-the-money puts were priced very high relative to their Black-Scholes values, while out-of-the-money calls were priced very low.

More than a year after the crash, this fear continues to affect option values.

What should you do if you think jumps are more likely to occur than the market thinks? If you expect a symmetric jump, buy short-term out-of-the-money options. Instead of stock, you can hold call options or more stock plus put options. Or you can sell at-the-money options. Instead of stock, you can hold more stock and sell call options. For a pure play on symmetric jumps, buy out-of-the-money calls and puts, and sell at-the-money calls and puts.

For up jumps, use similar strategies that involve buying short-term out-of-the-money calls, or selling short-term out-of-the-money puts, or both. For down jumps, do the opposite.

Interest Rate Changes

The Black-Scholes formula assumes a constant interest rate, but the yields on bonds with different maturities tell us that the market expects the rate to change. If future changes in the interest rate are known, we can just replace the short-term rate with the yield on a zero-coupon bond that matures when the option expires.

---

1. See John Cox and Stephen Ross, *Journal of Financial Economics* (January/March 1976).

2. See John Cox, Robert Merton, and Stephen Ross, *Journal of Financial Economics* (January/March 1976).

SUPPOSE YOU WANT TO SHORT A STOCK BUT YOU FACE PENALTIES IF
YOU SELL THE STOCK SHORT DIRECTLY...YOU CAN SHORT IT INDIRECTLY
BY HOLDING PUT OPTIONS, OR BY TAKING A NAKED SHORT POSITION
IN CALL OPTIONS.

But, of course, future changes in the interest rate are uncertain. When the stock's volatility is known, Robert Merton has shown that the zero-coupon bond yield will still work, even when both short-term and long-term interest rates are shifting.[3] At a given point in time, we can find the option value by using the zero-coupon bond yield at that moment for the short-term rate. When both the volatility and the interest rate are shifting, we will need a more complex adjustment.

In general, the effects of interest rate changes on option values do not seem nearly as great as the effects of volatility changes. If you have an opinion on which way interest rates are going, you may be better off with direct positions in fixed-income securities rather than in options.

But your opinion may affect your decisions to buy or sell options. Higher interest rates mean higher call values and lower put values. If you think interest rates will rise more than the market thinks, you should be more inclined to buy calls, and more inclined to buy more stocks and sell puts, as a substitute for a straight stock position. If you think interest rates will fall more than the market thinks, these preferences should be reversed.

Borrowing Penalties

The rate at which an individual can borrow, even with securities as collateral, is higher than the rate at which he can lend. Sometimes his borrowing rate is substantially higher than his lending rate. Also, margin requirements or restrictions put on by lenders may limit the amount he can borrow.

High rates and limits on borrowing may cause a general increase in call option values, since calls provide leverage that can substitute for borrowing. The interest rates implied by option values may be higher than lending rates. If this happens and you have borrowing limits but no limits on option investments, you may still want to buy calls. But if you can borrow freely at a rate close to the lending rate, you may want to get leverage by borrowing rather than by buying calls.

When implied interest rates are high, conservative investors might buy puts or sell calls to protect a portfolio instead of selling stock. Fixed-income investors might even choose to buy stocks and puts, and sell calls, to create a synthetic fixed-income position with a yield higher than market yields.

Short-Selling Penalties

Short-selling penalties are generally even worse than borrowing penalties. On U.S. exchanges, an investor can sell a stock short only on or after an uptick. He must go to the expense of borrowing stock if he wants to sell it short. Part of his expense involves putting up cash collateral with the person who lends the stock; he generally gets no interest, or interest well below market rates, on this collateral. Also, he may have to put up margin with his broker in cash, and may not receive interest on cash balances with his broker.

For options, the penalties tend to be much less severe. An investor need not borrow an option to sell it short. There is no uptick rule for options. And an investor loses much less interest income in selling an option short than in selling a stock short.

Penalties on short selling that apply to all investors will affect option values. When even professional investors have trouble selling a stock short, we will want to include an element in the option formula to reflect the strength of these penalties. Sometimes we approximate this by assuming an extra dividend yield on the stock, in an amount up to the cost of maintaining a short position as part of a hedge.

Suppose you want to short a stock but you face penalties if you sell the stock short directly. Perhaps you're not even allowed to short the stock directly. You can short it indirectly by holding put options, or by taking a naked short position in call options. (Though most investors who can't short stock directly also can't take naked short positions.)

When you face penalties in selling short, you often face rewards for lending stock to those who want to short it. In this situation, strategies that involve holding the stock and lending it out may dominate other strategies. For example, you might create a position with a limited downside by holding a stock and a put on the stock, and by lending the stock to those who want to short it.

Trading Costs

Trading costs can make it hard for an investor to create an option-like payoff by trading in the underlying stock. They can also make it hard to create a stock-like payoff by trading in the option. Sometimes they

---

3. Robert Merton, *Bell Journal of Economics and Management Science* (1977).

can increase an option's value, and sometimes they can decrease it.

We can't tell how trading costs will affect an option's value, so we can think of them as creating a "band" of possible values. Within this band, it will be impractical for most investors to take advantage of mispricing by selling the option and buying the stock, or by selling the stock and buying the option.

The bigger the stock's trading costs are, the more important it is for you to choose a strategy that creates the payoffs you want with little trading. Trading costs can make options especially useful if you want to shift exposure to the stock after it goes up or down.

If you want to shift your exposure to the market as a whole, rather than to a stock, you will find options even more useful. It is often more costly to trade in a basket of stocks than in a single stock. But you can use index options to reduce your trading in the underlying stocks or futures.

Taxes

Some investors pay no taxes; some are taxed as individuals, paying taxes on dividends, interest, and capital gains; and some are taxed as corporations, also paying taxes on dividends, interest, and capital gains, but at different rates.

The very existence of taxes will affect option values. A hedged position that should give the same return as lending may have a tax that differs from the tax on interest. So if all investors faced the same tax rate, we would use a modified interest rate in the option formula.

The fact that investor tax rates differ will affect values too. Without rules to restrict tax arbitrage, investors could use large hedged positions involving options to cut their taxes sharply or to alter them indefinitely. Thus tax authorities adopt a variety of rules to restrict tax arbitrage. There may be rules to limit interest deductions or capital loss deductions, or rules to tax gains and losses before a position is closed out. For example, most U.S. index option positions are now taxed each year—partly as short-term capital gains and partly as long-term capital gains— whether or not the taxpayer has closed out his positions.

If you can use capital losses to offset gains, you may act roughly the same way whether your tax rate is high or low. If your tax rate stays the same from year to year, you may act about the same whether you are forced to realize gains and losses or are able to choose the year you realize them.

But if you pay taxes on gains and cannot deduct losses, you may want to limit the volatility of your positions and have the freedom to control the timing of gains and losses. This will affect how you use options, and may affect option values as well. I find it hard to predict, though, whether it will increase or decrease option values.

Investors who buy a put option will have a capital gain or loss at the end of the year, or when the option expires. Investors who simulate the put option by trading in the underlying stock will sell after a decline, and buy after a rise. By choosing which lots of stock to buy and which lots to sell, they will be able to generate a series of realized capital losses and unrealized gains. The tax advantages of this strategy may reduce put values for many taxable investors. By a similar argument, the tax advantages of a simulated call option may reduce call values for most taxable investors.

Dividends and Early Exercise

The original Black-Scholes formula does not take account of dividends. But dividends reduce call option values and increase put option values, at least when there are no offsetting adjustments in the terms of the options. Dividends make early exercise of a call option more likely, and early exercise of a put option less likely.

We now have several ways to change the formula to account for dividends. One way assumes that the dividend yield is constant for all possible stock price levels and at all future times, Another assumes that the issuer has money set aside to pay the dollar dividends due before the option expires. Yet another assumes that the dividend depends in a known way on the stock price at each ex-dividend date.

John Cox, Stephen Ross, and Mark Rubinstein have shown how to figure option values using a "tree" of possible future stock prices.[4] The tree gives the same values as the formula when we use the same assumptions. But the tree is more flexible, and lets us relax some of the assumptions. For example, we can put on the tree the dividend that the firm will pay for each possible future stock price at each future time. We can also test, at each node of the tree,

---

4. John Cox, Mark Rubinstein, and Stephen Ross, "Option Pricing: A Simplified Approach," *Journal of Financial Economics* Vol. 7 (1979), 229-263.

whether an investor will exercise the option early for that stock price at that time.

Option values reflect the market's belief about the stock's future dividends and the likelihood of early exercise. When you think that dividends will be higher than the market thinks, you will want to buy puts or sell calls, other things equal. When you think that option holders will exercise too early or too late, you will want to sell options to take advantage of the opportunities the holders create.

Takeovers

The original formula assumes the underlying stock will continue trading for the life of the option. Takeovers can make this assumption false.

If firm A takes over firm B through an exchange of stock, options on firm B's stock will normally become options on firm A's stock. We will use A's volatility rather than B's in valuing the option.

If firm A takes over firm B through a cash tender offer, there are two effects. First, outstanding options on B will expire early. This will tend to reduce values for both puts and calls. Second, B's stock price will rise through the tender offer premium. This will increase call values and decrease put values.

But when the market knows of a possible tender offer from firm A, B's stock price will be higher than it might otherwise be. It will be between its normal level and its normal level increased by the tender offer. Then if A fails to make an offer, the price will fall, or will show a smaller-than-normal rise.

All these factors work together to influence option values. The chance of a takeover will make an option's value sometimes higher and sometimes lower. For a short-term out-of-the-money call option, the chance of a takeover will generally increase the option value. For a short-term out-of-the-money put option, the chance of a takeover will generally reduce the option value.

The effects of takeover probability on values can be dramatic for these short-term out-of-the-money options. If you think your opinion of the chance of a takeover is more accurate than the market's, you can express your views clearly with options like these.

The October 19 crash is the opposite of a takeover as far as option values go. Option values then, and since then, have reflected the fear of another crash. Out-of-the-money puts have been selling for high values, and out-of-the-money calls have been selling for low values. If you think another crash is unlikely, you may want to buy out-of-the-money calls, or sell out-of-the-money puts, or do both.

Now that we've looked at the 10 assumptions in the Black-Scholes formula, let's see what role, if any, they play in portfolio insurance strategies.

PORTFOLIO INSURANCE

In the months before the crash, people in the U.S. and elsewhere became more and more interested in portfolio insurance. As I define it, portfolio insurance is any strategy where you reduce your stock positions when prices fall, and increase them when prices rise.

Some investors use option formulas to figure how much to increase or reduce their positions as prices change. They trade in stocks or futures or short-term options to create the effect of having a long-term put against stock, or a long-term call plus T-bills.

You don't need synthetic options or option formulas for portfolio insurance. You can do the same thing with a variety of systems for changing your positions as prices change. However, the assumptions behind the Black-Scholes formula also affect portfolio insurance strategies that don't use the formula.

The higher your trading costs, the less likely you are to create synthetic options or any other adjustment strategy that involves a lot of trading. On October 19, the costs of trading in futures and stocks became much higher than they had been earlier, partly because the futures were priced against the portfolio insurers. The futures were at a discount when portfolio insurers wanted to sell. This made all portfolio insurance strategies less attractive.

Portfolio insurance using synthetic strategies wins when the market makes big jumps, but without much volatility. It loses when market volatility is high, because an investor will sell after a fall, and buy after a rise. He loses money on each cycle.

But the true cost of portfolio insurance, in my view, is a factor that doesn't even affect option values. It is the mean reversion in the market: the rate at which the expected return on the market falls as the market rises.[5]

---

5. For evidence of mean reversion, see Eugene Fama and Kenneth French, "Permanent and Temporary Components of Stock Prices," *Journal of Political Economy* Vol. 96 No. 2 (April 1988), 246-273; and James Poterba and Lawrence Summers, "Mean Reversion in Stock Prices: Evidence and Implications," *Journal of Financial Economics* Vol. 22 No. 1 (October 1988), 27-60.

Mean reversion is what balances supply and demand for portfolio insurance. High mean reversion will discourage portfolio insurers because it will mean they are selling when expected return is higher and buying when expected return is lower. For the same reason, high mean reversion will attract "value investors" or "tactical asset allocators," who buy after a decline and sell after a rise. Value investors use indicators like price-earnings ratios and dividend yields to decide when to buy and sell. They act as sellers of portfolio insurance.

If mean reversion were zero, I think that more investors would want to buy portfolio insurance than to sell it. People have a natural desire to try to limit their losses. But, on balance, there must be as many sellers as buyers of insurance. What makes this happen is a positive normal level of mean reversion.

THE CRASH

During 1987, investors shifted toward wanting more portfolio insurance. This increased the market's mean reversion. But mean reversion is hard to see; it takes years to detect a change in it. So investors did not understand that mean reversion was rising. Since rising mean reversion should restrain an increase in portfolio insurance demand, this misunderstanding caused a further increase in demand.

Because of mean reversion, the market rise during 1987 caused a sharper-than-usual fall in expected return. But investors didn't see this at first. They continued to buy, as their portfolio insurance strategies suggested. Eventually, though, they came to understand the effects of portfolio insurance on mean reversion, partly by observing the large orders that price changes brought into the market.

Around October 19, the full truth of what was happening hit investors. They saw that at existing levels of the market, the expected return was much lower than they had assumed. They sold at those levels. The market fell, and expected return rose, until equilibrium was restored.

■ FISCHER BLACK

is a Partner of Goldman Sachs, where he develops quantitative strategies for the firm's clients. Before joining Goldman Sachs in 1984, he was Professor of Finance at M.I.T.'s Sloan School of Management. He is the co-originator, with Myron Scholes, of the well-known Black-Scholes Option Pricing Model.

MEAN REVERSION AND STOCK VOLATILITY

Now that we've explained mean reversion, how can you use your view of it in your investments?

If you have a good estimate of a stock's volatility, the stock's expected return won't affect option values. Since the expected return won't affect values, neither will mean reversion.

But mean reversion may influence your estimate of the stock's volatility. With mean reversion, day-to-day volatility will be higher than month-to-month volatility, which will be higher than year-to-year volatility. Your volatility estimates for options with several years of life should be generally lower than your volatility estimates for options with several days or several months of life.

If your view of mean reversion is higher than the market's, you can buy short-term options and sell long-term options. If you think mean reversion is lower, you can do the reverse. If you are a buyer of options, you will favor short-term options when you think mean reversion is high, and long-term options when you think it is low. If you are a seller of options, you will favor long-term options when you think mean reversion is high, and short-term options when you think it's low.

These effects will be most striking in stock index options. But they will also show up in individual stock options, through the effects of market moves on individual stocks and through the influence of "trend followers." Trend followers act like portfolio insurers, but they trade individual stocks rather than portfolios. When the stock rises, they buy; and when it falls, they sell. They act as if the past trend in a stock's price is likely to continue.

In individual stocks, as in portfolios, mean reversion should normally make implied volatilities higher for short-term options than for long-term options. (An option's implied volatility is the volatility that makes its Black-Scholes value equal to its price.) If your views differ from the market's, you may have a chance for a profitable trade.

Article 14

STANDARD DEVIATIONS OF STOCK PRICE RATIOS IMPLIED IN OPTION PRICES

HENRY A. LATANÉ AND RICHARD J. RENDLEMAN, JR.*

THE OPTION PRICING MODEL derived by Black and Scholes (B-S) is a path breaking work in the area of contingent claim pricing. Of the five variables which are necessary to specify the model, all are directly observable except the standard deviation of returns from the underlying stock.[1] Due to its rigorous theoretical underpinnings and minimum reliance on subjectively determined inputs, the model has gained a great deal of popularity in both the academic and investment communities.

In an empirical test, B-S demonstrated that the model can be used effectively to determine whether call options are properly priced if one uses an estimate of the standard deviation which is based upon an ex post series of returns from the underlying stock. However, they showed that the actual standard deviation which would result over the life of an option would be a better input into the model if it were known in advance. Accordingly, they suggested that the usefulness of the model depends to a great extent upon investors' abilities to make good forecasts of this parameter.[2]

In this paper we derive standard deviations of continuous price relative returns which are implied in actual call option prices on the assumption that investors behave as if they price options according to the Black and Scholes model. A weighted average of these implied standard deviations (ISDs) is employed as a measure of market forecasts of return variability. These weighted implied standard

---

* Willis Professor of Investment Banking, and Research Assistant, Graduate School of Business Administration, University of North Carolina, Chapel Hill.

1. See Fischer Black and Myron Scholes, "The Pricing of Options and Corporate Liabilities," *Journal of Political Economy*, May/June 1973. The exact form of the Black and Scholes model is given below.

$$w = xN(d1) - ce^{-r(t^*)}N(d2)$$

$$d1 = \frac{\ln(x/c) + (r + \frac{1}{2}v^2)t^*}{v\sqrt{t^*}}$$

$$d2 = d1 - v\sqrt{t^*}$$

where w = call price
x = stock price
c = option's exercise price
t^* = number of time periods until maturity
r = continuous risk free interest rate per period
v = standard deviation of continuous returns from the underlying stock measured over one time period.
$N(\cdot)$ = cumulative normal density function

2. See Fischer Black and Myron Scholes, "The Valuation of Option Contracts in a Test of Market Efficiency," *Journal of Finance*, May, 1972.

deviations (WISDs) are used as the basis for many of the empirical tests in this paper. Specifically (a) we explore the usefulness of the WISD in reducing risk in hedged positions assuming weekly portfolio reallocations and in identifying relatively over and under-priced options, (b) we compare WISDs with the ex post standard deviations of log price relatives for the same stocks calculated over several time periods, and (c) we investigate the stability of the cross sectional average of the WISDs and the tendency for all WISDs to move together over time. These explorations throw considerable light on the ability of investors to make good forecasts of return variability and on the effectiveness of the B-S model.

DERIVATION OF THE WISD

Although it is impossible to solve the B-S equation directly for the standard deviation in terms of an observed call price and other variables, one can use numerical search to closely approximate the standard deviation implied by any given option price. Such a procedure is used to find an implied standard deviation which equates the right-hand side of the B-S equation given in footnote (1) within ± $.001 of the actual call price for a sample of observed call option prices which are described below. In some cases the implied standard deviation is impossible to calculate because the option's price falls below that which is consistent with the theory. In these instances, it may be possible to derive reasonablly good standard deviation estimates if the effects of dividend payments, transaction costs, taxes, and timing differences in the trading of options and stock are considered. However, we ignore these complicating, but admittedly, often important considerations in computing implied standard deviations, and accordingly omit such options from the remainder of the analysis.

As a basis for our tests we use actual closing option and stock prices as reported in the *Wall Street Journal* for 24 companies whose options traded on the Chicago Board Options Exchange for the 38 weeks (39 weekly observations) beginning October 5, 1973 and ending June 28, 1974. Companies were eliminated from the sample if at the end of any week in the period it was impossible to calculate implied standard deviations for at least two options traded in their stock.

The time remaining on an option is assumed to be the number of calendar days remaining until the option matures. All ISDs are calculated on a daily basis but converted to monthly standard deviations by multiplying each by the square root of 365/12. This type of transformation is appropriate when the returns from one period to the next are independent (which is assumed in the Black and Scholes model).

The risk free interest rate is calculated as the daily continuous return which would result from holding the treasury bill whose payment date corresponds most closely with the maturity date of a given option. This rate is multiplied by the time until maturity to arrive at the riskless rate of return which could be realized over the life of an option. The price of a treasury bill is based upon the mean of the bid and asked rates quoted in the *Wall Street Journal*.

If the assumptions underlying the Black and Scholes model were completely valid and the option market were completely efficient, then at any point in time all options on a particular stock would be priced with the same monthly standard deviation. As a practical matter, however, it is not likely that this will be the case, even in a market which is highly efficient. This is due to the fact that some options are more dependent upon a precise specification of the standard deviation than others.[3] For options such as those which are in the money with little time to maturity, an exact specification of the standard deviation hardly matters. However, for other types of options it may be very important.

It would be unreasonable to expect option prices for a given company to reflect the arithmetic average of implied standard deviations from all options on its stock which are traded at a particular point in time. The ISDs on those options whose prices are the least sensitive to a precise specification of the standard deviation are likely to be unrepresentative of the market's underlying expectation. Implied standard deviations on such options could take on a wide range of values within a narrow range of option prices, and accordingly, should not be given as much weight as ISDs of options in which the standard deviation is a more important factor. Therefore, we use a weighted average implied standard deviation (WISD) in which the ISDs for all options on a given underlying stock are weighted by the partial derivative of the B-S equation with respect to each implied standard deviation.[4]

RISKLESS HEDGING AND SHORT TERM CONVERGENCE

A trading model based upon the Black and Scholes riskless hedge is simulated to test the validity of employing the WISD as a proxy for market expectations. In this test we determine whether actual option prices have a tendency to converge to those which reflect the WISD on their underlying stock at particular points in time. In addition we analyze the risk characteristics of "riskless hedges" which are reallocated weekly and employ the WISD and other measures of return variability to determine the proper mix of options and stock to employ in such hedges.

According to Black and Scholes, if one purchases 100 shares of stock and writes $1/(\partial w/\partial x)$ options against the stock (see the notation in footnote 1), rebalancing the portfolio continuously over time, then a riskless hedge is formed which should yield the risk free rate of interest if options are properly priced.[5] The investment which is required for such hedges is $x - w/(\partial w/\partial x)$. If options are over-priced,

---

3. This was suggested to us by Willard T. Carleton.

4. The form of the weighting system is

$$\text{WISD}_{it} = \left[\sum_{j=1}^{N} \text{ISD}_{ijt}^2 \cdot d_{ijt}^2 \right]^{.5} \cdot \left[\sum_{j=1}^{N} d_{ijt} \right]^{-1}$$

where WISD_{it} = Weighted average implied standard deviation for company i in period t. $i = 1$ to 24, $t = 1$ to 39.

ISD_{ijt} = Implied standard deviation for option j of company i in period t. n denotes the number of options analyzed for company i and is always greater than or equal to 2.

d_{ijt} = Partial derivation of the price of option j of company i in period t with respect to its implied standard deviation using the Black and Scholes model.

5. Fischer Black and Myron Scholes, "The Pricing of Options and Corporate Liabilities," page 643.

then this type of investment should yield more than the risk free rate. Similarly, if options are under-priced, the hedge should yield less.

When engaging in riskless hedging, an investor must use estimates of standard deviations for two purposes. The first involves determining the sensitivity of an option's price to movements in the underlying stock and, hence, determining the number of options to write against the stock. The second purpose is to determine an option's justified price. If hedges are created which are approximately riskless, then returns greater than the risk free rate should result if an investor's estimate of the standard deviation of returns from the underlying stock allows him to recognize over-priced options. In addition, if options which are written in such hedges are recognized to be under-priced, then the investment should yield less than the risk free rate if the standard deviation is a good measure of the market's forecast. This idea serves as the basis for our tests to determine whether the WISD is a good measure of the standard deviation employed in the actual option market.

To test the risk characteristics of B-S hedges and short term convergence, several standard deviation measures are used to determine hedge weights and the justified prices of options at the beginning of each week. This weighting and selection process can be based (1) individual option ISDs, (2) underlying stock WISDs, and (3) ex post standard deviations. The set of possible criteria combinations is shown in Table 1. For example, the entry 3.2 indicates that hedge weights are determined by using the ex post standard deviation while options are selected as being over or under-priced by using the WISD.

Options are selected as being over or under-priced by re-pricing them using a particular standard deviation. As a result, criteria combinations 1.1, 2.1 and 3.1 are inoperative since, by definition, the ISD is the standard deviation which would result in an option's actual price.

The use of ISDs for hedge weights makes it likely that the riskless characteristics

TABLE 1

CRITERIA COMBINATIONS

Hedge Weights		Option Selection		
		Individual Option's ISD	Underlying Stock's WISD	Ex Post Standard Deviation*
		(1)	(2)	(3)
ISD:	(1)	1.1	1.2	1.3
WISD:	(2)	2.1	2.2	2.3
Ex Post:	(3)	3.1	3.2	3.3

*The standard deviation of monthly log price relative returns calculated over the four-year period ending September 30, 1973.

of the hedged position will be maintained, even if there is no tendency for option prices to converge to those reflecting a particular standard deviation. The extent to which the other estimates will affect the risk characteristics of the hedged position cannot be assessed until the results of our tests are examined. However, if a particular hedge weighting scheme produces returns which are obviously too risky to be consistent with the theory of riskless hedging, then it would not be possible to make an a priori estimate of the return which would result from such a hedge.

With these standard deviation inputs and the assumption that option prices should immediately converge to those indicated by the B-S model, the option in a particular stock indicating the highest potential return from the hedged position is chosen as the most over-priced, while that projecting the lowest return is considered to be the most under-priced. Both under and over-priced options are analyzed separately, with the assumption that the market's use of the WISD as a proxy for the variability of returns from the underlying stock should be reflected in higher returns for strategies employing WISDs for price projections when over-priced options are hedged, and lower returns for such hedges when under-priced options are employed. We consider the use of standard deviations which are based upon a historical series of price relative retuns to be a naive strategy against which the returns resulting from the use of WISDs can be compared.

We assume that the most over and under-priced options are written at market prices and repurchased a week later. The return on a treasury bill (assuming a constant rate of interest throughout the week) is subtracted from the return which is realized from each hedge. These weekly excess returns are averaged across all 24 companies at the end of each week, except in those few cases when an option which is assumed to be written does not trade the next week. In theory, the excess returns should be zero if options are properly priced, or if the method by which a justified price is determined is unable to distinguish between over and under-priced options (assuming that the hedges are approximately riskless). The mean and standard deviations of these average weekly excess returns which are realized from holding an equal dollar amount in hedges of each company are summarized in Tables 2A and 2B for the various criteria combinations.

Note that the standard deviation of the weekly portfolio excess returns from criteria 3.2 and 3.3 are very high for both over and under-priced option portfolios when compared with the other types of portfolios. This indicates that hedges which employ the ex post standard deviation to determine the mix of options and stock are not close to being riskless.[6] As a result, we feel that it would be impossible to

6. The reason that this occurs is that low-priced options are often very sensitive to a precise specification of the standard deviation when determining the number of options to write in a riskless hedge. The partial derivative of the Black and Scholes equation with respect to the stock price is the area under the normal distribution cutting off at the $d1$ term. One divided by this value indicates the number of options to write. When the area is small to begin with, a small change in its value resulting from an improper specification of the standard deviation can result in a very large change in the number of options written. When the ex post standard deviation is used to determine the number of options to write in a hedged position, the returns which are often produced are obviously too inconsistent with the theory of riskless hedging to be of any empirical value. If one observation involving an extreme return of this kind had been omitted from portfolios of over-priced options employing criteria combination 3.2, the mean excess portfolio return would have been reduced to .25606 (from .43253) and the standard deviation to 1.05187 (from 1.35497).

TABLE 2A

SUMMARY OF EXCESS RETURNS FROM RISKLESS HEDGES EMPLOYING OVER-PRICED OPTIONS

Criteria Combination	Weekly Portfolio Mean Excess Return	Standard Deviation of Weekly Excess Returns	Standard Deviation/$\sqrt{38}$	t Statistic
1.2	.00820*	.01729	.00280	2.93
1.3	.00788*	.01517	.00246	3.20
2.2	.03665*	.09772	.01585	2.31
2.3	.03496*	.09839	.01596	2.91
3.2	.43253	1.35497	.21981	1.97
3.3	.32499	1.01397	.16449	1.98

TABLE 2B

SUMMARY OF EXCESS RETURNS FROM RISKLESS HEDGES EMPLOYING UNDER-PRICED OPTIONS

Criteria Combination	Weekly Portfolio Mean Excess Return	Standard Deviation of Weekly Excess Returns	Standard Deviation/$\sqrt{38}$	t Statistic
1.2	$-$.00572*	.01304	.00212	$-$2.70
1.3	$-$.00110	.01384	.00225	$-$0.44
2.2	$-$.02822*	.07000	.01136	$-$2.48
2.3	$-$.01932	.06458	.01047	$-$1.85
3.2	$-$.12024	1.01397	.16449	$-$1.81
3.3	$-$.01353	1.26890	.20586	$-$0.07

t statistic computed by dividing the mean excess return by the standard deviation of the excess returns/$\sqrt{38}$.

* Significantly different from zero at the 5% level.

predict the magnitude of the excess returns resulting from such portfolios and omit them from consideration in the remainder of the analysis. On the other hand, the return variability of hedged portfolios employing the ISD of each individual option is low, especially when compared with the variability of returns from typical common stock portfolios. The standard deviations of portfolio returns from hedges employing the WISD are somewhat higher. However, we feel that they are not so high as to preclude the prediction of mean excess returns which result from such hedges.

If there is no tendency for options to converge upon prices which reflect a particular standard deviation estimate, then one would expect the mean excess return from a strategy employing that estimate to be zero. Our results show that all of the portfolios employing WISDs to make price projections produce mean excess returns which are significantly different from zero at the 5% level. The direction of difference is exactly that which would be expected if the WISD is a good estimate of short run market expectations. In addition, the mean returns from portfolios employing the WISD are consistently higher than those using the ex post standard deviation (for price projections) for over-priced options and lower for those which are under-priced. Ignoring the portfolios employing ex post standard deviations to determine hedge weights, the probability of four out of four comparisons being favorable on a random basis is only 1/16. With these results we feel that the WISD based upon the Black and Scholes model is useful, not only in determining proper hedged positions, but also in identifying relatively over and under-priced options.[7] In addition, the results demonstrate the validity of using the WISD as a measure of the standard deviation expected by the market for the returns on a particular stock.

WISDs Versus Actual Standard Deviations

A major goal of this paper is to test the ability of investors to make good estimates of return variability from common stocks. Market efficiency does not imply that ex ante expectations necessarily equal ex post realizations. However, efficiency in the options market does suggest that standard deviations which are used to price options bear some semblance to the actual variability of returns from the underlying stocks. To test the relationship between weighted average implied standard deviations and actual return variability, correlations are run on the following series of standard deviation measures:

1. The WISD averaged over the 38 week sample period (39 observations) for each of the 24 companies.
2. The standard deviation of monthly log price relative returns calculated over the four-year period ending September 30, 1973 for each company.
3. The standard deviation of weekly log price relative returns calculated over the 38 week sample period time adjusted to a monthly basis for each of the 24 companies.
4. The standard deviation of monthly log price relatives for each of the 24 companies calculated over the two-year period ending March 31, 1975.

Series 2 represents standard deviations which would be known at the beginning of the sample period. One would expect WISDs to be correlated with this series if investors use historical data to estimate standard deviations as inputs into the B-S model. However, if investors feel that the pattern of return variability should change substantially from that which was experienced in the past, then it is likely that the correlation between WISDs and those of series 2 would be low.

---

7. The closing prices of options and stock may not be representative of the prices at which one could transact due to possible timing differences in their trading. As a result, some options will appear to be over or under-priced and will create apparent excess returns from hedged positons which could not be obtained in practice. Therefore, it is difficult to determine the magnitude of actual average weekly excess returns which could have resulted from hedging strategies similar to those simulated in this study.

If investors make good forecasts of standard deviations, then there should be a high degree of correlation between WISDs and standard deviations which are calculated over the sample period and into the future (series 4). If investors are short sighted and can only make good estimates of return variablility into the immediate future, then the highest degree of correlation should be between WISDs

TABLE 3

WEIGHTED AVERAGE IMPLIED STANDARD DEVIATIONS (AVERAGED OVER THE SAMPLE PERIOD) VS. ACTUAL STANDARD DEVIATIONS OF STOCK PRICE RATIOS

Company	Series 1	Series 2	Series 3	Series 4
Atlantic Richfield	.08474	.07531	.15166	.06713
Avon	.11954	.04949	.14743	.12105
Bethlehem Steel	.09404	.06764	.09742	.06892
Brunswick	.16606	.10627	.14050	.15870
Eastman Kodak	.07857	.04048	.07349	.06761
Exxon	.07191	.03955	.07894	.05817
Ford	.07288	.05761	.07831	.07575
Great Western Financial	.15174	.08566	.17157	.13745
Gulf and Western	.11368	.09859	.09121	.09077
INA	.08373	.07389	.07232	.07504
International Harvester	.10274	.05755	.09325	.06832
ITT	.11865	.07640	.11839	.06494
Kresge	.10345	.06436	.11296	.08926
Loews	.11990	.09614	.14594	.09652
McDonalds	.12305	.07029	.13702	.09978
Merck	.07105	.04815	.06863	.05233
Monsanto	.10469	.05608	.11054	.08703
North West Airlines	.14343	.09306	.10403	.10594
Polaroid	.13868	.08117	.11961	.13848
RCA	.12525	.07643	.09794	.07276
Sperry Rand	.11186	.08023	.09944	.06565
Texas Instruments	.11698	.07107	.11705	.07993
Upjohn	.11281	.07312	.12137	.10595
Xerox	.08177	.05355	.08578	.06828
Mean	.10880	.07050	.11310	.08820

Correlation Matrix

	Series 1	Series 2	Series 3	Series 4
Series 1	1.00000	.74890	.68618	.82667
Series 2	.74890	1.00000	.46327	.55754
Series 3	.68618	.46327	1.00000	.74391
Series 4	.82267	.55754	.74391	1.00000

* Series 1. The WISD averaged over the 38 week sample period (39 observations)

Series 2. The standard deviation of monthly log price relative returns calculated over the four-year period ending September 30, 1975

Series 3. The standard deviation of weekly log price relative returns calculated over the 38 week sample period time adjusted to a monthly basis

Series 4. The standard deviation of monthly log price relatives calculated over the two year period ending March 31, 1975.

and series 3. The correlations between the ex post series themselves should give an indication of whether WISDs or historical estimates are better predictors of future return variability. Table 3 presents the four series of standard deviations, their means, and their correlation matrix.

The highest correlation is between the WISDs and series 4 which indicates that the implied standard deviations are highly correlated with a series of actual standard deviations which were calculated partially into the future. Note that both series 3 and 4 are more positively correlated with the WISDs than with ex post standard deviations calculated before the sample period. During this period, WISDs were better estimates of future return variability than ex post standard deviations which were calculated from historical data.

There is no claim that the relative magnitudes of the various correlation ratios in Table 3 will prove to be stable over time. However, there seems to be little doubt that the average WISD for individual stocks is significantly correlated both with the ex post and ex ante standard deviations of price relative returns.

It appears impossible to determine whether options were generally over or under-priced during the sample period by comparing the mean values of the various standard deviation measures. The average value of the series of WISDs is clearly higher than either series of ex post standard deviations employing monthly data (series 2 and 4). This indicates that options were over-priced during the sample period. However, the average value of standard deviations calculated over the sample period using weekly data is higher than the average value of WISDs which suggests that options were generally under-priced. Negative serial correlation of the weekly data, possibly caused by outlying observations, may well explain this latter result. If so, the preponderance of evidence would be toward options being over-priced.

The evidence for options being over-priced is supported by the results of Tables 2A and 2B in which the grand mean of the weekly excess returns from four criteria combinations of hedged portfolios containing both over and under-priced options is .00417.[8] In addition, the absolute value of the mean return of portfolios containing over-priced options is higher than that of portfolios containing under-priced options for every criteria combination. All of these hedges are constructed by buying stocks and selling options. As a result, the consistently positive excess returns suggest that options were over-priced in terms of the Black and Scholes model during the time period under review.

STABILITY OF THE WISDs

In the previous section we analyzed the average value of WISDs for the various stocks over the sample period. In this section we examine the individual WISDs calculated at the end of each week in order to gain insights into the stability of the standard deviation forecasts made in the options market.

Table 4 presents the cross sectional averages of the WISDs in each week and corresponding Black and Scholes prices for a typical option whose terms are given in the table.

8. We omitted the returns of criteria combinations 3.2 and 3.3 in order to be consistent with the earlier analysis.

TABLE 4

CROSS SECTIONAL AVERAGES OF THE
MONTHLY WISDs FROM WEEK 1 (OCTOBER 5,
1973) THROUGH WEEK 39 (JUNE 28, 1974)
AND CORRESPONDING VALUES OF A TYPICAL
CALL OPTION*

Week	Average WISD	Value of Call Option
1	.11056	$12.63
2	.12597	14.08
3	.13724	15.14
4	.13423	14.86
5	.13288	14.73
6	.12722	14.20
7	.12850	14.32
8	.13322	14.76
9	.13103	14.56
10	.12358	13.86
11	.12829	14.30
12	.12870	14.34
13	.12115	13.63
14	.12439	13.93
15	.11625	13.17
16	.11235	12.80
17	.10483	12.10
18	.09913	11.56
19	.10027	11.67
20	.09474	11.15
21	.08895	10.61
22	.08878	10.59
23	.09418	11.10
24	.09698	11.36
25	.09319	11.00
26	.10070	11.71
27	.09614	11.28
28	.09612	11.28
29	.09219	10.98
30	.09680	11.34
31	.08895	10.61
32	.09005	10.71
33	.09966	11.61
34	.10082	11.72
35	.10398	12.01
36	.09800	11.45
37	.09463	11.14
38	.10331	11.95
39	.10844	12.44

* Assumptions about the terms of the call option:
Monthly standard deviation is the average WISD
Stock price is $100
Exercise price is $100
Annual interest rate is 8% (or .00667 per month)
Time remaining until maturity is 6 months

The standard deviations range from a high of .13724 to a low of .08878. Option prices corresponding to these values are, respectively, $15.14 and $10.59. We feel that the degree of difference among the various option prices suggests that the market's standard deviation estimates tend to be inconsistent over time, or alternatively, that the Black and Scholes model does not fully capture the process determining option prices in the actual market. The following analysis should shed more light on these issues.

A test for systematic movements in WISDs is made by running the following regression for each company in the sample.

$$\text{WISD}_{it} = a_i + B_i\text{CWISD}_t$$

where WISD_{it} = Weighted average implied standard deviation for company i in period t. $i = 1$ to 24, $t = 1$ to 39.

CWISD$_t$ = Cross sectional average of WISDs in period t.

With an average R^2 of 63.25% there appears to be a very strong tendency for the standard deviations which are used to price options to move together over time. This could be interpreted as a tendency on the part of investors to alter their

TABLE 5

RESULTS OF REGRESSING AN INDIVIDUAL COMPANY'S WISD AGAINST THE CROSS SECTIONAL AVERAGE

Company	a	B	R^2	Standard Error
Atlantic Richfield	−.03243	1.07676	.71445	.01081
Avon	.10209	.16047	.06145	.00998
Bethlehem Steel	−.02338	1.07917	.60137	.01396
Brunswick	−.08365	2.29461	.80410	.01799
Eastman Kodak	.03813	.33790	.52636	.00508
Exxon	.01126	.55749	.68093	.00607
Ford	−.04199	1.05481	.76857	.00921
Great Western Financial	−.04059	1.76759	.77195	.01528
Gulf and Western	−.02360	1.26144	.83520	.00888
INA	−.02515	1.00066	.59236	.01318
International Harvester	−.05057	1.40905	.88076	.00823
ITT	.05088	.63008	.52300	.00954
Kresge	−.00066	.95713	.69862	.00998
Loews	.03204	.80768	.48633	.01318
McDonalds	.04776	.69254	.46448	.01180
Merck	−.01423	.82079	.77149	.00711
Monsanto	−.03695	1.30190	.77587	.01114
North West Airlines	−.01721	1.47609	.81925	.01103
Polaroid	.08515	.49085	.18754	.01627
RCA	.00028	1.14836	.75116	.01048
Sperry Rand	−.00745	1.09619	.79934	.08714
Texas Instruments	−.03651	1.41062	.72258	.01390
Upjohn	.02642	.79405	.55173	.01136
Xerox	.04103	.37416	.39237	.00739
			Mean	.63254

estimates about the variability of returns from stocks at different points in time. During some periods, investors may feel that stocks in general are more risky than on other occasions. Nevertheless, they tend to make reasonable estimates of risk over longer time periods as evidenced by the results of the previous section. To accept this explanation, one must believe that the B-S model generally captures the process employed by investors when determining option prices even though their standard deviation estimates are not constant over time.[9]

Alternatively, we feel that, on occasion, option prices may be bid up or down due to changes in the return prospects of stocks in general. As unhedged investors become more optimistic about a stock's expected return, they may find the leverage provided by call options to be quite advantageous and be willing to pay a premium for such securities.

Expected returns from the underlying stock do not enter the Black and Scholes model. However, this does not imply that expected returns are not a factor in the market. To the extent that transaction costs, margin requirements, and a lack of a well developed put market prohibit continuous portfolio rebalancing and the exploitation of arbitrage opportunities involving puts and calls, it is possible that option prices are partially determined by investors or speculators who do not hedge or continuously rebalance their portfolios.[10]

In the option pricing models of Sprenkel, Ayres, Boness, and others, it is either implicitly or explicitly assumed that investors buy and hold options until they mature. These models determine the price of an option as its discounted expected maturity value. Unfortunately, none of these models provides an adequate theoretical basis for determining an option's required rate of return. Nevertheless, it is obvious that an option's expected maturity value depends upon the expected return from the underlying stock.

The mathematics of the Black and Scholes model imply that any increase in an option's value which is caused by an increase in the expected return from the underlying stock is offset by an increase in the option's required rate of return. However, if investors do not increase the required rate of return on the option by the amount which is implied by the Black and Scholes model, then the option's price will be affected by changes in return expectations.

Research is under way using an alternative option pricing model to test whether the systematic changes in option prices could have been caused by changes in return expectations. In any event, we feel that our evidence suggests that factors determining expected standard deviations (or mean returns) not captured in the Black and Scholes model systematically affect all option prices.

9. In order to derive the Black and Scholes model it must be assumed that the actual standard deviation of returns from the stock and that which is expected by investors are identical and constant through time.

10. Black and Scholes derived their model under the assumption that investors create riskless hedges between options and stock. In addition, they derived their equation by using the capital asset pricing model. Although they did not make the assumption that investors continuously rebalance their portfolio in the alternative derivation, such behavior is implied if investors attitudes toward risk are assumed to remain constant through the duration of the option contract. Whether investors choose a portfolio with no risk, as in the alternative derivation, or at a desired "Beta" level, an option investment must be continuously rebalanced among stock and/or a riskless security in order to hold the risk characteristics of the portfolio constant through time.

SUMMARY AND CONCLUSIONS

We have described a methodology for estimating the standard deviation which is used to price options in a given stock under the assumption that the option market is dominated by investors who behave as if they employ the Black and Scholes model. These weighted average implied standard deviations for individual stocks averaged over the sample period are significantly correlated with actual standard deviations of stock price ratios calculated over various time periods. In particular, the WISD is generally a better predictor of future variability than standard deviation predictors based on historical data.

Tests of a trading model suggest that the Black and Scholes model can be used effectively to determine whether individual options are properly priced for short term riskless hedging. However, the instability of weighted average implied standard deviations resulting from factors which appear to affect all options in the same way, indicates that the model may not fully capture the process determining option prices in the actual market.

REFERENCES

Ayres, H. F., "Risk Aversion in the Warrant Markets," in P. Cootner, ed., *The Random Character of Stock Market Prices* (MIT Press, Cambridge, Mass.), 497–505.

Black, F. and Scholes, M., "The Pricing of Options and Corporate Liabilities," *Journal of Political Economy*, May/June, 1973.

—— and ——. "The Valuation of Option Contracts in a Test of Market Efficiency," *Journal of Finance*, May, 1972.

Boness, A. J., "Elements of a Theory of Stock-Option Value," *Journal of Political Economy*, April 1964.

Merton, R. C., "Theory of Rational Option Pricing," *Bell Journal of Economics and Management Science*, Spring, 1973.

Samuelson, P. A., and Merton, R. C., "A Complete Model of Warrant Pricing that Maximizes Utility," *Industrial Management Review*, Winter, 1969.

Sprenkle, C. M., "Warrant Prices as Indicators of Expectations and Preferences," in P. Cootner, ed., *The Random Character of Stock Market Prices* (MIT Press, Cambridge, Mass.) 412–474.

Article 15

THE PRICING OF COMMODITY CONTRACTS*

Fischer BLACK

Sloan School of Management, M.I.T., Cambridge, Mass. 02139, U.S.A.

Received July 1975, revised version received July 1975

The contract price on a forward contract stays fixed for the life of the contract, while a futures contract is rewritten every day. The value of a futures contract is zero at the start of each day. The expected change in the futures price satisfies a formula like the capital asset pricing model. If changes in the futures price are independent of the return on the market, the futures price is the expected spot price. The futures market is not unique in its ability to shift risk, since corporations can do that too. The futures market is unique in the guidance it provides for producers, distributors, and users of commodities. Using assumptions like those used in deriving the original option formula, we find formulas for the values of forward contracts and commodity options in terms of the futures price and other variables.

1. Introduction

The market for contracts related to commodities is not widely understood. Futures contracts and forward contracts are often thought to be identical, and many people don't know about the existence of commodity options. One of the aims of this paper is to clarify the meaning of each of these contracts.[1]

The spot price of a commodity is the price at which it can be bought or sold for immediate delivery. We will write p for the spot price, or $p(t)$ for the spot price at time t.

The spot price of an agricultural commodity tends to have a seasonal pattern: it is high just before a harvest, and low just after a harvest. The spot price of a commodity such as gold, however, fluctuates more randomly.

Predictable patterns in the movement of the spot price do not generally imply profit opportunities. The spot price can rise steadily at any rate lower than the storage cost for the commodity (including interest) without giving rise to a profit opportunity for those with empty storage facilities. The spot price can fall during a harvest period without giving rise to a profit opportunity for growers, so long as it is costly to accelerate the harvest.

---

*I am grateful for comments on earlier drafts by Michael Jensen, Myron Scholes, Edward Thorp, and Joseph Williams. This work was supported in part by the Center for Research in Security Prices (sponsored by Merrill Lynch, Pierce, Fenner & Smith Inc.) at the Graduate School of Business, University of Chicago.

[1]For an introduction to commodity markets, see Chicago Board of Trade (1973).

The futures price of a commodity is the price at which one can agree to buy or sell it at a given time in the future without putting up any money now. We will write x for the futures price, or $x(t, t^*)$ for the futures price at time t for a transaction that will occur at time t^*.

For example, suppose that it is possible today to enter into a contract to buy gold six months from now at \$160 an ounce, without either party to the contract being compensated by the other. Both parties may put up collateral to guarantee their ability to fulfill the contract, but if the futures price remains at \$160 an ounce for the next six months, the collateral will not be touched. If the contract is left unchanged for six months, then the gold and the money will change hands at that time. In this situation, we say that the six month futures price of gold is \$160 an ounce.

The futures price is very much like the odds on a sports bet. If the odds on a particular baseball game between Boston and Chicago are 2:1 in favor of Boston, and if we ignore the bookie's profit, then a person who bets on Chicago wins \$2 or loses \$1. No money changes hands until after the game. The odds adjust to balance the demand for bets on Chicago and the demand for bets on Boston. At 2:1, balance occurs if twice as many bets are placed on Boston as on Chicago.

Similarly, the futures price adjusts to balance demand to buy the commodity in the future with demand to sell the commodity in the future. Whenever a contract is opened, there is someone on each side. The person who agrees to buy is long the commodity, and the person who agrees to sell is short. This means that when we add up all positions in contracts of this kind, and count short positions as negative, we always come out with zero. The total long interest in commodity contracts of any type must equal the total short interest.

When the two times that specify a futures price are equal, the futures price must equal the spot price,

$$x(t, t) \equiv p(t). \tag{1}$$

Expression (1) holds for all times t. For example, it says that the May futures price will be equal to the May spot price in May, and the September futures price will be equal to the September spot price in September.

Now let us define the three kinds of commodity contracts: forward contracts, futures contracts, and option contracts. Roughly speaking, a forward contract is a contract to buy or sell at a price that stays fixed for the life of the contract; a futures contract is settled every day and rewritten at the new futures price; and an option contract can be exercised by the holder when it matures, if it has not been closed out earlier.

We will write v for the value of a forward contract, u for the value of a futures contract, and w for the value of an option contract. Each of these values will depend on the current futures price $x(t, t^*)$ with the same transaction time t^* as the contract, and on the current time t, as well as on other variables. So we will write $v(x, t)$, $u(x, t)$, and $w(x, t)$. The value of the short side of any contract will be just the negative of the value of the long side. So we will treat v, u, and w as the values of a forward contract to buy, a long futures contract, and an option to buy.

The value of a forward contract depends also on the price c at which the commodity will be bought, and the time t^* at which the transaction will take place. We will sometimes write $v(x, t, c, t^*)$ for the value of a long forward contract. From the discussion above, we know that the futures price is that price at which a forward contract has a current value of zero. We can write this condition as

$$v(x, t, x, t^*) \equiv 0. \tag{2}$$

In effect, eq. (2) says that the value of a forward contract when it is initiated is always zero. When it is initiated, the contract price c is always equal to the current futures price $x(t, t^*)$.

Increasing the futures price increases the value of a long forward contract, and decreasing the futures price decreases the value of the contract. Thus we have

$$\begin{aligned} v(x, t, c, t^*) > 0, \quad &x > c, \\ v(x, t, c, t^*) < 0, \quad &x < c. \end{aligned} \tag{3}$$

The value of a forward contract may be either positive or negative.

When the time comes for the transaction to take place, the value of the forward contract will be equal to the spot price minus the contract price. But by eq. (1), the futures price $x(t, t^*)$ will be equal to the spot price at that time. Thus the value of the forward contract will be the futures price minus the spot price,

$$v(x, t^*, c, t^*) = x - c. \tag{4}$$

Later we will use eq. (4) as the main boundary condition for a differential equation describing the value of a forward contract.

The difference between a futures contract and a forward contract is that the futures contract is rewritten every day with a new contract price equal to the corresponding futures price. A futures contract is like a series of forward contracts. Each day, yesterday's contract is settled, and today's contract is written with a contract price equal to the futures price with the same maturity as the futures contract.

Eq. (2) shows that the value of a forward contract with a contract price equal to the futures price is zero. Thus the value of a futures contract is reset to zero every day. If the investor has made money, he will be given his gains immediately. If he has lost money, he will have to pay his losses immediately. Thus we have

$$u(x, t) \equiv 0. \tag{5}$$

Technically, eq. (5) applies only to the end of the day, after the futures contract has been rewritten. During the day, the futures contract may have a positive or negative value, and its value will be equal to the value of the corresponding forward contract.

Note that the futures price and the value of a futures contract are not at all the same thing. The futures price refers to a transaction at times t^* and is never zero. The value of a futures contract refers to time t and is always zero (at the end of the day).

In the organized U.S. futures markets, both parties to a futures contract must post collateral with a broker. This helps to ensure that the losing party each day will have funds available to pay the winning party. The amount of collateral required varies from broker to broker.

The form in which the collateral can be posted also varies from broker to broker. Most brokers allow the collateral to take the form of Treasury Bills or marginable securities if the amount exceeds a certain minimum. The brokers encourage cash collateral, however, because they earn the interest on customers' cash balances.

The value of a futures customer's account with a broker is entirely the value of his collateral (at the end of the day). The value of his futures contracts is zero. The value of the collateral posted to ensure performance of a futures contract is not the value of the contract.

As futures contracts are settled each day, the value of each customer's collateral is adjusted. When the futures price goes up, those with long positions have money added to their collateral, and those with short positions have money taken away from their collateral. If a customer at any time has more collateral than his broker requires, he may withdraw the excess. If he has less than his broker requires, he will have to put up additional collateral immediately.

Commodity options have a bad image in the U.S., because they were recently used to defraud investors of many millions of dollars. There are no organized commodity options markets in this country. In the U.K., however, commodity options have a long and relatively respectable history.

A commodity option is an option to buy a fixed quantity of a specified commodity at a fixed time in the future and at a specified price. It differs from a security option in that it can't be exercised before the fixed future date. Thus it is a 'European option' rather than an 'American option'.

A commodity option differs from a forward contract because the holder of the option can choose whether or not he wants to buy the commodity at the specified price. With a forward contract, he has no choice: he must buy it, even if the spot price at the time of the transaction is lower than the price he pays.

At maturity, the value of a commodity option is the spot price minus the contract price, if that is positive, or zero. Writing c^* for the exercise price of the option, and noting that the futures price equals the spot price at maturity, we have

$$w(x, t^*) = x - c^*, \quad x \geqq c^*, \\ = 0, \quad\quad x < c^*. \tag{6}$$

Expression (6) looks like the expression for the value of a security option at maturity as a function of the security price.

2. The behavior of the futures price

Changes in the futures price for a given commodity at a given maturity give rise to gains and losses for investors with long or short positions in the corresponding futures contracts. An investor with a position in the futures market is bearing risk even though the value of his position at the end of each day is zero. His position may also have a positive or negative expected dollar return, even though his investment in the position is zero.

Since his investment is zero, it is not possible to talk about the percentage or fractional return on the investor's position in the futures market. Both his risk and his expected return must be defined in dollar terms.

In deriving expressions for the behavior of the futures price, we will assume that taxes are zero. However, tax factors will generally affect the behavior of the futures price. There are two peculiarities in the tax laws that make them important.

First, the IRS assumes that a gain or loss on a futures contract is realized only when the contract is closed out. The IRS does not recognize, for tax purposes, the fact that a futures contract is effectively settled and rewritten every day. This makes possible strategies for deferring the taxation of capital gains. For example, the investor can open a number of different contracts, both long and short. The contracts that develop losses are closed out early, and are replaced with different contracts so that the long and short positions stay balanced. The contracts that develop gains are allowed to run unrealized into the next tax year. In the next year, the process can be repeated. Whether this process is likely to be profitable depends on the special factors affecting each investor, including the size of the transaction costs he pays.

Second, the IRS treats a gain or loss on a long futures position that is closed out more than six months after it is opened as a long-term capital gain or loss, while it treats a gain or loss on a short futures position as a short-term capital gain or loss no matter how long the position is left open. Thus if the investor opens both long and short contracts, and if he realizes losses on the short contracts and gains on the long contracts, he can convert short-term gains (from other transactions) into long-term gains. Again, whether this makes sense for a particular investor will depend on his transaction costs and other factors.

However, we will assume that both taxes and transaction costs are zero. We will further assume that the capital asset pricing model applies at each instant of time.[2] This means that investors will be compensated only for bearing risk that cannot be diversified away. If the risk in a futures contract is independent of the risk of changes in value of all assets taken together, then investors will not have to be paid for taking that risk. In effect, they don't have to take the risk because they can diversify it away.

The usual capital asset pricing formula is

$$E(\tilde{R}_i) - R = \beta_i[E(\tilde{R}_m) - R]. \tag{7}$$

In this expression, $\tilde{R}_i$ is the return on asset i, expressed as a fraction of its initial value; R is the return on short-term interest-bearing securities; and $\tilde{R}_m$ is the return on the market portfolio of all assets taken together. The coefficient β_i is a measure of the extent to which the risk of asset i cannot be diversified away. It is defined by

$$\beta_i = \text{cov}\,(\tilde{R}_i, \tilde{R}_m)/\text{var}\,(\tilde{R}_m). \tag{8}$$

The market portfolio referred to above includes corporate securities, personal assets such as real estate, and assets held by non-corporate businesses. To the extent that stocks of commodities are held by corporations, they are implicitly included in the market portfolio. To the extent that they are held by individuals and non-corporate businesses, they are explicitly included in the market portfolio. This market portfolio cannot be observed, of course. It is a theoretical construct.

Commodity contracts, however, are not included in the market portfolio. Commodity contracts are pure bets, in that there is a short position for every long position. So when we are taking all assets together, futures contracts, forward contracts, and commodity options all net out to zero.

Eq. (7) cannot be applied directly to a futures contract, because the initial value of the contract is zero. So we will rewrite the equation so that it applies to dollar returns rather than percentage returns.

Let us assume that asset i has no dividends or other distributions over the period. Then its fractional return is its end-of-period price minus its start-of-period price, divided by its start-of-period price. Writing P_{i0} for the start-of-period price of asset i, writing $\tilde{P}_{i1}$ for its end-of-period price, and substituting from eq. (8), we can rewrite eq. (7) as

$$E\{(\tilde{P}_{i1} - P_{i0})/P_{i0}\} - R = [\text{cov}\,\{(\tilde{P}_{i1} - P_{i0})/P_{i0}, \tilde{R}_m\}/\text{var}\,(\tilde{R}_m)]$$
$$\times [E(\tilde{R}_m) - R]. \tag{9}$$

[2]For an introduction to the capital asset pricing model, see Jensen (1972). The behavior of futures prices in a model of capital market equilibrium was first discussed by Dusak (1973).

Multiplying through by P_{i0}, we get an expression for the expected dollar return on an asset,

$$E(\tilde{P}_{i1} - P_{i0}) - RP_{i0} = [\mathrm{cov}\,(\tilde{P}_{i1} - P_{i0}, \tilde{R}_m)/\mathrm{var}\,(\tilde{R}_m)][E(\tilde{R}_m) - R].$$

(10)

The start-of-period value of a futures contract is zero, so we set P_{i0} equal to zero. The end-of-period value of a futures contract, before the contract is rewritten and its value set to zero, is the change in the futures price over the period. In practice, commodity exchanges set daily limits which constrain the reported change in the futures price and the daily gains and losses of traders. We will assume that these limits do not exist. So we set $\tilde{P}_{i1}$ equal to $\Delta \tilde{P}$, the change in the futures price over the period,

$$E(\Delta \tilde{P}) = [\mathrm{cov}\,(\Delta \tilde{P}, \tilde{R}_m)/\mathrm{var}\,(\tilde{R}_m)][E(\tilde{R}_m) - R].$$

(11)

In effect, we have applied expression (10) to a futures contract, and have come up with expression (11), which refers to the change in the futures price. For the rest of this section, we can forget about futures contracts and work only with the futures price.

Writing β^* for the first factor on the right-hand side of eq. (11), we have

$$E(\Delta \tilde{P}) = \beta^*[E(\tilde{R}_m) - R].$$

(12)

Expression (12) says that the expected change in the futures price is proportional to the 'dollar beta' of the futures price. If the covariance of the change in the futures price with the return on the market portfolio is zero, then the expected change in the futures price will be zero,[3]

$$E(\Delta \tilde{P}) = 0, \quad \text{when} \quad \mathrm{cov}\,(\Delta \tilde{P}, \tilde{R}_m) = 0.$$

(13)

Expressions (12) and (13) say that the expected change in the futures price can be positive, zero, or negative. It would be very surprising if the β^* of a futures price were exactly zero, but it may be approximately zero for many commodities. For these commodities, neither those with long futures positions nor those with short futures positions have significantly positive expected dollar returns.

3. Futures prices and spot prices

When eq. (13) holds at all points in time, the expected change in the futures price will always be zero. This means that the expected futures price at any time t' in the future, where t' is between the current time t and the transaction time

---

[3]In the data she analyzed on wheat, corn, and soybean futures, Dusak (1973) found covariances that were close to zero.

M

t^*, will be equal to the current futures price. The mean of the distribution of possible futures prices at time t' will be the current futures price.[4]

But the futures price at time t^* is the spot price at time t^*, from expression (1). So the mean of the distribution of possible spot prices at time t^* will be the current futures price, when eq. (13) always holds.

Even when (13) doesn't hold, we may still be able to use eq. (12) to estimate the mean of the distribution of possible spot prices at time t^*. To use (12), though, we need to know β^* at each point in time between t and t^*, and we need to know $E(\tilde{R}_m) - R$.

A farmer may not want to know the mean of the distribution of possible spot prices at time t^*. He may be interested in the discounted value of the distribution of possible spot prices. In fact, it seems plausible that he can make his investment decisions as if β^* were zero, even if it is not zero. He can assume that the β^* is zero, and that the futures price is the expected spot price.

To see why this is so, note that he can hedge his investments by taking a short position in the futures market. By taking the right position in the futures market, he can make the β of his overall position zero. Assuming that the farmer is not concerned about risk that can be diversified away, he should make the same investment decisions whether or not he actually takes offsetting positions in the futures market.

In fact, futures prices provide a wealth of valuable information for those who produce, store, and use commodities. Looking at futures prices for various transaction months, participants in this market can decide on the best times to plant, harvest, buy for storage, sell from storage, or process the commodity. A change in a futures price at time t is related to changes in the anticipated distribution of spot prices at time t^*. It is not directly related to changes in the spot price at time t. In practice, however, changes in spot prices and changes in futures prices will often be highly correlated.

Both spot prices and futures prices are affected by general shifts in the cost of producing the commodity, and by general shifts in the demand for the commodity. These are probably the most important factors affecting commodity prices. But an event like the arrival of a prime producing season for the commodity will cause the spot price to fall, without having any predictable effect on the futures price.

Changes in commodity prices are also affected by such factors as the interest rate, the cost of storing the commodity, and the β of the commodity itself.[5] These factors may affect both the spot price and the futures price, but in different ways.

Commodity holdings are assets that form part of investors' portfolios, either directly or indirectly. The returns on such assets must be defined to include

---

[4]The question of the relation between the futures price and the expected spot price is discussed under somewhat different assumptions by Cootner (1960a, 1960b) and Telser (1960).

[5]Some of the factors affecting changes in the spot price are discussed by Brennan (1958) and Telser (1958).

such things as the saving to a user of commodities from not running out in the middle of a production run, or the benefit to anyone storing the commodity of having stocks on hand when there is an unusual surge in demand. The returns on commodity holdings must be defined net of all storage costs, including deterioration, theft, and insurance premiums. When the returns on commodity holdings are defined in this way, they should obey the capital asset pricing model, as expressed by eq. (7), like any other asset. If the β of the commodity is zero, as given in eq. (7), then we would expect the β^* of a futures contract to be approximately zero too, as given in eq. (12). And vice versa.

The notion that commodity holdings are priced like other assets means that investors who own commodities are able to diversify away that part of the risk that can be diversified away. One way this can happen is through futures markets: those who own commodities can take short positions, and those who hold diversified portfolios of assets can include long positions in commodity contracts.

But there are other ways that the risk in commodity holdings can be largely diversified away. The most common way for risk to be spread is through a corporation. The risk of a corporation's business or assets is passed on to the holders of the corporation's liabilities, especially its stockholders. The stockholders have, or could have, well diversified portfolios of which this stock is only a small part.

Thus if stocks of a commodity are held by a corporation, there will normally be no need for the risk to be spread through the futures market. (There are special cases, however, such as where the corporation has lots of debt outstanding and the lenders insist that the commodity risk be hedged through the futures market.) There are corporations at every stage in a commodity's life cycle: production, distribution, and processing. Even agricultural commodities are generally produced by corporations these days, though the stock may be closely held. Any of these corporate entities can take title to the stocks of commodities, no matter where they are located, and thus spread the risk to those who are in the best position to bear it. For example, canners of tomatoes often buy a farmer's crop before the vines are planted. They may even supply the vines.

This means that a futures market does not have a unique role in the allocation of risk. Corporations in the commodity business play the same role. Which kind of market is best for this role depends on the specifics of such things as transaction costs and taxes in each individual case. It seems clear that corporations do a better job for most commodities, because organized futures markets don't even exist for most commodities. Where they do exist, most of the risk is still transferred through corporations rather than through futures markets.

Thus there is no reason to believe that the existence of a futures market has any predictable effect on the path of the spot price over time. It is primarily the storage of a commodity that reduces fluctuations in its price over time.

M.

Storage will occur whether or not there is any way of transferring risk. If there were no way to transfer risk, the price of a seasonal commodity might be somewhat higher before the prime production periods than it is now. But since there are good ways to transfer risk without using the futures market, even this benefit of futures markets is minimal.

I believe that futures markets exist because in some situations they provide an inexpensive way to transfer risk, and because many people both in the business and out like to gamble on commodity prices. Neither of these counts as a major benefit to society. The big benefit from futures markets is the side effect: the fact that participants in the futures markets can make production, storage, and processing decisions by looking at the pattern of futures prices, even if they don't take positions in that market.

This, of course, assumes that futures markets are efficient. It assumes that futures prices incorporate all available information about the future spot price of a commodity. It assumes that investors act quickly on any information they receive, so that the price reacts quickly to the arrival of the information. So quickly that individual traders find it very difficult to make money consistently by trading on information.

4. The pricing of forward contracts and commodity options

We have already discussed the pricing of futures contracts and the behavior of futures prices. In order to derive formulas for the other kinds of commodity contracts, we must make a few more assumptions.

First, let us assume that the fractional change in the futures price over any interval is distributed log-normally, with a known variance rate s^2. The derivations would go through with little change if we assumed that the variance rate is a known function of the time between t and t^*, but we will assume that the variance rate is constant.

Second, let us assume that all of the parameters of the capital asset pricing model, including the expected return on the market, the variance of the return on the market, and the short-term interest rate, are constant through time.

Third, let us continue to assume that taxes and transaction costs are zero.

Under these assumptions, it makes sense to write the value of a commodity contract only as a function of the corresponding futures price and time. If we did not assume the parameters of the capital asset pricing model were constant, then the value of a commodity contract might also depend on those parameters. Implicitly, of course, the value of the contract still depends on the transaction price and the transaction time.

Now let us use the same procedure that led to the formula for an option on a security.[6] We can create a riskless hedge by taking a long position in the

[6]The original option formula was derived by Black and Scholes (1973). Further results were obtained by Merton (1973).

option and a short position in the futures contract with the same transaction date. Since the value of a futures contract is always zero, the equity in this position is just the value of the option.

The size of the short position in the futures contract that makes the combined position riskless is the derivative of $w(x, t)$ with respect to x, which we will write w_1. Thus the change in the value of the hedged position over the time interval Δt is

$$\Delta w - w_1 \Delta x. \tag{14}$$

Expanding Δw, and noting that the return on the hedge must be at the instantaneous riskless rate r, we have the differential equation[7]

$$w_2 = rw - \tfrac{1}{2}s^2 x^2 w_{11}. \tag{15}$$

Note that this is like the differential equation for an option on a security, but with one term missing. The term is missing because the value of a futures contract is zero, while the value of a security is positive.

The main boundary condition for this equation is expression (6).[8] Using standard methods to solve eqs. (15) and (6), we obtain the following formula for the value of a commodity option:

$$w(x, t) = e^{r(t - t^*)}[x N(d_1) - c^* N(d_2)], \tag{16}$$

$$d_1 = \left[\ln \frac{x}{c^*} + \frac{s^2}{2}(t^* - t) \right] \Big/ s\sqrt{(t^* - t)},$$

$$d_2 = \left[\ln \frac{x}{c^*} - \frac{s^2}{2}(t^* - t) \right] \Big/ s\sqrt{(t^* - t)}.$$

This formula can be obtained from the original option formula by substituting $xe^{r(t - t^*)}$ for x everywhere in the original formula.[9] It is the same as the value of an option on a security that pays a continuous dividend at a rate equal to the stock price times the interest rate, when the option can only be exercised at maturity.[10] Again, this happens because the investment in a futures contract is zero, so an interest rate factor drops out of the formula.

[7] For the details of this expansion, see Black and Scholes (1973, p. 642 or p. 646).

[8] Another boundary condition and a regularity condition are needed to make the solution to (15) and (6) unique. The boundary condition is $w(0, t) = 0$. The need for these additional conditions was not noted in Black and Scholes (1973).

[9] Thorp (1973) obtains the same formula for a similar problem, related to the value of a security option when an investor who sells the underlying stock short does not receive interest on the proceeds of the short sale.

[10] Merton (1973) discusses the valuation of options on dividend-paying securities. The formula he obtains (f. 62) should be eq. (16), but he forgets to substitute $xe^{r(t - t^*)}$ for x in d_1 and d_2.

Eq. (16) applies to a 'European' commodity option, that can only be exercised at maturity. If the commodity option can be exercised before maturity, the problem of finding its value becomes much more complex.[11] Among other things, its value will depend on the spot price and on futures prices with various transaction dates before the option expires.

Eq. (16) also assumes that taxes are zero. But if commodity options are taxed like security options, then there will be substantial tax benefits for high tax bracket investors who write commodity options.[12] These benefits may be passed on in part or in full to buyers of commodity options in the form of lower prices. So taxes may reduce the values of commodity options.

Compared with the formula for a commodity option, the formula for the value of a forward contract is very simple. The differential equation it must satisfy is the same. Substituting $v(x, t)$ for $w(x, t)$ in eq. (15), we have

$$v_2 = rv - \tfrac{1}{2}s^2 x^2 v_{11}. \tag{17}$$

The main boundary condition is eq. (4), which we can rewrite as

$$v(x, t^*) = x - c. \tag{18}$$

The solution to (17) and (18) plus the implicit boundary conditions is

$$v(x, t) = (x - c)\, e^{r(t - t^*)}. \tag{19}$$

Expression (19) says that the value of a forward contract is the difference between the futures price and the forward contract price, discounted to the present at the short-term interest rate. It is independent of any measure of risk. It does not depend on the variance rate of the fractional change in the futures price or on the covariance rate between the change in the futures price and the return on the market.

[11]See Merton (1973) for a discussion of some of the complexities in finding a value for an option that can be exercised early.
[12]For a discussion of tax factors in the pricing of options, see Black (1975).

References

Black, F., 1975, Fact and fantasy in the use of options, Financial Analysts Journal 31, July/Aug.
Black, F. and M. Scholes, 1973, The pricing of options and corporate liabilities, Journal of Political Economy 81, May/June, 637–654.
Brennan, M.J., 1958, The supply of storage, American Economic Review 48, March, 50–72.
Chicago Board of Trade, 1973, Commodity trading manual (Board of Trade of the City of Chicago, Chicago, Ill.).
Cootner, P.H., 1960a, Returns to speculators: Telser versus Keynes, Journal of Political Economy 68, Aug., 396–404.
Cootner, P.H., 1960b, Rejoinder, Journal of Political Economy 68, Aug., 415–418.

Dusak, K., 1973, Futures trading and investor returns: An investigation of commodity market risk premiums, Journal of Political Economy 81, Nov./Dec., 1387– 1406.

Jensen, M.C., 1972, Capital markets: Theory and evidence, Bell Journal of Economics and Management Science 3, Autumn, 357–398.

Merton, R.C., 1973, The theory of rational option pricing, Bell Journal of Economics and Management Science 4, Spring, 141–183.

Telser, L., 1958, Futures trading and the storage of cotton and wheat, Journal of Political Economy 66, June, 233–255.

Telser, L., 1960, Returns to speculators: Telser versus Keynes, Reply, Journal of Political Economy 67, Aug., 404–415.

Thorp, E., 1973, Extensions of the Black–Scholes options model, Bulletin of the International Statistical Institute, Proceedings of the 39th Session, 522–529.

Article 16

Valuation of American Futures Options: Theory and Empirical Tests

ROBERT E. WHALEY*

ABSTRACT

This paper reviews the theory of futures option pricing and tests the valuation principles on transaction prices from the S&P 500 equity futures option market. The American futures option valuation equations are shown to generate mispricing errors which are systematically related to the degree the option is in-the-money and to the option's time to expiration. The models are also shown to generate abnormal risk-adjusted rates of return after transaction costs. The joint hypothesis that the American futures option pricing models are correctly specified and that the S&P 500 futures option market is efficient is refuted, at least for the sample period January 28, 1983 through December 30, 1983.

FUTURES OPTION CONTRACTS NOW trade on every major futures exchange and on a wide variety of underlying futures contracts. The Chicago Mercantile Exchange, the Chicago Board of Trade, the New York Futures Exchange, and the Commodity Exchange now collectively have more than twenty options written on futures contracts, where the underlying spot commodities are financial assets such as stock portfolios, bonds, notes and Eurodollars, foreign currencies such as West German marks, Swiss francs and British pounds, precious metals such as gold and silver, livestock commodities such as cattle and hogs, and agricultural commodities such as corn and soybeans. Moreover, new contract applications are before the Commodity Futures Trading Commission and should be actively trading in the near future.

With the markets for these new contingent claims becoming increasingly active, it is appropriate that the fundamentals of futures option valuation be reviewed and tested. Black [5] provides a framework for the analysis of commodity futures options. Although his work is explicitly directed at pricing European options on forward contracts, it applies to European futures contracts as well if the riskless rate of interest is constant during the futures option life.[1] The options currently

* Associate Professor of Finance, University of Alberta and Visiting Associate Professor of Finance, University of Chicago. This research was supported by the Finance Research Foundation of Canada. Comments and suggestions by Fred D. Arditti, Warren Bailey, Giovanni Barone-Adesi, Bruce Cooil, Theodore E. Day, Thomas S. Y. Ho, Hans R. Stoll, and a referee and an Associate Editor of this *Journal* are gratefully acknowledged.

[1] Cox, Ingersoll, and Ross [11, p. 324] demonstrate that the price of a futures contract is equal to the price of a forward contract when interest rates are nonstochastic.

trading, however, are American options, and only recently has theoretical work begun to focus on the American futures option pricing problem.[2]

The purpose of this paper is to review the theory underlying American futures option valuation and to test it on transaction prices from the S&P 500 equity futures option market. In the first section of the paper, the theory of futures option pricing is reviewed. The partial differential equation of Black ([5]) is presented, and the boundary conditions of the American and European futures option pricing problems are shown to imply different valuation equations. For the American futures options, efficient analytic approximations of the values of the call and put are presented, and the magnitude of the early exercise premium is simulated.

In the second section of the paper, the American futures option valuation principles are tested on S&P 500 futures option contract data for the period January 28, 1983 through December 30, 1983. Included are an examination of the systematic biases in the mispricing errors of the option pricing models, a test of the stationarity of the volatility of the futures price change relatives, and a test of the joint hypothesis that the American futures option models are correctly specified and that the S&P market is efficient. The paper concludes with a summary of the major results of the study.

I. Theory of Futures Option Valuation

An option on a futures contract is like an option on a common stock in the sense that it provides its holder with the right to buy or sell the underlying security at the exercise price of the option. Unlike a stock option, however, a cash exchange in the amount of the exercise price does not occur when the futures option is exercised. Upon exercise, a futures option holder merely acquires a long or short futures position with a futures price equal to the exercise price of the option. When the futures contract is marked-to-market at the close of the day's trading, the option holder is free to withdraw in cash an amount equal to the futures price less the exercise price in the case of a call and the exercise price less the futures price in the case of a put. Thus, exercising a futures option is like receiving in cash the exercisable value of the option.

A. Assumptions and Notation

Black [5] provides the groundwork for futures option valuation. Although his work is directed at pricing a European call option, it is general in the sense that the partial differential equation describing the dynamics of the call option price through time applies to put options as well as call options and to American options as well as European options. The assumptions necessary to develop Black's partial differential equation are as follows:

---

[2] Following Black's [5] seminal article, Moriarity, Phillips, and Tosini [18], Asay [1], Wolf [24], and others discussed the European futures option pricing problem. Other than the studies by Whaley [22] and Stoll and Whaley [21], the theoretical work on American futures options is unpublished and includes studies by Ramaswamy and Sundaresan [19] and Brenner, Courtadon, and Subrahmanyam [9].

(A1) There are no transaction costs in the option, futures, and bond markets. These include direct costs such as commissions and implicit costs such as the bid-ask spread and penalties on short sales.

(A2) Markets are free of costless arbitrage opportunities. If two assets or portfolios of assets have identical terminal values, they have the same price, and/or, if an asset or portfolio of assets has a future value which is certain to be positive, the initial value (cost) of the asset or portfolio is certain to be negative (positive).

(A3) The short-term riskless rate of interest is constant through time.

(A4) The instantaneous futures price change relative is described by the stochastic differential equation,

$$dF/F = \mu \, dt + \sigma \, dz,$$

where μ is the expected instantaneous price change relative of the futures contract, σ is the instantaneous standard deviation, and z is a Wiener process.

Assumptions (A1) and (A2) are fairly innocuous. Transaction costs are trivial for those making the market in the various financial assets, and available empirical evidence suggests investors behave rationally. Assumption (A3) may appear contradictory, since some futures options are written on long-term debt instrument futures contracts[3] where the driving force behind the volatility of the futures price change relatives is interest rate uncertainty. The two interest rates are, to some degree, separable, however. Assumption (A3) describes the behavior of the short-term interest rate on, say, Treasury bills, while the volatility of T-bond futures prices, for example, is related to the volatility of the long-term U.S. Treasury bond forward rate.[4] Assumption (A4) describes the dynamics of the futures price movements through time. It is important to note that no assumption about the relationship between the futures price and the price of the underlying spot commodity has been invoked.[5] The valuation results presented in this section, therefore, apply to any futures option contract, independent of the nature of the underlying spot commodity.

---

[3] The Chicago Board of Trade, for example, lists options on U.S. T-bond and T-note futures contracts.

[4] A priori, the assumption of constant short-term interest rate is untenable for all option pricing models. A constant short-term rate implies a constant, flat term structure, with interest rate uncertainty having no bearing on the volatility of the underlying asset prices. Such is hardly the case. The validity of such option pricing models, however, need not be evaluated on the basis of their assumptions and can be judged on the merits of their predictions.

[5] Note that Assumption (A4) defines the dynamics of the futures price movements with no reference to the relationship between the futures price and the price of the underlying spot commodity. Whether such an assumption is more appropriate for the futures price dynamics or the underlying spot commodity dynamics is an open empirical question.

Assumption (A4) is consistent with the assumption that the underlying spot price, S, follows the stochastic differential equation.

$$dS/S = \alpha \, dt + \sigma \, dz,$$

where α is the expected relative spot price change, and σ is the instantaneous standard deviation if there is (a) a constant, continuous riskless rate of interest, r, and (b) a constant, continuous

For expositional purposes, the following notation is adopted in this study to describe futures options and their related parameters:

F = current futures price

F_T = random futures price at expiration

$C(F, T; X)[c(F, T; X)]$ = American [European] call option price

$P(F, T; X)[p(F, T; X)]$ = American [European] put option price

$\varepsilon_C(F, T; X)[\varepsilon_p(F, T; X)]$ = early exercise premium of American call [put] option

r = riskless rate of interest

T = time to expiration of futures options

X = exercise price of futures options.

B. Solution to Futures Option Pricing Problem

Under the above-stated assumptions, Black demonstrates that, if a riskless hedge can be formed between the futures option and its underlying futures contract, the partial differential equation governing the movements of the futures option price (V) through time is

$$\tfrac{1}{2}\sigma^2 F^2 V_{FF} - rV + V_t = 0. \tag{1}$$

This equation applies to American call ($C = V$) and put ($P = V$) options, as well as European call ($c = V$) and put ($p = V$) options. What distinguishes the four valuation problems is the set of boundary conditions applied to each problem.

C. European Futures Options

The boundary condition necessary to develop an analytic formula for the European call option is that the terminal call price is equal to the maximum value of 0 or the in-the-money amount of the option, that is, $\max(0, F_T - X)$. Black shows that, when this terminal boundary condition is applied to Equation

---

proportional rate of receipt (payment), d, for holding the underlying spot commodity. To show this result, apply Ito's lemma to the cost-of-carry relationship, $S_t = F_t e^{-(r-d)(T-t)}$, where F_t is defined in (A4). The expected futures price change relative, μ, is equal to the expected spot price change relative less the difference between the riskless rate of interest and the continuous rate of receipt, $\alpha - (r - d)$, and the standard deviation, σ, is the same for both the underlying spot commodity and futures price changes.

The interpretation of d depends on the nature of the underlying spot commodity. For example, in the foreign currency futures market, d represents the foreign interest rate earned on the investment in the foreign currency. For agricultural commodity futures, d is less than zero and represents the rate of cost for holding the spot commodity (i.e., storage costs, insurance costs, etc.), and for stock index futures, d represents the continuous proportional dividend yield on the underlying stock portfolio.

A continuous proportional dividend yield assumption may not be appropriate for a stock index since dividend payments are discrete and have a tendency to cluster according to the day of the week and the month of the year. With uncertain discrete dividend payments during the futures' life, the cost-of-carry relationship between the prices of the stock index and stock index futures is unclear, however, as long as (A4) holds for the futures price dynamics, the option pricing relationships contained in the paper will hold.

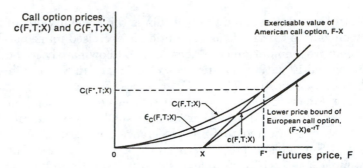

Figure 1. European and American Call Option Prices As a Function of the Underlying Futures Contract Price.

(1) where $c = V$, the value of a European call option on a futures contract is

$$c(F, T; X) = e^{-rT}[FN(d_1) - XN(d_2)], \qquad (2)$$

where $d_1 = [\ln(F/X) + 0.5\sigma^2 T]/\sigma\sqrt{T}$, and $d_2 = d_1 - \sigma\sqrt{T}$, and where $N(\ \ )$ is the cumulative univariate normal distribution. When the lower boundary condition for the European put, $\max(0, X - F_T)$, is applied to the partial differential Equation (1), the analytic solution is

$$p(F, T; X) = e^{-rT}[XN(-d_2) - FN(-d_1)], \qquad (3)$$

where all notation is as it was defined above.

D. American Futures Options

The European call formula (2) provides a convenient way of demonstrating that the American call option may be exercised early. As the futures price becomes extremely large relative to the exercise of the option, the values of $N(d_1)$ and $N(d_2)$ approach one, and the European call value approaches $(F - X)e^{-rT}$. But, the American option may be exercised immediately for $F - X$, which is higher than the European option value. Thus, the American call option may be worth more "dead" than "alive"[6] and will command a higher price that the European call option.

Figure 1 illustrates the value of the American call option's early exercise privilege. In the figure, F^* represents the critical current futures price level where the American call option holder is indifferent about exercising his option immediately or continuing to hold it. Below F^*, the value of the early exercise premium, $\varepsilon_C(F, T; X)$, is equal to the difference between the American and European call functions, $C(F, T; X) - c(F, T; X)$. Above F^*, $\varepsilon_C(F, T; X)$ is equal to $(F - X) - c(F, T; X)$. Note that as the futures price becomes large relative to the exercise price, the European call option value approaches $(F - X)e^{-rT}$, and the early exercise premium approaches $(F - X)(1 - e^{-rT})$. In other words, the maximum

---

[6] Merton [17] demonstrates that, because the exercisable value of an American call option on a nondividend-paying stock, $S - X$, is always below the lower price bound of the corresponding European option, $S - Xe^{-rT}$, the American call option is always worth more alive than dead, and, therefore, will not be exercised early.

value the early exercise premium may attain is the present value of the interest income which can be earned if the call option is exercised immediately.

Unlike the European option case, there are no known analytic solutions to the partial differential Equation (1), subject to the American call option on a futures contract boundary condition, $C(F, t; X) \geq \max(0, F_t - X)$ for all $0 \leq t \leq T$, and, subject to the American put option on a futures contract boundary condition, $P(F, t; X) \geq \max(0, X - F_t)$ for all $0 \leq t \leq T$. Usually, the valuation of American futures options has resorted to finite difference approximation methods.[7] Ramaswamy and Sundaresan [19] and Brenner, Courtadon, and Subrahmanyam [9], for example, use such techniques. Unfortunately, finite difference methods are computationally expensive because they involve enumerating every possible path the futures option price could travel during its remaining time to expiration.

Whaley [23] adapts the Geske-Johnson [13] compound option analytic approximation method to price American futures options. In addition to being computationally less expensive than numerical methods, the compound option approach offers the advantages of being intuitively appealing and easily amenable to comparative statics analysis. Unfortunately, even though the compound option approach is about twenty times faster than numerical methods, it is still not inexpensive because it requires the evaluation of cumulative bivariate and cumulative trivariate normal density functions.

The analytic approximation of American futures option values used in this study is that derived by Barone-Adesi and Whaley [3]. The method is based on MacMillan's [16] quadratic approximation of the American put option on a stock valuation problem and is considerably faster than either the finite difference or the compound option approximation methods.

The quadratic approximation of the American call option on a futures contract, as provided in Barone-Adesi and Whaley [3], is

$$C(F, T; X) = c(F, T; X) + A_2(F/F^*)^{q_2}, \quad \text{where} \quad F < F^*, \quad \text{and}$$

$$C(F, T; X) = F - X, \quad \text{where} \quad F \geq F^*, \quad (4)$$

and where $A_2 = (F^*/q_2)\{1 - e^{-rT}N[d_1(F^*)]\}$, $d_1(F^*) = [\ln(F^*/X) + 0.5\sigma^2 T]/\sigma\sqrt{T}$, $q_2 = (1 + \sqrt{1 + 4k})/2$, and $k = 2r/[\sigma^2(1 - e^{-rT})]$. F^* is the critical futures price above which the American futures option should be exercised immediately (see Figure 1) and is determined iteratively by solving

$$F^* - X = c(F^*, T; X) + \{1 - e^{-rT}N[d_1(F^*)]\}F^*/q_2. \quad (4a)$$

Although the valuation equation may appear ominous, its intuition is simple. For a current futures price below the critical stock price, F^*, the American call value is equal to the European value plus the early exercise premium, as approximated by the term, $A_2(F/F^*)^{q_2}$. Above F^*, the worth of the American call is its exercisable proceeds.

---

[7] The first applications of finite difference methods to option pricing problems were by Schwartz [20] who valued warrants written on dividend-paying stocks and by Brennan and Schwartz [7] who priced American put options on nondividend-paying stocks. These techniques are reviewed in Brennan and Schwartz [8] and Geske and Shastri [15].

The only parameter to the American option formula (4) which requires computational sophistication beyond that required for the European formula (2) is the determination of the critical futures price F^*. To this end, Barone-Adesi and Whaley [3] provide an algorithm for solving (4a) in five iterations or less.

The quadratic approximation of the American put option on a futures contract is

$$P(F, T; X) = p(F, T; X) + A_1(F/F^{**})^{q_1}, \quad \text{where} \quad F > F^{**}, \quad \text{and}$$

$$P(F, T; X) = X - F, \quad \text{where} \quad F \leq F^{**}, \tag{5}$$

and where $A_1 = -(F^{**}/q_1)\{1 - e^{-rT}N[-d_1(F^{**})]\}$, $q_1 = (1 - \sqrt{1 + 4k})/2$, and where all other notation is as it was defined for the American call, F^{**} is the critical futures price below which the American futures option should be exercised immediately and is determined iteratively by solving

$$X - F^{**} = p(F^{**}, T; X) - \{1 - e^{-rT}N[-d_1(F^{**})]\}F^{**}/q_1. \tag{5a}$$

E. Simulation of Early Exercise Premium Values

To demonstrate plausible magnitudes of the early exercise premium on American futures options, the European and American models prices were computed for a range of option pricing parameters. The results are reported in Table I. It is interesting to note that out-of-the-money futures options have negligible early exercise premiums. For example, when the futures price (F) is 90, the riskless rate of interest (r) is 8 percent, and the standard deviation of the futures price relatives (σ) is 0.15, an out-of-the-money call option with an exercise price (X) of 100 and a time to expiration (T) of 0.5 years has an early exercise premium of 0.0106, only slightly more than 1 percent of the American option price. Even at-the-money options have small early exercise premiums which account for only a small percentage of the option price. Only when the option is considerably in-the-money does the early exercise premium account for a significant proportion of the price of the option.

In summary, the theory of futures option valuation suggests that the early exercise privilege of American futures options contributes meaningfully to the futures option value. The simulation results, based on option pricing parameters that are typical for S&P 500 futures option contracts, suggest that this is true, but only for in-the-money options.

II. Empirical Tests

In this section, the performance of the American futures option pricing models is analyzed using transaction information for S&P 500 equity futures options. After the description of the data in the first subsection, the implied standard deviation methodology is discussed. Volatility estimates are made using nonlinear regression of observed futures option prices on model prices. The third subsection presents an examination of the systematic patterns in the models prediction errors. This analysis is motivated by the evidence reported in the stock option

Table I

Theoretical European and American Futures Option Values: Exercise Price (X) = 100

Futures Option Parameters[a]	Futures Price (F)	Call Options			Put Options		
		European $c(F, T; X)$[b]	American $C(F, T; X)$[c]	Early Exercise Premium $\varepsilon_C(F, T; X)$	European $p(F, T; X)$[b]	American $P(F, T; X)$[c]	Early Exercise Premium $\varepsilon_P(F, T; X)$
$r = 0.08$	80	0.0027	0.0029	0.0002	19.6067	20.0000	0.3933
$\sigma = 0.15$	90	0.2529	0.2547	0.0018	10.0549	10.1506	0.0957
$T = 0.25$	100	2.9321	2.9458	0.0137	2.9321	2.9458	0.0137
	110	10.1752	10.2627	0.0875	0.3732	0.3756	0.0024
	120	19.6239	20.0000	0.3761	0.0199	0.0204	0.0005
$r = 0.12$	80	0.0027	0.0030	0.0003	19.4116	20.0000	0.5884
$\sigma = 0.15$	90	0.2504	0.2533	0.0029	9.9549	10.1153	0.1605
$T = 0.25$	100	2.9029	2.9257	0.0228	2.9029	2.9257	0.0228
	110	10.0740	10.2205	0.1465	0.3695	0.3734	0.0039
	120	19.4286	20.0000	0.5714	0.0197	0.0205	0.0008
$r = 0.08$	80	0.3956	0.3986	0.0030	19.9996	20.2032	0.2036
$\sigma = 0.30$	90	1.9817	1.9913	0.0096	11.7837	11.8543	0.0707
$T = 0.25$	100	5.8604	5.8878	0.0274	5.8604	5.8878	0.0274
	110	12.2527	12.3237	0.0710	2.4507	2.4624	0.0116
	120	20.4776	20.6470	0.1694	0.8737	0.8790	0.0053
$r = 0.08$	80	0.0583	0.0603	0.0020	19.2740	20.0000	0.7260
$\sigma = 0.15$	90	0.8150	0.8256	0.0106	10.4229	10.6044	0.1815
$T = 0.50$	100	4.0637	4.1099	0.0463	4.0637	4.1099	0.0463
	110	10.6831	10.8584	0.1753	1.0752	1.0887	0.0134
	120	19.4105	20.0018	0.5913	0.1947	0.1991	0.0043

[a] The notation used in this column is as follows: r = riskless rate of interest; σ = standard deviation of the futures price change relative; and T = time to expiration.
[b] The European futures option values are computed using the Black [5] pricing equations.
[c] The American futures option values are computed using the Barone-Adesi and Whaley [3] analytic approximations.

pricing tests. In the fourth subsection, the hypothesis that the standard deviation of futures price change relatives is the same across call and put options is tested. The final subsection presents the results of a joint test of the hypothesis that the American futures option pricing models are correctly specified and that the S&P 500 futures option market is efficient.

A. Data

The data used in this study consist of transaction information for the S&P 500 equity futures and futures option contracts traded on the Chicago Mercantile Exchange (CME) from the first day of trading of the S&P futures options, January 28, 1983, through the last business day of the year, December 30, 1983. The data were provided by the CME and are referred to as "Quote Capture" information. Essentially, the data set contains the time and the price of every transaction in which the price changed from the previously recorded transaction. Bid and ask prices are also recorded if the bid price exceeds or the ask price is below the price at the last transaction. The volume of each transaction and the number of transactions at a particular price are not recorded.

Two exclusionary criteria were applied to the Quote Capture information. First, bid and ask price quotes were eliminated because they do not represent prices at which there were both a buyer and seller available to transact. Both sides of the market transaction were necessary within the market efficiency test design. Second, futures options with times to expiration in excess of 26 weeks were excluded. The trading activity in these options and their underlying futures contracts was too sparse to warrant consideration with the market efficiency test. What remained was a sample of 28,736 transactions, 21,613 in the nearest contract month, and 7,123 in the second nearest contract month.

The futures option pricing models require the futures price at the instant at which the option is traded. To represent the contemporaneous futures price, the futures price at the trade most closely preceding the futures option trade is used. Because the S&P 500 futures market was so active during the investigation period, the average time between the futures and the subsequent futures option transactions was only 21 seconds.

Table II offers a summary of the characteristics of the transactions contained in the 232-day sample period. Of the 28,736 transactions, 15,063 were call option transactions and 13,763 were puts. The at-the-money options appear to have been the most active, with 55 percent of the call option trades and 50 percent of the put option trades being at futures prices ±2 percent of the exercise price. Out-of-the-money options were more active than in-the-money options: 25 percent of total trades to 20 percent of total trades for calls and 42 percent to 8 percent for puts, respectively. Over 64 percent of the transactions were on options with maturities of less than 8 weeks, verifying that most of the trading activity was in the nearest contract month.

The yield on the U.S. Treasury bill maturing on the contract month expiration day[8] was used to proxy for the riskless rate on interest. The yields were computed

---

[8] S&P 500 futures option contracts expired the third Thursday of the contract month until the June 1984 contract. Beginning with the June 1984 contract, the third Friday of the month is the expiration day.

Table II

Summary of S&P 500 Futures Option Transactions during the Period January 28, 1983 through December 30, 1983

Futures Price/ Exercise Price (F/X)	No. of Transactions			Time to Expiration (in weeks) (T)	No. of Transactions		
	Call	Put	Both		Call	Put	Both
$F/X < 0.90$	11	2	13	$T < 2$	2,307	2,234	4,541
$0.90 \leq F/X < 0.92$	77	9	86	$2 \leq T < 4$	2,375	2,190	4,565
$0.92 \leq F/X < 0.94$	339	42	381	$4 \leq T < 6$	2,567	2,211	4,778
$0.94 \leq F/X < 0.96$	1,014	191	1,205	$6 < T < 8$	2,480	2,064	4,544
$0.96 \leq F/X < 0.98$	2,281	773	3,054	$8 < T < 10$	1,708	1,623	3,331
$0.98 \leq F/X < 1.00$	4,091	2,615	6,706	$10 \leq T < 12$	1,479	1,371	2,850
$1.00 \leq F/X < 1.02$	4,260	4,252	8,512	$12 \leq T < 14$	1,255	1,164	2,419
$1.02 \leq F/X < 1.04$	1,783	2,559	4,342	$14 \leq T < 16$	337	445	782
$1.04 \leq F/X < 1.06$	830	1,524	2,354	$16 \leq T < 18$	222	173	395
$1.06 \leq F/X < 1.08$	241	875	1,116	$18 \leq T < 20$	175	90	265
$1.08 \leq F/X < 1.10$	78	453	531	$20 \leq T$	158	108	266
$1.10 \leq F/X$	58	378	436				
All	15,063	13,673	28,736	All	15,063	13,673	28,736

daily on the basis of the average of the T-bill's bid and ask discounts reported in the *Wall Street Journal.*

B. Implied Standard Deviation Methodology

The American futures option pricing models have five parameters: F, X, T, r, and σ. Of these, four are known or are easily estimated. The exercise price, X, and the time to expiration, T, are terms of the futures option contract, and the futures price, F, and the riskless rate of interest, r, are easily accessible market values. The troublesome parameter to estimate is the standard deviation of the futures price change relatives.

The methodology used to estimate the standard deviation of the futures price change relative is described in Whaley [22, pp. 39–40]. Observed futures option prices, V_j, were regressed on their respective model prices, $V_j(\sigma)$, that is,

$$V_j = V_j(\sigma) + \varepsilon_j. \tag{6}$$

where ε_j is a random disturbance term,[9] each day during the sample period. All transaction prices for the day were used in each regression. The number of transactions used to estimate σ in a given day ranged from 30 to 300, with the average number being 124. The estimates of σ ranged from 0.1009 to 0.2176, with the average being approximately 0.1555.

The time series of standard deviation estimates indicates that the volatility of the S&P 500 futures price relatives declined during 1983. During the first 116 trading days of the sample period, the average estimate of σ using the American model was 0.1711, while, during the last 116 days of the period, it was 0.1399. It is interesting to note that, during the same two subperiods, the S&P 500 Index rose by 15.07 percent and −0.65 percent, respectively.[10]

C. Tests for Systematic Biases

One way in which the performance of an option pricing model may be evaluated is by examining its mispricing errors for systematic tendencies. Whaley [22] demonstrates that, when the early exercise premium of the American call option on a dividend-paying stock is accounted for in the valuation model, the exercise price and time to expiration biases which had been documented for the European model disappear. Geske and Roll [14] later verify this result and also attempt to explain the variance bias. Here, the variance bias is not of concern since there is only one underlying commodity. The ability of the American futures option models to eliminate the first two biases, however, should be examined.

The tests for systematic biases in the futures option pricing models involved clustering and then averaging the price deviations by the degree the option is in-

---

[9] The relationship between observed and model prices is not exact and is affected by: (a) model misspecification; (b) nonsimultaneity of futures and futures option price quotations; and (c) the bid-ask spread in the futures and futures option markets. If the residuals in the nonlinear regression (6) are independent and normally distributed, the resulting value of σ is the maximum likelihood estimate.

[10] This evidence is consistent with the notion that the variance rate depends on the price of the underlying asset.

Table III

Summary of Average Mispricing Errors of American Futures Option Pricing Models by the Option's Moneyness (F/X) and by the Option's Time to Expiration in Weeks (T) for S&P 500 Futures Option Transactions during the Period January 28, 1983 through December 30, 1983

	$C - C(F, T; X)$				$P - P(F, T; X)$			
	$T < 6$	$6 \leq T < 12$	$T \geq 12$	All T	$T < 6$	$6 \leq T < 12$	$T \geq 12$	All T
$F/X < 0.98$	-0.0630[a]	-0.1372	-0.0872	-0.1028	-0.1064	-0.0914	-0.1056	-0.1014
	(1,221)	(1,760)	(741)	(3,722)	(593)	(335)	(89)	(1,017)
$0.98 \leq F/X < 1.02$	-0.1228	-0.0775	0.0073	-0.0924	-0.0816	-0.0196	0.1336	-0.0406
	(4,452)	(2,858)	(951)	(8,351)	(3,999)	(2,193)	(675)	(6,867)
$F/X \geq 1.02$	0.0577	0.1175	0.0702	0.0806	0.1286	0.1906	30.3060	0.1929
	(1,486)	(1,049)	(455)	(2,990)	(2,043)	(2,530)	(1,216)	(5,789)
All F/X	-0.0757	-0.0599	-0.0120	-0.0606	-0.0191	0.0808	0.2287	0.0537
	(7,249)	(5,667)	(2,147)	(15,063)	(6,635)	(5,058)	(1,980)	(13,673)

[a] The average deviation of the observed option price from the model price for the 1,221 call option transaction prices with in-the-moneyness (F/X) less than 0.98 and time to expiration (T) less than 6 weeks is −0.0630.

the-money of the option and by the option's time to expiration. Table III contains a summary of the results for the 15,063 call option and the 13,673 put option transactions in the sample.

Both a "moneyness" bias and a "maturity" bias appear for the call option transaction prices of the sample. The moneyness bias is just the opposite of that reported for stock options.[11] The further the call option is in-the-money, the lower is the model price relative to the observed price (i.e., out-of-the-money calls are overpriced by the model and the in-the-money calls are underpriced). This is true for the American models when all maturities are clustered together and when the intermediate-term and long-term options are considered separately. For the short-term options, the greatest mispricing occurs for the at-the-money calls, which appear dramatically underpriced relative to the model [e.g., for the American call option pricing model, the average value of $C - C(F, T; X)$ is −0.1228].

The maturity bias for the calls is also just the opposite of that reported for call options on stocks. Here, the model prices are higher than the observed prices for short-term options and are lower than observed for long-term options. The relationship is not consistent across the moneyness groupings, however. For out-of-the-money calls, the mispricing is greatest for the intermediate term options with the model considerably overstating observed values [e.g., the average $C - C(F, T; X)$ is −0.1372], and, for in-the-money options, the mispricing is still greatest for the intermediate term options, but with the models understating observed values [e.g., the average $C - C(F, T; X)$ is 0.1175]. Overall, however, the maturity bias does not appear to be as serious as the moneyness bias for the sample of call option transaction prices.

The average price deviations for the put options appear to have a more orderly pattern, with the relationships between average price deviation and the moneyness and maturity of the options monotonic. Like the call option results, the maturity bias takes the form of short-term options being underpriced relative to the model and long-term options being overpriced. Unlike the call option results, however, the maturity bias is almost as serious as the moneyness bias, and the moneyness bias takes the form of out-of-the-money options being overpriced relative to the model and in-the-money options underpriced. (Recall the put option is in-the-money where $F/X < 1$.) A possible explanation of this latter result is that floor traders engage in conversion/reversal arbitrage using the European put-call parity relationship,[12]

$$c(F, T; X) - p(F, T; X) = (F - X)e^{-rT}. \tag{7}$$

[11] See, e.g., Black [4] or Whaley [22].

[12] The European put-call parity relationship can be found in a variety of papers, including Black [5], Moriarity, Phillips, and Tosini [18], Asay [1], and Wolf [24]. In all of these studies, the futures contract underlying the option contract is treated like a forward, but no problems arise because the European option can be exercised only at expiration.

For American futures options, the assumption of equivalence between forward and futures contract positions can lead to erroneous statements about futures option pricing. Some of these results are outlined in Ramaswamy and Sundaresan [19]. Stoll and Whaley [21] derive the put-call parity relationship for American futures options.

If the put-call parity relationship (7) is actively arbitraged, overpricing of in-the-money call options should result in overpricing of out-of-the-money put options, and underpricing of out-of-the-money call options should result in underpricing of in-the-money put options, or vice versa.

One final note about the results in Table III is worthwhile. During the period examined, put options were overpriced on average while call options were underpriced. Obviously, this result is sensitive to the volatility estimate used to price the options, but, nonetheless, the difference between the average mispricing errors of the put and call option formulas would be approximately the same even if a different estimate of σ were used. This peculiarity indicates that the market's assessment of the volatility of the relative futures price changes may be greater for puts than for calls and provides the motivation for the tests in the next subsection.

D. Stationarity of Volatility Estimates Across Options

To test the hypothesis that the standard deviation of futures price change relatives is the same in the pricing of call and put options on the S&P 500 futures contracts, the ratio,

$$R = [SSE_C(\sigma_C) + SSE_p(\sigma_p)]/SSE(\sigma), \qquad (8)$$

was computed each day during the sample period. In (8), $SSE_C(\sigma_C)$ is the sum of squared errors realized by estimating the nonlinear regression (6) using only the call option transaction prices during the day, and $SSE_p(\sigma_p)$ is the sum of squared errors using only the put option prices. $SSE(\sigma)$ is the sum of squared errors using both the call and put option prices. If the residuals of the regressions are independent and normally distributed, Gallant [12] shows that the test statistic,

$$F = (n - 2)(1 - R), \qquad (9)$$

is approximately distributed, $F_{1,n-2}$.[13] The results of these tests are reported in Table IV.

The test results indicate that the null hypothesis that the volatility estimates are equal for calls and puts is rejected in 75 percent of the cases for the American model. The standard deviation of futures price relatives implied by call option prices is lower, on average, than that implied by put option prices. The cause of this anomaly is difficult to determine. One possible explanation is that the stochastic process governing the futures price movements is ill-defined, so the option pricing models are misspecified. Another is that perhaps two separate clienteles trade in call options and in put options. But, this latter explanation fails to account for the floor traders who could costlessly benefit from such a clientele arrangement.

Regardless of the explanation, the anomaly may be only transitory. The only fact established so far is that the futures option pricing models do not adequately explain the observed structure of option prices. It may well be the case that the

[13] Barone-Adesi [2] uses a similar maximum likelihood test to compare the structural forms of competing option pricing models.

Table IV

Frequency Distribution of Non-Rejection/Rejection
of the Null Hypothesis that the Standard Deviations
Implied by Option Prices Are Equal for Call-and-Put
Options Using S&P 500 Futures Option Transaction
Prices during the Period January 28, 1983 through
December 30, 1983

Hypothesis[a,b]	Frequency
H_O: The standard deviation of the futures price relatives for call options is equal to the standard deviation for put options.	59
H_A: The standard deviation of the futures price relatives for call options is *not* equal to the standard deviation for put options.	173
Total	232

[a] The probability level used in the evaluation of the test statistics is 5 percent.

[b] The test statistic for the hypothesis test is $F = (n - 2)(1 - R)$, where n is the number of option transactions and $R = [SSE_c(\sigma_C) + SSE_p(\sigma_p)]/SSE(\sigma)$. Assuming the residuals are independent and normally distributed, the ratio F is approximately distributed as $F_{1,n-2}$.

market is mispricing S&P 500 futures options and that abnormal risk-adjusted rates of return may be earned by trading on the basis of the models' prices.

E. Market Efficiency Test

The systematic biases reported in Table III and the σ-anomaly reported in Table IV may result because the futures option pricing models are misspecified or because the S&P 500 futures option market is inefficient or both. One way of attempting to isolate the two effects is to test whether abnormal rates of return after transaction costs may be earned by trading futures options on the basis of the models' prices. If abnormal returns after transaction costs can be earned, it is likely to be the case that the market is inefficient. The price deviations, systematic or not, signal profit opportunities. If abnormal profits cannot be earned, there are no grounds for rejecting the null hypothesis that the model is correctly specified and that the S&P 500 futures option market is efficient.

The market efficiency test design involved hedging mispriced futures options against the underlying futures contract. Each day options were priced using the American futures option pricing models and the standard deviations estimated from *all* of the previous day's transaction prices.[14] Because no estimate of σ was available for the transactions of the first day of the sample period, January 28, 1983, the first day's transactions were eliminated, and only 231 days and 28,493 options remained in the sample.

[14] Because both call and put option transaction prices are used in the daily regression to estimate the σ, the estimate is, in essence, an average of the estimates implied by call and puts separately.

Each of the 28,493 option transactions was examined to see whether the option was undervalued or overvalued relative to the futures option pricing models. The hedge formed at that instant in time[15] depended on the nature of the transaction price:

Nature of Transaction Price	Futures Option Position	Futures Position
Undervalued call	Long 1 contract	Short $\delta C/\delta F$ contracts
Overvalued call	Short 1 contract	Long $\delta C/\delta F$ contracts
Undervalued put	Long 1 contract	Long $-\delta P/\delta F$ contracts
Overvalued put	Short 1 contract	Short $-\delta P/\delta F$ contracts

where the partial derivatives of the call and put option prices were computed using valuation Equations (4) and (5).

Two types of hedge portfolios were considered in the analysis. The first was a "buy-and-hold" hedge portfolio. Each hedge was formed according to the weights described above and was held until the futures option/futures expiration or until the end of the sample period, whichever came first. At such time, the futures option/futures positions were closed, and the hedge profit was computed. The second was the "rebalanced" hedge portfolio. Here, the initial hedge composition was the same as the buy-and-hold strategy, but at the end of each day, the futures position was altered to account for the change in the futures option's hedge ratio. The difference between the profits of these two hedge portfolio strategies was, therefore, the net gain or loss on the intermediate futures position adjustments within the rebalanced portfolio.[16]

Note that the hedge portfolios are assumed to be held until the option's

[15] The hedge portfolio strategy assumed that the hedge is formed at the prices which signalled the profit opportunity. This was done for two reasons. First, floor traders have the opportunity to transact at these prices. If a sell order at a price below the model price enters the pit, the floor trader can buy the options and then hedge his position within seconds using the futures. Second, the transaction price for retail customers may be handled by simply adding the bid-ask spread to the price which triggered a buy and subtracting the bid-ask spread from the price which triggered a sell.

[16] To illustrate the mechanics of the buy-and-hold and rebalanced hedge portfolio strategies, consider the following example. A call option with an exercise price of $100 and with two days to expiration is priced at $1, where its theoretical price is $1.50 and its hedge ratio is 0.8. The current futures price is $100. Because the call is underpriced relative to the model, it is purchased, and 0.8 futures contracts are sold. The net investment of both the buy-and-hold and rebalanced hedge portfolios is, therefore, $1 (i.e., one option contract times $1 per contract).

By the end of the day before expiration, the futures price rises to say, $102. At the new futures price, the model price is $3.00 and the hedge ratio is 0.9. Since the hedge ratio has changed, 0.1 more futures contracts must be sold in order to maintain the riskless hedge of the rebalanced portfolio. The additional futures contracts are assumed to be bought or sold at the day's closing price, in this case $102.

Now, suppose that on the following day, the futures expires at $106, and the futures option at $6.00 (i.e., the futures price $106 less the exercise price $100). The buy-and-hold hedge portfolio profit would be computed as the option position profit, $6 − 1 = $5, plus the futures position profit, $-0.8 \times (\$106 - 100) = -\$4.80$, or $0.20 in total. The rebalanced hedge portfolio profit is computed as the $0.20 buy-and-hold profit plus the net gain (loss) on the intermediate futures position change, $-0.1 \times (\$106 - 102) = -\$0.40$, or $-\$0.20$ in total.

expiration. This is unlike the empirical procedures used in the stock option market efficiency tests which assume that an option position is opened at one price and then closed at the next available price. If the option pricing models have systematic mispricing tendencies, an option which is undervalued on one day is likely to be undervalued on the next. By holding the option position open until expiration, at which time the observed and model prices converge to the same value, there is some assurance that the prospective option mispricing profits are being captured.

In Table V, the average cost, profit, and rate of return of the hedge portfolios formed on the basis of the American futures option prices are presented. When no minimum size restriction was placed on the absolute price deviation, 28,493 hedge portfolios were formed. On an average, the number of futures contracts in each hedge at formation was 0.442 (1.442 less one futures option contract). The average investment cost of each hedge was −$46.75 (−0.0935 × $500),[17] indicating that, on an average, money was collected when the hedge portfolios were formed.

The average profit for the buy-and-hold hedge portfolio was $88 (0.1760 × $500), and the average rebalanced hedge portfolio profit was $77.85. The daily rebalancing of the futures position lowered overall hedge profits. On the other hand, the standard deviation of the buy-and-hold profit was 1.9302 compared with 0.8574 for the rebalanced portfolio profits.[18] The daily rebalancing of the futures position decreased the volatility of the hedge profits portfolio by more than 55 percent.

Immediately to the right of the rebalanced portfolio profit column is a column with break-even transaction cost rates. These numbers represent the average of the transaction cost rate per contract sufficient to eliminate rebalanced portfolio profit. In other words, if the transaction cost rate was less than $57.60 (0.1152 × $500) per contract, the average portfolio profit was greater than zero. Note that the transaction costs were assumed to be paid only on the contracts bought or sold when the portfolio was formed. The overall net effect of the incremental transaction costs on the intermediate daily rebalancing of the futures position of the hedge portfolios was assumed to be equal to zero.[19]

The rebalanced portfolio excess rate of return column contains the average rate of return and the net of any interest carrying charge. If the option in the hedge portfolio was purchased, the excess rate of return of the hedge was equal to the rate of return on the hedge less the riskless rate of interest. If the option was sold, interest was assumed to be earned on the proceeds from the sale, so the excess rate of return on the hedge was equal to the rate of return on the hedge plus the riskless rate of interest. The excess rate of return for the rebalanced

---

[17] The value for the S&P 500 futures and futures options are index values. The dollar worth of the contract is obtained by multiplying the index value by $500.

[18] The standard deviations are not reported, but they can be inferred from the reported numbers of observations and the t-ratios.

[19] To account for the transaction costs of the daily readjustment of the futures position within each portfolio separately would dramatically overstate the role of transaction costs within the hedge portfolio because, at the end of the day, some hedges will require that futures contracts be purchased and some that futures be sold. The net overall daily adjustment in the futures position would likely be near zero, so no intermediate transaction costs were imposed.

Table V

Average Cost, Profit, and Rate of Return of Hedge Portfolios by Size of Absolute Price Deviation from the American Futures Option Pricing Models for S&P 500 Futures Option Transaction Prices during the Period January 31, 1983 through December 30, 1983

Minimum Absolute Price Deviation	No. of Observations	Average Investment[a]	Average No. of Contracts[b]	Buy-and-Hold Portfolio Profit[c]	Rebalanced Portfolio Profit[d]	Break-Even Transaction Cost Rate[e]	Rebalanced Portfolio Excess Rate of Return[f]	Rebalanced Portfolio Excess Return after Transaction Costs[g]	Relative Systematic Risk[h]
All $|\Delta|$	28,493	−0.0935	1.442	0.1760 (15.39)[i]	0.1557 (30.64)	0.1152	0.0905 (35.77)	0.0696 (27.78)	0.1193 (2.11)
$|\Delta| \geq 0.05$	22,850	−0.1035	1.441	0.2054 (15.83)	0.1854 (31.41)	0.1372	0.1026 (38.48)	0.0850 (32.21)	0.0745 (1.27)
$|\Delta| \geq 0.10$	17,596	−0.1160	1.437	0.2444 (16.24)	0.2181 (30.70)	0.1615	0.1164 (39.91)	0.1006 (34.81)	0.0375 (0.59)
$|\Delta| \geq 0.15$	13,116	−0.1370	1.430	0.2507 (14.07)	0.2424 (27.53)	0.1802	0.1247 (37.69)	0.1099 (33.48)	0.0924 (1.30)
$|\Delta| \geq 0.20$	9,521	−0.1200	1.425	0.2607 (12.18)	0.2696 (23.82)	0.2006	0.1309 (33.64)	0.1168 (30.20)	0.1632 (1.98)

[a] The cost of the hedge portfolio is equal to the option price if the option is purchased and minus the option price if the option is sold. The futures position involves no net investment.

[b] The average absolute number of option and futures contracts in the hedge.

[c] The buy-and-hold portfolio profit assumes the hedge is formed and held until the expiration of the contracts or the end of the sample period.

[d] The rebalanced portfolio profit is equal to the buy-and-hold profit plus (less) the net gains (losses) from the futures position adjustments made during the option's life.

[e] The break-even transaction cost per contract sufficient to eliminate the rebalanced portfolio profit.

[f] The rate of return of the rebalanced hedge portfolio less the riskless rate of interest.

[g] The excess rate of return of the rebalanced hedge portfolio after a $10 per contract transaction cost.

[h] The relative systematic risk is estimated by regressing the excess rate of return of the hedge on the relative futures price changes over the same period.

[i] The values in parentheses are t-ratios for the null hypothesis that the parameter is equal to 0.

portfolio using all of the transactions was 9.05 percent and is significantly greater than zero.

Before proceeding with a description of the remaining two columns, it is worthwhile to point out three facts about the excess rates of return for the rebalanced hedge portfolio. First, the excess return did not fall very much if the proceeds from the futures option sales were assumed to earn no interest. In this case, the average excess rate of return was 8.41 percent, with a t-ratio of 33.49. Second, the excess rate of return for the American model was only slightly higher than it was for the European model. For the latter model, the average return was 8.91 percent, with a t-ratio of 35.03. This evidence is consistent with the simulation results in the last section. Finally, the use of Student t-ratios to evaluate the significance of the excess rates of return is appropriate since the return distributions were symmetric and only slightly leptokurtic.

The column labelled excess rate of return after transaction costs incorporated a $10 per contract transaction cost assumption. Such a fee is probably appropriate for a floor trader.[20] The average excess rate of return after transaction costs was 6.96 percent, again significantly greater than zero.

The final column contains estimated slope coefficients from the regression of rebalanced portfolio excess rates of return on the futures price change relatives over the corresponding period. In essence, this regression is intended to evaluate the effectiveness of the portfolio rebalancing at maintaining a riskless hedge. For the entire sample of hedge portfolio, the relative systematic risk is significantly positive at the 5 percent level, however its magnitude, 0.1193, is very small.

Table V also contains the hedge portfolio profit characteristics when minimum absolute option price deviations of 0.05, 0.10, 0.15, and 0.20 were imposed. Naturally, the higher was the demanded absolute price deviation, the fewer were the option transactions to qualify as hedge portfolio candidates. In the case where the minimum absolute deviation was set equal to 0.10, for example, only 17,596 hedges were formed.

With all of the price deviation strategies reported in Table V, the average excess rates of return are significantly greater than zero. For floor traders,

---

[20] Actually, the assumed $10 per contract overstates the transaction costs a floor trader might face. The only transaction cost paid by floor traders is a clearing fee, which is on order of $1.50 per contract. The $10 per contract assumption, therefore, presents a conservative view of the floor trader's hedge portfolio profits after transaction costs.

Two other institutional considerations are worthy of note. The transaction cost rates in this market are quoted on a "round-turn" basis. That is, a $50 per contract commission charge covers the cost of entering the market at the time of purchase or sale and the cost of closing the position at a subsequent date. For futures contract positions, the broker charges all of the commission when the position is closed, and, for futures option positions, half the commission is charged when the position is opened and half when it is closed.

Since commission rates are negotiated between each customer and his or her broker, it is difficult to assess what are representative commission charges for the various futures/futures option customers. Large institutional customers such as mutual funds typically pay commissions at a rate of $20 to $30 per contract and are allowed to post margin requirement in the form of interest-bearing T-bills. Smaller customers likely pay commissions of $50 or more, and are also allowed to the T-bill margin-posting privilege. Some brokers quote lower rates for small customers, but demand margin money in the form of cash.

demanding a minimum price deviation of 0.05 is reasonable since they face only the cost of clearing their transactions, which is considerably less than $25 per contract. When such a minimum price deviation was imposed, the average hedge portfolio excess rate of return was 10.26 percent before clearing costs and 8.50 percent after a $10 per contract clearing cost was applied to both the futures option and futures transactions. Retail customers, however, not only face the commission rates imposed by their broker, but also the bid-ask spread imposed by the market maker. Assuming a commission rate of $50 per contract and a bid-ask spread of $50 per option contract, demanding a minimum price deviation of 0.20 is reasonable. However, in this case, the average break-even transaction cost rate was 0.2006, so the retail customer would have earned about $0.30 per hedge after transaction costs.

In the previous section, systematic mispricing errors related to the moneyness of the option were documented. For this reason, the option transactions were categorized by the type of option and by the degree to which the option is in-the-money. The results are reported in Table VI. Most of the abnormal profits associated with the trading strategy appear to be concentrated in out-of-the-money put options. The average excess rate of return after the floor trader's clearing costs was 16.88 percent. In comparison, none of the other option categories had an average return greater than 3 percent after clearing costs.

One plausible explanation for this result is that more than 72 percent out-of-the-money put options were overpriced (see Table III) and thus sold within the trading strategy. Over the period January 31, 1983 through December 30, 1983, the S&P 500 Index rose from 145.30 to 164.93, indicating that writing out-of-the-money puts would have been profitable indeed. But, the put options sold within the hedge strategy were balanced against short positions in the futures, so what was gained on the put transactions should have been lost on the futures transactions. Moreover, the estimated systematic risk for the hedge portfolios in this category was significantly negative, indicating that, if anything, not enough put options were sold to immunize the portfolio against movements in the underlying futures price. The overall upward market movement in the equity market during the examination period must, therefore, be discounted as a potential explanation of the market inefficiency.

Although the results of Table VI indicate that floor traders could profit by writing out-of-the-money puts, it is doubtful whether retail customers could profit by such a strategy. As was noted in Table II, at-the-money options enjoyed the greatest volume of activity and, therefore, probably experienced the lowest bid-ask spread. Out-of-the-money S&P 500 futures options have less liquidity, and it is not uncommon to find the bid-ask spread as high as 0.15 or 0.20. Assuming a commission rate of $50 per contract and a bid-ask spread of $50 per contract takes the average profit from $159.70 per hedge to an average gain after transaction costs of $45.40.

Overall, the results reported in Tables V and VI provide evidence that the joint hypothesis that the American futures option valuation models are correctly specified and that the S&P 500 futures option market is efficient is refuted for the period January 31, 1983 through December 30, 1983, at least from the

Table VI
Average Cost, Profit, and Rate of Return of Hedge Portfolios by the Moneyness of the Option for S&P 500 Futures Option Transaction Prices during the Period January 31, 1983 through December 30, 1983

Futures Option Category	No. of Observations	Average Investment[a]	Average No. of Contracts[b]	Buy-and-Hold Portfolio Profit[c]	Rebalanced Portfolio Profit[d]	Break-Even Transaction Cost Rate[e]	Rebalanced Portfolio Excess Rate of Return[f]	Rebalanced Portfolio Excess Return after Transaction Costs[g]	Relative Systematic Risk[h]
Calls $F/X < 1$	7,736	-1.0521	1.339	-0.0077 (-0.34)[i]	0.0204 (2.34)	0.0160	0.0432 (7.00)	0.0159 (2.60)	0.7339 (5.25)
Calls $F/X \geq 1$	7,150	0.5963	1.670	0.1052 (4.60)	0.1284 (16.81)	0.0763	0.0295 (12.58)	0.0206 (8.84)	0.4858 (9.02)
Puts $F/X < 1$	3,620	-1.9300	1.646	0.0975 (2.98)	0.0497 (1.95)	0.0273	0.0186 (3.99)	0.0074 (1.61)	0.4150 (3.66)
Puts $F/X \geq 1$	9,987	0.8208	1.286	0.3979 (21.53)	0.3194 (37.46)	0.2518	0.1968 (42.10)	0.1688 (36.42)	-0.7379 (-7.56)

[a] The cost of the hedge portfolio is equal to the option price if the option is purchased and minus the option price if the option is sold. The futures position involves no net investment.

[b] The average absolute number of option and futures contracts in the hedge.

[c] The buy-and-hold portfolio profit assumes the hedge is formed and held until the expiration of the contracts or the end of the sample period.

[d] The rebalanced portfolio profit is equal to the buy-and-hold profit plus (less) the net gains (losses) from the futures position adjustments made during the option's life.

[e] The break-even transaction cost per contract sufficient to eliminate the rebalanced portfolio profit.

[f] The rate of return of the rebalanced hedge portfolio less the riskless rate of interest.

[g] The excess rate of return of the rebalanced hedge portfolio after a $10 per contract transaction cost.

[h] The relative systematic risk is estimated by regressing the excess rate of return of the hedge on the relative futures price changes over the same period.

[i] The value in parentheses are *t*-ratios for the null hypothesis that the parameter is equal to 0.

Table VII

Average Cost, Profit, and Rate of Return of Hedge Portfolios by Subperiod for S&P 500 Futures Option Transaction Prices during the Period January 31, 1983 through December 30, 1983

Subperiod	No. of Observations	Average Investment[a]	Average No. of Contracts[b]	Buy-and-Hold Portfolio Profit[c]	Rebalanced Portfolio Profit[d]	Break-Even Transaction Cost Rate[e]	Rebalanced Portfolio Excess Rate of Return[f]	Rebalanced Portfolio Excess Return after Transaction Costs[g]	Relative Systematic Risk[h]
1/31/83–4/21/83	9,846	−0.0509	1.454	−0.1758 (−8.73)[i]	0.0308 (7.01)	0.0271	0.0047 (1.56)	−0.1024 (−4.13)	0.8848 (15.40)
4/22/83–7/14/83	8,237	−0.1623	1.450	0.5118 (22.84)	0.3884 (55.08)	0.2682	0.2067 (50.06)	0.1876 (39.82)	0.8641 (5.66)
7/15/83–10/6/83	6,001	−0.1902	1.423	0.2323 (8.86)	0.0953 (7.25)	0.0780	0.0737 (10.97)	0.0515 (7.72)	−0.2587 (−0.90)
10/7/83–12/30/83	4,409	0.0710	1.430	0.2588 (14.55)	0.0968 (4.49)	0.0740	0.0879 (12.48)	0.0567 (8.14)	−1.769 (−4.52)

[a] The cost of the hedge portfolio is equal to the option price if the option is purchased and minus the option price if the option is sold. The futures position involves no net investment.

[b] The average absolute number of option and futures contracts in the hedge.

[c] The buy-and-hold portfolio profit assumes the hedge is formed and held until the expiration of the contracts or the end of the sample period.

[d] The rebalanced portfolio profit is equal to the buy-and-hold profit plus (less) the net gains (losses) from the futures position adjustments made during the option's life.

[e] The break-even transaction cost per contract sufficient to eliminate the rebalanced portfolio profit.

[f] The rate of return of the rebalanced hedge portfolio less the riskless rate of interest.

[g] The excess rate of return of the rebalanced hedge portfolio after a $10 per contract transaction cost.

[h] The relative systematic risk is estimated by regressing the excess rate of return of the hedge on the relative futures price changes over the same period.

[i] The values in parentheses are t-ratios for the null hypothesis that the parameter is equal to 0.

standpoint of floor traders who stood ready to transact based on model prices. From a retail customer's standpoint, however, it is doubtful whether abnormal profits after transaction costs could have been earned.

In Table VII, the option transactions in four separate subperiods are considered. In the first subperiod, the average excess rate of return on the hedge portfolio was 0.47 percent, insignificantly different from zero. In the remaining three subperiods, the excess rate of return was significantly greater than zero, with the return highest in the second subperiod and second highest in the final subperiod. In other words, there does not appear to be any indication that the market became more efficient during 1983. Whether floor traders can continue to earn abnormal rates of return after clearing costs by buying undervalued and selling overvalued S&P 500 futures options must await further empirical investigation.

III. Summary and Conclusions

The purpose of this paper is to review the theory underlying American futures option valuation and to test the theory in one of the recently developed futures option markets. The theoretical work begins by focusing on the partial differential equation of Black [5] and by discussing how the boundary conditions to the equation imply different structural forms to the pricing equations. Although no analytic solutions to the American futures option pricing problems are provided, efficient analytic approximations are presented. Simulations of futures option prices using the European and American models and plausible option pricing parameters show that the early exercise premium of the American futures option has a significant impact on pricing if the option is in-the-money.

The empirical work focuses on transaction prices for S&P 500 equity futures options during the first 232 trading days of the market's existence, the period from January 28, 1983 through December 30, 1983. The major empirical results are as follows:

1. A moneyness bias and a maturity bias appear for the American futures option pricing models. For calls, the moneyness bias is the opposite of that reported for stock options—out-of-the-money options are underpriced relative to the model and in-the-money options are overpriced. For puts, just the reverse is true—out-of-the-money puts are overpriced relative to the model and in-the-money puts are underpriced. The maturity bias is the same for both the calls and the puts—short time-to-expiration options are underpriced relative to the model and long time-to-expiration are overpriced, but the bias appears more serious for put options than for call options.
2. The standard deviation implied by call option transaction prices is lower, on average, than that implied by put option prices.
3. A riskless hedging strategy using the American futures option pricing models (as well as the European futures option pricing models) generates abnormal risk-adjusted rates of return after the transaction costs paid by floor traders or large institutional customers. If a retail customer was to try to capture the profits implied by the futures option mispricing, however, transaction costs will likely eliminate the hedge portfolio profit opportunities.

REFERENCES

1. M. R. Asay. "A Note on the Design of Commodity Contracts." *Journal of Futures Markets* 2 (Spring 1982), 1–7.
2. G. Barone-Adesi. "Maximum Likelihood Tests of Option Pricing Models." *Advances in Futures and Option Research* 1, forthcoming, 1985.
3. —— and R. E. Whaley. "Efficient Analytic Approximation of American Option Values." Working Paper No. 15, Institute for Financial Research, University of Alberta, 1985.
4. F. Black. "Fact and Fantasy in the Use of Options." *Financial Analysts Journal* 31 (July/August 1975), 36–41, 61–72.
5. ——. "The Pricing of Commodity Contracts." *Journal of Financial Economics* 3 (January–March 1976), 167–79.
6. —— and M. Scholes. "The Pricing of Options and Corporate Liabilities." *Journal of Political Economy* 81 (May–June 1973), 637–59.
7. M. J. Brennan and E. S. Schwartz. "The Valuation of American Put Options." *Journal of Finance* 32 (May 1977), 449–62.
8. ——. "Finite Difference Methods and Jump Processes Arising in the Pricing of Contingent Claims: A Synthesis." *Journal of Financial and Quantitative Analysis* 13 (September 1978), 461–74.
9. M. Brenner, G. R. Courtadon, and M. Subrahmanyam. "Option on Stock Indices and Stock Index Futures." Working Paper, New York University, 1984.
10. G. Courtadon. "The Pricing of Options on Default-Free Bonds." *Journal of Financial and Quantitative Analysis* 17 (March 1982), 75–100.
11. J. C. Cox, J. E. Ingersoll, and S. A. Ross. "The Relation Between Forward and Futures Prices." *Journal of Financial Economics* 9 (December 1981), 321–46.
12. R. Gallant. "Nonlinear Regression." *American Statistician* 29 (May 1975), 73–81.
13. R. Geske and H. E. Johnson. "The American Put Valued Analytically." *Journal of Finance* 39 (December 1984), 1511–24.
14. R. Geske and R. Roll. "Isolating the Observed Biases in American Call Option Pricing: An Alternative Estimator." Working Paper, Graduate School of Management, UCLA, 1984.
15. R. Geske and K. Shastri. "Valuation by Approximation: A Comparison of Alternative Valuation Techniques." *Journal of Financial and Quantitative Analysis* 20 (March 1985), 45–71.
16. L. W. MacMillan. "Analytic Approximation for the American Put Option." *Advances in Futures and Options Research* 1, forthcoming, 1985.
17. R. C. Merton. "The Theory of Rational Option Pricing." *Bell Journal of Economics and Management Science* 4 (Spring 1973), 141–83.
18. E. Moriarity, S. Phillips, and P. Tosini. "A Comparison of Options and Futures in the Management of Portfolio Risk." *Financial Analysts Journal* 37 (January–February 1981), 61–67.
19. K. Ramaswamy and S. M. Sundaresan. "The Valuation of Options on Futures Contracts." Working Paper, Graduate School of Business, Columbia University, 1984.
20. E. S. Schwartz. "The Valuation of Warrants: Implementing a New Approach." *Journal of Financial Economics* 4 (January 1977), 79–93.
21. H. R. Stoll and R. E. Whaley. "The New Options: Arbitrageable Linkages and Valuation." *Advances in Futures and Options Research* 1, forthcoming, 1985.
22. R. E. Whaley, "Valuation of American Call Options on Dividend-Paying Stocks: Empirical Tests." *Journal of Financial Economics* 10 (March 1982), 29–57.
23. ——. "On Valuing American Futures Options." *Financial Analysts Journal* (forthcoming) and Working Paper No. 4, Institute for Financial Research, University of Alberta, 1984.
24. A. Wolf. "Fundamentals of Commodity Options on Futures." *Journal of Futures Markets* 2 (1982), 391–408.

Article 17

The pricing of options on debt securities

The route from pricing options on equities is a straight one, but the differences between the two are significant.

Mark Pitts

While managers of equity portfolios have long been acquainted with traded options, managers of debt portfolios frequently find the emerging markets in debt options difficult to understand. Furthermore, while much of our knowledge of equity options can be transferred directly to the debt option markets, this is not true for one of the most difficult questions that must be addressed, namely, the fair value of an options contract. That question is the subject of this article.

I shall show that equity option models are not directly applicable to debt options, but that we can use them in an altered form to value options on some debt securities. We should note at the outset, however, that an equity option model altered to take into account the characteristics of a debt security will not result in all cases in a good model for valuing debt options. These cases are discussed in more detail in the sections that follow.

OPTIONS ON ACTUALS AND OPTIONS ON FUTURES

Traded options on debt securities fall into two large categories: options on actual (or spot) debt securities and options on futures contracts on debt securities.[1] Options on actuals are probably the more familiar, since the equity options market has traditionally been based on actual securities. If a call option on an actual security is exercised, the owner of the option acquires a long position in the actual security; if a put option is exercised, the owner delivers the actual security.

1. Footnotes appear at the end of the article.

In many ways, options on futures are similar to options on actual securities — although they are not similar to futures contracts. The only significant difference between an option on an actual and an option on a future is that the underlying instrument in the latter case is a futures contract rather than a spot security. Thus, if a call is exercised, the owner of the option acquires a long position in the underlying futures contract and the option writer acquires the offsetting short position in the same futures contract. If a put option on futures is exercised, the owner of the option acquires a short position in the futures contract, and the option writer acquires a long position in the contract. Naturally, any prior positions in the same futures contract held by either party may be totally or partially cancelled out as a result of exercising the option.

For example, suppose that an owner of one put option on December Treasury bonds has previously established a long position in two December T-Bond futures contracts. If he decides to exercise the put, he acquires a short position in December T-Bonds that, when netted against his prior position, leaves him long one December futures contract.

Another difference between options on actuals and options on futures arises from the way in which spot prices and futures prices are quoted. For instance, a quote of 80 on an actual Treasury bond means that one can establish a long position in the actual bond for a price of 80% of par, or $80,000 for a bond with a $100,000 face value. On the other hand, if a futures contract in the same bond is quoted at 80, one can establish a long position in the futures contract essentially for free. The only "cost" in establishing a long position in futures is the initial margin, which is more in the nature of a good-faith deposit than of an actual cost. Therefore, a futures price of 80 does not mean that it costs 80% of the face amount to establish a long position in futures.

This method of quoting futures prices carries over to options on futures. For example, a call option on a futures contract on Treasury bonds struck at 80 does not mean that the owner of the option will pay the seller of the option $80,000 if the option is exercised; it simply means that the owner of the option has the right to establish a long futures position at 80, and the option writer is obligated to take the offsetting short futures position at 80.

Generally, an exchange would effect this transaction by establishing the futures positions at 80, and then immediately marking each position to market. For instance, if futures prices are currently at 85 and a call struck at 80 is exercised, the owner of the option acquires a long futures position at 80 and the writer of the option acquires a short futures position at 80. The exchange then immediately marks each position to market, meaning that the long receives 5 points ($5,000) in cash and the short position pays in 5 points, and the respective futures positions are reestablished at the prevailing futures price of 85.[2]

Finally, an option cannot "outlive" the underlying instrument: The expiration date of an option on a futures contract must be on or before the delivery date of the futures contract. In contrast, the expiration date for an option on an actual security is theoretically unlimited in the case of an equity option, and limited only by the maturity date of the underlying fixed-income security in the case of a debt option.

We do have a special case in which a European option on an actual security and a European option on a futures contract on the same security both expire on the futures delivery date. Here, the option on the actual and the option on the futures (with the same strike price) have the same value, even if one option is currently deep in-the-money and the other is currently deep out-of-the-money. This equality of value occurs because arbitrage will force futures prices and spot prices to converge on delivery date; therefore, the futures and the actual become one and the same instrument at the only point at which the option can be exercised.[3] Hence, there can never be any advantage to owning one option over the other.

RISKLESS HEDGE VALUATION

The riskless hedge model is the most widely accepted model for valuing options. Basically, the riskless hedge model involves working backward from the expiration date using a risk-free portfolio to derive the value of the option today. This technique underlies the Black-Scholes [2] model for equity options, the Black [1] model for options on commodity futures, and the binomial option model developed by Cox, Ross, and Rubinstein [5].

To illustrate the technique, we suppose the objective is to value a call option.

The riskless hedge models implicitly assume that the current value of the call option will depend on the current price of the underlying security. This assumption is reasonable since, with all other relevant factors held constant, one would expect the value of a call to increase when the price of the underlying security increases, and decrease when the price of the underlying security decreases — but usually not by equal amounts.

The riskless hedge models are based on a portfolio that is long one unit of the underlying security and short just enough calls so that the value of the portfolio will not change for infinitesimally small moves in the price of the underlying security, in effect creating a "riskless hedge." We can think of the resulting portfolio as a risk-free asset that, in equilibrium, will grow in value at the risk-free rate of return. Using this equilibrium argument and starting at option expiration, when the value of the option is easily derived, we can work *backward* through time to derive the value of the option in the current period, i.e., the value of the option "today."

Before explaining how we would apply the riskless hedge technique to options on debt securities, let us use a simple example to illustrate how investors use it to value options on equities. The following one-branch binomial model captures the essence of the riskless hedge model.[4]

Assume for now that the underlying security is a share of stock that pays no dividends until after the option expires. As shown in Figure 1, the current stock price is $81 and at option expiration (one month hence) the price will either rise to $83 or fall to $79. We assume that the interest rate is 1% per month. The objective in this example is to find the current value of a European call option with a strike price of $80.

Naturally, it is easy to find the value of the option at expiration if we know what the price of the stock will be at that time — the value of a call is just the price of the stock minus the strike price, or zero, whichever is larger. In this example, the value of the option will be $3 if the stock price rises to $83, and $0 if it declines to $79 (at which point the option would expire worthless). These option values appear in parentheses below the expiration prices in the figure.

The valuation problem is one of finding the

FIGURE 1

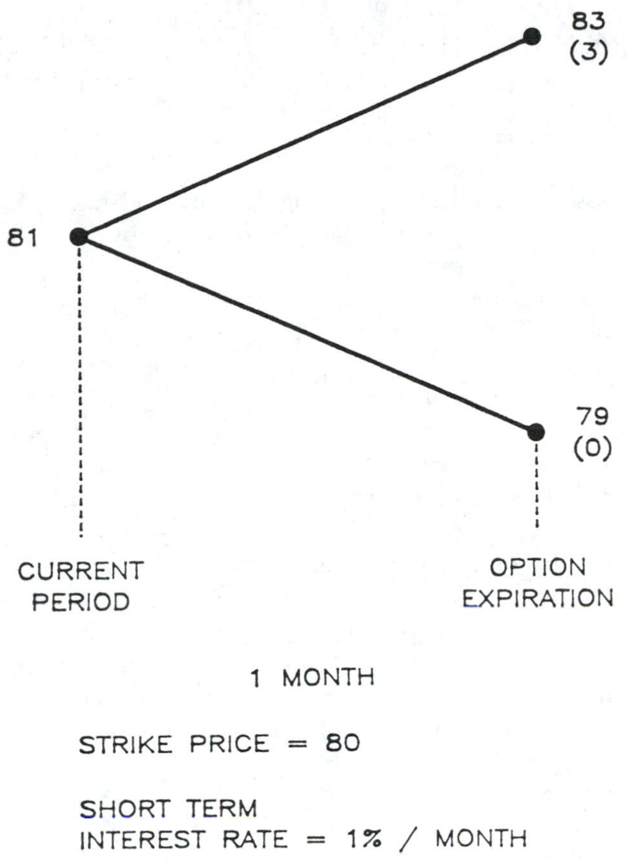

current fair value of the option with the stock price currently at $81. The riskless hedge technique enters here. To apply the technique, consider the following risk-free portfolio that can be purchased in the current period:

Portfolio = Long 1 Stock Share and Short 4/3 Call Options.

We assume that options contracts are completely divisible so that shorting 4/3 calls poses no problem. Also, we ignore taxes, transaction costs, and margin requirements. The portfolio is riskless because its value will be the same whether the stock price advances to 83 or declines to 79.

As shown in Table 1, if the stock price rises by the end of the period to $83, the liability associated with the short call position is $4 (i.e., $3 × [4/3]). On the other hand, if the stock price declines to $79, the options will expire worthless and there will be no associated liability. Adding the value of the long stock position to the liability of the short call position gives the resulting portfolio value of $79, regardless of which direction the stock moves!

Stock Price	Value of Stock	Liability of 4/3 Calls	Portfolio Value
Rises to 83	$83	($4)	$79
Declines to 79	$79	0	$79

This risk-free portfolio is a risk-free asset and must, in equilibrium, return no more than, and no less than, the risk-free rate of return (i.e., the T-Bill rate or the rate on some other totally risk-free investment). If the portfolio returned more than the risk-free rate, no one would buy T-Bills; they would buy the risk-free portfolio instead. If it returned less than the risk-free rate, arbitrageurs would short the risk-free portfolio (i.e., short the stock and buy 4/3 calls) and invest the proceeds at a rate higher than their effective "borrowing" cost, thus reaping risk-free profits.

Given that the risk-free portfolio will be worth $79 in one month, and given that the portfolio must grow in value by 1% per month (the assumed risk-free rate), its value must be $78.22 today (since 79/1.01 = 78.22). By the construction of the portfolio we can also see that the cost, or value, of the portfolio is the cost of one share of stock minus the premium received for the 4/3 calls. Equating these two expressions for the cost of the portfolio, we obtain:

$78.22 = (Price of 1 Share of Stock)- [(4/3) × (Price of 1 Call)].

Since the price of the stock is $81 at the time the portfolio is created this reduces to

$78.22 = 81 − [(4/3) × (Price of 1 call)].

Consequently, the current price of a call option must be $2.085. The problem has been solved.

The implications of the riskless hedge models for options on actuals are several.[5] Briefly, holding other factors constant:

1. If the price of the underlying security increases, the value of a call increases, but the value of a put decreases.
2. A higher strike price implies a higher value for the put option, but a lower value for the call option.
3. If the rate of interest for borrowing and lending over the life of the option is higher, the value of a call will be higher, but the value of a put will be lower.
4. If the volatility of the price of the underlying security is higher, the value of both the put and the call will be higher.
5. A longer time until expiration implies a greater value for both the American call and put options.

Finally, the most surprising result:

6. The drift, or trend, in the price of the underlying security has no effect on the value of either put or call options. (This means, for example, that with other factors equal, the value of a call on a stock with a strong upward trend will be the same as the value of a call on a stock with a strong downward trend.)

These results apply to options on actuals and are equally true for options on futures contracts, except that, with other factors held constant, a higher short-term interest rate for borrowing and lending over the life of the option on a futures contract decreases the value of the call as well as the value of the put.

The following sections will show how to generalize the equity option model to deal with options on debt securities. Not surprisingly, it turns out that the foregoing rules are also true for options on debt securities.

ASSUMPTIONS UNDERLYING THE EQUITY OPTION MODELS

We are now in a position to answer one of the most frequently asked questions about debt options, namely, why can't we use equity option models to value options on debt securities?

The answer is straightforward. Like most other mathematical models in finance, the riskless hedge model is based upon many simplifying assumptions. Since the model was originally constructed specifically for equity options, some of the underlying assumptions are unrealistic for options on debt securities. Hence, if equity option models were applied directly to debt securities, the resulting theoretical values would be misleading indicators of true option values.

While there are many variants of the riskless hedge model, the most widely used is the Black-Scholes model for options on (actual) equity securities. To clarify the limitations of the equity option models when applied to options on debt securities, let us examine the assumptions that underlie the Black-Scholes formula:

Assumption 1. Taxes, transaction costs, margin, and other frictions can be ignored.

Assumption 2. When the markets are open, the security underlying the options contract is traded continuously and its price can change very rapidly, but cannot jump. In other words, the price-time relationship is a continuous function. When the markets are closed, the price cannot change; thus, it is assumed that the opening price each day will equal the previous closing price.

Assumption 3. Proportional changes in price are normally distributed.

Assumption 4. The rate of interest for very short-term borrowing and lending over the life of the option is fixed and known.

Assumption 5. The option cannot be exercised prior to expiration.

Assumption 6. The underlying security will not make payouts of any kind during the life of the option.

Assumption 6 can be relaxed using the modification of the Black-Scholes formula proposed by Merton [6] that allows for payouts that are proportional to the price of the underlying security.

Examination of these assumptions will show why it is inappropriate to apply equity option models to debt securities. Perhaps the most inappropriate is Assumption 6, since the underlying securities on all options on actual debt securities that currently trade in any size are coupon-bearing. Furthermore, since accrued interest is continuously adding to the (full) price of a bond, accrued interest is essentially a continuous payout to the holder of the debt security. Thus, Assumption 6 will almost always be violated for options on actual debt securities, even if coupons are not paid during the life of the option. Moreover, since coupons are fixed in dollar amount and not proportional to the price of the debt security, Merton's modification of the formula is of little help. In the next section we show how to modify the riskless hedge models to account for coupon flows.

Now let us turn to the assumptions about the price of the underlying security (Assumptions 2 and 3). Since full price (i.e., quoted, or flat, price plus accrued interest) exhibits a saw-toothed pattern through time, it would be unrealistic to think of full price as the variable that exhibits normally distributed price changes (Assumption 3). Furthermore, because full price will immediately plunge to a lower level when coupons are paid, Assumption 2 would necessarily be violated as well. Thus, we should think of the "price" for options on debt securities as the flat price of the underlying security.

Unfortunately, another question arises upon deeper reflection. Is it reasonable to assume that even the flat price fulfills Assumption 3, i.e., that proportional changes in the flat price are normally distributed? If proportional price changes are normally distributed, negative prices are precluded, but negative yields may result since no upper bound is placed on prices.

For example, if a 10-year, 8% note sells at any price above 180 (the undiscounted sum of all future cash flows), the associated yield to maturity is negative. This result would be unreasonable since an investment in cash would dominate an investment in the note. As we show in later sections, the riskless hedge model can be modified so that both negative prices and negative yields are prohibited.

Assumption 4 states that the short-term rate of interest for borrowing and lending over the life of the option is constant. Since interest rate changes are the variables that drive price changes on debt securities (or vice versa), it would be ridiculous in some cases to hold the short-term rate of interest constant while the price of the underlying debt security is allowed to vary.

Suppose, for example, that we are considering a 1-year American option on a 1-year debt security. To hold the rate of interest for very short-term borrowing constant over the 1-year period and let the price (or yield) of the 1-year instrument vary would constitute a gross departure not only from reality but also from equilibrium. On the other hand, if the underlying instrument is a long-term bond, Assumption 4, while not totally realistic, is less likely to invalidate the resulting theoretical value. The conclusion of this paper proposes other solution techniques to provide partial solutions to this and other problems that are ignored in the riskless hedge models.

Finally, it is also usually assumed that the option cannot be exercised prior to expiration (Assumption 5). With debt options, as well as equity options, this is usually not the case. Subsequent discussion will indicate how the binomial model can be modified to allow for early exercise.

Thus, Assumptions 3 through 6 are particularly inappropriate for options on debt securities and may produce unrealistic values for those options. In the next section we show how to deal with some of these problems for options on actual debt securities, while in the subsequent section we modify the model for options on futures on debt securities.

RISKLESS HEDGE VALUATION OF OPTIONS ON ACTUAL DEBT SECURITIES[6]

When a riskless hedge model is used to value options on equities, we assume that proportional changes in price are normally distributed. In the binomial model, for example, this assumption, together with the other inputs to the model, dictates the shape and dispersion of the binomial tree. In practice, the tree has a very large number of branches, with the highest possible price much higher than the current price, and the lowest possible price approaching zero. As noted above, this construction will lead to problems if applied to debt securities since negative yields to maturity will result.

We can resolve this problem by an alternative approach, which is probably already more intuitive for those involved in the fixed-income markets. Instead of constructing the binomial tree in terms of price, we construct it in terms of yield. The assumption that proportional changes in yield, rather than price, are normally distributed precludes the possibility of a negative yield, but yields will have no bound on the upside — a realistic touch that fixed-income managers will be able to appreciate. As yields rise higher and higher, bond prices fall very low but will never go below zero. If yields fall very low and approach zero, bond prices become very high but never exceed the sum of the undiscounted cash flows.

Now let us return to the one-branch binomial model to show how this approach works for an option on an (actual) 8% 20-year bond currently selling at 81. For simplicity, let us assume that coupons are paid once a month, resulting in a yield to maturity on the bond of approximately 10.236%.

By the end of the month (at which time the option expires), we let the yield to maturity either rise by 25 basis points to 10.486% or fall by 25 basis points to 9.986%. As in our previous example, the strike price is 80 (a yield to maturity of 10.380%); however, we assume coupons are paid just before option expiration and, therefore, no interest has accrued if the option is exercised and full price equals flat price. (It is common practice to quote the strike price in terms of a flat price, but to require the buyer to pay full price if the option is exercised. Consequently, the actual strike price exhibits a saw-toothed pattern over time.) The very short-term rate of interest for borrowing and lending over the life of the option is 1% per month. Figure 2a illustrates these assumptions.

The problem, as before, is to find the fair value of a call option, except that now it is a call on a bond instead of a call on a share of stock. The first step in the process is to convert yields to prices — a simple matter since the yield to maturity uniquely determines the price.

Figure 2b shows the tree in (flat) prices that corresponds to the tree in yields. Remember that the bond is aging over time: When we calculate prices at option expiration, the underlying security is an 8% 19-year-11-month bond.[7]

We are now in a position to proceed in a manner similar to that used in valuing an equity option. As before, we will construct a risk-free portfolio (long the underlying bond and short call options) and impose the equilibrium condition that a risk-free portfolio return the risk-free rate of return. An important difference in this case will be the coupon received by the holder of the risk-free portfolio. As we have as-

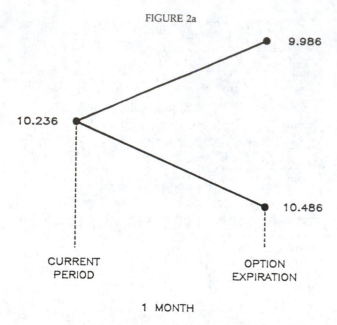

FIGURE 2a

9.986

10.236

10.486

CURRENT
PERIOD

OPTION
EXPIRATION

1 MONTH

STRIKE YIELD = 10.380

SHORT TERM
INTEREST RATE = 1% / MONTH

FIGURE 2b

82.856
(2.856)

81

79.256
(0)

CURRENT
PERIOD

OPTION
EXPIRATION

1 MONTH

STRIKE PRICE = 80

SHORT TERM
INTEREST RATE = 1% / MONTH

sumed that coupons are paid monthly, this means that the bond pays a coupon of .667 points each month.

Starting at expiration, we can fill in the values of the option for a given price of the underlying bond. If yields fall to 9.986% and prices rise to 82.856, a call struck at 80 is obviously worth 2.856. If yields rise to 10.486% and prices fall to 79.256, the option expires worthless. These values appear in parentheses in Figure 2b beneath the bond prices at expiration.

Consider now the following risk-free portfolio:

Portfolio = Long 1 8% 20-Year Bond and Short 1.2605 Call Options.

As illustrated in Table 2, this portfolio is risk-free because its value at the end of one month is predetermined. If yields rise, the options expire worthless and the value of the portfolio is 79.923 (i.e., 79.256 for the bond and .667 in coupon income). If yields fall, each short call is equivalent to a liability of 2.856 points, or 3.60 points for the short option position as a whole. Combined with the bond and the coupon income, this gives a net value of 79.923.

TABLE 2

Yields	Value of Bond	Liability of 1.2605 Calls	Coupon Payment	Portfolio Value
Fall to 9.986	82.856	(3.60)	.667	79.923
Rise to 10.486	79.256	0	.667	79.923

We can easily calculate the cost of purchasing the risk-free portfolio. It is just the cost of buying the bond in the current period, minus the price received for each call. Letting c denote the price of each call we have

$$Cost = 81 - 1.2605\, c .$$

If the portfolio will be worth 79.923 in one month, and if it must return the risk-free rate of return, then its cost must be the discounted value of 79.923. That is,

$$Cost = 79.923/1.01 = 79.1317 .$$

Equating these two expressions for the cost, and solving for c, we obtain

$$c = 1.4822 .$$

In other words, the option must be worth 1.4822 percentage points of par.

When we examined the riskless hedge model applied to options on equities, we showed how each relevant factor affected the value of the option. Each factor has the same effect when applied to options on debt securities.

RISKLESS HEDGE VALUATION OF OPTIONS ON FUTURES ON DEBT SECURITIES[8]

With the foundation laid in the previous section, we can show how to apply the riskless hedge model to options on futures contracts on debt securities. For convenience, we will assume that Figure 2a represents the possible quoted *futures* yields, but make no assumption whatsoever about the possible yields for actual debt securities.

Conversion of yields to prices requires a procedure that differs from the procedure used in the last section. For futures on coupon-bearing securities, the established method for linking quoted futures prices to quoted futures yields is to use the price-yield function of a standard non-aging instrument, such as a 20-year 8% bond.[9] Thus, to derive the appropriate tree of futures prices, we simply find the price of a 20-year 8% bond that corresponds to each of the yields shown in Figure 2a. (For simplicity we retain the assumption of monthly coupon payments.) Since there is no aging, we do not use a 19-year-11-month bond to obtain the prices at option expiration.

Figure 3 displays the futures prices. Note that the values of the option at expiration appear in parentheses below the futures prices at expiration.

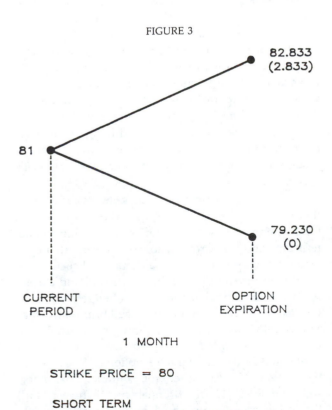

FIGURE 3

81

82.833
(2.833)

79.230
(0)

CURRENT PERIOD

OPTION EXPIRATION

1 MONTH

STRIKE PRICE = 80

SHORT TERM INTEREST RATE = 1% / MONTH

For call options on futures on debt securities, the risk-free portfolio is comprised of a long position in futures contracts and a short position in options. Unlike the risk-free portfolio for options on actual debt securities, however, the holder of this risk-free portfolio receives no coupon income. Although the bond that is deliverable in satisfaction of the futures contract may make periodic coupon payments, and the quoted price may be derived from the price-yield function for a coupon-bearing security, a long position in futures does not entitle the holder to receive coupons.

This is not to say that coupons are completely irrelevant in the context of pricing options on futures. Obviously, coupons are a major factor in the cost-of-carry and have a major impact upon the current futures price; in turn, the current futures price has a predominant impact on the price of the option. On the other hand, since the coupon payment is not received by the holder of the risk-free portfolio, it never enters the calculations. In other words, since the coupon is already incorporated into the prevailing futures price, it need not be explicitly considered in the option valuation procedure.

With this fact in mind, we consider the following risk-free portfolio:

Portfolio = Long 1 Futures Contract and Short 1.2718 Calls.

Table 3 demonstrates that this portfolio is, indeed, riskless and its value will be *negative* 1.770 whether futures yields rise or fall.

TABLE 3

Futures Yields	Margin Flow	Liability of 1.2718 Calls	Portfolio Value
Fall to 9.986	1.833	(3.603)	(1.770)
Rise to 10.486	(1.770)	0	(1.770)

A negative final value for the risk-free portfolio may seem paradoxical, but the paradox is resolved when we calculate the cost of establishing the portfolio. Since futures are "free," there are no economic costs associated with establishing the long futures position. Nevertheless, revenue is raised when the calls are sold. Thus, there is no cost in establishing the risk-free portfolio; in fact, we are paid to establish it. A position in the risk-free portfolio in the earlier cases was like a long position in a risk-free asset (i.e., we were lenders). Now the risk-free position is like a short position in a risk-free asset (i.e., we are borrowers).

Fortunately, the foregoing considerations do not complicate the valuation process. The rate of return on the portfolio must, in equilibrium, equal the risk-free rate. Thus, the present value of the portfolio must be the discounted value of -1.770. The value of the portfolio, however, is also equal to the cost of the calls. Denoting the price of the calls as c, we have

$$1.2718(-c) = -1.770/1.01 ,$$

or equivalently,

$$c = 1.378 .$$

AMERICAN OPTIONS

The foregoing sections have not dealt with the problems raised by the assumption that the options cannot be exercised prior to expiration (Assumption 5). The right to early exercise can only increase the value of an option: Obviously, it cannot decrease the value of the option since the holder is not obligated to exercise early and can always wait until expiration to exercise when this is a more favorable alternative.

The practical means by which an option can be Americanized is simple, especially in light of the highly mathematical treatment it receives in the academic press. We proceed to value an American option almost exactly as before — construct a tree of possible yields, derive the tree of possible prices, and fill in the option values at expiration. We then use the riskless hedge argument to step back through time. The only difference is that the resulting option value each time we move back one step is either the value derived from the riskless hedge procedure or the value of immediate exercise, whichever is greater. This process guarantees that the final value of the option reflects the possibility that the option may be exercised at any point up to, and including, the expiration date.

To illustrate, consider the example in the last section for options on futures contracts. To show that we might want to exercise early in this example, we will have to use an extremely high interest rate. Suppose, for illustrative purposes, that the interest rate is 50% per month. Then the last equation becomes:

$$1.2718 c = 1.770/1.50 .$$

Solving for c, the value of the call, we find c = .928. If the call is exercised immediately, however, it is worth 1 point (81-80). Therefore, the derived value of .928 cannot be correct if early exercise is allowed, and we should ignore it. In all subsequent calculations, 1 point should be considered the correct option value for this point in the binomial tree.

Admittedly, an example that depends upon such a high interest rate is unrealistic. There are, however, many realistic examples in which early exercise is optimal. The possibility of early exercise will gen-erally be greatest for in-the-money options and, in the case of call options on actuals, options on securities with high coupon payments. On the other hand, high volatility and a long time to expiration will tend to decrease the chances of immediate exercise by causing the value of the option to exceed its intrinsic value. As the foregoing example shows, the short-term rate of interest for borrowing and lending over the life of the option also plays a role in early exercise. In this particular example, an increase in the short-term rate made early exercise the optimal policy. The issue is not always as clear-cut for options on actual debt securities, but one general rule remains the same: Those factors that make early exercise more advantageous also make the American option more valuable than its European counterpart.

Finally, a model that accounts for the early exercise privilege of American options not only produces a theoretical value for the American option, but also provides the only general method by which we can determine when to exercise the option. The option should be exercised as soon as the value of immediate exercise exceeds the value of the option if immediate exercise were not allowed.

PROBLEMS, COMPLICATIONS, AND CONCLUSION

We have made the implicit assumption in each of our examples that the short-term rate of interest for borrowing and lending over the life of the option is constant (Assumption 4). This assumption can be relaxed, but in order to use the riskless hedge, we must assume that the short-term rate is a known function of the rate (or price) of the underlying security. Consequently, more complicated yield curve movements such as parallel shifts or snap-ups and snap-downs can be incorporated into the model.

Since interest rates are the driving variable behind the price of debt securities, we must treat any assumption about the short-term rate of interest with extreme care.

First, any assumption that we make concerning this rate must be consistent with the possible rates for the underlying security. For example, a high short-term rate and an extremely low long-term rate might mean that long-term debt is a dominated security — clearly, an unrealistic scenario. A second and closely related problem is that the riskless hedge models do not take into consideration the equilibrium structure of the yield cruve. There are, however, a number of more complex models that start by modeling the yield curve and derive the value of options on debt securities as a by-product. (See, for example, Cox, Ingersoll, and Ross [4] and Brennan and Schwartz [3].) While the more complicated models are frequently more theoretically sound, they are almost always more difficult to implement and require many additional assumptions.

In conclusion, the riskless hedge models provide a relatively simple means of valuing options on debt securities. They are not, however, appropriate for all debt options. A 3-month option on a 20-year bond futures contract can be reasonably valued using the riskless hedge, but the model would be totally inappropriate for a 1-year option on a 1-year bond. As is always the case with option models, the most critical step is to decide whether the underlying assumptions are, or are not, reasonable for the particular option that must be valued.

[1] In this paper we limit the discussion to options that are currently traded in size on an exchange or over the counter. Thus, for example, we do not explicitly consider the call provision attached to most long bonds.

[2] One can also think of an option on a futures contract as an option struck at $0 on the *value* of the futures contract (not to be confused with the price of the futures contract). In the foregoing example, the value of the contract at 80 is 5 points when futures prices are at 85.

[3] This is somewhat idealized in that it assumes that there is only one security that can be delivered in satisfaction of the futures contract and that there is a single moment at which delivery must be made. However, the established exchanges generally allow the short futures position some choice as to deliverable instrument and time of delivery.

[4] See Cox, Ross, and Rubinstein [5] for a rigorous development of the binomial model. The reader who is already familiar with the binomial model and riskless hedge models for options on equities can proceed to the next section without loss of continuity.

[5] Proof of each conjecture appears in Black and Scholes [2].

[6] For a more detailed analysis of debt options and the binomial model, see Pitts [7].

[7] Note that the tree in Figure 2a was constructed for yields on 20-year 8% instruments, not 19-year-11-month 8% instruments and, therefore, the conversion to prices is not as simple as we have indicated. This is probably of little importance in the example at hand; one could think of the yields in Figure 2a as yields on "long" instruments trading at a discount. Obviously, this technique becomes highly questionable for options with long lives.

[8] For more details on this subject see, Pitts [7].

[9] The quoted price determines the daily mark to market. The actual sale price, i.e., the amount of money that changes hands at delivery, will depend upon which one of several bonds are delivered. The literature published by the exchanges describes these considerations in detail.

REFERENCES

1. Fischer Black. "The Pricing of Commodity Contracts." *Journal of Financial Economics* (January/March 1976), pp. 167-179.

2. Fischer Black and Myron Scholes. "The Pricing of Options and Corporate Liabilities." *Journal of Political Economy* (May/June 1973), pp. 637-654.

3. Michael Brennan and Eduardo Schwartz. "Savings Bonds: Theory and Empirical Evidence." Monograph 1979-4, Salomon Brothers Center for the Study of Financial Institutions, 1980.

4. John Cox, Jonathan Ingersoll, and Stephen Ross. "A Theory of the Term Structure of Interest Rates." Working Paper, Stanford University, 1978.

5. John Cox, Stephen Ross, and Mark Rubinstein. "Option Pricing: A Simplified Approach." *Journal of Financial Economics* (September 1979), pp. 229-263.

6. Robert Merton. "Theory of Rational Option Pricing." *Bell Journal of Economics and Management Science* (1973), pp. 141-181.

7. Mark Pitts. "An Introduction to the Pricing of Options on Debt Instruments." Chapter 3 in *Winning the Interest Game: A Guide to Debt Options*, Frank J. Fabozzi (editor), Probus Publishing Co., 1985.

Article 18

Beyond Plain Vanilla:
A Taxonomy of Swaps

Peter A. Abken

Since their introduction over a decade ago, swaps have become an important tool for financial risk management. Generally, swaps alter the cash flows from assets or liabilities into preferred forms. Basic swaps have branched into many variants, some more popular and successful than others, each geared toward meeting specific customer needs in various markets. The author describes the features and typical applications of many variants of the four basic swap types—interest rate, currency, commodity, and equity.

Swap contracts of various kinds have become a mainstay of financial risk management since their introduction in the late 1970s. In the most general terms, a swap is an exchange of cash flows between two parties, referred to as counterparties in the parlance of swap transactions. Swaps, which transform the cash flows of the underlying assets or liabilities to which they are related into a preferred form, have been used in conjunction with positions in debt, currencies, commodities, and equity. Most swap agreements extend from one to ten years, although many have been arranged for much longer periods.[1]

The key players responsible for originating and propelling the swaps market are money center banks and investment banks. These institutions benefit from the fee income generated by swaps, which are off-balance-sheet items, and by the spreads that arise in pricing swaps. Innovations in the swaps market, as in other financial services areas, may be characterized as a Darwinian struggle, in which competition heats up and margins narrow as a particular kind of swap becomes accepted and widely used. Such swaps are disparagingly said to be trad-ed "like commodities." That is, little value is added by the dealer in structuring a swap and bringing counterparties together; consequently, little return is realized for the service of intermediation or position taking.

Perhaps the most basic, and most popular, swap involves the conversion of interest payments based on a floating rate of interest into payments based on a fixed rate (or vice versa). Because many variants of interest rate and other swaps have emerged over the years, this most basic type has become known as the "plain vanilla" swap.[2] As swap forms take on plain vanilla status, the firms that originated them are compelled to develop new types of swaps to regain their margins, amounting to monopoly rents, on new products. Some swap variations succeed, while others languish or fail.

In this article the plain vanilla swap is a starting point for a detailed taxonomy of the various species and subspecies of swaps. Swap variants are classified along cladistic principles, categorized and compared in terms of their features and applications. Examples illustrate many of the important types of swaps.

The Market

A Brief History. Before taking a detailed look at swaps, an overview of the market will help put their proliferation into perspective. Although some swaps had been arranged in the late 1970s, the first major transaction was a 1981 currency swap between IBM and the World Bank. This deal received widespread attention and stimulated others.

The currency swap actually evolved from a transaction popular in the 1970s, the parallel loan agreement, that produced cash flows identical to a swap's. For example, in one of these agreements a firm in the United States borrows a million dollars by selling a coupon bond and exchanges (swaps) this amount for an equivalent amount of deutsche marks with a German firm, which borrows those deutsche marks in its domestic market. This is the initial exchange of principal. Thereafter, the U.S. firm makes mark-denominated coupon payments and the German firm makes dollar-denominated coupon payments. Upon maturity of the underlying debt, the firms swap principal payments. These firms have effectively borrowed in one another's capital markets, although for a variety of reasons (such as foreign exchange controls or lack of credit standing in foreign markets) they could not borrow directly. As Clifford W. Smith, Charles W. Smithson, and Lee Macdonald Wakeman (1990a) point out, the problems with such an agreement were that default by one firm does not relieve the other of its contractual obligation to make payments and that the initial loans remain on-balance-sheet items during the life of the agreement for accounting and regulatory purposes. The currency swap, on the other hand, stipulates that a default terminates the agreement for both counterparties and, in general, limits credit-risk exposure to the net cash flows between the counterparties, not the gross amounts. This type of currency swap is essentially a sequence of forward foreign exchange contracts.[3]

Following the 1981 currency swap, the first interest rate swap, in mid-1982, involved the Student Loan Marketing Association (Sallie Mae). With an investment bank acting as intermediary, Sallie Mae issued intermediate-term fixed rate debt, which was privately placed, and swapped the coupon payments for floating rate payments indexed to the three-month Treasury bill yield. Through the swap, Sallie Mae achieved a better match of cash flows with its shorter-term floating rate assets.[4] At the end of 1982, the combined notional principal outstanding for interest rate and currency swaps stood at $5 billion. Notional principal is the face value of the underlying debt upon which swap cash flows are based.

The commodity swap made its appearance in 1987, when it was approved by a number of U.S. banking regulators (see Schuyler K. Henderson 1990 and Krystyna Krzyzak 1989b, c). Banks had been prohibited from direct transactions in commodities or related futures and forward contracts. In 1987 the Office of the Comptroller of the Currency permitted Chase Manhattan Bank to act as a broker in commodity swaps between an Asian airline and oil producers. Shortly afterward Citicorp also obtained approval for engaging in commodity swaps through its export-trading subsidiary. Regulations were further relaxed in February 1990 to allow national banks to use exchange-traded futures and options to hedge commodity swap positions. However, much commodity swap activity took place offshore because of uncertainties about the Commodity Futures Trading Commission's (CFTC) view of commodity swaps. The CFTC undertook a study of off-exchange transactions in February 1987 to determine whether they came under the CFTC's regulatory jurisdiction. In July 1989 the CFTC established criteria that would exempt commodity swaps from its regulatory oversight.[5] Since the CFTC's decision commodity swap activity has been increasing in the United States. As of early 1990, commodity swaps outstanding totaled about $10 billion in terms of the value of the underlying commodities (Julian Lewis 1990, 87).

Equity swaps are the newest variety, first introduced in 1989 by Bankers Trust. Based on both domestic and foreign stock indexes, these instruments may take complex forms, such as paying off the greater of two stock indexes against a floating rate of interest. The mechanics of such instruments and their advantages will be discussed below.

The Size of the Market. As of year-end 1989, the size of the worldwide swaps market, as measured by the dollar value of the notional principal, stood at $2.37 trillion. This figure does not include commodity or equity swaps, but these new types of swap have relatively small amounts outstanding compared with interest rate and currency swaps. The International Swap Dealers Association (ISDA), a trade organization, periodically surveys its members, who include most of the major swap dealers. Table 1 displays the survey results for swaps in various categories. The

The author is an economist in the financial section of the Atlanta Fed's research department. He is grateful to many people in the swaps market for assistance with his research for this article. He would particularly like to thank Charles W. Smithson and James M.F. MeVay of Chase Manhattan Bank and Ron Slivka of Salomon Brothers. However, any errors are the author's responsibility.

Table 1
U. S. Dollar Interest Rate Swaps
1985-89*

Survey Period	End User			ISDA User			Total		
	Contracts	Notional Principal	Average Contract	Contracts	Notional Principal	Average Contract	Contracts	Notional Principal	Average Contract
1985	5,918	$141,834	$23.97	1,061	$28,348	$26.72	6,979	$170,182	$24.38
1986	10,752	$235,829	$21.93	3,330	$76,921	$23.10	14,082	$312,750	$22.21
1987	16,871	$379,880	$22.52	7,472	$161,637	$21.63	24,343	$541,517	$22.25
1988	20,381	$484,272	$23.76	8,968	$243,894	$27.20	29,349	$728,166	$24.81
1989	23,324	$622,602	$26.69	13,303	$371,144	$27.90	36,627	$993,746	$27.13
Total Interest Rate Swaps 1987-89									
1987	23,768	$476,247	$20.04	10,359	$206,641	$19.95	34,127	$682,888	$20.01
1988	35,031	$668,857	$19.09	14,529	$341,345	$23.49	49,560	$1,010,203	$20.38
1989	50,193	$955,492	$19.04	23,635	$547,108	$23.15	73,828	$1,502,600	$20.35

* All dollar amounts are in millions of dollars in U.S. dollar equivalents.

Source: International Swap Dealers Association Market Survey.

interest rate swap market, involving swaps denominated in one currency, composed roughly two-thirds of the market, or $1.5 trillion as of year-end 1989. Of that amount, two-thirds consisted of U.S. dollar swaps, the most prevalent kind of swap. The average contract size was $20.35 million and $27.13 million for total and total dollar interest rate swaps, respectively. Currency swap market data are given in Table 2. The U.S. dollar is less dominant among currency swaps, for which it represents 41 percent of the total, compared with its 66 percent share of interest rate swaps. For the years during which the survey has been conducted, swaps of every type have grown rapidly.[6]

In all categories the position of the end users has been a multiple of those of the swap dealers. Interdealer swaps arise mainly in connection with hedging activities. A certain amount of double counting is therefore involved in the aggregate figures because one swap can set up a number of others as counterparties hedge their positions.

The latest ISDA survey reveals that the most active category for new swaps originated during the period January 1 to June 30, 1990, was non-U.S. dollar interest rate swaps, which grew by 26.4 percent. U.S. dollar swaps increased by 8.2 percent in this period. In contrast, total currency swaps rose by 2.9 percent, with U.S. dollar currency swaps contracted increasing by 4.6 percent. These semiannual growth rates show considerable variability over time and thus do not indicate trend movements. Further discussion of the ISDA survey results appears below in the section on currency swaps.

Interest Rate Swaps

Interest rate swaps account for the most volume in the swaps market, as seen in the previous section. The explanation to follow covers many of the numerous features that can modify the plain vanilla swap. Though discussed in detail only in relation to interest rate swaps, these alternate forms actually or potentially apply to currency, commodity, and equity swaps as well; they can be combined in innumerable ways to alter any kinds of cash flows.

The basic fixed-for-floating interest rate swap involves a net exchange of a fixed rate, usually expressed as a spread over the Treasury bond rate corresponding to the swap maturity, for a floating rate of interest. That floating rate is tied or indexed to any of a number of short-term interest rates. The London Interbank Offered Rate (LIBOR) is the most common.[7] Other rates include the Treasury bill rate,

the prime rate, the Commercial Paper Composite, the Certificate of Deposit Composite, the federal funds rate, the J.J. Kenney index, and the Federal Home Loan Bank System's Eleventh District cost-of-funds index. The Eleventh District index has been used mainly by thrift institutions in California.[8] The J.J. Kenney index is based on short-term tax-exempt municipal bond yields.

The fixed rate payer (and floating rate receiver) is said to have bought a swap or to have "gone long" a swap. Similarly, the floating rate payer (and fixed rate receiver) is said to have sold a swap or "gone short" a swap. Swaps are quoted by a dealer (or broker) usually in terms of the spread over the Treasury security of comparable maturity. For example, a swap with seven-year time to maturity, or tenor, might be quoted at 65-72. The dealer is offering to buy a swap (pay fixed) at a rate that is 65 basis points above the seven-year Treasury yield, and offering to sell a swap (receive fixed) at 72 basis points over that yield.[9] The dealer is therefore collecting a 7 basis point margin for standing between the counterparties.

Like floating rate notes, the floating rate payments on a swap do not necessarily match the timetable of the floating rate index.[10] The payment may be based on the average of the underlying index during some specified interval. The point at which the floating rate is established, based on the floating rate at that time or over some previous period, is termed the reset date. This date is not necessarily the same as the settlement date, when payment on the swap is made to the other counterparty. If reset and settlement dates do not coincide, the swap is said to be paid in arrears, which is also a common convention for floating rate notes. The floating rate may be reset daily, weekly, monthly, quarterly, or semiannually, while typically the settlement dates fall monthly, quarterly, semiannually, or annually (Anand K. Bhattacharya and John Breit 1991, 1158).

As over-the-counter instruments, interest rate swap terms are open to negotiation. The conventional way to quote a swap rate is relative to the floating rate index "flat." That is, a swap counterparty would pay the fixed rate and receive LIBOR. Swaps can also be arranged to include a spread above or below the floating rate—for example, LIBOR + 10 basis points. In addition, fixed rate payers and floating rate payers can agree to making payments at different periods—quarterly floating rate payments versus semiannual fixed rate payments.[11] However, swap counterparties usually prefer net transactions so that only a difference check passes between them, thereby limiting credit exposure. In the section below the first alteration of the basic plain vanilla structure that is considered encompasses different treatments of a

Table 2
U. S. Dollar Currency Swaps
1987-89*

Survey Period	End User			ISDA User			Total		
	Contracts	Notional Principal	Average Contract	Contracts	Notional Principal	Average Contract	Contracts	Notional Principal	Average Contract
1987	4,665	$129,181	$27.69	1,366	$33,425	$24.48	6,031	$162,606	$26.96
1988	6,777	$201,374	$29.71	2,297	$68,103	$29.66	9,074	$269,477	$29.70
1989	9,078	$257,748	$28.39	3,414	$96,418	$28.24	12,492	$354,166	$28.35
Total Currency Swaps 1987-89									
1987	5,173	$294,608	$28.47	1,439	$71,006	$24.67	6,612	$365,614	$27.65
1988	7,724	$469,092	$30.37	2,547	$164,550	$32.30	10,271	$633,642	$30.85
1989	11,270	$647,516	$28.73	4,015	$222,182	$27.67	15,285	$869,698	$28.45

* All dollar amounts are in millions of dollars in U.S. dollar equivalents.

Source: International Swap Dealers Association Market Survey.

swap's notional principal. The second general variation outlined allows for specially tailored coupon structures, and the discussion includes consideration of option-like features. Third, different types of underlying instruments—in particular, asset swaps and their uses in creating synthetic assets—are examined. Finally, option structures are discussed, including options on swaps, known as swaptions.

Variations on Notional Principal. The plain vanilla swap is nonamortizing. Nonamortizing swaps, known as "bullet" swaps, have a constant underlying notional principal upon which interest payments are made. This structure is easily modified to accommodate any kind of predictable changes in the underlying principal. Uncertainty about the future amount of the principal, which frequently arises with mortgage-backed securities, is usually better handled using option features, which will be discussed shortly.

Amortizing, Annuity, and Mortgage Swaps. Amortizing swaps are typically used in conjunction with mortgage loans, mortgage-backed securities, and automobile- and credit-card-backed securities. All of these tend to involve repayment of principal over time. In general it is difficult to match the amortization schedule of a swap, which usually cannot be changed after its initiation, against the amortization rate on these assets or liabilities; thus, the swapholder runs the risk of being over- or underhedged. A particular example of an amortizing swap is discussed in more detail in the section below on asset swaps. One specific kind is the mortgage swap, which is simply an amortizing swap on mortgages or mortgage-backed securities. The extreme form of an amortizing swap, in which the notional principal diminishes to zero as the principal of a fixed rate mortgage does, is an annuity swap.

Accreting Swaps. The flip side of an amortizing swap is an accreting swap, which, as its name suggests, allows the notional principal to accumulate during the life of the swap. Both amortizing and accreting swaps are sometimes also called sawtooth swaps. The accreting swap arises commonly with construction finance, in which a construction company or developer has a floating rate drawdown facility with a bank. That is, a line of credit may be tapped that would lead to increasing amounts of floating rate borrowing. An accreting swap would convert those floating rate payments into fixed rate payments, although again there is a risk of not exactly matching notional principal amounts at each settlement date. It is possible to create amortizing or accreting swaps from bullet swaps of varying tenor instead of arranging a swap specifically with the desired characteristics.

Seasonal Swaps and Roller Coasters. Finally, amortizing and accreting notional principals can be combined to form a seasonal swap, which allows the notional principal to vary according to a counterparty's seasonal borrowing needs such as those retailers typically experience. A swap that allows for periodic or arbitrary but predictable swings in notional principal is called a roller coaster.

Variations on Coupon Payments. Altering cash flows of underlying securities is one of the primary functions of swaps. In the following section a number of important types of swaps that accomplish this end are discussed, including those with option-like features.

Off-Market Swaps. The plain vanilla swap is also characterized as a par value swap. That is, the fixed rate for the swap is established such that no cash payment changes hands when the swap is initiated. The term *par value* derives from the swap's being viewed as a hypothetical exchange of fixed for floating rate bonds. When arranged at market interest rates, both bonds are equal to their face values (par value). Nonpar, or off-market, swaps involve fixed or floating rates that are different from the par value swap rates. Differences in the fixed rate above or below the par value swap rate entail a cash payment to the fixed rate payer from the floating rate payer if the fixed rate coupon is above the par value swap rate, and vice versa if it is below. The payment's amount is the present value of the difference between the nonpar and par value swap fixed rate payments. Swap counterparties commonly perform this kind of calculation in the process of marking an existing swap to market. An existing swap may be terminated (if permitted in the swap agreement) by such a marking to market of the remaining swap payments. High or low coupon swaps, as off-market swaps are alternatively called, are created simply by doing the calculation at the outset and making or receiving the appropriate payment. One reason for engaging in this type of swap is to change the tax exposure of underlying cash flows. Another is that spreads above or below the floating rate index can be introduced. John Macfarlane, Janet Showers, and Daniel Ross (1991) explain the mechanics of this variation.

Basis Swaps. A basis swap is an exchange of one floating rate interest payment for another based on a different index. Consider an example in which a bank, First SmartBucks, has invested in two-year floating rate notes that pay the bank one-month LIBOR plus 100 basis points. First SmartBucks has funded this purchase by issuing one-month certificates of deposit. The problem is that LIBOR and the CD rate will not track each other perfectly, exposing

First SmartBucks to a so-called basis risk; it may pay more on its CDs than it receives from its floating rate notes. The problem is solved by entering into a basis swap with a swap dealer, who will pay the one-month CD rate in exchange for LIBOR. Chart 1 illustrates the transaction. Aside from the initial fee for the swap, the cost of this hedging transaction manifests itself as a 10 basis point spread under the CD rate received from the dealer. This hedge may also be less than perfect, however, because the dealer probably would use the Certificate of Deposit Composite, which may not track First SmartBucks's CD rate perfectly, to index his payments. Nevertheless, the swap is likely to mitigate the original basis risk.

Yield Curve Swaps. The yield curve swap, a variant of the basis swap, typically is an exchange of interest payments indexed to a short-term rate for ones tied to a long-term rate. For example, a counterparty could contract to make semiannual floating rate payments based on six-month LIBOR and receive floating rate payments indexed to the prevailing thirty-year Treasury bond yield, less a spread to the swap dealer.[12] The ten-year Treasury bond yield has also been used for yield curve swaps on the long end, as well as three-month LIBOR on the short end.

Yield curve swaps gained popularity in early 1988 when the yield curve began to flatten—that is, when long rates fell relative to short rates (Krzyzak 1988, 29). Savings and loan institutions were major users of this new swap because they found it useful for adjusting the interest rate exposures of their portfolios (see asset swaps below). These swaps were also well suited to speculating on shifts in the yield curve while hedging against changes in its level. Finally, these instruments were combined with a new kind of floating rate debt, called FROGs (floating rate on governments), to transform the FROG's coupon into LIBOR. The coupon was reset semiannually and tied to the yield on newly issued Treasury bonds.[13] This strategy reportedly achieved a lower cost of funding than a standard LIBOR floating rate issue.

Caps, Floors, and Collars. A floating rate payer can combine option contracts with a swap to tailor the maximum size of potential swap payments. Interest rate caps, floors, and collars are instruments closely related to swaps that can alter swap cash flows.[14] As an example, consider a plain vanilla swap with a fixed rate of 8 percent (the swap rate). At a reset date, a rise in the floating rate above 8 percent would obligate the floating rate payer to pay the counterparty the net amount of the notional principal outstanding times the difference between the actual floating rate—say, 10 percent—and the swap rate. By buying a 9 percent cap of the same maturity as the swap the user would never pay more than one percentage point above the swap rate. The cap could be obtained from another counterparty, or it could be bundled with the swap in one transaction. However, buying a cap from another counterparty introduces an additional credit risk.

Chart 1
A Basis Swap

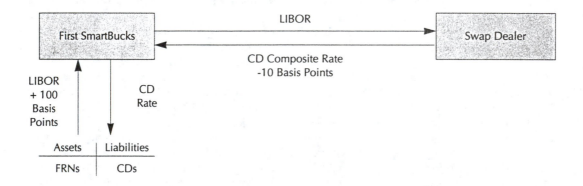

First SmartBucks transforms LIBOR interest coupons into CD composite rate payments via a basis swap.

A counterparty who sells (or writes) a cap is obligated to pay the excess over the cap's strike rate (9 percent in this example). The purchaser in return pays a cap "premium" up front. In fact, caps are sequences of interest rate options with maturities that match the schedule of floating rate payments. Analogous to caps, interest rate floors pay off whenever the floating interest rate falls below the prespecified floor level. To defray some or all of the cost of buying a cap, the floating rate payer could sell a floor with a strike rate less than the swap rate. Such a sale would create an interest rate collar. Thus, rather than paying for the protection of the cap outright, the floating rate payer could give up part of the payments from the swap resulting from large declines in the floating rate below the swap rate. That is, the maximum possible payment from the other swap counterparty would effectively be the difference of the swap rate and the floor strike rate times the notional principal.

Synthetic Swaps. The "collaring" of a swap suggests that a floating rate payer could completely offset a swap by buying a cap and selling a floor that both have strike rates equal to the swap rate. Similarly, a fixed rate payer could nullify a swap by selling a cap and buying a floor with strike rates equal to the swap rate. In these cases the floating rate payer would, in effect, be buying a "synthetic" swap and the fixed rate payer would be selling one. However, swaps are not usually unwound in this way because it is generally cheaper simply to buy or sell the corresponding swap; caps and floors may not be sufficiently liquid at the desired strike rates to execute these transactions at reasonable prices. (That is, an illiquid—infrequently traded—cap or floor would be quoted with large spreads.) Nevertheless, arbitrage between the swap and cap/floor markets is possible and does occur if rates for these instruments get too far out of line.

Participating Swaps. A hybrid version of the fixed rate swap and interest rate cap allows a counterparty to benefit partially from declining rates while not requiring any up-front payment as with a cap. Consider an example using LIBOR. The counterparty would receive LIBOR to pay its floating rate debt. In turn, instead of paying a fixed interest rate as for a plain vanilla swap, a higher fixed rate is established (above the swap rate), which is the maximum rate the counterparty would pay if LIBOR rises above that level. However, if LIBOR falls below this maximum rate, the counterparty's payment would decline less than one-for-one with LIBOR. For example, the swap terms could stipulate that a one percentage point drop in LIBOR would reduce the swap payment by one-half percentage point. The so-called

participation rate in this case is 50 percent. In other words, the counterparty would participate in 50 percent of any decline in LIBOR below the maximum rate. The maximum rate and the participation rate are set to price the swap at zero cost upon initiation. The price of this swap's option feature is paid by giving up part of the gains from falling rates.

The participating swap can also be structured to have the counterparty pay LIBOR and receive payments indexed to a fixed schedule. That is, a minimum rate would be specified in the swap, with payments above that minimum determined by the product of the prevailing LIBOR multiplied by the participation rate. A counterparty might want to use such a swap in conjunction with its floating rate assets. Participating swaps can be structured for any interest rates and are also used for currencies and commodities.

Reversible Swaps and Roller Coasters. Reversible swaps and roller coasters are a couple of exotic variants on swap structures. A reversible swap allows a counterparty to change status from floating rate payer to fixed rate payer or vice versa at some point during the life of the instrument. The roller coaster takes this concept a step further by having the counterparties reverse roles at each settlement date. Distinct from the earlier type of roller coaster involving variations in notional principal, this one has been used in only a limited number of transactions.

Zero Coupon Swaps. As its name implies, all payments on one side of the swap come at the end in one "balloon" payment, while the other side makes periodic fixed or floating rate payments. One use of zero coupon swaps is to transform the cash flows from zero coupon bonds into those of fixed coupon bonds or floating rate bonds, or vice versa.

Asset Swaps. Asset swaps are precisely what their name suggests. They effectively transform an asset into some other type of asset, such as the conversion of a fixed rate bond into a floating rate bond. The conversion results in synthetic securities because of the swap's effects. The analysis of asset swaps actually contains nothing new. The earlier example of First SmartBucks's use of a basis swap, exchanging LIBOR for the CD Composite rate, was a type of asset swap. Asset swaps are usually considered in connection with portfolio management and are low-cost tools for changing the characteristics of individual securities or portfolios.

Bhattacharya (1990) discusses an interesting application of asset swaps to a particular kind of mortgage-backed security. The collateral behind mortgage-backed securities is subject to prepayment. For example, homeowners may pay off their mortgage principals early in the event they move or mortgage rates drop sufficiently. Collateralized Mortgage Obligations (CMOs) repackage mortgage cash flows into a variety of securities that carry different prepayment risks. Planned Amortization Class (PAC) bonds are structured to have amortization schedules more predictable than those of other CMO classes. However, the risks are nevertheless sufficient to make PAC bonds trade at fairly wide spreads over corresponding Treasury securities. PAC bonds have been popular candidates for amortizing asset swaps that convert the bonds' fixed coupons into floating rate payments tied to any index. These asset swaps have the potential to make PAC bonds attractive to a broader class of investors and consequently channel more funds to the mortgage market. Such swaps may be a more cost-effective means of altering the characteristics of mortgage-backed securities than having an even broader array of such securities being issued.

As a tool for bond portfolio management, asset swaps can change a portfolio's exposure to interest rate risk. The value of a portfolio, and of any bonds within it, fluctuates with shifts in interest rates, tending to fall as market rates rise and vice versa. The sensitivity to interest rate risk is measured by a portfolio's duration, which is based on the future timing and size of its cash flows.[15] A portfolio manager can extend a portfolio's duration, increasing its volatility with respect to interest rate movements, by entering into asset swaps to receive fixed rate cash flows and to pay floating rate cash flows. Conversely, a portfolio can be protected or "immunized" against interest rate movements by contracting to make fixed rate cash flows and receive floating rate. The intuition here is that the more a portfolio's (or security's) cash flows move with current market rates, the closer its value will stay to face value. Money market funds, for example, experience little change in asset value because they have very short duration. In contrast, a fund consisting of long-term zero coupon bonds, which have durations equal to their maturities, would have extremely volatile asset values.

Asset swaps are particularly useful for adjusting a portfolio when securities sales would result in capital losses. For example, a portfolio manager would be reluctant to change the portfolio's duration by selling off bonds that are "under water" (currently valued below par). As just discussed, an asset swap is ideal for this kind of adjustment.[16] As another example, some bonds cannot be traded because they were purchased from an underwriter through a private placement to avoid registration and other costs associated with public issues. Using an asset swap obviates the need to trade the underlying security to alter interest rate exposure.

Forward and Extension Swaps. Forward swaps are analogous to forward or futures contracts as hedging instruments. The difference is that forward or futures contracts hedge cash flows at a single point in the future whereas forward swaps (and swaps generally) hedge streams of cash flows. Extension swaps are an application of forward swaps.

Forward Swaps. Financial managers, such as corporate treasurers, often want to hedge themselves against rising interest rates when considering a future debt issue. For example, selling a new issue of bonds may be necessary to refund outstanding corporate bonds that mature in one year. The yield on that issue is unknown today but could be locked in using a forward or deferred swap. If rates have risen when the outstanding bonds mature, the firm sells the swap, realizing a gain equal to the present value

---

"As a tool for bond portfolio management, asset swaps can change a portfolio's exposure to interest rate risk."

---

of the difference between the cash flows based on the current swap rate and those based on the lower fixed rate of the forward swap. This gain would offset the higher coupon payments on the newly issued fixed rate bond; the effective rate paid would be the same as the forward swap rate.

However, a fall in rates would translate into a loss on the forward swap upon sale, although the newly issued fixed rate bond would itself carry a lower rate. The effective rate on the fixed rate issue would again be the forward swap rate, neglecting differences in transactions costs. The forward swap in this example is used as a hedging tool, establishing a certain fixed rate today instead of an unknown fixed rate at the future date for debt issuance.

Extension Swaps. An extension swap is merely a forward swap appended to an existing swap before its term ends to extend it by some additional period (Jeffry Brown 1991, 127). If the forward swap is arranged based on current forward interest rates, the extension swap would be obtained at no cost. However, if a counterparty wants the forward swap rate to match an outstanding swap's rate, an up-front cash payment (or receipt) might be necessary to compensate for the change in market rates since the outstanding swap's origination. The extension swap in this case would be a type of off-market swap.

Swaptions. The earlier discussion of amortizing swaps and the example of an asset swap involving a PAC bond emphasized the risk inherent in mismatches of principal with notional principal. The amount of principal is not always perfectly predictable, especially for many new types of asset-backed securities. Option contracts are designed to handle contingencies of this kind, and, not surprisingly, a market has developed for options on swaps, known as swaptions. (There is also a market for op-

---

"For hedging applications, perhaps the swaption's most basic use is to give a swap counterparty the option to cancel a swap, at no further cost beyond the initial swaption premium."

---

tions on caps and floors, which, as one might guess, are called captions and floortions.)

Like any option, swaptions entail a right and not an obligation on the part of the buyer. Unfortunately, the nomenclature for swaptions is confusing, so the details are often simply spelled out in talking about them. A call swaption (a call option on a swap or payer swaption) is the right to buy a swap—pay a fixed rate of interest and receive floating. A put swaption (put option on a swap or receiver swaption) is the right to sell a swap—pay floating and receive fixed. The swaption on the plain vanilla swap is the most common, although swaptions can be written on more complicated swaps. Both the maturity of the swaption and the tenor of the underlying swap, which commences at a stipulated future date, must be specified. Also like options, swaptions come in both American and European varieties. The European swaption, which accounts for about 90 percent of the market, may be exercised only upon its maturity date, whereas the American swaption may be exercised at any time before maturity (Robert Tompkins 1989, 19). Only European swaptions will be considered in this discussion, unless otherwise noted.

A call swaption would be exercised at maturity if the swaption strike rate—the fixed rate specified in the contract—is lower than the prevailing market fixed rate for swaps of the same tenor. The swaption could be closed out by selling the low fixed rate swap obtained through the swaption for a gain, rather than entering into that swap. Similar reasoning applies to the decision to exercise a put swaption.

Swaptions are quite different from caps and floors, although these instruments are frequently used in similar situations. A swaption involves one option on a swap, while a cap (or floor) represents a series of options expiring at different dates on a floating interest rate. In addition, cap prices depend partly on the volatility of near-term forward rates, whereas swaption prices reflect the volatility of future swap rates, which in turn are averages of more distant, less volatile forward rates. Consequently, swaptions are much cheaper than caps or floors. Like options, swaptions require up-front payments, but these have recently fallen in the range of 20-40 basis points as compared with 200-300 basis points for caps or floors (Krzyzak 1989a, 13). American swaptions would be slightly more costly than European swaptions because of the additional right to exercise the instrument before maturity.

Callable, Puttable, and Reversible Swaps. For hedging applications, perhaps the swaption's most basic use is to give a swap counterparty the option to cancel a swap, at no further cost beyond the initial swaption premium. A fixed-for-floating swap bundled together with a put swaption is known as a callable swap. The swap can be canceled upon the maturity of the embedded swaption if, for example, interest rates have fallen. Exercising the swaption creates an offsetting floating-for-fixed swap. A floating-for-fixed swap combined with a call swaption is called a puttable swap. The swap can be terminated if interest rates have risen—that is, if a higher fixed rate could be received from a new swap.

Another example of a swaption application involves the PAC bond considered earlier. The amortizing swap to pay fixed and receive floating could be hedged against the possibility that the rate of amortization is faster than that structured in the swap. A put swaption purchased along with the original fixed-for-floating swap would (partially) hedge this risk. The purchaser would buy a swaption(s) in the amount necessary to partially offset the underlying swap in order to cover the potential additional amortization of principal. An American swaption would be appropriate for this application.

The reversible swap described earlier can be synthesized by a fixed-for-floating plain vanilla swap combined with put swaptions for twice the notional principal of the underlying swap. Assuming a swaption has the same notional principal amount as the swap, the first swaption cancels the existing swap and the second creates a floating-for-fixed swap upon maturity, running for the remaining term of the original swap.

Extendable Swaps. As the name suggests, an extendable swap contains the option to lengthen its term at the original swap rate. Such a swap simply amounts to an ordinary swap with a swaption expiring at the end of the swap's tenor. Note the difference between an extendable swap and an extension swap. The former gives the holder the option to extend a swap; the latter is a commitment. The same distinction applies to swaptions and forward swaps.

Leveraged Buyout Hedging. Another application of swaptions has been in leveraged buyouts, in which a firm's management takes on large amounts of debt to "take a firm private." Lenders, such as commercial banks, often require the firm to hedge its debt, which typically is floating rate. A call swaption with a strike rate at a level the firm could safely meet would accomplish this end. Should the floating rate rise sharply, the swaption would be exercised, converting the remaining floating rate payments to manageable fixed rate payments. However, lenders involved in leveraged buyout financing often prefer to sell caps because a swaption, if exercised, makes its writer a counterparty to a highly leveraged (and often low-rated) firm. A cap writer faces no credit risk from the cap buyer.

Synthetic Straight Debt. A final example of swaption usage is in stripping callable debt. This strategy has been popular in the swaption market's brief history. Corporate bonds are frequently issued with options allowing the issuer to refinance the debt issue at a lower coupon if interest rates fall before the bonds mature. The issuer usually cannot exercise the embedded call until after some prespecified date. The callable debt's buyer has effectively written a call option on the price of the bond to the issuer, the firm. If bond prices rise above the strike price of the calls (implying that interest rates have fallen sufficiently), the issuer has the right to call the bonds away after paying the strike price.

Because many participants in these markets have believed that the calls attached to these bonds are undervalued, the following arbitrage strategy developed. Firms wanting fixed rate debt issued callable bonds and "stripped" the embedded call options by selling call swaptions, with the net result of creating synthetic noncallable or "straight" bonds at a lower yield than that prevailing on comparable fixed rate bonds. The yield reduction stemmed from selling the undervalued bond market calls at a profit in the swap market.[17]

As an illustration of the basic strategy, assume the bond is callable at par. That is, if at the call date the relevant interest rate is at or below the original coupon rate, the bond will be called. To strip the call option, the issuer writes a put swaption, which, if exercised, obligates the firm to pay fixed and receive floating on a swap commencing on the bond's first call date and ending at the bond's maturity date. In this example the swaption strike would be set to the bond's coupon rate. If interest rates fall, the put swaption is exercised. In turn, the firm would call its debt and simultaneously issue floating rate debt, whose coupon payments would be met by the floating rate payments coming from the swap counterparty. On balance, the firm would continue to make fixed rate payments, though to the swap counterparty instead of to the bondholders. There are many variations on this strategy. Also, embedded put options can be stripped from bonds in a similar way.[18]

The Size of the Swaption Market. As of year-end 1989, $79.7 billion in U.S. dollar and non-U.S. dollar swaptions was outstanding, as measured by the value of the underlying notional principal.[19] The market grew 118 percent compared with the figure for year-end 1988, the first year the survey included swaptions. The size of the caps, collars, and floors market was considerably larger. For year-end 1989, the total U.S. dollar and non-U.S. dollar value of the notional principal for caps, collars, and floors was $457.6 billion, representing a 57 percent increase over the previous year's figure.

Non-U.S. Dollar Denominated Interest Rate Swaps. The interest rate swap market is active worldwide. About one-third of interest rate swaps outstanding involved currencies other than the U.S. dollar. Table 3 reports the latest International Swap Dealers Association survey results for year-end 1989 reflecting swaps involving a single currency. The dollar equivalent of the notional principal outstanding is shown, ranked by currency. The Japanese yen is a distant number two to the U.S. dollar, accounting for 8.5 percent of the market. The British pound and deutsche mark are next in order, with the New Zealand dollar ranking last.

Table 3
Interest Rate Swaps
as of December 31, 1989*

Currency	U.S. Dollar Equivalent	End-User Counterparty (percent)	ISDA Counterparty (percent)	Currency as Percentage of Total ($1,502.6 billion)
U.S. Dollar	$993,746	62.65	37.35	66.14
Yen	$128,022	52.25	47.75	8.52
Sterling	$100,417	60.13	39.87	6.68
Deutsche Mark	$84,620	61.46	38.54	5.63
Australian Dollar	$67,599	84.35	15.65	4.50
French Franc	$42,016	89.92	10.08	2.80
Canadian Dollar	$29,169	87.66	12.34	1.94
Swiss Franc	$28,605	55.65	44.35	1.90
European Currency Unit	$18,988	58.51	41.49	1.26
Dutch Guilder	$5,979	65.14	34.86	.40
Hong Kong Dollar	$2,149	60.12	39.88	.14
Belgian Franc	$835	79.16	20.84	.06
New Zealand Dollar	$444	82.66	17.57	.03

* All dollar amounts are in millions of dollars in U.S. dollar equivalents.

Source: International Swap Dealers Association Market Survey.

Currency Swaps

Basic currency swaps were described earlier in connection with their evolution from parallel loan agreements. The fixed-for-fixed currency swap is the most rudimentary type of swap and is roughly equivalent to a series of forward foreign exchange contracts. For example, a firm could borrow yen at a fixed interest rate and swap its yen-dominated debt for fixed rate dollar-denominated debt. The exchange rate for converting cash flows throughout the life of the swap would be established at the outset. Forward foreign exchange contracts, if they were available in long-dated maturities, could also lock in the exchange rate for future cash flows.

All of the features enumerated for interest rate swaps can be applied singly or in combination to swaps involving different currencies. A number of applications of currency swaps are discussed below.

Currency Coupon Swaps. One of the currency swap's early variants is the currency coupon swap, otherwise known as the cross-coupon swap. This swap is like a plain vanilla swap in which the fixed interest rate is paid in one currency while the floating rate is paid in another. However, the principal involved in the transaction is usually exchanged as well.

An Example. Consider a hypothetical transaction between a U.S. firm, USTech, and a British bank, Brit-Bank. A U.S. swap dealer intermediates the transaction, in part because this institution has the relevant credit information about the swap counterparties that they lack individually. USTech is setting up a British subsidiary and issuing dollar-denominated floating rate bonds tied to LIBOR to finance this operation. USTech wants to hedge itself on two counts, though: first, it wants protection against foreign exchange rate fluctuations because the subsidiary's sales revenue will be in sterling but will be needed to service the dollar-denominated floating rate debt; second, USTech prefers to make fixed rate payments. A currency coupon swap would enable the firm to make sterling-denominated fixed rate payments while receiving dollar-denominated LIBOR, which it would pass to its floating rate bondholders. On the other hand, BritBank would like sterling-denominated fixed rate cash flows instead of dollar-denominated LIBOR payments from floating rate notes that it holds in a portfolio within its trust department. The bank wants the fixed rate sterling cash flows to extend the duration of its portfolio.

As is typical of currency swaps, this one involves exchanges of principal at the beginning and end of the swap. The dealer collects his margin on the fixed rate side of the swap. Like the fixed rate currency swap, the exchange rate for the currency coupon swap is established at the outset and prevails at each of the subsequent settlement dates. Payments at those dates are for the gross amounts of the cash flows, not the net amount as with interest rate swaps, although some swaps stipulate that net amounts be exchanged.

European Currency Unit Swaps. The European Currency Unit (ECU) has become an increasingly important "currency" in the Eurobond market. If progress is made toward monetary union of the European Community (EC), the ECU may become European markets' official unit of account. It currently is valued as a weighted average of twelve EC currencies. Although growing rapidly, the number of outstanding ECU-denominated bonds constitutes only about 4 percent of the outstanding amount of publicly issued Eurobonds (Graham Bishop 1991, 72.) Cross-coupon ECU swaps have been used to transform both principal and coupon payments denominated in the ECU into other currencies and vice versa.

Terry Shanahan and Jim Durrant (1990) discuss an example in which a U.S. multinational firm needed to finance subsidiaries in France, Belgium, and the Netherlands. The firm borrowed in the Eurobond market by floating ECU-denominated fixed rate debt and converted the issue via a cross-coupon swap into floating rate debt with payments in French francs, Belgian francs, and Dutch guilders. The firm exchanged the principal, consisting of a basket of currencies in proportion to each currency's share in the ECU, raised from the bond buyers. In return, the firm received an equivalent value of the three currencies from the swap counterparty. During the life of this five-year swap, the firm received annual ECU coupon payments from the counterparty, which the firm passed on to the bondholders, and it made annual floating rate payments in guilders and Belgian francs and semiannual floating rate payments in French francs to the counterparty. Upon maturity of the swap, the initial transfer of principal was reversed. The counterparty exchanged ECU principal for repayment in the three currencies from the U.S. firm. In turn, the firm redeemed its bonds with the ECU payment from the counterparty.

Swapping Illiquid Bonds and Private Placements. A major impetus for the growth of currency swaps has been and continues to be the portfolio management of illiquid securities. The earlier discussion of portfolio duration adjustment showed a basic rationale for using swaps, which holds particularly true in the Eurobond market, where many bonds lack the liquidity to be traded readily. In addition, for internationally diversified portfolios, bond trading may be desired to change portfolios' exposures to exchange rate fluctuations. Currency swaps fulfill portfolio managers' needs for such risk management.

Currency (and interest rate) swaps have been especially useful in managing portfolios of privately placed bonds. In terms of a number of costs to the issuer, these bonds are significantly cheaper than publicly placed bonds. Use of privately placed bonds avoids the public disclosure and registration requirements as well as compliance with U.S. accounting regulations; it also minimizes legal costs, reduces underwriting costs, and speeds placement. Yet such securities appeal to a much narrower class of investors because of their illiquidity.

In April 1990 the Security and Exchange Commission approved Rule 144A, which greatly simplifies disclosure requirements for private placement issuers (Franklin Chu 1991, 55). Non-U.S. corporations that need to fund their U.S. subsidiaries will find it much easier to raise capital through private placements. The disadvantages of holding these relatively illiquid securities is expected to be lessened both by the use of swaps in portfolio management and by the growth of a secondary market for private placements (Brady 1990, 86).

The Size of the Market. The U.S. dollar is the preeminent currency in the currency swaps market. Table 4 shows that the dollar has a 41 percent share in the currency swaps market, followed by the Japanese yen with a 23 percent share. The Swiss franc, Australian dollar, and German mark occupy the next ranks, with the Hong Kong dollar taking the smallest share of the market for the surveyed currencies.

Commodity Swaps

Commodity swaps are straightforward extensions of financial swaps, though a number of institutional factors make commodity swapping much riskier than the financial variety. As mentioned earlier, only about $10 billion in notional value has been transacted in this relatively new market. However, commodity prices historically have been much more volatile than financial asset prices, and volatility tends to promote the development and use of hedging instruments. Commodity swaps' volume has reportedly doubled in the past year and is expected to do so

Table 4
Currency Swaps
as of December 31, 1989*

Currency	U.S. Dollar Equivalent	End-User Counterparty (percent)	ISDA Counterparty (percent)	Currency as Percentage of Total ($869.7 billion)
U.S. Dollar	$354,166	72.78	27.22	40.72
Yen	$201,145	71.83	28.17	23.13
Swiss Franc	$64,823	77.42	22.58	7.45
Australian Dollar	$61,768	70.77	29.23	7.10
Deutsche Mark	$53,839	79.93	20.07	6.19
European Currency Unit	$39,948	83.06	16.94	4.59
Sterling	$33,466	74.11	25.89	3.85
Canadian Dollar	$32,580	81.72	18.28	3.75
Dutch Guilder	$10,132	82.53	17.47	1.17
French Franc	$8,435	88.74	11.26	.97
New Zealand Dollar	$5,818	81.90	18.10	.67
Belgian Franc	$2,997	86.89	13.11	.34
Hong Kong Dollar	$583	90.39	9.61	.07

* All dollar amounts are in millions of dollars in U.S. dollar equivalents.

Source: International Swap Dealers Association Market Survey.

again in 1991 (Janet Lewis 1990, 207). Another impetus is likely to be the resolution of some regulatory uncertainties, as discussed above. Energy-related commodities hedged via swaps to date include crude oil, heating oil, gasoline, naphtha, natural gas, jet fuel, maritime diesel fuel, and coal. Swap maturities have ranged from one month to five years. A relatively smaller number of swaps have been arranged for gold and for base metals, mainly copper and aluminum, as well as a few in nickel and zinc (Brady 1990, 87).

The most popular commodity swap has been the plain vanilla fixed-for-floating swap, very much akin to the plain vanilla interest rate swap. End users turn to swaps for hedging for essentially the same reasons that they take positions in commodity futures contracts. Their pricing decisions can be based on a known future cost of inputs or revenue from outputs, allowing the appropriate margins to be built in. The end users avail themselves of hedging instruments to transfer the risk to others who specialize in managing that risk.[20] Exchange-traded futures and options contracts tend to be liquid for contracts with time to maturity of only a few months. Hedging large positions farther out in time would cause the futures prices to move against the hedger, raising the cost of the hedge. In contrast, over-the-counter oil swaps are well suited to hedging intermediate-term risks that cannot be handled by simple positions in futures having relatively short maturity. At the same time, the implication is that swap intermediaries face greater risks because of difficulties they encounter in hedging their swap positions (see Janet Lewis 1990). Oil trading firms have an advantage in acting as dealers because they also carry out transactions in the underlying commodities, giving them additional flexibility in hedging.

A commodity swap may be important as a hedge for a firm that is considering financing a project using debt.[21] The same is true for interest rate and currency swaps as well, but commodity prices are notoriously volatile, giving lenders ample reason to require a commodity swap hedge.[22] In other words, swaps can increase a firm's ability to borrow.

An Example. A U.S. producer of oil, TexOil, Inc., sells oil at the spot price but wants to hedge against any large drops in the price of oil that would make production uneconomical. Another counterparty, a charter luxury liner company, Luv-Boats Ltd., wants to hedge the proceeds from advanced ticket sales for the coming year. Maritime diesel fuel, purchased at the spot price, is a major operating cost for LuvBoats's ships. Chart 2 depicts a pair of plain vanilla swaps with a swap dealer intermediating the transaction.

As with any kind of swap transaction, a dealer does not necessarily need an offsetting counterparty to enter into a swap with another counterparty. The swap involving LuvBoats Ltd. is actually tied to the price of No. 2 heating oil, which is a more actively traded commodity than maritime diesel. The spread to the counterparty is lower because the swap dealer can better hedge its position, for example by using No. 2 heating oil futures contracts. LuvBoats is willing to bear some basis risk—the risk that maritime diesel and heating oil price movements will be less than perfectly correlated—to avoid paying the dealer a larger spread to index a swap to the price of maritime diesel. TexOil receives a fixed price of $25 per barrel of crude from the swap dealer, while LuvBoats pays a fixed amount of 74 cents per gallon of heating oil. Since the swap's origination, oil and refined product prices have declined, resulting in a $4.52 per barrel net payment to TexOil and a 9 cent per gallon net payment from LuvBoats at the current payment date.

Oil swaps can assume more complex forms. For example, they can be combined with currency and interest rate swaps to convert uncertain, dollar-denominated spot market purchases of oil into fixed deutsche mark payments. To meet regulatory guidelines, commodity swaps require the inclusion of caps and floors, although these are usually set at prices far from the prevailing commodity price and thus are unlikely to be reached. Caps, collars, floors, participating swaps, swaptions, and many other instruments have been adapted to the commodity markets. Also, oil and other commodity swaps typically reset based on daily averages of spot market prices for the underlying commodity. Averaging tends to make the floating side of a swap have a better correspondence with actual spot market purchases by the counterparties. A swap reset based on a single day's price would be less likely to be representative of such purchases.

Equity Swaps

Equity swaps are the newest type of swap and are a subset of a new class of instruments known as synthetic equity.[23] Equity swaps generally function as an asset swap that converts the interest flows on a bond portfolio into cash flows linked to a stock index. The stock indexes that have been used include the Standard and Poor's (S&P) 500, the Tokyo Stock Price Index (TOPIX) and Nikkei 225 (Japan), the Chambre des Agents de Change (CAC) 240 (France), the Financial Times Stock Exchange (FTSE) 100 (United Kingdom), the Toronto Stock Exchange (TSE) 300 (Canada), as well as others (see

**Chart 2
Commodity Swaps**

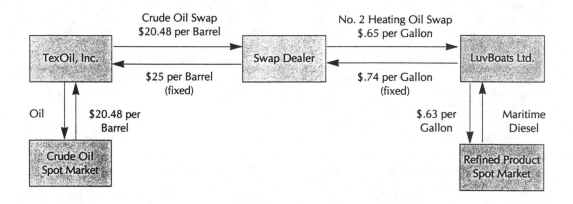

TexOil receives $25 per barrel and pays the spot price for crude oil. LuvBoats receives the spot price for No. 2 heating oil and pays a fixed price for heating oil. LuvBoats in turn buys maritime diesel at the spot price for diesel. There are 42 gallons in a barrel.

Salomon Brothers, Inc. 1990; Saul Hansell 1990; and Richard Metcalfe 1990, 40). Linking portfolio performance to an index means that dividends are not received as with actual equity ownership; the portfolio tracks only the capital gain component of the underlying stocks.

One of the advantages of using a synthetic swap is that transactions costs are mitigated, especially in dealing with less liquid foreign stock markets (Hansell 1990, 56). On the other hand, such swaps are also illiquid, which implies that their use be predicated on a buy-and-hold strategy for an investment portfolio. Equity swaps have been structured to have one- to five-year tenors and usually have quarterly or semiannual reset dates.

The mechanics of an equity swap are similar to the workings of other kinds of swaps. Typically, an investor will swap either fixed or floating rate interest payments for payments indexed to the performance of a stock index such as the S&P 500. If the index appreciates during the interval between settlement dates, the investor receives a payment from the counterparty equal to the rate of appreciation times the swap's notional principal. At the same time, the investor pays, for example, LIBOR less a spread representing the margin to the dealer. Actual settlement would involve only the difference between these bases. In the event the S&P 500 falls, the investor would pay the rate of depreciation times notional principal and LIBOR less a spread. Of course, the investor is receiving LIBOR or another floating rate from his or her investment portfolio. The net result of the swap is that the portfolio's income behaves like that of an index equity portfolio.

A variation of the basic equity swap—the asset allocation swap—links the equity side of the swap to the maximum of two indexes. For example, the swap agreement could stipulate that the counterparty receive the maximum of the rate of appreciation (or pay the maximum rate of depreciation) on the S&P 500 or Nikkei 225 at each settlement date. This kind of swap effectively swaps a portfolio into a foreign stock portfolio or domestic stock portfolio instantly, without transactions costs (apart from those associated with the swap). There are many other possibilities for asset allocation swaps. As another example, the swap could be indexed to the maximum of the S&P 500 or a bond index. Index options could be embedded in the swaps to trade away upside exposure in exchange for downside protection from index moves.

Conclusion

Swaps are but one kind of instrument that has been spawned in the profusion of financial innovation during the last two decades.[24] In the most general terms, swaps are contracts that transform cash flows from underlying assets or liabilities. They have been designed to incorporate great flexibility in that task and hence are frequently described as instruments that tailor cash flows. This article encompasses the four basic types of swap: interest rate, currency, commodity, and equity. Each group in turn branches into a variety of forms that can accommodate virtually any application. However, novelty does not guarantee success. The most successful swaps have frequently been the simplest, plain vanilla variety.

Swaps integrate credit markets. By the nature of their function, swaps can link money markets (short-term financing) and capital markets (long-term financing). Swaps also play a significant role in the so-called globalization of financial markets because they obviate the need for many investors to carry out transactions in underlying foreign securities, thereby contributing to the international diversification of portfolios. International arbitrage of securities and swaps markets is left to those participants who have the lowest transactions costs, increasing global market efficiency.

Swaps are an important tool for simplifying financial transactions that cross national borders. At the same time, they pose potential risks to the stability of financial markets. Recent concern about the strength of both banks and investment banks has focused the attention of swap market participants on counterparties' creditworthiness, upon which the financial obligations contracted through a swap agreement depend.[25]

However, part of the reason that swaps evolved was to reduce the credit exposure of counterparties involved in similar financial arrangements. Swaps generally confine credit risk to exposure to the net difference in cash flows, not the gross amounts or exposure of underlying principal, and defaults have been rare occurrences.[26] The implementation of the Basle Agreement in 1992 will establish more uniform capital standards for the world's commercial banks and should help to further reduce credit risks in the swap market.[27]

1. Shirreff (1989) reports that swaps with thirty-year maturities or "tenors" have been arranged. Such long-lived swaps typically involved counterparties with top credit ratings or relied on third-party credit enhancements.

2. Wall and Pringle (1988) discuss the plain vanilla swap in detail and consider the reasons for using swaps.

3. A forward contract commits the buyer to purchase the underlying asset at a prespecified price (the forward price) upon maturity of the contract. A call option gives the buyer the right, but not the obligation, to purchase an underlying asset at a prespecified price on or sometime before the maturity date of the option. The put gives the corresponding right to sell at a prespecified price. These instruments will be described further at appropriate places in the exposition.

4. See McNulty and Stieber (1991) for a more detailed account.

5. See Henderson (1990) for details about the CFTC's criteria.

6. The growth may be exaggerated by these figures because the number of survey respondents, not reported in the tables, has also been increasing. However, the ISDA points out that the major swap dealers have consistently participated in their surveys.

7. See Kuprianov (1986) for a background discussion of Eurodollar futures and LIBOR.

8. See McNulty and Stieber (1991, 100-101) for information about the Eleventh District cost-of-funds rate.

9. A basis point is a hundredth of a percentage point.

10. Ramaswamy and Sundaresan (1986) analyze floating rate securities and discuss the characteristics of such securities.

11. See Macfarlane, Showers, and Ross (1991) for a discussion of nonstandard swap terms. This article gives a detailed account of swap terminology and conventions.

12. Ordinarily, comparisons of yields along the yield curve are made using instruments of comparable default risk. Yield curve swaps exchange floating payments on debt bearing different default risks. Because the underlying three-month Eurodollar time deposit is default risky, LIBOR is greater than the riskless three-month Treasury bill yield. The swap therefore exchanges credit spreads as well as yield curve spreads.

13. See Goodman (1991, 160-61) for details about this strategy.

14. See Abken (1989) for an introduction to these instruments.

15. See Bodie, Kane, and Marcus (1989) for an introduction to duration analysis.

16. This example is cited by Bhattacharya (1990, 56).

17. Goodman (1991) and Brown and Smith (1990) discuss call monetization using several strategies. Forward swaps may also be used for this purpose. Brown and Smith discuss many subtleties of these strategies.

18. Krzyzak (1988, 29; 1989a, 9) reports that the embedded calls were overvalued and that call monetization was used to undo the expensive call. In this case, call monetization would not be an arbitrage.

19. Chew (1991) discusses recent activity in the non-U.S. dollar swaptions markets, particularly deutsche mark instruments.

20. This point of view is not universal or uncontroversial. Williams (1986) argues that risk aversion has nothing to do with the use of futures. Rather, futures contracts reduce transactions costs in dealing with underlying commodities. His model assumes that all futures market participants are risk neutral.

21. Also, Smith, Smithson, and Wilford (1990) discuss a conflict between stockholders and bondholders of a corporation, known as the underinvestment problem, that swaps can mitigate.

22. See Spraos (1990) for a case study of a complex copper swap required in part for this reason.

23. Other examples of synthetic equity include over-the-counter equity options, public warrant issues, and bonds containing equity options. See Hansell (1990). Index-linked certificates of deposit were a retail form of synthetic equity offered by a number of commercial banks and savings and loans in 1987.

24. See Finnerty (1990) for a comprehensive survey of financial innovations since the 1970s.

25. Krzyzak (1990) and Brady (1991) describe the concerns and difficulties experienced by low-rated swap dealers in dealing with higher-rated counterparties. See Abken (1991) for a model of swap valuation in which swaps are subject to default by the participating counterparties.

26. Aggarwal (1991) reports several sources giving a figure of $35 million in write-offs resulting from swap defaults as of year-end 1988. The collapse of Drexel, Burnham, Lambert in 1989 brought with it potential defaults on its swap book. Most of these swaps were closed out or rearranged with other swap dealers, avoiding defaults that would have shaken the swaps market. See Perry (1990) for an account of the Drexel collapse and its aftermath on the swaps market. Evans (1991) reports that U.S. and foreign banks face potential defaults of up to $1 billion because of to a British court ruling that nullifies swap contracts with about 80 British municipalities.

27. See Wall, Pringle, and McNulty (1990) for a discussion of the Basle Agreement and its treatment of swaps under the new capital standards. Levis and Suchar (1990) give further discussion and detailed examples.

References

Abken, Peter A. "Interest-Rate Caps, Collars, and Floors." Federal Reserve Bank of Atlanta *Economic Review* 74 (November/December 1989): 2-24.

_____. "Valuation of Default-Risky Interest-Rate Swaps." Federal Reserve Bank of Atlanta working paper, forthcoming, 1991.

Aggarwal, Raj. "Assessing Default Risk in Interest Rate Swaps." In *Interest Rate Swaps*, edited by Carl R. Beidleman, 430-48. Homewood, Ill.: Business One Irwin, 1991.

Bhattacharya, Anand K. "Synthetic Asset Swaps." *Journal of Portfolio Management* 17 (Fall 1990): 56-64.

_____, and John Breit. "Customized Interest-Rate Risk Agreements and Their Applications." In *The Handbook of Fixed Income Securities*, 3d ed., edited by Frank J. Fabozzi, 1157-89. Homewood, Ill.: Business One Irwin, 1991.

Bishop, Graham. "ECU Bonds: Pioneer of Currency Union." *Euromoney* (January 1991): 71ff.

Bodie, Zvi, Alex Kane, and Alan J. Marcus. *Investments*. Homewood, Ill.: Richard D. Irwin, Inc., 1989.

Brady, Simon. "How to Tailor Your Assets." *Euromoney* (April 1990): 83-89.

_____. "Time Runs Out for Low-Rated Swappers." *Euromoney* (February 1991): 9-10.

Brown, Jeffry P. "Variations to Basic Swaps." In *Interest Rate Swaps*, edited by Carl R. Beidleman, 114-29. Homewood, Ill.: Business One Irwin, 1991.

Brown, Keith, and Donald J. Smith. "Forward Swaps, Swap Options, and the Management of Callable Debt." *Journal of Applied Corporate Finance* 2 (Winter 1990): 59-71.

Chew, Lillian. "Strip Mining." *Risk* 4 (February 1991): 20ff.

Chu, Franklin J. "The U.S. Private Market for Foreign Securities." *Bankers Magazine* (January/February 1991): 55-60.

Evans, John. "British Court Rules Swaps by Municipalities Illegal." *American Banker*, January 25, 1991, 13.

Finnerty, John D. "Financial Engineering in Corporate Finance: An Overview." In *The Handbook of Financial Engineering*, edited by Clifford W. Smith and Charles W. Smithson, 69-108. Grand Rapids, Mich.: Harper Business, 1990.

Goodman, Laurie S. "Capital Market Applications of Interest Rate Swaps." In *Interest Rate Swaps*, edited by Carl R. Beidleman, 147-74. Homewood, Ill.: Business One Irwin, 1991.

Hansell, Saul. "Is the World Ready for Synthetic Equity?" *Institutional Investor* (August 1990): 54-61.

Henderson, Schuyler K. "A Legal Eye on Hedging's Newest Club." *Euromoney* (May 1990): 95-96.

Krzyzak, Krystyna. "Don't Take Swaps at Face Value." *Risk* 1 (November 1988): 26-31.

_____. "Swaptions Deciphered." *Risk* 2 (February 1989a): 9-17.

_____. "From Basis Points to Barrels." *Risk* 2 (May 1989b): 8-12.

_____. "Copper-Bottomed Hedge." *Risk* 2 (September 1989c): 35-39.

_____. "Swaps Survey: Around the Houses." *Risk* 3 (September 1990): 51-57.

Kuprianov, Anatoli. "Short-Term Interest Rate Futures." Federal Reserve Bank of Richmond *Economic Review* (September/October 1986): 12-26.

Levis, Mario, and Victor Suchar. "Basle Basics." *Risk* 3 (April 1990): 38-39.

Lewis, Janet. "Oil Price Jitters? Try Energy Swaps." *Institutional Investor* (December 1990): 206-8.

Lewis, Julian. "The Bandwagon Starts to Roll." *Euromoney* (May 1990): 87-94.

Macfarlane, John, Janet Showers, and Daniel Ross. "The Interest-Rate Swap Market: Yield Mathematics, Terminology, and Conventions." In *Interest Rate Swaps*, edited by Carl R. Beidleman, 233-65. Homewood, Ill.: Business One Irwin, 1991.

McNulty, James E., and Sharon L. Stieber. "The Development and Standardization of the Swap Market." In *Interest Rate Swaps*, edited by Carl R. Beidleman, 97-113. Homewood, Ill.: Business One Irwin, 1991.

Metcalfe, Richard. "Out of the Shadows." *Risk* 3 (October 1990): 40-42.

Perry, Phillip M. "Drexel Redux? Credit Quality Is a Hot Topic." *Corporate Risk Management* (May/June 1990): 27-29.

Ramaswamy, Krishna, and Suresh M. Sundaresan. "The Valuation of Floating-Rate Instruments: Theory and Evidence." *Journal of Financial Economics* 17 (December 1986): 251-72.

Salomon Brothers, Inc. "Equity-Linked Index Swaps." Sales brochure, 1990.

Shanahan, Terry, and Jim Durrant. "Driving Factors." *Risk* 10 (November 1990): 14ff.

Shirreff, David. "Where Others Fear to Tread." *Risk* 8 (September 1989): 11-16.

Smith, Clifford W., Charles W. Smithson, and Lee Macdonald Wakeman. "The Evolving Market for Swaps." In *The Handbook of Financial Engineering*, edited by Clifford W. Smith and Charles W. Smithson, 191-211. Grand Rapids, Mich.: Harper Business, 1990.

Smith, Clifford W., Charles W. Smithson, and D. Sykes Wilford. "Financial Engineering: Why Hedge?" In *The Handbook of Financial Engineering*, edited by Clifford W. Smith and Charles W. Smithson, 126-37. Grand Rapids, Mich.: Harper Business, 1990.

Spraos, Paul B. "The Anatomy of a Copper Swap." *Corporate Risk Management* 2 (January/February 1990): 8, 10.

Tompkins, Robert. "Behind the Mirror." *Risk* 2 (February 1989): 17-23.

Wall, Larry D., and John J. Pringle. "Interest Rate Swaps: A Review of the Issues." Federal Reserve Bank of Atlanta *Economic Review* 73 (November/December 1988): 22-37.

Wall, Larry D., John J. Pringle, and James E. McNulty. "Capital Requirements for Interest-Rate and Foreign-Exchange Hedges." Federal Reserve Bank of Atlanta *Economic Review* 75 (May/June 1990): 14-27.

Williams, Jeffrey. *The Economic Function of Futures Markets*. New York: Cambridge University Press, 1986.

Article 19

Interest Rate Swaps: A Review of the Issues

Larry D. Wall and John J. Pringle

Interest rate swaps have gained considerable importance in capital markets in the six years since they were introduced. This article questions some of the conventional views regarding the use of interest rate swaps and presents information on swaps' pricing, risks, and regulation.

In the last two decades a myriad of new instruments and transactions have brought about significant changes in financial markets. Some of these innovations have attracted considerable publicity; stock index futures and options, for example, were an important element in the studies of the October 19, 1987, stock market crash.[1] However, not all of these new developments are well-known to the public. One recent innovation that is quietly transforming credit markets is interest rate swaps—an agreement between two parties to exchange interest payments for a predetermined period of time.

The interest rate swap market began in 1982. By 1988 the outstanding portfolios of 49 leading swap dealers totaled $889.5 billion in principal, of which $473.6 billion represented new business in 1987.[2] Reflecting their rapid growth, swaps have gained considerable importance in the capital markets. Thomas Jasper, the head of Salomon Brothers' swap department, has estimated that 30 to 40 percent of all capital market transactions involve an interest rate, foreign-exchange, or some other type of swap.[3]

Their rapid growth is one reason swaps have generated considerable interest among academics, regulators, accountants, and market participants alike. Paramount among the questions surrounding swaps are the reasons for their use and the basis of their pricing. Regulators are also keenly concerned with the risks swaps pose to financial firms, while accountants are debating appropriate reporting. This article reviews the current literature and presents some new research on interest rate swaps. Among the issues addressed are the workings of interest rate swaps, the reasons that firms use such swaps, the risks associated with interest rate swaps, the pricing of these swaps, the regulation of participants in the swap market, and the disclosure of swaps on firms' financial statements.

What Is an Interest Rate Swap?

Interest rate swaps serve to transform the effective maturity (or, more accurately, the repricing interval) of two firms' assets or liabilities. This type of swap enables firms to choose from a wider variety of asset and liability markets without having to incur additional interest rate risk, that is, risk that arises because of changes in market interest rates. For instance, a firm that traditionally invests in short-term assets, whose

The authors are, respectively, a senior economist in the financial section of the Atlanta Fed's Research Department and a professor of finance at the University of North Carolina at Chapel Hill. They wish to thank William Curt Hunter and Peter Abken for their comments.

returns naturally fluctuate as the yield on each new issue changes, may instead invest in a long-term, fixed-rate instrument and then use an interest rate swap to obtain floating-rate receipts. In this situation, one firm agrees to pay a fixed interest rate to another in return for receiving a floating rate.

Interest rate swaps have fixed termination dates and typically provide for semiannual payments. Either interest rate in a swap may be fixed or floating.[4] The amount of interest paid is based on some agreed-upon principal amount, which is called the "notional" principal because it never actually changes hands. Moreover, the two parties do not exchange the full amounts of the interest payments. Rather, at each payment a single amount is transferred to cover the net difference in the promised interest payments.

An example of an interest rate swap is provided in Chart 1. Atlanta HiTech agrees to pay Heartland Manufacturing a floating rate of interest equal to the London Interbank Offered Rate (LIBOR), which is commonly used in international loan agreements.[5] In return, Heartland Manufacturing promises to pay Atlanta HiTech a fixed 9.18 percent rate of interest. The swap transaction is ordinarily arranged at current market rates in order for the net present value of payments to equal zero. That is, the fixed rate on a typical interest rate swap is set so that the market value of the net floating-rate payments

exactly equals the market value of the net fixed-rate payments. If the swap is not arranged as a zero-net-present-value exchange, one party pays to the other an amount equal to the difference in the payments' net present value when the swap is arranged.

Chart 2 demonstrates three aspects of the swaps market: converting floating-rate debt to fixed-rate debt, converting a floating-rate asset to a fixed-rate asset, and using an intermediary in the swap transaction. In Chart 2, Widgets Unlimited can issue short-term debt but is averse to the risk that market interest rates will increase. To avoid this risk, Widgets enters into a swap in which it agrees to pay the counterparty a fixed rate of interest and receive a floating rate. This arrangement resembles long-term, fixed-rate debt in that Widgets' promised payments are independent of market interest rate changes. If market interest rates rise, Widgets will receive payments under the swap that will offset the higher cost of its short-term debt. Should market rates fall, though, under the terms of the swap Widgets will have to pay its counterparty money.

The combination of short-term debt and swaps is not identical to the use of long-term debt. One difference is that Widgets' interest payments are not truly fixed. The company is protected from an increase in market rates but not from changes in its own risk premium. The swap

Chart 1.
An Interest Rate Swap without a Dealer

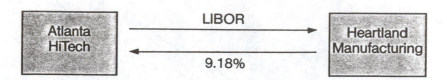

In this example, Atlanta HiTech agrees to pay Heartland Manufacturing a floating rate of interest equal to the London Interbank Offered Rate. In return, Heartland agrees to pay Atlanta HiTech a fixed 9.18% rate of interest. These two companies do not actually exchange the full amounts of the interest payments, but at each payment, a single amount is transferred to cover the net difference in the promised interest payments.

would not compensate Widgets if its own cost of short-term debt increased from LIBOR-plus-0.5 percent to LIBOR-plus-0.75 percent. If the cost of short-term debt to Widgets decreased to LIBOR-plus-0.30 percent, however, the cost of the debt issue would fall by 0.20 percent. In addition, the counterparty to the combination generally does not provide the corporation with the interest rate option implicit in many bonds issued in the United States, whereby they can be called in at a fixed price regardless of current market rates. Call options allow issuers to exploit large changes in market interest rates.[6] In contrast, standard interest rate swap contracts may be unwound or canceled only at prevailing market interest rates.

The other swap user in this example illustrates a swap's potential to convert a floating rate asset to one in which the rate is fixed. One-State Insurance, a small life insurance company, has long-term, fixed-rate obligations but would like to invest part of its portfolio in short-term debt securities. OneState Insurance can invest in short-term securities without incurring interest rate risk by agreeing to a swap in which the insurer pays a floating rate of interest and receives a fixed rate of interest. This combination provides the insurance company with a stream of income that does not fluctuate with changes in short-term market interest rates.

This example also demonstrates the usefulness of an intermediary in a swap. Although Widgets and OneState Insurance could have entered into a swap agreement with each other, in this example (see Chart 2), both Widgets Unlimited and OneState Insurance actually have a swap agreement with DomBank. Numerous large commercial and investment banks as well as insurance companies have entered into the swap market as intermediaries. DomBank is compensated in an amount equal to the difference between what is received on one swap and what is paid under the other one. In this example, the fee is equal to 10 basis points.

Using DomBank is advantageous to Widgets and OneState Insurance for two reasons. First, the use of an intermediary reduces search time in establishing a swap agreement. DomBank is willing to enter into a swap at any time, whereas Widgets and OneState Insurance might take several days to discover each other, even with a broker's help. Second, an intermediary can reduce the costs of credit evaluation. Either of the participants in an interest rate swap may become bankrupt and unable to fulfill their side of the contract. Thus, each swap participant should understand the credit quality of the other party. In this example, Widgets and OneState are not familiar with each other, and each would need to undertake costly credit analysis on the other before agreeing to deal directly. However, total credit analysis costs are significantly reduced since both parties know the quality of DomBank and DomBank knows their respective credit standings.

Reasons for Interest Rate Swaps

Why do two firms agree to swap interest payments? They could either acquire assets or

Chart 2.
An Interest Rate Swap with a Dealer

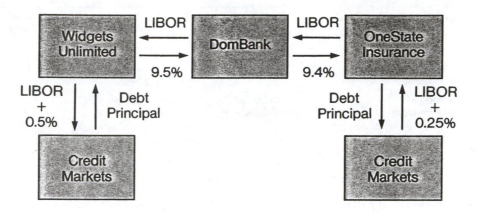

This chart demonstrates three aspects of the swaps market:

(1) Converting floating-rate debt to fixed-rate debt (Widgets Unlimited)
(2) Converting floating-rate assets to fixed-rate assets (OneState Insurance)
(3) Using an intermediary (DomBank) to facilitate the swap

issue liabilities with their desired repricing interval (or maturity) and eliminate the need to undertake a swap. An early explanation for swaps was that they reduce corporations' funding costs by allowing firms to exploit market inefficiencies.[7] Although this explanation remains popular with some market participants, academic analysis has questioned the ability of market inefficiencies to explain the existence and growth of the swap market. Several other explanations for the swap market's popularity that do not rely on market inefficiency have also been provided. The next section of this article presents both original research and a review of recent literature to determine alternative reasons for the surge in use of interest rate swaps.

Quality Spread Differential. The cost savings explanation of swaps claims that swaps allow corporations to arbitrage quality spread differentials. A *quality spread* is the difference between the interest rate paid for funds of a given maturity by a high-quality firm—that is, one with low credit risk—and that required of a lower-quality firm. The quality spread *differential* is the difference in quality spreads at two different maturities. Table 1 provides the calculation of the quality spread differential based on the example provided in Chart 1. Atlanta

HiTech, which has a AAA rating, can obtain short-term financing at six-month LIBOR-plus-0.20 percent or fixed-rate financing at 9.00 percent. Heartland Manufacturing can obtain floating-rate funding at six-month LIBOR-plus-0.70 or fixed-rate funds at 10.20 percent. For floating-rate funding, the quality spread, or difference in rates, between the two firms is 50 basis points, but it widens to 120 basis points for fixed-rate funding. The difference in quality spread, or the quality spread differential, in this example is 70 basis points.

The quality spread differential may be exploitable if Atlanta HiTech desires floating-rate funds and Heartland Manufacturing seeks a fixed rate. Table 2 shows how the quality spread differential is exploited through an interest rate swap. Atlanta HiTech issues fixed-rate debt, and Heartland issues floating-rate debt. Then the two firms enter into an interest rate swap. The net result is that Atlanta HiTech obtains funds at LIBOR minus 18 basis points and Heartland obtains fixed-rate funds at 9.88 percent. Compared with their cost of funds had they not used the interest rate swap strategy, this result represents a 38 basis point savings for Atlanta HiTech and a 32 basis point savings for Heartland. Note that the division of the gain in this

Table 1.
Numerical Example of a Quality Spread Differential

	Atlanta HiTech	Heartland Manufacturing	Quality Spread
Credit rating	AAA	BBB	
Cost of Raising Fixed-Rate Funding	9.00%	10.20%	1.20%
Cost of Raising Floating-Rate Funding	6-month LIBOR plus 0.20%	6-month LIBOR plus 0.70%	0.50%
Quality Spread Differential			0.70%

example is arbitrary and that the two parties could split the gains differently. However, the total gains to the swapping parties will always equal the quality spread differential—70 basis points in this example.

Table 2 clearly demonstrates the ability of swaps to help exploit apparent arbitrage opportunities. However, some observers question whether arbitrage opportunities actually exist. Stuart Turnbull (1987) argues that swaps are zero-sum games in the absence of market imperfections and swap externalities. He also suggests that quality spread differentials may arise for reasons that are not subject to arbitrage. Clifford W. Smith, Charles W. Smithson, and Lee Macdonald Wakeman (1986) note that, even if quality spread differential arbitrage were possible, such activity by itself would not explain swap market growth. In fact, the annual volume of new swaps should be declining as arbitrage becomes more effective.

If the quality spread differential is not entirely the result of market inefficiencies, why does it exist? In a 1987 research paper, the authors of this article point out that quality spread differentials could arise for a number of reasons, including differences in expected bankruptcy costs. Because the expected discounted value of bankruptcy-related losses increases at a faster pace for lower-rated corporations than for higher-rated ones, quality spreads increase with maturity. In this case, the lower initial cost of swap financing is offset by higher costs later.

Alternatively, Jan G. Loeys (1985) suggests that quality spread differentials could arise as

risk is shifted from creditors to shareholders. Creditors have the option of refusing to roll over their debt if the firm appears to be riskier than when the debt was incurred, and short-term creditors have more opportunities to exercise this option. Thus, the creditors of a firm that issues short-term debt bear less risk than the creditors of a firm that issues long-term debt. If the creditors of firms that issue short-term debt bear less risk, the equity holders and long-term creditors necessarily bear more risk.

A third possible explanation for the quality spread differential involves differences in short- and long-term debt contracts. Long-term contracts frequently include a variety of restrictive covenants and may incorporate a call option that is typically not present in short-term debt contracts. The differences in these contract provisions may be reflected in the interest rates charged on various debt contracts. For example, Smith, Smithson, and Wakeman point out that the long-term corporate debt contracts issued by U.S. firms in domestic markets typically have a call provision that is not adjusted for changes in market interest rates. However, long-term debt contracts issued in the Eurobond markets frequently have call provisions that adjust call prices for market rate changes. Thus, quality spread differentials will reflect differences in contract terms if they are calculated using domestic U.S. market rates for lower-quality firms and Eurobond rates for higher-quality firms.

In a forthcoming paper, one of the authors of this article suggests that the quality spread dif-

Table 2.
Numerical Example of a Swap's Ability to Reduce a Firm's Cost of Funding

	Atlanta HiTech	Heartland Manufacturing
Direct Funding Cost		
Fixed-rate funds raised directly by Atlanta HiTech	(9.00%)	
Floating-rate funds raised directly by Heartland		(6-month LIBOR + 0.70%)
Swap Payments		
Atlanta HiTech pays Heartland floating rate	(LIBOR)	LIBOR
Heartland pays Atlanta HiTech fixed rate	9.18%	(9.18%)
All-in cost of funding	LIBOR - 0.18%	9.88%
Comparable cost of equivalent direct funding	LIBOR + 0.20%	10.20%
Savings	38 basis points	32 basis points

ferential may reflect differences in the agency costs associated with short- and long-term debt. Agency costs arise because managers, owners, and creditors have different interests, and managers or owners may take actions that benefit themselves at the expense of the other parties and at the expense of total firm value. In particular, Larry D. Wall notes that the owners of firms that issue long-term, noncallable debt create an incentive to underinvest and to shift investments from low-risk to high-risk projects.[8] A firm may underinvest in new projects because most of the benefit of some projects is received by creditors in the form of a reduced probability that the firm will default. Owners will prefer a high-risk project to a low-risk project because they receive the gains on successful high-risk projects while creditors may suffer most of the losses if the projects fail. Creditors recognize the incentives created by long-term debt and demand a higher risk premium in compensation. The problems created by long-term debt may be reduced or eliminated by short-term debt, that is, debt which matures shortly after the investment decision.[9] An interest rate swap allows lower-quality firms to issue short-term debt while avoiding exposure to changes in market interest rates. Thus, the combination of short-term debt and swaps may be less costly than long-term debt.

In their 1987 paper, the authors also point to another agency cost—that of liquidating insolvent firms—which may be reduced by using short-term debt. Insolvent firms have an incentive to underinvest because, according to David Mayers and Clifford W. Smith (1987), creditors receive almost all of the benefit. Creditors of these firms can reduce the costs associated with underinvestment by taking control of the firm as soon as possible after the firm becomes insolvent. However, creditors may not gain control of a firm until it fails to make a promised debt payment. Short-term debt may hasten creditors' gaining control when a firm has adequate funds to pay interest but lacks the resources to pay interest on its debt and repay the principal.

According to Wall and John J. Pringle, the quality spread differential is not exploitable to the extent that it arises from differences in the expected costs of bankruptcy, shifts in risk from creditors to equityholders, or actual differences in contract terms. However, the quality spread differential can be exploited to the extent that it arises from agency costs. Moreover, arbitrage may eliminate differentials that arise from market inefficiencies, whereas one firm's swap does not reduce the potential agency cost savings to another firm. Thus, agency cost explanations could provide at least a partial explanation for the continuing growth of the swap market.

An important question facing the quality spread differential-based explanations is the extent to which the differential reflects exploitable factors. The authors note that the various explanations of the quality spread differential are not mutually exclusive. For example, if the differential is 70 basis points, then perhaps only 30 basis points may be exploitable.

One empirical study that has some bearing on the quality spread differential is by Robert E. Chatfield and R. Charles Moyer (1986). This study examines the risk premium on 90 long-term puttable bonds issued between July 24, 1974, and August 2, 1984, and a control sample of 174 nonputtable bonds. The put option on long-term, floating-rate debt gives creditors the option to force the firm to repay its debt if the firm becomes riskier.[10] The study finds that the put feature reduces the rate that the market requires on long-term debt by 89 basis points for the bonds in the sample. Chatfield and Moyer provide strong evidence that at least part of the quality spread differential does not arise due to inefficiencies in the markets for short- and long-term debt. However, the observed savings arising from the put feature may be attributable to some of the factors discussed earlier, including bankruptcy costs, risk shifting from creditors to equityholders, and agency costs. Thus, the Chatfield and Moyer results cannot be used to determine the magnitude of agency-cost savings available through interest rate swaps.

Other Explanations. Several explanations for the increased use of the interest rate swap market which do not depend on exploiting the quality spread differential are available. One is that swaps may be used to adjust the repricing interval (or maturity) of a firm's assets or liabilities in order to reduce interest rate risk. For example, a firm may start a period with an acceptable degree of exposure to changes in market interest rates. Subsequently, though, it desires a change in its exposure because of shifts in its product environment or in the volatility of interest rates. Swaps provide a low-cost method of making immediate changes in exposure to market interest rates. For example, suppose that a firm is initially fully hedged with respect to interest rate changes but that a subsequent change in its product markets increases its revenues' sensitivity to interest rates. This company may be able to offset the increased sensitivity by entering into a swap whereby it agrees to pay a floating rate of interest, which better matches revenues, and receives a fixed rate of interest to cover payments on its outstanding debt.[11]

Smith, Smithson, and Wakeman (1987a) suggest that swaps may allow firms greater flexibility in choosing the amount of their outstanding debt obligations. In particular, reducing debt levels may be a problem if swaps are not used. To reduce its outstanding long-term debt, a firm may need to pay a premium (that is, the call price may exceed the current market value of the debt). On the other hand, if it issues short-term debt without a swap, it may be exposed to adverse changes in market interest rates. However, by issuing a combination of

---

"Swaps provide a low-cost method of making immediate changes in exposure to market interest rates."

---

short-term debt and swaps, the firm avoids the need to pay a premium to retire debt and simultaneously eliminates its exposure to changes in market interest rates.

Marcelle Arak and others (1988) present a general model in which firms will choose the combination of short-term debt and interest rate swaps over short-term debt; long-term, fixed-rate debt; and long-term, variable-rate debt. The model suggests that the combination will be preferred if the firm expects higher risk-free interest rates than does the market, the firm is more risk-averse than the market with respect to changes in risk-free rates, the firm expects its own credit spread to be lower than that expected by the market, and the borrower is less risk-averse to changes in its credit spread than is the market. The researchers also note that not all four conditions need to be met at the same time.

Arak and her colleagues' model is very broad and could include the agency cost models as subsets. An additional implication of their model is that firms may use swaps to exploit information asymmetries. Suppose that a company desires fixed-rate financing to fund a project. It could issue long-term debt, but, if management thought that the company would soon receive a better credit rating, issuing long-term debt would force the firm to pay an excessive risk premium. By issuing short-term debt, the firm could obtain a lower cost of long-term funds in the future when its credit rating improved. However, this strategy would expose the firm to interest rate risk. By instead issuing a combination of short-term debt and interest rate swaps the firm's managers can exploit their information about the true credit risk of the firm

---

"One limitation of the nonarbitrage explanation of swaps is that they provide only one reason for floating-rate payers to enter into swaps, namely, the ability to change the maturity structure of the firm's assets and liabilities."

---

without exposing the organization to changes in market interest rates.[12] When the good news comes, the firm's floating rate payments to outside creditors falls while its payments under the swap remain the same, thus reducing the firm's total financing costs. One important limitation of this explanation is that it applies only to firms that expect improved credit ratings in the near future.

In yet another alternative to the quality spread differential explanation, Loeys points out that swaps may allow firms to exploit differences in regulation. He notes that Securities and Exchange Commission (SEC) registration requirements raise the cost of issuing bonds in the United States by approximately 80 basis points above the cost of issuing bonds in the Eurobond markets. However, not all firms have access to the Eurobond market. Thus, the costs of obtaining fixed-rate funding may be reduced

by having companies with access to the Eurobond market issue long-term debt and then enter into a swap with firms that lack access to but prefer fixed-rate funding. Smith, Smithson, and Wakeman, observing that a variety of regulations differ across countries in ways that can be exploited, refer to this explanation as tax and regulatory arbitrage.

A Review of the Explanations. The various explanations of interest rate swaps discussed above are not mutually exclusive, since different firms may use swaps for different reasons. One of the most popular explanations of interest rate swaps—that they allow arbitrage of the quality spread differential—is also the explanation with the weakest theoretical support. The other explanations are all theoretically plausible. Unfortunately, published empirical evidence on the reasons for using swaps is almost nonexistent. Linda T. Rudnick (1987) provides anecdotal evidence that reductions in financing costs are one of the primary reasons that firms enter into interest rate swaps. In research currently in progress, the authors of this article are examining the financial characteristics of firms that reported the use of swaps in the notes to their 1986 financial statements.

One limitation of the nonarbitrage explanations of swaps is that they provide only one reason for floating-rate payers to enter into swaps, namely, the ability to change the maturity structure of the firm's assets and liabilities. Moreover, this single explanation fails to provide a sound reason for a firm to issue long-term, fixed-rate debt and then enter into a swap agreement. If a company does issue long-term debt and then enters into a swap agreement as a floating-rate payer, either fixed-rate payers are sharing part of their gains with the floating-rate payer or floating-rate payers obtain some as yet undiscovered benefit from swaps.

Risks Associated with Swaps

Interest rate swap contracts are subject to several types of risk. Among the more important are interest rate, or position, risk and credit risk. Interest rate risk arises because changes in market interest rates cause a change in a swap's value. Credit risk occurs because either party may default on a swap contract. Both participants in a swap are subject to each type of risk.

Interest Rate Risk. As market interest rates change, interest rate swaps generate gains or losses that are equal to the change in the replacement cost of the swap. These gains and losses allow swaps to serve as a hedge which a company can use to reduce its risk or to serve as a speculative tool that increases the firm's total risk. A swap represents a hedge if gains or losses generated by the swap offset changes in the market values of a company's assets, liabilities, and off-balance sheet activities such as interest rate futures and options. However, a swap is speculative to the extent that the firm deliberately increases its risk position to profit from predicted changes in interest rates.

The determination of whether and how to use a swap is straightforward for a firm that is a user, one which enters into a swap agreement solely to adjust its own financial position.[13] First, the company evaluates its own exposure to future changes in interest rates, including any planned investments and new financings. Then, its views on the future levels and volatility of interest rates are ascertained. Firms wishing greater exposure to market rate changes enter into swaps as speculators. Alternatively, if less exposure is desired, the company enters into a swap as a hedge.

The problem facing a dealer—a firm that enters into a swap to earn fee income—is more complicated. A dealer may enter into a swap to hedge changes in market rates or to speculate in a manner similar to users. However, a dealer may also enter a swap to satisfy a customer's request even when the dealer wants no change in its interest rate exposure.[14] In this case, the dealer must find some way of hedging the swap transaction.

The simplest hedge for one swap transaction by a dealer is another swap transaction whose terms mirror the first swap. An example of this arrangement is given in Chart 2, in which the dealer's promised floating-rate payments of LIBOR to Widgets Unlimited is exactly offset by OneState's promise to pay LIBOR. Similarly, the fixed payments to OneState Insurance are covered by Widgets' promised fixed payments, and DomBank is left with a small spread. This combination of swaps is referred to as a *matched pair*. One problem with relying on matched

pairs to eliminate interest rate risk is that the dealer is exposed to interest rate changes during the time needed to find another party interested in a matching swap. Another problem is that the dealer may be relatively better at arranging swaps with fixed-rate payers and, thus, have problems finding floating-rate payers to execute the matching swap (or vice versa).

An alternative to hedging one swap with another swap is to rely on debt securities, or on futures or options on debt securities, to provide a hedge. Steven T. Felgran (1987) gives an example whereby a dealer agrees to pay a fixed rate and receive a floating rate from a customer. The dealer uses the floating-rate receipts to support a bank loan, which is then used to purchase a Treasury security of the same maturity and value as the swap. Any gains or losses on the swap are

---

"One problem with relying on matched pairs to eliminate interest rate risk is that the dealer is exposed to interest rate changes during the time needed to find another party interested in a matching swap."

---

subsequently offset by losses or gains on the Treasury security. Felgran does note one problem with using Treasury securities to hedge a swap: the spread between them and interest rate swaps may vary over time.[15] According to Felgran, dealers are unable to hedge floating-rate payments perfectly. Sources of risk include differences in payment dates and floating-rate reset days, disparities in maturity and principal, and "basis risk," that is, the risk associated with hedging floating payments based on one index with floating payments from another index.

Using the futures market to hedge swaps also entails certain drawbacks. Wakeman points to the "additional risk created by the cash/futures basis volatility." He also notes that matching the fixed-rate payments from a swap with the Treasury security of the closest maturity may not be optimal when the Treasury security is thinly traded. As an alternative he suggests that "on-the-run" (highly liquid) Treasury issues be used for hedging. The investment amount and type of issues to be used may be determined applying a duration matching strategy. Still, this approach is unlikely to eliminate interest rate risk for the swap dealer since duration matching provides a perfect hedge only under very restrictive assumptions.

Credit Risk. Aside from interest rate and basis risk, both interest rate swap participants are subject to the risk that the other party will default, causing credit losses. The maximum amount of the loss associated with this credit risk is measured by the swap's replacement cost, which is essentially the cost of entering into a new swap under current market conditions with rates equal to those on the swap being replaced.

"Aside from interest rate and basis risk, both interest rate swap participants are subject to the risk that the other party will default, causing credit losses."

A simple example can demonstrate the credit risk of swaps. Suppose that Widgets Unlimited agrees to pay a fixed rate of 9.5 percent to Dom-Bank, and in return Widgets will receive LIBOR on a semiannual basis through January 1994. If the market rate on new swaps maturing in January 1994 falls to 8 percent, the swap has positive value to DomBank—that is, DomBank would have to pay an up-front fee to entice a third party to enter into a swap whereby DomBank receives a fixed rate of 9.5 percent. DomBank will suffer a credit loss if Widgets becomes bankrupt while the rate is 8 percent and pays only a fraction of its obligations to creditors. On the other hand, if the rate on swaps maturing in January 1994 rises to 10.5 percent and DomBank defaults, Widgets may suffer a credit loss.

This example demonstrates that both of the parties to an interest rate swap may be subject to credit risk at some time during the life of a swap contract. However, only one party at a time may be subject to credit risk. If rates in the above example fall to 8 percent, DomBank can suffer credit losses, but Widgets is not exposed to credit risk. That is, the swap has negative value to Widgets when the market rate is 8 percent; Widgets would be happy to drop the swap agreement if DomBank were to go bankrupt. In practice, though, Widgets is unlikely to receive a windfall from DomBank's failure. The swap contracts may provide for Widgets to continue making payments to DomBank or, if the contract is canceled, provide for Widgets to pay DomBank the replacement cost of the swap.[16]

One way of reducing the credit risk associated with swaps is for the party to whom the swap has negative value to post collateral equal to the swap's replacement cost. Some swaps provide for collateral but most do not. According to Felgran, swap collateralization is of uncertain value because such documentation has yet to be adequately tested in court. Moreover, some parties that would be happy to receive collateral are themselves reluctant to post it when swap rates move against them. Certain commercial banks in particular have a strong incentive to avoid collateralization. Such institutions take credit risks in the ordinary course of business and are comfortable with assuming credit risk on interest rate swaps. Investment bankers, on the other hand, are typically at risk for only short periods of time with their nonswap transactions and are not as experienced in evaluating credit risk. Thus, the continued presence of credit risk in the swap market strengthens the relative competitive position of commercial banks.

Several simulation studies have explored the magnitude of the credit risk associated with individual swaps or matched pairs of swaps. Arak, Laurie S. Goodman, and Arthur Rones (1986) examine the credit exposure—or maximum credit loss—of a single interest rate swap to determine the amount of a firm's credit line that is used by a swap.[17] They assume that short-term rates follow a random walk with no drift; in other words, the change in short-term rates does not depend on the current level of or on past changes in short-term rates. After the swap begins, the floating-rate component of the swap is assumed to move one standard deviation each year in the direction of maximum credit exposure. The standard deviation of interest rates is calculated using 1985 data on Treasury issues. Their results suggest that until the swap matures, maximum annual credit loss on swaps is likely to be between 1 and 2 percent of notional principal.

J. Gregg Whittaker (1987b) investigates the credit exposure of interest rate swaps in order to develop a formula for swap pricing. Using an options pricing formula to value swaps and assuming that interest rates follow a log-normal distribution and volatility amounts to one standard deviation, Whittaker finds that the maximum exposure for a 10-year matched pair of swaps does not exceed 8 percent of the notional principal.

The Federal Reserve Board and the Bank of England studied the potential increase in credit exposure of a matched pair of swaps.[18] The study's purpose is to develop a measure of the credit exposure associated with a matched pair of swaps that is comparable to the credit exposure of on-balance sheet loans. The results are used to determine regulatory capital requirements for interest rate swaps. The joint central bank research assumes that for regulatory purposes the swaps' credit exposure should be equal to its current exposure, that is, the replacement cost plus some surcharge to capture potential increases in credit exposure. The investigation uses a Monte Carlo simulation technique to evaluate the probabilities associated with different potential increases in credit exposure.[19] Interest rates are assumed to follow a log-normal, random-walk distribution with the volatility measure equal to the 90th percentile value of changes in interest rates over six-month intervals from 1981 to mid-1986. The credit exposure of each matched pair is calculated every six months and the resulting exposures are averaged over the life of the swap. The study concludes with 70 percent confidence that the average potential increase in credit exposure will be no greater than 0.5 percent of the notional principal of the swap per complete year; at the 95 percent confidence level it finds the average credit risk exposure to be no greater than 1 percent of the notional principal.

Terrence M. Belton (1987) follows this line of research in analyzing the potential increase in swap credit exposure, but he uses a different method of simulating interest rates. Belton estimates a vector autoregressive model over the period from January 1970 to November 1986 to estimate seven different Treasury rates. (Vector autoregressive models estimate current values of some dependent variables, in this case interest rates at various maturities, as a function of current and past values of selected variables. Belton uses current and past interest rates as explanatory variables.) Changes in the term structure are then simulated by drawing a set of random errors from the joint distribution of rates and solving for future values at each maturity. In effect, Belton's procedure allows the historical shape in the yield curve and historical changes in its level and shape to determine the value of various interest rates in his simulations. Belton's analysis differs from prior studies in that he uses stochastic, or random,

"[S]everal ways of estimating the increased credit exposure associated with matched pairs of swaps . . . might not be applicable to swap portfolios."

default rates rather than focusing exclusively on maximum credit exposure. His results imply that the potential increase in credit exposure of swaps caused by rate changes can be covered by adding a surcharge of 1 percent to 5 percent of the notional principal to the current exposure for swaps with a maturity of 2 to 12 years.

While the foregoing analyses suggest several ways of estimating the increased credit exposure associated with matched pairs of swaps, these approaches might not be applicable to swap portfolios. Starting with the assumption that dealers use matched pairs of swaps and that the swaps are entered into at market interest rates, Wall and Kwun-Wing C. Fung (1987) note that the fixed rate on the matched pairs will change over time as interest rates move up and down. Wall and Fung point out that if rates have fluctuated over a certain range, a bank may have credit exposure on some swaps in which it pays a fixed rate and on others in which it pays a floating rate. In this case, an increase in rates generates an increase in the credit exposure of swaps in which the dealer pays a fixed rate but also causes a decrease in the exposure of swaps in which the dealer pays a floating rate. Similarly, a decrease in rates will increase the exposure on the swaps in which the dealer pays a floating rate and decrease exposure on those in which the dealer pays a fixed rate.[20]

In a more empirical vein, Kathleen Neal and Katerina Simons (1988) simulate the total credit exposure of a portfolio of 20 matched pairs of interest rate swaps. The initial portfolio is generated by originating one pair of five-year swaps per quarter from the fourth quarter of 1981 through the fourth quarter of 1986 at the prevailing interest rate. For the period 1987

"[T]he maximum exposure on a matched pair of swaps is unlikely to exceed a small fraction of the swap's notional principal."

---

through 1991, the interest rates are generated randomly based on the volatility observed in historical rates.[21] The maturing matched pair is dropped each quarter from the sample and a new five-year swap is added to the portfolio at the simulated interest rates. After running "several thousand" simulations and assuming a portfolio of interest rate swaps with a notional principal of $10 million, Neal and Simons find the average maximum credit loss to be $185,000 and the 90th percentile exposure, $289,000.

No single correct approach is available to determine the expected credit exposure on an interest rate swap. The results may be influenced by the assumptions that are made about the distribution of future interest rates. However, several studies using different methodologies have reached the conclusion that the maximum exposure on a matched pair of swaps is unlikely to exceed a small fraction of the

swap's notional principal. Moreover, the analysis of a single matched pair may overstate the expected exposure of a swap portfolio. Therefore, additional simulations of portfolio analysis risk may be appropriate to determine the risk exposure of swap dealers. Dominique Jackson (1988) reports that a survey of 71 dealers showed that 11 firms had experienced losses with "total write-offs accounting for $33 million on portfolios which totaled a notional (principal) of $283 billion."

How Should Swaps Be Priced?

In addition to considering the reasons for engaging in swaps and the attendant risks, the literature on interest rate swaps addresses two important pricing questions: (1) how should the overall value of a swap be established, and (2) what spread between higher-rated and lower-rated firms is appropriate to cover swap credit risk? James Bicksler and Andrew H. Chen (1986) provide an analysis of a swap's overall value. They suggest that an interest rate swap be treated as an exchange of a fixed-rate bond for a floating-rate bond. According to this approach, the fixed-rate payer has in effect sold a fixed-rate bond and purchased a floating-rate bond. Bicksler and Chen suggest that pricing an interest rate swap is essentially the same as pricing a floating-rate bond.

Insight into the appropriate spreads between high- and lower-rated firms can be obtained by comparing the quality spreads on bonds versus those on swaps. Patrick de Saint-Aignan, the chairman of the International Swap Dealers Association and a managing director at Morgan Stanley, remarks that, "There's a credit spread of 150 basis points in the loan market but of only 5 to 10 basis points in swaps."[22] However, Smith, Smithson, and Wakeman (1987a) note that the risk exposure, as a proportion of notional principal for swaps, is far less than the exposure on loans. Lenders have credit exposure for all principal and interest payments promised on the loan, whereas a swap participant's credit exposure is limited to the difference between two interest rates. Thus, the credit risk borne by swap dealers is a far smaller proportion of the (notional) principal than that assumed by lenders.

Belton also addresses the question of appropriate spreads to compensate for swaps' credit risk by considering the default premium required to compensate one party for the expected value of the default losses from the other. For low-risk firms—companies with a 0.5 percent probability of default in one year and zero payment on default—the required premium is 0.70 basis points for a two-year swap and 3.02 basis points for a ten-year swap. For below-investment-grade firms—with a 2 percent probability of default per year and zero payment on default—the required premium ranges from 2.83 basis points for a two-year swap to 14.24 basis points for a ten-year swap. The differences in default premium of 2 to 14 basis points found by Belton for swaps is approximately in the 5 to 10 basis point range of the credit spread charged in swaps markets.

Whittaker (1987b) applies his options pricing method for calculating swaps' credit risk to the issue of swap pricing. He views a swap as a set of options to buy and sell a fixed-rate bond and a floating-rate bond. In his model default by the fixed-rate payer is analogous to a decision to exercise jointly a call option to purchase the fixed-rate bond and a put option to sell a floating-rate security. From this perspective, the decision to exercise one option is not independent of the decision to exercise another. Thus, one option may be exercised even though it is unprofitable to do so, provided that it is sufficiently profitable to exercise the other option. He then estimates the value of these options and suggests that "the market does not adequately take account of the exposure and pricing differentials across varying maturities." However, Whittaker claims that his results may not necessarily imply that the market is on average underpricing swap credit risk.

One limitation of the above studies is that they fail to combine into an integrated framework the distribution of interest rates and the credit risk associated with swaps. A conceptually superior approach to interest rate swap valuation begins by separating the payments. The result looks like a series of forward contracts in which the floating-rate payer agrees to buy a zero-coupon Treasury security from the fixed-rate payer. This forward contract may then be decomposed into two options, one in which the floating-rate payer buys a call from the fixed-

rate payer on the zero-coupon Treasury security and one in which the floating-rate payer sells a put on the security to the fixed-rate payer.

Unfortunately, the options derived from this analysis cannot be valued using standard options pricing formulas because both options are subject to credit risk. Herb Johnson and René Stulz (1987) analyze the problem of pricing a single option subject to default risk. However, swaps are a series of linked options whose payments in one period are contingent on the terms of the swap contract being fulfilled in prior periods. Thus, as Smith, Smithson, and Wakeman (1987b) suggest, to derive an optimal default strategy for swaps requires analysis of compound option issues similar to those discussed by Robert Geske (1977) for corporate coupon bonds.

"[T]he interest rate swap market is subject to remarkably little regulation and does not have a central exchange or even a central clearing mechanism."

The theoretical and pedagogical advantages of splitting a swap into a series of default-risky options are that the decomposition clearly illustrates the primary determinants of swap value: the distribution of the price of default-risk free bonds (interest rates), the possibility of default by either participant, and the linked nature of the options through time. The practical problem with the decomposition is that developing a pricing formula is not straightforward.

Requirements Imposed on Swaps

Regulation. In contrast to most other financial markets in the United States, the interest rate swap market is subject to remarkably little regulation and does not have a central exchange or even a central clearing mechanism. The terms of a swap agreement are determined by the parties to the contract and need not be disclosed. Nor does the existence of a swap need to be disclosed at the time the agreement is executed. (The financial statements' disclosure requirements for individual firms are discussed later in this article.) While certain regulators have a general responsibility for the financial soundness of some participants in the swap market, no public or private organization has overall responsibility for its regulation.

In general, this lack of regulation has not resulted in any major problems. Legislatures could make one potentially valuable contribution, though, by providing specific statutory language on the treatment of swap contracts when one party defaults. Market participants are currently waiting for the courts to determine

---

"Like regulatory requirements, accounting standards for swaps are minimal at best, owing largely to their rapid development."

---

if default procedures will follow the language of the swap contract or if the courts will impose some other settlement procedure. For example, many swaps are arranged under a master contract between two parties that provides for the netting of payments across swaps. This clause is desirable because it reduces the credit risk borne by both parties. However, the risk exists that a bankruptcy court will ignore this clause and treat each swap separately.

Even though the swap market is not subject to regulation, individual participants are. In particular, federal banking regulators in the United States are including interest rate swaps in the recently adopted risk-based capital standards. These standards are designed to preserve and enhance the safety and soundness of commercial banks by requiring them to maintain capital commensurate with the levels of credit risk they incur.[23]

Banks' capital standards first translate credit exposure on swaps into an amount comparable to on-balance sheet loans. The loan equivalent amount for swaps is equal to the replacement cost of the swap plus 0.5 percent of the notional principal. This loan equivalent amount is then multiplied by 50 percent to determine a risk-adjusted asset equivalent. Banks are required to maintain tier-one (or core) capital equal to 4 percent of risk-adjusted assets and total capital equal to 8 percent by 1992.[24]

The central banks of 12 major industrial powers have agreed to apply similar risk-based capital requirements to their countries' financial firms.[25] However, these standards do not apply to U.S. investment banks or insurance companies. Thus, capital requirements are not being applied to all swap dealers. Some market participants are concerned that the standards will place dealers that are subject to capital regulation at a competitive disadvantage.[26]

Accounting. Like regulatory requirements, accounting standards for swaps are minimal at best, owing largely to their rapid development. Existing accounting standards provide a general requirement that a firm disclose all material matters but do not require a company to disclose its participation in the interest rate swap market. Different firms appear to be following many of the same rules in accounting for the gains and losses under swap contracts, but some important discrepancies exist in practice.

Keith Wishon and Lorin S. Chevalier (1985) note that swap market participants generally do not recognize the existence of swaps on their balance sheets, a practice which is consistent with the treatment of futures agreements. However, they aver that the notes to the firm's financial statements should disclose the existence of material swap agreements and discuss the swap's impact on the repricing interval of the firm's debt obligations. Harold Bierman, Jr. (1987) recommends that firms also disclose the transaction's effects on their risk position.

Another issue at the inception of some swap contracts is accounting for up-front payments. Wishon and Chevalier believe that any up-front payments that reflect yield adjustments should be deferred and amortized over the life of the swap. While acknowledging that payers appear to be following this policy, the researchers note that some recipients have taken the position that all up-front fees are arrangement fees and may be immediately recognized in income. Bierman argues that yield-adjusting fees cannot be distinguished from others. Thus, all fees should be treated in the same manner. He further maintains that the most appropriate treatment is to defer recognition and amortize the payments over the life of the contract.

According to Wishon and Chevalier, regular payments and receipts under a swap agreement are frequently recorded as an adjustment to interest income when the swap is related to a particular debt issue. Though the receipts and payments are technically not interest, this approach is informative, especially if footnote disclosure is adequate. They report, nonetheless, that changes in the market value of the swap are generally not recognized in the income statement if gains and losses are not recognized on the security hedged by the swap. This treatment parallels that of futures, which meets the hedge criteria in the Financial Accounting Standards Board's Statement Number 80, "Accounting for Futures Contracts."

Another issue arising during the life of an interest rate swap is the presentation of the credit risk. For a nondealer, credit risk may not be material and, therefore, need not be reported. However, Wishon and Chevalier argue that the credit risk taken by a dealer is likely to be material and should be disclosed.

Some firms may enter into swaps as a speculative investment. Wishon and Chevalier contend that speculative swaps should be accounted for in the same manner as other speculative investments. Among the alternatives they discuss are using either the lower of cost or market method of valuation, with writedowns only for losses that are not "temporary," and the lower of cost or market in all cases. Both approaches are flawed. The treatment of some swap losses as "temporary" is inappropriate because objective and verifiable predictions of changes in interest rates are impossible.[27] Yet using the lower-of-cost-or-market method of valuation in all cases will always result in a swap's being valued at its historical low, an excessively conservative position. Probably the best approach is to report the swap's replacement cost and to recognize any gains or losses in the current period.

Bierman suggests that, when a speculative swap is terminated prior to maturity, the gain or loss should be recognized immediately. However, no consensus exists on the treatment if the swap is a hedge. Wishon and Chevalier report widespread disagreement on the appropriate treatment of a swap's termination. One common approach would defer and amortize any gains or losses on the swap over the life of the underlying financial instrument. The other calls for immediate recognition of any gains or losses. The treatment of gains or losses on futures hedges suggests that the deferral and amortization of early swaps termination is appropriate.

Eugene E. Comiskey, Charles W. Mulford, and Deborah H. Turner (1987-88), surveying the financial statements of the 100 largest domestic banks in 1986, discovered that some banks are deferring gains or losses in accordance with hedge accounting treatment even though hedge accounting would not be permitted in similar circumstances for futures.[28] They also found that five banks disclosed their maximum potential credit loss in the extremely unlikely event that every counterparty defaulted on all swaps that were favorable to the bank.

The Financial Accounting Standards Board issued an Exposure Draft of a proposed Statement of Financial Accounting Standards titled "Disclosures about Financial Instruments." The statement proposes disclosing a variety of new information about financial instruments, including the maximum credit risk; the reasonably possible credit loss; probable credit loss; the amount subject to repricing within one year, one to five years, and over five years; and the market value of each class of financial instrument. This statement specifically includes interest rate swaps in its definition of financial instruments. If, when, and in what form this proposal will be adopted is unclear.

Commercial banks in the United States are currently required to disclose the notional principal on their outstanding interest rate swap portfolio to the federal bank regulators.[29] It would seem that regulators should also consider requiring disclosure of the replacement cost of outstanding swaps given that replacement cost is an element of the risk-based capital standards.

Conclusion

This article surveys the literature and some research in progress on interest rate swaps. The extremely rapid growth of the market has left academics trying to explain the existence of the market and the pricing of these instruments, regulators attempting to determine what risks these instruments pose to financial firms, and accountants endeavoring to determine how institutions should report their use of swaps. Evidence is beginning to accumulate to dispel some of the early misconceptions about this market, but far more analysis remains before interest rate swaps can be fully understood.

[1]See Abken (1988) for a review of the studies of the stock market crash.

[2]The size of the interest rate swap market is typically stated in terms of the notional principal of the outstanding swaps. See the explanation of interest rate swap transactions for a discussion of the role of the notional principal. Refer to Jackson (1988) for a discussion of the size of the interest rate and currency swap markets.

[3]See Celarier (1987): 17. This estimating appears to encompass the effect of both interest rate swaps and a related instrument called a currency swap. A *currency swap* is an arrangement between two organizations to exchange principal and interest payments in two different currencies at prearranged exchange rates. For example, one corporation agrees to pay a fixed amount of dollars in return for receiving a fixed number of Japanese yen from another corporation. This article focuses on interest rate swaps, and hereafter the term *swaps* will be used as a synonym for interest rate swaps. Beckstrom (1986) offers a discussion of different types of swaps.

[4]Both fixed-rate interest payment to floating-rate payment swaps and floating-rate to floating-rate swaps whereby, for example, one party pays the London Interbank Offered Rate (LIBOR) while the other party pays the commercial paper rate, are observed in the market.

[5]LIBOR is the most common floating rate in interest rate swap agreements, according to Hammond (1987).

[6]However, the call option is not a free gift provided by the bond market to corporations. Corporations pay for this call option by paying a higher rate of interest on their bonds.

[7]See Bicksler and Chen (1986) as well as Whittaker (1987a) and Hammond (1987) for further discussion.

[8]See Myers (1977); Bodie and Taggart (1978); and Barnea, Haugen, and Senbet (1980).

[9]Long-term, callable debt may also reduce the agency problems of underinvestment and risk shifting problems. However, Barnea, Haugen, and Senbet point out that callable debt does not eliminate the underinvestment problem. Wall (forthcoming) suggests that callable bonds may not solve the risk shifting problem in all cases and also notes that short-term debt will solve both problems if it matures shortly after the firm makes its investment decision.

[10]Investors may also have an incentive to exercise the put option on fixed-rate bonds when interest rates increase. An easy way to control for this feature is to focus exclusively on floating-rate bonds. However, Chatfield and Moyers' study contained fixed-rate, puttable bonds. Their research controlled for the interest rate feature of the put option on these bonds by including a variable for the number of times per year the coupon rate on a bond adjusts and a measure of interest rate uncertainty.

[11]Bennett, Cohen, and McNulty (1984) discuss the use of swaps for controlling interest rate exposure by savings institutions.

[12]Robbins and Schatzberg (1986) suggest that callable bonds are superior to short-term debt in that they permit firms to signal their lower risk and to reduce the risk borne by equityholders. However, their results depend on a specific example. Wall (1988) demonstrates that the call-

able bonds may fail to provide a separating equilibrium if seemingly small changes are made to their example.

[13]This analysis does not consider the use of the futures, forward, and options markets. See Smithson (1987) for a discussion of the various financial instruments that may be used to control interest rate risk.

[14]The dealer may enter into a swap for a customer even though the dealer desires a change in exposure in a direction opposite to the swap.

[15]Indeed, some variation in the spread should be expected since the Treasury yield curve incorporates coupon interest payments and principal repayments at the maturity of the swap whereas the swap contract provides only for periodic interest payments.

[16]Widgets would probably prefer to cancel the contract and enter into a new swap contract with a different party. Otherwise, market rates could increase above 9.5 percent and then DomBank might be unable to make the promised payments. See Henderson and Cates (1986) for a discussion of terminating a swap under the insolvency laws of the United States and the United Kingdom.

[17]One way that banks typically limit their risk to individual borrowers is to establish a maximum amount that the organization is willing to lend to the borrower, called the borrower's credit line. The amount of a credit line used by a loan is the principal of the loan; however, the amount of the line used by a swap is less clear since a swap's maximum credit loss is a function of market interest rates.

[18]See also Muffet (1987).

[19]The Monte Carlo technique involves repeated simulations wherein a key value, in this case an interest rate, is drawn from a random sample.

[20]Consider two matched pairs of swaps. For the first matched pair the bank agrees to two swaps: 1) the bank pays a fixed rate of 11 percent and receives LIBOR on the first swap, and 2) the bank pays LIBOR and receives 11 percent. For the second matched pair the bank pays and receives a 9 percent fixed rate for LIBOR. Assume that the notional principal, maturity, and repricing interval of all swaps are equal. If the current market rate for swaps of the same maturity is 10 percent, the bank has credit exposure on the 9 percent fixed-rate swap in which it pays a fixed rate of interest and has credit exposure on the 11 percent fixed-rate swap in which it pays a floating rate of interest. If the market rate on comparable swaps increases to 10.5 percent, credit exposure increases on the 9 percent swap in which the dealer pays a fixed rate and decreases on the 11 percent swap in which the dealer pays a floating rate. Given the assumptions of this example, the change in exposure is almost zero when the market rate moves from 10 percent to 10.5 percent.

[21]The paper does not explain how swap replacement values and interest rate volatility were calculated.

[22]David Shirreff (1985): 253.

[23]The standards do not include any framework for evaluating the overall interest rate risk being taken by banking organizations.

[24]The standards effective in 1992 define core (tier-one) capital as common stockholders equity, minority interest in the common stockholders' equity accounts of con-

solidated subsidiaries, and perpetual, noncumulative preferred stock. (The Federal Reserve will also allow bank holding companies to count perpetual, cumulative preferred stock.) Total capital consists of core capital plus supplementary (tier-two) capital. Supplementary capital includes the allowance for loan and lease losses; perpetual, cumulative preferred stock; long-term preferred stock, hybrid capital instruments including perpetual debt, and mandatory convertible securities; and subordinated debt and intermediate-term preferred stock.

[25] The framework for risk-based capital standards has been approved by the Group of Ten countries (Belgium, Canada, France, the Federal Republic of Germany, Italy, Japan, the Netherlands, Sweden, the United Kingdom, and the United States) together with Switzerland and Luxembourg.

[26] Pitman (1988) discusses the capital standards' implications for various swap market participants.

[27] If the predicted changes in interest rates were subject to objective verification, that would suggest that arbitrage opportunities exist. That is, investors may be able to earn a profit with no net investment (financing the purchase of one debt security with the sale of another) and without assuming any risk (since objective verification proved that interest rates will move in the predicted direction). However, efficient markets theory implies that the market will immediately compete away any arbitrage opportunities.

[28] Deferral of gains or losses on futures is permitted only if the future is designated as a hedge for an "existing asset, liability, firm commitment or anticipated transactions," according to Comiskey, Mulford, and Turner, 4, 9.

[29] See Felgran (1987) for a listing of the top 25 U.S. banks by notional principal of swaps outstanding.

References

Abken, Peter A. "Stock Market Activity in October 1987: The Brady, CFTC, and SEC Reports." Federal Reserve Bank of Atlanta Economic Review 73 (May/June 1988): 36-43.

Arak, Marcelle, Arturo Estrella, Laurie Goodman, and Andrew Silver. "Interest Rate Swaps: An Alternative Explanation." Financial Management 17 (Summer 1988): 12-18.

Arak, Marcelle, Laurie S. Goodman, and Arthur Rones. "Credit Lines for New Instruments: Swaps, Over-the-Counter Options, Forwards and Floor-Ceiling Agreements." Federal Reserve Bank of Chicago, Conference on Bank Structure and Competition, 1986, 437-56.

Barnea, Amir, Robert A. Haugen, and Lemma W. Senbet. "A Rationale for Debt Maturity Structure and Call Provisions in the Agency Theoretic Framework." Journal of Finance 35 (December 1980): 1223-34.

Beckstrom, Rod. "The Development of the Swap Market." In Swap Finance, vol. 1, edited by Boris Antl, 31-51. London: Euromoney Publications Limited, 1986.

Belton, Terrence M. "Credit-Risk in Interest Rate Swaps." Board of Governors of the Federal Reserve System unpublished working paper, April 1987.

Bennett, Dennis E., Deborah L. Cohen, and James E. McNulty. "Interest Rate Swaps and the Management of Interest Rate Risk." Paper presented at the Financial Management Association meetings, Toronto, October 1984.

Bicksler, James, and Andrew H. Chen. "An Economic Analysis of Interest Rate Swaps." Journal of Finance 41 (July 1986): 645-55.

Bierman, Harold, Jr. "Accounting for Interest Rate Swaps." Journal of Accounting, Auditing, and Finance 2 (Fall 1987): 396-408.

Black, Fischer, and Myron Scholes. "The Pricing of Options and Corporate Liabilities." Journal of Political Economy 81 (1973): 637-59.

Bodie, Zvi, and Robert A. Taggart. "Future Investment Opportunities and the Value of the Call Provision on a Bond." Journal of Finance 33 (September 1978): 1187-1200.

Celarier, Michelle. "Swaps' Judgement Day." United States Banker (July 1987): 16-20.

Chatfield, Robert E., and R. Charles Moyer. " 'Putting' Away Bond Risk: An Empirical Examination of the Value of the Put Option on Bonds." Financial Management 15 (Summer 1986): 26-33.

Comiskey, Eugene E., Charles W. Mulford, and Deborah H. Turner. "Bank Accounting and Reporting Practices for Interest Rate Swaps." Bank Accounting and Finance 1 (Winter 1987-88): 3-14.

Federal Reserve Board and Bank of England. "Potential Exposure on Interest Rate and Exchange Rate Related Instruments." Unpublished staff paper, 1987.

Felgran, Steven D. "Interest Rate Swaps: Use, Risk and Prices." New England Economic Review (November/December 1987): 22-32.

Geske, Robert. "The Valuation of Corporate Liabilities as Compound Options." Journal of Financial and Quantitative Analysis 12 (1977): 541-52.

Hammond, G.M.S. "Recent Developments in the Swap Market." Bank of England Quarterly Review 27 (February 1987): 66-79.

Henderson, Schuyler K., and Armel C. Cates. "Termination Provisions of Swap Agreements under U.S. and English Insolvency Laws." In Swap Finance, vol. 2, edited by Boris Antl, 91-102. London: Euromoney Publications Limited, 1986.

Jackson, Dominique. "Swaps Keep in Step with the Regulators." Financial Times, August 10, 1988, 22.

Johnson, Herb, and René Stulz. "The Pricing of Options with Default Risk." Journal of Finance 42 (June 1987): 267-80.

Loeys, Jan G. "Interest Rate Swaps: A New Tool For Managing Risk." Federal Reserve Bank of Philadelphia Business Review (May/June 1985): 17-25.

Mayers, David, and Clifford W. Smith. "Corporate Insurance

and the Underinvestment Problem." *Journal of Risk and Insurance* 54 (March 1987): 45-54.

Muffet, Mark. "Modeling Credit Exposure on Swaps." Federal Reserve Bank of Chicago, *Conference on Bank Structure and Competition,* 1987, 473-96.

Myers, Stewart C. "Determinants of Corporate Borrowing." *Journal of Financial Economics* 5 (November 1977): 147-76.

Neal, Kathleen, and Katerina Simons. "Interest Rate Swaps, Currency Swaps, and Credit Risk." *Issues in Bank Regulation* (Spring 1988): 26-29.

Pitman, Joanna. "Swooping on Swaps." *Euromoney* (January 1988): 68-80.

Robbins, Edward Henry, and John D. Schatzberg. "Callable Bonds: A Risk Reducing, Signalling Mechanism." *Journal of Finance* 41 (September 1986): 935-49.

Rudnick, Linda T. "Discussion of Practical Aspects of Interest Rate Swaps." Federal Reserve Bank of Chicago, *Conference on Bank Structure and Competition,* 1987, 206-13.

Shirreff, David. "The Fearsome Growth of Swaps." *Euromoney* (October 1985): 247-61.

Smith, Clifford W., Charles W. Smithson, and Lee Macdonald Wakeman. "The Evolving Market for Swaps." *Midland Corporate Finance Journal* 3 (1986): 20-32.

_____ , _____ , and _____ . "The Market for Interest Rate Swaps." University of Rochester Working Paper Series No. MERC 87-02 (May 1987a).

_____ , _____ , and _____ . "Credit Risk and the Scope of Regulation of Swaps." Federal Reserve Bank of Chicago, *Conference on Bank Structure and Competition,* 1987b, 166-85.

Smithson, Charles W. "A LEGO® Approach to Financial Engineering: An Introduction to Forwards, Futures, Swaps, and Options." *Midland Corporate Finance Review* 4 (Winter 1987): 16-28.

Stulz, René M., and Herb Johnson. "An Analysis of Secured Debt." *Journal of Financial Economics* 14 (December 1985): 501-21.

Turnbull, Stuart M. "Swaps: A Zero Sum Game?" *Financial Management* 16 (Spring 1987): 15-21.

Wakeman, Lee Macdonald. "The Portfolio Approach To Swaps Management." Chemical Bank Capital Markets Group unpublished working paper, May 1986.

Wall, Larry D. "Interest Rate Swaps in an Agency Theoretic Model with Uncertain Interest Rates." *Journal of Banking and Finance* (forthcoming).

_____ . "Alternative Financing Strategies: Notes Versus Callable Bonds." *Journal of Finance* 43 (September 1988): 1057-65.

_____ , and Kwun-Wing C. Fung. "Evaluating the Credit Exposure of Interest Rate Swap Portfolios." Federal Reserve Bank of Atlanta Working Paper 87-8 (December 1987).

_____ , and John J. Pringle. "Alternative Explanations of Interest Rate Swaps." Federal Reserve Bank of Chicago, *Conference on Bank Structure and Competition,* 1987, 186-205.

Weiner, Lisabeth. "Dollar Dominates Swaps, Survey Shows: Deals in U.S. Currency Outstrip Yen, Deutsche Mark by Far." *American Banker,* February 26, 1988, 2.

Whittaker, J. Gregg. "Interest Rate Swaps: Risk and Regulation." Federal Reserve Bank of Kansas City *Economic Review* (March 1987a): 3-13.

_____ . "Pricing Interest Rate Swaps in an Options Pricing Framework." Federal Reserve Bank of Kansas City unpublished working paper RWP 87-02. Presented to the Financial Management Association Meetings, Las Vegas, October 1987b.

Wishon, Keith, and Lorin S. Chevalier. "Interest Rate Swaps— Your Rate or Mine?" *Journal of Accountancy* (September 1985): 63-84.

Article 20

The Pricing
of Swaps

8.1 OVERVIEW

In this chapter, we consider how swap banks price swaps. (We assume that the swap bank is acting as a dealer in swaps and hence as a counterparty to the swap rather than as a swap broker.) The pricing of the swap is important for both the swap bank and the corporate user. The corporate user might want to compare the pricing of swaps offered by several swap banks and compare the all-in cost of these swap alternatives to the all-in cost of other financing and/or other risk-management opportunities available to it.

The bank's pricing will hinge on a number of things. These include:

1. the maturity of the swap;
2. the structure of the swap;
3. the availability of other counterparties with whom the bank can offset the swap;
4. the creditworthiness of the client counterparty;
5. the demand and supply conditions for credit generally and for swaps in particular in all countries whose currencies are involved in the swap; and
6. any regulatory constraints on the flow of capital that influence the efficiency of the markets.

The market for swaps consists of short-dated swaps—those under two years—and long-dated swaps—those over two years. The market for short-dated swaps is largely an interbank market and of little interest to corporate end users. To the degree that corporate end users have a need for short-term hedges, they can usually construct very efficient hedges by using interest-rate and exchange-rate futures and/or FRAs. In addition, since short-dated swaps can easily be replicated from FRAs and Eurodollar futures, it is not surprising that short-dated swaps are usually priced off a futures strip. A **futures strip**, the reader will recall, is a sequence of futures contracts. The most important group of futures for pricing short-dated swaps are the Eurodollar futures that are traded on the International Monetary Market (IMM). Short-dated swaps priced off IMM Eurodollar futures contract and that use IMM settlement dates are called **IMM swaps**. The logic of pricing short-dated swaps off the IMM strip parallels the pricing of FRAs as it was discussed in Chapter 5 and we do not take it up again. Instead, this chapter concentrates on long-dated swaps.

The pricing of interest-rate swaps is the chapter's first topic and starts with the plain vanilla fixed-for-floating rate swap based on bullet transactions. The analysis then progresses slightly by introducing amortization and payment frequency considerations. The examples assume that the swap bank offsets its swaps in the U.S. Treasury and/or Eurodollar markets until such time as it can offset the swaps with other counterparties. After completing a look at the pricing of interest-rate swaps, the pricing of currency swaps is discussed. The plain vanilla currency swap, which is called an exchange of borrowings, is examined first and is followed by **amortizing currency swaps** and pricing complications introduced by off-market transactions. Finally, the pricing of fixed-for-fixed rate currency swaps created through a combination of a fixed-for-floating interest rate swap and a fixed-for-floating exchange of borrowings (currency swap) is considered.

It is important to understand that in the discussion of swap pricing that follows, bid-ask spreads that range to 25 basis points are employed. Swap spreads of this magnitude were typical in swap bank pricing in the mid 1980s, but have narrowed considerably during the last few years. Spreads of 10 basis points or less are more realistic today. In any case, the actual size of the spread used in our examples is not very important to understanding the principles involved.

For the corporate reader interested in discussing a swap with a swap bank, we have included the membership list of the International Swap Dealers Association as an appendix to this chapter. This is the most complete list currently available of firms actively involved in making markets in swaps. For each swap bank, we have included the firm's name and address. We have deliberately left out phone numbers and contact points because these change from time to time.

8.2 INDICATION PRICING SCHEDULES: THE INTEREST-RATE SWAP

Swap banks regularly prepare indication pricing schedules for use by their capital market personnel. These schedules provide swap dealers with guidelines for pricing swaps and they are updated frequently to take account of changing market conditions. Prices take the form of interest rates and are stated in terms of basis points (bps). Each basis point is one-one hundredth of one percent. In the case of dollar-based interest rates, the fixed-rate side of the swap is usually stated as a spread over prevailing yields on on the run U.S. Treasury securities. On the runs are the securities of a given maturity that were most recently auctioned. For example, five years ago the Treasury auctioned 10-year notes. With the passage of time, these 10-year notes have become five-year notes. If the Treasury was now to auction a new issue of five-year notes, then there would be at least two five-year T-note issues simultaneously trading. The most recent issues (the on the runs) have the more current coupon and tend to be more liquid then the older issues. The floating-rate side is most often taken to be LIBOR flat. The pricing structure assumes bullet transactions. That is, as with Treasury securities, it is assumed that the principal is repaid in a lump sum at maturity.

A minor complication introduced by this pricing scheme is that the interest rate on the fixed-rate side of a swap is quoted as a semiannual **bond equivalent yield**. Bond equivalent yields are based on a 365-day year. The floating-rate side is usually tied to LIBOR. LIBOR is quoted as an annual money market yield. Money market yields are based on a 360-day year. This difference in yield conventions often necessitates some conversions to make the rates more directly comparable. This issue will be addressed shortly.

In the early days of swaps, it was quite common for the swap bank to require a front-end fee for arranging the swap. The front-end fee was negotiable and could run as much as one-half of a percentage point. The justification for the front-end fee was the time it took to write the swap documentation and the time it took to work with the client to design a swap that would accomplish the client's objectives. With the increasing standardization of swaps, front-end fees have all but disappeared. Today, a front-end fee will only be imposed when some fancy financial engineering is required or when the client is purchasing a special option-like feature. Front-end fees have never been common on interbank swaps.[1]

Consider a typical indication pricing schedule for swaps with various maturities as depicted in Table 8.1. The prices indicated are for fixed-for-floating interest-rate swaps and assume semiannual compounding (sa). Although we always state interest rates on an annual basis, it is customary to call an annual rate of interest compounded semiannually a semiannual rate. For example, the phrase "a semiannual rate of 8 percent" means an annual interest rate of 8 percent that is compounded semiannually. The phrase "an annual rate of 8 percent" means an annual interest rate of 8 percent that is compounded annually.

Let us consider a simple example: A corporation has determined that it can sell $25 million of five-year nonamortizing debt at par by offering a semiannual coupon of 9.675 percent.[2] It prefers floating-rate liabilities to fixed-rate liabilities and approaches the capital markets group of our swap bank to arrange an interest-rate swap. Call this corporate client Counterparty 1.

The swap bank has been asked to pay fixed rate and receive floating rate. Since the bank has been asked to pay fixed rate, the bank offers to pay 9.26 percent (five-year TN rate + 34 bps) in exchange for six-month LIBOR flat. The corporate client's net cost of funds,

TABLE 8.1
Indication Pricing for Interest Rate Swaps

Maturity	Bank Pays Fixed Rate	Bank Receives Fixed Rate	Current TN Rate
2 years	2-yr TN sa + 20 bps	2-yr TN sa + 45 bps	8.55 percent
3 years	3-yr TN sa + 25 bps	3-yr TN sa + 52 bps	8.72 percent
4 years	4-yr TN sa + 28 bps	4-yr TN sa + 58 bps	8.85 percent
5 years	5-yr TN sa + 34 bps	5-yr TN sa + 60 bps	8.92 percent
6 years	6-yr TN sa + 38 bps	6-yr TN sa + 66 bps	8.96 percent
7 years	7-yr TN sa + 40 bps	7-yr TN sa + 70 bps	9.00 percent
10 years	10-yr TN sa + 50 bps	10-yr TN sa + 84 bps	9.08 percent

Note: The schedule assumes semiannual rates and bullet transactions.
　　　 TN denotes the Treasury note rate.

after the interest-rate swap, appears to be LIBOR + 0.415 percent (9.675% + LIBOR − 9.260%). This is not, however, quite correct. Because the fixed-rate sides are bond equivalent yields, the difference between them, 0.415 percent, is also a bond equivalent. This difference cannot be added directly to LIBOR without first converting it to a money market yield equivalent. Remember, six-month LIBOR is quoted as a semiannual money market yield (MMY) and based on the assumption of a 360-day year, while the fixed-rate side of a fixed-for-floating rate swap is quoted as a semiannual bond equivalent yield (BEY) and based on the assumption of a 365-day year. (We discussed the differences in yield conventions in Chapters 2 and 3.) The importance of the difference in yield conventions when pricing swaps now becomes apparent. For this reason, we will reiterate some of what has already been said on this subject—but now in the context of swap pricing.

To combine these values correctly, we must transform the fixed-rate differential, 0.415 percent, to its money market yield equivalent. The conversion formula appears as Equation 8.1.[3] This conversion is simple because both six-month LIBOR and the swap coupon are semiannual rates. When the payment frequencies are mismatched (annual versus semiannual, for example) the conversions are somewhat more complex.

$$\text{MMY differential} = \text{BEY differential} \times \frac{360}{365} \qquad \textbf{(8.1)}$$

$$= 0.415 \text{ percent} \times \frac{360}{365}$$

$$= 0.409 \text{ percent}$$

The final floating-rate cost of funding for this corporate client is then LIBOR + 0.409 percent. The cash flows associated with this swap are depicted in Exhibit 8.1. As it happens, had this corporate client borrowed directly in the floating-rate market, it would have been required to pay LIBOR plus 1.25 percent. The client thus enjoyed a cost savings by engaging in the swap.

The swap bank above would look for an opportunity to offset this swap with another swap. Until it can do so, however, the bank will hedge in T-notes and Eurodollars (or T-bills). For example, since the swap bank has agreed to pay fixed rate and receive floating rate, it might short $25 million (market value) six-month Treasury bills and use the proceeds from this sale to purchase $25 million (market value) of five-year Treasury notes.[4] The bank can obtain the securities for the short sale by a reverse repurchase agreement (reverse) with another institution. In a reverse, the bank "purchases" a security from another party and agrees to "sell" the security back to this same party at a specific later date for a specific price. (The repo/reverse market is discussed more fully in Chapter 3.)

An alternative way to obtain securities for a short sale exists when the swap bank holds a portfolio of Treasuries separate and distinct

EXHIBIT 8.1. Cash Flows Between Counterparty 1 and Swap Bank

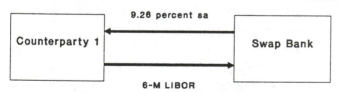

($25 million notional principal)

from its swap operations. For example, the portfolio might represent an investment portfolio that the bank manages either for itself or for its clients, or the swap bank might be a market maker in Treasuries (known as a government securities dealer). These portfolios can serve as the source of the securities that the swap bank sells short. The swap desk will pay other departments of the bank for these securities. The cost of these intrabank borrowings is called the **transfer pricing rate** (TPR). The transaction may be viewed as equivalent to a reverse repurchase agreement between departments within the bank. For purposes of this text, we assume that the TPR is the prevailing rate on Treasuries of the maturity borrowed. In practice, the TPR will usually be at a premium to Treasuries. The cash flows for the swap bank are depicted in Exhibit 8.2.

The swap bank prefers to offset the swaps to which it is a counterparty with matching swaps with other counterparties. The Treasury/Eurodollar positions represent hedges placed only until such time as a matched swap can be arranged. It is important to note that if the swap bank hedges in T-bills, as opposed to Eurodollars, it will have a residual basis risk because LIBOR and the T-bill rate are not perfectly correlated. This point is addressed more fully in the next chapter.

Suppose now that another corporate client approaches the swap bank in need of $30 million of fixed-rate dollar financing. This firm has a comparative advantage in the floating-rate (LIBOR) market. It can sell semiannual five-year nonamortizing floating rate notes (FRNs) at par by paying six-month LIBOR plus 150 basis points. Through the

EXHIBIT 8.2. Cash Flows After Offset in Government Securities Market

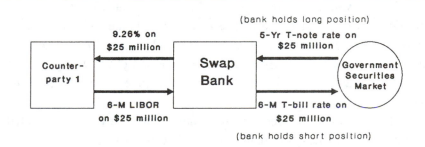

vehicle of the swap, the corporate client would like to convert this floating-rate liability into a fixed-rate liability. The swap bank is asked to receive fixed rate and pay floating rate. Call this corporate client Counterparty 2.

The swap bank has been asked to receive fixed rate and pay floating rate. Assume that the indication pricing schedule depicted in Table 8.1 is still in effect. Since the bank has been asked to receive fixed rate, it would require that Counterparty 2 pay 9.52 percent (five-year TN rate + 60 bps) in exchange for the bank paying six-month LIBOR flat. To calculate Counterparty 2's net cost of funds, we must first convert the floating-rate spread over LIBOR (1.5 percent), which is stated on a money market basis, to a bond equivalent basis. Equation 8.1 allowed us to move from a bond equivalent yield to a money market yield; in this case, we need to move in the opposite direction. Equation 8.2 allows us to move from a money market yield to a bond equivalent yield. Again, this conversion is simple because both rates are already stated on a semiannual basis. If the payment frequencies were mismatched, the conversions would be more complex.

$$\text{BEY differential} = \text{MMY differential} \times \frac{365}{360} \qquad (8.2)$$

$$= 1.5 \text{ percent} \times \frac{365}{360}$$

$$= 1.521 \text{ percent}$$

The conversion renders the value 1.521 percent. Counterparty 2's net cost of funds, after the interest-rate swap, is then 11.041 percent (LIBOR + 1.521 percent − LIBOR + 9.52 percent). As it happens, this firm could have borrowed fixed-rate funds directly at a cost of 11.375 percent. Thus, this client has also enjoyed a benefit from its swap.

The cash flows between the bank and Counterparty 2 are depicted in Exhibit 8.3. The swap bank could offset its position with Counter-

EXHIBIT 8.3. Cash Flows Between Counterparty 2 and Swap Bank

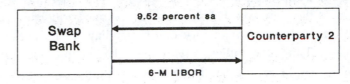

($30 million notional principal)

party 2 by selling $30 million (market value) of five-year Treasury notes short and by using the proceeds from this short sale to purchase $30 million (market value) of six-month T-bills.

Notice that the bank's cash flows with Counterparty 2 are very nearly the mirror image of the bank's cash flows with Counterparty 1. In fact, if the swap bank lifts its Treasury market positions which it is using to hedge its swap with Counterparty 1, it will only require a $5 million position in Treasuries/Eurodollars to hedge the interest-rate exposure that stems from its swap with Counterparty 2. The flows, from the swap bank's perspective, are depicted in Exhibit 8.4.

EXHIBIT 8.4. Cash Flows Between Counterparties and Swap Bank with Residual Position in Government Securities

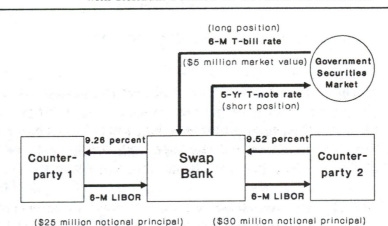

The indication pricing schedule used to price the swaps made between the swap bank and Counterparties 1 and 2 assumes that the swaps are of the plain vanilla fixed-for-floating rate variety and that the counterparties have a satisfactory credit standing in the eyes of the swap bank. Thus, the indication pricing schedule provides starting prices only. To the extent that the swap will require a special structure, or that a counterparty's credit standing is not first rate, or that the swap exposes the bank to special risks, the swap pricing will have to be adjusted to reflect these factors. Price adjustments can take the forms of a wider swap bid-ask spread or a front-end fee or both. Front-end fees, however, are no longer typical except when special financial engineering is required or when the swap incorporates an option-like feature. In the latter case, the front-end fees are best viewed as option premiums.

For example, if Counterparty 1, who is paying the equivalent of LIBOR plus 0.409 percent, desired a rate cap of 12.5 percent, the swap bank would likely oblige; but it would add a front-end fee and/or raise the floating rate payment. Suppose this particular swap bank will oblige Counterparty 1's request for a rate cap, but it will require a front-end fee of one-quarter point (25 basis points) and increase the counterparty's rate to LIBOR plus 0.550 percent. Similar fees and adjustments would be made if the counterparty required a call feature, a put feature, a rate floor, and so on.

8.3 ADJUSTMENTS TO INDICATION PRICING

The indication pricing schedule assumes that payments are to be made semiannually and that all transactions are bullet transactions. It is not unusual for one or both of these assumptions to fail. When this happens, an adjustment in pricing must be made.

We will first consider the pricing adjustments necessitated by a failure of the nonamortizing bullet-transaction assumption. Following this, we will consider the adjustments necessitated by a failure of the semiannual payment assumption.

8.3.1 Amortizing Loans: Duration versus Average Life

The indication pricing schedule assumes that the swap is nonamortizing so that the interest payments are calculated on the same notional principal throughout the term of the swap. Suppose instead that the swap bank's client requires a swap that is based upon amortizing principal. Any number of amortizing schedules are possible. For example, the client might require:

1. that the notional principal underlying the swap be reduced by a fixed dollar amount each year (often called a sinking fund schedule);

2. that the notional principal be reduced by a fixed dollar amount each year beginning after some defined **grace period** during which no amortization of notional principal occurs; or

3. that the principal amortize at an increasing rate as is customary with mortgage-type amortization schedules (perhaps the client is a savings and loan looking to hedge the interest-rate risk associated with its mortgage portfolio).

As already described, most swap banks price the fixed-rate side of an interest-rate swap as a spread over Treasury securities. Treasury debt is always nonamortizing. That is, the Treasury pays periodic (semiannual) interest but does not repay any principal on a Treasury note or bond until such time as the note or bond matures. At maturity, the Treasury repays all principal in a single transaction. Given the nonamortizing nature of Treasury securities, it is not appropriate to base the price of an N-year amortizing swap on the prevailing yield of an N-year nonamortizing Treasury security.

Operatives in the debt markets, including commercial banks, investment banks, and government securities dealers, know that, all other things being equal, the longer the maturity associated with a given debt instrument, the more price sensitive the debt instrument will be to fluctuations in yield levels. It is partly for this reason that long-term debt instruments are regarded as more risky than short-term debt instruments. This fact forms the foundation for one well-known, though not universally accepted, explanation for the shape of the Treasury yield curve—the liquidity preference theory—which holds that the yield on a debt instrument is directly related to its price sensitivity to interest-rate fluctuations.[5] However, it has also long been known that maturity alone is not the sole determinant of a debt instrument's price sensitivity to changes in interest rates. A second, and very important, determinant is the speed with which the debt principal amortizes. Other less important factors include the size of the coupon payments, the frequency of the coupon payments, and the yield presently afforded by the instrument.

In 1938, Frederick Macaulay developed a measure of price sensitivity to yield changes that incorporates all five of the factors that influence price sensitivity. This measure is known as duration. Some of the uses of duration were discussed in Chapters 2 and 4 but we have not yet attempted to apply the concept to the pricing of swaps.

Assuming equal basis point changes in yield, two debt instruments with identical durations will have identical interest-rate sensitivities. In addition, the ratio of two debt instruments' durations is an accurate measure of their relative price sensitivities to equivalent yield changes when such price sensitivity is stated on a percentage basis. Duration, which is measured in years and denoted here by D, is a weighted-average time to the maturity of the instrument. The weights are the ratios of the present values of the future cash flows (including both interest and principal) to the current market price of the instrument. The current price of the instrument is, of course, the sum of the present value of all future cash flows associated with the instrument.

The duration formula from Chapter 2 is repeated here as Equation 8.3.

$$D = \sum_{t}^{m \cdot T} W_t \cdot (t/m) \qquad (8.3)$$

$$\text{where} \quad W_t = \frac{CF(t/m) \cdot (1 + y/m)^{-t}}{\sum_{t} CF(t/m) \cdot (1 + y/m)^{-t}}$$

$$t = 1, 2, 3, \ldots m \cdot T$$

$CF(t/m)$ = Cash flow at time t/m (time measured in years).

y = Present yield on instrument.

m = The number of payment periods per year.

Because of its long-standing role as a measure of a debt instrument's price sensitivity to fluctuations in yield (interest-rate risk), it seems logical to use duration in the pricing of the fixed-rate side of interest-rate and currency swaps. Unfortunately, duration has proven unsatisfactory for this purpose. The duration equation allows one to determine an instrument's duration if one knows its yield. A problem occurs when the instrument's duration and the appropriate yield—which is the fixed rate of interest used for the swap coupon—are both not known.

One widely used solution to pricing the fixed-rate side of a swap is to use a weighted-average measure of the times at which notional principal is amortized where the weights are formed without reference to yield. **Average life** is such a measure.[6]

The average life of an instrument is found by forming the product of the principal repayment and the time at which that principal repayment will be made. These products are then added and the sum is divided by the notional principal at the start of the swap. The average life formula appears as Equation 8.4.

$$AL = \frac{\Sigma P(t) \cdot t}{IP} \qquad (8.4)$$

AL = average life.

$P(t)$ = principal repaid (or cancelled) at time t.

IP = initial principal (principal at start of swap).

It is important to remember that in interest-rate swaps the principal repayments are only notional. The notional nature of the principal, however, does not affect the calculation of the average life.

Let's consider a simple example: Suppose a firm requires an amortizing swap with an initial notional principal of $9.5 million and a term of nine and one-half years with semiannual payments. The principal will amortize under a semiannual sinking-fund type schedule with notional principal payments of $0.5 million each.[7] Thus, the first payment is due at time 0.5, the second is due at time 1.0, and so on until the last—which is due at time 9.5. The first product is formed by multiplying $0.5 million by 0.5; the second is formed by multiplying $0.5 million by 1; and so on.

These products are then added to get 47.5 million. Finally, this sum is divided by the initial notional principal of 9.5 million to get an average life of five years. Thus, the swap has an average life of five years. The calculation of this average life is repeated below.

Time		Principal Repaid		Product
0.5	×	$0.5 M	=	$0.25 M
1.0	×	$0.5 M	=	$0.50 M
.	.	.	.	.
.	.	.	.	.
.	.	.	.	.
9.5	.	$0.5 M	.	$4.75 M
			Sum	47.50 M

$$AL = 47.5 \div 9.5 = 5 \text{ years}$$

Once the average life has been determined, the swap is treated as though it is equivalent to a T-note that has a maturity equal to the swap's average life. The next step is to look at the indication pricing schedule for the pricing of swaps of this term. This particular swap would be priced from the five-year T-note. While the average life of an amortizing instrument is not the same as its term to maturity, the average life of a nonamortizing instrument, such as a T-note, is identical to its term to maturity.

Suppose the five-year T-note is currently yielding 8.75 percent. Using the duration formula, we find that the five-year T-note has a duration of 3.98. Using the same yield to calculate the duration of the amortizing swap, we find that the swap has a duration of 3.93. Thus, the duration of the swap and the duration of the T-note with the same average life are nearly the same—although not necessarily identical.

When pricing swaps, an important argument in favor of the use of average life, as opposed to duration, lies in the treatment of interest. With a typical debt instrument, interest payments flow only one way. With a swap, interest payments flow two ways and are therefore largely offsetting. The offsetting nature of the interest payments suggests a strong argument for focusing on the principal alone—which is precisely what average life does.

With the widespread stripping of coupon-bearing Treasury securities to create zero coupon Treasury products, sufficient liquidity has developed in zero coupon Treasuries for the emergence of a well-defined zero coupon yield curve. The zero coupon yield curve depicts the relationship between the yields on zero coupon Treasuries and their respective maturities. Zero coupon securities are unique in that their duration, average life, and maturity are identical.

At present, many swap banks use the zero coupon yield curve as the basis of their swap hedging operations but continue to price their swap products off the conventional yield curve. It is likely that in time swap banks may switch to pricing their swap products off the zero coupon yield curve. Some already do. In keeping with common practice, however, we will continue to use coupon-bearing Treasuries for our pricing discussion.

8.3.2 Semiannual Rates versus Other Payment Frequencies

Interest-rate swaps priced as a spread over Treasuries assume semiannual interest payments. When the bank's client requires annual payments, as opposed to semiannual payments, the bank must adjust the fixed rate of interest to reflect this difference.

Consider again the case of Counterparty 2, which had approached the swap bank for a five-year fixed-for-floating interest-rate swap. This party would pay fixed rate and receive floating rate. The bank quotes a semiannual fixed rate of 9.52 percent (five-year TN + 60 bps). Counterparty 2 now indicates that it prefers annual fixed-rate payments although it still wishes to receive semiannual floating-rate payments based on six-month LIBOR.

The swap bank is agreeable but must now determine the annual rate that is equivalent to a semiannual rate of 9.52 percent. The procedure for determining the equivalent annual rate is founded on basic time value arithmetic. That is, we calculate the annual interest rate that would provide the same future value, for a given starting sum, as would the semiannual rate. This calculation appears as Equation 8.5.

$$r_{an} = \left(1 + \frac{r_{sa}}{2}\right)^2 - 1 \qquad (8.5)$$

In Equation 8.5, r_{an} denotes the annual interest rate and r_{sa} denotes the semiannual interest rate. More generally, an interest rate stated on one payment frequency can be converted into an interest rate stated on another payment frequency by using the relationship given in Equation 8.6.

$$r_m = m \cdot \left[(1 + \frac{r_z}{z})^{z/m} - 1\right] \qquad (8.6)$$

r_m = Annual rate of interest assuming m compoundings per year.
r_z = Annual rate of interest assuming z compoundings per year.

In this more general formulation, m would be 1 if the rate r_m were annual; z would be 2 if the rate r_z were semiannual; and so on. These conversions ignore the issue of reinvestment risk. Reinvestment risk is the risk that income received from an investment will be reinvested at a rate that differs from the rate that prevailed at the time the investment was acquired. The swap bank can be expected to attach a premium to its swap pricing when the swap structure gives rise to reinvestment risk. This risk, however, is small in comparison to other risks that are discussed shortly and so we will ignore it.

Now let's return to Counterparty 2. Counterparty 2 requires a payment schedule that provides for annual, rather than semiannual, payments of fixed-rate interest. The bank calculates the annual interest rate using Equation 8.6.

$$r_1 = 1 \cdot [(1 + .0952/2)^{2/1} - 1] = 9.747\%$$

The swap bank now offers its client a fixed-for-floating rate swap in which the bank would pay semiannual interest to the client at the rate of six-month LIBOR in exchange for the client's annual payments to the bank at the rate of 9.747 percent.

There is one additional problem with this swap from the swap bank's perspective. Since the bank pays the client semiannually but the client only pays the bank annually, there is a payment mismatch that exposes the bank to considerable credit risk. For example, suppose that the floating-rate side is initially set at 8.5 percent and that six months after the swap documents are executed, the bank pays its counterparty client $1.275 million—calculated as one-half of 8.5% on $30 million. Next, suppose that, six months later, the counterparty client defaults at the time the counterparty is due to make its first payment to the bank. While the counterparty's default frees the bank from its obligation to make the current and future interest payments, as per the rights of set-off contained in the terms and conditions of the swap agreement, the bank has already made its first payment to the counterparty. It must now utilize the swap's default provisions to try to recover its losses.

This example illustrates the extra level of risk associated with entering into swaps that have payment timing mismatches. We will consider this problem again, and the steps the swap bank might take to alleviate it, in Chapter 9. One final point is, however, in order. Because payment timing mismatches increase the risk exposure of the swap bank, we might expect that the swap bank will insist on additional compensation from its counterparty client. For example, the bank might add a few basis points to the fixed rate its counterparty client is required to pay.

It is important to note that there is almost always some credit risk to the swap bank from its swap activities. While the rights of set-off relieve the swap bank from making payments to its counterparty should the counterparty default, the default does not relieve the swap bank of its commitments to other counterparties—including those with whom the bank has matched the defaulted swap. Thus, credit risk is very real even when the timing of the payments are perfectly matched. Clearly, however, mismatched timing of payments amplifies credit risk.

8.4 MARKET IMBALANCES AND PAY/RECEIVE RATE ADJUSTMENTS

The difference between the fixed rate a swap bank must receive and the fixed rate it is willing to pay at any given average life is its bid-ask spread for swaps with that average life. In preparing its indication pricing schedules and implied spreads, the swap bank must take several things into consideration. Of major importance, of course, are the competitive pressures of the market. The swap bank must offer competitive swap pricing if it is to attract rate-conscious corporate clients.

Suppose that the swap bank using the indication pricing schedule appearing in Table 8.1 finds that it is attracting considerable five-year average life fixed-for-floating swap activity on the bank-pays-fixed-rate side but very little swap activity on the other side. The swap bank prefers to offset its swaps with other swaps rather than resorting to hedging in the cash market for Treasury securities. Looking again at the bank's current pricing for five-year average life swaps, it can be seen that the bank needs to attract additional swap activity on the bank-receives-fixed-rate side. At present, the bank's base pricing requires the Treasury note rate plus 60 basis points (TN + 60 bps) from fixed-rate payers. The bank can attract additional activity on the bank-receives-fixed-rate side by lowering the fixed rate it requires of fixed-rate paying counterparties. For example, it could lower its price on five-year average life swaps to the Treasury note rate plus 58 basis points. At the same time, it might lower the rate that it will pay so as to discourage new swaps on the bank-pays-fixed-rate side until such time as it can fully offset its existing portfolio of swaps. For example, it might lower its bank-pays rate to the Treasury note rate plus 31 basis points. These pricing adjustments are summarized in Table 8.2.

By frequently adjusting its pay/receive rates, the swap bank is able to attract additional counterparties on the side of the market it prefers and to thereby correct market imbalances. In more extreme cases, the swap bank might find that some of the counterparties attracted to its prevailing rate are themselves swap banks who have developed imbalances on the other side of the fixed-for-floating-rate market.

TABLE 8.2
Pay/Receive Pricing Adjustments to
Correct Market Imbalances

	Maturity	Bank-Pays Fixed Rate	Bank-Receives Fixed Rate	Current TN Rate
Old	5 years	5-yr TN sa + 34 bps	5 yr TN sa + 60 bps	8.92 percent
New	5 years	5-yr TN sa + 31 bps	5 yr TN sa + 58 bps	8.92 percent

8.5 INDICATION PRICING SCHEDULES: CURRENCY SWAPS

In the plain vanilla currency swap, the counterparty client wants to swap a fixed-rate obligation in one currency for a floating-rate obligation in another currency. By using a currency swap in conjunction with an interest-rate swap, we can convert a fixed-rate obligation in one currency to a fixed-rate obligation in another currency or, alternatively, we can use a currency swap in conjunction with an interest-rate swap to convert a floating-rate obligation in one currency to a floating-rate obligation in another currency.

This section concentrates on the pricing of fixed-for-floating-rate currency swaps. The swap bank's international capital markets team will estimate appropriate pay and receive fixed rates for all of the currencies in which the bank makes a market. All rates are against six-month LIBOR flat. The fixed rates may be stated on an annual or a semiannual basis and the adjustment from annual to semiannual or vice versa is exactly the same as that described in our discussion of rate adjustments for interest-rate swaps. Assume that the rates in the following examples are all stated on a semiannual basis.

In the case of currency swaps, indication pricings are often stated as a mid-rate to which some number of basis points is added or subtracted depending on whether the swap bank is to receive or pay fixed rate. Such a schedule is depicted for deutschemark-to-dollar rates in Table 8.3.

The structure of the DM-to-USD indication pricing schedule in

TABLE 8.3
Indication Pricing for
Deutschemark-to-Dollar Swaps

Maturity	Mid-Rate
2 years	6.25% sa
3 years	6.48% sa
4 years	6.65% sa
5 years	6.78% sa
6 years	6.88% sa
7 years	6.96% sa
10 years	7.10% sa

Note: The rates above are mid-rates. To these rates, deduct one-eighth percent (12.5 bps) if the bank is paying fixed rate. Add one-eighth percent (12.5 bps) if the bank is receiving fixed rate. All principal transactions are assumed to be bullet transactions.

Table 8.3 is typical of currency swaps, although the size of the bid-ask spread (25 basis points) is excessive by current standards. The swap bank would likely offer similar schedules for the other major hard currencies including the Swiss franc, French franc, British pound, Canadian dollar, and Japanese yen.

As already mentioned, the rates in Table 8.3 are mid-rates. The actual pay/receive rates are found by deducting/adding the appropriate premium to the mid-rate. For straight U.S. dollar interest-rate swaps, the indication pricing schedule depicted in Table 8.1 lists both the bank's pay and receive rates. Nevertheless, we can obtain a mid-rate for interest-rate swaps by simply taking the average of the pay and receive rates. For example, for the five-year interest-rate swap the mid-rate is 9.39 percent—calculated as (9.26 + 9.52) ÷ 2.

Consider now a simple example: A German firm approaches our swap bank looking to convert a DM 35 million five-year semiannual fixed-rate liability into a floating-rate dollar liability. The swap bank offers an exchange of borrowings (straight currency swap) at the current spot exchange rate of 1.75 DM/USD. At the current exchange rate, the principal is $20 million. Since the bank will be paying fixed rate, the rate is found by taking the five-year mid-rate and deducting one-eighth of one percent. This calculation produces a rate of 6.655 percent (6.78 − 0.125). Thus, the German counterparty client would pay the swap bank six-month LIBOR on principal of $20 million and the swap bank would pay the German firm 6.655 percent sa on DM 35 million.

Unlike an interest-rate swap, in which there is no exchange of principals, there is often an exchange of principals in the straight currency swap. That is, at the commencement of the swap, the German firm would exchange its DM 35 million for the bank's $20 million. For the next five years, the two parties would pay each other interest at the rates indicated. After five years, the two parties would re-exchange principals at the same exchange rate used for the initial exchange of principals (i.e., 1.75 DM/USD). The straight currency swap clearly involves three separate cash flows:

1. the initial exchange of principals;
2. the interest payments; and
3. the re-exchange of principals.

These are depicted in Exhibits 8.5, 8.6, and 8.7.

As with interest-rate swaps, the swap bank makes its profit on currency swaps from its bid-ask spread. For this swap bank, the spread is currently one-quarter point (25 basis points) since the bank is adding and subtracting one-eighth point from its mid-rate. The bank is, of course, looking to offset its exchange-rate and interest-rate exposures. These exposures are most easily offset by finding another counterparty client with matching needs. Such a client would be looking to exchange 20 million five-year floating-rate dollars for fixed-rate deut-

EXHIBIT 8.5. Currency Swap (Exchange of Borrowings)
Initial Exchange of Principals

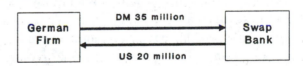

EXHIBIT 8.6. **Currency Swap (Exchange of Borrowings)**
Interest Flows Between Exchanges of Principals

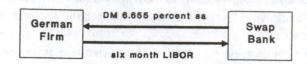

EXHIBIT 8.7. **Currency Swap (Exchange of Borrowings)**
Reexchange of Principals

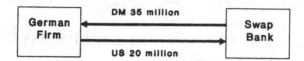

schemarks. Assuming the bank has such a client immediately available, the bank would offer to swap the currencies at the current spot exchange rate of 1.75 DM/USD. The bank would pay this second counterparty six-month LIBOR flat in exchange for the second counterparty client paying the bank DM 6.905 percent sa.

By offsetting the currency and interest exchanges with a second counterparty with cash flow needs that match those of the first, the bank is fully hedged against fluctuations in both exchange rates and interest rates. Of course, the bank may not be able to immediately identify a counterparty with matching needs. In this case, the bank might want to construct temporary hedges by using other instruments such as FRAs, FXAs, DIFFs, currency futures, and/or positions in Treasuries and foreign debt. We address these considerations more fully in Chapter 9.

In the event that the bank experiences a demand imbalance on one side of the currency swap market, the bank will have to raise or lower its mid-rate. For example, suppose that the bank experiences a surge in demand for currency swaps by clients who want to pay five-year fixed-rate deutschemarks and receive floating-rate dollars. To discourage this side of the market and encourage the other, the bank will raise its five-year mid-rate from 6.78 percent to say 6.85 percent.

Determining the correct mid-rates to serve as the basis of swap pricing is typically a function of a swap bank's international capital markets group. **Capital markets groups** operate with an international perspective and continuously monitor the capital markets worldwide. They watch their own banks' swap portfolios closely and adjust rates quickly when they suspect that an imbalance is developing. A capital markets group may find, for instance, that they must lower the bank's four-year mid-rate while simultaneously raising the bank's five-year mid-rate.

8.6 CURRENCY SWAPS WITH NO INITIAL EXCHANGE OF BORROWING

The straight currency swap involves an initial exchange of principals and an eventual re-exchange of principals. Not all currency swaps involve two exchanges of principals. Let us consider such a case.

Suppose it is now 1 February 1989. As a consequence of an earlier financing, a firm is committed to making semiannual floating-rate (six-month LIBOR) dollar payments on an amortizing loan for four more years. The payment dates are 1 August and 1 February. By the nature of the firm's business, the firm receives revenue in deutschemarks. The firm's current payment schedule is depicted in Table 8.4.

Recent fluctuations in the DM/USD exchange rate and U.S. interest rates have caused the firm's management to become increasingly concerned about its dollar liabilities and have led the firm to look for a way to convert its floating-rate dollar liabilities to fixed-rate deutschemark liabilities. At the same time, it would like to lock in the current DM/USD exchange rate (1.75 DM/USD) for all future exchanges. The swap bank offers a currency swap with no initial exchange of principals. The bank offers to pay LIBOR on the amortizing balance and to pay $0.5 million every six months. The swap has an average life of two and one-half years, and the bank's current mid-rate for two and one-half year deutschemarks is 6.365 percent. In exchange for the bank's paying LIBOR, the bank requires the firm to pay the bank 6.49

TABLE 8.4
Amortization Schedule of Dollar Loan

Date	Loan Balance Before Payment	Loan Balance After Payment	Payment Amount
1 Feb 1989	–	$4.0 million	—
1 Aug 1989	$4.0 million	$3.5 million	$0.5 million + LIBOR
1 Feb 1990	$3.5 million	$3.0 million	$0.5 million + LIBOR
1 Aug 1990	$3.0 million	$2.5 million	$0.5 million + LIBOR
1 Feb 1991	$2.5 million	$2.0 million	$0.5 million + LIBOR
1 Aug 1991	$2.0 million	$1.5 million	$0.5 million + LIBOR
1 Feb 1992	$1.5 million	$1.0 million	$0.5 million + LIBOR
1 Aug 1992	$1.0 million	$0.5 million	$0.5 million + LIBOR
1 Feb 1993	$0.5 million	$0.0	$0.5 million + LIBOR

percent (mid-rate plus 12.5 basis points). In addition, the bank will pay the firm $0.5 million every six months in exchange for the firm's payments to the bank of 0.875 million deutschemarks every six months. This latter sum reflects principal translations at a DM/USD exchange rate of 1.75. These payments are depicted in Table 8.5.

The counterparty client's dollar commitments to its earlier financing source (third-party lender) are now assured. The bank will pay its counterparty client $0.5 million + LIBOR flat every six months and the counterparty client will then pay this identical sum to its creditor.

TABLE 8.5
Currency Swap Payment Schedule

Date	Bank Pays Counterparty Client	Counterparty Client Pays Bank
1 Feb 89	—	—
1 Aug 89	$0.5 million + LIBOR	DM 0.875 million + 6.49 percent
1 Feb 90	$0.5 million + LIBOR	DM 0.875 million + 6.49 percent
1 Aug 90	$0.5 million + LIBOR	DM 0.875 million + 6.49 percent
1 Feb 91	$0.5 million + LIBOR	DM 0.875 million + 6.49 percent
1 Aug 91	$0.5 million + LIBOR	DM 0.875 million + 6.49 percent
1 Feb 92	$0.5 million + LIBOR	DM 0.875 million + 6.49 percent
1 Aug 92	$0.5 million + LIBOR	DM 0.875 million + 6.49 percent
1 Feb 93	$0.5 million + LIBOR	DM 0.875 million + 6.49 percent

The client's net liability is now to pay DM 0.875 million plus 6.49 percent sa. That is, it has a fixed-rate deutschemark commitment—exactly what it was looking for. It is now fully hedged with respect to exchange rates and interest rates.

Unlike the straight currency swap, which is best understood as an exchange of borrowings, this currency swap is best viewed as a series of forward contracts all made at the current spot rate of 1.75 DM/USD with the normal forward-spot exchange-rate differential incorporated in the interest payments made by the counterparties.

8.7 OFF-MARKET PRICING

Just as it is frequently necessary to make pricing adjustments to interest-rate swaps for payment frequencies that differ from those assumed in the indication pricing schedules and for amortization schedules that differ from those assumed in the indication pricing schedules, it is also frequently necessary to make pricing adjustments for variations in currency swap requirements. The straight currency swap assumes semiannual payments and bullet transactions. If the currency swap requires annual fixed-rate payments instead of semiannual payments, the annual equivalent rate for the semiannual rate would be determined again by using Equation 8.6. If the swap is an amortizing one, the appropriate rate would be found employing average life rather than maturity (as with the currency swap in the preceding example). There is one additional adjustment that is often necessary in the case of currency swaps. This occurs when the swap is **off-market**.

The need for an off-market swap arises when a firm has an existing liability at a rate that differs from that which is currently prevailing in the market. Consider the following case: A U.S. firm is committed to making semiannual interest payments to holders of its deutschemark bonds that were issued five years ago. The bond principal covers DM 18 million, all of which will be repaid at maturity in 10 more years. The bond carries a fixed coupon of 9.50 percent. The U.S. firm wants to swap this liability for a floating-rate dollar liability. Its purpose is to eliminate exchange-rate risk. Note that this swap requires no initial exchange of principals and is similar in this regard to the case discussed in the preceding section.

The swap bank's current indication pricing schedule (Table 8.3) calls for the bank to pay a fixed rate of DM 6.975 percent sa (mid-rate less 12.5 basis points) against six-month LIBOR flat. However, the counterparty client, which is the U.S. firm in this case, requires the bank to pay DM 9.50 percent. Any rate other than DM 9.50 percent will leave a residual exchange-rate risk for the U.S. firm. This swap calls for off-market pricing.

The trick to pricing off-market swaps is to create cash flow patterns with equivalent present values. This requires that we exploit our knowledge of the 10-year U.S. fixed rate and the 10-year DM fixed rate. We use mid-rates for this purpose. The latter is 7.10 percent (Table 8.3) and the former is 9.75 percent (Table 8.1).

The first step is to determine the rate differential between that which the bank's counterparty client requires and that which the bank would ordinarily pay. The differential, in this case, is 2.525 percent—calculated as 9.50 percent less 6.975 percent. That is, the client requires that the bank pay a premium of 2.525 percent on the DM fixed-rate side.

The next step is to determine the dollar-rate premium that has the same present value as this 2.525 percent DM premium. Since this DM payment takes the form of an annuity, we can compute the present value of the payment using present value annuity arithmetic. The necessary relationship is given by Equation 8.7.[8]

$$PVA = PMT \times \{[1 - (1 + R/m)^{-m \cdot n}] \div R/m\} \qquad (8.7)$$

PVA = Present value of the annuity.
PMT = Annuity payment.
  R = Mid-rate (for deutschemarks).
  n = Term of swap (number of years to maturity of swap).
  m = Frequency of interest payments.

The values of PMT, R, m, and n are, in this case, 2.525, 7.10

percent, 2, and 10, respectively. Plugging these values into Equation 8.7 provides a present value of 35.725.

Now use this present value to determine the dollar-interest premium. To obtain the dollar-interest premium Equation 8.7 is again employed but this time the current mid-rate for dollars is used for R (9.75 percent). Substitute the value 35.725 for PVA and solve for PMT. The value of PMT that solves this particular case is 2.836. This value is interpreted as the dollar-rate premium on this off-market transaction. However, this rate premium was derived from fixed-rate bond equivalent yields and, consequently, cannot be added directly to LIBOR. An adjustment must first be made. Use Equation 8.1 to make the necessary adjustment. The adjustment provides a yield premium of 2.797 percent that can be added directly to LIBOR. The swap will then call for the bank to pay its counterparty client deutschemarks at the semiannual fixed rate of 9.50 percent in exchange for the counterparty client paying the bank dollars at the rate of six-month LIBOR plus 2.797 percent. At maturity, the parties will exchange principals at an exchange rate of 1.75 DM/USD (the spot rate at the time the swap is negotiated). The cash flows associated with this swap are depicted in Exhibits 8.8 and 8.9. The bank may also look to collect a front-end fee if any special financial engineering is required in designing the swap or evaluating the client's needs.

The client firm is now fully hedged against exchange-rate fluctuations. The deutschemark payments, including both interest and principal, that it must make to its creditor (the third-party lender) are perfectly matched by the bank's payments to its client firm. The client firm's net position consists of its LIBOR plus 2.797 percent payments to the bank. It need no longer concern itself at all with the DM/USD exchange rate.

EXHIBIT 8.8. Off-Market Pricing of Currency Swap
Interest Flows Between Counterparty and Bank

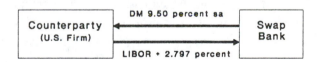

EXHIBIT 8.9. Off-Market Pricing of Currency Swap
Terminal Exchange of Principals

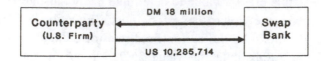

Note: In this swap, the only exchange of principals occurs at the termination of the swap agreement. This exchange takes place at the spot rate which prevailed at the time the swap was negotiated, i.e., 1.75 DM/US.

8.8 A NOTE ON THE PRICING OF CIRCUS SWAPS

The swap pricing discussed in this chapter has provided for the pricing of fixed-for-floating interest-rate swaps and fixed-for-floating currency swaps. The corporate user, however, might require a swap to convert fixed-rate payments in one currency to fixed-rate payments in another currency or, alternatively, to convert floating-rate payments in one currency to floating-rate payments in another currency. As mentioned in Chapter 7, fixed-for-fixed rate and floating-for-floating rate currency swaps can be engineered by combining a fixed-for-floating interest-rate swap with a fixed-for-floating currency swap. When both of the floating rates are LIBOR, these combinations are often called **circus swaps**.

The pricing of circus swaps directly follows from the mechanics of the two swap components. Consider one last time the off-market swap discussed in the previous section. The U.S. firm has swapped a 9.50 percent fixed-rate deutschemark commitment for LIBOR plus 2.797 percent. This same client can now convert its dollar floating-rate payments to fixed-rate payments using the rates in Table 8.1. That is, the bank will pay its counterparty client LIBOR + 2.797 percent in exchange for the client paying the bank the "bank-receives" rate of 9.92 percent plus 2.836 percent. The end result for the counterparty client is a fixed-rate semiannual payment of 12.756 percent USD.

No additional adjustments for principal are required since the principal in an interest-rate swap is purely notional. The interest flows

EXHIBIT 8.10. Off-Market Circus Swap
Currency Swap Component

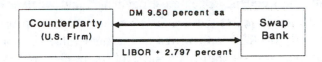

EXHIBIT 8.11. Off-Market Circus Swap
Interest-Rate Swap Component

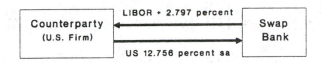

EXHIBIT 8.12. Off-Market Circus Swap
Net Interest Flows

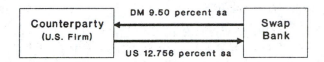

from the currency portion of this off-market circus swap are depicted in Exhibit 8.10 (this repeats Exhibit 8.8). The interest flows from the interest-rate portion of the circus swap are depicted in Exhibit 8.11. The net cash flows from the combined components of the circus swap are depicted in Exhibit 8.12.

8.9 SUMMARY

The pricing of swaps is a complex undertaking. Typically, a swap bank's capital markets group is charged with developing and periodically revising indicative swap pricing schedules for both the interest-rate and the currency swaps in which the bank makes a market.

These schedules provide base rates. The base rates are adjusted to reflect any special features the client requires, the creditworthiness of the client, the frequency of interest payments, and whether the swap will be at-market or off-market. The arithmetic of swap pricing depends heavily on the mathematics of the time value of money.

Short-dated swaps are usually priced off a futures strip. When the pricing vehicle is the IMM's Eurodollar contract and the swap uses IMM settlement dates, the swap is called an IMM swap. Dollar-based long-dated swaps are usually priced as a spread over Treasuries of similar maturity. This assumes that the swap is nonamortizing. When the swap involves amortization of principal, an alternative measure of the swap term must be used. The most frequently used of such measures is the average life of the swap.

The swap banker must monitor the bank's swap portfolio on a continuous basis. While temporary hedges are often constructed through positioning in the Government securities market, futures, and other hedging media, the optimal long-term goal is to match all swaps. This matching is often achieved by writing a swap with a second counterparty or by writing a swap with another swap bank on an interbank basis. When one side of the bank's swap portfolio becomes out of line with the other side, the bank can adjust its bid and asked prices to attract activity to the deficient side and/or make the surplus side less attractive.

A need for off-market pricing arises whenever a client of the bank requires a swap to be written at a rate that differs from the prevailing swap rates. This situation is most likely to arise when a firm seeks to transform the type of interest rate or the currency associated with an existing obligation. The off-market pricing adjustments are made with the aid of present value arithmetic.

Circus swaps, by combining interest-rate and currency swaps, allow the end-user to convert fixed-rate debt in one currency to fixed-rate debt in a different currency, or to convert floating-rate debt in one currency to floating-rate debt in another currency. These swaps are priced in exactly the same fashion as other swaps but the pricing is a two-stage process.

REFERENCES AND SUGGESTED READING

Arak, M., L. S. Goodman, and J. Snailer. "Duration Equivalent Bond Swaps: A New Tool," *Journal of Portfolio Management*, 26-32 (Summer 1986).

Fage, P., *Yield Calculations*, London: Credit Swiss First Boston, October 1986.

Gay, G. D. and R. W. Kolb. "Removing Bias in Duration Based Hedging Models: A Note," *Journal of Futures Markets*, 4:2, 225-228 (Summer 1984).

Kopprasch, R., J. Macfarlane, D. Ross, and J. Showers. "The Interest Rate Swap Market: Yield Mathematics, Terminology and Conventions," in *The Handbook of Fixed Income Securities* (2d ed), edited by F. Fabozzi and I. Pollock.

Leibowitz, M. L. "The Dedicated Bond Portfolio in Pension Funds—Part II: Immunization, Horizon Matching and Contingent Procedures," *Financial Analysts Journal*, 47-57 (Mar/Apr 1986).

Macaulay, F. R. *Some Theoretical Problems Suggested by the Movement of Interest Rates, Bond Yields, and Stock Prices in the United States since 1856*, New York: Columbia University Press for the National Bureau of Economic Research, (1938).

Nadler, D. "Eurodollar Futures/Interest Rate Swap Arbitrage," Quantitative Strategies Group, Shearson Lehman Hutton, April 1989.

Weston J. F. and T. E. Copeland. *Managerial Finance*, 8th ed., New York: Dryden Press, (1986).

ENDNOTES

[1]Interbank swaps are swaps made between swap banks. Banks enter into interbank swaps for a variety of purposes including:

1. to hedge other bank positions;
2. to close a gap;
3. to speculate on the direction of interest rates and exchange rate; and
4. to better manage their own swap portfolios.

[2]The corporation will, of course, also encounter some flotation costs in the form of underwriting fees. While these flotation costs must be factored in to obtain the firm's all-in cost in any actual financing, we ignore them here in order to concentrate on the pricing of swaps.

[3]For a fuller discussion of yield conversions and yield conventions, see Chapters 2 and 3. For more detail, see Fage (1986).

[4]When the swap bank's objective is simply to hedge a swap until a matched swap can be booked or until the swap can be assigned to another party, the bank will often hedge the swap in T-note and Eurodollar (or T-bill) futures. This is important as futures hedges, like swaps themselves, are off-balance sheet positions while cash

market positions are on-balance sheet positions. This use of futures to hedge un-matched swaps is discussed more fully in Chapter 9.

⁵The liquidity premium theory explains the shape of the yield curve in terms of ever greater interest-rate risk associated with ever greater maturities on U.S. Treasury securities. Greater risk requires higher levels of interest as compensation.

⁶For an examination of the relationship between duration and average life, see Leibowitz (1986).

⁷A sinking fund is a program involving the periodic set aside of a fixed sum to provide for the eventual retirement of an outstanding debt or preferred stock issue.

⁸For a discussion of the arithmetic of annuities, see Chapter 2. For a more detailed discussion, see Weston and Copeland (1986).

Section III

Equity Market Applications

One of the great financial innovations of recent years has been the emergence of stock index futures. This market has flourished because it offers exciting speculative opportunities and provides powerful techniques for reducing financial risk. In his study, "Managing Stock Market Risk with Stock Index Futures," Charles S. Morris shows how to use futures to control stock market risk. As Morris notes, stock index futures offer new techniques for handling stock market risk. However, for the unwary, they also present new risks.

Portfolio insurance consists of a set of techniques in which traders use financial derivatives to protect the value of a stock portfolio. In essence, traders take an existing portfolio and trade derivatives against the portfolio to insure that the entire value of the stock/derivatives portfolio will not fall below a specified level. This insurance, of course, has a cost in the form of reducing the upside potential for the portfolio.

Peter A. Abken, in "An Introduction to Portfolio Insurance," shows the basic ideas that underlie portfolio insurance. As Abken discusses, portfolio insurance strategies may be implemented directly by purchasing put options. Alternatively, many portfolio insurers prefer to use a strategy of trading stock index futures to simulate the results of buying put options.

The actual implementation of the dynamic hedging strategies in portfolio insurance can be complicated. Thomas O'Brien clarifies the implementation of portfolio insurance in his article, "The Mechanics of Portfolio Insurance." As O'Brien explains, the dynamic hedging approach of insuring a portfolio by trading futures requires careful monitoring of the position to achieve the desired results.

In the strictest sense, a portfolio insurance strategy guarantees that the value of a portfolio will not fall below a specified level over a given time horizon. When strategies are implemented via dynamic hedging, there exists a possibility that the dynamic strategy may not achieve the idealized goal of maintaining the specified portfolio value with certainty. Mark Rubinstein explores the issues involved in implementing portfolio insurance in his paper, "Alternative Paths to Portfolio Insurance."

In financial markets, there is no free lunch, and the lunch of portfolio insurance like all others has a cost. In their article, "Assessing the Costs of Portfolio Insurance," Richard J. Rendleman, Jr. and Richard W. McEnally explain the sources of these costs. As McEnally and Rendleman explain, having a high guaranteed value for a given portfolio means a considerable loss in long-run expected return on the portfolio. By insuring against only the worst outcomes it is possible to maintain much of the expected return inherent in an uninsured portfolio. Not surprisingly, McEnally and Rendleman find a tradeoff between the degree of insurance and the expected return on the portfolio.

While stock index futures and trading strategies based upon them have become very popular, they certainly have their critics. Many have even blamed stock index arbitrage as being responsible for the Crash of 1987. (See the next section for articles on equity derivatives and the crash.) Mark Rubinstein believes that alternative financial derivatives may come to be more important than futures in equity markets. In his paper, "Market Basket Alternatives," Rubinstein explores some of the strongest competitors for futures, such as index participations and market basket securities.

Article 21

Managing Stock Market Risk With Stock Index Futures

By Charles S. Morris

Stock market investments always have been risky because stock returns are volatile. Stock returns are volatile because investors continually assess the effects of economic events on firm values. Some events are specific to an individual firm and therefore affect only that firm's stock price. Other kinds of events affect virtually all firms, causing the value of the entire market to change. For example, when the stock market collapsed on October 19, 1987, the price of nearly every publicly traded stock fell.

Stock investors traditionally have managed the volatility of returns due to firm-specific events by diversifying their portfolios. But diversification cannot reduce the volatility of returns caused by marketwide events like the October 1987 collapse. To protect themselves from mar-

ketwide events, stock investors traditionally have had to sell some of their portfolio and to buy other, less risky securities or to buy stocks that are influenced less by marketwide events. Such methods, however, are often costly and inconsistent with desired investment strategies.

The development over the past decade of stock index futures has given investors in stocks a new and better way to manage stock market risk. This article explains how stock index futures allow investors to manage risk by hedging the exposure of stock portfolios to marketwide events. The first section of the article discusses how stock market risks have traditionally been managed. The second section describes stock index futures and discusses the growth of stock index futures trading. The third section shows how stock index futures are used to manage market risk and explains their advantages over traditional methods of managing market risk. The fourth section discusses some of the limitations of managing risk with stock index futures.

Charles S. Morris is a senior economist at the Federal Reserve Bank of Kansas City. Julia Reigel, a research associate at the bank, assisted in the preparation of this article.

Traditional forms of risk management

Investments in stocks are risky because their returns are uncertain. Stock returns are uncertain because stock prices and dividends vary over time. Volatility in prices and dividends comes from two sources. One source is economic events specific to individual firms. The second source is economic events that affect every firm in the economy. Investors have generally found it more difficult to manage the second type of stock market risk.

Events unique to a specific firm are the primary source of volatility in an individual firm's stock returns. Indeed, the volatility in returns caused by firm-specific events is called *firm-specific* risk. For example, if a pharmaceutical company discovers a new drug, its stock price may rise. This company's discovery, however, would not directly affect any other company's stock price. If the company does not get approval to market the drug from the Food and Drug Administration, only that company's stock price would fall.

The stock returns of individual firms are also affected by marketwide events that affect the stock returns of all firms in the economy. The volatility in returns caused by marketwide events is called *market risk*. For example, an increase in interest rates might lower the earnings outlook for virtually every firm in the economy, causing all stock prices to fall.

Investors manage risk by choosing the amount of risk they are willing to incur. Some investors are willing to bear relatively high levels of risk, while others are not. In general, investors will not choose to minimize risk because there are costs to reducing risk. Because the risk and the expected return of an investment are inversely related, the main cost of reducing risk is a lower expected return.

To successfully manage risk, investors must independently manage both firm-specific risk and market risk. Firm-specific risk is traditionally managed by holding a diversified portfolio of stocks. Diversification can reduce risk because events specific to an individual firm have no direct effect on other firms. For example, suppose an investor invests in the stocks of a pharmaceutical company and an oil company. If the oil company happens to discover a new oil field and the pharmaceutical company has a new drug petition denied, the increase in the oil company's stock price could offset some or all of the decrease in the pharmaceutical company's stock price. As a result, the volatility of a diversified portfolio's returns is likely to be lower than that of any of its component stocks.

Diversification across stocks, however, cannot reduce market risk. For example, if an increase in interest rates causes all stock prices to fall, the change in one firm's stock price could not offset the change in another firm's stock price. Even the value of a completely diversified portfolio that contains every traded stock—that is, the stock market as a whole—would fall. Thus, investors must use other methods to manage market risk.

Market risk can be managed in two ways using traditional risk management techniques. One way is to adjust the share of stocks in an investment portfolio.[1] For example, an investor can decrease a portfolio's exposure to market risk by decreasing the share of stocks in the portfolio and increasing the share of other assets, such as bonds. A second way to reduce market risk is to sell stocks that have a large amount of market risk and buy stocks with a small amount of market risk. For example, the value of an S&L is very sensitive to changes in interest rates, while the value of a retail grocery store is not. Thus, an investor who has a portfolio that includes S&L stocks could reduce the portfolio's exposure to market risk by selling the S&L stocks and buying retail grocery stocks.

In contrast to diversification, these traditional methods for managing market risk are often costly and inconsistent with desired investment strategies. Adjusting portfolio shares is often inconsistent with a strategy of investing heavily in stocks. For example, the manager of a stock mutual fund must invest in stocks, but the manager cannot do so and simultaneously reduce market risk by selling stocks.

Substituting low market-risk stocks for high market-risk stocks also has several problems. First, very few stocks have a small amount of market risk because all firms are affected by marketwide events, such as changes in interest rates. Second, stocks that have a small amount of market risk might not fit into an investor's overall investment strategy. For example, an investor who has detailed knowledge about S&Ls but very little knowledge about retail grocery stores would not want to sell S&L stocks and buy retail grocery stocks. Finally, a stock with a small amount of market risk might have a large amount of firm-specific risk.

An introduction to stock index futures

The limitations of the traditional methods of managing market risk have led investors to search for new risk management techniques. Since they began trading in 1982, stock index futures have become an extremely popular tool for managing market risk. This section provides an overview of stock index futures, highlighting some of their similarities and differences with other types of financial futures.

What are stock index futures?

A financial futures contract is an agreement between two parties to buy or sell a financial asset, such as a Treasury bond or foreign currency, at a given time in the future for a predetermined price. Stock index futures are financial futures contracts in which the underlying asset is a group of stocks included in one of the major stock price indexes such as the Standard & Poor's 500 Composite Stock Price Index.

In a financial futures contract, nothing is exchanged when the contract is written because it is only an agreement to make an exchange at a future date. In a typical futures contract, the buyer of the contract agrees to take delivery of the underlying asset at the agreed price when the contract expires. The seller of the contract agrees to deliver the asset at the agreed price on the expiration date.

In most financial futures contracts, physical delivery of the asset rarely occurs. Indeed, in some futures contracts, delivery is not even permitted. In most financial futures contracts, a buyer or seller settles the contract by taking an offsetting position in the same futures contract before delivery. For example, a buyer of a March Treasury bond futures contract can offset the position by selling a March Treasury bond futures contract before the expiration date of the contract.

Stock index futures are one type of futures contract that requires traders to settle contracts by taking an offsetting position. The reason that delivery is not permitted in stock index futures is that it would be impractical for a person who, say, sells an S&P 500 index futures contract to deliver all 500 stocks in exactly the proportion in which they make up the index. Although delivery is not allowed, there is a "delivery" or expiration date for stock index futures contracts. On this date, any unsettled contracts are settled by taking an offsetting position at the price of the underlying index.

Although delivery of the underlying stocks is not allowed in stock index futures contracts, thinking about the contract as if delivery were allowed may make the concept of a stock index future more intuitive. For example, if in March an investor were to buy a June S&P 500 index futures contract, the investor would simply be agreeing to buy in June the 500 stocks in the proportion in which they make up the index. Similarly, if an investor were to sell a June S&P 500 index futures, the investor would simply be agreeing to sell the stocks in June.

Profits and losses in stock index futures

As in other futures markets, traders in stock index futures will generally earn profits or suffer losses when they settle a contract. To make a profit, futures traders must sell futures for a higher price than they pay. Whether a stock index futures trader gains or loses, therefore, depends on two conditions: whether futures were initially bought or sold, and whether the price of the futures contract rises or falls between the time the initial contract is established and the time an offsetting position is taken.

A buyer of stock index futures makes a profit when the futures price rises and suffers a loss when the futures price falls. Suppose, for example, on March 10 an investor buys a June S&P 500 index futures contract for $300 per unit of the contract, and on April 20 settles the position by selling a June S&P 500 index futures contract for $305.[2] Under these circumstances, the investor would make a profit of $5 per unit

because he offset his position by selling a futures contract for $5 more than he paid.[3] On the other hand, if the price falls to $297 on April 20, the investor would lose $3 per unit because he offset the position by selling a futures contract for $3 less than the original purchase price.

In contrast, a seller of stock index futures suffers a loss when the futures price rises and makes a profit when the futures price falls. Suppose on March 10 an investor sells a June S&P 500 index futures contract for $300 per unit of the contract, and on April 20 settles the position by buying a June S&P 500 index futures contract for $305. The investor would suffer a loss of $5 because he offset his position by buying a contract for $5 more than he initially received from selling the contract. On the other hand, if the price falls to $297 on April 20, the investor would make a profit of $3 because he offset his position by buying a contract for $3 less than he initially received from selling the contract.

Growth in stock index futures trading

Stock index futures are one of the more recent financial futures. Stock index futures are used primarily by institutional investors, such as stock mutual funds, pension funds, and life insurance companies. The first stock index futures contract began trading in February 1982, when the Kansas City Board of Trade introduced a contract based on the Value Line Index. This contract was soon followed by a futures contract based on the S&P 500 index, which began trading on the Chicago Mercantile Exchange in April 1982. A futures contract based on the New York Stock Exchange Composite Index began trading on the New York Futures Exchange in May 1982. Although other contracts have begun

CHART 1

Open interest in S&P 500 index futures

Thousands of contracts

Note: Values are monthly averages of daily open interest in the nearest S&P 500 index futures contract with at least one month until expiration.

Source: Data Resources Inc.

trading since 1982, the S&P 500 index futures is the most popular stock index futures contract.[4]

Despite their relatively short history, stock index futures have gained widespread acceptance by stock market investors. One measure of activity in a stock index futures contract is open interest in the contract—the number of contracts not yet offset by opposite transactions. Chart 1 shows the open interest in the S&P 500 index futures contract from June 1982 to December 1988. Although open interest in S&P 500 index futures is fairly volatile, the trend is clearly upward. From June 1982 to December

1987, open interest rose at an average rate of 250 percent per year. While open interest has not grown much since the end of 1987, it has remained very high, suggesting that stock index futures remain popular among investors.[5]

Managing market risk with stock index futures

Stock index futures have been successful because they have opened up new dimensions for managing market risk through hedging. In contrast to traditional methods of managing market risk, hedging with stock index futures is relatively inexpensive and is consistent with most investment strategies.

Why stock index futures can hedge market risk

Investors face market risk when marketwide events cause the value of their stock portfolios to change. The market risk of a portfolio is usually measured as the volatility of that part of the portfolio's returns that is correlated with the returns of the overall stock market.

To hedge market risk, an investor must be able to take a position in a hedging asset such that profits or losses on the hedging asset offset changes in the value of the stock portfolio when marketwide events occur. For example, when marketwide events cause the value of an investor's portfolio to fall, the investor needs to make a profit on the hedging asset. The risk reduction from hedging is not free, however. Because risk and expected return are inversely related, the primary cost is that the investor's expected return will also fall.

Stock index futures can hedge market risk effectively because changes in stock index futures prices will generally be highly correlated with changes in stock portfolio values caused by marketwide events.[6] That is, when marketwide events cause the value of the stock portfolio to change, these same events will cause stock index futures prices to change. As a result, the investor can use changes in the value of a stock index futures contract to offset—that is, to hedge—changes in the value of his portfolio caused by marketwide events.

The more diversified the portfolio, the greater the correlation between the value of the portfolio and the price of stock index futures. The reason is that the primary source of risk in a well-diversified portfolio is market risk. That is, diversification eliminates most of a portfolio's firm-specific risk. For example, Chart 2 shows the value of a well-diversified stock portfolio and the price of the S&P 500 index futures.[7] The portfolio is considered to be well diversified because market risk accounts for 99 percent of its total risk.[8] As expected, the futures price and portfolio value follow each other quite closely. Because of this close relationship, stock index futures should be very effective at hedging the risk of this portfolio.

How stock index futures hedge market risk

In general, investors who hold stock portfolios hedge market risk by selling stock index futures.[9] An investor in a stock portfolio that contains market risk suffers a loss when the market falls because the value of his portfolio will also fall. But if the market falls, stock index futures prices will fall as well. When the market falls, therefore, an investor needs to make a profit from falling futures prices to offset the loss on his portfolio. Since sellers of futures make a profit when futures prices fall, the investor would hedge by selling futures. Similarly, when the market rises, the losses on the futures contract at least partly offset the profits on the original stock portfolio. Thus, by selling stock index futures, investors can reduce the price volatility of their portfolios caused by marketwide events.[10]

The reduction in price volatility that can be achieved by hedging is shown in Chart 3. This chart compares the values of the well-diversified portfolio and the same portfolio hedged by sales of S&P 500 index futures.[11] The value of the hedged portfolio is clearly less variable than the

CHART 2

Diversified portfolio value and futures price

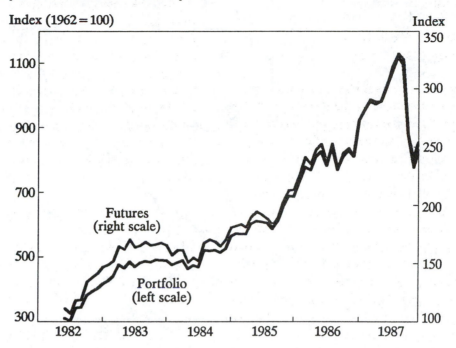

Note: The futures price is the price of the nearest S&P 500 index futures contract with at least one month until expiration. The portfolio consists of stocks of the largest firms on the New York Stock Exchange (NYSE). These firms have a market capitalization (stock prices time shares outstanding) equal to 10 percent of the NYSE capitalization.

Sources: The futures prices are from Data Resources, Inc. The portfolio values are from the Center for Research in Securities Prices.

value of the unhedged portfolio. In fact, the volatility of returns on the hedged portfolio, measured by its variance, is 91 percent lower than the volatility of the returns on the unhedged portfolio. The effectiveness of the hedge in reducing market risk is easily seen in October 1987, the month of the stock market collapse. From the end of September 1987 to the end of October 1987, the value of the unhedged portfolio fell 19 percent, while the value of the hedged portfolio fell only 6 percent.

Advantages of stock index futures over traditional techniques

Managing market risk by hedging with stock index futures does not suffer from the same problems associated with traditional methods of managing market risk. Stock index futures are relatively inexpensive and are consistent with desired investment strategies.

Relative to traditional methods of managing market risk, stock index futures are inexpen-

CHART 3

Hedging market risk

Index (1962 = 100)

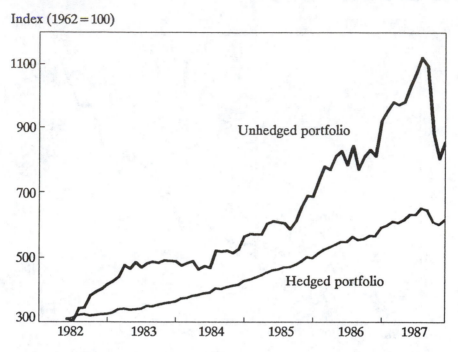

Note: The portfolio consists of stocks of the largest firms on the New York Stock Exchange (NYSE). These firms have a market capitalization (stock prices times shares outstanding) equal to 10 percent of the NYSE capitalization. The hedged value is the value of the minimum-risk hedged portfolio of stocks using the nearest S&P 500 index futures contract with at least one month until expiration.

Sources: The futures prices are from Data Resources, Inc. The portfolio values are from the Center for Research in Securities Prices.

sive because the transaction costs of establishing a futures position are low. When a position is established, the only outlays are broker fees and an initial margin deposit with the broker.[12] The fees paid to brokers and traders are quite small. For example, the cost of establishing and settling a position in an S&P 500 index futures contract is only $25.[13] Because a single S&P 500 index futures contract is worth 500 times the futures price, the total value of a contract that costs, say, $300 would be $150,000, and the $25

fee would be less than .02 of a percent of the underlying value of the contract. The initial margin is also relatively small—the margin on an S&P 500 index futures contract used for hedging purposes is $4,000. The cost of meeting the initial margin requirement is very small because investors generally can earn interest on the initial margin by using U.S. government securities to meet the margin requirement.[14]

Hedging market risk with stock index futures is also consistent with most investment strategies. In contrast to traditional methods of managing market risk, an investor who hedges market risk with stock index futures does not have to alter the composition of his portfolio. For example, stock fund managers do not have to sell part of their portfolios to reduce market risk. Nor would an investor in S&L stocks have to sell his stocks and buy low market-risk stocks with which he might not be familiar. To manage market risk by hedging with stock index futures, the investor simply has to sell the correct amount of stock index futures contracts.

Limitations of stock index futures

Despite the advantages of hedging market risk with stock index futures, there are some limitations. One important limitation is that stock index futures provide no protection against firm-specific events. In addition, the investor can be exposed to other forms of risk.[15]

Basis risk

Hedging with futures allows investors to reduce, but generally not to completely eliminate, risk. Basis risk is the risk that remains after a portfolio has been hedged. Because stock index futures only hedge market risk, firm-specific risk is the primary source of basis risk in a portfolio hedged with stock index futures.[16]

The basis risk of a hedged stock portfolio will be high when the portfolio contains a large proportion of firm-specific risk. That is, stock index futures will not be very effective in reducing the overall risk of a relatively undiversified portfolio. The reason is that firm-specific events generally have no impact on the value of the market and therefore will not affect futures prices. Because fluctuations in portfolio values due to firm-specific events are not related to futures prices, stock index futures will not provide a good hedge for these changes in portfolio values.[17]

The significance of basis risk is shown in Charts 4 and 5. Chart 4 compares the value of a relatively undiversified stock portfolio and the price of the S&P 500 index futures contract. In contrast to the well-diversified portfolio (Chart 2) in which firm-specific risk accounted for just 1 percent of total risk, firm-specific risk accounts for 34 percent of the total risk of the portfolio in Chart 4.[18] The futures price and portfolio value are related, but not nearly as closely as are the futures price and well-diversified portfolio value.

Because the value of the relatively undiversified portfolio and the futures price are not closely related, stock index futures should be less effective at hedging the total risk of this portfolio. Chart 5 compares the values of the unhedged portfolio and the same portfolio hedged by sales of S&P 500 index futures.[19] The variance of returns on the hedged portfolio is just 27 percent lower than that of the unhedged portfolio. The relative ineffectiveness of the hedge is easily seen in October 1987. From the end of September 1987 to the end of October 1987, the value of the hedged portfolio fell 24 percent, only slightly less than the 29 percent decline in the value of the unhedged portfolio.

New risks

One new type of risk involved in futures trading is marking-to-market risk. This is the risk that arises because futures traders have to cover their futures losses at the end of each day. All futures exchanges require every unsettled futures position to be marked to market every

CHART 4

Undiversified portfolio value and futures price

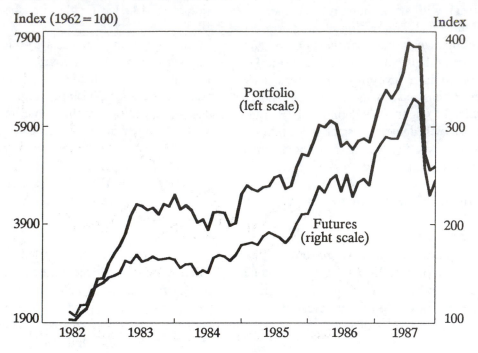

Note: The futures price is the price of the nearest S&P 500 index futures contract with at least one month until expiration. The portfolio consists of stocks of the smallest firms on the New York Stock Exchange (NYSE). These firms have a market capitalization (stock prices times shares outstanding) equal to 10 percent of the NYSE capitalization.

Sources: The futures prices are from Data Resources, Inc. The portfolio values are from the Center for Research in Securities Prices.

night and settled daily. That is, at the end of each day, funds are transferred from individuals who lose on their contracts to individuals who gain on their contracts so that buyers and sellers actually realize the gains and losses from daily price changes as they occur. A problem could occur for those who suffer losses on their futures position, though, because they must make immediate cash outlays. Although losses on stock index futures contracts are generally offset by gains on the stock portfolio being hedged, investors usually do not receive those gains as they occur. Therefore, investors would either have to liquidate some of their investments and lose the associated income flows or pay interest on borrowed funds to cover their futures losses as they occur.

A second type of risk involved in futures trading is managerial risk. Managerial risk, broadly defined, is the risk stock index futures will be used inappropriately and result in greater, rather than less, risk. This is really a "catch all" category that accounts for anything else that can go wrong with a hedging program.

CHART 5
Hedging an undiversified portfolio

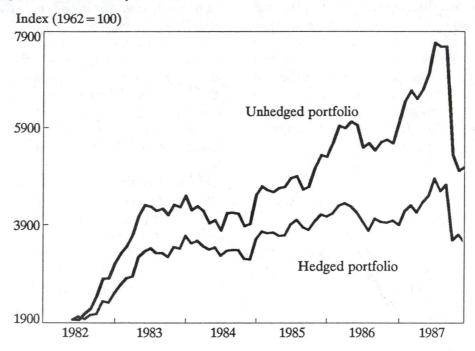

Index (1962 = 100)

Note: The portfolio consists of stocks of the smallest firms on the New York Stock Exchange (NYSE). These firms have a market capitalization (stock prices times shares outstanding) equal to 10 percent of the NYSE capitalization. The hedged value is the value of the minimum-risk hedged portfolio of stocks using the nearest S&P 500 index futures contract with at least one month until expiration.

Sources: The futures prices are from Data Resources, Inc. The portfolio values are from the Center for Research in Securities Prices.

One major reason that managerial risk arises is that stock index futures can be used for speculative purposes. In addition to being good assets for hedging market risk, stock index futures are also good assets for speculating on stock market movements for two reasons. First, it costs very little to establish a futures position, and second, stock index futures are just as risky as the market. An institution that wants to hedge with futures must have internal controls to make sure those responsible for hedging are not speculating.

Managerial risk also arises because hedging strategies involving stock index futures can become complicated. Because they can be complicated, it is possible for managers to make incorrect decisions that significantly lower a portfolio's value. For example, suppose a manager wants to minimize the market risk of a stock portfolio, but he overhedges by selling too many futures contracts. If the market were to rise, the losses on the futures position could be much greater than the gains on the portfolio. Thus, when overhedged, the riskiness of a portfolio is greater than the minimum level of risk and the expected return is less than that associated with the minimum level of risk. In fact, the riskiness of an overhedged portfolio can even be greater than the riskiness of the unhedged portfolio. To control this risk, it is important that managers understand the complexities of hedging with stock index futures, the capabilities and limitations of a hedging program, and the need to continually monitor hedging programs.

Conclusion

Stocks have always been relatively risky investments. While investors in stocks have always been able to manage the firm-specific risk component of total risk through diversification, managing the market risk component has traditionally been costly and inconsistent with desired investment strategies. The development of stock index futures, however, has provided investors in stocks with a new, low-cost tool for managing market risk. As a result, stock index futures are one of the most successful financial innovations of recent years. They have become an essential part of virtually every stock portfolio manager's tool kit for managing market risk.

This article showed how stock index futures can be used successfully to manage market risk. It must be remembered, though, that hedging with stock index futures can be complex, and investors must thoroughly examine all aspects of stock index futures and hedging techniques before implementing a hedging strategy.

Endnotes

[1] In a sense, adjusting the share of stocks in an investment portfolio is diversification, but it is diversification across different types of assets as opposed to diversification across different stocks. Throughout this article, diversification means diversification across different stocks.

[2] Actually, the quoted price of a futures contract itself is an index. The value of an S&P 500 index futures contract is $500 times the level of the index. The value of one unit of the contract, therefore, is 1/500 of the total value of the contract, or $1 times the level of the index. The total value of one contract at $300 per unit is $150,000 (500 units times $300 per unit).

[3] Because the contract is for 500 units, the actual profit is $2,500 (500 units times $5 per unit).

[4] The Value Line Index, Standard and Poor's 500 Composite Stock Price Index, and New York Stock Exchange Composite Index contracts are each worth $500 times the index level. A contract equal to $250 times the Major Market Index is traded on the Chicago Board of Trade exchange, and a contract equal to $100 times the Value Line Index (Mini Value Line) is traded on the Kansas City Board of Trade exchange.

[5] One reason open interest has leveled off is that many traders have shied away from trading stock index futures since the stock market collapsed in October 1987.

[6] These changes are highly correlated because both are highly correlated with changes in the value of the overall market. As discussed in the text, market risk is measured by the correlation between portfolio returns and market returns. Stock index futures prices are highly correlated with the value of the market because (1) broad stock indexes, such as the S&P 500 index, are used to measure the value of the market, and (2) stock index futures prices are highly correlated with the underlying index.

The price of any futures contract is always highly correlated with the price of the underlying asset. The theoretical relationship between the price of a futures contract and the price of its underlying asset is known as the cost-of-carry theory of futures prices. Prices do deviate slightly from cost of carry, though, because of transaction costs and capital market imperfections. For a detailed discussion of the relationship between stock index futures prices and stock prices, see Bradford Cornell and Kenneth R. French, "The Pricing of Stock Index Futures," *The Journal of Futures Markets* (Spring 1983), pp. 1-14.

7 The best stock index futures contract for hedging a particular stock portfolio is the futures contract whose price is most correlated with the value of the portfolio. Stock prices move together, though, so most of the stock indexes—and therefore most of the stock index futures prices—move together. Thus, for the purposes of these examples, it makes little difference which futures contract is used. The S&P 500 index futures contract is used in all examples because it is by far the most popular of the stock index futures contracts.

8 Total risk is measured by the variance of the portfolio's total monthly returns over the period from July 1982 to December 1987. Market risk is measured by the variance of the predicted returns from a regression of the portfolio's monthly returns on market returns over the same period. For a discussion of how market risk is measured, see Thomas E. Copeland and J. Fred Weston, *Financial Theory and Corporate Policy*, 2d ed., (Reading, Mass: Addison-Wesley Publishing Co., 1983).

The S&P 500 index is used to measure market returns. Theoretically, the market portfolio contains every asset in the economy. Since it is not possible to observe the true market returns, however, an imperfect measure must be used. While there are many broad stock indexes that can be used to measure market returns, the various indexes generally move together. As a result, the qualitative conclusions reached in the text remain the same as long as one of the broad indexes is used to measure market returns.

9 Although this section describes how stock index futures hedge market risk, stock index futures are also often used for reasons other than purely hedging market risk. Some strategies, such as stock selection and market timing, are used in an attempt to outperform the market. Portfolio managers also use stock index futures to give them more flexibility in liquidating a portfolio. For more information on these strategies, see Stephen Figlewski, *Hedging with Financial Futures for Institutional Investors: From Theory to Practice* (Cambridge, Mass.: Ballinger Publishing Co., 1986) pp. 115-54. Stock index futures are also used in portfolio insurance strategies. For a discussion of portfolio insurance, see Peter A. Abken, "An Introduction to Portfolio Insurance," *Economic Review*, Federal Reserve Bank of

Atlanta (November/December 1987), pp. 2-25. Finally, stock index futures are used by arbitragers who try to make a profit from discrepancies between actual stock index futures prices and the prices that would be predicted from the cost-of-carry theory of futures prices. For a discussion of index arbitrage, see John J. Merrick, Jr., "Fact and Fantasy About Stock Index Futures Program Trading," *Business Review*, Federal Reserve Bank of Philadelphia (September/October 1987), pp. 13-23.

10 Although investors in stock portfolios generally sell stock index futures to hedge their portfolios, there are times when they buy stock index futures. For example, a portfolio manager who wants to purchase some stocks but does not expect to have the necessary funds for several days faces the risk that the market will rise in the interim. The manager could hedge the risk that arises from changes in the market by buying futures. If the market rises, the loss from having to pay a higher price for the stocks will at least be partly offset by the profit on the futures. On the other hand, if the market falls, the profit from buying the stocks at a lower price will at least be partly offset by the loss on the futures.

11 For simplicity, this example assumes that the investor wants to minimize risk. In general, investors would not *minimize* the risk of a stock portfolio with stock index futures. The reason is that the expected return on such a portfolio is the risk-free rate, which the investor could get at a much lower cost by simply investing in Treasury bills. The example also ignores the effects of margin requirements, transaction costs, taxation, accounting practices, and regulatory requirements on the value of the hedged portfolio, all of which could affect the value of the hedge and the hedging strategy. The prices are end-of-month data, and the futures price is on the nearest contract with at least one month until expiration.

The example does not account for the possibility that risk could be reduced further by (1) using futures with contract months that are further out, or (2) estimating the number of contracts to sell over shorter time periods and then adjusting the number of contracts to account for the changes. On the other hand, the example could be overstating the degree of risk reduction because the number of contracts sold is estimated from actual price data over the hedging period, whereas investors must estimate the number of contracts using data from periods prior to the hedging period.

12 The margin on a futures contract is "good faith" money deposited with a broker to assure him that losses can be covered in the event of adverse price movements.

13 See Arnold Kling, "Futures Markets and Transaction

Costs," in Myron L. Kwast, ed., *Financial Futures and Options in the U.S. Economy: A Study by the Staff of the Federal Reserve System* (Washington, D.C.: Board of Governors of the Federal Reserve System, 1986), pp. 41-54.

[14] The minimum initial margin and the minimum level that must be maintained are set by the exchanges and are changed from time to time. The margin level depends on factors such as the volatility of the price of the underlying instrument. Margins also may depend on whether a person is just buying or selling futures alone or is buying or selling futures to establish a hedge. The margin on an outright purchase or sale of an S&P 500 index futures for speculative purposes is $6,500. Although investors can earn interest on the initial margin by depositing U.S. government securities, they can not earn interest on additions to the margin account because additions must be made with cash. Cash is required because additions are for losses on a contract that are transferred to the accounts of parties that have gained from price movements.

[15] One risk that individuals do not have to be concerned about is the risk of the opposite party defaulting on a futures contract. The reason is that every futures exchange has a clearing organization that is a party to every futures contract in order to guarantee the integrity of the contract. In effect, then, the clearing house is the seller in every contract bought and the buyer in every contract sold.

[16] Hedging a stock portfolio with stock index futures will completely eliminate risk only if the values of the portfolio and the futures are perfectly correlated. In general, the correlation is not perfect for two reasons. The primary reason is that most portfolios contain firm-specific risk. In addition, though, stock index futures do not even provide full protection from marketwide events because the value of the market is not perfectly correlated with the value of the futures contract. In other words, even if an investor were to diversify away all firm-specific risk and hold the market portfolio, the hedged portfolio would still contain some residual, or basis, risk.

[17] Although stock index futures are less effective at hedging the total risk of a portfolio with a relatively large share of firm-specific risk, they are equally effective at hedging the market risk of portfolios with large or small shares of firm-specific risk.

[18] Firm-specific risk is measured by the variance of the residual returns from a regression of the monthly portfolio returns on the S&P 500 index returns over the period from July 1982 to December 1987.

[19] The qualifications and assumptions that applied to the hedge of the well-diversified portfolio in Chart 3 also apply to this example (see note 11).

Article 22

An Introduction to Portfolio Insurance

Peter A. Abken

Portfolio insurance is distinguished from other types of hedging by its continuous adjustments of the investment position. Like other forms of hedging, however, portfolio insurance does not perform perfectly, as was amply demonstrated during the stock market crash of October 19.

The stock market crash on October 19, 1987, and subsequent market turmoil heated up debate over two relatively new trading techniques, stock-index arbitrage and portfolio insurance. While both are types of so-called program trading that involve use of stock-index futures contracts, stock-index arbitrage has come to be the better known of the two. This article attempts to demystify portfolio insurance by explaining this portfolio management technique and by illustrating its performance in recent market history. Consideration is also given to whether, as some market observers allege, portfolio insurance destabilized the stock market and exacerbated the crash.

Portfolio insurance (PI) programs have been offered by major banks, brokerage firms, insurance companies, and specialized PI firms. These insurance programs have attracted large institutional users, primarily pension funds. Compared with the potential market, however, portfolio insurance is still relatively obscure. Before the stock market crash in October 1987, estimates of asset values covered by portfolio insurance programs ranged from $60 billion to $100 billion. Even so, insured portfolios constituted only a small percentage of total pension fund assets.

This article presents the basic theoretical and practical aspects of portfolio insurance. It also reports simulations of portfolio insurance using the Standard and Poor's (S&P) 500 index as the underlying portfolio. Two different kinds of PI implementations are considered: the index/ Treasury bill and index/futures methods. The latter is of particular interest both because it is the actual method most commonly used and because the literature on portfolio insurance has not treated it in any depth. The article concludes with a discussion of the recent controversy surrounding portfolio insurance.

The author, a specialist in futures and options markets, is an economist in the financial section of the Atlanta Fed's Research Department. He thanks Steven Feinstein for helpful comments and both Sharon Fleming and Allison Smith for excellent research assistance.

Hedging Instruments

A review of the underlying financial instruments facilitates discussion about portfolio

insurance. The standard means for implementing portfolio insurance strategies uses stock-index futures contracts, usually the S&P 500 contract traded on the Chicago Mercantile Exchange (CME). An alternative to this approach would be simply to employ stock-index option contracts. Both futures and option contracts are referred to as derivative assets because their value depends on the value of an underlying asset, in this case a unit of the S&P 500 index.[1] A unit or "share" of the S&P 500 index is a portfolio of stocks that is identical in composition to the index. In general, a futures contract establishes a certain price at the time of purchase (sale) for deferred delivery of a specified quantity of a commodity or asset. By purchasing an S&P 500 futures contract, which is referred to as taking a *long* position in the contract, the buyer is obligated to take future delivery of the cash value of the S&P 500 index upon expiration of the contract.[2] Selling a contract, or taking a *short* position, binds the seller to pay the cash value. The obligation to make actual payment can be nullified at any time if an investor simply takes an opposite position in futures; for example, an investor could buy a futures contract if one had been previously sold, and vice versa. Gross profit on a long or short futures position solely depends upon the difference between the value of the initial futures position and its final value.

The usefulness of stock-index futures for hedging the value of a portfolio will be discussed below in detail. For now, suffice it to say that the essence of a hedging operation entails taking a futures position whose value is negatively correlated with the asset or commodity being hedged. Suppose, for instance, that a portfolio manager wants to protect a portfolio from a drop in value until some future date when the portfolio will be sold. The manager could sell stock-index futures that expire at the time he intends to liquidate the portfolio, so that for every dollar the portfolio loses (gains) in value, the short futures position gains (loses) a dollar. Obviously, although this procedure entails no risk of loss, it also presents no opportunity for gain. Using futures in this way sacrifices all "upside" potential for the portfolio. In fact, as will be demonstrated below, holding a short futures position against a portfolio is equivalent to liquidating the portfolio and holding only cash, or more precisely, holding a risk-free asset.

A portfolio's upside potential is retained by a stock-index put option, which gives the purchaser the *right* but not the *obligation* to sell the underlying units at a specified price upon expiration of the contract. (A call option gives the purchaser the corresponding right to buy.) The price specified in an option contract is known as the exercise or striking price. For an index option, the exercise price is a particular index value.

Unlike futures contracts, option contracts offer asymmetric payoffs. For example, the value of a portfolio of stocks held along with a stock-index put option may fall below the exercise price at the time of the option's expiration. This portfolio loss will result in an opposite, offsetting gain in the value of the put option, an outcome similar to that for a short index futures position. However, a rise in the portfolio's value above the exercise price is offset only by the cost of the option. Thus, this kind of option strategy, commonly known as a protective put, both "insures" a portfolio and permits it to participate in rising markets. The price of the option, or the option premium, represents the cost of the portfolio insurance.

The use of index puts in conjunction with an index portfolio is one means of creating an insured portfolio, but it has several limitations. Exchange-traded index options have a maximum maturity of nine months and are offered only for a limited number of exercise prices. Furthermore, such options may be exercised not only upon expiration, but at any time after purchase. This last feature of a so-called American option is not needed for the type of portfolio insurance generally practiced; the extra flexibility it offers to the option holder adds to the cost of the option. For these reasons, the portfolio insurance strategies considered below will involve the creation of European put options, which may be exercised only at expiration.

The Put Option as Insurance

As mentioned above, the combination of a long index put option with a unit of the S&P 500 index creates one type of portfolio insurance. For a better intuitive understanding of this relationship, the widely used payoff diagram may be helpful (see Chart 1). The diagram illustrates the range of returns available to an insured portfolio. Its horizontal axis indicates the index price at expiration of the put, and the vertical axis shows the return to the portfolio. A long position in the index is represented by line A, which intersects the horizontal axis at 200, the price at which the index was originally purchased. At expiration, every dollar rise above this purchase price corresponds to a dollar in capital appreciation by the portfolio; conversely, every dollar drop below 200 represents capital losses. Line A therefore reflects the returns to the uninsured S&P 500 portfolio. Line B depicts the returns to an index put option whose exercise price is 200. If the index price climbs to 200 or higher, the put expires unexercised, worthless. The option is said to have expired "at-the-money" (final index price equals the exercise price) or "out-of-the-money" (final index price exceeds the exercise price). The constant negative return represents the cost of the put, the put premium, which is the maximum loss that can be realized from a long put. On the other hand, if the index price is below 200, the put ends "in-the-money" and its return rises dollar for dollar with the drop in the index price.

By summing vertically the returns to the long index (line A) and long index put (line B) positions, the payoff line for the insured portfolio, line C, is derived. The maximum loss below 200 is limited to the put premium, while above 200 the portfolio rises dollar for dollar with a rise in the index price. Notice, however, that the return to the insured portfolio for index prices above 200 is shifted downward by the amount of the put premium—the cost of portfolio insurance. The "upside capture" on the insured portfolio is less than 100 percent of the return on its uninsured counterpart due to the initial investment in the index put.

In view of this cost, portfolio insurance should be seen as a way of trading off upside potential for downside protection. Electing to insure a portfolio therefore alters its return distribution. The decision to buy insurance depends on the portfolio's objectives. As reason would suggest, funds geared toward investors who are more risk-averse than average would choose insurance.[3] Besides the very serious practical questions about the effectiveness of these insurance strategies during turbulent markets, there is

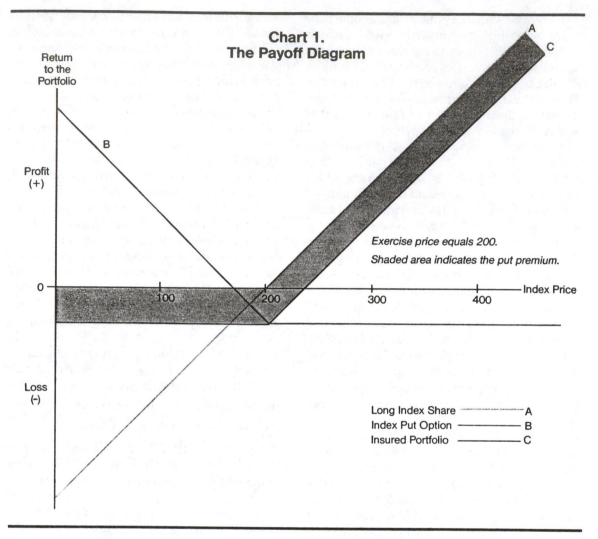

Chart 1.
The Payoff Diagram

Return to the Portfolio

Profit (+)

0

Loss (−)

Index Price

100   200   300   400

Exercise price equals 200.

Shaded area indicates the put premium.

Long Index Share ⋯⋯⋯⋯ A
Index Put Option ———— B
Insured Portfolio ———— C

some controversy about whether simpler, traditional strategies are more cost-effective. This issue is complex and unresolved, and is beyond the scope of this article.

The index put option in Chart 1 was chosen to be "at-the-money"; that is, its exercise price equals the purchase price of the index portfolio. The insured portfolio finishes with a loss at expiration when the index itself ends unchanged from its initial value, as the cost of the put option must be subtracted. By choosing an index put option whose exercise price exceeds the purchase price of the index portfolio, the investor trades off greater downside protection—a higher floor for the portfolio return—against smaller potential upside returns. This approach accords with the insurance analogy since choosing a higher exercise price is like reducing the size of the insurance deductible, thus increasing the

insurance and raising its cost. Similarly, reducing the exercise price raises the deductible and lowers the cost of insurance.

Factors Affecting the Cost of Insurance

The exercise price is but one of several determinants of the insurance cost. For the purposes of this analysis, there are two general kinds of factors that influence the cost of portfolio insurance: (1) those bearing on the value of put options and (2) those arising from the implementation of the insurance, namely, transactions costs. Option valuation factors are discussed here and the second category is deferred until later.

The Black-Scholes option pricing model provides the standard framework for approaching questions of option valuation. For highly accessible discussions of this model, see Clifford W. Smith, Jr. (1977) and John C. Cox and Mark Rubinstein (1985), among others. The underlying assumptions for the Black-Scholes model are quite restrictive; for example, the model assumes that the stock price does not make discrete jumps.[4] Even so, the model has proved to be reasonably accurate despite real world violations of those assumptions. According to the Black-Scholes model, put and call prices may be expressed as functions of five variables: (1) the current stock price, (2) the exercise price, (3) the time to expiration of the option, (4) the risk-free interest rate, and (5) the volatility of the stock price. Note that unlike stocks, which embody the market's expectations concerning future earnings, options contain no expectational factors except for the stock price's volatility. As will be seen below, this unobservable volatility must be estimated, making it the greatest obstacle in determining the value of options.

Option prices change as the underlying variables fluctuate. At any time before expiration, call prices rise with increases in the stock price, the time to expiration, the interest rate, and the volatility; they fall with increases in the exercise price. Put prices rise with increases in the exercise price and the volatility; they fall with increases in the stock price and the interest rate. A lengthening of the time to expiration has an ambiguous impact on put prices. In evaluating these effects, it is assumed that when a change in any particular variable is considered, all other variables remain constant.

An intuitive understanding of the relationships noted above facilitates discussion of option pricing and portfolio insurance. A higher stock price before the option expires reduces the put price because it lowers the probability that the put will end in-the-money. Assuming all other variables—including the volatility and the current stock price—remain unchanged, a higher exercise price increases the likelihood that the put will expire in-the-money. This greater probability raises the put price. A higher stock price volatility also increases the put price. On the one hand, given a fixed current stock price, greater dispersion of future stock prices cannot drive the put price any lower than zero. This is so because put prices, like stock prices, have limited liability to the owner: no matter how much the stock price exceeds the exercise price at expiration, the put has the same zero value. On the other hand, higher volatility, by definition, also broadens the range of lower stock prices that may occur at expiration. Greater dispersion of future stock prices raises the put's value, for the stock price at expiration is now more likely to fall below the exercise price.

As for the effect of interest rates on the pricing of put options, a higher rate lowers put prices because, before expiration, the greater interest rate diminishes the value of the exercise price for the put holder. More precisely, the present discounted value of the exercise price drops with a rise in interest rates, so that the put's future payoff, should it expire in-the-money, is worth less at the current time.

"(U)nlike stocks . . . options contain no expectational factors except for the stock price's volatility. . . . (V)olatility must be estimated, making it the greatest obstacle in determining the value of options."

Lengthening the time to expiration has an ambiguous effect on put prices. An increase in the time to expiration reduces put prices if the ratio of the stock price to the exercise price is small. In other words, the more in-the-money the put is, the less value the prospective receipt of the exercise price will have since the payment is further out in the future. This price-reducing effect may be dominated by a second effect, however. The longer the time to expiration, the greater will be the variability of the stock price over the life of the option, which, everything else being constant, boosts the probability that the put will expire in-the-money. For a sufficiently high ratio of stock price to exercise price, this second effect will overwhelm the first, so that lengthening the time to expiration raises put prices.

Creation of a Replicating Portfolio

To this point, the present discussion of portfolio insurance has focused on combining an actual index option with a portfolio to achieve the desired insurance. For the reasons cited earlier—short maturities, limited exercise prices, and early exercise rights—this protective put approach has its drawbacks. Fortunately, the same end can be reached by another method that provides greater flexibility than outright purchase of a put. This method entails "synthetically" creating an insured portfolio using a technique known as dynamic hedging. While the protective put strategy is generally quite familiar to financial market participants, dynamic hedging is less well understood and thus more likely to evoke an aura of mystery.

"Modern option pricing theory is based partly on the principle that any option position can be duplicated or replicated by systematically adjusting another portfolio that consists solely of stocks and bonds."

In a sense, the techniques of portfolio insurance are a by-product of theoretical advances in option pricing. Modern option pricing theory is based partly on the principle that any option position can be duplicated or replicated by systematically adjusting another portfolio that consists solely of stocks and bonds. The original Black-Scholes equation for the price of a European call option was derived in this way in their 1973 article. Only much later were the principles used in a practical implementation, notably by Mark Rubinstein and Hayne E. Leland (1981), which led to the development and widespread institutional use of portfolio insurance. To understand what synthetically created options are, one must first review some theoretical details, which again are discussed with emphasis on the underlying intuition.

As mentioned earlier, options are derivative assets, and so they do not depend on market participants' expectations concerning future values. Furthermore, the Black-Scholes model is developed in such a way that it is unnecessary to consider market participants' attitudes toward risk. The value of an option before expiration may be expressed as the present discounted value of its expected payoff at expiration.[5] The expectation is a mathematical, not a psychological, one, so that the expected payoff reflects the probability that the option will expire in-the-money. The relevant probabilities are determined by the five variables enumerated above: the current stock price, interest rate, volatility, exercise price, and time to expiration. Thus, given an estimate of the volatility, option valuation is entirely a mechanical process.

To make this discussion more concrete, consider the following example of the synthetic creation of an insured index portfolio. The elements needed for this task are the uninsured index portfolio and Treasury bills (the risk-free asset). The object is to form a portfolio consisting of one unit or share of the S&P 500 and one S&P 500 index put. The value of this portfolio at the time of expiration can be symbolically represented as:

$$S^* + P^* = \text{MAX} [S^*, K^*], \qquad (1)$$

where S, P, and K are respectively the index price, the put price, and the exercise price. The asterisks denote the value of these variables at the time of expiration. Omission of the asterisks indicates that these variables take on their current values. This equation simply states that the insured portfolio will be worth the greater of S^* or K^*. That is, if S^* exceeds K^*, the put expires worthless and the portfolio value is S^*; otherwise the put expires in-the-money, offsetting the decline in S^* below K^*, and the portfolio value is K^*.

Things are much more complicated prior to expiration. The formula for the *current* insured portfolio value is:

$$S + P = DF \cdot E (S^* + P^*), \qquad (2)$$

where DF represents a discount factor, which converts the future expected value of the insured portfolio into a current value, and E symbolizes the current expected value of the insured portfolio at the expiration date. DF depends on the interest rate and the time to expiration. The expectation denoted by E may be thought of as an averaging of all the values that the insured portfolio can have at the time of expiration. Some values have higher probabilities than others and thus have greater weight in the computed average. Again, it bears emphasizing that the probabilities depend only on the current values of the five underlying "inputs" into the option pricing equation. In other words, the range of possible insured portfolio values is constrained by these input variables.

Thanks to Black and Scholes's ingenuity, equation (2) can be written in terms of the five underlying variables:[6]

$$S + P = S \cdot N_1 + K \cdot DF \cdot N_2. \qquad (3)$$

Only currently observed variables and the volatility appear in the equation, which is expressed in a simplified notation to emphasize the key variables. The protective put (long index share/long index put) on the left-hand side of the equation has the same value as the replicating portfolio of the index and Treasury bills on the right-hand side. $S \cdot N_1$ represents the dollar amount of the index held and $K \cdot DF \cdot N_2$ the dollar amount of T-bills. Adjustments to the composition of the index/T-bill portfolio over time are made so that the value of the replicating portfolio matches the value of the protective put. This adjustment process is referred to as dynamic hedging, which contrasts with traditional static hedging strategies such as taking a fixed position in short futures or holding a fixed proportion of a portfolio in bonds or bills.

$K \cdot DF$ is the present discounted value of the exercise price. It has an alternative interpretation as the floor for the value of an insured portfolio any time before expiration; K is the floor at expiration.[7] Any desired index put on the left-hand side can be created by an appropriate choice of the exercise price K. The first term on the right-hand side, $S \cdot N_1$, represents the present discounted expected value of the index S* at the expiration date, given that S* exceeds the exercise price K, that is, the put expires out-of-the-money. This so-called conditional expectation is a weighted average of all possible future values of the index that are greater than K. Analogously, the second term on the right-hand side, $K \cdot DF \cdot N_2$, is the present discounted value of K, given that S* turns out to be

less than or equal to K, that is, the put finishes in-the-money.

A more immediate sense of how the replicating portfolio mimics a protective put can be developed through a consideration of extreme values that N_1 and N_2 can take. The variables N_1 and N_2 are complicated functions of the five underlying variables; they embody terms for conditional expectations and probabilities. As N_1 approaches zero, N_2 approaches one, and vice versa. Technically, these variables are known as cumulative normal distribution functions, which take values that range from zero to one. As the underlying variables change—for example, as the stock price or its volatility changes—the values of N_1 and N_2 vary, resulting in shifts in the composition of the replicating portfolio that maintain its equality with the protective put. If

---

"Adjustments to the composition of the index/T-bill portfolio over time are made so that the value of the replicating portfolio matches the value of the protective put. This adjustment process is referred to as dynamic hedging."

---

the current index price S is very much greater than K, the put is likely to expire out-of-the-money (worthless), and so N_1 is approximately equal to one and N_2 approximately zero. Hence, the current values of the insured portfolio and the index are close. Conversely, if the current index price is very much less than K, the put is "deep" in-the-money and the current insured portfolio value is close to $K \cdot DF$.

The value of N_1 plays a pivotal role in portfolio insurance. It will henceforth be referred to as the option delta, which is the standard name given to this variable. As the index price rises, so does delta; the probability that the synthetic put will expire out-of-the-money increases. The option delta has another important interpretation: it indicates what fraction of the index to hold in the replicating portfolio. Similarly, N_2

indicates the fraction of the maximum current investment in Treasury bills, that is, K·DF. Thus, as delta increases and the index rises, the replicating portfolio is shifted out of Treasury bills and into the index by selling bills and using the proceeds to buy the index. Conversely, as delta decreases and the index falls, the replicating portfolio is shifted the other way by selling the index and using the proceeds to buy bills. At expiration, the portfolio is invested entirely in the index or entirely in T-bills.

Although the composition of the replicating portfolio changes over time as the five underlying variables fluctuate, its current value equals the current value of a long index/long put portfolio because both offer the same payoff at the expiration date. It is in this respect that the replicating portfolio is equivalent to the protective put. The two portfolios are exactly equivalent only if the replicating portfolio is adjusted continuously over time. The continuously-adjusted replicating portfolio is said to be self-financing because once the initial investment is made, no further cash flows come from outside the portfolio. The protective put is also obviously self-financing in that, after the initial purchase of the index share and the index put, no further cash flows arise until the expiration date. The complications that occur due to *discontinuously adjusted* replicating portfolios are discussed below.

For the insured portfolio, part of the initial investment goes toward the purchase of a put, necessarily reducing the portfolio's upside potential. The upside capture for the replicating portfolio will be the same as that for an index-put portfolio. The cost is not an actual payment for the put, but the opportunity cost of holding part of the portfolio in Treasury bills. The greater the level of the floor, the higher are the exercise price and put premium and the smaller is the upside capture.

Using Index Futures. Although theoretically feasible, index/T-bill replicating portfolios are not used in practice. Instead, most insured portfolios are implemented using S&P 500 index futures contracts. The transactions costs for using the latter are about one-third less than for Treasury bills. Furthermore, the futures market is more liquid than the stock market, as order executions to buy or sell futures are transacted faster than those for the underlying S&P 500 itself.

The key to understanding the futures implementation is to see that a portfolio combining one share of the index with a short future is theoretically equivalent to holding a Treasury bill. In fact, a short future/long index portfolio is sometimes referred to as a synthetic money market instrument. This equivalence is based on what is known as a cost-of-carry model for futures. Buying an index share and simultaneously selling a futures contract short creates a hedged, (nearly) riskless portfolio because the futures contract fixes the selling price. What should the rate of return on a riskless asset be? By arbitrage, any assets of equal risk and maturity should earn the same rate of return. Thus, the hedged index portfolio should earn the T-bill rate. Further details about creating synthetic money market instruments are presented in the appendix to this article.

Using futures instead of T-bills simply involves an additional step in setting up and adjusting a replicating portfolio. The initial index/T-bill portfolio contains some proportion of bills, based on equation (3). For the futures version, the portfolio holds the entire share of the index and has an appropriate number of short futures contracts in order to create the bill position. In the event that the index rises after the portfolio is established, the short futures position is reduced by buying futures contracts, resulting in a smaller synthetic bill position. On the other hand, a falling index induces more futures sales to lessen the portfolio's exposure to the market, thus placing more of the portfolio in synthetic bills.

> *"For the futures version, the portfolio holds the entire share of the index and has an appropriate number of short futures contracts in order to create the . . . synthetic bill position."*

Practical Considerations

This section develops in greater depth the background needed to understand the index/T-bill and index/futures implementations of portfolio insurance. Before examining simulations run on actual historical data, some additional preliminary topics are discussed. These are intended to give a more detailed view of the mechanics of running an insured portfolio and to help in interpreting the simulation results. These topics will also help to illuminate the channels through which portfolio insurance may have affected the underlying stock market, particularly during the October 19 crash.

Sources of Error and Risk in Portfolio Replication. In practice, the floor provided by portfolio insurance can be rather soft. Inaccuracies in protective put replication arise from a number of sources. Nonconformity of real-world stock and stock-index price movements with those assumed in an option pricing model, as well as the possible inadequacy of the model itself, presents a source of error and risk to the insured portfolio owner.

The adaptation of theory to practice gives rise to replication errors, the differences between the values of the actual replicating portfolio and the theoretical insured portfolio (that is, long index/long put). Discontinuous adjustment to the composition of the insured portfolio necessarily produces replication errors, both gains and losses, which add to the uncertainty about insured portfolio performance. This adjustment process is referred to as rebalancing the portfolio. There are many possible rebalancing criteria that offer different trade-offs between more accurate replication of a long index/long put portfolio and the transactions costs that accrue due to rebalancing. According to the Black-Scholes model, one necessary condition for perfect replication is that rebalancing must occur *continuously* over time; however, even if this were possible, transactions costs would render such rebalancing prohibitively expensive. Thus, actual replicating portfolios will not match their theoretical potentials. For the purpose of this exposition, the simulated insured portfolios were rebalanced daily.

Replication errors are particularly serious when stock prices "jump" to a new level. During such sharp market moves, there is no opportunity to rebalance the insured portfolio. Due to the trade-offs involved in managing an insured portfolio, achieving a firm floor is difficult in practice. This obstacle poses a serious risk to the holder of an insured portfolio.

Mentioned above were the problems associated with estimating volatility.[8] Furthermore, the volatility may change over time, adding to uncertainty about the cost of portfolio insurance. The volatility estimate is usually revised whenever the insured portfolio is rebalanced.

For portfolios whose composition is not identical to the index, there also exists a basis risk. This risk refers to the less than perfect positive correlation between movements in the values of the portfolio and (discounted) long futures. Even for exact index portfolios, a basis risk is

---

"Nonconformity of real-world stock and stock-index price movements with those assumed in an option pricing model, as well as the possible inadequacy of the model itself, presents a source of error and risk to the insured portfolio owner."

---

still present if the put option expiration date does not coincide with the futures expiration. Nonsynchronous expiration dates also gives rise to an interest rate risk. The S&P 500 index futures contracts can be readily traded only in contract maturities of no longer than four months. Furthermore, these short-maturity contracts, being more liquid, are traded with lower transactions costs. Portfolio insurance programs, however, typically run from one to five years. Hence, the futures position must be "rolled over" at relatively frequent intervals. The difference in the expiration dates for the PI program and futures contracts creates a mismatch between the interest rate appropriate for the replicating portfolio and the short-term interest rate implied by the futures position. Thus, using futures generally entails both basis risk and interest rate risk.

The simulation runs discussed below are intended as an illustration of portfolio insurance, not as an evaluation of its efficacy. A more sophisticated modeling effort would be needed to capture many of the subtleties involved in running real-world insured portfolios.[9] Actual portfolio insurance providers do not simply let their programs run on automatic. Instead, much judgment comes into play, particularly in estimating the unobservable option volatility. Judgment is likewise instrumental when an insurer wishes to profit from futures mispricing and timing of rollovers, to decide on the timing and criteria for rebalancing, and, for some insurers, to switch among different methods for creating the insurance. These complications make actual implementation of portfolio insurance as much an art as a science.

"Actual portfolio insurance providers do not simply let their programs run on automatic. Instead, much judgment comes into play. . . . These complications make actual implementation of portfolio insurance as much an art as a science."

Some Refinements. To simplify the exposition thus far, it has been assumed that the index does not pay dividends. Because the simulations presented below use actual index data, the option pricing model needs to account for dividend payments. The insured portfolios to be examined will create European, payout-unprotected puts, that is, puts that protect only the capital appreciation component of the index return, not the dividend component. To value a dividend-unprotected put, it was assumed that the future dividend payments and their timing are known with certainty. Each index price was adjusted by subtracting the present discounted value of all future dividend payments remaining between the current date and the expiration date. In theory, stock prices fall by the amount of the dividend payment on their ex-dividend dates; the same is true of the index, which

experiences dividend distributions almost daily from its constituent stocks. The dividend-adjusted index was used in the Black-Scholes option formula to evaluate the value of delta. Both insured and uninsured index portfolios receive dividends, which are reinvested in T-bills. Bear in mind that variations in the dividend flow from the index account for only a minor proportion of the variations in the total returns on the insured and uninsured portfolios.

The simulations reported below compare insured with uninsured index portfolios. In order to make the two comparable, both were constructed to start with the same initial investment, which was the current index value for each simulation period. (Establishing an insured portfolio of the index and T-bills, or the index with short futures, is conceptually equivalent to allocating part of the funds toward paying the put premium and the remainder toward buying the index). Details concerning the method of equating the initial values of both portfolios are discussed in Mark Rubinstein (1984) and in F.J. Gould and C.B. Garcia (1987). All portfolios used daily closing prices for the S&P 500 index and futures. Unless otherwise noted, daily interest rates were computed from the outstanding T-bill that matured immediately after the S&P 500 futures expired. The expiration dates used in the simulations were taken to be the first trading day during the delivery month for the expiring S&P 500 futures contract. Transactions costs were incorporated in the Black-Scholes model using the Leland (1985) method of augmenting the estimated option volatility. The assumed transactions costs of adjusting the insured portfolio are taken to be 1 percent of the volume of transactions for the index/T-bill version and 0.33 percent for the index/futures. These figures are consistent with those reported in Rubinstein (1984), Ethan S. Etzioni (1986), and Garcia and Gould (1987). The relative cost advantage of futures assumed here is fairly conservative.

Another detail that deserves mention is that the cash flows associated with a futures position are ignored in the simulations. Futures contracts are marked to market daily, which means that gains (or losses) to the futures position are received (or paid) daily. In managing an actual insured portfolio, some provision must be made to handle these cash flows, particularly the out-

Table 1.
An Example of an Index/T-Bill Insured Portfolio,
September 3, 1986 - September 16, 1986*

Date	Uninsured Portfolio	Percent Change	Insured Portfolio	Percent Change	Delta	Synthetic Put Price**	Stock	Bills	Interest Rate
9/3	250.08	.00	250.08	.00	.278	11.38	66.60	183.48	5.25
9/4	253.86	1.51	250.90	.33	.377	9.09	91.58	159.53	5.22
9/5	250.54	.18	250.00	-.03	.302	11.44	72.27	177.63	5.28
9/8	248.24	-.73	249.51	-.23	.248	13.08	58.95	190.31	5.28
9/9	247.81	-.91	249.45	-.25	.221	13.12	52.31	196.87	5.27
9/10	247.23	-1.14	249.39	-.28	.204	13.56	48.13	200.96	5.22
9/11	235.38	-5.88	247.50	-1.03	.119	24.94	26.69	220.10	5.28
9/12	230.90	-7.67	247.05	-1.21	.083	29.11	18.42	227.90	5.26
9/15	232.20	-7.15	247.20	-1.15	.092	27.94	20.47	225.99	5.23
9/16	232.02	-7.22	247.22	-1.14	.088	28.13	19.43	227.06	5.20

*   *The portfolio is rebalanced daily.*

** *The expiration date for the synthetic put is December 1, 1986.*

flows. Either a separate fund of cash instruments (T-bills) is set aside for this purpose, or part (say, 5 percent) of the insured portfolio is held in T-bills. A somewhat more complicated accounting scheme would have been needed in the simulations to keep track of the interest earned (or forgone) on the gains (or losses) to the futures position. However, including this accounting would have only a minor effect on the simulation results.

Two Examples of Insured Portfolios

The Index/T-Bill Version. Table 1 provides a detailed comparison of the daily changes in sample insured and uninsured S&P 500 index portfolios. The insured portfolio uses the index/T-bill implementation; its transactions costs were set to zero for this example. Both portfolios are initiated on September 3, 1986, and have initial index values of 250.08. The insured portfolio contains a synthetic put that expired on December 1, 1986, and that was constructed to insure to a maximum (theoretical) loss of zero percent of the initial portfolio value. The zero percent floor applies to the insured portfolio value as of the expiration date. Prior to that date, as can be seen, the portfolio can fall

below the floor level, although capital losses will be less than those on the uninsured portfolio.

During the ten-trading-day period reported in the table, the S&P 500 fell sharply, experiencing a very large 4.8 percent decline on Thursday, September 11, from the previous day's close. This produced a 42 percent drop in delta, which triggered a 45 percent reduction in the insured portfolio index holdings. The proceeds from the partial index liquidation were used to increase bill holdings. Due to this gradual daily shifting of index holdings to bills, the insured portfolio had lost 1.0 percent of its value from September 3 as compared with a 5.9 percent loss on the uninsured index itself. Another way to view this process is to note that the synthetic put value rose over this period as the index fell, thus providing partial insurance during the market's decline.

Over the full insurance period, the actual index turned out to be almost unchanged, finishing on December 1 at 249.05. The uninsured portfolio (which includes accumulated dividends and interest) was up 0.41 percent, while the insured portfolio was down 0.60 percent. As expected, the insured portfolio was less volatile than the index: the maximum loss for the uninsured portfolio was 7.8 percent as opposed to a

Table 2.
An Example of an Index/Futures Insured Portfolio,
September 3, 1986 - September 16, 1986*

Date	Uninsured Portfolio	Percent Change	Insured Portfolio	Percent Change	Delta	Synthetic Put Price**	Stock	Bills	Synthetic Interest Rate	Futures Basis
9/3	250.08	.00	250.08	.00	.278	11.38	66.60	183.48	8.54	2.27
9/4	253.86	1.51	251.17	.44	.377	9.09	91.58	159.68	8.10	2.07
9/5	250.54	.18	250.83	.30	.302	11.44	72.27	178.46	5.71	.98
9/8	248.24	-.73	249.25	-.33	.248	13.08	58.95	190.18	8.93	2.31
9/9	247.81	-.91	249.46	-.25	.221	13.12	52.31	197.02	8.12	1.93
9/10	247.23	-1.14	249.63	-.18	.204	13.56	48.13	201.35	7.37	1.59
9/11	235.38	-5.88	249.07	-.40	.119	24.94	26.69	220.02	2.68	-.28
9/12	230.90	-7.67	249.25	-.33	.083	29.11	18.42	230.47	0.74	-.97
9/15	232.20	-7.15	249.19	-.35	.092	27.94	20.47	228.36	1.21	-.79
9/16	232.02	-7.22	249.28	-.32	.088	28.13	19.43	229.48	0.94	-.87

* The portfolio is rebalanced daily.

** The expiration date for the synthetic put is December 1, 1986.

maximum loss of 1.5 percent for the insured; the maximum gains were 1.5 percent and 0.3 percent, respectively. Again, downside protection comes at the expense of upside performance.

The Index/Futures Version. Table 2 repeats the portfolio comparisons given in Table 1, but instead of index/bill implementation the insured portfolio uses index/futures. The synthetic put prices and option deltas are identical to those in Table 1, because the T-bill rate was still used in the Black-Scholes equation. Transactions costs are again assumed to be zero for this example. Differences between the two simulations arise because of mispricing of the futures. Both Etzioni (1986) and John J. Merrick, Jr. (1987b) discuss the empirically observed tendency for index futures price changes to "overshoot" index price changes. In other words, when the index price is rising (falling), the futures price tends to increase (decrease) more than proportionately. As a result of mispricing, the value of the synthetic bill position on a given day will differ from the value of the T-bill position on that day. The reported daily interest rates on the synthetic bill are clearly more volatile than the corresponding T-bill rates. This is true not only for this small sample but also over the entire history of the S&P 500 index futures. The volatility tends to be greatest during the contract's delivery month, which is why the expiration date for the insurance period was chosen to be the first trading day of the delivery month.

Underpriced futures contracts imply that bill yields are lower and bill prices are higher. Additional futures sales during a market decline are therefore equivalent to purchasing low (and possibly negative) yielding synthetic bills. During the market drop on September 11, the synthetic rate dropped from 7.37 percent the previous day to 2.68 percent, and continued to fall on the next day to 0.74 percent. As can be seen in the "Futures Basis" column, the decline in yield corresponds to a dipping of the S&P December futures price below the S&P 500 index (that is, a negative basis). This occurrence is not uncommon, despite the fact that it represents a stock-index arbitrage opportunity.[10]

The value of the synthetic bill component of the insured portfolio on September 11 exceeded the value of the corresponding actual bill component reported in Table 1. This disparity appears simply because the synthetic bills bought before September 11 were cheaper than the actual T-bills; that is, the synthetic yield was greater than the actual bill yield. After September 11, the pricing relationship reversed so that if the insured portfolio had been liquidated at the close of business on September 11, capital gains would have accrued to the synthetic bills. The superior performance of the index/futures portfolio over the index/T-bill portfolio resulted because futures were initially overpriced and later underpriced during the first half of September 1986. From September 3 to the close on September 11, the index/futures insured portfolio was down only 0.40 percent as compared with a decline of 1.03 percent for the index/T-bill portfolio.

During the course of the insurance period, it turned out that the synthetic rate was more often than not below the actual bill rate. The cumulative impact of the futures mispricing caused the index/futures insured portfolio to finish below the index/T-bill insured portfolio. At expiration on December 1, 1986, the index/T-bill insured portfolio was 0.60 percent below its initial value, while the index/futures insured portfolio was down 1.06 percent. Discontinuous trading results in cumulative errors in the replicating portfolio, so that, as in these cases, the portfolio performances will virtually always deviate from their theoretical potentials.

Simulations Using Historical Data

Tables 3 through 5 report simulation results for insured and uninsured S&P 500 index portfolios spanning different periods and using different implementations and insurance floors. Table 3 displays the results for portfolio simulations that ran one-year insured portfolios with starting dates from January 1974 to January 1986. The daily yield on the current one-year T-bill was used in the daily option pricing. Most portfolios were simulated over 253 trading days, and the insured portfolios, with - 5, 0, and 3 percent floors, were rebalanced daily. Most items in the table are self-evident. For any time period, the uninsured S&P 500 index and insured portfolio data and statistics are read by row. The final S&P 500 index value is less than the S&P portfolio value (the "Final Portfolio" column) because the latter includes accumulated dividends and interest on those dividends. The uninsured S&P portfolio is directly comparable with the various insured portfolios.

All percentage changes are taken relative to the initial portfolio values, which by construc-

tion are the same for all portfolios. The "Portfolio Percent Change" column gives the total change from the initial to final dates. The "Maximum Percent Change" column gives the maximum cumulative change in portfolio that occurred during the life of the portfolio. Similarly, the "Minimum Percent Change" column indicates the lowest cumulative percentage change from the initial portfolio value.

Finally, the "Cost" column reports the difference between a given insured portfolio's final return (under "Portfolio Percent Change") and the uninsured portfolio's final return (in the same column). Again, the cost can be thought of as being analogous to funds allocated to purchasing a put, so that less remains for investment in the index. The cost actually arises because part of an insured portfolio's value is placed in T-bills, which necessarily results in forgone capital and dividend returns when the uninsured portfolio appreciates faster than T-bills. The cost, therefore, is actually an opportunity cost associated with creating an insured portfolio. On the other hand, when the insured portfolio loses value relative to the floor level, the cost of holding an insured portfolio will be negative, that is, the insurance pays off.

As an example of insured and uninsured portfolio performance during a rising market, consider the January 2, 1986, to December 31, 1986, holding period in Table 3. All portfolios started at the initial index value of 209.59. The uninsured portfolio appreciated by 19.65 percent by December 31, whereas all insured portfolios underperformed this rate of appreciation, as expected. The - 5 percent floor portfolio had, in effect, the largest deductible and consequently had the next best return of 12.67 percent, 6.99 percentage points less than the uninsured portfolio's cumulative change. Reducing the deductible, by lifting the floor, raised the opportunity cost of insurance considerably. The cumulative returns on the 0 percent and 3 percent floor portfolios were, respectively, 9.39 and 5.08 percent. The synthetic creation of a protective put also dampened fluctuations in insured portfolio values over the lives of the portfolios, as is readily seen in the maximum and minimum cumulative percentage change columns.

The January 3, 1977, to December 30, 1977, period gives an example of portfolio performance during a declining market. Because the

Table 3.
Insured vs. Uninsured Index Portfolios*
(Transactions Costs Included)

Index/T-Bill Version

Portfolio	Floor Level	Initial Index	Final Index	Final Portfolio	Portfolio Percent Change	Maximum Percent Change	Minimum Percent Change	Cost
January 3, 1974 - December 31, 1974 **253 Trading Days**								
S&P 500	***	97.68	68.56	72.39	-25.90	2.83	-33.32	***
-5%	92.80	***	***	94.45	-3.31	1.13	-5.44	-22.60
0%	97.68	***	***	99.79	2.16	2.16	-1.64	-28.06
+3%	100.61	***	***	101.84	4.26	4.26	-0.81	-30.16
January 2, 1975 - December 31, 1975 **253 Trading Days**								
S&P 500	***	70.23	90.19	94.08	33.93	39.04	-0.19	***
-5%	66.72	***	***	84.99	21.02	28.25	-0.15	12.91
0%	70.23	***	***	80.59	14.74	21.83	-0.08	19.20
+3%	72.35	***	***	76.00	8.21	13.97	-0.01	25.72
January 2, 1976 - December 31, 1976 **253 Trading Days**								
S&P 500	***	90.90	107.46	111.51	22.65	22.65	1.86	***
-5%	86.36	***	***	104.77	15.26	15.65	1.32	7.39
0%	90.90	***	***	101.73	11.91	12.24	0.88	10.74
+3%	93.63	***	***	97.30	7.04	7.20	0.46	15.62
January 3, 1977 - December 30, 1977 **252 Trading Days**								
S&P 500	***	107.00	95.10	99.83	-6.72	-1.20	-11.59	***
-5%	101.65	***	***	100.80	-5.80	-0.89	-6.42	-0.92
0%	107.00	***	***	106.94	-0.06	-0.06	-2.29	-6.66
+3%	110.21	***	***	110.16	2.96	2.96	-0.46	-9.67
January 3, 1978 - December 29, 1978 **252 Trading Days**								
S&P 500	***	93.82	96.11	101.43	8.09	17.91	-6.47	***
-5%	89.13	***	***	95.11	1.37	12.93	-4.73	6.71
0%	93.82	***	***	93.31	-0.55	10.49	-2.60	8.64
+3%	96.64	***	***	95.03	1.28	6.92	-1.07	6.80
January 2, 1979 - December 31, 1979 **253 Trading Days**								
S&P 500	***	96.73	107.94	113.91	17.74	19.63	0.25	***
-5%	91.89	***	***	106.93	10.54	13.87	-0.58	7.20
0%	96.73	***	***	105.66	9.24	12.35	-0.14	8.51
+3%	99.63	***	***	103.75	7.26	10.10	0.35	10.48
January 2, 1980 - December 31, 1980 **253 Trading Days**								
S&P 500	***	105.76	135.76	142.42	34.63	38.54	-5.73	***
-5%	100.47	***	***	134.19	26.88	31.32	-5.53	7.75
0%	105.76	***	***	132.10	24.90	29.26	-4.79	9.73
+3%	108.93	***	***	129.59	22.53	26.80	-4.18	12.10

Table 3 continued

Portfolio	Floor Level	Initial Index	Final Index	Final Portfolio	Portfolio Percent Change	Maximum Percent Change	Minimum Percent Change	Cost
			January 2, 1981 - December 31, 1981 253 Trading Days					
S&P 500	***	136.34	122.55	129.71	-4.88	1.66	-13.53	***
-5%	129.52	***	***	128.67	-5.63	1.02	-8.39	0.75
0%	136.34	***	***	136.95	0.45	0.85	-3.58	-5.32
+3%	140.43	***	***	141.91	4.08	4.08	-2.58	-8.96
			January 4, 1982 - December 31, 1982 253 Trading Days					
S&P 500	***	122.74	150.64	148.06	20.60	21.87	-12.93	***
-5%	116.60	***	***	138.92	13.18	15.08	-9.09	7.42
0%	122.74	***	***	138.26	12.64	14.45	-6.41	7.96
+3%	126.42	***	***	137.05	11.66	13.42	-4.79	8.95
			January 3, 1983 - December 30, 1983 253 Trading Days					
S&P 500	***	138.34	164.93	172.40	24.59	28.91	1.48	***
-5%	131.42	***	***	159.01	14.94	20.18	0.55	9.65
0%	138.34	***	***	153.75	11.14	16.05	0.43	13.45
+3%	142.49	***	***	148.07	7.03	10.92	0.37	17.56
			January 3, 1984 - December 31, 1984 253 Trading Days					
S&P 500	***	164.04	167.24	175.18	6.77	7.93	-7.28	***
-5%	155.84	***	***	166.25	1.35	3.23	-7.10	5.42
0%	164.04	***	***	166.08	1.25	2.91	-4.39	5.52
+3%	168.96	***	***	166.21	1.32	2.88	-2.38	5.45
			January 2, 1985 - December 31, 1985 253 Trading Days					
S&P 500	***	165.37	211.28	219.67	32.81	33.03	-0.99	***
-5%	157.10	***	***	207.71	25.60	26.04	-0.74	7.21
0%	165.37	***	***	203.62	23.13	23.55	-0.52	9.28
+3%	170.33	***	***	198.39	19.97	20.37	-0.32	12.85
			January 2, 1986 - December 31, 1986 253 Trading Days					
S&P 500	***	209.59	242.17	250.82	19.65	24.95	-2.70	***
-5%	100.11	***	***	236.14	12.67	18.18	-2.05	6.99
0%	209.59	***	***	229.28	9.39	14.74	-1.39	10.26
+3%	215.88	***	***	220.23	5.08	10.60	-0.76	14.58

* *The portfolios are rebalanced daily.*

uninsured portfolio ended 6.72 percent below its initial value, all synthetic puts finished in-the-money. The - 5, 0, and 3 percent floor portfolios had cumulative final returns of - 5.80, - 0.06, and 2.96 percent respectively. These returns happen to be quite close to their floor values. Due to replication errors, returns for these portfolios during other down-market years are sometimes greater or smaller than their targeted floors. Notice that even before the insured portfolios' expiration dates, some degree of protection was obtained from market declines, since the minimum cumulative percentage changes are not as large as the -11.59 percent drop for the uninsured portfolio.

Tables 4 and 5 give simulation results for three-month insurance periods (see pp. 20-23). The two tables are identical in all respects, except that Table 4 represents the index/T-bill version of portfolio insurance while Table 5 represents the index/futures version. Each insurance period coincides with the final three months for each of the S&P 500 index futures contracts issued, beginning with the March 1983 contract. The T-bill expiring immediately after the futures contract was matched with the futures in doing each simulation, and the daily yield on that bill was used in pricing the option in both tables. The tables include insured portfolios with 0 and - 5 percent floors. The full simulation results for Tables 1 and 2 are given in the last block of entries in Tables 4 and 5.

In the sample considered in Tables 4 and 5, futures mispricing turns out to be substantial. In 14 out of 36 simulated insured portfolios, the cost of the index/futures version exceeded that of the index/T-bill version, despite the transactions cost advantage of using futures. These simulations were also recomputed setting transactions costs to zero, as in Tables 1 and 2. Differences between the two implementations now arise solely because of mispricing.[11] The results (not included in the tables) indicate that 18 out of 36 index/futures simulations are higher-cost compared with their index/T-bill counterparts. The simulations reveal that index futures mispricing is empirically important and can offset the cost advantage of using futures. This conclusion is tempered by the caveats offered above concerning simulations and by the conservative estimate for the futures cost advantage.

To the extent that the mispricing is systematic and predictable, the replication strategy can be adjusted to compensate for the mispricing. Merrick (1987b) discusses a procedure to correct for predictable mispricings. To some degree, judgment and discretion exercised in insuring a portfolio using futures would be expected to mitigate the costs arising from disadvantageous mispricing.

Insurers particularly want to protect against catastrophic market declines, and this is precisely where the usefulness of portfolio insurance is problematic. The mispricing phenomenon became acute during the October 19, 1987, stock market crash. One prominent portfolio insurer hesitated in selling futures as the market declined because of the steep discount on the futures below the index. The firm hoped for a realignment of futures and index prices, which did not occur due to the breakdown in arbitrage, and eventually sold less than half the futures contracts that their programs called for.[12] Other insurers were probably in a similar bind at the time. As a result, insured portfolios fell below their floor levels. The accompanying box discusses the issues and presents currently available information on the role of portfolio insurance in the October crash (see p. 19).

Conclusion

The term portfolio insurance is a misnomer, as the recent market crash has made abundantly clear. This article has shown how the most common implementation of portfolio insurance is a specialized form of hedging using stock-index futures. As is well known to practitioners, hedging is generally not without risk, and portfolio insurance strategies are no exception.

The dynamic adjustments associated with portfolio insurance distinguish it from other types of hedging. Frequent changes to the short futures position, or alternatively to the index and T-bill positions, are made to replicate synthetically a portfolio insured by an index put (a protective put). The success of this hedging strategy in providing downside protection depends on a host of factors, which have been discussed in this article. Actual insured portfolio performance may fail to achieve the prespecified floor rate of return. One reason, highlighted above, is that futures prices frequently differ substantially from their theoretically predicted values. Futures mispricing contributes to the uncertainty regarding insured portfolio performance and cost.

The mispricing that occurred during the October 19 stock market crash was unprecedented, as were practically all aspects of that financial collapse. As critics were quick to point out, portfolio insurance did not perform as expected. However, the partial failure of the insurance was a consequence of structural frictions in both the stock and futures markets, not of the insurance technique per se. Since the market collapse, the number of clients using portfolio insurance has shrunk, reportedly by half of the pre-October level, in terms of asset values covered.[13] Whether portfolio insurance recovers its appeal remains an open question. What is clear is that major institutional changes that transform trading into a more highly automated process would improve the effectiveness of PI strategies. Over recent years, advances in computer technology have revolutionized trading in traditional as well as in new securities and financial instruments and will surely continue to do so. Portfolio insurance is an outgrowth of progress in financial theory and practice, and is but one example of the evolutionary development of the marketplace.

Appendix

The relationship between the index price and the futures price is determined by the net cost of holding a hedged long position in the S&P 500 index. The opportunity cost of this investment is assumed to be the risk-free rate, that is, the interest rate on Treasury bills of comparable maturity. Selling an S&P 500 futures contract against a share of the S&P 500 index renders the long index position riskless because at expiration, due to the convergence of futures and index prices, the gain (or loss) on the long index position will be exactly offset by the loss (or gain) on the short futures position. In equilibrium, investors will be indifferent between holding a perfectly hedged position in the index and holding an equivalent position in T-bills.

The cost-of-carry relationship may be expressed as follows:

$$\frac{365}{\tau} \left[\left(\frac{F - I}{I}\right) + \frac{D}{I} \right] = r,$$

where F is the current futures price, I the current index price, D the present discounted value of anticipated dividends, r the annualized risk-free rate, and τ the time to expiration of the futures contract. The first term in brackets is the futures basis, expressed as a fraction of the index. The second term is the expected dividend yield. The annualized sum of these two yields is equal to the annualized risk-free rate. In other words, the holder of the hedged index position receives the capital appreciation locked in by the futures contract and the dividends paid by the stocks contained in the index up until expiration of the futures contract.

Given the values of the other variables, the equilibrium value of the futures price is determined. A futures basis greater than the equilibrium basis implies a risk-free arbitrage opportunity which entails selling the relatively overpriced future and buying the underpriced index. Conversely, a futures basis smaller than the equilibrium basis induces arbitrage, which involves buying the underpriced future and selling (or selling short) the overpriced index. See John J. Merrick, Jr. (1987a) for an introduction to stock-index arbitrage, and Hans R. Stoll and Robert E. Whaley (1985) for a discussion of practical aspects of carrying out the arbitrage.

Portfolio Insurance and the Crash of October 1987

The stock market crash on Monday, October 19, 1987, has raised questions both about how effectively portfolio insurance limited downside risk and about its possible systemic repercussions to the underlying stock market. On October 19, "Black Monday," the Dow Jones Industrial Average plunged a record 508 points (22 percent) and the S&P 500 Index dropped 57.6 points (20.5 percent), proportionately almost as much. In the following weeks, both stock-index arbitrage and portfolio insurance were widely blamed for exacerbating the market's turmoil.

Some critics have raised a well-founded concern that the *interaction* of portfolio insurance and stock-index arbitrage may be destabilizing. Stock-index arbitrage should be thought of as a trading link between the futures and stock markets that aligns index futures and stock index prices. Stock-index arbitrage is a straightforward form of arbitrage: buying a good or asset in a market where it is cheap and selling it in a market where it is dear. If the futures price is sufficiently below (above) the index price, arbitrageurs buy (sell) the futures and sell (buy) the index. In theory, ensuring that the "law of one price" holds cannot be destabilizing; in practice, however, the volume and timing of stock-index arbitrage could conceivably contribute to intraday volatility. Coupling index arbitrage with portfolio insurance may create destabilizing price movements. The critics' argument goes as follows: A large market decline triggers futures selling by portfolio insurers, which drives the futures price down relative to the index price. This in turn sets off arbitrage trading because the futures become underpriced relative to the index. Stock-index arbitrageurs buy the futures and sell short a basket of stocks that replicates the current composition of the index. Stock sales by arbitrageurs drive the index price down. Thus, stock-index arbitrage transmits the selling pressure from futures to the stock market. Arbitrage-induced price declines in the stock market then induce further portfolio-insurance futures selling, setting off a downward price spiral between the stock and futures markets.

What actually happened on October 19 is more complicated than the above scenario. Right at the opening of trade on "Black Monday," the S&P 500 futures market was exposed to great selling pressure. After the previous Friday's 106 point decline on the Dow, portfolio managers and others may have anticipated further futures selling by insurers and tried to get their own futures and stock sales in ahead of them.

The chaotic market conditions on Black Monday led to a breakdown of stock-index arbitrage because it became very risky. The volatility in both the futures and stock markets made it difficult to know what the current futures and index prices were. Trades based on incorrect prices could translate into large losses on what theoretically are riskless transactions. The record trading volume of 605 million shares on the New York Stock Exchange (NYSE) also compounded the risk, as orders could not be executed immediately and simultaneously in the two markets. The NYSE "uptick" rule restricted opportunities to sell stock short during the huge market decline on October 19. Arbitrageurs who executed their stock market trades by short selling had to wait for component stock prices to rise before having their sell orders executed. Severe order backlogs developed on the NYSE.

Preliminary survey data collected by the regulatory agency that oversees stock-index futures trading, the Commodity Futures Trading Commission (CFTC), indicate that index arbitrage constituted only 9 percent of total NYSE volume on that day. On the following day, after the Chicago Mercantile Exchange temporarily suspended trading in stock-index futures, the NYSE effectively banned arbitrage by prohibiting brokerage houses from executing orders through direct computer links to the exchange floor; arbitrage trading dropped to 2 percent of volume.[1]

According to preliminary CFTC trader position data, futures selling by institutional investors accounted for a greater volume of trades in the S&P 500 futures than stock-index arbitrage: their futures sales on October 19 represented between 12 and 24 percent of that day's total volume in the S&P 500 contract and between 19 and 26 percent on October 20.[2] Portfolio insurance-related futures sales were a portion of that hedging-related activity. Only careful study of market events surrounding the crash may uncover what role portfolio insurance played in the market turmoil.

Notes

[1] U.S. Commodity Futures Trading Commission, *Interim Report on Stock Index Futures and Cash Market Activity During October 1987*, November 9, 1987, p. 74.
[2] Ibid.

Table 4.
Insured vs. Uninsured Index Portfolios*
(Transactions Costs Included)
Index/T-Bill Version

Portfolio	Floor Level	Initial Index	Final Index	Final Portfolio	Portfolio Percent Change	Maximum Percent Change	Minimum Percent Change	Cost
			January 31, 1983 - March 1, 1983					
			22 Trading Days					
S&P 500	***	144.51	150.88	151.49	4.83	4.83	-1.03	***
-5%	137.28	***	***	150.16	3.91	3.91	-0.88	0.92
0%	144.51	***	***	145.08	0.39	0.48	-0.15	4.43
			March 3, 1983 - June 1, 1983					
			64 Trading Days					
S&P 500	***	152.30	162.55	164.36	7.92	10.23	-1.58	***
-5%	144.68	***	***	161.12	5.79	8.14	-1.22	2.13
0%	152.30	***	***	154.28	1.30	2.75	-0.25	6.62
			June 3, 1983 - September 2, 1983					
			66 Trading Days					
S&P 500	***	163.98	165.00	166.86	1.75	4.54	-2.12	***
-5%	155.78	***	***	164.06	0.05	3.67	-2.85	1.70
0%	163.98	***	***	163.41	-0.35	1.72	-0.92	2.10
			September 7, 1983 - December 1, 1983					
			62 Trading Days					
S&P 500	***	167.89	166.49	168.25	0.21	3.24	-2.89	***
-5%	159.50	***	***	166.42	-0.88	2.42	-2.95	1.09
0%	167.89	***	***	168.77	0.52	0.99	-0.40	-0.31
			December 5, 1983 - March 1, 1984					
			62 Trading Days					
S&P 500	***	165.54	158.19	160.01	-3.34	2.68	-5.79	***
-5%	157.26	***	***	157.66	-4.76	2.00	-5.27	1.42
0%	165.54	***	***	166.16	0.37	0.96	-0.58	-3.71
			March 5, 1984 - June 1, 1984					
			64 Trading Days					
S&P 500	***	159.24	153.24	155.14	-2.57	2.46	-4.48	***
-5%	151.28	***	***	152.94	-3.95	1.38	-4.66	1.38
0%	159.24	***	***	160.05	0.51	0.54	-0.78	-3.08
			June 5, 1984 - September 4, 1984					
			65 Trading Days					
S&P 500	***	154.34	164.88	166.85	8.11	9.82	-3.53	***
-5%	146.62	***	***	163.87	6.17	8.07	-3.38	1.93
0%	154.34	***	***	158.51	2.70	4.48	-0.93	5.41
			September 6, 1984 - December 3, 1984					
			63 Trading Days					
S&P 500	***	164.29	162.82	164.73	0.27	4.53	-1.16	***
-5%	156.08	***	***	162.05	-1.36	3.13	-1.44	1.63
0%	164.29	***	***	166.00	1.04	1.38	0.05	-0.77

Table 4 continued

Portfolio	Floor Level	Initial Index	Final Index	Final Portfolio	Portfolio Percent Change	Maximum Percent Change	Minimum Percent Change	Cost
			December 5, 1984 - March 1, 1985					
			61 Trading Days					
S&P 500	***	163.38	183.23	185.17	13.34	13.34	-0.83	***
-5%	155.21	***	***	182.18	11.51	11.58	-0.77	1.83
0%	163.38	***	***	176.08	7.78	7.83	-0.25	5.56
			March 5, 1985 - June 3, 1985					
			64 Trading Days					
S&P 500	***	182.06	189.32	191.36	5.11	5.22	-2.88	***
-5%	172.96	***	***	189.37	4.02	4.23	-2.30	1.09
0%	182.06	***	***	184.44	1.31	1.54	-0.55	3.80
			June 5, 1985 - September 3, 1985					
			64 Trading Days					
S&P 500	***	190.04	187.91	189.97	-0.04	3.47	-2.36	***
-5%	180.54	***	***	187.45	-1.36	2.61	-2.22	1.33
0%	190.04	***	***	190.54	0.26	1.22	-0.56	-0.30
			September 5, 1985 - December 2, 1985					
			63 Trading Days					
S&P 500	***	187.37	200.46	202.46	8.05	9.11	-3.33	***
-5%	178.00	***	***	199.66	6.56	7.66	-2.92	1.49
0%	187.37	***	***	194.52	3.82	4.88	-0.74	4.24
			December 4, 1985 - March 3, 1986					
			62 Trading Days					
S&P 500	***	200.86	225.42	227.49	13.25	13.98	1.11	***
-5%	190.82	***	***	223.82	11.43	12.17	0.82	1.82
0%	200.86	***	***	216.05	7.56	8.28	0.07	5.69
			March 5, 1986 - June 2, 1986					
			63 Trading Days					
S&P 500	***	224.38	245.04	247.12	10.13	11.41		***
-5%	213.16	***	***	242.35	8.01	9.31	-0.01	2.12
0%	224.38	***	***	232.17	3.47	4.71	0.01	6.66
			June 4, 1986 - September 2, 1986					
			64 Trading Days					
S&P 500	***	245.51	248.52	250.65	2.09	3.99	-4.42	***
-5%	233.23	***	***	246.66	0.47	2.39	-3.67	1.63
0%	245.51	***	***	245.47	-0.02	0.87	-0.75	2.11
			September 4, 1986 - December 1, 1986					
			63 Trading Days					
S&P 500	***	250.08	249.05	251.12	0.41	1.51	-7.83	***
-5%	237.58	***	***	246.01	-1.63	1.10	-5.10	2.04
0%	250.08	***	***	249.38	-0.28	0.33	-1.21	0.69

* The portfolios are rebalanced daily.

Table 5.
Insured vs. Uninsured Index Portfolios*
(Transactions Costs Included)

Index/Futures Version

Portfolio	Floor Level	Initial Index	Final Index	Final Portfolio	Portfolio Percent Change	Maximum Percent Change	Minimum Percent Change	Cost
			January 31, 1983 - March 1, 1983					
			22 Trading Days					
S&P 500	***	144.51	150.88	151.53	4.83	4.83	-1.03	***
-5%	137.28	***	***	150.05	3.83	3.83	-0.91	0.99
0%	144.51	***	***	143.46	-0.73	0.16	-0.85	5.55
			March 3, 1983 - June 1, 1983					
			64 Trading Days					
S&P 500	***	152.30	162.55	164.36	7.92	10.23	-1.58	***
-5%	144.68	***	***	161.81	6.25	8.61	-1.07	1.67
0%	152.30	***	***	154.54	1.47	3.60	-0.26	6.45
			June 3, 1983 - September 2, 1983					
			66 Trading Days					
S&P 500	***	163.98	165.00	166.86	1.75	4.54	-2.12	***
-5%	155.78	***	***	163.96	-0.01	3.87	-3.14	1.77
0%	163.98	***	***	161.77	-1.35	1.97	-2.15	3.10
			September 7, 1983 - December 1, 1983					
			62 Trading Days					
S&P 500	***	167.89	166.49	168.25	0.21	3.24	-2.89	***
-5%	159.50	***	***	166.04	-1.10	2.47	-3.47	1.31
0%	167.89	***	***	167.78	0.06	0.91	-1.00	0.28
			December 5, 1983 - March 1, 1984					
			62 Trading Days					
S&P 500	***	165.54	158.19	160.01	-3.34	2.68	-5.79	***
-5%	157.26	***	***	156.65	-5.37	2.06	-6.09	2.03
0%	165.54	***	***	166.26	0.43	1.21	-1.08	-3.77
			March 5, 1984 - June 1, 1984					
			64 Trading Days					
S&P 500	***	159.24	153.24	155.14	-2.57	2.46	-4.48	***
-5%	151.28	***	***	152.65	-4.14	1.39	-5.24	1.57
0%	159.24	***	***	160.07	0.52	0.83	-1.13	-3.10
			June 5, 1984 - September 4, 1984					
			65 Trading Days					
S&P 500	***	154.34	164.88	166.85	8.11	9.82	-3.53	***
-5%	146.62	***	***	164.12	6.34	8.24	-3.72	1.77
0%	154.34	***	***	159.60	3.41	5.25	-1.69	4.70
			September 6, 1984 - December 3, 1984					
			63 Trading Days					
S&P 500	***	164.29	162.82	164.73	0.27	4.53	-1.16	***
-5%	156.08	***	***	162.00	-1.39	3.17	-1.68	1.66
0%	164.29	***	***	165.22	0.57	1.37	-0.36	-0.30

Table 5 continued

Portfolio	Floor Level	Initial Index	Final Index	Final Portfolio	Portfolio Percent Change	Maximum Percent Change	Minimum Percent Change	Cost
				December 5, 1984 - March 1, 1985				
				61 Trading Days				
S&P 500	***	163.38	183.23	185.17	13.34	13.34	-0.83	***
-5%	155.21	***	***	182.58	11.75	11.82	-0.85	1.59
0%	163.38	***	***	177.48	8.63	8.70	-0.42	4.71
				March 5, 1985 - June 3, 1985				
				64 Trading Days				
S&P 500	***	182.06	189.32	191.36	5.11	5.22	-2.88	***
-5%	172.96	***	***	189.50	4.09	4.30	-2.72	1.02
0%	182.06	***	***	186.66	2.53	2.68	-1.38	2.59
				June 5, 1985 - September 3, 1985				
				64 Trading Days				
S&P 500	***	190.04	187.91	189.97	-0.04	3.47	-2.36	***
-5%	180.54	***	***	187.78	-1.19	2.89	-2.19	1.15
0%	190.04	***	***	191.79	0.92	2.08	-0.75	-0.96
				September 5, 1985 - December 2, 1985				
				63 Trading Days				
S&P 500	***	187.37	200.46	202.46	8.05	9.11	-3.33	***
-5%	178.00	***	***	199.80	6.64	7.74	-3.16	1.42
0%	187.37	***	***	196.48	4.86	5.94	-1.03	3.19
				December 4, 1985 - March 3, 1986				
				62 Trading Days				
S&P 500	***	200.86	225.42	227.49	13.25	13.98	1.11	***
-5%	190.82	***	***	224.42	11.73	12.47	0.87	1.52
0%	200.86	***	***	217.44	8.25	8.98	0.08	5.00
				March 5, 1986 - June 2, 1986				
				63 Trading Days				
S&P 500	***	224.38	245.04	247.12	10.13	11.41		***
-5%	213.16	***	***	243.10	8.34	9.65	-0.09	1.79
0%	224.38	***	***	232.76	3.73	4.99	0.33	6.40
				June 4, 1986 - September 2, 1986				
				64 Trading Days				
S&P 500	***	245.51	248.52	250.65	2.09	3.99	-4.42	***
-5%	233.23	***	***	246.26	0.30	2.30	-4.16	1.79
0%	245.51	***	***	245.11	-0.16	1.31	-1.10	2.26
				September 4, 1986 - December 1, 1986				
				63 Trading Days				
S&P 500	***	250.08	249.05	251.12	0.41	1.51	-7.83	***
-5%	237.58	***	***	245.40	-1.87	1.21	-5.49	2.29
0%	250.08	***	***	247.83	-0.90	0.44	-0.90	1.32

* The portfolios are rebalanced daily.

Notes

[1]Rubinstein (1987, p. 73) defines a derivative asset as "an asset whose payoffs are completely determined by the prices or payoffs of other underlying assets." The underlying asset discussed in the article is the S&P 500 index, which is a value-weighted index of 500 stocks selected by the Standard and Poor's Corporation. The weight of each stock in the index is the ratio of the market value of outstanding shares for that stock to the market value of all outstanding shares for the 500 stocks.

[2]The actual cash value of the S&P 500 futures contract is 500 times the index value. For expositional convenience, it is assumed that the underlying asset size for either futures or option contracts is equal to one index unit.

[3]See Leland (1980).

[4]In addition to the assumption cited as an example in the text, other important assumptions of the model that will be discussed in more detail are that trading in stock and options takes place continuously, that the stock volatility is constant, and that the stock pays no dividends.

[5]The rate of interest used in discounting future values is the risk-free rate. Technically, the choice of the risk-free rate is only appropriate for a world of risk-neutral investors, in which equilibrium expected rates of return on *all* assets equal the risk-free rate. However, the Black-Scholes call option pricing equation is valid for any degree of risk aversion because the equation's derivation is based on the valuation of a riskless hedge portfolio of stock and calls. Smith (1976, pp. 22-23) and Jarrow and Rudd (1983, chapters 7 and 8) discuss the so-called risk neutrality argument. Although the interpretations regarding present discounted values offered in this section of the article are strictly correct only for a risk-neutral world, the value of the insured portfolio in terms of the underlying variables is correct for any degree of risk aversion.

[6]Smith (1976) contains an excellent exposition of the solution technique for call options.

[7]K•DF dollars invested in T-bills will increase to K dollars by the expiration date due to the accumulation of interest.

[8]There is no one method for estimating volatility. All existing techniques are ad hoc. The volatility calculations used for the simulations employed a 30-trading-day moving average of the squared log (dividend-adjusted) index price relatives.

[9]A study by Garcia and Gould (1987) is a comprehensive simulation that attempts to evaluate the cost of portfolio insurance. Ad hoc procedures are used to ensure a firm floor. They conclude that "the evidence does not indicate that a dynamically balanced, insured portfolio will over the long run outperform a static mix portfolio" (p. 44). They claim that their method is biased in favor of portfolio insurance, but certain aspects of their procedure, particularly their stop-out rule, may bias the results the other way.

[10]There has been concern expressed in the financial press about the apparent inadequate liquidity of the S&P 500 futures contract. See Falloon (1987, p. 63). Addressing a related issue, Rubinstein (1987, p. 84) considers various hypotheses for the apparent mispricing of index futures, and states: "I am forced to the conclusion that even today the growth in index futures trading continues to outstrip the amounts of capital that are available for arbitrage."

[11]Because, in fact, a long index/short futures portfolio is not riskless, the implied interest rate will usually exceed the T-bill rate. See Kawaller (1987). This interest rate differential may partly explain the apparent mispricing.

[12]See Anders (1987).

[13]See Wallace (1987).

References

Anders, George. "Portfolio Insurance Provided Cold Comfort." *Wall Street Journal*, October 28, 1987.

Black, Fischer, and M. Scholes. "The Pricing of Options and Corporate Liabilities." *Journal of Political Economy* 81 (May-June 1973): 637-59.

Bookstaber, Richard. "The Use of Options in Performance Structuring." *Journal of Portfolio Management* 11 (Summer 1985): 36-50.

Boyle, Phelim P., and David Emanuel. "Discretely Adjusted Option Hedges." *Journal of Financial Economics* 8 (September 1980): 255-82.

Cox, John C., and Mark Rubinstein. *Options Markets.* Englewood Cliffs, N.J.: Prentice-Hall, 1985.

Etzioni, Ethan S. "Rebalance Disciplines for Portfolio Insurance." *Journal of Portfolio Management* 13 (Fall 1986): 59-62.

Falloon, William. "Will PI Be Strangled by Illiquidity?" *Intermarket* 4 (November 1987): 63.

Garcia, C.B., and F.J. Gould. "An Empirical Study of Portfolio Insurance." *Financial Analysts Journal* 43 (July-August 1987): 44-54.

Jarrow, Robert A., and Andrew Rudd. *Option Pricing.* Homewood, Ill.: Richard D. Irwin, 1983.

Kawaller, Ira G. "A Note: Debunking the Myth of the Risk-Free Return." *Journal of Futures Markets* 7 (1987): 327-31.

Leland, Hayne E. "Who Should Buy Portfolio Insurance." *Journal of Finance* 35 (May 1980): 581-94.

_____. "Option Pricing and Replacement with Transaction Costs." *Journal of Finance* 60 (December 1985): 1283-301.

Merrick, John J., Jr. "Fact and Fantasy about Stock Index Futures Program Trading." Federal Reserve Bank of Philadelphia *Business Review* (September/October 1987a): 13-25.

_____. "Portfolio Insurance with Stock Index Futures." Working Paper No. 434, Salomon Brothers Center for the Study of Financial Institutions, New York University, August 1987b.

Rubinstein, Mark. "Alternative Paths to Portfolio Insurance." *Financial Analysts Journal* 41 (July-August 1984): 42-52.

_____. "Derivative Assets Analysis." *Journal of Economic Perspectives* 1 (Fall 1987): 73-93.

_____, and Hayne E. Leland. "Replicating Options with Positions in Stock and Cash." *Financial Analysts Journal* 37 (July-August 1981): 63-72.

Smith, Clifford W., Jr. "Option Pricing: A Review." *Journal of Financial Economics* 3 (January-March 1976): 3-51.

Stoll, Hans R., and Robert E. Whaley. "Expiration Day Effects of Index Options and Futures." *Monograph Series in Finance and Economics,* No. 1986-3, Salomon Brothers Center for the Study of Financial Institutions, New York University, 1986.

U.S. Commodity Futures Trading Commission. *Interim Report on Stock Index Futures and Cash Market Activity During October 1987 to the U.S. Commodity Futures Trading Commission.* The Division of Economic Analysis, The Division of Trading and Markets, November 9, 1987.

Wallace, Anise C. "A Suspect in Market's Plunge." *New York Times,* December 1, 1987.

Article 23

The mechanics of portfolio insurance

It works . . . at least in theory.

Thomas J. O'Brien

Although dynamic replication portfolio insurance is not designed to work in anything but an orderly market, it is useful still to understand how the concept should work if the market is orderly. This paper shows in explicit detail how dynamic portfolio insurance should work in theory when the market is orderly. The purpose is to clarify the mysterious "miracle." While the papers referenced below convey the general ideas in applied portfolio insurance, they omit many mechanical details, including the potential drawbacks of insurance even in an orderly market. Some modest progress toward clarifying the mechanics can be found in Sharpe (1985) and Singleton and Grieves (1984), but many practitioners still need considerably more detail on the process. A major objective of this study is to show in more detail just how the principle of dynamic portfolio insurance works, including the use of index futures.

By way of introduction, in 1980 Leland provided a provocative solution to insuring a portfolio against loss below a specified floor: One can insure, in theory and in an orderly market, via a trading strategy based rigidly upon calculated values from option pricing theory. To those who did not quite grasp the relationship of trading, options, and Leland's portfolio insurance, Rubinstein and Leland provided clarification in a 1981 paper. There they explained how a portfolio manager could theoretically act out, or "role play," the Black–Scholes model (1973).

The manager replicates an option through a process of continually revising, in a prescribed manner, the proportions of a portfolio consisting of the underlying asset and the riskless asset. Indeed, Rubinstein and Leland indicate that the replication strategy is helpful in understanding options. The concept implements a version of Pozen's protective put option (1978), extended to an entire portfolio, using a synthetic "portfolio" put option manufactured through "dynamic" trading.

With the introduction of exchange-traded index put options, it seemed theoretically possible for an investor to use these contracts to insure well-diversified portfolios, especially index funds. Nevertheless, investors have not used the option market, for five reasons.

First, adequate contracts, corresponding to the horizons of the institutional managers seeking protection, have not been introduced. Second, the traded options are American, and prices therefore reflect the risk and privilege of early exercise; portfolio insurers with fixed horizon dates do not need to pay this cost. The insurance Leland had in mind is "European," in that it applies to a fixed horizon date corresponding to the expiration time of a European option. The insurance does not apply to times before or after the horizon. Third, there are position limits for exchange-traded puts. Fourth, insurance floors often need to be tailored at a level that is different from the fixed striking prices of traded options.

Fifth, and perhaps most significant, the cost of

THOMAS J. O'BRIEN, who is not related to John O'Brien of Leland, O'Brien, Rubinstein Associates, Inc., is Associate Professor of Finance in the School of Business, University of Connecticut at Storrs (CT 06268). He gratefully acknowledges that this paper grew from a previous analysis with Richard J. Rendleman, Jr., of the University of North Carolina at Chapel Hill, whose comments on this paper have helped improve the presentation as well. The author is also grateful for the support provided for the earlier project by McMillion/Eubanks, Inc., of Greensboro, NC, and for this project by the Center for Research and Development of Financial Services of the University of Connecticut (Neil B. Murphy, Director).

insuring via the exchange-traded puts is clear, but the dynamic trading approach sometimes is presented in such a way as to give the illusion of producing the insurance out of thin air. See, for example, Wallace's discussion (1982) of the "miracle" of portfolio insurance via dynamic option replication. Nothing in any of the theoretical literature by Leland and Rubinstein, however, suggests any miracles; the nature of the product simply seems to obscure the costs. Yet this literature, including a more recent paper by Ferguson (1986), has managed to convey the seemingly miraculous benefits of the dynamic trading approach without covering the mechanics or costs in sufficient detail.

Attracted to the "miracle" of portfolio insurance via dynamic trading, practitioners have nevertheless been puzzled by the sophistication of the concept: Besides the complex mathematical nature of the underlying option pricing theory, the strategy calls for buying more stock when the market is going up and selling off some stock as the market goes down. This strategy is contrary to many practitioners' intuition. Moreover, many practitioners believe that the whipsaw potential of buying high and selling low is a drawback in the practical application of the theory.

Practitioners also have been skeptical about the potential amount of trading and thus trading costs that the dynamic approach would entail. To address the trading cost problem, Rubinstein (1985) has argued that index futures could be used as a trading vehicle synthetic to reduce trading costs substantially. Rubinstein's idea also suggests that the insurance can be "obtained" from an advisory that is physically separated from the portfolio to be insured; the insured portfolio itself does not have to be traded, and the portfolio manager can rely upon the advisory's expertise to produce the counter-intuitive "miracles."

Finally, practitioners have been concerned with the possibility of a large gap opening in the market that would prevent the continual trading application at just the time when insurance would be most desirable. Indeed, there has been some concern about the role that insured portfolios themselves would play in exaggerating a market panic. Sellers of portfolio insurance had discounted the possibility of something like a 1929 crash ever happening again, until, of course, October 19, 1987. Unfortunately, a full accounting of what happened to insured portfolios on that day and in the ensuing turbulent weeks had not emerged by the time editorial schedules necessitated completion of this paper.

The device used in my mechanics analysis is a four-date example in the Cox–Ross–Rubinstein (1979) and Rendleman-Bartter (1979) multi-period, two-state

option-theoretic intuition of the Black–Scholes theory. This framework permits an extension of the Rubinstein-Leland (1981), Sharpe (1985), and Singleton and Grieves (1984) treatments of portfolio insurance to more periods and more details.

This analysis exposes one aspect of dynamic portfolio insurance that, although not miraculous, is rather remarkable (as long as the market remains orderly): An investor can specify a trading plan that both meets the insurance objective and is entirely "self-financing," regardless of the path taken by random stock prices. This is the insight of Black and Scholes (1973).

On the other hand, the portfolio insurance cannot be miraculously manufactured at zero cost, even in a theoretical world of zero trading costs. The cost is the forgone returns. This paper gives some details on determining these opportunity costs relative to uninsured equity positions. A more rigorous discussion of the costs relative to optimal asset allocation positions can be found in Rendleman and McEnally (1987).

STOCK PRICE (UNDERLYING PORTFOLIO) DYNAMICS

The stock price dynamics that underlie the mechanics analysis appear in Figure 1. As the topic is "portfolio" insurance, we may also wish to interpret the dynamics in Figure 1 as characteristic of the *underlying* portfolio in the insurance program. This underlying portfolio with the insurance attached will be referred to as the *insured* portfolio, although sometimes it will be more convenient for me to refer to the underlying portfolio as simply the stock.

The tree diagram in Figure 1 depicts a three-period (or four-date), two-state process, where the movement in an upstate is 1.2 times the current value,

FIGURE 1

STOCK PRICE (UNDERLYING PORTFOLIO VALUE) DYNAMICS

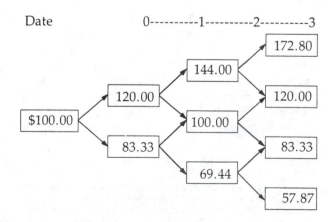

and the movement in a downstate is 1/1.2 times the current value. This kind of process is described in Rendleman and Bartter (1979), in their intuitive explanation of the kind of dynamics used in the derivation of the Black–Scholes option model.

OPTION VALUATION AND DYNAMICS

In this framework, options are valued via a "no-arbitrage" argument — start with the expiration-time option price possibilities, and work backward to determine the previous option values. The options in the demonstration are assumed to expire at the end of Period 3. From top to bottom, the potential expiration-time values for a put option with a strike price of $100 would be $0, $0, $16.67, and $42.13. Assuming a risk-free rate of 0.02 per period, these equilibrium "no-arbitrage" put option values are shown in Figure 2.

These option values would correspond to Black–Scholes values if we had a very large number of periods in the tree diagram. The simplified theory of option pricing used here, like that of Black–Scholes, is based on the notion of no-arbitrage, riskless hedging.

FIGURE 2

PUT OPTION DYNAMICS IF STRIKE PRICE = $100.00

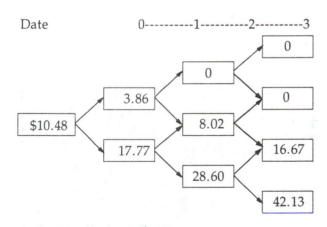

Date   0---------1---------2---------3

PORTFOLIO INSURANCE VIA PURCHASED OPTIONS

Before covering dynamic replication insurance, let us first consider insurance via protective puts. If put options for expiration at Time 3 with a strike price of $100.00 are available, a manager who wishes to insure the portfolio (the stock) for $100.00 at Time 0 for the horizon at the end of Period 3 can simply purchase a protective put for $10.48. The tree diagram of the insured portfolio, which appears in Figure 3, is simply the sum of the underlying portfolio value (stock value) and the put value for each of the potential states of nature.

FIGURE 3

INSURED PORTFOLIO DYNAMICS

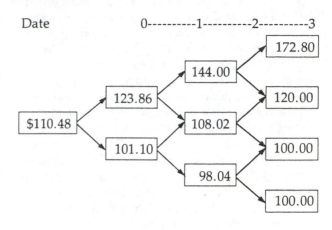

Date   0---------1---------2---------3

To insure the portfolio at $100.00 via a put in this example, we will need beginning capital of $110.48; $100.00 to put into the underlying portfolio and $10.48 to pay for the put (the insurance premium). In this situation we get one full share of action if share value is above the insurance floor. Later we will see how we can insure at the same level of capital that we start with, or at a higher level, with corresponding costs of forgone upside participation.

Before turning to dynamic replication of the action in Figure 3, we note without proof that the same price dynamics as in Figure 3 apply to a combination of a $100.00 face value riskless asset with a maturity date at the expiration time and a call option with a strike price of $100.00. The Time 0 riskless asset value is $100.00/(1.02)^3 = $94.23, and the call option value will be $16.25. Again, $110.48 is required to insure at $100.00 via this synthetic approach. Thus, the riskless asset plus call option combination is an alternative, synthetic way to create an insured portfolio. Of course, not all managers can employ this method, as someone must hold the stocks.

DYNAMIC REPLICATION

The basic dynamic trading approach involves replicating the insured portfolio's price action with an ever-changing combination of positions in the underlying portfolio and the riskless asset. The underlying portfolio/riskless asset positions are used to create an insured portfolio consisting of a (synthetic) riskless asset plus call option. The proportions allocated to the underlying portfolio and the riskless asset change every period, so that the dynamic insurance strategy requires a significant amount of trading. Later, we will see how the same replication is accomplished (approximately) with either a stock portfolio and short stock futures positions or the riskless asset and long stock futures.

The number of units of the underlying portfolio that must be held long at any given moment will be given by the call option's "delta," the reciprocal of how many calls it takes to hedge a unit of the underlying portfolio. The call deltas in Figure 4 tell us the number of units of the underlying portfolio to hold. The amount of the riskless asset to hold is determined by subtracting the value of the held units of the underlying portfolio from the total value of the insured portfolio.

For example, at Time 0, the insurance strategy requires 0.6206 units of the underlying portfolio at $100.00 per unit for $62.06, plus $110.48 − 62.06 = $48.42 in the riskless asset. Thus 0.6206 is *not* the proportion of the dynamic hedging portfolio allocated to the underlying portfolio. Insured portfolio proportions can be found in a manner that is similar in principle to the method in Benninga and Blume [1985, Equation (1)].

The detailed, trade-by-trade, mechanics of the

FIGURE 4

CALL OPTION DELTAS

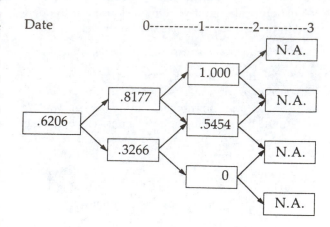

dynamic hedging strategy in Figure 5 shed light on the mysteries of portfolio insurance via dynamic trading. Note first that the scheme is self-financing. The purchase of units of the underlying portfolio can always be made with proceeds from the riskless asset

FIGURE 5

DYNAMIC REPLICATION OF INSURED PORTFOLIO

```
                                                                              172.80
                                                                              Insd Port      = 172.80
                                                                              1 sh at 172.80 = 172.80
                                                                                 0 Bills             0
                                                                                 Total          172.80

                                         144.00  Insd Port  =  144.00
                                         = .8177 shs x 144 + 26.25
                                         Buy .1823 shs at 144
                                         Sell 26.25 Bills
                                                                              120.00
                                         New Portfolio:                       Insd Port      = 120.00
                                         1 sh at 144      =   144.00          Either
                120.00  Insd Port  = 123.86     0 Bills             0         1 sh at 120    = 120.00
                = .6206 shs x 120 + 49.39       Total          144.00            0 Bills             0
                Buy .1971 shs at 120                                             Total          120.00
                Sell 23.65 Bills
                                         100.00  Insd Port  =  108.02         or
                New Portfolio:           = Either① .8177 shs x 100 + 26.25    .5455 shs at 120 = 65.46
                .8177 shs at 120  =  98.12   or   ② .3266 shs x 100 + 75.36      Bills          54.54
  100.00          Bills             25.74  if① sell .2722 shs at 100             Total         120.00
                  Total            123.86        buy 27.22 Bills
  Buy .6206 shs   62.06                     if② buy .2189 shs at 100
  Buy Bills       48.42                          sell 21.89 Bills             83.33
    Total        110.48  83.33  Insd Port  = 101.10                          Insd Port      = 100.00
                         = .6206 shs x 83.33 + 49.39  New Portfolio:          Either
                                                 .5455 shs at 100  =  54.55   .5455 shs at 83.33 = 45.46
                         Sell .2940 shs at 83.33    Bills             53.49      Bills             54.54
                         Buy 24.50 Bills            Total            108.02      Total            100.00
                                                                             or
                         New Portfolio:                                      0 shs                    0
                         .3266 shs at 83.33 =  27.22                            Bills            100.00
                           Bills             73.88                              Total           100.00
                           Total            101.10
                                         69.44  Insd Port  =  98.04
                                         =.3266 shs x 69.44 + 75.36           57.87
                                                                             Insd Port      = 100.00
                                         Sell .3266 shs at 69.44             0 shs                    0
                                         Buy 22.68 Bills                        Bills            100.00
                                                                               Total           100.00
                                         New Portfolio:
                                         0 shs                    0
                                           Bills             98.04
                                           Total            98.04
```

sales, and vice versa. For convenience, the price of the underlying stock is given in the upper left-hand corner of each box.

Note also that the units of the underlying portfolio correspond to the call option deltas in Figure 4. Further, note that the stock-plus-put dynamics of Figure 3 can be replicated only with a starting portfolio value of $110.48 — insurance costs $10.48, the Time 0 price of the put. No miracle here, a point also stressed by Singleton and Grieves (1984).

Another way of looking at the cost is the forgone return on the upside. In this example the manager gets only one share of action on the upside in lieu of 1.1048 shares of action that could have been obtained with an uninsured portfolio. The upside value capture ratio is 1/1.1048, or about 91%.

Finally, note especially the middle event at the end of Period 2 in Figure 5, when the value of the underlying portfolio returns to $100.00 from either the previous downstate or the previous upstate. As $100.00 was the Time 0 beginning value of the underlying portfolio, we can compare the value of the insured portfolio, $108.02, with that at Time 0, $110.48. This is the often-discussed "whipsaw," viewed as one of the practical problems of applying the theory in the real world.

In the context of the dynamic allocation strategy, however, this "whipsaw" is part of the plan. It is not so much a problem as it is the natural reduction of the insured portfolio value over time, all else equal, as gradual payment for the insurance. Rather than regarding dynamic portfolio insurance as some kind of miracle with the practical application problem of the whipsaw, it is more appropriate to understand that the whipsaw is the missing cost element of the portfolio insurance "miracle." This point is made as well by Asay and Edelsburg (1986). Of course, the market turbulence after October 19, 1987, might have caused a whipsaw for insured portfolios that was several orders of magnitude greater than the one that theory allows for. In such a case, a more practical perspective has to be taken on the whipsaw issue.

THE USE OF FUTURES

Rubinstein (1985) based his insight on the use of index futures to implement dynamic insurance upon the assumption that the portfolio to be insured is well-diversified. Ideally, the insured portfolio would be an index fund. One of the arguments against the use of exchange-traded put options to insure, in fact, is that the underlying portfolio is not necessarily the index; this argument applies also to the use of index futures in dynamic insurance strategies.

Nevertheless, the low cost and convenience of trading index futures relative to trading the actual portfolio make the basis risk of using the index futures to cross-hedge a fairly well-diversified portfolio a problem that can be lived with. For convenience here, we will assume that the underlying portfolio is the index portfolio.

Portfolio insurance in this case is created dynamically by using the index futures to create a synthetic position in either the riskless security or the underlying portfolio. The dynamics shown in Figure 3 can be replicated by putting 100% of the portfolio into the underlying portfolio and then creating an (adjustable) synthetic riskless asset out of a portion with some short futures positions. Alternatively, we could duplicate the same dynamics by putting 100% of the capital into the riskless asset and then create an (adjustable) synthetic position in the underlying portfolio out of a portion with some long futures positions.

In this section, I demonstrate the use of futures under the ideal assumption that the futures are always priced according to their correct theoretical value in terms of the underlying index. For convenience, I assume a constant interest rate environment, so that the theoretically correct futures price for contract delivery n periods hence will at any time be equal to the spot price of the underlying commodity times $(1 + r)^n$, where n is the number of periods until delivery, and r is the risk-free interest rate per period.

First let us look at the situation where index futures are available with the same delivery date as the horizon date of the insurance program. The theoretically correct futures price dynamics are shown in Figure 6, corresponding to the underlying portfolio dynamics in Figure 1. Note that the end-of-last-period futures prices in Figure 6 are the same as the spot

FIGURE 6

DYNAMICS OF A CORRECTLY VALUED FUTURES CONTRACT FOR DELIVERY AT TIME 3

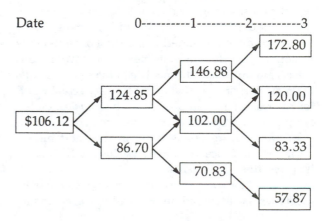

Date   0----------1----------2----------3

prices, as this is the delivery time of the futures.

In the dynamic replication with combinations of the underlying portfolio and short futures positions, we must determine the number of short index futures contracts to establish by $1/[1 + r]^{(n - 1)}$ times the quotient of the level of the riskless asset needed and the current price of the underlying stock. For example, at Time 0, we should short $1/[(1.02)^2]$ times [48.42/100.00], which is 0.4654 contracts. The details of the entire replication, similar to Figure 5, are available from the author on request.

In this replication, as the underlying portfolio value rises, some of the short positions are covered, and as the underlying portfolio value falls, additional short positions are taken. These transactions correspond to coming out of the riskless asset and into the underlying portfolio in upswings, and vice versa in downswings.

Typically, futures contracts will not be available for long-horizon insurance programs. If, for example, the insurance program of Figure 3 were envisioned to have a one and one-half year horizon, the investor might have to use a sequence of three six-month index futures contracts. It is still perfectly general to short futures contracts in the amount of $1/[(1 + r)^{(n - 1)}]$ times the quotient of the level of the riskless asset needed and the price of the underlying stock. In this example, however, n is always equal to 1, as the futures delivery date is always one period away.

At Time 0, the six-month futures price is $100.00 \times 1.02 = \$102.00$; we will short $1/[1.02^0]\, (= 1)$ times 48.42/100.00 = 0.4842 futures. At the end of the first period, if the stock is $120.00 (the upstate), we will have 1.1048 shares at $120.00 minus 0.4842 times ($120.00 − 102.00), for a total of $123.86; if the stock is $83.33 (the downstate), we will have 1.1048 shares at $83.33 minus 0.4842 times ($83.33 − 102.00), for a total of $101.10. These Time 1 amounts are exactly in accordance with the insurance plan of Figure 3. The subsequent details of the insurance program using short-term futures are straightforward. We shall now revert to using long-term futures for consistency.

As described so far, the strategy does call for some trading in the underlying portfolio. Units of the underlying portfolio have to be sold to cover futures losses, and futures gains must be reinvested into units of the underlying portfolio. The strategy actually calls for the sale of a small portion of the physical underlying portfolio when values have risen, with a more than offsetting reversing trade in the short futures positions, and vice versa when values of the underlying portfolio have fallen.

In actual practice, we can accomplish the same dynamics as discussed above, without ever trading the original position in the underlying portfolio, by borrowing to cover losses on futures while shorting more futures to hedge the retained excess position in the portfolio in upstates, and by investing futures profits into the riskless asset and shorting fewer futures to compensate for being underinvested in the portfolio in downstates.

For example, if the underlying portfolio value goes to $120.00 at Time 1, then, instead of selling $1.1048 − 1.0322 = 0.0746$ units of the underlying portfolio and shorting 0.2103 futures, we may maintain 1.1048 shares and borrow the $8.72 to cover the futures loss. The new short futures position should be 0.2814 instead of 0.2103. (The entire trading mechanics of this approach are available from the author.) Of course, the borrowing must be repaid at the horizon. The important thing is that the strategy replicates the same insured portfolio's price dynamics as shown in Figure 3.

It is also possible to put on a portfolio insurance program that has the same price dynamics but consists only of long positions in cash and long positions in the index futures. The mechanics of this alternative are easy. We invest fully in cash and then go long futures contracts in an amount determined by dividing the call delta by $(1 + r)^{(n - 2)}$. Futures gains and losses are simply paid out of the cash. (The mechanics of this alternative are also available from the author.)

Rubinstein (1985) implied that the flexibility of choosing between the long portfolio/short futures and long cash/long futures approaches allows users to dismiss the problem of futures mispricing, and even to take advantage of it. On the other hand, a manager who has a long stock portfolio to insure may not have the flexibility to sell everything and convert to cash.

Regardless of which approach is chosen at the beginning, all flexibility of capitalizing on futures mispricing is lost. Over time we will have to go long more futures positions in rising markets and short more in falling markets, no matter which approach we had selected in the beginning. If futures are typically overpriced in rising markets when we go to buy, and underpriced in falling markets when we go to sell, then this is a problem. Just how much of a problem this represented on October 19, 1987, has yet to be determined. Perhaps there is more flexibility in this respect when using short-term futures or traded puts and calls.

USING TRADED PUTS AND CALLS

While generally it is not possible to buy traded options with an expiration time long enough to coincide with typical insurance program horizons, we can use the traded puts and calls as part of a dynamic trading insurance program. For example, consider a call with a striking price of $95.00 that expires at Time 2. The call's equilibrium Time 0 price is $12.12; the Time 1 contingent prices are $21.87 in the upstate and $2.50 in the downstate. We can solve, using simultaneous equations, for the originating number of shares to go long and the number of calls to write, so that we get $123.86 in the Time 1 upstate and $101.10 in the Time 1 downstate. The answer will be to go long 1.249 shares and sell 1.191 calls. Naturally, the amount of initial capital necessary still turns out to be $110.48. We can then reallocate at Time 1, possibly liquidating all the option positions and rolling forward into other options or futures.

Etzioni (1986), a practicing insurer, indicated in a presentation at an American Stock Exchange Option Colloquium that in reality traded puts are sometimes too overvalued in the market to be useful as a trading vehicle this way. He also said that in actual practice the use of traded calls poses technical problems of another type, an issue beyond the scope of this paper.

TARGET INSURANCE LEVELS AND PORTFOLIO INSURANCE COSTS

So far, we have conveniently assumed that the manager has $110.48 and wishes to insure for $100.00. The horizon action above the insurance floor was for that of a full share, representing a "cost" of about 9% of the upside appreciation potential, relative to 100% investment in the underlying portfolio. We may often wish to insure for the starting amount or higher. The target must always be less than the future value of the starting amount (at the risk-free rate), and, the higher the target, the larger the loss of upside participation.

Let us examine the case where we start out with $100.00 and wish to insure at $100.00. In this case, the manager needs to buy m shares and m put options, such that the total expended for the position equals $100.00 and such that the number of puts purchased times their striking price equals the target insurance amount, $100.00. Even though the insurance may be accomplished via dynamic replication, we can look at the problem as if protective puts were being used.

We must know the theoretical put values for various striking prices over a relevant range. The Table supplies some relevant Time 0 put option values, all generated the same way as the one in Figure 2. The table also gives the corresponding m value, such that m times the put's striking price equals the insurance target floor of $100.00. Finally, the table gives the total costs of buying m shares and m puts. The

TABLE

ANALYSIS OF INSURING AT TARGET LEVEL

Strike Price (K)	Put Price (P)	m (m*K = $100.00)	Total Cost (= m*($100.00 + P)1
$100.00	$10.48	1.0000	$110.48
. . .	. . .	. . .	. . .
105.00	12.80	0.9524	107.43
. . .	. . .	. . .	. . .
110.00	16.38	0.9090	105.80
. . .	. . .	. . .	. . .
119.00	19.41	0.8403	100.34
120.00	19.64	0.8333	99.70
. . .	. . .	. . .	. . .

manager must select that "row" of the table for which the total cost figure equals $100.00.

In our example, the objective would be achieved for a put with a striking price between $119.00 and $120.00. For simplicity, let us say the put with the $120.00 striking price is closest. We buy 0.8333 shares at $100.00 per share and 0.8333 puts at $19.64 for an approximate expenditure of $100.00. It should be clear now that, if longer-horizon traded puts with set exercise prices were available, we might still prefer dynamic replication because of the ability to tailor the insurance floor by creating an option with the desired striking price.

The insured portfolio dynamics for the selected strategy are given in Figure 7. These dynamics of course can be replicated. The portfolio is insured against loss below $100.00, but the upside capture has been reduced to 0.8333 of what it would have been if the original $100.00 had been put entirely into the stock. This 0.1667 participation give-up is one way to view the cost of portfolio insurance. The higher the target floor — and it can be above the original stake, guaranteeing a fixed interest rate — the greater will be the participation give-up. The give-up also depends on the stock's volatility and the risk-free interest rate.

FIGURE 7

INSURED PORTFOLIO DYNAMICS FOR $100.00 TARGET FLOOR

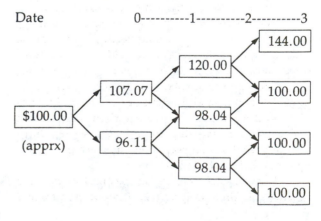

Finally, let us see what would happen if we started with $100.00 and used the deltas in Figure 4 to determine the number of shares to hold in the basic stock–bill insurance program. We would start off with bills in the amount of $100.00 minus the stock investment of $62.06, or $37.94. The details of the replication are available on request.

Whichever horizon state occurs, the insured portfolio ends up exactly $11.12 less what it would have been in the insured portfolio cases of Figures 3 and 5. Here is another way to see the insurance cost. The present value of $11.12, discounting at the 2% risk-free rate per period, is $10.48, the Time 0 price that would have been paid for a put with a $100.00 striking price. We can think of this situation as insuring at a $100.00 target and starting with $100.00, but paying a fixed cost for the insurance at the end of the program.

Essentially, the investor is "short" the price of the protection — the price of the put — and this amount must be repaid with interest. Of course, the floor in this example, net of the future value of the insurance cost, is $88.88. As pointed out earlier, if we start with $100.00 and really want a $100.00 horizon insurance floor, we must put on a different program with costs in terms of reduction of upside participation.

SUMMARY AND CONCLUDING REMARKS

This article has presented a line of analysis designed to clarify the mysteries of the basic portfolio insurance concept. A simplified abstraction of reality shows that portfolio insurance works. With an understanding of the mechanics and cost concepts presented here, the analyst may proceed to consider aspects of real-world application.

There are many periods and possible horizon states in actual practice, rather than the four used in the example here. Therefore, the Black–Scholes model is the starting point for calculating deltas and expected insurance costs in the real world. Advanced applications would try to make use of extensions to the Black–Scholes model to factor in the impact of certain real-world issues. Such extensions include work by Merton (1973) to factor in uncertain interest rates, by Leland (1985) to factor in trading costs — and futures mispricing can be viewed as a trading cost (Hill, Jain, and Wood, 1988) — by Johnson and Stulz (1987) to factor in default risk, and by Hull and White (1987) to factor in uncertain volatilities. Clarification of the impact of these real-world issues on horizon outcomes will be welcome.

In the simple, abstract environment assumed here, dynamic portfolio insurance has been shown to work. No guarantee can be made that dynamic replication will be effective against a catastrophe that occurs during a time when the market is closed, or against a "market meltdown" during trading hours, possibly exacerbated by insurance programs. Indeed, the macro-effect of dynamic insurance on the market is still in question. (The words of this concluding paragraph were written prior to October 19, 1987!)

REFERENCES

Asay, M., and C. Edelsburg. "Can a Dynamic Strategy Replicate the Returns of an Option?" *Journal of Futures Markets* 6, Spring 1986, pp. 63-70.

Benninga, S., and M. Blume. "On the Optimality of Portfolio Insurance." *Journal of Finance* 40, December 1985, pp. 1341-1352.

Black, F., and M. Scholes. "The Pricing of Options and Corporate Liabilities." *Journal of Political Economy* 81, May-June 1973, pp. 637-654.

Cox, J., S. Ross, and M. Rubinstein. "Option Pricing: A Simplified Approach." *Journal of Financial Economics* 7, September 1979, pp. 229-263.

Etzioni, E. "Rebalance Disciplines for Portfolio Insurance." *Journal of Portfolio Management* 13, Fall 1986, pp. 59-62.

Ferguson, R. "How to Beat the S&P 500 (Without Losing Sleep)." *Financial Analysts Journal* 42, March/April 1986, pp. 37-46.

Gatto, M., R. Geske, R. Litzenberger, and H. Sosin. "Mutual Fund Insurance." *Journal of Financial Economics* 8, September 1980, pp. 283-317.

Hill, J., A. Jain, and R. Wood. "Portfolio Insurance: Volatility Risk and Futures Mispricing," *Journal of Portfolio Management*, Winter 1988, pp. 23-29.

Hull, J., and A. White. "The Pricing of Options with Stochastic Volatilities," *Journal of Finance* 42, June 1987, pp. 281-300.

Johnson, H., and R. Stulz. "The Pricing of Options with Default Risk," *Journal of Finance* 42, June 1987, pp. 267-280.

Leland, H. "Option Pricing and Replication with Transaction Costs." *Journal of Finance* 40, December 1985, pp. 1283-1301.

——. "Who Should Buy Portfolio Insurance?" *Journal of Finance* 35, May 1980, pp. 581-594.

Merton, R. "Theory of Rational Option Pricing," *Bell Journal of Economics and Management Science* 3, Spring 1973, pp. 141-183.

Pozen, R. "The Purchase of Protective Puts by Financial Institutions." *Financial Analysts Journal* 34, July/August 1978, pp. 47-60.

Rendleman, R., and B. Bartter. "Two-State Option Pricing." *Journal of Finance* 34, December 1979, 1093-1110.

Rendleman, R., and R. McEnally. "Assessing the Costs of Portfolio Insurance." *Financial Analysts Journal* 43, May-June 1987, pp. 27-37.

Rubinstein, M. "Alternative Paths to Portfolio Insurance." *Financial Analysts Journal* 41, July/August 1985, pp. 42-52.

Rubinstein, M., and H. Leland. "Replicating Options with Positions in Stock and Cash." *Financial Analysts Journal* 37, July/August 1981, pp. 63-72.

Sharpe, W. "Portfolio Insurance," in *Investments*. Englewood Cliffs, N.J.: Prentice-Hall, Inc., 1985, pp. 509-514.

Singleton, C., and R. Grieves. "Synthetic Puts and Portfolio Insurance Strategies." *Journal of Portfolio Management* 10, Spring 1984, pp. 63-69.

Wallace, A. "Marketing a 'Miracle' Model." *Institutional Investor* 16, September 1982, pp. 101-106.

Article 24

by Mark Rubinstein

Alternative Paths to Portfolio Insurance

Portfolio insurance is equivalent to a securities position comprised of an underlying portfolio plus an insurance policy that guarantees the portfolio against loss through a specified policy expiration date. Under true portfolio insurance, the probability of experiencing a loss is zero; the position's return is dependent solely on the ending value of the underlying portfolio, regardless of interim movements in portfolio value; and the expected rate of return is greater than that on any other strategy possessing the first two properties.

European payout-protected puts could be used to provide perfect portfolio insurance. The investor would select a put option on the underlying portfolio such that exercising the put would yield just enough to make up for any decline in portfolio value plus the initial cost of the option. Unfortunately, European options are not available on listed exchanges in the U.S.

In their absence, portfolio insurance may be approximated by using listed options or by a systematic dynamic asset allocation strategy employing either cash and the underlying portfolio or a replicating futures position. Because the longest effective maturities of listed options are two or three months, a portfolio insurance strategy of any reasonable length will be susceptible to interim movements in the underlying portfolio, hence will generally have lower expected returns than true portfolio insurance. Dynamic asset allocation strategies designed to replicate a long-term European protect put come closest to perfect portfolio insurance.

PORTFOLIO INSURANCE, in its purest and simplest form, is equivalent to a securities position comprised of an underlying portfolio plus an insurance policy that guarantees the insured portfolio against loss through a specified policy expiration date. Should the underlying portfolio (including any income earned and reinvested in the portfolio but deducting the cost of buying the insurance) experience a loss by the policy expiration date, the insurance policy can be used to refund the

Mark Rubinstein is Professor of Finance at the Graduate School of Business of the University of California at Berkeley and a principal of Leland O'Brien Rubinstein, Associates.

The author thanks Hayne Leland for his helpful comments.

This article was awarded first prize in the 1984 Institute for Quantitative Research in Finance competition.

amount of the loss. On the other hand, should the underlying portfolio show a profit, all profit net of the cost of the insurance is retained.

Consider a portfolio with the same composition as the Standard & Poor's 500 and suppose it is covered by an insurance policy that has one year until expiration. The S&P 500 is at 100 at the start of the policy, and the one-year insurance policy costs $3.33. After buying the insurance, an investor with $100 has $96.67, which can buy 0.9667 "shares" of the S&P 500.

Table I shows the pattern of returns this investor will realize at the end of the year. The *minimum* value of the insured portfolio is $100; there will be no loss, even after the cost of the insurance is deducted. On the upside, the value of the insured portfolio depends on the behavior of the full $100 investment in the S&P 500. Because the insured portfolio owns 0.9667 shares of the S&P 500, its value on the upside

Table I Pattern of Returns from Portfolio Insurance After One Year

Value of S&P 500 with Dividends Reinvested	Value of Insured S&P 500 Portfolio
$ 75	$100
80	100
85	100
90	100
95	100
100	100
105	101.50
110	106.34
115	111.17
120	116
125	120.84
130	125.67

will always be 0.9667 times the value of the S&P 500 with dividends reinvested (e.g., 125 × 0.9667 = 120.84). This number is sometimes referred to as the "upside capture."

Properties of Insured Portfolios

The return pattern of the insured portfolio has several important properties:

(A) The probability of experiencing any losses is zero.

(B) The return on any profitable position will be a predictable percentage of the rate of return that would have been earned by investing all funds in the S&P 500.

(C) If the portfolio is restricted to investments in the S&P 500 and cash loans, if the expected rate of return on the S&P 500 exceeds the return on cash, and if the insurance is fairly priced, then among all investment strategies possessing properties (A) and (B), the insured portfolio strategy has the highest expected rate of return.

Stop-loss orders are perhaps the simplest examples of investment strategies that have property A (ignoring jumps through the stop-limit price) but lack property B. To implement a stop-loss order strategy, one invests the entire $100 in the S&P 500 and instructs the broker to sell out completely and convert to cash if the S&P 500 (with dividends reinvested) falls so low that a conversion to cash, given then current interest rates, would result in a value of exactly $100 at the end of the year.

Clearly, this strategy possesses property A. However, the value of the portfolio is not completely determined by the level of the S&P 500. If, midway through the year, the S&P 500 fell low enough to trigger the conversion into cash,

then the return on the portfolio from then on would be entirely unrelated to the S&P 500.

It is easy to devise other strategies that have both properties A and B but lack C. Suppose an investor is restricted to "buy and hold" positions using only the S&P 500 and cash and wants to maximize expected rate of return while insuring against a loss. If the interest rate is 10 per cent, he can invest $90.91 in cash and $9.09 in the S&P 500. Now, even if the S&P 500 falls to zero, he would just break even (since $90.91 × 1.1 = $100). If the expected rate of return on the S&P 500 is 16 per cent, the overall expected rate of return from following this strategy would be 10.5 per cent (= (90.91 × 10%) + (9.09 × 16%)).

The proof that portfolio insurance satisfies property C, hence must have a higher expected rate of return than the buy and hold strategy, will not be reproduced here.[1] However, it will be demonstrated by example in the course of the discussion.

Why Purchase Portfolio Insurance?

Clearly, anyone who wants to insure against any losses while maximizing expected return is a candidate for the purchase of portfolio insurance.[2] Equally clearly, for every investor who purchases portfolio insurance there needs to be an investor who sells it.[3] We are thus led to conclude that intelligent buyers of portfolio insurance are typically more sensitive to downside risk than the average investor.

For either the buyer or seller of portfolio insurance, property B still holds: The return from the insured portfolio (S&P 500 plus insurance policy) will be fully determined by the return from the underlying portfolio (S&P 500) at the insurance expiration date. The path taken to reach this level of return will have no effect on the outcome.

Outcomes of "path-dependent" strategies are usually much more difficult to describe and evaluate than those of "path-independent" strategies.[4] That is, predicting returns from path-dependent strategies requires knowledge of many more factors. It is also difficult to see why an investor would want his return to be influenced by intermediate levels of the index, apart from their cumulative effect on the ending level of the index.

The remainder of this article focuses on the purchase of portfolio insurance—specifically, how is it done?

---

1. Footnotes appear at end of article.

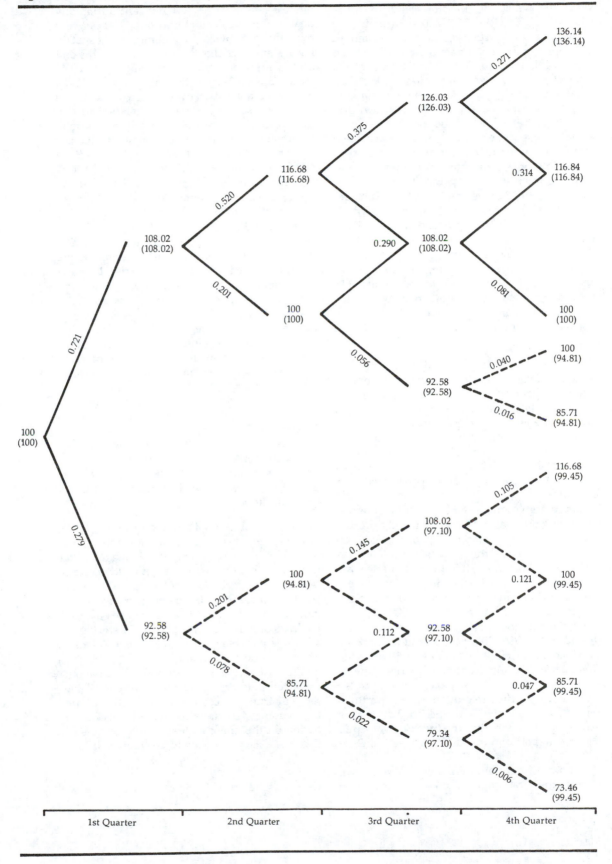

Alternative Paths

We assume that the investor wants to insure against losses in the S&P 500 with dividends reinvested. We further assume the economic environment that gives rise to the Black-Scholes option valuation formula.[5] In particular, the interest rate is known and constant, the dividend yield of the S&P 500 is known and constant, the volatility of the S&P 500 is known and constant, the value of the S&P 500 moves smoothly over time without jumps or gap openings, there are no opportunities for riskless arbitrage profits, and transaction costs are zero.

In the interest of comparability, we will assume that the interest rate is 10 per cent per year, the expected rate of return on the S&P 500 is 16 per cent, the dividend yield on the S&P 500 is 5 per cent, and the (arithmetic) volatility of the S&P 500 is 18 per cent.[6]

Each technique for creating portfolio insurance is designed to be 100 per cent reliable in preventing losses. Our comparison will focus on differences in path-independence and expected rate of return.

Stop-Loss Orders

The analysis of stop-loss orders as a method for approximating portfolio insurance is complicated by path-dependence. Suppose, for instance, that the investor executes a stop-loss order at the end of each quarter. To keep things as simple as possible without sacrificing the main elements of the problem, suppose that the S&P 500 (with dividends reinvested) moves either up or down by a fixed percentage over each quarter.

Figure A gives the S&P 500's pattern of movement over the year, given its assumed expected rate of return and volatility.[7] Both the S&P 500 and the value of the stop-loss portfolio (in parentheses) begin at $100. In each quarter, the probability of the index moving up by 8.02 per cent is 0.721, and the probability of the index moving down by 7.42 per cent is 0.279.

As the stop-loss portfolio starts out fully invested in the S&P 500, both the index and the portfolio are at either 108.02 or 92.58 after the first quarter. During the second quarter, however, path-dependence appears. If the index moved up in the first quarter, the portfolio remains fully invested in the S&P 500 during the second quarter; whether the index moves up or down, the portfolio tracks it to either 116.68 or 100.

If, on the other hand, the index moved down during the first quarter, the stop-loss order

would be triggered. It is easy to see why. The interest rate must be 2.41 per cent during any quarter if it is to compound out to 10 per cent over the year while remaining at a constant level. If the portfolio is down to 92.58 at the end of the first quarter, it can only reach 99.45 ($= 92.58 \times 1.0241^3$) by the end of the year, even if it is invested in cash over the remainder of the year. Because this ending level is less than 100, the stop-loss order is executed and the portfolio reverts for the remainder of the year to 100 per cent cash. At the end of the second quarter, the portfolio is thus at 94.81 ($= 92.58 \times 1.0241$). The dashed lines in Figure A indicate that the portfolio has been stopped out.

When the index is at 100, there is a 0.201 probability (0.721×0.279) that the portfolio will be at 100 and a 0.201 probability (0.279×0.721) that it will be at 94.81. That is, although the index may reach the same level either by moving up and then down or by moving down and then up, the same is not true of the portfolio. The *path* by which the index reaches 100 leads to different values for the stop-loss portfolio.

To evaluate a stop-loss order as a method for creating portfolio insurance, it is necessary to measure its expected rate of return, given its degree of path-dependence. Path-dependence can be measured by the expected absolute deviation of the rate of return conditional on the level of the index; the appendix illustrates the calculation. Perfect portfolio insurance requires that path-dependence be zero; the stop-loss order has a path-dependence of 3.14 per cent. Table II lists the nine distinct possible outcomes from the stop-loss strategy considered above.

European Payout-Protected Puts

The stop-loss strategy is path-dependent, but it *is* a step in the right direction. It suggests that there may be a way to transfer systematically between the S&P 500 and cash to generate portfolio insurance. By moving *gradually* into stock from cash as the stock price goes up, and *gradually* out of stock into cash as the stock price falls, it is possible to generate the equivalent of an insured position in stock.[8]

Alternatively, if one-year European payout-protected puts on the S&P 500, were available, these instruments could provide perfect portfolio insurance. An investor would select a put option on the index with striking price K such that K satisfies the following equality:

$$P(K) = K - S.$$

Here, P is the price of the put (shown above as a

Table II Possible Outcomes of Stop-Loss Strategy

Value of S&P 500 with Dividends Reinvested	Stop-Loss Portfolio Return	Probability
$136.14	36.14%	0.270
116.68	16.68%	0.314
116.68	−0.56%	0.105
100.00	0.00%	0.081
100.00	−0.56%	0.121
100.00	−5.19%	0.040
85.71	−0.56%	0.047
85.71	−5.19%	0.016
73.46	−0.56%	0.006

function of its striking price) and S is the concurrent level of the S&P 500 index.[9] If the index, with dividends reinvested, were to fall below its initial level by the end of the year, it could be sold by exercising the put at price K; this would be just enough to make up for the index decline and the initial cost P of the put.

This strategy is 100 per cent reliable in preventing losses. In addition, because the payoff of such a put would be solely dependent on the year-end level of the S&P 500 (with dividends reinvested), the protective put position would be completely path-independent. Assuming, as before, that the S&P 500 has an arithmetic expected rate of return and a volatility of 16 and 18 per cent, respectively, the striking price of the put would need to be 103.45 to provide insurance against losses. The expected rate of return on the insured portfolio (S&P 500 plus put) is 14.30 per cent.[10] The payoff pattern given in Table I is from just this strategy.

Of course, the investor must pay for the index put out of his initial $100. The ratio of the initial S&P 500 level to the striking price of the put is 0.9667 (100/103.45). The investor thus ends up with 0.9667 shares of the S&P 500 and 0.9667 puts, each at a striking price of 103.45. He must invest $3.33 ($3.45 × 0.9667) in puts and $96.67 in the S&P 500.

Several other types of instruments can be used to effect the same pattern of returns. From the European put-call parity relation, we know that a protective put is equivalent to a *fiduciary call* (purchased call plus cash), where the call has the same time to expiration and striking price as the put.[11] Moreover, with known rates of interest, a European put (or call) on the S&P 500 is equivalent to a European put (or call) on S&P 500 futures contracts, provided the expiration date of the option coincides with the delivery date of the underlying futures contracts.[12] Perfect portfolio insurance could be provided by either a *protective index futures put* or a *fiduciary index futures call*.

If a one-year European payout-protected option were available on each stock in the S&P 500, these instruments could be used to insure the S&P 500 by insuring each stock in the portfolio against loss for the year. However, use of conventional options on individual stocks leads to path-dependent outcomes with lower expected rates of return than index option strategies.[13]

Unfortunately, currently listed index options do not have the terms we have assumed. First, all listed options are *American*. American options can be exercised at any time before expiration, whereas European options can be exercised only at expiration. Because American options have every advantage of European options (they can be turned into European options by holding them to expiration) as well as the increased flexibility of early exercise, American options should be more expensive than otherwise identical European options. Second, listed options are not protected against dividends. As a result, they can be used to insure the capital appreciation component of stock returns, but not the dividend component. Third, all listed options have maturities of less than nine months. Because almost all trading volume is concentrated in the nearest maturities, the longest effective maturities are about three months for index futures options and two months for index spot options.[14] Finally, listed options have highly standardized striking prices that do not typically match the striking prices needed for portfolio insurance. This, combined with the advisability of early exercise of some American options, means that no American options of particular striking prices may survive in the market, even though European options of the same striking price would.

Sequential Short-Term Index Options

Although the listed markets do not offer options with the proper terms, there may still be some way of using these options to approximate portfolio insurance. In order to focus on the most significant feature of listed index options, we will assume that payout-protected European options are available in maturities of less than a year.

If six-month payout-protected European options were available, an investor could approximate portfolio insurance by rolling over a position in index puts every six months. He might start with a protective put that would insure the portfolio against loss over the first six months. If, at mid-year, the S&P 500 has declined so that it pays to exercise the put, the investor will buy another protective put to insure the portfolio over the next six months. At worst, by the end of the year, he should break even.

But suppose the S&P 500 rises over the first six months, so that the put is not exercised. In this case, the investor would buy a put that will insure the portfolio's mid-year value with a deductible equal to the profit earned over the first six months.

Figure B illustrates this strategy when the year is divided into four (binomial) intervals. Using the Black-Scholes formula, the striking price of the purchased six-month put at the beginning of the year is $103.86 (in brackets). After two quarters, the S&P 500 index is at 85.71, 100 or 116.68. In each case, the striking price of the six-month put purchased next is different.

When the index is at 85.71 or 100, the portfolio has just broken even over the first six months; the investor can't afford to lose money over the next six months. He must purchase a put with the same striking price relative to the stock price as the put he purchased at the beginning of the year.[15] When the index is at 116.68, however, such conservatism is not needed. Now, the investor can afford to lose $12.34 during the next six months and still break even at the end of the year. He can purchase a put with a striking price considerably below the current value of the portfolio.

This strategy is 100 per cent reliable in preventing losses, but it does suffer from path-dependence. Its expected rate of return, moreover, will usually fall short of the expected rate of return that could be achieved with a one-year protective European put, if one were available or could be created from a dynamic asset allocation strategy. Table III (which assumes the year is divided into 144 binomial intervals) provides estimates of the magnitudes of path-dependence and rate of return for different roll-over periods. As the roll-over becomes more frequent, the path-dependence increases and the expected rate of return decreases.

The limited availability and liquidity of listed striking prices that are distant from the money, and the five-point intervals at which they are listed, force the investor to be more conservative in practice than he might want to be.[16] Suppose that striking prices are only available in

Table III Path-Dependence and Expected Rates of Return for Roll-Over of Short-Term Protective European Puts*

Roll-Over Period	Path-Dependence	Expected Rate of Return
one year	0.00%	14.30%
six months	1.50 (1.67%)	14.04 (13.74%)
four months	2.12 (2.39)	13.96 (13.63)
three months	2.56 (2.90)	13.90 (13.53)
two months	2.97 (3.45)	13.86 (13.44)
stop-loss orders	3.73	14.70

* These results are particularly sensitive to the assumptions that volatility is known in advance and that there are no jump movements in the S&P 500 index.

three-point intervals and the deepest out-of-the-money put available is at most eight points out-of-the-money (relative to an S&P 500 level of 100). The numbers in parentheses in Table III show the degree to which this constraint increases path-dependence and reduces expected rate of return.

Real-World Considerations

The discussion so far has ignored complications created by American options, uncertain interest rates, uncertain volatility, jumps in security price movements, apparently mispriced securities, and transaction costs.

American Options

As building blocks for portfolio insurance, even long-term American index puts pose an unfortunate dilemma: It is either impossible to provide path-independence and 100 per cent reliability in preventing losses, or the insurance must be purchased at an excessive price!

As noted, if it is to insure a portfolio against loss, the index put must have a striking price K such that P(K) = K − S. Because of the possibility of early exercise, however, this the lowest price an American option can have. Furthermore, if the option is priced properly, it would pay to exercise it immediately.

If the put were worth less than K − S, an investor could earn a riskless arbitrage profit by buying the put and the underlying stock and then immediately exercising the put to receive K > P + S. If the put were worth exactly K − S, the investor who exercised the option immediately would get the full benefit of the put and also be able to start earning interest on the net receipt of K − S. By pricing the put at its exercisable value, the market implies that the interest that can be received through early exercise of the put outweighs its time value.

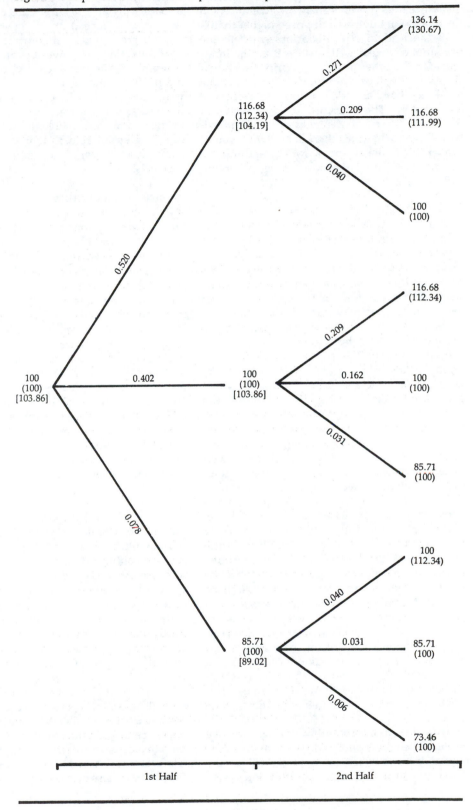

1st Half   2nd Half

Using American puts to generate portfolio insurance thus presents an awkward choice. On the one hand, buying a put priced higher than K − S can lead to a portfolio loss equal to the premium over parity (P − (K − S)) if the index falls. On the other hand, a put priced such that P = K − S will be overpriced, inasmuch as the insurance purchaser doesn't plan to exercise it immediately. The investor must steer between Scylla and Charybdis; as he avoids one difficulty, he approaches the other. In brief, the American put purchaser pays for something he doesn't want—the right to exercise the option early.

Uncertain Interest Rates

In all the strategies we have considered, except the use of long-term European payout-protected index options, uncertain interest rates increase the difficulty of predicting upside returns. The strategies' ability to protect against loss is unaffected, however, if care is taken to measure changes in interest rates and to factor these changes into the ongoing strategy.

In the case of the stop-loss strategies, for example, declining interest rates during the year translate into a shorter time to the stopout point. For the sequential option strategies (since option prices are partly determined by interest rates) uncertainty regarding interest rates increases the uncertainty regarding the prices that must be paid for options at future dates; nevertheless, changes in the option prices offset interest rate changes, preserving full loss protection.

Within the context of Black-Scholes assumptions, there is no reason to distinguish between options and their replicating dynamic asset allocation strategies; both produce identical results. With uncertain interest rates, however, dynamic strategies no longer have the power to replicate long-term European options exactly. Nonetheless, dynamic strategies that transfer holdings between stock and cash can hedge changes in interest rates over the year. Proper implementation using one-year Treasury bills as the hedging instrument (cash) should make conventional dynamic strategies less susceptible to shifts in shorter-term rates than either the stop-loss or sequential option strategies.

Dynamic option replication strategies can be implemented by using index futures. A purchased index futures contract, if held to the delivery date, implicitly embodies a long position in the index coupled with an equal amount of borrowing at a risk-free rate over the life of the contract. Instead of selling stock and lending the proceeds (as in conventional dynamic asset allocation), the investor can sell futures to accomplish similar ends by much simpler means. If the futures delivery date is less than a year, however, it will be necessary to roll over the futures hedge during the year. The strategy is thus more susceptible to uncertainty surrounding upside returns than conventional dynamic asset allocation utilizing one-year Treasury bills.

Uncertain Volatility

In practice, the source of the greatest difference between options and dynamic strategies is uncertain volatility. Not only does predicted volatility have an important effect on option prices but, of all their determinants, it is the most difficult to measure. Purchasing an index option amounts to insuring against fluctuations in the volatility of the index through the expiration date of the option. Proper implementation of the replicating dynamic asset allocation strategy retains full loss protection, but the upside capture now depends on the realized volatility over the year. The greater the volatility, the less the upside capture. This introduces a form of path-dependence into the outcome.

Sequential option strategies are exposed to a similar form of path-dependence. The prices of options to be purchased at future dates are dependent on the market's future predictions of volatility.

Security Price Jumps

As noted, stop-loss strategies may be threatened by jumps in security prices. For this reason, as contingent immunization (a form of stop-loss order applied to bond portfolio management) is practiced, the position remains 100 per cent invested in the actively managed bond portfolio as long as the stopout point is sufficiently distant. However, when the stopout point comes into view, the active portfolio is gradually transferred into the immunized portfolio.

In the case of dynamic asset allocation, this gradual transition to cash is an automatic and continuous feature. Because the portfolio will tend to be invested mostly in cash just before a jump that could create a loss, jumps will be less of a problem. The additional conservatism required of stop-loss orders to prevent losses from jumps will tend to equalize the expected rates of return from the stop-loss and dynamic asset allocation strategies.

Mispriced Securities

The investor who believes he can identify mispriced index futures, index options or even conventional options on common stocks may want to consider different approaches to portfolio insurance at different times. For example, when index calls are underpriced relative to index puts, he should give preference to fiduciary calls in place of protective puts as a means of creating portfolio insurance. If he thinks he can identify relatively underpriced calls on individual stocks, he may want to use a portfolio of fiduciary calls on individual stocks, despite the disadvantages of this strategy. If index futures appear to be underpriced, the preferred method may be to buy futures against a position in cash, rather than selling futures against a long position in the index.

Transaction Costs

By far the most liquid spot index option contracts are the S&P 100 options traded on the CBOE, which now comprise in total about 33 per cent of all CBOE options volume—typically representing trades to more than 20 million shares of the index per day (about $3 billion). The S&P 500 index futures traded on the CME are also highly liquid, representing trades to over 25 million shares per day (about $3.750 billion).

Currently, almost all trading volume for both index futures and options is concentrated in the nearest maturing contracts. As a result, it is necessary in the case of large trades to turn over options hedges about once every two months and futures hedges about once every four months to obtain sufficient liquidity. For options, we assume a 2 per cent one-way commission and a 1 per cent one-way spread give-up for a total one-way transaction cost of 3 per cent—about 12 cents on a $4 option, or about 0.08 per cent of the spot index. Additional costs from terminating index options at their expiration are ignored, because of their cash resettlement feature. For futures, we estimate a round-trip commission of $30 per contract and a $25 spread give-up for a total round-trip transaction cost of 0.07 per cent of the spot index price.

With a turnover of six times per year for a sequential options strategy, the total annual options transaction cost is 0.48 per cent of the spot index price. For dynamic asset allocation using index futures, turnover comes from two sources—from rolling the futures over three times per year (each time on an average of half the index portfolio) and from the requirements of dynamic asset allocation (which, based on simulation, is roughly 50 per cent per year). In total, futures would need to be bought or sold on 2.5 times the value of the index portfolio, which in turn implies a total annual futures transaction cost of 0.18 per cent of the spot index price.

Conventional dynamic asset allocation, which requires transferring assets between S&P 500 stocks and Treasury bills, is estimated from experience to cost 0.56 per cent of the spot index price.

In summary, conventional dynamic asset allocation is only slightly more expensive than a sequential index options strategy (0.56 per cent versus 0.48 per cent per annum). Dynamic asset allocation implemented with index futures is the cheapest, at about one-third this cost.

Conclusion

Long-term European payout-protected index options provide perfect portfolio insurance, but they do not currently exist in exchange-traded markets. Until they do, it will be necessary to use other instruments to approximate portfolio insurance on broad-based stock market indexes.

Stop-loss order strategies suffer from extreme path-dependence. Sequential index option strategies are also path-dependent and have a lower expected rate of return than perfect portfolio insurance. Of all the methods examined above, dynamic asset allocation, which attempts to replicate a long-term European protective put, seems to come closest to perfect portfolio insurance. ∎

Appendix

Calculating Path-Dependence

For each ending level of the index, make the best possible estimate of the portfolio rate of return. On average, as Table AI shows, the realized portfolio rate of return may be expected to err by 3.14 per cent. At worst—if the index ends at 116.68—the error may be expected to be 6.47 per cent.

The overall expected rate of return on the stop-loss strategy is calculated by summing the products of the second and third columns of Table II in the text. This results in 14.57 per cent.

Table AI Calculation of Path-Dependence

Value of S&P 500 with Dividends Reinvested	Conditional Portfolio Expected Value	Expected Absolute Deviation	Probability
$136.14	$136.14	0.00	0.271
116.68	112.37	6.47	0.418
100.00	98.85	1.35	0.243
85.71	98.28	1.74	0.062
73.46	99.45	0.00	0.006

Path Dependence = $(0.418 \times 6.47) + (0.243 \times 1.35)$
$+ (0.062 \times 1.74)$
$= 3.14\%$

Example: When S&P 500 = 116.68:

$$112.37 = \frac{(0.314 \times 116.68) + (0.105 \times 99.45)}{0.314 + 0.105}$$

$$6.47 =$$
$$\frac{[0.314 \times |116.68 - 112.37|] + [0.105 \times |99.45 - 112.37|]}{0.314 + 0.105}$$

For a very close approximation of the results from continuous S&P 500 movements, divide the year into 50 equally spaced intervals with binomial moves over each interval.[17] In this case, the path-dependence and expected rate of return are 3.73 and 14.70 per cent, respectively. With a continuous process, the stop-loss order could be executed at exactly 100; in that case, the stop-loss strategy would be 100 per cent reliable in preventing losses.

Also of interest for the stop loss strategy are the stopout probability, which is 40 per cent, and the expected time to stopout, which is 0.76 of a year (roughly, the beginning of the fourth quarter).

Footnotes

1. The proof of this proposition is contained in an unpublished note by Hayne Leland.
2. For a more complete treatment, see Hayne Leland, "Who Should Buy Portfolio Insurance?" *Journal of Finance*, May 1980.
3. It is hypothesized that an investor who sells portfolio insurance wants to maximize the probability of obtaining a specified level of profit (the insurance premium in the case of a no-loss policy). In compensation for this, the investor must absorb all losses in the index.
4. For a proof that rational, risk-averse investors in a complete-markets, random-walk, time-additive utility environment should prefer path-independent to path-dependent strategies, see John C. Cox and Hayne Leland, "A Characterization of Path-Independent Policies." For the special case of investors who maximize the terminal value of

their wealth at the end of a specified horizon, the intuition behind their proof is easily grasped. Suppose the only thing an investor cares about is the amount of wealth he will have at his horizon date and he has no reason to be concerned about the implications of past outcomes for future returns (the random walk assumption). Then, if he can achieve path-independent outcomes for the pattern of returns that he desires at his horizon date, he will prefer these to path-dependent outcomes. The additional uncertainty from path-dependence is uncompensated risk. It is as though, in addition to his desired outcome of $120.84, the investor had to flip a coin to determine whether he receives $5 more or $5 less. No risk averter would willingly accept this gamble.

5. See Fischer Black and Myron Scholes, "The Pricing of Options and Corporate Liabilities," *Journal of Political Economy*, May–June 1973.
6. The Black-Scholes option pricing formula uses the logarithmic or continuous volatility (the standard deviation of the *natural logarithm* of one plus the rate of return) as an input, rather than the arithmetic or discrete volatility (the standard deviation of the rate of return). In our case, the S&P 500 is assumed to have an arithmetic mean and volatility of 16 and 18 per cent, respectively. Assuming lognormality of its rate of return, this translates into a logarithmic volatility of 15.5 per cent.
7. Formulas for transforming the mean and volatility of a lognormal security price process into the sizes and probabilities of the up and down moves of a discrete binomial process are given in John C. Cox, Stephen A. Ross and Mark Rubinstein, "Option Pricing: A Simplified Approach," *Journal of Financial Economics*, September 1979.
8. See M. Rubinstein and H. Leland, "Replicating Options with Positions in Stock and Cash," *Financial Analysts Journal*, July/August 1981.
9. Readers familiar with options may wonder if a striking price K can be chosen satisfying this equation. If the put were American (permitting early exercise), then the striking price would be so high that the put should be immediately exercised. But the put under consideration here is European (it cannot be exercised early), so its price must only satisfy $P > Kr^{-t} - S$, which permits its price to fall such that $P < K - S$ prior to expiration. Here, r is one plus the annual rate of interest and t is the time to expiration. Since a protective European put is always worth $S + P$, it follows that at no time in its life can the value of this position fall below Kr^{-t}. This implies that if, at any time during its life, the put were converted into cash, the investor could realize a minimum $Kr^{-t} \times r^{t} = K$ by the expiration date.
10. This technique for calculating the expected rates of return of European options is developed in Mark Rubinstein, "A Simple Formula for the

Expected Rate of Return of an Option over a Finite Holding Period" (Working paper #119, Research Program in Finance, Institute of Business and Economic Research, University of California at Berkeley, March 1984).

11. If S is the stock price, C the call price, P the price of an otherwise similar put, r one plus the annual rate of interest, t the time to expiration of the options, and K their common striking price, according to the put-call parity relationship, at all times during the lives of the options:

$$P + S = C + Kr^{-t}.$$

The left-hand side of this equation is a protective put and the right-hand side is a fiduciary call.

12. Because neither the European spot call nor the European futures call can be exercised early, and because the spot and futures prices must be equal on the expiration date of the options, the cash flows received from either option must be identical.

13. See Mark Rubinstein, "Alternative Paths to Portfolio Insurance: A Detailed Analysis" (Expanded version of this article, May 1984).

14. The most active listed index options, the CBOE S&P 100 options, are not even listed with maturities beyond three months. A casual glance at the *Wall Street Journal* reveals that about 90 per cent of the volume in listed index puts is concentrated in puts with less than 40 days to expiration, with negligible volume in puts with more than 60 days to go.

15. Observe that when the index is at 85.71, the striking price of the next six-month put, relative to the index level is 103.86. (= 89.02/85.71).

16. To preserve reliability at three-point intervals, the investor must buy puts at slightly higher striking prices than optimal. Moreover, when the S&P 500 rises, the eight-point limitation will also force one to buy options at higher than optimal striking prices.

17. With 50 intervals, the minimum number of separate nodes at the end of the tree is 51 and the maximum number is 2^{50} or 123 trillion. In the stop-loss strategy, the number of different ending nodes turns out to be 638.

Article 25

by Richard J. Rendleman, Jr. and Richard W. McEnally

Assessing the Costs of Portfolio Insurance

Before purchasing portfolio insurance, the investor should consider the cost of coverage—in particular, the cost the marketplace extracts for bearing portfolio insurance risk. One way to gauge this cost is to compare the results from portfolio insurance with those from a reasonable alternative portfolio management strategy.

Portfolio insurance suffers in comparison with an "optimal" portfolio designed to maximize the rate of growth of portfolio value over time. Over a variety of assumptions for market volatility, interest rate, time horizon and insured floor, the insured portfolio can expect a lower continuously compounded rate of growth than a comparable optimal portfolio. The insured portfolio is also more likely than the optimal portfolio to achieve only the guaranteed minimum return.

The economic cost of portfolio insurance can be substantially reduced by lowering the minimum return requirement and by lengthening the horizon over which the insurance program is implemented. Furthermore, portfolio insurance (at least as conventionally implemented) comes closest to offering optimal results when investors are highly risk averse.

PORTFOLIO INSURANCE is an asset management technique that provides a minimum floor on portfolio value while allowing the portfolio to benefit from rising security prices. It is one of the most successful investment management innovations of our time, having attracted over $50 billion dollars of portfolio assets in the five or so years since its inception. Its potential ability to capture upside returns while protecting against downside loss has become increasingly attractive, especially to private employee benefit plans, in light of a protracted bull market and recent pension accounting changes.

A plan sponsor or other investment policy-maker deciding whether to use portfolio insurance must compare the benefits and costs of the technique. The benefit is straightforward; de-

pending on the way it is structured, portfolio insurance can virtually guarantee that a portfolio will not incur losses in excess of a specified percentage, will not have negative returns, or will not experience returns below some positive level. The cost may be measured in terms of forgone returns. This cost has two elements— one associated with the pure price the market extracts for providing the insurance (i.e., for bearing the risk that insurance lays off), the other due to the frictions, imperfections and market price pressure effects encountered in implementation of the technique.

This article addresses the first and more fundamental cost element—the cost the market demands for bearing portfolio insurance risk.[1] In the process, we will outline a method for addressing four questions that should be considered in insuring any portfolio.

- What is the probability that the portfolio will earn no more than its insured floor return?

Richard Rendleman, Jr. is Professor of Finance and Richard McEnally is Meade Willis Professor of Investment Banking at the School of Business Administration of The University of North Carolina at Chapel Hill.

1. Footnotes appear at end of article.

- What are the expected returns and utilities of return of the insured portfolio versus those of a reasonable alternative strategy?
- What are the probabilities that the insured portfolio or the alternative will have the higher returns?
- Over the long run, how will the accumulation of value from the insured portfolio stack up against the alternative?

Because portfolio insurance is a conservative strategy, the question of how risk averse one must be to justify insurance is also explored.

We compare the results from an insurance strategy with those from an alternative strategy that maximizes expected utility according to an "everyman's" utility function—or, for those who find the notion of expected utility unappealing, so that it maximizes the expected rate of accumulation of portfolio value. We then extend the analysis to compare portfolio insurance with strategies that are more conservative or more aggressive in their approach to optimal portfolio composition.

Portfolio Insurance, Plain and Fancy

The basic concept of portfolio insurance is extremely straightforward: Purchase a "protective put" that allows a portfolio to be sold for a price sufficient to yield the minimum required return, and invest the remaining funds conventionally.

Suppose an investor starts with $1.00 and wants to insure that his portfolio has a minimum return of, say, 5 per cent. Suppose further that one unit of a market index can be purchased for $0.9097 and that a "European" put on this index (i.e., a put exercisable only at expiration) has a strike price of $1.05 and is available in the marketplace for $0.0903. (The origin of these numbers is explained below.) The investor could then purchase one put for $0.0903 and buy a unit of the index with the $0.9097 remaining. If the index declines or simply fails to rise above $1.05 by the end of the period, the investor can use the put to sell the index for $1.05, thereby achieving the required 5 per cent return. If the value of the index at the end of the period exceeds $1.05, the put expires worthless, but the investor is left with a portfolio whose value exceeds $1.05.

The higher the actual value of the index, the greater the value of the investor's portfolio. However, the investor's ending capital will never be more than 90.97 per cent of the capital of someone who simply bought the index outright, because only this fraction of the $1.00 is invested in the index. For example, the investor could have used his $1.00 to purchase outright 1.0993 ($1.00/$0.9097) units of the index; if the index then rose to $1.1826, the investor would have a terminal wealth of $1.30 (or $1.1826 × 1.0993), representing a 30 per cent return, versus the insured portfolio's terminal wealth of $1.1826 (the value of the index, or 1.30 × 0.9097) and 18.26 per cent return.[2] The difference—$0.1174, or 11.74 percentage points—is due to the cost of portfolio insurance.

The investment outcomes from portfolio insurance can also be achieved with calls and fixed income investment. Suppose the risk-free interest rate is 10.52 per cent (the annualized equivalent of a 10 per cent continuously compounded rate). According to the standard put-call parity relationship, a call on the index exercisable at $1.05 should sell for $0.0499.[3] The investor could therefore purchase one call on the index and invest the remaining $0.9501 (or $1.00 − $0.0499) at the risk-free rate. At the end of the period, this portfolio would have a minimum value of $1.05 (or $0.9501 × 1.1052). If the index rose above $1.05, then the $1.05 could be used to exercise the call, leaving the investor in the same position he would have been in had he purchased the protective put.

In practice, listed protective puts or calls are not normally used to insure portfolios. For one thing, it is virtually impossible to obtain puts or calls that have exactly the right period to expiration, exercise price, etc., needed for a particular insurance strategy. For another, most puts and calls readily available to U.S. investors—i.e., "American" puts and calls—are exercisable at any time, rather than only at expiration, as with "European" options. The early exercise feature of American options is valuable under some conditions and increases their prices, but it is not a feature needed for insuring portfolios. Therefore, the use of American options would unduly increase the cost of portfolio insurance. Fortunately, there are viable alternatives to listed options for insuring portfolios.

In principle, it is possible to replicate exactly the return outcomes from European options by *continuously* rebalancing a package of assets between the associated equity security or securities and risk-free assets such as Treasury bills.[4] This process is referred to as the creation of "synthetic options"; when applied to portfolio insurance it is often called Dynamic Asset Allocation.[5] The process involves maintaining a stock-bill balance such that the value of the portfolio has exactly the same sensitivity to changes in the value of the stock market index (or other underlying risky asset) as it would have had it been insured with protective European puts. The portfolio will be rebalanced toward the risky asset if the value of the risky asset increases, and it will be rebalanced toward bills if the value of the risky asset decreases. Intuitively, as the portfolio increases in value, equity commitment can be increased; with poor performance, more funds must be placed in Treasury bills, or the equivalent, in order to assure the target return.

Futures contracts on market indexes provide still a third way of implementing portfolio insurance. The objective is still to replicate the value sensitivity of a portfolio insured with European options. If the underlying portfolio is fully invested in common stocks, a short position in futures will dampen the volatility of the overall portfolio. If the value of the portfolio rises, the short position is reduced to increase equity exposure; with a drop in the value of the portfolio, increasing the short position in futures decreases downside loss. This approach is often referred to as "dynamic hedging." Compared with synthetic options, it confines trading to the highly liquid futures market and minimizes disruptive shifts in the composition of the portfolio being insured.

In evaluating the economic costs of portfolio insurance, the differences in these three approaches are not critical, because their differences lie in implementational efficiency, rather than in their effects on the fundamental risks and returns of the insured portfolio. Indeed, any fundamental differences in outcomes would give rise to arbitrage opportunities that a well functioning market would quickly eliminate. Our analysis therefore focuses on operations in stocks, European options and bills, rather than in synthetic options or futures. This approach, a standard one, should not reduce the generality or relevance of the results.

Criteria for Assessing Portfolio Insurance
The downside risk from portfolio insurance is exercising the protective put and obtaining only the minimum return. An obvious first criterion for evaluating portfolio insurance, therefore, is the probability or frequency of this occurring. In other words, how often will the insured portfolio do no better than its guaranteed return?

The remaining criteria evaluate the outcomes of portfolio insurance in comparison with those achieved under some alternative strategy. One alternative, the one we initially employ, is the "optimal" portfolio in the sense that it maximizes the expected logarithmic utility of outcomes and maximizes the expected growth rate of portfolio assets over time.

The idea of forming portfolios to maximize expected utility has never met with overwhelming enthusiasm among practicing portfolio managers. Nevertheless, maximizing expected utility is the standard paradigm for analysis of decisions in financial economics, and it is one that provides the foundations of modern portfolio theory. The utility function, or relation between utility and investment outcomes, we use is the logarithmic utility function—a member of the set of utility functions sometimes known as "isoelastic" because they treat utility as being independent of the absolute amount of wealth involved. This property has obvious appeal in dealing with investor decisions in the abstract.[6] It asserts that the utility of an outcome is equal to the (natural) logarithm of the outcome, hence that utility varies in proportion to the change in the logarithm of the outcome. It thus implies that, while positive outcomes are liked and negative outcomes are disliked, a given absolute amount of downside outcome is disliked more than the same amount of upside outcome is liked; it also implies that constant absolute increases in outcomes give less and less utility.

Consider the following holding period returns (i.e., the ratios of ending portfolio values to beginning portfolio values, or rate of return plus one)—0.90, 1.10, 1.20 and 1.21. The natural logarithms of these values are -0.1054, 0.0953, 0.1823 and 0.1906. The loss of 10 per cent (holding period return of 0.90) reduces utility more than the gain of 10 per cent (holding period return of 1.10) increases it. Doubling of the rate of return from 10 to 20 per cent (holding period return of 1.20) does not double the utility of the outcome (2×0.0953 is greater than 0.1823). Because of risk aversion, the rate of return would have to increase from 10 to 21 per cent to double the utility ($2 \times 0.0953 = 0.1906$, which is also the logarithm of the holding period return of 1.21).

The logarithmic utility function is frequently regarded as an "everyman's" utility function because it appears to be generally consistent with many of the economic decisions people are observed to make.[7] More to the point, given reasonable inputs regarding risks and returns of marketable securities, portfolios constructed to maximize expected logarithmic utility (that is, to maximize the sum of the probabilities of a holding period outcome times the logarithm of that outcome) fall well within the realm of "reasonable" composition by most standards.

This strategy for constructing portfolios has an alternative justification, one that may appeal more to those not comfortable with the notion of expected utility maximization: Selecting a portfolio to maximize the expected natural logarithm of its end-of-period value is equivalent to maximizing the portfolio's expected continuously compounded rate of return—its rate of growth of value. A decision-maker who regards expected utility maximization as irrelevant but who wishes to see the portfolio grow at the fastest rate possible should structure it exactly as though the objective is to maximize expected logarithmic utility.

Perhaps the most interesting feature of the strategy is that, over the long run, the probability approaches 1.0—i.e., certainty—that a portfolio managed according to the logarithmic strategy will accumulate more wealth than any significantly different strategy involving the same assets. For this reason it is frequently referred to as the "growth-optimal" strategy. Although the relevant "long run" may be too long for some portfolio managers, the strategy may be appropriate for retirement funds and endowments, whose assets are committed for relatively long periods of time. Another significant feature of the logarithmic strategy is that it never risks the loss of a portfolio's original capital: It will never select an asset mix for which there is any positive probability that a portfolio's end-of-period value will be zero or less.

One criterion for evaluating portfolio insurance is how much expected utility, or expected rate of portfolio growth, is given up by using the insurance strategy rather than the optimal strategy. A second is the probability that the insured portfolio will have higher returns than the optimal portfolio, or the reverse. The third criterion is the comparative wealth accumulation from the two strategies over multiple-year horizons.

Assumptions and Method

We ignored taxes and transaction costs and assumed the probability distribution of returns on risky assets to be lognormal. We used the same assumptions about asset returns to construct insured portfolios and growth-optimal portfolios. We assumed first a 16 per cent, then a 12 per cent, annual expected arithmetic return on the common stock investment alternative; an annual arithmetic standard deviation of either 20 per cent or 18 per cent; and a risk-free borrowing/lending rate of either 10 or 6 per cent compounded continuously. The common stock investment alternative will be referred to as "stock," with the understanding that it may consist of any package of risky assets. Similarly, the risk-free asset will occasionally be referred to as "bills," although other securities might qualify.

The risk assumptions, the 16 per cent return assumption and the 10 per cent interest rate assumption are taken from Robert Ferguson's article, "How to Beat the S&P 500 (without losing sleep)" (*Financial Analysts Journal*, March/April 1986). These numbers are used for convenience and because they carry the imprimatur of an advocate of portfolio insurance. The analysis can easily be conducted with alternative assumptions. It is important to emphasize, though, that the analysis is forward-looking, employing expectations about probability distributions of asset returns, rather than historical outcomes.[8]

We computed holding period returns for various insurance programs and for optimally constructed portfolios involving the same assets. The insured portfolios had horizons of either one or three years and guaranteed minimum annual returns of 5 per cent, zero or −5 per cent. Each insurance program implicitly involved the purchase of a specific European put option, with the remainder of the funds being allocated to stock. All options were priced according to the Black-Scholes model.[9]

We determined optimal portfolio compositions using a computer program that, in brief, takes as its inputs the expected return and volatility of a risky asset, the price of a European call option on this asset and the maturity and strike price of the call, the riskless rate of interest, and information on the investor's utility function.[10] The program then determines the optimal allocation among the risky asset, the

Table I Expected Logarithmic Utility of Alternative Portfolio Strategies

Assumptions[a]				Expected Utility[b] — Optimal			Portfolio Weights							
							Insured		Optimal Buy-Hold				Optimal Continuous Reallocation	
Minimum Return (per cent)	Stock Volatility (per cent)	Interest Rate (per cent)	Time Horizon (years)	Insured	Buy-Hold	Continuous Reallocation	Stock	Put	Stock	Call	Put	Bill	Stock	Bill
5	20	10	1	0.1164	0.1338	0.1346	0.9097	0.0903	1.7651	0.0000	0.0803	−0.8454	1.4282	−0.4282
									0.9556	0.0444	0.0000	0.0000		
0	20	10	1	0.1228	0.1342	0.1346	0.9534	0.0466	1.6153	0.0000	0.0334	−0.6487	1.4282	−0.4282
									0.9318	0.0682	0.0000	0.0000		
−5	20	10	1	0.1266	0.1344	0.1346	0.9754	0.0246	1.5342	0.0000	0.0157	−0.5499	1.4282	−0.4282
									0.9102	0.0898	0.0000	0.0000		
5	18	10	1	0.1186	0.1407	0.1426	0.9423	0.0757	2.3352	0.0000	0.1157	−1.4508	1.7577	−0.7577
									0.9238	0.0762	0.0000	0.0000		
0	18	10	1	0.1257	0.1417	0.1426	0.9630	0.0370	2.0637	0.0000	0.0453	−1.1090	1.7577	−0.7577
									0.8834	0.1166	0.0000	0.0000		
−5	18	10	1	0.1298	0.1422	0.1426	0.9817	0.0183	1.9215	0.0000	0.0200	−0.9416	1.7577	−0.7577
									0.8462	0.1538	0.0000	0.0000		
5	20	6	1	0.0669	0.0977	0.1005	0.8029	0.1971	2.5028	0.0000	0.3734	−1.8770	1.5201	−0.5201
									0.9788	0.0212	0.0000	0.0000		
0	20	6	1	0.0800	0.0994	0.1005	0.9182	0.0818	1.8939	0.0000	0.0851	−0.9790	1.5201	−0.5201
									0.3957	0.0605	0.0000	0.0000		
−5	20	6	1	0.0868	0.1000	0.1005	0.9580	0.0420	1.7321	0.0000	0.0361	−0.7682	1.5201	−0.5201
									0.9096	0.0904	0.0000	0.0000		
5	20	10	3	0.1226	0.1342	0.1346	0.9136	0.0864	1.6604	0.0000	0.0739	−0.7344	1.4282	−0.4282
									0.8781	0.1219	0.0000	0.0000		
0	20	10	3	0.1281	0.1344	0.1346	0.9703	0.0297	1.5096	0.0000	0.0213	−0.5309	1.4282	−0.4282
									0.8143	0.1857	0.0000	0.0000		
−5	20	10	3	0.1303	0.1344	0.1346	0.9907	0.0093	1.4438	0.0000	0.0066	−0.4505	1.4282	−0.4282
									0.7400	0.2592	0.0000	0.0000		

a. Assumptions include an expected stock return of 0.16 per annum except in the third panel, where the expected stock return is approximately 0.12. All values enter the computations in discrete form except for the interest rates, which enter in continuously compounded form.

b. Because of the utility function assumption, these values correspond to the expected continuously compounded portfolio returns.

call option and the safe asset, assuming that the portfolio composition is maintained without revision until the maturity date of the option. A transformation of the optimal solution using the put-call parity relationship provided an economically equivalent solution for a portfolio involving a European put rather than a call.

We also determined the optimal allocation of the portfolio between stock and the riskless asset under a policy of continuous portfolio revision, and the logarithmic expected utility and expected rate of asset growth from such a policy. Although such a portfolio could not be maintained in practice, it serves as a useful point of reference because it shows the highest level of performance available to the investor in a frictionless environment.[11]

Results

Table I summarizes the results regarding portfolio composition, expected utility and the expect-

ed growth rate of assets. The top section assumes a one-year insurance program, annual stock return volatility of 20 per cent and an annual interest rate of 10 per cent. The second section is based on volatility of 18 per cent. The third section assumes the original 20 per cent volatility and one-year insurance program, but decreases the interest rate and stock return assumptions to 6 and 12 per cent, respectively. Finally, the last section involves a three-year insurance program and the original volatility and return assumptions.

The first row of figures, for example, pertains to an insurance program designed to guarantee a 5 per cent return over a one-year horizon under the assumptions of 20 per cent annual market volatility, a 10 per cent continuous interest rate and a 16 per cent expected market return. The "portfolio weights" for this insurance program represent an investment of $0.9097 in risky assets for every dollar of initial capital and the purchase of a put costing $0.0903. (These figures formed the basis of our earlier example.)

The composition of an *optimal* portfolio consisting of stock, the put option and the safe asset calls for borrowing $0.8454 per dollar of initial capital and investing $1.7651 in stock and $0.0803 in a put. Given an initial price of $0.9097, the $1.7651 investment in stock represents the purchase of 1.94 units of stock ($1.7651/$0.9097); inasmuch as 1.10 units ($1.00/$0.9097) could have been purchased with the initial dollar of capital, an additional 0.84 unit (or 1.94 − 1.10) is purchased through leverage. The investment of $0.0803 in a put option represents a put on 0.89 unit ($0.0803/$0.0903). The put option covers the downside risk associated with the 0.84 unit of stock purchased with borrowed funds plus an option to sell an additional 0.05 unit. Although the optimal portfolio weights appear much different from those of the insurance program, the optimal portfolio nevertheless contains an element of insurance.

The table also shows the weights for an economically equivalent portfolio involving calls rather than puts. Here the optimal solution calls for an investment of $0.9556 in stock and $0.0444 in calls. The call option contributes leverage to the portfolio without the risk of ruin.

The last two columns of the table show the optimal allocation between stock and the safe asset assuming continuous portfolio revision. The optimal portfolio policy involves borrowing $0.4282 and investing a total of $1.4282 in stock. Under this strategy, the portfolio is revised continuously to maintain constant portfolio weights. This constant rebalancing enables the investor to avoid the risk of ruin despite the use of leverage.

The figures for expected utility show that the insured portfolio in the first row is associated with an expected logarithmic utility of 0.1164. This corresponds to an expected continuously compounded rate of growth of 11.64 per cent, or an equivalent annually compounded geometric mean return of 12.34 per cent (100 × [Exp(0.1164) − 1]). The corresponding optimal stock-option-bill portfolio provides an expected logarithmic utility of 0.1338, corresponding to an expected continuously compounded rate of asset growth of 13.38 per cent, or an equivalent geometric mean return of 14.31 per cent. The difference between the two geometric mean returns is 1.97 per cent, or 197 basis points.

Inasmuch as "one-hundred-fifty basis points is nothing to sneeze at," a 197 basis point differential represents a significant give-up in the annual compound return.[12]

The remainder of the table essentially echoes the message in the first row. The only major departures occur when the minimum rate of return for the insured portfolio is reduced, when the return environment is less favorable, and when the investment horizon is extended.

In each of the panels, when the minimum return is reduced to zero or −5 per cent, the insured investor gains in terms of expected logarithmic utility or portfolio growth in comparison with the optimal strategies. Relaxing the minimum return constraint allows the insured portfolio to act more like a conventional stock portfolio. Thus a more aggressive portfolio composition moves the portfolio in the direction of optimality.

In the second panel, where the volatility of the market is reduced from 20 to 18 per cent, utility or expected growth increases under both strategies. However, the gain is greater for the optimal than for the insurance strategy. As intuition might suggest, portfolio insurance is relatively more valuable to risk-averse investors in more volatile markets.

The third panel, where the interest rate and expected market return are both reduced by approximately 4 percentage points, to 6 and 12 per cent, portrays circumstances closer to the recent market environment. It is hardly surprising that, in this lower return environment, expected growth declines under both insured and optimal strategies. What is surprising is the high cost of the insured portfolio compared with the optimal portfolios. With a zero minimum return target, for example, the expected return of the insured portfolio is only 0.0800, versus 0.0994 for the buy-and-hold optimal portfolio. Compare this 0.0194 difference with the 0.0114 difference at this minimum return level in the 10 per cent rate, 16 per cent return environment. The insured strategy fares especially poorly in the low return environment when its minimum return target is 5 per cent, which is close to the 6 per cent interest rate. Under these circumstances, the insured strategy gives up 0.0308 to the optimal strategy. Low returns require that relatively more insurance be purchased to guarantee the minimum, leaving less of the portfolio to participate in upside markets. This effect is especially pronounced

Table II Probabilities of Selected Returns from Insured and Optimal Portfolios

Assumptions				Probability That			
Minimum Return (per cent)	Stock Volatility (per cent)	Interest Rate (per cent)	Time Horizon (years)	Insured = Minimum	Optimal < Minimum	Insured > Optimal	Optimal > Insured
5	20	10	1	0.53	0.42	0.42	0.58
0	20	10	1	0.32	0.35	0.35	0.65
−5	20	10	1	0.20	0.26	0.42	0.58
5	18	10	1	0.48	0.48	0.48	0.52
0	18	10	1	0.28	0.36	0.44	0.56
−5	18	10	1	0.16	0.27	0.41	0.59
5	20	06	1	0.82	0.45	0.45	0.55
0	20	06	1	0.48	0.43	0.57	0.43
−5	20	06	1	0.29	0.34	0.41	0.59
5	20	10	3	0.31	0.33	0.36	0.64
0	20	10	3	0.13	0.20	0.37	0.63
−5	20	10	3	0.05	0.12	0.37	0.63

when the target is high compared with the interest rate; in the first row of this panel, for example, nearly 20 per cent of the insured portfolio goes to purchase insurance.

By extending the investment horizon from one to three years, in the last panel, the level of expected utility or portfolio growth increases considerably for the insured strategy. With a 16 per cent expected stock return, the probability that the three-year return will fall below a specified rate such as a 5 per cent annual return is much lower than the probability that the one-year return will fall below the same annual rate. As a result, the effective annualized cost of insuring a portfolio to earn a given annualized return is reduced. This reduction enables the portfolio to grow at a higher rate, or earn a higher level of expected utility, over the longer horizon.

Probability Distributions

In addition to examining the probability distributions of portfolio outcomes at the end of a one-year insurance period, it is interesting to consider the distributions of outcomes over longer periods. In constructing such multiperiod distributions, we assumed that a given portfolio is reallocated each year according to its original proportions.[13] The multiperiod return distributions are based on 1,000 simulated multiperiod outcomes, rather than on analytical results.

Table II gives four probabilities for each set of assumptions in Table I. For example, the first row shows that the probability of the insured portfolio only equaling the guaranteed mini-

mum return of 5 per cent is 0.53. The return from the optimal portfolio has a 0.42 probability of returning this minimum or less. The insured portfolio should outperform the optimal portfolio 42 per cent of the time under this set of assumptions; conversely, the optimal portfolio's returns will exceed those of the insured portfolio with a 0.58 probability.

From the table, it is evident that lower minimum return requirements reduce considerably the probability of attaining only the minimum return; at the same time, however, the optimal portfolio tends to outperform the insured portfolio at lower minimum required returns. The probability of the portfolio achieving only the minimum return escalates dramatically when the minimum returns are high compared with available market returns.

Over a three-year time horizon, the probability of the insured portfolio achieving only the minimum return is considerably less than over the one-year horizon. Over the longer horizon, however, the optimal portfolio tends to outperform the insured portfolio more often.

Figures A, B and C portray the complete probability distributions of portfolio outcomes for periods of one, 10 and 20 years, given the assumptions used in the first row of the tables. Figure A, illustrating one-year periods, captures much of the information in Table II; in addition, it shows that, even though the return of the optimal portfolio could theoretically approach a 100 per cent loss, this is an unlikely practical result; 99 per cent of the time, the return of this portfolio will exceed −29 per cent.

Figures B and C extend the analysis, showing

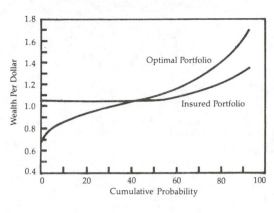

Figure A   Probability Distribution After One Year

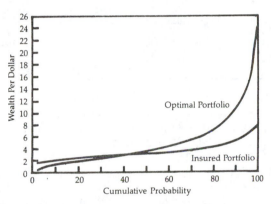

Figure B   Probability Distribution After 10 Years

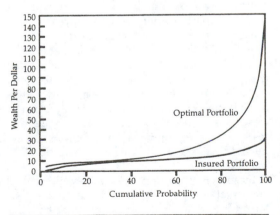

Figure C   Probability Distribution After 20 Years

simulated probability distributions of portfolio outcomes after 10 and 20 years. These figures illustrate two general relations. First, as the number of years in the investment horizon increases, the probability that the optimal strategy will outperform the insured strategy also increases; for the 10 and 20-year periods, these probabilities are approximately 66 and 70 per cent.[14] Second, the upside give-up associated with the insurance strategy becomes much more pronounced as the period of analysis is extended; the average terminal portfolio values (not evident from the figures) are $5.47 and $27.15 for the optimal strategy over 10 and 20 years, respectively, while the expected portfolio values for the insured strategy are only $3.44 and $11.39. For every initial dollar invested, the simulated optimal portfolio values exceed $24.08 and $143.23 for the 10 and 20-year periods, respectively, in 2 per cent of cases. Corresponding values for the insured strategy are $7.70 and $30.32. On the downside, however, the second percentile cutoff points are $0.88 and $1.65 for the optimal strategy and $1.80 and $4.45 for the insured strategy. The *worst* of 1,000 simulated outcomes are $0.44 and $0.68 for the optimal strategy and $1.63 and $3.01 for the insurance program.

Over the long run, the probability becomes quite high that the optimal strategy will significantly outperform the insurance strategy. However, for the small percentage of the time that the optimal strategy underperforms the insurance strategy, it does much worse.

Alternative Attitudes toward Risk

The analysis so far has focused entirely on the logarithmic utility function. Some investment decision-makers may look at the probability distributions of returns depicted in Figures A through C and feel that the risks seem too large (in which case a more conservative utility function would be appropriate) or that more risk can be tolerated (suggesting that a more aggressive utility function is justifiable).

The remaining analysis compares the one-year, 5 per cent minimum return insurance program described in the first row of Table I with an optimal strategy that assumes greater or lesser degrees of investor risk aversion.

The aggressiveness or conservativeness of the utility function is controlled by the "coefficient of relative risk aversion," a number that measures the investor's aversion to risk. A coeffi-

Table III Optimal and Insured Portfolios for Various Levels of Risk Aversion

Risk-Aversion Coefficient	Expected Utility		Optimal Portfolio Weights			
	Insured	Optimal	Stock	Call	Put	Bill
0.2	0.1270	0.2853	13.6518	0.0000	1.3281	−13.9798
			0.2654	0.7346	0.0000	0.0000
0.4	0.1242	0.1891	6.3927	0.0000	0.5661	−5.9855
			0.6869	0.3121	0.0000	0.0000
0.6	0.1215	0.1583	3.6998	0.0000	0.2834	−2.9832
			0.8432	0.1568	0.0000	0.0000
0.8	0.1189	0.1432	2.4588	0.0000	0.1531	−1.6119
			0.9153	0.0847	0.0000	0.0000
1.0	0.1164	0.1338	1.7651	0.0000	0.0803	−0.8454
			0.9556	0.0444	0.0000	0.0000
2.0	0.1054	0.1107	0.6678	0.0000	−0.0085	0.3407
			0.7535	−0.0047	0.0000	0.2512
3.0	0.0963	0.1000	0.4119	0.0000	−0.0123	0.6004
			0.5360	−0.0068	0.0000	0.4708
4.0	0.0886	0.0927	0.3020	0.0000	−0.0103	0.7082
			0.4055	−0.0057	0.0000	0.6002
5.0	0.0820	0.0870	0.2411	0.0000	−0.0077	0.7666
			0.3185	−0.0042	0.0000	0.6858
6.0	0.0764	0.0821	0.1943	0.0000	−0.0080	0.8137
			0.2750	−0.0044	0.0000	0.7295
7.0	0.0715	0.0779	0.1686	0.0000	−0.0062	0.8376
			0.2314	−0.0034	0.0000	0.7720
8.0	0.0672	0.0740	0.1427	0.0000	−0.0066	0.8640
			0.2097	−0.0037	0.0000	0.7940
9.0	0.0634	0.0705	0.1262	0.0000	−0.0061	0.8799
			0.1879	−0.0034	0.0000	0.8154
10.0	0.0601	0.0673	0.1143	0.0000	−0.0051	0.8908
			0.1662	−0.0028	0.0000	0.8867

cient of zero indicates that the investor is risk-neutral. A coefficient of 1.0 indicates logarithmic utility. An investor whose aversion to risk is characterized by a coefficient between zero and 1.0 would be more aggressive than a logarithmic expected utility maximizer, while an investor with a coefficient above 1.0 would be more conservative.[15]

Table III provides an analysis of optimal portfolio proportions and levels of expected utility for the one-year, 5 per cent minimum return insurance program. It shows optimal portfolio proportions for investors with coefficients of relative risk aversion ranging from 0.2 to 10.0; the values associated with the coefficient of 1.0—the logarithmic utility function—are repeated for comparative purposes.

Consider the optimal portfolios associated with risk-aversion coefficients between 0.2 and 1.0, representing utility functions more aggressive than the logarithmic. For these utility functions, optimal put option portfolios consist of levered stock positions that are protected from ruin through the purchase of puts. The amount of leverage and the proportion of the portfolio allocated to put options increase as the inves-

tor's aversion to risk decreases. Economically equivalent portfolios involving call options require an allocation of portfolio funds between stock and calls, with the proportion invested in calls increasing as the investor's aversion to risk decreases.

For the risk-aversion coefficients in the range of 0.2 to 1.0, the levels of expected utility for optimal portfolios are much higher than those of the insured portfolios. For example, if the coefficient of relative risk aversion is 0.2, the optimal stock-option-bill portfolio provides a level of expected utility equal to 0.2853, while the expected utility of the insured portfolio is only 0.1270. Expected utility numbers are difficult to interpret in isolation, but inasmuch as the level of expected utility for the optimal portfolio is over twice that of the insured portfolio, it is obvious that the insured portfolio is not close to being optimal. This is also true, but to a lesser extent, for all the utility functions characterized by risk-aversion coefficients in the 0.4 to 1.0 range.

Inasmuch as portfolio insurance represents a conservative approach to investing, it is not surprising that this strategy would be very suboptimal for aggressive investors characterized by relatively high risk tolerance. But what about conservative investors, those with risk-aversion coefficients of 2.0 or greater?

As Table III shows, optimal put portfolios for conservative investors generally involve an investment in both stock and bills in conjunction with a small put option writing position. Equivalent portfolios with call options involve investment in slightly more stock and less bills, along with a small call option writing position. Although the optimal portfolios offer higher levels of expected utility than their insured counterparts, the difference in expected utility is not nearly as large as for portfolios tailored for more aggressive investors. If one takes a conservative approach to investing, a portfolio insurance program is not optimal, but it comes close to providing a level of utility associated with the best potential use of portfolio assets. It is interesting to note, however, that for the conservative investor, the best use of portfolio assets involves writing puts rather than buying puts.

Although it is not evident from Table III, it can be shown that the assumptions underlying the analysis imply that an investor with a coefficient of relative risk aversion equal to 1.428 would choose to hold an all-stock portfolio. A more aggressive investor would always choose to lever a stock portfolio and purchase protective puts—an action that amounts to taking out some portfolio insurance—while a more conservative investor would choose to allocate his investment between stock and bills while simultaneously writing puts. These general relations hold no matter what specific risk-aversion coefficient is assumed.[16] ■

Footnotes

1. For a discussion of the debate over implementational costs, see "Investors Rush for Portfolio Insurance," *Wall Street Journal*, October 14, 1986, p. 6.
2. The 0.9097 is frequently called the "upside capture" because it shows the fraction of the *ending value* of the speculative asset that is captured by the insured portfolio when the asset ends up above the strike price. Note, however, that the fraction of the *return* on the speculative asset that is attained by the insured portfolio is considerably less than the upside capture.
3. The put-call parity equation is developed in H. R. Stoll, "The Relationship between Put and Call Option Prices," *Journal of Finance*, December

1969, pp. 801–824 and in R. C. Merton, "The Relationship between Put and Call Option Prices: Comment," *Journal of Finance*, March 1973, pp. 183–184.
4. See H. Leland and M. Rubinstein, "Replicating Options with Positions in Stock and Cash," *Financial Analysts Journal*, July/August 1981, pp. 63–72; C. Singleton and R. Grieves, "Synthetic Puts and Portfolio Insurance," *Journal of Portfolio Management*, Spring 1984, pp. 63–69; and M. Rubinstein, "Alternative Paths to Portfolio Insurance," *Financial Analysts Journal*, July/August 1985, pp. 42–52.
5. "Dynamic Asset Allocation" is a registered service mark of Leland O' Brien Rubinstein Associates.
6. The logarithmic utility function is also a member of the set of generalized logarithmic utility functions. For an exposition, see M. Rubinstein, "The Strong Case for the Generalized Logarithmic Utility Model as the Premier Model of Financial Markets," *Journal of Finance*, May 1975, pp. 551–571.
7. As observed by Leonard Savage in his classic, *The Foundations of Statistics* (New York: John Wiley & Sons, 1954), p. 94. The properties of the logarithmic utility function have been extensively documented. See for example R. McEnally, "Latané's Bequest: The Best of Possible Portfolio Models," *Journal of Portfolio Management*," Winter 1986, pp. 21–30.
8. While testing alternative strategies with historical data can yield useful insights, the results tend to be highly period-specific. See, for example, "The Role of Optimal Portfolio Insurance in Optimal Asset Allocation," *Stock Index Strategist* (a publication of Donaldson Lufkin Jenrette), April 1986, which shows computed returns (ex dividend) of 7.1 per cent per year for an insured strategy versus 6.3 per cent for the S&P 500 over the period 1973–85. Such a result (which even the most fervent advocate of portfolio insurance should find troublesome) reflects the time period investigated and may be attributed to initiating the experiment at a time of pronounced market weakness.

One advantage claimed for portfolio insurance over more conventional strategies is that it does not require expectations about risky asset returns. This is not true. Insuring portfolios in the absence of European options requires expectations about the volatility of risky asset returns in order to price the implicit put or call and thereby structure the portfolio. Errors in forecasting can have significant impacts on outcomes. See Rubinstein, "Alternative Paths," *op. cit.* for a discussion of this point.
9. See F. Black and M. Scholes, "The Pricing of Options and Corporate Liabilities," *Journal of*

Political Economy, May/June 1973, pp. 637–654. To facilitate the comparison of this article's results with those of Ferguson, we employed arithmetic volatilities rather than logarithmic volatilities. The pricing of options according to Black-Scholes requires that the arithmetic volatilities be transformed into their logarithmic equivalents. With an expected stock return of 16 per cent, the logarithmic equivalent of Ferguson's arithmetic volatility of 0.2 is 0.1841, while his 0.18 volatility becomes 0.1660.

10. The program is described in R. Rendleman, "Optimal Long-Run Option Investment Strategies," *Financial Management*, Spring 1981, pp. 61–76.

11. Given the assumption that options are priced according to Black-Scholes, the use of options is not necessary with continuous portfolio reallocation. See Rendleman, "Optimal Long-Run Strategies," *op. cit.*

12. Ferguson makes this observation in "How to Beat the S&P," *op. cit.*, p. 38.

13. The annual reallocation of portfolio assets back to the original mix requires the assumption that the probability distributions of all portfolio assets are not expected to change. Even if one can reasonably anticipate change, the optimal *current* allocation under any isoelastic utility function will be unaffected, provided the returns on portfolio assets are independent over time. In practice, of course, weights would be altered to reflect changed probability distributions.

14. At horizons of 50 and 100 years, the probabilities increase to 80 and 91 per cent, respectively. The analysis thus supports the notion that probability approaches 1.0 over the long run that the logarithmic strategy will outperform any significantly different strategy using the same assets. The convergence to 1.0 can be slow, however.

15. The utility function employed here takes the form:

$$U[H] = E\,[(H^{1-y} - 1)/(1 - y)],$$

where H denotes the portfolio's holding period return and y is the coefficient of relative risk aversion. This function is equivalent to the logarithmic utility function when the coefficient of relative risk aversion equals 1.0.

16. An observation made by Hayne Leland in "Who Should Buy Portfolio Insurance?" *Journal of Finance*, May 1980, pp. 581–594, is consistent with this analysis. Leland states an investor should buy insurance if his risk tolerance increases with wealth more rapidly than that of the average investor and/or his expectations are more optimistic than average. The analysis here cannot address the first point because the isoelastic utility functions assume risk tolerance is independent of wealth. His second point, however, is similar to our observation than an aggressive investor should buy insurance.

Suppose the average investor has a logarithmic utility function. It can be shown that this investor will want to hold the market portfolio if its expected arithmetic return is 14.33 per cent (see Rendleman, "Optimal Long-Run Strategies," *op. cit.*). If the average investor is also characterized as one who holds the market portfolio, then the market-clearing equilibrium expected return for stocks is 14.33 per cent. An investor who expects a 16 per cent return (as is assumed in this article) would be more optimistic than the average, hence should purchase portfolio insurance. Note also that the optimal strategy for the highly risk-averse investor does not involve portfolio insurance.

Article 26

by Mark Rubinstein

Market Basket Alternatives

Several exchange and government-sponsored studies of the stock market crash of 1987 pointed, rightly or wrongly, to program trading as one of its accessories. At the same time, they accepted the growing need for financial institutions to trade large diversified portfolios of assets, and they called for innovation to find some means of preserving this benefit while reducing the potential for these trades to destabilize the market. This article examines alternative methods to facilitate simultaneous execution of trades of a large standardized diversified portfolio of stocks.

It is assumed that an ideal market basket vehicle would (1) represent an important component of risk borne generally by investors; (2) have low tracking error; (3) have a continuous market through time; (4) have low creation costs; (5) have low trade execution costs; (6) have low inventory carrying costs; (7) preserve or enhance tax benefits; (8) have full collateralization; (9) pass through voting rights; (10) be offered in small enough unit size to appeal to small investors; (11) have a predetermined long life before forced liquidation or turnover; (12) not provide incentive to manipulate prices illegally; (13) be part of a related system of securities permitting desirable variations in patterns of returns; (14) not be subject to various miscellaneous security regulations; (15) possess a number of desirable trading features; (16) be simply described to potential investors and have readily accessible price quotations; (17) be consistent with existing securities regulation; and (18) remove all basket-motivated trading away from the individual securities comprising the basket.

This framework is used to compare established alternatives—open-end index funds of either the mutual or bank trust variety, stock index futures and program trades—with the recently developed "index participations" traded on the Philadelphia and American stock exchanges and with proposals currently being examined by the SEC—the "market basket securities" of the Chicago Board Options Exchange and the "exchange stock portfolios" of the New York Stock Exchange. One or more of these newer basket alternatives are likely to become the most actively traded U.S. equity instruments. Moreover, the winners of this competitive experiment in market innovation will set standards for basket trading of foreign equities and other types of securities.

PROGRAM TRADING has developed a bad reputation.[1] Even before the stock market crash of 1987, newspapers routinely blamed large movements in market prices on programs. After the crash, the use of programs to facilitate futures-index arbitrage, despite its profitability, was abandoned by most large investment houses, with considerable publicity. Several exchange and government-

---

1. Footnotes appear at end of article.

Mark Rubinstein is Professor of Finance at the University of California at Berkeley and a Principal of Leland O'Brien Rubinstein Associates.

The author thanks Robert Ferguson, Larry Harris, Hayne Leland and John O'Brien for their helpful comments, and notes that this article has benefited greatly from a working paper, "The Economics of Cash Index Alternatives," by Larry Harris.

S&P 500 Index and S&P 500 Portfolio Index are trademarks of Standard & Poor's Corporation.

sponsored studies of the crash rightly or wrongly pointed to program trading as one of its accessories. At the same time, they accepted the growing need of financial institutions to trade large diversified portfolios of assets and called for some means of preserving this benefit while reducing the potential for market destabilization.

This invitation to innovate was eagerly pursued by several exchanges. They saw not only an opportunity to respond constructively to flaws in market structure exposed by the crash, but also an opening to enlarge their own competitive turf. The Philadelphia Stock Exchange, known for its successful innovation in currency options, filed with the SEC the first proposal to trade "index participations" (IPs). This filing was followed quickly by similar proposals from the American Stock Exchange and the Chicago Board Options Exchange. Although the CBOE later withdrew its IP proposal, it filed a second proposal to trade "market basket securities" (MBS). The New York Stock Exchange has filed its own proposal to trade "exchange stock portfolios" (ESPs), a market basket similar to the CBOE's MBS.[2]

Despite an unresolved squabble over regulatory turf, IPs on the PHLX and the AMEX began trading under SEC registration on May 12, 1989. On August 18, 1989, the U.S. Court of Appeals of the Seventh Circuit ruled that the newly listed IPs fall under CFTC, not SEC, jurisdiction. As a result, existing investors will be forced to close their positions. However, this victory for the futures exchanges could retrospectively be seen as a minor skirmish in a long-drawn-out battle that may eventually involve the Supreme Court and Congress. In contrast, the CBOE and NYSE proposals have not been opposed by the futures exchanges. As they continue to undergo refinement in the registration process, final approval seems likely before the end of 1989.

All these proposals attempt to facilitate the simultaneous execution of trades of a large standardized, diversified portfolio of stocks. In this author's opinion, one or more of these baskets are likely to become the most actively traded U.S. equity instruments. Moreover, the winners of this competitive experiment in market innovation will set standards for basket trading of foreign equities and other types of securities.

A Wish List

In examining market basket alternatives, we should keep in mind the features we might want. Without further justification, this article assumes that an ideal market basket vehicle would have the following characteristics.

(1) It would represent an important component of risk borne generally by investors.

(2) It would have low tracking error with respect to capital gains and payouts. Tracking error can take the form of discounts or premiums relative to fair value, differential performance due to failure to hold all underlying securities or due to maintenance of cash balances, and differential performance due to non-simultaneous transactions in the underlying securities.

(3) It would have a continuous market through time for basket sales and purchases. Such a market would provide reliable cash-out prices prior to commitment to trade.

(4) It would have low creation costs. Such costs are increased by a requirement that any long position be matched by an offsetting short position held by another investor. They include trade execution costs incurred in the original purchase of components of the underlying basket and registration and organization costs of a financial intermediary set up to manage securities underlying the basket.

(5) It would have low trade execution costs for the basket itself and for the component securities in the basket. Execution costs include SEC and exchange fees, brokerage, the effective bid/ask spread, market impact, clearing costs and rollover costs.

(6) It would have low inventory carrying costs—costs of receiving securities into inventory, holding them in inventory and selling them out of inventory. These costs include custodial settlement and carrying charges, accounting expenses, management fees, dividend payout expenses, rollover costs forced by maturity of inventoried securities and basket readjustment costs due to redefinition of the underlying target portfolio.

(7) It would preserve or enhance tax benefits obtained from positions in the individual components of the basket. For example, one would hope that a separate basket entity not be taxed as a corporation, that the intercorporate dividends-received deduction be retained on basket payouts, and that there be no taxation of unrealized profits.

(8) It would have full collateralization. This implies that there is no risk that a buyer (seller)

will default on subsequent obligations to a seller (buyer).

(9) It would "pass through" the voting rights accompanying direct ownership of the securities underlying the basket.

(10) It would be offered in small enough units to appeal to small investors, not just large institutional investors.

(11) It would have a predetermined long life before forced liquidation or turnover.

(12) It would not provide incentives to manipulate illegally the prices of other securities, or provide incentives for investors to time basket transactions to benefit at the expense of other investors holding the same basket.

(13) It would be part of a related system of securities, which would permit desirable variations in patterns of returns. For example, related securities might permit investors to split rights to dividends and interest from capital gains, or to split upside or downside rights to capital gains from the remaining returns of the basket.

(14) It would not be subject to various miscellaneous security regulations. Such regulations or industry practice include the short-sale uptick rule, inability to earn interest on the proceeds of short sales, special qualifications for investors to trade or brokers to advise trading in the basket, position or exercise limits, and high margin requirements or frequent marking-to-market.

(15) It would possess a number of desirable trading features. These include quick settlement, block trading facilities, direct hedgability with the securities underlying the basket and cross-collateralization with similar basket securities.

(16) It would be simply described to potential investors, have readily accessible price quotations and prominent newspaper listing and require minimal revision of back-office procedures and computer programs.

(17) It would be consistent with existing securities regulation.

(18) It would remove all basket-motivated trading away from the individual securities or risks comprising the basket.

Established Market Basket Vehicles

The goals of basket trading are currently accomplished primarily through open-end index funds of either the mutual or bank trust variety, through stock index futures and options contracts and through program trades.

Index Funds

Index funds with multiple holders essentially centralize the basket holdings of many investors. These funds can offer investors reduced transaction costs by matching separate deposits and redemptions.[3] Using proprietary mathematical models, many index funds trade tracking error off against reduction in transaction costs by holding an inventory of cash to minimize trading should the next investor demand a redemption. In so doing, index funds act as their own crossing market, thereby removing some of the burden from stock exchange specialist systems.

Index funds may also be able to obtain favored executions through the market power created by their large size, although this advantage may be offset by the greater market impact of their trades. Index funds also reap any advantages from economies of scale in receiving securities into inventory, holding them in inventory and selling them out of inventory. Finally, at the cost of some default risk, index funds can enhance their returns through securities lending, an opportunity not open to most individual investors.[4]

But open-end index funds fall short of the ideal basket trading instrument. Unlike closed-end investment companies or exchange-traded stock, they do not provide a ready intraday market for deposits and redemptions with a continuous series of available transaction prices. Investors may not know with sufficient certainty the cash-out value of a redemption before they must commit to it.[5] They are not given this opportunity with good reason: If they were given this information before they agreed to redeem, they could profit at the expense of the remaining investors in the fund by redeeming shares when they have reason to believe that net asset values overstate the prices to be realized in subsequent transactions in the individual stocks.

Index funds add fidelity relative to the underlying index by passing dividends through to investors. Funds with more than one shareholder, however, do not pass through the voting rights of their component securities.[6] For some institutional investors, this is a significant drawback. Some consider the exercise of voting rights to be a social responsibility, and some believe these rights can be used to influence management in a way that would be favorable to stock price.

Furthermore, to control tracking error at times

of change in composition of the underlying index, index funds are forced to incur transaction costs and to impose realized capital gains or losses on taxable investors.[7] The performance of index funds will tend to fall short of the index for another reason as well: New stocks added to the index may immediately rise in value after announcement of their inclusion, and index funds can usually realize, at best, only a portion of this increase.

Finally, index funds have not met with much success with small investors. Vanguard Index Trust, the largest publicly held index fund available to small investors (minimum initial account size of $3,000), had only $1.52 billion in assets at the close of trading on June 30, 1989, an amount estimated to exceed by two times the *aggregate* assets of all other publicly available U.S. index mutual funds.

Index Futures

Stock index futures provide a very liquid intraday market, which index funds lack. Like index funds, however, they act as a crossing market, taking much of the burden away from stock exchange specialists. Only when an order imbalance extends beyond the liquidity provided by futures market-makers does trading pressure spill over, via index arbitrage, into the stock market.

As long as a significant order imbalance does not exist, execution costs in stock index futures are thought to be between 1/6th and 1/10th of a comparable program trade.[8] Execution costs are lower for several reasons. Traders in individual stocks need to protect themselves against both systematic and nonsystematic risk. The purely firm-specific, idiosyncratic nature of nonsystematic risk cannot be hedged by holding other stocks. Yet it is just this source of risk that is most likely to be coupled with information-based trading. Apart from changes in the basis, market-makers in index futures need hedge only against systematic risk, and effective hedges can be constructed from relatively small diversified portfolios of stock, or from other index-related instruments. Market-makers also have much less to fear from information traders, who are less likely to know something significant about the market as a whole than to have information about a single stock.[9] Market-makers in individual stocks may quote large spreads because their activity forces them to bear an inventory containing significant nonsys-

tematic risk; in contrast, the inventories of index futures traders are automatically diversified.

The low margins required for index futures, together with one-day settlement, mean that investors can move quickly and easily into and out of the market in size. Trading demand for index portfolios is high and concentrated in just a few short-term instruments. For example, the daily trading volume (in terms of the dollars to which the volume is a right) in just one index futures contract, the near-term S&P 500 index future, is comparable to the daily dollar trading volume on the NYSE. The resultant economies of scale and competition among hundreds of floor traders make this market among the most liquid in the world.

But stock index futures also fall short of the ideal basket trading instrument. Their most serious deficiency stems from being in zero net supply. This means that it is possible to create a long position in the underlying index only if another investor is willing to go short. This seriously limits the size of the open interest. While there are billions of dollars of natural longs, the opposing billions of dollars of natural shorts do not exist. The natural position for an investor is long, because we live in a world where assets are in positive net supply.

To this simple intuitive observation, we can apply a little standard academic finance thinking. Suppose we lived in an economy of identical individuals, where there were slight economies of scale in trading securities. There would be a huge demand for index funds, but no demand for short selling or index futures. These instruments take on interest to the extent individuals differ with respect to preferences or beliefs.

Suppose that differences in preferences tend to be long-term, while differences in beliefs are short-lived. Differences in preferences might be partially satisfied by side-bets using futures or by differential positions in the underlying cash assets. Institutions with fiduciary responsibilities, which are accustomed to holding legal title to the underlying assets, are unlikely to maintain semipermanent positions in futures over the long term. This means that the role of futures in institutional trading will remain limited, as it has so far, to short-term portfolio adjustments.[10]

Stock index futures also suffer as market basket instruments because they are tied to the underlying cash index only by their contractual terms at maturity. Prior to maturity, futures prices can exhibit substantial discounts or premiums to fair value, which expose holders of open positions to unwanted risk entirely unrelated to their investment objectives. If futures of the desired maturity existed, this uncertainty could be eliminated by closing out the futures position at maturity. Unfortunately, because the futures market is liquid only in the shortest maturities, longer-term investors must keep rolling existing contracts over into new contracts near maturity, each time being uncertain in advance about the basis. Moreover, even if the basis were predictable, the futures price reflects anticipated dividends, rather than the actual realization of dividends; open positions thus bear another type of risk—uncertainty about this difference, which is also typically unrelated to the objectives of investors.

Even if dividends were predictable and futures always priced at fair value, the purchase of a future would be akin to buying the underlying index by borrowing its value at a rate of interest. So a future, in effect, forces the buyer to couple his basket trade with a loan he may not want, either because he has no desire to borrow or does not find the implied interest rate attractive. We should also remember that stock index futures are not forward contracts. With uncertainty about future interest rates, both the buyer and seller are exposed to another typically unwanted source of risk: The daily resettlement procedure makes terminal values from futures positions dependent on the fluctuating path of short-term interest rates during the holding period.

Current margin regulations for index futures do not allow an institution that holds the stocks underlying the future to use these stocks as collateral backing the futures position. In addition, because futures are marked-to-market, the institutional hedger who holds the underlying basket and is short futures is faced with the daily problem of finding cash for variation margin. In practice, such a hedger must maintain a cash reserve; moreover, should stocks rise sufficiently, the hedger will be forced to liquidate stock to meet the unfavorable marks—even though he remains perfectly hedged. At these times, to make matters even worse, the longer five-day settlement procedure normally used for stocks can become a real inconvenience, because losses on short futures must be settled the next business day.

Any derivative asset, such as a stock index future, that settles in cash at maturity provides

investors with an incentive to manipulate illegally the index value on which the cash settlement is based. For a very large multibillion-dollar investor in index futures, only a comparatively small amount of capital might be required to move the closing cash index level at maturity by a sufficient amount to bring a substantial net profit.

Collateralization of index futures is only partial, particularly as margin deposits are now only about 2.5 to 4 per cent of the value of the futures obligation. Both the buyer and seller rely on the integrity of the clearing back-up mechanism. Even with the remote possibility of default, conservative institutions such as pension funds still find this an important issue and, as a result, do not hold large portions of their assets in the form of cash matched against long index futures, or in the form of stock matched against permanent short positions in index futures.

The collateralization issue is more significant in a market collapse than in a sudden market increase. In a suddenly rising market, although losses will fall on the shoulders of shorts and sellers of futures, most investors will find themselves suddenly much better off. Thus the brokerage firms and investment houses that are the members of the clearing corporations, which provide the capital behind the back-up mechanism, should be able to pick up the pieces. Because these firms have a vested interest in the integrity of the clearing mechanism, they may even be willing to go beyond their contractual commitment to the clearing corporations and provide additional capital, if necessary. In contrast, in a market collapse, these very firms may suddenly find themselves in a precarious financial position and be unwilling or unable to go the extra distance to keep the clearing mechanism functioning.

In a market crisis, worries about collateralization can have a nasty circular feedback. As the collapse deepens, before the clearing mechanism fails, hedged sellers of index futures are tempted to close out positions by buying back futures and selling stock. This in turn places further selling pressure on the underlying securities, which further deepens the collapse.

Program Trading
Program trades, with the assistance of the NYSE Super-DOT trading system, provide a reasonably efficient means of trading large baskets of securities. However, a *standardized* basket, given sufficient demand for trading, should

afford improvements. Below we discuss some recent proposals.

Index Participations

On February 26, 1988, following two years of development, the Philadelphia Stock Exchange officially filed its application with the SEC to trade a new basket product called an "index participation" (IP).

In many ways, an IP transaction is similar to a short sale of stock. In a short sale, the seller borrows stock from another investor and sells the stock in return for cash equal to its market value. (As such, short sales are zero-net-supply positions with a variable open interest that is not directly related to the outstanding supply of the underlying stock.) The short seller leaves the proceeds as collateral with his broker and additionally deposits margin usually equal to 50 per cent of the value of the proceeds. (The buyer is also usually able to purchase the stock with 50 per cent margin.) The short seller's account is periodically marked-to-market, and he (as well as the buyer) is subject to additional margin deposits should the stock move against him.

While the short position is open, the short seller compensates the lender for any dividend payments; these payments to the lender are not available for treatment as an intercorporate dividends-received tax deduction, because they are not dividends actually paid by an issuing corporation. The lender of the stock loses voting rights. But the lender (or the lender's broker) receives any interest on the proceeds of the short sale while the position is open; this serves as an incentive for the lender to permit his securities to be lent out.

The short seller can close out his position by covering (buying back the stock and returning it to the lender). He may be forced to do so if his broker can no longer find a source to lend the stock. Although the buyer is never forced to close his position (provided he can finance maintenance margin), he can do so at any time simply by selling the purchased stock.

IP Delivery

IPs differ from short sales of individual stocks in two major ways. First, the asset underlying an IP is not a single stock, but rather a well defined portfolio of stocks, such as the S&P 500.

The second difference relates to the timing and method of delivery of the underlying securities from the seller to the buyer. At the opening of the position, as in a short sale, the seller receives cash equal to the market value of the IP (which should approximate the market value of the underlying portfolio). In return, however, the seller only *promises* to deliver the underlying portfolio at specific times in the future, at the option of the buyer.

This contrasts with an ordinary stock transaction in which the buyer and seller complete the entire transaction at its initiation. It contrasts with a forward contract, where the entire exchange between buyer and seller is postponed until a specific date in the future. And it contrasts with a call option contract in which the seller receives the option premium at initiation and, possibly, an additional amount (the striking price) at a future date. With an IP, the seller receives up front everything he is ever going to receive from the transaction, and the buyer receives nothing until prespecified times in the future.

Only the buyer, however, can decide when and if subsequent delivery is to take place. For example, the AMEX has two index participations (called "equity index participations" or EIPs) on the S&P 500 (500 value-weighted stocks) and on the Major Market Index (20 price-weighted stocks). In each case, the buyer can require a cash-out settlement at quarterly intervals (third Fridays of March, June, September and December), based on the opening value of the index underlying the IP on the cash-out Friday.

In lieu of cash, block buyers can request physical delivery of the underlying securities. Sellers who are holders of open positions on these Fridays must then face the prospect of an involuntary forced liquidation on very short notice. This feature seems designed as a compromise between the need for some provision tying an IP down to its underlying index and the need to minimize the risk of buyers and sellers being forced to terminate their positions.[11]

Because the IP seller does not deliver the securities until a future date, he does not need to find another investor to lend him the securities. This means that the seller earns full interest on the proceeds he receives from the sale of the IP. Sellers of futures and calls also receive most of the interest on the proceeds of their implicit short position, although indirectly, through the pricing of these instruments. Unlike a future (or a short sale of stock), however, short IP positions are not subject to uncertain cash inflows and outflows due to marking-to-market (apart from maintaining the maintenance margin level above 30 per cent).[12]

Advantages and Disadvantages

Compared with index funds, IPs do not require management fees or inventory carrying costs for the underlying basket of securities. Indeed, because of the contractual arrangements, neither the buyer nor the seller need ever hold the component securities in the basket. However, a hedger who holds the securities in the underlying basket against short IPs may want to revise his stock holdings to reduce cross-hedge risk as the composition of the underlying index changes.

IPs also have some advantages over futures. In essence, they come a step closer to providing buyers with legal title to the underlying securities. Realized dividends are passed through; the long-term buyer is not forced to roll over his position (as he has full control over maturity); physical delivery of the underlying assets can be requested; and higher margins provide greater assurance that future obligations will be met.[13]

From the seller's point of view, the buyer has no future obligation; the buyer fully discharged his obligation at the initiation of the position by paying the seller the full value of the IP. Only the seller has a future obligation. Therefore, IPs are effectively fully collateralized in a falling market; just prior to a market collapse, sellers must have on deposit with their brokerage house at least 100 per cent of the value of their obligation. Only in a rapidly rising market might this collateral prove insufficient. But, as pointed out earlier, it is precisely under these circumstances that the integrity of the clearing corporation is likely to be assured by its members.

IPs also have a number of flaws, which could cause them them to lose out to alternatives such as futures and exchange stock portfolios. Interest of the largest institutional investors is dampened by position limits, which currently restrict investment in an IP to less than $500 million. Also, like futures, IPs fail to pass through voting rights.

Most importantly, IPs (again like futures) are in zero net supply, so open interest is limited by the willingness of investors to maintain short positions. IPs are most attractive to long-term buyers and least attractive to long-term sellers. The offsetting long-term seller could be even harder to locate than the short-term seller needed in the futures market.

Investors can take a short futures position with a small amount of margin. Not only do IPs require that the proceeds of the sale be left as collateral with the broker, but, as in a short sale, the seller must put up an additional 50 per cent of the value of the IP. Sellers must also be prepared for forced liquidation at the end of each quarter. Furthermore, whenever IP prices fall below their current cash settlement value, arbitrageurs could buy IPs and force settlement. Sellers do not have a symmetric right to force settlement; IP prices can easily wander above index levels, creating an undesirable and uncertain premium without creating an arbitrage opportunity.[14] The short seller (even one who attempts to hedge by holding the underlying securities) faces potentially unlimited upside losses.

The Evidence So Far

As of this writing, IPs have been trading for 74 business days. Initial trading volume has been lower than expected, typically less than 10,000 contracts ($30 million, or about 200 equivalent S&P 500 index futures contracts) per day on the AMEX and much lower on the PHLX. Almost all the trading has been by market-makers and specialists, using IPs to hedge their positions. Both the AMEX and PHLX have had almost no outside customer business. An early article in the *New York Times* attributes the low volume to lack of interest from brokerage firms, which see IPs as, if anything, primarily a retail product.[15]

IPs are seen as a confusing hybrid of options, stocks, futures and mutual funds requiring some back-office investment in accounting procedures and considerable broker education. At the same time, from a legal point of view, the continued existence of IPs has been in question. Successful suits were filed by the Chicago Mercantile Exchange and the Chicago Board of Trade claiming that IPs are inherently futures contracts and therefore should fall under CFTC rather than SEC jurisdiction. The CFTC informed the SEC that it also supports this position, but has not yet sought legal remedy. The Investment Company Institute has filed a letter of objection with the SEC claiming that IPs are inherently mutual funds and should therefore come under the provisions of the 1940 Investment Company Act.[16] As if this were not enough, the PHLX has gone on public record accusing the AMEX of literally copying its SEC submission, but it has yet to take any legal action.

Exchange Stock Portfolios

On January 11, 1989, the CBOE resubmitted to the SEC a modified proposal to trade a basket of stocks. The NYSE filed a similar proposal on June 1, 1989. Even now, the final features of these proposals remain subject to further revision as the exchanges await the SEC's response.

The CBOE calls its proposed new trading instrument a "market basket security" (MBS), and the NYSE calls its instrument an "exchange stock portfolio" (ESP). In somewhat simplified terms, an MBS or ESP permits an exchange similar to that of a common stock, except a standardized portfolio of stocks is exchanged in place of a single stock. Both the CBOE and NYSE chose the S&P 500 as their first standardized portfolio; the CBOE also proposes to trade an MBS based on the S&P 100. As these proposals are similar, only one—exchange stock portfolios—will be discussed in detail.

The seller of a S&P 500 ESP (who has not entered a subsequent closing transaction the same day) must be prepared to deliver, five business days after the trade, a basket of stocks consisting of x_1 shares of IBM, x_2 shares of AT&T, x_3 shares of Exxon, etc., where x is set equal to a multiplier times the weight of each stock in the "S&P 500 Portfolio Index." This weight will be *approximately* equal to the stock's weight in the S&P 500—the current number of outstanding shares divided by the current S&P 500 divisor. With the S&P 500 near 312, one ESP would be worth about $5,000,000 (= 312 × 16,000).

The S&P 500 Portfolio Index differs from the S&P 500 in order to accommodate standardized basket trading. First, to reduce rebalancing required to liquidate a basket position whenever the composition of the underlying index changes, the S&P 500 Portfolio Index will not be changed as frequently as the S&P 500. Minor changes in the S&P 500 will be allowed to accumulate and will be reflected in a revised S&P 500 Portfolio Index only once a calendar quarter, or at the time a significant change in the S&P 500 occurs. Second, fractional weights will be rounded to the nearest share. Because of rounding to the nearest share (rather than to the nearest round lot), almost all securities in the basket will involve portions of non-round lots. The large minimum size of the basket is dictated in part by the need to include all 500 stocks in

the S&P 500 in roughly their current proportions, where the largest stock exceeds the smallest stock by a factor of about 3000 per cent. (The CBOE proposal has a smaller minimum trade size of about $1,500,000.)

Trading Mechanism

The New York Stock Exchange has developed a very innovative ESP floor-trading environment designed to pool large amounts of market-making capital from its existing stock specialists and proprietary member firms. A "Basket Book Broker" (BBB) will coordinate trading in ESPs. Currently, 462 of the S&P 500 stocks are listed on the NYSE. The remaining 38 AMEX and OTC stocks in the index (approximately 3 per cent of index capitalization) will be given a combined "mini-basket" quote by the BBB. Except for that (and to correct an error position), the BBB will not be allowed to trade for his own account.

Every 15 seconds during the trading day, the bids and asks at each of the specialist posts in these stocks, together with the mini-basket quote, will be aggregated in proportion to the stocks' weights in the S&P 500 Portfolio Index. This aggregated first-tier bid and ask, good for one ESP basket, will be entered into the BBB's limit order book. In addition, the specialists will also set a second-tier aggregated quote good for three ESP baskets, which will also be entered into the book.[17]

In addition, "Competitive Basket Market-Makers" (CBMM), representing NYSE individual members or member firms and meeting a $10 million minimum capital requirement, will be obligated to make a two-sided market with a maximum quote spread of two index points during normal market conditions. CBMMs will be allowed to trade on behalf of customers as well as for their own accounts. CBMMs will have no obligation to maintain a floor presence, but will be able to trade from upstairs terminals. The entire limit order book will be open not only to floor traders, but also to CBMM upstairs terminals. Thus, in an unprecedented rule change, information about the depth of the market for ESPs—limit order size at various prices away from the current market, as well as the current bid-ask quote—will be available to all direct market participants.

Orders with a minimum tick size of 0.01 index points can be entered. Orders will be filled according to price and time, but without the usual priority given to size.[18] Market orders in size will "walk the book," in the sense that they will be filled against several opposing limit orders at the displayed price of each limit order.

The combined effect of these innovations will be to concentrate large amounts of market-making capital in ESPs. If the specialist first-tier quote is hit, for example, a public customer selling IBM may find himself (without ever being informed) on the opposite side of an ESP purchase. It would not be surprising to find the bid-ask spread and market-impact execution costs of ESPs rivaling those in the index futures market.

Because an MBS or ESP transaction is so similar to the simultaneous entry but separate execution of shares of several common stocks (a program trade), the CBOE and the NYSE have requested margin and settlement provisions similar to those for common stocks. Unlike other derivative securities, market basket securities and exchange stock portfolios do not create open interest; the exchanges therefore believe that position limits are not appropriate. Finally, the CBOE and the NYSE have sought exemption from the short-sale uptick rule.

One interesting complication arises from the necessity to record a purchase price for each stock in the basket for tax and accounting purposes. If, for example, one stock in a purchased basket were subsequently sold, the seller might need to set an initial purchase price to establish a basis for tax purposes. This could be done by recording the transaction prices of the securities in the S&P 500 Portfolio Index at the time just preceding the basket transaction. The NYSE has decided not to use this approach because the computer systems available to investors may not be capable of recording the transaction prices of all stocks in the S&P 500 Portfolio Index at unanticipated times during the day. Instead, the NYSE plans to assume that all recorded transaction prices for the individual securities will be taken from the closing transactions for the day of the trade.

For example, suppose for the sake of argument that there are only two securities in the basket—A and B, the first weighted by 100 and the second weighted by 200. At 11:00, A is selling for $20 per share and B is selling for $30 per share. The net asset value of the basket, based on these prices, is $8,000 [= (20 × 100) + (30 × 200)]. For many reasons, the actual transaction price for the basket might be somewhat higher or lower. Suppose it is $8,007. At 4:00, the close of trading for the day, the last transaction prices are $19 for A and $31 for B. The net asset value of the basket based on these prices is

$8,100 [= (19 × 100) + (31 × 200)]. The buyer will receive (and the seller will deliver) 100 shares of A and 200 shares of B. For this, the buyer will pay $8,007. For bookkeeping purposes, the buyer assumes that he has purchased 100 shares of A at $19 per share and the 200 shares of B at $31 per share. The difference between the closing net asset value of the basket and the actual transaction price of the basket is $93 (= 8,100 − 8,007).

It is unclear exactly how this "clearance cash adjustment" will be handled for tax purposes. One possibility is that the tax basis for each stock will be reduced by the factor 8007/8100. More likely, the $93 will be considered an intraday short-term capital gain (loss) for the buyer (seller) on the basket itself. In other words, the buyer will regard the transaction as the purchase of a basket security at 11:00 for $8,007 and the sale of the basket security at 4:00 in exchange for shares worth, at that time, $8,100.

Advantages

For index fund investors who desire to buy or sell a portfolio closely approximating the composition of the S&P 100 or S&P 500, CBOE market basket securities and NYSE exchange stock portfolios will have advantages over program trading. In contrast to program trades, ESPs provide simultaneous execution across all securities in the basket at an intraday price known before the transaction occurs. ESPs also visibly separate investors according to their motivation for trading: Investors with special information about individual stocks will continue to trade those stocks, while investors with overall portfolio objectives will tend to trade basket securities.

This means that the spread portion of transaction costs should be lower for investors using baskets than for those who continue to trade in individual stocks through program trades. This difference in spreads should be enlarged even further by a circular second-order effect: Because most remaining orders in individual stocks will now contain a larger proportional component of information-based trades, the spreads on individual stocks will tend to increase, providing yet further incentive for using exchange stock portfolios rather than program trades.[19]

Trading in exchange stock portfolios should also reduce market instability. Specialists trading in individual stocks will be less likely to confuse orders motivated by overall portfolio adjustment with orders motivated by information about individual stocks. This should permit them to make more orderly markets, particularly during times of large sale or purchase imbalances. Much of the imbalance that would occur will be absorbed by the market-makers handling basket securities.

With the replacement of S&P 500 program trading by lower-cost market basket trades, the basis in the S&P 500 index futures market should become less variable and more closely attuned to fair value. It will simply be too easy for an investor to buy or sell the physical S&P 500 through a basket trade should the futures become mispriced. Most arbitrage-based program trades do not complete transactions in all S&P 500 securities, leaving open some cross-hedge risk. The NYSE and CBOE baskets provide virtually perfect replication. The closer approximation of the futures basis to fair value will itself reduce the amount of arbitrage-based program trading between futures and stocks. This will in turn simplify trading at individual stock specialist posts.

The index-arbitrage trading that remains should focus primarily on baskets and individual stocks. The difference between a basket trade and a program trade in the individual stocks (where delivery of the physicals occurs at the same time and dividends are identically treated) is much less than the difference between a futures and a program trade (where delivery of the physicals occurs at different times and dividends are treated differently). As a result, index arbitrage between baskets and individual stocks should be much easier to accomplish, less profitable and therefore less frequent.

Program trading may continue to be a significant factor in the market because it allows trading of a non-standardized basket. Even small index funds may prefer a program trade to an S&P 500 basket trade that forces them to hold small numbers, perhaps non-round lots, of several stocks.[20] ■

Footnotes

1. Here program trading is defined as the simultaneous entry, but separate execution, of orders in stocks in proportion to their relative representation in major indexes. During the first four months of 1989, program trades on the NYSE accounted for approximately 10 per cent of daily volume. About half this volume was due to index arbitrage.
2. Yet another market basket proposal has been filed by a private firm, Leland O'Brien Rubinstein Associates. This proposal will not be examined here.

3. Many large bank trust commingled index funds operate an explicit internal crossing market. Investors seeking redemption indicate their intention to sell, and the index fund manager is requested to postpone the redemption until a matching cash depositor can be found. The largest funds use crosses to handle about 50 per cent of redemptions. Investors planning to transfer their assets from one index fund to another are also able to save transaction costs by redemption and deposit in kind.

   Many commingled funds attempt to measure the transaction costs incurred by the fund as the result of each deposit and redemption. This cost is charged against the corresponding deposit or redemption, which spares the other investors from bearing turnover costs created by another party. The commissions component is easy to measure. To the extent a cross cannot be arranged, the market impact and spread components can be subsumed in the commissions by transacting through brokers at guaranteed market closing prices. In contrast, mutual funds, which are under an obligation to treat all investors equally, can only have a basis-point charge that is the same for all investors. However, this charge can be omitted for deposits and redemptions made in kind.
4. Securities lending is practical only for index funds of sufficient size and stability. Typically, the fund must reach a size of at least $1 billion before securities lending becomes a worthwhile alternative.
5. A few index funds are set up to permit intraday redemptions and deposits for an extra fee. Intraday deposits are handled by a cash deposit with the fund followed by an immediate purchase of the underlying basket securities, which determines the new investor's ownership proportion of the commingled fund. But even in this case, the investor must commit in advance to buy into the fund before knowing the price.
6. Commingled index funds operated by bank trust departments, because of their fiduciary obligation, are not allowed to delegate voting rights to investors in the fund.
7. For example, during 1988 the S&P 500 experienced 62 divisor changes. For exact replication, it would have been necessary to revise the composition of an index fund on most of those occasions. It becomes practical to hold all S&P 500 securities only when the size of the index fund exceeds $50 million.
8. Estimates of the market impact of program trades can be found in S. Grossman, "Trading Technology and Financial Market Stability" (Working paper 17-89, Rodney L. White Center for Financial Research, University of Pennsylvania).

9. Hans Stoll estimates that 43 per cent of a typical specialist's spread reflects a charge to protect himself against adverse information. The remaining portion of the spread derives from order-processing costs and inventory holding costs. See "Inferring the Components of the Bid-Ask Spread: Theory and Empirical Tests," *Journal of Finance*, March 1989.

10. On a typical day—May 11, 1989—the volume of trading across all four U.S. exchanges (NYFE, CME, KC and CBT) was equivalent to $7.2 billion—roughly one-third that day's open interest of $22.9 billion. The ratio of daily dollar trading volume to outstanding dollar value of shares on the NYSE is less than 1/200. The much faster turnover in the futures market indicates that index futures are used primarily for short-term trading purposes. Moreover, the outstanding market value of publicly available index funds (including those aimed at both retail investors and large institutions) was at least $175 billion—more than eight times the open interest in index futures. (This figure does not include possibly large amounts held by private index funds.)

11. PHLX IPs (called "cash index participations" or CIPs) are based on two portfolios not identical to, but nonetheless designed to track, the S&P 500 and the Dow Jones Industrial Average. In addition to quarterly cash-out, buyers of CIPS have the right to a daily cash-out based on closing prices at a sacrifice of a premium of one-half of 1 per cent.

12. There are some other less significant differences between short sales and IPs. During the quarter, dividends on stocks in the underlying index that go ex-dividend during the quarter are accumulated on paper. A cash amount equal to the total is paid by the seller to the buyer on the second Friday of the quarterly cash-out month. Thus IPs trade with rights to accrued dividends. Note that this is somewhat less than the terminal value from dividends received by a comparable index fund, because the index fund will be able to receive returns during the quarter from reinvestment of the dividends as they are paid. While individual stocks are quoted with a one-eighth tick size, IPs are quoted with a $0.01 minimum increment. S&P 500 EIPs, trading in round lots of 100, will look like ordinary stocks with the value of one EIP equal to 1/10th the value of the index. Compared with S&P 500 index futures, which trade in round lots of 500, the minimum invest-

ment in IPs will be 1/50th the size, or about $3,000 at current index levels—well within the range of small investors. Like index futures and options, IPs continue to trade until 4:15 EST, 15 minutes after the underlying stocks close. While stocks settle in five business days, cash-settled IPs settle in one business day. IPs also have explicit position limits (150,000 round lots for either the S&P 500 or Major Market Index IP) and are cleared through the Options Clearing Corporation.

13. Although IPs are essentially perpetual instruments from the buyer's point of view, the PHLX and the Options Clearing Corporation reserve the authority, upon one year's notice, to force closure of all open IP positions. This authority may be invoked if the open interest in CIPs becomes too low to justify continued exchange listing.

14. Closed-end investment companies provide a more extreme example. In this case, neither the buyer nor short seller can force settlement. As a result, closed-end companies often sell at significant discounts or premiums to net asset value.

15. "New Form of Index Trading has Foes in Powerful Places," *New York Times*, May 18, 1989.

16. Letter by Matthew Fink, representing the Investment Company Institute, to Richard Ketchum, Director of the Division of Market Regulation, SEC, December 19, 1988. The letter states that exemptive relief from the provisions of the 1940 Act would be required in a number of areas. For example, exemption would be required for EIPs to be redeemable less frequently than daily, or for CIPs to be redeemable on a daily basis only in cash, and not in kind.

17. Aggregate specialist quotes can be provided only after all 462 stocks have opened for trading. According to the NYSE, during the first 100 trading days of 1989, all 462 stocks were open for trading 89.5 per cent of the time after 10:00 EST.

18. The one exception is that the first and second-tier aggregated specialist bids and offers will have priority over other orders placed earlier if they are placed at the same price.

19. For a formal model consistent with the conclusion reached here, see A. Subrahmanyam, "A New Rationale for Markets in Baskets of Stocks" (Working paper 10-89, Anderson School of Management, UCLA, April 1989).

20. Based on current prices, Exxon has the highest weighting in the NYSE ESP, with about 3100 shares, while about 160 stocks in the basket have weights of less than 100 shares.

Section IV
Equity Derivatives
and the Crash

On October 19, 1987, the stock market sustained its greatest single-day loss of the twentieth century, losing about 22 percent of its value. This contrasted with a 12 percent drop that signaled the beginning of the Great Depression. Naturally, an event of this magnitude has called forth an analysis of trading unprecedented in the history of financial markets. Many observers believe that active markets in equity derivatives were responsible for the severity of the crash. This section explores the role of equity derivatives in the crash and discusses some changes in stock market structure that emerged from reflection on the crash.

Lawrence Harris focuses on the difference between S&P 500 cash and futures prices during the crash in his article, "The October 1987 S&P 500 Stock-Futures Basis." No-arbitrage conditions link cash and futures prices through the cost-of-carry relationship—at least when markets function normally. Harris documents that the market certainly did not function normally during the period of the crash. In essence, prices fell so quickly and information lagged so far behind the quickly changing prices, that the equity market ground to a halt. As a result, the normal linkages between the futures and cash markets were entirely disrupted.

Gilbert W. Bassett, Jr., Virginia Grace France, and Stanley Pliska explore the relationship between cash and futures prices on the day of the crash in their paper, "The MMI Cash-Futures Spread on October 19, 1987." The MMI stock index futures contract trades on the Chicago Board of Trade, and the MMI (Major Market Index) is a stock market index that closely mirrors movements in the Dow Jones Industrial Averages. Like Harris, Bassett, France, and Pliska find a severe disruption in the normal price relationship between the cash and futures markets.

G. J. Santoni analyzes some of the claims that have been advanced about the Crash of 1987 in his article, "The October Crash: Some Evidence on the Cascade Theory." According to the "cascade theory," trading strategies popular in the futures market (stock index arbitrage and portfolio trading) generated sell orders in response to the initial large drop in stock prices. The selling of futures generated a further drop in the stock market, due to the normal linkages between cash and futures prices. This subsequent stock market drop triggered yet more sales of stock index futures and options, leading in turn to a greater drop in the stock market. This cycle repeated itself throughout the day on October 19, 1987, causing prices to cascade downward. Santoni weighs the evidence on the cascade theory and finds it lacking. Nonetheless, many observers continue to believe the cascade theory and these beliefs have probably led to changes in trading rules in the stock and stock derivatives markets.

Mark Rubinstein considers the connection between the Crash of 1987 and one popular stock index derivatives trading strategy in his paper, "Portfolio Insurance and the Market Crash." Rubinstein finds that portfolio insurance strategies were probably not important in fueling the crash. He then goes on to consider the performance of portfolio insurance strategies during the crash and finds them lacking. As a consequence, Rubinstein suggests that portfolio insurance will probably move away from dynamic trading strategies and begin to seek implementation through the direct trading of options.

The Crash of 1987 led to considerable debate over the cause of the crash and to a search for measures to prevent future market breaks. One of the major changes in trading rules that resulted is the implementation of planned trading halts in periods of large price movements. These measures are called "circuit breakers," and are explored by James T. Moser in his article, "Circuit Breakers." Moser explains how circuit breakers function and analyzes the likely effects of this new system of trading halts. In sum, he finds that circuit breakers limit access to markets and may impair liquidity. While admitting that circuit breakers may have some merit, Moser is at pains to stress that circuit breakers also impose costs on the markets.

Article 27

The October 1987 S&P 500 Stock-Futures Basis

LAWRENCE HARRIS*

ABSTRACT

Five-minute changes in the S&P 500 index and futures contract are examined over a ten-day period surrounding the October 1987 stock market crash. Since nonsynchronous trading problems are severe in these data, new index estimators are derived and used. The estimators use the complete transaction history of all 500 stocks. Nonsynchronous trading explains part of the large absolute futures-cash basis observed during the crash. The remainder may be due to disintegration of the two markets. Even after adjustment for nonsynchronous trading, the index displays more autocorrelation than does the futures and the futures leads the index.

THE RELATION BETWEEN THE S&P 500 index futures market and the underlying cash market always has been of interest to investors, academics, and regulators. Recently, it became the focus of much new attention when volatility in these markets increased. One aspect of the relation between these two markets is the basis spread, the difference between the value of the underlying cash index and the futures price. The basis is studied because it is a key determinant of whether arbitrage opportunities exist, because variance in the basis is a measure of how well integrated the two markets are, and because the basis is related to tests for causality among the prices in the two markets.

The basis is normally calculated by subtracting the futures price from the most recent value of the S&P 500 index. The result, however, is unlikely to be the best measure of the true price relation between the two markets because the index often is not the best measure of the current value of the S&P 500 stocks. The S&P 500 index, which is a value-weighted sum of the most current stock prices, is subject to nonsynchronous trading problems. The index lags behind the true value of the underlying S&P 500 stocks when any of the constituent stocks have not recently traded since underlying stock values may change between trades. If the futures price is contemporaneously correlated with the underlying aggregate S&P 500 stock value, the index will lag behind the futures price. Nonsynchronous

* Associate Professor of Finance and Business Economics, University of Southern California. Numerous individuals were very helpful in providing me the data necessary to undertake this study. They include J. Kimball Dietrich, of the U.S. Department of the Treasury (visiting), Kenneth Lehn, Chief Economist of the U.S. Securities and Exchange Commission, Bill MacDonald of the SEC, Ken Cone of the Chicago Mercantile Exchange, Jeremy Evnine of Wells Fargo Investment Advisors, and others unknown to me. Their assistance is greatly appreciated. The final version of the paper benefited from discussions in seminars at the SEC, the CFTC, the Fuqua School at Duke, and the Graduate School of Business at NYU. Other editorial suggestions were also provided by the editor, the referee, and Eduardo Schwartz. All remaining errors and all opinions are mine only. Partial financial support for this research was provided by the Mid America Institute for Public Policy Research, for which I am grateful.

trading also causes the index to be more autocorrelated and less volatile than the underlying aggregate stock value. If the nonsynchronous trading problem is ignored, spurious conclusions about volatility, market efficiency, and the relation between the futures and cash markets can be obtained and arbitrage opportunities can be falsely identified.

The nonsynchronous trading problem is greatest when prices are analyzed over short time intervals, such as are examined in studies of intraday data, and when trading is thin. Both conditions apply to detailed studies of market performance during the October 1987 crash. The crash probably will be best understood by studying intraday data, and, due to institutional factors and/or investor behavior, trading became thin at precisely those times when timely information would have been most useful. These considerations strongly suggest that better measures of the underlying values of the S&P 500 stocks be constructed and used. This paper derives such measures, compares them to the index, and uses them to analyze the relation between the two markets.

The new index measures are obtained directly from transactions data which identify the time and price of every trade. Briefly, each transaction price change is decomposed into a systematic component and a nonsystematic component. The systematic component is further decomposed into a sum of systematic price changes, one for each time interval spanned by the transaction price change. The systematic price changes, which are common to all transaction price changes spanning a given interval, are estimated as parameters using weighted sum of squares. The results are used to estimate what prices would have been observed had all securities traded. These are then used to compute an adjusted index. In effect, the estimation method obtains information from those stocks that did trade to determine the implied value of the underlying index.

The results suggest that part, but by no means all, of the large futures basis observed during the week of October 19–23 can be explained by nonsynchronous trading. The remainder may be due to disintegration (decoupling) of these two markets in which risk in the S&P 500 stocks is traded. The disintegration may have resulted when traders could not execute sell orders in the cash markets, when effective means of conducting arbitrage became unavailable (because of either order and confirmation channel congestion or regulation), and when the Chicago Mercantile Exchange halted trading in the futures contract.

Several studies have considered the effects of nonsynchronous trading on portfolio returns. These include Fisher [6], Dimson [4], Scholes and Williams [11], Cohen, Maier, Schwartz, and Whitcomb [2], Cohen, Hawawini, Maier, Schwartz, and Whitcomb [3], and, most recently, Atchison, Butler, and Simonds [1] and Shanken [12]. None of these studies, however, considers estimation solutions to nonsynchronous trading problems which can be executed using transactions data. Cohen et al. [2, 3] suggest that nonsynchronous trading may be only one of several market frictions which cause positive serial autocorrelation. Perry [10] and Atchison et al. [1] provide empirical and theoretical studies which imply that nonsynchronous trading, by itself, cannot account for the observed autocorrelation in daily index returns. The empirical analyses in this paper show that portfolio returns are autocorrelated even after the effects of nonsynchronous trading are explicitly removed.

Several studies consider the "causal" relation between stock index and index futures markets. Finnerty and Park [5], Kawaller, Koch, and Koch [7, 8], and Stoll and Whaley [13] all show that "causality" runs from the futures to the cash markets. However, as the authors are aware, the result may be caused by the lag that nonsynchronous trading induces into indices. This study shows that, even after the effect of nonsynchronous trading is removed, the futures price strongly leads the cash index.

MacKinley and Ramaswamy [9] provide a detailed theoretical and empirical study of the S&P 500 index-futures arbitrage conditions. They find that fifteen-minute changes in the computed index are more autocorrelated than changes in the futures and attribute this to nonsynchronous trading in the index stocks. Although they discuss how nonsynchronous trading can lead to the perception of arbitrage opportunities, they do not provide a method for eliminating the effect. This paper provides a method that can be implemented in real time.

The remainder of this paper consists of four sections. In Section I, the new method for computing indices from nonsynchronous data is motivated, derived, and presented. Section II describes the sample and experimental design of the empirical investigation into the S&P 500 index cash/futures relation surrounding October 19. Section III presents and describes the results. A summary with interpretations is provided in the last section, along with a discussion of the policy implications.

I. Methodology

Before presenting the weighted least-squares method for determining the aggregate market value of a stock portfolio from nonsynchronous trade prices, it is useful to introduce concepts and notation by discussing the standard definition of portfolio valuation. Portfolio value at time t, S_t, is normally computed as the sum over all N portfolio stocks of the number of shares held in each stock i, q_i, times the most recently observed price as of time t, P_{it}:

$$S_t = \sum_{i=1}^{N} q_i P_{it}.\text{[1]}$$ (1)

For now, assume that prices, if observed, are observed at discrete intervals.

Let S_t^*, the aggregate value of the portfolio, be defined by

$$S_t^* = \sum_{i=1}^{N} q_i V_{it},$$ (2)

where V_{it} is the value of a share of firm i at time t. Assume that this value equals the observed price when the price is observed. In general, share value differs from the last observed price if the latter is old. S_t^* is related to S_t as follows:

$$S_t^* - S_t = \sum_{i=1}^{N} q_i (V_{it} - P_{it}) = \sum_{i=1}^{N} q_i \Delta_{k_{it}} V_{it} \equiv A_t,$$ (3)

[1] The S&P 500 index is computed from (1) with $q_i = Q_i/DIV$, where Q_i is the total number of shares outstanding for stock i and DIV is a divisor published by S&P. The index is $1/DIV$ of the last-observed-price aggregate value of all S&P 500 stocks. It is a value-weighted index because the relative change in the index, $(S_t - S_{t-1})/S_{t-1}$, can be expressed as the value-weighted sum of the constituent stock returns.

where Δ_k is the k-period difference operator and k_{it} is the number of periods since the last price was observed for security i. ($k_{it} = 0$ if the price is observed at t.) If prices for all stocks are observed at time t, S_t is equal to S_t^*. Otherwise, S_t lags S_t^*. This expression shows that S_t^* can be estimated if A_t, the nonsynchronous trading adjustment, can be estimated.

The method presented here uses a simple one-factor representation of the value-generating process to estimate the nonsynchronous trading adjustment. Assume that values are generated by the following process:

$$\Delta \log(V_{it}) = f_t + e_{it}, \tag{4}$$

where f_t is the common factor and e_{it} is assumed to be zero-mean firm-specific variation. If a set of factor estimates $\{\hat{f}_t\}$ is available, unobserved multiperiod changes in value can be estimated by

$$\Delta_{k_{it}} \hat{V}_{it} = P_{it} \exp(\sum_{i=1}^{k_{it}} \hat{f}_{t-i+1}), \tag{5}$$

where P_{it}, the most recently observed price as of time t, was observed k_{it} periods ago. Equations (3) and (5) reduce the problem of estimating S_t^* to one of estimating the underlying factor changes from nonsynchronous data.

The factor estimation method used in this study uses weighted least squares to allocate variance to the various intervals spanned by a price change. Motivation and interpretation of the method are best established by first considering a simple one-period problem.

The one-period percentage change in observed portfolio value, $\%\Delta S_t = (S_t - S_{t-1})/S_{t-1}$, can be computed by solving the following minimization problem:

$$\min_{f_t} \sum_{i=1}^N w_i (\%\Delta P_{it} - f_t)^2, \tag{6}$$

where $w_i = q_i P_{it-1}/S_{t-1}$ is the value weight of stock i in the portfolio. The minimizing value of f_t, $\hat{f}_t = \sum w_i \%\Delta P_{it} / \sum w_i = \sum q_i \Delta P_{it}/S_{t-1}$ is identically equal to $\%\Delta S_t$,

This minimization problem has a weighted least-squares regression interpretation which is nearly identical to (4):

$$\%\Delta P_{it} = f_t + e_{it}, \quad i = 1, \cdots, N, \tag{7}$$

where e_{it} is a firm-specific residual with variance proportional to $1/w_i$. This specification does not realistically represent the value-generating process (which may include multiple factors, non-unit factor loadings, and different firm-specific variance components); nor is it meant to. It is a consequence only of the definition of portfolio value. It does, however, suggest that factor estimates can be interpreted as percentage changes in portfolio value if value weights are used in weighted least-squares estimation.[2]

---

[2] More realistic factor models can be used in a nonsynchronous trading analysis within the framework presented in this article. In particular, multiple factors, non-unit loadings, realistic firm-specific variances, and information about bid/ask spreads can be incorporated. After examining the results obtained from the simple model presented here, it seems unlikely that a more complex model would yield results leading to different conclusions. Moreover, factor estimates obtained from more

Estimation of the factors from nonsynchronous data is accomplished using a multiperiod generalization of this simple regression model:

$$\Delta_{k_{it}} \log(P_{it}) = \sum_{j=1}^{K_{it}} f_{t-j+1} + e_{it}, \tag{8}$$

for all observed P_{it} in a cross-sectional sample of $i = 1, \cdots, N$ and a time-series sample of $t = t_0, \cdots, T$, with the variance of the firm-specific residual, e_{it}, proportional to $1/w_i$. If there are large numbers of independent observations at each time t, and if the price changes are small so that $\Delta \log(P)$ is approximately equal to $\%\Delta P$, $\hat{f}_t$ estimates $\%\Delta S_t^*$. (The latter condition is generally met in transactions data, even during the crash.)

The remainder of this section provides a brief discussion of several technical issues that arise when equation (8) is estimated. A complete presentation can be found in the Appendix.

Until now, all transactions, if observed, were assumed to occur at discrete intervals. In fact, they occur and are observed in continuous time. Failure to account for this characteristic of the data wastes information that can be used to obtain a better solution of the nonsynchronous trading problem. The Appendix describes and motivates a simple modification of equation (8) which allows extraction of this information from transaction prices that fall in the middle of an observational interval.

If there are a large number of intervals to be analyzed ($T - t_0$ is large), it is not practical to analyze them all at once. This would require computing and inverting a $T - t_0$ dimensional matrix of sums of squares and cross-products. Instead, a rolling regression spanning K intervals is used. The implementation is described fully in the Appendix.

Two types of nonsynchronous trading adjustments can be obtained from the rolling regressions: a current information adjustment and a perfect foresight adjustment. The current information adjustment for time t is computed using only the factor estimates of the regression whose leading edge is at t. This adjustment can be computed in real time using only those prices available at or before time t. The perfect foresight adjustment is computed using the factor estimates obtained from the middle interval of each rolling regression and therefore depends on future as well as past price changes. Although the perfect foresight measure may be the best measure of index value for testing certain hypotheses about investor behavior, other hypothesis tests requiring a measure which reflects only information available to investors as of time t are best examined using the current information adjustment. The empirical section describes the relation between the two measures and their differential implications for the future/cash basis.

Useful measures of uncertainty about index price changes and of uncertainty in index levels due to the nonsynchronous trading problem can be obtained from the inverse sum of squares and cross-products matrix of the regression. These measures, which quantify index precision and the loss in information due to nonsynchronous trading, are more fully described in the Appendix.

---

complex models cannot be interpreted as estimates of the change in portfolio value. (This property, though, is not necessary to the nonsynchronous trading analysis.)

II. Sample

The stock sample consists of all primary market trades of each S&P 500 stock from the open of trading on Monday, October 12, 1987 to the close of trading on Friday, October 23. The data, which come from SIAC via the Securities and Exchange Commission, include the date, time, price, and shares traded for each transaction on each exchange in the United States. The transaction time is the exact second when a trade was executed in the DOT system or when a record of it was read by an exchange card reader. Only primary market transactions are used since the S&P 500 index is computed only from primary prices. The primary markets for all S&P 500 stocks opened at 9:30 A.M. EST and closed at 4:00 P.M. except on the last sample day, when they all closed at 2:00 P.M. Some of the stocks traded later (except on Friday, October 23) on the Pacific Exchange. The NYSE is the primary market for 462 of the S&P 500 stocks, AMEX for eight, and the NASDAQ National Market System for the remaining 30. Shares outstanding (used to compute market weights) for each of the S&P 500 stocks are obtained from the October 1987 Standard and Poor's *"500" Information Bulletin*, and, where appropriate, the shares outstanding and/or prices are adjusted for all stock splits, stock dividends, new issues, and announced repurchases.[3]

The futures sample consists of all prices recorded by the CME market recorders in the December 1987 S&P 500 index for the corresponding sample period. Trade opened at 9:30 A.M. EST and closed at 4:15 P.M. EST except on the last day, when it closed at 2:00 P.M. EST. Each record includes the exact second that the price was entered by the recorder. On Tuesday, October 20, the exchange closed for about one hour near midday. Futures traders at the CME received reports of the S&P 500 index, computed from SIAC data, with no more than a thirty-second lag (even if the Composite Tape is running late).

The sample period is divided into 765 discrete intervals consisting of seventy-eight five-minute intervals for each full day (6.5 hours × 12 intervals/hour), fifty-four five-minute intervals for the last Friday, and nine overnight intervals. In the Appendix it is shown that only the first and last prices (if available) in each interval for a given stock are informative. Accordingly, the analysis is conducted using only these prices.

The first and last prices within an intraday interval are easy to identify, but two additional comments about the last and first daily intervals are necessary. First, although the exchanges nominally close at 4:00, many trades are recorded as late as 4:10 because trading in a crowd did not stop or because there are lags in the floor recording process. If the last trade of the day was recorded after 4:00, it is used as the last trade in the last interval and, for the purposes of the statistical analyses, its time is taken as 4:00. Second, the opening trade is often

---

[3] My computations of the S&P 500 index are consistently 0.3 points less than those reported in the November issue of Standard and Poor's *"500" Information Bulletin*. The difference almost certainly is due to inaccuracies in the number of shares outstanding. I obtained information about share changes from *Standard and Poor's Corporation Records, Current News Edition*, from the *Wall Street Journal*, and by comparing the numbers of shares outstanding reported in the October and November issues of the *"500" Information Bulletin*. Since the differences are small and consistent, they do not materially affect the analyses.

not recorded until some time after the nominal start of trade at 9:30. If a trade was recorded in the first five minutes, it is classified as the opening trade and its time is taken as 9:30. The first daily interval therefore covers the time between the first trade of the day (if recorded before 9:35) and 9:35. The overnight interval covers the time between 4:00 (or the last trade if recorded after 4:00) and the first trade of the day (if recorded before 9:35). To ensure that the futures data are compatible when overnight comparisons are made, the overnight change in the futures price is computed from the last price before 4:00 to the first opening price. (Both prices were recorded in the last and first minutes, respectively, on each trading day in the sample.)

Although some time series in the data set start at 9:30 on Monday, October 12, the first results concerning index levels reported in this paper start at interval 38 (Monday, October 12, 12:35–12:40). The delay occurs because index computation requires all prices. The last S&P 500 stock to open on that Monday first traded at 12:37. The regression analysis, which is designed to operate on incomplete data, uses all of the data starting from the Monday open. (Had closing prices for Friday, October 9 been available, the time-series results could have been extended back to the Monday open.)

III. Results

A. Overview

The CME December 1987 S&P 500 index futures contract price and the cash S&P 500 index are plotted by five-minute intervals in Figure 1. During the week

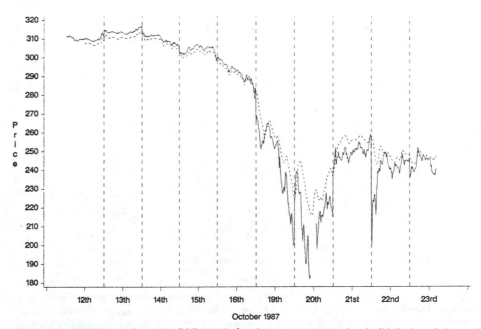

Figure 1. CME December 1987 S&P 500 index futures contract price (*solid line*) and the cash S&P 500 index (*broken line*), plotted by five-minute intervals.

of October 12–19, the two time series tracked each other very closely until Friday, when the futures started to trade at a discount to the cash. During the next week, the relation significantly deteriorated, with the basis ranging from −60 to +10 points. Two not necessarily exclusive explanations can account for the breakdown in the basis: nonsynchronous trading and disintegration.

If prices are nonsynchronous, the index will lag the underlying value of the S&P 500 stocks. (The lag is especially obvious on Figure 1 near the open of trading on October 19 and 20.) If that value is more currently reflected in futures price, and if it changes quickly, the basis will widen in the direction of change. This was generally observed between late Friday, October 16, and midmorning on Tuesday, October 20. Figure 2 presents time plots of two measures of trade frequency: the value-weighted mean number of intervals (and fractions of intervals) since the last trade was observed for stocks on the S&P 500 list, and the fraction of the total market value of the S&P 500 stocks which did not trade in a given interval. The time periods in which trading is least frequent correspond to those with the greatest absolute basis.

Under the disintegration hypothesis, the basis breaks down when mechanisms that integrate these two markets for fundamentally the same risk fail. This could have been the case during much of the week of October 19–23, when traders could not always execute sell orders in the cash markets, when effective means of conducting index arbitrage were unavailable (either because of order and

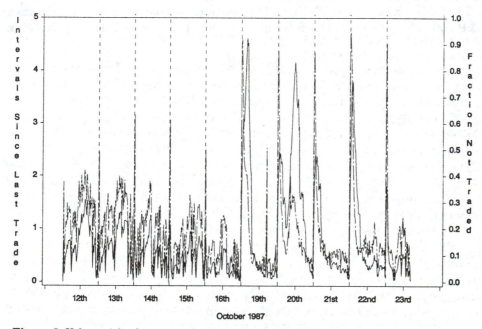

Figure 2. Value-weighted mean number of intervals, including fractional intervals, since the last trade was observed for stocks on the S&P 500 list (*solid line*) and the fraction of the total market value of the S&P 500 stocks which did not trade in a given interval (*broken line*). Each interval is five minutes long, except for the first interval of each day, which corresponds to the period between the preceding 4:00 close and the opening transaction, if observed before 9:35.

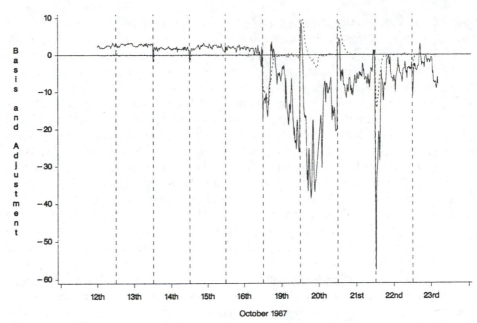

Figure 3. CME December 1987 S&P 500 index futures basis (*solid line*) and the perfect foresight nonsynchronous index adjustment (*broken line*), plotted by five-minute intervals. The current information adjustment, if plotted, would lie almost exactly on the perfect foresight adjustment. The basis is futures price minus the cash index.

conformation channel congestion or regulation), and when the CME halted trading in the futures contract.

The methods developed in this paper provide the tools for measuring how much of the abnormal basis was due to nonsynchronous trading. Time plots of the basis (futures minus cash) and of the perfect foresight nonsynchronous index adjustment are presented in Figure 3. (The current information adjustment, if plotted, would lie almost exactly on the perfect foresight adjustment.[4]) If nonsynchronous trading explained all of the variation in the basis, the basis and the adjustment would track each other very closely at a distance of about 2.5 points. (The actual distance depends on expected dividend yields and carrying costs.) The plots show that the adjustment explains some of the variation in the basis, especially near market openings. Much of the remaining variation, however, remains unexplained. It may be due to market disintegration.

Figure 4 plots the estimated standard errors of the perfect foresight index adjustment and of the estimated change in the S&P 500 index implied by the perfect foresight estimated factor. As noted in the Appendix, the standard errors obtained from the regression analysis are not the actual standard errors of estimators (since the variance weights used in the regression do not correspond

---

[4] In all of the results reported, there is very little difference between the current information adjustment and the perfect foresight adjustment. This implies that the cross-section is large enough that estimation error is not a significant source of time-series variation in the factor estimates. Current information alone appears to be sufficient to accurately estimate the factors in this sample.

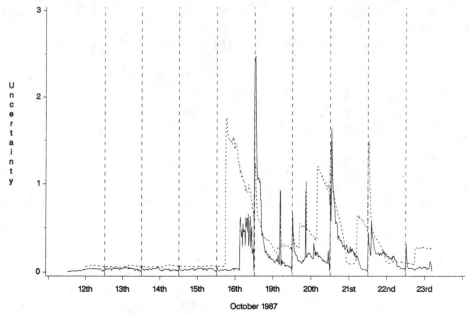

Figure 4. Estimated standard error of the perfect foresight index adjustment (*solid line*) and of the estimated change in the S&P 500 index, implied by the perfect foresight estimated factor (*broken line*). These standard errors obtained from the regression analysis are not the actual standard errors of estimators since the variance weights used in the regression do not correspond to the actual firm-specific component variances.

to the actual firm-specific component variances). They do, however, show that uncertainty due to nonsynchronous trading occurs when it is expected, given the time-since-last-trade data plotted in Figure 2.

B. Correlations, Lead-Lag Relations, and Autocorrelations

Quantitative measures of the tracking performance of the index and the adjusted indices are presented in Table I. The results confirm that the adjusted indices track the futures better than does the S&P 500 index. When prices are most volatile, the perfect foresight-adjusted index is generally closest to the futures price, the current information-adjusted index is second-closest, and the index is farthest away. Otherwise, all three measures of the index are nearly coincident. (If prices are nonsynchronous, the index will accurately represent value if value does not change very quickly.) Although the mean differences are not large, paired *t*-tests show that the mean basis distances for the adjusted indices are generally significantly smaller than for the index. The differences between the perfect foresight and the current information indices are also often significant.

Further evidence suggesting that the adjusted indices more closely approximate the aggregate underlying value of the S&P 500 stocks than does the S&P 500 index can be found by examining correlations. Since the futures contract and the S&P 500 index both price the same risks, changes in their values should be

Table I

Distance Measures of the Basis (Futures−Index) between the CME December 1987 S&P 500 Index Futures and the S&P 500 Index, and the Two Adjusted Indices[a]

Sample	N	Mean Basis			Mean Absolute Basis			Root Mean-Squared Basis		
		Index	Current Adjusted	Perfect Adjusted	Index	Current Adjusted	Perfect Adjusted	Index	Current Adjusted	Perfect Adjusted
All	717	−3.60	−3.36	−3.31	5.88	5.62[b]	5.57[bc]	9.44	8.91[b]	8.83[bc]
Week 1	356	2.07	2.10	2.11	2.12	2.13	2.14[c]	2.22	2.22	2.23[c]
Week 2	361	−9.20	−8.75	−8.65	9.60	9.06[bc]	8.96[bc]	13.12	12.37[b]	12.25[bc]
12th	40	2.36	2.36	2.37	2.36	2.36	2.37	2.39	2.38	2.39
13th	79	2.79	2.77	2.77	2.79	2.77	2.77	2.81	2.79	2.79
14th	79	1.70	1.75	1.76	1.72	1.75	1.76	1.77	1.78	1.79
15th	79	2.07	2.14	2.16	2.11	2.14	2.16	2.20	2.21	2.22
16th	79	1.56	1.60	1.60	1.73	1.75	1.76	1.86	1.86	1.87
19th	79	−10.55	−8.18	−7.83	10.89	9.30[b]	9.04[bc]	13.08	11.84[b]	11.79[bc]
20th	69	−16.99	−18.00	−18.10	17.88	18.12	18.14	20.61	20.70	20.67
21st	79	−5.57	−6.68	−6.74	6.15	6.76[b]	6.81[b]	6.68	7.40[b]	7.43[b]
22nd	79	−8.76	−7.30	−7.08	8.76	7.30[bc]	7.08[bc]	13.65	10.89[b]	10.39[bc]
23rd	55	−3.30	−3.00	−2.96	3.51	3.16[b]	3.13[b]	4.44	3.99[b]	3.96[b]

[a] The current information-adjusted index is the index plus an adjustment for nonsynchronous trading that is computed from lagged and contemporaneous information only. The adjustment for the perfect foresight-adjusted index is obtained using leading data as well. The measures are computed from data observed at five-minute intervals starting at market open.

[b] Mean significantly different from the corresponding index basis mean using a paired t-test with a one-sided significance level of five percent.

[c] Mean significantly different from the current adjusted basis mean using a paired t-test with a two-sided significance level of five percent.

correlated. Nonsynchronous trading in the cash market, however, tends to break up that correlation. The adjusted indices therefore should be more highly correlated with changes in the futures price than is the index. Results reported in Panel A of Table II confirm this prediction. For the sample as a whole and every time subsample, both adjusted measures are more closely correlated with the futures than is the index.

Information about the time relation between the futures and cash markets can be obtained by examining cross-correlations. Modeling nonsynchronous trading is very important in this analysis because, even if the relation is completely contemporaneous, nonsynchronous trading will cause the futures price to lead the computed index. This argument suggests that the lagged changes in the futures should be more highly correlated with current changes in the index than with those of the adjusted indices. However, if in the true causal relation, the futures leads the cash (as might be expected given the lower transactions costs and greater liquidity in the futures markets), lagged futures should be less highly correlated with the current index than with the current adjusted indices. This is because the index contains noise induced by nonsynchronous trading. The results (Table II, Panel B and Figure 5) show that the futures leads all measures of the index. In the first week of the sample, when noise due to nonsynchronous trading is not great, the lead correlations (negative lags of the futures) are greatest for the S&P 500 index, as predicted. In the second week, the lead correlations are initially greatest for the adjusted indices, consistent with the noise prediction. There is little evidence of the cash leading the futures in any of the measures (Table II, Panel C).

An interesting implication of the cross-correlation between the current changes in the various indices and the leads and lags of changes in the futures is that lagged adjustments have no predictive power for futures prices. This can be seen most clearly in Figure 6, in which the sample cross-correlation functions are plotted for current values of the two adjustments with leads and lagged changes in the futures. These results show that the futures market "sees through" (is efficient with respect to) noise due to nonsynchronous trading.

One prediction of the nonsynchronous trading analysis is that the S&P 500 index should be positively autocorrelated. In five-minute data (Table III and Figure 7), it is very autocorrelated (0.697 for the whole sample) and, as expected, the adjusted indices are less correlated. The autocorrelation in the adjusted series, however, is still quite large (0.527 for perfect foresight adjustment) relative to the autocorrelation in the futures (0.143). These results suggest that many stock specialists attempted to maintain price continuity. They also show that serious problems would result if the nonsynchronous trading problems were modeled using time-series methods which assume that the underlying index value follows a random walk.

The nonsynchronous data analysis predicts that the index should catch up with its underlying value as trades are observed. This implies that the adjustments should lead the index. The results (Table IV and Figure 8) confirm this prediction. The current adjustments are correlated with the lagged and current values of the index change (because the adjustments are computed partly from lagged and current index changes) and with leads of the index change, as expected. Note

Table II

Correlations of Changes in the S&P 500 Index, the Adjusted Indices, and the Index-scaled Estimated Factors, with Changes in the CME December 1987 Futures Price[a]

Sample	N	S&P 500 Index	Index with Current Information Adjustment	Index with Perfect Foresight Adjustment	Estimated Factor Change, Current Information	Estimated Factor Change, Perfect Foresight
Panel A: Correlations with Contemporaneous Changes in the Futures Price						
All	716	0.196	0.347	0.444	0.371	0.431
Week 1	356	0.587	0.682	0.690	0.683	0.671
Week 2	360	0.172	0.332	0.438	0.359	0.425
12th	40	0.670	0.711	0.732	0.761	0.725
13th	79	0.667	0.719	0.739	0.751	0.743
14th	79	0.528	0.737	0.750	0.753	0.768
15th	79	0.633	0.734	0.769	0.771	0.772
16th	79	0.574	0.654	0.641	0.615	0.587
19th	79	0.182	0.393	0.429	0.428	0.405
20th	68	0.177	0.296	0.367	0.304	0.332
21st	79	0.249	0.576	0.641	0.607	0.656
22nd	79	0.039	0.195	0.444	0.246	0.448
23rd	55	0.355	0.639	0.630	0.660	0.583
Panel B: Correlations with First Lagged Changes in the Futures Price						
All	715	0.259	0.403	0.391	0.394	0.369
Week 1	355	0.531	0.421	0.434	0.433	0.426
Week 2	360	0.248	0.411	0.397	0.402	0.372
12th	39	0.726	0.544	0.550	0.583	0.540
13th	79	0.328	0.213	0.216	0.239	0.200
14th	79	0.300	0.298	0.329	0.307	0.322
15th	79	0.614	0.496	0.509	0.505	0.488
16th	79	0.610	0.477	0.484	0.478	0.482
19th	79	0.364	0.417	0.434	0.435	0.381
20th	68	0.323	0.489	0.502	0.491	0.456
21st	79	0.203	0.399	0.325	0.400	0.318
22nd	79	0.057	0.406	0.370	0.358	0.355
23rd	55	0.344	0.138	0.178	0.203	0.170
Panel C: Correlations with First Lead Changes in the Futures Price						
All	715	0.001	0.040	0.047	0.045	0.030
Week 1	355	0.005	0.055	0.033	0.040	−0.013
Week 2	360	0.000	0.039	0.049	0.046	0.033
12th	39	0.352	0.454	0.390	0.405	0.266
13th	79	−0.143	0.069	0.027	0.039	−0.017
14th	79	−0.189	−0.173	−0.201	−0.183	−0.248
15th	79	0.201	0.224	0.218	0.238	0.179
16th	79	−0.066	−0.007	−0.026	−0.025	−0.072
19th	79	0.033	−0.015	0.001	0.013	−0.036
20th	68	−0.062	0.069	0.064	0.061	0.046
21st	79	−0.170	−0.005	−0.004	−0.038	−0.033
22nd	79	−0.025	−0.043	−0.023	−0.029	−0.038
23rd	55	0.046	0.285	0.300	0.340	0.306

[a] The changes for each day are computed over five-minute intervals with the preceding overnight change included.

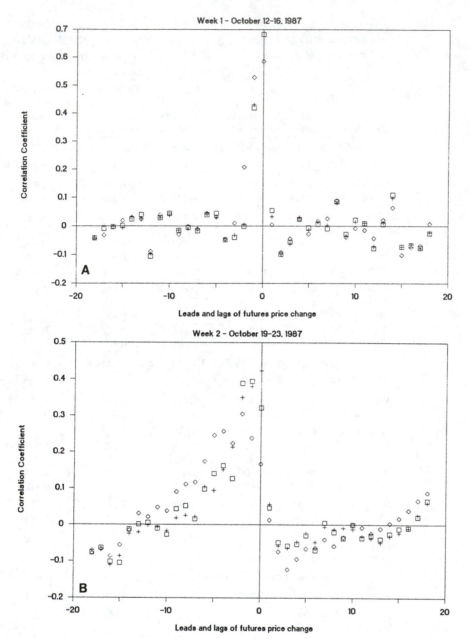

Figure 5. Cross-correlations, current five-minute changes in the S&P 500 index and in the two adjusted indices with leads and lags of changes in the CME December 1987 S&P 500 index futures. There are 356 five-minute and overnight intervals plotted. Positive correlations to the left of zero indicate that the futures leads the indices. The *diamonds* plot correlations of S&P 500 index changes with leads and lags of changes in the futures price. The *boxes* plot cross-correlations for changes in the current information foresight index, while the *pluses* plot cross-correlations for changes in the perfect foresight index.

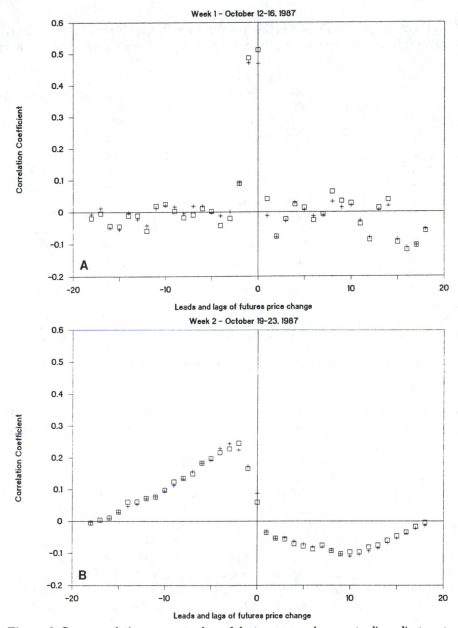

Figure 6. Cross-correlations, current values of the two nonsynchronous trading adjustments with leads and lags of five-minute changes in the CME December 1987 S&P 500 index futures price. There are 356 five-minute and overnight intervals plotted. Positive correlations to the left of zero indicate that the futures leads the adjustments. The *boxes* plot the perfect foresight adjustment correlations, while the *pluses* plot the current information adjustment correlations.

Table III

First Autocorrelation Coefficients for Changes in the CME December 1987
S&P 500 Index Futures Price, the S&P 500 Index, the Adjusted Indices, and
the Index-Scaled Estimated Factors[a]

Sample	N	CME December 1987 Futures	S&P 500 Index	Index with Current Information Adjustment	Index with Perfect Foresight Adjustment	Estimated Factor Change, Current Information	Estimated Factor Change, Perfect Foresight
All	726	0.143	0.697	0.458	0.527	0.562	0.559
Week 1	356	0.059	0.372	0.190	0.205	0.234	0.151
Week 2	371[b]	0.145	0.755	0.496	0.574	0.613	0.614
12th	39	0.290	0.635	0.385	0.406	0.477	0.343
13th	79	−0.065	0.026	0.054	0.051	0.097	0.011
14th	79	−0.082	0.154	0.013	0.034	0.073	0.022
15th	79	0.338	0.398	0.132	0.190	0.207	0.170
16th	79	0.001	0.454	0.292	0.278	0.288	0.167
19th	79	−0.025	0.554	0.248	0.325	0.383	0.426
20th	79[b]	0.286	0.873	0.819	0.851	0.873	0.850
21st	79	−0.030	0.654	0.422	0.386	0.377	0.401
22nd	79	0.132	0.777	0.379	0.645	0.602	0.644
23rd	55	0.195	0.447	0.107	0.135	0.198	0.121

[a] The changes for each day are computed over five-minute intervals with the preceding overnight change included.

[b] The futures sample is eleven observations smaller due to the halt of trading near midday on Tuesday, October 20.

that this does not imply that the adjustments predict future changes in value. They predict past changes in value which have not yet been incorporated into the observed index.

Further evidence of the nonsynchronous trading-induced lags in the index can be found in Figure 9, in which the root mean-squared cross-basis function is plotted. The cross-basis is the difference between the index and a lagged or lead value of the futures. The minimum of this function indicates at what lag the relation between the futures and the index is closest. In the first week of the sample, this relation was closest for the contemporaneous basis. It is quite flat because prices did not change very much that week (Friday excepted). In the second week the minimum for the index is found at lag 5 of the futures and between lags 2 and 3 for the adjusted indices. This shows that the adjustments take out some of the lag observed in the index during the week, but not all.

IV. Summary, Interpretations, and Conclusions

This paper derives new estimators of the underlying value of a stock portfolio which abstract from nonsynchronous trading problems by using the complete transaction history of all stocks in the portfolio. The methods are applied to the S&P 500 index for a ten-day period surrounding the October 1987 stock crash.

Nonsynchronous trading can explain part of the large absolute futures-cash basis observed during the crash, but not all of it. Much of the unusually large

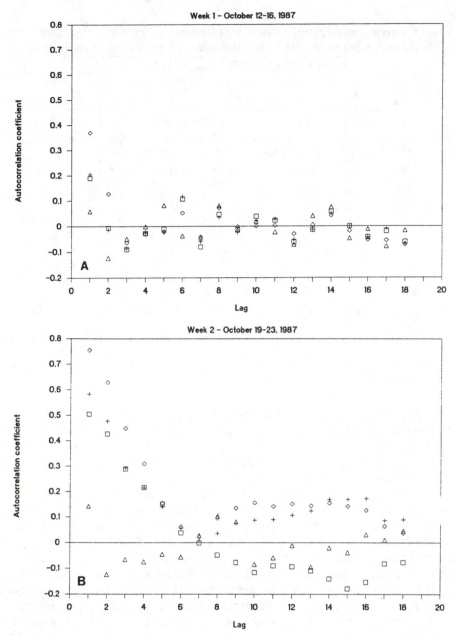

Figure 7. Autocorrelation coefficients for five-minute changes in the CME December 1987 S&P 500 index futures (*triangles*), in the S&P 500 index (*diamonds*), in the perfect foresight-adjusted index (*boxes*), and in the current information adjustment (*pluses*). There are 356 five-minute and overnight intervals plotted.

basis may be due to the disintegration of the two markets caused by capacity and/or regulatory disruptions in the trade processes.

The large index autocorrelations observed in the second week, even after adjustment for serial correlation, and the long lagged relation between the index

Table IV

Correlations of the Current Information and Perfect Foresight Adjustments to the S&P 500 Index with Changes in the Index[a]

Sample	N[b]	First Lagged Index		Contemporaneous Index		First Lead Index	
		Current	Perfect	Current	Perfect	Current	Perfect
All	727	0.473	0.449	0.516	0.485	0.474	0.457
Week 1	356	0.296	0.294	0.711	0.643	0.482	0.423
Week 2	371	0.506	0.481	0.540	0.510	0.501	0.487
12th	40	0.321	0.348	0.758	0.784	0.660	0.596
13th	79	0.364	0.353	0.699	0.693	0.414	0.392
14th	79	0.205	0.214	0.631	0.561	0.458	0.415
15th	79	0.358	0.365	0.737	0.638	0.517	0.485
16th	79	0.243	0.253	0.873	0.893	0.518	0.418
19th	79	0.252	0.252	0.286	0.276	0.230	0.234
20th	79	0.606	0.529	0.588	0.512	0.506	0.450
21st	79	0.636	0.618	0.749	0.751	0.733	0.748
22nd	79	0.471	0.466	0.536	0.517	0.530	0.543
23rd	55	0.312	0.304	0.436	0.421	0.377	0.372

[a] The changes for each day are computed over five-minute intervals with the preceding overnight change included.

[b] Number of observations for the contemporaneous correlation. The lead and lag correlations have one less observation for the sample as a whole, for week 1 and for October 12.

and the futures during this week suggest that the futures market leads the cash market and that the cash market is not as efficient (as measured by serial correlations) over short intervals as is the futures market. Alternatively, these results may be interpreted as evidence that specialists were providing price continuity and that its provision took time.

These results may be more compelling than similar ones obtained in earlier studies since this study explicitly controls for the lagged cross-correlations and serial correlations which nonsynchronous trading introduces into the data. This study analyzes a very short sample period, but the results may be very strong because of the extraordinary variation in that sample.

A full analysis of why and how the crash occurred requires a much broader study than that presented here. However, the partial elimination of nonsynchronous trading as an explanation for the large basis reduces the set of possible causes and clarifies the problem. A reasonable interpretation of the results suggests that the crash might not have been as large as it was had more orderly trade mechanisms been maintained. In particular, the partial elimination of futures arbitrages due to exchange regulation, to congestion in the order and confirmation systems, and to other difficulties associated with executing sale orders in the cash market removed a potentially significant flow of buy orders from the futures market. Moreover, these same difficulties may have increased the number of sell orders coming into the futures market even though it traded at a significant discount. These two factors may have caused larger drops in the futures than might otherwise have been observed. This may have had a very significant effect

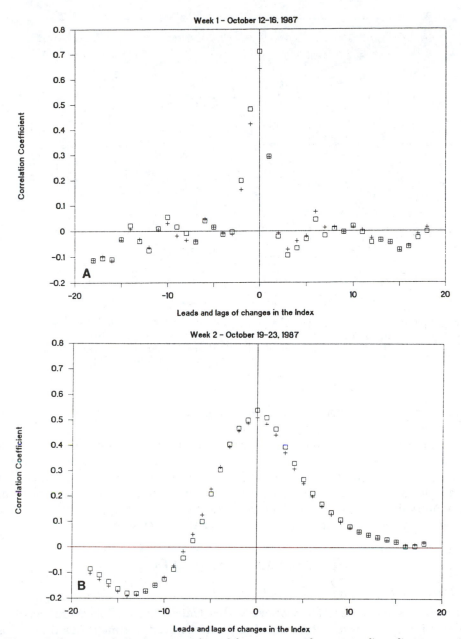

Figure 8. Cross-correlations, current values of the two nonsynchronous trading adjustments with leads and lags of five-minute changes in the S&P 500 index. There are 356 five-minute and overnight intervals plotted. Positive correlations to the right of zero indicate that the adjustments lead the index. The *boxes* plot the perfect foresight adjustment correlations, while the *pluses* plot the current information adjustment correlations.

on the overall performance of the two otherwise integrated markets since the evidence strongly suggests that the cash market follows the futures market.

This interpretation of the results suggests that future problems can be at least partially eliminated if capacity limits to the flow of information are raised. In

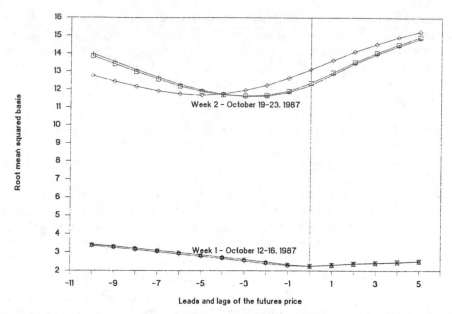

Figure 9. Root mean-squared cross-basis. The cross-basis is the difference between the index and a lead or lag of the futures price. The *diamonds* plot the cross-basis computed using the S&P 500 index, the *boxes* plot the cross-basis computed using the perfect foresight-adjusted index, while the *pluses* plot the cross-basis computed using the current information-adjusted index.

particular, orders, confirmations, and transaction reports on the ticker tape should all arrive at their destinations instantly.

Also, the requirement that specialists maintain continuous markets should be relaxed somewhat in the direction of broad market moves. In practice, this could be done by monitoring the difference between the percentage price change in a specialist's stock and the percentage change in some market index over the same time interval. This relaxation of the requirement to maintain continuous markets should be offset by requiring specialists to quote tighter spreads.

Appendix: Methodological Details

A. Intra-Interval Prices

The discussion in Section I assumes that transactions, if observed, occur at discrete intervals. In fact, they occur and are observed in continuous time. This can cause problems when estimating (8). Suppose that the regression is estimated using only the last transaction price, if available, from each of the $T - t_0$ time intervals. This simple and common practice destroys useful information concerning when within the interval the price is observed. For example, let measurement intervals be five minutes long and suppose that only two prices are observed in intervals $t - 2$ to t: one at 0.5 minutes into interval $t - 2$ and the other at one minute into interval t. It would be inappropriate to allow the implied price change to equally influence the estimation of f_{t-1} and f_t, as would happen using this simple practice. Doing so would allocate too much variation to interval t, which is hardly spanned by the price change, and none to interval $t - 2$, which is mostly spanned by the price change. This problem can be partly solved by allocating variance in proportion to the span of the observed price change over that interval. For the above example, (8) would be modified to read: $(P_t - P_{t-2})/P_{t-2} = 0.9f_{t-2} + f_{t-1} + 0.2f_t + e_t$. This allocation method can be justified if we assume that prices within an interval are generated by Gaussian diffusion with constant variance.[5]

Although this allocation method would permit all transaction prices to be used in the estimation, it is best not to use them all since doing so unnecessarily increases estimator variance. All information about the total factor change within a given interval is contained only in the first and last transactions in that interval. The use of intermediate transactions increases noise because the intra-interval factor variance decomposition is done with error; it is assumed to be proportional to the total factor change over the interval.[6] Therefore, the model is estimated using only first and last interval prices, if available.[7]

[5] Suppose that f^b, f^a, and f are random variables such that $f^b + f^a = f$ with f^b and f^a uncorrelated. Interpret f as the change in the factor over the entire interval, f^b as the change in the factor before a price is observed, and f^a as the change in the factor after the price is observed. We want to know the conditional mean of f^b given f. It is $E(f^b|f) = cov(f^b, f)/var(f) f$, which can be reduced to $var(f^b)/var(f) f$ since f^b and f^a are uncorrelated. If the factor evolves at a uniform rate, the ratio of variances is equal to the fraction of time in the interval past when the price is observed.

[6] Using the intermediate price increases estimation error because the intra-interval variance is poorly modeled. This can be illustrated in the following example. Suppose that price change d_1 spans the subinterval from 0 to x and price change d_2 spans the subinterval from x to 1, $0 < x < 1$. Let these price changes be generated from the following model:

$$d_1 = f_1 + e_1,$$

$$d_2 = f_2 + e_2,$$

where f_1, f_2, e_1, and e_2 are uncorrelated and e_1 and e_2 have variances respectively equal to x and $(1 - x)$ and f_1 and f_2 have variances respectively equal to sx and $s(1 - x)$, where s is some positive constant. Consider the problem of estimating $f = f_1 + f_2$ given d_1 and d_2. The variance decomposition procedure implies the following regression model:

$$d_1 = xf + n_1,$$

$$d_2 = (1 - x)f + n_2.$$

The OLS estimator of f is $\hat{f} = b_1 d_1 + b_2 d_2$, where $b_1 = x/[x^2 + (1 - x)^2]$ and $b_2 = (1 - x)/[x^2 + (1 - x)^2]$. The mean-squared error in this estimator has two components. The first component is due to the fact that f_1 and f_2 are not equal to xf and $(1 - x)f$, respectively. This component is equal to $(b_1^2 - 1)sx + (b_2^2 - 1)s(1 - x) + b_1^2 x + b_2^2(1 - x)$. The second component is due to the noise caused by e_1 and e_2. This component is equal to $[x^3 + (1 - x)^3]/[x^2 + (1 - x)^2]^2$. For all x, this second component is greater than or equal (at $x = 0.5$) to one, which is the total estimator mean-squared error of $\hat{f} = d_1 + d_2$, the best estimator.

[7] An additional example provides further intuition for why the first transaction in each interval should be included in the analysis. Suppose that prices are observed at the beginning of interval $t - 1$, 0.5 minutes into interval t, and at the end of interval t. The intermediate transaction, which would be ignored if we only examined the last transaction in each interval, clearly contains useful information about the decomposition of total variance between the two intervals.

B. Uncertainty Measures

Useful measures of uncertainty can be obtained from the estimated variance-covariance matrix of the regression model estimates. The estimated standard error of $\hat{f}_t$, however, must be interpreted with caution since it reflects the value weights used in the estimation and not the actual variance of the firm-specific variance components. It is, however, positively related to the extent of nonsynchronous trading and is therefore useful as an ordinal measure of factor uncertainty due to nonsynchronous trading.[8] An ordinal measure of uncertainty in the index due to nonsynchronous trading can also be obtained from the estimator variance-covariance matrix since the nonsynchronous trading adjustment, A_t, computed using (3) and (5), is approximately a linear sum of the factor change estimates. The approximation error is very small since the second and higher order terms in the expansion of the exponential function in (5) are very small. The estimated standard error of this sum is a measure of the uncertainty in the index due to nonsynchronous trading.

C. Rolling Regressions

Since the number of intervals to be analyzed is large, it is not practical to analyze them all at once. Instead, a rolling regression spanning K intervals is used. In order to preserve as much information as possible, the rolling regression is started at interval 1, spanning only that interval. In the next step, intervals 1 and 2 are analyzed and, in the next, intervals 1 to 3. The analysis continues in this manner until the regression spans intervals 1 to K, after which the next regression spans intervals 2 to $K + 1$. The regression then steps through the data until intervals $T - t_0 - K$ to $T - t_0$ are analyzed, at which point the analysis is finished.[9]

D. Estimator Precision

Simulated data were created and analyzed using this new econometric method. The results (not reported) confirm that the machine algorithms are accurate and that the method is able to recover underlying factors from nonsynchronous data, even when the data are far less synchronous than actual stock market prices. There is, however, an upper bound on estimator precision as the cross-sectional sample increases for a given interval length. The bound is due to unmodeled intra-interval variation associated with observations which arrive in the middle of an interval. The proportional allocation rule for this variation proposed above

---

[8] If cardinal measures are desired, they can be computed from estimates of the variance of firm-specific variance components since the weighted least-squares estimator is a linear function of the data. Note also that, if there is no nonsynchronous trading, the portfolio values would be known with certainty but not the underlying factor values. Uncertainty about the factor values depends on the number of stocks in the portfolio and on their weighting within the portfolio.

[9] The rolling regressions use a span of sixty-one intervals. A comparison of results from smaller regressions spanning a maximum of fifteen and thirty-one intervals suggests that little would be gained from using a longer span. The factor estimate for interval t used for computing perfect foresight adjustments is taken from the 61st rolling regression if $t \leq 31$, from the $t + 30$th rolling regression if $31 \leq t \leq 735$, and from the 735th regression if $t \geq 735$.

raises, but cannot fully remove, this bound. If the cross-sectional sample is large, overall precision (per unit of time) can be increased by decreasing the analysis interval length. The simulation results and the results reported above showing near equivalence of the two adjustment methods suggest that in this study it is unlikely that estimator noise is a large source of variation relative to variation due to the underlying factor.

REFERENCES

1. Michael D. Atchison, Kirt C. Butler, and Richard B. Simonds. "Nonsynchronous Security Trading and Market Index Autocorrelation." *Journal of Finance* 42 (March 1987), 111–18.
2. Kalman J. Cohen, Steven F. Maier, Robert A. Schwartz, and David K. Whitcomb. "On the Existence of Serial Correlation in an Efficient Securities Market." *TIMS Studies in the Management Sciences* 11 (1979), 151–68.
3. Kalman J. Cohen, Gabriel Hawawini, Steven F. Maier, Robert A. Schwartz, and David K. Whitcomb. "Friction in the Trading Process and the Estimation of Systematic Risk." *Journal of Financial Economics* 12 (August 1983), 263–78.
4. E. Dimson. "Risk Measurement When Shares Are Subject to Infrequent Trading." *Journal of Financial Economics* 7 (June 1979), 197–226.
5. Joseph E. Finnerty and Hun Y. Park. "Does the Tail Wag the Dog?: Stock Index Futures." *Financial Analysts Journal* 43 (March 1987), 57–58.
6. Lawrence Fisher. "Some New Stock Market Indexes." *Journal of Business* 39 (January 1966), 191–225.
7. Ira G. Kawaller, Paul D. Koch, and Timothy W. Koch. "The Extent of Feedback Between S&P 500 Futures Prices and the S&P 500 Index." Working paper, Chicago Mercantile Exchange, 1987.
8. ———. "The Temporal Price Relationship between S&P 500 Futures and the S&P 500 Index." *Journal of Finance* 42 (December 1987), 1309–29.
9. A. Craig MacKinlay and Krishna Ramaswamy. "Index-Futures Arbitrage and the Behavior of Stock Index Futures Prices." *Review of Financial Studies* 1 (Summer 1988), 137–58.
10. Philip R. Perry. "Portfolio Serial Correlation and Nonsynchronous Trading." *Journal of Financial and Quantitative Analysis* 20 (December 1985), 517–23.
11. Myron Scholes and Joseph Williams. "Estimating Betas from Nonsynchronous Data." *Journal of Financial Economics* 5 (December 1977), 309–27.
12. Jay Shanken. "Nonsynchronous Trading and the Covariance-Factor Structure of Returns." *Journal of Finance* 42 (June 1987), 221–31.
13. Hans R. Stoll and Robert E. Whaley. "The Dynamics of Stock Index and Stock Index Futures Prices." Working paper, Owen Graduate School of Management at Vanderbilt University, 1987.

Article 28

The MMI Cash-Futures Spread on October 19, 1987

Gilbert W. Bassett, Jr.
Associate Professor of Economics
University of Illinois at Chicago

Virginia G. France
Assistant Professor of Finance
University of Illinois at Urbana-Champaign

Stanley R. Pliska*
Professor and Chairman of the Department of Finance
University of Illinois at Chicago

*This research was supported by a grant from the Educational Research Foundation of the Chicago Board of Trade. We would like to thank Jen Chin Chen for research assistance, and Ted Doukas who provided the MMI data.

Abstract

On Monday, October 19, 1987, the day of the record stock market decline, the stable spread relationship between stock market indices and their associated futures contracts apparently ceased to exist. For considerable periods of time throughout the day, the futures contracts sold at deep discounts to the value of the indices. The size of the spread was unprecedented and it has received considerable publicity since October 19. The discussion has ranged from the mere observation that the size of the large negative basis was a singular event emerging out of the unusual conditions of the 19th to the possibility that the spread actually played a causal role in setting off and determining the severity of the crash.

The extent to which there actually were discrepancies between the price of futures and stocks at approximately the same time is considered in this paper. The MMI futures contract and its constituent stocks are examined to see whether the large spread was due to the last-trade method used to compute the cash value of the index and, hence, whether there was in fact an actual real-time discount between futures and stocks. Further, the minute-by-minute price movements of each of the stocks is used to test the sensitivity of the spread to slight changes in the time path of reported prices.

The analysis shows that the large discount between the cash value and the price of the futures contract during the opening two hours of trading occurred because Friday prices were being used to estimate the values of unopened stocks. During the rest of the day, the large spread was mostly due to the rapid change in prices. The spread diminishes when the cash value and futures price are compared at about the same time. The large reported spread is, therefore, misleading because prices in the stock and futures markets at about the same time were not far apart from one another.

I. Introduction

On Monday, October 19, 1987, the day of the record stock market decline, the stable relationship between the price of stock index futures and the

Figure 1.   The MMI spread, October 19, 1987

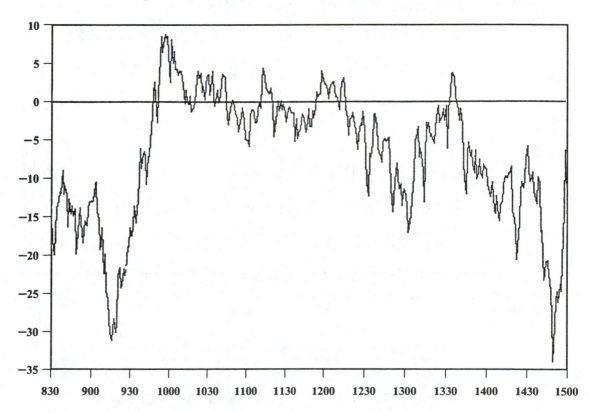

value of the constituent stocks in the indices apparently ceased to exist. For considerable periods of time throughout the day, the futures contracts sold at deep discounts to the value of the indices. Figure 1 depicts the difference between the value of the Major Market Index (MMI) contract and the cash value of its constituent stocks; the spread on the previous trading day is shown in Figure 2.[1] The size of the spread for the MMI as well as other index futures was unprecedented and it has received considerable publicity since October 19. The discussion has ranged from the mere observation that the size of the spread was a singular event emerging out of the unusual conditions of the 19th to the possibility that the spread actually played a causal role in setting off and determining the severity of the crash.[2]

The extent to which there actually were discrepancies between the price of the MMI futures contract and its constituent stocks at approximately the same time on the day of the market crash is considered in this report. The evidence in Figure 1 is not by itself conclusive evidence for the existence of different prices in the two markets at about the same time. One reason for

Figure 2.   The MMI spread, October 16 and 19, 1987

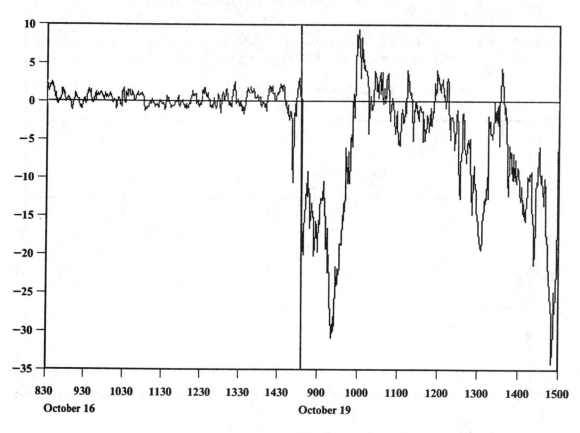

[1]The terms *cash-futures spread, spread, basis,* and *basis spread* have all been used to refer to the difference between the cash value and futures price of a stock index contract. In this report, the term *spread* will usually be used to refer to the cash value-futures difference; it should not be confused with the price differences of contracts in different months.
[2]See Edwards [1988] for an overview of the government reports on the crash.

this is related to the way the value of the cash index is computed. Another reason is related to the behavior of the spread when prices are changing rapidly. Either of these factors can generate a large spread even when conditions are similar in the futures and stock markets.[3]

The spread shown in Figure 1 is based on an estimate of the market index value that is computed using the most recently traded prices of the stocks in the index; see Figure 3 for the cash and futures values on the 19th. This means that the estimated cash value of the index will not necessarily be an accurate measure of the current value of the futures contract when index stocks do not trade. Since prices were changing rapidly and there were gaps in trading, especially at the open, it is possible that the large spread was due to the last-trade method used to estimate the cash value of the index and that there was not an actual real-time discount between futures and stock values.

The possibility that the spread on the 19th was a result of gaps in stock

Figure 3. The MMI futures prices and cash values, October 19, 1987

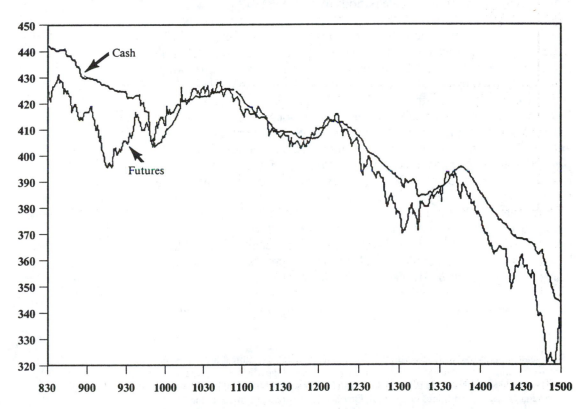

[3]The issue here is not whether arbitrage was feasible on the 19th. In the chaotic conditions of the day, there was no reasonable expectation that trades would be executed, and so arbitrage opportunities were probably nonexistent. Arbitrage, however, is only a sufficient condition for prices in two markets to be about the same. If prices were being influenced by similar information, then we would expect prices in the two markets to be approximately the same even in the absence of any arbitrage.

trading has been investigated previously. It is considered in the government reports that were issued in the aftermath of the crash and also in Harris [1987]. The studies have focused on the S&P 500 futures contract and they have examined transactions on intervals as short as five minutes.

In this report, the MMI futures contract, which is based on 20 stocks, will be examined. The minute-by-minute price movements of each of the stocks and the futures contract will be examined in order to assess the extent to which there were discrepancies between the value of the futures contract and the associated stocks.

The previous studies have found that the bias due to infrequent trading and delayed openings cannot account for all the time periods on the 19th when there was a large negative spread. From the time (10:23) at which all stocks had opened until right before the close, there were no large time intervals in which the MMI stocks did not trade. The cash value of the index was, therefore, being computed with recent price information of the stocks and yet, as shown in Figure 1, the large spread was not confined to the opening.[4] This has led some to conclude that values in the two markets departed from each other for considerable periods of time on the 19th.

The large spread combined with continuous trading does not necessarily mean, however, that values in the two markets were different at about the same period of time. When prices are changing rapidly, the spread can increase if there are only slight differences in the time paths of prices in the two markets. This is illustrated in Figure 4, which shows the spread between prices in two markets increasing even though conditions in the two markets at about the same time (that is, within a few periods of one another) are almost the same. Only minor changes in the time path of prices can give the appearance of a large spread if prices are changing rapidly. If prices are stable, a large spread means that there are large price differences in the two markets. Such differences will not be sensitive to slight changes in the time paths of prices in the two markets due to reporting delays or slight differences in the speed with which new information is incorporated into prices. In a rapidly changing market, however, such slight differences will lead to large spreads even though prices in the markets are similar at the same time.[5]

The sensitivity of the spread to slight changes in reporting conditions or in

---

[4]The situation on the next day when there was also a large spread was quite different. Even after the opening, there were long periods of time when some of the MMI stocks did not trade. For example, IBM did not trade between 10:30 annd 12:26; see the SEC [1988] report for a description of trading conditions on Tuesday, October 20. We are only looking at the 19th in this report because, after the open, trading was fairly continuous, and continuous trading is needed to compute the window-width spreads in Section III.

[5]The sensitivity of the spread to slight differences in the times when stock and futures prices are compared may be due to what Kleidon [1988] calls *stale prices*. Prices are stale when there is a difference between the price of a security at the time of order submission and order execution. This will occur when prices are changing rapidly and can lead to the appearance of large spreads at the short time scales that are considered in this paper.

Figure 4.   Example of a large spread with prices close together

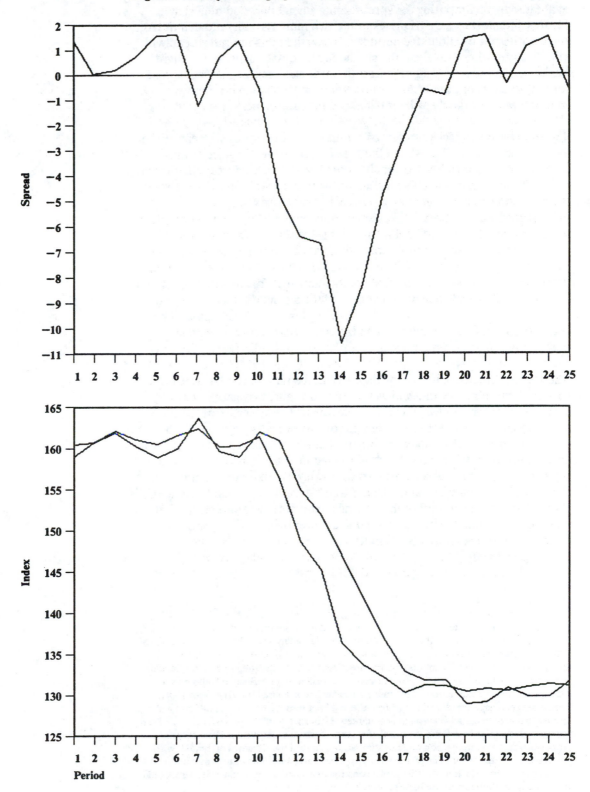

the speed with which information is transmitted to changing prices will be evaluated by recomputing the spread using a neighborhood of nearby futures and stock prices.[6] If prices in the two markets really did depart from one another for considerable periods of time, then this revised spread will still be large. Alternatively, if the spread is found to be sensitive to slight variations in the time path of prices, then the existence of the large spread for long periods of time would not be evidence that values in the two markets were markedly different at about the same time.[7]

The data base for stocks consists of minute-by-minute prices for each of the 20 MMI securities. The data on the MMI stocks were extracted from transaction data on all NYSE stocks, which were obtained from the Francis Emory Fitch Company. The price at each minute was taken as the price of the first listed transaction during that minute; if there was no trade, the price record was left blank. Transaction data on the MMI futures contract were provided by the CBOT. The price of the futures at minute t was taken as the price of the first reported trade during the minute.

Section II describes the open on Monday morning. This covers the first two hours of trading and ends with the open of the last MMI stock at 10:23 (all times are Chicago time). Reasonable assumptions about the values of not-yet-opened stocks are shown to explain the large spreads that were observed during this time period.

The spread during the rest of the day is described in Section III. The first part presents evidence that shows that the bias caused by gaps in trading cannot explain the large spreads after the open. There were simply not enough gaps or gaps of sufficient length for there to be a large bias in the cash value of the MMI index; trading in the MMI stocks after the open was fairly continuous. The second part of the section shows, however, that the large spread during much of this part of the day is sensitive to slight changes in the time paths of the stocks and futures prices. The existence of a large spread during most of the afternoon did not, therefore, mean that values in the markets were far from one another for extended periods of time. Concluding comments are in the final section.

---

[6]Stoll and Whaley [1988] found that since the inception of futures trading the MMI and S&P 500 futures returns have tended to lead stocks by about 5 and sometimes 10 minutes even after returns have been purged of infrequent trading effects. The analysis was based on a time series of 5-minute intraday returns.

[7]It should be noted that the analysis will not directly concern the question of whether futures prices played a causal role in the crash. It is conceivable that short lead-lag relations between the prices in the two markets occur because traders act in one market based on price information coming from the other market. Alternatively, lead-lag relations could exist in the absence of any direct link between the two markets. If the two markets are totally isolated from one another, there will exist lead-lag relations if new information is translated into new prices in one market more rapidly than in the other market. Some of the scenarios presented for the crash require the existence of large differences in prices in the stock and futures markets for lengthy periods of time. If the large spread is sensitive to slight changes in the price series, then these scenarios for the crash will be less likely.

**II. The Open
8:30–10:30**

Table 1 lists the 20 MMI stocks and the times and prices at which they opened on Monday morning. It also shows the price of the last transaction from the previous trading day on Friday. The opening period lasted from 8:30 to 10:23 when the last MMI stock, Exxon, opened. This means that until 10:23 the cash value of the index was utilizing prices of stocks from the previous Friday close. The gap between the last trade prices on Friday and the opening prices on Monday shows that the value of unopened stocks was being biased by the higher Friday prices.

Table 1. MMI stocks

Company Name	Symbol	First trade Time—Oct 19	First trade Price—Oct 19	Last trade Price—Oct 16
Merck & Co.	MRK	9:47	162.00	184.00
Intern. Bus. Mach.	IBM	9:43	124.00	135.00
Phillip Morris	MO	9:48	90.00	102.63
Du Pont	DD	9:51	90.00	98.50
Dow Chemical	DOW	8:48	85.50	88.00
Gen. Motors	GM	8:49	65.38	66.00
Procter & Gamble	PG	8:51	82.00	85.00
Johnson & Johnson	JNJ	8:52	75.00	79.00
Minnesota Mng & Mfg	MMM	8:55	64.00	69.25
Chevron	CHV	8:47	47.50	49.50
Mobil	MOB	8:32	40.88	42.75
Exxon	XON	10:23	40.00	43.50
Eastman Kodak	EK	9:40	76.00	92.13
General Elec.	GE	9:30	42.00	50.75
Intern. Paper	IP	8:44	41.00	45.75
Coca Cola	KO	8:54	36.25	39.75
Sears Roebuck	S	9:58	36.88	41.00
USX	USX	8:35	32.25	34.00
American Tel & Tel	T	8:36	28.38	30.25
American Express	AXP	8:31	28.88	32.00

To determine the extent to which the last-trade index was biased by the use of Friday prices, several alternative indices were computed. These alternatives did not use information from Friday to estimate the value of unopened stocks. Instead, the value of unopened stocks was estimated using information on stocks that were trading and that therefore reflected market conditions on Monday. An illustration of the method used to estimate the values at the open will be presented after first introducing the following notation.[8]

Let t_i denote the minute when the ith MMI stock began trading and let $Z(t)$

---

[8]The estimated prices of the unopened stocks are based on only the distribution of the opened stocks—we did not use betas or the correlations within the portfolio of MMI stocks or between MMI and other stocks. We suspect that this additional information would not change our conclusions about the spread at the opening. Such an analysis is needed, however, for analyzing events on Tuesday when the gaps in trading were much more numerous and lengthy than on Monday.

denote the set of MMI stocks that opened prior to time t. A minute-by-minute price series

$$P_i(t), t = t_i, t_{i+1}, t_{i+2}, \ldots$$

for each of the opened MMI stocks was constructed by filling in any trading gaps with last-trade prices. (Prior to 10:23, there were two gaps of four minutes, one gap of three minutes, and all other gaps for opened MMI stocks were two minutes or less).

For each opened stock, the price relative to 10:23 was computed for each minute

$$r_i(t) = P_i(t)/P_i(10:23), \qquad t_i < t < 10:23,$$

where $P_i(t)$ denotes the price of stock i at minute t.[9] Finally, the distribution of price changes of the opened stocks at time t is denoted by $D(t)$ where

$$D(t) = \{r_i(t)|i\varepsilon Z(t)\} \qquad 8:30 < t < 10:23.$$

The price changes of the unopened stocks are estimated using the minimum, the average, and the maximum of the price change distribution. The average provides an estimate of central tendency, while the maximum and minimum provide bounds on the values of unopened stocks. The index value is then computed using the estimated values of unopened stocks and the actual prices of trading stocks. The estimation method is explained in the following example.

Example

To illustrate how the values of unopened stocks were estimated, consider the following simple example of an index that is just the ordinary average of three stocks. Table 2 shows the illustrative data for the periods prior to the time that all stocks open. It also shows the previous close of each stock as well as the index value based on a last-trade index. The two features of the 19th that are included in the illustrative data are the delayed openings and the lower prices at the open compared to the previous close.

The 10:23 time at which all MMI stocks had opened corresponds in this example to period 5. Stock A begins trading at the open of trading, stock B does not open until period 3, and stock C does not open until period 5. This means that until period 5 the last trade index value is being computed using at least one price from the previous close.

Tables 2B and 2C show the price changes of the index stocks relative to period 5. Also shown are the minimum, average, and maximum values of

[9]This procedure makes the price change distribution sensitive to the stock prices at exactly 10:23. An alternative would have been to use an average price around 10:23 and thereby smooth out any large price changes that occurred at the exact 10:23 minute. The price changes of the individual stocks around 10:23 are, however, not large and it did not seem that the use of a smoothed price series would alter the price change distribution.

Table 2. Example

(A) Price data

Period	Stock A	B	C	Index value
prev. close	52	105	77	78.00
1	50	—	—	77.33
2	49	—	—	77.00
3	48	100	—	75.00
4	46	98	—	73.67
5	47	95	75	72.33
6	45	94	75	71.33

(B) Price changes relative to period five

Period	Stock A	B	C
1	50/47	—	—
2	49/47	—	—
3	48/47	100/95	—
4	46/47	98/95	—
5	47/47	95/95	75/75

(C) Distribution of price changes

Period	Stock A	B	C	Min	Ave	Max
1	1.06	—	—	1.06	1.06	1.06
2	1.04	—	—	1.04	1.04	1.04
3	1.02	1.05	—	1.02	1.035	1.05
4	0.98	1.03	—	0.98	1.005	1.03
5	1.00	1.00	1.00			

(D) Estimated stock values*

Period	Stock A	B	C
1	50	1.06×95	1.06×75
2	49	1.04×95	1.04×75
3	48	100	1.035×75
4	46	98	1.005×75
5	47	95	75

Estimated index values*

Period	Stock A	B	C	Index value
1	50	100.7	79.5	76.73
2	49	98.8	78	75.27
3	48	100	77.625	75.21
4	46	98	75.375	73.13
5	47	95	75	72.33
6	45	94	75	71.33

*Using the average of the price change distribution

(E) Estimated index values

Period	Min	Ave	Max	Last trade
1	76.73	76.73	76.73	77.33
2	75.27	75.27	75.27	77.00
3	74.83	75.21	75.58	75.00
4	72.50	73.13	73.75	73.67
5	72.33	72.33	72.33	72.33

the price change distribution. Each row of the table determines $D(t)$, the distribution of price changes of those stocks that had already opened.

The estimates of the values of the not-yet-opened stocks are shown in Table 2D. The estimates are computed using the average of the price change distribution. For example, at period 3, there are two opened stocks. These two stocks were trading during period 3 at prices that were on average 3.5 percent higher than at period 5. Since the price of stock C at period 5 is 75, its estimated value at period 3 using this average of opened stocks is $1.035 \times 75 = 77.625$. The table shows how the values of the unopened stocks at other times were estimated.

Table 2E shows the estimated index values using the average and also the minimum and maximum values of the distribution of opened stocks. It illustrates the differences that can exist between the last-trade index and estimated indices that use information on only opened stocks.

The method used to construct estimated values for unopened stocks and the MMI index is identical to that shown in the example except that there are 20 rather than 3 stocks and there are 113 (minutes) rather than 5 periods before all stocks begin trading.

Figure 5.   MMI spread at the open, last trade and average of trading stocks

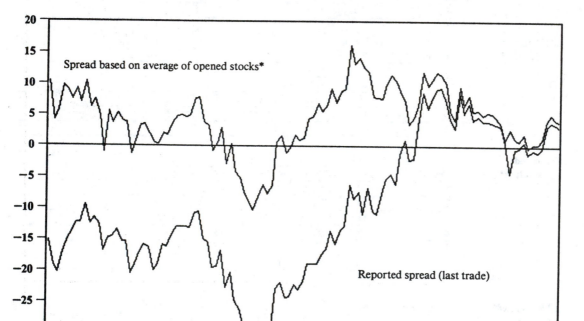

*See description in text

Figure 5 shows the spread at the open that results when the prices of the unopened stocks are estimated using the mean or average of the $D(t)$ distribution; Figure 6 shows the corresponding value of the index. The estimated value of each unopened stock, $P_i(t)$, $t < t_i$, is given by

$$P_i(t) = a(t)P_i(10{:}23)$$

where $a(t)$ is the mean or average of the price change distribution $D(t)$. The value of the MMI index was computed by summing the actual and estimated prices of the index stocks and dividing by 3.18322, the MMI divisor that was valid on October 19.[10]

Figures 5 and 6 show that the cash and futures prices track far better than when the last-trade cash index is computed with Friday prices. This occurs because the cash value of the index is being estimated using only the information from Monday the 19th.

Figure 6. MMI estimated cash value at the open using the average of trading stocks

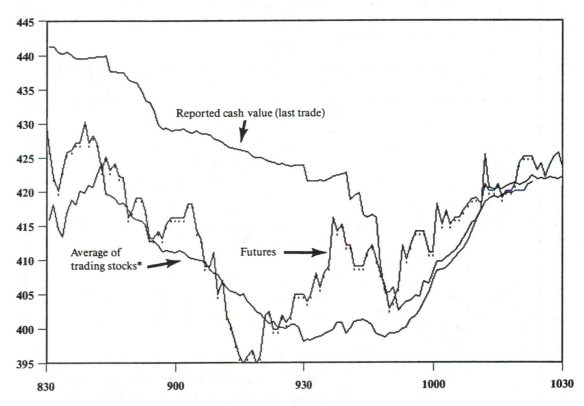

*See description in text

[10]The MMI, like the Dow Jones Industrial Average that it was designed to mimic, is just a scaled summation of stock prices. This differs from other indices (e.g., the S&P 500) that are based on the total value of outstanding shares of stock. The MMI method means that the index is influenced most by high-priced stocks (IBM and Merck) and least by low-priced stocks, even if the total value of outstanding shares is large (e.g., AT&T).

Figure 7 shows the estimated value of the index that results when the minimum and maximum values of the price change distribution are used to estimate the values of unopened stocks. As in the illustrative example, the upper bound on $P_i(t)$ for $t < t_i$ is given by

$$P_i(t) = \max\{D(t)\}P_i(10:23)$$

and similarly for the minimum estimate of $P_i(t)$. Using these maximum and minimum estimates yields the minimum and maximum estimates of the index shown in Figure 7. It shows that throughout most of the opening two hours the futures contract traded within the upper and lower estimates of the futures contract value.

Figure 7.   MMI estimated cash value, using the max and min of trading stocks

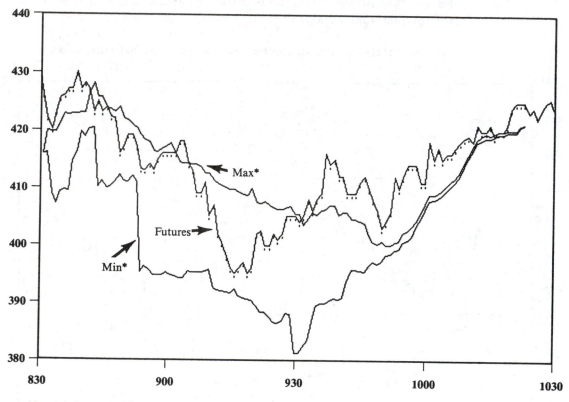

*See description in text

The estimates of the futures index value derived from Monday price information provide persuasive support for the position that the large spread at the opening was not due to different values in the futures and stock markets. The higher Friday prices included in the last trade-based estimate of the futures contract caused it to overstate the value of the index. This finding, using minute-by-minute transaction data, is similar to that in the government reports on the crash where transactions were examined at five-minute and longer intervals.

III. The Spread from 10:30 to 15:00	The first part of this section presents evidence that shows that trading gaps were not long enough or numerous enough to account for the large spread after the open. The second part examines the sensitivity of the spread to slight changes in the time path of futures and stock prices.
Trading Gaps	Summary data on gaps in trading are presented in Table 3 and Figure 8. Table 3 shows for each MMI stock the number of minutes during each half hour when there were no transactions. For example, IBM traded in all but two minutes in the half hour after 12:30. The table shows that each MMI stock traded in about 80 percent of the minutes during the day. (The only long trading gap occurred for Merck, which did not trade for a period of 28 minutes in the hour after 2:00). The half-hour pattern of trading for most of the stocks remained constant until just prior to the close.

Figure 8 shows the frequency of all gaps. It shows that there were very few gaps longer than three minutes. The figure reveals that there was fairly continuous trading in all of the MMI stocks. This continuous trading means that the kind of reasoning used to explain the large spread at the open cannot be used to account for the large spreads observed during the rest of the trading day.

Further evidence for continuous trading is provided by a comparison of the last-trade index and another index based on a look ahead at a stock's next transaction price. The bias caused by infrequent trading in a next-trade index will be equal in magnitude but opposite in sign to the bias of the standard last-trade estimate. The numerical difference between the two

Table 3. Nontrading minutes by half hour

Time	MRK	IBM	MO	DOW	PG	DD	JNJ	MMM	GM	EK	GE	IP
10:30–10:59	3	0	4	4	2	4	9	6	8	3	4	2
11:00–11:29	4	0	2	2	5	7	2	6	3	3	4	7
11:30–11:59	8	1	5	8	4	7	1	4	3	1	1	9
12:00–12:29	4	0	4	4	5	5	5	5	5	3	1	7
12:30–12:59	9	2	4	4	3	10	10	5	5	4	6	1
1:00–1:29	7	1	7	7	12	11	12	7	3	15	4	5
1:30–1:59	3	0	3	3	4	10	4	8	3	2	5	3
2:00–2:30	12	1	3	6	2	8	6	1	2	3	3	2
2:30–3:00	22	2	4	3	7	5	3	2	0	8	2	5

Time	XON	KO	CHV	MOB	S	X	T	AXP	Total	Pct.
10:30–10:59	5	9	7	19	9	7	5	2	112	18.7
11:00–11:29	8	11	7	6	14	7	8	1	107	17.8
11:30–11:59	7	7	8	11	18	12	11	2	128	21.3
12:00–12:29	5	5	9	9	15	10	4	2	107	17.8
12:30–12:59	15	14	3	5	11	4	1	3	119	19.8
1:00–1:29	10	6	14	15	18	5	5	4	168	28.0
1:30–1:59	4	5	6	5	7	3	1	3	82	13.7
2:00–2:30	2	6	7	3	12	1	0	4	84	14.0
2:30–3:00	9	2	9	3	9	6	0	4	105	17.5

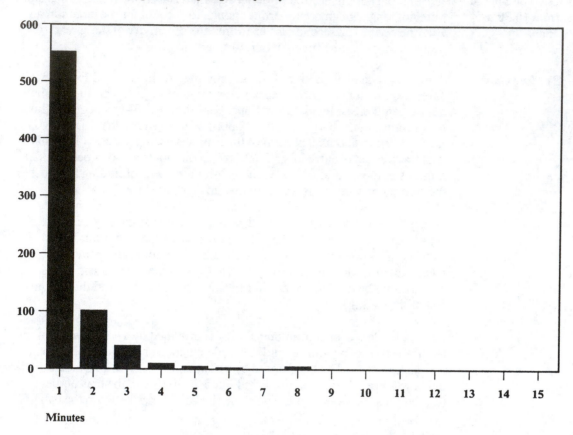

Figure 8.   Gap length frequency

Minutes

There was one gap of 28 minutes.

estimates will indicate the times when stocks were trading infrequently and with large price differences between subsequent trades.

Figure 9 depicts the difference between the last- and next-trade estimates of the index value. The difference is seen to be negligible during most of the day. It reaches a maximum of only about 4 points. This is far smaller than the spread of 15 and more points using the last-trade estimate. The large spread would, therefore, still exist if the cash value of the index was computed using a next-trade index. The large spread evidently is not explained by the bias caused by nontrading stocks.

The evidence in Figure 10 is similar. The figure depicts the spread between the MMI futures price and an estimate of the cash value that is computed at only those times when all MMI stocks have recently traded. At such times, there will be little bias from untraded stocks and the spread should be near zero. The gaps in the picture correspond to the times when there was at least one MMI stock that had not traded for five or more minutes. At all other times, every MMI stock has traded within the past four minutes. The figure shows the spread that results at only the times when all of the MMI stocks have recently traded. It shows that the spread is still large; it is

Figure 9. The difference between next and last trade indices

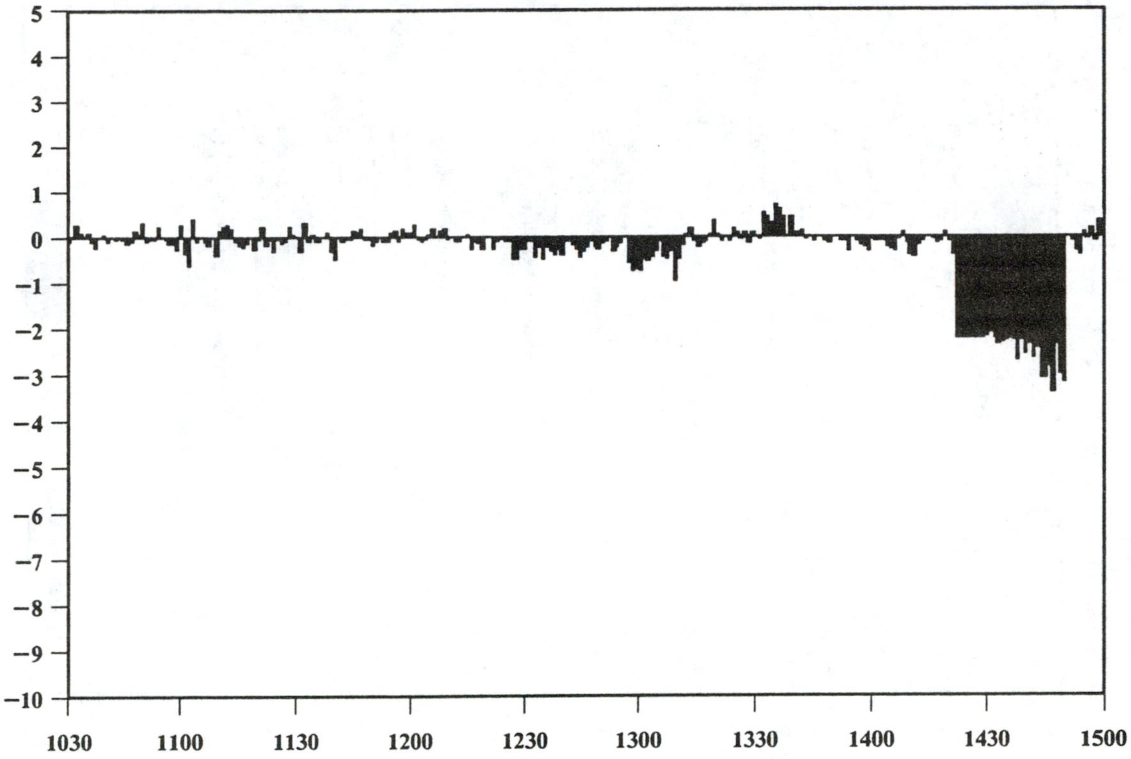

Vertical axis measures next-trade index minus last-trade index

again about 15 points in the early afternoon and about 25 points near the close. The figure shows again that the large spread after the open cannot be associated with any bias from untraded stocks. When every MMI stock is trading, there is still a large difference between the reported futures and stock prices.

The large spread recorded after all stocks had opened could not have been due to the bias of the last-trade-based estimate of the index value. The trading gaps were not long enough for the last-trade index to become a biased estimate of real-time conditions in the stock market. The next-trade index, which should have the opposite bias, still leaves a large negative spread. Further, the large spread exists when attention is restricted to only those times when trading in all MMI stocks was nearly continuous.

Window-Width Spreads

As suggested in the introduction, the large spread combined with continuous trading does not by itself imply that futures and stock values were significantly different at about the same time. Slight differences in the time paths of futures and stock prices coupled with steep price trends can generate pictures that show a large spread existing for long periods of time. The misleading impression from the picture is a large and persistent divergence in prices when, in fact, the prices in the two markets are close

Figure 10. MMI estimated spread, using only recent prices of all stocks

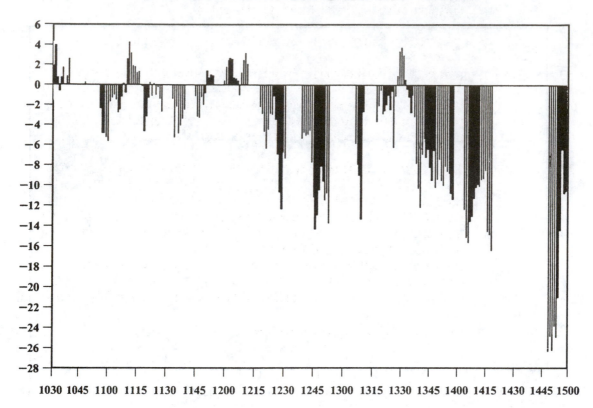

together. We examine this possibility by examining the sensitivity of the spread to slight changes in the time paths of the futures and stock prices.

The cash value of the MMI contract at minute t is denoted by $M^*(t)$. This series was made continuous (minute-by-minute) by using last-trade prices of the stocks that did not trade during a minute. (As explained above, the nearly continuous trading after the open means that the series is not strongly dependent on the use of last-trade prices; a next-trade or interpolation-based index would lead to essentially the same continuous price series.)[11] The price of the futures contract at time t is denoted by $F(t)$. Except for three different minutes, the contract traded in every minute during the trading day; the series was made continuous using previous trades for the minutes when the contract was not traded.

The sensitivity of the spread to slight variations in the time paths of prices is measured by what is called a *window-width spread*. The window width is measured by a parameter w that measures the length of the time interval on

[11]A continuous price series is needed to compute the window-width spread. While such a series can be constructed for prices on Monday, it cannot be done for the next day because the trading gaps preclude reasonable estimates (using anything other than the futures contract itself) of stock values during the extended gaps in trading.

which the two price series are compared. The window-width spread of
length w is denoted by $s_w(t)$ and it is defined as

$$s_w(t) \;=\; \min\{\,|F(\tau) - M^*(\tau')|: \tau \varepsilon t(w),\; \tau' \varepsilon t(w)\}$$

where $t(w)$ is the interval $[t - w, t + w]$. The spread $s_w(t)$ is necessarily
decreasing in w and, at $w = 0$, it is identical to the usual spread. It measures
the minimum difference between the cash and futures prices for any two,
possibly different, times between $t - w$ and $t + w$. We will examine window-
width spreads with w set at 5 and 10 minutes.

The sensitivity of the usual spread to changes in the price paths in the two
markets is indicated by the size of $s_w(t)$ as a function of w. If small values of
w eliminate the spread, then only slight shifts in the time paths of the
futures and stock prices can account for the size of the spread. Contrary to
the impression given by Figure 1, this would mean that futures and stocks,
while being considerably different at *exactly* the same minute, were actually
close together within a few minutes of each other. Conversely, if the spread
stays large as w increases, then slight changes in the time paths will not
account for the large spread. This would be the best evidence for genuine

Figure 11. Window-width spread, 5 minutes

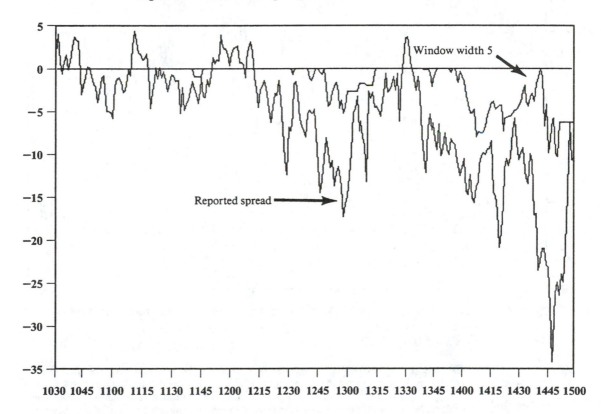

discrepancies between the futures and stock prices over extended time periods.[12]

Figures 11 and 12 depict the window-width spreads using $w = 5$ and $w = 10$ minutes. The 5-minute window width eliminates most of the spread that existed between noon and 1:30. The large spread that existed during the last hour of trading is reduced but is still substantial with this window. Using a 10-minute window eliminates the spread in the last hour except for short time periods at about 2:20 and right before the close.

IV. Conclusions   First, the large reported spread on Monday morning was primarily due to the delayed opening of the MMI stocks. The cash value of the MMI index computed using Monday morning price information (rather than the previous Friday closing prices) does not exhibit a large discount from the futures price.

Figure 12.   Window-width spread, 10 minutes

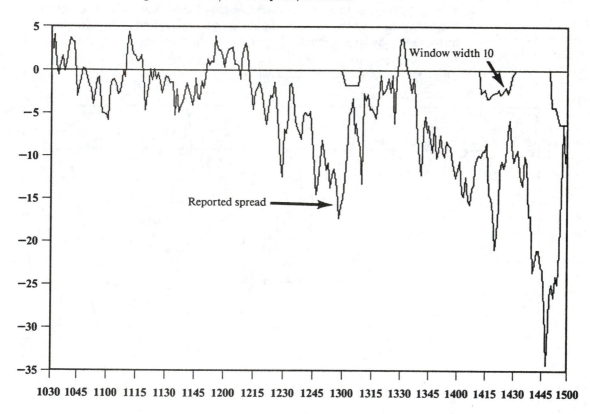

[12]A better, but more complicated, way to measure the sensitivity of the spread to slight shifts in the time paths of prices would be to compute a "nearby" cash price of the futures contract using nearby prices for the individual stock prices. That is, instead of perturbing the cash value of the index by $\pm w$ minutes, a range of cash values would be computed using $(\Sigma P_i(t + \tau) | -w < \tau < w)$. When this estimate was evaluated for selected minutes, it did not give very different values than the window-width spreads using $M^*(t)$, and we, therefore, used the simpler method.

Second, during the rest of the day, the gaps in trading were not large enough or numerous enough to account for the spread. The spread stays large when the cash value of the index is recomputed in a number of different ways designed to minimize the impact of gaps in trading.

Third, for much of the trading day, the futures and stock prices were close together at about the same time despite the fact that the instantaneous spread stayed large for extended periods. An exception to this occurred in the last hour of trading when futures traded below stocks even after allowing a 10-minute period for the prices to come in line with one another.

Finally, it should be noted that we have not considered the reason why asset values fell by over 20 percent on the 19th. Our findings support the position that the futures and stock prices tended to move together and stay at comparable (and falling) levels on the day of the market crash. Since the large spread was due to gaps at the open and to rapid, but not perfectly correlated, price changes in the futures and stock markets, the hypothesis that the large spread played a causal role in the events of the 19th is not supported or it has to be combined with the dubious assumption that investors perceived different price behavior when none existed. Alternatively, other explanations for the crash that do not rely on price differences at about the same time in the futures and stock markets must be examined as possible causes of the crash.

References

"Analysis of Trading on the Chicago Board of Trade's Major Market Index Futures Contract on October 20, 1987." Commodity Futures Trading Commission, January 4, 1988a, mimeo.

Edwards, F.R. "Studies of the 1987 Stock Market Crash: Review and Appraisal." Center for the Study of Futures Markets. Working Paper CSFM-#168, 1988.

"Final Report on Stock Index Futures and Cash Market Activity During October 1987." Commodity Trading Futures Commission, January 1988b, mimeo.

Harris, L.J. "The October 1987 S&P 500 Stock-Futures Basis." *The Journal of Finance* 44(1)(1989), pp. 77–100.

Kleidon, A.W. "Arbitrage, Nontrading, and Stale Prices: October 1987." 1988, mimeo.

Stoll, H.R., and R.E. Whaley. The Dynamics of Stock Index and Stock Index Futures Returns." Futures and Options Research Center, Duke University, Working Paper No. 88-101, 1988.

"The October 1987 Market Break." A Report by the Division of Market Regulation, U.S. Securities and Exchange Commission, February 1988.

Article 29

G. J. Santoni

G. J. Santoni is a senior economist at the Federal Reserve Bank of St. Louis. Thomas A. Pollmann provided research assistance.

The October Crash: Some Evidence on the Cascade Theory

"It's the nearest thing to a meltdown that I ever want to see."
John J. Phelan, Jr., Chairman of the New York Stock Exchange

THE record one-day decline in stock prices on October 19, 1987, stripped roughly 22 percent from stock values. More disconcerting, however, were the speed of the adjustment, the tumultuous trading activity in financial markets and the uncertainty that prevailed during the week of October 19. These aspects of the crash bore a surprising resemblance to previous financial panics that many thought were historical artifacts outmoded by modern regulatory and surveillance systems as well as by advances in the financial sophistication of market participants. The crash shocked this complacency and reawakened considerable interest in financial panics and their causes.

As with its 1929 predecessor, the list of popular explanations for the panic of 1987 runs the gamut from the purely economic and financial to the frailties inherent in human nature (see opposite page). Recently, a number of more-or-less official

investigating agencies have released reports about the October panic.[1] Generally speaking, these reports do not attempt to identify the reason for the decline in stock prices. Rather, they focus on the factors that characterized it as a panic: the *sharpness* of the decline on October 19 and the *tumultuous* trading activity that occurred on this day and during the following week.

Virtually all of the reports agree that the inability of the New York and other cash market exchanges to process the unprecedented volume of trades quickly contributed importantly to the market turmoil. They disagree widely, however, about the reasons for the sharpness of the decline.

The Brady Commission Report attributes the downward "cascade" in stock prices to programmed trading — more specifically, to the trading strategies known as index arbitrage and portfo-

---

[1] See, for example, the *Report of the Presidential Task Force on Market Mechanisms* (1988); U.S. General Accounting Office (1988); U.S. Commodity Futures Trading Commission (1988); and the report of Miller, Hawke, Malkiel and Scholes (1987).

Article 29   The October Crash: Some Evidence on the Cascade Theory—*Santoni*   **461**

Some Popular Notions Regarding the Crash of '87

"Wall Street has supplanted Las Vegas, Atlantic City, Monte Carlo and Disneyland as the place where dreams are made, where castles appear in the clouds. It was Pinocchio's Pleasure Island, where children (and the adults whose bodies they inhabited) could do and have whatever they wanted, whenever they wanted it.

But now it's morning and the binge seems to be over. Many have hangovers. Many have worse. The jackasses are clearly identifiable. And the rest of us, who pretended not to notice, are left with the job of cleaning up the mess."

> Robert B. Reich, *New York Times*
> (October 22, 1987)

"People are beginning to see that the five-year bull market of the Eighties was a new Gatsby age, complete with the materialism and euphoric excesses of all speculative eras. Like the Jazz Age of F. Scott Fitzgerald's . . ., the years combined the romance of wealth and youth with the slightly sinister aura of secret understandings."

> William Glaberson, *New York Times*
> (December 13, 1987)

"We've been through quite a few years in which we felt we had reached the millennium, which was high rewards and no risk. We are now understanding that that is not the case."

> Peter G. Peterson, *New York Times*
> (December 13, 1987)

"Ultimately, we will view this period as one in which we made a very important mistake. What we did was divorce our financial system from reality."

> Martin Lipton, *New York Times*
> (December 13, 1987)

"Investors knew that stocks were overpriced by any traditional valuation measure such as price/earnings ratios and price to book value. They also knew that the combination of program trading and portfolio insurance could send prices plummeting."

> Anise C. Wallace, *New York Times*
> (November 3, 1987)

"On Monday, October 19, Wall Street's legendary herd instincts, now embedded in digital code and amplified by hundreds of computers, helped turn a sell-off into a panic."

> David E. Sanger, *New York Times*
> (December 15, 1987)

"Futures and options are like barnacles on a ship. They take their life from the pricing of stocks and bonds. When the barnacles start steering the ship, you get into trouble, as we saw last week."

> Marshall Front, *Christian Science Monitor*
> (October 30, 1987)

"One trader's gain is another's loss, and the costs of feeding computers and brokers are a social waste."

> Louis Lowenstien, *New York Times*
> (May 11, 1988).

"We probably would have had only a 100- to 150-point drop if it hadn't been for computers."

> Frederick Ruopp, *Christian Science Monitor* (October 30, 1987)

"This [restrictions on programmed trading] will make it a market where the individual investor can tread without fear of the computers."

> Edward A. Greene, *New York Times*
> (November 3, 1987).

"In my mind, we should start by banning index option arbitrage and then proceed with other reforms which will restore public confidence in the financial markets. The public has every reason to believe that the present game is rigged. It is. Many would be better off in a casino since there people expect to lose but have a good meal and a good time while they're doing it."

> Donald Regan, U.S. Senate Hearing, Committee on Banking, Housing and Urban Affairs (May 24, 1988, pp. 76–77).

The Trading Strategies

Portfolio insurance is an investment strategy that attempts to insure a return for large portfolios above some acceptable minimum. For example, if the acceptable minimum return is 8 percent and the portfolio is currently returning 13 percent, the portfolio's managers may want to decrease the share of the portfolio held in bonds and cash, which are safe but yield relatively low returns, and increase the share of the portfolio held in higher-yielding stock. This increases the expected return of the portfolio but exposes it to more risk. On the other hand, a stock price decline that reduced the return of the portfolio to, say, 10 percent puts the return close to the minimum. In this event, the managers may want to reduce the risk exposure of the portfolio. This can be accomplished by reducing the share of the portfolio held in stock and increasing the shares held in cash and bonds.[1]

This strategy results in stock purchases when stock prices rise significantly and stock sales when stock prices decline significantly.[2] Initially, these portfolio adjustments typically are made by trading in stock index futures, because the transaction cost for large baskets of stock are lower in futures than in the cash market.[3]

Index arbitrage is a trading strategy based on simultaneous trades of stock index futures and the corresponding basket of stocks in the cash market. This trading strategy attempts to profit from typically small and short-lived price discrepancies for the same group of stocks in the cash and futures markets.

Cash and futures prices for the same stock or group of stocks typically differ. The difference — called the basis — results from the "cost of carrying" stocks over the time interval spanned by the futures contract. These costs depend on the relevant interest rate and the dividends the stocks are expected to pay during the interval. On occasion, the observed basis may diverge from the cost of carry. If so, arbitrageurs can expect to profit *if simultaneous trades* can be placed in the two markets — purchasing the relatively low-priced instrument and selling the relatively high-priced instrument. These trades move the basis back to the cost of carry.

---

[1]See Miller, Hawke, Malkiel and Scholes (1987), p. 12.

[2]The purpose of this paper is not to evaluate the wisdom of these trading strategies. Rather, it is to evaluate the proposition that they contributed importantly to the panic.

[3]For example, the transaction costs of trading one futures contract based on the Standard and Poor's 500 are about

$500 lower than trading the equivalent basket of stocks in the cash market. See Miller, Hawke, Malkiel and Scholes (1987), p. 11, and U.S. General Accounting Office (1988), p. 20.

---

lio insurance (see above for a discussion of these strategies).[2] This conclusion, however, is questioned seriously in reports filed by the Commodity Futures Trading Commission (CFTC) and Chicago Mercantile Exchange (CME).[3] These reports attribute the swift decline in stock prices to a massive revision in investors' perceptions of the fundamental determinants of stock prices.[4] Furthermore, since different rules govern trading in the cash and futures markets, a careful analysis of the effect of these different rules may better explain the evidence advanced by the Brady Commission in support of the cascade theory.[5]

This paper examines minute-by-minute price data gathered from the cash and futures market for stocks from October 15–23 to determine if the data are best explained by the cascade theory or the different trading rules in the two markets.

Resolving this issue is important because of the legislative and regulatory proposals spawned by the October panic. For example, the regulatory

---

[2]See the *Report of the Presidential Task Force on Market Mechanisms* (1988), pp. v, 15, 21, 29, 30 and 34–36.

[3]See U.S. Commodity Futures Trading Commission (1988), pp. iv, v, viii and 38–138 (especially p. 137); and Miller, Hawke, Malkiel and Scholes (1987), pp. 6, 8, 10–11, 41–43 and 55–56.

[4]See U.S. Commodity Futures Trading Commission (1988), p. ix; and Miller, Hawke, Malkiel and Scholes (1987), p. 6.

[5]See Miller, Hawke, Malkiel and Scholes (1987), pp. 21–23, 25, 37 and 49–50.

proposals advanced by the Brady Commission include:

(1) One agency to coordinate regulatory issues that have an impact across all financial markets;

(2) Unified clearing systems across related financial markets;

(3) Consistent margin requirements in the cash and futures markets;

(4) Circuit breaker mechanisms (such as price limits and coordinated trading halts); and

(5) Integrated information systems across related financial markets.[6]

Proposals 3 and 4 clearly reflect the Commission's belief that programmed trading contributed significantly to the panic. Furthermore, the action taken by the New York Stock Exchange (NYSE) to restrict use of its Designated Order Turnaround (DOT) system by program traders suggests that the officials of this exchange also subscribe to the Brady Commission's explanation.[7] This belief was reaffirmed more recently. Beginning February 4, 1988, the NYSE has denied use of the DOT system to program traders whenever the Dow Jones Industrial Average moves up or down by more than 50 points from its previous day's close.

THE CASCADE THEORY

The Brady Commission suggests that the stock market panic is best explained by the "cascade theory." This theory argues that "mechanical, price-insensitive selling" by institutions using portfolio insurance strategies contributed significantly to the break in stock prices.[8] In an effort to liquidate the equity exposure of their portfolios quickly, these institutions sold stock index futures contracts in the Chicago market. Such sales lowered the price of the futures contracts *relative* to the price of the equivalent basket of stocks in the New York cash market. The decline in the futures price relative to the cash price induced index arbitrageurs to purchase futures contracts in the Chicago market (which, in their view, were undervalued) and sell (short) the underlying stocks in

the New York market (which, in their view, were overvalued relative to futures). Thus, index arbitrage transmitted the selling pressure from the Chicago futures market to the New York cash market causing cash prices in New York to decline.

The story does not end here. According to the theory, the decline in cash prices triggered a further selling wave in the Chicago market by portfolio insurers that index arbitrageurs, again, transmitted to the New York market. This process was repeated time after time causing a "downward cascade" in stock prices.[9]

The Brady Commission suggests that support for the cascade theory can be found by examining the behavior of the spread (the basis) between the price of stock index futures contracts and the cash prices of the shares underlying the contracts.[10] The basis is normally positive. Stock index futures prices generally exceed cash prices because the net costs of carrying stock forward (interest cost less expected dividends) are typically positive.[11] During the panic, however, the basis turned negative. The Commission suggests that this observation is consistent with the cascade theory.

Chart 1 plots both the price of the December Standard and Poor's 500 futures contract and the Standard and Poor's index of 500 common stocks. The latter represents the cash price of the stocks underlying the futures contract. The data cover half-hour intervals during October 15–23, 1987. Chart 2 plots the basis — the difference between the two prices shown in chart 1. As one can see, the basis fell below zero in the late afternoon of October 16 and, with a few exceptions, remained negative for the rest of the week. In the Brady Commission's view, this evidence provides important support for the cascade theory.

THERE IS LESS TO THE CASCADE THEORY THAN MEETS THE EYE

The Negative Basis

As mentioned, proponents of the cascade theory suggest that their theory is supported by the nega-

---

[6]*Report of the Presidential Task Force on Market Mechanisms* (1988), p. vii.

[7]The DOT System is a high-speed, order-routing system that program traders use to execute simultaneous trades in the cash and futures markets.

[8]*Report of the Presidential Task Force on Market Mechanisms* (1988), p. v.

[9]*Ibid.*, pp. 15, 17, 21, 30–36 and 69. It is apparent that our knowledge of stock market panics has advanced considerably

in the 58 years since the 1929 crash. "Black Tuesday" was caused by a downward price "spiral." "Bloody Monday" was a "cascade."

[10]*Report of the Presidential Task Force on Market Mechanisms* (1988), pp. III.1–III.26, especially III.16–III.22.

[11]See Figlewski (1984), pp. 658–60; Burns (1979), pp. 31–57; Cornell and French (1983), pp. 2–4; Modest and Sundaresan (1983), pp. 22–23; Santoni (1987), pp. 23–25; Schwarz, Hill and Schneeweis (1986), pp. 326–46; Working (1977); Kawaller, Koch and Koch (1987), p. 1311.

Chart 1
Cash and December Futures

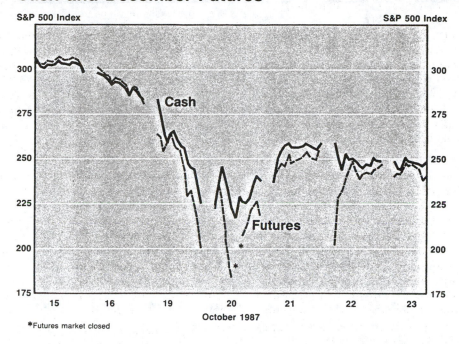

S&P 500 Index

S&P 500 Index

Cash

Futures

*

*

15   16   19   20   21   22   23

October 1987

*Futures market closed

Chart 2
Basis = December Futures – Cash

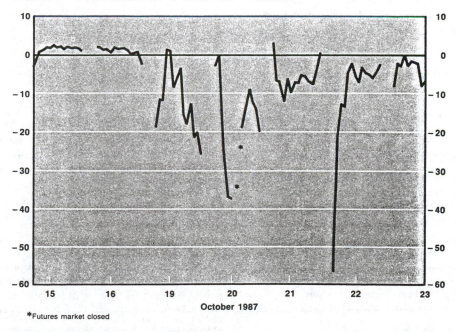

*

*

15   16   19   20   21   22   23

October 1987

*Futures market closed

Table 1

Calculating the Basis

Panel A

Assumptions:

$$D_t = \$1.00$$

$$g = 5.0\%$$

$$E_tD_{t+1} = D_t(1+g) = \$1.05$$

$$r = 11\%$$

(1) $P_t = E_tD_{t+1}/(r-g) = \$1.05/.06 = \$17.50$

(2) $E_tP_{t+1} = P_t(1+r) - E_tD_{t+1} = \$17.50(1.11) - \$1.05 = \$18.38$

(3) $B = E_tP_{t+1} - P_t = \$18.38 - \$17.50 = \$ .88$

Panel B

Assumptions: Same as A except $g' = 3.0\%$

(1) $P'_t = E_tD'_{t+1}/(r-g') = \$1.03/.08 = \$12.88$

(2) $E_tP'_{t+1} = P'_t(1+r) - E_tD'_{t+1} = \$12.88(1.11) - \$1.03 = \$13.27$

(3) $B' = E_tP'_{t+1} - P'_t = \$13.27 - \$12.88 = \$ .39$

where:

D_t = the current dividend

E_tD_{t+1} = the expected dividend at year end

P_t = the current share price

g = the expected growth rate in dividends

r = the relevant long-term interest rate

---

tive basis observed on the afternoon of October 16 and on subsequent trading days during the week of October 19. However, a negative basis does not necessarily support the cascade theory.

Panel A of table 1 calculates the current price of a stock, P_t, assuming that the currently observed dividend, D_t, is $1; the long-term interest rate, r, is 11 percent and the expected growth rate in dividends, g, is 5 percent.[12] Under these assumptions, the current price of the stock is $17.50(= $1.05/ [.11 − .05]). In addition, panel A calculates the expected price of the stock one year from now, E_tP_{t+1}. This expected price is the amount to which P_t would grow if invested at r less the dividend expected at the end of the year, E_tD_{t+1}.[13] This amount is $18.38(= $17.50[1.11] − $1.05). Assuming that arbitrageurs are rational and that transaction costs are very low, the basis between the price of a futures contract dated to mature in one year and the current cash price of the stock is the difference between the expected price of the stock one year from now and its current price, $.88(= $18.38 − $17.50).

Panel B performs similar calculations assuming that the expected growth rate in dividends, g, falls from 5 percent to 3 percent, while everything else

---

[12]See Brealey (1983), pp. 67–72.

[13]The example assumes that the yield curve is flat.

remains constant. Notice that this results in a decline in the current price of the stock from $17.50 to $12.88, a reduction of about 30 percent. Furthermore, since the expected price of the stock one year from now falls to $13.27, the basis falls to $.39(= $13.27 − $12.88). Other things the same, a decline in the expected growth rate of dividends causes a decline in the current price, the futures price and the basis. For reasons discussed later, futures prices typically respond to new information more rapidly than indexes of cash market prices. This was particularly so during the crash. In terms of our example, if the futures price declines immediately to $13.27 but cash prices adjust less quickly, the *observed* basis may be negative during the adjustment period. In short, there is no need for a special theory, like the cascade theory, to explain the behavior of the basis during the week of October 19.[14]

Irrational Price-Insensitive Traders

Stock prices declined throughout the day of October 19, 1987. The decline was particularly sharp in the afternoon (see chart 1). At about 1:30 p.m. EST, the price of a December S&P 500 futures contract was about 15 points lower than the cash prices of the stocks underlying the contract (that is, the basis was − 15 points, see chart 2). This means that liquidating the basket of stocks underlying the S&P 500 through futures market sales was about $7,500 more costly (before transaction costs) than liquidating the same basket in the cash market.[15] Yet, according to the cascade theory, portfolio insurers continued to liquidate in the futures market. In the words of the Brady Commission, this apparently anomalous behavior was the result of "mechanical price-insensitive selling." Put more bluntly, the theory attributes the observation to irrationality on the part of portfolio managers who, by most accounts — including those of the Brady Commission — are credited with being highly sophisticated financial experts.

The Missing Arbs

The cascade theory depends on index arbitrage activity to transmit selling pressure from the futures to the cash market. Yet, by all accounts, index arbitrage virtually ceased about 1:30 p.m. EST on October 19.[16] Cash market prices, however, fell sharply between 1:30 and the market's close. The S&P 500 index lost about 30 points during this time, while the Dow fell by more than 300 points. Furthermore, index arbitrage was severely restricted in subsequent trading days because the NYSE limited use of its DOT system by arbitrageurs. However, this did not prevent a further sharp decline in stock prices on October 26.

Foreign Markets and Previous Panics

The cascade theory fails to explain why stock market panics in foreign markets occurred at the same time as the U.S. panic. Programmed trading is virtually nonexistent in overseas markets. Yet these markets crashed as quickly and by as much as the U.S. market. Between October 16 and 23, for example, the U.K. stock market declined 22 percent, the German and Japanese markets fell 12 percent, the French market fell 10 percent and the U.S. market declined 13 percent. What's more, programmed trading dates back no further than 1982 when stock index futures contracts began trading. U.S. stock market panics have a much longer history. Since the cascade theory does not explain these other panics, there is some reason to be skeptical about its usefulness in explaining the latest U.S. panic.

AN ALTERNATIVE EXPLANATION: EFFICIENT MARKETS

A long-standing proposition in both economics and finance is that stock prices are formed in efficient markets.[17] This means that all of the relevant information currently known about interest rates, dividends and the future prospects for firms (the fundamentals) is contained in current stock prices. Stock prices change only when new information regarding the fundamentals is obtained by someone. New information, by definition, cannot be predicted ahead of its arrival; because the news is just as likely to be good as it is to be bad, jumps in stock prices cannot be predicted in advance.

If the efficient markets hypothesis is correct, past price changes contain no useful information

---

[14]See, in addition, Malkiel (1988), pp. 5–6.

[15]The value of a S&P 500 futures contract is $500 times the level of the index. Consequently, if the cash market index is about 255 and the futures market index is about 240 as they were at 1:30 p.m. EST on October 19, the value of the basis: B = $500(240) − $500(255) = − $7,500.

[16]See the *Report of the Presidential Task Force on Market Mechanisms* (1988), pp. vi, 32 and 40; U.S. General Accounting Office (1988), pp. 43 and 45–46; U.S. Commodity Futures Trading Commission (1988), pp. vi and 46.

[17]See Brealey and Meyers (1984), pp. 266–81; Malkiel (1981), pp. 171–79; Brealey (1983), pp. 15–18; Leroy (1982) and Fama (1970).

about future price changes. With some added assumptions, this can be translated into a useful empirical proposition. If transaction costs are low, the expected return to holding stock is constant and the volatility of stock prices does not change during the time period examined, the efficient market hypothesis implies that observed *changes* in stock prices will be uncorrelated. The sequence of price changes are unrelated; they behave as random variables. This is sometimes called "weak form efficiency."

This implication contrasts sharply with a central implication of the cascade theory. The cascade theory suggests that price changes in both the cash and futures markets are positively correlated with their own past. This follows from the theory's circularity which attributes sharp price declines to immediately preceding sharp declines.

The behavior of U.S. stock prices generally conforms to the efficient markets hypothesis in the sense that past changes in stock prices contain no *useful* information about future changes.[18] However, when data on stock price indexes are observed at very high frequency (intra-day but not day-to-day), changes in the level of *cash* market indexes are correlated and appear to lag changes in futures prices.[19] This behavior appears to favor the cascade theory. When differences in the "market-making" techniques employed in the cash and futures markets are taken into account, however, intra-day data from both markets reject the cascade theory, while, on the whole, they are consistent with the efficient markets hypothesis.[20]

Market-Making in the Cash Market

Trading on the NYSE is conducted by members who trade within an auction framework at posts manned by specialists.[21] Specialists' activities are concentrated on a particular group of stocks that are traded at a particular post. One of the main functions of a specialist is to execute limit orders for other members of the Exchange. A limit order is an order to buy (sell) a specified number of shares of a given stock when and if the price of the stock falls (rises) to some specified level. The spe-

cialist maintains a book in which these orders are recorded and to which only he has access. The ability to place a limit order with a specialist frees the broker who places the order from having to wait at the post for a price movement that may never occur.

For example, suppose the information contained in the specialist's book for shares of XYZ corporation is summarized in figure 1.[22] The demand curve aggregates the purchase orders that have been placed with the specialist. These include bids of $9\frac{7}{8}$ for 400 shares, $9\frac{3}{4}$ for 300 shares, etc. The supply curve aggregates the specialist's sell orders of 100 shares at $10\frac{1}{8}$, 200 shares at $10\frac{1}{4}$, etc. Brokers, standing at the post, trade XYZ shares with each other and the specialist. At any time, a broker may request a quote from the specialist who, given the information in figure 1, would respond "$9\frac{7}{8}$ for 400, 100 at $10\frac{1}{8}$." This indicates that the specialist has buy orders for 400 shares at $9\frac{7}{8}$ and sell orders for 100 shares at $10\frac{1}{8}$. If the buy and sell orders of the other brokers at the post are in balance at the current price, trading in XYZ shares will occur within the price range of $9\frac{7}{8}$ bid and $10\frac{1}{8}$ ask.[23]

Suppose, however, that a broker has a market buy order for 300 shares that he is unable to cross with a broker with sell orders for 300 shares at the quoted spread (in this case, at an ask price of $10\frac{1}{8}$ or less). Since the specialist's quote indicates that he will sell 100 shares at $10\frac{1}{8}$, the broker will respond "Take it." The broker has purchased 100 shares from the specialist at $10\frac{1}{8}$. Since the broker must buy another 200 shares, he will ask for a further quote. If nothing further has occurred, the specialist will quote "$9\frac{7}{8}$ for 400, 200 at $10\frac{1}{4}$." The broker will respond "Take it." The broker has satisfied the market buy order for 300 shares of XYZ. He purchased 100 shares at $10\frac{1}{8}$ and 200 shares at $10\frac{1}{4}$. Of course, the broker could have acquired 300 shares immediately by offering to pay a price of $10\frac{1}{4}$ but the cost would have been greater. Instead, it pays the broker to try to "walk up" the supply curve by executing a number of trades rather than jumping directly to the price that will get him 300 shares in

---

[18]Malkiel (1981), Brealey (1983) and Fama (1970).

[19]See Perry (1985); Atchison, Butler and Simonds (1987) and Harris (1988).

[20]See Grossman and Miller (1988) for a discussion of why trading rules many differ across the markets.

[21]Of course, the NYSE is not the only cash market for stocks, but it is a major market. Because of its relative size, the discussion focuses on this market.

[22]For purposes of exposition, the figure and discussion ignore the effect of "stops" and "stop loss orders" on the book.

[23]See Stoll (1985), Shultz (1946), pp. 119–44 and *The New York Stock Exchange Market* (1979), pp. 14–21 and pp. 30–31.

Figure 1
An Illustration of Limit Order Supply and Demand

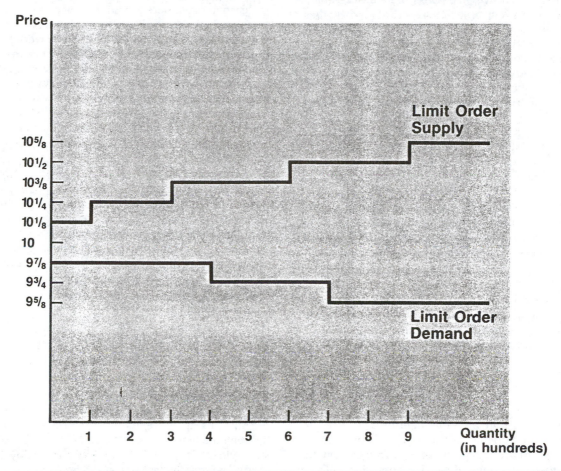

Notice that this process of "walking up" the supply curve or "walking down" the demand curve can generate a sequence of recorded transaction prices that run in the same direction. The larger the excess of market buy (or sell) orders is relative to the size of the specialist's limit orders at various prices, the longer the sequence of recorded transaction prices that run in the same direction and the greater the likelihood that re-

one trade.[24] Similar reasoning applies to situations in which excess market sell orders exist at the quoted spread.

corded price changes over the time interval are correlated. This situation is particularly likely to arise during panics when large order imbalances develop at quoted prices.

Specialist Rule 104

Specialists are required by rule SR 104 to maintain a "fair and orderly" market. More specifically, the rule states that

[t]he maintenance of a fair and orderly market implies the maintenance of price continuity with rea-

---

[24]Under NYSE rules, public orders have precedence over specialists' orders at the same price. See Stoll (1985), p. 7.

sonable depth, and the minimizing of the effects of temporary disparity between supply and demand.

In connection with the maintenance of a fair and orderly market, it is commonly desirable that a . . . specialist engage to a reasonable degree under existing circumstances in dealings for his own account when lack of price continuity, lack of depth, or disparity between supply and demand exists or is reasonably to be anticipated.[25]

For example, rule SR 104 requires the specialist to buy shares for his own account to assist the maintenance of an orderly market if, in his estimation, sell orders *temporarily* exceed buy orders at the existing market price and conversely. If these imbalances are truly temporary, the trades required by SR 104 will be profitable for the specialist; evidence indicates that specialists typically sell on up ticks in price and buy on down ticks.[26] If large order imbalances develop that threaten the orderliness of the market, the specialist may institute an opening delay or trading halt. The specialist needs the approval of a floor official or governor to do this and to establish a new opening price.[27]

The effect of SR 104 is to smooth what would otherwise be abrupt movements in stock prices, at least over short periods of time (a few minutes). Rather than allowing the price to move directly to some new level, specialist trading temporarily retards the movement. This can generate a sequence of correlated price changes.

Market-Making in the Futures Market

Trading in futures markets is governed by CFTC rules that require all trades of futures contracts to be executed openly and competitively by "open outcry." In particular, the trading arena, or pit, has no single auctioneer through whom all trades are funneled. Rather, the pit is composed of many traders who call out their bids and offers to each other. The traders are not required to stabilize the market. They may at any time take any side of a transaction even though this might add to an imbalance of buy and sell orders at the quoted price, and they may leave the pit (refuse to trade) at any time. At the time of the crash, there was no rule

regarding limit moves in the price of the Standard and Poor's futures contract.

These rules contain no requirement to smooth out movements in the price. Traders are free to move the price immediately to a new level. Unlike the cash market, there are no trading rules in futures markets that are likely to result in correlated price changes. Furthermore, since there were no rules that retarded price changes in the futures market, futures prices were free to adjust more quickly than cash prices so changes in futures prices may lead changes in cash prices.

Different Instruments

It is important to note that different instruments are traded in the cash and futures markets. Stock index futures contracts are agreements between a seller (short position) and a buyer (long position) to a cash settlement based on the change in a stock index's value between the date the contract is entered by the two parties and some future date.[28] The instrument underlying the futures contract is a large basket of different stocks, that is, the stocks contained in the Major Market Index, the Value Line Index, the S&P 500 Index, etc. No such instrument is traded in the cash market, where purchasing or selling 500 different stocks, for example, requires as many different transactions and can only be executed at significantly higher costs.[29]

The different instruments traded in the cash and futures markets have a further implication for the relationship between observed price changes between the two markets. The cash market prices shown in chart 1, as well as those examined by the Brady Commission, are measured by an index. The index is an average of the prices of all the stocks included in the index. When the index is observed at a very high frequency (say, minute-by-minute), some of the stocks included in the index may not have traded during the interval between observations. If not, the level of cash prices measured by the index includes some prices from previous observations. In other words, the index

---

[25]*Report of the Presidential Task Force on Market Mechanisms* (1988), p. vi–7. Rule 104 is taken seriously. See pp. vi–9.

[26]See Stoll (1985), pp. 35–36.

[27]It was the application of SR 104 that resulted in the opening delays and trading halts that occurred during the week of October 19. For stocks included in the S&P 500, these delays and halts averaged 51 minutes on October 19 and 78 minutes on October 20. See U.S. General Accounting Office (1988), p. 56.

[28]See Schwarz, Hill and Schneeweis (1986), p. 9.

[29]For example, the cost of trading one futures contract based on the Standard and Poor's 500 is about $500 lower than trading the equivalent basket of stocks in the cash market. See Miller, Hawke, Malkiel and Scholes (1987), p. 11, and U.S. General Accounting Office (1988), p. 20.

Table 2

Stale Prices and Correlated Changes in a Price Index: A Simple Example

Period	Share prices			Index[1]	Change in index
	A	B	C		
0	$10	$20	$30	100	
1	9	20	30	98.33	−1.67
2	9	18	30	95.00	−3.33
3	9	18	27	90.00	−5.00

[1]Index $= \dfrac{(A+B+C)/3}{\$20.00} \times 100$

includes some "stale" prices. The term used to describe this phenomenon is "nonsynchronous trading."

Typically, nonsynchronous trading does not create a serious measurement problem. Under normal conditions, a buy or sell order is executed in about two minutes on the NYSE. On October 16 and during the week of October 19, however, the time required to execute orders rose markedly.[30] On those days, the index contained a considerable number of stale prices.[31] The subsequent piecemeal adjustment of these stale prices for individual stocks could explain correlated changes in the level of the cash market index. This is shown in the table 2 example. The example assumes that the index is a simple average of the prices of three stocks (A, B and C) divided by the average price in period zero and multiplied by 100. The initial prices (in period zero) are equilibrium prices (i.e., they contain all currently available relevant information). Then, new information becomes available in period 1 that eventually will cause a 10 percent decline in all stock prices. If there is nonsynchronous trading, the revisions will occur piecemeal for each of the stocks. One example of this is shown in the table: the price of stock A falls in period 1, the price of stock B falls in period 2, etc. If the index is reported in each period, it will dis-

play positively correlated changes as shown in the table.

The stale price problem is not relevant for futures market prices; futures prices are actual prices. As a result, changes in futures prices will appear to lead changes in the cash market index if the index contains a substantial number of stale prices.

THE DIFFERENT IMPLICATIONS

The central feature of the cascade theory is that declines in cash and futures prices reinforced each other and led to further declines in both markets. The theory suggests that declines in the price of stock index futures contracts *caused* a decline in the cash prices of the underlying stocks, and this drop *caused* a further decline in the prices of index futures contracts. If the theory is correct, changes in cash prices will be positively correlated with past changes in the price of index futures and conversely. The cascade theory further implies that price changes in each market are positively correlated with their own past changes. This follows from the circularity of the theory which attributes sharp declines in stock prices to immediately preceding sharp declines. Finally, since the cascade theory contends that this specific behavior *caused* the panic, these correlations should be observed during the panic, but not at other times.

The efficient markets hypothesis suggests that market-making in the cash market and nonsynchronous trading could produce intra-day *cash* market price changes that are correlated. Furthermore, the hypothesis suggests that changes in futures prices may lead changes in cash prices. These implications are similar to the implications of the cascade theory. The two differ, however, in three important respects. Unlike the cascade theory, the efficient markets hypothesis suggests that:

(1) Changes in the price of stock index futures contracts are uncorrelated,
(2) Changes in cash prices do not lead changes in futures prices, and
(3) Relationships that exist across the two markets are not unique to the panic.

---

[30]See U.S. General Accounting Office (1988), p. 73.

[31]See Harris (1988); *Report of the Presidential Task Force on Market Mechanisms* (1988), p. 30; Miller, Hawke, Malkiel and Scholes (1987), pp. 21–22 and 34–35; U.S. Commodity Futures Trading Commission (1988), pp. v, 15 and B-1 through B-9.

TESTING THE TWO THEORIES

These theories are tested using minute-by-minute data on the level of the Standard and Poor's 500 index (S&P 500) and the price of the December 1987 Standard and Poor's 500 index futures contract (S&P 500 Futures). The level of the S&P 500 index represents the cash price of the stocks underlying the S&P 500 futures contract. All tests are conducted using first differences of the natural logs of the levels. This transformation of the data approximates one-minute percentage changes (expressed in decimals) in cash and futures market prices. The data cover the trading days immediately before, during and after the panic: October 16, 19 and 20.[32]

A few comments about the data are important. The NYSE, on which the great bulk of the stocks included in the S&P 500 index are traded, was open from 9:30 a.m. to 4:00 p.m. EST on the above days. The CME, which trades the S&P 500 futures contract, was open from 9:30 a.m. to 4:15 p.m. EST on October 16 and 19; on October 20, however, trading in the S&P 500 futures contract was halted from 12:15 p.m. to 1:05 p.m. EST. All tests reported here *exclude* the period on October 20 when trading in the futures market was halted.

Were Changes in Stock Prices Correlated?

Table 3 presents the results of a test (called a Box-Pierce test) based on the estimated autocorrelations of percentage changes in cash market prices. This test is designed to determine whether the data are significantly correlated, that is, whether current changes in cash market prices are related to their own past changes. Both theories discussed in this paper suggest that intra-day, high-frequency cash market price changes will be positively correlated, although the reasons for the positive correlation are considerably different. As a result, these data do not help discriminate between the two theories. If the data prove inconsistent with this implication, however, neither theory performs well in explaining the behavior of cash market prices.

The data in table 3 indicate that minute-to-minute changes in the S&P 500 Index are significantly correlated. Furthermore, the correlations are positive at least over the initial lag.[33]

Table 3

**Cash Market
(Autocorrelation Coefficients and Box-Pierce Statistics for First Differences of Logs of the Minute-by-Minute S&P 500 Index)**

Panel A: October 16, 1987 (9:30 a.m. – 4:00 p.m. EST)

To lag	Autocorrelation coefficient	Box-Pierce statistic[1]
1	.570*	112.09
2	.530*	209.00
3	.385*	260.14
6	.178*	333.81
12	−.148	352.51
18	−.208	406.39
24	−.072	462.80

Panel B: October 19, 1987 (9:30 a.m. – 4:00 p.m. EST)

To lag	Autocorrelation coefficient	Box-Pierce statistic[1]
1	.342*	37.78
2	.397*	88.69
3	.406*	141.93
6	.264*	237.78
12	.231*	345.66
18	.124	385.52
24	.054	396.34

Panel C: October 20, 1987 (9:30 a.m. – 4:00 p.m. EST)

To lag	Autocorrelation coefficient	Box-Pierce statistic[1]
1	.535*	84.15
2	.561*	176.68
3	.590*	279.02
6	.521*	548.61
12	.311*	845.55
18	.324*	1026.74
24	.250	1155.57

[1]Critical value for 24 lags is 33.20. A Box-Pierce statistic in excess of this indicates significant autocorrelation.
*Exceeds two standard errors

Table 4 presents the results of the same test for the December S&P 500 futures contract. The efficient markets hypothesis and the absence of specialist traders suggest that these changes are not correlated. Conversely, the cascade theory

---

[32]Minute-by-minute price data were also examined for October 15 and 21–23. In each case, the qualitative results were the same as those presented here.

[33]These correlations are analyzed further below.

Table 4

Futures Market (Autocorrelation Coefficients and Box-Pierce Statistics for First Differences of Logs of the Minute-by-Minute Price of the December S&P 500 Futures Contract)

Panel A: October 16, 1987 (9:30 a.m. – 4:15 p.m. EST)

To lag	Autocorrelation coefficient	Box-Pierce statistic[1]
1	.090	2.89
2	.035	3.33
3	−.047	4.12
6	−.020	8.25
12	−.020	16.02
18	.017	19.10
24	−.044	22.29

Panel B: October 19, 1987 (9:30 a.m. – 11:00 a.m. EST)

To lag	Autocorrelation coefficient	Box-Pierce statistic[1]
1	−.309*	8.49
2	.140	10.24
3	.005	10.24
6	−.131	15.41
12	.110	18.95
18	.043	21.69
24	−.020	23.13

Panel C: October 19, 1987 (11:00 a.m. – 4:15 p.m. EST)

To lag	Autocorrelation coefficient	Box-Pierce statistic[1]
1	−.072	1.63
2	.090	4.17
3	−.004	4.18
6	.091	7.21
12	.020	9.60
18	.073	14.95
24	.000	22.37

Panel D: October 20, 1987 (9:30 a.m. – 4:15 p.m. EST)

To lag	Autocorrelation coefficient	Box-Pierce statistic[1]
1	.029	.26
2	.022	.41
3	.042	.95
6	.046	4.22
12	−.071	9.28
18	.033	11.81
24	−.035	17.62

[1]Critical value for 24 lags is 33.20. A Box-Pierce statistic in excess of this value indicates significant autocorrelation.

*Exceeds two standard errors

predicts that percentage changes in the futures price will be positively correlated.

The data presented in table 4 are consistent with the efficient markets hypothesis, not the cascade theory. None of the test statistics for October 16 (panel A), October 20 (panel D) and for the bulk of the trading day on October 19 (panel C) indicate significant correlations at conventional significance levels. These price changes are serially uncorrelated.[34] Data for the first 90 minutes of trading on October 19 (panel B) are an exception. During this period, changes in the futures price were significantly correlated with the change the previous minute. This correlation, however, is negative, not positive as the cascade theory implies.[35] Thus, the evidence presented in table 4 is inconsistent with the cascade theory, while, on the whole, it conforms to the efficient markets hypothesis.

Is the Cash Market Efficient?

The table 3 results indicate that intra-day changes in cash market prices are correlated. Put another way, past price changes contain some information about future changes for the next few minutes. Is this information useful in the sense that it can be profitably exploited by traders? If so, it would suggest that cash market traders do not incorporate information efficiently. This, of course, would provide evidence against the efficient markets hypothesis.

In part, the answer to this question depends on the length of the time period over which the price changes are related. If the time period is short, shorter than the time required to execute a transaction, the information contained in past price changes cannot be exploited profitably and the cash market is efficient.

Table 5 helps answer this question. The table 5 data are estimates of the length of the lagged relationship between current and past cash market price changes for October 16, 19 and 20. The estimates were obtained by regressing the contemporaneous minute-to-minute price change on the 15 previous minute-to-minute price changes. Initially, this specification was identified as the unrestricted model. To determine whether the esti-

[34]The same result was obtained when data for October 15 and 21–23 were examined.

[35]This puzzling result for the first 90 minutes of trading on October 19 may be due to the fact that many stocks had not yet opened for trading on the NYSE and the rumors at that time that the SEC would call a trading halt. See Miller, Hawke, Malkiel and Scholes (1987), wire report summary.

Table 5

Estimated Lag Lengths in the Cash Market

Panel A: October 16, 1987 (9:30 a.m. – 4:00 p.m. EST)

$$\Delta LNC_t = -.003 + .401\Delta LNC_{t-1} + .343\Delta LNC_{t-2}$$
$$ (1.19) \quad (7.80)^* \qquad (6.51)^*$$

$\bar{R}^2 = .41$
DW = 2.00

Panel B: October 19, 1987 (9:30 a.m. – 4:00 p.m. EST)

$$\Delta LNC_t = -.016 + .123\Delta LNC_{t-1} + .228\Delta LNC_{t-2} + .242\Delta LNC_{t-3} + .112\Delta LNC_{t-4}$$
$$ (2.46)^* \quad (2.20)^* \qquad (4.14)^* \qquad (4.39)^* \qquad (1.99)^*$$

$\bar{R}^2 = .26$
DW = 2.01

Panel C: October 20, 1987 (9:30 a.m. – 4:00 p.m. EST)

$$\Delta LNC_t = -.001 + .107\Delta LNC_{t-1} + .173\Delta LNC_{t-2} + .258\Delta LNC_{t-3} + .174\Delta LNC_{t-4} + .153\Delta LNC_{t-5}$$
$$ (.132) \quad (1.82) \qquad (2.98)^* \qquad (4.52)^* \qquad (2.99)^* \qquad (2.60)^*$$

$\bar{R}^2 = .48$
DW = 2.02

*Statistically significant at the 5 percent level

mated coefficients are sensitive to the lag length and to identify statistically redundant lags, the lag structure was successively shortened by one lag. At each stage, the t-statistic for the coefficient of the most distant lag was examined. If the test indicated the coefficient was statistically insignificant, that lag was dropped and the equation was reestimated with one less lag. This process was repeated until the test rejected the hypothesis that the estimated coefficient of the most distant remaining lag was zero.[36]

The estimates shown in table 5 indicate that the lags ranged from about two minutes on October 16 to five minutes on October 20.[37] It requires about two minutes to execute a trade on the NYSE under normal trading conditions. During the panic, execution times ranged from about 10 to 75 minutes at times.[38] In view of this, the lags estimated in table 5 do not appear to be long enough to reject

the efficient markets hypothesis; also, since they varied over the period, it is doubtful that past price changes contained information that could be exploited by traders.

Did Stock Price Changes Reinforce Each Other Across Markets?

The central feature of the cascade theory can be tested by determining whether past price changes in the futures market help explain current price changes in the cash market and conversely. This is done by regressing the change in cash prices on past changes in cash prices; then, past changes in futures prices are added to the estimated regression equation to see if they improve the equation's explanatory power. An F-test is conducted to determine whether the addition of the futures market data significantly increases the cash price equation's coefficient of determination (R^2). The

---

[36]See Anderson (1971), pp. 223 and 275–76. It is possible that this test may reject some lags that are, in fact, significant if taken as a group. To control for this, F-tests were run with the lag length in the unrestricted model set at 15. The number of lags in the restricted model was set at 12 to determine if the three omitted lags were significant. The lags in the restricted model was then reduced to nine and the test repeated, etc.

[37]The lag had declined to about three minutes by October 23. The method used in this paper to estimate lag length has the

problem that the probability of rejecting the null hypothesis (the estimated coefficient is zero) when it is true rises as the lag length is reduced. Consequently, the true lag lengths may be shorter than those estimated in table 5. See Batten and Thornton (1983), pp. 22–23, and Anderson (1971), pp. 30–43.

[38]U.S. Government Accounting Office (1988), p. 73.

Table 6
Granger Tests

Day	Lags	F-statistic Futures → Cash	F-statistic Cash → Futures
October 16	2	17.61*	.76
October 19	4	4.46*	1.57
October 20	5	2.59*	.67

*Statistically significant at the 5 percent level

test is then reversed, with the change in futures prices as the dependent variable.

The results of this test are presented in table 6 for each of the trading days examined in this paper. The lag length employed on each day is the one identified by the table 5 test.[39] The results for cash market prices show that the addition of past changes in futures prices improve the regression estimates; this suggests that price changes in the futures market preceded those in the cash market. This result is consistent with both the cascade theory and the efficient markets hypothesis. Furthermore, it is not unique to the panic; it has been observed for intra-day price data during other periods as well.[40]

Other table 6 results, however, are inconsistent with the cascade theory. The inclusion of past changes in cash prices in the regressions that estimate the change in futures prices does not significantly improve the estimates. This rejects the notion that past changes in cash prices help explain changes in futures prices. This finding is inconsistent with the central feature of the cascade theory, which suggests the panic was caused by declines in cash and futures prices that became larger as they tumbled over each other on the way down.

CONCLUSION

This paper has examined the cascade theory, which has been advanced as an explanation of the October 1987 stock market panic. The theory relies on the notion that stock traders behave "mechanically," are "insensitive to price," and execute transactions in markets without regard to transaction costs. These assertions are inconsistent with the behavior of wealth-maximizing individuals. Not only are the theoretical underpinnings of the cascade theory weak, the data do not support the theory. Instead, the observed relationships that do exist between the markets are not unique to the crash and can be explained by a theory that relies on wealth maximizing behavior.

Almost 60 years later, the cause of the "Great Crash" in October 1929 is still being debated. Those with even longer memories know that there is little agreement about what caused the stock market panic in 1907. Although financial reforms followed each of these panics, history indicates that the reforms have done little to reduce the frequency or severity of panics. Without a reliable theoretical guide to the mechanics of a panic, any reform is no more than a "shot in the dark." The evidence presented in this paper suggests that the reforms advanced by proponents of the cascade theory are unlikely to alter this historical pattern.

REFERENCES

Anderson, Theodore W. *The Statistical Analysis of Time Series* (John Wiley and Sons, Inc., 1971).

Atchison, Michael D., Kirt C. Butler, and Richard R. Simonds. "Nonsynchronous Security Trading and Market Index Autocorrelation," *Journal of Finance* (March 1987), pp. 111–18.

Batten, Dallas S., and Daniel L. Thornton. "Polynomial Distributed Lags and the Estimation of the St. Louis Equation," this *Review* (April 1983), pp. 13–25.

Brealey, R. A. *An Introduction to Risk and Return from Common Stocks* (The MIT Press, 1983).

Brealey, Richard, and Stewart Meyers. *Principles of Corporate Finance* (McGraw-Hill, 1984).

Burns, Joseph M. *A Treatise on Markets: Spot, Futures, and Options* (American Enterprise Institute, 1979), pp. 31–55.

Cornell, Bradford, and Kenneth R. French. "The Pricing of Stock Index Futures," *Journal of Futures Markets* (Spring 1983), pp. 1–14.

Fama, Eugene F. "Efficient Capital Markets: A Review of Theory and Empirical Work," *Journal of Finance, Papers and Proceedings* (May 1970), pp. 383–417.

Figlewski, Stephen. "Hedging Performance and Basis Risk in Stock Index Futures," *Journal of Finance* (July 1984), pp. 657–69.

Grossman, Sanford J., and Merton H. Miller. "Liquidity and Market Structure," Princeton University Financial Research Center Memorandum No. 88 (March 1988).

[39]Hsiao (1981) uses a similar method. These lag lengths apply to the cash market. Analysis of the futures market suggests that the appropriate lag for this market is zero.

[40]See Kawaller, Koch and Koch (1987).

Harris, Lawrence. "Nonsynchronous Trading and the S&P 500 Stock-Futures Basis in October 1987" (University of Southern California Working Paper, processed January 11, 1988).

Hsiao, Cheng. "Autoregressive Modelling and Money-Income Causality Detection," *Journal of Monetary Economics* (January 1981), pp. 85–106.

Kawaller, Ira G., Paul D. Koch, and Timothy W. Koch. "The Temporal Price Relationship Between S&P 500 Futures and the S&P 500 Index," *Journal of Finance* (December 1987), pp. 1309–29.

Leroy, Stephen F. "Expectations Models of Asset Prices: A Survey of Theory," *Journal of Finance* (March 1982), pp. 185–217.

Malkiel, Burton G. "The Brady Commission Report," Princeton University Financial Research Center Memorandum No. 92 (May 1988).

_____. *A Random Walk Down Wall Street* (W. W. Norton and Company, 1981).

Miller, Merton H., John D. Hawke, Jr., Burton Malkiel, and Myron Scholes. *Preliminary Report of the Committee of Inquiry Appointed by the Chicago Mercantile Exchange to Examine the Events Surrounding October 19, 1987* (December 22, 1987).

Modest, David M., and Mahadevan Sundaresan. "The Relationship Between Spot and Futures Prices in Stock Index Futures Markets: Some Preliminary Evidence," *Journal of Futures Markets* (Spring 1983), pp. 15–41.

Perry, Philip R. "Portfolio Serial Correlation and Nonsynchronous Trading," *Journal of Financial and Quantitative Analysis* (December 1985), pp. 517–23.

Report of the Presidential Task Force on Market Mechanisms (U.S. Government Printing Office, January 1988).

Santoni, G. J. "Has Programmed Trading Made Stock Prices More Volatile?" this *Review* (May 1987), pp. 18–29.

Schwarz, Edward W., Joanne M. Hill, and Thomas Schneeweis. *Financial Futures* (Dow Jones-Irwin, 1986).

Shultz, Birl E. *The Securities Market and How It Works* (Harper and Brothers, 1946).

Stoll, Hans R. *The Stock Exchange Specialist System: An Economic Analysis.* Monograph Series in Finance and Economics (Salomon Brothers Center for the Study of Financial Institutions, New York University, 1985).

The New York Stock Exchange Market (New York Stock Exchange, June 1979).

U.S. Commodity Futures Trading Commission. *Final Report on Stock Index Futures and Cash Market Activity During October 1987* (U.S. Commodity Futures Trading Commission, January 1988).

U.S. General Accounting Office. *Financial Markets: Preliminary Observations on the October 1987 Crash* (U.S. General Accounting Office, January 1988).

Working, Holbrook. *Selected Writings of Holbrook Working* (Chicago Board of Trade, 1977).

Article 30

by Mark Rubinstein

Portfolio Insurance and the Market Crash

The market crash of October 19, 1987, undermined two preconditions of all portfolio insurance programs—(1) low transaction costs and (2) price continuity. As a result, although most portfolio insurance programs did not violate their minimum returns, many did not perform as well as expected. Differential performance across different programs probably had more to do with the size of the hedges in place at the time of the crash than with the amount of trading the program undertook. Conservative programs (say, 50 per cent hedged) probably outperformed more aggressive programs.

Did portfolio insurance itself contribute to the crash? Portfolio insurance accounted for perhaps 12 per cent of the dollar change in net sold positions on October 19. Is this substantial? It seems unlikely, given the many other significant events—the twin deficits, the falling dollar, uncertainty over the market system itself—that have been implicated in the press.

In the aftermath of the crash, portfolio insurance strategies are likely to be more difficult to implement and riskier in terms of predictability of outcome. We can expect to see fewer dynamic strategies, because of increased transaction costs, and greater use of options markets, which avoid the price discontinuity problem. We might also see a better balance between explicit buyers and sellers of insurance.

THE EVENTS OF THE week of October 19, 1987 have raised several questions concerning portfolio insurance and securities market regulation:

- How did the market crash affect the performance of portfolio insurance strategies?
- How did portfolio insurance strategies affect the crash?
- What, if anything, should be done to reduce the probability of market crashes in the future?
- How will portfolio insurance strategies be modified in the future?

At present, I have inadequate information to give a definitive answer to any of these questions. Even after all the study and analysis has been completed by regulatory agencies and academics, we may still not be sure we know the answers. Nonetheless, based on what I currently know or surmise, I will answer these questions as best I can.

How Did the Crash Affect the Performance of Portfolio Insurance Strategies?

Typical implementation of portfolio insurance has relied on two preconditions—low transac-

Mark Rubinstein is Professor of Finance at the Graduate School of Business of the University of California at Berkeley and a Principal of Leland O'Brien Rubinstein Associates.

The author thanks Tony Baker, Fischer Black, Michael Brennan, Larry Edwards, Jeremy Evnine, Bob Ferguson, Scott Grannis, Chris Hynes, Pete Kyle, Hayne Leland, Terry Marsh, Robert Merton, Merton Miller, David Modest, Girish Reddy, Richard Sandor and Andy Turner for their helpful conversations.

tion costs and more or less price-continuous markets.[1] Following an unbroken record of reliability reaching at least as far back as the Great Depression, these preconditions were suddenly and simultaneously violated on October 19, 1987.

Transaction Costs

Transaction costs consist of four components —commissions, bid-ask spread, market impact (moving prices through large transactions) and, for investors using index futures markets, differences between futures prices and "fair value." In spot, futures and options markets, bid-ask spreads widened substantially on October 19, and market impact (perhaps on the order of 1 per cent) was significant for investors selling either directly in the spot market or implicitly in futures and options markets. As a general rule, futures should sell above the spot index level. On October 19, however, S&P 500 futures sold (and closed at the end of the day) an average of about 10 per cent below the concurrently reported level of the spot S&P 500 index.

Unfortunately, even under normal market conditions, it is difficult to determine the fair value of an index future because of uncertainty surrounding the concurrent level of the spot index. The individual stocks in the index do not all trade (and thereby register new prices, which may revise the index) at the same time. Indeed, some components of the index commonly trade with lags of several minutes. As a result, the reported index at any time is a combination of prices drawn from different times during the day. My own research suggests that the S&P 500 is typically about five minutes old. To estimate fair value, one would instead like to know what the index would currently be if all the stocks in the index had just traded. During periods when the reported index is moving rapidly up or down, the lag can make it appear that the futures price is significantly different from fair value, when in reality the futures price is just reflecting the level the index would have if all stocks in the index were to trade simultaneously. The common observation that the futures market tends to lead the stock market confirms this view.

On October 19, the measurement problems created by the lag reached unprecedented proportions, primarily because of delayed openings in key S&P 500 stocks, sluggish trading due to order imbalances at intervals throughout the day, and attempts by specialists to absorb massive selling pressure. Compounding these problems was the apparent absence of program traders, who normally serve to transmit price changes between the spot and futures markets.[2] By the end of the day, while the S&P 500 was down 20 per cent compared with the previous day's close, the December S&P 500 futures contract was down 29 per cent.

As was also observed on October 20 and 21, with the relative inactivity of program trading, the futures market was effectively uncoupled from the spot market. Under these circumstances, it was understandable that different individuals observing the reported spot and futures prices would have drawn different conclusions: Some felt the basis (the difference between futures and spot prices) was in fact very large, while others believed that the unadjusted futures price provided the most reliable measure of the concurrent level the index would have if supply and demand imbalances were to be corrected for all stocks in the index.

The differential responses of individual portfolio insurers on October 19 can be traced to this source. If he believed transaction costs were very high, a sensible portfolio insurer would substantially reduce the number of futures contracts sold; if he thought transaction costs were low, large numbers of contracts would be sold.

Ironically, if transaction costs were at just the right level, it would not have mattered what the insurer did. For example, suppose selling futures imposed a transaction cost of 10 per cent and assume that an insurer started out the day with a sold futures position covering 10 per cent of his underlying portfolio. Suppose further that, with no transaction costs, every 1 per cent decline in the S&P 500 index would trigger a 2 per cent increase in sold futures in order to create an insured outcome. With the index falling 20 per cent on October 19, the insurer would then want to increase his sold futures position from 10 to 50 per cent (0.10 + 2 x 0.20), for an average hedge during the day of 30 per cent [(0.10 + 0.50)/2].

Now compare two extreme responses—an insurer who follows the strategy as if there were no transaction costs and an insurer who, estimating high transaction costs, stays pat and holds his hedge at 10 per cent. The first insurer will lose about 70 per cent (1 − 0.30) of the 20

---

1. Footnotes appear at end of article.

per cent decline, as well as losing 10 per cent of 40 per cent (0.50 − 0.10) in transaction costs, for a total loss of 18 per cent [(0.70 x 0.20) + (0.10 x 0.40)]. But the second insurer, who doesn't trade at all, will *also* lose 18 per cent (0.90 x 0.20). In other words, if transaction costs were in fact 10 per cent, it would not have mattered whether the insurer traded or not; exactly the same result would have occurred in either case.

Ten per cent would seem to be an upper bound on the level of transaction costs for a seller of futures on October 19, because the true contemporaneous S&P 500 was surely much lower than its reported value. Given that transaction costs were almost certainly lower than 10 per cent, an insurer who *knew in advance* that the index was going to fall 20 per cent would have been taking the right step by selling futures. At the beginning of the day, however—and even near the end, with one hour of trading remaining, when the DJIA had dropped 300 points—it was far from obvious that the DJIA would end the day down 508 points. If, to take an extreme example, the index had reversed itself, the insurer who had not traded would have ended up outperforming the insurer who traded, not only because he would have avoided large whipsaw costs, but also because he would have been spared relatively high transaction costs. Balancing these considerations against each other, I would guess that, even if transaction costs were as little as 3½ to 4 per cent, very little trading would have been advisable. Of course, after the fact, with the index down 20 per cent, anyone who had sold futures, even at high levels of transaction cost, would have realized superior performance.

A key issue in assessing the performance of portfolio insurance on October 19 is thus what the true level of transaction costs was for sellers of index futures. Studies of this question are currently under way, utilizing a time-stamped record of transactions in S&P 500 futures and constituent S&P 500 stocks. Such studies infer from the transaction prices of stocks that have traded information about the prices of other stocks that have been delayed in trading. Even after careful study of the available data, we may not be sure what transaction costs actually were on Black Monday.

Discontinuous Markets

During the life of many portfolio insurance strategies, adjustments are made to compensate for unexpected shifts in the realized volatility of the underlying asset. Generally speaking, if volatility is higher than expected, the hedge is increased to make the strategy more conservative; if volatility is lower than expected, the hedge is reduced to make the strategy more aggressive. Given a required minimum rate of return, these adjustments prevent the strategy from stopping out and being forced completely and permanently into cash to guarantee delivery of the minimum return. While an insurance strategy that is forced to stop-out may still be able to deliver the minimum return, it will fail to capture any portion of subsequent upside movement in the underlying index.

Unfortunately, even for insurance strategies where some forethought was given to the possibility of stopping-out, the discontinuity in the markets and the sudden increase in volatility experienced on October 19 made it virtually impossible to prevent stop-out by making the usual adjustments. Indeed, the 7 per cent gap-down opening at the beginning of the day, and the last 200-point move in the DJIA, occurred so quickly that it was probably impossible to execute the requisite number of futures transactions during those times. As a result, although few insurers missed the minimum return, they were stopped-out and forced into cash for the remainder of the life of their policies. In effect, the volatility that had been expected to occur smoothly over the entire planned life of the policy instead occurred in one day.

Effects

The dependency of typical portfolio insurance strategies on preconditions of low transaction costs and market continuity should have been well-known to both those marketing the strategy and those using the strategy on their own portfolios. Even the most elementary understanding of the implementation of portfolio insurance would make this obvious. Because these preconditions were severely violated on Black Monday, it should not be surprising that portfolio insurance strategies, even though they typically did not violate the minimum return, did not in many cases perform as expected. What came as a shock to most participants was not that portfolio insurance performed poorly, given the market environment, but that the preconditions were so suddenly and strongly violated in the market.

The comparative performance of alternative

portfolio insurers during the crash has been a topic of some interest. Despite the focus of attention on the amount of trading on October 19, I believe that differential performance depends primarily on the extent to which exchange-traded options were properly used to implement the insurance, the extent of the hedge already in place at the close of trading on October 16, and the extent to which it was possible to implement the insurance directly by trading stocks.

Although there were sound reasons not to implement portfolio insurance with options, policies properly relying on options instead of futures would nonetheless have been immune to the effects of high transaction costs and discontinuities. Once an option position is in place, it can be interpreted as providing the appropriate hedging adjustment automatically, without visible trading. Indeed, if purchased options were used to implement the strategy, with substantially expanding premiums resulting from the increase in perceived volatility, a portfolio insurer might even have shown a profit.

More importantly, conservative policies that started 50 per cent hedged, or originally aggressive policies that had become 50 per cent hedged because of the stock market decline over the previous two months, would have lost half as much as very aggressive policies just started with no hedge, even if they did no trading on October 19. The answer to the simple question, "How hedged were you going into Black Monday?" probably goes farther in explaining differential performance than any other factor.

Finally, insurers with access to the cash assets, even though they would have paid a large bid-ask spread in the stock market, could at least have avoided the additional unfavorable basis costs (if any) of using the futures market.

Ironically, the actions taken by a portfolio insurer in the futures market on Black Monday may have been of little importance by comparison. As we have seen, to the extent transaction costs were high, expected and to a large extent realized, losses may not have been greatly different whether one traded or not.

How Did Portfolio Insurance Strategies Affect the Crash?

Any investor who unexpectedly reduced his holdings of stock, shorted stock, covered long futures positions or increased open sold futures positions on October 19 contributed to the crash. Several regulatory agencies are currently gathering data in an attempt to align the amount of net sales with particular motivations. A proper analysis should focus on particular shifts in *net sold positions* as a percentage of the total shift in net sold positions in the stock and futures markets, rather than on an analysis of *trading volume*.

For example, an investor who began the day holding 1000 shares of stock and who bought 200 shares and sold 500 shares over the day, would have shifted his net position by 300 sold shares. To determine the total change in net sold stock positions over the day, these figures are value-weighted and added together across all investors selling shares on net during the day.

On Black Monday, about 162,000 S&P 500 futures contracts were traded for a total market value of about $22 billion. In addition, about 604,000,000 NYSE shares of stock were traded, with a market value of about $30 billion. Rough estimates of the dollar value of futures and stock sold by portfolio insurers on that day are $3.5 billion (26,000 contracts) and $2.5 billion, respectively. (I caution that these are very rough estimates, soon to become more accurate as the total size of portfolio insurance trades is made public.) Aggregating these figures together, portfolio insurers accounted for about 11½ per cent of the volume. Including trading on the American and regional exchanges and other index futures contracts, this figure may be reduced to about 9 per cent. If, say, three-quarters of the volume is accounted for by investors reducing their positions in stock and futures, then portfolio insurers would have accounted for about 12 per cent of the dollar change in net sold positions.

Is this "substantial"? It's difficult to say. It was well known from several sources that the amount of equities committed to portfolio insurance strategies was on the order of $60 to $80 billion before the crash. Therefore, one important mitigating factor is that much of the trading should have been anticipated by professional investors. Much more dangerous to the market are traders who unexpectedly revise their positions in the same direction, catching the market unprepared. Finally, it is well to remember that firms with portfolio insurance programs in place did not select these programs at random. For the most part, the programs were self-selected by the insurers' atypically strong desire to protect themselves against losses beyond a specified amount. Many of them might have been sellers during the week of the crash, even without a formal portfolio insurance strategy in place.

There is another important mitigating influence. As long as increases in transaction costs to portfolio insurers go hand-in-hand with rapid shifts in market values, these costs create a natural brake on the impact of portfolio insurance on market prices. A strong case can be made that transaction costs were very high on October 19. Under these conditions, a rational implementation of portfolio insurance would have stopped far short of implementing the full hedge that would have otherwise been called for. Indeed, this is precisely what happened.

We must also remember that the crash had many other potential causes that have been mentioned in the press. A partial list would include (1) the apparently unjustified and unprecedented rapid rise in market prices over the previous year, (2) the Dow's decline of 475 points during the two months previous to October 19, which left many investors poised to press the sell button, (3) fears of increasing interest rates and a resurgence of inflation, (4) dissatisfaction concerning the ability of Congress to control the federal deficit, (5) increasing protectionism in international trade, (6) fear of an increasing trade deficit, a fall in the dollar and a consequent withdrawal from U.S. markets of foreign investors, (7) reports of massive layoffs at securities brokerage firms during early October, (8) the apparent weakness of the executive branch of the federal government, as demonstrated by the Iran/Contra scandal and the failure to secure confirmation of Robert Bork to the Supreme Court, (9) fear of U.S. retaliation against escalating aggressive actions taken by Iran in the Persian Gulf, (10) proposed changes in the tax laws governing mergers and acquisitions, (11) fear that the mechanical structure of the market might fail going into October 19, and (12) observed failures of the structure during the crash.

This last concern was probably the most significant in precipitating the ensuing panic, as specialists closed trading in several large stocks because of order imbalances, as market-makers left the floors of the futures and options exchanges, as the capital of program traders dried up (uncoupling the futures and stock markets), as regulators considered trading halts, as the NYSE's SUPER DOT system for processing program trades experienced a massive mechanical failure because of system overload, as brokers throughout the country failed to answer phones and process clients' orders, as brokerage house and clearing firm failures became likely, and as banks became reluctant to extend loans to specialists and other traders.

The case that portfolio insurance was a substantial contributor to the market crash is also somewhat weakened by the fact that portfolio insurance currently plays a very small role in foreign markets, and yet the crash was international in scope. Finally, it is difficult to blame the subsequent prolonged increased volatility of the stock market on portfolio insurance. These observations strongly suggest that other, more important factors have been at work.

What Should be Done to Reduce the Probability of Crashes?

The continuing challenge to the design of securities markets has been to provide methods of liquid risk transfer among investors, while at the same time assuring the viability of the market mechanism permitting these transfers.

I am concerned that regulatory agencies will fall back on old remedies and fail to seek creative solutions to new problems. In recent years, it seems to me, our securities markets have undergone a significant change: Many large investors seem willing to buy or sell very large blocks of stock or index futures on short notice. Some of these may be portfolio insurers; most are investors attempting to shift their asset allocation for other reasons.

In large part, the willingness to make large trades can be attributed to reductions in the cost of trading. For example, in 1984 turnover on the NYSE reached 49 per cent, 2½ times greater than in 1975, and block trades represented 50 per cent of traded shares, about three times greater than in 1975. In addition, the introduction of index futures in 1982 and index options in 1983, as well as new technology-based methods of programmed trading, have increased the ease with which portfolios of stocks can be traded as a group.

In this new environment, without a substantial expansion of the capitalization of specialists and market-makers, the possibility of exchanges becoming overwhelmed with orders on one side of the market is more likely. There are some proposals for changing the market mechanism, which would reduce this possibility and at the same time increase market liquidity. We should embrace any of these changes immediately.

Formalized Voluntary "Sunshine" Trading

Suppose that, before the S&P 500 futures market opens, you plan to sell 5000 futures contracts at 11:00 if the index stays near its current level. If formal "sunshine" trading were allowed, you would be able to post these intentions on a bulletin board at the Chicago Mercantile Exchange before the opening of the market at 8:30; your trading intentions would also be carried via computer to broker-dealers all around the country. To prevent price manipulation, you would be required, as a sunshine trader, to carry out the trade if your stated conditions were met.

Many large traders, such as portfolio insurers, whose trades are not motivated by information may be attracted to sunshine trading as a way of creating a more orderly market to handle the other side of their trades. While the advisability for an investor of this form of trading is controversial among professionals, it should nonetheless be encouraged; voluntary advance disclosure of trading intentions can only enhance liquidity, compared with the alternative of suddenly surprising the market with a large order.

While the proposal submitted by the New York Futures Exchange to the CFTC concerning disclosure of trading intentions has not yet been approved, I believe the CFTC is likely to permit this type of trading in index futures when computer systems have been revised by data vendors to carry notification of sunshine trades. Unfortunately, vendors of prices may not voluntarily revise their software to carry such notification until there are sunshine trades to announce; so the proposal seems stymied at this juncture. I would hope that the parties involved would be encouraged to work together to make formalized sunshine trading a reality.

Sunshine trading should also be permitted on other markets. Many exchanges may actively resist sunshine trading proposals because such trading tends to lead to a matching of public orders with each other, thereby circumventing the intermediation role played by specialists and market-makers.

Periodic Single-Price Auctions

The closest thing to an ideal single-price auction occurs at the opening on the NYSE. Supplies and demands are aggregated and executed at a single price—the lowest accepted bid and the highest accepted offer (which are the same). All market orders, limit orders to buy higher than that price, and limit orders to sell lower than that price are filled. If a trading imbalance occurs, the imbalance is announced and investors have a chance to change their orders.

Single-price auctions should be held at other times during the trading day, not just at the open. Like sunshine trading, single-price auctions take the pressure off the specialists or market-makers and reduce the damage to their capital during times of rapid price change in the same direction. Again, however, this is a proposal that may be resisted by exchanges because it also leads to circumvention of the normal intermediation services performed by specialists and market-makers.[3]

Side-by-Side Trading of Related Securities

Consider trading an underlying stock and its associated options contracts at the same physical location. Hedged positions would be easier to execute, economies of scale and the reduction of information trading should reduce transaction costs, and illegal trading practices would be more easily detected. Of course, the trading of options and stocks together would entail a major restructuring of those markets and would face considerable opposition from entrenched interests.[4]

Reduced Margin for Fully-Hedged Futures Positions

There seems to be little reason to increase margin requirements for investors who are completely hedged, because these investors are already effectively 100 per cent margined.[5] For example, an investor who holds a diversified portfolio of common stocks should be able to sell futures covering a large portion of the value of the stock portfolio with very little, if any, required margin. Mechanisms should be in place that would allow that investor to pledge his stock portfolio as collateral and meet calls for variation margin by temporarily borrowing against that collateral, with the requirement that he liquidate his stock portfolio as needed in an orderly fashion.

During the week of October 19, several hedgers were forced to sell stock at a discount to raise variation margin due the next business day. Under this proposal, hedgers would be allowed to borrow temporarily to meet variation margin and to liquidate their stock to pay off the loan under the normal five-day stock-settlement procedure.

Alignment of Margin Requirements

I have wondered for some time why initial and maintenance margins on exchange-traded common stocks were 50 per cent and 30 per cent, respectively, while speculative maintenance margins in index futures contracts, prior to October 19, were about 7 per cent. Futures positions are resettled every day, but the marking-to-the-market of maintenance margins on stocks is quite similar. The typical individual stock is clearly more risky than a stock market index, but this relatively small differential in risks hardly justifies such a large differential in margin requirements. The truth is that margin requirements are to a large extent an accident of history, in part the result of the division of the regulation of financial instruments between the SEC and the CFTC.

Increases in Speculative Margin or Capital Requirements

The lower the level of speculative margin requirements, during times of normal market volatility, the easier it is for investors to take positions and the greater the liquidity of the market. During times of high volatility, however, investors with little margin may become overextended and be forced to sell or buy, compounding the problems that arise when the market has to absorb a lot of volume from one direction. Or investors such as specialists and market-makers may simply be forced to step aside because of inadequate capitalization. Ironically, as we have recently witnessed, the very provisions that lead to high liquidity in times of normal volatility can cause liquidity to dry up during periods of high volatility.

The level of initial speculative margin required for S&P 500 futures contracts was raised from $10,000 per contract before October 19 to its current level of $20,000 per contract, or to about 12 per cent of the value of the stock underlying the contract. Many individuals believe that this requirement is still too low. Should this requirement be raised?

Many products are purposely engineered with specific stochastic failure rates built in. For example, it simply does not pay to manufacture a car that will never break down. This same principle applies to the market for stocks. After over 50 years of more or less uninterrupted service, the market finally experienced two or three days when it failed to function as usual and came close to a total breakdown. Should we re-engineer the market to reduce further the probability of failure, or should we save costs during normal times and be content with the current built-in failure rate? The answer will depend both on the extent of the damage incurred during a failure and the expected frequency of failure.

In general, because speculative margin requirements should depend on the volatility of underlying assets, margin should be raised above normal levels during times of high volatility, such as we are now experiencing. This provides a case for temporarily increasing required margin for stocks as well as for unhedged options and futures. However, I believe it is a mistake to change margin requirements without ample warning, particularly during a period when the market is very vulnerable to sudden large changes in prices. Increasing requirements at these times can easily increase instability.

Although increases in speculative futures margins may be advisable, I suggest that forced sales by speculators in index futures to cover variation margin played a small role in the market crash. By contrast, sales by margined investors in the stock market almost surely played a much larger role, if for no other reason than that the market value of outstanding shares is far larger than the market value of the assets underlying the open interest in index futures.

Increasing speculative margin requirements obviously involves a tradeoff, in terms of liquidity, between low-volatility and high-volatility environments. Other proposals, such as the one described below, would reduce liquidity with little compensating benefit.

Price–Move Limits for Index Futures

Thirty-point limits were imposed on S&P 500 index futures contracts on October 23 and remain in force as of this writing. It has been argued that such limits (1) provide more time for investors to raise variation margin, (2) reduce the potential size of errors made by floor traders, thereby substantially reducing the likelihood in fast-moving markets of a floor trader bringing down his clearing firm to make up for his own bankruptcy, (3) provide time for clearing firms to reassess the credit they should extend to investors whose accounts they guarantee, (4) reduce the tendencies of investors who know they are in default to "double-up" their bets before they are forced to stop trading, (5) reduce the probability that an investor will voluntarily default on a futures position, (6) give the futures market time to adjust calmly to quickly moving prices and thereby reduce the magnitude of price whipsaws when investors are acting under panic, (7) prevent the index futures market from being blamed for abetting substantial declines in the stock market, and (8) represent an historically accepted way of controlling the magnitude of price changes in futures markets.

These arguments are far from compelling. No price-limit rule is going to be able to distinguish between a panicked reaction and a fundamentally justified price change. In the latter case, price limits trap investors into positions, substantially increasing their risk. A sequence of price-limit moves in the same direction can impose huge unavoidable losses. In the extreme, we have the infamous example of the Hong Kong Stock Exchange, which shut down trading for a week, thereby trapping many investors into untenable positions.

A further problem with limits is the tendency of the limit to act as a price magnet: As the futures price approaches the limit, the actions of investors, all fearful of being locked into their positions, drive the price even further toward the limit.

Finally, just as in the case of margins, I believe it is a mistake to impose or strengthen price limits during periods of sudden increases in market volatility. For example, in the first four days after October 19, the S&P 500 index futures price at the open gapped down 18.25 points, up 20.5 points, up 23.75 points and down 48.25 points in daily succession. It thus appeared that the 30-point limit imposed on the fifth day was very likely to be triggered (although, fortuitously, it was not). If the futures market had subsequently moved strongly up, we might have seen hedged investors with sold futures positions desperately buying back futures and selling stocks to meet variation mar-

gin. With the relative absence of program trading, this could have pushed futures prices toward their limit, while at the same time causing stock prices to fall.

How Will Portfolio Insurance Strategies be Modified?

In many cases, portfolio insurance strategies did not perform as expected during the market crash because of unexpected and sudden increases in transaction costs and large discontinuities in market prices. I believe it is prudent to presume that the probability of witnessing these kinds of markets again, at least for the near future, is much higher than one would have thought before the crash.

In addition, to providers of portfolio insurance, both index futures and options markets are for the time being much less useful than before the crash. Trading volume in both these markets has been cut in half, bid-ask spreads have widened, margin requirements for hedgers have been increased, price-move limits have been imposed on index futures, and the regulatory environment continues to be highly uncertain.

Even so, with the doubling of stock market volatility and the events of the week of October 19 so savagely imprinted on investors' minds, the demand continues for some form of portfolio insurance that can be delivered under current conditions.

The preference-based case for dynamic strategies remains unchanged. That is (in general terms), those who are sufficiently more concerned about downside risk than the average investor should attempt to buy insurance. Those who are sufficiently less concerned about downside risk than the average investor should attempt to sell insurance. All others should buy and hold.[6]

Those who proclaim the death of preference-based motivations for dynamic strategies are presupposing an implausible reformation of natural human desires. Nonetheless, the nature of the dynamic strategies investors will follow in the future will differ in several important ways from the strategies employed before the crash.

Alternative Buying Strategies

Even before the crash, it seemed that many investors who had attempted to buy portfolio insurance had selected policies containing "too much insurance." For example, an investor might choose a one-year policy with a minimum rate of return of zero. Although he might start out about 65 per cent invested in equities and 35 per cent invested in cash, as the expiration date approached he might soon find his portfolio either with almost nothing invested in equities (if the stock market fell) or with almost 100 per cent in equities (if the stock market rose). As this began to happen, most investors would find some reason to ratchet back to a more balanced position. After the crash, when many insured investors were completely in cash, and required by the initial policy to remain in cash for some time, these investors showed their true intentions by quickly "reinsuring" and moving to a more balanced position. It was not that these investors did not want insurance; rather, they wanted much less insurance than indicated by their initially stated intentions.

The extreme insurance policies selected by many investors could only be justified by a correspondingly extreme aversion to downside risk. As their subsequent actions revealed, a more appropriate policy for them would have been one that moved more slowly out of equities and into cash as the market fell (perhaps with a minimum exposure to equities of 25 per cent) and moved more slowly from cash into equities as the market rose (perhaps with a maximum exposure to equities of 85 per cent). I expect to see more strategies of this type in the future.[7]

In addition, I expect to see a greater emphasis by pension funds on "surplus" insurance rather than pension fund asset insurance.[8] This form of portfolio insurance typically requires much less trading than purely asset-based insurance.

Explicit Selling of Insurance

As the purchase of portfolio insurance became popular, it was surprising that few investors explicitly wanted to sell insurance. The other side of the market, to some extent supplied by rebalancers and investors following tactical asset allocation, was not well-organized.

Today, because of increased volatility, the apparent price of insurance is much higher than it was before the crash. Moreover, even when (if?) realized stock volatility falls back to more traditional levels, realistic pricing of insurance will probably be higher than before the crash. Under these circumstances, I believe, the market is likely to be better balanced, with explicit sellers as well as purchasers of insurance.

Transaction-Cost-Sensitive Strategies

To the extent transaction costs increase, fewer investors should engage in dynamic strategies. Only investors with attitudes toward downside risk very different from those of the average investor should consider dynamic strategies, and the dynamic strategies they should select should require less trading. The minimum-and-maximum-exposure strategy, surplus insurance and insurance of balanced, rather than pure equity, portfolios have all reduced expected portfolio turnover. There will also be more implementation of portfolio insurance utilizing spot, rather than futures, markets, not only as a way of controlling the impact of the basis, but also in response to the reduced usefulness of the futures markets.

For some insurance strategies, higher transaction costs increase the barrier around the ideal hedge ratio until a trade is triggered. The size of this barrier is continually adjusted in an attempt to create an optimal tradeoff between the expected level of realized transaction costs and the accuracy of delivery of the target payoff pattern. This tends to reduce portfolio turnover during periods of high transaction costs. But this adjustment only goes partway toward reflecting the full impact of variable transaction costs, because it leaves the target payoff pattern unchanged. This target pattern was probably chosen under an assumption concerning the level of transaction costs. Insurers need to find a way to adjust the target as transaction costs change during the life of a policy.

Unfortunately, significantly variable transaction costs during the life of a policy substantially complicate the task of delivering a specified payoff pattern with accuracy. Both buyers and sellers of portfolio insurance, implemented either in the spot or futures markets, must learn to tolerate increased unpredictability of outcome.

Increased Use of Exchange-Traded Options

The second precondition of successful portfolio insurance using spot or futures markets is market price continuity. Listed options clearly provide a way around this problem. Protection against discontinuities may come at a price, but many insurers may find the benefits worth that price.[9]

Unfortunately, the size of an individual investor's (or group of investors') position in CBOE index options on the S&P 100 or S&P 500 on one side of the market is limited to 15,000 contracts in the near maturity.[10] This limit severely reduces the interest of the largest investors in implementation of portfolio insurance with options.

Implications

Under post-crash conditions, successful implementation of a systematic dynamic strategy is more difficult, requiring a mixture of trading in the underlying spot assets, in futures and in options. Uncertainty about the level of transaction costs, potential discontinuities in market prices and uncertainty in the regulatory environment increase the difficulty of predicting the outcome from any type of dynamic strategy. Understandably, the demand for portfolio insurance has fallen off. Moving forward, we are likely to see increased technological sophistication and a more balanced variety of dynamic strategies in the future. ∎

Footnotes

1. See M. Rubinstein and H. Leland, "Replicating Options with Positions in Stock and Cash," *Financial Analysts Journal*, July/August 1981, p. 66.
2. The capital of program traders able to take arbitrage positions by selling stock they already owned was for the most part absorbed by positions taken prior to the crash. Other program traders who rely on short selling were largely shut out by the short-sale up-tick rule. In addition, trading delays substantially increased the risk of arbitrage-related transactions.
3. For a much more detailed analysis of single-price auctions, see Steven Wunsch's discussion in Kidder, Peabody's *Stock Index Futures* commentary dated October 29, 1987.
4. See J. Cox and M. Rubinstein, *Options Markets* (Englewood Cliffs, NJ: Prentice-Hall, 1985), p. 86.
5. Prior to October 19, futures hedgers were required to deposit $5,000 per contract; now the requirement has been raised to $15,000 per contract.
6. Compared with investors who buy and hold, buyers (sellers) of insurance adopt strategies that systematically transfer wealth toward (away from) risky assets and away from (toward) less risky assets as the relative values of risky assets rise (fall), and do the opposite as risky asset values fall.
7. Well before the crash, investors were moving in this direction by selecting longer-term policies (which also tend to moderate trading in the early years of the policy), but even these investors would be faced with taking extreme positions near the end of the policy. Some insurance vendors have attempted to replicate these more complex policies with minimum and maximum exposures, but potential clients seemed to prefer the simplicity of the more extreme forms of insurance.
8. Surplus is defined as the difference or the ratio of the market values of the assets and liabilities of the pension fund.
9. In a Black-Scholes environment, options are priced as if investors are risk-neutral. But, by their assumption, price movements are continuous. In discontinuous markets, it is possible that options may be priced relative to their underlying assets with built-in risk premiums. This could raise the market prices of most options above their Black-Scholes values.
10. The limits are 25,000 contracts irrespective of maturity. However, longer-maturity options have poor liquidity, and positions greater than 15,000 contracts must be reduced to that number when the options become the nearest maturity contracts.

Article 31

Circuit breakers

These safety mechanisms are triggered by rapid or heavy market changes, and they can have unintentional effects on the financial system

James T. Moser

The "circuit breakers" that have gradually been added to financial markets since 1987 got their toughest test of the year yesterday. They passed.
—Wall Street Journal, July 24, 1990.

The limits "did exactly what they were supposed to do," he said.
—New York Times, July 24, 1990, quoting a trader.

Press reports describing the markets' encounter with circuit breakers on July 23, 1990, regarded them as successful. Their apparent criterion for success is the fact that the Dow Jones Industrial Average rose 60 points after encountering the circuit breaker. The experience from other markets suggests that circuit breakers do not usually produce dramatic price reversals. But, they do have effects. This article examines these effects.

Circuit breakers are mechanisms used by management to control activity in capacity-constrained systems. The term circuit breaker originates in electrical engineering to describe a pre-set switch that shuts down electrical activity in excess of a system's design capacity. The activation level of the breaker reflects an *ex ante* decision on the capability of the system.

Circuit breaker activation is inherently costly. The system engineer designing a circuit-breaker makes an *ex ante* choice between temporary loss of the use of the system and reductions in the likelihood of permanent dam-age to system integrity. Activation of a circuit breaker intentionally imposes costs that are expected to be less than losses realized by exceeding the system's capacity. Cost considerations naturally focus on the value the intended users can expect to obtain through their use of the system.

Activation of circuit breakers can also have unintentional costs. These have two sources. First, activation of circuit breakers can lead to unanticipated convenience losses. For example, system engineers may undervalue some activities lost when a circuit breaker is activated. Therefore, system users with a financial stake in its operation have incentives to increase system capacity by allowing increases in the activation levels of circuit breakers. It is these incentives that produce pressure to re-allocate financial resources toward increased investment in the system. Thus, when private interests are involved, the ability to re-allocate resources insures that unanticipated convenience losses will be infrequent and temporary.

Second, costs are also incurred when unplanned uses of the system are disrupted. System engineers focusing on anticipated uses will not incorporate the value of unanticipated uses into their circuit-breaker decisions. These value losses are recognized only when service interruption motivates increased investment by such users. When value losses fail to attract investment, system engineers are not moti-

James T. Moser is a senior economist at the Federal Reserve Bank of Chicago.

vated to include these losses in the circuit-breaker decision. I refer to these interests as *public*, to distinguish them from *private* interests that do lead to increased investment in the system.

In financial markets, the intended effect of circuit breakers is to halt trading when activity levels threaten market viability. Earlier circuit breaker policy was determined within the affected market by parties having private rather than public interests in the activation of circuit breakers. Exchanges, responding to these interests, developed three separate circuit breaker mechanisms. *Order-imbalance* circuit breakers are intended to protect the interests of market makers in specialist markets. *Volume-induced* circuit breakers are intended to protect the viability of back-office operations. *Price-change* circuit breakers are intended to bring excessive volatility under control.

Recent developments in financial markets have elevated the importance of public interests. Markets are increasingly characterized as inter-related. This inter-relatedness increases the importance of price information flowing between markets. This is particularly true between the stock markets and the markets for financial derivatives—options and futures.

Futures exchanges have developed standardized contracts for a variety of financial assets. Value changes in these contracts are closely linked to developments in their related asset markets. Thus, asset prices serve the public purpose of determining gains and losses in futures contracts. Futures exchanges and their customers have benefitted from the price information generated by asset markets. Activation of circuit breakers interrupts this information flow, decreasing the public value of the services rendered by asset markets.

Futures markets offer a distinct set of services including opportunities to manage risks and additional routes to price discovery. Circuit breakers activated in these markets similarly disrupt these services, lessening their value. The stock-index futures contract illustrates this. Prices for these futures contracts are for hypothetical baskets of stocks. Thus, a single quote determines the price of the futures basket, whereas in the asset market cash prices must be aggregated to produce a cash index. In addition, daily settlement in the futures market is in cash, greatly simplifying order processing. The simplicity of stock-index futures contracts produces an ideal instrument for institutions to manage systematic risk levels through simultaneous trading in asset markets and futures. Circuit breakers disrupt the normal synchronization of price changes between futures contracts and asset prices. This disruption amplifies the risk that gains realizable in one market may be unavailable to offset losses in the other market.

The current proliferation of derivative-asset markets with differing capacity constraints, combined with intensive intermarket trading, raises coordination issues that were less crucial in the past. Circuit breakers activated in one market now can affect several markets, not only the market in which they were activated. Thus, circuit breakers in financial markets can influence public interests. These public costs are realized in two ways. First, circuit breaker interruption of private markets serves to shift trading into markets that remain open. Such interruptions initiate a chain of events that ultimately generates demand for a lender of last-resort to supply liquidity to the financial system. Second, price-change circuit breakers shift credit risk to gaining positions that implicitly extend credit to loss positions. Their creditworthiness may decrease the quality of exchange guarantees of performance.

The next section describes the three types of circuit breakers. Then, I examine the history of circuit breaker activity. An analysis of the unintended result of price limits on liquidity demands and the quality of nonperformance guarantees follows.

Classification of circuit breakers

Circuit breakers are of three types. Each addresses a different design-capability issue. The first, the order-imbalance circuit breaker, occurs in specialist markets. Inequalities in the number of buy and sell orders are balanced by specialists trading for their own accounts. These trades maintain orderly markets by smoothing short-run order imbalances. Substantial order imbalances increase the risk born by specialists. This, in turn, jeopardizes orderly markets. The second type, volume-induced, occurs when order processing becomes uneconomic. At low volume, order processing does not meet costs. High volume impedes the ability of the exchange to effectively process orders. Markets close when either volume effect pushes trading costs to uneconomic levels. The third type, the price-triggered circuit breaker, closes markets when a given price level is reached. This last type originated in the futures markets. Such circuit breakers are called "price limits." Justifications of price limits are couched in terms of controlling "excessive" volatility.

Order-imbalance circuit breakers

Stock markets activate order-imbalance circuit breakers at the request of a specialist. The specialist asks for a suspension of trade in an individual stock when an order imbalance occurs. In these cases, suspension gives the specialist time to determine a market-clearing price based upon information obtained off the exchange floor. Following the price determination period, the market re-opens with the specialist taking a position at the newly determined price. The purpose of this circuit breaker is to protect the specialist from large losses.

Order imbalances were a problem in both the 1987 and 1989 breaks. In 1987, selling pressure at the October 19 opening prevented trading in 140 of the NYSE-listed stocks in the S&P 500 during the first half hour. In 1989, openings on October 16, 1989 were similarly delayed. (Most stocks were reported not opened during the first fifteen minutes of trading. Beginning 8:45 CT, stocks began opening and trading was reported at 9:15.) In both cases, the intended effect of the order-imbalance circuit breakers was to protect specialists from losses incurred by purchases in declining markets.

Activation of these circuit breakers have unintentional effects. Trading halts in individual stocks create uncertainty about the correct level of the aggregate indexes. This, in turn, tends to be reflected in the futures contract. As a result, the futures contract becomes more likely to encounter a price limit. (On October 16, 1989, it did hit the open limit—5 points down.) When a price limit is reached futures trading stops, shifting some trades to the stock exchange. These trades tend to aggravate any existing order-imbalance problems.

Volume-induced circuit breakers

The cost-effectiveness of order processing depends on the level of trading volume. At low trading levels, breakeven costs are not met. The determination of exchange trading hours recognizes that the fixed costs of operations must be covered by revenues generated from trading activities. Exchanges schedule closings based on expectations that additions to these fixed costs will not be adequately compensated. Thus, daily closes can be construed as activation of a circuit breaker.

Trading volume can surpass the ability of exchange back offices to process the paperwork required to document executed trades. When this happens, the effectiveness of order processing is reduced, producing additional costs as the need for correcting orders rises. These costs are expected to rise with trading volume. With these additional costs, exchange operations can become uneconomic and the exchange closes.

In 1968, the stock exchanges instituted a temporary four-day week during the last half of the year, closing on Wednesdays to increase the time available to process paperwork. Heavy volume in the period prior to the four-day week had led to increases in errors executing orders. These midweek closings insured that each five-trading-day delivery period included at least one nontrading day, allowing the back offices to catch up.

More recently, heavy volume appears to have complicated the order-matching activity of the specialists. Stock trading volume during the 1987 price break surpassed the ability of specialists to match orders. As a result, executions were not timely and the ticker lagged current trades. Changes instituted after 1987 substantially increased the capacity of the exchange to process orders to an estimated one billion shares daily. However, the trading suspensions that resulted from the volume on October 13, 1989, suggest a lower capacity. At the rate of trading in the last hour of October 13, daily volume would have been just over 703 million shares. Volume on October 16, 1989, the heaviest day of trading since October 1987, was 416 million shares. After processing the overhang from the previous Friday (most stocks were trading by 10:15), stock trading proceeded smoothly all day.

Price-limit circuit breakers

In futures markets, price limits restrict trading to a band of prices generally symmetrical above and below the previous trading day's settlement price.[1] The stated goals of circuit breaker policies have historically been to control volatility. More recently, price limits on stock index contracts have been set to coordinate price movements in the cash and futures markets. Price limits serve as market-closing rules because:

1) short trades (sales of futures contracts) are not offered on up-limit days—the market clearing price is higher; and

2) long trades (buying futures contracts) are not offered on down-limit days—the market clearing price is lower.

Historically, the rules committees of the futures exchanges incorporated price limits into trading rules in response to threatened regulatory intervention. That pattern suggests that price-triggered circuit breakers would not exist without potential regulatory intervention.

Past circuit breaker experience

This history of the price-limit form of circuit breaker demonstrates that price limits appear to resolve "political" volatility.[2] The imposition of price limits, an apparent impediment to the price discovery purpose of futures exchanges, coincides with threats to the independence of the exchanges. Rather than face increased regulatory oversight and lose their ability to resolve disputes internally, the exchanges accommodated pressures for regulation by self-imposing price limits.

Early history of price limits

The earliest occurrence of a price limit in futures trading was at the Dojima exchange in Japan during the early 18th century. Settlement in the *koku* "small futures" contract for rice was determined by the average of the previous three days' forward-closing prices. If this price deviated by more than a fixed amount from the cash price for rice, all contracts were either reversed out or delivered. This effectively discontinued trading in the contract by eliminating all futures positions. Also, the futures price was tied to the cash market, avoiding the potential criticism that futures trading caused problems in cash markets. Imposition of the rule came during a time when rice markets were described as "deteriorating." Deteriorating markets are often characterized by price volatility.

The first instance of a price limit rule in the United States came during the First World War. On February 1, 1917, Germany announced that its submarines would sink all ships found in the major Atlantic shipping lanes. Cotton prices for May delivery on the New York Cotton Exchange closed down by a record of over five cents a pound. By the following Monday, however, the market had recovered to within one and one-half cents of the earlier price. In subsequent weeks, futures prices continued to be extremely volatile. The threat of attacks on shipping continued to run down prices as traders feared lost access to the European markets. Cotton prices rose as markets responded to news of potentially large purchases of cotton for military uniforms. Congress responded by supplying flat-rate three percent war loss insurance—a substantial discount from the then-current Lloyd's of London quote of ten percent. Cotton prices reached an all-time high following the introduction of this subsidized insurance.

The futures exchanges trading cotton responded to this volatility in two ways. On June 20, 1917, the British Board of Trade closed down cotton futures trading and the New York Cotton Exchange increased margin requirements. Separately, the U.S. government requested a price limit on the cotton contract. On August 22, 1917, a three-cent price limit was imposed. This limit remained in effect for the duration of the war. Interestingly, there is no record of a limit day during this period.

Also during the First World War, the Food Administration froze prices on wheat to prevent profiteering in that commodity. This action closed down trading in wheat futures at the Chicago Board of Trade. However, other grain prices were not frozen and their corresponding futures contracts traded freely. Since these grains are partially substitutable for wheat, government policy regarding wheat induced volatility in other grains. Futures prices for these commodities reflected this volatility, attracting the attention of the Food Administration. As a result of this scrutiny, the Board of Trade instituted a two-cent per day price limit on the oat contract and the New York Mercantile Exchange introduced a three-cent per day price limit on soy bean oil contracts. These price limits were removed once trading in wheat futures resumed after the war.

Price limits were formalized in 1925 at the Chicago Board of Trade. The 1925 Annual Report reported a modification to all contracts allowing the Board of Directors to set price-change limits of five percent of the preceding day's average closing price, following a ten-hour notice period. (For comparison, a five percent limit on wheat in today's wheat contract comes to 18.9 cents per bushel. The present limit is twenty cents per bushel.) Determination of an emergency was left to the Board. Nevertheless, price limits retained their temporary character, to be used only in emergency situations.

Direct federal intervention in agricultural markets during peace time began in the early 1930s under the authority of the Agricultural Adjustment Act. The Federal Farm Board, attempting to maintain prices in spite of large supplies of wheat, opened long futures contracts in May 1931 and 1932 wheat. Uncertainty about government policy (including complaints that officials were manipulating prices in their own interests) increased the frequency of emergency use of price limits.

(A recent proposal by Robert Heller makes similar use of futures markets. He argues the current policy of supplying liquidity during a market break disrupts monetary policy. Instead he suggests the Fed supply liquidity directly by taking long futures positions. His use of futures contracts is reasoned from the same basis as the Federal Farm Board policy of six decades ago—both approaches avoid the problem of the federal government holding and disposing of assets. The experience of the 1930s suggests that careful consideration should be given to the problem of contract expiration.)[3]

Passage of the National Industrial Recovery Act in July 1933 opened the way for trade associations to enforce price stabilization agreements, with the federal government acting both as architect and enforcing partner. Application for these partnerships was made through the National Recovery Administration (NRA) with the agreements chartered through Executive Orders by President Franklin Roosevelt. The agreements came in the form of codes for fair competition.

Grain price volatility continued to be high after the Farm Board ceased its price manipulations. The drought of the period and uncertainty about government policy were contributing factors. This high volatility led to Department of Agriculture pressure in July 1933 for a fair-trade agreement among the grain exchanges. Pressure on the exchanges to comply came in the form of a proposal by the Agricultural Adjustment Administration and the Grain Futures Administration that would have empowered the Secretary of Agriculture to modify and enforce trading rules at the futures exchanges. The proposed authority included limits on individual trading, limits on daily price changes, and margin setting. The futures exchanges complied with the request and Executive Order No. 6648, entitled "Code of Fair Competition for Grain Exchanges and Members Thereof", was signed by President Roosevelt on March 20, 1934. The agreement, implemented the next day, included price limits which could not be exceeded, but did permit exchanges to set limits below the prescribed maximums.

The Supreme Court ruling in the Schechter Poultry Corporation case on May 27, 1935, declared the NRA codes unconstitutional. Following the Schechter decision, Congressional hearings began on the Commodity Exchange Act to broaden the scope of federal regulatory powers over the futures exchanges. These powers had previously been lodged within the Grain Futures Administration. Congressional discussion indicated the proposed Act would institutionalize the defunct NRA codes.

To thwart increased regulation, the Chicago Board of Trade incorporated permanent price limits on all its contracts. (At the same time, the Board of Trade also eliminated trading of options on futures, then called "priviledges [sic]." These were also targeted in Congressional hearings.) The action began the use of price limits as a standard contract feature. The Commodity Exchange Act later passed specifying only regulatory review, rather than expanded powers, over contract details—including price limits.

Circuit breakers in the 1980s

In 1982, futures contracts on stock indexes were introduced. The initial contracts, keeping with standard practice, were introduced with price limits. However, for the first time since the 1930s, these limits were dropped on objections from New York stock trading interests. In late 1984, price limits were dropped on all International Monetary Market contracts for foreign exchange.

The movement away from price limits continued until the market break of October 1987, when price limits were instituted on the S&P 500 contract. Three of the six commissions studying issues of the market break recommended significant regulatory changes. With regard to price limits the recommendations differ substantially. The Brady Commission recommended coordinated trading halts. While no specific method was proposed, the Commission indicated that price limits should be considered among the possible mechanisms. The NYSE "Katzenbach" study group said that price limits will not resolve market break issues. Their proposals focused on increasing the cost of trading to prevent speculation. They specifically proposed requiring delivery of stocks on stock-index futures contracts--increasing the cost of trading futures. The SEC study recommended against price limits on stock-index contracts. The SEC proposal suggested optional delivery of stock on index contracts, again increasing the cost of trading futures.

After the 1987 break, price limits were imposed on stock-index futures. The stated reason for these limits was to synchronize futures and cash prices. In 1988, the S&P 500 contract traded with a level-determined price limit. At levels below 275, the limit was 15 index points ($7500 per contract); between 275.05 and 325, the limit was 20 index points ($10,000 per contract); and, above 325, the limit was 25 index points ($12,500 per contract). Initial margins on these contracts were $15,000, twice the pre-break amount. In addition, a five-point limit was established at market opening. On reaching an opening limit, trading is suspended for two minutes and reopened at a new opening level. The opening limit rule holds only for the first ten minutes of trading.

The 1987 market break also led to introduction of price-triggered circuit breakers on the New York Stock Exchange. After a fall of 25 points in the Dow Jones Industrial Average (DJIA), the Sidecar program re-prioritized orders, giving priority to small (less that one million dollars) orders. After a decline of 250 points in the DJIA, the stock market would be closed for one hour. After a 400-point decline in the DJIA, the stock market would be closed for two hours. In addition, the DOT (Designated Order Turnaround) program would be shut down after a 50-point decline in the DJIA.

The mini-crash of October 1989

Recalling that the intent of these circuit breakers is to synchronize cash and futures markets, the events of October 13, 1989, provide a gauge for the usefulness of circuit breaker mechanisms. The evidence suggests that price limits did not synchronize these markets and may have routed dynamic-hedge trades into the stock market.

At 1:43 (CDT) negotiators announced the failure of financing for the proposed UAL buyout. The announcement sent the stock and index-futures markets into a steep decline. At 2:00 the DJIA was down 55 points. This corresponds to a 7.3 point drop in the S&P. Seven minutes later, the S&P futures contract hit its limit—12 points down. With futures trading suspended, the DJIA at 2:30 was down 114.76 points or roughly 15.3 S&P points. At 2:30, the futures contract reopened, but closed again fifteen minutes later—down 30 points. At the close of trading (3:00), the DJIA was down 190 points, or 25.3 S&P points. Quotes from the stock market clearly lagged behind those from the futures market. The circuit breakers do not appear to have kept prices in line.

Trading volume was affected by the circuit breakers. Figure 1 shows NYSE volume for half-hour intervals for 10/13/89 and 10/16/89. Volume at 1:30 on 10/13 was 125.52 million shares for the day, or 12.55 million shares per half-hour interval. The market response to the UAL announcement in the 1:30-2:00 interval increased volume to 17.48 million shares, or 39 percent above the average prior to 1:30 but still less than two of the previous half-hour intervals.

At 2:07 CDT futures trading was suspended for the remainder of the half-hour period. Minutes later Chicago Board Options Exchange (CBOE) closed without re-opening. Volume during that period was 45.86 million shares, 265 percent above the average and more than twice the busiest previous period. During the last half-hour of trading. volume was 396 percent above the average—nearly

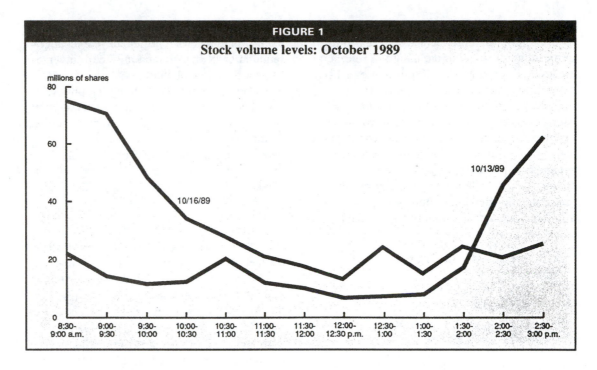

FIGURE 1

Stock volume levels: October 1989

millions of shares

four times the busiest period before 1:30. This trading might be explained as a response to new information and, therefore, independent of the incidence of circuit breakers but evidence in the Index futures pit suggests more was involved.

After limits were hit in the S&P 500 pit for the second time, a limited number of sell orders were executed at the limit price despite the disadvantageous price obtained there. Further, at the official 3:15 close of index trading, 2,000 sell orders worth $330 million were said to be outstanding. The pattern of selling in the Index pit indicates that traders were searching for reliable executions. The closest available substitute to selling stock-index futures is the sale of stock holdings. Thus, the substantial increase in stock volume can be related to the incidence of the CME circuit breaker. (See Figure 2).

The consequence of the volume increase may have been an increased difficulty in keeping up with the flow of orders. Heavy selling after 1:30 CDT produced suspensions in ten stocks with seven not re-opening. This suggests that stock markets were unable to handle the increased volume.

Finally, the evidence from the 1989 price break reveals three weaknesses. First, volume increases after price limits were encountered suggest these circuit breakers routed trades from the futures markets to the stock markets.

This is a serious concern. There is good evidence from the 1987 break that order imbalances are positively correlated with price changes. Policies tending to exacerbate the order-imbalance problem are likely to increase price volatility during price swings encountered in the future. Second, both the price lags reflected in the DJIA and the suspensions in stock trading indicate that the circuit breakers did not keep prices in line. Third, taking the $330 million overhang in the futures market to be intended to cover stock positions of institutional traders, at least one-third of a billion dollars went unhedged.

New circuit breakers in place

After the 1989 market break, price limits were revised. The following describes current limit procedures for the S&P contract. The five-point opening limit is retained. After the opening interval and at all levels of the index, current levels are: On a 12-point drop in the index prior to 2:30 PM (Central Time), trading is suspended for thirty minutes; on a 20-point drop in the index prior to 1:30 PM, trading is suspended for one hour; on a 30-point change (up or down), trading is suspended until 50 percent of S&P stocks (by capitalized value) are open for trading.

The NYSE also revised its circuit breakers to restrain program trading. After a 30-point drop in the DJIA, incoming orders are routed into the Sidecar for fifteen minutes. After a 75-point drop trading orders are Sidecar'd for thirty minutes. In addition, the CME rejects incoming S&P 500 contract orders after a 12-point drop in the S&P.

The emphasis on drops clarifies the purpose of recent price-linked, circuit-breaker policies. They do not resolve cash flow problems for the futures exchanges—else limits would be imposed on the upside as well. Nor do they control volatility—for the same reason. They do shield the futures exchanges from the criticism that futures trading pulls down stock prices.

Circuit breakers and the market for liquidity

Liquidity is the relative ease of matching buy and sell orders at recently observed prices. Sellers can always obtain liquidity by lowering offers to sell. The difference between the price they obtain and the previously observed prices they expected can be construed as the cost of liquidity. Buyers recognize that for some assets these costs may be high. Thus, their offers to buy incorporate the risk of encountering a high liquidity cost on the eventual sale of the asset. Buyers respond by adjusting bids downward.

Markets respond by organizing to keep liquidity costs low. They accomplish this through efficient matching of buy and sell orders backed up by methods to handle any order imbalances that may arise.

The market-making activity

Market making refers to the activity of matching buy and sell orders. In specialist markets such as the stock exchanges, orders to buy or sell arrive at a central post, are matched up by a specialist, and are posted as transactions. The specialist's order book is unbalanced when the number of buy and sell orders at the most recent price are unequal. When these order imbalances occur, exchange rules require the specialist to trade for his own position—buying in a declining market or selling in a rising market. Since these trades are aimed at re-balancing the order book, they may be loss trades for the specialist; that is, buying above the correct market price in a declining market or selling below in a rising market. These trades produce a balance of buy and sell orders and fulfill the specialist's re-

sponsibility of maintaining an orderly market. To facilitate this role, dealers have exchange-required capitalization and minimum inventories for their stock listings.

Under an interest-rate targeting policy, the Fed acts as a marketmaker in markets directly linked to reserve assets. Reserve policy effects credit levels so that a stable monetary policy depends on a stable market for reserves. To maintain this stability, the Fed acts as a specialist in reserves—both buying and selling to prevent order imbalances.

Links between financial markets

The Federal Reserve is affected by circuit breakers because markets for stocks, bonds, and futures contracts are fundamentally linked through the payments system and the market for reserves. To see this, consider the problem faced by the specialist after a steep decline in stock prices. In the process of buying stock to maintain an orderly market, losses have been encountered. In addition, inventories of stock, generally purchased on margin, have been marked down and require additional financing. Summing the financing needs of many specialists after declines of the magnitude experienced during the breaks of 1987 and 1989, one will generally observe a large increase in the demand for loanable funds. Institutions supplying funds to specialists respond by selling short-term Treasury securities to meet reserve requirements. Thus, the demand shock in the loanable funds market tends to destabilize markets for Treasury securities—orders to sell Treasury securities exceed buy orders.

Shocks to the loanable funds market are also felt as the margin accounts of mark-to-market assets are adjusted. Dynamic hedge trades in a declining market increase demand for Treasury securities placed in the initial margin accounts of long and short futures positions. Long and short positions marked to market add further shocks as losing positions sell Treasuries to generate funds required to cover calls for variation margin and winning positions invest cash balances in Treasuries. Over a period of time these shocks will net out. Nevertheless, lack of synchronicity induces short-term swings in the supply of liquidity.

Combining with these separate effects, stock-market specialists encountering losses from their market-making activities are seek-

FIGURE 2

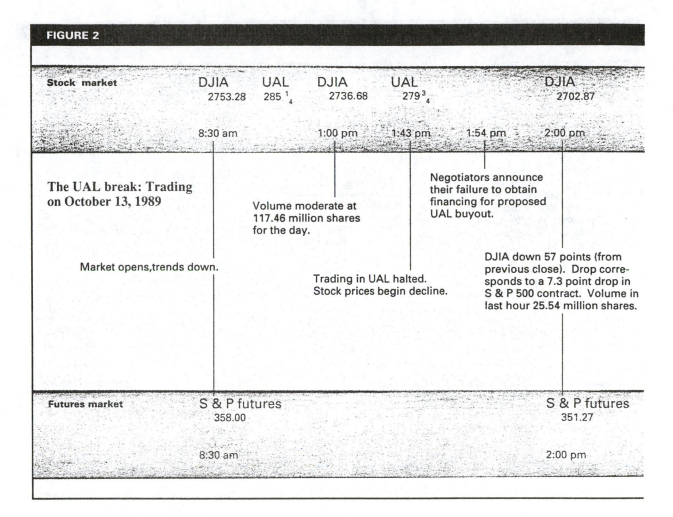

Stock market

| DJIA
2753.28 | UAL
285 $\frac{1}{4}$ | DJIA
2736.68 | UAL
279 $\frac{3}{4}$ | DJIA
2702.87 |

8:30 am   1:00 pm   1:43 pm   1:54 pm   2:00 pm

The UAL break: Trading on October 13, 1989

Volume moderate at 117.46 million shares for the day.

Negotiators announce their failure to obtain financing for proposed UAL buyout.

Market opens, trends down.

Trading in UAL halted. Stock prices begin decline.

DJIA down 57 points (from previous close). Drop corresponds to a 7.3 point drop in S & P 500 contract. Volume in last hour 25.54 million shares.

Futures market

| S & P futures
358.00 | S & P futures
351.27 |

8:30 am   2:00 pm

ing funds in a market subjected to volatile levels of liquidity. In its capacity as reserve specialist, the Federal Reserve supports liquidity by maintaining a balance between buy and sell orders for reserves and Treasury securities. This activity prevents short-run order imbalances from wringing liquidity from the system. The credit-demand shock from specialists' needs for funds are supported as the Fed adds reserves to the system.

Importantly, Fed policy must first distinguish between the real and monetary components of these shocks in the market for reserves. Facilitating the liquidity demands of a financial shock need not have real effects. Liquidity can be increased through purchases of Treasuries. Once the short-term credit needs of the payments system subside, reserve levels can then be reduced. These financial shocks can be identified by sharp market declines accompanied by volume and order-balancing problems. The timing of this credit accommodation requires consideration.

Circuit breakers interfere with trades needed to generate liquidity. The appropriate time for the Fed to begin the supply of liquidity is at the point when trading halts create an imbalance of buy and sell orders for reserves and Treasury securities.

Policy considerations for mixed real-monetary shocks differ. In these events, the Fed must consider both the need for credit accommodation through its order-matching activity and its monetary policy which is implemented through reserve-level choices. For example, liquidity operations after the 1987 break produced significant decreases in short-term rates. Reserves were left in the system after October 1987, giving permanence to the October liquidity operations. The 1989 break was followed by reports that the Fed would supply liquidity as in 1987. These reports were later disavowed. However, open market operations on October 16, 1989, did effect a modest temporary increase in the reserve base.

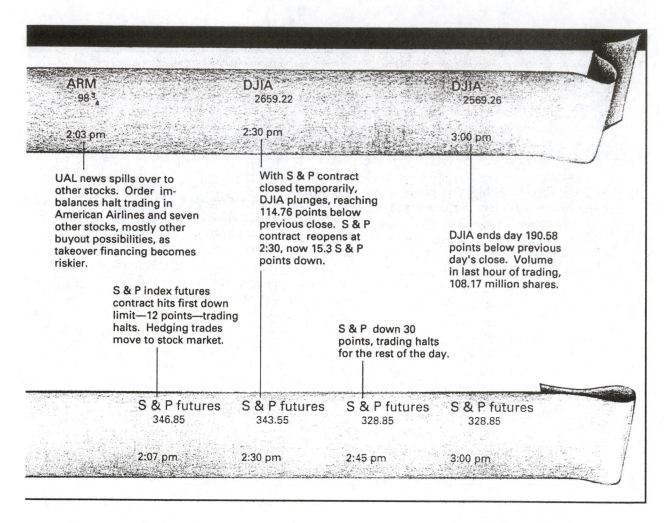

ARM
98 3/4
2:03 pm

DJIA
2659.22
2:30 pm

DJIA
2569.26
3:00 pm

UAL news spills over to other stocks. Order imbalances halt trading in American Airlines and seven other stocks, mostly other buyout possibilities, as takeover financing becomes riskier.

With S & P contract closed temporarily, DJIA plunges, reaching 114.76 points below previous close. S & P contract reopens at 2:30, now 15.3 S & P points down.

DJIA ends day 190.58 points below previous day's close. Volume in last hour of trading, 108.17 million shares.

S & P index futures contract hits first down limit—12 points—trading halts. Hedging trades move to stock market.

S & P down 30 points, trading halts for the rest of the day.

S & P futures
346.85
2:07 pm

S & P futures
343.55
2:30 pm

S & P futures
328.85
2:45 pm

S & P futures
328.85
3:00 pm

In terms of the effect on credit markets, the expectation of increased credit availability is key. Interest rates fell on October 16, evidencing market anticipation of increased purchases of Treasuries. Interest rates rose shortly afterwards as the Fed's response and its disclaimers became known.

Identification of a real component to a shock suggests consideration of a less temporary adjustment to the reserve level. Accommodation of temporary liquidity needs facilitates the allocation of capital. Failure to accommodate liquidity tends to hinder the reallocation of capital, delaying recovery from the real shock. Once temporary liquidity needs are met, reserve policy should then focus on real, relatively permanent aspects.

Effect of circuit breakers

Circuit breakers alter the effect of a market move on credit markets by altering cash flows. Trading halts have three effects on the flow of funds.

First, amounts marked to market based on prices recorded when trading was halted do not reflect market values—short positions record less gain in a price decline, long positions record less loss. Provided trading halts are synchronized across markets, amounts marked to market for related securities are similar causing no excess demand for loanable funds. Unsynchronized trading halts, on the other hand, tend to produce asymmetry in that losses and gains on related assets are unequal. The liquidity needs produced by losses incurred in one market cannot be covered by recognition of gains in related markets. Thus, nonsynchronized trading halts increase the demand for loanable funds and shift liquidity trades into those markets which remain open. This places greater stress on these markets.

Consider, for example, a specialist hedging his equity position with a short futures position in an index contract. A trading halt in the index futures contract can result in equity losses exceeding gains on futures. In an unrestricted market, the futures position, in this example, would generate needed cash to cover the financing needs of the stock position. A halt in futures trading reduces the flow of funds to the specialist, increasing dependance on borrowed funds. Inventory financing needs that cannot be met with gains from the futures contract must be covered by increased borrowing.

Second, positions not marked to market are affected like marked-to-market accounts. The difference is one of form, not result. Gains and losses on stocks or options are realized by unwinding the position. Circuit breakers halt trading and prevent unwinding of contracts. This restricts access to invested balances required to cover losses, realized elsewhere, increasing the demand for credit.

For example, traders holding UAL on 10/13 attempted to sell out after the 1:43 announcement. The halt in trading of that stock initiated a search for close substitutes for UAL stock. The nearest substitutes were other takeover stocks and transportations, particularly airlines. Order books for these stocks quickly became unbalanced. Three Big Board stocks halted trading temporarily: USAir Group, Delta Air Lines, and Philips Industries. Seven Big Board stocks halted and remained closed for the day: UAL, AMR, BankAmerica, Walt Disney, Capital Cities/ABC, Philip Morris, and Pacific Telesis. Sales again shifted; first to index futures, then to a broad range of stocks after the 15-point limit halted futures trading.

These first two effects of price limits derive from restrictions on investor access to liquidity. During market breaks when liquidity is most valuable, circuit breakers reduce the number of routes available for private resolution of liquidity needs. This tends to increase demand for a source of last resort to supply liquidity—a role many expect to be taken up by the Fed.

A third effect derives from responses to price uncertainty as clearinghouses re-consider prudential margin levels. The trade halt produced by a circuit breaker creates uncertainty about the market's actual volatility. Since margin levels are determined in response to estimates of price volatility, risk-averse clearinghouses are forced to estimate margin needs on a worst-case basis. This will tend to increase the margin levels required by prudent clearinghouses. Recognizing that further losses to customer accounts may be substantial, initial and variation margin levels are increased to prevent losses from spilling over from customer accounts into clearing-member accounts. This effect tends to decrease the supply of loanable funds by increasing use of Treasury securities to meet margin obligations.

Credit risk due to loss financing

The previous comments on circuit breakers emphasize problems induced by disruption to the flow of funds. Circuit breakers can also be viewed as shifting credit risk. Failure to record the full loss amount in a marked-to-market account implicitly extends an interest-free loan for a portion of the loss amount to the losing position. The amount of this loan is the difference between the amount marked to the settlement price and the amount marked to the true market price. The loan is extended to losing positions from gaining positions.

The amount of credit extended by these loans can be considerable. To illustrate, I will use the October 1989 market break. Taking the true futures price to be roughly the 10/16/89 opening, the true settlement price for the 117, 202 December contracts outstanding should have been 323.85. The difference between the actual settlement of 328.85 and the estimate of the true settlement is 5 S&P points. The amount of credit implicitly extended to short positions over the weekend of 10/14-10/15 was, therefore, $58.6 million or 3.3 percent of the value marked to market on 10/13.[4]

To gauge the risk to the financial system, we need to recall that futures clearinghouses provide performance guarantees for contracts trading on their affiliated exchanges. The quality of these guarantees depends on the amount of potential loss relative to equity. As potential losses increase relative to a fixed level of equity, the possibility of default rises, diminishing the quality of any guarantees. Book equity balances for the CME at the end of 1988 were $79.3 million. The $58.6 million implicitly lent to short positions is 73.9 percent of book equity.

The full implication for contract performance guarantees is not known. Threats to these guarantees will tend to shift trading away from the futures markets as the perceived quality of the guarantees declines. This tends to increase the credit needs of specialists operating in stock markets, requiring increases in reserves to meet these demands. Thus, the significance of the credit balance implied by price limits bears investigation. The policy issue is the viability of contract performance guarantees provided by the futures exchanges.

Conclusion

This article examines the effects of circuit breakers on the stability of the financial markets. Circuit breakers are classified into three types based on capacity issues: volume-triggered circuit breakers halt trading when volume exceeds order-processing capacity; order-imbalance circuit breakers halt trading when orders to buy or sell threaten the viability of the specialist; and price-limit circuit breakers halt trading when price changes are regarded as excessive. The history of price limits suggests they are introduced when futures exchanges are threatened with greater regulatory oversight.

This paper argues that circuit breakers reduce access to markets. This reduces the ability of markets to resolve needs for liquidity. Second, price limits extend credit to loss positions in futures and options markets. Since clearinghouses guarantee contract performance, these guarantees may be threatened by large credit balances.

On several recent occasions, circuit breakers have proved of some value in market crises. But it must be remembered that their value is not costless, nor their benefits without limit.

FOOTNOTES

[1]A notable exception to price-limit symmetry is found in the stock-index contracts. These are discussed in the next section.

[2]This term is from Joseph A. Grundfest, Commissioner of the Securities and Exchange Commission.

[3]The Heller proposal is in Heller, R., "Have the Fed Support Stock Market, Too," *Wall Street Journal*, October 27, 1989, p. A14. An analysis of the 1930s experience is in

Moser, James T., "Public Policy Intervention Through Futures Market Operations," forthcoming in the *Journal of Futures Markets*.

[4] The 10/16 open price is probably too high. Opening contract prices on that date encountered the CME open limit of five points, preventing realization of a lower price on the S&P contract. Thus, our estimate may significantly underestimate the amount of credit extended.

Section V
Debt Market Applications

Financial institutions, such as savings and loan associations and commercial banks, face considerable interest rate risk in acting as financial intermediaries. For example, most savings and loan associations hold portfolios of real estate mortgages which they finance with short-term deposits. If interest rates rise, a portfolio of long-term assets funded by short-term liabilities will lose value—unless the manager of the portfolio takes steps to protect the value of the portfolio. Created in the mid-1970s, interest rate derivatives provide powerful tools for managing interest rate risk. Probably more than any other application, the power and proven usefulness of debt market derivatives has fueled the explosion of financial derivatives in the last 20 years.

Interest rate futures began trading only in 1975, and the first techniques for using these new instruments for hedging risk were adapted from proven techniques developed for physical commodities. In a seminal article, "The Hedging Performance of the New Futures Market," Louis H. Ederington, showed how to apply these hedging techniques to debt instruments. Essentially the technique requires the manager to view the debt instrument and the interest rate futures as a two-asset portfolio. The manager chooses the number of futures contracts to trade to minimize the risk of the two-asset portfolio. As such, this technology is a direct outgrowth of portfolio diversification.

One drawback of the portfolio approach to hedging is that it does not fully consider the interest rate sensitivity of the instrument that is to be hedged. Robert W. Kolb and Raymond Chiang try to account for the interest rate sensitivity of the instrument to be hedged in their article, "Improving Hedging Performance Using Interest Rate Futures." Kolb and Chiang argue that the duration (a measure of how a bond's price will change for a change in yields) of the underlying instrument must be considered in deriving the appropriate hedging strategy.

A bond portfolio is considered to be immunized if its value is insensitive to changes in interest rates. For example, if a zero net worth balance sheet has assets and liabilities with equal durations, a rise in interest rates will cause asset and liability values to fall by the same amounts. In "Immunizing Bond Portfolios with Interest Rate Futures," Gerald D. Gay and Robert W. Kolb show how a given portfolio can be immunized by trading interest rate futures against the portfolio. Because futures markets exhibit great liquidity and low trading costs, it is often more efficient to implement immunization strategies with futures. Also, if the immunization is to be conducted with futures, the cash portfolio can be left undisturbed.

One of the great advantages of swaps is their flexibility, due in large part to the fact that a swap can be designed for a specific application. Laurie S. Goodman demonstrates the wide range of corporate applications for swaps in her article, "The Use of Interest Rate Swaps in Managing Corporate Liabilities." Goodman shows that swaps can be used to hedge the future issuance of debt, and she catalogs the many ways that swaps can be used to change the risk profile of existing liabilities.

Robert Einzig and Bruce Lange provide a real-world examination of the use of swaps in a corporate environment in their article, "Swaps at Transamerica: Applications and Analysis." One of the main advantages of swaps is the ability for both swap partners to exploit their comparative advantages. Einzig and Lange begin their article by explaining how they engaged in an interest rate swap with a European bank that helped both counterparties reduce their cost of funds. They go on to consider other applications of swaps, and they try to show all of the potential complications the swap user will face in real applications.

Peter A. Abken considers three important types of interest rate risk management in his article "Interest-Rate Caps, Collars, and Floors." In each technique, a risk manager uses debt derivatives to limit the effects of interest rate fluctuations. An interest rate cap, for example, effectively places a ceiling on the level of interest rates that a lender must pay. Similarly, a floor places a lower bound on the effective rate of a transaction. Finally, a collar consists of a cap and a floor. Applying these strategies consists of creating a series of options with expirations on successive dates over the life of the debt obligation.

A strip is a package of futures with expirations on successive dates. For example, a position of 3 Eurodollar futures, with one contract expiring in each of three expiration months (e.g, March, June, and September), would be a Eurodollar strip. In his article, "Interest Rate Swaps versus Eurodollar Strips," Ira G. Kawaller shows that a Eurodollar strip is essentially similar to a certain kind of interest rate swap. In many applications, Kawaller shows, the choice between the swap and the strip will depend on the pricing.

A LYON is a "liquid yield option note." As the name implies, a LYON is a debt instrument with option characteristics. In particular, a LYON is a zero coupon, convertible, callable, puttable bond. Understanding the pricing of a LYON requires coming to grips with the option portion of the bond's value. John J. McConnell and Eduardo S. Schwartz apply principles of option pricing in their article, "LYON Taming." They also discuss how the special features of a LYON give rise to management opportunities for both the holder and the issuer. For example, converting a LYON to common stock discards any remaining option value held by the owner. A decision to convert the bond must weigh the advantages of conversion against the loss of the remaining option value.

A bull floating rate note is a floating rate note that increases the rate on the note when interest rates fall and decreases the rate when interest rates rise. Because the rate of interest on a bull floater moves inversely with interest rates, these instruments are sometimes called inverse floaters. By contrast, a bear floater resets the interest rate in the same direction as the movement in market rates, but changes the interest rate by more than the move in the reference interest rate. Both bull and bear floaters offer payoff characteristics not available through other instruments. As such they require a special analysis, which Donald J. Smith provides in his article, "The Pricing of Bull and Bear Floating Rate Notes: An Application of Financial Engineering."

Much of the corporate debt issued today is callable, giving the issuer the right to retire the debt under terms specified in the bond contract. The call feature of a bond constitutes an option imbedded in the bond. In the context of managing callable debt from the issuer's point of view, Keith C. Brown and Donald J. Smith consider the array of debt derivatives suitable for this management task. Their paper, "Forward Swaps, Swap Options, and the Management of Callable Debt," focuses on using interest rate swaps with delayed starting dates to preserve the value of the call option built into a callable debt issue.

Article 32

The Hedging Performance of the New Futures Markets

LOUIS H. EDERINGTON*

ORGANIZED FUTURES MARKETS in financial securities were first established in the U.S. on October 20, 1975 when the Chicago Board of Trade opened a futures market in Government National Mortgage Association 8% Pass-Through Certificates. This was followed in January, 1976 by a 90 day Treasury Bill futures market on the International Monetary Market of the Chicago Mercantile Exchange. In terms of trading volume both have been clear commercial successes and this has led to the establishment, in 1977, of futures markets in Long Term Government Bonds and 90-day Commercial Paper and, in 1978, of a market in One-Year Treasury notes and new GNMA markets.

The classic economic rationale for futures markets is, of course, that they facilitate hedging—that they allow those who deal in a commodity to transfer the risk of price changes in that commodity to speculators more willing to bear such risks. The primary purpose of the present paper is to evaluate the GNMA and T-Bill futures markets as instruments for such hedging. Obviously it is possible to hedge by entering into forward contracts outside a futures market, but, as Telser and Higinbotham [19] point out, an organized futures market facilitates such transactions by providing a standardized contract and by substituting the trustworthiness of the exchange for that of the individual trader.

In the futures market, price change risk can be eliminated entirely by making or taking delivery on futures sold or bought, but few hedges are concluded in this manner.[1] The major problem with making or taking delivery is that there are only four delivery periods per year for financial security futures so it is often

---

* Associate Professor, Georgia State University. The author would like to acknowledge the helpful comments of Bruce Fielitz, Ed Ulveling, and Jerome Stein. This research was supported in part by the Bureau of Business and Economic Research of Georgia State University.

[1] It should perhaps be noted that in the GNMA market there would, however, be some uncertainty regarding the amount one would need to hold to make delivery. The futures contract is for $100,000 of GNMA 8% Pass-Through Certificates. Since prepayment on these certificates might occur prior to delivery, there is some uncertainty regarding the quantity one would need to hold at present in order to deliver $100,000 of certificates. This is mitigated by the fact that one can deliver certificates of between $97,500 and $102,500 face value with the deficiency or excess to be settled in cash but some uncertainty remains. In addition, the person who accepts delivery of GNMA futures faces uncertainty regarding the type and relative market value of the certificates to be received. While trading is in 8% certificates, certificates of any mortgage rate can be delivered as long as the quantity delivered is equivalent to $100,000 of 8% certificates assuming a thirty year certificate with total prepayment at the end of twelve years. Since the market doesn't always accept such arbitrary prepayment assumptions, it may be cheaper to deliver 6½% or 9% or some other certificates. Indeed, it has generally been cheaper to deliver 9% certificates [6]. Consequently, those accepting delivery may not receive $100,000 of 8% certificates or their market equivalent. This also means that at delivery the futures price for GNMA's will generally remain somewhat below the cash price.

It should also be noted that over the observed period, January 1976 through July 1977, futures prices were below cash prices except for a few occasions within a few weeks of delivery. Purchasers of

impossible to hedge in this manner over the desired time period. Moreover, the desired time period may change or may be uncertain. The most common hedge, therefore, is one in which the seller (buyer) of the futures contract cancels his delivery commitment by buying (selling) a contract of the same future prior to delivery. It is this type of hedge, in which futures positions are liquidated by offsetting trades, which has received the most attention in the hedging literature and is examined in this paper.

In order to illustrate such a hedge and the potential of the new markets for risk avoidance, let us suppose that on September 16, 1977 a mortgage lending institution committed itself to a future loan at a set interest rate. Suppose, further, it was the lender's intention to finance this loan by issuing or selling $100,000 of 30 year GNMA Pass-Through Certificates with an 8% coupon rate which were selling at that time (September 16, 1977) at $99,531 or an effective yield of 8.02%.[2] Fearing that interest rates would rise and GNMA prices would fall by the time it actually sold its certificates, the mortgagor decided to hedge against this risk by selling December 1977 GNMA futures which were trading at $98,219 or an effective yield of 8.20% on September 16.[3] This transaction is summarized in the top half of Table 1.

In this particular case, our firm's fears of an interest rate rise were realized and the hedge was successful. By October 14, 1977, when the firm closed its loan and sold the GNMA certificates, cash market yields had risen 17 basis points to 8.19%. However, futures market yields had also risen 15 basis points to 8.30% so, as shown in Table 1, the futures market gain largely offset the cash market loss. This is a short hedge. If an individual or firm plans to purchase GNMA's, T-Bills, or some other security in the future, it could attempt to protect against the contingency of a decline in interest rates by buying GNMA or T-Bill futures, i.e., entering a long hedge. In this particular example, the hedge was successful because cash and futures prices both fell, but this may not always be the case.

There is not perfect agreement in the futures market literature as to what hedging is or why it is undertaken. The paper begins in Part I, therefore, with a survey of three major theories of hedging: the traditional theory, the theories of Holbrook Working, and the portfolio theory. The portfolio theory, which the author finds superior to the other two, suggests a method for measuring the hedging effectiveness of a futures market and this measure is used in Part II to evaluate the GNMA and T-Bill futures markets. These financial security futures are compared with each other and with two more established and heavily traded

---

GNMA or T-Bill futures could therefore lock-in a lower price as well as a certain price but sellers of futures would have to be willing to lock-in a loss. On GNMA's, for example, the futures price averaged 1.9 below the cash price two months before delivery over the observed period and ranged from 1.1% below the cash price to 2.5% below.

[2] GNMA yields are calculated on the assumption of a prepayment after 12 years. The published market yields also take into account, as the face yields do not, that there is an interest free delay of 15 days in payments of principal and interest.

[3] Note that if the firm were to wait until December and make delivery, it would lock in exactly this price and yield but if it closes the hedge prior to delivery the price and yield are still somewhat uncertain.

At the present time there is no good data on what sort of firms are hedging in the market so this example is hypothetical. In addition, there are regulatory constraints on the participation of banks and S & L's (See Ederington and Plumly, 1976).

Table 1

A Possible Short Hedge Based on Actual Prices

Cash Market	Futures Market
September 16, 1977	
Makes mortgage commitment and makes plan to sell $100,000 face value of GNMA 8% Certificates	Sells one December futures contract at $98,219
Current price $99,531	
October 14, 1977	
Sells GNMA 8% certificates ($100,000 face value)	Buys one December futures contract at $97,156
Current price $98,281	

Results:		
Loss from delay on cash market		$1250
Gain on futures market		1063
Net Loss		$ 187

futures markets: corn and wheat. The portfolio theory also provides a method for measuring the costs of hedging and these costs are examined for the two financial security futures. The article closes with a summary of the conclusions and some observations on possible future research in futures in Part III.

I. Theories of Hedging

A. *Traditional Hedging Theory*

While traditional hedging theory predates the work of Working and the application of portfolio theory to hedging, it continues to be important. Indeed, it is the traditional theory which underlies almost all the early "How To" articles on hedging which accompanied the establishment of the GNMA and T-Bill futures markets.[4]

Traditional hedging theory emphasizes the risk avoidance potential of futures markets. Hedgers are envisioned as taking futures market positions equal in magnitude but of opposite sign to their position in the cash market as in the example in Table 1. For instance, holders of an inventory of X units would protect themselves against the loss from a decline in the cash price by selling X futures of the same commodity or security. When the inventory is sold, futures contracts would be purchased canceling both positions.

If the cash or spot prices at times t_1 and t_2 are P_s^1 and P_s^2 respectively, the gain or loss on an unhedged position, U, of X units is $X[P_s^2 - P_s^1]$, but the gain or loss on a hedged position, H, is $X\{[P_s^2 - P_s^1] - [P_f^2 - P_f^1]\}$ where the f subscript denotes the futures price. Traditional theory argues that spot and futures prices generally move together so that the absolute value of H is less than U or that $\text{Var}(H) < \text{Var}(U)$. This question is often discussed in terms of the change in the cash price versus the change in the "Basis," where the basis is defined as the difference between the futures and spot prices so that the change in the basis is

[4] Examples are the Chicago Board of Trade's "Hedging in GNMA Interest Rate Futures" (1975) and articles by Smith [6], Jacobs and Kozuch [10], Sandor [5], Stevens [8], and Duncan [5].

$\{(P_f^2 - P_s^2) - (P_f^1 - P_s^1)\}$ or $-\{(P_s^2 - P_s^1) - (P_f^2 - P_f^1)\}$. A hedge is viewed as perfect if the change in the basis is zero. It is commonly argued that the basis and changes in the basis are small because of the possibility of making or taking delivery, hence $\text{Var}(H) < \text{Var}(U)$. The question of smallness is, of course, relative. While it is true that delivery possibilities limit changes in the basis, a range for variation obviously remains.

Certainly, the familiar theory of adaptive expectations implies that if futures prices reflect market expectations they should not normally match changes in cash prices. According to the theory of adaptive expectations

$$E_n^2 - E_n^1 = a[P_s^2 - E_2^1] + u$$

where E_n^2 and E_n^1 represent the cash prices expected to prevail in period n as of periods 2 and 1 respectively and E_2^1 represents the price which had in period 1, been expected to prevail in period 2. If one assumes that $P_f^2 = E_n^2$ and $P_f^1 = E_n^1$, one obtains

$$P_f^2 - P_f^1 = a[P_s^2 - P_s^1] - a[E_2^1 - P_s^1]$$

If, therefore, no change in spot prices is expected between periods 1 and 2 ($E_2^1 = P_s^1$) and a $\neq$ 1, this theory implies that any change in the spot price will be accompanied by a proportional but unequal movement of the futures price. If, on the other hand, cash prices change in exactly the manner which had been expected ($P_s^2 = E_2^1$), then certainly there will be no change in futures prices.

While it is clear that the basis changes so that most traditional hedges are not perfect, Working [20] complained that many writers of the time were conveniently ignoring this fact:

> *A major source of mistaken notions of hedging is the conventional practice of illustrating hedging with a hypothetical example in which the price of the future bought or sold as a hedge is supposed to rise or fall by the same amount that the spot price rises or falls.* [20, pp. 320–321.]

In perusing articles and pamphlets on hedging in GNMA's and T-Bills, I have been surprised to note that many continue to follow the same practice almost 25 years later. This includes not only publications of the exchanges and brokerage houses and articles in trade publications, such as *Savings and Loan News* [16] and *The Mortgage Banker* [10], but also articles in the *Review of the Federal Reserve Bank of St. Louis* [18] and the *Federal Home Loan Bank Board Journal* [15]. In these articles, any caveat that cash and futures price changes may not be equal is relegated to a footnote or a discussion of cross-hedging.

B. *Working's Hypothesis*

Working [20 and 21] challenged the view of hedgers as pure risk minimizers and emphasized expected prfit maximization. In his view hedgers functioned much like speculators, but, since they held positions in the cash market as well, they were concerned with relative not absolute price changes. Instead of expecting cash and futures prices to move together, he argued that "most hedging is done in expectation of a change in spot-futures price relations [20]." Holders of a long position in the cash market would, according to Working, hedge if the basis was expected to fall and would not hedge if the basis was expected to rise.

C. *Portfolio and Hedging Theory*

By viewing hedging as a simple application of basic portfolio theory Johnson [11] and Stein [17] were able to integrate the risk avoidance of traditional theory with Working's expected profits maximization. Johnson and Stein argued that one buys or sells futures for the same risk-return reasons that one buys any other security. While traditional theory argued that hedgers should always be completely hedged and Working's hypothesis indicated (though he realized such was not always the case) that hedgers would be completely hedged or unhedged, the application of portfolio theory allowed Johnson and Stein to explain why hedgers would hold both hedged and unhedged commodity stocks.

While the portfolio model of hedging may contain nothing which is new to those in the finance field, it is less familiar to analysts of commodity futures markets and has experienced a somewhat slower acceptance in this field. Since we will use this model to evaluate the GNMA and T-Bill futures as hedging instruments in the next section, let us briefly summarize its important characteristics.

One difference between this and the more familiar portfolio model is that cash and futures market holdings are not viewed as substitutes. Instead, spot market holdings, X_s, are viewed as fixed and the decision is how much of this stock to hedge. Following Johnson and Stein, let us restrict our attention to the case in which the potential hedger holds only one spot market commodity or security. Since spot market holdings are exogenous, any interest payments may also be viewed as predetermined and therefore irrelevant to the hedging decision. Letting U represent once again the return on an unhedged position,

$$E(U) = X_s E[P_s^2 - P_s^1] \tag{1}$$

$$\text{Var}(U) = X_s^2 \sigma_s^2 \tag{2}$$

Let R represent the return on a portfolio which includes both spot market holdings, X_s, and futures market holding[5], X_f.

$$E(R) = X_s E[P_s^2 - P_s^1] + X_f E[P_f^2 - P_f^1] - K(X_f) \tag{3}$$

$$\text{Var}(R) = X_s^2 \sigma_s^2 + X_f^2 \sigma_f^2 + 2 X_s X_f \sigma_{sf} \tag{4}$$

where

X_s and X_f represent spot and futures market holdings.

$K(X_f)$ are brokerage and other costs of engaging in futures transactions including the cost of providing margin.

$\sigma_s^2, \sigma_f^2, \sigma_{sf}$ represent the subjective variances and the covariance of the possible price changes from time 1 to time 2.

Note that the portfolio, whose returns are represented by R, may be a portfolio which is either completely are partially hedged. There is no presumption, as in traditional theory, that $X_f = -X_s$ (in which case $R = H$). Indeed cash and futures market holdings may even have the same sign.

Let $b = -X_f/X_s$ represent the proportion of the spot position which is hedged. Since in a hedge X_s and X_f have opposite signs, b is usually positive.

$$\text{Var}(R) = X_s^2\{\sigma_s^2 + b^2\sigma_f^2 - 2b\sigma_{sf}\} \quad \text{and} \tag{5}$$

$$\begin{aligned} E(R) &= X_s\{E(P_s^2 - P_s^1) - bE(P_f^2 - P_f^1)\} - K(X_s, b) \\ &= X_s\{(1 - b)E(P_s^2 - P_s^1) + bE(P_s^2 - P_s^1) - bE(P_f^2 - P_f^1)\} \\ &\quad - K(X_s, b) \end{aligned} \tag{6}$$

or, letting $E(\Delta b) = E\{P_f^2 - P_s^2 - (P_f^1 - P_s^1)\}$ represent the expected change in the basis,

$$E(R) = X_s[(1 - b)\,E(S) - b\,E(\Delta B)] - K(X_s, b) \tag{7}$$

where $E(S) = E(P_s^2 - P_s^1)$ is the expected price change on one unit of the spot commodity.

If the expected change in the basis is zero, then clearly the expected gain or loss is reduced as $b \to 1$. It is also obvious that expected changes in the basis may add to or subtract from the gain or loss which would have been expected on an unhedged portfolio $\{E(U) = X_s E(S)\}$.

Holding X_s constant, let us consider the effect of a change in b, the proportion hedged, on the expected return and variance of the portfolio R.

$$\frac{\partial\,\text{Var}(R)}{\partial b} = X_s^2\{2b\sigma_f^2 - 2\sigma_{sf}\} \tag{8}$$

so the risk minimizing b, b^*, is

$$b^* = \frac{\sigma_{sf}}{\sigma_f^2} \tag{9}$$

$$\frac{\partial E(R)}{\partial b} = -X_s[E(\Delta B) + E(S)] - \frac{\partial K(X_s, b)}{\partial b} \tag{10}$$

Since $E(\Delta B)$ and $E(S)$ may be either positive or negative, the opportunity locus of the possible combinations of $E(R)$ and $Var(R)$, which are shown in figure 1, may lie in either the first or second quadrant or both. Moreover, as b increases one moves either clockwise or counterclockwise around the locus depending on the sign of equation 10.

In this model there is no riskless asset. Treasury bills, which are usual candidate for a riskless asset, are themselves being hedged. One may wish to liquidate a position in bills prior to maturity in which case there is a price risk however small. Consequently, the optimal b, $\hat{b}$, will be that associated with the point on the indifference curve which is just tangent to the highest indifference curve, II′. Not only need $\hat{b}$ not equal one as traditional hedging theory presumed, but $\hat{b}$ may be greater than one, in which case one takes a greater position in the futures than in the cash market, or $\hat{b}$ may be less than zero, in which case one takes the same position (either short or long) in both the spot and futures markets.[5]

---

[5] Since one would normally assume that $\sigma_{sf} > 0$, $b^* > 0$ but since b may be either increasing or decreasing as one moves counterclockwise around the opportunity locus, the portion of the locus above b^* may represent either $b < b^*$ or $b < b^*$.

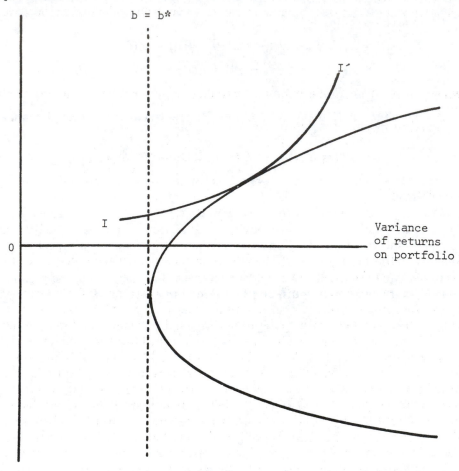

Expected return
on portfolio

b = b*

I´

I

Variance
of returns
on portfolio

0

Figure 1

II. Evaluating the GNMA and T-Bill Futures Markets

The purpose of this section is to estimate the effectiveness of the new futures markets in reducing the risk associated with a cash position in GNMA's or T-Bills based on the market experience to date and to estimate the costs of hedging (the impact on expected returns).

While traditional theory indicates that the risk reduction to be achieved by hedging can be measured by comparing the variance of the change in the basis to the variance of the change in the cash price, this presumes that $b = 1$ which as shown above may not be the case. Fortunately, portfolio theory also provides a measure of hedging effectiveness. While the risk reduction achieved by any one hedger depends on the chosen b, the futures markets' potential for risk reduction can be measured by comparing the risk on an unhedged portfolio with the minimum risk that can be obtained on a portfolio containing both spot and forward securities. This minimum risk is represented by the left most point of the opportunity locus in figure 1, and corresponds to the variance of the return on a portfolio where b equals the b^* defined in equation 9. The measure of hedging effectiveness used in this paper is, therefore, the percent reduction in the variance or

$$e = 1 - \frac{\text{Var}(R^*)}{\text{Var}(U)}$$

where $\text{var}R^*$ denotes the minimum variance on a portfolio containing security futures.

Substituting equation 9 into equation 5 yields

$$\text{Var}(R^*) = X_s^2 \left\{ \sigma_s^2 + \frac{\sigma_{sf}^2}{\sigma_f^2} - 2\frac{\sigma_{sf}^2}{\sigma_f^2} \right\} = X_s^2 \left(\sigma_s^2 - \frac{\sigma_{sf}^2}{\sigma_f^2} \right)$$

Consequently

$$e = \frac{\sigma_{sf}^2}{\sigma_s^2 \sigma_f^2} = \rho^2$$

where ρ^2 is the population coefficient of determination between the change in the cash price and the change in the future's price.

In order to judge the market's effectiveness at reducing risk, we estimated e using the sample coefficient of determination, r^2, for hedges of two arbitrary lengths (two and four weeks) and using the sample variances and sample covariance of the two and four week price changes over the observed period to estimate b^* as well as σ_s^2, σ_f^2 and σ_{sf}. As noted above, the GNMA and T-Bill markets were established in October 1975 and January 1976 respectively. Since it seemed prudent to allow the markets to gain some depth before analyzing them, weekly data collection for the GNMA market began in January 1976 and for the T-Bill market in March 1976. Both data sets were continued through December 1977. For comparison purposes we also collected data (January 1976—December 1977) and calculated e for two established and heavily traded futures: corn and wheat.[6]

For T-Bill cash prices, 90-day T-Bill prices were consistently used because they were readily available. This ignores the fact that over the hedge period the term to maturity of any T-Bills held will decline. Actual hedgers would need to adjust their b according to the term of the T-Bills held and the length of the hedge [5].

Since a hedger can buy futures with near or distant delivery dates, hedges in futures with a delivery date in 3 months or less (the nearby contract), in 3 to 6 months, in 6 to 9 months, and in 9 to 12 months were evaluated separately.[7] It could be argued that one's expectations of the near future will be affected more by unexpected changes in the cash price than one's expectation of the more distant futures, and this is supported by some work on adaptive expectations using forward rates from the term structure [12]. Consequently, we hypothesize that e will decline as one considers more distant contracts.

[6] The futures prices were weekly closing prices as reported in the *Wall Street Journal*. For the spot price of wheat, we used the price of #2 Kansas City hard and for corn we used the price of #2 Chicago yellow as reported in the *Journal*.
[7] Two or four week periods in which the nearby contract expired were dropped from the sample. During the harvest season, futures contracts are available for every other month for corn and wheat, so the time periods for these differ somewhat from those for GNMA's and T-Bills.

Table 2
Two Week Hedges

The Futures Contract	Estimated e	Estimated b*
8% GNMA's (46 observations)		
The Nearby Contract	.664	.801*
3 to 6 Month Contract	.675	.832
6 to 9 Month Contract	.677	.854
9 to 12 Month Contract	.661	.852
90 Day Treasury Bills (41 observations)		
The Nearby Contract	.272	.307*
3 to 6 Month Contract	.256	.237*
6 to 9 Month Contract	.178	.143*
9 to 12 Month Contract	.140	.116
Wheat (45 observations)		
The Nearby Contract	.898	.864*
2 to 6 Month Contract	.889	.815*
4 to 8 Month Contract	.868	.784*
6 to 10 Month Contract	.841	.778*
Corn (45 observations)		
The Nearby Contract	.649	.915
2 to 6 Month Contract	.605	.905
4 to 8 Month Contract	.541	.868
6 to 10 Month Contract	.450	.764

* Significantly different from 1 at .05 level.

In addition, it is hypothesized that e will be greater for four week than for two week hedges because absolute changes in cash prices should generally be greater and futures prices would have more time to respond (if there is a lag) over the longer period.

The results for two week hedges are shown in Table 2 and the results for four week hedges are shown in Table 3. The most striking result is the marked superiority of the GNMA market to the T-Bill market particularly for the shorter hedges. While it appears less effective than the wheat market, the GNMA market compares quite favorably with the corn market as a hedging instrument. With the puzzling exception of hedges in the nearby contract for a four week period, the T-Bill market appears rather ineffective in reducing exposure to price change risk particularly over the shorter period. Indeed, if one followed the prescription of traditional theory and set $b = 1$, the hedged T-Bill portfolio would have been more risky than the unhedged portfolio in all cases except for four week hedges in the nearby contract. The author feels that this may be due to the fact that the T-Bill rate is closely related to the federal funds rate which, given current Federal Reserve operating procedures, is basically controlled by the Fed over short periods. If short-run changes in T-Bill rates are viewed as induced by monetary authorities, market participants may see no need to adjust their expectations of future rates.

While the author is unaware of any way to statistically test this hypothesis, the

Table 3

Four Week Hedges

The Futures Contract	Estimated e	Estimated b*
8% GNMA's (23 observations)		
The Nearby Contract	.785	.848
3 to 6 Month Contract	.817	.993
6 to 9 Month Contract	.799	1.019
9 to 12 Month Contract	.780	1.035
90 Day Treasury Bills (21 observations)		
The Nearby Contract	.741	.651*
3 to 6 Month Contract	.571	.427*
6 to 9 Month Contract	.406	.242*
9 to 12 Month Contract	.369	.228*
Wheat (21 observations)		
The Nearby Contract	.918	.917
2 to 6 Month Contract	.921	.862*
4 to 8 Month Contract	.909	.840*
6 to 10 Month Contract	.887	.843*
Corn (21 observations)		
The Nearby Contract	.725	1.021
2 to 6 Month Contract	.666	1.011
4 to 8 Month Contract	.608	.969
6 to 10 Month Contract	.560	.887

* Significantly different from 1 at .05 level.

results in Tables 1 and 2 are certainly consistent with the hypothesis that e will be larger for the longer hedges. This difference in hedging effectiveness appears particularly pronounced for the financial security futures.

The hypothesis that short-term hedges in nearby contracts are more effective than hedges in more distant contracts appears to hold for all except the GNMA market.

In estimating e we also estimated b^*.[8] These estimates, which are also reported in the Tables, are themselves of interest since traditional theory implies that $b^* = 1$. In most cases b^* was significantly different from 1 and in general was less than 1. The hypothesis that $b^* = 1$ is therefore rejected.

Since these are ex-post estimates of b^* and since hedgers may be unable because of the individuality of the futures contract to achieve the desired b, the question of the sensitivity of e to the chosen b is one of some importance. To address this question, we calculated e or r^2 for b's ten percent greater and lower than those shown in Tables 1 and 2. For hedges in either GNMA's or T-Bills, in either the nearby or the next closest contract, and over either a two or four week period, raising or lowering b ten percent from the estimated b^* resulted in a reduction in e of approximately 1%. We conclude, therefore, that these results are not very sensitive to small deviations in b.

[8] Let us note again that hedgers in T-Bills must adjust these estimates of b^* to reflect the term to maturity and the hedging period of their own portfolio.

While real cross-hedging was not considered, the effectiveness of the GNMA futures market in hedging positions in 6½% and 9% certificates was examined. As mentioned earlier, one can deliver these certificates to satisfy a futures contract and an earlier study (Ederington and Plumly, 1976) indicated that, at least in 1976, it would have been cheaper to deliver 9% certificates than 8% certificates and more expensive to deliver 6½% certificates. For this reason we expected e to be higher for 9% than for either 8 or 6½% certificates. This proved to be the case for all two-week hedges. Indeed, for all futures contracts e was highest for a hedge against 9% certificates, lower for 8% certificates, and lowest for 6½% certificates. For hedges in the nearby contract over a two week period, for instance, the measures of e were .820, .664, and .662 respectively.

Having found that, at least for GNMA's, one can lower the risk (as measured by the variance) associated with holding securities by holding futures, attention is now turned to the impact of hedging on expected returns. Two points are clear from equation 7. One, expected returns are lowered by the amount of the brokerage and other costs associated with the futures. Two, if the expected change in the basis is zero and $0 < b < 1$, partial hedging reduces the gain or loss associated with an unhedged position $\{X_s E(S)\}$. Attention is therefore centered on the term, $E(\Delta B)$. The important question is whether over the long run $E(\Delta B)$ will tend to be consistently negative or positive i.e., whether the expected value of the expected change in the basis is positive or negative. Since the basis must be approximately zero at the delivery date,[9] $E(\Delta B)$ will generally be positive if the current cash price exceeds the current futures price and will generally be negative if the futures price exceeds the cash price.

The longer the hedge and the closer the delivery date, the closer this relationship between $E(\Delta B)$ and the initial basis should be. The question basically reduces, therefore, to whether there is any reason to anticipate that in the long-run futures prices will generally be above or below cash prices.

Over the observed period, cash prices on GNMA's and T-Bills consistently exceeded futures prices (except occasionally at delivery). To provide an idea of what changes in the basis might have been expected during this period, the average change in the basis as a percent of the cash price (for comparison) was calculated for four week hedge periods.[10] The results are shown in Table 4.[11] As expected, the average change in the basis was positive so that over this period the change in the basis tended to add to (subtract from) the expected returns of those taking a long (short) position in the futures market.[12] In addition, it is interesting to note that for GNMA's the average change in the basis tended to vary inversely with the length of the futures contract. Since the risk reduction

---

[9] If it is cheaper to deliver GNMA certificates with a mortgage rate other than 8%, the basis for GNMA's will not be eliminated completely. A negative basis remains depending on the difference in costs.

[10] The average change for four weeks is not exactly double the change for two weeks because the periods do not completely overlap since periods in which the nearby contract matured were eliminated.

[11] The author does not feel that corn and wheat provide a meaningful comparison in this case because the basis on these varies with the time till harvest and storage costs.

[12] Note that when the basis is negative, those who take a long position in the futures market and take delivery lock in the lower buying price and higher interest rate. Those who are short and make delivery lock-in a selling price which is below the current selling price.

Table 4

Average Change in the Basis
Over 4 Week Periods
January 1976 (March for T-Bills)—December 1977

	Average Change in the Basis as a % of the Cash Price	
Futures Contract	GNMA Certificates	Treasury Bills
The Nearby Contract	.271%	.184%
3 to 6 Month Contract	.162%	.220%
6 to 9 Month Contract	.133%	.161%
9 to 12 Month Contract	.098%	.164%

was approximately the same for all four contracts, this suggests that long (short) hedgers would have been well advised to hedge in the nearby (distant) contract.

While over the observed period cash prices on GNMA's and T-Bills consistently exceeded futures prices so that positive changes in the basis could generally be expected, this was not always the case in 1978 and may not be the case in the future. The author is much more reluctant to accept Table 4 as a guide to the future than Tables 2 and 3. The crucial question is whether futures prices are unbiased measures of market expectations of future spot rates or whether they are biased downward by "normal-backwardation." There isn't enough data to answer this question since the lower futures prices to date could simply reflect consistent expectations of rising interest rates.

There continues to be a theoretical and empirical debate over "normal backwardation," the Keynes-Hick argument from which the liquidity premium theory of the term structure was developed.[13] However, it is questionable whether evidence from other futures markets is applicable to GNMA and T-Bill markets. Hick's argument [8, pp. 136–139] was that most hedgers of agricultural commodities maintain a long position in the cash and a short position in the futures market so that there is a weakness on the demand side of the futures market which speculators will not step in and absorb until the futures price is sufficiently low so that the expected favorable price change will compensate for the risk. Since it is an open question whether hedgers in GNMA's and T-Bills are generally long or short, the existence and sign of any liquidity premium in these markets is less certain.

For the T-Bill market there is an additional consideration. Since one can satisfy the delivery commitment by delivering longer T-Bills on which all but three months have elapsed, the possibility of riskless arbitrage should theoretically keep the futures rates close to the forward rates implicit in the term structure.[14] If, therefore, there are liquidity premiums in the term structure they should be reflected in the futures market. While there is still debate on this point, the bulk of recent evidence indicates that the term structure does contain liquidity premiums [7 and 9]. For T-Bills, therefore, it may be that futures prices normally tend to be below cash prices so that $E(\Delta B)$ is generally positive.

[13] See Peck, Section 1 [4], Burger, Lang and Rasche [3], Fama [7], and Cornell [4].

[14] While this should theoretically be the case, surprisingly large differences between future and forward rates have been observed [2].

III. Conclusions and Observations

The conclusions of this study may be summarized as follows:

1. The decision to hedge a cash or forward market position in the futures market is no different from any other investment decision—investors hedge to obtain the best combination of risk and return. Basic portfolio theory, which best explains when and how much holders of financial portfolios will wish to hedge, encompasses both the traditional hedging theory and Working's theory as special cases.

2. The implication of many "How-To" articles in the popular financial press that hedges in GNMA's and T-Bills are perfect because cash and futures prices change by equal amounts is completely indefensible.

3. Contrary to traditional hedging theory (but consistent with the theory of adaptive expectations), our empirical results indicate that even pure risk-minimizers may wish to hedge only a portion of their portfolios. In most cases the estimated b^* was less than one.

4. Based on the experience to date, the GNMA futures market appears to be a more effective instrument for risk avoidance than the T-Bill market particularly for short-term (i.e., two-week) hedges.

5. Both the GNMA and the T-Bill market appear to be more effective in reducing the price change risk over long (four-week) than over short (two-week) periods.

6. While changes in the basis were generally positive over the observed period (adding to the return on long hedges and subtracting from that on short hedges), the financial futures markets have not been in existence long enough to tell whether this is the usual case because of "normal backwardation" or whether it merely reflects expectations during the observed period.

A number of unanswered questions and topics for future research regarding futures markets in financial securities obviously remain. One which the author regards as particularly important is the effectiveness of the new futures markets for cross-hedging, i.e., for reducing the risk of portfolios containing securities other than GNMA's or T-Bills. Since mortgage lenders must often commit themselves months before the funds are lent, the effectiveness of the GNMA future in hedging against changes in conventional mortgage rates (or in the cost of funds) seems to be an important unanswered question. [However, our results are appropriate if the lender plans to finance the mortgages by issuing GNMA Pass-Through Certificates as in Table 1.] Unfortunately, the only data series for local mortgage rates of which the author is aware—the Federal Home Loan Bank Board series—measures the rate on loans made and these loans may reflect commitments made months ago. What are needed are localized data on new commitments.

REFERENCES

1. P. W. Bacon, and R. E. Williams, 1976. "Interest Rate Futures: New Tool for the Financial Manager," *Financial Management* (Spring, 1976), pp 32–38.
2. B. Branch, 1978. "Testing the Unbiased Expectations Theory of Interest Rates." Paper presented at 1978 annual meeting of the Eastern Finance Association.
3. A. E. Burger, R. W. Lang, and R. H. Rasche, 1977. "The Treasury Bill Futures Market and Market Expectations of Interest Rates," *Review* of the Federal Reserve Bank of St. Louis, Vol 59, No. 6, pp 2–11.

4. Bradford Cornell, 1977. "Spot Rates, Forward Rates and Exchange Market Efficiency," *Journal of Financial Economics* (August, 1977), pp 55–60.

5. W. H. Duncan, 1977. "Treasury Bill Futures—Opportunities and Pitfalls," *Review* of the Federal Reserve Bank of Dallas (July, 1977).

6. L. E. Ederington, and W. E. Plumly, 1976. "The New Futures Market in Financial Securities," Futures Trading Seminar Proceedings, Vol IV, Chicago Board of Trade.

7. E. F. Fama, 1976. "Forward Rates as Predictors of Future Spot Rates," *Journal of Financial Economics* (Oct., 1976), pp 361–378.

8. J. R. Hicks, 1946. *Value and Capital* (London: Oxford University Press) second edition.

9. T. E. Holland, 1965. "A Note on the Traditional Theory of the Term Structure of Interest Rates on Three-and-Six-Month Treasury Bills," *International Economic Review* (September, 1965), pp 330–36.

10. S. F. Jacobs, and J. R. Kozuch, 1975. "Is There a Future for a Mortgage Futures Market," *The Mortgage Banker.*

11. L. L. Johnson, 1960. "The Theory of Hedging and Speculation in Commodity Futures," *Review of Economic Studies.* Vol 27, No. 3, pp 139–51.

12. J. B. Michaelsen, 1973. *The Term Structure of Interest Rates* (New York: Interest Educational Publishers).

13. J. H. McCulloch, 1975. "An Estimate of the Liquidity Premium," *Journal of Political Economy* (February, 1975), pp 95–119.

14. A. E. Peck, 1977. *Selected Writings on Futures Markets,* Vol II (Chicago: Board of Trade of the City of Chicago).

15. R. L. Sandor, 1975. "Trading Mortgage Interest Rate Futures," *Federal Home Loan Bank Board Journal* (September, 1975), pp 2–9.

16. B. Smith, 1976. "Trading Complexities, FHLBB Rules Impede Association Activity," *Savings and Loan News* (January, 1976).

17. J. L. Stein, 1961. "The Simultaneous Determination of Spot and Futures Prices," *American Economic Review,* Vol LI, No. 5.

18. N. A. Stevens, 1976. "A Mortgage Futures Market: Its Development, Uses, Benefits and Cost," *Review* of the Federal Reserve Bank of St. Louis (April, 1976).

19. L. G. Telser, and H. N. Higinbotham, 1977. "Organized Futures Markets: Costs and Benefits," *Journal of Political Economy* (October, 1977), Vol 85, pp 969–1000.

20. H. Working, 1953. "Futures Trading and Hedging," *American Economic Review* (June, 1953), pp 314–343.

21. _____. 1962. "New Concepts Concerning Futures Markets and Prices," *American Economic Review* (June, 1962), pp 431–459.

Article 33

Improving Hedging Performance Using Interest Rate Futures

Robert W. Kolb and Raymond Chiang

Robert W. Kolb is Assistant Professor of Finance at Emory University. Raymond Chiang is Assistant Professor of Finance at the University of Florida. The authors would like to thank the Center for Econometrics and Decision Sciences at the University of Florida for its financial support.

■ Effective hedging of interest rate risk depends on four key factors:

1. The maturity of the hedged and hedging instrument;
2. The coupon structure of the hedged and hedging instruments;
3. The varying risk structure of interest rates; and
4. The changes in the term structure of interest rates.

Many practical guides to hedging interest rate risk use examples in which equal face value amounts of the hedged and hedging instrument are employed [1, 5, 6, 10, 13]. For a hedger seeking to minimize interest rate risk, this is almost always incorrect. The only time it is correct is when all four factors mentioned above are perfectly matched.[1] Under any other circumstances a better hedge can be devised.[2]

In the past, when interest rates have fluctuated relatively little, naive approaches to hedging interest rate risk have served relatively well. Today, with extremely volatile interest rates affecting bankers, investors, corporations, and underwriters to a much greater extent than ever before, the development of more efficient hedging techniques has become crucial. Furthermore, the recent development of interest rate futures markets with standardized contracts has enriched the hedging opportunities of all market participants and lowered the cost of hedging. This paper formulates more efficient hedging rules and illustrates their application and usefulness.

More Efficient Hedging Techniques

Upon entering the futures market to hedge some interest rate risk, the hedger knows the maturity and

---

[1]When the four factors match perfectly, the hedged and hedging instruments will respond in the same way to interest rate changes (factors 1 and 2), and they will experience the same changes in their risk and term structures (factors 3 and 4). The conceptual background is common to the bond immunization literature. See [2].

[2]See [5] and [14] for another approach to developing more efficient hedging strategies. The "portfolio approach" attempts to minimize the variance of the value of the entire hedge over its life; [14] also develops an approach similar in spirit to ours.

coupon structure of the hedged and hedging instruments. He does not know the changes in the risk and term structure of interest rates that will occur while the hedge is in effect. (If he could know the future course of interest rates, the prospective hedger would not hedge anyway. He would simply alter his portfolio to profit from the rate changes that were about to occur.)

Because these two elements are unknown when the hedge is initiated, it is impossible to guarantee in advance that the hedge will be perfect. (A perfect hedge is one that leaves the hedger's wealth unchanged.) If changes in the term and risk structure are assumed known, it is possible to derive a hedge ratio that protects against interest rate risk caused by a mismatch of maturity and coupon between the hedged and hedging instrument.

All hedging strategies make some implicit assumption about the kinds of interest rate changes that will occur, and any hedging rule implies beliefs about the future course of interest rates. In the derivation of our hedge ratio, we explicitly assume that the yield curve remains flat for the life of the hedge. (Throughout the paper we ignore the difference between the yield to maturity and the expected return, which is tantamount to assuming that both instruments have zero default risk.) We make this assumption for several reasons. First, it helps to make the mathematics tractable. Second, a flat yield curve is a convenient approximation to the more realistic case of a yield curve that has "shape," but that maintains the same shape, changing only its level.

The basic strategy revolves around choosing some number of units (N) of futures contract j to hedge one unit of asset i with the goal that, over the life of the hedge:

$$\Delta P_i + \Delta P_j (N) = 0, \qquad (1)$$

where P_i and P_j are, respectively, the values of the bond to be hedged and the futures contract. Clearly, for any given interest rate shock the size of ΔP_i and ΔP_j depends on the sensitivity of i and j to a change in interest rates. Our problem, then, is to choose the number of futures contracts to trade (N) to balance out the different interest rate sensitivities of i and j, and thereby to preserve the truth of Equation (1). (Note that the technique hedges against a single interest rate shock.) As the equation implies, the perfect hedge we wish to find is the hedge that makes wealth invariant to a change in interest rates.

One important and useful measure of a financial asset's sensitivity to interest rates is its duration (D), which we may define as:

$$D_k = \frac{\sum\limits_{t=1}^{K} \dfrac{tC_{kt}}{(R_k)^t}}{\sum\limits_{t=1}^{K} \dfrac{C_{tk}}{(R_k)^t}} \qquad (2)$$

where C_{kt} = the tth period cash flow from asset k;
　　　$R_k = 1 + r_k$;
　　　r_k = yield to maturity on k; and
　　　K = term to maturity.

This is the duration measure as developed by Macaulay. (For an exposition of the concept, see [14]; [9] gives an account of duration's development.)

In Equation (2) the denominator is simply the price of asset k. The numerator is the present value of a single cash flow (C_{kt}) multiplied by (t), the number of periods until the payment is received. The result, duration, is the negative of the asset's price elasticity with respect to a change in the discount factor (R_k).

We show in the appendix that to hedge one unit of asset i with financial futures contract j one should trade N units of j, where N is given by:

$$N = \frac{-\bar{R}_j P_i D_i}{\bar{R}_i FP_j D_j} \qquad (3)$$

where $R_F = 1 +$ the risk-free rate;
　　　$\bar{R}_j = 1 +$ the rate expected to obtain on the asset *underlying* futures contract j;
　　　$\bar{R}_i = 1 +$ the expected yield to maturity on asset i;
　　　FP_j = the price agreed upon in the futures contract for title to the asset *underlying* j;
　　　P_i = the price of asset i expected to prevail on the planned termination date of the hedge;
　　　D_i = the duration of asset i expected to prevail on the planned termination date of the hedge; and
　　　D_j = the duration of the asset *underlying* futures contract j expected to prevail on the planned termination date of the hedge.

The Treasury Bill Futures Contract

Treasury bill futures contracts call for the delivery of $1,000,000 face value of 90-day Treasury bills upon maturity of the futures contract. Consequently, for every Treasury bill hedge $D_j = \frac{1}{4}$ year. Prices of

Treasury bill futures are quoted according to the IMM Index, which is simply 100 − bank discount rate. (See [10] for an exposition of the IMM Index.) This is not a true yield, and it requires conversion to $\bar{R}_J$. For example, if the IMM Index is 87.47, the bank discount rate is 12.53% which is equivalent to a true yield of 13.576%, or an $\bar{R}_J = 1.13576$. This means that:

$$FP_J = \frac{\$1,000,000}{(\bar{R}_J)^{0.25}} . \quad (4)$$

For a hedge with a Treasury bill futures contract, N is given by the simpler expression:[3]

$$N = \frac{-4(\bar{R}_J)^{1.25} P_1 D_1}{\bar{R}_1 (\$1,000,000)} . \quad (5)$$

The values needed to calculate N in Equation (5) are easily determined from the *Wall Street Journal*.

The Treasury Bond Futures Contract

The Treasury bond futures hedge is slightly more complicated because of the fact that Treasury bonds have coupons. Treasury bond futures contracts call for the delivery of $100,000 face value of 8% coupon Treasury bonds having a maturity of at least 15 years, or at least 15 years to their first call date. Bonds with a coupon other than 8% may be delivered to fulfill the futures contract subject to an adjustment. Long maturity bonds having an 8% coupon may be delivered against the futures contract with no adjustment. Generally, it is cheapest to deliver the longest maturity lowest coupon Treasury bond against the future contract.

From discussions with representatives of the Chicago Board of Trade, it appears that the market is well aware of this fact. For the most recent month on record, the bonds delivered were all of maturity in excess of 21 years. The *Wall Street Journal* reports implicit yields assuming a 20-year 8% coupon bond. The futures market, however, must price the actual bond that is to be delivered if it is efficient. Currently, the longest-maturity lowest-coupon bonds mature between 2005 and 2010 and have a coupon of 10%. To be consistent with the values reported in the *Wall Street Journal*, we assume an 8% 20-year bond for delivery against the futures contract.

In the *Wall Street Journal*, Treasury bond futures prices are quoted in "points and 32^{nd}s of par." A futures price of 71–24 means that the price is 71 24/32% of par. As for the whole contract par = $100,000, a futures price quoted as 71 24/32 would correspond to an $FP_J = \$71,750$ (71 24/32% × $100,000 = $71,750). Because Treasury bonds have coupons, D_J varies with $\bar{R}_J$. The exhibit provides a table of D_J and $\bar{R}_J$ for selected bonds with prices between 60-00 and 100-00 assuming a 20-year maturity and an 8% coupon. The values in the exhibit make it easy to calculate N for the Treasury bond futures hedge with Equation (3).

How to Apply the Hedging Rules

To illustrate the hedging rules developed, consider a portfolio manager who learns on March 1 that he or she will receive $5 million to invest on June 1 in AAA corporate bonds with a coupon rate of 5% and a maturity of 10 years. The manager finds current AAA yields attractive, and he or she wishes to lock in that rate for June 1 investment by trading in the futures market now. There are two possibilities. In the first case, rates on the hedged and hedging instruments change by the same amount, while in the second, they change by different amounts. For the two alternatives we can examine the hedging actions and outcomes for the naive strategy (face value dollar for face value dollar) and the method developed earlier, which we call the price-sensitivity (PS) strategy.

Case 1

Assume the following rates obtain:[4]

	Treasury Bill Futures	Treasury Bond Futures	AAA
March 1	8.00	8.50	9.50
June 1	7.58	8.08	9.08

As of March 1, when the hedge is initiated, the price expected to hold June 1 for the AAA bond must be $717.45 ($P_1$), given the current rate of 9.5%. Its duration (D_1) on June 1 will be 7.709 years. We can now calculate the hedge ratio (N) for hedging with Treasury bill futures from Equation (5):

---

[3]Note that N is calculated to hedge the position as of some one moment — the planned termination date of the hedge. $\bar{R}_1$ and $\bar{R}_J$ are the rates expected at that time, and the P_1 and D_1 are the price and duration expected to prevail at that time, given $\bar{R}_1$.

[4]Numerically these Treasury bond yields are the same as those used in an example of a perfect hedge in [7], page 8. We assume, however, that the rates are the true rates, corresponding to the $\bar{R}_J$ and the $\bar{R}_1$. Compare our results with that of the CBT example.

Exhibit. Prices, Yield, and Durations for 20-year 8% Treasury Bonds

Price	R̄	D	Price	R̄	D	Price	R̄	D
60– 0	1.1449	7.746	73–24	1.1167	8.804	87–16	1.0962	9.655
60– 8	1.1443	7.768	74– 0	1.1163	8.821	87–24	1.0959	9.668
60–16	1.1437	7.789	74– 8	1.1158	8.839	88– 0	1.0955	9.682
60–24	1.1431	7.810	74–16	1.1154	8.856	88– 8	1.0952	9.696
61– 0	1.1425	7.831	74–24	1.1150	8.873	88–16	1.0949	9.709
61– 8	1.1419	7.853	75– 0	1.1145	8.890	88–24	1.0946	9.723
61–16	1.1413	7.874	75– 8	1.1141	8.906	89– 0	1.0942	9.737
61–24	1.1407	7.894	75–16	1.1137	8.923	89– 8	1.0939	9.751
62– 0	1.1401	7.916	75–24	1.1133	8.939	89–16	1.0936	9.764
62– 8	1.1395	7.937	76– 0	1.1129	8.956	89–24	1.0933	9.778
62–16	1.1390	7.957	76– 8	1.1125	8.972	90– 0	1.0930	9.791
62–24	1.1384	7.977	76–16	1.1121	8.989	90– 8	1.0927	9.804
63– 0	1.1378	7.998	76–24	1.1117	9.006	90–16	1.0924	9.818
63– 8	1.1373	8.018	77– 0	1.1113	9.022	90–24	1.0921	9.832
63–16	1.1367	8.039	77– 8	1.1109	9.038	91– 0	1.0918	9.844
63–24	1.1361	8.060	77–16	1.1105	9.054	91– 8	1.0915	9.858
64– 0	1.1356	8.079	77–24	1.1101	9.070	91–16	1.0912	9.871
64– 8	1.1351	8.099	78– 0	1.1097	9.087	91–24	1.0909	9.884
64–16	1.1345	8.120	78– 8	1.1093	9.102	92– 0	1.0906	9.897
64–24	1.1340	8.139	78–16	1.1089	9.119	92– 8	1.0903	9.910
65– 0	1.1334	8.159	78–24	1.1085	9.134	92–16	1.0900	9.923
65– 8	1.1329	8.179	79– 0	1.1082	9.150	92–24	1.0897	9.936
65–16	1.1324	8.199	79– 8	1.1078	9.166	93– 0	1.0984	9.949
65–24	1.1318	8.219	79–16	1.1074	9.181	93– 8	1.0891	9.962
66– 0	1.1313	8.238	79–24	1.1070	9.187	93–16	1.0888	9.975
66– 8	1.1306	8.256	80– 0	1.1066	9.213	93–24	1.0885	9.987
66–16	1.1303	8.277	80– 8	1.1063	9.228	94– 0	1.0882	10.000
66–24	1.1298	8.296	80–16	1.1059	9.244	94– 8	1.0879	10.013
67– 0	1.1293	8.315	80–24	1.1055	9.259	94–16	1.0876	10.026
67– 8	1.1288	8.334	81– 0	1.1051	9.275	94–24	1.0873	10.038
67–16	1.1283	8.353	81– 8	1.1048	9.290	95– 0	1.0871	10.051
67–24	1.1278	8.372	81–16	1.1044	9.305	95– 8	1.0868	10.063
68– 0	1.1273	8.391	81–24	1.1041	9.320	95–16	1.0865	10.075
68– 8	1.1268	8.410	82– 0	1.1037	9.335	95–24	1.0862	10.088
68–16	1.1263	8.428	82– 8	1.1033	9.350	96– 0	1.0859	10.100
68–24	1.1258	8.447	82–16	1.1030	9.365	96– 8	1.0856	10.113
69– 0	1.1253	8.466	82–24	1.1026	9.380	96–16	1.0854	10.125
69– 8	1.1248	8.484	83– 0	1.1023	9.395	96–24	1.0851	10.137
69–16	1.1244	8.502	83– 8	1.1019	9.410	97– 0	1.0848	10.149
69–24	1.1239	8.521	83–16	1.1016	9.425	97– 8	1.0845	10.162
70– 0	1.1234	8.539	83–24	1.1012	9.439	97–16	1.0843	10.174
70– 8	1.1229	8.558	84– 0	1.1009	9.454	97–24	1.0840	10.186
70–16	1.1225	8.576	84– 8	1.1005	9.469	98– 0	1.0837	10.198
70–24	1.1220	8.594	84–16	1.1002	9.484	98– 8	1.0835	10.210
71– 0	1.1216	8.611	84–24	1.0998	9.498	98–16	1.0832	10.222
71– 8	1.1211	8.629	85– 0	1.0995	9.512	98–24	1.0829	10.234
71–16	1.1207	8.647	85– 8	1.0991	9.527	99– 0	1.0826	10.246
71–24	1.1202	8.665	85–16	1.0988	9.542	99– 8	1.0824	10.257
72– 0	1.1197	8.683	85–24	1.0985	9.556	99–16	1.0821	10.269
72– 8	1.1193	8.700	86– 0	1.0981	9.570	100– 0	1.0816	10.292
72–16	1.1189	8.718	86– 8	1.0978	9.584	100– 8	1.0813	10.304
72–24	1.1184	8.735	86–16	1.0975	9.598	100–16	1.0811	10.316
73– 0	1.1180	8.753	86–24	1.0972	9.612	100–24	1.0808	10.327
73– 8	1.1175	8.770	87– 0	1.0968	9.627			
73–16	1.1171	8.787	87– 8	1.0965	9.640			

The exhibit presents prices, discount rates, and durations for a wide variety of Treasury bonds assuming 20 years to maturity and an 8% coupon paid semi-annually. These values of R̄$_J$ and D$_J$ may be used in Equation (3) for the calculation of the proper hedge ratio N.

Prices are presented in "points and 32nds of par" to correspond to the *Wall Street Journal* listings. To calculate N the prices in the exhibit must be converted to FP$_J$. For bonds with prices not in the table, one may simply interpolate.

$$N = \frac{-4(1.08)^{1.25}(-\$717.45)(7.709)}{(1.095)(\$1,000,000)} = 0.022244. \quad (6)$$

This means that 0.022244 Treasury bill futures contracts should be traded for each bond. As the manager knows he or she will have $5 million to invest, expecting the price of the bond to be $717.45 on June 1, he or she is planning to buy 6,969.1268 bonds ($5,000,000/$717.45). Consequently, he or she should buy 155.0213 Treasury bill futures contracts (6,969.1268 × 0.022244).[5]

Given the interest rate changes shown above, the price of the bond on June 1 is $739.08, not the expected $717.45. For the manager buying the bonds on June 1, this represents an opportunity loss of $21.63 on each bond, and $150,742.21 on the entire position. Let us now compare the hedging effectiveness of the two strategies: the naive vs. the PS.

According to the naive strategy, one will trade one dollar of face value in the futures market per dollar of bonds. The naive hedge is to buy five Treasury bill futures contracts, whereas the PS strategy recommends 155.0213 contracts. When the rates drop from 8.00 to 7.58%, this generates a gain on a futures contract of $956.02:

$$\frac{\$1,000,000}{(1.0758)^{0.25}} - \frac{\$1,000,000}{(1.08)^{0.25}} = \$956.02.$$

For the naive strategy the total gain in the futures market is $4,780.10, while for the PS strategy it is $148,203.46. The following table depicts the results:

Bond Market Opportunity Loss	Treasury Bill Futures Market	
	Naive Strategy	PS Strategy
−$150,742.21	+$4,780.10	+$148,203.46
ERROR	−$145,962.11	−$2,538.75

The PS strategy is not perfect, losing $2,539 because of the fact that the change in rates was discrete. The error from the naive strategy, though, is 57.5 times the error from the PS strategy.

Part of the explanation for this difference in the performance of the two strategies stems from the short maturity and absence of coupons of Treasury bills. The naive strategy should be closer in dollar amount

---

[5]The cost of a Treasury bill futures contract is negligible. It takes $60 in transactions costs and a margin of $1,000 for daily resettlement for one contract ($1 million in denomination). In our example, we assume interest rates change at the end of the hedge period. With interest rates changing frequently in the real world, the manager will need a small amount of cash for daily resettlement, and rebalancing will be necessary.

to the performance of the PS strategy using Treasury bond futures, for Treasury bonds more closely match the maturity and coupon structure of the bond being hedged. To hedge with Treasury bond futures, the correct hedge ratio is given by Equation (3):

$$N = \frac{-(1.085)(-\$717.45)(7.709)}{(1.095)(\$96,875)(10.143)} = 0.005577.$$

To implement the hedge with Treasury bond futures, we will trade 38.8667 (0.005577 × 6,969.1268) contracts according to the PS strategy, and 50 contracts according to the naive strategy (the Treasury bond future contract is for $100,000 face value of bonds).

From the exhibit one observes that a drop in rates from 8.5 to 8.08% causes the futures price to rise from $96,875 to $100.750, for a gain of $3,875 per contract. For the two strategies this gives the following hedging results:

Opportunity Loss	Treasury Bond Futures Market	
	Naive Strategy	PS Strategy
−$150,742.21	+$193,750.00	+$150,608.46
ERROR	+$43,007.79	−$133.75

In this case, the error of the naive strategy is 321.6 times that of the PS strategy, but the dollar difference between the two is smaller, as the price sensitivity of Treasury bonds is closer to that of the bond being hedged than is the case with Treasury bills. The PS strategy is almost perfect, hedging 99.91% of the $150,742.21 opportunity loss in the bond market.

Case 2

This case allows the rates to change by different amounts from the same original starting point. Assume now that the following rates obtain:

	Treasury Bill Futures	Treasury Bond Futures	AAA
March 1	8.00	8.50	9.50
June 1	7.58	8.08	9.25

As long as the starting rates are all the same, the hedge ratios will all be the same as above. For the futures, the rates conform to the previous sample, but the yield change for the bonds has been decreased. With a rate of 9.25% the price of the bond will be $730.24 on June 1. For the bond position the total opportunity loss is \$89,135.13 (6,969.9268 × \$12.79). For the Treasury bill hedge the new results are:

Bond Market Opportunity Loss	Treasury Bill Futures Market	
	Naive Strategy	PS Strategy
−\$89,135.13	+\$4,780.10	+\$148,203.46
ERROR	−\$84,335.03	+\$59,068.33

For the Treasury bond hedge the result would be:

Bond Market Opportunity Loss	Treasury Bill Futures Market	
	Naive Strategy	PS Strategy
−\$89,135.13	+\$193,750.00	+\$150,608.46
ERROR	+\$104,614.87	+\$61,473.33

In both cases, the PS strategy gives a smaller error. If rates change by different amounts on the hedged and hedging instruments, it is possible for the naive strategy to outperform the PS strategy, but that would occur only by infrequent coincidence. This possibility notwithstanding, the naive hedger subjects himself or herself to considerable risk that the hedger following the PS strategy can avoid.

Some Final Hints

The PS strategy presented here provides a rational procedure for hedging interest rate risk by trading in the Treasury bill and Treasury bond futures market. The method takes account of differences between the maturity and coupon structures of the hedged and hedging instruments. With a flat yield curve and an infinitesimal change in interest rates, the PS strategy results in a perfect hedge. In the real world one cannot expect the PS strategy to provide a perfect hedge, for rates change constantly by discrete amounts, and the term structure is not flat. Yet the method we develop can be expected to improve hedging performance in actual trading.

To apply the PS strategy, it is better to use a futures instrument with a maturity and coupon structure matching that of the bond to be hedged. (That is why the error was smaller with the Treasury bond hedge.) The method can also be applied to bond portfolios by simply using portfolio values, durations, and interest rates. Finally, as rates vary over time, the hedging performance can be improved by periodic rebalancing of the hedge. The PS strategy is designed to hedge against a single interest rate shock. Hedging performance can be improved by periodic recalculation of N and by adjusting the hedge accordingly. The frequency of rebalancing depends upon the size of the position,

transactions costs of changing the hedge, and the anticipated volatility of interest rates.

References

1. P. Bacon and R. Williams, "Interest Rate Futures: New Tool for the Financial Manager," *Financial Management* (Spring 1976), pp. 32–38, reprinted in G. Gay and R. Kolb, eds., *Interest Rate Futures: Concepts and Issues,* Richmond, Robert F. Dame, Inc., 1981.
2. G. Bierwag, G. Kaufman, and C. Khang, "Duration and Bond Portfolio Analysis: An Overview," *Journal of Financial and Quantitative Analysis* (November 1978), pp. 671–682.
3. J. Cox, J. Ingersoll, and S. Ross, "A Re-Examination of Traditional Hypotheses about the Term Structure of Interest Rates," University of Chicago Working Paper (November 1980).
4. J. Cox, J. Ingersoll, and S. Ross, "A Theory of the Term Structure of Interest Rates," University of Chicago Working Paper (August 1978).
5. L. Ederington, "The Hedging Performance of the New Futures Market," *Journal of Finance* (March 1979), pp. 157–170, reprinted in G. Gay and R. Kolb, eds., *Interest Rate Futures: Concepts and Issues,* Richmond, Robert F. Dame, Inc., 1981.
6. W. Feller, *An Introduction to Probability Theory and Its Applications,* Volume II, New York, John Wiley & Sons, 1971.
7. "Hedging Interest Rate Risks," Chicago, Chicago Board of Trade, 1977.
8. J. Ingersoll, J. Skelton, and R. Weil, "Duration Forty Years Later," *Journal of Financial and Quantitative Analysis* (November 1978), pp. 627–650.
9. "An Introduction to the Interest Rate Futures Market," Chicago, Chicago Board of Trade, 1978.
10. E. Kane, "Market Incompleteness and Divergences between Forward and Futures Interest Rates," *Journal of Finance* (May 1980), pp. 221–234, reprinted in G. Gay and R. Kolb, eds., *Interest Rate Futures: Concepts and Issues,* Richmond, Robert F. Dame, Inc., 1981.
11. R. Kolb and R. Chiang, "Duration, Immunization, and Hedging with Interest Rate Futures," *Journal of Financial Research* (forthcoming), reprinted in G. Gay and R. Kolb, eds., *Interest Rate Futures: Concepts and Issues,* Richmond, Robert F. Dame, Inc., 1981.
12. A. Loosigian, *Interest Rate Futures,* Princeton, N.J., Dow Jones Books, 1980.
13. R. McEnally, "Duration as a Practical Tool for Bond Management," *Journal of Portfolio Management* (Summer 1977), pp. 53–57
14. R. McEnally and M. Rice, "Hedging Possibilities in the Flotation of Debt Securities," *Financial Management* (Winter 1979), pp. 12–18, reprinted in G. Gay and R. Kolb, eds., *Interest Rate Futures: Concepts and Issues,* Richmond, Robert F. Dame, Inc., 1981.

15. "Treasury Bill Futures," Chicago, International Monetary Market, 1977.

Appendix. Derivation of Hedge Ratios

Assume:

1. That the yield curves are flat for each instrument, so that all future payments associated with an instrument are appropriately discounted at a single rate — the instruments' yield to maturity; and

2. That cash flows occur on a futures contract immediately upon a change in its value, which corresponds to the current institutional arrangement of daily resettlement.

Notation

Instrument i is to be hedged by financial futures contract j, where:

P_i, P_j = the value of instruments i and j, respectively;

C_{it}, C_{jt} = the tth period cash flows for instrument i and for the financial asset underlying financial futures contract j, respectively;

FP_j = the price specified for the delivery of the instrument in futures contract j;

D_i, D_j = Macaulay's duration measure for instrument i and the asset underlying financial futures contract j, respectively;

R_F = 1 + the risk-free rate;

$\tilde{R}_i, \bar{R}_i$ = 1 + the yield to maturity on i and the expected value of $\tilde{R}_i$, respectively;

$\tilde{R}_j, \bar{R}_j$ = 1 + the yield to maturity on the asset underlying financial futures contract j expected to obtain at the planned termination date of the hedge, and the expected value of $\tilde{R}_j$, respectively;

R_j^* = the yield to maturity implied by FP_j for the instrument underlying financial futures contract j;

N = the hedge ratio to be derived — the number of futures contracts j to trade to hedge a one-unit position in asset i; and

I, J = the term to maturity of asset i and the term to maturity of the financial asset underlying futures contract j.

The goal of the hedge is to insure, insofar as possible, that as of the planned termination date of the hedge:

$$\Delta P_i + (\Delta P_j) N = 0. \qquad (A\text{-}1)$$

To find N we must solve the equation:

$$\frac{dP_i}{dR_F} + \frac{dP_j}{dR_F} N = 0. \qquad (A\text{-}2)$$

As i is a bond, its price is given at any time by:

$$P_i = \sum_{t=1}^{I} \frac{C_{it}}{(R_i^*)^t}. \qquad (A\text{-}3)$$

At any time the value of the futures contract is given by (ignoring the problem of Jensen's Inequality):

$$P_j = \sum_{t=1}^{J} \frac{C_{jt}}{(\bar{R}_j)^t} - \sum_{t=1}^{J} \frac{C_{jt}}{(R_j^*)^t}. \qquad (A\text{-}4)$$

Equation (A-4) has an important economic interpretation. When one purchases a futures contract, one agrees to pay the futures price, FP_j, at the maturity of the futures contract, in exchange for the series of flows C_{jt}. Consequently, it must be the case that:

$$FP_j = \sum_{t=1}^{J} \frac{C_{jt}}{(R_j^*)^t}. \qquad (A\text{-}5)$$

It is reasonable to agree to pay FP_j only if one believes, at the time of entering the futures contract, that $\bar{R}_j = R_j^*$. Otherwise one of the parties to the futures contract expects a loss. Consequently, at the time of entering the futures contract, $P_j = 0$ for Equation (A-4). Later, during the life of the futures contract, it may be that $\bar{R}_j \neq R_j^*$, and then $P_j \neq 0$.

Substituting (A-3) and (A-4) into (A-2) gives:

$$\frac{d \sum_{t=1}^{I} \frac{C_{it}}{(\bar{R}_i)^t}}{d \bar{R}_i} \frac{d \bar{R}_i}{d R_F} +$$

$$\frac{d \left[\sum_{t=1}^{J} \frac{C_{jt}}{(\bar{R}_j)^t} - \sum_{t=1}^{J} \frac{C_{jt}}{(R_j^*)^t} \right]}{d \bar{R}_j} \frac{d \bar{R}_j}{d R_F} N = 0, \qquad (A\text{-}6)$$

from which we derive:

$$\frac{1}{\bar{R}_i} \sum_{t=1}^{I} \frac{-t C_{it}}{(\bar{R}_i)^t} \frac{d\bar{R}_i}{dR_F} +$$

$$\frac{N}{\bar{R}_j} \sum_{t=1}^{J} \frac{-t C_{jt}}{(R_j)^t} \frac{d\bar{R}_j}{dR_F} = 0. \qquad (A\text{-}7)$$

Solving for N, we find

$$N = -\frac{\bar{R}_j}{\bar{R}_i} \frac{\sum_{t=1}^{I} \frac{t C_{it}}{(\bar{R}_i)^t} \frac{d\bar{R}_i}{dR_F}}{\sum_{t=1}^{J} \frac{t C_{jt}}{(\bar{R}_j)^t} \frac{d\bar{R}_j}{dR_F}}. \qquad (A\text{-}8)$$

Equation (A-8) is a general expression for N applying to any bond i and any futures contract j. Recall Macaulay's duration measure, D, is:

$$D_i = \frac{\displaystyle\sum_{t=1}^{I} \frac{tC_{it}}{(\bar{R}_i)^t}}{\displaystyle\sum_{t=1}^{I} \frac{C_{it}}{(\bar{R}_i)^t}}. \qquad (A-9)$$

Substituting (A-3) and (A-9) into (A-8) gives:

$$N = \frac{-R_j P_i D_i}{\bar{R}_i FP_j D_j} \frac{\dfrac{d\bar{R}_i}{dR_F}}{\dfrac{d\bar{R}_j}{dR_F}}. \qquad (A-10)$$

Note that, in Equation (A-10), P_i, D_i, FP_j, and D_j are all evaluated as of the planned termination date of the hedge. Because we have assumed that the yield curve is flat, they are the prices and durations that will obtain at current rates.

Assuming $d\bar{R}_i/dR_F$ and $d\bar{R}_F$ can be estimated, those estimates should be included in the computation of N for improved hedging performance. For illustrative purposes, we assume $d\bar{R}_i/dR_F = d\bar{R}_j/dR_F$, so Equation (A-10) becomes:

$$N = \frac{-\bar{R}_j P_i D_i}{\bar{R}_i FP_j D_j}, \qquad (A-11)$$

and Equation (A-11) is used for the computation of N throughout the paper.

Article 34

Immunizing Bond Portfolios With Interest Rate Futures

Robert W. Kolb and Gerald D. Gay

■ The concept of duration has attained a significant place in the finance literature since its introduction by Macaulay more than forty years ago.[1] During the same time, duration has attained unparalleled acceptance as a practical technique for the management of bond portfolio risk.[2] Because of the important role of duration in bond portfolio management, it is crucial that duration oriented strategies be implemented as effectively and efficiently as possible.

To that end this paper explains the important role that interest rate futures can play in bond portfolio management. Basically, the strategy advanced here maintains that, by trading interest rate futures in conjunction with the holding of a bond portfolio, one can effectively adjust the duration of the bond portfolio. Further, if the duration of the portfolio is adjusted by using interest rate futures, the holdings of the bond portfolio itself need not be altered. This means that the portfolio manager may maintain the bond portfolio itself without disturbing favored maturities or issues. Since the bonds in the portfolio are not traded, one avoids the problem of a lack of marketability of the bonds. Also, the transaction costs associated with adjusting the duration are much lower if one uses interest rate futures, and the task can be accomplished with little or no capital, since one must make only a margin deposit to trade the futures contract. Finally, the technique of using interest rate futures for duration adjustment is compatible with all of the more sophisticated duration techniques that have been developed recently.

The authors gratefully acknowledge the support of the Chicago Board of Trade Foundation in the conduct of this research.

[1] For reviews of the history and development of the concept of duration see Weil [34], Ingersoll, Skelton, and Weil [23], and Bierwag, Kaufman, and Khang [2].

[2] McEnally [31] provides a useful introduction to the concept of duration and its applicability to bond portfolio management.

Duration and Immunization

Macaulay introduced the concept of duration (D) which he defined as:

$$D_i = \sum_{t=1}^{m} \left[\frac{\frac{tC_{it}}{(1 + K_i)^t}}{P_i} \right] \qquad (1)$$

where C_{it} = cash flow from the ith financial instrument at time t,

K_i = the instrument's yield to maturity,

t = an element of a time vector ranging over the time to maturity,

P_i = the instrument's price.

It can be proven that D_i is the negative of the instrument's price elasticity with respect to a change in the discount factor $(1 + K_i)$. From this it follows that, for infinitesimal changes in $(1 + K_i)$:

$$\Delta P_i = -D_i \frac{\Delta(1 + K_i)}{(1 + K_i)} P_i \qquad (2)$$

For discrete changes in the discount factor, (2) holds as a close approximation. Although (1) strictly applies to a single instrument, the duration of a portfolio (D_p) with N assets each having weight W_i in the portfolio is given by:

$$D_p = \sum_{i=1}^{N} W_i D_i \qquad (3)$$

So defined, the concept of duration has two distinct uses. The first case, which can be called the "Bank Immunization Case," assumes that one agent holds both an asset and liability portfolio of equal value. Then, as Equation (2) suggests, by setting the duration of the asset and liability portfolios equal, any change in K affects both portfolios equally.[3] Consequently, the portfolio holder incurs no wealth change due to a shift in interest rates. In an important sense, he can be said to be "immunized" against interest rate changes.[4] The

second use of duration, for the "Planning Period Case," is directed toward a portfolio holder who has some planning period in mind, after which he plans to liquidate the portfolio. By setting the duration of the portfolio equal to the time remaining until the end of the planning period, the investor can guarantee a certain minimal rate of return.[5] If interest rates fluctuate, the return may be higher over the life of the planning period, but it cannot be less. If rates rise over the planning period, this generates a capital loss, but it also creates an offsetting benefit because the reinvestment rate, at which the cash throw-off from the portfolio can be reinvested, is higher. Exactly the opposite trade-off occurs if rates fall.[6]

As has been well recognized, Equations (1) and (2) rely on some unrealistic assumptions. Strictly speaking, Equation (1) is correct only if the term structure is flat, since it implicitly discounts all future cash flows at the uniform rate K. In itself, this difficulty is surmountable by simply re-defining D_i as D_i^* to take account of term structures with shape:

$$D_i^* = \sum_{t=1}^{M} \left[\frac{\frac{tC_{it}}{\prod_{j=1}^{t} (1 + K_j)}}{\sum_{t=1}^{M} \frac{C_{it}}{\prod_{j=1}^{t} (1 + K_j)}} \right] \qquad (4)$$

where K_j = the appropriate one-period rate for the jth period.

D_i^* allows for each flow to be discounted at a unique rate commensurate with its true discount rate as given by the term structure.

A second deeper difficulty emerges from Equation (2), which also implicitly assumes that when rates change, all rates change by the same amount. Even if D_i^* is allowed to accommodate term structure shape,

---

[3] As a practical matter, measuring the duration of a bank's assets and liabilities is at best a difficult process. Demand deposits, for example, represent a case where it is not at all obvious how to measure duration. However, the problems with measuring duration affect the traditional "bonds only" approach and the "bonds and futures" approach, to be developed here, equally. Here we assume equal values in the asset and liability portfolios. This is only for convenience. The analysis can be extended to the more general case with ease.

[4] Grove [21] analyzes this type of portfolio immunization. In a perfect market, the individual investor could trade bonds costlessly, thereby achieving "homemade immunization." Institutional concern with immunization, like firm concern with leverage, stems from market imperfections.

[5] Fisher and Weil [17] discuss planning period immunization. This technique was later elaborated by Kaufman [26], in which the nature of the trade-off between capital gains/losses and reinvestment rates is discussed.

[6] The immunization guarantees that the return will be at least as large as the promised return, Fisher and Weil [17]. As Bierwag and Khang [5] show, this means that an immunized portfolio stochastically dominates a single bond. Further, a portfolio of coupon bonds, with duration equal to the planning period, stochastically dominates a pure-discount bond with maturity equal to the planning period. This is the case, since the realized yield equals the promised yield for the pure discount bond. For the immunized coupon-bond portfolio one may realize a return greater than the promised yield, but one cannot realize a lower yield. This consideration should give pause to those portfolio managers who welcome the issuance of pure-discount bonds by J.C. Penney, Pepsi, and others.

Equation (2) assumes that all rate changes preserve the same shaped yield curve. The parallel, or additive, shifts of the yield curve presupposed by (2) are, of course, the rare exception, not the rule. Instead, non-shape preserving term structure changes, or twisting yield curves, are more normal. Even so, the situation is perhaps not desperate. It can be shown that an appropriate duration hedging formulation exists for any given yield curve twist. However, the impending twist must be correctly anticipated, and the duration strategy adjusted accordingly, if the immunization is to be perfect.[7] This fact offers small comfort for two reasons. First, no one knows what yield curve twist is about to occur. Second, if one did know he would simply trade on this knowledge and would not be concerned with immunization.

In the final analysis, then, one cannot use the duration techniques to guarantee perfect immunization. This is clear from a consideration of the Bank Immunization Case. Assume some difference in coupon and maturity structure of the asset and liability portfolios. (If no differences exist, one has a net zero position and no discussion of immunization need be undertaken. The portfolio is of necessity perfectly immunized.) Also assume any desired duration measure and that the durations of the asset and liability portfolios are matched. Then some yield curve twist is possible that will generate a wealth change.

In spite of the fact that perfect immunization cannot be guaranteed, the practical consequence is small. Elaborate simulation of different yield curve twists leads to the conclusion that the use of Macaulay's duration (D_i of Equation (1)) is very effective in achieving nearly perfect immunization.[8] Also, the immunization is made more nearly perfect by matching the maturities of the asset and liability portfolios in the Bank Immunization Case, and by matching the maturity of the portfolio to the planning period in the Planning Period Case.[9]

No matter which measure of duration is used, the immunization holds only for a single instantaneous change in rates that occurs when either the asset portfolio duration equals that of the liability portfolio (the Bank Immunization Case), or when the duration of the portfolio equals the planning period (the Planning Period Case). But, durations of instruments change due to (1) the mere passage of time or (2) a shift in yields. These two factors mean that the originally initiated immunization condition cannot be preserved, without re-adjusting the portfolio. Maintaining the immunization condition at all times necessitates continuous adjustment. But this is costly, so for practical purposes, portfolios are only re-adjusted periodically. In the light of this need for re-adjustment, the cost and practicality of the adjustment process requires attention.

Duration and Interest Rate Futures

In the strictest sense, futures contracts do not have a price, which means that they have no duration either, since the duration Equation (1) involves division by the price. The fact that future contracts have no price *per se* can be seen from the fact that one need not pay anything to enter a futures contract. Rather the "futures prices" that are quoted are better thought of as expected future prices for their respective underlying instruments at the time of delivery. For an interest rate futures contract (j), this expected future price (FP_j) depends upon the promised yield to maturity that is expected to prevail on the underlying instrument at the delivery date (K^*) and the cash flows (C_{jt}) associated with that underlying instrument. Thus, for any interest rate futures contract:

$$FP_j = \sum_{t=0}^{M} \frac{C_{jt}}{(1 + K^*)^t} \qquad (5)$$

Note here that the index for the summation runs over the period from the delivery date ($t = 0$) to the maturity of the underlying instrument. Equation (5) treats futures contracts as though they are forward contracts, in spite of significant institutional differences between the two contracts. Further, recent research [14, 24] has shown that futures and forward prices need not be equal even in perfect markets, if interest rates are stochastic. Recent evidence [12] has shown that these differences are very small, even insignificant, for the foreign currency market. Consequently, we ignore the difference between futures and forward contracts.[10]

---

[7]Bierwag and Kaufman [1] derive more sophisticated measures for duration to immunize against non-additive interest rate shocks. Kolb and Chiang [28] treat interest rate futures contracts similarly.

[8]The fact that Macaulay's duration measure assumes a flat term structure, contrary to fact, is not of great empirical significance. Gifford Fong Associates [20] presents results from elaborate simulations showing that the Macaulay duration measure performs as well as the complex duration measures for a wide variety of cases.

[9]Fong and Vasicek [18] show that immunization is made more nearly perfect when bonds maturing close to the planning horizon are used in the portfolio. In other words, the following strategy is recommended: Minimize the variance of the portfolio payment dates about the portfolio duration subject to the constraint that the duration = planning horizon.

[10]Existing studies of interest rate futures market efficiency substantiate the very close relationship between forward yields and futures yields. Since these efficiency studies proceed by comparing returns on futures and forward contracts, and generally find them to be equal [30, 32, 33], forward and futures contracts are very close substitutes and are essentially similar in their institutional respects. For further justification of this position, see Kolb [27], Chapter IV.

The question can then be raised: What is the relationship between the forward or futures price and the expected future spot price to prevail at the maturity of the forward or futures contract? Under certain conditions, the forward or futures price equals the expected future spot price. Fischer Black [6, p. 167] analyzes forward and futures price behavior in a CAPM setting and shows that: "If changes in the futures price are independent of the return on the market, the futures price is the expected spot price." This must be the case if there is no systematic risk, since only the bearing of systematic risk is compensated in an efficient market. With no systematic risk (and ignoring transaction costs), the holding of a forward or futures contract is a pure zero sum game. As Black shows [6] such a situation requires that the equilibrium forward or futures price must equal the expected future spot price.

The key issue then becomes whether futures contracts exhibit systematic risk. While the question has not been fully resolved, the best available evidence concludes that the systematic risk of futures contracts is zero [15]. In accordance with this evidence, this analysis assumes that the futures and forward contracts are essentially similar in their institutional features and that they exhibit no systematic risk. Consequently, forward and futures prices may be interpreted as the market's best estimate of the futures spot price to prevail upon delivery.

From Equation (5) for infinitesimal changes in K*:

$$\Delta FP_j = -D_j \frac{\Delta(1 + K^*)}{(1 + K^*)} FP_j \qquad (6)$$

Note here, however, that D_j is the duration of the underlying financial instrument that is expected to prevail at the delivery date. This means that D_j is based on K*, the yield on the underlying instrument expected to prevail on the delivery date of the futures contract:

$$D_j = \sum_{t=1}^{M} \left[\frac{\dfrac{tC_{jt}}{(1 + K^*)^t}}{\displaystyle\sum_{t=1}^{M} \dfrac{C_{jt}}{(1 + K^*)^t}} \right] \qquad (7)$$

So while the futures contract itself does not have a duration, its price sensitivity depends upon the duration and yield of the underlying instrument that is expected to prevail on the delivery date.

Earlier changes in the duration of a financial instrument were said to be a function of changes in yields and the passage of time. When one considers the dura-

tion of the instrument underlying a futures contract, two related points are evident. First, D_j of Equation (7) clearly depends upon changes in K*. Second, D_j does not change with the passage of time over the life of the futures contract. This differentiates Equations (2) and (6). D_j cannot change over the life of the futures contract, barring changes in K*, because the maturity of the deliverable instrument is fixed by the terms of the futures contract. This fact helps to make futures contracts particularly useful for the implementation of immunization strategies.

The similarity of duration measures for bonds (1) and futures contracts (7) makes clear the susceptibility of futures contracts to all analyses that have been applied to a "bonds only" approach. In the context of portfolio immunization, futures contracts also suffer basis risk [13], can be applied to immunizing for multiple planning periods [4], and can be used in active and passive management strategies [3].

Available Futures Contracts

Futures contracts are currently available on T-bills, -notes, and -bonds, GNMAs (certificate delivery and collateralized depository receipts), certificates of deposit, Eurodollars and commercial paper (30 and 90 day maturities). Most immunization strategies concern portfolios of non-mortgage related instruments, so GNMA futures will not be considered. Currently, markets for commercial paper and T-note futures contracts are extremely thin.[11] Since T-bill and T-bond contracts enjoy very robust futures markets, and since they lie at the two ends of the duration spectrum, they appear to be the most applicable for the implementation of immunization strategies.

A T-bill futures contract calls for delivery of $1,000,000 face value of T-bills having 90 days remaining until maturity. Since T-bills are pure discount instruments, their duration, as given by Equation (7), will always be equal to M, which is 90 days or .25 years. This will be the same for every T-bill, no matter what its yield. For T-bonds the situation is more complex. To fulfill a T-bond futures contract, one may deliver any T-bond not maturing and not callable within 15 years from the time of delivery. This means that several different bonds are deliverable. For example, in February 1982, 18 different T-bonds were deliverable, with call or maturity dates ranging from 16 to 24 years and coupons ranging from 3½ to 15¾%. Clearly the prices and durations of these deliverable instru-

---

[11]Recently both commercial paper contracts showed zero open interest on the CBT. The open interest on 2-year 8% Treasury notes was 630 contracts on the COMEX.

ments vary widely. The rules of the Chicago Board of Trade (CBT), the largest T-bond futures market, specify price differentials based on which bond is actually delivered.[12] However, usually one bond is cheapest to deliver and the futures market tends to trade to that bond [9]. Consequently, the duration of the underlying T-bond must be computed from Equation (7). For greatest accuracy, it should be computed for the T-bond that is cheapest to deliver.[13]

How to Immunize with Interest Rate Futures

Here two examples are presented, one for the Planning Period Case and one for the Bank Immunization Case. In Exhibit 1, three bonds are considered, along with the T-bill and T-bond futures contracts. The Exhibit reflects the assumption of a flat yield curve and instruments of the same risk level.[14] Since the yield curve is flat, duration is appropriately calculated by Equation (1) or (7). Only parallel shifts in the yield curve are considered in these examples, and all market imperfections are ignored.

The Planning Period Case. Assume a $100 million bond portfolio of Bond C with a duration of 9.285 years. Assume now that the portfolio duration is to be shortened to 6 years to match the planning period. The shortening could be accomplished by selling Bond C and buying Bond A until the following conditions are met:

$$W_A D_A + W_C D_C = 6 \text{ years}$$
$$W_A + W_C = 1$$

where: W_I = percent of portfolio funds committed to asset I.

---

[12]For these rules see CBT [11]. The calculation of the invoice price requires conversion factors from Financial Publishing Co. [16].

[13]For sample durations based on a 20 year 8% T-bond, see [29], Appendix.

[14]The constant yields of Exhibit 1 are consistent with this assumption of homogeneous risk. One may think of the bond portfolio as consisting of U.S. Treasury issues. However, the argument of the paper does not require the assumption of uniform yields, but only parallel shifting yield curves.

Exhibit 1. Instruments Used in the Analysis

	Coupon	Maturity	Yield	Price	Duration
Bond A:	8%	4 yrs.	12%	885.59	3.475
Bond B:	10%	10 yrs.	12%	903.47	6.265
Bond C:	4%	15 yrs.	12%	463.05	9.285
T-Bond Futures:*	8%	20 yrs.	12%	718.75	8.674
T-Bill Futures:*	—	¼ yr.	12%	972.07	.25

*For purposes of comparability, we assume face values of $1000 for these instruments.

This means that 56.54% of the $100 million must be put in Bond A, the funds coming from the sale of Bond C. Call this Portfolio 1.

Alternatively, one could adjust the portfolio's duration to match the 6 year planning period by trading interest rate futures. For Portfolio 2, the problem is to continue to hold $100,000,000 in Bond C, yet to achieve the same price action as Portfolio 1. If Portfolio 2 is to be comprised of Bond C and T-bill futures, the T-bill futures position must be chosen to satisfy the condition:

$$\Delta P_P = \Delta P_C N_C + \Delta FP_{TBILL} N_{TBILL}$$

where:
P_P = value of the portfolio,
P_C = price of bond C,
FP_{TBILL} = T-bill futures price,
N_C = number of C bonds,
N_{TBILL} = number of T-bills.

Applying the same price change formula (2) to the portfolio value, Bond C, and the T-bill futures:

$$-D_P \frac{\Delta(1 + r)}{(1 + r)} P_P = [-D_C \frac{\Delta(1 + r)}{(1 + r)} P_C] N_C$$
$$+ [-D_{TBILL} \frac{\Delta(1 + r)}{1 + r} FP_{TBILL}] N_{TBILL}$$

which reduces to:

$$D_P P_P = D_C P_C N_C + D_{TBILL} FP_{TBILL} N_{TBILL}$$

Since the goal is to mimic Portfolio 1, which has a total value of $100,000,000 and a duration of 6 years, it must be that:

$$P_P = \$100,000,000$$
$$D_P = 6$$
$$D_C = 9.285$$
$$P_C = \$463.05$$
$$N_C = 215,959$$
$$D_{TBILL} = .25$$
$$FP_{TBILL} = 972.07$$

Solving for $N_{TBILL} = -1,351,747$ indicates that this many T-bills (assuming $1,000 par value) must be sold short in the futures market. Since T-bill futures are denominated in $1,000,000 face value, this technique requires that 1,352 contracts be sold.

The same technique used to created Portfolio 2 can be applied using a T-bond futures contract, which gives rise to Portfolio 3. Solving:

$$D_P P_P = D_C P_C N_C + D_{TBOND} FP_{TBOND} N_{TBOND}$$

for N_{TBOND} gives $N_{TBOND} = -52,691$. Since T-bond futures contracts have a face value denomination of $100,000, 527 T-bond futures contracts must be sold.

Exhibit 2. Portfolio Characteristics for the Planning Period Case

		Portfolio 1 (Bonds Only)	Portfolio 2 (Short T-bill Futures)	Portfolio 3 (Short T-bond Futures)
Portfolio Weights	W_A	56.54%	—	—
	W_C	43.46%	100%	100%
	W_{CASH}	0	0	0
Number of Instruments	N_A	63,844	0	—
	N_C	93,856	215,959	215,959
	N_{TBILL}	—	(1,351,747)	—
	N_{TBOND}	—	—	(52,691)
Value of each Instrument	$N_A P_A$	56,539,608	—	—
	$N_C P_C$	43,460,021	99,999,815	99,999,815
	$N_{TBILL}\ FP_{TBILL}$	—	1,313,992,706	—
	$N_{TBOND}\ FP_{TBOND}$	—	—	37,871,656
	Cash	371	185	185
Portfolio Value $(N_A P_A + N_C P_C + cash)$		100,000,000	100,000,000	100,000,000

For each of the three portfolios, Exhibit 2 summarizes the relevant data.

Now we assume an instantaneous drop in rates for all maturities from 12% to 11%. Assume also that all coupon receipts during the six-year planning period can be re-invested at 11% until the end of the planning period.[15] With the shift in interest rates the new prices become:

$$P_A = 913.57$$
$$P_C = 504.33$$
$$FP_{TBILL} = 974.25$$
$$FP_{TBOND} = 778.13$$

Exhibit 3 presents the effect of the interest rate shift on portfolio values, terminal wealth at the horizon (year 6), and on the total wealth position of the portfolio holder.

As Exhibit 3 reveals, each portfolio has the same response to the shift in yields. The slight differences that can be observed are attributable to either (1)

rounding errors or (2) the fact that the duration price change formula holds exactly only for infinitesimal changes in yields. The largest difference (between terminal values for Portfolios 1 and 2) is only .29%, which reveals the effectiveness of the alternative strategies.

The Bank Immunization Case. Assume that a bank holds a $100,000,000 liability portfolio in Bond B, the composition of which is fixed. Bonds A and C are available for its asset portfolio, and the bank wishes to hold an asset portfolio that will protect the wealth position of the bank from any change as a result of a change in yields.

Five different portfolio combinations illustrate different means to achieve the desired result:

Portfolio 1: Hold Bond A and Bond C (the traditional approach)

Portfolio 2: Hold Bond C, SELL T-bill futures short

Portfolio 3: Hold Bond A, BUY T-bond futures

Portfolio 4: Hold Bond A, BUY T-bill futures

Portfolio 5: Hold Bond C, SELL T-bond futures short

For each portfolio, the full $100,000,000 is put in a bond portfolio (and is balanced out by cash). Portfolio 1 exemplifies the traditional approach of immunizing

---

[15]In reality the re-investment rate is not certain. No matter what re-investment rates prevail, the "bonds only" and "bonds with futures" immunization give the same terminal wealth. Consequently, the assumption of an 11% re-investment rate merely simplifies the example without any loss in generality.

Exhibit 3. Effect of a 1% Drop in Yields on Realized Portfolio Returns

	Portfolio 1	Portfolio 2	Portfolio 3
Original Portfolio Value	100,000,000	100,000,000	100,000,000
New Portfolio Value	105,660,731	108,914,787	108,914,787
Gain/Loss on Futures	-0-	(2,946,808)	(3,128,792)
Total Wealth Change	5,660,731	5,967,979	5,785,995
Terminal Value of All Funds at t=6	197,629,369	198,204,050	197,863,664
Annualized Holding Period Return Over 6 Years	1.120234	1.120776	1.120455

by holding an all bond portfolio with no futures contracts added. Portfolios 2 and 5 are comprised of the highly volatile Bond C, and that volatility is offset by selling interest rate futures. By contrast, the low volatility Bond A is held in Portfolios 3 and 4. In conjunction with Bond A, the overall interest rate sensitivity is increased by buying interest rate futures. The composition of these five portfolios is presented in Exhibit 4.

Now assume an instantaneous drop in rates from 12 to 11%, affecting all maturities. Exhibit 5 presents the effect on each of the portfolios. As the rows reporting wealth changes reveal, all five methods are comparable in their performance. The small differences that exist are due to rounding errors and the discrete change in interest rates.

Transaction Costs

One important concern in the implementation of immunization strategies is the transaction costs involved. As one wishes to re-adjust the immunized position over time, the commission charges, marketability, and liquidity of the instruments involved become increasingly important. These considerations highlight the practical usefulness of interest rate futures in bond portfolio management.

Consider as an example the transaction costs associated with the different immunization portfolios for the Planning Period Case. Starting from the initial position of $100,000,000 in Bond C, and wishing to shorten the duration to 6 years, Exhibit 6 shows the trades necessary and the estimated costs involved. To implement the "bonds only" traditional approach of Portfolio 1, one must sell 122,103 bonds of type C and buy 63,844 bonds of type A. Assuming a low commission charge of $2 per bond, this results in a total cost of $371,894. By contrast one could sell 1,352 T-bill futures contracts to immunize Portfolio 2, or sell 527 T-bond futures contracts for Portfolio 3, at total costs of $20,280 and $7,905, respectively. (Additionally one would have to deposit approximately $2,000,000 mar-

Exhibit 4. Liability Portfolio and Five Alternative Immunizing Asset Portfolios

		Liability Portfolio	Portfolio 1 (Bonds Only)	Portfolio 2 (Short T-bill Futures)	Portfolio 3 (Long T-bond Futures)	Portfolio 4 (Long T-bill Futures)	Portfolio 5 (Short T-bond Futures)
Portfolio	W_A	0	51.98%	0	100%	100%	0
Weights	W_B	100%	0	0	0	0	0
	W_C	0	48.02%	100%	0	0	100%
	W_{CASH}	0	0	0	0	0	0
Number	N_A	0	58,695	0	112,919	112,919	0
of	N_B	110,684	0	0	0	0	0
Instruments	N_C	0	103,704	215,959	0	0	215,959
	N_{TBILL}	0	0	(1,242,710)	0	1,148,058	0
	N_{TBOND}	0	0	0	44,751	0	(48,441)
	$N_A P_A$	0	51,979,705	0	99,999,937	99,999,937	0
	$N_B P_B$	99,999,673	0	0	0	0	0
	$N_C P_C$	0	48,020,137	99,999,815	0	0	99,999,815
	Cash	327	158	185	63	63	185
	$N_{TBILL} P_{TBILL}$	0	0	(1,208,001,110)	0	1,115,992,740	0
	$N_{TBOND} P_{TBOND}$	0	0	0	32,164,781	0	(34,816,969)
	Portfolio Value	100,000,000	100,000,000	100,000,000	100,000,000	100,000,000	100,000,000

Exhibit 5. Effect of a 1% Drop in Yields on Total Wealth

	Liability	Portfolio 1	Portfolio 2	Portfolio 3	Portfolio 4	Portfolio 5
Original Portfolio Value	100,000,000	100,000,000	100,000,000	100,000,000	100,000,000	100,000,000
New Portfolio Value	105,910,526	105,923,188	108,914,788	103,159,474	103,159,474	108,914,788
Profit/(Loss) on Futures	0	—	(2,709,108)	2,657,314	2,502,766	(2,876,427)
Total Wealth Change (On Portfolio Plus Futures)	5,910,527	5,923,188	6,205,680	5,816,788	5,662,240	6,038,361
Total Wealth Change (Asset-Liability Portfolio)	—	12,622	295,154	(93,738)	(248,286)	127,835
% Wealth Change	—	.00013	.00295	(.00094)	(.00248)	.00128

Exhibit 6. Transaction Costs for the Planning Period Case

	Portfolio 1	Portfolio 2	Portfolio 3
Number of Instruments Traded			
Bond A	63,844	—	—
Bond C	(122,103)	—	—
T-Bill Futures Contracts	—	1,352	—
T-Bond Futures Contracts	—	—	527
One Way Transaction Cost			
Bond A @ $2	127,688	—	—
Bond C @ $2	244,206	—	—
T-Bill Futures @ $15	—	20,280	—
T-Bond Futures @ $15	—	—	7,905
Total Cost of Becoming Immunized	$371,894	$20,280	$7,905

gin for the T-bill strategy or $800,000 for the T-bond strategy. But this margin deposit can be in the form of interest earning assets.)

Clearly, there is a tremendous difference in transaction costs between trading the cash and futures instruments. In an extreme example of this type, the transaction cost for the "bonds only" case is prohibitive, amounting to almost .4% of the total portfolio value.[16] But also it is practically impossible for another reason. The volume of bonds to be traded is enormous, exceeding any reasonable volume for bonds of even the largest issue. The superior marketability and liquidity of the futures market is clearly evident. The 1,352 T-bill futures contracts are about 10% of the daily volume or .5% of the current open interest. Likewise, the 527 T-bond futures constitute only 1% of daily volume and .2% of the current open interest. The evident ability of the futures market to absorb the kind of activity involved in this example demonstrates the practical usefulness of interest rate futures in managing bond portfolios.

Summary

To date, immunization strategies for bond portfolios have focused on all bond portfolios. This paper has shown that interest rate futures can be used in conjunction with bond portfolios to provide the same kind of immunization. The method advocated here works equally well for both types of immunization: the Planning Period Case and the Bank Immunization Case.

Note that all of the examples assumed parallel shifting yield curves. If the change in interest rates brings about non-parallel shifts in the yield curve, then the "bonds only" and "bonds-with-futures" approaches will give different results. Which method turns out to be superior would depend upon the particular pattern of interest rate change that actually occurred.

[16]Gushee [22] recommends two "bonds only" strategies which involve high transaction costs.

References

1. G. Bierwag and G. Kaufman, "Coping with the Risk of Interest Rate Fluctuations: A Note," *Journal of Business* (July 1977), pp. 364–370.

2. G. Bierwag, G. Kaufman, and C. Khang, "Duration and Bond Portfolio Analysis: An Overview," *Journal of Financial and Quantitative Analysis* (November 1978), pp. 671–682.

3. G. Bierwag, G. Kaufman, R. Schweitzer, and A. Toevs, "The Art of Risk Management in Bond Portfolio Management," *Journal of Portfolio Management* (Spring 1981), pp. 27–36.

4. G. Bierwag, G. Kaufman, and A. Toevs, "Immunization for Multiple Planning Periods," unpublished, 1979.

5. G. Bierwag and C. Khang, "An Immunization Strategy Is a Minimax Strategy," *Journal of Finance* (May 1979), pp. 389–399.

6. F. Black, "The Pricing of Commodity Contracts," *Journal of Financial Economics* (January/March 1976), pp. 167–179.

7. Z. Bodie and V. Rosansky, "Risk and Return in Commodity Futures," *Financial Analysts Journal* (May/June 1980), pp. 27–39.

8. Chicago Board of Trade, "An Introduction to the Interest Rate Futures Market," Chicago 1978.

9. Chicago Board of Trade, "An Introduction to Financial Futures," Chicago, 1980.

10. Chicago Board of Trade, "Financial Instruments Markets: Cash Futures Relationships," Chicago, 1980.

11. Chicago Board of Trade, "Understanding the Delivery Process in Financial Futures," Chicago, 1980.

12. B. Cornell and M. Reinganum, "Forward and Futures Prices: Evidence from the Foreign Exchange Markets," *Journal of Finance* (December 1981), pp. 1035–1045.

13. J. Cox, J. Ingersoll, and S. Ross, "Duration and the Measurement of Basis Risk," *Journal of Business* (January 1979), pp. 51–61.

14. J. Cox, J. Ingersoll, and S. Ross, "The Relation Between Forward Prices and Futures Prices," *Journal of Financial Economics* (December 1981), pp. 321–346.

15. K. Dusak, "Futures Trading and Investor Returns: An Investigation of Commodity Market Risk Premiums,"

Journal of Political Economy (November 1973), pp. 1387–1406.

16. Financial Publishing Company, "Treasury Bond and Note Futures Conversion Tables," Publication No. 765, Boston, 1980.

17. L. Fisher and R. Weil, "Coping with the Risk of Interest Rate Fluctuations: Returns to Bondholders from Naive and Optimal Strategies," *Journal of Business* (October 1971), pp. 408–431.

18. G. Fong and O. Vasicek, "A Risk Minimizing Strategy for Multiple Liability Immunization," unpublished, 1980.

19. G. Gay and R. Kolb (eds.) 1982. *Interest Rate Futures: Concepts and Issues.* Robert F. Dame, Inc., Richmond, Virginia.

20. Gifford Fong Associates, "Immunization: Definition and Simulation Study," unpublished, 1979.

21. M. A. Grove, "On Duration and the Optimal Maturity Structure of the Balance Sheet," *The Bell Journal of Economics and Management Science* (Autumn 1974), pp. 696–709.

22. C. Gushee, "How to Hedge a Bond Investment," *Financial Analyst Journal* (March/April 1981), pp. 44–51.

23. J. Ingersoll, J. Skelton, and R. Weil, "Duration Forty Years Later," *Journal of Financial and Quantitative Analysis* (November 1978), pp. 627–650.

24. R. Jarrow and G. Oldfield, "Forward Contracts and Futures Contracts," *Journal of Financial Economics* (December 1981), pp. 373–382.

25. E. Kane, "Market Incompleteness and Divergences Between Forward and Futures Interest Rates," *Journal of Finance* (May 1980), pp. 221–234.

26. G. Kaufman, "Measuring Risk and Return for Bonds: A New Approach," *Journal of Bank Research* (Summer 1978), pp. 82–90.

27. R. Kolb, 1982. *Interest Rate Futures: A Comprehensive Introduction,* Robert F. Dame, Inc., Richmond, Virginia.

28. R. Kolb and R. Chiang, "Duration, Immunization, and Hedging with Interest Rate Futures," forthcoming, *Journal of Financial Research* (1982).

29. R. Kolb and R. Chiang, "Improving Hedging Performance Using Interest Rate Futures," *Financial Management* (Autumn 1981), pp. 72–79.

30. R. Kolb, G. Gay, and J. Jordan, "Are There Arbitrage Opportunities in the Treasury-Bond Futures Market?" forthcoming, *The Journal of Futures Markets* (Fall 1982).

31. R. McEnally, "Duration as a Practical Tool for Bond Management," *The Journal of Portfolio Management* (Summer 1977), pp. 53–57.

32. R. Rendleman and C. Carabini, "The Efficiency of the Treasury Bill Futures Market," *Journal of Finance* (September 1979), pp. 895–914.

33. A. Vignola and C. Dale, "The Efficiency of the Treasury Bill Futures Market: An Analysis of Alternative Specifications," *Journal of Financial Research* (Fall 1980), pp. 169–188.

34. R. Weil, "Macaulay's Duration: An Appreciation," *Journal of Business* (October 1973), pp. 589–592.

Article 35

THE USE OF INTEREST RATE SWAPS IN MANAGING CORPORATE LIABILITIES

by Laurie S. Goodman, Eastbridge Capital

A s a result of the high and volatile interest rates of the early 1980s, companies began to emphasize active management of their liabilities as well as their assets. Issuers started to realize that the type of debt used and its maturity could make a considerable difference in their funding costs. At the same time, a number of new risk management products—futures, options, swaps, and caps—made it possible for corporate treasurers to manage their liabilities more actively. They began to understand that debt could be readily transformed to take advantage of changing market conditions. Rates on floating-rate debt could be fixed by using futures or swaps, floating debt could be capped, fixed rates could be transformed into floating rates, and issuers could hedge the cost of a new issue by fixing or capping the rate. Corporate treasurers also discovered that the cheapest way to issue a given variety of debt was not always the most straightforward. Issuers have sometimes found opportunities to make initial debt offerings in one form and then, with the use of risk management products, to convert that debt into the desired form, thereby producing a lower all-in cost of funds.

In this article, I shall discuss the corporate uses of one of the most widely used risk management products: interest rate swaps. The principal roles that swaps have assumed in corporate liability management can be summed up in the following three:

1. reducing the cost of current issuance,
2. locking in the cost or spread on an expected future issue, and
3. hedging the corporate exposure to interest rates by altering the cash flows on an existing liability.

In the process of allowing corporations to manage interest rate exposures and reduce funding costs, the growth of the interest rate swap market has contributed significantly to the further integration of the fixed-rate and floating-rate debt markets. As a result of corporate attempts to exploit pricing differences between these markets, many of the financing "arbitrage" opportunities described below are no longer available. For example, while the combination of floating debt with a swap has at times been considerably cheaper than issuing fixed debt, the disparities are not nearly as great as they were reported to be five years ago. Thus, while some of the funding techniques presented here may still be used on a fairly regular basis, most should probably be regarded as "window-of-opportunity" arbitrages that appear only from time to time—and are thus available to only the most opportunistic corporate treasurers.[1]

---

1. This article considers the economics of various swap transactions, but does not address tax and accounting issues. An issuer would want to take these into account before making a final decision as to what form the debt will take.

EXHIBIT 1   USING SWAPS AND SWAPTIONS TO TRANSFORM DEBT

Transformed Debt	Original Debt				
	(1) Floating Rate	(2) Fixed rate Non-callable Non-putable	(3) Callable Fixed Rate Debt	(4) Putable Fixed Rate Debt	(5) Non-Conventional
(1) Floating rate debt	X	Vanilla Swap	Callable Swap	Putable Swap	FROG + yield Curve Swap
(2) Fixed rate non-callable non-putable debt	Vanilla Swap	X	Callable Swap + Vanilla Swap or Swaption	Putable Swap + Vanilla Swap	Inverse Floater + Vanilla Swap or FROG + yield curve swap + vanilla swap
(3) Callable fixed rate debt	swaption + vanilla swap	swaption	X	not economical	not economical
(4) Putable fixed rate debt swaption + vanilla swap	swaption	two swaptions	X	not economical	
(5) Non-conventional debt	not economical	not economical	not economical	not economical	X

This exhibit shows how swaps can transform one type of debt to another. The original form of the debt is given in the colums, the transformed debt in the rows. The entry in the cell shows the swap requirements that are necessary to accomplish the transformation. Thus, callable fixed rate debt (Column 3) can be transformed into floating rate debt (Row 1) via a callable swap (Column 3, Row 1). An "X" indicates no transformation is necessary. "Not economical" means the transformation has never made sense economically—the transformed debt has never been cheaper than the original.

REDUCING THE COST OF A CURRENT ISSUE

By using the swap market, companies have obtained their desired financing at a lower cost than issuing the desired debt directly. For example, if a firm wants to issue fixed-rate noncallable debt, it has at least five choices:

1. issue the fixed-rate debt directly;
2. issue floating-rate debt and swap the floating-rate debt into fixed-rate debt;
3. issue callable fixed-rate debt and enter into a callable swap or write an option on a swap;
4. issue putable fixed-rate debt and enter into a putable swap; or

5. issue an unconventional instrument and enter into a swap to obtain the equivalent of a fixed-rate bond.

Exhibit 1 illustrates each of these funding strategies, as well as a number of others. For example, to obtain fixed-rate noncallable debt (row 2), any of the original debt issues listed in the top row can be transformed by adding the features of the cell that intersects the applicable column and row 2. Thus, an issue of callable fixed-rate debt (column 3) can be transformed into noncallable fixed-rate debt (column 3, row 2) by entering into a callable swap or writing an option on a swap (also known as a "swaption").

The choice among the five alternatives outlined above will depend primarily on which is cheapest for the issuer. Although the development of competitive markets over time should limit the cost differences among such financing alternatives, issuers should nonetheless consider all possibilities to ensure their achieving the lowest cost of funds in fixed-rate *noncallable* debt. That is, pricing inefficiencies arise from time to time, and thus issuers should examine all of the alternatives across row 2 to be sure of gaining the lowest-cost means to this method of funding.

In addition, many issuers will want to investigate the other funding opportunities that are available, while bearing in mind the necessary trade-offs. For example, issuers should weigh the cost of issuing fixed-rate noncallable debt against the cost of issuing callable fixed-rate debt in order to evaluate the cost of purchasing the right to call the debt. They might also want to see how much issuing a put bond might lower the required coupon on an issue. In terms of Exhibit 1, after finding the lowest-cost funding method in each row, issuers may also want to compare the various rows as alternative financing strategies. Thus, an issuer interested in ending up with some form of fixed-rate debt should compare the low-cost entry in row 2 with those in rows 3, 4, and 5.

As we proceed in this article, we will first look at the various ways of creating straight fixed-rate debt with no embedded options. Then we will consider ways of creating floating-rate debt, callable fixed-rate debt, and putable fixed-rate debt. All the techniques discussed in these pages, I should point out, have been used in the market. Some, though, have been used only sparingly, and thus seem to have been appropriate only for a special set of market conditions. The "arbitrage" financing techniques in the first part of this article are all premised on some kind of market mispricing. As the swap market further integrates the fixed and floating debt markets, the cost reductions achieved by issuing synthetic debt should become increasingly hard to find.

Creating Synthetic Optionless Fixed-Rate Debt

The interest rate swap market provides a variety of ways to create noncallable fixed-rate debt using original debt of another form. Such synthetic fixed-rate debt is most often created in one of two ways: (1) if the original bond is a floater, it can be combined with a conventional (or "plain vanilla") swap to convert floating payments to fixed; or (2) if the original bond is callable, it can be combined with the sale of a callable swaption. Less frequent variations use putable bonds and unconventional bonds as the original underlying instrument.

Transforming Floating-Rate Debt Into Synthetic Fixed-Rate Debt. Companies with credit ratings lower than AA have taken advantage of opportunities to achieve cheaper fixed-rate financing by using floating-rate debt plus swaps instead of conventional fixed-rate issues. These opportunities arise from sizeable differences in the relative credit spreads between the fixed-rate market and the floating-rate market. Firms with a lower credit rating often pay a smaller spread over a more highly rated borrower in the floating market than in the fixed market.

To illustrate how swaps have been used to take advantage of this disparity, assume that an issuing firm would have to pay a fixed rate of 200 basis points over a 10-year Treasure (T_{10}). Alternatively, it could issue a floating-rate note (FRN) at LIBOR + 50 bp. Assume also that the swap rate it faces is T_{10} + 70 bp. The firm could arrange LIBOR-based financing and swap the proceeds for fixed at an interest rate equal to the 10-year Treasury + 70 bp. By so doing, the firm would obtain "synthetic" fixed financing of T_{10} + 120 bp, calculated as follows:

Instrument	Action	Cash Flow
FRN	Firm pays	LIBOR + 50 bp
Swap	Firm receives	(LIBOR)
	Firm pays	T_{10} + 70bp
Synthetic Fixed	Net payment	T_{10} + 120 bp

When this net payment is compared with an original fixed-rate issue of T_{10} + 200 bp, the net saving is 80 bp.[2]

If the firm issues a floating-rate note as illustrated above, the payment on the synthetic fixed-rate instrument is locked in. Typically, however, the firm chooses to issue floating-rate debt in which the credit spread is reset each period. Examples of this include short-term issues in the Euromarket and commercial paper market. In these instances, the firm has not actually locked in a rate beyond the first period. The borrowing rate can be

---

2. For a much more detailed and precise attempt to calculate the cost savings from this kind of financing "arbitrage," see the next article in this issue ("Swaps at Transamerica: Analysis and Applications," by Robert Einzig and Bruce Lange). Among other important points made by Einzig and Lange, this article demonstrates that creating synthetic fixed-rate debt with swaps sometimes imposes considerable refunding and basis risk that is often ignored in popular accounts of the benefits of swaps.

EXHIBIT 2
USING CALLABLE SWAPS
TO CREATE SYNTHETIC
NON-CALLABLE DEBT

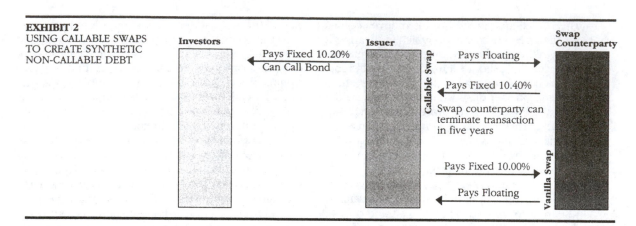

decomposed into two parts—a base interest rate and a credit spread. As the base interest rate rises, the rate received on the swap (and paid on the commercial paper) will also rise. Changes in the firm's credit standing are unhedged. Thus, if the firm-specific credit spread narrows (the firm's credit quality improves), then the firm will achieve a lower cost for subsequent periods. If the firm-specific credit risk widens, the firm will end up with a higher cost for subsequent periods. If a firm expects its credit spread to remain constant or to narrow, a series of short-term borrowings will be preferable to a floating-rate note. In choosing that option, however, the firm is bearing the risk that its credit spread will widen.

Corporate treasurers should be aware that short-term borrowings usually have a lower credit spread than floating-rate notes, as credit spreads generally increase with maturity. Thus, when a corporate treasurer is comparing the cost of a commercial paper issue plus a swap to a fixed-rate financing, the cost savings will appear to be misleadingly large, as he has not locked in the credit spread. The cost of doing so is the cost differential between a floating-rate note and short-term borrowings.[3]

Transforming Callable Debt Into Noncallable Debt Using Callable Swaps. Callable swaps have often

been used together with callable bonds to create synthetic noncallable debt. The reason: Bond investors may demand less for the call option inherent in a callable bond than such an option will bring in the swap market.[4] An issuer generally pays a premium to investors (in terms of a higher interest rate than otherwise) for the right to call the original bond after a stated period of time, say, 10 years. In essence, the issuer has purchased a call option. Having purchased this call option, the issuer is thus in a position to *sell* an equivalent call option—but in the form of an option to call (or terminate) an interest rate swap. In this way, some issuers have been able to obtain noncallable debt at lower cost.

The mechanics of this transaction, which can best be illustrated by means of a simple example, actually involve entering into two swaps. Say that a firm issues a 10-year note that can be called at par after five years. The note is sold to yield 10.20%. This option may add 20 bp to the cost of the debt. In other words, if the firm issued a non-callable bond, it would pay only 10.00%. But as we shall see, the issuer will ultimately be better off by issuing the callable debt.

Along with the callable issue, the firm executes two transactions in the swap market. It enters into a callable swap—a swap with an option to call or terminate the

---

3. Actually, many firms may make a deliberate decision to use short-term financing rather than a floating-rate note. There are two possible reasons for this. First, short-term financing plus a swap allows a firm to achieve a fixed base interest rate plus a floating credit spread. There is no other combination of instruments available which can achieve this result. (See Marcelle Arak, Arturo Estrello, Laurie Goodman, and Andrew Silver, "Interest Rate Swaps: An Explanation," *Financial Management*, Summer 1987 for a complete explanation.) Second, short term paper plus a swap fixes an interest rate while avoiding agency costs. If a firm has only long-term debt (either fixed rate or floating rate notes), the firm would have an incentive to shift toward more risky projects because bondholders share the downside, but not the upside. Short-term debt requires the firm to go to the markets each period to be re-evaluated and hence saves these agency costs. This argument is developed by Larry R. Wall, "Interest Rate Swaps, an Agency Theoretic Model with Uncertain Interest Rates," *Journal of Banking and Finance* (in press).

4. There is considerable anecdotal support, as well as some academic evidence, that corporate bond investors have "underpriced" the option they give corporations on the typical bond. Investors might, however, rationally charge less than "fair value" for granting such an option. A failure by corporate management to exercise the option efficiently (by exercising as soon as the bond price exceeds the call price by an acceptable margin) would cause investors to underestimate its true value. (For a discussion of the optimal bond refunding strategy, see Alan Kraus, "An Analysis of Call Provisions and the Corporate Refunding Decision," *Midland Corporate Finance Journal*, Vol. 1 No. 1 (Spring 1983).

The amount of refunding activity in the last 7-8 years would suggest underpricings of the call option by bond market investors should become increasingly scarce over time. Moreover, the growth of markets for callable swaps and swaptions (those with surrogate call provisions) should further act to erase large call pricing disparities between the swaps and bond markets.

swap after five years. The firm pays the floating rate and receives a fixed rate of 10.40%. For illustrative purposes, we further assume that the fixed rate on a vanilla swap is 10.00%, which means that the counterparty to the callable swap is willing to pay 40 bp per annum for the right to terminate the swap after five years. Because the swap counterparty will terminate the swap only if rates decline—that is, if it can enter into a new swap and pay less than 10.40%—the counterparty has effectively purchased a call on the debt.

The net effect is that the issuing firm pays a net floating rate of interest of LIBOR minus 20 bp. In order to transform the debt into fixed rate, the issuer can then enter into a plain vanilla swap in which it agrees to receive floating and pay fixed. Assuming the fixed interest rate is 10.00%, the firm ends up with a net interest cost of 9.80% (10.20% on the bond less 10.40% on the swaption plus 10.00% on the vanilla swap), which is 20 bp less than it would have cost to issue the non-callable debt directly. (This series of transactions is illustrated in Exhibit 2.)

Let's also look at the transactions from the perspective of the issuer and the swap counterparty under different interest rate scenarios:

Scenario	Issuer	Swap Counterparty	Result
Interest rates are higher after five years.	No action on bond.	No action. Both swaps remain outstanding.	Issuer has ended up with 10-year fixed rate money.
Interest rates are lower after five years.	Bond is called. Issuer funds floating.	Swap in which issuer pays floating and receives fixed is called. Swap in which issuer pays fixed and receives floating remains outstanding.	Issuer has ended up with 10-year fixed rate money.

Thus, a callable swap is simply a swap in which the fixed payer (the counterparty) has the right of early termination without penalty. In either scenario, the issuer has achieved 10-year fixed rate financing.

Other variants of this structure are, of course, possible. For example, rather than receiving 10.40% per annum on the callable swap, the bond issuer could receive 10% plus 2.00%-2.25% of the par value of the bond as an upfront fee. In this case, the firm is paying the same 10.20% to issue debt as initially, but has traded away its call option for a fee of 2.00%-2.25%.

Transforming Callable Debt Into Noncallable Debt Using Swaptions. Thus far we have discussed how to achieve fixed-rate financing by transforming callable debt into noncallable debt using callable swaps. The same result can be achieved using "swaptions." A swaption is an option providing a counterparty the right, but not the obligation, to enter into an interest rate swap at a future date. A callable bond and a swaption can be used to create fixed-rate funding to the call date and synthetic fixed-rate financing from the call date to the maturity date. As with the use of callable swaps described above, the use of swaptions to convert callable into noncallable debt is likely to be undertaken only if and when the call feature is priced more cheaply by the bond market than by the swap market.

In order to create five-year noncallable debt, one funding technique uses callable debt with a final maturity of five years and a "back-end fixed" swaption—that is, an option to enter into a swap to pay fixed and receive floating extending from the call date to the maturity date on the notional amount of the debt. If the call can be exercised after year 3, the swaption would allow the issuer to pay fixed from year 3 to year 5. Alternatively, an issuer could achieve the same result by issuing longer maturity (10-year) debt with a call in five years and a "back-end floating" swaption to enter into a swap to pay floating and receive fixed for the balance of the 10-year maturity. A "back-end fixed" swaption simply means that the issuer pays fixed and receives floating if the swaption is exercised. With a "back-end floating" swaption, the issuer pays floating and receives fixed.

Let's look at an example of callable debt and a "back-end fixed" swaption. Assume an issuer wants five-year fixed-rate funding. He can create it by issuing a five-year bond, callable at par after three years, and selling a back-end fixed swaption. This swaption provides the buyer with the option to enter into a two-year interest rate swap commencing in three years. The back-end fixed swaption would commit the issuer to pay fixed and receive floating if desired by the counterparty. We show the results below:

Scenario	Swap	Issuer	Result
Interest rates are higher after three years.	The swaption is not exercised.	The issuer does not call the bond.	Issuer has five-year fixed rate money.
Interest rates are lower after three years.	The swaption is exercised. The issuer pays fixed and receives floating for years four and five.	The issuer calls the bond and funds floating for years four and five.	Issuer has five-year fixed rate money.

Note that, under either scenario, the issuer has obtained five-year fixed-rate money.

EXHIBIT 3
USING PUTTABLE SWAPS
TO CREATE SYNTHETIC
NON-CALLABLE DEBT

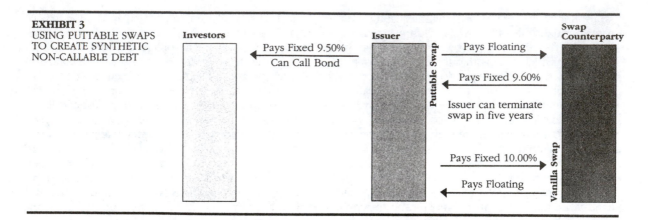

An issuer could also obtain noncallable debt by issuing a 10-year note callable at par after five years and selling a "back-end floating" swaption. This swaption would allow the buyer the option to enter into a five-year swap, commencing in five years. The back-end floating swaption would commit the issuer to pay floating and receive fixed. Here are the results under the two interest rate scenarios:

Scenario	Swap	Issuer	Result
Interest rates are higher after five years.	The swaption is exercised. Issuer pays floating and receives fixed from years 6-10.	The issuer does not call the bond.	Issuer has five-year fixed-rate money. Over years 6-10, the issuer has floating money.
Interest rates are lower after five years.	The swaption is not exercised.	Issuer calls the bond.	Issuer has five-year fixed-rate money.

Again, the issuer has achieved fixed-rate funding for five years under either interest rate scenario.

One advantage of this structure is that if the swaption is exercised, and the issuer does not call the bond, he still has the call option. That is, the swaption does not extinguish the call on the bond. This option can be exercised if rates move down in the future.

In all of these alternatives, the issuer obtains synthetic noncallable debt. The choice among these alternatives will depend on how costly the embedded call option is relative to the back-end fixed swaption, the back-end floating swaption, and the callable swap.

Transforming Putable Debt Into Optionless Debt

Putable swaps paired with put bonds have occasionally been used by issuers wanting to issue noncallable debt as cheaply as possible. They are used less frequently than callable swaps. With a put bond the investor purchases the right to put the bond back to the issuing firm—an option which becomes more valuable to the investor as interest rates rise. For example, assume a firm issues a 10%, 10-year bond with a put that can be exercised after five years. If after five years rates had risen to 12%, the investor would put the bond back to the issuer and reinvest at the 12% rate. Naturally, from an investor's perspective, a 12% reinvestment rate is preferable to the 10% rate implicit in the bond. If rates fall, the put bond remains outstanding.

To the extent investors are willing to pay more for the put feature than the price of the put in the swap market, a put bond can be combined with a putable swap to create inexpensive noncallable debt. With a put bond, as suggested above, the issuer writes an option. He can then buy a putable swap to offset the exposure created by the put in the bond. But, once again, this would make sense only if the issuer can realize more by selling the put option on the bond than he must pay for the put on the swap he purchases.

This funding strategy, as illustrated in Exhibit 3, is achieved by using two swaps. In the putable swap, the issuer receives a fixed rate and pays a floating rate. The fixed rate the issuer receives is lower than the rate on a vanilla swap, reflecting the fact that the issuer can terminate the swap if rates rise. The issuer will terminate the swap if he can receive a higher rate than 9.60% at the expiration of the option—in other words, if interest rates have risen. The vanilla swap converts the then-floating rate payments of LIBOR less 10 bp into fixed payments. The issuer pays an effective interest rate on the noncallable, nonputable debt of 9.90%—9.50% on the bond less 9.60% on the swaption plus 10.00% on

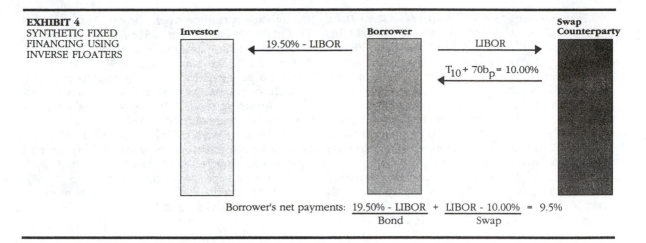

EXHIBIT 4
SYNTHETIC FIXED FINANCING USING INVERSE FLOATERS

Investor ← 19.50% - LIBOR — Borrower — LIBOR → Swap Counterparty

$T_{10} + 70b_p = 10.00\%$ ←

Borrower's net payments: $\underline{19.50\% - LIBOR}$ + $\underline{LIBOR - 10.00\%}$ = 9.5%
                                              Bond   Swap

the vanilla swap. This is 10 bp cheaper than optionless debt with the same characteristics.

Under our alternative interest rate scenarios:

Scenario	Issuer	Swap Counterparty	Result
Interest rates are higher after five years.	Bond is put to issuer.	Swap for issuer to pay floating and receive fixed is terminated. Swap for issuer to pay fixed and receive floating remains standing.	Issuer has 10-year fixed-rate money.
Interest rates are lowest after five years.	No action.	Both swaps remain outstanding.	Issuer has 10-year fixed rate money.

Note that a putable swap is a swap in which the fixed-rate receiver (in this case, the issuer) has the option to walk away from the swap.

Creating optionless debt from put bonds is an arbitrage-driven transaction—that is, it is done only if the optionless debt can be created synthetically more cheaply than it can be issued directly.

Transforming Unconventional Debt

Inverse Floaters Into Fixed-Rate Debt. Another, less frequently used method of obtaining fixed-rate financing is through the use of an inverse floating rate security. An inverse floater is an instrument that pays a pre-specified interest rate minus LIBOR. This is generally coupled with a swap in which the issuer receives fixed and pays floating.

We can illustrate this transaction with an example viewed from the issuer's perspective (see Exhibit 4). We assume the floater pays 19.50% minus LIBOR. The swap spread in this example would be T_{10} + 70 bp or 10.00%.

Instrument	Action	Cash Flow
FRN	Firm pays	19.50% – LIBOR
Swap	Firm receives	(10.00%)
	Firm pays	LIBOR
Synthetic Fixed	Net payment	9.50%

Using an inverse floater plus a vanilla swap, the issuer has locked in a coupon payment of 9.5%. The coupon payments on a new fixed-rate issue would be 10.0%. Thus, the borrower has saved 50 bp over a traditional bond.

With this sort of funding strategy, a cap is necessary to protect against very high rates. Without a cap, if LIBOR happened to rise above 19.5%, the investor would owe the issuer money. Obviously, the issuer could not logistically collect from the investor. Thus, the issuer can buy a cap that will enable him to be paid if rates go above 19.50%. This cap is far out of the money, and the protection is very inexpensive.

This structure attracted a great deal of interest when introduced in 1986. Investors initially did not realize that it was equivalent to holding a long position in *two* fixed-rate bonds and a short position in a floating-rate instrument. They could easily recreate this position by purchasing a fixed-rate bond and entering into a swap in which the investor received fixed and paid floating. Investors showed interest in the security because they were convinced short rates would drop. When LIBOR rates fell, the coupon on an inverse floater increased. But once investors realized how easily this strategy could be replicated, it was priced fairly and there were no new issues.

Transforming FROGS Into Fixed-Rate Debt.
There is one other kind of unconventional debt that has been transformed into fixed-rate debt. FROGS are floating-rate notes with coupons based on the 30-year treasury rate that are reset quarterly or semi-annually. They have typically been combined with "yield curve" swaps in order to produce floating-rate debt. In a yield curve swap, floating payments are exchanged at two different points of the yield curve. This debt can then be transformed into fixed-rate debt with a vanilla swap.

To see how this works, assume that a firm issues a FROG that pays the 30-year Treasury rate, reset every six months (UST), minus 115 bp. The issuer enters into a yield curve swap in which he pays six-month LIBOR and receives the 30-year Treasury rate, reset every six months, less a fixed spread (say 105 bp). (This is called a "yield curve" swap because floating-rate payments indexed to the short end of the market are being exchanged for floating rate payments indexed to the long end of the yield curve.)

As shown below, the issuer has essentially locked in floating-rate financing:

Instrument	Action	Cash Flow
FROG	Firm pays	UST – 115 bp
Swap	Firm receives	(UST – 105 bp)
	Firm pays	LIBOR
Synthetic Floating	Net payment	LIBOR – 10 bp

This synthetic floating-rate instrument can be converted to fixed-rate payments by means of a vanilla swap in which the issuer pays the three-year Treasury rate (T_3) + 70 in exchange for LIBOR (as shown below).

Instrument	Action	Cash Flow
Synthetic Floating	See above	LIBOR – 10 bp
Vanilla Swap	Firm receives	(LIBOR)
	Firm pays	T_3 + 70 bp
Synthetic Fixed	Net payment	T_3 + 60 bp

FROGs, in fact, were initially created out of the desire to locate counterparties for yield curve swaps. Firms were enticed to issue FROGs and swap for LIBOR funding—a transaction that generated sub-LIBOR financing for the issuer.

FROGs were very popular investments in mid-1988 as a yield curve strategy, in large part because the average spread between 30-year Treasuries and LIBOR during 1983-87 was 125 bp. At 115 basis points (which was 10 basis points less than historical levels), these notes became very attractive. Moreover, investors who preferred (or were required) to purchase only short-term securities were able to obtain a short-term instrument reset off a long-term rate—a combination not previously available.

Ex-post, however, FROGs have turned out not to be attractive investments. If the yield curve had steepened, FROGs would have performed well. With the yield curve flattening and inverting in 1989, FROGs have performed poorly and no new issues have come to market since late 1988.

Creating Floating-Rate Debt

We now consider funding alternatives that have enabled issuers to create synthetic floating-rate debt. The two most common alternatives are as follows: (1) a fixed rate optionless bond plus a vanilla swap and (2) a callable bond plus a callable swap. Less commonly used alternatives include put bonds combined with putable swaps and FROGs combined with yield curve swaps. We examine each of these in turn.

Synthetic Floating Using Vanilla Swaps

Companies with well-known names and high credit ratings have taken advantage of very inexpensive fixed-rate financing in the Eurobond market.[5] In fact, many of these entities have been foreign banks that actually prefer floating-rate financing because their loan portfolio is primarily floating rate. To see how an issuer might create synthetic floating-rate assets, we start by assuming that the firm can raise 10-year fixed-rate funds at only 50 bp over the 10-year Treasury (T_{10}) bond rate. The swap rate is LIBOR against T_{10} + 70 bp. Using the swap market, the firm can create synthetic floating-rate debt at LIBOR minus 20 bp. If the firm issued the debt directly, it would issue at LIBOR. This is illustrated below:

Instrument	Action	Cash Flow
Fixed Rate Bond	Firm pays	T_{10} + 50 bp
Swap	Firm receives	T_{10} + 70 bp
	Firm pays	LIBOR
Synthetic Fixed	Net payment	LIBOR – 20 bp

5. For a discussion of the cost savings from Eurobond financing, see Wayne Marr and John Trimble, "The Persistent Borrowing Advantage in Eurodollars: A Plausible Explanation," which appeared in the Summer 1988 issue of this journal.

Thus, the firm ends up paying LIBOR minus 20 bp for its funds, 20 bp less than the cost of issuing new floating rate debt at LIBOR flat.

Transforming Callable Debt into Floating-Rate Debt. Issuers can create synthetic floating-rate financing by using a callable bond and a callable swap. The rate on this financing will be less than on a straight floating-rate issue whenever the issuer is able to purchase a call option from investors (the call option that is embedded in the debt) for substantially less than the swap market is willing to pay for the call option.

The mechanics of this transaction are similar to those described in the previous section for transforming callable debt into noncallable debt. The firm issues callable debt and enters into a callable swap (as illustrated earlier in Exhibit 2). The difference in this case is that there is no vanilla swap.

Let us consider the payoffs from this combination under different scenarios. If rates are higher at the call date than they were at the time of issue, neither the bond nor the swap will be called, and the issuer will obtain floating funding until maturity. If rates are lower at the call date than at issue, the issuer will call the bond. The counterparty will terminate the swap. Thus, if rates go down, the issuer will have floating money until the call date.

The issuer, then, has issued floating-rate funding for a period either to call or to maturity. If interest rates are lower, the issuer has locked in floating rate debt for only the time until the call. If interest rates go up, he locks in floating-rate money until maturity—a desirable situation.

Transforming Putable Debt into Floating-Rate Debt. Putable debt can be transformed into floating-rate debt by pairing a put bond with a putable swap. This is similar to transforming putable debt into optionless fixed-rate debt (as illustrated in Exhibit 3). In this case there is no need for the vanilla swap.

Let us now consider the payoffs from this combination under different scenarios. Assume a firm issues 10-year money, putable at the investor's option after year 5. If rates turn out to be higher at the put date than at the issue date, the bond will be put and the swap in which the issuer pays floating and receives fixed will be terminated. The issuer can raise new floating rate money during years 6-10 at par. Thus, the issuer has floating money over the 10-year period. If rates decline, the bond remains outstanding and the swap remains outstanding. The net result

here is also floating-rate money over the 10-year period.

Transforming FROGs Into Floating-Rate Debt. FROGs are frequently transformed into floating-rate rather than fixed-rate debt. This is done by pairing a FROG with a yield curve swap. The issuer pays the long-term Treasury rate less a spread on the FROG. Again, the long-term rate is reset every six months. The issuer then enters into a yield curve swap in which he pays six-month LIBOR and receives the long-term Treasury rate, reset every six months, less a spread.

Creating Callable Debt

Issuers with access to the U.S. long-term fixed-rate debt markets have generally not found it economical to replicate callable debt. However, there are certain issuers, such as U.S. savings and loan associations, that have been unable to borrow economically in these markets. These issuers have occasionally used the swap market to transform fixed- and floating-rate debt into long-term callable debt. In other instances, issuers that do have access to the corporate market prefer instead to issue debt using a medium-term note strategy, with which they can bring a small issue or an odd amount to market. Medium-term notes are noncallable.

Long-term callable debt can be created from long-term noncallable fixed-rate debt by purchasing a back-end floating swaption. If rates decline, the swap will be activated and the issuer will pay floating and receive fixed. Consider an issuer of five-year noncallable debt who has purchased a back-end floating swaption for years four and five. If rates remain high, the issuer will have five-year debt. If rates decline, the issuer will have three-year fixed-rate debt.

A floating-rate issue can be transformed into fixed-rate debt through combination with a vanilla swap and then be made callable by purchasing a back-end floating swaption.

Creating Putable Debt

We now consider a synthetic alternative to a put bond issued in the marketplace. The most common synthetic put bond is constructed by combining a callable bond issue with the sale of both a back-end fixed swaption and a back-end floating swaption. By holding both these options, the swap counterparty has a one-time right either (1) to make the issuer pay the fixed-rate versus receiving floating (by exercising the back-end fixed swaption) or (2) to make the issuer receive fixed (by exercising the back-end floating swaption) and pay floating.

The swap counterparty, to repeat, purchases two options. The effect of one (the back-end fixed swaption) is to cancel the embedded option on the call, and the effect of the other (the floating swaption) is to create the put that is inherent in a putable bond.

Let us use the example of a five-year issue, callable in three years. At the end of three years, the results under alternative interest rate scenarios are shown below:

Scenario	Swap	Issuer	Result
Interest rates rise higher after three years.	Issuer caused to receive fixed and pay floating for years four and five.	No action.	Issuer has ended up with three-year followed by two-year floating-rate money.
Interest rates are lower after three years.	Issuer caused to pay fixed and receive floating for two years.	Issuer calls issue, funds floating-rate.	Issuer has ended up with five-year rate money.

As with a regular put bond, if rates fall the issuer has ended up with five-year fixed-rate money. If rates rise the issuer has ended up with three years of fixed funding and two years of floating funding.

The major difference between a synthetic put bond and a real put bond is that, with a synthetic put bond, the issuer has to raise funds in the floating-rate market if rates fall. With a real put bond, the issuer has to borrow in the floating rate market if rates rise. This is important to some issuers, such as banks and finance companies, that are more concerned about funding in a higher-rate than in a lower-rate environment.

Note that whatever cost savings can be achieved by using a synthetic rather than a straightforward put bond depend upon investors' pricing the call option for less than the swap market. By contrast, swap counterparties will pay full value for that call and a further significant premium for the right to buy the put.

A less commonly used variation on the synthetic put bond has been accomplished by issuing fixed-rate noncallable debt and selling a back-end fixed swaption. This eliminates the arbitrage opportunity in the call option. Assume the debt is issued for a five-year period, and the back-end fixed swaption can be exercised at the end of year three. The swaption will be exercised and the issuer will have received fixed and paid floating for years four and five if rates are lower.

This transaction could also be done by using floating-rate debt as the initial issue. Such debt could then be transformed into fixed debt by means of a five-year swap. It could then be further transformed into a synthetic put bond with a back-end fixed option.

LOCKING IN THE COST OF A FUTURE ISSUANCE

While the major use of swaps centers on altering the character of a current bond issue, issuers also apply strategies involving the swap market to expected future issuances. For example, a company that expects rates to rise may want to lock in a fixed cost on a future issuance by using a forward swap (also known as a "delayed start" swap). A corporate treasurer who expects interest rates to remain steady or decline while credit spreads widen may wish to lock in a generic credit spread by means of a "spread lock." We examine each of these in turn.

Forward Swaps

A forward swap is exactly like a regular interest rate swap transaction, except that the accruals begin on a future date—normally the expected date of the bond issuance. A forward swap is usually combined with a floating-rate issue in order to lock in a fixed rate.

Consider the following example. A firm enters into a three-month forward swap agreeing to pay the current five-year Treasury rate plus 75 bp. In return, the firm will receive six-month LIBOR. The notional amount of the swap will be the same as that of the anticipated debt issue. In three months the firm issues floating-rate debt. Six months after the issuance, the first payments are exchanged. The firm pays the fixed rate available at the time the swap was entered into and receives six-month LIBOR. The LIBOR payment is used to pay the interest on the floating-rate debt.

The net cost of the issuance will be the fixed rate on the swap plus the difference between six-month LIBOR and the floating rate at which the firm issues its debt. If the firm issues floating-rate debt at six-month LIBOR + 25 bp, its all-in funding cost will be the five-year Treasury yield plus the 75 bp swap spread plus the 25 bp margin on the floating-rate debt. Note that the only component not locked in is the margin on the floating-rate debt.

If the firm later issues floating-rate debt off a different index from LIBOR, it can realize cost savings but will incur basis risk. If, for example, the firm issues floating-rate debt at the commercial paper rate, the cost of funds to the firm will be less than the five-year Treasury yield plus 75 bp, reflecting the fact that the commercial paper rate is below LIBOR.

Forward swaps are most attractive for issuers that like the current level of interest rates and expect a rate increase in the future, but do not currently need funding. Entering into a forward swap locks in the rate without forcing the issuer to fund immediately.

Spread Locks

A spread lock allows an issuer to fix the credit spread without fixing the base rate. Thus, a spread lock can be viewed as a tool to hedge the general level of corporate spreads. A spread lock is most effective when a firm knows it will have to come to market within a relatively short time—two or three months.

In a spread lock, the issuer agrees to enter into a swap deal at a specified spread to Treasuries but delays fixing the base Treasury rate for a period ranging up to two or three months. In other words, the issuer must fix the base interest rate by the end of the period, but may choose to fix the rate anytime within that period. When the base rate is eventually fixed, the pre-specified swap spread is added to arrive at the fixed rate payable on the swap. If Treasury rates fall over near term, the firm is able to take advantage of the decline.

To see how a spread lock would work, assume that a firm wants a spread lock for the next two months. At the end of the two-month period—or earlier if Treasury rates look attractive in the interim—the firm issues floating-rate debt and takes down the swap (in which it pays fixed and receives floating). Assume that the fixed swap spread is 80 bp and its issuing rate is LIBOR + 25bp. The firm will, on net, pay the Treasury rate prevailing at the time the swap is taken down plus 105 bp (80 + 25).[6]

A spread lock will be used if the firm does not expect rates to rise, but is concerned that credit spreads may widen. Issuers should note, however, that the spread lock does not hedge their firm-specific credit spread, but rather a general credit market spread.

MANAGING CORPORATE INTEREST RATE EXPOSURES BY ALTERING THE CASH FLOWS ON AN EXISTING LIABILITY

Companies can also use swaps to alter the cash flow on an existing liability, in a variety of ways: (1) by entering into a swap in order to fix the payment on an existing floating liability; (2) by entering into a swap in order to turn an existing fixed payment security into a floating-rate liability, and (3) by entering into a forward swap to lock in attractive interest rates after the call date on existing debt with in-the-money call options.

Fixing a Payment on a Floating-Rate Issue

A firm can convert a floating rate issue into a fixed-rate instrument by using a swap in which the issuer receives floating and pays fixed. The fixed rate is the then-prevailing fixed rate. Thus, when interest rate levels look attractive and a firm feels vulnerable to higher rates, it can lock its floating debt into a fixed rate through the use of the swap market.

Converting an Existing Fixed-Rate Bond

Similarly, a firm that has initially issued fixed-rate debt can also convert that debt to floating rate through the swap market. In this instance, the firm pays floating and receives fixed. If market rates have changed, the fixed rate at which the firm issued the debt is different from the prevailing fixed rate. The firm can either receive the fixed rate prevailing in the swap market, or match its own funding cost with an upfront payment if rates have declined or with an upfront receipt if rates have risen.

This is not, it is important to note, a means of escaping high-coupon debt in a declining rate environment. It does, however, provide a way for the firm to benefit from a further future reduction in rates.

To give an example, we assume that three years ago a firm issued fixed-rate 10-year noncallable debt at 11%. The firm now wishes to convert this debt to floating-rate debt. The swap market is such that the firm currently would have to pay LIBOR to receive 70 bp over the rate on seven-year Treasury notes (T_7+70 bp, or 9.70%). If the firm entered into a market swap, its cash flows would be as follows:

---

6. A spread lock is typically offered at a 2-4 bp premium over the straight swap. The premium exists because of the swap counterparty's hedging cost. The swap counterparty will short Treasury securities and invest the proceeds in short- term instruments until the swap is taken down. The negative carry during the hedge period is figured into the quoted spread. Thus, 150 bp of negative carry for two months is $0.25 per $100 par, or 2.5 bp for a seven-year issue.

Instrument	Action	Cash Flow
Bond	Firm pays	11.00%
Swap	Firm receives	(9.70%)
	Firm pays	LIBOR
Synthetic Floater	Net payment	LIBOR + 130 bp

Instrument	Action	All-in Cost
Bond	Firm pays	8.00%
Swap	Firm receives	(9.70%)
	Firm pays	LIBOR
	Firm receives $8.50 upfront	(170 bp)
Synthetic Floater	Net payment	LIBOR – 170 bp

Note that the firm is paying LIBOR + 130 bp. The large increment over LIBOR reflects the fact that the firm has above-market (11%) noncallable debt outstanding. It cannot escape this obligation. If rates decline further, however, the LIBOR financing will prove more attractive than the fixed rate financing. If rates increase, the reverse will be true.

Alternatively, the firm could enter into an off-market swap in which it pays an upfront amount in order to pay LIBOR and receive 11% on the swap. The upfront payment would reflect the 130 bp per annum, capitalized into an upfront sum, as shown below:

Instrument	Action	All-in Cost per Annum
Bond	Firm pays	11.00%
Swap	Firm receives	(11.00%)
	Firm pays	LIBOR
	Firm pays upfront $6.50	130 bp
Synthetic Floater	Net payment	LIBOR + 130 bp

Note the present value of the all-in costs is roughly the same if the firm accepts a market swap or an off-market swap.

If rates have risen and the issuer is convinced they have peaked, it may want to swap an outstanding fixed-rate issue into a floating-rate obligation. This allows the issuer to benefit from lower rates in the future. The issuer could opt for a swap at market rates, or for an off-market swap in which it accepts a below-market rate on the swap plus an upfront payment.

To give an example, let's assume that three years ago a firm had issued 8.00% debt for 10 years. In the swap market, this firm could pay LIBOR and receive T_7 + 70 bp, or 9.70%. If the firm agreed to a swap at now-current rates, its cash flows would be as follows:

Instrument	Action	Cash Flow
Bond	Firm pays	8.00%
Swap	Firm receives	(9.70%)
	Firm pays	LIBOR
Synthetic Floater	Net payment	LIBOR – 170 bp

The net payment of LIBOR minus 170 bp reflects the fact that the firm had below-market debt on its books.

If the firm wanted an off-market swap, the all-in cost would be as follows:

In both cases, the firm's all-in cost is the same. With an off-the-market swap, the firm is compensated for accepting a below-market rate on the swap.

Thus, if converting fixed-rate debt to floating-rate debt is designed only to take advantage of an expected fall in rates, any fall or rise that has already occurred will be built into the price of the swap. Nonetheless, if further changes in rates are anticipated, a review of outstanding liabilities is in order.

Locking in Attractive Interest Rates on Existing High-Coupon Debt

Forward swaps can be used to lock in future rates on outstanding callable debt. To see how this can be done, assume that a firm has 14.00% debt outstanding, originally issued in 1984. The debt matures in 10 years, or 1994. It is callable in 1991. If the notes were currently callable, the issuer would call the bond and refinance with lower-cost debt. However, since the notes are not callable for some years, the company must leave the bonds outstanding until the call date and continue to pay the 14.00% coupon.

If the company feels that interest rates will rise by 1991 and eliminate some or all of the benefits of today's relatively low interest rates, the issuer can execute a forward swap. Essentially, this would lock in current forward rates. In other words, the firm can enter into a three-year swap effective two years from now in which it agrees to pay fixed and receive floating. We will assume here that the firm can lock in a 10% fixed rate on this swap.

This strategy leaves the company with a great deal of flexibility on the call date. If interest rates turn out to be lower than 14% on the call date, the firm could refinance on a floating-rate basis. The floating payments on the debt would be offset by payments on the swap. The firm's all-in cost would be the 10% fixed rate plus (minus) its issuing cost above (below) LIBOR.

If the firm wanted to refinance at a fixed rate, the forward swap could be sold. The cash settlement to (or by) the issuer will be equal to the present value of the difference between the forward rate swap and the market rate for new swaps with a three-year maturity. If rates turn out to be higher than 10%, the issuer will receive a payment. If rates prove to be lower than 10.0%, the issuer will pay the cash settlement from the sale of the swap.

There is a third alternative, as well. Say the firm wants to refinance with a fixed rate, but rates are lower and the issuer is reluctant to buy out the forward swap. As an alternative, it could enter into an offsetting spot transaction. To see how this might work, assume the fixed rate is 9%, and the firm has locked in a 10% forward swap. The forward swap can be offset on the call date as follows:

Instrument	Action	Cash Flow
Original Bond	Called	
New Bond	Firm pays	9.00%
Forward Swap	Firm receives	(LIBOR)
	Firm pays	10.00%
New Swap	Firm receives	(9.00%)
	Firm pays	LIBOR
Fixed + Swap	Net payment	10.00%

Note that the firm has locked in the 10% rate. The rate on the new bond is 9.00%, and the 1% per annum loss on the forward swap takes the form of a higher net payment.

So far we have assumed that the interest rates on the call date are below 14% and that the issue will be called. The forward swap does not affect the company's ability to leave the issue outstanding if rates are above 14% on the call date. In this instance, if the issuer chooses to leave the issue outstanding, it could sell the forward swap. The windfall profit on the forward swap would be the difference between the then-current market rates for a three-year period. Thus, the forward swap locks in the "intrinsic value" of the call option.[7] It does not, however, extinguish the option. And it can gain further value in the future if rates rise sufficiently.

CONCLUSION

The primary corporate uses of interest rate swaps are to reduce corporate exposures to interest rate movements by altering the cash flow pattern of outstanding debt, to reduce the cost of a current issuance by "arbitraging" disparities between debt and swap markets, and to lock in the cost or spread of an expected future issue. Historically, much of the corporate use of swaps has centered on reducing the cost of a current issue. Prior to the introduction of swaps, companies had to issue debt into the ultimately desired form. For example, companies wanting long-term fixed-rate noncallable debt had to include all the desired features in the issue itself. There was no way to transform callable debt into noncallable or putable debt.

With swaps, however, debt can be easily and inexpensively transformed from one form into another. Issuers have sometimes been able to obtain the desired form of debt synthetically at a lower cost than by a direct issuance. This arises, in part, because the swap market allowed issuers to take advantage of differential pricing between the new issue bond market and the swap market. Call options, for example, appear to be cheaper in the bond market than in the swap market. Floating-rate issues can be less expensive than fixed-rate issues for lower-rated issuers. In addition, certain new structures can give investors their desired risk-return trade-off while allowing the issuer to end up with what looks like conventional debt.

Issuers can also lock in the cost of a future issue through a forward swap. Spread locks can be used to lock in generic credit spreads. Finally, the swap market allows issuers to transform floating rates on outstanding debt into fixed rates, and fixed rates into floating (although off-market swaps are generally necessary to equate cash flows on a new swap with those on the old debt).

Swaps, in short, are highly versatile and cost-effective instruments for managing corporate liabilities. They have transformed liability management into a more active undertaking, one that involves not only evaluating what is desirable for current issuances, but also re-evaluating past issues and anticipating those of the future.

---

7. The "intrinsic value" is the value of the option if exercised immediately.

■ LAURIE GOODMAN

is a Vice President at Eastbridge Capital, a firm specializing in money management and asset-liability consulting. Prior to joining Eastbridge, Dr. Goodman was a strategist in the fixed-income research groups at Goldman Sachs and Citibank. She has published extensively on instruments and alternatives for managing risk in fixed-income markets.

Article 36

SWAPS AT TRANSAMERICA: ANALYSIS AND APPLICATIONS

*by Robert Einzig,
Transamerica Corporation and
Bruce Lange,
Security Pacific Corporation**

It is understandable that swaps should be viewed with some suspicion by the corporate financial officer. Isn't the promotion of swaps by commercial and investment banks just another way of packaging their services to make them appear more attractive to a potential client—even while swaps themselves provide little added value? After all, there is no such thing as a free lunch, so why expect one from swaps? The reaction of the financial officer trained in quantitative methods is likely to be still more skeptical. Any advantage gained by a swap is assumed to conceal either the assumption of more risk or greater expense.

In looking for corporate financing opportunities, whether in the swaps market or elsewhere, we have always been concerned to understand the nature of the opportunity presented. Our conviction that capital markets are highly efficient makes our examination of possible advantages particularly painstaking.

The first swap transactions into which we entered appeared to offer an advantage deriving from a form of inefficiency that has been characterized as a "comparative advantage." It appeared that major European banks with excellent reputations, well known in their own countries and in the Euromarkets, could borrow at long term in those markets more cheaply than we could—and could even borrow at short term more advantageously as well. But their relative advantage was clearly greater in issuing long-term securities, where there was reportedly strong interest by investors. The assets of such banks, however, were typically on a short-term floating-rate basis, thus making long-term funding inappropriate. This pattern was exactly opposite the position of many companies, particularly in the U.S., which have long-term needs for funds at fixed rates but can generally borrow advantageously in the short-term markets at floating rates. By having these European banks borrow long term while we borrowed short term, and then swapping the interest rate obligations with each other, both of us were able to reduce our cost of funds and increase our ability to match the maturity of the interest rates on our assets and liabilities.

---

* A version of this article will appear in the forthcoming book, *The Handbook of Currency and Interest Rate Risk Management*, edited by Robert Schwartz and Clifford Smith (New York Institute of Finance, 1990). Printed here with permission of the publisher.

ALTHOUGH SOME INTERNATIONAL FINANCING BARGAINS HAVE INDEED BEEN
ERASED THROUGH COMPETITION, WE NEVERTHELESS CONTINUE TO BELIEVE
THAT BOTH TEMPORARY AND LONGSTANDING DIFFERENCES
IN HISTORICAL INSTITUTIONAL ARRANGEMENTS BETWEEN COUNTRIES WILL
CONTINUE TO CREATE FINANCING OPPORTUNITIES.

Whether such advantages are likely to persist in competitive capital markets is a matter of some controversy. Some observers have argued that this comparative advantage cannot explain satisfactorily the explosion in size of the swap markets.[1] As more and more firms attempt to take advantage of such arbitrage opportunities, such information disparities between markets should become ever smaller. Although we agree with the general thrust of this reasoning—and would add that many such international financing bargains have indeed been erased through competition—we nevertheless continue to believe that both temporary and longstanding differences in historical institutional arrangements between countries will continue to create financing opportunities. They are not likely to be around for long, but such "windows of opportunity" will arise from time to time to provide financing bargains for alert financial officers.

We also recognize that there are longer-term advantages of swaps as debt instruments that permit borrowers to separate the risk and credit elements in these interest costs.[2] In fact, the bulk of the paper that follows focuses on these continuing advantages of swaps. We first consider the cost advantages of swaps and weigh them against the basis risk, counterparty credit risk, and corporate credit and liquidity risk that swaps often impose. We then emphasize the flexibility of swaps as well as the speed with which they can be arranged and terminated. Important elements of such flexibility are the ability of the corporation to separate credit risk from rate risk, to maintain asset quality while enhancing investment returns, and to obtain rate protection for non-debt instruments. We also provide examples of general purpose swaps to show specific uses to which swaps have been put and the analysis performed by us at the time. The analysis and examples are provided in a form that we believe the typical corporate financial practitioner can both understand and use. We hope that our enthusiasm for using the swap instrument to take advantage of continuing market imperfections or unusual opportunities as they arise is evident in our discussion.

BACKGROUND IN THE USE OF SWAPS

Transamerica was one of the first major corporations to participate in the fledgling swaps market of the early 1980s. Transamerica's first swap transaction was executed in August 1981. Since then the swap portfolio has grown to more than $1.3 billion. While the size of the portfolio is not exceptional, what is unusual is the breadth of uses the swaps have served. During this period, Transamerica was a diversified organization whose major operations included commercial and consumer finance, life insurance, property and casualty insurance, insurance brokerage, manufacturing, transportation, and leasing. All of these businesses have used the swap markets; however, they have been used for varying purposes based on the differences in the requirements of each industry.

No one example can convey adequately the merits of swaps without placing them within a conceptual framework. To do so, we show the underlying problem in each case to which a swap provided a solution. We also include situations in which swaps were considered but rejected. Much of the following discussion is specific to Transamerica's point of view (i.e., that of an A-rated diversified financial services company) and assumes that the counterparty is a bank.

From this perspective there are three reasons for the use of swaps at Transamerica:

1. reduced cost of funds,
2. rapid execution of transactions, and
3. increased flexibility in debt management.

The examples assembled below support the contention that savings are achieved. These savings, however, are not always achieved without some risk. The most obvious risk results from the need to refund short-term debt. (By funding short, a company effectively gives the lender an option on its own creditworthiness—one that is not provided by long-term debt or a revolving credit arrangement.) Financing structures have, nevertheless, been available whereby Transamerica has achieved unequivocally better rates than by issuing comparable "plain vanilla" public debt. These structures have typically been funded swaps in which long-term debt was issued in conjunction with a swap (for example, fixed-rate Eurodollars swapped into commercial paper).

The cost saving of swaps is relatively easy to determine; the simplicity and speed with which transactions may be accomplished are less obvious advantages. A borrower using a swap may lock in a fixed rate with little or no lead time. There is no lengthy registration process and documentation

---

1. For a good exposition of the argument, see Clifford W. Smith, Charles W. Smithson, and D. Sykes Wilford, "The Growth of the Swaps Market," Chapter 8 in *Managing Financial Risk*, New York: Harper & Row, (1989), pp.213-28.

2. See M. Arak, A. Estrella, L. Goodman and A. Silver, "Interest Rate Swaps: An Alternative Explanation," *Financial Management* 17 (Summer 1988), pp. 12-18.

often can be accomplished after the fact. Speed may not be a major advantage of swaps when other alternatives exist (such as shelf registrations) and may, in fact, create problems if the major issues relating to documentation are not resolved in advance. Less controversial is the speed advantage of a swap in the ability to reverse out of a fixed rate position in a matter of minutes, either by terminating an existing swap or by reversing it. While a similar result might be achieved by the repurchase of bonds, this is a cumbersome and often expensive process. Swaps have consequently added a new dimension to debt management.

The ability to terminate a position rapidly leads to the last reason that Transamerica has participated in the swap market. Swaps have provided additional flexibility in debt management by increasing the number of options available. Part of the flexibility arises from the formation of a market that has reduced transaction costs and transaction times to the point where restructuring a debt portfolio is a practical alternative. Prior to swaps, restructuring was always a theoretical possibility, but the traditional repurchase of debt normally led to investors demanding substantial premiums for disrupting their portfolios. The development of a number of major market makers running dynamically hedged books has created an extremely competitive market. A market maker in interest rates will, by definition, deal at market prices to terminate or modify an existing agreement. The complex hedging techniques used by market makers also can be applied to produce tailor-made interest rate agreements (forward swaps, amortizing swaps, zero coupon swaps, etc.) for corporate use.

Another aspect of flexibility is related to the nature of the instrument itself rather than to increases in the efficiency and flexibility of the interest rate markets. A swap is a contractual agreement to exchange certain payments and no principal is at risk. As a result, liquidity risk and much of the credit risk are isolated from rate risk. An entity that cannot borrow on a cost-effective basis in the fixed-rate debt markets can use swaps to separate risk elements and thereby reduce rate risk without paying the full premium for long-term funding. For certain of Transamerica's independently leveraged subsidiaries (unrated subsidiaries that borrow without the benefit of a parent company guarantee) this flexibility has been the prime motivation and has generated more transactions than any other factor.

THE COST ADVANTAGES OF SWAPS AND THEIR RISKS

Cost savings is a common explanation for the rise of the swap market. Certainly Transamerica would not have entered into so many agreements without some readily discernible economic advantage.

In the standard example of a swap, party A swaps short-term and therefore floating-rate debt into a fixed interest payment (unfunded swap), and party B swaps long-term fixed-rate debt into a floating interest payment (funded swap). An alternative is possible: party A swaps funded floating-rate debt into fixed rate. When long-term debt is matched to a swap, the liquidity risk of refunding is eliminated and the swap is funded. This contrasts with an unfunded swap into a fixed rate, in which case the underlying debt is short term. Because of this difference in refunding risk, the two type of swaps are analyzed separately.

For most corporations, a bank acts as an intermediary and writes swaps directly off its own book, or portfolio, without attempting to match the counterparties directly. The bank collects as a minimum the bid/offer spread—that is, the difference between the bank's fixed receipt on the one side and its fixed payment on the other. Transamerica has saved the amount of this spread, which amounts to about five to ten basis points, by arranging swaps between different subsidiaries with offsetting requirements for fixed and floating debt. Seven transactions of this type, totalling $90 million, have been executed.

For analytic purposes, unfunded swaps into a fixed rate are compared with medium-term, noncallable, fixed-rate public debentures. The benchmark for funded swaps into a floating rate is commercial paper. This procedure has the flaw of comparing long- and short-term instruments, albeit with comparable interest rate risk profiles. A combination of quantitative adjustment and qualitative considerations is needed to address this problem.

A cost comparison appears on the surface simple enough. The foremost elements when considering the cost advantage of a swap are as follows:
- the basis risk between the experienced cost of floating-rate borrowing and the index used for the swap;
- the credit risk introduced by the counterparty;
- the liquidity risk inherent if short-term debt is used to provide the underlying funding when the alternative is long-term funded debt.

FOR SWAPS IN WHICH TRANSAMERICA RECEIVES THE FLOATING SIDE,
THERE HAVE BEEN ADVANTAGES TO PAYING THE VERY SHORT END
OF THE CURVE (30 DAY) ON THE UNDERLYING DEBT AND RECEIVING PAYMENT
BASED ON SIX MONTH ROLLOVERS.

Basis Risk. In the simplest case, where the floating swap payable/receivable is indexed to commercial paper, the only basis risk is the spread against the Federal Reserve Composite commercial paper rate at which Transamerica issues (the "H15 CP" index most commonly used in swap agreements). A six-month LIBOR swap receipt is usually specified to offset interest expense which approximates the 30-day H15 CP rate. Only 5 percent of Transamerica's swaps from floating into fixed use commercial paper as an index and the other 95 percent use six-month LIBOR. In contrast, all of Transamerica's swaps into a floating rate use 30-day CP as the index. As a consequence, there is basis risk only for the unfunded swap portfolio.

The reasons Transamerica has used LIBOR-based swaps are these:

■ Transamerica's back-up lines use LIBOR as an index. The use of LIBOR as an index for back-up agreements means that the maximum cost of the fixed-rate payment will be the differential, if any, between the LIBOR received and paid. If, for example, the swap calls for a LIBOR receipt and the payment of a fixed rate of 10%, and the back-up agreement calls for LIBOR plus 1/4%, the maximum cost of the long-term funds to the corporation would be 10.25%.

■ The market for LIBOR-based swaps has been the most liquid, permitting tighter spreads and more economical early termination.

■ For swaps in which Transamerica receives the floating side, there have been advantages to paying the very short end of the curve (30 day) on the underlying debt and receiving payment based on six month rollovers. This will be the case in a stable, falling, or slowly rising interest rate environment. While we would expect that this advantage is already incorporated into the underlying price of the swap, prior to 1988 this does not seem to have been the case. According to our survey of the market, during the period 1982-1987, Transamerica usually would have had a fixed payment approximately 25-30 basis points higher than if we had been prepared to accept the commercial paper rate (converted to a money market yield) reset and compounded every 30 days. It is estimated that the average actual advantage on Transamerica's swap portfolio between 1982 and 1987 was approximately 60 basis points, for a net saving of 30-35 basis points.

Where the financial officer wants to position his company on the risk-reward continuum is, of course, a matter of individual determination—one that will likely be based upon the company's views about the probable future relationship between CP and LIBOR as well as the future steepness of the yield curve in relation to interest rate movements. We should point out, however, that when doing an analysis of the cost effectiveness of combining a commercial paper issue with a LIBOR-based swap, it is useful to subtract the current spread between LIBOR- and CP-based swaps. This allows for a direct comparison between LIBOR- and CP-based swaps.

Counterparty Credit Risk. This risk is typically small for a corporate user. In contrast, a market maker, even if only at risk for a small net position, may have considerable risk to one counterparty due to offsetting positions. Risk has been limited at Transamerica by ensuring that no one bank dominates the portfolio. For analytic purposes, we add a small adjustment of 2 basis points for credit risk which mimics the cost banks use when analyzing transaction profitability.

Liquidity Risk. Transamerica's policy is to provide 100% back-up coverage for all short-term debt swapped into fixed rates. Essentially the argument is that short-term debt plus a revolving credit agreement plus a swap is the equivalent of noncallable, fixed-rate funded borrowing. This partially addresses the argument that swaps provide lower cost fixed-rate funds by placing the burden of credit and liquidity on the unfunded participant. Credit commitment costs, in consequence, are added when performing a cost analysis.

Two Cases

We now turn to two examples (the first describing an unfunded swap into fixed, the second a funded swap into floating) intended to illustrate our procedures for adjusting financing costs to reflect basis, credit, and liquidity risk. It is worth stressing that these examples represent the opportunities facing a typical A-rated corporate debt issuer. The rates and spreads used, while also typical, are of course subject to the conditions of the market as related to a particular issuer. In Transamerica's case, medium-term notes have frequently been used to reduce the cost of fixed public debt, thereby decreasing the advantage of unfunded swaps into a fixed rate. Alternatively, commercial paper has often been issued at a greater spread under the H15 CP rate, increasing the cost savings of unfunded swaps.

EXAMPLE 1

COST COMPARISON BETWEEN PUBLIC DEBT OF AN A-RATED COMPANY AND COMMERCIAL PAPER SWAPPED INTO A FIXED RATE

1. Issue CP backed by revolving credit agreements
2. Swap floating rate payments (6 month LIBOR) into fixed rate payments
3. Adjust for counterparty credit risk
4. Adjust for basis/yield curve pick-up between the floating rate payments on the underlying funding (1 month CP) and the floating rate swap receipts (6 month LIBOR)

ASSUMPTIONS
- 3 Year Treasury: 8.50%
- 3 Year Swap Indexed to 6 Month LIBOR: Pay Treasuries Plus 0.75% / Pay 9.25% Receive 6 Month LIBOR

- Commercial Paper Issuance Commissions: 0.05%
- Spread Under the H15 CP Rate at which CP is Issued: 0.05%
- Revolving Credit Agreement Fee: 0.12%
- Adjustment for Counterparty Credit Risk: 0.02%
- Adjustment for Basis/Yield Curve Pick-Up Between 1 Month CP Rate and 6 Month LIBOR (approximates the reduction in the fixed swap payment if the floating receipts were the H15 CP rate): 0.27%
- All-in Cost to Issue Non-Callable Fixed Rate Public Debt: Pay Treasuries Plus 0.80% / Pay 9.30%

Net Savings from Swapping CP into Fixed Rate Debt

Fixed Swap Payment	−9.25%
CP Issuance Commissions	−0.05%
CP Issuance Spread under H15	0.05%
Revolving Credit Agreement Fee	−0.12%
Counterparty Credit Risk	−0.02%
Adjustment for Basis/Yield Curve	0.27%
Net Fixed Rate Cost of Swapped CP	**−9.12%**
Save Cost of Public Fixed Rate Debt	9.30%
Net Savings	**0.18%**

EXAMPLE 2

COST COMPARISON BETWEEN COMMERCIAL PAPER AND PUBLIC DEBT OF AN A-RATED COMPANY SWAPPED INTO FLOATING PAYMENTS INDEXED TO COMMERCIAL PAPER

1. Issue fixed rate non-callable public debt
2. Swap fixed rate debt payments into floating rate payments
3. Adjust for counterparty credit risk

ASSUMPTIONS
- 3 Year Treasury: 8.50%
- 3 Year Swap Indexed to 1 Month H15 CP: Receive Treasuries Plus 0.40%/Receive 8.90%—Pay H15 CP

- Commercial Paper Issuance Commissions: 0.05%
- Spread Under the H15 CP Rate at which CP is Issued: 0.05%
- Revolving Credit Agreement Fee: 0.12%
- Adjustment for Counterparty Credit Risk: 0.02%
- All-in Cost to Issue Non-Callable Fixed Rate Public Debt: Pay Treasuries Plus 0.80%/Pay 9.30%

All-In Cost of Fixed Rate Non-Callable Debt Swapped into Synthetic Commercial Paper

Payments	
Floating Swap Payment	H15 CP
Fixed Debt Coupon	9.30 %
Adjustment for Counterparty Credit Risk	0.02 %
Total Payments	**H15 CP + 9.32 %**
Receipts	
Fixed Swap Receivable	−8.90 %
Net Cost	**H15 CP + 0.42%**

All-In Cost of Commercial Paper

Interest Cost	H15 CP - 0.05 %
Revolving Credit Agreement	0.12 %
CP Issuance Commissions	0.05 %
	H15 CP + 0.12%
Net Additional Cost of Synthetic Commercial Paper	**0.30%**

The first example demonstrates a net savings of 18 basis points from creating synthetic fixed-rate debt by issuing commercial paper in combination with a LIBOR-based swap. Measurement of the savings is complicated by both basis risk (from commercial paper to LIBOR) and yield curve risk (floating receipts indexed to the six month point on the curve while funding resets monthly). Such risks could be eliminated, however, by swapping against 30-day commercial paper instead of LIBOR; and the net cost savings in Example 1 would still equal 18 basis points (the 27 basis point adjustment for basis/yield curve risk would not be included, but the fixed swap payment would be reduced by the same amount from 9.25% to 8.98%).

The second example shows net additional *costs* of 30 basis points from using the reverse strategy: creating synthetic commercial paper by issuing fixed-rate public debt and swapping into floating. Excluding the effect of the spread between the swap bid and offer rates (eight basis points), the savings in Example 1 are about equal to the additional costs in Example 2. The fixed swap payment in Example 1 would be four basis points lower if the quote were from the middle of the market and net savings would rise from 18 basis points to 22 basis points. Similarly, the fixed swap receivable in Example 2 would be four basis points higher and the net additional cost would drop from 30 basis points to 26 basis points.

A clear understanding of this distinction is central to developing a corporate policy for the use of swaps. In one case costs are reduced by funding in the short term markets (when compared against the cost of fixed funded debt) even after adjustments that include the cost of back-up lines of credit. This appears logical, given that a revolving credit agreement to lend money to Transamerica at a fixed spread over a floating index is obviously not as secure as actually having the funds at a fixed cost.

In summary, it appears that 22 to 26 basis points is the additional cost for an A-rated corporate borrower to remove credit and liquidity risks. The exact trade-off between cost and liquidity depends on the credit quality of the borrower. The similarity between the cost savings from swapping short-term debt into fixed-rate debt and the added costs of swapping funded fixed debt to floating-rate debt only holds approximately true for an A-rated company. The cost of short-term debt and swaps do not change significantly with the rating of the corporate borrower, even though the AAA borrower can issue fixed-rate public debt at an appreciably better rate than an A-rated company. The consequence of this structure is that highly creditworthy corporate borrowers will generally be advantaged when considering swaps from fixed-rate funded debt into floating, and vice versa for less highly rated companies.

Two More Examples

As a further example, consider a corporation which can issue public debt 30 basis points more cheaply, at an all-in spread of 50 basis points over Treasuries instead of 80, but whose commercial paper costs are only 5 basis points cheaper. The swap spread would likely be identical. Examples 3 and 4 illustrate how such a borrower would view his alternatives from the same perspective as the analysis that Transamerica performs. The unfunded swap into a fixed rate is at a four basis point disadvantage to public debt while funded debt swapped into floating is only eight basis points more expensive than commercial paper.

Summary of Cost Savings. The essential point which emerges from the preceding discussion for a company such as Transamerica is that an unfunded swap into a fixed payment will achieve a cost savings relative to fixed-rate public debt in return for assuming modest additional risk. Transamerica has experienced savings in excess of 50 basis points, part of which is due to the pick-up between LIBOR and CP. Savings are substantially larger for Transamerica's unrated independently leveraged subsidiaries.

The corollary of the previous argument is that swaps from domestic fixed rate debt into a floating rate payment would normally increase Transamerica's cost of funds—so this structure has not been used. While Transamerica has entered into funded swaps, these have typically been done to take advantage of sporadic opportunities in overseas markets. In general, a fixed rate payment has been swapped into a floating coupon. These cost savings are *not* directly a result of the swap market; instead, they arise from the underlying debt issue. The swap permits efficient access to a specific dollar or non-dollar market using fixed or floating debt, regardless of which type meets Transamerica's requirements at that time.

Transamerica has been able to achieve funded floating debt at all-in rates below the H15 Federal Reserve Composite for commercial paper. As an

EXAMPLE 3

COST COMPARISON BETWEEN PUBLIC DEBT OF AN AAA-RATED COMPANY AND COMMERCIAL PAPER SWAPPED INTO A FIXED RATE

1. Issue CP backed by revolving credit agreements
2. Swap floating rate payments (6 month LIBOR) into fixed rate payments
3. Adjust for counterparty credit risk
4. Adjust for basis/yield curve pick-up between the floating rate payments on the underlying funding (1 month CP) and the floating rate swap receipts (6 month LIBOR)

ASSUMPTIONS
- 3 Year Treasury: 8.50%
- 3 Year Swap Indexed to 6 Month LIBOR: Pay Treasuries Plus 0.75% / Pay 9.25% Receive 6 Month LIBOR

- Commercial Paper Issuance Commissions: 0.05%
- Spread Under the H15 CP Rate at which CP is Issued: 0.10%
- Revolving Credit Agreement Fee: 0.09%
- Adjustment for Counterparty Credit Risk: 0.02%
- Adjustment for Basis/Yield Curve Pick-Up Between 1 Month CP Rate and 6 Month LIBOR (approximates the reduction in the fixed swap payment if the floating receipts were the H15 CP rate): 0.27%
- All-in Cost to Issue Non-Callable Fixed Rate Public Debt: Pay Treasuries Plus 0.50% / Pay 9.00%

Net Cost from Swapping CP into Fixed Rate Debt

Fixed Swap Payment	−9.25 %
CP Issuance Commissions	−0.05 %
CP Issuance Spread under H15	0.10 %
Revolving Credit Agreement Fee	−0.09 %
Counterparty Credit Risk	−0.02 %
Adjustment for Basis/Yield Curve	0.27 %
Net Fixed Rate Cost of Swapped CP	**−9.04%**
Save Cost of Public Fixed Rate Debt	9.00 %
Net Cost	**−0.04%**

EXAMPLE 4

COST COMPARISON BETWEEN COMMERCIAL PAPER AND PUBLIC DEBT OF AN AAA-RATED COMPANY SWAPPED INTO FLOATING PAYMENTS INDEXED TO COMMERCIAL PAPER

1. Issue fixed-rate non-callable public debt
2. Swap fixed-rate debt payments into floating rate payments
3. Adjust for counterparty credit risk

ASSUMPTIONS
- 3 Year Treasury: 8.50%
- 3 Year Swap Indexed to 1 Month H15 CP: Receive Treasuries Plus 0.40% / Receive 8.90%—Pay H15 CP

- Commercial Paper Issuance Commissions: 0.05%
- Spread Under the H15 CP Rate at which CP is Issued: 0.10%
- Revolving Credit Agreement Fee: 0.09%
- Adjustment for Counterparty Credit Risk: 0.02%
- All-in Cost to Issue Non-Callable Fixed-Rate Public Debt: Pay Treasuries Plus 0.50%/Pay 9.00%

All-In Cost of Fixed Rate Non-Callable Debt Swapped into Synthetic Commercial Paper

Payments	
Floating Swap Payment	H15 CP
Fixed Debt Coupon	9.00 %
Adjustment for Counterparty Credit Risk	0.02 %
Total Payments	**H15 CP + 9.02%**
Less Receipts	
Fixed Swap Receivable	−8.90 %
All-In Cost of Synthetic CP	**H15 CP + 0.12%**

All-In Cost of Commercial Paper

Interest Cost	H15 CP - 0.10 %
Revolving Credit Agreement	0.09 %
CP Issuance Commissions	0.05 %
All-In Cost of CP	**H15 CP + 0.04%**
Net Additional Cost of Synthetic Commercial Paper	0.08%

example, a subsidiary issued New Zealand dollar debentures which were swapped into an all-in rate of 2 basis points below the H15 CP composite. While for our unfunded swaps the savings come at the expense of some additional limited risk, this New Zealand debt swap is unequivocally less costly than issuing commercial paper at an all-in cost of 14 basis points over the composite (including back-up costs and commissions). There is the added benefit of having obtained a funded borrowing instead of relying on revolving credit agreements with their possible contingencies. The reduction in funding risk offsets the increased risk elsewhere in our portfolio from entering into unfunded swaps. In fact, replacing the same amount of (1) commercial paper with fixed-rate funded debt swapped into floating and (2) fixed-rate funded debt with commercial paper swapped into fixed results in exactly the same refunding risk as the original debt portfolio without the swaps. Interest expense is reduced because the underlying fixed-rate funding is less costly.

TRANSACTION SPEED

The swap market enables a borrower to lock in a rate with little or no lead time. This may be an advantage when fixed debt is required but there is little or no prior knowledge of the exact timing of the requirement.

In 1987, for example, Transamerica purchased Borg Warner Acceptance Corporation. A major restructuring of Transamerica over the period 1985-1987 had increased debt capacity at a time when cash from the sale of assets was being used to pay down debt. Surplus equity generated by the restructuring (relative to our targeted single A rating) could have been used for the acquisition but the actual funds were provided by debt. The acquisition analysis had assumed a given cost for fixed-rate borrowing and this established a maximum target. While acquisition negotiations were proceeding, interest rates were rising rapidly causing concern that the interest rate goal would not be met. Until the acquisition was completed, however, it was not prudent to hedge the risk. Once the purchase was finalized, $200 million in interest rate swaps were used immediately to lock in the rates on a portion of the debt.

From a corporate perspective, rapid execution is largely a function of reduced credit risk relative to money borrowed. This permits a more relaxed attitude to documentation. To understand why the concern over credit is limited it is important to realize that initially there is no credit risk. Risk does not develop until rates move appreciably, and then only if rates shift in your favor. No principal is at risk and credit exposure is limited to the amount by which a position has moved "into the money."

Take, for example, a case in which the corporate counterparty declares bankruptcy the day that it enters into an interest rate agreement. Assuming that the bank had maintained a balanced book, the bank's book becomes unbalanced once the agreement is terminated. The situation may be rectified simply by replacing the terminated position with a new one at the same rate, provided interest rates have not moved in the interim. The bank loses only transaction costs, which are small, and the income anticipated for acting as an intermediary in the transaction. Of course, as time elapses and markets move, it may not be possible to replace the position at the same rate. But the magnitude of the credit risk is small relative to that for money borrowed.

It is dangerous to emphasize the advantages of negotiating documentation after the fact considering the acrimony that can develop without a clear prior understanding between both parties. Establishing master agreements in advance, which then govern a series of individual rate swap agreements, can allay this concern. The problem with this approach, however, is that it may limit flexibility in choosing a counterparty or selecting the cheapest quotes. Perhaps the most practical compromise approach is to discuss in advance the following key points of the anticipated document.

Events of Default: The standard events of default are laid out in the International Swap Dealers Association Code of Standard Wording, Assumptions, and Provisions for Swaps.

Termination Events: These are circumstances that result in termination of the agreement, generally without fault by either party, and which lead to the payment of the market value of the swap to the party who is "in the money."

Reciprocity: A swap is a contractual agreement between two parties, both of whom face essentially the same credit risk. There is no reason why one party should receive greater protection from the document than the other unless the credit rating of the two parties is substantially different.

Termination of Existing Agreements

The interest rate swap market provides the means to reverse quickly out of fixed interest payments or receipts. This can be accomplished either by terminating a swap or by entering into a new agreement to offset an existing position.

Executing a new swap locks in a future net differential between the first and second instrument. In the case of a termination, the bank calculates the net cash flow that would result from offsetting swaps, and discounts the gain or loss forward. A single payment is then made to the party paying a less (or receiving a greater) than market coupon.

Three rationales for terminating positions have suggested themselves to Transamerica.

1. Restructure Debt Portfolio: The most obvious use is to reduce or increase the proportion of fixed to floating debt, either in response to changing liability requirements or to position a debt portfolio to take advantage of predicted interest rate movements.

2. Tax/Accounting Treatments: Termination of agreements may result in early recognition of gains or losses. Tax and accounting treatments are not always identical, and, of course, expert advice is recommended.

3. Hedge Anticipated Fixed Debt Issuance: A swap can be used to lock in the fixed coupon of a borrowing prior to actual issuance. At the time the coupon on the debt is set, the swap can be terminated and the cash gain or loss amortized over the life of the borrowing. To the extent that the spread over Treasuries for swaps tracks the same spread for corporate public debt, the hedge will also provide more complete protection than a comparable hedge directly against the appropriate Treasury security.

Over the last two years Transamerica has reversed out of $350 million in swaps. Of these $150 million were in response to changes in our businesses during 1986 that led to reduced requirements for fixed-rate debt. A further $200 million were terminated in 1987 with the net result of a payment to Transamerica of $13.5 million.

FLEXIBILITY

The diversity of potential uses makes it impossible to illustrate all of them, but examples are here provided of how Transamerica has used and, in some cases, rejected this product in representative situations.

Transamerica has taken advantage of the flexibility of swaps in three distinct situations: (1) to isolate credit considerations from the decision to pay fixed or floating interest rates, (2) to provide liquidity for regulatory purposes while moving out the yield curve to enhance investment returns, and (3) to protect against rate movements when the underlying liquidity is provided by an instrument other than debt.

Separation of Credit Risk from Rate Risk

Transamerica has a general policy of not guaranteeing the debt of subsidiaries. As a result, except for the finance subsidiary, which is separately rated, the premium for fixed-rate funded debt over and above the cost of short term debt has appeared prohibitive. These subsidiaries, which have included leasing, car rental and manufacturing companies, have been able to borrow variable-rate debt with liquidity backed by revolving credit agreements. The parent company, by either guaranteeing a swap or by entering into a swap which it then downstreams to the subsidiary through the use of an intra-company agreement, has been able to provide subsidiaries with fixed-rate debt at a cost comparable to that of an A-rated entity. Transamerica currently has in excess of $450 million of swaps arranged for this advantage alone.

Maintenance of Asset Liquidity While Enhancing Investment Returns

During Transamerica's ownership of Fred. S. James, an insurance brokerage company, it had outstanding an average of $100 million in short-term investments with the yield effectively indexed to the rate on Federal Funds. Regulatory constraints in each state limited investment of premiums collected but not yet remitted to the insurer to highly liquid assets generally placed with approved local depositaries. By swapping a portion of the floating rate obtained from these depositaries into a two-year fixed-rate receipt, the yield was increased to a level consistent with a longer maturity investment. Some interest rate risk was thereby assumed, as is the case in any decision to invest in a fixed-rate asset versus stay short. This interest rate risk is basically an opportunity cost: if short-term rates rise very rapidly above the fixed-rate agreed upon, the gains from this strategy would become opportunity losses as with any long-term investment. In this instance there was also basis risk (the actual investment returns were at the Fed Funds rate and the floating swap payable was LIBOR). Given the goal of extending asset maturity without compromising liquidity or regulation, a swap was the only available mechanism.

EXAMPLE 5
RATE PROTECTION FOR DARTS: INITIAL SITUATION

CP Rate	DARTS Dividends @ 76% of C $100.00	Fixed Swap Payment @ 9% of $115.15	Floating Swap Receipt @ CP on $115.15	Net Pre-Tax Swap Payment	Net After-Tax Swap Payment/ Receipt	Net After-Tax Cost
(1)	(2)	(3)	(4)	(5) (3-4)	(6) (5 × 66%)	(7) (2 + 6)
5.0	($3.80)	($10.36)	$ 5.76	($4.61)	($3.04)	($6.84)
6.0%	($4.56)	($10.36)	$ 6.91	($3.45)	($2.28)	($6.84)
7.0%	($5.32)	($10.36)	$ 8.06	($3.45)	($1.52)	($6.84)
8.0%	($6.08)	($10.36)	$ 9.21	($1.15)	($0.76)	($6.84)
9.0%	($6.84)	($10.36)	$10.36	$0.00	$0.00	($6.84)
10.0%	($7.60)	($10.36)	$11.52	$1.15	$0.76	($6.84)
11.0%	($8.36)	($10.36)	$12.67	$2.30	$1.52	($6.84)

Rate Protection for Non-Debt Instruments

Due to the separation of liquidity and rate risk, a swap may provide a hedge even if the risk is not directly related to a borrowing. The risk may come instead from an instrument for which fixed-rate debt is not an alternative. For example, the development of a market for Dutch Auction Rate Preferred Stock ("DARTS" are money market preferred stock for which the dividend is reset every 49 days) provided an attractive alternative to commercial paper for both borrower and lender, depending on their tax situations. A taxable investor is taxed only on a portion of the dividend and passes some of the savings on to the issuer. If the issuer is not currently taxable, the present value of this savings could more than offset the loss of the tax deduction for interest expense. The market was successful in attracting investors and rates were competitive. However, the dividend yield was, and continues to be, as volatile as short-term rates.

For analytic purposes, the dividend yield is usually compared to commercial paper yields and trades at a relatively fixed percentage of that rate, with the percentage being linked to the tax advantage. While rates were falling in 1985 and 1986, this was an advantage. But with increasing concern over the likelihood of rate increases, hedging was considered.

A specific hedge of DARTS has to take account of the differing tax consequences of swaps versus DARTS. Swap payments are tax deductible but dividends paid on the DARTS are not deductible for the issuer while only partially taxed for the investor. For this reason, the notional amount of the swap should be greater than the amount of outstanding preferred stock if it is to provide an *after-tax* hedge. In contrast, DARTS trade so as to yield some percentage of commercial paper yields, which implies that the swap should be against a notional principal less than the outstanding preferred stock value.

An Example. To allow for comparison with a "plain vanilla" fixed-dividend preferred stock issue, the following adjustments are necessary for a swap:

Assumptions:
Tax Rate - 34%
DARTS trade to yield 76% of commercial paper
Fixed swap against commercial paper @ 9.00%

a. Reduce the notional amount of the swap by a factor of 0.76/1.00 to match pre-tax commercial paper receipts from the swap with dividends paid to holders of the DARTS.

b. Increase the notional amount of the swap by a factor of 0.66 to compensate for the tax impact on the swap payments/receipts.

These assumptions produce an overall Net Adjustment Factor of 0.76/0.66 = 115.15%.

Example 5 illustrates how the notional principal of the swap should be made to equal 115.15% of the DARTS outstanding to obtain a full hedge. Various commercial paper rates are shown to illustrate the consistency of coverage.

It is evident from Example 5 that a 115.15% swap locks in the initial after-tax cost of DARTS. There does remain, though, a substantial risk that either the corporate tax rate or the yield of DARTS relative to CP will change. Such changes in turn influence the amount of the swap required for a perfect hedge. In practice, however, the approach outlined substantially reduces risk despite such changes. If, for example, the corporate tax rate increased to 40%, the hedge would then have to be increased to 126.6% (0.76/0.60) and the balance of the hedge (11.52%) would be at the rate prevailing at the time.

CONCLUSION

Pricing is a sufficient explanation for Transamerica's use of funded swaps. Transamerica's funded swaps have permitted opportunistic issuance of debt in offshore markets resulting in both cost savings and long-term funding of floating-rate debt.

Cost savings have also been achieved through the use of unfunded swaps. The major incentive for using unfunded swaps has been the additional flexibility they provide in structuring a large debt portfolio. One major benefit of this flexibility has been to provide reasonable fixed-rate borrowing to subsidiaries that otherwise would have faced excessive fixed-rate terms or have been limited to floating-rate debt.

The traditional explanation for the opportunity to create cheaper synthetic fixed-rate debt has been described as some form of "comparative advantage" in borrowing in certain markets. In the case of Transamerica's unfunded swaps into fixed rates, however, the standard market rates for interest rate swaps are more easily explained by the separation of liquidity and interest rate risk which that market provides. In effect, the borrower obtains cost savings by choosing to bear the risk of refunding.

The benefits that have been derived from the ability to terminate fixed-rate positions did not become apparent until after Transamerica already had a sizeable portfolio. This aspect has since proved to be of considerable value.

■ ROBERT EINZIG

has held a variety of positions at Transamerica since joining the company in 1971, including that of Vice President, Finance and Treasurer; and he continues to serve as an adviser to the company. Dr. Einzig holds a Ph.D. in Economics from the University of Michigan, and is presently an Adjunct Professor of Finance at the University of California at Berkeley.

■ BRUCE LANGE

is Vice President in the Treasury Department at Security Pacific Corporation, where he is involved in all aspects of the funding process. He was previously Director of Treasury Operations at Transamerica.

Article 37

Interest-Rate Caps, Collars, and Floors

Peter A. Abken

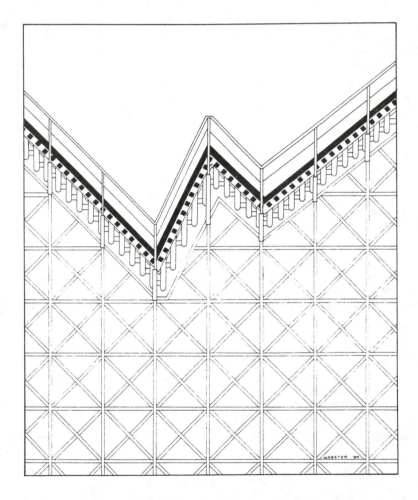

As some of the newest interest-rate risk management instruments, caps, collars, and floors are the subject of increasing attention among both investors and analysts. This article explains how such instruments are constructed, discusses their credit risks, and presents a new approach for valuing caps, collars, and floors subject to default risk.

Since the late 1970s interest rates on all types of fixed-income securities have become more volatile, spawning a variety of methods to mitigate the costs associated with interest-rate fluctuations. Managing interest-rate risk has become big business and an exceedingly complicated activity. One facet of this type of risk management involves buying and selling "derivative" assets, which can be used to offset or hedge changes in asset or liability values caused by interest-rate movements. As its name implies, the value of a derivative asset depends on the value of another asset or assets.

Two types of derivative assets widely discussed in the financial press and in previous *Economic Review* articles are options and futures contracts.[1] Another derivative asset that has become extremely popular is the interest-rate swap.[2] This article examines a group of instruments known as interest-rate caps, collars, and floors, which are medium- to long-term agreements that have proven to be highly useful for hedging against interest-rate uncertainties. In this regard, caps, collars, and floors can be thought of as insurance policies against adverse movements in interest rates.

Like interest-rate swaps, to which these instruments are closely related, caps, collars, and floors are designed to hedge cash flows over time rather than on a single date. The discussion below will show how caps, collars, and floors are related to each other, as well as how they may be constructed from the most basic derivative asset, the option. The article also shows the ways in which caps, collars, and floors are created in practice, along with the different kinds of intermediaries involved in the cap market.[3] The rationale for hedging is reviewed, as are examples of how caps, collars, and floors are used by different financial institutions. The last section of the article considers the credit risk associated with buying caps, collars, or floors and presents a new approach for determining the expected cost of default on these instruments.

The author is an economist in the financial section of the Atlanta Fed's Research Department. He thanks Igor A. Lamser of Noonan, Astley, and Pearce, Inc., for helpful discussions about the cap market and for providing data on cap rates.

What Is an Interest-Rate Cap?

An interest-rate cap, sometimes called a ceiling, is a financial instrument that effectively places a maximum amount on the interest payment made on floating-rate debt. Many businesses borrow funds through loans or bonds on which the periodic interest payment varies according to a prespecified short-term interest rate. The most widely used rate in both the caps and swaps markets is the London Interbank Offered Rate (LIBOR), which is the rate offered on Eurodollar deposits of one international bank held at another.[4] A typical example of floating-rate borrowing might be a firm taking out a $20 million bank loan on which the interest would be paid every three months at 50 basis points (hundredths of a percent) over LIBOR prevailing at each payment date. Other short-term rates that are used in conjunction with caps include commercial bank certificate of deposit (CD) rates, the prime interest rate, Treasury bill rates, commercial paper rates, and certain tax-exempt interest rates.

Data on the size of the cap market are sketchy. The International Swap Dealers Association (ISDA) conducted a survey of its members in March 1989, and 44 of the association's 97 members responded. Almost 90 percent of the respondents reported participating in the markets for caps, collars, floors, and options on swaps. As of year-end 1988, these members alone held 7,521 caps, collars, and floors, with a total notional principal of $290 billion. The volume conducted through 1988 was reported as having notional principal of $172 billion. These figures inflate the size of the market considerably because they are not adjusted for transactions among the dealers themselves, such as the purchase or sale of caps or floors to hedge existing positions in these instruments. On the other hand, the survey did not cover the entire market. Nonetheless, the figures probably still greatly overstate the size of the market, net of interdealer transactions or positions.[5] The interest-rate swaps market is vastly larger at over $1 trillion.

Most studies of caps concern agreements offered by commercial or investment banks to borrowers seeking interest-rate protection. These instruments are often tailored to a client's needs, and, particularly in the case of caps, may be marketable or negotiable. Caps, collars, and floors can also be manufactured out of basic derivative assets: options or futures contracts, or a combination of the two. The following discussion will define caps, collars, and floors in terms of option contracts, which are the simplest type of derivative asset.

Call and Put Options. An option is a financial contract with a fixed expiration date that offers either a positive return (payoff) or nothing at maturity, depending on the value of the asset underlying the option. At expiration, a call option gives the purchaser the right, but not the obligation, to buy a fixed number of units of the underlying asset if that asset's price exceeds a level specified in the option contract. The seller or "writer" of a call has the obligation to sell the underlying asset at the specified exercise or strike price if the call expires "in the money." The payoff on a call need not actually involve delivery of the underlying asset to the call buyer but rather can be settled by a cash payment. The caps market, for example, uses cash settlement. If the asset price finishes below the exercise price, the call is said to expire "out of the money."

Put options are analogous to calls. In this case, though, the purchaser has the right to sell, rather than buy, a fixed number of units of the underlying asset if the asset price is below the exercise price. The options discussed in this article will all be "European" options, which can only be exercised on the expiration date, as opposed to "American" options, which can be exercised any time before or at expiration. As will be seen, caps, floors, and collars are European-style option-based instruments, and the European interest-rate call option is the basic building block for the interest-rate cap.

Options on debt instruments can be confusing if it is unclear just what the option "price" represents. For debt instruments, the strike price is referred to as the strike level, reflecting an interest rate. Recall that the price of a debt instrument, such as a Treasury bill or CD, moves inversely with its corresponding interest rate; as the interest rate of a Treasury bill rises, its price falls. Thus, a call on a Treasury bill rate is effectively a put on its price. (To keep the exposition clear, all discussion will be in terms of options on interest rates. The strike price will be re-

ferred to as the strike level.) A call with a strike level of 8 percent (on an annual basis) on some notional amount of principal is effectively a cap on a floating-rate loan payment coinciding with the expiration of this option. (The notional amount of principal is a sum used as the basis for the option payoff computation. Cap, collar, and floor agreements do not involve any exchange of principal.)

Assume the call's payment date, known as the reset date, falls semiannually. If the interest rate is less than 8 percent on the reset date, the call expires worthless. If the interest rate exceeds 8 percent, the call pays off the difference between the actual interest rate and the strike level times the notional principal, in turn multiplied by the fraction of a year that has elapsed since purchase of the option. For example, if

---

"[C]aps, floors, and collars are European-style option-based instruments, and the European interest-rate call option is the basic building block for the interest-rate cap."

---

the actual rate of interest six months later were 10 percent and if the notional principal were $1 million, the payment received from the call writer would be 2 percent (the 10 percent actual rate minus the 8 percent strike level) x $1,000,000 x 180/360 = $10,000.

A put option on an interest payment works in a similar way and is the foundation for the interest-rate floor. The holder of a floating-rate loan could protect against a loss in interest income from the loan by buying an interest-rate put. A fall in the interest rate below the strike level of the put would result in a payoff from the option, offsetting the interest income lost because of a lower interest payment on the loan.

An option writer is basically an insurer who receives a premium payment from the option buyer when an option is created (sold). In fact, the option price is alternatively called the option premium. The same party can simultaneously write and buy options, thus creating an interest-rate collar. Before exploring this strategy further, option pricing must be reviewed briefly.

Option Pricing. An option's price before expiration depends on several variables, including the value of the underlying asset on which the option is written, the risk-free rate of interest (usually a Treasury bill that matures at the same time as the option), the time remaining before expiration, the strike price or level, and the volatility of the underlying asset price.[6] For later reference, readers should know how an option price changes in response to a change in an underlying variable, all other variables remaining constant. A call price rises (falls) when the underlying asset price, volatility, or time to expiration increases (decreases). It falls (rises)

"A cap can . . . be perceived as a series of interest-rate call options for successively more distant reset dates; a floor is a similarly constructed series of put options."

---

with an increase (decrease) in the exercise price. A put price rises (falls) with an increase (decrease) in the strike price or volatility. It falls (rises) with an increase (decrease) in the underlying asset price or interest rate. Unlike a call price, a put price is not unambiguously affected by an increase in the time to expiration, but the put price depends at any time on how far in or out of the money the put is.[7]

For an interest-rate call option, the higher the strike level compared to the current interest rate, the lower the option value. Choosing a high strike level (out-of-the-money) call is less expensive than buying an at-the-money or in-the-money call. Similarly, a low strike level (out-of-the-money) put is cheaper than one with a higher strike level.

This relationship between an option's strike level and its price (the amount the option is out of the money) is analogous to a large deductible

on an insurance policy. Such a policy is less likely to pay off and is therefore less expensive. Likewise, the cost of interest-rate "insurance" can be reduced by taking a large deductible— that is, buying an out-of-the-money option— and thereby protecting only against large, adverse interest-rate movements.

Creating an interest-rate collar is another method for reducing the cost of interest-rate insurance. The call-option premium for an interest-rate cap may be partially or completely offset by selling a put option that sets an interest-rate floor. For a floating-rate debt holder, the effect of this dual purchase is to protect against rate movements above the cap level while simultaneously giving up potential interest savings if the rate drops below the floor level.

If the cap and floor levels of a collar are narrowed to the extent that they coincide at the current floating interest rate—that is, both put and call options are at the money—the resulting collar is so tight that it is similar to a forward contract on an interest rate, which is a derivative asset that locks in the current forward rate. When the contract expires, the change in the contract's value that has occurred since the inception of the contract exactly offsets the change in the interest payment due. A rise in the floating-rate payment is matched by an equal gain in the interest paid to the contract holder; a fall in the floating-rate payment is balanced by an equal loss on the forward contract. In effect, a forward contract converts a floating-rate payment to a fixed-rate payment.

The discussion thus far has been about a single payment, yet, as mentioned earlier, actual cap, collar, or floor agreements are designed to hedge a series of cash flows, not just one. A cap can thus be perceived as a series of interest-rate call options for successively more distant reset dates; a floor is a similarly constructed series of put options. Assume that an interest payment on floating-rate debt falls due in three months, at the next reset date. If the interest rate on the reset date exceeds the strike level, the cap writer would make a payment to the cap buyer on a date to coincide with the cap buyer's own payment date on the underlying floating-rate debt.

A collar that consists of a series of at-the-money call and put options is equivalent to an interest-rate swap. Buying the cap and selling the floor transforms floating-rate debt to fixed-rate debt, whereas selling the cap and buying the floor switches fixed-rate debt into floating-rate debt. A swap that is constructed out of cap and floor agreements is called a *synthetic swap*. Caps brokers and dealers will sometimes determine rates on floors by deriving the rate from swap and cap rates, which come from instruments that are more actively traded than floors and therefore more accurately reflect current market values.

In practice, swaps are not usually put together from cap and floor agreements. Caps and floors are more readily tradable than swaps because credit risk is one-sided; swaps carry a credit risk that is two-sided in nature. Matching buyers and sellers for swaps is therefore more involved than for caps or floors.[8]

Examples of some caps, collars, and floors should help the reader understand their operation. As the foregoing single-payment-date discussion illustrates, creating these instruments amounts to an exercise in option pricing. One widely used option-pricing model, known as the Black futures option model, is used in the following examples.[9] Robert Tompkins (1989) explains caps pricing in terms of Black's model, and the examples that follow are loosely patterned on Tompkins' approach.

The chief virtue of the Black model is its simplicity and ease of use, even though it has a serious internal inconsistency when used to value debt options: the assumption that the short-term interest rate (that is, the Treasury bill rate) is constant. Options on short-term interest rates have value, though, only if those rates are less than perfectly predictable. In the last section of this paper, a more complex model that does not suffer from this shortcoming is used to price options.[10]

Eurodollar Futures and Forward LIBOR. In order to give realistic yet simple examples of caps, collars, and floors, this article assumes that the reset dates coincide with the expiration dates of Eurodollar futures contracts, which are traded at the Chicago Mercantile Exchange (CME) and the London International Financial Futures Exchange (LIFFE). Purchase of a Eurodollar futures contract locks in the interest payment on a $1 million three-month time deposit to be made upon expiration of the futures contract. The interest rate on the deposit is three-month LIBOR. On the other hand, the seller of a Eurodollar futures contract is obligated to pay the specified LIBOR-based interest payment at expiration.[11]

Eurodollar futures expire in a quarterly cycle two London business days prior to the third Wednesday of March, June, September, and December. The Chicago Mercantile Exchange currently offers contract expiration months extending four years, with only March and September contracts for the fourth year.[12] The interest rate implied by a Eurodollar futures price may be regarded as a forward interest rate, that is, the three-month LIBOR expected by the market to prevail at the expiration date for each contract.[13]

The Black model uses the futures price for a particular contract expiration month as an input to determine the value of a European call and put option on that contract. In the case of Eurodollar futures contracts, the add-on yield (100 minus the futures price) is plugged into Black's formula. Another crucial variable is the volatility, which is either estimated from the historical volatility of the Eurodollar futures yield or obtained as an implied volatility from traded Eurodollar futures options.[14] Chart 1 shows the recent behavior of both of these volatility measures. Again, higher volatility results in higher-cost call and put options and hence more expensive caps and floors.

Table 1 gives two-year cap, floor, and collar prices on three-month LIBOR for two arbitrarily chosen dates, June 19, 1989, and December 14, 1987, that give reset dates which coincide with Eurodollar futures expiration dates. The first date illustrates pricing during a relatively low volatility period when the term structure of LIBOR rates, as given by the "strip" of prices on successively more distant contracts, was just about flat. The market was predicting virtually no change in short-term interest rates over this two-year horizon. In panel A of Table 1, the contract expiration months are given along with the forward rates or add-on yields for each futures contract. The row labeled *time to expiration* shows the number of days from the creation of the cap, floor, or collar to the expiration date for each contract. Another input into Black's formula, the risk-free rate, is taken to be the Treasury bill or zero-coupon bond yield for which the

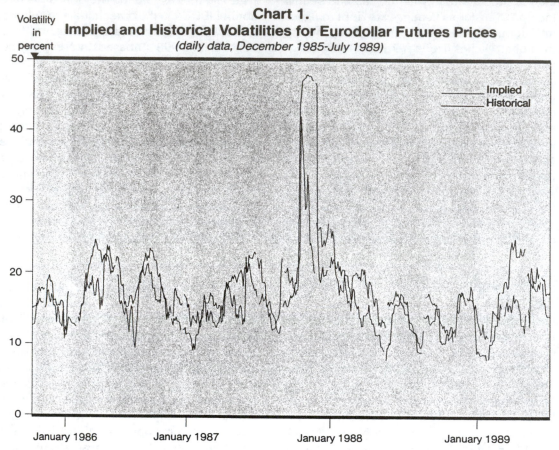

Chart 1.
Implied and Historical Volatilities for Eurodollar Futures Prices
(daily data, December 1985-July 1989)

Volatility in percent

Implied
Historical

January 1986 January 1987 January 1988 January 1989

Higher volatility, such as that exhibited around the time of the October 1987 stock-market break, results in more expensive caps, shown in Charts 2, 3, and 4.

Note: Gaps in Chart 1 result from missing observations.

Source: Chicago Mercantile Exchange.

expiration falls nearest to the futures expiration date.

The first example prices a two-year 10 percent cap, which consists of the sum of seven call options. At 10 percent, this cap is clearly out of the money. The computed call option price is expressed in basis points. The calls become progressively more expensive as the time to expiration increases, reflecting the rising time value of the calls. The shorter-maturity calls have little value because they are out of the money and, given the volatility, only a slight chance exists that they might finish in the money. Although the more distant calls are also out of the money, there is more time (and more uncertainty) about what LIBOR will do. Thus, their value is greater because of the higher probability that they might expire in the money. The sum of these calls is the cap rate, which is 147 basis points (rounded from 147.1).[15] For a three-month contract with a nominal face value of $1 million, a one-basis-point move is worth $25 ($1 million x .01% x 90/360). Translated into dollars, 147.1 basis points is $3,677.60 (147.1 x $25), which represents the dollar cost of placing a cap for two years on a $1 million loan. This example was computed ignoring the risk of default on the cap. It also assumes that payments at reset dates, if owed, are made at the time of the reset date.

Next, a slightly out-of-the-money 7.5 percent floor is shown. The total cost is 96 basis points, or $2,396.61. As mentioned above, the cost of interest-rate protection can be reduced by creating a collar, which is sometimes referred to as a ceiling-floor agreement. In this example,

Table 1.
Examples of Two-Year Cap, Floor, and Collar Prices on Three-Month LIBOR

Panel A: June 19, 1989; Volatility, 18 percent						
	September 1988	December 1988	March 1989	June 1989	September 1989	December 1989	March 1990
Time to expiration (days)	91	182	273	364	455	546	637
Forward rate	9.02	8.84	8.64	8.71	8.77	8.87	8.86
Risk-free rate	8.46	8.47	8.54	8.56	8.59	8.59	8.56
Call prices (10.0 percent strike)	5.3	10.3	12.9	19.9	26.5	34.1	38.1
Put prices (7.5 percent strike)	.6	4.7	11.8	15.4	18.6	20.6	24.2

10 percent cap	7.5 percent floor	Zero-cost collar
Cost in basis points: 147	Cost in basis points: 96	10 percent cap implies
Cost in dollars: $3,677.60	Cost in dollars: $2,396.61	7.85 percent floor

Panel B: June 19, 1989; Volatility, 18 percent						
	September 1988	December 1988	March 1989	June 1989	September 1989	December 1989	March 1990
Call prices (11 percent strike)	.4	2.2	3.8	7.6	11.8	16.9	20.3
Put prices (7 percent strike)	.1	1.3	4.7	7.2	9.5	11.2	13.9

11 percent cap	7 percent floor	Zero-cost collar
Cost in basis points: 63	Cost in basis points: 48	11 percent cap implies
Cost in dollars: $1,575.84	Cost in dollars: $1,198.08	7.19 percent floor

Panel C: December 14, 1987; Volatility, 25 percent						
	March 1988	June 1988	September 1988	December 1988	March 1989	June 1989	September 1989
Time to expiration (days)	91	182	280	371	455	553	644
Forward rate	8.09	8.34	8.62	8.88	9.11	9.31	9.48
Risk-free rate	6.09	6.79	7.11	7.51	7.66	7.79	7.92
Call prices (10 percent strike)	2.1	12.5	28.9	45.9	62.0	78.0	91.6
Put prices (7.5 percent strike)	16.2	23.0	26.8	29.0	30.5	32.9	34.8

10 percent cap	7.5 percent floor	Zero-cost collar
Cost in basis points: 321	Cost in basis points: 193	10 percent cap implies
Cost in dollars: $8,025.53	Cost in dollars: $4,829.68	8.05 percent floor

Note: Dollar amount is for $1,000,000 in notional principal.

selling a 7.5 percent floor would substantially reduce the cost of a 10 percent cap. The combination would cost about 51 basis points, or $1,281. However, by judiciously selecting the floor level—in this case, 7.85 percent—the price of the cap can be driven to zero.[16] Marketing people delight in explaining that downside interest-rate protection (the cap) can be obtained at no cost: just sell a floor.[17] Of course, though, this strategy carries a cost. The holder of an interest-rate collar has traded away potential savings on interest-rate declines below the floor. This caveat notwithstanding, a collar for which the floor exactly matches the cap will be referred to as a *zero-cost* collar.

Panel B illustrates how the cost of caps and floors falls by selecting more out-of-the-money levels. Increasing the cap by one percentage point to 11 percent reduces the cap rate substantially to 63 basis points, or $1,575.84. Decreasing the floor by half a percentage point to 7 percent more than halves the cost to 48 basis points, or $1,198.08. A zero-cost collar with an 11 percent cap effectively lowers the floor to 7.19 percent.

The final example, reflected in panel C of Table 1, shows prices for caps, collars, and floors during the relatively high volatility period after the October 1987 stock market break. As depicted in Chart 1, Eurodollar futures' volatility surged during and after the October 21 crash; the degree of fluctuation had abated greatly by late January, although it had not returned completely to precrash levels. The implied volatility was 25 percent on December 14, 1987, as compared to 18 percent on June 19, 1989, in the earlier examples. The 10 percent cap priced in panel C is substantially more costly than the one in panel A. The cost is 321 basis points, or $8,025.53. Another important factor contributing to the higher cost is the rising structure of LIBOR forward rates. Although the futures nearest to expiration indicate a forward rate of 8.09 percent as compared to 9.02 percent in the June 19, 1989, example, the distant futures for December 14, 1987, have forward rates that are well above those for June 19. The upward sloping term structure of interest rates for December 14 reinforces the effect of higher volatility on raising cap and floor rates. The floor is more expensive as well at 193 basis points, or $4,829.68. Interestingly, the zero-cost collar with a 10 per-

cent cap is only slightly more constraining with a floor of 8.05 percent as compared to 7.85 percent in the previous example, which exhibited low volatility and flat term structure.[18]

Caps, Collars, and Floors in Practice

At first sight, creating caps, collars, and floors would appear to be a simple matter because options are traded on the Eurodollar futures contract. Selecting the appropriate strike levels and expiration dates would appear to be all one needs to manufacture a cap, collar, or floor. However, as mentioned above, Eurodollar contracts extend into the future for at most four years (which nevertheless is an unusually large number of months for a futures contract). Eurodollar futures options traded at the Chicago Mercantile Exchange currently have expiration dates ranging out only two years, in a quarterly cycle that matches that of the Eurodollar futures contracts.[19]

Another limitation of Eurodollar futures options is that only contracts expiring within the three months or so from the current date are liquid, that is, they are the only ones that are actively traded so that their prices at any time reliably reflect equilibrium values. The options also are limited to strike levels in increments of 25 basis points, whereas the futures have increments of one basis point. Unlike Eurodollar futures and options, caps, collars, and floors have been created with maturities extending as much as 10 years. Furthermore, actual caps, collars, and floors can be created on any day, not just on futures and options expiration dates. The actual use of futures and options to fashion caps, collars, and floors is neither a straightforward nor a riskless matter.

The solution to this problem is the use of existing futures and options contracts to create the desired positions synthetically. Synthesizing an options position using options or futures contracts—or a combination of the two—requires not only taking appropriate positions in the existing liquid contracts but also altering that position over time so that the value of the actual position tracks or "replicates" the desired position. This process is known as *dynamic hedging*. Theoretically, the replicating portfolio of actual futures and options contracts can exactly match the value of, say, a cap sold to a counterparty.[20] In reality, managing a replicating portfolio is a risky and costly activity.[21] Tracking errors cumulate since costly trading cannot be conducted continuously as is theoretically required and because mismatches can occur with the expiration dates and possibly also with the interest rates involved. Using Eurodollar futures to hedge a cap based on the commercial paper rate exemplifies the latter.[22]

The Over-the-Counter Market

In view of the complexities and risks of dynamic-hedging strategies, most cap, collar, and floor users prefer over-the-counter instruments. Commercial and investment banks create these instruments themselves, possibly by manufacturing them through dynamic hedging. Nonfinancial users tend to rely on the expertise of these financial institutions and are willing to pay for the convenience of interest-rate risk management products issued through an intermediary. The intermediaries may also be more willing to bear the risks associated with hedging because of the scale of their operations. In fact, Keith C. Brown and Donald J. Smith (1988) describe the increasing involvement of banks in offering interest-rate risk management instruments as the reintermediation of commercial banking. Since the 1970s, commercial banks have played less of a role in channeling funds from lenders to borrowers. With the growth of interest-rate risk management, though, their intermediary role is being restored, albeit in a different form.

Commercial banks, particularly the largest money-center banks, are better able to absorb and control the hedging risks associated with managing a caps, collars, and floors portfolio, and these institutions are better able to evaluate the credit risks inherent in instruments bought from other parties. Credit risk arises because any counterparty selling a cap, for example, is obligated to make payments if the cap moves in the money on a reset date. That counterparty could go bankrupt at some point during the course of the cap agreement and would default on its obligation. (This issue is examined in detail in the last section of this article.) By taking positions in caps, collars, and floors, commercial banks—and to a lesser extent, investment banks—act as dealers by buying and selling to any counterparties. Within their portfolio or "book" of caps and floors, individual instruments partially net out, leaving a residual exposed position that the banks then hedge in the options and futures markets. Much trading of caps, collars, and floors consists of purchases and sales of these instruments to adjust positions and risk exposures, so much of the caps market's volume is generated by interdealer transactions. In addition to the dozen or so commercial and investment banks in New York and London that dominate the caps market, there are about half a dozen caps brokers, who do not take positions themselves but instead match buyer and seller.[23]

Caps, collars, and floors are usually sold in multiples of $5 million, but because of the customized nature of the over-the-counter market other amounts can be arranged. Most caps have terms that range from one to five years and have reset dates or frequencies that are usually monthly, quarterly, or semiannual. Caps based on three-month LIBOR are the most common and the most liquid or tradable. From the purchaser's point of view, buying a cap that matches the characteristics of the liability being hedged might seem best. Even strike levels and notional principal amounts can be chosen to vary over the term of an agreement in a predetermined way, but good fit comes at a price. Transactions costs are higher for such tailored products, as reflected by the larger difference between bid and offer rates on uncommon caps. This wider spread also increases the cost of removing caps by selling them before their term expires. Many users opt for a liquid cap and are willing to absorb the basis risk—the risk from a mismatch of interest basis or other characteristics—in order to avoid the higher cost of a less liquid instrument.

Caps and floors are usually available at strike levels within several percentage points of the current interest-rate basis and are most commonly written out of the money. Settlement dates typically occur after reset dates, upon maturity of the underlying instrument. For example, interest on a three-month Eurodollar deposit is credited upon maturity of the deposit. A cap on three-month LIBOR would have a three-month lag between a reset date and actual settlement. Most payments for caps are made up front, although they can also be amortized. When a cap and a floating-rate loan come from the same institution, the two are usually treated as a single instrument; thus, when the floating rate exceeds the strike level, payment is limited to the strike level and the cap does not pay off directly.[24]

Long-Term Caps. During the mid-1980s, early in the development of the caps market, longer-term caps were created directly from floating-rate securities rather than synthetically. Two kinds of floating-rate instruments were used: floating-rate CDs and floating-rate notes.[25] Floating-rate notes are debt obligations usually indexed to LIBOR, and floating-rate CDs are medium-term deposit instruments that are also typically indexed to LIBOR. The innovation that sparked much activity in the caps market was the issuance of capped floating-rate notes and CDs that in turn had their caps stripped off and sold as separate instruments sometimes known as "free-standing" caps.

As an illustration, consider the floating-rate CD. Banks use ordinary CDs as well as variable-rate CDs to acquire funds for the purpose of making loans and funding other balance-sheet assets. The capped floating-rate CD was promoted as a method of raising funds below LIBOR, the rate on an uncapped CD with a variable rate of interest. The reason is that, after issuing a capped floating-rate CD to a depositor, a bank could then sell the corresponding cap into the caps market and collect premium income. Because CDs of this type typically fund floating-rate loans, the bank would be fully hedged after selling the cap. Funding costs would be lowered if the premium for the cap on the floating-rate CD were less than the premium that the bank collected upon selling the cap into the market.[26] This method of creating or "sourcing" caps, floors, and collars—through capped floating-rate CDs and floating-rate notes—became extremely popular but was short-lived. Reportedly, the longer-term caps were gradually perceived to be undervalued, such that cap writers were not being compensated for the risks of having to make payments to cap holders if interest rates rose above strike levels.[27] Also contributing to the demise of this method of

sourcing was a flattening of the yield curve that made floating-rate borrowing less attractive and reduced cap prices. Today, few caps, collars, or floors are created beyond the five-year maturity.

Charts 2-4 give actual cap bid and offer rates, in basis points, quoted by one major caps broker in New York. The bid rate is the rate at which the broker is willing to buy a cap; the offer rate is the rate at which the broker sells a cap. The spread between the two represents the transactions costs of matching buyer with seller. Charts 2, 3, and 4, respectively, give the rates on two-year 8 percent, three-year 10 percent, and five-year 10 percent caps. These rates are just a sample; many other strike levels are available. The strike levels quoted change over time as interest rates change. Cap strike levels that move too far in the money or out of the money are discontinued and replaced by caps with strike levels that are in greater demand. All of these series are highly correlated. They are also correlated with the volatilities shown in Chart 1, which are a major determinant of cap values.[28]

The Motivation for Hedging and Some Hypothetical Examples

With some background on the caps, collars, and floors market, the use of interest-rate risk management instruments can now be put into perspective by briefly considering the nature of hedging. Caps, collars, and floors are often talked about in terms of an insurance analogy. They are instruments that can be used to hedge assets or liabilities and thus protect against loss resulting from interest-rate risk. In practice, though, distinguishing between hedging and speculating in interest-rate risk management is sometimes difficult, especially with option-based instruments. Discretion is required in selecting the timing of the hedge, the strike level, and the maturity of the instrument, all of which are usually predicated on some opinion of what interest rates and other variables are expected to do. Selling a cap or floor, for example, is a way to generate income on a fixed-income portfolio by collecting the premiums. The decision to sell often reflects a difference of opinion regarding the volatility implied by the

Chart 2.
Two-Year 8 Percent Cap Bid and Offer Rates
(daily data, March 1987-October 1988)

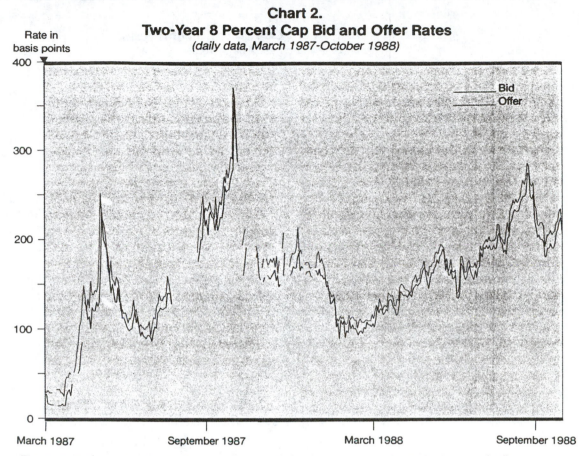

Rate in
basis points

The spread between the bid and offer rates represents the transactions costs of matching buyer and seller.

Note: Gaps in Charts 2, 3, and 4 reflect days for which rates were not available.

Source: Noonan, Astley, and Pearce, Inc.

cap or floor. If a money manager thinks a cap is overvalued because the market's expectation of volatility is higher than his or her own, then selling an out-of-the-money cap might be a good move. If the money manager's judgment about volatility is correct, even small upward moves in the interest rate may not wipe out all of the premium income. At the same time, the sale provides a limited hedge against small downward moves in rates, again because of the premium receipt.

Even determining the effect of hedging can be problematic, since a firm's purchase of a cap, for example, to hedge the interest-rate risk of a particular liability could increase the variability of the firm's net worth. The financial claim being hedged may itself help offset the variability of another financial claim on the balance sheet.

The net result of a specific hedge could be to increase the interest-rate risk exposure of the firm.

A more fundamental issue is why firms hedge in the first place. A basic insight derived from the economics of uncertainty is that risk aversion leads individuals to prefer stable income and consumption streams to highly variable ones. Given an assumption of risk aversion on the part of decision makers, one can show that their welfare or utility (that is, their economic well-being) is greater over time if they enjoy smooth income or consumption opportunities rather than erratic ones.[29] Hedging is a way of improving economic well-being by trading off income or consumption in good times for greater income or consumption in bad times. Thus, a hedging strategy serves a well-defined purpose

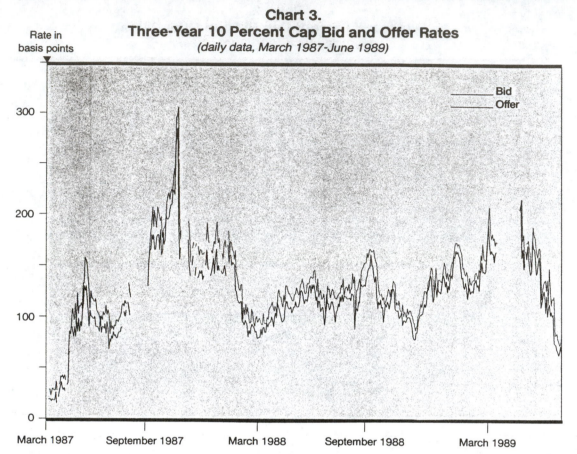

Chart 3.
Three-Year 10 Percent Cap Bid and Offer Rates
(daily data, March 1987-June 1989)

Rate in
basis points

——— Bid
——— Offer

300

200

100

0

March 1987   September 1987   March 1988   September 1988   March 1989

The rates depicted in Chart 3 are highly correlated with those in Charts 2 and 4, as well as with the volatilities in Chart 1.

Source: Noonan, Astley, and Pearce, Inc.

for risk-averse economic agents, such as farmers or a firm's owner-manager. The issue is less clear-cut for widely held corporations, which actually are the typical users of interest-rate risk-management tools. A corporation owned by a large number of stockholders need not operate like a risk-averse decision maker because each stockholder can insulate his or her wealth and consumption opportunities from risk, specific to the corporation's activities, by holding a diversified portfolio of assets.

Clifford W. Smith and René M. Stulz (1985) surveyed managers of widely held, value-maximizing corporations to determine the motivations behind hedging behavior. According to the researchers, managers engage in hedging of a firm's value for three basic reasons. The first explanation is tax-related; Smith and Stulz ar-

gue that, on average, a less variable pretax firm value implies a higher after-tax firm value than does a more variable pretax value. The reasoning turns on their assumption that the level of corporate tax liabilities grows at an increasing rate with rising pretax firm value because of the progressive structure of the tax code. Hedging helps reduce the variability of pretax firm value and therefore raises after-tax value. Second, Smith and Stulz maintain that hedging lowers the probability that the firm will go bankrupt and thus incur bankruptcy costs. Hedging firm value would benefit stockholders by reducing the expected future costs of bankruptcy that lower current firm value. A related point is that a firm's debt may often contain covenants that force the company to alter investment policies that the shareholders would like to see under-

Chart 4.

Chart 4.
Five-Year 10 Percent Cap Bid and Offer Rates
(daily data, March 1987-June 1989)

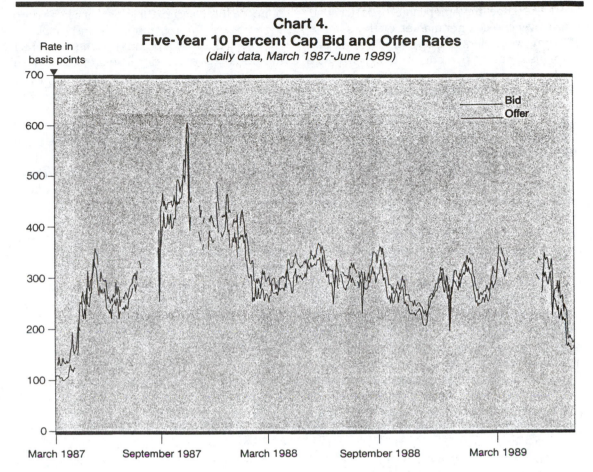

The longer expiration date on a five-year cap results in prices that are relatively higher than those on shorter-term caps.

Source: Noonan, Astley, and Pearce, Inc.

taken. Hedging reduces the likelihood of financial distress and the limitations on managers' discretion that bond covenants may impose. A third reason for hedging is that when managerial compensation is tied to the firm's value, managers may become more risk-averse in order to maintain that value.

Participants in the Caps, Collars, and Floors Market. While the precise social value of interest-rate risk management products is not fully understood in the case of widely held corporations, such products are clearly becoming increasingly popular among corporate treasurers and other financial managers. End users of caps, collars, and floors typically include firms seeking to limit exposure to adverse movements in short-term interest rates, such as a firm that sells commercial paper to fund its purchases of inventory.

Specific market participants are depository institutions, particularly savings and loan associations (S&Ls); corporations going through leveraged buyouts (LBOs) or taking on debt to fend off hostile takeovers; and real estate developers, who are often highly leveraged with floating-rate debt. Unfortunately, the only information about these applications is anecdotal. Also, compared to the potential market, the actual market is probably very small. Many potential users are unaware of or cautious about interest-rate risk management instruments.

Any user of interest-rate swaps is potentially also a user of caps, collars, and floors. Larry D. Wall and John J. Pringle (1988) conducted a systematic search of annual reports for 4,000 firms that used interest-rate swaps in 1986. The stocks of these firms were traded on the New York

Stock Exchange, the American Stock Exchange, or the over-the-counter market. Of this sample, 250 firms were identified as swaps market participants. Over 50 percent of this group were banks, savings and loans, and other financial services firms; commercial banks alone accounted for half of these. In addition, Wall and Pringle report that "the overwhelming majority of thrifts (59 percent), manufacturing firms (69 percent), and nonfinancial, nonmanufacturing firms (77 percent) are exclusively fixed-rate payers."[30] As a conjecture, the profile of caps, collars, and floor users may be quite similar to that for swaps users. The fact that credit risks for caps and floors are one-sided, however, suggests that firms with weaker credit ratings probably use caps and floors because they cannot gain access to the swaps market on favorable terms.

Anecdotal accounts from various sources illustrate how different end users employ caps, collars, or floors in their management of interest-rate risk. Many savings and loans, for instance, have been active users of these option-based instruments. The interest-rate risk confronting S&Ls, and depository institutions generally, may be considered in terms of their net interest margins, that is, the difference between the rates at which an institution lends and borrows. S&Ls are particularly vulnerable to changes in interest rates because maturities (or alternatively, the durations) of these institutions' assets, predominantly long-term mortgages, greatly exceed the maturities of their liabilities, most often short-term time and savings deposits. Thus, a rise in rates raises the interest expense on an S&L's short-term liabilities with possibly little increase in interest earnings on its mortgages. The net interest margin narrows and could very well become negative. One solution is to convert the floating-rate interest expense on the liabilities into fixed-rate payments via an interest-rate swap. The net interest margin would then become much more stable. However, a weak credit standing could make such a swap too expensive or unobtainable. A cap on the floating-rate liabilities could be an effective alternative. An S&L's credit rating would be irrelevant to a cap writer, who bears no credit exposure.[31]

As another example, consider a commercial bank's portfolio manager who is responsible for overseeing a portfolio of floating-rate notes.

Suppose this manager believes that a large drop in short-term interest rates, currently at about 8 percent, is about to occur. He wants to protect the portfolio's earnings and therefore buys an out-of-the-money 7 percent interest-rate floor. Concerned about the cost of this protection and reasonably convinced that rates will not rise substantially, he also decides to sell a 9 percent interest-rate cap to create a collar on the portfolio. This example highlights the discretion involved in selecting a hedge. A floor could have been in place all along, but maintaining a floor reduces a portfolio's return by the amount of the premium expense. Only when the manager has strong concerns about a drop in rates is the floor purchased.

As a final example, the corporate treasurer of a consumer products firm is worried about the prospects of a rise in interest rates because her company has recently undergone a leveraged buyout. The financing strategy for the LBO included heavy reliance on floating-rate debt secured from a syndicate of commercial banks. The firm's debt-to-equity ratio has soared, and even a modest rise in rates could bankrupt the company. After the LBO the firm's credit standing was downgraded by the rating services; consequently, access to the swap market is effectively foreclosed. Buying a two-year interest-rate cap to cover the firm's floating-rate exposure seems to be a prudent action.[32] The treasurer expects earnings will be more robust after a two-year interval. Also, the protection gained for a relatively short-term horizon makes sense because during this period the firm would be downsizing and reorganizing its operations.

Credit Risk

The earlier discussion of the over-the-counter market for caps, collars, and floors alluded to the risk of default inherent in these instruments. That risk is present because the seller of a cap or floor is agreeing to fulfill a contract in the event the cap or floor moves in the money on a payment date. Since the seller is a firm, whether a commercial bank, investment bank, or non-financial institution, its assets are limited, and thus the company is exposed to the possibility of bankruptcy. The probability of default is rather small for the typical caps, collar, or floor writer who also typically issues investment-grade bonds into the market. Moody's Investors Service, one of the major bond rating firms, recently released a study indicating that from 1970 to 1988 the average annual rate of default by issuers of investment-grade bonds was 0.06 percent, as compared to an average annual default rate of 3.3 percent for junk bond issuers.[33] Because the consequences of default can be financially damaging, default risk receives careful analysis, particularly by counterparties entering into caps and swaps agreements. This section of the article takes a detailed look at how default risk is evaluated and how it affects the pricing of caps, collars, and floors.

The first aspect of the problem is to consider the precise nature of the default risk or, alternatively, the credit exposure. If a cap is in the money on a floating-rate reset date, the owner of the cap expects to receive a payment from the cap writer, as reviewed above. If the writer is insolvent and thus fails to make the payment, the owner is again in an unhedged position and must make the full floating-rate payment, but this is not the only consequence of default. Provided the default does not occur on the final reset date, the cap was also hedging future reset dates, which upon default are also fully exposed. Thus, credit exposure depends on the time that default occurs in the life of a cap agreement. (Note that a parallel argument can be made for floors and collars.) The cost of default to the cap buyer is the cost of replacing the original cap with a new cap from another seller. If interest rates at the default date were identical to the initial interest rates and the volatility had not changed since the original cap was purchased, the replacement cost of the cap would be zero, ignoring transactions costs and differences in credit risks. That is, the cost of a new cap for the remaining reset dates would exactly equal the current market value of the existing cap (if default had not occurred).

The next and rather complex aspect of the credit risk question to consider concerns the method of assessing credit risk when a cap is sold. Bankruptcy of a cap writer has no impact on cap buyers as long as the cap stays out of the money and the cap buyer has no intention of selling the cap before its term ends. Default occurs only when a cap is in the money and the cap writer is bankrupt. The likelihood of bankruptcy may also be related to the level of interest rates and thus dependent on the future path of these rate movements. In addition, as just discussed, a cap's replacement cost is a function of where in the life of the cap agreement default occurs. All of these factors should be weighed in evaluating what the potential cost of default could be and how that should affect the price of a cap.

Marcelle Arak, Laurie S. Goodman, and Arthur Rones (1986) propose a method of computing credit exposure for caps, collars, and floors. Their approach amounts to considering different worst-case scenarios that are defined by the degree to which a cap can move in the money. For a cap the computed exposure de-

"The cost of default to the cap buyer is the cost of replacing the original cap with a new cap from another seller."

pends on the size of the upward movement in the interest rate that could occur during each reset interval. A cap's replacement value will tend at first to increase early in the life of the instrument and then to decrease toward the end of the contract. The credit exposure is taken to be the maximum replacement value computed at the reset dates. For example, if the interest-rate volatility based on three-month LIBOR is 10 percent (as measured by the annual standard deviation), over a three-month period the volatility is $0.10 \times \sqrt{(1/4)} = 5$ percent.[34] Assuming an initial 7 percent LIBOR, three months later the upward move would be to 7.35 [7.0 + (0.05 x 7.0)]. Given this rate and a further assumption that rates at all other maturities shifted in parallel, the cap replacement value is calculated. Another 5 percent upward move is then computed, giving a new LIBOR of 7.72 [7.35 + (7.35 x 0.05)] and again the replacement value is computed, and so forth. The credit exposure is the maximum value of the replacement cost during the cap agreement.

A more conservative evaluation of credit exposure might assume that rates rose by two standard deviations per year instead of one as in the previous example. At two-standard-deviation moves, the actual exposure would, on average, exceed the maximum computed amount only 2.5 percent of the time (as compared to exceeding it 16.5 percent of the time using a one-standard-deviation measure).[35] Arak, Goodman, and Rones give an example of the credit exposure on various collar agreements with a floor equal to 6 percent and a cap equal to 9 percent. For three-month reset intervals, the exposure is 0.44 percent of the notional principal (two-year collar), 0.82 percent (five-year collar),

"Computations based on worst-case scenarios implicitly overstate the actual incidence of default because of the arbitrary assumption about sequential interest-rate moves only in one direction."

and 2.68 percent (10-year collar).[36] By these researchers' calculations, the credit exposure on collars is rather small, especially compared to similar calculations for other instruments they consider, such as interest-rate swaps and forward contracts. These calculations are intended for commercial banks, which set credit limits for particular customers in order to manage the size of potential losses in the event of default. However, the method put forth by Arak, Goodman, and Rones is not useful for pricing caps—that is, for adjusting the price or rate for the anticipated cost of default. Computations based on worst-case scenarios implicitly overstate the actual incidence of default because of the arbitrary assumption about sequential interest-rate moves only in one direction. A more desirable approach would compute the "expected value" of default—the difference between caps not subject to default and those that are.

Caps as Default-Risky Options. Almost all of the option pricing models used to value caps ignore default risk. An exception is the model proposed by Herb Johnson and Stulz (1987), in which they derive formulas for default-risky or "vulnerable" puts and calls. Unfortunately, their formulas cannot be straightforwardly applied to caps, collars, or floors because of the time dimension involved in these options-based instruments. As has been emphasized, caps are a sequence of options—default-risky options. Fulfilling a given option contained in a cap depends on the absence of bankruptcy at earlier reset dates. If bankruptcy occurred earlier, the current option would not be honored by the cap writer. The sequential time dimension involved in valuing caps makes the mathematics formidably complex.[37]

This author has tackled the complexity of cap valuation by using computer-intensive methods to handle the intricate contingencies implied in cap, collar, floor, and swap agreements (Peter A. Abken [forthcoming]). His computer model avoids the contradictory assumption inherent in the Black model used for short-term debt options—that short-term interest rates are constant—but at the cost of trading off a simple analytical formula for a complicated computer algorithm. Nevertheless, the intuition behind the new model is simple and easily explained.

The value of a European option can be thought of as the average or expected value of its payoffs at expiration, discounted back to the present. Options are difficult to value because the payoff upon expiration is a "kinked," or discontinuous, function of the underlying asset price. A call option is worth zero if the underlying asset price at expiration is less than the strike price, and positive in value if the underlying asset price exceeds the strike price, increasing dollar for dollar with the amount above the strike. The Black-Scholes and Black formulas compute the value of a call as the expected value of the future payoffs.[38] Some payoffs are more likely to occur than others, and the formulas account for the probabilities associated with the payoffs.

Monte Carlo Simulation. One method for valuing options relies on extensive computations to determine the expected payoffs. Known as Monte Carlo simulation, this process was first applied to option pricing problems by Phelim P. Boyle (1977). The standard application involves stock option pricing. A stock price, on which an option is valued, is assumed to rise and fall randomly over time, although its value at any point can be described in terms of its statistical distribution, which is known or assumed. In standard problems the distribution for stock price changes is assumed to be fully characterized by its mean and variance. Using this information, artificial future stock-price paths, also known as *realizations,* can be created numerically by computer. By randomly generating a large enough number of price paths (tens of thousands, at a minimum) and evaluating the payoff on an option with a given strike price at a particular point in time—the option's expiration date—an average over these randomly generated payoffs can be made. The option price is given by appropriately discounting the expected future payoff into current dollars. Of course, the Black-Scholes formula accomplishes the same thing mathematically and is conceptually equivalent. To the penny, both methods will give the same price using identical assumptions regarding the statistical characteristics of stock price movements. The Monte Carlo method, though cumbersome, pays off in cases where the asset price moves in unusual ways, such as in random jumps—for example, due to a stock market crash. The Black-Scholes model rules out such movements by assumption. Cap valuation is another area where Monte Carlo methods offer a simplification over approaches that may not otherwise be mathematically tractable.

Three factors taken together contribute to the complexity of default-risky cap valuation. The first is that debt prices on instruments like Treasury bills or Eurodollar deposits vary with interest rates. Second, each constituent option in a cap is subject to default and must be valued as a default-risky option. Third, the payoff on a given option depends on the nonoccurrence of default on options from earlier periods.

The payoff of a vulnerable call option is the lesser of the firm's value or the default-free option payoff. The value of the firm is the market value of its equity (before including the value of its cap). If the value of the firm that sold the option is greater than the payoff, no default occurs. If the payoff exceeds the firm's value, the company defaults and the option holder receives the value of the firm—or some share of it, as determined by the bankruptcy courts—when

the company is liquidated. In view of the fact that a vulnerable call may pay off less, but never more, than a default-free call, the value of a vulnerable call must be less than the value of an otherwise comparable default-free call.

An additional consideration for cap valuation, as discussed above, is that default on a cap leaves the cap buyer unhedged. The exposure is the replacement value of the cap. Thus, default involves at a minimum replacement of the missed option payoff, and possibly the entire remaining value of the cap, if the firm wants to maintain the hedge. Thus, besides valuing default-risky call options, cap valuation must also evaluate such replacement costs.

The Elements of the Caps Model. To convey the basic ideas behind construction of the caps model, this section of the article sketches out

"An additional consideration for cap valuation . . . is that default on a cap leaves the cap buyer unhedged. The exposure is the replacement value of the cap."

the model, the technical details of which can be found in Abken (forthcoming). Three so-called state variables are computer-generated to implement the simulation. The options making up a cap are valued based on the underlying interest rate, as discussed earlier. The entire path of the term structure of interest rates is generated using the model developed by Stephen M. Schaefer and Eduardo S. Schwartz (1984). Two state variables are the difference or spread between the instantaneous rate and a consol rate (that is, the rate on a bond having infinite maturity), and the consol rate itself. All other intermediate-maturity discount bonds are derived by formula from these two inputs, which describe absolute and relative movements in interest rates at all maturities. The third state variable represents the value of the firm, which also fluctuates randomly over time, reflecting unpredictable changes in interest rates, earnings, and other variables that determine firm value.

The example to be considered is parallel to the one discussed earlier in Table I, but the focus is now on credit risk. The cap model will value two-year caps on a three-month interest rate. The cap consists of seven reset dates, at each of which the firm's value is compared to the call option payoff. Default-free and default-risky caps are valued. The difference in the price or rate for these otherwise identical caps is the credit spread for default risk. The example developed below illustrates how default risk is particularly sensitive to the correlation over time between firm value and interest-rate movements.

The parameter values for the Schaefer-Schwartz model were estimated from actual

---

"[D]efault risk is particularly sensitive to the correlation over time between firm value and interest-rate movements."

---

interest-rate data on one-month Treasury bill and 30-year bond yields, which served as proxies for the instantaneous interest rate and consol interest rate, respectively. The rates were sampled weekly on Fridays from January 1983 to August 1989. The reader is referred to Abken (forthcoming) for details concerning parameter estimation and other technical details concerning the model.

A simplification used in the simulations presented in this article is that whenever a default occurs—that is, when the firm value is less than the option payoff—the replacement value of the cap is not computed. Instead, the option payoff for that reset date is set equal to the negative of the payoff. In other words, the cap owner has to cover the full floating-rate interest payment for that date. Payoffs at future reset dates are assumed to be zero. Valuing a new cap at current rates would increase the cost of default com-

pared to the procedure used here; such valuation, however, would also require separate simulations at each occurrence of default.

More Examples. Table 2 gives the results of the simulations. Three panels of this table differ only in the degree that firm value is correlated with interest-rate movements. In the Schaefer-Schwartz model, there are two elements to this correlation. Firm value can be correlated with consol rate movements or spread movements, or both. (The Schaefer-Schwartz model assumes that the spread and consol rate are uncorrelated, which is supported by empirical research.) Correlation coefficients range from -1, perfect negative correlation, to 1, perfect positive correlation. Intuitively, a cap writer whose firm value is negatively correlated with interest-rate movements poses a greater credit risk than one that is positively correlated. For a given strike level, when interest rates are high, caps are more likely to be in the money and require a payment from the writer. A negative correlation therefore means that high interest rates are associated with low firm value; hence, default is more probable than it would be for zero or positive correlations. Also, empirically short- and long-term interest rates are positively correlated. Thus, a negative correlation of firm value and long-term interest rate would also be associated with a negative correlation between the firm value and interest-rate spread (defined as the short rate less the long rate).

Panel A gives the base case of zero correlation of firm value with the interest-rate spread and with the long-term interest rate. The annual default rate for this case is set to 0.13 percent by adjusting the initial value of the firm to give this rate as the outcome of the simulations.[39] The same initial firm value is then used in panels B and C, thereby yielding new default rates due to different correlations with the term structure variables. The initial term structure has a spread of 2.7 percentage points, which was the average spread over the sample period. The short-term interest rate is initially 8 percent and the cap is written at 9 percent. As in Table I, the option rates are given for each reset date. This table includes default-free and default-risky options; the sum over reset dates for each type is the cap rate. Because the default rate is so low, the discrepancies between default-free and default-risky option prices do not become significant

Table 2.
Default-Free and Default-Risky Cap Rates
Estimated by Monte Carlo Simulation, 9.0 Percent Two-Year Cap

Initial term structure: Short-term rate, 8.0 percent; Long-term rate, 10.7 percent

Panel A: Correlation of firm value with interest-rate spread: 0
Correlation of firm value with long-term rate: 0

Reset date number:	1	2	3	4	5	6	7
Time to expiration (weeks):	13	26	39	52	65	78	91
Default-free option rate:	7.94	17.99	26.95	35.57	43.98	51.87	59.86
Default-risky option rate:	7.94	17.99	26.95	35.53	43.81	51.34	58.71

Default-free cap rate:	244.16	Default-risky cap rate:	242.28
Standard deviation:	(1.45)	Standard deviation:	(1.43)
95 percent confidence interval:	(241.32, 247.00)	95 percent confidence interval:	(239.48, 245.08)

Credit spread in basis points:	1.89
Standard deviation:	(0.14)
95 percent confidence interval:	(1.62, 2.16)
Annual default rate:	0.13 percent

Panel B: Correlation of firm value with interest-rate spread: −0.5
Correlation of firm value with long-term rate: −0.5

Reset date number:	1	2	3	4	5	6	7
Default-free option rate:	7.94	17.99	26.95	35.57	43.98	51.87	59.86
Default-risky option rate:	7.94	17.98	26.79	34.98	42.19	48.15	53.51

Default-free cap rate:	244.16	Default-risky cap rate:	231.54
Standard deviation:	(1.45)	Standard deviation:	(1.35)
95 percent confidence interval:	(241.32, 247.00)	95 percent confidence interval:	(228.89, 234.19)

Credit spread in basis points:	12.63
Standard deviation:	(0.35)
95 percent confidence interval:	(11.94, 13.32)
Annual default rate:	0.71 percent

Panel C: Correlation of firm value with interest-rate spread: 0.5
Correlation of firm value with long-term rate: 0.5

Reset date number:	1	2	3	4	5	6	7
Default-free option rate:	7.94	17.99	26.95	35.57	43.98	51.87	59.86
Default-risky option rate:	7.94	17.99	26.95	35.57	43.98	51.87	59.86

Default-free cap rate:	244.16	Default-risky cap rate:	244.16
Standard deviation:	(1.45)	Standard deviation:	(1.45)
95 percent confidence interval:	(241.32, 247.00)	95 percent confidence interval:	(241.32, 247.00)

Credit spread in basis points:	0.0
Standard deviation:	(0.0)
95 percent confidence interval:	(0.0, 0.0)
Annual default rate:	0.0 percent

Note: Sample size for each panel: 50,000 independent draws. Cap rates expressed in basis points.

until the later reset dates. The default-free cap rate is 244.16 basis points, whereas the default-risky cap rate is 242.28. The difference of 1.89 basis points is the credit spread.

These figures are estimates and have an error associated with them. One can arbitrarily reduce that error by increasing the number of realizations used to compute the options. Quadrupling the number of realizations reduces the standard deviation by half. The simulations for each panel were generated by taking 50,000 independent sets of realizations of the state variables.[40] The standard deviation and 95 percent confidence intervals for each cap rate and the spread are reported in Table 2.

The simulation used to generate panel B was the same as that for panel A in all respects except that the correlation between firm value and interest-rate spread is −0.5 instead of zero, and the correlation between firm value and long-term rate is −0.5 instead of zero. The results show a substantial increase in the incidence of default. The base rate in panel A for zero correlations is 0.13 percent, whereas the negative correlations in panel B raise the default rate to 0.71 percent. The credit spread rises from 1.89 basis points to 12.63 basis points. As discussed previously, the reason is that firm value is likely to be low when interest rates are high. The cap writer has a greater chance of being insolvent when a payment is required. As a final example, the correlations in panel C take the opposite signs from those in panel B. The credit spread and annual default rate drop to zero. The greater chance of high firm value coinciding with cap payments reduces the likelihood of default by the cap writer; in this case, the incidence of default drops to zero.

The substantial increase in the credit spread exhibited in panel B may exaggerate default risk for two reasons. First, the cap is assumed to be unhedged by the firm. In other words, the company is taking a speculative position. Actual cap writers usually take offsetting positions in other caps or hedge by other methods, at least to some degree. Second, the model assumes that failure to cover cap payments is the only factor causing bankruptcy. For actual cap writers, the contingent liability posed by a cap is probably small compared to other items on the balance sheet. On the other hand, the computed credit spread may still be a good approximation if the cap serves as a proxy for the firm's overall balance sheet exposure to movements in interest rates.

No data on actual credit spreads are published. In conversations with the author, cap market participants place the credit spreads that have occurred in the range of 5 to 10 basis points for two- to three-year caps. The estimated spreads using the cap model are roughly in that range. Further research into actual credit spreads and refinements of the cap model should sharpen the estimation results and make the model more useful.

Conclusion

Interest-rate caps, collars, and floors are among the newest interest-rate risk management instruments. This article has given an exposition of these closely related instruments, which are options-based and designed to limit exposure to fluctuations in short-term interest rates on floating-rate assets or debt. Their applications are not limited to hedging. Like options, they are also convenient for speculating on interest-rate movements. In practice, however, the distinction between these two applications is rarely clear-cut. Several examples served to illustrate how financial managers use caps, collars, and floors.

The article also discussed the credit risks associated with caps, collars, and floors, which for the most part are over-the-counter contracts offered by one firm to another. Default risk is inherent in this kind of arrangement and can be priced. A new cap valuation model produced credit spreads that are not much different from those observed in the cap market between stronger and weaker credit risks among cap writers. Interest-rate risk management has been growing in importance for financial managers. This article may improve their understanding of the credit risk of caps, collars, and floors and help determine the cost of interest-rate protection.

Notes

[1] Recent *Economic Review* articles include Abken (1987), Feinstein and Goetzmann (1988), Kawaller, Koch, and Koch (1988), and Feinstein (1989).

[2] See Wall and Pringle (1988) for an introduction to interest-rate swaps.

[3] For brevity, the market for caps, collars, and floors will be referred to as the *cap market*.

[4] See Kuprianov (1986): 16-20, for a discussion of Eurodollar deposits and Eurodollar futures.

[5] The information on the ISDA survey was reported in *Risk* 2 (April 1989): 11.

[6] A detailed discussion of option pricing is beyond the scope of this article. A basic overview can be found in Abken (1987). See Cox and Rubinstein (1985) or Jarrow and Rudd (1983) for more thorough introductions to option pricing.

[7] See Abken (1987): 6, for more detail.

[8] See Henderson (1986) for further discussion.

[9] See Black (1976).

[10] To the author's knowledge, no published studies have compared the accuracy of different option-pricing models for pricing caps and related instruments. One reason may be that there are no publicly available data on these rates, and another is that these instruments are relatively new. Little empirical research exists on the adequacy of different interest-rate option-pricing models. Boyle and Turnbull (1989) use the Courtadon option-pricing model in evaluating collar rates, but they do not compare their rates with those from other models nor with actual market rates.

[11] Because the CME and most LIFFE Eurodollar futures are "cash-settled," a $1 million deposit is rarely made, but instead only the difference between the current, or spot, LIBOR and the contracted LIBOR times the notional principal actually changes hands.

[12] Prior to June 1989 contract months extended three years.

[13] A Eurodollar futures price is actually an index value that equals 100 minus the "add-on" yield (three-month LIBOR). Thus, the futures price and add-on yield move inversely with each other. See Kuprianov (1986): 16, for more detail on Eurodollar futures and short-term interest-rate futures generally. Both the add-on yield and the futures price are usually quoted in the financial press.

[14] See Feinstein (1989) for details on the estimation, interpretation, and uses of implied volatilities. The Eurodollar futures options are actually American options, but the early exercise feature has negligible value for the slightly out-of-the-money options usually used in estimating the implied volatilities with a European futures option formula.

[15] Sums in Table 1 may not add up due to rounding error. Cap rates are usually rounded to whole basis points. The dollar amounts are the exact amounts computed in constructing Table 1.

[16] Another way to create a zero-cost collar is to set the floor first and then determine the appropriate cap. The method discussed in the text is more common.

[17] Collars have also been offered that give the buyer a payment for taking the collar, that is, the value of the floor sold exceeds the cost of the cap purchased. See "NatWest Uses Incentives to Push Rate Collars," *American Banker*, August 2, 1989.

[18] These examples are consistent with the recent findings of Boyle and Turnbull (1989) in their examination of collars. Using a different option-pricing model than the Black model, they found that a 100 percent increase in the volatility causes the floor level to change by less than one basis point. If their findings are also valid for the Black model, most of the difference observed in the examples in the text is attributable to the difference in yield curves.

[19] Before March 1989, contract expiration dates had a maximum maturity of one year. See Chicago Mercantile Exchange (February/March 1989): 7.

[20] The term *counterparty* is standard terminology for the other party in a swap, cap, floor, or collar agreement.

[21] Another complication in using futures in a replicating portfolio is that futures contracts are marked to market daily. This situation may create cash flow problems since futures positions that lose value may be subject to frequent margin calls. Even though the replicating portfolio is used to hedge a cap, which matches it in value, the cash flows from the cap come only when it is sold and on interest payment dates.

[22] See Abken (1987) for more on the synthetic creation of options. Mattu (1986) gives examples of replicating portfolios for caps and floors.

[23] Shirreff (1986) gives an interesting though somewhat dated overview of the caps market and the various players in it.

[24] LeGrand and Fertakis (1986): 134.

[25] Floating-rate CDs are also called variable-rate CDs.

[26] See *Intermarket* (October 1986): 14, for an account of the first such sale of a cap from a capped floating-rate note (FRN). By selling a cap off an issue of $100 million in 12-year capped FRNs, Banque Indosuez of Paris lowered its interest rate by one-eighth of a point below LIBOR. Uncapped, the notes would have sold at LIBOR. The capped FRNs were issued at LIBOR plus three-eighths. On an annual basis, Indosuez therefore collected the equivalent of 50 basis points on the sale of its cap.

[27] Shirreff (1986): 29.

[28] The volatilities shown in Chart 1 are probably not the same as those used to generate the cap rates. The volatilities were obtained from a different source than the cap rates, but they should be highly correlated with the actual volatilities used to price the caps.

[29] Newbery and Stiglitz (1981) give a comprehensive discussion of risk aversion and the rationale for hedging.

[30] Wall and Pringle (1988): 22.

[31] The example given was described in terms of a "flow concept" of interest-rate risk, that is, the impact of a change in interest rates on the net interest margin. Another way to view interest-rate risk is in terms of a "stock concept," the change in the net worth of the firm. A parallel shift in the term structure of interest rates would reduce the value of an S&L's long-term mortgages more than it would reduce the value of its short-term liabilities. Net worth would be reduced or possibly turn negative. Purchasing a cap—an asset on the balance sheet—would offset loss of net worth

to some extent because it would gain value as interest rates rise. See Spahr, Luytjes, and Edwards (1988) for a good exposition of this application of caps and how they hedge interest-rate risk.

[32]Commercial banks underwriting debt for highly leveraged financings often require their floating-rate borrowers to buy caps for a portion of the debt. This hedging requirement may be stipulated in the loan covenant. See Richardson (1989): 12.

[33]See *Moody's Special Report* (1989).

[34]This method assumes that the interest rate follows a random walk with no "drift" (that is, deterministic trend movements). Changes in the interest rate from period to period are assumed to be normally distributed with constant variance (or standard deviation), implying that the statistical distribution of interest-rate movements may be completely characterized by only its mean and variance.

[35]These percentages are based on the properties of the normal distribution, which is assumed to describe interest-rate movements.

[36]Arak, Goodman, and Rones (1986): 452.

[37]Cap valuation can be formulated as a kind of compound option problem. See Geske (1977) to appreciate the complexities involved in valuing securities that are composed of sequences of options.

[38]In a discrete time model the expected value is a weighted average of all possible payoffs, each payoff multiplied by the probability of its occurring.

[39]According to Moody's study, the lowest investment-grade bonds, rated Baa (or BBB by Standard and Poor's), had average annual default rates over two-year horizons of 0.25 percent. A Standard and Poor's BBB-rated investment bank was reportedly at a disadvantage in writing caps compared to stronger writers. See Shirreff (1986): 34.

The 0.13 default rate used in the example was chosen to reflect the lower risk of default on a cap relative to a bond.

[40]The Monte Carlo simulations used a variance reduction technique called the method of antithetic variates (see Boyle [1977]). The total number of realizations was in fact 200,000 for each simulation, though only a fourth of that number came from independent draws from the random number generator. See Abken (forthcoming) for more details.

References

Abken, Peter A. "An Introduction to Portfolio Insurance." Federal Reserve Bank of Atlanta *Economic Review* 72 (November/December 1987): 2-25.

——————. "Valuing Default-Risky Interest Rate Caps: A Monte Carlo Approach." Federal Reserve Bank of Atlanta Working Paper (forthcoming).

Arak, Marcelle, Laurie S. Goodman, and Arthur Rones. "Credit Lines for New Instruments: Swaps, Over-the-Counter Options, Forwards and Floor-Ceiling Agreements." In *Proceedings of a Conference on Bank Structure and Competition.* Federal Reserve Bank of Chicago (May 1986): 437-56.

Black, Fischer. "The Pricing of Commodity Contracts." *Journal of Financial Economics* 3 (January/March 1976): 167-79.

Boyle, Phelim P. "Options: A Monte Carlo Approach." *Journal of Financial Economics* 4 (May 1977): 323-38.

Boyle, Phelim P., and Stuart M. Turnbull. "Pricing and Hedging Capped Options." *Journal of Futures Markets* 9 (February 1989): 41-54.

Brown, Keith C., and Donald J. Smith. "Recent Innovations in Interest Rate Risk Management and the Reintermediation of Commercial Banking." *Financial Management* 17 (Winter 1988): 45-58.

"Caps and Floors." *The Banker* (February 1989): 9.

Chicago Mercantile Exchange. *Market Perspectives.* Various issues.

Commins, Kevin. "Managing Interest Rate Risk." *Intermarket* (May 1987): 28-34.

Cox, John C., and Mark Rubinstein. *Options Markets.* Englewood Cliffs, N.J.: Prentice-Hall, 1985.

Feinstein, Steven P. "Forecasting Stock-Market Volatility Using Options on Index Futures." Federal Reserve Bank of Atlanta *Economic Review* 74 (May/June 1989): 12-30.

Feinstein, Steven P., and William N. Goetzmann. "The Effect of the 'Triple Witching Hour' on Stock Market Volatility." Federal Reserve Bank of Atlanta *Economic Review* 73 (September/October 1988): 2-18.

Geske, Robert. "The Valuation of Corporate Liabilities as Compound Options." *Journal of Financial and Quantitative Analysis* 12 (1977): 541-52.

Henderson, Schuyler K. "Securitizing Swaps." *International Financial Law Review* (September 1986): 31-34.

Jarrow, Robert A., and Andrew Rudd. *Option Pricing.* Homewood, Ill.: Richard D. Irwin, Inc., 1983.

Johnson, Herb, and René Stulz. "The Pricing of Options with Default Risk." *Journal of Finance* 42 (June 1987): 267-80.

Kawaller, Ira G., Paul D. Koch, and Timothy W. Koch. "The Relationship between the S&P 500 Index and S&P 500 Index Futures Prices." Federal Reserve Bank of Atlanta *Economic Review* 73 (May/June 1988): 2-10.

Kuprianov, Anatoli. "Short-Term Interest Rate Futures." Federal Reserve Bank of Richmond *Economic Review* (September/October 1986): 12-26.

LeGrand, Jean E., and John P. Fertakis. "Interest Rate Caps: Keeping the Lid on Future Rate Hikes." *Journal of Accountancy* (May 1986): 130-36.

Mattu, Ravi. "Hedging Floating Rate Liabilities: Locks, Caps and Floors." Chicago Mercantile Exchange Strategy Paper, 1986.

Moody's Special Report. "Historical Default Rates of Corporate Bond Issuers, 1970-1988." July 1989.

Newbery, David M.G., and Joseph E. Stiglitz. *The Theory of Commodity Price Stabilization: A Study in the Economics of Risk*. New York: Oxford University Press, 1981.

Richardson, Portia. "Put on Your Thinking Cap." *Intermarket* (March 1989): 10-13.

Schaefer, Stephen M., and Eduardo S. Schwartz. "A Two-Factor Model of the Term Structure: An Approximate Solution." *Journal of Financial and Quantitative Analysis* 19 (December 1984): 413-24.

Shirreff, David. "Caps and Options: The Dangerous New Protection Racket." *Euromoney* (March 1986): 26-40.

Smith, Clifford W., and René M. Stulz. "The Determinants of Firms' Hedging Policies." *Journal of Financial and Quantitative Analysis* 20 (December 1985): 391-405.

Spahr, Ronald W., Jan E. Luytjes, and Donald G. Edwards. "The Impact of the Uses of Caps as Deposit Hedges for Financial Institutions." *Issues in Bank Regulation* (Summer 1988): 17-23.

Sutherland, L. Frederick. "Squeezing Cash: How to Make an LBO Work." *Corporate Cashflow* (June 1988): 47-50.

Tompkins, Robert. "The A-Z of Caps." *Risk* 2 (March 1989): 21-23, 41.

Wall, Larry D. "Alternative Explanations of Interest Rate Swaps: A Theoretical and Empirical Analysis." *Financial Management* (forthcoming, 1989).

Wall, Larry D., and John J. Pringle. "Interest Rate Swaps: A Review of the Issues." Federal Reserve Bank of Atlanta *Economic Review* 73 (November/December 1988): 22-37.

Article 38

Ira G. Kawaller

Interest Rate Swaps versus Eurodollar Strips

An interest rate swap is essentially a contract between two parties, A and B. A calculates his interest obligation on the basis of a floating rate benchmark such as LIBOR. B calculates his obligation based on a known fixed rate. A periodic adjustment is made between the two parties, commensurate with the difference between the two obligations. A swap allows A to convert from a floating rate sensitivity to a fixed rate, and it does the opposite for B. In practice, such swaps are often designed to offset, or "hedge," existing rate exposures.

The Eurodollar futures contract sets rates on Eurodollar time deposits, beginning on a specific forthcoming date. As interest rates rise, futures prices will fall, and vice versa. The futures market participant can maintain either a long position (in which case he will benefit if yields fall) or a short position (which would benefit from rising yields). The participant will have to mark the contract to market on a daily basis and make daily cash settlements for changes in value.

Strips of Eurodollar futures are simply the coordinated purchase or sale of a series of contracts with successive expiration dates, the objective being to "lock in" a rate of return for a given term. The construction of the strip will depend on the prices of the contracts, the amount of principal plus interest received in each quarter and the number of days in each quarter. Actual return from a correctly constructed hedge should come very close to the expected return.

Both interest rate swaps and strips of Eurodollar futures contracts allow a manager to decrease (or increase) exposure to interest rate changes by converting a floating rate exposure to a fixed rate (or vice versa). With swaps, however, the precise fixed rate is readily identifiable. The ultimate outcome with interest rate strips is somewhat uncertain. This article provides a framework for making direct comparisons between Eurodollar strips and interest rate swaps. This will considerably ease the task of identifying the more attractively priced instrument.

Swaps

Figure A summarizes the standard, "plain vanilla" swap agreement. Here two counterparties enter into a contract whereby A calculates an interest rate expense obligation based on a floating interest rate benchmark and B calculates an obligation based on a known, fixed rate.

The amount of the interest expense for which A is responsible will clearly rise in a rising rate environment and fall with declining rates. In contrast, B's obligation is constant, based on the stated, notional amount specified by the swap agreement and the contractually determined fixed interest rate. The swap requires periodic interest payments whereby the difference between the two interest obligations (the net) is passed from the party with the greater obligation to the party with the lesser obligation.

Consider the case where A agrees to pay B based on the London Interbank Offered Rate (LIBOR) on three-month Eurodollar deposits, and B agrees to pay A based on a fixed, money market rate of 10 percent.[1] Assume a notional amount of $100 million for the swap and quarterly interest payments. With each fixing of LIBOR, A establishes his forthcoming interest obligation.

Figure A. Plain Vanilla Swap

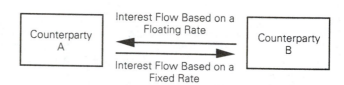

If LIBOR were equal to 10 percent at the first rate setting, for example, no cash adjustment would be made by either party. If LIBOR were 11 percent, counterparty A would pay B $250,000 (i.e., $100 million x 0.11 x $\frac{1}{4}$ – $100 million x 0.10 x $\frac{1}{4}$). If LIBOR were 9 percent, counterparty B would pay A $250,000 (i.e., $100 million x 0.09 x $\frac{1}{4}$ – $100 million x 0.10 x $\frac{1}{4}$). This process would continue for the term of the contract, following each reset of LIBOR.

If both A and B had no exposure to interest rates prior to executing the swap contract, the swap would expose A to the risk of higher short-term rates and the opportunity of lower rates; B's exposure would be the opposite. Often, however, counterparties will use swaps to offset existing exposures. In the first case, the swap is being used as a trading vehicle; in the second, it is being used as a hedge.

Eurodollar Strips

The Eurodollar futures contract sets rates on Eurodollar time deposits, commencing on a specific forthcoming date — the third Wednesday of March, June, September, or December, depending on the contract expiration month. Operationally, futures prices are derived by subtracting an interest rate (in percentage points, carried to two decimal places) from 100. As interest rates rise, futures prices will fall, and vice versa.

The face amount of the Eurodollar futures contract is one million dollars, and its maturity is three months.

---

[1]The terms of the swap will often relate the fixed rate to some benchmark (e.g., 300 basis points above five-year U.S. Treasuries). This allows a general swap agreement to be worked out where the pricing details will reflect market conditions at the time the deal is signed.

Table 1. Strip Hedge Objectives

Quarter	Amount to be Hedged (millions)	Quarterly Futures Interest Rate (%)	Days Per Quarter	Principal Plus Interest (end of quarter)
1	$100.00	7.21	91	$101.82
2	101.82	7.49	91	103.75
3	103.75	7.73	91	105.78
4	105.78	7.95	92	107.93

Table 2. Hedge Ratio Calculations*

Quarter	
1	($100.00 million x (0.0001) x $^{91}/_{360}$)/$25 = 101 contracts
2	($101.82 million x (0.0001) x $^{91}/_{360}$)/$25 = 103 contracts
3	($103.75 million x (0.0001) x $^{91}/_{360}$)/$25 = 105 contracts
4	($105.78 million x (0.0001) x $^{92}/_{360}$)/$25 = 108 contracts

*This hedge construction implicitly assumes that the rate on the Eurodollar strip will move point-for-point with the rate on the exposed instrument. Clearly this assumption may be modified by simply adjusting the hedge ratios by a factor designed to take into account the expected relative rate change.

Every basis-point move in the futures price (yield) translates to a value of $25 (= $1,000,000 x 0.0001 x 90/360). In general, movements in the Eurodollar futures market are closely correlated with yield movements in the underlying Eurodollar time deposit market, although changes are not precisely equal over any given period.

The futures market participant can maintain either a long position (hoping the market will rise in price and decline in yield) or a short position (hoping the market will decline in price and rise in yield). In either case, the participant will be obligated to mark the contract to market on a daily basis and make daily cash settlements for any change in value. This obligation can be terminated at any time by simply "trading out" of the position (i.e., making the opposite transaction to the initial trade). Upon expiration of the contract, any participant still maintaining contracts will make a final mark-to-market adjustment, with the final settlement price based on an average derived from a survey of London bankers who report their perceptions of the cash market three-month LIBOR to the Chicago Mercantile Exchange at the time of the survey.

Strips of Eurodollar futures are simply the coordinated purchase or sale of a series of futures contracts with successive expiration dates. The objective is to "lock in" a rate of return for a term equal to the length of the strip. For example, a strip consisting of contracts with four successive expirations would lock up a one-year term rate, eight successive contracts would lock up a two-year rate, and so on. As is the case with swaps, futures strips may be used to take on additional interest rate risk in the hope of making trading profits, or as an offset or hedge to an existing exposure.

Calculating Strip Yields

What is the term rate that can be expected to result form employing a strip of Eurodollar futures? And how should the hedge be constructed to achieve this rate?

The answers depend on the objectives of the strip creator with respect to the accruing interest. That is,

creation of a synthetic zero-coupon fixed income security would require one particular hedge construction, while creation of a synthetic coupon-bearing security would require another.

The Zero-Coupon Strip

Consider the problem of creating a one-year, zero-coupon strip with four successive contract expirations. Assume the prices for these contracts are 92.79, 92.51, 92.27, and 92.05, respectively. Under these conditions, the hedger would have four hedgeable events designed to lock up rates of 7.21 percent (100 – 92.79) in the first quarter, 7.49 percent (100 – 92.51) in the second quarter, 7.73 percent (100 – 92.27) in the third quarter, and 7.95 percent (100 – 92.05) in the fourth quarter.

To arrive at the number of contracts required for the hedge, the hedger would first determine the amount of principal plus interest at the end of each quarter. Assume the number of days in each of the quarters are 91, 91, 91 and 92, respectively. At the end of the first quarter, the principal plus interest would be calculated as the starting principal plus that principal multiplied by the first futures' interest rate (7.21 percent) multiplied by 91/360.[2] This end-of-quarter value would serve as the amount to be hedged in the second quarter. Table 1 illustrates the process over the four quarters, assuming an initial value of $100 million.

The number of contracts required is found by dividing the value per basis point of each quarter's amount to be hedged (the prior quarter's principal plus interest) by $25, which is the value of the basis point per futures contract. The actual hedge ratio would have to be rounded to a whole number, of course, as futures cannot be bought or sold in fractional units. Table 2 gives the calculations.

[2]The denominator, 360, reflects the convention that LIBOR is quoted as a money market rate, counting the actual number of days during the period in the numerator.

Table 3. Interest Rates Rise to 15 Percent

Quarter	Futures Results*	End-of-Quarter Balances
1	101 contracts x (85.00 – 92.79) x $2500 = –$1.97 million	100.00 million x (1 + 0.15 x $^{91}/_{360}$) – 1.97 million = $101.82 million
2	103 contracts x (85.00 – 92.51) x $2500 = –$1.93 million	101.82 million x (1 + 0.15 x $^{91}/_{360}$) – 1.93 million = $103.75 million
3	105 contracts x (85.00 – 92.27) x $2500 = –$1.91 million	103.75 million x (1 + 0.15 x $^{91}/_{360}$) – 1.91 million = $105.78 million
4	108 contracts x (85.00 – 92.05) x $2500 = –$1.90 million	105.78 million x (1 + 0.15 x $^{92}/_{360}$) – 1.90 million = $107.93 million

* As prices are reflective of percentage points, rather than basis points, the multiplier becomes $25 x 100, or $2500.

Table 4. Interest Rates Decline to 2 Percent

Quarter	Futures Results	End-of-Quarter Balances
1	101 contracts x (98.00 – 92.79) x $2500 = $1.32 million	100.00 million x (1 + 0.02 x $^{91}/_{360}$) + 1.32 million = $101.82 million
2	103 contracts x (98.00 – 92.51) x $2500 = $1.41 million	101.82 million x (1 + 0.02 x $^{91}/_{360}$) + 1.41 million = $103.75 million
3	105 contracts x (98.00 – 92.27) x $2500 = $1.50 million	103.75 million x (1 + 0.02 x $^{91}/_{360}$) + 1.50 million = $105.78 million
4	108 contracts x (98.00 – 92.05) x $2500 = $1.61 million	105.78 million x (1 + 0.02 x $^{92}/_{360}$) + 1.61 million = $107.93 million

Bond-equivalent Yields

Incorporating the concept of the bond-equivalent yield allows us to generalize from this specific example. The bond-equivalent yield for a strip of virtually any length (up to the maximum number of quarterly expirations available) can be derived from Equation 1.

Equation 1.

$$\left(1 + RF1\frac{DQ1}{360}\right)\left(1 + RF2\frac{DQ2}{360}\right) \cdots \left(1 + RFN\frac{DQN}{360}\right)$$
$$= (1 + Reff/P)^{(N \times P/4)}.$$

Here RF1, RF2, and RFN are the respective annual futures rates (100 minus the appropriate futures prices, expressed in decimals). DQ1, DQ2, and DQN are the days in each three-month period beginning with the third Wednesday of the respective future's expiration months.[3] N is the number of quarters in the strip. Reff is the effective annual bond-equivalent yield for the strip. P is the number of periods per year for which compounding is assumed.

The left-hand side of Equation 1 shows the effect of borrowing (or lending) for each quarter at the interest rate designated by the appropriate futures contract. The right-hand side incorporates the effective yield that would be required to generate the same principal plus interest by the end of the term. In all cases, effective yields are approximations, as the periods covered by the futures contracts may either overlap or have gaps.

Despite the fact that futures expire quarterly, one can calculate an effective term rate assuming any compounding frequency. Most likely, the choice of P would reflect the compounding assumptions implicit in the fixed rate quotation of an instrument to which the strip yield may be compared.

If, as in the above example, a one-year strip is arranged with contracts priced at 92.79, 92.51, 92.27, and 92.05, respectively, the target return is 7.93 percent.[4]

Tables 3 and 4 illustrate two extreme cases that demonstrate the robustness of this hedge.

For both tables, end-of-quarter balances are found by investing the initial $100 million at the spot LIBOR and adjusting the ending principal plus interest by the gains or losses on that quarter's hedge. This adjusted figure becomes the principal amount to be rolled over and reinvested. Such practice is consistent with the accounting tradition of allocating hedge results to the quarter for which the hedge is designed. (On a cash flow basis, hedge gains and losses for all contracts are generated daily, and variation margin adjustments are called for. Returns calculated from actual cash flows would therefore differ from the calculations shown.)

Table 3 assumes that LIBOR immediately skyrockets to 15 percent following the initiation of the hedge and remains there. Thus all futures are liquidated at 85.00. Table 4 assumes that LIBOR drops to 2 percent and remains there. Thus all futures are liquidated at 98.00. That both cases result in identical ending balances demonstrates the robustness of the hedge.

Real-World Considerations

It should be noted that the analysis above assumes perfect convergence between LIBOR and the Eurodollar futures rate each time a futures contract expires or is liquidated. A nonzero basis at the time of hedge liquidations could alter the results. The size of the alteration would depend on magnitudes and directions of the basis at liquidation.

---

[3]The number of days in the quarter should be measured by counting from the calendar day of the third Wednesday of the expiration month to that same calendar day three months later (e.g., March 17 to June 17, which measures 92 days).
[4]This result follows from an ending principal plus interest of $107.93 million one year after an initial principal of $100 million. It assumes that P equals one.

Table 5. Worst-Case Scenario

Quarter	Futures Results	End-of-Quarter Balances
1	101 contracts x (84.75 – 92.79) x $2500 = –$2.03 million	100.00 million x (1 + 0.15 x $^{91}/_{360}$) – 2.03 million = $101.76 million
2	103 contracts x (84.75 – 92.51) x $2500 = –$2.00 million	101.76 million x (1 + 0.15 x $^{91}/_{360}$) – 2.00 million = $103.62 million
3	105 contracts x (84.75 – 92.27) x $2500 = –$1.97 million	103.62 million x (1 + 0.15 x $^{91}/_{360}$) – 1.97 million = $105.58 million
4	108 contracts x (84.75 – 92.05) x $2500 = –$1.97 million	105.58 million x (1 + 0.15 x $^{92}/_{360}$) – 1.97 million = $107.65 million

For the long strip (that is, where the futures contracts are originally purchased), a LIBOR at liquidation higher than the rate implied by the futures contract would be desirable. A LIBOR below the futures rate would be undesirable. For the short strip, the opposite would apply.

It is worthwhile to look at some possible adverse market conditions that might apply when futures contracts are liquidated.[5] Assume, for example, that a long strip is created, as in the examples above. With LIBOR at 15 percent, assume the worst case of futures liquidation at 84.75, or a rate of 15.25 percent for each futures contract. The worst-case projected results differ from the results in Table 3 because of the somewhat greater futures losses in each quarter. The differences equal the number of contracts for that quarter's hedge times 25 basis points times $25 per basis point, as Table 5 shows. Because of the greater futures losses, a return of 7.65 percent results, rather than a bond-equivalent yield of 7.93 percent, as initially targeted.

The above calculation demonstrates that an adverse basis of 25 basis points at each hedge liquidation would lower the perfect convergence target by 28 basis points (7.93 – 7.65) — just about one-for-one. But this represents the results for what has been judged to be a worst-case scenario.

In many cases, the actual shortfall would be substantially smaller. It could be virtually negligible in the case where hedges are scheduled for liquidation at or near futures expiration dates. Furthermore, the basis conditions of hedge liquidation could be favorable, in which case the hedge performance would be better than that indicated by the perfect convergence calculation.

Extensions and Refinements

When considering a strip as an alternative to another fixed income security, the user should try to arrange the strip so that it mirrors the cash flow properties of the competing instrument as closely as possible. For example, if the alternative to the strip is a two-year swap, where the fixed payments are scheduled semiannually, the strip should be formulated to replicate semiannual cash disbursements.

Think about the two-year fixed income obligation as if it were a series of four six-month, zero coupon strips, where the bond-equivalent yield of each six-month strip would be calculated and implemented as explained above. The effective rate for the whole two-year period would reflect compounding of all substrip segments. The appropriate general formula is shown in Equation 2.

Equation 2.

$$(1 + BEY1/P)^t (1 + BEY2/P)^t ... (1 + BEYK/P)^t = (1 + R/P)^{Kt},$$

where

BEYi = the bond-equivalent yield of the ith substrip,
P = the assumed number of compounding periods per year,
t = the length of each substrip, in compounding periods and
K = the number of substrips.

Table 6 gives the characteristics relevant to the above synthetic two-year, semiannual-coupon, fixed income construction. Days per quarter are counted rigorously, from the third Wednesday of the expiration month to that calendar day three months later, and the two-quarter strip yields are calculated using the methodology of Equation (1).[6] Given the bond-equivalent yields from Table 6 and Equation 2, the annualized yield to maturity, r, is 9.18 percent.

Table 6. Two-Year, Semiannual-Coupon Synthetic

Contract Expirations	Futures Price	Days Per Quarter	Bond-Equivalent Yield (two-quarter strips)
1	91.22	90	
2	91.34	92	8.91
3	91.21	90	
4	91.04	92	9.08
5	90.87	92	
6	90.90	91	9.37
7	90.82	90	
8	90.75	91	9.37

As this synthetic construction is designed to mimic a security with semiannual coupons, the amount to be hedged in the first, third, fifth or seventh quarter will be the notional amount of the deal. For a $100 million deal, given the respective days in each of these quarters, the hedge ratios are 100, 100, 102 and 100 contracts, respectively (see Table 7). For the remaining quarters, (two,

---

[5]The existence of gaps or overlaps because of the futures expiration cycle can be considered as a special case contributing to this risk.

[6]P in Equation (1) is assumed here to be two, reflecting semiannual compounding.

Table 7. Hedge Construction for $100 Million in Semiannual-Coupon, Two-Year-Maturity Fixed Income Obligation

Quarter		Hedge Ratio
1	$100 million x 0.0001 x $^{90}/_{360}$/25 =	100
2	$100 million x (1 + 0.878 x $^{90}/_{360}$) x 0.0001 x $^{92}/_{360}$/25 =	104
3	$100 million x 0.0001 x $^{90}/_{360}$/25 =	100
4	$100 million x (1 + 0.879 x $^{90}/_{360}$) x 0.0001 x $^{92}/_{360}$/25 =	104
5	$100 million x 0.0001 x $^{92}/_{360}$/25 =	102
6	$100 million x (1 + 0.913 x $^{92}/_{360}$) x 0.0001 x $^{91}/_{360}$/25 =	103
7	$100 million x 0.0001 x $^{90}/_{360}$/25 =	100
8	$100 million x (1 + 0.918 x $^{90}/_{360}$) x 0.0001 x $^{91}/_{360}$/25 =	103

four, six and eight), the calculation takes the original notional amount plus the interest income from the prior quarter, based on that quarter's futures rate. That is, the hedge ratio for the second quarter depends on the futures rate locked up in the first quarter; the hedge ratio for the fourth quarter depends on the third quarter's future's rate; and so on. These calculations are shown in Table 7.

As was the case with the zero-coupon strip construction, the actual outcomes may differ somewhat from the calculated target because of rounding errors and the prospect of imperfect convergence. Thus appropriate allowance for some deviation from these calculations should be given when determining whether or not to choose a strip as the preferred transaction vehicle. With these considerations in mind, failure to choose the alternative with the more (most) attractive yield necessarily leaves money on the table and thus reflects a suboptimal market decision.

Conclusion

Constructing Eurodollar strip trades requires a certain amount of care. In particular, a strip should match as closely as possible the cash flow provisions of the competing alternative instrument. The payoff for making the correct calculation and implementing it properly is an incrementally superior return. There can be no question that choosing the more attractively priced alternative will necessarily enhance performance.

Ira G. Kawaller is vice president-director of the New York office for the Chicago Mercantile Exchange.

This article is reprinted from the September-October 1989 issue of *Financial Analysts Journal*, published by The Financial Analysts Federation, 1633 Broadway, New York, NY 10019.

Article 39

LYON Taming

JOHN J. McCONNELL and EDUARDO S. SCHWARTZ*

ABSTRACT

A Liquid Yield Option Note (LYON) is a zero coupon, convertible, callable, puttable bond. This paper presents a simple contingent claims pricing model for valuing LYONS and uses the model to analyze a specific LYON issue.

A LIQUID YIELD OPTION NOTE (LYON) is a complex security. It is a zero-coupon, convertible, callable, redeemable bond. The complexity of this security is further increased because the prices at which the issuer may call the bond and the prices at which the investor may redeem (or put) the bond escalate through time. Additionally, the bond contains call protection for the investor because the bond may not be called for a prespecified period of time after issuance unless the issuer's stock prices rises above a predesignated level.

This fascinating security was created by Merrill Lynch White Weld Capital Markets Groups in 1985. In the spring of 1985 Waste Management, Inc. and Staley Continental, Inc. were the first two issuers of this security, with Merrill Lynch acting as the underwriter.[1] Because of its novelty and complexity, potential issuers find this security difficult to analyze. Two issues are of paramount concern to LYON issuers. First, is the security "correctly" priced at the initial offering? The issuer is concerned that the security not be underpriced at the initial offering and the underwriter is concerned that the security not be overpriced. Second, the issuer is concerned that the security not be converted "too soon" after issuance. Issuers are concerned that premature conversion will dilute the issuer's earning per share and that the valuable tax savings associated with the LYON will be dissipated.

To address these concerns (and others) we were engaged to analyze the Liquid Yield Option Note. To do so, we developed a LYON pricing model using modern contingent claims pricing techniques. In developing the model we were especially concerned that it be commercially useable. Thus, our goal was to develop a model that is both rich enough to capture that salient ingredients of this complex security and simple enough to be implemented with an enhanced personal computer. Because of the complexity of the security, the final pricing equation can be solved only with numerical techniques. Thus, the focus of this paper is on the practical application of contingent claim pricing models that can be solved only with numerical techniques. The contribution of this paper is that it reports

* Purdue University and University of British Columbia, respectively. Thomas Patrick, Lynne Dinzole, Lee Coles, and Robert Moulton-Ely of Merrill Lynch White Weld Capital Markets Group were especially helpful to us in developing the ideas presented in this paper.

[1] Subsequently, LYONs were issued by the G. Heileman Brewing Co., Merrill Lynch & Co. and Joseph E. Seagram & Son, Inc. and others.

on an actual case situation in which numerical solution techniques were used to analyze a security pricing problem.

We first describe in some detail a specific LYON issue. We then present a pricing model which we shall refer to as the commercially-useable LYON pricing model. As will be quite evident, this simplified pricing model takes a number of liberties with the "state-of-the-art" in contingent claim pricing analysis.[2] Following our presentation of the commercially-useable LYON pricing model we discuss its limitations and simplifications and suggest ways in which the various limiting assumptions could be relaxed so as to yield a theoretically more sophisticated model. The benefit of a more sophisticated model is that it would likely increase the accuracy of the resulting analysis. The cost is that it would increase the difficulty of implementing and using the model. As it turns out, the commercially-useable LYON pricing model, although quite simple in comparison with a theoretically more sophisticated model, appears to work well in practice, in that the theoretical LYON prices generated with the simplified model closely tracked the reported market closing prices for both the Waste Management and the Staley Continental LYONs over the first several weeks following their issuance. Whether the accuracy of the simple model is sufficient for all commercial uses depends, of course, on the needs of the user.

Following our presentation of the simplified LYON pricing model we present our application of the model to the valuation of the Waste Management LYON. We then investigate the sensitivity of theoretical LYON values to changes in the characteristics of the issuer, the economic environment and the security. Finally, using the same data, we illustrate the way in which the model can be used to calculate the LYON's optimal conversion price. We end the paper with a brief summary and some concluding remarks.

I. The LYON

An appreciation of the LYON pricing model can perhaps best be gained by considering a specific issue. The one that we consider here was issued by Waste Management, Inc. on April 12, 1985.

According to the indenture agreement, each Waste Management LYON has a face value of $1,000 and matures on January 21, 2001. If the security has not been called, converted, or redeemed (i.e., put to the issuer) prior to that date, and if the issuer does not default, the investor receives $1,000 per bond. At any time prior to maturity (or on the maturity date), the investor may elect to convert the bond into 4.36 shares of Waste Management common stock. Additionally, however, the investor can elect to put the bond to Waste Management beginning on June 30, 1988, and on each subsequent anniversary date, at fixed exercise prices that escalate through time.[3] The put exercise prices are:

---

[2] An excellent survey of recent applications of contingent claims pricing analysis in corporate finance is provided by Mason and Merton [6].

[3] The investor must give Waste Management at least 30 days' notice and not more than 90 day's notice prior to exercising the put option.

Date	Put Price		Date	Put Price
June 30, 1988	$301.87		June 30, 1995	613.04
June 30, 1989	333.51		June 30, 1996	669.45
June 30, 1990	375.58		June 30, 1997	731.06
June 30, 1991	431.08		June 30, 1998	798.34
June 30, 1992	470.75		June 30, 1999	871.80
June 30, 1993	514.07		June 30, 2000	952.03
June 30, 1994	561.38			

Finally, Waste Management can elect to call the LYON at fixed exercise prices that escalate through time. Although the issuer may call the LYON immediately after issuance, the investor does receive some call protection because Waste Management may not call the bond prior to June 30, 1987 unless the price of the Waste Management common stock rises above $86.01.[4] On the LYON issue date, the Waste Management stock price was $52.125. The LYON call prices are:

Date	Call Price		Date	Call Price
At Issuance	$272.50		June 30, 1994	563.63
June 30, 1986	297.83		June 30, 1995	613.04
June 30, 1987	321.13		June 30, 1996	669.45
June 30, 1988	346.77		June 30, 1997	731.06
June 30, 1989	374.99		June 30, 1998	798.34
June 30, 1990	406.00		June 30, 1999	871.80
June 30, 1991	440.08		June 30, 2000	952.03
June 30, 1992	477.50		At maturity	1,000.00
June 30, 1993	518.57			

Additionally, if the LYON is called between the dates shown above, the call price is adjusted to reflect the "interest" accrued since the immediately preceding call date shown in the schedule.[5]

As our brief description indicates, analysis of a LYON is not a simple matter. To value a LYON it is necessary to take into account the unique characteristics of the security, the issuer, and the economic environment in which the security is issued. Furthermore, the security can be valued only if it is possible to identify the conversion and redemption strategies to be followed by investors and the call strategy to be followed by the issuer. In the spirit of Brennan and Schwartz [2], [4] and Ingersoll [5], we assume that the issuer follows a call policy that minimizes the value of the LYON at each point in time and that the investor follows conversion and redemption strategies that maximize the value of the LYON at each point in time. We refer to these as the optimal call, the optimal conversion, and the optimal redemption strategies, respectively. The optimal call, conversion, and redemption strategies depend upon, among other things, the bond's conver-

[4] Waste Management must give the investor at least 15 days' notice prior to exercising the call option.

[5] The imputed interest is computed by increasing the call prices at a rate of 9.0% per year compounded semiannually.

sion ratio and upon the call and redemption schedules specified in the bond's indenture agreement.

A. Optimal Conversion Strategy

Because the investor seeks to maximize the value of the LYON, the investor will never convert if the market value of the LYON is greater than the value of the stock into which the LYON can be converted. That is, the LYON will never be converted as long as its market value exceeds its conversion value. Contrarily, because the investor would receive an immediate gain from conversion, the investor would always convert if the value of the LYON were less than its conversion value. Thus, investors will optimally convert the LYON when the value of the security just equals its conversion value. As a consequence, the value of an outstanding LYON must be greater than its conversion value.

B. Optimal Redemption Strategy

On each redemption date the investor must choose between holding the LYON and putting it to the issuer for the prespecified redemption value. However, because the investor seeks to maximize the market value of the security, on any anniversary date the investor will not put the LYON to the issuer if the security's value is greater than its redemption price at that time. Contrarily, because the investor would receive an immediate gain from redemption, the investor would always redeem the LYON if the LYON value were less than its redemption price on any redemption date. Thus, investors optimally will redeem the LYON when the LYON's market value just equals its redemption value. At no time will the value of the LYON be less than its redemption value.

The redemption value, of course, is the exercise price of a put option. The twist here is that unlike a conventional put option, the exercise price of the put option imbedded in a LYON changes through time.

C. Optimal Call Strategy

On the one hand, because the issuer seeks to minimize the value of the LYON, the issuer will never allow the market value of the security to exceed its call price. On the other hand, the issuer will never call the LYON when its value is less than the call price because this would convey an immediate windfall gain to the investor. Thus, the issuer will optimally call the LYON when the LYON's market value just equals its call price. When the issuer calls the LYON, the investor can elect to receive either the cash call price or the conversion value of the security, whichever is greater. As a consequence, at any point in time, the value of a callable LYON will not exceed the greater of its call price or conversion value.

To determine the equilibrium value of the LYON, we assume that investors and issuers follow the optimal conversion, redemption and call policies and that each party expects the other also to follow the optimal strategy. Under the optimal strategies, the value of the LYON is bounded from above by the maximum of its call price and conversion value and it is bounded from below by the maximum of its redemption price and conversion value.

II. The LYON Pricing Model

To derive the LYON pricing model we assume that the value of the LYON depends upon the issuer's stock price (S) and that instantaneous changes in the issuer's stock price follow a diffusion process with constant variance (σ_s). That is,

$$dS = [S\mu - D(S, t)]dt + S\sigma_s dz_s \qquad (1)$$

where $S(t)$ is the issuer's stock price at time t; μ is the (possibly stochastic) instantaneous total expected return on the issuer's common stock; σ_s is the standard deviation of the rate of return on the issuer's common stock; and $D(s, t)$ is the total rate of dividends paid to stockholders at time t. In applications of the model, we allow dividend payments to take the general form

$$D(S, t) = d_y S + de^{g(t-t_0)} \qquad (2)$$

where d_y is the issuer's dividend yield; d is the issuer's dividend rate; g is the constant growth rate of dividends; and t_0 is the issue date of the LYON. This general form for dividend payments permits either a constant dividend yield (when $d = 0$) or a constant dividend growth rate (when $d_y = 0$).

We further assume that capital markets are perfect, that investors and issuers have costless access to all relevant information, and that the term structure of interest rates if flat and known with certainty. Then, given the usual arbitrage arguments, the value of the LYON must satisfy the partial differential equation

$$\tfrac{1}{2}\sigma_s^2 S^2 L_{ss} + [rS - D(S, t)]L_s + L_t - rL = 0 \qquad (3)$$

where r is the known, constant interest rate and subscripts represent partial derivatives.

Solution of (3) subject to four boundary conditions gives the theoretical value of the LYON. The boundary conditions follow from the optimal conversion, redemption and call strategies and from the maturity condition specified in the LYON contract.

A. The Maturity Condition

At the maturity date of the contract, the value of the LYON will be the greater of the conversion value or the face value of the contract:

$$L(S, T) = \text{Max}(C_r S, F) \qquad (4)$$

where C_r is the number of shares of the issuer's common stock into which the LYON can be converted (i.e., C_r is the conversion ratio and $C_r S$ is the conversion value of the LYON); F is the face value of the LYON at maturity (typically specified to be \$1,000); and T is the maturity date of the contract.

B. The Conversion Condition

At any point in time, the value of the LYON must be greater than or equal to its conversion value:

$$L(S, t) \geq C_r S \tag{5}$$

C. The Redemption (or Put) Condition

At any redemption date the value of the LYON must be greater than or equal to the then prevailing redemption price:

$$L(S, t_p) \geq P(t_p) \tag{6}$$

where $P(t_p)$ is the redemption (or put) price at time t_p.

D. The Call Condition

At every point in time, the value of the LYON must be less than or equal to the greater of the call price and the conversion value:

$$L(S, t) \leq \text{Max}\{C(t), C_r S\} \tag{7}$$

where $C(t)$ is the call price of the LYON at time t.

Partial differential equation (3) subject to the boundary conditions (4), (5), (6) and (7) gives the value of the LYON under our set of assumptions. Although there is no known closed form solution to this equation, the virtue of this simplified model is that it can be solved easily by means of numerical methods with an enhanced personal computer. In our applications of the model, the method of finite differences was used to solve (3) on an IBM personal computer. Solution of a typical problem required less than 10 minutes.

III. Discussion of the Simplified LYON Pricing Model

It is readily apparent that the commercially-useable LYON pricing model embodies a number of simplifying assumptions. These assumptions were dictated largely by the circumstances under which the model was developed. For the most part, however, the assumptions seem justifiable given the requirements of the model. In this section we discuss some of these assumptions in more detail, suggest ways in which the assumptions can be relaxed, and consider the costs and benefits of relaxing these assumptions.

Perhaps the most egregious assumptions are that the value of the LYON depends upon the value of the issuer's common stock rather than the total market value of the firm and that the term structure of interest rates is flat and known with certainty.

As an alternative to the assumption that the LYON value depends upon the value of the issuer's common stock which follows a diffusion process with constant variance, a theoretically more palatable assumption is that the total value of the firm follows a diffusion process with constant variance and that the LYON and the issuer's stock are both contingent claims that depend upon the total value of the firm. This assumption is theoretically more desirable because it would more appropriately capture the default risk of the LYON. The assumption that the value of the LYON depends upon the value of the issuer's common stock precludes the possibility of bankruptcy. Under this assumption, at the maturity date, the investor receives either the face value of the LYON or the conversion value, whichever is greater. Under the alternative assumption, the maturity condition would be altered such that the investor would receive either the greater of the conversion value of the security or the lesser of the face value of the bond or the total value of the firm.[6] Our simplifying assumption, by precluding bankruptcy, means that the simplified model overstates the value of the LYON. Quite clearly, the lower the probability of bankruptcy, the smaller the overstatement of value.

In actual applications of the model, we do, however, compensate for this overstatement of value. Rather than using the risk-free rate of interest as the discount rate, we use an intermediate-term interest rate that is grossed up to capture the default risk of the issuer. This higher discount rate tends to reduce the value of the LYON.[7]

The more vexing assumption is that the term structure of interest rates is flat and known with certainty. This assumption is vexing for two opposing reasons. On the one hand, one of the features of the LYON is the ability of the investor to put the LYON to the issuer at prespecified redemption prices. The redemption feature will be especially valuable if interest rates rise dramatically (and unexpectedly) during the life of the LYON. In that case, the investor would elect to cash in the LYON for the redemption price and invest the proceeds elsewhere. The assumption that future interest rates are known with certainty reduces the value of the put option and, consequently, tends to understate the value of the LYON.

On the other hand, the call option is especially valuable to the issuer if interest rates fall dramatically (and unexpectedly) in the future. In that case, the issuer would call the LYON and issue an alternative security with a lower "cost." For this reason, ignoring interest rate uncertainty tends to overstate the value of the LYON. Which of the two opposing interest rate effects is of greater importance in pricing the LYON depends, among other things, upon the call and redemption schedules specified in a specific indenture agreement. Of course, there are ways in which the model could be expanded to account for interest rate uncertainty. One possible approach, which has been successful in other contexts, is the two factor model of interest rate uncertainty developed by Brennan and Schwartz [3]. We should note that the simplified model does take into account the level of interest rates through the term, r, in equation (3) and changes in r do permit sensitivity analysis with respect to changes in this variable.

The disadvantage of the simplified LYON pricing model is that it may contain

[6] This assumes that the issuer has only two securities outstanding—common stock and the LYON. A model could be developed (as in Brennan and Schwartz [4]) which would allow for multiple senior securities.

[7] A second desirable feature of the alternative assumption is that it is more reasonable to assume that the value of the firm follows a process with constant variance than to assume that the value of the stock follows a process with constant variance. This is because the equity of the firm and all of the firm's senior securities can be considered contingent claims on the total value of the firm. If the total return on the firm follows a process with constant variance, the variance of return on equity must be stochastic because the existence of the firms' senior securities (including the LYON) will affect the stochastic process followed by the stock price.

errors in valuing the LYON and, because of the various opposing effects, the direction of the errors is unknown. The benefit of the simplified model is that it reduces substantially the difficulty of implementing the model. A theoretically more elegant model would encompass three stochastic variables—the value of the issuing firm and the two interest rate factors. Solution of a partial differential equation with three stochastic variables is substantially more difficult than solving a single variable model. Perhaps more importantly, though, are the reduced estimation demands of the simplified model. Implementation of a theoretically more complete model would require estimation of the total value of the firm and of the volatility of the total value of the firm and it would require estimation of the market price of interest rate risk and the parameters of the two factor interest rate process.

The degree to which a theoretically more sophisticated model would enhance the analysis is, of course, an empirical issue for which we do not have a ready answer. For most reasonably secure issuers a more appropriate accounting for default risk would probably have little effect on the theoretical LYON values. Additionally, as regards the question of introducing a stochastic interest rate, we can take comfort from the conclusions of Brennan and Schwartz [4]. They compare traditional convertible bond prices generated by means of a nonstochastic interest rate model with prices generated by means of a single factor stochastic interest rate process and conclude that " . . . for a reasonable range of interest rates the errors from the certain interest rate model are likely to be slight, and, therefore, for practical purposes it may be preferable to use this simpler model for valuing convertible bonds" (pp. 925–926). Thus, although the commercially-useable LYON pricing model is relatively simple, for most practical purposes it may well be more than adequate given the costs of implementing a more sophisticated model.

IV. Application of the LYON Pricing Model to Waste Management, Inc.

On April 12, 1985 the Waste Management LYON was issued at a price of $250.00 per bond. On April 11, 1985 the closing price of the Waste Management common stock was $52.125. On the issue day, the closing price of the Waste Management LYON was $258.75.

To apply the LYON pricing model to Waste Management, Inc. it was necessary to estimate the volatility of the company's common stock and to specify an appropriate interest rate. The common stock volatility used was the standard deviation of daily returns over the 100 trading days prior to issuance of the LYON. The estimated volatility is 30% per year. Whether this is the appropriate estimation period or technique is an open question—which we cannot resolve here—but sensitivity analysis does allow us to determine the likely impact of errors in the estimate of the stock price volatility.

The interest rate used is 11.21% per year. The rate was chosen because on the issue date this was the approximate yield of intermediate term bonds of the same risk rating as the Waste Management bond.

Table I

Waste Management Common Stock Prices, Theoretical LYON
Prices, And Reported LYON Market Prices from April 12, 1985
Through May 10, 1985

Date	Closing Stock Price	Closing LYON Market Price	High LYON Market Price	Low LYON Market Price	LYON Theoretical Price
April 12, 1985	$52¼	$258.75			$262.7
15	53	258.75	$260.0	$258.75	264.6
16	52⅝	257.5	257.5	257.5	263.7
17	52	—	—	—	262.1
18	52⅜	257.5	275.5	255.0	263.0
19	52¾	257.5	257.5	257.5	264.0
22	52½	257.5	257.5	257.5	263.3
23	53¼	260.0	260.0	257.5	265.3
24	54¼	265.0	265.0	262.5	267.9
25	54¼	265.0	265.0	262.5	267.9
26	54	265.0	265.0	265.0	267.2
29	53¾	260.0	265.0	260.0	266.6
30	52⅛	260.0	260.0	257.5	262.4
May 1, 1985	49¾	252.5	257.5	252.5	256.7
2	50½	250.0	252.5	250.0	258.4
3	50¾	252.5	252.5	252.5	259.0
6	50½	252.5	255.5	251.25	258.4
7	50⅞	255.0	256.25	252.5	259.3
8	50¾	253.75	257.5	253.75	259.0
9	51¼	255.0	255.0	253.75	260.3
10	53⅛	260.0	260.0	255.0	265.0

Finally, the dividend yield of the Waste Management common stock was specified as a constant 1.6% per year. This yield was chosen because the company's previous quarterly dividend payment was $.20 per share. With recent stock prices of approximately $50.00 per share, this dividend payment provides an annual yield of 1.6% (i.e., 4 × $.20/$50.00).

With these parameters, and the data given in the Waste Management prospectus, the theoretical LYON price on the issue date was $262.70. As the data in Table I indicate, over the first four weeks following issuance, the theoretical LYON prices closely track the reported market closing prices, although there is a tendency for the model prices to overstate slightly the reported closing prices. Whether this slight overstatement in prices is due to the simplicity of the model or due to an error in the estimation of the stock volatility is not known. Apparently, though, the model is sufficiently accurate to provide a rough guideline for the pricing of new LYON issues. Other LYON issuers would, of course, have different characteristics than Waste Management and would be issuing the security in other interest rate environments. For that reason it is interesting to investigate the sensitivity of the theoretical LYON value to changes in the values of the parameters used in the base case example.

Panel A of Table II illustrates the sensitivity of the LYON price to changes in the level of the issuer's stock price and to changes in the issuer's stock price volatility. It should come as no surprise that the LYON value increases mono-tonically with increases in the issuer's stock price and with increases in the volatility of the issuer's stock price. Additionally, as is the case with other stock price contingent claims, the LYON value is highly sensitive to changes in the volatility of the underlying stock. The result emphasizes the importance of accurate stock volatility measurement procedures—an area in which the volume of research now approaches that of a small cottage industry.

Panel B of Table II illustrates the sensitivity of LYON values to changes in the issuer's dividend yield. The table indicates that the LYON value declines monotonically with increases in the issuer's dividend yield. This occurs because a higher dividend yield implies a lower expected rate of stock price appreciation. Additionally, the value of dividends is not impounded in the LYON price because the LYON investor does not receive dividend payments. Perhaps somewhat surprisingly, the LYON values are not terribly sensitive to changes in the dividend yield. For example, for the base case stock price of $52.125, an increase in the dividend yield from 1.6% to 3.0% reduces the LYON value by only about $3.00 per bond.

In a separate analysis not shown here, LYON values were computed with the dividend specified to grow at a constant rate (rather than being specified as a constant yield). That analysis indicated that the theoretical LYON values are even less sensitive to major changes in the assumed dividend growth rate.

Panel C of Table II illustrates the sensitivity of the theoretical LYON values

Table II

Sensitivity Of The Theoretical LYON Values To Changes In The Issuer's Stock Price, Stock Price Volatility, And Dividend Yield And To Changes In The Interest Rate

A. Sensitivity of LYON Values To Changes In The Issuer's Stock Price Volatility

Stock Price[a] (per share)	Stock Price Volatility[b] (per year)				
	0.10	0.20	0.30	0.40	0.50
$46.00	$223.23	$236.01	$247.34	$257.22	$265.10
47.00	224.67	237.92	249.48	259.44	267.33
48.00	226.26	239.92	251.69	261.71	269.59
49.00	228.02	242.03	253.96	264.03	271.90
50.00	229.94	244.24	256.30	266.39	274.23
51.00	232.03	246.54	258.71	268.80	276.60
52.00	234.28	248.94	261.18	271.26	279.00
53.00	236.71	251.44	263.71	273.76	281.44
54.00	239.29	254.04	266.31	276.30	283.91
55.00	242.04	256.73	268.97	278.88	286.40
56.00	244.94	259.51	271.68	281.51	288.93
57.00	247.99	262.38	274.46	284.17	291.49
58.00	251.19	265.34	277.29	286.87	294.08
59.00	254.52	268.39	280.18	289.62	296.69

Table II—*continued*

B. Sensitivity of LYON Values To Changes In The
   Issuer's Dividend Yield

Stock Price[a] (per share)	Dividend Yield[c] (per year)			
	0.0%	1.6%	3.0%	5.0%
$46.00	$250.50	$247.34	$244.84	$241.34
47.00	252.72	249.48	246.90	243.28
48.00	255.00	251.69	249.03	245.31
49.00	257.34	253.96	251.24	247.40
50.00	259.74	256.30	253.52	249.58
51.00	262.20	258.71	255.87	251.83
52.00	264.72	261.18	258.29	254.16
53.00	267.30	263.71	260.78	256.57
54.00	269.93	266.31	263.34	259.05
55.00	272.62	268.97	265.96	261.61
56.00	275.36	271.68	268.65	264.25
57.00	278.14	274.46	271.40	266.96
58.00	280.98	277.29	274.22	269.74
59.00	283.86	280.18	277.10	272.60

C. Sensitivity of LYON Values To Changes In The Interest
   Rate

Stock Price[a] (per share)	Interest Rate[d] (per year)				
	7.21%	9.21%	11.21%	13.21%	15.21%
$46.00	$301.36	$264.73	$247.34	$235.80	$228.43
47.00	302.19	266.38	249.48	238.27	231.13
48.00	303.07	268.10	251.69	240.82	233.91
49.00	304.01	269.89	253.96	243.43	236.75
50.00	305.00	271.74	256.30	246.10	239.66
51.00	306.04	273.66	258.71	248.85	242.63
52.00	307.14	275.64	261.18	251.66	245.66
53.00	308.29	277.69	263.71	254.53	248.75
54.00	309.49	279.81	266.31	257.46	251.90
55.00	310.76	281.98	268.97	260.45	255.11
56.00	312.07	284.22	271.68	263.50	258.38
57.00	313.44	286.51	274.46	266.60	261.70
58.00	314.87	288.87	277.29	269.77	265.07
59.00	316.35	291.29	280.18	272.98	268.49

[a] Base case stock price is $52.125 per share.
[b] Base case stock price volatility is 0.20 per year.
[c] Base case dividend yield is 1.6% per year.
[d] Base case interst rate is 11.21% per year.

to changes in the discount rate. As we would anticipate, the LYON value declines monotonically as the interest rate increases.

In evaluating our example LYON we have proceeded as if the terms of the contract were given and have analyzed the sensitivity of the LYON value to the issuer's stock price volatility and dividend payment policy and the level of interest rates. However, the more likely situation is one in which these parameters are given and the issuer wishes to analyze the effect of changes in the terms of the contract on the LYON price. The LYON pricing model permits an analysis of the various tradeoffs between the terms of the contract and the LYON price. For example, the issuer may wish to examine the effect on the LYON price of changes in the conversion ratio or of changes in the schedules of put prices and call prices specified in the LYON indenture.

Illustrating the sensitivity of the theoretical LYON value to changes in the conversion ratio and the redemption and call schedules is a somewhat more complicated procedure because there exists an infinite number of possible ratios and schedules. However, to give some indication of the sensitivity of the LYON price to changes in the redemption and call schedules, Table III presents values of the LYON with and without the call and redemption features. Column 1 gives the issuer's stock price, Column 2 presents the value of the LYON with the redemption and call schedules as specified in the Waste Management prospectus, Column 3 gives the value of the LYON without the call option (but with the redemption option), Column 4 gives the value of the LYON without the redemption option (but with the call option), and Column 5 gives the value of the LYON without the call option and without the redemption option. Thus, Column 5 gives the value of a zero-coupon convertible bond.

As the table indicates, the call option is valuable to the issuer. When the call option is removed, the LYON value increases. Similarly, the redemption option is valuable to the investor. When the redemption option is removed, the LYON value declines. The two effects are not symmetric. Removal of the call feature in the base case increases the value of the LYON by about $20.00, whereas removal of the redemption option reduces the value of the LYON by almost $50.00. Nevertheless, when both features are removed (in Column 5) the LYON value is almost the same as when the LYON contains both features. Obviously, the value of the LYON is not merely the sum of the values of its individual components. Each of the features of this complex security interacts with the others to determine the security's value.

V. The Optimal Stock Price to Convert a LYON

An important feature of the LYON is that issuers may deduct the imputed interest costs of the security without any offsetting cash outflow to investors. This tax shelter may be valuable to LYON issuers. Once the LYON is converted, however, this tax shield disappears. For this reason, LYON issuers may be concerned that investors will convert their LYON prematurely.

At any point in time, the investor can choose to convert the LYON. In deciding whether to convert, the investor weighs the value of the dividends he gives up by continuing to hold the LYON against the value of the downside risk protection that he gives up by converting the LYON to the issuer's common stock. The downside risk protection is provided by the redemption option held by the investor.

In general, when the dividend yield of the issuer's stock is relatively low, the benefits of conversion (to obtain the dividend) also will be relatively low. In the

Table III

Analysis Of The Value Of A LYON With And Without The Call And Redemption Options

Stock Price[a] (per share)	Callable Redeemable[b] LYON (per bond)	Noncallable Redeemable LYON (per bond)	Callable Nonredeemable LYON (per bond)	Noncallable Nonredeemable LYON (per bond)
$45.00	$245.28	$264.85	$181.94	$244.08
46.00	247.34	267.26	186.48	246.92
47.00	249.48	269.72	191.02	249.79
48.00	251.69	272.22	195.58	252.69
49.00	253.96	274.76	200.14	255.63
50.00	256.30	277.34	204.72	258.60
51.00	258.71	279.96	209.30	261.60
52.00	261.18	282.62	213.89	264.63
53.00	263.71	285.31	218.49	267.69
54.00	266.31	288.04	223.10	270.78
55.00	268.97	290.81	227.72	273.90
56.00	271.68	293.61	232.34	277.05
57.00	274.46	296.44	236.98	280.22
58.00	277.29	299.31	241.62	283.43
59.00	280.18	302.22	246.27	286.66
60.00	283.13	305.15	250.93	289.92

[a] Base case stock price is $52.125 per share.
[b] This column represents the base case. The call and redemption schedules in the base case are taken from the Waste Management LYON prospectus (see Section I).

extreme, when the underlying common stock pays no dividend, there is no incentive for the investor ever to convert the LYON into common stock. Similarly, for low dividend paying stocks there is relatively little incentive for the investor to convert the LYON into common stock. However, even for low dividend paying stocks, if the stock price rises high enough, it will be so far above the put price that the downside protection provided by the investor's put option become negligible. In that case, the investor will decide optimally to convert to common stock.

The LYON pricing model can be used to calculate the stock price at which it is optimal to convert a LYON. The optimal conversion stock price is the price at which the investor is just indifferent between holding the LYON and converting to common stock. At any stock price above this critical point, the investor is better off to convert to common stock. At any stock price below this critical point, the investor is better off holding the LYON.

The critical conversion stock price is that price at which the present value of the future dividends forgone by continuing to hold the LYON just equals the present value of the downside protection forgone if the investor converts to common stock. The present value of the downside protection forgone is the expected loss to the investor if he converts now and the conversion value of the LYON at maturity (if the investor had held the LYON) turns out to be less than the security's face value at that date.

In most cases, the critical conversion stock price would imply a LYON value that exceeds the specified call price. Thus, in most cases, if issuers follow the call policy that minimizes the value of the LYON, the issuer would call the bond prior to the point at which the investor would optimally convert. To calculate the stock price at which it is optimal for the investor to convert, it is necessary to assume that the issuer follows a policy of never calling the bond or, alternatively, to assume that the bond is noncallable. With this assumption, the critical stock price can be determined by solving equation (3) subject to boundary conditions (4), (5) and (6). At the critical stock price, the value of the LYON is equal to its conversion value. As an illustration, Column 2 of Table IV displays the stock price at which it would be optimal for an issuer to convert the Waste Management LYON on each anniversary date. At the issue date (or immediately thereafter) the stock price would have to increase to $129.50 per share. As time progresses, the critical stock price increases. The critical stock price increases for two reasons. First, as time passes, the present value of the dividends forgone by holding the LYON declines. Secondly, because the redemption prices of the LYON increases through time, the value of the downside risk protection for holding the LYON increases. Both of these effects reduce the incentive to convert. However, with two years remaining to maturity, the optimal conversion price declines. This occurs because the critical conversion stock price at the maturity date of the LYON equals the bond's face value divided by the conversion ratio. In this case that critical value is $1,000/4.36 = $229.36. Because the optimal conversion value previously calculated is above that level, the critical price declines as the term-to-maturity of the bond becomes shorter.

Table IV presents the optimal conversion price for one set of parameters. However, the model is flexible. Issuers that are concerned about premature

Table IV

The Stock Price At Which It Is Optimal To Convert A Waste Management LYON

Anniversary Date	Optimal Conversion[a] Stock Price (per share)
At Issue	$129.50
June 30, 1985	132.00
June 30, 1986	145.00
June 30, 1987	158.50
June 30, 1988	173.50
June 30, 1989	194.50
June 30, 1990	217.00
June 30, 1991	238.50
June 30, 1992	257.00
June 30, 1993	273.00
June 30, 1994	287.00
June 30, 1995	301.50
June 30, 1996	316.00
June 30, 1997	329.50
June 30, 1998	339.00
June 30, 1999	340.00
June 30, 2000	317.50
January 21, 2001	229.36

[a] Data used to calculate the optimal conversion stock price are taken from the base case example and the Waste Management LYON prospectus.

conversion could use the LYON pricing model to test the sensitivity of the optimal conversion price to changes in the terms of the contract and to changes in dividend policy.

VI. Conclusion

Following the pathbreaking work by Black and Scholes [1] and Merton [7], contingent claims pricing methodology has been applied to the pricing and analysis of a wide variety of securities—put options, convertible bonds, warrants, forward contracts, futures contracts, mortgage-backed securities and many others. Models for analyzing some of these securities give rise to closed-form solutions. Models for many others can be solved only with numerical techniques. Those models with closed-form solutions—especially stock option pricing models—have been readily adopted by practical market participants. Those models requiring numerical solution techniques have not yet met wide acceptance, probably because of limitations imposed by the lack of availability of the computer hardware and software needed to implement the models. In this paper we report on one case in which numerical solution techniques were used in a practical situation to solve a simplified model for pricing and analyzing a complex security. Presumably, as more powerful personal computers evolve and as the availability of the software used with numerical solution techniques increases, market practitioners will find other situations in which contingent claims pricing models that can be solved only with numerical techniques can be of use in analyzing complex securities.

REFERENCES

1. F. Black and M. S. Scholes. "The Pricing of Options and Corporate Liabilities." *Journal of Political Economy*, 81 (May–June 1973), 637–59.
2. M. J. Brennan and E. S. Schwartz. "Convertible Bonds: Valuation and Optimal Strategies for Call and Conversion." *Journal of Finance*, 32 (December 1977), 1699–1715.
3. ———. "A Continuous Time Approach to the Pricing of Bonds." *Journal of Banking and Finance*, 3 (July 1979), 133–55.
4. ———. "Analyzing Convertible Securities." *Journal of Financial and Quantitative Analysis*, 15 (November 1980), 907–29.
5. J. E. Ingersoll, Jr. "A Contingent-Claims Valuation of Convertible Securities." *Journal of Financial Economics*, 4 (May 1977), 289–382.
6. S. P. Mason and R. C. Merton. "The Role of Contingent Claims Analysis in Corporate Finance." in *Recent Advances in Corporate Finance*, E. I. Altman and M. G. Subrahmanyam, Editors, Homewood, IL: Richard D. Irwin, 1985.
7. R. C. Merton. "The Theory of Rational Option Pricing." *Bell Journal of Economics and Management Science*, 4 (Spring 1973), 141–83.

DISCUSSION

SCOTT P. MASON*: This paper by John McConnell and Eduardo Schwartz (M&S) concerns the pricing of Liquid Yield Option Notes (LYONs) through an application of Contingent Claims Analysis (CCA). The paper is an excellent example of the art of striking a balance between rigor and practicality in applying CCA to real-world problems. I will try to keep my comments consistent with this "trade-off" spirit of the paper since it is easy to describe (as M&S do) more rigorous or elegant approaches to the LYON pricing problem.

The approach that M&S take is to treat the LYON as a single security which is a function of the firm's stock price. As discussed in the paper, it would be more complete to recognize the role of interest rate uncertainty but the trade-off between the practicality and increased accuracy of this approach is questionable. At this junction I might have explored the possibility of viewing the LYON as a callable/puttable unit comprised of a risky zero coupon bond and a warrant which requires the use of the bond as scrip to exercise. The merit of this approach is to underscore the fact that the LYON is made up of a warrant, not a call option, and therefore has a dilutive effect on the firm's equity. It is also true that with this approach the discount rate for the risky discount bond must be specified as opposed to a discount rate for the entire LYON.

Furthermore, with regards to M&S's specification of a single risk adjusted discount rate for the LYONs problem, I would have specified the short risk free rate of interest as time dependent in a manner consistent with the implied forward rates in the U.S. Treasury term structure. I would have then priced the

---

* Harvard University

risky zero coupon bond off the yield of the risk free zero coupon bond of the same maturity, possibly making the spread a function of time and the level of the stock price.

The contribution of M&S's work is its case-like treatment of the many practical problems of applying CCA to the pricing of an actual complex security. My comments simply serve to point out that there is more than one way to approximate the CCA approach to the LYONs pricing problem.

Article 40

The Pricing of Bull and Bear Floating Rate Notes: An Application of Financial Engineering

Donald J. Smith

Donald J. Smith is an Assistant Professor of Finance and Economics at the School of Management, Boston University, Boston, MA.

■ Financial engineering can be described as the construction of a security or a portfolio of securities with an otherwise unavailable risk-return configuration. A classic example of financial engineering is the recent issuance of floating rate notes (FRNs) with nontraditional coupon reset formulas. A traditional FRN resets the coupon rate periodically at some fixed margin over (or under) a reference index rate, for example, LIBOR + 0.25%. Since 1986, a number of FRNs have been issued with reset formulas at some fixed rate minus the reference rate. These can be called bull or inverse floaters or, as named by some issuers, yield curve notes— see Ogden [8] for further institutional details. The idea is that an investor who is "bullish" on bond prices would be attracted to a security that has a coupon rate that moves inversely to the market rate.

SallieMae (the Student Loan Marketing Association) has issued several bull floaters, including the initial one that had a reset formula of 17.20% - LIBOR. Albert Lord, the chief financial officer of SallieMae, said at the time (April 1986):

> *"The formula worked out that the bull floater, or yield curve note, plus the swap resulted in us paying 17.20% and receiving fixed rate funds pegged to Treasuries. The end cost of funds, including the cost of the cap, was very competitive—below the five-year Treasury rate"* [9].

An earlier version of this paper was presented under the title "The Pricing of Innovative Floaters" at the Southwestern Finance Association Meeting, March 1988, San Antonio, TX, and at the Western Finance Association Meeting, June 1988, Napa, CA. The author thanks the discussants at those sessions, Robert Daigler and Clifford Smith, respectively, and Keith Brown for their comments and suggestions.

Evident in this quote is the contention that SallieMae was able to financially engineer a synthetic fixed rate below the comparable Treasury yield by combining the bull floater with interest rate swap and cap agreements.

Bear floaters, which reset at a multiple of the reference rate minus some fixed rate, followed. For instance, Mellon Bank in June 1986 issued three-year, floating rate certificates of deposit (CDs) with a coupon reset formula of twice LIBOR minus 9.12%. In principle, an investor who is "bearish" on bond prices would be attracted to this security, since the coupon rate rises by more than the increase in the market rate. A *Wall Street Journal* article [7] describing the issue observed:

> *"From the point of view of the issuer, the CD offers conventional floating-rate financing. That's because, like many similar offerings, the CD's structure involves an interest rate swap that eliminates the unusual features of the interest rate on the CDs, leaving Mellon with conventional floating-rate financing ....A swap official at another firm said such a transaction could leave the issuer with a financing cost of about half a percent below LIBOR."*

The intent of this article is to analyze these financially engineered structures and to develop equilibrium pricing conditions for bull and bear floating rate notes. Pricing here means the determination of the fixed rate component in the coupon reset formula for a par-value FRN, e.g., the fixed rates of 17.20% and 9.12% in the above examples. The methodology is to construct a synthetic fixed-rate portfolio containing the bull or bear floater and interest rate swap, cap, and floor agreements. Equilibrium pricing will be such that the synthetic fixed rate equals an explicit fixed rate alternative. Otherwise, there would be an opportunity for profitable arbitrage.

I. An Example of Equilibrium Pricing on a Bull Floater

Assume that a firm can issue a five-year, semi-annual payment, fixed coupon note which is priced at par value to yield 10%. The firm also can issue a five-year, par-value, floating rate note with a semi-annual coupon reset formula of six-month LIBOR plus 0.25%. Both types of traditional debt are assumed to have the same documentation and transaction costs and are neither callable nor puttable. In sum, the notes are identical on all dimensions except the fixity of the coupon payments on the first alternative.

Assume further that the firm can enter into par-value, five-year, semi-annual settlement interest rate swaps to either pay or receive a fixed rate of 9.75% versus six-month LIBOR.[1] Such a "fixed-floating" swap is simply a net exchange of coupon cash flows based on a common notional principal amount, see Loeys [6], Felgran [5], Bicksler and Chen [2], or Arnold [1] for institutional details on interest rate swaps. A par-value swap entails no initial cash payment; at each subsequent settlement date a payment is made or received for the annual rate difference, adjusted for the fraction of the year elapsed and multiplied by the notional principal. The fixed rate on the swap is assumed to be 9.75%, to rule out the possibility of obtaining a lower cost of funds by issuing one type of traditional debt and directly swapping into the other.

Now suppose that the firm considers issuing a five-year bull floater at par value. The bull floater would have a coupon reset formula of X - LIBOR. The problem is to determine the break-even fixed rate, X_B, such that if $X < X_B$, the firm would be able to lower its cost of funds vis-a-vis the traditional alternatives. An initial approximation for X_B is 19.75%. To see this, let the bull floater be issued at 19.75% - LIBOR, and the firm agree to receive 9.75% and to pay LIBOR on an interest rate swap having a notional principal equal to the par value of the FRN. At each semi-annual payment date the cost of funds (COF) is:

$$COF = 19.75\% - LIBOR - (9.75\% - LIBOR) = 10\%. \quad (1)$$

Since the LIBORs cancel by design, the firm appears to obtain a synthetic fixed rate of 10%, which equals the explicit fixed rate alternative. A break-even rate of 19.75% is only approximate, however, since it neglects the non-negativity constraint on the bull floater. If LIBOR is above 19.75%, the coupon rate is zero, but the firm is still obligated to pay LIBOR on the swap. For example, if LIBOR is 21%, the net settlement payment on the swap is 11.25%. Therefore, the synthetic fixed rate is 10% only for LIBOR ≤ 19.75%, and rises above 10% if LIBOR > 19.75%.

The firm could resolve this problem by purchasing a five-year, semi-annual settlement, interest rate cap on

---

[1]The assumption that the firm can either pay or receive at the same fixed rate neglects the swap market-maker's bid-ask spread. In fact, a firm will pay a slightly higher fixed rate than it would receive. The bid-ask spread has narrowed considerably in recent years, due to competition, and is now on the order of ten basis points. The assumption in the paper simplifies the analysis.

six-month LIBOR at a strike rate of 19.75% for a notional principal equal to the par value of the bull floater. An interest rate cap agreement is in effect a series of over-the-counter, European, cash settlement put options.[2] The buyer of the cap pays an up-front premium, an amount quoted as a percentage of the contractual notional principal. In return, the cap writer agrees to pay to the buyer at each settlement date the excess of the variable reference rate (typically LIBOR) over the strike rate, adjusted for the fraction of the year elapsed, times the notional principal. If the reference rate is at or below the cap strike rate, no payment is made. With such a cap agreement, the firm would receive cash flows whenever LIBOR exceeds 19.75% in sufficient amount to keep the net interest payments constant at 10%.

The purchase price of a cap agreement, as with any option, will depend on the level of the strike rate, the time to maturity, and the current and expected future levels and volatility of the reference rate. In this example, a cap on LIBOR at 19.75% might well be a deep-out-of-the-money option and, therefore, not very expensive. Nevertheless, the premium when amortized over the five-year funding period will raise the overall cost of funds above 10%. So, the bull floater would have to be priced somewhat below 19.75% at break-even, to compensate for the cost of the cap agreement. The investor, in effect, must pay for the non-negativity constraint.

Since the price of a cap agreement is a function of the strike rate, a closed-form solution to the equilibrium fixed rate component to the coupon reset formula is unobtainable. In any case, to complete the example, suppose that a five-year, semi-annual settlement cap on six-month LIBOR at a strike rate of 19.50% costs 96 basis points, that is, 0.96% of the notional principal. The amortized cost of the cap is then about 25 basis points per year, calculated as a ten-period annuity using 5% per period as the interest rate and annualizing the per-period cost. Therefore, if the firm issues a par-value bull floater at 19.50% - LIBOR, pays LIBOR and receives 9.75% fixed on an interest rate swap, and buys a cap on LIBOR at 19.50% at an up-front premium of 96 basis points, the cost of funds in each period can be summarized as:

$$
\begin{aligned}
COF &= Max(0, 19.50\% - LIBOR) - (9.75\% - LIBOR) \\
&\quad + 0.25\% - Max(0, LIBOR - 19.50\%) \\
&= 10\% \ .
\end{aligned} \tag{2}
$$

Exhibit 1 graphically depicts the terms in Equation (2). Panel A-1 shows the first term, the coupon rate on the bull floater, to be constrained to non-negative values. Panel A-2 shows that the payoff on the swap, the second term, is in effect a forward rate agreement. If LIBOR is above 9.75%, the firm pays the counterparty; if LIBOR is below 9.75%, the firm receives the rate difference. Panel A-3 includes the amortized cost of the cap, the third term, and the receipts on the cap when LIBOR exceeds 19.50%, the fourth term. These cash flows are vertically summed in Panel A-4 to represent the synthetic fixed rate cost of funds of 10%. Since that equals the explicit cost of traditional fixed rate debt, 19.50% represents the equilibrium pricing on the bull floater.

Now suppose that the firm can in fact issue a par-value bull floater at 18.50% - LIBOR. The cost savings, or arbitrage gain, will be somewhat less than 100 basis points, however. First, the premium on a cap at a strike rate of 18.50% will always be higher than at a strike rate of 19.50%. That raises the amortized cost to some degree. Second, the interest rate swap entails bearing the credit risk of the counterparty. If the counterparty were to default when the fixed rate on a replacement swap is less than 9.75%, the cost of funds would rise above 10%. This can be seen by shifting the payoff line on the swap Panel A-2 of Exhibit 1 to the left. Also, there is credit risk on the cap agreement since the firm pays the purchase price at origination and depends on future receipts from the counterparty. Therefore, the expected cost savings should reflect the expected default losses on the swap and cap agreements.

II. An Example of Equilibrium Pricing on a Bear Floater

The firm might also consider issuing a bear floater with a coupon reset formula of the form: $2 \times LIBOR - Y$. Assume the same rate environment as in the previous section. Now the firm would solve for Y_B, the break-even fixed rate component, such that if $Y > Y_B$ a cost savings is obtained. An initial approximation for Y_B is 9.50%. To obtain a synthetic fixed rate, the firm would issue a par-value bear floater at $2 \times LIBOR - 9.50\%$ and enter *two* interest rate swaps to pay the fixed

[2]A cap agreement is typically documented as a series of put options on an underlying time deposit to conform to Internal Revenue Service regulations for the taxation of exchange-traded options. In practice, many market participants refer to a cap as a "call option on the rate." See Smith [12] for a discussion of the equivalence between a put on a price and call on the rate.

Exhibit 1. Bull Floater

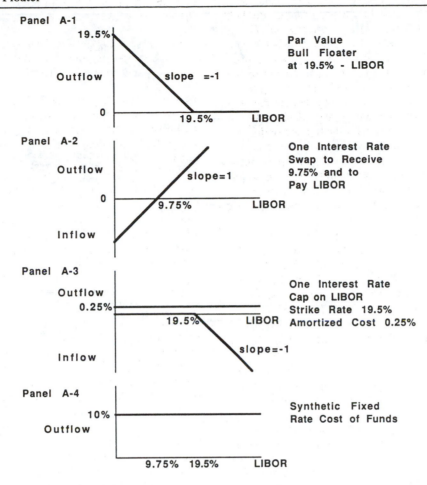

Panel A-1

19.5%

Outflow

slope = -1

0

19.5%   LIBOR

Par Value
Bull Floater
at 19.5% - LIBOR

Panel A-2

Outflow

slope=1

0

9.75%   LIBOR

Inflow

One Interest Rate
Swap to Receive
9.75% and to
Pay LIBOR

Panel A-3

Outflow

0.25%

19.5%   LIBOR

Inflow

slope=-1

One Interest Rate
Cap on LIBOR
Strike Rate 19.5%
Amortized Cost 0.25%

Panel A-4

10%

Outflow

9.75% 19.5%   LIBOR

Synthetic Fixed
Rate Cost of Funds

rate of 9.75% and to receive LIBOR on each. The cost of funds for each period would be:

$$COF = 2(LIBOR) - 9.50\% + 2(9.75\% - LIBOR)$$
$$= 10\% . \qquad (3)$$

Note that the firm could use just one swap that has a notional principal of twice the par value of the bear floater.

The non-negativity constraint on the bear floater becomes binding at low market rates, particularly when LIBOR < 4.75% if the reset formula is 2 × LIBOR - 9.50%. Therefore, the structure in Equation (3) provides only quasi-fixed funding. If LIBOR is 4%, the coupon rate on the bear floater is zero while the firm pays the counterparty 5.75% on each of two swaps, for a total cost of funds of 11.50%. The firm can complete

the structure with the purchase of an interest rate floor agreement. A floor agreement is in effect a series of over-the-counter, European, cash settlement call options.[3] The holder of the floor receives payments from the writer whenever the reference rate is below the strike rate, but none when it is at or above the strike rate. An up-front premium, quoted as a percentage of the notional principal, is paid to the floor writer by the buyer.

---

[3]A floor agreement is typically documented as a series of call options on a time deposit but referred to by market participants as a "put option on the rate." See Brown and Smith [3] for further discussion of interest rate caps and floors.

Exhibit 2. Bear Floater

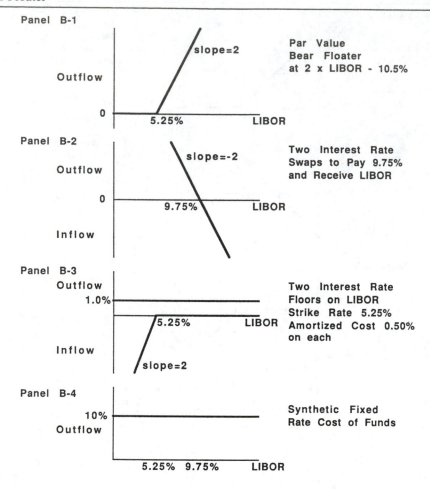

Panel B-1

Outflow

0

5.25% LIBOR

slope=2

Par Value
Bear Floater
at 2 x LIBOR - 10.5%

Panel B-2

Outflow

0

9.75% LIBOR

Inflow

slope=-2

Two Interest Rate
Swaps to Pay 9.75%
and Receive LIBOR

Panel B-3

Outflow
1.0%

5.25% LIBOR

Inflow

slope=2

Two Interest Rate
Floors on LIBOR
Strike Rate 5.25%
Amortized Cost 0.50%
on each

Panel B-4

10%

Outflow

5.25% 9.75% LIBOR

Synthetic Fixed
Rate Cost of Funds

The initial approximation for Y_B at 9.50% will be too low, since the amortized cost of a floor on LIBOR at a 4.75% strike rate will raise the all-in synthetic fixed rate above 10%. As in the bull floater example, a closed-form solution for the break-even rate is unobtainable because the purchase price of floor agreement depends on the specific strike rate, among other factors. Assume, in any case, that a five-year, semi-annual settlement floor on six-month LIBOR at a strike rate of 5.75% costs 193 basis points, i.e., 1.93% of the notional principal. That translates to an amortized cost of about 50 basis points per year.

The portfolio that obtains a synthetic fixed rate of 10% in any rate environment consists of: a par-value bear floater at 2 × LIBOR - 10.50%, two interest rate swaps to pay 9.75% and receive LIBOR, and two inter-est rate floors at a strike rate 5.25%. The cost of funds can be summarized as:

$$COF = Max[0, 2 \times LIBOR - 10.50\%]$$
$$+ 2(9.75\% - LIBOR) + 2(0.50\%)$$
$$- 2[Max(0, 5.25\% - LIBOR)]$$
$$= 10\% . \qquad (4)$$

The first term is the coupon rate on the bear floater, which is restricted to non-negative values. The second term is the payoff on the two interest rate swaps. The third and fourth terms are the amortized cost and the cash receipts from the two interest rate floors. These cash flows are displayed in Exhibit 2. Note that the use of two swap and floor agreements, each having a notional principal equal to the par value of the bear floater, doubles the slope of the payoff lines in Panels B-2 and B-3.

III. Generalized Equilibrium Pricing of Bull and Bear Floaters

The numerical examples in the previous sections can now be generalized to cover the equilibrium pricing of any floating rate note. A general expression for the coupon reset formula on an FRN is:

$$C = AR + B, \qquad (5)$$

where C is the periodic coupon rate, R is the variable reference rate (e.g., LIBOR), and A and B are parameters. A traditional FRN has a coupon reset formula of the form $C = R + M$, where M is the fixed margin over (or under) the reference rate. Hence, a traditional FRN is a special case where $A = 1$ and $B = M$. A traditional fixed rate note is another special case where $A = 0$ and $B = F$, where F represents the fixed rate cost of funds. Bull floaters are those for which $A < 0$ and bear floaters are those for which $A > 1$. Another possible class, which can be called quasi-fixed (or quasi-floating), includes FRNs for which $0 < A < 1$. Parameter A is defined as the characteristic parameter since it determines the type of FRN. Parameter B is the fixed rate component to the formula and is the subject of the equilibrium pricing analysis.

The fixed rate on par-value interest rate swaps is assumed to be $F - M$ and the floating rate is the reference rate R. This eliminates the possibility of financial savings from issuing one type of traditional debt and then directly swapping into the other. All FRNs have a non-negativity constraint that $C \geq 0$. For now, however, consider a fully unrestricted floater. While this permits the possibility that the investor would be required to make coupon payments to the issuer when $C < 0$, it provides a base line to analyze the implications of the non-negativity constraint. Let the superscript u indicate an unrestricted floater.

Proposition I. On a par-value unrestricted floater with a linear coupon reset formula of the form $C^u = AR + B^u$, the equilibrium pricing condition is that $B^u = (1 - A) F + AM$ for any A.

This proposition can be demonstrated by combining the unrestricted floater with (the absolute value of) A interest rate swaps to obtain a synthetic fixed rate

portfolio. The cost of funds (COF) in each subsequent period will be:

$$COF = AR + B^u + A[(F - M) - R]. \qquad (6)$$

The characteristic parameter A will indicate the type (pay-fixed or receive-fixed) and number of swaps needed in the portfolio. If $A > 0$, as on a quasi-fixed or bear floater, the firm will pay the fixed rate of $F - M$ and receive the floating rate of R on A swaps. If $A < 0$, as on a bull floater, the firm becomes the fixed-receiver on (the absolute value of) A swaps. The notional principal of each swap is the par value of the floater. If A is a non-integer, the firm could enter just one swap but set the notional principal equal to (the absolute value of) A times the par value. Regardless of the sign of A, the variable reference rate in Equation (6) drops out, leaving a synthetic fixed rate equal to $B^u + A (F - M)$. The necessary condition for the absence of an arbitrage opportunity is that this synthetic fixed rate equals the explicit fixed rate alternative, F. Equating the two and rearranging terms obtains the equilibrium pricing condition in Proposition I.[4]

Interest rate caps and floors are needed in order to deal with the rate environments when the coupon payment would be negative on a hypothetical unrestricted floater. The non-negativity constraint becomes binding on bull floaters at high levels of the reference rate, requiring caps, and on bear floaters at low levels, requiring floors. Let $Z_{cap}(X)$ and $Z_{floor}(X)$ stand for the amortized costs of a cap and floor, respectively, having a strike rate of X and a notional principal equal to the par value of the FRN. The payoff on a cap on R at a strike rate of X is $Max[0, R - X]$ and the payoff on a floor is $Max[0, X - R]$. Let the superscript r indicate a restricted floater.

Proposition II. On a par-value floater with a linear coupon reset formula of the form $C^r = AR + B^r$ restricted to non-negative values, the equilibrium pricing condition is:

---

[4] An equivalent result obtains if the structure is intended to create a synthetic floating rate. For any A, the cost of funds on the FRN combined with $(1 - A)$ swaps is $AR + B^u + (1 - A) [R - (F - M)]$. If $A < 1$, the firm receives the fixed rate; if $A > 1$ the firm pays the fixed rate. The cost of funds reduces to $B^u + R + M - (1 - A)F - AM$. In the absence of profitable arbitrage opportunities that variable rate must equal the explicit floating rate of $R + M$. Therefore, $B^u = (1 - A)F + AM$ for any A.

$$B^r = \begin{cases} (1 - A) F + AM + A[Z_{cap}(-B^r/A)] & \text{if } A < 0, \quad (7) \\ (1 - A) F + AM & \text{if } 0 \le A \le 1, (8) \\ (1 - A) F + AM - A[Z_{floor}(-B^r/A)] & \text{if } A > 1. \quad (9) \end{cases}$$

These results are obtained by combining the FRN for any A with interest rate swaps and caps (or floors) to create a synthetic fixed rate portfolio. For a bull floater when $A < 0$, the net cost of funds in any period is:

$$COF = Max[0, AR + B^r] + A[(F - M) - R] \\ - A[Z_{cap}(-B^r/A)] + A\{Max[0, R - (-B^r/A)]\}. \quad (10)$$

The first term is the coupon rate on the bull floater, restricted to non-negative values. The second term is the net payoff on (the absolute value of) A receive-fixed swaps. The third term is the amortized cost of (the absolute value of) A interest caps at a strike rate of $-B^r/A$, chosen to become in-the-money exactly when the non-negativity constraint on the bull floater becomes binding. The fourth term is the receipt on the caps whenever $R > -B^r/A$. Notice that, when $R \le -B^r/A$, the first term is $AR + B^r$ and the fourth term is zero. When $R > -B^r/A$ the first term is zero and the fourth is $AR + B^r$. Therefore, for any R, Equation (10) reduces to:

$$COF = AR + B^r + A[(F - M) - R] - A[Z_{cap}(-B^r/A)]. \quad (11)$$

This expression is set equal to F to rule out any arbitrage opportunities and, after rearranging terms, the condition for $A < 0$ in Proposition II is obtained.

For a bear floater when $A > 1$, a synthetic fixed rate results from combining the FRN with A pay-fixed swaps and A interest rate floors. The net cost of funds for each period is:

$$COF = Max[0, AR + B^r] + A[(F - M) - R] \\ + A[Z_{floor}(-B^r/A)] - A\{Max[0, (-B^r/A) - R]\}. \quad (12)$$

The non-negativity constraint on the bear floater becomes binding at $R < -B^r/A$, so the strike rate on the floor agreements is set at that level.

When $R \ge -B^r/A$, the first term, the coupon rate on the FRN, is $AR + B^r$ and the fourth term, the payoff on the floors, is zero. When $R < -B^r/A$, the first term is zero but the fourth becomes $AR + B^r$. Combined with the second and third terms, the settlement on the swaps and the amortized cost of the floors, the net cost is reduced to:

$$COF = AR + B^r + A[(F - M) - R] \\ + A[Z_{floor}(-B^r/A)]. \quad (13)$$

The variable reference rate R drops out, providing a synthetic fixed rate that must equal F in order to eliminate any arbitrage opportunities. Rearranging terms obtains the equilibrium condition of $A > 1$ Proposition II.

The non-negativity constraint on a quasi-fixed floater when $0 < A < 1$ is never binding so interest rate floors are unnecessary. In Proposition II then, B^r equals B^u, the pricing condition for an unrestricted floater. Notice that on both bull and bear floaters, B^r is less than B^u. In equilibrium, the issuer is compensated for the amortized costs of the caps or floors via a lower coupon rate. In other words, the investor pays for the advantage of the non-negativity constraint by accepting a lower coupon rate than if the FRN had been fully unrestricted.

It should be emphasized that the pricing conditions in Proposition II are not closed-form solutions for B^r, since the amortized costs of the caps and floors depend on the specific strike rate, which is $-B^r/A$. However, the required strike rates on the caps and floors in practice are likely to represent deep-out-of-the-money options on the reference rate. Then, the amortized costs are likely to be small, and B^u, for which there is a closed-form solution, will be a reasonably good approximation for equilibrium pricing.

IV. The Pricing Sensitivity of Bull and Bear Floaters

The traditional FRN market started in the 1970s in response to the increasing volatility in interest rates. Given no change in the underlying credit worthiness of the issuer or in the marketability of the security, a traditional FRN should trade at par value on each reset date. The minimization of price volatility compared to a fixed rate note for the same maturity is its salient feature. The relative price sensitivity of bull and bear floaters, however, will be quite different than traditional fixed and floating rate instruments because of their innovative coupon reset formulas.

The price sensitivity of bull and bear floaters can be initially examined by returning to the numerical examples of the first sections. The equilibrium pricing of the bull floater is 19.50% - LIBOR, where in the notation of the previous section $F = 10\%$, $R = LIBOR$, $M = 0.25\%$, and $Z_{cap}(19.50\%) = 0.25\%$. Substitution into the result in *Proposition II* for $A = -1$ obtains $B^r = 19.50\%$. The equilibrium pricing for the bear floater is $2 \times LIBOR - 10.50\%$. Then, for $A = 2$, $B^r = -10.50\%$ assuming $Z_{floor}(5.25\%) = 0.50\%$.

Now suppose that on a reset date with four years remaining until maturity, market rates in general rise. In particular, assume that a four-year, par-value, fixed rate note would have a coupon rate, F', equal to 11%. LIBOR too has risen, but a par-value traditional FRN can still be issued with a reset formula of LIBOR + 0.25%. The fixed rate on four-year, par-value interest rate swaps would now be 10.75% versus LIBOR.

The equilibrium pricing on a new bull floater for $A = -1$ will reflect the higher market rates and will be approximately 21.50% - LIBOR. This assumes that the amortized cost of the requisite cap is still 25 basis points. The cap strike rate is higher, from 19.50% to 21.50%, but so is the current market rate. Those factors offset, and in the absence of a formal cap pricing model a better assumption is unavailable. The equilibrium pricing on a new bear floater for $A = 2$ will now be approximately 2 × LIBOR - 11.50%. This also assumes that the amortized cost of the floor agreements remains at 0.50%. A higher strike rate on the floor, from 5.25% to 5.75%, is presumed to offset the higher level for LIBOR.

The key point of this simulation, albeit approximate, is that an investor in the original bull floater experiences an opportunity loss of about 200 basis points per year for the remaining four years. Given the increase in market rates from 10% to 11%, the market price of a bull floater at 19.50% - LIBOR will fall to about 93.67, where par value is 100 and the new fixed rate is used to discount the 100-basis-point-per-period loss over the eight semi-annual periods. On the other hand, an investor in the original bear floater at 2 × LIBOR - 10.50% experiences an opportunity gain of about 100 basis points per year. Therefore, the market price will rise to about 103.17. Uncharacteristic to bond pricing conventions, market rates and the price of a bear floater will be positively related.

Exhibit 3 shows the results for repeating this numerical simulation for a range of market rates, which are represented by the new fixed rate on a par-value, four-year note. The amortized costs of the cap and floor agreements are assumed to remain at 0.25% and 0.50%, respectively. The traditional fixed and floating rate instruments represent the usual choice set for an investor. A quasi-fixed floater $(0 < A < 1)$ would have a price-yield curve that falls between those two. Since there is nothing new about its price sensitivity, it is not surprising that quasi-fixed floaters have not appeared in the marketplace. The bull floater, however, is much more price-sensitive than a traditional fixed rate note. Intuitively, this is because a higher (lower) market rate

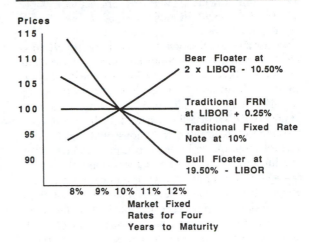

Exhibit 3. Simulated Price Sensitivities

both lowers (raises) future coupon cash flows and raises (lowers) the discount rate at which those cash flows are valued. A bear floater has a wholly atypical price-yield configuration. This is because a higher (lower) market rate raises (lowers) future coupon cash flows by more than the change in the discount rate used to value them.

The price sensitivities in Exhibit 3 can also be interpreted as implied durations.[5] A bull floater appears to have a higher duration (i.e., price elasticity with respect to rate changes) than a fixed rate note of comparable maturity, while a bear floater will have a negative duration. These attributes can be generalized by substituting the equilibrium pricing conditions from Proposition II into the general expression for the coupon reset formula that $C' = AR + B'$, as follows:

$$C' = \begin{cases} A[R + M + Z_{cap}] + (1-A)F & \text{if } A < 0, \quad (14) \\ A[R + M] + (1-A)F & \text{if } 0 \le A \le 1, \quad (15) \\ A[R + M - Z_{floor}] + (1-A)F & \text{if } A > 1. \quad (16) \end{cases}$$

The strike rate of $-B'/A$ on the amortized costs of the caps and floors is dropped for simplicity. In this setting the coupon rate on a general floater is replicated by a portfolio of rate-restricted traditional FRNs and fixed

---

[5]This approach to calculating the implied durations by means of the duration of a replicating portfolio was first seen by the author in Yawitz [13].

rate notes. The terms A and $(1 - A)$ represent the portfolio weights. From the investor's perspective, negative weights imply short positions and positive weights imply long positions.

A bull floater for any $A < 0$ is replicated by purchasing $(1 - A)$ fixed rate notes and selling (the absolute value of) A "capped" floaters. These "capped" floaters have a coupon reset formula of $R + M + Z_{cap}$, which is higher than on a traditional FRN to offset the maximum rate. This maximum rate is $-F(1 - A)/A$ to correspond to the non-negativity constraint that $C^r \geq 0$. The duration of the bull floater can be inferred from the duration of the replicating portfolio. That will be $(1 - A)$ times the duration of a fixed rate note, which is easily calculated, less (the absolute value of) A times the duration of the "capped" floater. The duration of a "capped" floater depends on the proximity of the current coupon rate to the maximum. If the current rate is well below the ceiling, such that the cap is a deep-out-of-the-money option, the duration of the "capped" floater will be close to that of the traditional FRN. A traditional FRN, without a maximum rate, can be assumed to have a short duration equal to the time until the next reset date.[6] As the current rate nears the maximum, the pricing sensitivity of the "capped" floater increases. When the constraint becomes binding, the "capped" floater acts like a fixed rate note and has a comparable duration.

This approach can be clarified with the numerical example. The bull floater at 19.50% - LIBOR can be replicated by an investor via a long position in two fixed rate notes at 10% and a short position in an FRN at LIBOR + 0.50% that has a maximum rate of 20%. Given a remaining maturity of four years, each fixed rate note has a (Macaulay) duration of 3.39 years. If LIBOR is well below 20%, the "capped" floater will have a duration of about 0.50 years. Therefore, the implied duration of the bull floater is approximately 6.28 years. Note that in the earlier exercise the price of the bull floater falls from 100 to about 93.67 when the market rate rises from 10% to 11%. That percentage price change corroborates an implied duration of over six years, despite a maturity of only four years.

A bear floater for $A > 1$ is replicated by long positions in A "floored" floaters and short positions in

(the absolute value of) $1 - A$ fixed rate notes. These "floored" floaters have a reset formula of $R + M - Z_{floor}$, which is lower than that of a traditional FRN to reflect the (non-zero) minimum coupon rate. This minimum rate is again specified by $-F(1 - A)/A$ to correspond to $C^r \geq 0$. In the numerical example the bear floater at $2 \times$ LIBOR - 10.50% can be replicated by buying two FRNs at LIBOR - 0.25%, subject to a 5% minimum rate, and by selling one 10% fixed rate note. The duration of the bear floater will be two times the duration of the "floored" floater minus the duration of the fixed rate note. The price sensitivity of the "floored" floater will be similar to a traditional FRN, namely the time to the next reset date, except when the minimum constraint is binding. In other than low-rate environments, the implied duration of a bear floater is likely to be less than zero because of the negative weight of the long-duration fixed rate note in the replicating portfolio. That gives the uncharacteristic positive relationship between market rates and the price of a bear floater, as shown in Exhibit 3.

V. Summary and Conclusions

The issuance of bull and bear floaters in recent years is a prototypical example of financial engineering—the construction of a security with a risk-return configuration otherwise unavailable. The anecdotal evidence is that issuers have been able to lower their cost of funds by issuing the bull or bear floater, and then transforming that debt to traditional fixed or floating rate funding via interest rate swap, cap, and floor agreements. The option-like cap or floor agreements are needed to offset the non-negativity constraint on the underlying security. A bull floater combined with receive-fixed interest rate swaps and cap agreements creates a synthetic fixed rate. A bear floater combined with pay-fixed swaps and interest rate floor agreements also creates a synthetic fixed rate security. A synthetic (traditional) floating rate note could be created instead by altering the number of swaps, caps, and floors.

The initial issuers of a new instrument can exploit arbitrage opportunities. This is a common pattern in financial market innovation. As time passes, those exploitable arbitrage opportunities diminish as learning (reverse engineering) takes place, which leads to the entry of other issuers. Rates and prices are adjusted to reduce or eliminate the arbitrage gain. For instance, institutional investors realize that they can create synthetic bull and bear floaters themselves by combining traditional instruments with swaps, caps, and floors.

---

[6]This necessarily assumes that neither the credit risk of the issuer nor the marketability of the securities has changed. See Yawitz, et al. [14] for analysis of the duration of floating rate notes when the credit risk changes.

The equilibrium, or break-even, pricing conditions are those for which the implicit rate on a synthetic structure for both issuers and investors equals the explicit alternative.

An innovative security must be able to transcend the initial arbitrage motivation to attain a lasting presence in the financial marketplace. The unique properties of bull and bear floaters, i.e., their price sensitivities, will have to become the motivating force for issuers and investors. Bull floaters are more sensitive to market rate movements than fixed rate notes of comparable maturity. In fact, the implied duration of a bull factor is typically longer than its maturity. The market price of a bear floater has the atypical characteristic of being positively related to market rates. That implies a negative duration. The addition of bull or bear floaters, then, can dramatically alter overall portfolio price sensitivity. Therefore, bull and bear floating rate notes potentially have a role in interest rate risk management strategies. The question is whether that role can be carried out more efficiently than it could with more traditional products such as futures and options contracts. The early evidence is negative. After an initial flurry in 1986 and 1987, the new-issues market in bull and bear floating rate notes appears to be thinning. Perhaps this is just a further statement of financial market efficiency and the hit-miss process of innovation.

References

1. T. Arnold, "How To Do Interest Rate Swaps," *Harvard Business Review* (September/October 1984), pp. 96–101.

2. J. Bicksler and A. Chen, "An Economic Analysis of Interest Rate Swaps," *Journal of Finance* (July 1986), pp. 645–655.

3. K. Brown and D. Smith, "Recent Innovations in Interest Rate Risk Management and the Reintermediation of Commercial Banking," *Financial Management* (this volume).

4. B. Cornell, "Pricing Interest Rate Swaps: Theory and Empirical Evidence," working paper, UCLA, April 1986.

5. S. Felgran, "Interest Rate Swaps: Use, Risk, and Prices," *New England Economic Review* (November/December 1987), pp. 22–32.

6. J. Loeys, "Interest Rate Swaps: A New Tool for Managing Risk," *Federal Reserve Bank of Philadelphia Business Review* (May/June 1985), pp. 17–25.

7. A. Monroe, "Mellon Issues CDs with Interest Rate Keyed to the Libor," *Wall Street Journal* (June 6, 1986).

8. J. Ogden, "An Analysis of Yield Curve Notes," *Journal of Finance* (March 1987), pp. 99–110.

9. S. Priestley, "Engineering Swaps," *Euromoney Corporate Finance* (April 1986), pp. 25–28.

10. K. Ramaswamy and S. Sundaresan, "The Valuation of Floating Rate Securities," *Journal of Financial Economics* (December 1986), pp. 251–272.

11. C. Smith, C. Smithson, and L. Wakeman, "The Evolving Market for Swaps," *Midland Corporate Finance Journal* (Winter 1986), pp. 20–32.

12. D. Smith, "Putting the Cap on Options," *Euromoney Corporate Finance* (January 1987), pp. 20–21.

13. J. Yawitz, "Pricing and Duration of Inverse Floating Rate Notes." Financial Strategies Group, Goldman Sachs (March 1986).

14. J. Yawitz, H. Kaufold, T. Macirowski, and M. Smirlock, "The Pricing and Duration of Floating Rate Bonds," *The Journal of Portfolio Management* (Summer 1987), pp. 49–56.

Article 41

FORWARD SWAPS, SWAP OPTIONS, AND THE MANAGEMENT OF CALLABLE DEBT

*by Keith C. Brown,
University of Texas at Austin and
Donald J. Smith, Boston University*

Companies issuing intermediate- to long-term fixed-rate bonds generally choose to attach call provisions to those issues. Such a call provision gives management the *option* to buy back the bonds (usually at a slight premium over par) after a specified period of "call protection." After the call protection period, if interest rates have fallen below the rate on the outstanding issue, management can reduce its cost of funds by calling and refunding the issue with lower-cost debt.[1]

A good deal of academic work has been devoted to the problem of when a corporation should call its outstanding bond issues. The consensus to date is that it is optimal to exercise the refinancing option as soon as the bond trades in the market at a price sufficiently greater than its contractual call price to cover the transactions costs of refunding.[2] This decision rule and the supporting analysis are based, of course, on the assumption that it is possible to call the bond whenever it is advantageous to the issuer—that is, the bond is no longer "call-protected."

The problem this paper addresses is somewhat different: What if interest rates have fallen significantly since the bond was originally placed, but the call provision cannot be exercised for several more years?

A callable bond that is still in its deferment, or protection, period contains what amounts to a European-style, but unmarketable option. It is like a

European option, which cannot be exercised until maturity, in the sense that its exercise must be deferred to a future "call" date. Further, since it is attached to the underlying bond, it cannot be sold directly as a separate instrument.

The option's current value to the issuer—that is, the value of the option if exercised today—is roughly equivalent to the difference between the price of the callable bond and the price of the same issue if it were noncallable. Alternatively, the intrinsic value of the option can be thought of as the present value of the cost savings that management could achieve by retiring the issue at the date of first call and then issuing a (noncallable) fixed-rate issue at today's lower interest rates.[3]

As the holder of this surrogate call option on interest rates, management has three choices: (1) it can wait until the protection period ends, thus risking future increases in rates (which would reduce the current value of the call option) while benefiting from further declines; (2) it can take steps to preserve the value of the option until it can be exercised by hedging against future increases in rates; or (3) it can attempt to find a way to effectively "sell" the option to a third party.

Taking the first approach, management can capture part of the value of the call feature immediately by refunding the entire outstanding debt

---

1. Financial theorists have argued that, in a capital market free from "imperfections," the inclusion of such covenants would be a matter of indifference to issuers. That is, in a world without taxes, transaction costs, and informational "asymmetries," the cost of the call to issuers in the form of higher interest rates required by bond market investors should equal the expected benefits.

However, several recent studies have presented cogent explanations for the pervasiveness of callable bonds based on the tax and informational asymmetries that exist between the firm's various agents and investors. See, for instance, Z. Bodie and B. Taggart, "Future Investment Opportunities and the Value of the Call Provision on a Bond," *Journal of Finance* 33 (September 1978), pp. 1187-1200, A. Barnea, R. Haugen and L. Senbet, "A Rationale for Debt Maturity Structure and Call

Provisions in the Agency Theory Framework," *Journal of Finance* 35 (December 1980), pp. 1223-1234 and I. Brick and B. Wallingford, "The Relative Tax Benefits of Alternative Call Features in Corporate Debt," *Journal of Financial and Quantitative Analysis* 20 (March 1985), pp. 95-105.

2. On this point, see A. Kraus, "The Bond Refunding Decision in an Efficient Market," *Journal of Financial and Quantitative Analysis* 8 (December 1973), pp. 793-806. For a less technical version of the same, see "The Corporate Refunding Decision," *Midland Corporate Finance Journal* (Stern Stewart & Co., publisher), Vol. 1 No. 1 (Spring 1983).

3. Assuming a common coupon rate and maturity date.

through a tender offer or open market repurchase program while issuing new noncallable bonds as replacements. There are, however, major uncertainties in implementing such a bond repurchase program. In the case of a tender offer, management fixes the repurchase price (typically at a significant premium over market), but has no direct control over the quantity of bonds that are actually tendered.[4] With a direct market repurchase, by contrast, management faces considerable uncertainty about the average price necessary to buy back the outstanding bonds, especially in the case of large debt issues. Moreover, to the extent management is forced to pay a price above the call premium, such buyback strategies effectively give away much of the current option value—which derives from the firm's right to retire the debt at a fixed price over par.[5]

Over the last few years, investment and commercial banks have promoted the use of interest rate swaps with delayed starting dates (or "forward swaps") and options on swaps ("swaptions") as ways of reducing the uncertainty attending the above refunding strategies. As a number of scholars have pointed out, an interest rate swap is essentially a series of over-the-counter forward contracts, wherein two counterparties agree to exchange fixed for floating payments based on a notional principal amount.[6] Because of their forward-like structure, swaps are ideal vehicles for hedging "symmetric" interest rate risks—for example, situations in which an increase in rates leads to a proportionate decrease in the value of the asset and vice versa. Companies seeking to realize the current value of their embedded call options, presumably to protect against rises in market rates between now and the call date, can use either a forward swap or a swap option in a hedging scheme similar to those using exchange-traded futures and options on futures.

The key difference between the use of swaps and exchange-traded instruments in call management is that swaps are flexible, negotiated contracts that can be tailored by a market-maker to match the dates and amount of the targeted call provision. That flexibility can be used to improve the hedge by reducing its basis risk. Further, it allows callable debt

management strategies for deferment periods extending beyond the relatively short delivery dates of available futures contracts. In sum, the swap-based hedging techniques described in this paper represent advances over both traditional capital market refunding strategies and the use of exchange-traded financial futures and options.

FORWARD SWAPS AND CALLABLE DEBT

Forward swaps can be used to manage callable debt in two different ways. First, management can preserve the value of an (in-the-money) option to call its own debt by entering into an "on-market" forward swap—that is, a delayed-start swap agreement at the prevailing market (forward) swap rate set to begin at the date of first call. This would effectively "lock in" the current level of interest rates until the call exercise date. Alternatively, it can choose a forward swap rate different from the current rate (thus creating an "off-market" forward swap) and thereby capture immediately (or "monetize") the present value of the bond's call option.

Preserving the Value of the Call With an On-Market Forward Swap

Let us start by assuming that if rates have fallen significantly since a callable bond was originally issued, management would choose to sell the call option (thereby locking in current rates) if it could indeed be separated from the host bond. The problem arises from the fact that the embedded call cannot be separated and sold as such.

This is a classic hedging problem: rates could rise or fall by more than is generally expected during the time until the call date. If rates rise, the call option loses value; if rates fall, the call gains value. Management's concern is that interest rates might rise prior to the call date, reducing or even wiping out the value of the option. If management is uncomfortable with the uncertainty of these outcomes, a negatively correlated position in another instrument can be acquired to serve as a hedge. The objective

---

4. Bond tender offers are, on average, only 76% successful at obtaining the desired number of outstanding instruments. See J. Finnerty, A. Kalotay and F. Farrell, *Evaluating Bond Refunding Opportunities*, Hagerstown: Ballinger Publishing (1988).

5. Note that exercising an option that could be sold on the market captures only the "intrinsic value" and forgoes the remaining "time value." This approach can lead to a deadweight loss in the option's value due to the extinguishment of

the benefits associated with potential exercise features. See M. Livingston, "Measuring the Benefit of a Bond Refunding: The Problem of Non Marketable Call Options," *Financial Management* 16 (Spring 1987), pp. 38-40.

6. For a background discussion on the swap market, see C. Smith, C. Smithson and L. Wakeman, "The Evolving Market for Swaps," *Midland Corporate Finance Journal* Vol. 3 No. 4 (Winter 1985).

THE DESIGN FLEXIBILITY AND EASE OF OPERATIONAL MANAGEMENT OF
INTEREST RATE SWAP CONTRACTS CAN ALSO BE USED TO REDUCE THE
BASIS RISK IN THE HEDGING STRATEGY THAT OFTEN ATTENDS THE USE OF
FINANCIAL FUTURES.

EXHIBIT 1
MARKER EVENTS IN THE
CALL MANAGEMENT
PROBLEM

Years			
0	2	4	7
Original Issue Date	Current Date	Call Date	Maturity Date

---

of the hedge is to smooth the range of future payoffs, if not indeed to "lock in" the future value of the asset. (It should be noted, however, that one can only hedge against unexpected changes because the forward rates used in hedging already reflect market expectations.)

The most obvious means of hedging the interest rate risk is to take a short position in a financial futures contract. The short position would gain when interest rates rise and thus futures prices fall. An alternative would be to buy a put option on the futures contract. The put option, which upon exercise allows the holder to acquire a short position in the futures contract at the strike price, would also appreciate in value as rates rise.

The problem with exchange-traded futures and futures options, however, is often the absence of a suitable contract. The call date on the bond can be several years away, but liquidity in the futures market (and indeed the availability of the futures option) usually is limited to the nearest delivery months. Also, futures contracts require frequent managerial attention to deal with the margin account and daily mark-to-market valuation and settlement.

Forward interest rate swaps, by contrast, are over-the-counter, directly negotiated instruments that represent the hedging equivalent of financial futures contracts. In particular, as we shall demonstrate later, a "pay-fixed" forward swap is functionally equivalent to a short position in futures in terms of reducing the interest rate risk in the future value of the call option. Moreover, the design flexibility and ease of operational management of interest rate swap contracts can also be used to reduce the basis risk in the hedging strategy that often attends the use of financial futures.

A Simple Case. A numerical example will be useful to illustrate the use of forward swaps to preserve the call rate. Suppose that two years ago a corporation issued $100 million in seven-year 12% coupon bonds at par value. Assume also that the bonds pay coupons semi-annually, the issue was originally callable at par in four years, and two years remain in the call protection period. (See Exhibit 1.)

Now suppose that an on-market, $100 million notional principal forward swap is available such that the corporation could pay 10.25% and receive six-month LIBOR for three years, starting two years from now. This forward swap is simply a deferred-start transaction. The deferral period corresponds to (and is set to equal) the time remaining in the call protection period; and the maturity (or "tenor") of the swap corresponds to the remaining maturity on the underlying bonds as of the call date. There is no initial cash settlement on the transaction, hence the term "on-market" swap. (As we will discuss later, an "off-market" swap would require an initial payment from one counterparty to another.)

This on-market forward swap agreement will appreciate in value if interest rates rise over the next two years by more than had been generally expected (as reflected in the forward swap rate). The gain on the swap, like that on a comparable short position in interest rate futures, would offset the decline in the value of the call option. Unlike the use of futures, however, the timing of the forward swap can be set to match exactly the call and maturity dates—an outcome that would only occur by coincidence with standardized, exchange-traded futures.

Pricing Forward Swaps. The fixed rates on forward swaps are determined by the rates available in the current swap spot market—that is, for swaps that begin at once. Suppose that a company could simultaneously enter a five-year, pay-fixed swap at 9.75% and a two-year, receive-fixed swap at 9.00%, both versus six-month LIBOR. As illustrated in Exhibit 2, that combination of swaps effectively constructs a three-year, pay-fixed (since the initial LIBOR flows cancel) swap that is deferred for two years. Unless the two-year and five-year fixed rates are identical (which is highly unlikely), there will be a remaining fixed rate payment or receipt during the initial "stub" period.

Pricing the forward swap, then, is basically an exercise in the time value of money. The problem is to transfer the first four cash payments forward in time and spread them evenly amongst the latter six. In practice this is done using implied forward rates

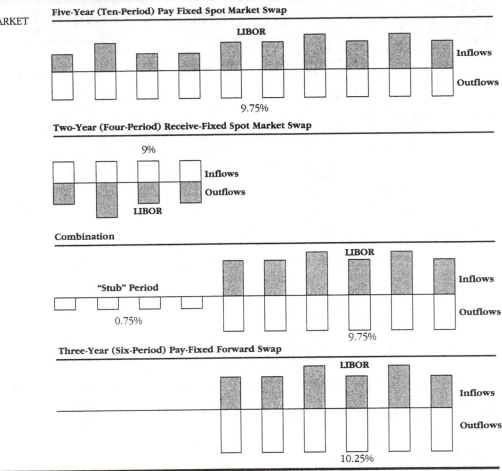

EXHIBIT 2
PRICING AN ON-MARKET
FORWARD SWAP

Five-Year (Ten-Period) Pay Fixed Spot Market Swap

Two-Year (Four-Period) Receive-Fixed Spot Market Swap

Combination

Three-Year (Six-Period) Pay-Fixed Forward Swap

derived from a zero-coupon swap yield curve. Here, and in the continuation of this example that follows, we simply assume that the result of that exercise is a forward swap fixed rate of 10.25%.

The effectiveness, and inherent risks, of this forward swap hedging strategy can be demonstrated by considering the various decisions that must be made at the call date in two years. First, management must decide whether to call the underlying debt. It is reasonable to assume that it will do so only if the fixed-rate cost of funds for the remaining three years turns out to be lower than 12%. Second, if the debt is called, management must decide if it will refinance with fixed- or floating-rate debt. Third, it must decide if it will retain the swap or close it out by entering into an offsetting, receive-fixed swap. If management wants to continue with fixed-rate funding, then

the second and third decisions are not independent: If the swap is closed out, the firm can just issue fixed-rate notes; but if the swap is retained, management will have to issue LIBOR-based floating-rate debt to obtain a net fixed-rate cost of funds.

A Digression on The Relationship between Swap and Bond Spreads. At this point it is necessary to introduce some notation to describe the relevant market rates prevailing at the call date in two years. Following market conventions, we decompose all fixed rates into the Treasury yield (T) for a comparable maturity (in this case, three years) and a spread over that Treasury yield. For example, the three-year fixed-rate cost of funds is denoted T + BS, where BS stands for "bond (market) spread." In a similar fashion, the fixed rate on a three-year swap (versus six-month LIBOR) is denoted T + SS, where

EXHIBIT 3
CALL VALUE PRESERVATION
USING AN ON-MARKET
FORWARD SWAP

	Treasury Yield (T)			
	9%	10%	11%	12%
Refunding Fixed Rate (T + BS)	9.75%	10.75%	11.75%	12.75%
Decision	Call	Call	Call	Not Call
Value of the Call Option	$1,125,000	$625,000	$125,000	0
Swap Fixed Rate (T + SS)	9.50%	10.50%	11.50%	12.50%
Gain on the Forward Swap	− $375,000	$125,000	$625,000	$1,125,000
Total Gain	$750,000	$750,000	$750,000	$1,125,000
Present Value	$3,822,034	$3,761,539	$3,702,522	$5,467,406

Numerical Example Assuming BS = 0.75%, CS = 0.25%, and SS = 0.50%
Value of the Call Option (as an Annuity) = (12% − Refunding Fixed Rate) × ($1/2$) × $100 Million,
Gain on the Forward Swap (as an Annuity) = (Swap Fixed Rate − 10.25%) × ($1/2$) × $100 Million
Total Gain = Value of the Call Option plus the Gain on the Forward Swap
Present Value (as of the Call Date) of the Total Gain per Semi-Annual Period for Six Remaining Semi-Annual Periods, Discounted at the Refunding Fixed Rate

SS means "swap (market) spread." The reset rate for a three-year floating rate note is LIBOR + CS, where CS stands for "credit (market) spread."[7]

When the swap market is "in equilibrium," the general relationship between these three spreads is that SS = BS − CS—that is, the swap spread equals the bond spread minus the credit spread. We assume that the corporation at the call date in two years can either issue fixed-rate debt at T + BS or floating-rate debt at LIBOR + CS. Then suppose that it issues fixed-rate debt and also enters a swap agreement to receive a fixed rate of T + SS and to pay LIBOR. Its net "synthetic" floating-rate cost of funds would be LIBOR + (BS − SS) since the fixed Treasury yield (T) cancels out. In equilibrium, that floating rate should equal the explicit floating rate of LIBOR + CS; and simple algebra tells us that BS − SS = CS.[8]

The Effectiveness of Forward Swaps as a Hedge. Exhibit 3 shows the results of the forward swap hedge assuming four different interest rate outcomes. On the call date, Treasury yields are allowed to range from 9% to 12% (while bond credit and swap spreads are assumed to remain fixed, and in equilibrium, at BS = 0.75%, CS = 0.25%, and SS = 0.50%).

For example, if the three-year Treasury yield turns out to be 10% at the time of the call date, the corporation is assumed (1) to call and refund its 12% debt with a three-year fixed-rate note at 10.75% and (2) to close out its pay-fixed 10.25% forward swap by entering into a three-year receive-fixed swap at 10.50%. As shown in Exhibit 3 (third row, second column), the value of exercising the call option expressed as a six-period (three-year) annuity turns

---

7. BS and CS represent the issuing corporation's marginal risk relative to the Treasury yield and LIBOR in the fixed- and floating-rate markets, respectively. Those spreads depend largely on default risk, but also reflect any differing degrees of marketability, taxation, and so forth. Note that there is no particular reason for BS to equal CS since the former is expressed relative to risk-free Treasuries and the latter to "bank-risk," or LIBOR.

8. This discussion abstracts from the bid-ask spread on swaps in practice. Since the swap market-maker, typically a commercial or investment bank, will need to cover the credit risk inherent in the transaction as well as other hedging and regulatory (e.g., capital adequacy) costs, it will always quote a higher receive-fixed rate than its pay-fixed rate. The bid-ask spread has narrowed markedly in recent years as testimony to the competitiveness of the swap market and now ranges between 4-10 basis points.

out to be $625,000 per period (or [12.00% − 10.75%] × 1/2 × $100 million). The value of the forward swap hedge is also positive because management is able to close out the 10.25% pay-fixed forward swap with a 10.50% receive-fixed swap; and the per period savings are $125,000 per period ([10.50% − 10.25%] × 1/2 × $100 million) for the six remaining semi-annual periods. The sum of the two sources of gain, the call and the hedge, is an annuity of $750,000. The present value of that annuity, as of the call date, is $3,761,539, calculated using the 10.75% fixed rate cost of funds as the discounting factor.

The salient features of the call rate preservation strategy are apparent in this simulation exercise. As shown in Exhibit 3, the payoffs on closing out the pay-fixed forward swap are negatively correlated with the value of the call option. For the given values of BS, CS, and SS, the strategy "locks in" the future gain for varying levels of market rates. (Actually, the "locked in" value is a nominal annuity, the present value of which depends on the level of the rate used for discounting.) Notice, however, that although the net gain is constant when it is optimal to call the existing debt (that is, when the refunding rate is less than the existing rate), the gains rise when it is not optimal to call (i.e., when rates rise above 12%). This means that the forward swap strategy, in effect, "overhedges" the risk.

This "overhedging" arises from the use of a symmetric-payoff instrument like a futures contract or swap agreement to hedge an "asymmetric" or one-sided risk exposure. This asymmetric exposure in turn arises from the fact that management's option to call its bond has a minimum value of zero. (Remember that the issuer effectively paid for the call right in the form of a higher interest rate when it issued the bonds.) If the refunding rate exceeds 12%, the call option value falls to zero but is never negative; but the value of the forward swap hedge continues to rise proportionally with increases in rates above 12%.

If management wanted to eliminate (or at least minimize) this overhedging effect, then it would have to substitute the use of an asymmetric (or option-like) hedging instrument to offset its one-sided exposure. As we will show later in this paper, call monetization strategies using swap options instead of swaps can be used to accomplish this end.

The Problem of Basis Risk. The forward swap hedge, as illustrated in Exhibit 3, immunizes the corporation against changes in future Treasury yields. But, it is important to recognize that the amount of the future gain—and thus the effectiveness of the hedge—depends on the corporation's future refunding rates. Specifically, it depends on the firm-specific risk spreads represented by BS and CS, as well as on the swap spread SS.

Suppose that the credit standing of the corporation deteriorates at the time of the call date, such that BS rises to 0.95% while SS remains at 0.50%. The value of the call option falls for any level of T, while the payoff on closing out the swap hedge is unchanged. This shift in the bond spread relative to the swap spread lowers the net gain either as a future annuity or as a present value.

This type of basis risk is common in hedging programs. In effect, such hedging programs reduce general market interest rate risk while continuing to bear some spread risk. The assumption underlying these strategies is that the variance in the spread over Treasuries will be much less than the variance in the Treasury yield itself. Nevertheless it should be clear that the hedge does entail risk. As a worst-case scenario, suppose that the combined Treasury yield and swap spread remain less than 10.25%, and thus the forward swap can only be closed out at a loss, while the bond spread rises such that the call option value falls to zero. The corporation would be worse off for having hedged than not.

To assess the level of basis risk, it is instructive to break the annuity gain of $750,000 per period in our example into two components: a non-random part that depends on the existing coupon rate vis-a-vis the forward swap rate, and a random part that depends on the bond and swap spreads at the future call date. The first part is $875,000 per period, calculated as (12% − 10.25%) × 1/2 × $100 million. That amount is known with certainty at the current date when the hedging strategy is undertaken since both rates are observable. The second part, in general, is (SS − BS) × 1/2 × $100 million. In Exhibit 3, where it is assumed that SS = 0.50% and BS = 0.75%, this second amount is −$125,000 per period. Adding the two gives the annuity gain of $750,000. The key point here is that (SS − BS), the difference between the swap and bond market spreads over Treasuries, is the source of basis risk in the hedging program. (In a later section, we will examine some empirical evidence attesting to the size and variance of these spreads.)

Basis Risk Also Affects The Call Decision. Up to this point, we have assumed that when the call

EXHIBIT 4
PRICING AN OFF-MARKET
FORWARD SWAP

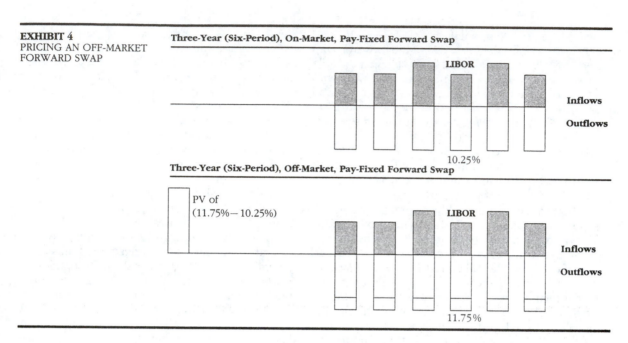

date arrives, the decision whether to call or not is made simply by comparing the current three-year fixed rate to the existing coupon rate; that is, if T + BS is less than 12%, management calls the bonds. Management also, however, has two other alternatives. It can call the debt and refund in the floating-rate market at LIBOR + CS and retain the swap to pay 10.25% and receive LIBOR. That alternative yields a net fixed-rate cost of funds of 10.25% + CS (since the LIBOR-based cash flows cancel). Or, it can choose not to call, maintain the 12% debt and close out the swap. That entails receiving T + SS while paying 10.25%; and the net cost of funds would be 12% + [10.25% – (T + SS)].

Given this analysis, the decision to call or not depends on a comparison of 10.25% + CS to 12% + [10.25% – (T + SS)]. Simplifying that comparison, the decision rule becomes to call if T + SS + CS is less than 12%. If swap markets are in equilibrium (and thus BS = SS + CS), then the two decision rules—one based on the fixed spread and one on the floating-plus-swap spread—will yield identical call decisions. If swap markets are not in equilibrium, then the two rules could produce conflicting decisions.

The importance of this last result is that there can be circumstances when a corporation appears to be making a sub-optimal call decision if only the fixed-rate cost of funds is observable. For instance, suppose that T = 11.30%, BS = 0.75%, CS = 0.20%,

and SS = 0.40% on the call date. The fixed-rate refunding alternative of 12.05% would indicate that the call option has a value of zero and that calling the debt would be irrational. At the same time, however, the (likely short-lived) disequilibrium in the swap market would allow the firm to call the debt, refund at LIBOR + 0.20%, and pay 10.25% on the forward swap, obtaining a net fixed rate of 10.45%. That strategy generates a six-period annuity gain of $775,000 per period, whereas not calling the debt and simply closing out the swap by agreeing to receive the current swap fixed rate of 11.70% against the payments of 10.25% generates an annuity gain of only $725,000. Naturally, in an efficient capital market one would not expect disequilibrium conditions like this to persist.

In summary, the future value of the firm's embedded call option depends on future interest rates. That risk exposure can be hedged in principle by short positions in financial futures contracts or by the use of pay-fixed forward swaps. While the forward swap can lock in some of the current value of the call option—although only the amount that reflects the generally expected level of future rates—there is still basis risk. In this context, the basis risk is represented by the relationship between the (fixed-rate) bond spread, the (floating-rate) credit spread, and the swap market spread. Unexpected changes in those spreads can reduce the effectiveness of the hedge.

EXHIBIT 5
CALL MONETIZATION USING
AN OFF-MARKET FORWARD
SWAP

	Treasury Yield (T)			
	9%	10%	11%	12%
Refunding Fixed Rate (T + BS)	9.75%	10.75%	11.75%	12.75%
Decision	Call	Call	Call	Not Call
Value of the Call Option	$1,125,000	$625,000	$125,000	0
Swap Fixed Rate (T + SS)	9.50%	10.50%	11.50%	12.50%
Gain on the Forward Swap	− $1,125,000	− $625,000	− $125,000	$375,000
Total Gain	0	0	0	$375,000
Present Value	0	0	0	$1,822,469

Numerical Example Assuming BS = 0.75%, CS = 0.25%, and SS = 0.50%
Value of the Call Option (as an Annuity) = (12% − Refunding Fixed Rate) × ($\frac{1}{2}$) × $100 Million.
Gain on the Forward Swap (as an Annuity) = (Swap Fixed Rate − 11.75%) × ($\frac{1}{2}$) × $100 Million
Total Gain = Value of the Call Option plus the Gain on the Forward Swap
Present Value (as of the Call Date) of the Total Gain per Semi-Annual Period for Six Remaining Semi-Annual Periods,
Discounted at the Refunding Fixed Rate

Monetizing the Call Value with an Off-Market Forward Swap

The use of an on-market, pay-fixed forward swap effectively locks in the future value of the call option, subject to the basis risk mentioned above. That future value, as we have seen, is an annuity that reflects the difference between the existing coupon rate and the forward swap rate multiplied by the principal. For instance, in Exhibit 3, the annuity (or semi-annuity) is a cost savings of $750,000 per period for six remaining semi-annual periods.

Call monetization, by contrast, refers to strategies that transform this deferred annuity into a single current cash payment that is equal to the present value of the series of payments. To return to our earlier example, management could monetize the value of the call by entering into a pay-fixed forward swap at 11.75% for three years instead of using the on-market

forward swap with a fixed rate of 10.25%. Of course, the corporation would be willing to pay the higher fixed rate only if it receives something in return—in fact, an immediate payment for the present value of the annuity represented by the difference between the rates. That annuity is $750,000 ([11.75% − 10.25%] × 1/2 × $100 million) for six semi-annual periods.

The actual amount of cash that the corporation will receive upon agreeing to the off-market forward swap will depend on the discount factors used to calculate the present value. Typically, a commercial bank is the counterparty to these swaps. The bank should view this off-market transaction as a combination of an on-market forward swap and a loan agreement. The on-market swap calls for no immediate exchange of cash; however, the bank is effectively lending the corporation a specific amount now and later expects to be repaid in six installments of $750,000. Based on this reasoning, the appropriate

---

9. Notice that if the corporation enters an off-market forward swap to pay fixed at less than 10.25%, it would effectively be making a deposit to the bank. Then, the bank's lower deposit rates would be used for discounting, thereby raising the amount of the requisite immediate payment.

discount factors are the bank's lending rate for zero-coupon transactions ("bullet" loans) maturing in 2 1/2 to 5 years (See Exhibit 4).[9]

The Effectiveness of an Off-Market Forward Hedge. The implications of hedging the call value with an off-market, forward swap are apparent in Exhibit 5 (which, like Exhibit 3, also assumes BS = 0.75%, CS = 0.25%, and SS = 0.50%, and T ranging from 9% to 12%). The structure by design has transferred the future gain of $750,000 per period to the current date. In cases when it would be optimal to call the debt (for example, when Treasury yields turn out to be 9, 10, or 11%), the value of the call option is completely offset by the loss on the forward swap. If rates rise to 12% or higher (and thus the call option's value falls to zero), there is a gain on the forward swap, thus leading to the same asymmetric outcome associated with the use of on-market swaps. As explained earlier, this overhedging phenomenon arises from the use of forward-based instruments with symmetric payoffs to hedge one-sided risks.

This strategy also contains the same basis risk that attends the use of on-market forward swaps: namely, that which results from possible changes in the relationship between the swap spread and the bond spread (SS − BS). The future annuity gain would be reduced for any level of T, and even could be negative, if BS turns out to be higher than 0.75% or SS lower than 0.50%.

For example, assume that on the current date the expected future values for BS, CS, and SS are 0.75%, 0.25%, and 0.50%, as in Exhibits 3 and 5. These expectations would likely be based on current spreads and the assumption of swap market equilibrium. In this case, the off-market forward swap rate of 11.75% is simply the one that makes the expected annuity gain zero (at least, over that range of interest rates when the call would be exercised). The corporation could have chosen any number of other forward rates—12%, for instance, to match the existing coupon rate.

In short, the choice of a different forward rate merely transfers the certain portion of the annuity gain from a future value to a present value, but it does not remove the basis risk.

SWAP OPTIONS AND CALLABLE DEBT[10]

Another way of monetizing the current value of the bond's embedded call option is through the use of swap options (also known as "swaptions"). In contrast to hedges with off-market forward swaps, the use of swaptions has the advantage of reducing the overhedging problem that affects forward swap-based hedging schemes. But these benefits are also accompanied by one new drawback: because the strategy requires the callable debt issuer to sell a swap option, the swaption holder must decide when to exercise the option, thereby introducing—as we shall see—another dimension of risk into the problem.

Because the market for options on swaps is not as well developed as the swap market itself, it might be helpful to begin this section with a brief description of the product. Broadly speaking, in exchange for a front-end premium, the holder of a swap option has the right, but not the obligation, to enter into a swap on or before a specific exercise date. The agreement also specifies which counterparty pays the fixed rate. By convention, the holder of the right to enter into a pay-fixed swap is said to own a call option; and the holder of the right to enter a receive-fixed swap is said to have a put. Finally, the swaption contract also designates the amount of notional principal, the level of the fixed rate (i.e., strike rate) and the particular index used to represent the floating rate (e.g., six-month LIBOR).

To extend the example of the previous section, assume once again that the firm holds an option to call its original $100 million of 12% debt and that it would like to convert this asset into cash today. But, because the call feature is attached to the bond, it cannot be sold separately nor can it be exercised for another two years. What can be sold today is an option on a swap market transaction.

Monetizing the bond option in this context involves selling a swap option having terms set as closely as possible to those of the original debt issue. Specifically, the firm would sell a put option (i.e., the right to receive the fixed rate) on a three-year swap, exercisable in two years with a strike rate of 12% and notional principal of $100 million. In this case, the two-year expiration date on the swaption matches that on the bond option while the three-year swap tenor matches the difference between the bond's call date and its maturity.

Like the off-market forward swap strategy discussed earlier, the sale of a swap option converts the benefits of the call into an immediate receipt of cash.

---

10. The discussion in this section is an expanded version of a portion of our article "The Swap-Driven Deal," *Intermarket* 6 (March 1989), pp. 15-19.

EXHIBIT 6

SEMI-ANNUAL FUNDING COST WITH THE SWAP OPTION-BASED CALL MONETIZATION STRATEGY

Treasury Yield (T)	Bond Spread (BS)	Swap Spread (SS)		
		0.25%	0.50%	0.75%
10.5%	0.50%	$6,125,000	$6,000,000	$5,875,000
	0.75%	6,250,000	6,125,000	6,000,000
	1.00%	6,375,000	6,250,000	6,125,000
11.0%	0.50%	$6,125,000	$6,000,000	$5,875,000
	0.75%	6,250,000	6,125,000	6,000,000
	1.00%	6,375,000	6,250,000	6,125,000
11.5%	0.50%	$6,125,000	$6,000,000	$6,000,000
	0.75%	6,125,000	6,000,000	6,000,000
	1.00%	6,125,000	6,000,000	6,000,000
12.%	0.50%	$6,000,000	$6,000,000	$6,000,000
	0.75%	6,000,000	6,000,000	6,000,000
	1.00%	6,000,000	6,000,000	6,000,000

In this display, the funding cost is calculated as: **(Funding Rate)** $\times$ **(1/2)** $\times$ **($100 million)** where Funding Rate = Min[12%, (T + BS)] + Max[0, 12% – (T + SS)].
Decisions: (i) Call option on bond is exercised if (T + BS) < 12%, (ii) Swap option is exercised if (T + SS) < 12%.

The swap option strategy, however, is complicated by an unknown that does not present itself with the forward swap hedge. In the case of the swaption hedge, when the call date arrives two years later, there are two decisions to be made (or two options that can be exercised) by two different parties: (1) management may decide to call and refinance its original debt; and (2) the swap option holder must decide at that point whether to enter into a receive-fixed swap on the designated terms.

The complicating factor is not the presence of two separate parties in the decision process, but rather the fact that their decisions will be based on movements in two different interest rates. As in the case of forward swaps, the firm's decision to refund at the call date will be determined by the prevailing level for three-year fixed-rate debt in relation to the 12% coupon it is currently paying. On the same call date, the swaption holder will evaluate the economic merits of entering into a three-year swap to receive the fixed rate of 12% based on the prevailing three-year swap rate.

Generally speaking (that is, if interest rates are the only factor), a firm that has chosen to monetize its debt option through the sale of a swaption faces four different possible outcomes:

1. The bond is called if (T + BS) < 12%
   The swap option is exercised if (T + SS) < 12%,
2. The bond is called if (T + BS) < 12%
   The swap option is not exercised if (T + SS) ≥ 12%,
3. The bond is not called if (T + BS) ≥ 12%
   The swap option is exercised if (T + SS) < 12%,
4. The bond is not called if (T + BS) ≥ 12%
   The swap option is not exercised if (T + SS) ≥ 12%.

Whether the options are exercised either independently or simultaneously depends once again on the relationship between BS and SS. Thus, as with the forward swap-based alternative, the basis risk between the bond and swap market yields becomes an important factor.

The Effectiveness of the Hedge Using Swaptions. In Exhibit 6, we have calculated the semi-annual funding cost to the firm employing this swap option-based monetization strategy under several representative interest rate outcomes. For purposes of this analysis, we also assume that if management chooses to call its original debt, it will issue new three-year fixed-rate debt having a coupon rate of (T + BS). Also, if the swap option holder chooses to exercise its contract, the firm—which would then be forced into paying a 12% fixed swap rate in exchange for LIBOR—will counterbalance its position with an offsetting receive-fixed swap at (T + SS).[11]

---

11. Under these assumptions, the post-call date funding cost can be expressed in an annual percentage rate as follows: Min[12%, (T + BS)] + Max[0, 12% – (T + SS)].

EXHIBIT 7
PAYOFF DIAGRAMS
ILLUSTRATING THE
RELATIONSHIP BETWEEN
FORWARD SWAPS AND
SWAP OPTIONS

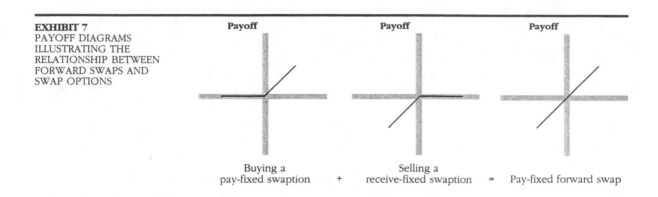

The most intriguing thing about the display is that it indicates that the firm's funding cost could be either higher, lower, or the same as its present expense depending on the relationship between the credit spreads in the swap and bond markets. More precisely, notice that the semi-annual funding cost will remain at its current level of $6 million if the prevailing rates in both markets exceed 12% at the call date. In this case, neither option will be exercised and so the firm simply will continue to repay its original debt issue. Alternatively, notice that even when (T + BS) and (T + SS) are both below 12%—implying that both options will be exercised—the funding cost will still be $6 million *as long as the swap and bond spreads are equal.*

On the other hand, whenever SS < BS, the funding cost to the firm will increase any time it is optimal to exercise the swap option (i.e., when (T + SS < 12%). And, as we have suggested, it can be profitable to exercise the swap option even when it doesn't make sense to refund the bond. Conversely, if BS < SS, the funding cost may be reduced below the $6 million level. The important point here, once again, is that while the sale of the swaption can provide a hedge against general movements in Treasury yields, it does not protect the firm against changes in the relationship between BS and SS.

Management may be justified in having some confidence in the stability of the spread differential, in which case its assessment of the amount of basis risk would be relatively low. For instance, in the preceding examples we assumed that the initial spreads were SS = 0.50% and BS = 0.75%. Without

reason to believe otherwise, the company might expect this differential of −0.25% to continue through the call date. In such a case, a conservative firm might actually set the strike rate on the swaption it sells 25 basis points lower (i.e., at 11.75%). This decision would result in a lower premium received, but reduce the firm's exposure to future changes in the spread differential.

Before leaving the subject of swaptions, it is instructive to compare the front-end premiums generated by the sale of swaptions to the cash payments accompanying the use of off-market forward swaps. By extending the well-known "put-call-futures" parity relationship, we can show that entering into the pay-fixed side of a three-year off-market swap two years forward at the rate of 11.75% is equivalent to the following transactions: (1) buying a pay-fixed option that can be exercised in two years on an 11.75% three-year swap; and (2) selling a receive-fixed option on the same swap.[12] (The pay-off diagrams illustrating put-call parity are shown in Exhibit 7.) Because both of these options carry the same strike rate, which is greater than the assumed on-market forward swap rate of 10.25%, only the latter option will be in-the-money upon issue.

What this exercise reveals is that the forward swap monetization strategy effectively requires the firm to purchase an out-of-the-money pay-fixed swap option that it does not really need to hedge changes in the value of its call provision. As demonstrated earlier, the off-market forward swap overhedges the firm's call option relative to the sale of a swaption. And, because the forward swap strategy involves the purchase of this

12. For a detailed discussion of the theoretical foundations for this result, see H. Stoll, "The Relationship Between Put and Call Option Prices," *Journal of Finance* 24 (December 1969), pp. 801-824 and E. Moriarty, S. Phillips and P. Tosini, "A Comparison of Options and Futures in the Management of Portfolio Risk," *Financial Analysts Journal* 37 (January/February 1981), pp. 61-67.

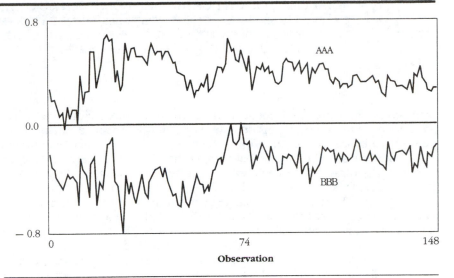

EXHIBIT 8
DIFFERENCES BETWEEN SWAP AND BOND CREDIT SPREADS (I.E., SS — BS) FOR SEVEN-YEAR UTILITY BONDS RATED AAA AND BBB

In this display, Observations 1, 74 and 148 refer to the calendar dates January 10, 1986, June 5, 1987 and November 4, 1988, respectively.

unnecessary option, the premium the firm receives from the use of forward swaps must always be less than that generated by the sale of swaptions.

THE BASIS RISK IN SWAP-BASED STRATEGIES

In the previous sections, we have demonstrated that all of the swap-based approaches to callable debt management provide an explicit hedge against unanticipated movements in Treasury rates during the protection period. What we have also emphasized, however, is that the general level of interest rates is not the only factor determining the effectiveness of the hedging strategy. The difference between swap and bond credit spreads (i.e., SS – BS) at the call date—which, of course, is not known at the time the initial decision is made—will also play a significant role. This source of uncertainty, which we call basis risk, arises from the issuing firm's attempt to "sell" its debt option through a parallel transaction in the swap market.

To get a better sense of the extent to which this credit spread differential changes over time, we analyzed several different series of weekly swap and bond yields from Salomon Brothers' *Bond Market*

Roundup during the period spanning January 10, 1986 to November 4, 1988.[13] To calculate bond market spreads, we used the average yield-to-maturity (i.e., T + BS) on seven-year utility bond indices in two different Standard & Poor's credit rating classes: AAA and BBB. These data were then adjusted by subtracting the yield on seven-year Treasury bonds in order to isolate the bond credit spread component. Each of these adjusted series was then compared to weekly quotes of the fixed-rate credit spread (SS) for seven-year U.S. dollar interest rate swaps using three-month LIBOR as the floating rate. Exhibit 8 shows the resulting spread differential series for the 148 observations in the data set.

As the graph rather strikingly illustrates, the relationship between the swap and bond markets, as measured by (SS – BS), has not been stable over time. For the AAA and BBB rating classes, the range between the maximum and minimum values was 72 and 84 basis points, respectively. This represents a considerable degree of volatility considering that the historical bond yield differential between the two credit grades is typically only about 150 basis points.[14] Consequently, even if it is assumed that the credit rating of the firm doesn't change during the

---

13. We are indebted to Dave Hartzell for furnishing us with this data.
14. See J. Bicksler and A. Chen. "An Economic Analysis of Interest Rate Swaps." *Journal of Finance* 41 (July 1986), pp. 645-655.

call protection period, movements in this basis risk component can generate considerable uncertainty about the ultimate effectiveness of the hedge.

There is also another potential complication in that changes in the spread differential documented in Exhibit 8 appear to vary considerably across the two credit grades. (In fact, the correlation between the spread differentials for AAA-rated and for BBB-rated debt in this sample was only 0.258.) This means that if the credit quality of the firm should deteriorate after any of the swap-based management strategies are initiated, the degree of basis risk volatility at the beginning of the hedge will be an unreliable indication of what it can expect on the call date.

CONCLUDING COMMENTS

The events of the last several years have created a tremendous demand for new tools and strategies designed to manage a corporation's exposure to interest rate movements. Interest rate swaps are among the most prominent of the new products introduced by investment and commercial banks during the past decade. Although the ability of swaps to transform current cash flows has received a great deal of recent attention, little has been written about some of their more creative uses.

In this paper, we explain how interest rate swaps with delayed starting dates can be used to preserve the value of the call option built into a seasoned callable debt issue. We also demonstrate how such instruments offer protection against movements in the underlying term structure of Treasury rates. In so doing, however, they leave the firm exposed to potentially volatile movements in the risk premium differential between swap and credit markets. Finally, we also show how the basic hedge, as well as one involving options on swaps, can be modified to allow the company, in effect, to detach the call feature from the original bond and sell an otherwise unmarketable asset.

Perhaps the most critical advantage of the swap-based hedging strategies—at least, relative to the exchange-traded financial futures and options that can be used to accomplish the same end—is that swaps and swaptions can be tailored to meet the exact requirements of the end user. This kind of flexibility is one of the primary by-products of the ongoing search in our capital markets for innovative solutions to traditional problems. On the downside, however, it must also be recognized that the more specialized the structure, the less liquid it is likely to be. The lack of liquidity, in turn, makes the default potential of the financial intermediary a concern that must be carefully evaluated. Further, our evidence on bond and swap spread volatility indicates that, over the past three years, the basis risk inherent in these strategies would have been large and unpredictable.

■ KEITH BROWN

is the Allied Bancshares Centennial Fellow and Assistant Professor of Finance at the University of Texas. He is a Chartered Financial Analyst and formerly worked as a Senior Consultant to the Corporate Professional Development Department at Manufacturers Hanover Trust Company.

■ DONALD SMITH

is Associate Professor of Finance and Economics at Boston University. Professor Smith also has worked as a Senior Consultant to the Corporate Professional Development Department at Manufacturers Hanover, and is currently involved in executive training programs at a number of financial institutions.

Section VI
Foreign Exchange Applications

Long before the advent of exchange-traded financial futures in the early 1970s, there was a robust forward market in foreign exchange. In the last 20 years however, the range and power of foreign exchange derivatives has expanded tremendously. The articles in this section explore the problem of foreign exchange risk and show how foreign exchange derivatives can be used to manage risk.

The first paper in the section, "The Nature and Management of Foreign Exchange Risk," by Niso Abuaf, introduces the major issues of FOREX (foreign exchange) risk management. Abuaf reviews the recent history of foreign exchange fluctuations and discusses techniques for forecasting foreign exchange rates. Finally, Abuaf presents a guide to the different instruments available for hedging foreign exchange risk. He presents this data in a table that shows the different instruments and the advantages and disadvantages of each.

In "Identifying, Measuring, and Hedging Currency Risk at Merck," Judy C. Lewent and A. John Kearney explain how FOREX risk management can be conducted at a large pharmaceutical firm. The authors show how to identify the foreign exchange risk that faces the company. After identifying the risk, the managers must determine whether direct action to reduce the risk is required. This direct management of the risk, often through trading derivative instruments such as futures and options, is called hedging. The decision to hedge is not automatic, but depends on analyzing the costs and benefits of attempting to manage the risk.

In his article, "Foreign Exchange Options: The Leading Hedge," Niso Abuaf reviews the many uses of foreign exchange options. Abuaf begins by considering the usefulness of FOREX options for hedging contingent risk exposure, which arises when a firm may incur foreign exchange risk at a future date, but the risk is not yet certain. He also considers the ways in which FOREX options allow investors to structure the exact risk and return profiles that they desire. On the whole, Abuaf finds that FOREX options are more powerful instruments than FOREX forwards or futures.

Article 42

The Nature and Management of Foreign Exchange Risk

Niso Abuaf,
Chase Manhattan Bank*

Since the 1970s, exchange rate volatility has increased markedly and, with it, the levels of foreign exchange risk. In fact, fluctuations in financial variables such as exchange rates and interest rates have produced capital gains and losses so large as to swamp many companies' operating results. In response, many financial managers have turned to hedging as well as to more active risk management strategies in the foreign exchange markets. In this article, I review the theoretical and practical issues involved, while citing actual market experience since 1973. With this as background, I then go on to discuss current forecasting techniques and risk management strategies.

Before the main issues are addressed, however, let me offer a few definitions of key terms. First, care should be exercised when using the term "risk." In popular usage, risk is the possibility of an outcome that is less favorable than expected. This is not the definition used either in the finance literature or in this article. Here risk is defined as the dispersion of possible values, favorable or not, around those values that are expected. Foreign exchange risk is the chance that fluctuations in the exchange rate will change the profitability of a transaction from its expected value.

Second, *real* exchange rate risk should be considered apart from *nominal* exchange rate risk. Fluctuations in exchange rates that are not matched by offsetting changes in price levels at home and abroad are changes in the real exchange rate (or, alternatively, deviations from purchasing power parity (PPP)). It is only changes in real exchange rates that affect a country's international competitive position and the underlying profitability of its businesses. As such, they are crucial in both corporate and governmental decisions.

The Recent Foreign Exchange Experience

Many economists have been surprised by the recent volatility of foreign exchange rates and by the persistence of deviations from purchasing power parity (which they call "misalignment"). Milton Friedman, for example, has argued that exchange rates should be unstable only if fundamental economic variables—most notably, national monetary policies, economic growth rates, interest and inflation rate differentials, and current account imbalances—are also unstable. But such arguments have overlooked the extent to which exchange rates behave like asset prices. The prices of financial assets are extremely sensitive to news; they adjust very quickly to reflect new information about the intrinsic value of the underlying asset. The variability of this news by itself increases the volatility of financial asset prices. Moreover, because financial assets, unlike goods, can be almost costlessly stored or traded, their prices are more volatile than those of goods. Exchange rates, accordingly, have been more volatile than goods prices.

This section summarizes well-documented

*I would like to acknowledge the support of the Chase Manhattan Bank, where this research was carried out. I also wish to thank R.L. Slighton, C.W. Slighton, J.R. Zecher for helpful comments, criticisms, and suggestions; D. Chew and C.B. Pantuliano for editorial assistance, and K. Holmes for research support.

Past monthly changes [in exchange rates] are not useful in forecasting future monthly changes, and the expected change in the monthly exchange rate is thus zero.

observations of exchange rate movements, most of which are consistent with this "asset market" view of exchange rate determination.

Volatility Has Been High Compared to Market Fundamentals and Is Increasing.

The most striking observation about exchange rates since 1973 is that monthly exchange rate changes have been more volatile than changes in the observed values of the fundamental determinants. Monthly changes in exchange rates have been within ± 6 percent, with a few approaching ± 12 percent, while reported inflation differentials have not exceeded ± 2 percent.[1]

Moreover, the daily volatility of most currencies, with the exception of the Japanese yen, had increased until the September 1985 "Group of Five" meeting. Due to coordinated intervention, there has been a marked decline in volatility since then—with a few exceptions.[2] Though the reasons for this increase in volatility are not completely clear, part of the explanation may be the increasing deregulation and integration of the financial markets, along with increased uncertainty about the international financial system. By contrast, the daily volatility of the Japanese yen seems to have declined since 1984, especially when compared to the volatilities of other currencies. This is probably due to day-to-day smoothing operations by the Japanese authorities.

There is Almost No Correlation Between Successive Changes in Exchange Rates.

Along with the increased volatility since 1973, monthly changes in exchange rates have been uncorrelated over time and have tended to average zero. This absence of statistically detectable trends suggests that past monthly changes are not useful in forecasting future monthly changes, and that the expected change in the monthly exchange rate is thus

zero. The econometric evidence also shows that weekly changes are uncorrelated. Daily changes, however, appear to be weakly correlated. This could happen if news that affects exchange rates takes a few days to be fully absorbed by the markets (or if central banks intervene to attempt to reverse market trends).

Spot and Forward Rates Move Together.

Spot and forward rates tend to move together. In fact, a regression of the change in the DM/$ forward rate on the change in the DM/$ spot rate results in a coefficient estimate of 0.98, with a standard error of 0.01 and an adjusted R^2 of 0.98.[3] The statistical properties of changes in spot rates, the fact that these changes cannot be predicted by lagged forward rates or discounts, and the high correlation of these changes with changes in forward rates support the hypothesis that most exchange rate changes are unexpected and are thus the result of market adjustments to new information.[4]

Deviations From Purchasing Power Parity Persist For Long Periods.

Along with a weaker short-run link with the fundamentals since 1973, there have been persistent deviations from purchasing power parity (PPP) that have lasted, on average, about five years. One possible explanation is that exchange rates react to shocks quickly while price levels adjust slowly. In the long run, however, both exchange rates and price levels will tend to adjust to absorb shocks. The best available estimate of this rate of adjustment is 2 to 4 percent per month.

Deviations from PPP, as mentioned earlier, are changes in real exchange rates. The real exchange rate can be defined as:

$$E = SP^*/P \tag{1}$$

where S is the nominal exchange rate in terms of home currency per foreign currency, P^* is the foreign price level and P is the home price level. If PPP

1. In fact, some analysts argue that exchange rate changes have more frequent outliers than changes in their fundamental determinants. Formally, academics characterize exchange rate changes as having "fat tails," that is, as compared to the normal distribution function.

2. Volatility may be defined in various ways. Here, it is simply defined as the absolute value of the daily percentage changes times 15.8, the square root of 250, which is the approximate number of trading days in a year. The constant 15.8 annualizes the daily volatility calculations.

3. The residuals do not signal any autocorrelation or other econometric problems. The data are monthly from February 1975 to March 1985.

4. If changes in spot rates had been expected, then such changes would be highly correlated with lagged forward premiums and discounts, and uncorrelated with contemporaneous changes in forward rates. Since this is not so, we infer that spot and forward rates jointly respond to the same news.

It is clear that substantial deviations from PPP do happen; further, they have lasted, on average, five years during the period of floating rates.

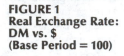

FIGURE 1
Real Exchange Rate:
DM vs. $
(Base Period = 100)

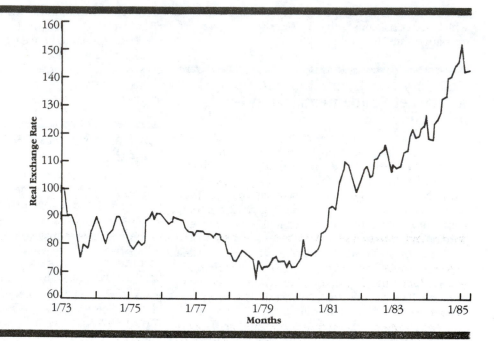

holds, then a change in P*/P should be exactly offset by a change in S, yielding a constant E.

In the short run, movements in real exchange rates reflect primarily changes in the nominal exchange rate rather than changes in relative inflation differentials. Hence, real exchange rate risk in the short run is difficult to distinguish from the risk of changes in nominal exchange rates.

To demonstrate this relationship between real and nominal exchange rate changes, Figure 1 plots the real exchange value of the mark against the dollar. By definition, an upward movement in the index implies that the mark is depreciating in real terms, and a downward move implies a real appreciation. If the years between 1973 and 1977 are taken as the base period, the dollar has been clearly overvalued with respect to PPP in the early 1980s.

In PPP calculations, however, the choice of the base period is always difficult. In this case, for example, if the 1950s were instead chosen as the base period, then the dollar in the early 1980s would not be considered overvalued. To illustrate this point, Figure 2 plots the trade-weighted real exchange value of currencies of the major U.S. trading partners *vis-a-vis* the dollar. (Note that an upward movement in this graph implies a real *depreciation* of the dollar.)

Regardless of the choice of the base period,

however, it is clear that substantial deviations from PPP do happen; further, they have lasted, on average, five years during the period of floating rates. That is, as can be seen in a graphical analysis of various real exchange rates, the real exchange rate tends to wander away from some agreed-upon base level for approximately five years on average. This average embodies both the magnitude of past shocks and the speed of adjustment towards PPP. As such, the predictive ability of this average is quite limited.

There are several reasons for deviations from PPP. Actual or expected changes in central bank reactions and monetary and fiscal policies are predominant. Differential productivity growth in various countries also result in deviations from PPP. And under certain conditions, such as the imposition of capital controls, these deviations can become permanent.

Correlations with Market Fundamentals Are Unstable and Sometimes Curious.

Explanations for movements in exchange rates are hampered by the extremely weak and unstable relationship over the past decade between changes in exchange rates and the major macroeconomic

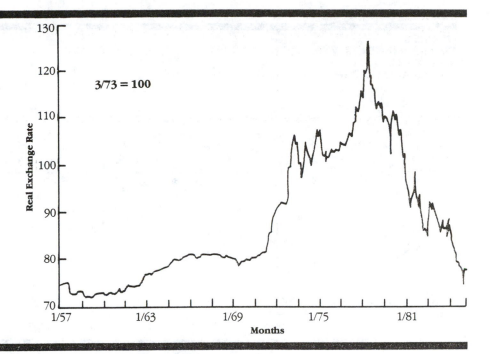

FIGURE 2
U.S. Trade-Weighted Real Exchange Rate Index

3/73 = 100

variables. Some of this may be due to the inconsistency of economic relationships over time; some may be due to the role of swiftly changing expectations.

For example, contrary to theoretical arguments by monetarist economists, the actual correlation between relative changes in the money supply and in exchange rates has been almost nonexistent in the monthly data of the industrialized countries. The correlation does seem to hold, however, for countries subject to extremely high inflation. In such cases, high monetary growth seems to be a reliable predictor of a sharply depreciating currency.

Another weak, though often asserted, correlation is that between relative current account balances and exchange rate changes. Most models maintain that an improvement in the home current account implies an appreciation of the home currency and, conversely, that large trade deficits cause depreciations. The gist of the argument is that a current account surplus increases domestic holdings of foreign exchange reserves, thereby raising the price of the home currency. That is, for domestic residents willingly to own a greater proportion of foreign assets, the relative price of those assets must fall.

Figure 3 plots the quarterly percentage changes in the DM/$ rate against changes in the difference between the ratio of the current account to GNP for the U.S. and the same ratio for Germany over the period 1973-1985. If the theory posited above were true, we would expect larger relative current account surpluses (deficits) to be reflected in an appreciating (depreciating) currency. This expectation is not borne out in Figure 3.

Similarly, attempts to find a stable relationship between interest rates (whether daily, weekly or monthly), oil prices, and exchange rate changes have failed. Table 1, which lists the elasticities of various exchange rates with respect to oil price changes, illustrates the instability of some econometric relationships. Except in the case of Britain, signs of oil prices changes driving exchange rate movements are visible in 1983, not at all in 1982, and only faintly detectable in 1984 and 1985. In 1982, the stability of oil prices may explain the inability of statistical tests to pick up a relationship. As for 1984, it is possible that most countries learned how to hedge their oil exposures while Britain did not because of the size of its oil endowment. Countries that are oil poor relative to the U.S. should experience an appreciation of their currencies when oil prices decrease. (In Table 1, this relationship would appear as a positive

FIGURE 3
Change in the DM/$
Rate vs. Change in
Current-Account Proxy

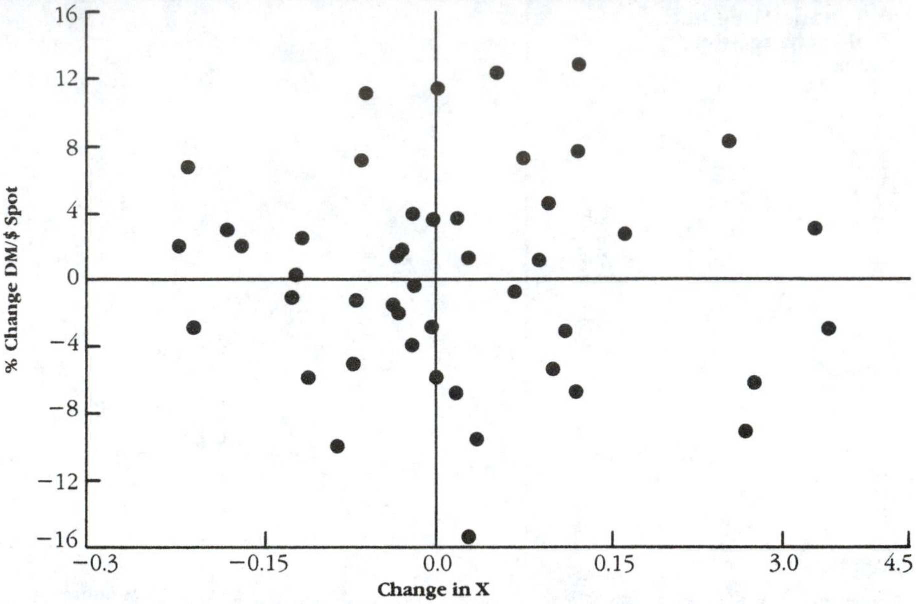

X = German (current
account/GNP) − U.S.
(current account/GNP)

TABLE 1
Foreign Exchange Rate
Elasticities with Respect
to Oil Price Changes

Sample	1982	1983	1984–85
DM/$	.0166	−.0874[c]	−.0809
	(.0915)	(.0428)	(.0739)
YEN/$	.0459	−.0754[b]	−.0524
	(.1172)	(.0434)	(.0467)
SF/$	.0489	−.1563[c]	−.0931[a]
	(.1171)	(.0479)	(.0671)
BP/$	−.0144	−.1268[c]	−.1190[b]
	(.0888)	(.0449)	(.0699)
FF/$	−.0165	−.0672[a]	−.0980[a]
	(.0876)	(.0452)	(.0720)
LIT/$	.0535	−.0825[c]	−.0639
	(.1753)	(.0407)	(.0666)

Standard errors are in parentheses.
Data are daily. The 1985 sample ends on February 6.
DM, YEN, SF, BP, FF and LIT, respectively, stand for the German mark, Japanese yen, Swiss franc, British
pound, French franc and Italian lira.
[a,b,c] Denote significance at the 10, 5 and 2.5% levels for a two-tailed t-test.

number because of the way exchange rates are defined.) The converse is true for the U.K. because it is endowed with oil (and would be shown as a negative number in Table 1). Let us call this the "oil-to-currency" effect.

Yet, the fact that oil is priced in dollars introduces a complication. When the dollar appreciates (and, thus, foreign currencies depreciate relative to the dollar), oil producers may be prompted to reduce their dollar oil prices to foreign buyers to keep local currency oil prices more or less constant (thus giving rise to a negative number in Table 1). This relation-

There is good reason to believe that U.S. monetary policy is more unstable than its German counterpart. Hence, the dollar might be a riskier asset than the DM. This suggests that the DM/$ forward rate would overvalue the DM compared to the expected future spot rate.

TABLE 2 Estimates of Currency Betas	Sample	1982	1983	1984–85
	YEN/$	1.027 (.0496)	.8044 (.0390)	.0436 (.0241)
	SF/$	1.134 (.0356)	.9727 (.0385)	.8544 (.0191)
	BP/$	.7272 (.0412)	.5179 (.0589)	.9012 (.0321)
	FF/$	.9533 (.0412)	.9525 (.0657)	.9650 (.0090)
	LIT/$	.9629 (.0790)	.8519 (.0264)	.9015 (.0170)

Data are daily: The 1985 data end on March 28.
All coefficients are significant at least at the 2.5% level (two-tailed test).
See Table 1 for additional notes.

ship can be called the "dollar-to-currency" effect.

The oil-to-currency effect implies a positive relationship for all except the British pound. The dollar-to-oil effect implies a negative relationship for all. Table 1 suggests that, contrary to conventional wisdom, the dollar-to-oil effect dominates. Even for the pound, it might be argued that were it not for the dollar-to-oil effect, the pound would not be as sensitive to oil price changes as it seems to be. Note that both the first and second effects for the pound are in the negative direction. For the other currencies, the effects tend to cancel out.

Correlations Across Rates Are Often Unstable.

Movements in one exchange rate are not independent of movements in another. Such relationships, however, are not stable. Correlations among currency movements can be measured using the concept of "beta (β)," a regression coefficient, which is formulated as follows:
$$\Delta S = \beta \, \Delta S_{DM/\$}$$
where Δ is the percentage change, S is the exchange rate in foreign currency units per dollar, $S_{DM/\$}$ is the DM/$ exchange rate and β is a constant. Note that the DM/$ rate is chosen as the anchor only for convenience. Table 2 presents estimates of various currency betas over several periods.

As exhibited in the cases of SF and yen, betas are unstable over time. In particular, the Japanese authorities in 1984-85 seem to have been trying to dampen currency movements. It appears that the yen has not been allowed to depreciate against the dollar as much as European currencies, possibly to prevent trade sanctions against Japan by the U.S. or even Europe. The mildness of this depreciation is made up when the dollar depreciates, for then the yen is not allowed to appreciate against the dollar by as much as the European (EMS) currencies. Casual observation suggests that the betas of other EMS currencies are roughly around 1.0 for DM/$ changes of no more than 10 percent in absolute value. For larger changes, EMS betas drop below 1.0.[5]

Forward Rates May Have Stable or Fluctuating Biases.

Forward rates may continuously under- or overpredict future spot rates. These biases may be due to the risk characteristics of the underlying economies. For instance, there is good reason to believe that U.S. monetary policy is more unstable than its German counterpart. Hence, the dollar might be a riskier asset than the DM. This suggests that the DM/$ forward rate would overvalue the DM compared to the expected future spot rate. In fact, most recent econometric evidence, discussed in more detail later, suggests that forward rates are actually biased predictors of future spot rates. If the riskiness of the

5. It is interesting that the Swiss beta is lower in 1984-85 than in 1982. The explanation for the previously larger Swiss beta was that the SF market was not as deep as the DM market and produced larger swings. Apparently, this is no longer true, either because of central bank intervention or deeper markets.

It is important to remember that the volatility of exchange rates, even though high, is not significantly different from that of the prices of other financial assets.

underlying economies fluctuates, so would the bias in the forward rate.

There is an additional source of fluctuating biases. Currencies that are not allowed to float freely, such as the Mexican peso, exhibit a special statistical characteristic that has come to be known as the "peso problem." When the market expects the peso to be sharply devalued, but does not know the exact date of the devaluation, the forward discount on pesos is not as large as the expected devaluation. Hence, the forward peso continuously undervalues the peso through a series of negative forecast errors for dates preceding the devaluation. And for dates subsequent to the devaluation, the forward rate overvalues the peso through a large positive forecast error. Thus, a series of small negative forecast errors followed by a large positive forecast error, or its converse, has come to be called the peso problem.

Biases similar to the peso problem may also exist for the exchange rates of more or less freely floating currencies. This is especially true when there is uncertainty about both the timing and actual occurence of major economic or political events—for example, the unexpected election of a political candidate likely to change a country's monetary and fiscal policies.

The Implications

Just as in the stock market, foreign exchange analysts use various techniques alleged to provide an edge in forecasting financial prices such as exchange rates and stock prices. If such techniques did prove to be effective forecasting tools, it would imply that the users of such techniques could generate profits above the fair market rate of return. While this sometimes may occur, it generally does not. And there is good reason to be skeptical about apparent free lunches: it is not rational to share successful forecasting methods with others because doing so would reduce per-capita profits.

In this section we discuss the efficient markets hypothesis (EMH)—loosely, the notion that there is no free lunch—and its implications for foreign exchange forecasting. In the critical light of EMH, we then assess the usefulness of the technical and econometric analyses that are currently used to forecast exchange rates.

There Is No Free Lunch: The Efficient Markets Hypothesis

The dismal forecasting performance of econometric models, as well as the very limited horizon of technical models, add further credence to the efficient markets hypothesis. In its so-called "strong" form, the EMH states that financial asset prices, such as exchange rates, fully reflect *all* information. Investors therefore cannot consistently earn extraordinary profits by exploiting any sources of information, even that of insiders. Less extreme versions of the hypothesis state that only *publicly* available information, including all past price performance, is already reflected in the current price.

The strong form of the hypothesis is based on the observation that financial assets can be easily traded by numerous well-informed traders who make decisions continuously.[6] For this reason, financial prices are extremely sensitive to news and immediately adjust to reflect all available information about the major determinants of an asset's value. In turn, the strength of these expectations affects the volatility of the financial asset's price.

In the long run, financial prices do turn out to be consistent with market fundamentals. In the short run, however, financial prices are rather "noisy," whether because of shifts in expectations, institutional movements in and out of the market, or other unsystematic factors. Nevertheless, it is important to remember that the volatility of exchange rates, even though high, is not significantly different from that of the prices of other financial assets.

For reasons discussed previously, efficient market theorists contend that the apparent departures from market fundamentals do not necessarily imply that the market is inefficient. Such departures do not offer consistent opportunities to earn extraordinary profits (on a risk-adjusted basis).

In judging the efficient markets hypothesis, it is perhaps better to think of market efficiency as the description of a process rather than a static condition of the market at each point in time. It is, in fact, almost impossible for investors to make extraordinary profits using only publicly available information. Those who do make such profits possess superior forecasting skills and their economic return may be viewed as a "monopoly rent." Aside from these ex-

---

6. It also assumes that these assets can be stored without cost.

In the absence of capital controls, arbitrage dictates that the home currency must be at a forward discount that is approximately equal to the difference between home and foreign interest rates.

ceptions, many other traders invest in information gathering and processing; and they make economic profits on their positions if their judgments are borne out. Such traders help ensure that the market reflects all available information.

A corollary of the EMH is the validity of the random walk model (or some variant thereof). The model holds that the best predictor of future asset prices is the current asset price, perhaps with some adjustment for the expected growth of the asset. There are two types of random walk models: those with and those without "drift." Drift stands for the expected growth of the asset in question.

Are Current Rates Adjusted for Interest Differentials the Best Forecasters of Future Spot Rates?

Price changes have two components: the expected and the unexpected. In the case of equities, stock prices move at a rate appropriate to their risk class (the expected component) together with a random term (the unexpected component). The unexpected component can only be random because new information, by definition, arrives randomly. From this, it follows that stock prices behave according to the random walk model with a drift term (which reflects, again, an expected rate of growth in the asset's price).[7]

This model is also applicable to the foreign exchange market. One can either invest a dollar at home or, alternatively, convert it to foreign currency, invest it abroad, and repatriate it at the end of the investment period. The functioning of arbitrageurs who are indifferent between holding domestic and foreign assets ensures that the above two investment strategies produce the same rate of return. That is, we would expect the home currency to depreciate by an amount approximately equal to the difference between domestic and foreign interest rates.[8] For example, if home interest rates are 200 basis points below foreign rates, then one expects the home currency to appreciate by 2 percent.

This relationship is known as the *uncovered interest rate parity* theorem. In essence, it is the ran-

dom walk model with drift, in which the drift (or expected) term is the differential between home and foreign interest rates. The unexpected term is the arbitrageurs' judgmental error.[8]

Aha, the Corresponding Forward Rate Is the Best Forecaster of Future Spot Rates!

One twist in the foreign exchange markets that must be accounted for is the forward market. In the absence of capital controls, arbitrage dictates that the home currency must be at a forward discount that is approximately equal to the difference between home and foreign interest rates.[9] For instance, if foreign annual interest rates are 300 basis points above home rates, then the foreign currency must be at a 3 percent annual forward discount. Otherwise, there would be arbitrage opportunities through the forward market.

Because speculators take forward positions which reflect their views, it can be argued that forward rates should be unbiased predictors of future spot rates.[10] In fact, some authors have coined the term "forecasting efficiency" to indicate that forward exchange rates are the best available forecasters of the future spot rate.

Or Maybe the Best Forecaster of Future Spot Rates Is the Current Rate.

Unfortunately, the most satisfying simple model of exchange rate movement turns out to be the random walk model without drift, which implies that the best forecaster of all future spot rates is the current spot rate. The forecasting superiority of the spot rate over the forward rate is especially prominent in the short run, but gradually disappears as the forecasting horizon is lengthened.

What Really Forecasts Future Spot Rates Best?

There is increasing evidence that forward rates, and hence the random walk model with drift, are not unbiased predictors of future spot rates. This may be due to the existence of a risk premium that arises from restrictions on the free substitution of home

7. Expressed in the form of an equation, the random walk model with drift is as follows: $s_t = u + s_{t-1} + e_t$, where s is the natural log of the underlying asset price. subscripts t and t-1 denote the time at which a variable is measured, u is the drift term (expected component) and e (unexpected component) is a normally, independently distributed error term with mean zero and constant variance. Note that since s_t and s_{t-1} are in logs, their difference is the expected growth rate of the asset, u. And e represents the unexpected growth of the asset.

8. The uncovered interest rate parity theorem, which is simply a reworking of the equation for the random walk model with drift, can be formulated as follows: $s_{t-1} = (i - i^*) + s_t + e_{t+1}$, where s_{t-1} and s_t are the logs of the exchange

rate in terms of home currency per unit of foreign currency at times t+1 and t, respectively; i and i* are the home and foreign interest rates; and e_t, the unexpected component, is a normally, independently distributed error term with mean zero and constant variance.

9. In equation form, $_tf_{t+1} - s_t = i - i^*$, where $_tf_{t+1}$ is the log of the forward rate set at time t for delivery at time t+1.

10. This assumes there is no risk premium in international capital markets—either because of risk neutrality or because assets can be readily substituted.

When central banks attempt to dampen price changes that would otherwise take place, they make exchange rate behavior look like the slow spread of new information.

and foreign assets, or from investors' demand for a higher expected return for holding more risky currencies. The evidence is that current exchange rates predict future spot rates better than do forward rates; forecast errors, as measured by the mean absolute errors for example, are smaller when current rates are used.

Further, there is evidence that the random walk model without drift has better forecasting performance than such models, even when econometric models use actual values for the independent variables. This is well documented for forecasting horizons of up to a year. Hence, the empirical evidence suggests that the best simple predictor of future spot prices is the driftless random walk model.

This finding poses a problem because the driftless random walk model is extremely unsatisfactory from a theoretical perspective. In fact, this implies a money-making strategy (which I discuss later) and is inconsistent with long-term PPP.

Technical Analysis May Work in the Very Short Run.

Technical analysis is a vague term but is here defined as a body of analysis for forecasting the price of a financial asset solely on the basis of that asset's own price history. Common forms of technical analysis include models with names such as "momentum," "slope," "moving average," and "head and shoulders." Most of these models forecast only the direction of price movements.

A momentum model is based on the idea that a price, such as an exchange rate, will continue to move up if it has been rising in the past, and vice versa. Another theory defines a peak as a resistance area. If the market again approaches a peak, after having moved down from it, it is said to be "testing" the resistance area. If it "pierces" the resistance area, it is likely to move up for a while. If it backs away, it is likely to go down some more. Resistance areas are also formed on the downside.[11]

Technical analysis can be successful only if successive price changes are correlated. There is some support for technical analysis from a number of mechanisms that cause price changes to be positively autocorrelated. These include mass psychol-

ogy, in the form of price changes feeding upon themselves, and the slow spread of new information. The existence of central banks that "lean against the wind" is another such mechanism. When central banks attempt to dampen price changes that would otherwise take place, they make exchange rate behavior look like the slow spread of new information.

For example, if there is market pressure for the exchange rate to move by 10 percent and the central bank instead allows only a series of 2 percent changes in stages, these small changes would be positively autocorrelated, whereas a once-and-for-all 10 percent jump does not have to be correlated with subsequent changes. Furthermore, technical analysis may pick up certain factors that escape classical statistical methods. For instance, technical analysis might be better at signaling certain discrete "jumps," such as a European Monetary System realignment.

Indeed, there is evidence that technical models have predictive power, especially in intra-day trading. However, their predictive power for periods of a month or longer does not seem strong. If information spreads in a few days, and if information in technical models is quickly disseminated, it is possible to have daily but not monthly autocorrelations.

If a technical model signals that a market will go up—and if enough people act on this signal—the market will go up by an amount corresponding to the information embodied in the technical signal. But because financial markets react quickly to news, it is unlikely that any worthy news will take a month or longer to be disseminated. Thus, the very use of technical models in the short run invalidates their use in the longer run.

Econometric Analysis Has Been Disappointing In The Short To Medium Run.

The exchange rate is an asset price that equilibrates various markets. When asset holders' expectations change with respect to the factors that affect those markets, the exchange rate also adjusts to reflect the new expectations. Attempts to uncover this process have produced several theoretical models of exchange rate determination, ranging from simple monetary theories to more complex portfolio bal-

---

11. There are also less common forms of technical analysis. Sophisticated econometric techniques such as Box-Jenkins analysis that use a price series' own history for forecasting are philosophically no different from the more traditional forms of technical analysis. However, Box-Jenkins-like autoregressive methods forecast the magnitude of change as well as the direction of change.

ance formulations. Econometric analysis is generally used to substantiate the superiority of one model over another. Thereafter comes forecasting.

With econometric forecasting of exchange rates, however, a number of problems arise. First, we do not have a satisfactory theory to explain the formation of expectations. Moreover, we cannot accurately measure expectations—not surprisingly, since expectations are not directly observable (that is, when we are unable to measure accurately the variables that go into an econometric forecasting model, we cannot place much faith in the forecast itself). Second, any knowledge embodied in an econometric or technical model should already be embodied in the market price of a financial asset. Thus, the use of a model should not give its user an edge over other market participants. Third, the true underlying model that drives the world has not yet been uncovered. And fourth, the data needed to build econometric models of foreign exchange rates are inadequate. Statistics collected for this purpose usually are not timely or of the desired frequency. They are often inaccurate and generally do not reveal enough about institutional factors such as interventions and financial flows. Institutional factors may not be important in the determination of foreign exchange rates in the long run. Nevertheless, a large jump in the demand for foreign exchange by a large corporation on any given day will move the exchange rate on that day. And for traders whose profitability hinges on intra-day movements, that is important.

On balance, then, given the current state of the art, econometric models are not very useful for forecasting exchange rates in the short to medium term—that is, up to five years—though forecasting performance improves with the length of the horizon. Still, the longer-run forecasting capabilities of econometric modeling may be useful for other purposes, if only for focusing management's attention on the likely economic consequences of future exchange rate changes.

Risk Management Strategies

Though faced with ever greater exchange rate risk, financial managers can nevertheless reduce their exposure to such risk. Some of the available means for managing exchange risk are the consolidation of foreign exchange receivables and payments, hedging, and diversification.

Consolidate Receivables and Payables

The obvious first step in the management of foreign exchange exposure is to consolidate foreign currency receivables and payables. This gives management a clearer picture of foreign exchange exposures and avoids unnecessary covering costs.

In addition, correlations among currency movements can be exploited. Suppose, for example, that the current spot rates are 2.00 DM/$ and 150 yen/$, with receivables consisting of 200,000 DM and payables consisting of 15,000,000 yen in matched maturities. At current exchange rates, the yen payables are offset by the DM receivables. If management does not expect exchange rates to change, then no hedging transactions are necessary.

This would also be true if exchange rates change and the yen Beta equals one; that is, if changes in the yen were accompanied by the same percentage change in the value of the DM. If, however, the yen Beta is less than one, the DM receivables do not fully hedge the yen payables when the dollar appreciates because the depreciation of the DM exceeds the depreciation of the yen. Put differently, the yen has appreciated against the DM. Conversely, if the dollar depreciates, the mark receivables more than fully hedge the yen payables. In fact, it can be shown that one can be fully hedged by altering the DM position by the amount y, where:

$y = x (1 - Beta)$ and where x is the expected change in the DM/$ exchange rate. That is, if x equals 0.10 (that is, the dollar appreciates by 10 percent), and Beta is 0.5, the DM position should be increased by 5 percent (y = .05).

Hedging Is Relevant.

The second step in foreign exchange exposure management is assessing and, if necessary, hedging the remaining exposure to exchange risk. The selection of an appropriate risk management strategy depends on management's view of what constitutes risk. The prevailing view, among practitioners at least, is that the primary purpose of exchange risk management is to reduce the variability of the firm's profits—whether measured by cash flows or conventionally reported dollar earnings—caused by changes in exchange rates. Financial academics, however, have long argued that reducing the variability of a company's returns, while leaving the expected level of those returns unchanged, should

Reducing the overall risk profile of the firm is relevant to shareholders if only because risk affects the perceptions and behavior of other corporate stakeholders such as employees, managers, lenders, and suppliers.

have little effect on the value of the firm. This view of risk management focuses on risk in the equity markets and considers a security or a firm's operations risky only to the extent that the firm's activities move in tandem with the market as a whole. Well-diversified international investors, so the argument goes, should not be willing to pay a premium for corporate hedging activities which they can easily duplicate for themselves simply by adjusting their portfolios. According to this view, although hedging to reduce overall variability of profits may be important to executives compensated on the basis of short-term earnings, it is largely a matter of "irrelevance" to shareholders.

I take issue with this argument, first of all, because it underestimates the importance of information, transaction costs, and other sources of friction in the operation of markets. These factors may make it costlier for market participants to hedge certain risks than for the firm to do so. In this article, I begin with the assumption that hedging does have value for shareholders (in part because it is so widely observed). Reducing the overall risk profile of the firm—stemming from fluctuations in commodity prices, high fixed costs, high financial leverage, as well as exchange rate swings—is relevant to shareholders if only because risk affects the perceptions and behavior of other corporate stakeholders such as employees, managers, lenders, and suppliers.[12] By reducing the total risk or variability of the firm, hedging transactions reduce the exposure of a range of corporate constituencies; and this in turn may increase the value of shareholders' claims.

Use Passive Strategies If You Cannot Forecast Nominal Rates.

For protection against the risk arising from currency volatility, there are a number of passive strategies that either totally or partially hedge a firm's foreign exchange exposure. These strategies are particularly useful when management has little confidence in its ability to forecast. In general, these strategies try to avoid risk at almost all cost. By contrast, active strategies—those which entail participation in the foreign exchange market based on a view of currency

movements—require some appetite for risk.

Some passive strategies ensure a minimum level of profits and, at the same time, allow the opportunity for more. But at the least, passive strategies are beneficial because they insure positions and insulate the firm's income from undesirable foreign exchange moves. These strategies, with the exception of using futures, also avoid the costs involved in managing positions.

Passive strategies use a variety of financial instruments, including forwards, futures, swaps, and options. Other widely used techniques are leading and lagging, borrowing and lending, currency matching, and commodity hedging. (Only a few examples are illustrated below, but the pros and cons of each technique are outlined in the Appendix to this article.) Because the characteristics of foreign exchange risk tend to differ by time horizon, the appropriate strategies for the short, medium, and long term also vary.

Use Readily Available Instruments in the Short Term.

The evidence presented above suggests that in the short term (less than one year), most movements in nominal exchange rates are largely unanticipated. Moreover, prices at home and abroad do not adjust quickly to offset nominal exchange rate changes (thereby causing deviations from PPP). And finally, nominal interest rate differentials across countries are not matched by subsequent and offsetting exchange rate changes.

This evidence implies that there is *real* foreign exchange risk in the short term. In turn, this leads directly to business risk by affecting both unhedged monetary and nonmonetary positions arising out of commercial transactions and dividend flows. This type of currency risk is sometimes referred to as "transaction" risk.

Because foreign exchange forecasting is so unreliable in the short term, transaction risk should be (and is easily) hedged by using the available financial instruments and techniques mentioned above. Of course, there is a cost attached to these procedures. For example, the cost of forward covering is best represented as the difference between the bid-ask spread in the forward contract and in the spot markets.[13]

---

12. For an extensive discussion of this point, see Alan Shapiro and Sheridan Titman, "An Integrated Approach to Corporate Risk Management," *Midland Corporate Finance Journal*, Vol. 3 No. 2 (1985).

13. This, however, is a controversial matter. Some authors argue for the difference between the current spot and the forward rate. Others believe cost should be viewed as the difference between the forward contract and the spot

In order for FASB 52 to provide an accurate representation of true economic value, all items on the balance sheet must be marked to market.

Match Assets and Liabilities in the Medium Term and Use Actual or Synthetic Instruments.

In the medium term—say, one to five years—foreign exchange risk encompasses both transaction and translation risks. Translation risk relates to the effects of nominal exchange rate changes on balance sheet exposures. Firms try to manage such exposures by matching assets and liabilities in a particular currency as well as by using the above-mentioned techniques and instruments. Nevertheless, such efforts have limited effectiveness because of transaction costs and various constraints.

An understanding of translation exposure requires knowledge of accounting rules and regulations such as FASB 8 and FASB 52. For instance, the more recent, and more relevant, FASB 52 rule states that all translation must be carried out at the prevailing spot rates when the accounting statements are prepared. By contrast, FASB 8 translates monetary items at the exchange rate on the reporting date and nonmonetary items at the exchange rates prevailing at the time of acquisition. Another difference between the two rules concerns the separation of foreign exchange income from operating income. FASB 8 reports translation gains and losses in current income, blurring the distinction between operating income and foreign exchange income. FASB 52, on the other hand, incorporates foreign exchange gains and losses in an equity account (except for certain aspects of the operations of foreign subsidiaries that use a certain "functional" currency as reported in FASB 8).

For the purpose of judging a firm's economic value, FASB 52 is incomplete unless it is accompanied by thorough inflation accounting at home and abroad. In order, then, for FASB 52 to provide an accurate representation of true economic value, all items on the balance sheet must be marked to market. To illustrate, consider a foreign subsidiary located in an inflationary environment where price increases are fully matched by local currency depreciation (such that PPP is maintained). To the extent that the fixed assets of the subsidiary are valued at historical book value and translated at current exchange rates, translation according to FASB 52 will understate the value of these fixed assets. Because share prices are likely to reflect real economic performance rather than that indicated by translated accounting earnings, it might be argued that accounting exposure should not be a matter of concern. Nonetheless, translation exposure can have some important effects. Accounting conventions affect tax payments, royalty payments, executive compensation, and various other contractual obligations.

Try to Forecast Real Exchange Rates in the Long Term.

Long-term exchange risk (more than five years), also known as "real" or "economic" exchange risk, arises from permanent secular changes in real exchange rates and from permanent differences in real returns across countries. Such changes influence the profitability of various production locations around the globe and are critical to decisions about foreign production and investment.

It is very difficult to hedge real exchange risk in the marketplace with any precision. Explicit instruments for such operations are either nonexistent or thinly traded. Nevertheless, there are some, admittedly crude, approaches to hedging economic exchange risk. For example, a U.S. multinational sourcing some of its components in Brazil will face reduced profitability if the real exchange value of the cruzado appreciates—that is, if Brazilian prices (wages and other costs) rise faster than the rate of cruzado depreciation. To protect itself, the company can construct a hedge by buying Brazilian cruzados forward, together with forward contracts of Brazilian commodities. Or it can buy forward cruzados and Brazilian real assets.

The problem with these strategies, however, is that long-dated forward markets for the cruzado and for Brazilian commodities are probably extremely thin. One alternative is to borrow in the U.S. and lend in Brazil. But these sets of transactions are too cumbersome to be economical. Yet another alternative is to attempt to forecast real exchange rates, particularly since long-term real exchange rates are probably easier to forecast than short-term rates.

Under certain assumptions, an improvement in overall home productivity points to a real appreciation of the home currency. This suggests that when

rate at maturity. Still others vote for the difference between the forward rate and the expected future spot rate. Ultimately, though, the cost of the forward cover is the income of units that provide this cover. This income is the bid-ask spread, and it is this cover that has to be compared to the alternative of transacting in the spot market.

Despite persuasive arbitrage arguments, real rates of interest may be consistently different across countries, even after adjusting for exchange rate changes. Perhaps the reason is that there is risk associated with being long in a certain country.

TABLE 3 Spot and Forward Rates for the BP and SF on 3/22/85	Sample	Spot	30 Days	90 Days	180 Days
	$/BP	1.1740	1.1692	1.1623	1.1594
	$/SF	.3663	.3674	.3696	.3743

multinationals produce abroad, they should invest in industries with higher than average expected productivity growth. Such a strategy helps to ensure that the cost of the components sourced in these countries remains competitive.

Use Active Strategies If You Have A View.

At the opposite end of passive strategies in the risk-management spectrum are those that maximize expected value regardless of risk. Examples of some active management strategies, which are geared toward achieving a profit target at the expense of incurring some risk, are discussed below.

Borrow Low, Lend High.

As shown above, the current spot rate may be a better predictor of future spot rates than the corresponding forward or futures rates (as predicted by the random walk model). Although even this relationship is not precise, it can be exploited if investors are willing to bear some risk. The strategy is to make buy or sell decisions in the forward markets based on the assumption that, on average, the current spot rates will prevail in the future.

To illustrate, consider the spot and forward rates for the British pound (BP) and the Swiss Franc (SF) in Table 3. Note that the pound is at a discount and the SF is at a premium throughout the forward horizon of 30 to 180 days. For the 180-day horizon, the forward rates imply that the pound is at a 2.48 percent per year discount, and the SF is at a 4.36 percent per year premium. Under the above strategy, which essentially bets on the current spot rate against the forward rate, the company should take a long forward position in pounds and a short forward position in SFs. In essence, this means taking a long forward position in BPs because forward BPs are incorrectly cheaper than spot BPs. That is, in the relevant future, the spot BP will not be as cheap as the forward rates indicate but, instead, will be just as expensive as the current spot rate. The converse is true for the SF. The strategy expects to make profits of .0048c/BP, .0117c/BP and .0146c/BP on the 30-, 90- and 180-days contracts, respectively.

Such a strategy, incidentally, is virtually identical to borrowing in countries with low interest rates and lending in countries with high interest rates. Borrowing in Switzerland is the same as being short Swiss bonds. At maturity, SFs must be bought to pay one's liabilities; and this is thus identical to shorting forward SFs. Similarly, lending in the U.K. means that one is long British bonds, which is equivalent to being long in forward pounds.

Under these circumstances, it is no wonder that international arbitrage and the figures given in the table indicate that annualized British and Swiss interest rates are approximately 248 basis points higher, and 436 basis points lower, than U.S. rates, respectively. Another example: when 15-year interest rates were 8 percent for the SF and 17 percent for the US$, the World Bank was funding some of its operations in the Swiss franc. The Bank calculated that the breakeven point would occur at a 9 percent annual rate of appreciation for the SF vis-a-vis the dollar. Over 15 years, this would compound to a 364 percent appreciation, or a change to $1.75/SF from the 48c/SF prevailing at the time. Since the World Bank reasoned that this was an unlikely outcome, they accepted the risk and funded in SFs.

But let me offer one caveat in betting against the forward rate. In doing so, one maintains naked positions in the forward markets. Put differently, the expected return of this strategy may be viewed as a reward to the risk associated with the strategy. Despite persuasive arbitrage arguments, real rates of interest may be consistently different across countries, even after adjusting for exchange rate changes. Perhaps the reason is that there is risk associated with being long in a certain country. This risk can be mitigated in two ways: first, by using foreign exchange options, which put a limit on losses; and, second, by using a portfolio approach to currency management.

Use the Portfolio Approach to Exploit Correlations, or Lack Thereof, among Currency Movements.

The portfolio approach takes advantage of the correlations, or lack thereof, among various ex-

International portfolio diversification pays off if national financial markets are sufficiently segregated.

change rate changes. For example, we know that movements in the Dutch guilder (DG) and the German mark (DM) are highly correlated vis-a-vis the dollar. If Dutch interest rates suddenly go up, the portfolio approach suggests that one should borrow marks and lend guilders. This is a less risky strategy than borrowing dollars and lending guilders because it involves uncertainty in only one exchange rate—that is, the DM/DG. By contrast, borrowing US$ and lending DG entails uncertainty in two exchange rates: the $/DM and DM/DG. (Here, it is useful to think of the DM as a price leader and the DG as a price follower.)

While it is useful to exploit high degrees of co-movements, managers can reduce overall variability when there are low degrees of co-movement between returns on different assets or markets. This can be done by diversifying away from a single market or asset toward several markets or assets. For example, if returns on French securities, after accounting for exchange rate changes, have almost no correlation with returns on Australian securities, a U.S. investor could reduce the overall variability of his portfolio by holding both French and Australian securities. This is similar to selling life insurance to a diverse group of people.

International portfolio diversification pays off if national financial markets are sufficiently segregated. If they are, arbitrage relationships such as PPP may not hold while returns, measured in the home currency of the investor, may be uncorrelated. The risk of this approach is that correlations among the returns of various assets may be unstable over time. Even so, the evidence suggests that international portfolio diversification does pay off by reducing risk when an expected return is the main goal, or by increasing expected return when a specific level of risk is kept under control.

Concluding Comments

The facts about exchange rate behavior summarized in this article suggest that it is difficult to forecast exchange rates with any degree of confidence. The reason is that exchange rate movements are largely unanticipated and are more volatile than market fundamentals. In addition, correlations with market fundamentals and among rates are unstable. Though there is a gradual move towards purchasing power parity—at an average of about 4 percent a month—this is nonetheless not a very useful forecasting paradigm, given the volatility of foreign exchange rates. Even forward rates may not be accurate forecasters because of built-in biases and because of the rapidity with which new information hits the markets.

Because of this difficulty in forecasting exchange rates, corporate treasurers are well advised to hedge net exposures by using readily available (or synthetically constructing) hedging instruments such as forwards, swaps, and options. The markets for these instruments are usually very deep for tenors of one to two years, and are deepening for maturities of up to 15 years—especially in the major currencies. It is noteworthy that these instruments can also allow corporate treasurers to exploit borrowing or investment "windows" across the globe while reducing foreign exchange risk.

In managing longer-term, economic exposures, however, there is more room for economic analysis and perhaps even forecasting—despite the risks. For instance, if exchange rates are misaligned according to most PPP calculations, then treasurers might want to position themselves so as to benefit from a shift of rates back toward PPP. Similarly, interest rate differences might indicate certain borrowing or lending strategies even after accounting for possible exchange rate adjustments. It also might be wise to reduce production costs by sourcing overseas in industries where the expected productivity growth of the sourced component is higher than the overall rate of productivity growth in the source country. More adventurous corporate treasurers can attempt to exploit correlations among currency movements and to benefit from the insights provided by some of the more esoteric econometric techniques—although these should also be used with caution.

Niso Abuaf
is Vice President and Economist for the Chase Manhattan Bank. Dr. Abuaf follows the foreign exchange markets and designs new products having option- and futures-like features. He has taught micro and macroeconomics, as well as money and banking, at the University of Chicago's Graduate School of Business, where he received his Ph.D. in International Finance.

Instruments	Description	Pros	Cons
Forwards	An almost custom-made contract to buy or sell foreign-exchange in the future, at a presently specified price.	Maturity and size of contract can be determined individually to almost exactly hedge the desired position.	Use up bank credit lines even when two forward contracts exactly offset each other.
Futures	A ready-made contract to buy or sell foreign exchange in the future, at a presently specified price. Unlike forwards, futures have a few maturity dates per year. The most common contracts have maturity dates in March, June, September, or December. But, these contracts are almost continuously traded on organized exchanges. Contract sizes are fixed.	No credit lines required. Easy access for small accounts. Fairly low margin requirements. Contract's liquidity guaranteed by the exchange on which it is traded.	Margin requirements cause cash-flow uncertainty and use managerial resources.
Options	A contract that offers the right but not the obligation to buy or sell foreign exchange in the future, at a presently specified price. Unlike forwards and futures, options do not have to be exercised. Available on an almost custom-made basis from banks or in ready-made form on exchanges.	Allow hedging of contingent exposures and taking positions while limiting downside risk and retaining upside potential for profit. Also permit tradeoffs other than risk versus expected return.	Since an option is like insurance coupled with an investment oportunity, its benefits are not readily observable, leading some to conclude that it is "too expensive."
Swaps	An agreement to exchange one currency for another at specified dates and prices. Essentially, a swap is a series of forward contracts.	Versatile, allowing easy hedging of complex exposures.	Documentation requirement might be extensive.

Techniques	Description	Pros	Cons
Borrowing and lending	Creates a synthetic forward by borrowing and lending at home and abroad. For example, a long forward foreign-exchange position is equivalent to borrowing at home, converting the proceeds to foreign exchange and investing them abroad. The converse holds for a short forward foreign-exchange position.	Useful when forwards, futures or swaps markets are thin—particularly for long-dated maturities.	Utilizes costly managerial resources. May be prohibited by legal restrictions.
Commodity hedging	Going short (long) a commodity contract denominated in a foreign currency to hedge a foreign-exchange asset (liability).	Commodity markets are usually deep, particularly for maturities up to a year.	Price changes of commodities, in terms of home currency, may not exactly offset price changes in the asset (liability) to be hedged. Commodity hedging may not be possible for maturities of over one year.
Leading and lagging	Equating foreign-exchange assets and liabilities by speeding up or slowing down receivables or payables.	Avoids unnecessary hedging costs.	Appropriate matches may not be available. Utilizes costly managerial resources.
Matching	Equating assets and liabilities denominated in each currency.	Avoids unnecessary hedging costs.	Appropriate matches may not be available.

Article 43

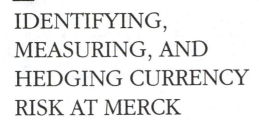

IDENTIFYING, MEASURING, AND HEDGING CURRENCY RISK AT MERCK

by Judy C. Lewent and A. John Kearney, Merck & Co., Inc.

The authors would like to thank Francis H. Spiegel, Jr., Senior Vice President and CFO of Merck & Co., Inc., and Professors Donald Lessard of M.I.T. and Darrell Duffie of Stanford for their guidance throughout.

The impact of exchange rate volatility on a company depends mainly on the company's business structure, both legal and operational, its industry profile, and the nature of its competitive environment. This article recounts how Merck assessed its currency exposures and reached a decision to hedge those exposures. After a brief introduction to the company and the industry, we discuss our methods of identifying and measuring our exchange exposures, the factors considered in deciding whether to hedge such risks, and the financial hedging program we put in place.

AN INTRODUCTION TO THE COMPANY

Merck & Co., Inc. primarily discovers, develops, produces, and distributes human and animal health pharmaceuticals. It is part of a global industry that makes its products available for the prevention, relief, and cure of disease throughout the world. Merck itself is a multinational company, doing business in over 100 countries.

Total worldwide sales in 1989 for all domestic and foreign research-intensive pharmaceutical companies are projected to be $103.7 billion. Worldwide sales for those companies based in the U.S. are projected at $36.4 billion—an estimated 35% of the world pharmaceutical market; and worldwide sales for Merck in 1989 were $6.6 billion. The industry is highly competitive, with no company holding over 5% of the worldwide market. Merck ranks first in pharmaceutical sales in the U.S. and the world, yet has only a 4.7% market share worldwide. The major foreign competitors for the domestic industry are European firms and emerging Japanese companies.

Driven by the need to fund high-risk and growing research expenditures, the U.S. pharmaceutical industry has expanded significantly more into foreign markets than has U.S. industry as a whole. In 1987, the leading U.S. pharmaceutical companies generated 38% of their sales revenues overseas; and 37% of their total assets were located outside the U.S. In contrast, most U.S. industry groups report foreign sales revenues in the range of 20% to 30%. Merck, with overseas assets equal to 40% of total and with roughly half of its sales overseas, is among the most internationally-oriented of U.S. pharmaceutical companies.

The U.S. pharmaceutical industry also differs in its method of doing business overseas. In contrast to U.S. exporters, who often bill their customers in U.S. dollars, the pharmaceutical industry typically bills its customers in their local currencies. Thus, the effect of foreign currency fluctuations on the pharmaceutical industry tends to be more immediate and direct.

The typical structure is the establishment of subsidiaries in many overseas markets. These subsidiaries, of which Merck has approximately 70, are typically importers of product at some stage of manufacture, and are responsible for finishing, marketing, and distribution within the country of incorporation. Sales are denominated in local currency, and costs in a combination of local currency for finishing, marketing, distribution, administration, and taxes, and in the currency of basic manufacture and research—typically, the U.S. dollar for U.S.-based companies.

EXHIBIT 1
MERCK SALES INDEX

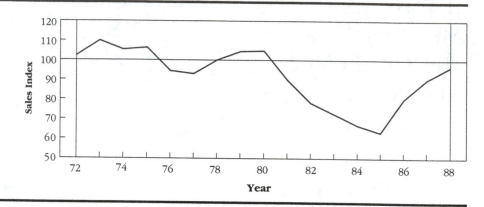

IDENTIFICATION AND MEASUREMENT OF EXPOSURE

It is generally agreed that foreign exchange fluctuations can affect a U.S. company's economic and financial results in three ways:

1. By changing the dollar value of net assets held overseas in foreign currencies (known as "translation" exposures) or by changing the expected results of transactions in non-local currencies ("transaction" exposures).

2. By changing the dollar value of future revenues expected to be earned overseas in foreign currencies ("future revenue" exposures).

3. By changing a company's competitive position—for example, a competitor whose costs are denominated in a depreciating currency will have greater pricing flexibility and thus a potential competitive advantage ("competitive" exposures).

Competitive exposures have been the subject of much of the recent academic work done on exchange risk management. Such exposures are best exemplified by the adverse effect of the strong dollar on the competitive position of much of U.S. industry in the early 1980s. This was true not only in export markets but also in the U.S. domestic market, where the strengthening U.S. dollar gave Japanese and European-based manufacturers a large competitive advantage in dollar terms over domestic U.S. producers.

For the pharmaceutical industry, however, the pricing environment is such that competitive exposure to exchange fluctuations is generally not significant. The existence of price controls through-

out most of the world generally reduces flexibility to react to economic changes.

Hence, Merck's exposure to exchange tends to be limited primarily to net asset and revenue exposures. The potential loss in dollar value of net revenues earned overseas represents the company's most significant economic and financial exposure. Such revenues are continuously converted into dollars through interaffiliate merchandise payments, dividends, and royalties, and are an important source of cash flow for the company. To the extent the dollar value of these earnings is diminished, the company suffers a loss of cash flow—at least over the short term. And, as discussed in more detail later, the resulting volatility in earnings and cash flow could impair the company's ability to execute its strategic plan for growth.

With its significant presence worldwide, Merck has exposures in approximately 40 currencies. As a first step in assessing the effect of exchange rate movements on revenues and net income, we constructed a sales index that measures the relative strength of the dollar against a basket of currencies weighted by the size of sales in those countries.[1] When the index is above 100%, foreign currencies have strengthened versus the dollar, indicating a positive exchange effect on dollar revenues. When the index is below 100%, as was the case through most of the 1980s, the dollar has strengthened versus the foreign currencies, resulting in income statement losses due to exchange.

As Exhibit 1 illustrates, the index was relatively stable from 1972 to 1980. But, as the dollar strengthened in the early 1980s, the index declined to the

---

1. The index uses 1978 as its base year. The currency basket excludes hyperinflationary markets where exchange devaluation is measured net of price increases.

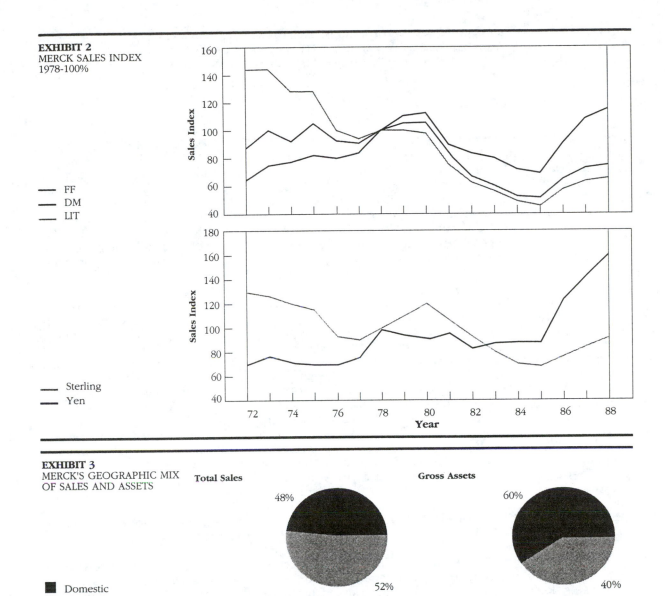

EXHIBIT 2
MERCK SALES INDEX
1978=100%

— FF
— DM
— LIT

— Sterling
— Yen

EXHIBIT 3
MERCK'S GEOGRAPHIC MIX
OF SALES AND ASSETS

Total Sales

Gross Assets

48%

52%

60%

40%

■ Domestic
▨ Foreign

60% level, resulting in a cumulative exchange reduction in sales of approximately $900 million. But, then, as the dollar weakened in the later 1980s, the index increased to roughly 97%, returning to its 1972-1980 range.

But, as Exhibit 2 also shows, although the overall index returned as of 1988 to the earlier range, not all currencies have moved together against the dollar. The strengthening in the yen and the deutschemark has offset the decline of historically weaker currencies such as the Italian lira and French franc, while the British pound is very near 1978 levels.

RESOURCE ALLOCATION

Given the significant exchange exposure of our net overseas revenues, as reflected by our experience in early 1980s, we next decided to review the company's global allocation of resources across currencies and, in the process, to determine the extent to which revenues and costs were matched in individual currencies. Our analysis (the main findings of which are illustrated in Exhibit 3) revealed that the distribution of Merck's assets differs somewhat from the sales mix, primarily because of the concentration of research, manufacturing, and headquarters operations in the U.S.

On the basis of this analysis, it was clear that Merck has an exchange rate mismatch. To reduce this mismatch, we first considered the possibility of redeploying resources in order to shift dollar costs to a different currency. This process would have involved relocating manufacturing sites, research sites, and employees such as headquarters and support staff. We soon reached the conclusion, however, that because so few support functions seemed appropriate candidates for relocation, a move would have had only a negligible effect on our global income exposure. In short, we decided that shifting people and resources overseas was not a cost-effective way of dealing with our exchange exposure.

HEDGING MERCK'S EXPOSURES WITH FINANCIAL INSTRUMENTS

Having concluded that resource deployment was not an appropriate way for Merck to address exchange risk, we considered the alternative of financial hedging. Thinking through this alternative involved the following five steps:

1. Exchange Forecasts. Review of the likelihood of adverse exchange movements.

2. Strategic Plan Impact. Quantification of the potential impact of adverse exchange movements over the period of the plan.

3. Hedging Rationale. Critical examination of the reasons for hedging (perhaps the most important part of the process).

4. Financial Instruments. Selection of which instruments to use and how to execute the hedge.

5. Hedging Program. Simulation of alternative strategies to choose the most cost-effective hedging strategy to accommodate our risk tolerance profile (an ongoing process supported by a mathematical model we have recently developed to supplement our earlier analysis).

STEP 1: Projecting Exchange Rate Volatility

Our review of the probability of future exchange rate movements was guided by four main considerations:

(1) The major factors expected to affect exchange rates over the strategic plan period—for example, the U.S. trade deficit, capital flows, the U.S. budget deficit—all viewed in the context of the concept of an "equilibrium" exchange rate.

(2) Target zones or government policies designed to manage exchange rates. To what extent will government policies be implemented to dampen exchange rate volatility, particularly "overshooting," in the future?

(3) Development of possible ranges for dollar strength or weakness over the planning period.

(4) Summary of outside forecasters—a number of forecasters were polled on the outlook for the dollar over the plan period.

Our review of outside forecasters showed they were almost evenly split on the dollar's outlook. Although almost no one predicted a return to the extremes of the early 1980s, we nonetheless concluded that there was a potential for a relatively large move in either direction.

We developed a simple method for quantifying the potential ranges that reflects the following thought process:

■ Except for 1986, the upper limit of the year-to-year move in average exchange rates for the deutschemark and the yen has been about 20%. We used this as the measure of potential volatility in developing the probabilistic ranges in the forecast. (The deutschemark, incidentally, was used as a proxy for all European currencies.)

■ The widest ranges would likely result from one-directional movements—that is, 5 years of continued strengthening or weakening.

■ However, as the effect of each year's movement is felt in the economy and financial markets, the probability of exchange rates' continuing in the same direction is lessened. For example, if the dollar were to weaken, the favorable effects on the trade balance and on relative asset values would likely induce increased capital flows and cause a turnaround.

Based in part on this concept of exchange rate movements as a "mean-reverting" process, we developed ranges of expected rate movements (as shown in Exhibit 4) by assigning probabilities to the dollar continuing to move along a line of consecu-

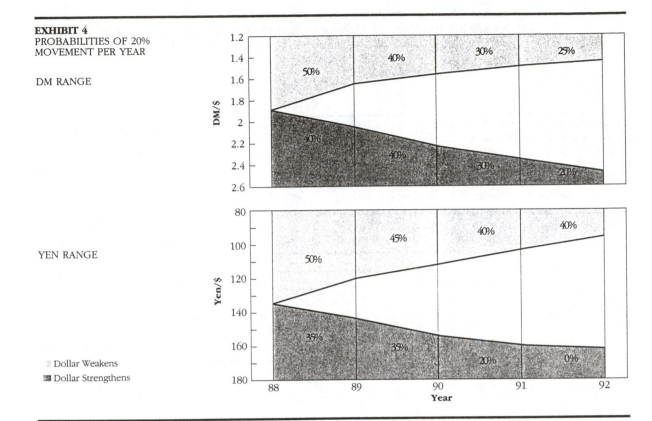

EXHIBIT 4
PROBABILITIES OF 20%
MOVEMENT PER YEAR

DM RANGE

YEN RANGE

☐ Dollar Weakens
▓ Dollar Strengthens

tive years' strengthening or weakening. For example, the dollar was considered to have a 40% probability of strengthening by 20% versus the DM in 1989. If the dollar does appreciate by 20% in 1989, then we also assume that the probability of its strengthening by a further 20% in 1990 is also 40%, but that the chance of this pattern continuing in 1991 is only 30% and falls to 20% in 1992.

Such ranges represent our best guess about the likely boundaries of dollar strength or weakness. The actual probability of exchange rate movements reaching or exceeding these boundaries is small, but the use of such extreme rates allows us to estimate the extent of our exposure. These exchange boundaries were also used in quantifying the potential impact of unfavorable exchange rate movements on our Strategic Plan.

STEP 2: Assessing the Impact on the 5-Year Strategic Plan

To assess the potential effect of unfavorable exchange rates, we converted our Strategic Plan into U.S. dollars on an exchange neutral basis (that is, at the current exchange rate) and compared these cash flow and earnings projections to those we expected to materialize under both our strong dollar and weak dollar scenarios. (See Exhibit 5.)

Further, we measured the potential impact of exchange rate movements on a cumulative basis as well as according to the year-to-year convention that is standard in external reporting. Exhibit 6 shows the effect of translating the year-to-year data from Exhibit 5 on a cumulative basis. (The total bar represents the cumulative variance, while the top portion represents the variance as determined by the change in rates from one period to the next.) Because it looks beyond a one-year period, the cumulative exchange variance provides a more useful estimate of the size of the exchange risk associated with Merck's long-range plan. Use of a cumulative measure also provides the basis for the kind of multi-year financial hedging program that, as we eventually determined, is appropriate for hedging multi-year income flows.

EXHIBIT 5
UNHEDGED NET INCOME
1989-1992

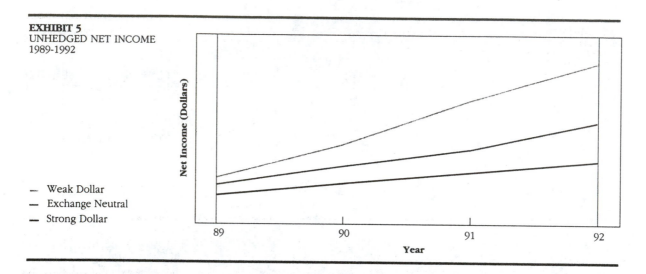

— Weak Dollar
— Exchange Neutral
— Strong Dollar

EXHIBIT 6
EXCHANGE IMPACT
STRONG DOLLAR
SCENARIO

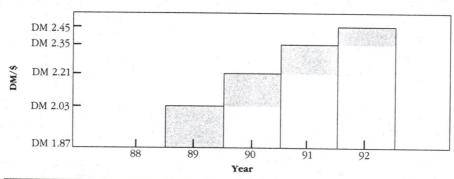

Total Bar represents cumulative exchange impact. Shaded area represents year-on-year impact.

STEP 3: Deciding Whether to Hedge the Exposure

Over the long term, foreign exchange rate movements have been—and are likely to continue to be—a problem of volatility in year-to-year earnings rather than one of irreversible losses. For example, most of the income statement losses of the early 1980s were recouped in the following three years. The question of whether or not to hedge exchange risk thus becomes a question of the company's own risk profile with respect to interim volatility in earnings and cash flows.

The desirability of reducing earnings volatility due to exchange can be examined from both external and internal perspectives.

External Concerns. These center on the perspective of capital markets, and accordingly in-volve matters such as share price, investor clientele effects, and maintenance of dividend policy. Although exchange fluctuations clearly can have material effects on reported accounting earnings, it is not clear that exchange-related fluctuations in earnings have significant effects on stock price. Our own analysis (as illustrated in Exhibit 7) suggests only a modest correlation in recent years between exchange gains and losses and share price movements, and a slight relationship in the strong dollar period—the scenario of greatest concern to us.

Industry analysts' reports, moreover, tend to support our analysis by arguing that exchange gains and losses are at most a second-order factor in determining the share prices of pharmaceutical companies. While invariably stressing the importance of new products as perhaps the most critical share price variable, analysts

THE KEY FACTORS THAT WOULD SUPPORT HEDGING AGAINST EXCHANGE
VOLATILITY ARE . . . THE LARGE PROPORTION OF THE COMPANY'S OVERSEAS
EARNINGS AND CASH FLOWS; AND THE POTENTIAL EFFECT OF VOLATILITY ON
OUR ABILITY TO EXECUTE OUR STRATEGIC PLAN.

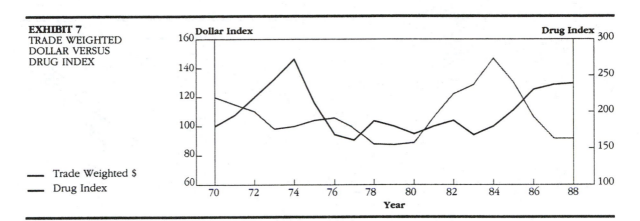

EXHIBIT 7
TRADE WEIGHTED
DOLLAR VERSUS
DRUG INDEX

—— Trade Weighted $
—— Drug Index

also often comment on the regulated price environment overseas (which, as we pointed out earlier, limits competitive exposure by reducing the effect of exchange changes on sales volume).[2]

With respect to investor clientele, exchange would seem to have mixed effects. To the extent that some investors—especially overseas investors—see Merck's stock as an opportunity for speculating on a weak dollar, hedging would be contrary to investors' interests. But, for investors seeking a "pure play" on the stocks of ethical drug companies, significant exchange risk could be undesirable. Thus, given this potential conflict of motives among investors, and recognizing our inability to ascertain the preferences of all of Merck's investor clienteles (potential as well as current), we concluded that it would be inappropriate to give too much weight to any specific type of investor.

On the issue of dividend policy, we came to a somewhat different conclusion. Maintaining Merck's dividend, while probably not the most important determinant of our share price, is nevertheless viewed by management as an important means of expressing our confidence in the company's prospective earnings growth. It is our way of reassuring investors that we expect our large investment in future research (funded primarily by retained earnings) to provide requisite returns. And, although both Merck and the industry in general were able to maintain dividend rates during the strong dollar period, we were concerned about the company's ability to maintain a policy of dividend *growth*

during a future dollar strengthening. Because Merck's (and other pharmaceutical companies') dividend growth rates did indeed decline during the strong dollar 1981-1985 period, the effect of future dollar strengthening on company cash flows could well constrain future dividend growth. So, in considering whether to hedge our income against future exchange movements, we chose to give some weight to the desirability of maintaining growth in the dividend.

In general, then, we concluded that although our exchange hedging policy should consider capital market perspectives (especially dividend policy), it should not be dictated by them. The direct effect of exchange fluctuations on shareholder value, if any, is unclear; and it thus seemed a better course to concentrate on the objective of maximizing long-term cash flows and to focus on the potential effect of exchange rate movements on our ability to meet our internal objectives. Such actions, needless to say, are ultimately intended to maximize returns for our stockholders.

Internal Concerns. From the perspective of management, the key factors that would support hedging against exchange volatility are the following two: (1) the large proportion of the company's overseas earnings and cash flows; and (2) the potential effect of cash flow volatility on our ability to execute our strategic plan—particularly, to make the investments in R & D that furnish the basis for future growth. The pharmaceutical industry has a very long planning horizon, one which reflects the complexity

2. Some analysts have also claimed to detect an inverse relationship between drug stock prices and inflation that also acts to reduce currency exposure. Drug stocks, as this reasoning goes, are growth stocks and generally benefit from low inflation because the discount factor used to price growth stocks declines under low inflation which increases shareholder value. Likewise a high inflation environment will depress share prices for growth stocks. Since generally high inflation leads to a weaker dollar, the negative impact of high inflation would over time limit the positive effect of a weaker dollar and the reverse would also be true.

EXHIBIT 8
ALTERNATIVE HEDGING
INSTRUMENTS

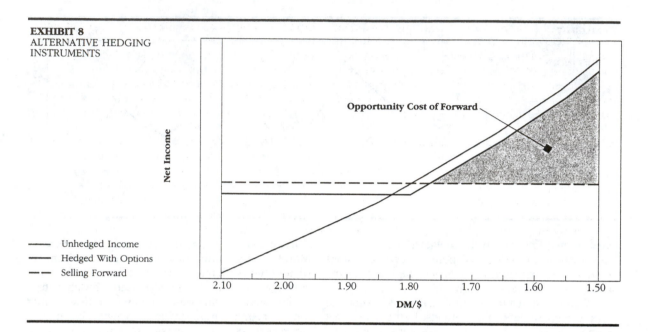

of the research involved as well as the lengthy process of product registration. It often takes more than 10 years between the discovery of a product and its market launch. In the current competitive environment, success in the industry requires a continuous, long-term commitment to a *steadily increasing* level of research funding.

Given the cost of research and the subsequent challenges of achieving positive returns, companies such as Merck require foreign sales in addition to U.S. sales to generate a level of income that supports continued research and business operations. The U.S. market alone is not large enough to support the level of our research effort. Because foreign sales are subject to exchange volatility, the dollar equivalent of worldwide sales can be very unstable. Uncertainty can make it very difficult to justify high levels of U.S. based-research when the firm cannot effectively estimate the pay-offs from its research. Our experience, and that of the industry in general, has been that the cash flow and earnings uncertainty caused by exchange rate volatility leads to a reduction of growth in research spending.

Such volatility can also result in periodic reductions of corporate spending necessary to expand markets and maintain supportive capital expenditures. In the early 1980s, for example, capital expenditures by Merck and other leading U.S. pharmaceutical companies experienced a reduction in rate of growth similar to that in R & D.

Our conclusion, then, was that we should take action to reduce the potential impact of exchange volatility on future cash flows. Reduction of such volatility removes an important element of uncertainty confronting the strategic management of the company.

STEP 4: Selecting the Appropriate Financial Instruments

While we will not discuss the various hedging techniques in detail, we do wish to share the thought processes that led us to choose currency options as our risk management tool. Our objective was to select the most cost-effective hedging instrument that accommodated the company's risk preferences.

Forward foreign exchange contracts, foreign currency debt, and currency swaps all effectively fix the value of the amount hedged regardless of currency movements. With the use of options, by contrast, the hedging firm retains the opportunity to benefit from natural positions—albeit at a cost equal to the premium paid for the option. As illustrated in Exhibit 8, under a strong dollar scenario (based on 1988 spot rates and forward points), Merck would prefer a forward sale because the contract would produce the same gains as the option but without incurring the cost of the option premium. But, under the weak dollar scenario, both the unhedged and the option positions would be preferred to hedging with the forward contract.

A CERTAIN LEVEL OF OPTION PREMIUMS COULD BE JUSTIFIED AS THE COST OF
AN INSURANCE POLICY DESIGNED TO PRESERVE OUR ABILITY TO CARRY
THROUGH WITH OUR STRATEGIC PLAN.

Given the possibility of exchange rate movements in either direction, we were unwilling to forgo the potential gains if the dollar weakened; so options were strictly preferred. We also concluded, moreover, that a certain level of option premiums could be justified as the cost of an insurance policy designed to preserve our ability to carry through with our strategic plan.[3]

STEP 5: Constructing a Hedging Program

Having selected currency options as our hedging vehicle and designated the 5-year period of our strategic plan as our hedging horizon, we then considered several implementation strategies, including:

Varying the term of the bedge. That is, using year-by-year rather than multi-year hedging.

Varying the strike price of the foreign exchange options. For example, out-of-the-money options were considered as a means of reducing costs.

Varying the amount. That is, different percentages of income could be covered, again, to control costs.

After simulating the outcome of alternative strategies under various exchange rate scenarios, we came to the following decisions: (1) we would hedge for a multi-year period, using long-term options to protect our strategic cash flow; (2) we would not use far-out-of-the-money options to reduce costs; and (3) we would hedge only on a partial basis and, in effect, self-insure for the remainder.

We continue to refine this decision through our use of increasingly more sophisticated modeling. Recognizing this as a quantitative process whereby decisions can be improved by application of better techniques, Merck has been developing (with the guidance of Professor Darrell Duffie of Stanford University) a state-of-the-art computer model that simulates the effectiveness of a variety of strategies for hedging. The model is a Monte Carlo simulation package that presents probability distributions of unhedged and hedged foreign income for future periods (the shortest of which are quarters). By so doing, it allows us to visualize the effect of any given hedging policy on our periodic cash flows, thus permitting better-informed hedging decisions.

The model has six basic components:

1. Security Pricing Models: State-of-the-art financial analytics are used to calculate theoretical prices for various securities such as bonds, futures, forwards, and options.[4]

2. Hedging Policy: We can specify a variety of hedging policies, with each representing a portfolio of securities to buy or sell in each quarter. The number of hedging policies is essentially unlimited, reflecting a variety of hedge ratios, proxy currencies, accounting constraints, security combinations, etc. For example, the model permits us to compare a hedging program of purchasing options that cover the exposures of the 5-year planning period and holding them until maturity with the alternative of a dynamic portfolio revision strategy. A dynamic hedge would involve not only the initial purchase of options, but a continuous process of buying and selling additional options based on interim changes in exchange rates.

3. Foreign Income Generator: Before simulating changes in hedging policy, however, we start by building our strategic plan forecast of local currency earnings into the model. The model then generates random earnings by quarter according to a specified model of forecast projections and random forecast errors. This process provides us with an estimate of the variability of local currency earnings and thereby allows us to reflect possible variations versus plan forecasts with greater accuracy.

4. Exchange Rate Dynamics: The model uses a Monte Carlo simulator to generate random exchange rates by quarter. The simulator allows us to adjust currency volatilities, rates of reversion, long-term exchange rates, and coefficients of correlation among currencies. We can test the sensitivity of the simulator to stronger or weaker dollar exchange rates by modifying the inputs. We can also use the Monte Carlo simulation package to re-examine the development of exchange scenarios and ranges described earlier.[5]

---

3. It was also recognized that to the extent hedge accounting could be applied to purchased options, this represents an advantage over other foreign currency instruments. The accounting ramifications of mark-to-market versus hedge accounting were, and remain, an important issue and we have continued to monitor developments with respect to the ongoing controversy over accounting for currency options.

4. In pricing options, we have the choice of using the Black-Scholes model or an alternative highly advanced valuation model. These models provide reasonably reliable estimates of the expected true cost, including transaction fees, of the option program. Although Black Scholes is the predominant pricing model in pricing many kinds of options, alternative models appear to have an advantage in the pricing of long-dated currency options. Black Scholes implicitly assumes that the volatility of exchange rates grows exponentially with time to maturity. General-

ly speaking, the further out the expiry date, the higher the price. The alternative model has a sophisticated approach in its assumption of a dampened exponential relationship between time to maturity, expected volatility, and price. For this reason, in the case of long-dated options, the Black Scholes model generally overstates option prices relative to the alternative model.

5. The model will also have the ability to simulate historic exchange trends. The model will have access to a large database of historic exchange rates. We will be able to analyze the impact of hedging on a selected time period, for example, the strong dollar period of the 1980's. Or, we can have the model randomly select exchange rate movements from a historical period, resulting in a Monte Carlo simulation of that period.

EXHIBIT 9
MERCK FOREIGN
CASH FLOW
UNHEDGED VS. HEDGED*

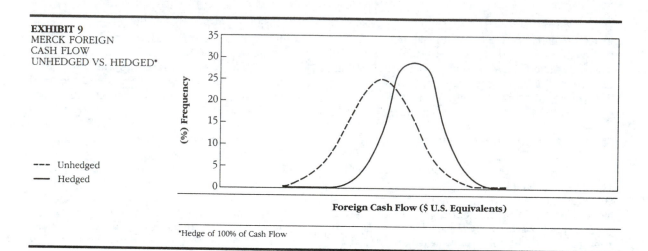

--- Unhedged
— Hedged

*Hedge of 100% of Cash Flow

5. Cash Flow Generator: The model collects information from each of the above four components so as to calculate total cash flow in U.S. dollars by quarter for each random scenario.

6. Statistical and Graphical Output: The quarterly cash flow information for each of a large number of scenarios is collected and displayed graphically in frequency plots, and in terms of statistics such as means, standard deviations, and confidence levels. Exhibit 9 provides an example of the graphical output from our simulator, comparing distributions of unhedged and hedged cash flows. In this case, the hedged curve assumes 100% of Merck's exposure has been covered through the purchase of foreign currency options. Given the pattern of exchange rate movements simulated, the hedging strategy has shifted the hedged cash flow distribution to the right, cutting off a portion of unfavorable outcomes. In addition, the hedged cash flow distribution has a higher mean value as well as a lower standard deviation. Therefore, in this scenario, hedging would be preferable to not hedging, resulting in higher returns as well as lower risk. (Again, of course, the trade-off is the initial cost of the option premiums that would have to be balanced against

the improved risk/return pattern.) Other scenarios may indicate that a lower hedge ratio or not hedging is the preferred strategy.

In sum, the model provides Merck with a powerful tool to determine the optimal strategy for reducing our exposure to foreign currency risk. The simulator allows us to analyze a wide range (in fact, an infinite number) of exchange scenarios, hedging policies, and security combinations. This in turn gives us the ability to select the hedging policy that is both cost-effective and consistent with our desired risk profile.

CONCLUSION

Identifying a company's exchange risk and reaching a decision with respect to what action, if any, should be taken requires extensive analysis. We believe that, as a result of this kind of analysis of Merck's currency exposures, we have developed an appropriate financial hedging plan—one that provides management with what amounts to an insurance policy against the potentially damaging effect of currency volatility on the company's ability to carry out its strategic plan. We continue to refine the actual implementation process as we move forward.

■ JUDY LEWENT AND JOHN KEARNEY

are Vice President and Treasurer, and Assistant Treasurer, respectively, of Merck & Co., Inc. Ms. Lewent has spent nine years ᵗ Merck and Mr. Kearney has been with the company 20 years.

Article 44

Foreign Exchange Options: The Leading Hedge

Niso Abuaf, *Salomon Brothers Inc*

Foreign exchange options (FXOs) can serve international financial managers in several ways. First, FXOs are essential to hedging "contingent" foreign exchange exposures—the kind of exposure which arises, for example, when a U.S. contractor bids for a contract denominated in a foreign currency. Second, FXOs are used in active foreign exchange exposure management—that is, those cases in which management chooses to take a position on the direction or the volatility of currency movements. In this more speculative use, options can limit downside risk while retaining upside potential for profit. Forwards or futures, by contrast, do not allow the investor to take a view and cap losses at the same time. Third, using FXOs in portfolio management allows managers to construct portfolios according to the specific risk-return profile they desire. Conventional financial instruments allow managers to make tradeoffs only between the risk (or variance) and the return of a portfolio. FXOs, however, make possible the more complex trade-offs described later in this article.

Hedging Contingent Exposures in Foreign Currency

Contingent foreign exchange exposures arise when there is the possibility, but not the certainty, of future receipts or payments in a foreign currency. This usually occurs, as mentioned above, when a bid is submitted for a contract denominated in a foreign currency. In such cases, the firm may wish to hedge its potential receivables at the time the bid is submitted.

To hedge contingent payables or receivables in foreign currencies, foreign exchange options can be used either alone or in combination with forward or futures contracts. Forward or futures contracts alone,

however, cannot be used to hedge contingent payables or receivables. In hedging contingent receivables, for example, the simple forward sale of foreign exchange (equal to the amount of the bid) is not a solution to the risk problem because the bidder's foreign currency exposure depends on whether the bid is eventually accepted. If the bid is accepted after the firm sells the foreign exchange forward, then the firm is indeed hedged. But if the bid is not accepted and the firm has already sold forward the anticipated amount of foreign currency, the firm has a "naked" short position in the foreign currency. It has taken a speculative rather than a hedged position; and if the foreign currency appreciates, the firm loses. But, if the firm does not sell forward the anticipated foreign currency and the bid is accepted, the firm finds itself in an uncovered long position. In this situation, it takes a loss if the foreign currency depreciates.

Contingent foreign exchange receivables also come about as the result of disposals of foreign subsidiaries, uncertain foreign sales, and uncertain dividend remittances from abroad, to name just a few possibilities. For example, the central banks of Portugal, Spain, Turkey, and Yugoslavia usually receive remittances from guest workers in Germany. These remittances depend on such factors as economic conditions in Germany, the prevailing exchange rate, the wedge between the prevailing official exchange rate and the parallel market rate, and so forth. These central banks also usually have debt-servicing liabilities denominated in dollars. They may need to hedge their contingent deutschemark receivables in terms of their certain dollar liabilities.

Options can solve these problems because the exercise of options is voluntary and contingent upon prevailing economic conditions. There are two basic

There are two basic methods of dealing with contingent receivables: (1) buy a put option on the foreign currency or (2) sell the foreign currency forward and simultaneously buy a call option.

methods of dealing with contingent receivables: (1) buy a put option on the foreign currency or (2) sell the foreign currency forward and simultaneously buy a call option. And, as can be demonstrated using the "option parity theorem," they are perfectly equivalent strategies.[1]

If using the first method, the purchase of a put option, one must buy the put such that the timing, quantity, and strike price of the option corresponds to that of the bid. If the timing of the receivable is uncertain even in the event the bid is won, then the bid should be hedged with American rather than European options. The maturity of the options should reflect the upper end of the uncertain timing range. The quantities and strike prices can take on a range of values depending on management's desired risk-return profile.

The premium on the put option is sometimes viewed as the cost of buying insurance against possible exchange rate fluctuations in the event the bid is accepted. If the bid is accepted and the foreign currency depreciates, the firm offsets the loss in the value of the foreign currency by exercising the put option. In fact, however, the put option also provides additional profit opportunities. If the foreign currency depreciates and the bid is rejected, the hedger can exercise the option and profit by selling the foreign exchange for dollars. (Of course, if the foreign currency appreciates, the firm will let the put option expire in either case.) In this sense, the option premium consists of both an investment value and a hedging value. Only the hedging value of the option premium should be incorporated into the cost of submitting the bid—provided, of course, that this hedging value can be calculated.

Using another, fully equivalent hedging strategy, the firm can sell the foreign currency forward, and simultaneously buy a call on the foreign currency, with matching quantities, exercise prices, and expiration dates.[2]

If the bid is accepted and the foreign currency depreciates, the forward transaction fully hedges the firm, which simply lets the call expire. In the event that the foreign currency appreciates, the firm's forward contract covers its receipts, and it exercises the call for additional profits. If the bid is rejected, however, and the foreign currency appreciates, the call fully hedges the firm's short forward position. Should the foreign currency depreciate, the firm lets the call option expire and buys spot foreign currency to cover its forward position.

Contingent Payables

Contingent payables in foreign exchange come about as the result of transactions such as stock tender offers, merger and acquisition tenders to foreign companies, pending foreign law suits, and probable foreign dividend payments. Such payables, like contingent receivables, are also properly hedged with foreign exchange options.

Once again, there are two equivalent techniques for hedging contingent payables in foreign exchange: (1) buy a call option on foreign exchange or (2) simultaneously buy a long forward contract on the foreign currency and a put option. To be fully hedged, it is assumed that the exercise price and the maturity of the option contracts match those of the corresponding forward contracts. However, as already noted, this need not always be the case.

If the contingent payable materializes, the long forward covers it. If the contingent payable does not materialize, the put covers the long forward position. As in the earlier hedging example, these two methods also allow for situations where additional profits are possible.

Active Management of Foreign Exchange Exposure

Various option strategies can provide complex risk-return trade-off profiles that would not be available through other instruments. Among these are straddles and spreads.

---

1. According to the option parity theorem, buying a European call and selling a European put is equivalent to being long forward:

buy call+sell put=long forward.

If the foreign currency appreciates relative to the exercise price, it is profitable to exercise the call. Conversely, if the foreign currency depreciates relative to the strike price, the buyer of the put exercises his option, forcing the seller of the put to buy the foreign exchange at the exercise price. Thus the simultaneous purchase of a call and sale of a put at the same exercise price is similar to the purchase of a forward contract at that exercise price. Note, however, that this equivalence is perfect only for European options which can be exercised only at maturity, not before. The equivalence is not perfect for American options, which can be exercised before maturity and can hence result in a position in the foreign currency before the maturity of the forward contract.

Rearranging the terms above:

buy call+short forward=buy put.

Here, algebraically changing the sign of a term, when its position vis-a-vis the equal sign changes, is equivalent to transforming a long position to a short position, and conversely.

2. See note 1.

The most important determinant of the fair actuarial value of this insurance is the expected volatility of the underlying currency. If one's expectation of this volatility is lower than the market's, one buys this insurance.

Straddles

A straddle is formed by simultaneously buying or selling puts and calls. The purchase of a straddle is equivalent to buying both a put and call at the same time; sale of a straddle is the same as simultaneously selling a put and call.

Straddles are bought or sold when management has specific expectations about the future variability of exchange rates, but not about the direction of those movements. Specifically, management buys a straddle when it believes a currency will either appreciate or depreciate beyond a specific point.[3]

Similarly, a straddle is sold if management thinks that currency movements will be limited within a specific range. For example, the firm may sell a straddle if it thinks that the volatility of the value of a certain currency will drop below market expectations, possibly because of expected central bank intervention. Conversely, the firm may buy a straddle if it expects volatility to rise above market expectations—as the result, say, of expected increases or decreases in money supply growth.

Figure 1c illustrates the profit opportunities provided by buying a straddle in the case of exchange rate movements below S_3 and above S_4. To see why a straddle provides this payoff profile, remember that the purchase of a straddle is equivalent to the simultaneous purchase of a call option and a put option with identical terms. The profit profile of buying a call option at exercise price X is illustrated by Figure 1a. At spot exchange rates X and lower, the call is not exercised, so the loss equals the price of the option, c. At spot exchange rates above S_1, the option is sufficiently in the money to more than cover its cost. Between X and S_1, the option is in the money, though not by enough to cover its cost. Similarly, figure 1b illustrates the profit profile of buying a put option.

Return once more to Figure 1c, which, again, illustrates the profit profile of a straddle purchase. Since buying a straddle is the simultaneous purchase of a put and a call, figure 1c is the vertical sum of figures 1a and 1b. Buying a straddle, incidentally, should not be viewed as providing a "free lunch." The price of the straddle incorporates the market's assessment of the *variability* of the exchange rate.

The buyer of the straddle profits only if the exchange rate moves plus or minus a certain percentage, $[(S-X)(100)/X]$, or $[(X-S)(100)/X]$, beyond X. The *seller* of the straddle accepts that risk for a lump sum.

The profit profile of *selling* a straddle is the mirror image of figure 1c around the horizontal axis. An investor would write a straddle if he believed that the volatility of the currency would drop by more than the market expects, possibly as a result of expected central bank intervention to stabilize the exchange rate.

Just as in buying a straddle, writing a straddle does not imply a free lunch. Writing a straddle is quite risky because the investor is writing both a naked call and a naked put. He has no protection against large moves in the value of the currency in either direction, thus implying a potential for unlimited loss.

As figure 1 suggests, buying a straddle is equivalent to buying insurance, with a deductible, against large movements either up or down in the value of the underlying security. Profit opportunities or bargains exist, however, only if this insurance (1) can be bought for less than its fair actuarial value or (2) can be sold for more than its fair actuarial value.

The most important determinant of the fair actuarial value of this insurance is the expected volatility of the underlying currency. If one's expectation of this volatility is lower than the market's, one buys this insurance. But, if one's expectation of this volatility is lower than the market's, one sells this insurance. The side whose expectations are correct more often profits in the long run. So if someone thinks he can judge a currency's future volatility better than the market, he can buy or write straddles.

Spreads

A spread is the simultaneous purchase of one option and sale of another on the same underlying security in which the two options differ only in time to expiration or in strike price. Vertical spreads are formed by varying only the strike price; horizontal spreads (also called "time" or "calendar" spreads) are formed by varying the time to maturity. These spreads are so named because options differing in exercise price are listed vertically in the published option quotations, and options differing in maturity

---

3. As shown below, this point is a function of the exercise prices of the individual options in the straddle, and the option premiums.

Straddles are bought or sold when management has specific expectations about the future variability of exchange rates, but not about the direction of those movements.

FIGURE 1
Profit Profile of Buying a Straddle

(a) Buying a Call

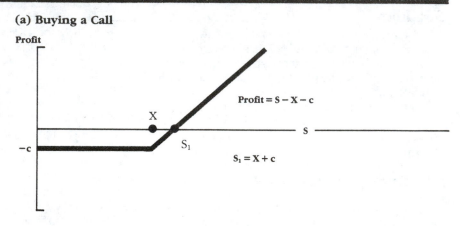

Profit $= S - X - c$

$S_1 = X + c$

(b) Buying a Put

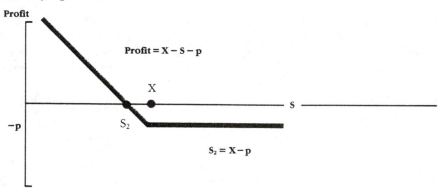

Profit $= X - S - p$

$S_2 = X - p$

(c) Buying a Straddle

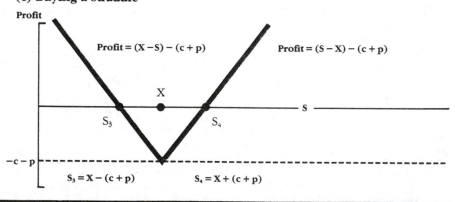

Profit $= (X - S) - (c + p)$

Profit $= (S - X) - (c + p)$

$S_3 = X - (c + p)$

$S_4 = X + (c + p)$

are listed horizontally.

When traders think that certain options are mispriced, they try to make a profit by establishing a spread—that is, by buying the low-priced option and selling the high-priced one. The following example, using three-month and six-month foreign exchange options, illustrates how traders detect arbitrage opportunities.

FIGURE 2
Profit Profile of a 6-3
Month Spread

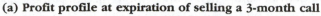

(a) Profit profile at expiration of selling a 3-month call

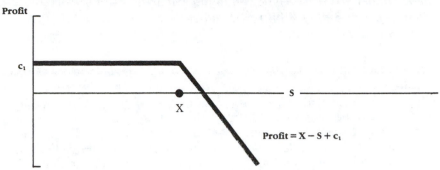

$$\text{Profit} = X - S + c_1$$

(b) Profit profile at 3 months of buying a 6-month call

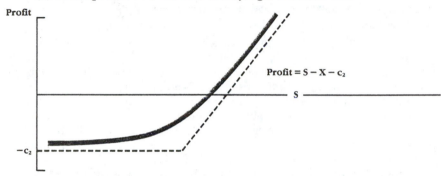

$$\text{Profit} = S - X - c_2$$

(c) Profit profile at 3 months of a 6-3 month spread

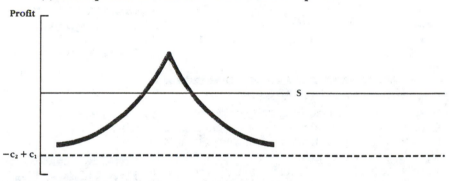

First, the implied variances of 3-month and 6-month FXOs are calculated by using the option pricing models together with current option prices to "back out" the market's implicit estimate of expected variance. Second, the implied variance of 3-month FXOs is used to compute the theoretical value of 6-month FXOs. If the theoretical value of 6-month FXOs is higher than the actual value, then 6-month FXOs must be underpriced and 3-month FXOs must be overpriced. Following the adage "buy low, sell high," the trader buys 6-month FXOs and sells 3-month FXOs. The same trader could also arrive at the same result by comparing the implied variances of 3-month versus 6-month FXOs. The FXO with the higher implied variance is the one that is overpriced.

But this is not an entirely riskless activity. First,

If an international portfolio manager buys protective puts to cover his international investments, he can totally eliminate his downside risk at the expense of reducing his upside potential by the amount of the premium paid for the puts.

minimal as it might be, a spread might incur a loss. The maximum loss is called the "basis" of the spread, and is discussed in further detail below. Second, variance may not be a stationary process—that is, the relationship between the variance of 3-month and 6-month FXOs may change over time—creating potential losses for those who use the past as their guide to speculating on the future.

Horizontal Spreads

Figure 2 illustrates the profit of a horizontal spread formed by selling a 3-month call and by buying a 6-month call, both at the same exercise price. The profit profile, at expiration, of selling a 3-month is straightforward and is presented in part (a). The profit profile, at 3 months, of buying a 6-month call is given in part (b). (The broken lines are the asymptotes of the profit profile.) The solid line represents the actual profit profile, reflecting the fact that options command a time premium. The profit profile of the spread, at 3 months, is the vertical sum of parts (a) and (b). The maximum loss of the spread equals the premium of the 6-month call minus the premium of the 3-month call. This is called the "basis" of the spread.

The Simple Vertical Spread

The simple vertical spread is formed by buying an option with one exercise price (X_1) and selling another option with the same maturity date as the first, but at a different exercise price (X_2). Figure 3 illustrates the profit profile of buying a call at X_1, and selling a call at $X_2 (X_2 > X_1)$. The profit profile from selling a call at X_1 and buying a call at X_2 is the negative counterpart of figure 3.[4]

The Butterfly Spread

This is formed by selling two options, one with a high exercise price and one with a low exercise, and buying two options at the exercise price in between the two. Figure 4 illustrates the profit profile of a butterfly spread formed by selling two calls at X_1 and X_3, and by buying two calls at $X_2 [X_1 > X_2 > X_3; X_2 = (X_1 + X_3)/2]$.

The Sandwich Spread

A sandwich spread is the opposite of a butterfly spread. It is formed by buying two options, one with a high exercise price and one with a low exercise price, and selling two options at the exercise price in between the two. The profit profile of a sandwich spread formed by buying two calls at X_1 and X_3, and selling two calls at X_2 is the negative of figure 4 and is given in figure 5.

Note that the profit profiles of sandwich and butterfly spreads somewhat resemble those of straddles. The difference is that, unlike straddles, sandwich and butterfly spreads limit the potential profits and losses. Like straddles, sandwich and butterfly spreads can be used to take positions when one's expectation of the future volatility of a currency's change is different from that of the market's. The earlier economic arguments about the scarcity of free lunches also apply to butterfly and sandwich spreads.

Other Spreads

In addition to the above, there is a wide variety of option strategies, including diagonal spreads (a combination of vertical and horizontal spreads) and others. Just as in the earlier strategies, these are used when the expectation about the currency's future volatility is different from the market's or when it is believed that a particular option is mispriced.

The Use of Options in Portfolio Management

Modern portfolio theory holds that the performance of a portfolio of assets can be characterized by two variables: risk and return. It is possible to increase the expected return of a portfolio by accepting more risk and to reduce the risk of a portfolio by accepting lower expected return. The traditional technique of levering a portfolio up or down (by using forwards markets, for example) yields a trade-off between risk and return.

So, if an international portfolio manager completely covers all of his foreign exchange posi-

---

4. When referring to spreads, the first quantity represents the option that one is long in.

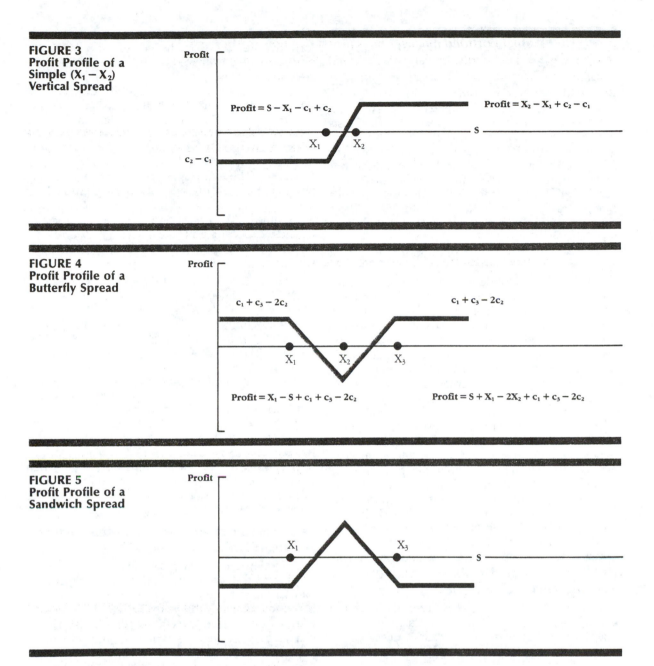

FIGURE 3
Profit Profile of a
Simple $(X_1 - X_2)$
Vertical Spread

Profit

$Profit = S - X_1 - c_1 + c_2$

$Profit = X_2 - X_1 + c_2 - c_1$

X_1 X_2

S

$c_2 - c_1$

FIGURE 4
Profit Profile of a
Butterfly Spread

Profit

$c_1 + c_3 - 2c_2$

$c_1 + c_3 - 2c_2$

X_1 X_2 X_3

$Profit = X_1 - S + c_1 + c_3 - 2c_2$

$Profit = S + X_1 - 2X_2 + c_1 + c_3 - 2c_2$

FIGURE 5
Profit Profile of a
Sandwich Spread

Profit

X_1 X_3

S

tions by buying forwards or futures contracts, he locks in his expected return, and eliminates his downside risk at the expense of removing any upside potential. Similarly, an international portfolio manager can choose to be only partially covered, reducing both the mean and the variance of the portfolio.

Options, however, open the door to other trade-offs. For example, if an international portfolio manager buys protective puts to cover his international investments, he can totally eliminate his downside risk at the expense of reducing his upside potential by the amount of the premium paid for the puts.

Partially Hedging Payables or Receivables

Consider the case of U.S. domestic exporters who hold contracts for future delivery to a foreign country in the currency of that country. These exporters know that while their manufacturing costs are largely denominated in dollars, a selling price quoted in a foreign currency may fetch fewer (or more) dollars at delivery than when the contract was written. Similarly, American importers of foreign goods, with contracts for future delivery quoted in a foreign currency, face the possibility of a future change in their costs due to exchange rate fluctuations.

Of course, the exporter or importer can sit back and do nothing, accepting whatever exchange rate prevails at the time of delivery. Doing nothing, however, can mean large losses for the exporter if the foreign currency depreciates (or large gains if the currency appreciates). Many firms therefore seek to protect themselves from foreign exchange risk by selling all of the foreign exchange receivables forward. Doing so, however, means placing a ceiling on the exporter's profit. Alternatively, the exporter could buy puts on the foreign exchange. This procedure would allow the exporter to ensure minimum profits while retaining the possibility of larger profits. Similarly, an American importer of foreign goods, holding contracts for future delivery in a foreign currency, also could do nothing, go long in the forwards, or buy call options on foreign exchange. Of these alternatives, foreign exchange options may well be the best strategy for tailoring portfolios according to individual preferences and beliefs.

Buying Calls and Puts for Active Portfolio Management

Some finance theorists have recently suggested that it may be profitable to bet against the forward rate. They argue that current exchange rates forecast future spot rates more accurately than do forward rates, and that it is thus profitable to bet against the forward rate based on the current spot rate. The problem with this strategy is, of course, that it is quite risky.

To illustrate, suppose that the deutschemark (DM) is currently trading at $0.54. If 3-month DMs are selling at $0.55, this strategy dictates that one should go short in forward DMs. If, as indicated by the strategy, the DM ends up very close to $0.54 in the future, then one makes a profit of $.01 per DM. However, if the future spot price of the DM ends up above $0.55, then one incurs a loss. Conversely, if spot pound is selling at $1.61 and forward pounds are selling at $1.60, then one goes long on forward pounds, expecting a profit of $.01 per pound. The risk is again substantial, and losses result if the future spot price falls below $1.60.

Options, however, limit the downside risk, allowing the active manager to take a view. Put differently, if the forward DM is at $0.55, one goes short in DMs and simultaneously purchases a call for $0.55, thereby putting a cap on losses. Conversely, if the forward pound is at $1.60, then one goes long on forward pounds, simultaneously buying a put on pounds for $1.60, thus putting a cap on losses.

This strategy is usually used in the context of a portfolio of currencies, because most currency movements are correlated. When returns on securities are correlated, using a number of securities in a portfolio allows risk/return profiles that are superior to the risk-return profile of a single security. When options are used in such a context, risk-return profiles can attain shapes that would otherwise be impossible.

A Potent Instrument

Foreign exchange options, in sum, are a potent instrument for coping with today's highly volatile financial environment. Options enable managers to hedge contingent foreign exchange exposures, to take a view on the direction and volatility of exchange rate movements while limiting downside risk, and to tailor portfolio outcomes in new ways.

Niso Abauf

is Senior Research Associate at Salomon Brothers, Inc. Dr. Abuaf follows the foreign exchange markets and designs new products having option- and futures-like features. He has taught micro- and macroeconomics, as well as money and banking, at the University of Chicago's Graduate School of Business, where he received his Ph.D. in International Finance.

Sources

I. Introduction: Financial Derivatives and Financial Engineering

1. Smith, Jr., Clifford W., Charles W. Smithson, and D. Sykes Wilford, "Managing Financial Risk," *Journal of Applied Corporate Finance*, 1:4, Winter 1989, pp. 27-48.

2. Finnerty, John D., "Financial Engineering in Corporate Finance: An Overview," *Financial Management*, 17:4, Winter 1988, pp. 14-33.

3. Rubinstein, Mark, "Derivative Assets Analysis," *The Journal of Economic Perspectives*, 1:2, Fall 1987, pp. 73-93.

4. Abken, Peter A., "Globalization of Stock, Futures, and Options Markets," Federal Reserve Bank of Atlanta *Economic Review*, July/August 1991, pp. 1-22.

II. Derivative Instruments: Theory and Pricing

A. Forwards and Futures

5. Kolb, Robert W., "Pricing Financial Futures: An Introduction," written for this volume.

6. Kawaller, Ira G., Paul Koch, and Tim Koch, "The Relationship Between the S&P 500 Index and S&P 500 Index Futures Prices," CME Financial Strategy Paper, (Chicago: Chicago Mercantile Exchange, 1988). This article also appeared as Federal Reserve Bank of Atlanta *Economic Review*, May/June 1988, pp. 2-9.

7. Kawaller, Ira G., "Determining the Relevant Fair Value(s) of S&P 500 Futures: A Case Study Approach," CME Financial Strategy Paper, (Chicago: Chicago Mercantile Exchange, 1991).

8. Kawaller, Ira G. and T. Koch, "Cash-and-Carry Trading and the Pricing of Treasury Bill Futures," *The Journal of Futures Markets*, 4:2, Summer 1984, pp. 115-123.

B. Options

9. Rendleman, Richard J., Jr., and Brit J. Bartter, "Two-State Option Pricing," *Journal of Finance*, 34, 1979, pp. 1093-1110.

10. Black, F. and M. Scholes, "The Pricing of Options and Corporate Liabilities," *Journal of Political Economy*, 81:3, Part 1, 1973, pp. 637–654.

11. Black, Fischer, "How We Came Up With the Option Formula," *Journal of Portfolio Management*, Winter 1989, pp. 4–8.

12. Black, Fischer, "Fact and Fantasy in the Use of Options," *Financial Analysts Journal*, Vol. 31:4, 1975, 36–41 and 61–72.

13. Black, Fischer, "How to Use the Holes in Black–Scholes," *Journal of Applied Corporate Finance*, 1:4, Winter 1989, pp. 67–73.

14. Latané, Henry A., and Richard J. Rendleman, Jr., "Standard Deviations of Stock Price Ratios Implied in Option Prices," *Journal of Finance*, Vol. 31, 1976, pp. 369–381.

C. Options on Futures

15. Black, Fischer, "The Pricing of Commodity Contracts," *Journal of Financial Economics*, 3:1/2, September 1976, pp. 167–179.

16. Whaley, R., "Valuation of American Futures Options: Theory and Empirical Tests," *Journal of Finance,* 41:1, March 1986, pp. 127–150.

17. Pitts, Mark, The Pricing of Options on Debt Securities," *Journal of Portfolio Management*, Vol. 9, Winter 1985, pp. 41–50.

D. Swaps

18. Abken, Peter A. "Beyond Plain Vanilla: A Taxonomy of Swaps," Federal Reserve Bank of Atlanta *Economic Review*, March/April 1991, pp. 12–29.

19. Wall, Larry D. and John J. Pringle, "Interest Rate Swaps: A Review of the Issues," Federal Reserve Bank of Atlanta *Economic Review*, 1988, pp. 22–40.

20. Kapner, Kenneth R. and John F. Marshall, "The Pricing of Swaps," Chapter 8 of Kapner, Kenneth R. and John F. Marshall, *The Swaps Handbook*, (New York: New York Institute of Finance), 1990, pp. 319–350.

III. Equity Market Applications

21. Morris, Charles S., "Managing Stock Market Risk with Stock Index Futures," Federal Reserve Bank of Kansas City *Economic Review*, June 1989, pp. 3–16.

22. Abken, P., "An Introduction to Portfolio Insurance," Federal Reserve Bank of Atlanta *Economic Review*, 72:6, November/December 1987, pp. 2-25.

23. O'Brien, T., "The Mechanics of Portfolio Insurance," *Journal of Portfolio Management*, 14:3, Spring 1988, pp. 40-47.

24. Rubinstein, M., "Alternative Paths to Portfolio Insurance," *Financial Analysts Journal*, 41:4, July-August 1985, pp. 42-52.

25. Rendleman, Jr., Richard J. and Richard W. McEnally, "Assessing the Costs of Portfolio Insurance," *Financial Analysts Journal*, Vol. 43:3, May/June 1987, pp. 27-37.

26. Rubinstein, Mark, "Market Basket Alternatives," *Financial Analysts Journal*, 45:5, September/October 1989, pp. 20-29, 61.

IV. Equity Derivatives and the Crash

27. Harris, L., "The October 1987 S&P 500 Stock-Futures Basis," *Journal of Finance*, 44:1, March 1989, pp. 77-99.

28. Bassett, G., V. France, and S. Pliska, "The MMI Cash-Futures Spread on October 19, 1987," *The Review of Futures Markets*, 8:1, 1989, pp. 118-138.

29. Santoni, G. J., "The October Crash: Some Evidence on the Cascade Theory," Federal Reserve Bank of St. Louis, *Review*, May/June 1988, pp. 18-33.

30. Rubinstein, Mark, "Portfolio Insurance and the Market Crash," *Financial Analysts Journal*, 44:1, January/February 1988, pp. 38-47.

31. Moser, James T., "Circuit Breakers," Federal Reserve Bank of Chicago *Economic Perspectives*, 14:5, September/October 1990, pp. 2-13.

V. Debt Market Applications

32. Ederington, L., "The Hedging Performance of the New Futures Market," *Journal of Finance*, 34:1, March 1979, pp. 157-170.

33. Kolb, R. and R. Chiang, "Improving Hedging Performance Using Interest Rate Futures," *Financial Management*, 10:4, 1981, pp. 72-79.

34. Gay, G. and R. Kolb, "Immunizing Bond Portfolios with Interest Rate Futures," *Financial Management*, 11:2, Summer 1982, pp. 81-89.

35. Goodman, Laurie S., "The Use of Interest Rate Swaps in Managing Corporate Liabilities," *Journal of Applied Corporate Finance*, 2:4, Winter 1990, pp. 35–47.

36. Einzig, Robert and Bruce Lange, "Swaps at Transamerica: Applications and Analysis," *Journal of Applied Corporate Finance*, 2:4, Winter 1990, pp. 48–58.

37. Abken, P., "Interest-Rate Caps, Collars, and Floors," Federal Reserve Bank of Atlanta *Economic Review*, 72:6, November/December 1989, pp. 2–24.

38. Kawaller, Ira G., "Interest Rate Swaps versus Eurodollar Strips," *CME Financial Strategy Paper*, (Chicago: Chicago Mercantile Exchange, 1987).

39. McConnell, John J. and Eduardo S. Schwartz, "LYON Taming," *Journal of Finance*, 41:3, 1986, pp. 561-577.

40. Smith, Donald J., "The Pricing of Bull and Bear Floating Rate Notes: An Application of Financial Engineering," *Financial Management*, 17:4, Winter 1988, pp. 72–81.

41. Brown, Keith C. and Donald J. Smith, "Forward Swaps, Swap Options, and the Management of Callable Debt," *Journal of Applied Corporate Finance*, 2:4, Winter 1990, pp. 59–71.

VI. Foreign Exchange Applications

42. Abuaf, Niso, "The Nature and Management of Foreign Exchange Risk," *Midland Corporate Finance Journal*, 4:3, Fall 1986, pp. 30–44.

43. Lewent, Judy C. and A. John Kearney, "Identifying, Measuring, and Hedging Currency Risk at Merck," *Journal of Applied Corporate Finance*, 2:4, Winter 1990, pp. 19–28.

44. Abuaf, Niso, "Foreign Exchange Options: The Leading Hedge," *Midland Corporate Finance Journal*, 5:2, Summer 1987, pp. 51–58.